Gale 30.95

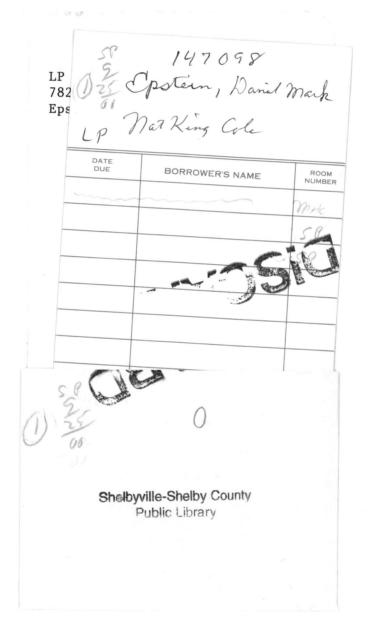

NAT KING COLE

G·K
Hall
&Cº

NAT KING COLE

DANIEL MARK EPSTEIN

G.K. Hall & Co. • Thorndike, Maine

Additional copyright information may be found on page 703.

Published in 2000 by arrangement with
Farrar, Straus and Giroux, LLC

G.K. Hall Large Print Core Series.

The text of this Large Print edition is unabridged.
Other aspects of the book may vary from the original edition.

Set in 16 pt. Plantin.

Printed in the United States on permanent paper.

Library of Congress Cataloging-in-Publication Data

Epstein, Daniel Mark.
    Nat King Cole / Daniel Mark Epstein.
        p. (large print) cm.
    ISBN 0-7838-9012-5 (lg. print : hc : alk. paper)
    1. Cole, Nat King, 1917–1965.   2. Singers — United States
    — Biography.   3. Large type books.   I. Title.
ML420.C63 E67 2000
782.42164′092—dc21
    [B]   00-026026

For my mother, Louise Tillman Epstein,
And her brother, Paul Tillman,
Who always loved this music

CONTENTS

PART THREE
America

PART FOUR
This World and the Next

PART ONE
Chicago

THE KID — CHICAGO, 1935

The kid was wearing a light green gabardine suit that draped his long, slender frame so loosely it looked like the first high-note blast of a trumpet might blow his coat off. His mouth was set, his dark face brooding like the rain-filled clouds on that warm night in September. Approaching the bandstand with a flat-footed, pigeon-toed shamble, he held his head down and to one side, his slanted eyes averted, as if afraid to meet the gaze of several thousand dancers, jazz lovers, and curiosity seekers who filled the Savoy Ballroom.

The kid was shy, and he was amazingly bold. He was the one the young dancers had come to see. They came to hear him play, the boy who would be King, a skinny sixteen-year-old pianist who dared to go up against Earl Hines in the Battle of Rhythm. In 1935 Hines was King of the Ivories, pianist without peer, leader of the hottest dance band on the South Side of Chicago, which was the jazz mecca of America at the very moment the music had achieved a peak of perfection it could not sustain or regain, ever. The music would never be better.

Earl Hines smiled at the people. They called him Gatemouth because of his long smile, full of teeth. He had a dapper pencil-thin mustache and wide-set eyes with high arched brows. He grinned at the jitterbugs on the dance floor, and he smiled

11

up at the slim kid who was whispering orders to his sidemen setting up on their side of the double bandstand.

Gatemouth beamed at the crowd of thousands milling and jostling on the half-acre dance floor of the Savoy Ballroom. The bar in the northwest corner of the room was busy serving drinks to parties at the tables around the three sides of the dance floor. There were 3,000 people in the joint already and it would hold 6,000, at 40 cents a head. It was 30 cents a head before 8:30, when the show was to begin, but most folks couldn't get to the Savoy much before the show started. Gatemouth smiled at his competitor, but the youngster, self-absorbed, earnest, did not smile back, not because he was rude or hostile but because he was going about his business.

Earl Hines may have wondered if this very skinny, very black kid with the slanted eyes and bad complexion knew how to smile. A woman leaned over and whispered in Earl's ear. Wasn't there something about this boy, anyway, a power lurking? Wasn't there a kind of sweetness and vulnerability in his young face, his lean athletic carriage, his thick, soft hair? He was, well, he was adorable, that was the word, like a lion cub. You couldn't help but like him whether or not he could play a bit of piano . . .

You could hardly help liking the kid, and right now Gatemouth was trying. He was trying like hell not to like him, tonight's rival in the Battle of Rhythm. The King of the Ivories could not figure out just how this had happened, how he, a master pianist and bandleader, thirty-two years old, at

12

the top of his game, had been matched against this kitten half his age, this child who was up past his bedtime. The fledgling band would play the first set, Hines's band would follow, and so they would alternate, all night, competing for the crowd's applause. What harebrained publicist, what backstabbing promoter would have put him in this position. Ed Fox of the Grand Terrace? Eddie Plique or Harry Englestein of the Savoy?

What could Hines possibly win from this beanpole kid and his high school band? It was as if Jack Dempsey, in the full glare of Madison Square Garden, should be pitted against some half-starved club fighter from Des Moines. If he beat him up, the crowd's heart would go out to the victim. If he didn't, if the youngster scored *any* points off the old man, he'd look like a young hero . . . Gatemouth smiled at the Savoy. He had been set up. Money was changing hands. Money was always changing hands. Gatemouth was the property of Ed Fox of the Grand Terrace, on loan from the Terrace to the Savoy for two nights in September, the 7th and 8th. Last night the show had gone from 9 to 4 a.m. after the election of the "mayor" of Bronzeville, an annual popularity contest on the South Side. Folks had called this area Bronzeville since the blacks had settled here at the turn of the century.

Hines had been so busy he might not have noticed the little two-by-five-inch ad on page four of the *Chicago Defender* that day:

Battle of Rhythm
Sunday, Sept. 8th

13

Earl Hines and his Orchestra
vs.
Nat Cole, Chicago's Young Maestro,
And his Rogues of Rhythm
2————Bands————2

Gatemouth had to admit it was good marketing. His orchestra was the premier dance band in the Midwest, with nightly network broadcasts from the Terrace Ballroom, and dozens of recordings on the Victor label. And the kid? Somehow he was already famous in Chicago. Almost a year earlier, October 6, 1934, the Negro newspaper the *Chicago Defender* had published a headshot of the fifteen-year-old in a white collar and dark necktie, pouting pretty much like he was doing now, under the words "Plenty Hot," over the news story that "Nat" Cole had "started out a few years ago as just another musician, but today he is known as the leader of one of the hottest bands in the Middle West." Started out a few years ago! How old was he then? Nine? Ten? Now everybody knew that the kid and his band were battling every Sunday afternoon at the Warwick Hall against an older high school bandleader, Tony Fambro. They called Tony "Little Duke" because he modeled his band on Ellington's.

Jazz was bigger than any varsity sport on the South Side of Chicago in 1935. Any boy who could blow five notes on a horn or pluck a fiddle string or bang a pot wanted to be in a band. There were dozens of these outfits, hundreds of them. Somehow Nat Cole, playing in clubs and dance halls from childhood, had set himself apart, above

14

the rest of them.

Everybody liked him, liked to hear him play piano. He had a following. And somebody "up there" liked him too, it seemed, somebody in the upper echelon of the *Chicago Defender*, the weekly newspaper that was the voice, the conscience and the guiding spirit of the South Side. They kept printing his name and his picture in the "Stage-Screen-Drama" section of the paper. On December 15, 1934, they had printed Nat Cole's picture again, this time the brooding, intense face in three-quarter profile, in white tie. It was to publicize the *Defender*'s Midnight Show at the Regal Theatre. This was the seventh annual Christmas Basket Show, all proceeds to go to needy families.

Cole's name already was being used to sell seats in the largest theater on the South Side of Chicago.

"You are sure to like his playing," wrote the journalist, "for he is a second Earl Hines."

Gatemouth smiled, reflectively. Was there enough room in Chicago for another Earl Hines?

GATEMOUTH

To know Nat Cole you must first know Earl Hines, his artistic father.

Earl's teeth were like the white keys of a piano. They called him Gatemouth because his mouth was like the pearly gates and he was always smiling. He smiled because he loved to play piano and he was almost always playing. Sometimes he smiled so hard the muscles in his face would freeze and the smile would stick on his face for an hour or so after the show was over. One of his sidemen would have to massage the smile off his face.

Musicians were already beginning to call Earl Hines "Fatha" at age thirty-two because he had given birth to a style — more than a style, a virtual language — of jazz piano. There were wicked rumors that Hines had an invisible third hand, that he had made a pact with the Devil. Men who had never seen him up close, envious musicians, said that Gatemouth had cut the "webs" between his fingers with a razor blade, so as to give him the extra stretch needed to manage those tenth-interval trills.

Every kid pianist in the Midwest copied Earl Hines.

Little Nat Cole learned to play jazz piano by listening to Gatemouth on the radio. And when the radio blew a tube the boy would sneak out of his apartment on Prairie Avenue, run several blocks through the dark, and stand outside the Grand Terrace nightclub, under the elevated train, and listen to Earl's piano live from there. It inspired him to precocious mastery of jazz.

Hines, too, had been a prodigy, mastering the Czerny exercises and playing Chopin preludes by the age of eleven in Duquesne, Pennsylvania. By the time he was fourteen Hines was winning prizes and getting his picture in the paper. He was drawn to popular music. Earl was living with his Aunt Sadie Phillips when he was in high school, and she dabbled in light opera. Musicians like Eubie Blake and Noble Sissle, renowned pianist/composer Lucky Roberts, and singer Lois Deppe liked to visit Sadie and play on her piano. That is how Earl first heard ragtime and blues.

Mr. Deppe the jazz singer was so impressed with the boy's command of the keyboard he persuaded Earl's father to let him come and live at Lieder House. This was a sort of cabaret and inn in Pittsburgh. There, for fifteen dollars a week, Earl accompanied the singer. Soon Hines organized a band called the Symphonian Serenaders. He watched other pianists. Jim Fellman taught him to make "tenths" with his left hand. Johnny Waters of Detroit could stretch tenths with his *right* hand while playing a little melody with the middle fingers. Young Earl watched, and listened, and stretched his growing hands.

Deppe took him on the train to visit Lucky Roberts in New York. The titanic composer of "Junk Man Rag" lived in a three-room apartment furnished exclusively with pianos. Talk about the musicians' skill in terms of *quantity* must have

17

started with Lucky, who did indeed play a *lot* of piano. He had great big hands, and fingers bigger than most people's thumbs. Lucky would break down your piano. He could, and would, break down anybody's piano, when he got warmed to his work on numbers like "Maple Leaf Rag" or "The Crazy Blues." He made money writing show tunes, most of which went to buy pianos, which he regarded as a disposable commodity like shirt collars and umbrellas. He had a piano for every day of the week, for every mood. To walk through Lucky's rooms was to survey the wreckage of his musical epiphanies.

Earl Hines and Lois Deppe watched Lucky roll up his sleeves and attack one of his torn-out pianos in pursuit of some uncommonly syncopated boogie-woogie; the men ducked and dodged piano keys as they came flying across the room.

By the time Earl Hines arrived in Chicago in 1924 at age twenty, he had recorded eight sides for Gennet, including his own "Congaine," and Lucky's "Isabel." He had formed his own band with Benny Carter on sax and "Cuban" Bennet blowing trumpet. And at twenty-one, Gatemouth had forged a piano style that surpassed that of James P. Johnson and rivaled the work of the great Jelly Roll Morton, the self-styled "Originator of Jazz."

Ferdinand Joseph Morton, a.k.a. Ferdinand La Menthe and "Jelly Roll," born in Louisiana in 1885, moved to Chicago a year before Hines. In the sporting houses of New Orleans's red-light district, Storyville, Jelly Roll fused ragtime, blues, and marches into a foot-stomping, finger-snapping dance music for the piano. His left hand would "stride" out bass rhythms like the drums and saxhorns of a marching band (*oomp-cha, oomp-cha*) while his right hand fingered syncopated melodies and high obbligati.

It was Jelly Roll's stride style of piano that folks danced to in sporting houses and gin mills from New Orleans to Biloxi, in roadhouses and at rent parties from Jacksonville to Mobile, from St. Louis to Kansas City, from San Francisco to Detroit, as Jelly rambled for twenty years before hauling up to Chicago in the summer of 1923.

Jelly Roll came swaggering into a house party and musicians made way for him like the Red Sea parting for Moses. He was a slender and light-skinned Creole, a dapper man utterly without humility. As he took over the piano he would throw his head back and proclaim: "I am the *great* Jelly Roll Morton." Then he would turn his head to the crowd and flash them a smile that lit up the 30-point diamond set in his front tooth. He would pound the keyboard hard with block chords in both hands to establish his authority, then lightly tease with a seductive melody as he again shouted, "I am the great Jelly Roll!" Then the voodoo thunder of the striding bass would start in the left hand and a double-note obbligato or trill in the right hand on a knockout tune like "King Porter Stomp." As he played, Jelly Roll would scream, "I invented jazz! Yes I did! *I* did that!" But by then everybody would be jumping and swinging around the room, and the music was so good nobody cared who had invented it.

Jelly Roll may have created jazz piano. But

Gatemouth Earl Hines was the first grand master of the art, bringing to that complex, many-voiced instrument the volume and harmonic richness it deserves. He drew upon three hundred years of European chording and counterpoint to embellish the dance music of New Orleans. He would free his left hand from the chains of the stride bass, without missing a beat of dance rhythm, using his left to make melodies and harmonies from one end of the keyboard to the other. Upward glissandos, octave slides, he played with a nimble left hand so free of his right that it was hard to believe there was only one man at the piano.

Jelly heard Earl Hines playing solo at the Elite No. 2 Club in Chicago in 1924, before Gatemouth went on the road with Carroll Dickerson's band. A few years later he might have heard Earl at the Sunset Café, a mob-controlled nightclub on 35th and Calumet, playing duets with Louis Armstrong, numbers such as "Muggles" and "Weather Bird Rag."

There in the Sunset Café in 1927 and 1928 the twenty-one-year-old keyboard genius and the twenty-seven-year-old archangel of the trumpet created the seminal rhythmic language of ensemble jazz.

It is fitting that the central act of creation was not a solo or a chorus but a duet: high jazz was born by Satchmo's horn out of Gatemouth's piano. Listening to the masterpieces recorded in those years, "Skip the Gutter" or "West End Blues," you cannot separate rhythm from melody, or divorce the inspiration of the piano from the trumpet's. They greet each other, trade phrases

20

and solos, they harmonize. They fall in love, fight, and make up again. If Jelly Roll Morton heard them at the Sunset Café, or later at the Warwick Hall, where Gatemouth and Satchmo tried, and failed, to start their own gangsterless nightclub, Jelly might well have wondered what God had wrought, what his own invention had come to. These young men were breaking the old wood into kindling and setting the house on fire.

On his birthday, December 28, 1928, Earl Hines and his ten-piece band opened Ed Fox's brand-new Grand Terrace, a Chicago nightclub and dance hall at Oakwood and South Parkway Boulevard. Customers sat on different terrace-like levels on either side of the bandstand. Owner and manager Fox was a stocky Jew with close-cropped hair, a flat nose, and a triangular smile. He had ambitions to be a music impresario.

Puffing on a cigar, he told Hines, "I have a hundred thousand dollars," back when that much could buy more than a million can now. "I'm going to run this place for one year. Whether anybody comes in here or not, you're going to get your money."

For the twenty-three-year-old pianist this was a dream come true. He bought a three-piece suit and a beaver coat. He bought kid gloves and a big gold ring. His contract with Fox guaranteed Gatemouth $150 a week, rain or shine. It was a fortune. Earl and his band began recording for Victor records in 1929. Summers the band toured, playing St. Louis and Earl's hometown, Pittsburgh. WSBC radio began broadcasting

Earl's performances at the Grand Terrace.

In 1932, when business was booming at the Grand Terrace, Al Capone sent five men to pay Ed Fox a visit. They entered without knocking. The first man went straight to the cash register. One stood outside the front door, on guard, one on either side of the building, while the lieutenant of the squad led Fox to the back office.

"We're going to take twenty-five percent," Capone's man told Fox.

"You must be losing your mind," the club owner replied.

When the visitor softly explained that Fox needed protection, and that his wife and little boys also needed protection, Ed Fox found himself without the heart to refuse it.

From that point forward Fox had a partner in the gold mine that was the Grand Terrace, and Earl Hines had two bosses, one of whom was scarface Al Capone. Police never came near the speakeasy. Gangs would come in and try to outspend one another. Al Capone would drop by the club. Earl said hello to him at the door. Capone would lift his hand to straighten the handkerchief in Earl's breast pocket and later Gatemouth would find a hundred-dollar bill there. It was during the reign of Al Capone that Earl Hines got his three-thousand-dollar Bechstein piano. Band members Jimmie Mundy and Trummy Young were amazed how Earl could break strings in the Bechstein with the power of his left hand. Later they would hammer at the Bechstein with their fists and they couldn't do it.

Capone began to think of Gatemouth as property. When Hines went on the road with his band, two bodyguards accompanied him everywhere because Scarface was worried a rival gang might injure Hines to hurt Capone. When the pianist protested he didn't need two bodyguards, Capone shrugged and said it was no big deal, he had thirty of them himself.

Now Gatemouth smiled at the boy called Nat Cole. Did he really want to be a second Earl Hines? Did he know the cost?

During the rule of the gangsters in the 1930s Earl Hines's dream became a nightmare. He was a black songbird in a gilded cage. Hines was one of many great musicians chained to a certain nightclub or theater the way antebellum Negroes were chained to a plantation. The jazz slave masters were mobsters: Owney Madden of Harlem's Cotton Club, Johnny Lazia of Kansas City, and Al Capone in Chicago. The bandstand at the Cotton Club even featured white columns, with a backdrop that depicted the slave quarters and weeping willows of a Southern mansion. The mob network controlled the bookings and salaries of such jazz luminaries as Cab Calloway, Duke Ellington, Jimmie Lunceford, Louis Armstrong, and Earl Hines.

But while Fox and others at the Grand Terrace were getting rich, Gatemouth found himself shackled to a $150-per-week contract that was built to outlast Chicago itself. Through his front man Ed Fox, Capone had a covenant with Hines that would not even allow him to use his own name if he left the Grand Terrace without permis-

23

sion. The contract existed *in perpetuo:* if Fox died, Gatemouth would be the widow's chattel; if she died, the eldest son would inherit the pianist . . .

If it wasn't the gangsters it was the musicians' union complicating Earl's life. Jealous musicians without steady work resented Earl's arrangement with the Grand Terrace. They would mutter under their breath: "Everybody standing around the mail box / While Gatemouth got his pension with Mister Ed Fox." It was bad enough having Al Capone ordering him around, but he was damned if the union was going to tell him where he could play.

So in May of 1933, when the union suspended Hines for playing a nonunion café in St. Louis, he tried to ignore it. He needed money. A month later he played a nonunion gig at a dance in Danville, Illinois, and the union suspended him for a year. That hurt him, and he spent much of the summer of 1933 in the appeal process, getting his colleagues to forgive and reinstate him.

And if it wasn't the gangsters, or the union, it was the women, flirting, distracting, double-timing, loving and leaving him in joy or misery. But that was another story . . .

Through all the toil and trouble Hines at least had his music, his piano, and the orchestra to nourish and sustain him. And he enjoyed the company of bandmates who were great musicians in their own right: Walter Fuller and George Dixon on trumpets, Trummy Young and Louis Taylor on trombones, Budd Johnson and Jimmy Mundy on saxophones, plus Omer Simeon and Darnell Howard, versatile on clarinets and saxes.

Now they were all standing around at the Savoy Ballroom, smoking, drinking, joking, waiting for this new kid Cole to hit the keys and make music. That's what they were all here for, the music, to play it and hear it and dance to it. None of them were getting rich from it.

It was almost nine o'clock, and soon the kid had to begin. A stream of automobiles crawling bumper to bumper north and south on South Parkway Boulevard was unloading passengers — girls in black satin dresses, guys in loose pinstripes and shiny wing-tip shoes. Incredibly, the crowd was still filing into the ballroom, three, four thousand of them, laughing, jostling under the lighted beams of the high ceiling, eddying around the square columns with the plaster Corinthian capitals, maneuvering for a little ground on the dance floor with a clear view of the stage.

There stood the announcer, Eddie Plique, a thin white guy with a pinched face, dark eyes, and a square chin, holding a crumpled piece of paper. Over the din at the Savoy, Eddie Plique introduced the meager band of high school boys that would throw the first punch of the evening . . . "Ladies and gentlemen, Nat Cole and his Royal Dukes!" Applause. "On saxophone, Andrew Gardner, on trumpet, Charles Gray . . . Russell Shores on drums . . . on bass, Mr. Henry Fort, on trombone John Dawkins . . . and last but not least, the Prince of Ivories, Nat 'Schoolboy' Cole!"

At the sound of Cole's name, a roar of affection arose from the audience, and Earl Hines knew he was in trouble. The Schoolboy had the home-court advantage. If this scant band of amateurs

25

could play jazz at all, then it would take enormous finesse and tact for Hines's fourteen-piece orchestra to survive the night with any dignity. It was David vs. Goliath.

Could the kid play? Gatemouth watched the boy as he sat sweating under the bright lights of the bandstand, fronting his ragged orchestra of dented horns, dressed in ill-fitting green suits like their leader's, gripping their instruments in terror as if the dancers were about to open fire on them. What would they play?

The kid jerked his left hand in the air and dropped it. There sounded the dull sputtering of an alto saxophone, and they were off running, the kid nodding on the beat, his arms hanging at his sides as the muted trumpet stated the theme. It was Gatemouth and his arranger Quinn Wilson's version of "Sweet Georgia Brown." Hines might have known the battle of rhythm would be fought with his own weapons. The kid knew him by heart. Maybe he would just echo the master, roughly, in respectful homage. That wouldn't be so bad. Or would it?

"No gal made has *got* a *shade* on . . . sweeet Georgia Brown . . ." No vocal, just the simple tune played by the muted trumpet in a steady moderate tempo and a little doubling at the end of the chorus but nothing too ambitious. Then the sax returned to take over the next chorus, blurting the melody, chewing it up a little while the trumpet harmonized in the fourth line, or commented with obbligati in the fifth and sixth. It wasn't very good playing but it wasn't quite embarrassing either . . .

Then the crowd that had been murmuring and

26

restless grew still. There was a perceptible strain-ing of attention as they heard, somewhere a long way off, ever so faintly through the dense forest of horn growls and blasts, drumrolls, and thumping bass, a ripple of harmony. There was a clear harp in the distance that moved toward them rapidly as the young man at the piano began to brush his long hands lightly over the keys, looking at the crowd slyly out of the corners of his eyes. It was the kid, Nat Cole, entering the Savoy Ballroom through the last bars of the second chorus, come to rescue his schoolboy band from adolescent aimlessness and confusion.

The next chorus was all his, and Cole pounced on it, grabbing up the theme with his right hand in bright clear octaves while keeping a solid stride rhythm with his left hand. That was good, a fine copy of the master, Gatemouth, but how far could he go with it? The crowd was bouncing, nodding in time, and some were calling out encourage-ment. At the fifth bar Cole hit the high note and slid down off it into the middle register with the grace of an otter. Then he bounced back to play three more measures the same, maintaining the melody line within the cascade of glissandos, and the crowd began clapping in time. At the ninth bar the kid threw his right hand far east to grab what-ever notes he could find up there and came down with clams, cherrystones, raw noise. But it hardly mattered as Nat cut the notes into double-eighths, sixteenths. All the while that stride rhythm kept going strong, rocking in the bass, Earl's men were staring and all the kids in the ballroom were on their feet dancing.

Gatemouth smiled in wonder at the kitten on the keys. It would be a long night. The kid had the gift, no question. But how bad did he want it, the music, the moments of glory, the trouble — gangsters, unions, the women? He might have the gift, but he was going to have to fight for it. Tonight and forever.

Who was Nat Cole, this boy who would be King?

FLIGHT OUT OF EGYPT

He was born in Montgomery, Alabama, on St. Patrick's Day, March 17, 1919, and christened Nathaniel Adams Coles. At fifteen he would drop the s from his surname. The authorities in Alabama were lax about recording the births of Negro babies in those days. So there is no birth certificate. Family members recalled the day because of the Irish connection. But in years to come the year of birth would be a matter of dispute, and then dismay for Nathaniel's biographers. The young man would claim birth in 1915, 1916, or 1917, on his marriage license, or in filing with Selective Service, making himself whatever age suited his immediate purposes.

We might still be in a quandary over Nathaniel's birth date except for the diligence of the census taker. Early in 1920 he knocked on the door of the five-room bungalow at 1524 St. Johns Street, where Nathaniel had been born, and found the infant in his lovely mother's arms. She had a round, bright face and slanted eyes like the infant's. Perlina Adams Coles, twenty-eight, informed the census taker that she and her husband, Edward James Coles, thirty-three, were the parents of four children: Eddie Mae, ten; Edward D., eight; Evelina, five; and the babe in arms Nathaniel, age nine months. There would have been twice that number but they died in infancy.

On his broad tablet the census taker also wrote down that the head of the household, Edward, was by profession a wholesale grocer. This was a sensible job for a man with six mouths to feed, because when you are in the food business your family will not go hungry. He was a skilled butcher.

But Edward James had a deep desire to leave the grocer's trade, a desire that was more than an ambition — it was a true vocation. He wanted to serve the Lord, as had his late father-in-law Dan Adams. Edward wanted to preach the gospel in his own church.

How much sacrifice he and his family would have to undergo in order for Edward Coles to realize this dream, we can only guess. We know little about the family's years in Alabama. They lived in a one-story frame house in a poor black neighborhood where the older children went to grammar school. Edward and Perlina's parents were all deceased. Except for Edward's brother Henry they had no relatives in Montgomery. Reverend Dan Adams, who died in 1905, had three sisters, named Comfort, Patience, and Mercy, and brothers named Ruben, Ben, and Joseph, who lived in Birmingham. Years later Nathaniel's sister Evelyn (as Evelina called herself) recalled a trip to Birmingham in 1923. That was the day they said goodbye to Perlina's cousin Hattie Goines Thomas and her daughters, just before leaving Alabama forever, so Papa could serve the Lord in Chicago, Illinois.

Sometime between the census man's visit in 1920, and the spring of 1923, the wholesale grocer Edward Coles decided to give up the comforts of his native Alabama and move his wife and four children to the chilly city of Chicago. This was a bold, romantic move, if not downright foolhardy at his age, to seek a new career in a strange city. Rents for three-room railroad flats on the South Side, where they were bound to live, were astronomical — hundreds a month. There is no evidence that Edward's career as a minister was much more than a dream in 1923, when he uprooted his family and put them on the train to Chicago. We know he had been a "deacon" of the Beulah Baptist Church in Montgomery, reading the lessons, preaching from time to time. Whether he had been ordained as a salaried minister of the Baptist Church before 1923 is a matter of doubt.

They were joining the Great Migration of African-American families from Dixie to the North. Some called it the Flight Out of Egypt, echoing Exodus. Between 1916 and 1919 a half million black Americans left the Southern states for Northern cities. A million more would follow in the twenties.

Although little is known about the Coleses' life in Montgomery, a good deal is known about Alabama in the early 1920s, just after American soldiers returned from World War I. The state was a brutal place for a black man to raise his family. Montgomery had flourished in the bosom of the Confederacy, and many of its citizens seemed unconvinced the North had won the Civil War. The KKK was in its heyday. Beatings and lynchings of blacks were common. A man of color who was fortunate enough not to be lynched or beaten could not expect work for pay equal to the white man's, or equal schooling for his children, or comparable housing.

There was every reason to leave Alabama, and a number of reasons to go to the Windy City. By the time Edward Coles considered it, there was a thriving neighborhood of Alabama blacks on the South Side. Word came home that the streets were paved with gold, the air was filled with music, and, as Langston Hughes said, "the midnight was like day." Chicago was the destination for black families from Alabama, Louisiana, Mississippi, and Arkansas. By the mid-twenties a hundred thousand blacks had gone to Chicago from the South. For many it was the Promised Land. There were jobs. Companies such as the Illinois Central Railroad, the Bessemer steel mills, and the Swift and Armour meat factories welcomed the nonunionized black workers, recruiting the newcomers to break the back of the white unions.

Maybe Edward Coles did have a paying job waiting for him in the Baptist Church in Chicago when he arrived there in 1923. It appears unlikely. The Reverend Coles was not a man to play fast and loose with the truth, and all his life he would tell how he had come to Chicago in that year "to organize the Second Progressive Baptist Church." This was a chapel of the "storefront" variety, two blocks south of the Coleses' first-floor flat on Prairie Avenue. Likely the butcher-evangelist, with a family of six to feed and high rent, chopped meat in the slaughterhouses every hour he was not preaching or asleep.

He had a strong melodious voice, stamina, and a dramatic presence in the pulpit. In that neighborhood of Alabama refugees, Reverend Coles rapidly saved enough souls and preached well enough to make the collection plate ring, fill the pews, and pay himself a living wage. Soon he was a full-time minister of the gospel. His fame grew. A few blocks south at 45th and Dearborn, some fellow Baptists had established the Truelight Baptist Church in 1924. With greater resources, and their own corner church seating two hundred, they invited Reverend Coles to join forces, and he agreed.

So by 1925 Reverend Coles, in the role he longed for, had leapt into the void, risked everything, and landed on his feet by the Grace of the Lord. He was a minister of the Baptist Church and his devoted wife, Perlina, played piano for the choir on Sundays. His four children were attending good schools in the neighborhood, wearing clothes which, if not in the height of fashion, were at least patched to withstand the severe winters. They would never go hungry.

Yet the move from subtropical Alabama to the icebox of Chicago had taken a toll, and the struggle was far from over. Though the family would never admit they were poor, that is what they were, subsisting in that drafty, cracked first-floor flat on Prairie Avenue, poor as church mice.

The eldest child, Eddie Mae, quiet and obedient, had been doing double duty as schoolgirl and nursemaid from the day Perlina began packing to leave Montgomery. Dutiful, maternal as first daughters tend to be in large families, Eddie Mae was on call for her mother day and night, supervising the younger children while her mother shopped, washed clothes, or slept. She cooked and cleaned. In a pinch she could run the household.

Deprived of the Alabama sunlight, the blooming fifteen-year-old began to wither and fade. When the wind was from the northeast it blew bitterly across Lake Michigan and down Prairie Avenue, buffeting the girl as she made her way to school. In the cold winter of 1925, Eddie Mae was so weakened she got pneumonia. Without the medical care she might have gotten in some other part of town, Eddie Mae Coles struggled for breath and passed away.

She left a painful void in the heart of the family, and in Reverend Coles a keen desire to justify the great distance he had traveled to serve the Lord.

On a dark, hard winter day they buried the elder daughter. To cope, Edward threw himself into the work of merging his church with the Truelight Baptist, while Perlina fought to conquer a sorrow greater than any she had ever known. She might have lost her reason but for her faith, and the duty to comfort her younger children, who were grief-stricken and frightened by the specter of mortality.

By instinct the mourning woman would focus her attention on the baby, Nathaniel, the most vulnerable, holding him close so that no harm might come to him.

SCHOOLBOYS

He was a cheerful, agreeable little boy with a wide smile and twinkling eyes, and his mother and sisters adored him. He idolized his older brother, Eddie, and tried to copy him. But they were different. Handsome Eddie had round eyes like his father, and a sly grin; Eddie was boisterous, outgoing, a clown. Nat, on the other hand, was shy and reflective; he spoke with difficulty, stammering, lisping — but what he said was often surprising.

At the end of a long day when he had heard his mother warn him, time and again, to stand clear of the hot potbellied stove, the child heard his father lecture them on the almighty power of the Lord.

"The Lord," the Reverend Coles announced at the dinner table, "can do anything you can think of, move the mountains, dry up the seas, anything . . ."

And a little voice piped up from the other end of the table. "Oh, can he? Anything?" asked the youngest.

"Anything," said the preacher, nodding kindly.

"I b-bet he can't sit down on that hot stove b-bare naked," said Nathaniel.

So the child displayed even at that early age a wit that could make everyone laugh while letting the air out of a platitude.

The Reverend Coles could laugh heartily but he

preferred the jokes not to be made at God's expense. The Devil and the Good Lord battled night and day over the souls of children in South Side Chicago, where gangsters fortified the economy with bootlegging, drug traffic and prostitution, gambling and loan-sharking. The speakeasy was the Devil's headquarters and jazz was his music. The Coleses' apartment building stood only a short stroll from 35th and State Street, Chicago's "gay white way," the Pullman Café, the Vendome, the Grand Theater, and seventy more jazz clubs and dance halls. Temptation was all around them the minute they stepped out the door.

Reverend Coles was not about to lose his war with the Devil on his home ground. A strict disciplinarian, the Reverend insisted upon a high level of propriety. His children must respect and obey their parents, their teachers, and the law; they must love the Lord; they must be loyal to each other; they must avoid bad company and wicked influences; and they must always work — work as hard as possible at the job that needed to be done.

He would send Nathaniel on an errand, to the cobbler to pick up his resoled dress shoes. Dreamy Nathaniel would be back in ten minutes, empty-handed, having left the claim ticket on the piano.

"Use your head, boy," growled his father. "Do the job right. Use your head or you're going to use your feet. You're going to keep coming and going until you use your head and do the job right."

He insisted upon this kind of common sense. And if gentle persuasion failed the Reverend would resort to main force.

As a boy Eddie was pressed into service as or-

36

ganist for the church choir. One day during a long rehearsal, the little musician sat and gazed wistfully out the window at some boys playing ball. Asked for the ninth time to play "Go Down, Moses," or "Swing Low," Eddie balked. He launched into a jazz rendition of "The Volga Boatmen."

This was the climax of an argument that had been raging at home for some time, over the moral purpose of music. Summoned to the pastor's office, the young rebel was reprimanded, spanked, and suspended from choir duty. Not too long after this his little brother Nathaniel replaced him.

Nathaniel and Eddie were alike only in their passion for sports and music. They shared a bedroom in the apartment. The Coleses had an upright piano in the living room, and a radio with glowing amber tubes. Mama's piano played gospel. The radio blew jazz.

All the Coles children learned to play piano at their mother's knee. At twelve, Eddie was already known in the neighborhood for his skill as a pianist and tuba player. He listened in pride and wonder as his four-year-old brother Nat plunked the keys. With both hands the child played "Yes, We Have No Bananas." Hearing the song on the radio, he had picked it out on the keyboard. Nat liked to conduct the radio as he had seen the bandleaders do in Washington Park using a pencil or ruler instead of a baton.

The autumn after Eddie Mae died, Nathaniel's mother walked him around the corner to the Felsenthal Elementary School, at 41st and Calumet, and left him at the door with tearful good-byes. As soon as he could get his hands on a piano he played his theme song, "Yes, We Have No Bananas," and other tunes, to the amazement of his teachers, and the delight of his classmates, who danced merrily around him.

Music — hymns and gospel — was as central to the family's life as prayer, just as music was the heartbeat of Chicago's South Side. The education Perlina began in the home was enthusiastically continued out of doors.

Eddie would soon find himself in a band uniform, a member of the newsboys' band. He earned extra dimes for the family by delivering the *Chicago Defender*, which was the bulletin and the conscience of the South Side. The weekly journal brought courage and solidarity to the African-American community in those years of struggle. And the *Defender*'s engagement in Chicago's life did not end with words on a page. The publisher, Robert Abbott, was so enlightened that he understood the interdependence of art and commerce — that the cultural and economic healths of a people go hand in hand. Abbott knew that music was a key, if not *the* key, to the moral victory everyone worked and prayed for in Bronzeville.

Music inspired the children, just as books did, and it gave them joy in discipline. So in 1925 Robert Abbott went out and looked for the best music teacher and bandmaster he could find, to organize, instruct, and lead a marching band picked from the army of boys who delivered the *Defender* newspaper.

That man was major N. Clark Smith, famous for founding the great bands, orchestras, and chamber ensembles at the Tuskegee Institute in Alabama. The broad-shouldered Major wore double-breasted suits, a pince-nez on a cord, and a handlebar mustache.

Smith was also known as the author of hymns published in Chicago by Lyon and Healy, including "Steal Away to Jesus" and "Couldn't Hear Nobody Pray." Mme. Ernestine Schumann-Heink, a diva with the Chicago opera, donated a house at 32nd and Michigan Avenue. The Major soon transformed the home into a music school and rehearsal hall. Samuel Insull, a Chicago utilities magnate, arranged with Lyon and Healy's music store to supply enough oboes, flutes, English horns, trumpets, trombones, etc., to outfit a seventy-five-piece symphony orchestra.

In that neighborhood, where Louis Armstrong was tuning up his trumpet to high C, where the sound of Jimmie Noone's rippling clarinet and the cascades of Earl Hines's piano solos poured from cabaret windows day and night, every child wanted to play. The Major had no trouble finding volunteers for his band. They fought over the hot instruments like the trumpet and saxophone, but a boy would settle for a piccolo or a tuba, anything to get him into the band, marching in parades from one end of town to the other, in the smart uniforms with gold braid. In no time the ensemble included boys named Lionel Hampton, Ray Nance, Milt Hinton, Bill Oldman, and Eddie Coles.

When Smith was not leading his newsboy band he was hard at work in his new job as bandmaster and music instructor at Wendell Phillips High

School, where Eddie Coles was a freshman. The school, a magnificent edifice of red brick, stood at the head of Prairie Avenue, only a short walk from the Coles apartment, visible through the limbs of stately trees on either side of the street. Bass player Milt Hinton and bandleader Lionel Hampton would recall in old age what they learned in the Wendell Phillips band room. The Major stressed the importance of sight-reading and music theory, but he also made a routine practice of "ear training," so that a player might never take the pitch of a note for granted or commit the sin of playing out of tune. These and other lessons Major N. Clark Smith taught Eddie Coles, whose brother Nathaniel was only a few steps behind him.

Nathaniel Coles was so tall for his age and so precocious, musically, that no one outside of the family ever knew how old he was. Milt Hinton, jolly, large-eyed wizard of the bass fiddle, was in Eddie Coles's class at Phillips though he was born in 1910, two years before Eddie. (Hinton lost two years in transferring from a school in Vicksburg.) Hinton remembers that young Nat Coles used to come to his house once a week to take piano lessons with Mrs. Hinton, after Perlina had taught Nat all she could. The next thing Hinton knew, the kid was showing up in Smith's band room at Wendell Phillips. Somehow Nat managed to persuade the Major to give him a clarinet part in the newsboys' band though he was not yet a newsboy. Hinton recalls that many of the other band members who were sixteen or seventeen years old were angry that this freshman got a clarinet. Hinton himself had to stagger around under a tuba!

Hinton tells the story, laughing, at the age of eighty-seven; the interviewer does not presume to correct him, does not dare to explain that Nathaniel Coles, at the time of the incident, 1928, was not a freshman at Wendell Phillips. He was a fourth-grade student at Felsenthal Elementary, and all of nine years old.

As the elder son, Eddie would lead the rebellion against their stern, pious father. But Nathaniel stood right behind his brother. Entering his teens, Eddie decided he had felt the sting of his father's belt on his backside for the last time. The Reverend kept several of these brown straps hanging in the closet for this purpose. Eddie plotted with Nat to steal the belts, and together they disposed of them in a trash bin behind the laundry around the corner.

The next time the Reverend went for the straps he had more than one reason to be angry.

"Who took the straps?" he asked Nathaniel, the delinquent at hand. And Nat, in a moment of inspiration, spoke the half-truth that his brother, Eddie, had taken them. This so distracted the Reverend he dismissed Nat with a suspended sentence. The father paused to reflect on the value of whipping his boys, and he seems to have given it up then, much to the benefit of the younger.

Mostly the battle was fought on the grounds of music and education. It was a bitter irony to Reverend Coles that his devoted wife, Perlina, had given the boys the ammunition to attack and torment him. He was a man of some learning,

41

hard-earned, and had a great respect for books and education. His dream for his children — one of his reasons for moving North — was for them to go to college. They could become doctors, lawyers, teachers; perhaps one might even become a minister like himself.

Music had seduced, overwhelmed them, spoiling their interest in reading, writing, arithmetic, and prayer. From the day Eddie learned to play boogie-woogie piano he began to lose interest in school. From the hour he learned to pluck a bass, the jazz clubs began to beckon to him in the night. He started climbing out the bedroom window. And who could stop him?

Eddie was no more than thirteen years old when he began escaping to play paying gigs in nightclubs, after his parents had gone to sleep. Nobody knew it at first but his little brother Nathaniel, who at six wanted to go along and play piano too — and he could *play* piano at age six. Eddie would explain to Nat that he couldn't come now but someday he *could* come along, if only he could keep their secret, so that Eddie could get rich and famous, and then they might play together in their own band . . .

The truth is that the dignified red-brick school at the end of Prairie Avenue, Wendell Phillips High, even with Major Smith presiding over the music classes, was no match for the great university of the Bronzeville Jazz Emporiums. What there was to be learned in those smoky caves in that moment of history could not be learned anywhere else on earth, before or since.

The timing of the Coleses' arrival in Chicago

was crucial, providential. It coincided precisely with the greatest gathering of musical genius America has ever known, in its most creative decade. Louis Armstrong arrived in Chicago in the summer of 1922 to join King Oliver's Dixieland band at Lincoln Gardens. Jelly Roll Morton came to town in 1923 to record with the New Orleans Rhythm Kings and stayed to organize his Red Hot Peppers. Gatemouth Earl Hines set down roots soon after Jelly Roll. The enchanting clarinetist Jimmie Noone had come up at about the same time as King Oliver, to play with him.

The jazz train roared into Chicago in 1923, bearing the avatars of the Golden Age of Jazz, brass, reeds, and rhythm, and the Coles brothers were on that train. The boys had the musical instinct to realize it, and all the Reverend's sermons and lectures and whippings were powerless to prevent it. Their fate was sealed.

By the time Eddie was sneaking out the bedroom window to gig at the Apex or the Pullman Café, Fats Waller was playing piano at the Vendome, Eddie South (the "Dark Angel of the Violin") was at the Moulin Rouge Café, and Cab Calloway was singing at the Grand Theater. Satchmo and Gatemouth had commenced their epoch-making duets and duels at the Sunset Café.

How could a young musician sleep with such a racket all around him, within walking distance?

Over on South State Street the commercial area from 31st to 39th streets was known as "the Stroll." Black and white "sports" came from all over town dressed in their finery to see and be seen in the glaring neon and arc light of the cabaret and theater district. A short five-block walk north from 39th Street would bring Eddie to the corner of 35th and State. This was the heart of Bronzeville and the center of "sporting life" on the South Side of Chicago. The Monogram Theater, a vaudeville house, stood on the east side of State Street. Ma Rainey sang there, and Stovepipe Johnson. If you wanted to see a picture show you could take in a Mack Sennett at the State Theatre, or a serial such as *The Perils of Pauline*, with mood music by a sleepy pianist and tipsy drummer.

But the real action was in the notorious cabarets, like the Sunset and Al Capone's all-night Plantation Café. These were called the "black-and-tans" after an old slang phrase used during Reconstruction to describe Republican leagues of blacks and whites. In these clubs the races mingled, listened to jazz bands, flirted. The chief attraction for slumming white customers was the spectacle of blacks and whites dancing together. It was dangerous, erotic. In a segregated city such clubs were essential channels for interracial contact. Jazz rhythm provided a structure for chaotic emotions; jazz harmony assuaged the fear of racial violence. The music, served up with bootleg whiskey, was a quick solution for the disorder and antagonism of urban life. Glorified by some as "the embodiment of culture," the cabarets were damned by others as "immoral entertainment of the lowest type." The black press railed against the flesh trade along the Stroll, especially what was called "the white plague": white men in search of colored women, and white female hookers looking for customers among black men. Interracial prostitution was big business in the neighborhood.

Handsome, big for his age, an impulsive comedian, Eddie Coles could go wherever he wanted. He went to the Apex Club, where pudgy, light-skinned Jimmie Noone was purling fantasies on his clarinet. He went to Capone's Plantation Café and listened to the Dixie Syncopators. "Wailing, pulsating," *Variety* called them, "jazz with no conscience," so loud you could listen to it in the alley half a block away — Barney Bigard crying out on tenor sax, the amazing Kid Ory following him on trombone. Variety warned that white women were not safe in the club. This must have been because of the white gangsters in there, as most of the black men were on the pavement outside selling gin for $3.00 a pint and bonded bourbon for $8.00, or they were up on the bandstand playing jazz for the dancers.

Eddie loved to watch the dancers at the Plantation do the Snake Hips, the Itch, the Grind, and the Mess Around. Now and then the joint would get raided, but it was all in fun; the thrill of drinking in a black-and-tan that might be busted added a certain spice to the experience.

On Christmas night of 1926, several hundred men and women at the Plantation were doing a dance called the Black Bottom, which required strenuous movements below the waist. Twenty policemen burst through the doors led by a Detective Shoemaker. The Chief of Detectives described the dance as an immoral exhibition, "particularly vicious in its effect upon white women."

Of course, the police also said the dancers of the Black Bottom had been drinking intoxicating beverages. They found bottles under the tables and on top of the tables. As a member of a religious family, a minister's son, Eddie Coles was probably not present in the Plantation on Christmas night of 1926. But it was a scene he would have found familiar.

Catercorner from the Plantation was the glowing neon of the Sunset Café, where Eddie wanted to go most of all because that is where he could hear cornetist Louis Armstrong. Louis was so loud and clear that you could hear him even if you couldn't see him. But it was much better to see him because he was so funny. Louis was such a natural clown that it took people a while to realize he was a genius. With his saucer-shaped bright eyes and his big lips pulled back over his white teeth in a grin and his hair combed down into bangs, he looked funny. And with his round belly, Louis looked about six months pregnant. He did crazy things with his horn too. He could make it sound like a police siren, a foghorn, a sick dog, a thunderstorm. He could make it sound like a trombone, a clarinet, or a saxophone, mocking every instrument in the orchestra.

When Louis first came to Chicago he was playing second cornet to King Oliver at Lincoln Gardens on 31st Street. Musicians came from all over town to check it out and they could have died laughing. Louis was about twenty-three and he looked like a big kid in a black tuxedo. King Oliver would play a chorus on his cornet while Louis sat in his chair looking like he was bored, or asleep.

Suddenly he would jump out of his chair and blow four bars or eight bars on his horn that were either a perfect echo of King Oliver or the perfect answer, and then he would sit down again, on his sheet music. That was part of what was so hilarious, the way Louis sat on his sheet music while everyone else read the notes. He'd sit and grin at the audience and wink his eyes and then leap up again and play like an angel.

It was funny, and it was scary — the way Oliver and Armstrong were playing, taking duet breaks, improvising, riffing off each other without colliding harmonically, never looking at the book. They were the talk of the town. Young Bix Beiderbecke couldn't figure it out, nor could Paul Whiteman, or the whole membership of the colored musicians' union, Local 208. They packed the Lincoln Gardens nightly to hear King Oliver and Satchelmouth Armstrong playing the "Weather Bird Rag" and "Alligator Hop," trading harmonic breaks like Dixieland twins.

Louis wore these thick-soled police-issue shoes that made a clomping sound as he walked into a room. He walked with a bounce like a six-year-old kid trying to get attention. He got plenty. First thing you knew, every cornet player in Chicago was wearing ugly black shoes like Louis, talking like him, trying to play like him. Nobody could play like him. When he sang "When you're smiling" he could make you laugh and cry at the same time while giving you this sunny moment of perfect peace. You would never know that he was already playing with Al Capone's gun to his head.

Armstrong was incredibly kind and generous

47

with everyone, especially children. They called him Pops. He lived around the corner, only a few blocks away from the Coleses, at 421 East 44th Street with his second wife, Lil Hardin, a pianist. On warm summer afternoons you could see Armstrong strolling through the alleys of Bronzeville in a white undershirt, khaki pants, white socks, and black slippers, carrying his trumpet case, the children following behind him like the Pied Piper. He would stop in somebody's kitchen yard, sit on a swing, and declare, "I want you kids to listen to some pretty tunes." Then he would take the trumpet from the case, fix a mute on it, and begin to blow. Pops would swing back and forth and play for the children for an hour, sometimes two hours. That was how he practiced. Then he'd hand out dimes to the kids to pay them for their time.

If Eddie Coles was lucky, he might squeeze in the back door of the Sunset Café and hear Pops play trumpet in Carroll Dickerson's band, with Gatemouth Earl Hines on piano, Pete Briggs on bass, the legendary Honoré Dutry on trombone, and Tubby Hall on drums. If Eddie caught Pops's eye, the great man would smile on him in benediction.

For the time being, his little brother Nathaniel would have to settle for the stories Eddie told, in the wee hours, of his escapades along the Stroll and his encounters with the jazz giants. But it would not be long before Nathaniel gained the freedom to enter that fabulous world on his own.

On July 13, 1927, Duke Ellington's "Black and Tan Fantasy" was on the radio. So was Al Jolson's

"Me and My Shadow." Babe Ruth was on a pace to hit sixty home runs, and Al Capone was on a pace to make $105 million, the highest income ever recorded by a private citizen — $35 million more than Henry Ford ever made in his best year. Charles Lindbergh was still beaming from his triumph over the Atlantic Ocean.

And on that day in the sultry heat of the Chicago summer, Perlina Coles gave birth to a new baby boy. They named him Isaac, the Hebrew word for laughter. It was a time of celebration for the family, a life-affirming event that at last subdued the lingering grief over Eddie Mae's passing.

For Nathaniel Coles this was a time of growth and the promise of freedom. He was no longer the baby of the family or the main object of his mother's attention and concern. His gentle sister Evelyn, at twelve, was the right age to help with the newborn. Young Nat would be free to run after Eddie.

But Eddie had plans of his own that could not always include Nathaniel, no matter how well he played piano or how tall he was for his age. Eddie was rapidly spinning out of control. The presence of a newborn sibling was enough to push him out of the nest. According to his own account, it was in the school year after Isaac's birth that Eddie Coles got his first big career break. A bandleader named Vernie Robinson invited the high school bass fiddler to join his orchestra, the Syncopators, to play an engagement in Madrid.

Eddie could not leave Wendell Phillips and go to Spain without his parents' permission, if not their blessing. And so he set the case before them that night over dinner. The Reverend Coles did a slow burn and then exploded. Perlina, nursing the baby, listened as Edward the Elder railed against jazz, bass fiddles, Spain, against modernity itself and the wicked Syncopators. When her husband had finished, mild Perlina simply said they should let the boy go and play his music. He was almost a man. Eddie pleaded. This was the chance of a lifetime.

Loving his brother as he did, Nathaniel must have been appalled by the quarrel. He would hate to see Eddie go away. But wasn't it true that here there were too many mouths to feed? And out there was the chance to play, to learn, to make money and see the world? The Reverend was obstinate in his refusal to let Eddie leave school. Perlina was equally stubborn, knowing in her heart nothing could hold her son back.

According to Eddie Coles, one of his aunts (was it Aunt Patience or Aunt Mercy?) visiting from Birmingham at last influenced the Reverend to change his mind.

So in a matter of months Nathaniel went from being the baby of the family to being the elder son, with a room and window all to himself. No longer would he have to fight Eddie for the piano.

Every morning Nat got dressed next to the stove. He would walk out the door with his lunch in his hand, down Prairie Avenue to 41st Street, and turn east, passing under the street trestle of the South Side branch of the elevated. Sometimes the train came thundering overhead and he would count the cars. His head was full of music, piano, trumpet, human voices, and the elevated train made a kind of music too. He went to the four-room schoolhouse around the corner every day, attending to his reading and writing and arithmetic dutifully, obediently, but without enthusiasm, because he could not wait to get back to the piano.

BUD BILLIKEN DAYS

Letters came from Eddie Coles in 1928 with strange postmarks: from Spain; from Portugal, where the band broke up in Lisbon. He joined a road show directed by Lou Douglas that took the young bass player from Italy to Russia. Eddie would not come home that year or the next.

Meanwhile ten-year-old Nathaniel was growing so fast they could scarcely keep him in shoes and breeches. Because he was shyer than Eddie, or due to better surveillance, Nat had not yet crept out the window into the starry night of jazz. He would find his way with less open rebellion than Eddie. Nat was a boy wonder, a virtuoso adored in a neighborhood that cherished and cheered its children.

On a rainy Saturday afternoon in late November 1928, Nat joined a parade of four thousand youngsters marching from the *Chicago Defender*'s building at 35th and Indiana, bound along South Parkway for the Regal Theatre. They were all card-carrying members of the Bud Billiken Club, and there wasn't a child in Bronzeville who wished to be anywhere else.

The boys and girls danced and splashed in the puddles. The Wendell Phillips High School band led the way playing "It Ain't Gonna Rain No More" and "We Choose to Be Billikens," ahead of a squad of patrolmen. Behind the police guard rolled the flag-draped automobiles of publisher Robert S. Abbott and his lawyer, Nathan McGill, escorted by two motorcycle cops.

The windows and sidewalks of houses along the parade route thronged with spectators who cheered as Robert Abbott passed by. Fifty cars wrapped with blue crepe and red ribbon followed Abbott's, honking their horns, and in each car at least six children could be seen hanging out the windows singing and shrieking at the tops of their voices.

The next division of the parade was the marching foot soldiers of Billikens from the Wabash Avenue YMCA, the South Side Boys Club, and groups from Jackson, Douglas, Mosley, Forrestville, and a dozen more neighborhood playgrounds. "The rain did not dampen the spirit of these youngsters who marched through the rain and mud to the Regal Theatre," wrote a reporter from the *Defender*. A siren wailed from the ambulance of W. T. Brown's funeral company, attracting hundreds more citizens to the crowd that mobbed the sidewalks along the way.

The children were marching to Bud Billiken's First Regal Party in the magnificent theater on 47th Street. Four hours of entertainment would begin with "Garbage" Rodgers the comedian, then came Sammy Williams playing the pipe organ. At two o'clock they showed a Lon Chaney movie. After that the Regal Symphony played the overture from *Rose Marie*, and curtains opened on the stage show: Garbage Rodgers in a one-act play, followed by musical acts that included the Harlem Red Hots, the Regalettes, and Albertine

53

Pickens. Then came the Bud Billiken hour: a shoelacing contest, a dancing contest, a barrel-boxing contest in which the boys had to stand in barrels and try to knock each other down, and finally a greased-pole climb. A five-dollar bill was stuck on top the slick pole as a prize.

After the prizes had been awarded, Robert Abbott thanked the children for making the day a success. He announced that many surprises were in store for them in the months and years ahead. "We are planning a picnic for this summer," announced Abbott, "if you remain loyal Billikens." He urged the children to write letters around the state, expanding the community of Billikens.

"There is no color line in the Billiken Club. Kids of all races may join and enjoy the same privileges."

The publisher was as good as his word, and Nathaniel found a great deal to look forward to in his years as a club member. Abbott never tired of looking for new ways to educate and entertain the black children of Chicago. Bronzeville was populated by families like the Coleses that had fled the Southern workhouses and lynch mobs in order to make a better life. As Milt Hinton says: "It was not the idlers or the no-goods that took their families all that way to Chicago." The way they helped each other — in housing, job hunting, and child care — was inspiring and often ingenious. At the center of this movement was the *Chicago Defender*, Abbott's newspaper.

Back in 1923 Abbott decided it would be a good idea to have a children's column. Ten-year-old Willard Motley (later to write *Knock on Any Door*) was first editor of the column, named "The Billiken" after the Chinese guardian angel of children. A photo of Motley, wearing horn-rimmed glasses and an eyeshade, appeared under the masthead. The page featured jokes, puzzles, cartoons, and stories — and, most important, the exchange of letters between Bud Billiken pen pals. Any child could become a member just by writing to ask for a free membership card and button. It was the Mickey Mouse Club of its time.

When young Motley complained that his column was interfering with his schoolwork, the grown-up David W. Kellum took over. Kellum edited the page for twenty-five years, during which the Billikens numbered more than a quarter of a million children from Chicago to Africa; its members included Lionel Hampton, Milt Hinton, Ray Nance, and Nathaniel Coles. Kindly, slender Kellum, with his narrow, wise face and bright bespectacled eyes, eventually became Bud Billiken to the children who read his page.

Bud Billiken would see to it that Nathaniel and his friends *always* had something to look forward to: a parade, a party, a theater show, concert, or picnic. Even after the stock market crashed in October 1929 and so many fathers were out of work, Bud Billiken was faithful. Dempsey Travis, who grew up with Nat, says that next to Christmas the children most looked forward to the Billiken Day Picnic in August and the Thanksgiving and Easter parties at the Regal Theatre. These were the gala seasonal events of the 1930s. But hardly a month went by without a movie, concert, or stage show for the children.

As we know from his hiring of Major Smith to lead the newsboys' band, Robert Abbott understood the role of music in the life of the South Side. So did Bud Billiken. He gave his children the chance to hear the great jazz performers of the day in live performance. And Bud would give hopeful musicians like Nat Coles their moment in the spotlight, a chance to play on the million-dollar stage of the Regal Theatre, for the applause of thousands.

On a hot saturday morning in August of 1931, Perlina Coles sat in a rocking chair fanning herself. She was seven months pregnant with her sixth child. Eddie was still in Europe playing bass for Noble Sissle's band; Evelyn, now sixteen, sulked because the Reverend would not let her go dancing at the Savoy Ballroom; the Reverend was writing his sermon for the next day. It would be nice if Nathaniel would help with little Isaac, but Nathaniel was going to the Bud Billiken Picnic in Washington Park.

From the sirens of the motorcycle police and ambulances, and the squads of Cadillacs blowing their horns up and down South Parkway just before parade time, you would have thought a city block had caught fire.

The parade of 35,000 children and parents was three miles long; starting at 35th Street, it ended at the duck pond at 52nd Street in the park. A twenty-five-piece band from the South Side Boys Club, a drum and bugle corps of Boy Scouts, flowery floats with *tableaux vivants*, buses, trucks, and fancy touring cars rolled by, followed toward the rear by a flag-draped maroon-colored Lincoln limousine. In the limo sat Bud Billiken, his son, his secretary, and the Billikens' chief patron, undertaker W. T. Brown.

And in the car behind them rode the great Duke Ellington.

Nathaniel was glad to be tall, as he darted along the parade route to gaze at Edward Kennedy Ellington. Duke rode in an elegant red Pierce-Arrow sedan with his parents and his son Mercer, who was Nat's age. The Duke stood up and bowed as the crowd cheered him. His manager, Irving Mills, surveyed the crowd, wondering how many would come to the show at the Oriental Theatre.

Another official car followed, bearing the most generous patrons, the Vinebergs of L. Fish Furniture, Abe Tannenbaum of the Five-Cent-to-a-Dollar Store, and behind them came the marching ranks of happy Billikens.

The crowd of 35,000 poured into the park, jamming around a huge wooden platform set up near the duck pond. Radio comedians Amos 'n' Andy headlined the list of hosts; Lightnin' was there too and Tim Moore (later known as Kingfish) to make the folks laugh. Under the noonday sun everyone would cheer and dance to the music of Lucky Millinder and his Cotton Club Band; one of their own, Lucky had gone to Wendell Phillips. Now he was Al Capone's "man with the band" in Cicero. There were chocolate ice-cream bricks by the thousands and candy bars by the truckload. There would be a bathing beauty contest and a basketball game and fried chicken and potato salad. But the highlight of the day for boys like Nathaniel was the Duke and his band.

They called him Duke but at thirty the handsome bandleader was already the "King of Jazz." His natural gifts were prodigious, awe-inspiring. Tall, clean-featured, with his pencil mustache, he looked like movie star, like a Melanesian god. Master pianist, composer, arranger, conductor — the aristocratic Ellington was all of these things because he wanted to be, he *could* be, not because he had to. Before this he was a prize-winning graphic artist and made a living at that. With his looks he might have acted on the stage. It seemed unfair that Nature would lavish so many gifts on one black man when so many were deserving. How lucky for them he chose to play music, today, for the crowd at Washington Park.

What would the Duke play? In an effort to hear, Nathaniel pressed through the crowd as close to the wooden stage as he could get. To please the Billikens the Duke would perform tunes they had heard on the radio, jump tunes like "Tiger Rag" and "Hot and Bothered." To get the dancers limbered up, he kicked things off with a chase number like "Hot Feet," its scat vocals answered by the trumpet of Freddy Jenkins for a couple of choruses, then working up to a blistering duet of Joe Nanton's wah-wah trombone and Wellman Braud's double-time walking bass.

After a few songs the kids were hysterical. When Duke had gotten them quieted down he played his new hit, "Mood Indigo." The sweet, melancholy sound of Artie Whetsol's trumpet soared out over the trees into the summer sky and clear to the horizon. Returning to weave harmony with Nanton's trombone and Barney Bigard's low clarinet, that blue-shaded trumpet created a longing in the audience that transcended sadness, stole them away and brought them home again.

Duke played the piano but it was hard to hear through the crowd in the open air. Besides, the orchestra was Duke's instrument. They played and played, but for that crowd it would never be enough. As thrilled as Nathaniel had been to hear the Duke, he was so sad when the band packed up and the day was over — thrilled and sad and full of longing.

Nat wanted to be a bandleader, a pianist and composer like Duke Ellington. So he spent every spare minute of his waking life practicing piano or daydreaming about it. He did his best to help his father out by playing the organ in church. And the flock liked to hear this boy improvise, as he delivered gospel variations that expressed the emotional cadences of the Reverend's sermons. But it was jazz, "too much on the hot side," Nathaniel would recall, and this made his father scowl. "Tone it down, son, or take the consequences."

He would take the consequences, as his brother Eddie had. But in the autumn of 1931, twelve-year-old Nathaniel Coles did not wish to trouble his parents. Times were never harder than in 1931 — nine million people out of work and twenty-three hundred bank failures — and another baby was on the way. Every morning Nat went to school. Every afternoon he practiced piano. At night, listening to Earl Hines on the radio, live from the Grand Terrace, a few blocks away, he was tempted to climb out the window; but he was a good boy.

On October 15, 1931, his mother gave birth to another son, Lionel. But all Nathaniel could think about was the Thanksgiving Party that Bud Billiken had promised. Everybody in town was talking about it. Earl Hines was the greatest jazz pianist in the world; he could play more piano in a minute than anyone else could play in an hour. Nat idolized him. Now old Bud had persuaded Earl, his moaning saxophones, his wailing cornets, and his laughing trombones to play for the Billikens at the Thanksgiving Party at the Regal.

He would get to hear Earl Hines live. And maybe Hines would hear *him*, Nat Coles, during the show's talent contest, which he planned to enter. Billikens who could sing, dance, play an instrument, or juggle would take their turns on the million-dollar stage of the Regal. The twenty afforded the most applause would each win a fat turkey donated by the South Center Department Store. If Nat could bring home a pink turkey for Thanksgiving by playing jazz piano it might lighten everyone's spirits.

The Regal Theatre, which would be the scene of Nat's early triumphs, was a pleasure dome of oriental splendor. Built in 1928, a boom year at the height of movie mania, the Regal was designed to inspire fantasies of imperial wealth and romance, if not delusions of grandeur. The style was Spanish baroque; the great recessed arch over the marquee and the double arabesques of the facade showed heavy Moorish influence. The outer lobby alone was larger than most theaters. Fifteen hundred people could stand waiting there, under a vaulted ceiling composed of 69,000 crystals that shed a dazzling light, before a wide marble staircase that led to the mezzanine.

From the lobby you passed into a foyer with ornate plaster cornices and a marble floor like a grand checkerboard. Here were the coatroom, candy counter, and rest rooms. And there were leather chairs and couches, and romantic paintings. The statue of Sira, the pretty black girl, stood bare-armed in her Roman dress, inspecting the brand on her shoulder that marked her as a slave. You passed the slave girl to enter the theater.

The Regal auditorium had 3,500 seats covered in red velvet. Your eyes lifted to the dome, shaped like an inverted daisy, a sky-wide tent of gay damask stripes with folds and slits through which you could glimpse the midnight heavens. The walls were bronze-colored, the side boxes were silk-draped. Poles on either side of the stage appeared to support this "tent." The stage curtains were trimmed with rhinestones that glittered in the radiance of an electric-lighted crown, high in the center of the proscenium.

Under this dome Nathaniel would see Hines play for the first time. On this stage Nat would play for his first great audience.

At last the day arrived.

On Saturday morning, November 21, 1931, Nathaniel rose early to get in line at the Regal. The crowd began forming at eight o'clock and he did not want to miss his chance to play in the contest. He stood under the marquee and watched as the parade of 2,000 arrived at 47th Street from the West Side, buses, trucks, marching bands, and, in a flag-draped car at the head of the procession, Dave Kellum, Bud Billiken himself.

The doors opened at noon, and the crowd pressed into the lobby. At one o'clock the theater seats were all taken. A fire marshal, a battalion chief, and two dozen policemen were called to the theater to maintain order. The marshal asked the children if they would share their seats with the boys and girls outside. When they agreed, the doors opened again and another 3,000 children squeezed into the auditorium.

They watched an *Our Gang* comedy and a Western called *Riders of the Purple Sage*. They heard Hortense Hall play the Barton organ. According to reporters, by the time Earl Hines and his band took the stage there were 8,000 people under the dome of the Regal Theatre and another 4,000 listening outdoors.

Hines and his men all dressed in white from collar to shoes, except for dark four-in-hand ties. Hines sat sideways at the piano with his knees pointing out, and he smoked a cigarette while he played. Great handfuls of notes, rivers of notes poured from the white piano, making his solo instrument equal at times to the whole orchestra.

There is no record of what Hines played for Nathaniel and the other Billikens that Saturday afternoon — maybe "Everybody Loves My Baby" or "Black Bottom Stomp." But it is certain that Nat had never seen or heard anything like it. Long after this he would copy Earl Hines — the cigarette, the sideways seat at the piano, the rivers of notes.

When Hines and his orchestra were gone from the stage it was time for the amateur hour. Forty contestants were vying for the twenty turkeys, so there was little hope the great man would stick around to hear Nat Coles. Yet the boy waited his turn, thrilled to be following Hines on that stage, sharing Hines's audience, playing Hines's piano. His pulse raced, he bit his nails. As each contestant heard his name announced, he entered the spotlight to sing or play, and the crowd welcomed the newcomer with warm applause. But soon came the verdict. The performers the crowd loved got foot stomping, cheers, and loud clapping. Those they disliked got silence, or sometimes booing, though Bud Billiken discouraged this as poor sportsmanship. Bud would give you a pat on the back or hand you a fat turkey.

What did Nat play for the crowd of 8,000 under the Regal's dome? Probably something he had heard Earl do on the radio, something simple like "Sweet Sue" or "Basin Street Blues." From the moment his hands hit the keyboard the crowd knew the turkey was his.

According to the Coles family legend, "every year Nat won the Thanksgiving turkey," so that Perlina could practically figure this into the household budget. The earliest photograph of the boy shows him smiling broadly, in a group of Billikens, dressed in a suit, holding a fresh turkey. Though we lack the exact dates, it is safe to say that Nat's efforts in these tournaments, which he may have entered as early as 1929, and continued as late as 1933, met with growing enthusiasm and echoing applause. Cheered first as a child prodigy, he became a crowd favorite, a pianist to watch, a rising star. If he stopped competing for turkeys at age thirteen it was because he no longer could be considered an amateur.

But on the Saturday evening of November 21, 1931, Nat Coles, coming home with the turkey, received a hero's welcome. Even his father the Reverend must have been pleased, and not only for the bounty. The cash donations from Bud Billiken's Thanksgiving Party would be given to charity, to feed Chicago's unemployed of all races. Playing jazz, his son had served the Lord.

ON THE TOWN

After sharing the spotlight with Earl Hines, playing for the applause of 8,000 at the Regal Theatre, Nathaniel was not quite the same boy.

If he had been content with his schedule of classes, piano lessons, and household chores, pleasing his parents while dreaming of glory, now he was not. He was impatient to enter the world he wanted, that wanted him. If his parents had been concerned that he might follow in his brother Eddie's footsteps, now they had good reason. By the time Nathaniel encountered Hines again on the Regal stage a year later, November 19, 1932, his imitation of the master was adept because he had been studying Hines up close.

He had begun climbing out his bedroom window in the night. Now it was his turn to walk under the neon lights of "the Stroll" and hear the music coming from the "black-and-tan" cabarets. Louis Armstrong was in town from February till June 1933 playing one-nighters under the direction of Zilner Randolph, all over town, including the new Panama Café on South Prairie Avenue.

Unlike Eddie, Nathaniel had a favorite destination very close to home, the Grand Terrace Ballroom on South Parkway, one block north from his house, where Hines and his orchestra played almost every night.

Shy and poor, Nathaniel could neither pay nor

talk his way into the mob-controlled Grand Terrace. So in good weather he stood in the alley south of the long brick building to hear the clear octaves of Hines's solos. And if it rained Nat went to stand under the tracks of the elevated that passed east and west over the alley. You could hear the music almost as well from there unless a red-eye train roared overhead.

Sometimes he would go alone, and other times he went with friends, other teenage musicians. They might meet at 35th Street and South Parkway, near the granite shaft with four bronze figures of Negro soldiers, the memorial to heroes of the Colored Regiment who died in France. The boys would stroll, look at women, and argue about music. They would smoke cigarettes and maybe drink a little gin. After listening to Earl Hines they might walk down to 47th, a corner alive with people at all hours. Down the small side streets you could smell smoke of chicken and spareribs barbecuing over wood fires; you could smell sweet potato pie and gumbo, mustard greens and chitterlings. Little shops sold mystic charms and potions, mojos and John the Conquer Root. Blues music moaned from the taverns.

Despite his stammering shyness Nat was developing a subtle power of leadership. His ambition was like a magnet — other boys wanted to play music with him, hang out with him.

He entered Wendell Phillips High in September of 1933 nearly grown, six feet tall, and a schoolmate recalls that he already had the attraction of a high school football star. Though not exactly handsome, the boy was striking, with his wide-set, slanted eyes, shy smile, and very graceful physique that flattered whatever he wore. According to one account, the Coles boys were so poor they wore secondhand army and navy trousers, but Nat made his clothes look good. Though he was a good sandlot baseball player he was not a varsity athlete. His charisma was not the glow of a sports hero. It was the halo of the musician he had found on the stage of the Regal Theatre. Girls swooned over him, and other boys spoke of him in hushed tones with a mixture of awe and envy.

A review of his high school record shows he was taking what was then called a "general science sequence" and "his classes included English, Geometry, Botany, Spanish, Physical Education and Music. His music grades were about par with his other grades and he took only the required music classes." School principal Byron Minor states that "he was satisfactory in scholarship. He was not an honor student; neither was he failing." Mr. Minor is discreet, officially bound to be no more specific, but seems eager to add that "Nat was already playing professionally in South Side night clubs." This extracurricular activity, like football, might explain away mediocre scholarship. Tim Black sat in the seat in front of Nat every morning in homeroom. He remembers that Nat was polite and rather shy, and music was all he and his friends ever talked about.

Byron Minor is very specific about one matter and it is illuminating. Nathaniel Coles entered Phillips High School in September 1933 and attended there until 1934. He entered again in the autumn of 1934, and on November 28, 1934, he left school, never to return. Record clerk Henry Springs affirms: "He left, he did not go to another school . . . he would have graduated in 1936 but we have no record of his returning . . . Nat was a dropout."

Tim Black recalls the day Reverend Coles came to school with Nat to discuss an alternative schedule that might enable the boy to stay in school while he kept working. After all, it was the Great Depression. The principal was understanding but firm: there would be no exceptions for child prodigies at Wendell Phillips. The boy would go to school like other boys or not at all.

His parents' worst fears would be justified. Measuring himself against his wandering brother, young Nat would not stay in high school a month longer than Eddie had.

For Nathaniel this was a period of intense growth as a musician, and increasing pressure at home, as the young adult sought his identity, fought for his freedom. He made a pact with his father: he could play jazz on his own time if he would play hymns in church on Sunday. But the tension was still irksome. His parents worried. Where did the money come from for all the cigarettes he was smoking? High school was a drudgery and a bore but he went, dutifully, while he could. And in one way we know Wendell Phillips helped Nat Cole's musical education. That was in the band room of Walter Henri Dyett.

Major N. Clark Smith, the band director, had moved away to St. Louis. But his student, Captain Walter Dyett, carried on his work. Born in 1901, the Captain graduated from the University of California, where he was first violinist in the symphony. He played violin, clarinet, and bassoon in churches and concert halls around Chicago, but his greatest contribution was as a teacher and bandleader.

The Captain was much like his mentor, Major Smith, but not so patient. Sad-eyed, slender, the Captain was famous for his quick temper and his colorful language. Over the years his pupils included Ray Nance, Johnny Griffin, Benny Green, Ahmad Jamal, and the pianist Dorothy Donegan. He was so good, Tim Black recalls, he would throw kids out of class, and they would *beg* him to let them back, as mean as he was. The late Dorothy Donegan said: "His ear was so sensitive he could hear a mosquito piss on a bale of cotton. Out of a hundred-piece band he could tell just who made the mistake. You'd know it because he would stare at you with his one good eye and make you feel like a snail. Music was a matter of life and death." If he could not get through to them any other way the Captain would throw his baton. He was notorious for his accuracy with the baton.

There is a great deal of anecdotal evidence from Donegan, Tim Black, Gwendolyn Dyett (Walter's widow), and others that Nathaniel Coles's musical training, particularly sight-reading and ear training, took place under that hard taskmaster, Walter Henri Dyett.

But Nathaniel was burning the candle at both ends. If Captain Dyett caught him catnapping in the rhythm section of the band, it was because the boy wonder was going to "night school." In 1934 Nat Coles was enrolled in the swinging University of the Bronzeville Jazz Emporiums. The repeal of Prohibition in December 1933 created a momentary euphoria in the depths of the Depression. For a while the golden hooch and jazz in the cabarets flowed more freely than ever. New clubs opened and an exodus of musicians to New York left room for newcomers in the South Side bands.

Nat could hang out at the Midnight Club on South Indiana, and sit in with clarinetist Jimmie Noone and Franz Jackson on tenor sax. Whenever young Benny Goodman was in town he would be there too in the wee hours studying Jimmie Noone, trying to capture Noone's wailing, lyrical soul tone. But Goodman could never quite get it. "His sound was so beautiful he made my efforts sound like I was playing a set of plumbing pipes," said Franz Jackson. Nathaniel loved gentle Jimmie, especially the way he intoned "Sweet Loraine."

Nat could follow Noone to the Lido, or the Sunset Café, or when Jimmie entered a battle of the bands against Hines at the Savoy. In the Cotton Club on the top floor of the Arcade Building, Nat could hear Walter Barnes's band, or the twelve-piece orchestra of fiddler Erskine Tate. Downtown on 51st Street the old master clarinetist Johnny Dodds was blowing Dixieland with his Rhythm Kings at the New Plantation Café.

Who could go home to bed with so much jazz all around? Jabbo Smith was winding his trumpet at the brand-new Panama Café at the corner of South Prairie and 58th. Nat was earning a name for himself: in any of these joints the young virtuoso might be asked to sit in, for a number or a set.

Then there were the pretty girls in the floor shows at the Little Chicago Theater and the Club De Lisa. Everybody was talking about the young dancer from East St. Louis who was packing them in at the Little Chicago Theater, the "sinuous Nadine Robinson." Her name was all over the *Chicago Defender*, which described her as "a stand-out tap dancer with perfect rhythm." Nat would have to have a look at Nadine Robinson, as we shall see.

In the winter 1934 Eddie Coles returned to Chicago from his long apprenticeship in Europe. Jack Ellis reports in his January 27 column that "Eddie Coles is playing bass for Noble Sissle at the College Inn, Sherman Hotel in Chicago." Eddie was not home for long, because he was still Sissle's bass man and the band was touring the Midwest. But he must have been impressed, if not stunned, by his kid brother's progress as a pianist. Events of the rest of that year prove that by now the kid could play piano with the best of them.

In fact it would not be surprising if the events of 1934 inspired Eddie not only with pride in his little brother but with a measure of envy. Eddie liked seeing his own name in the paper. By Christmas his fifteen-year-old brother Nat's name (changed from Coles to Cole) was a house-hold word to the readers of the *Chicago Defender* and his brooding face was familiar from photos on the entertainment page.

During the winter and spring of 1934 Nat was organizing his own band, the Royal Dukes. Bassist Henry Fort recalls getting a phone call from Nat in January, asking him to join, and then attending

71

the first rehearsal in Nat's home on South Prairie. Soon the ten-piece band, featuring vocalist Arthur Hicks, was rehearsing and performing in basements, lofts, and dance halls all over the South Side. We hear stories of the Royal Dukes appearing then, without pay or fanfare, on a covered pavilion *outside* the Savoy Ballroom while a show went on within. This suggests a great tolerance on the management's part, as well as the loan of a piano. The young pianist-bandleader was getting a lot of encouragement from everybody in Bronzeville but his father; Nathaniel and his band were welcome to perform that summer at concerts at the Regal and the Savoy that drew enormous crowds and press coverage.

In the competitive world of music, Nat Cole's combo must have had some high visibility triumphs in the summer of 1934. For on October 6, Nat's picture appeared dead center of the "Stage-Screen-Drama" section of the *Chicago Defender*, under the large-type caption "Plenty Hot." The article under the photo says that "today he is known as the leader of one of the hottest bands in the Middle West. His individual capers before the band inspired critics to call him 'a second Cab Calloway' already." If Nat cut capers he was aping his older brother — Eddie Coles was the clown of the family.

The photographer who went to Prairie Avenue to get the headshot of the "second Cab Calloway" discovered no clown but a very intense, tall young man dressed in his navy-blue Sunday suit and a necktie under a neatly pinned collar. Efforts to make him smile were in vain. The large mouth was pursed, tense. The wide-set eyes above the broad nose burned with an intensity of undifferentiated emotion, hot, "plenty hot," a heat of desire, rage, and ferment. And there were odd premature lines in the brow and transverse lines under the eyes as if from lack of sleep.

A professional witness of character, the photographer sees the uniqueness of a face as well as its type. Here was the furious adolescent, the boy impatient for a man's dignity. But there was something else, clearly, that set this fellow apart. It lay behind the rage in the eyes, a certain humor of perception, a knowingness that says to the cameraman: "I know you, and you must understand this is not really me, not yet." This touch of humor made him appealing; without it he was just one more angry kid from the South Side of Chicago.

Nathaniel and his family were thrilled to see his picture in the paper, alongside a "Backstage" column that spoke of Eddie South, the famous bandleader, Ed Fox, the notorious manager of the Grand Terrace, and the great Jimmie Lunceford and his band, who were coming to the Regal on Sunday. Jimmie Lunceford was one of Nat's heroes. It must have been a heady experience for the boy to see his picture above the huge ad for Jimmie and his Harlem band. If he was seeing their names, they were seeing his.

Malcolm Smith had something to do with Nat Cole's publicity. The young promoter, a stringer for the *Pittsburgh Courier*, specialized in entertainment for the high school and college set. That autumn Smith was organizing Sunday dances at the

Warwick Hall on 47th Street. He had been drumming up interest in Tony "Little Duke" Fambro and his band. Tony was eighteen, and his boys played imitations of Ellington. But Smith's efforts to market him were not paying off. Nat Cole was generating the sort of heat and light the promoter needed.

Smith, a part-time newsman, had close friends at the *Defender*. He got Leon Foster to take a publicity photo of Cole, and then convinced Julius Adams, the *Defender*'s managing editor, to make a splash for "the greatest young star of the junior set," according to Adams. After the photo appeared in the paper, Smith hired Cole and his Royal Dukes to play against Tony Fambro and his Jungle Rhythm Orchestra every Sunday afternoon at the Warwick. All through October and November the bands battled, Nat Cole in the rhythmic style of Earl Hines against Tony Fambro in the high manner of Ellington.

Nat joined the union, Local 208 of the American Federation of Musicians.

Nat Cole's ear was so good he was able to memorize entire arrangements of Hines tunes and teach them to his band members. Some of the orchestrations were tricky and it drove him crazy when he couldn't get them exactly right.

Listening in the alley behind the Grand Terrace one night, Nathaniel met a youngster from Detroit named Timmie Rogers. A high school dropout, Timmie ran away with a band called Floyd Ray's Ginger Snaps and worked as a clown, an acrobat, and a hoofer. He was a live wire. He had gangly arms and legs and big laughing eyes and an

74

enormous mouth that was always smiling, clucking, and chuckling. Timmie could not stand still but was forever pacing, shuffling, or shifting his weight from foot to foot. Now he was dancing and clowning between Earl Hines sets at the Grand Terrace.

Timmie Rogers's comic mobility was a perfect contrast to Nat Cole's intense calm.

"I love that tune 'Rosetta,' " said Nat Cole, lighting a cigarette.

"Yeah, man," said Timmie, and he shuffled his feet, clucking in appreciation. "That's a sweet tune."

"I can't play it," said Nat, puffing defiantly.

"Can't nobody play it but Earl Hines," said Timmie.

"If I could read it, I could play it," Nat declared.

"We'll see about that."

Rogers talked to somebody in the band, who talked to Earl's arranger, Cecil Irwin, who smuggled Rogers the sheet music of "Rosetta." He handed it to Nathaniel Coles, who soon was playing the ballad at Warwick Hall and elsewhere. People started calling Nat's band the Rogues of Rhythm.

"They were rogues," said neighbor Dempsey Travis, "because they stole from Earl Hines."

The family that gathered around the dinner table for Thanksgiving on November 22, 1935, was, like many families, bound by love and torn by strife. Eddie was home for two weeks with his new wife, Thelma, before going back on the road. The marriage would end as swiftly as it had come

75

about. He was playing bass with Sissle at the French Casino, and when his name appeared in the paper it was for gambling, philandering, or other behavior unbecoming a minister's son. Nathaniel, whose career was taking off like a rocket, had decided to quit high school. The rivalry between the boys was masked by pride and deep affection. The Reverend felt defeated by their united front and did not know whether to blame Eddie, Nathaniel, or the corrupt nature of the times.

Nat was preparing for his biggest opportunity yet. David Kellum (his old friend Bud Billiken) had invited the pianist to perform at the Regal's sixth annual Christmas Basket Show. Nathaniel would not say very much to Eddie about this for fear of seeming boastful. But everybody knew about it. On December 15, a week after Eddie left with Sissle for Cleveland, Nat's photograph appeared again in the middle of the *Defender*'s entertainment page, this time twice the size of the earlier picture. In a city where hundreds of career musicians were scrambling for attention, the fifteen-year-old pianist was receiving a vast amount of it.

There was accidental irony in the article that describes the "well-known young pianist and student of Wendell Phillips," because on the Wednesday after Thanksgiving, Nathaniel had quit school. Few people were surprised. This was the Depression and the young man was making money playing music full-time. But it was a source of great sadness at home. His sister Evelyn might accompany him to the Regal Theatre at midnight, but his parents would not.

At midnight on Friday, December 14, 3,000 people filled the red seats under the "tented" dome of the Regal. Nat watched from the wings. David Kellum welcomed the audience. Then A. N. Fields, another writer for the *Defender*, introduced Ed Kelly, the mayor of Chicago.

"It is a pleasure," said the mayor. "I think this is a worthy cause."

The great Carroll Dickerson's orchestra kicked off the stage show, making the chorus dancers strut their stuff. Ethel Waters sang "Stormy Weather" and "Moonglow," and Mae Alix sang "St. Louis Blues." There were trios and quartets, a dancer on roller skates, and comics by the dozen, mugging, clowning, jiving. There were stars of stage and radio, and two more orchestras to last until 4 a.m.

But no one was greeted more warmly than the young pianist who had appeared on this stage repeatedly as a striving amateur. At last he was in his element, performing with fellow professionals, his peers. Nat Cole had arrived.

During the winter and spring of 1935 Nat could be heard jamming "in every joint on the South Side," according to guitarist Les Paul. The red-haired musician from Wisconsin, nineteen years of age, felt an instant rapport with the black pianist, who became Paul's guide to Bronzeville. The after-hours clubs were wide open, democratic. Musicians of all ages and races mingled freely. There they might glimpse Earl Hines or pianist Teddy Wilson. If you were good enough, you might play with anybody, you might be heard by anybody.

Louis Armstrong was back from Paris, sick and depressed. For three years he had been traveling all over the world in flight from the long arms of Crime Incorporated — Al Capone and New York's Owney Madden. Louis had blown his trumpet until his lips oozed blood. Now the doctor was telling him not to play for six months. The IRS was on his case, and Lil Armstrong, his ex-wife, was suing him for back alimony. Nat Cole and Les Paul hung out with Louis Armstrong, and the two teenagers helped to cheer him up.

In the company of young Louis Armstrong, Nat, Les Paul, and Timmie Rogers would be welcome almost anywhere. They would jam at the Club De Lisa on South State Street, where pianist Albert Ammons led the Rhythm Kings. Beautiful Nadine Robinson was dancing there. Art Tatum, the one-eyed piano wizard, was in residence at the Three Deuces, in the Swing Room downstairs from the main club on North State Street. Tatum, twenty-five, was already renowned for his speed on the keyboard and his ornate melodic inventions, on his way to being called the greatest jazz pianist of all time. Nat Cole first met Tatum in the Swing Room. They jammed and jousted and jived all night until 5:30 a.m., when Les Paul had to show up for his job at the radio station. Curious about where the fair-skinned guitarist had to go at such an hour, Tatum allowed himself to be led, by Nat Cole, to the studios of station WJJD. There the man they would call the greatest pianist listened to Rhubarb Red, as Paul called himself on the air, broadcast country and western tunes on his hillbilly show. "That kid is a cowboy," declared Art Tatum, as if he had suspected it all along.

Up all night studying jazz in this company, Nat slept into the afternoon, much to his parents' dismay. Then he would round up the high school boys in his band, George Skinner, Henry Fort, Andrew Gardner, Charlie Murphy, Russell Shores, and the rest, and they practiced until evening the numbers they would play on the weekend.

How good were they? On Easter Sunday, the Savoy Ballroom was nearly empty because every jitterbug in Bronzeville was at the Warwick dancing to the Royal Dukes' music. The Savoy's manager had to go over to the Warwick to see with his own eyes who was stealing his clientele. That was when the manager, Harry Engelstein, vowed he would lure Nat Cole away from Malcolm Smith.

And so it went until mid-June of 1935, when school was out and Nat's band could rehearse in earnest, full-time. They practiced in a room upstairs from the musicians' union hall at 39th and South State, from eleven to five; according to Jack Ellis, "when he turns that five-part brass loose, the bricks in the wall begin to jump around."

As a bandleader Nathaniel had precocious abilities. "Nat seemed much older," said bassist Henry Fort. "He was serious and so intense and nervous he bit his fingernails. He was authoritative without being dictatorial, and he was able to whip a bunch of undisciplined teenagers into a music unit in less than sixty days. His objective was to make us sound like Earl 'Fatha' Hines; Earl was Nat's idol.

"Nat could sit down at a piano and tell the horn player to play a B-flat here or a C there, and believe it or not, it came out perfect . . . If someone hummed a tune around Nat, before the last sixteen bars were finished, he would pick up the tune and play it as if it were his own. At rehearsal when the band played a number Nat hadn't heard yet, he usually got up and directed. Then he could sit down at the piano and play that number a second time around as if he had written the arrangement, which was phenomenal."

Under such leadership the Royal Dukes rapidly reached an astonishing performance level. Soon they were so popular among youngsters that Malcolm Smith was able to book them on a summer tour of Illinois. The announcement of the tour in the *Defender* links the Coles brothers' names for the first time in print: "Nate (schoolboy bandleader) Cole is the brother of 'Jelly' Coles in Noble Sissle's band." Eddie and his wife had wintered in New York. But now Eddie was breezing in and out of Chicago with Sissle, and keeping an eye on his kid brother's success.

Before going on the road with his band for the first time, Nat said goodbye to Louis Armstrong. In late June, Armstrong was also going on tour, and there was a party for him at one of their all-night spots, the Clef Club on Michigan Avenue. Now Louis was well enough to blow his trumpet, so he played. Lil Armstrong played the piano too, and Albert Ammons and his band performed. The next week Nat Cole and his Royal

Dukes followed Louis Armstrong at the Clef Club, so the boys could try out their repertoire on a live audience before leaving town.

That summer the Royal Dukes entertained in Aurora, the big railroad town on the Fox River. They made music in high school gyms and clubs in Joliet, traveling by train past the lime quarries and coal mines. Wide-eyed and fascinated, the city boys chugged south through farmland to play Kankakee, but there disaster struck. In the heat of the summer sun the kids stripped down to take a swim in the Kankakee, the long river that rises near South Bend, Indiana, flowing rapidly southwest into Illinois. One of them, a trumpet player now remembered only as "Rail," got caught in the undertow, went under, and the boys could not find him. He was never seen again.

According to Henry Fort, Mama Perlina Coles was so upset when she heard about the drowning that she contacted her son Eddie. In a gesture that the Reverend Coles might have likened to pouring goose grease on a kitchen fire, the worried mother begged her eldest son to leave Noble Sissle's band (a top band of the era), come home to Chicago, and take Nathaniel under his wing.

The idea appealed to Eddie for more than one reason. He and Nat might make beautiful music together if the kid hadn't grown too big for his breeches. At sixteen the "schoolboy" had a bigger name in Chicago than Eddie had at twenty-five.

Next thing you knew, Nat Cole would be going up against Earl Hines himself in a Battle of the Bands at the Savoy Ballroom.

81

THE SAVOY BALLROOM —
SEPTEMBER 8, 1935

It was not yet midnight and Gatemouth Earl Hines had heard about all he wanted to hear of Nat Cole's piano. The hysterical applause the kid was getting from the crowd of 5,000 on the dance floor was unreal, unfair; it was downright ugly.

Hines and his Grand Terrace Orchestra had rendered their first set of the evening with ease and grace. They did tunes like the rocking "Fat Babes" with its trombone trio, and "Copenhagen," and the flag-waver "That's a Plenty," nothing fancy. They just played good solid swing music for the folks to dance to. The gift of Hines's piano to an orchestra was a matter of atmosphere, musical weather. His speed and dynamic control enabled him to surround the ensemble, lay green grass under it, spread a clear sky over it with sunshine or stars, or blow like a hurricane through an out-chorus. The delicate high descants of his piano could make a light spring rainstorm; then he would descend in bass decrescendos to violent thunder.

Tonight Earl left most of the solo work to Trummy Young's trombone and the trumpets of Walter Fuller and George Dixon. They played like the professionals they were, in their tailored white suits and black bow ties; they performed like

82

gentlemen, and the crowd responded with polite applause.

But the kid was challenging Gatemouth with every song he played, mimicking, riffing lengthily, shamelessly, grandstanding, showing off. And the crowd loved it. If he played the Fats Waller tune "Ain't Misbehavin' " he would wink and play quintuplet quarter notes, and the girls would scream. Mostly he played Earl Hines's own numbers like "Rock and Rye" and "Harlem Lament," and the crowd roared its approval as if it could not tell this was a cheap imitation or did not care. As Gatemouth smoked a cigarette and waited his turn, he smiled at the crowd in the Savoy Ballroom. But he was losing his famous sense of humor. He was going deaf from the applause for his opponent.

Sometime after midnight, some say, Hines got angry. It might have been in the middle of one of his own sets, as he looked out beyond the spotlights and saw the crowd using his show time to refill their glasses at the bar in the corner, or sitting at side tables resting their legs so they could jitterbug all the harder to the Rogues of Rhythm.

Hines had been playing a flag-waver, something like "Sensational Mood," with a bright tempo and a bang-up trumpet solo and vocal by Fuller. It should have gotten the lindy dancers swinging from the ceiling but didn't, and after the outchorus Hines lit a cigarette. The room got quiet for a minute, about as quiet as any ballroom can get with 5,000 people in it drinking and waiting for the band to play.

Gatemouth smiled at the people. He smiled at

83

Nathaniel, who was watching his every movement. The kid had a gift, no question. But how bad did he want it — the music, the glory, the trouble that came with it? He showed promise, had a gift — but tonight he was going to have to fight for it. Hines knew what he would do.

The King of the Ivories set the glowing coal of his cigarette under the toe of his shoe and crushed it. He called out to Budd Johnson and George Dixon, "Angry!" He shouted to Jimmie Mundy and Darnell Howard, "Angry!" and they echoed their leader. Soon all twelve musicians were muttering to one another as they picked up horns and drumsticks and wet their reeds. "Angry! Angry!" Father Hines had decided to take off his gloves and teach the boy some piano.

Light flashed on the brass of the trumpets, trombones, and saxophones, light glinted on the high-hat cymbals beside the drums. And light gleamed in the eye of Gatemouth Hines as he struck up his Grand Terrace Orchestra to play "Angry."

The song, written by the brothers Henry and Merrit Brunies, had been a hit a decade earlier. There were words to "Angry" but now nobody could remember them, because the piece had become the moral property of Earl Hines, a showcase for his unearthly virtuosity. Without a word of English the tune in its moderate tempo tells the story of a lover's complaint, beginning with the introductory verses, a dialogue between moaning saxophones and a sharp-tongued, hot-tempered trumpet.

After the head count the music seemed to start

84

out of nowhere, abruptly, the mock sadness of two alto saxophones played by Darnell Howard and Omer Simeon. Moaning, explaining, apologizing for some misdeed, the saxes met the quick trumpet of George Dixon, interrupting, accusing. "I'm angry. You *know* I'm angry," snapped the muted trumpet. "Wah, wah, wah, wah, wah," said an abject saxophone.

A few more bars of this, and Hines stepped in to take over the argument for the trumpet. Everyone fell silent but the piano man, with the soft brushwork of Wally Bishop's drums behind him.

What followed was a valedictory of such furious eloquence that nobody now would believe it if the performance had not been recorded.

Hines would play two solo choruses, each thirty-two measures long, the two joined so seamlessly they sounded like one sixty-four-bar composition. He entered with moody flatted third chords, in the "locked hands" style (both hands playing the same chords) but quickly began gathering up pieces of the theme, a short middle-register glissando here, a high trill there, keeping a steady rhythm with single bass notes or low block chords. By the start of the second eight, Earl was easing into the major melody with a spare stride rhythm — not a lot of notes, just enough to state the lover's complaint. This heated up after the sixteenth bar, rising to some jarring high trills at the height of the bridge and the blaring octave chords that folks called Earl's "trumpet tones." No mistake — he was angry. But the emotion was under control. By the last eight bars of the chorus he had settled back down into the stride rhythm of the coda.

But it wasn't over, not by a long shot. What the audience had heard was admirable, even remarkable, piano playing that no other man could excel and few could match. But Earl was holding back. The crowd could feel it, as the pianist dodged the final resolving notes of the chorus in the last two measures, reaching up with his right hand to grab some piercing high-octave "trumpet" notes and trills, reaching into a second chorus where he would show you just how angry he really was.

If anyone had been dancing, now they stood still. If anyone had been whispering or clinking ice in a glass, now they fell silent. What was happening on the bandstand commanded the total attention of anyone lucky enough to be there. The first chorus had been no more than a quiet warning about what would follow. After four measures of the second chorus Earl began hurling notes, piano notes by the handful, by the bucket, by the barrel — not just any notes but the perfect ones. He played furious torrents and thick forests of notes, eighths and sixteenths; he cut them up so fine you could hardly tell they were notes anymore and not fluid ideas, like the grains of millet in Zeno's paradox.

He raced through the second four bars in one wild run that began high in the treble, sixteenth notes dizzily descending to the bass and then zigzagging home to the middle register. But this was child's play compared to the run he would make after the bridge, the bridge that took fire from the locked hand countermelodies that wove through the previous measures. You would have thought there was little left after the climax of the bridge, but then it came: a cyclone of notes, a daring breakneck ascending run that covered the whole length of the keyboard in two measures — not a "slide" or glissando, but rather a fully articulated scale, about forty-five distinct notes in less than three seconds.

Now there was little left of the solo but the turnback to the out-chorus, the trumpets, the saxes, and the clarinets. The anger was spent. The audience whispered and exchanged glances, wondering if they could believe their ears.

Earl Hines smiled at Nat Cole in a fatherly way, glad to show there wasn't another man on earth who could play *that* much piano.

Nonetheless, Nat and his Rogues of Rhythm remained high-spirited. After all, they were the darlings of the crowd, the young heroes of Bronzeville. Earl's piano was overwhelming but the applause was not. In his musical fury, he had left the audience behind.

When his turn came again Nathaniel took his place at the piano bench. Now he sat tall; he appeared to have grown into the suit of green gabardine. At last he was smiling, with a certain satisfaction that he had provoked this outburst from Fatha Hines, smiling with apt humility in his role, but without apology. He knew very well he could not match Hines note for note — not tonight, maybe never. But there might be a better way to the crowd's heart.

Gatemouth wondered, as did everyone else in the Savoy, what the kid would do next. Surely he would not have the gall to play "Angry" back at him, though desperate contenders were known to throw such roundhouse punches, mocking each other's hit songs and the like.

So perhaps Earl was relieved, then amazed, when he heard the simple, straightforward stride rhythm of the piano playing the opening verse of "Rosetta." Earl had written the lovely ballad himself, with help from Henry Woode, and "Rosetta" had become Earl's theme song. It was at once the most beautiful song Hines ever wrote, and wholly untypical of his style. Gatemouth was complex, percussive. His effects were architectural. "Rosetta" was soft, lyrical, with the easy grace of simplicity. He had many ways of performing it, as solo, as vocal, as ensemble instrumental, and all of them were good.

Now the kid lightly played eight bars and turned it over to the saxophones for the chorus:

> *Rosetta, I'll be waiting*
> *Oh not for teasing*
> *But only for you*
>
> *Rosetta, never leave me*
> *I'll be always*
> *Always the one for you*

There was no vocalist but the words were well known. So by the time the trumpets entered at the bridge some folks were singing softly the theme of love lost, of knowledge gained through suffering. "While you made me learn / Learn to forget / All those things that could keep us apart . . ." But at the turnback line the crowd grew still again, because the second chorus belonged to the piano player.

Like a burst of sunbeams from a dark sky came the high-octave notes of the first measure, and nobody could keep from smiling. The kid was playing a lovely, happy melody that was not "Rosetta," and yet it was, too, a perfect descant, a countermelody to Hines's famous tune. If you carried "Rosetta" in your head now you couldn't help but hear Nathaniel's voice as a duet with Earl's — high and low, young and old. And all the while that left hand was pumping bass notes in a stride rhythm as sure and rocking as Jelly Roll Morton's.

Soon the dancers were on their toes and jitterbugging. They hardly noticed when the kid hit an octave trill at the bridge and held it, eight bars, while his bass hand took over the melody. They did not care because they were too busy dancing.

But Gatemouth noticed and smiled approvingly. The kid was paying him homage, not with a bushel basket of notes but with a simple sweet bouquet of them. He was winning the crowd over the same way, with vibrant charm and incomparable rhythm, never giving them a note more than the dance demanded. Something was going on here in the late summer of 1935 that Gatemouth could not wholly understand because he was the wrong age. And it had to do with rhythm. Rhythm had always been boss in Chicago jazz. Now almost overnight the Golden Age of Jazz had become the Swing Era.

Nathaniel Coles had stolen Earl Hines's theme song and made it his. Now he was stealing everyone's heart.

BROTHERS

In the wee hours of the morning, the music columnist for the *Defender* left the Savoy Ballroom wondering how he would describe the "battle." Writer Jack Ellis loved the musician's phrase "boil it down to a low gravy" used to encourage a band to find the essence of a theme or rhythm. Now Ellis would use the expression diplomatically to cover this Battle of the Bands. He wished to offend no one, neither the dignity of Earl Hines nor several thousand young fans of Nat Cole.

He wrote: "Earl Father Hines and Nat Cole's cats swung down to a low gravy at the Savoy," evenly praising the show as a whole. Word was out that Nat's Rogues had won, so the legend has come down to us that Hines lost his crown that night to the kid. Smiling Jack Ellis hesitates: "No, Nat didn't wash Earl, but he was in his collar all night." More jazz lingo, meaning that if Nat did not knock Earl down, he staggered him. Tim Black recalls: "Nat was no Earl Hines, but he was our guy. We gave him our best, knowing we'd be back in school talking about it the next day."

More solid evidence of Nathaniel's success that night is that the management of the Savoy wanted him back. He and the Rogues of Rhythm played the Ballroom all by themselves on Sunday, September 22, and the very next Sunday they squared off there against another wunderkind, twenty-one-year-old Ray Nance, and his band. Nance, a violinist and trumpeter, studied at Phillips with Major Clark Smith before leading his own sextet for several years at Dave's Café and the Midnight Club. All the Savoy engagements were competitive and high-profile. For an entire month Nat Cole's name was in every issue of the *Defender*.

We do not know if Eddie Coles was in Chicago that September. He was still traveling with Noble Sissle when he got wind of his kid brother's triumphs at the Savoy. We can only imagine the swirl of emotions and motives that caused Eddie to leave his gainful job with Sissle in October of that year to join his brother's band in Chicago. Surely his mother's appeal to him in August was a factor. Certainly he wanted to have a hand in his brother's fast-breaking career. No doubt he smelled money.

Eddie left Sissle's band on the road in Rochester, New York, in mid-October, returning home. Events of the next year indicate a fruitful collaboration between the brothers, as well as a classic power struggle. The boys had a childhood dream of making music together. Now that dream would be tested against the harsh realities of the jazz marketplace and the volatile chemistry of the brothers' personalities, ambition, and desire for control.

As the eldest son, almost a decade older than Nathaniel, Eddie Coles felt the rights of seniority, experience, and maturity. At first this would be hard for Nat to dispute, mild-mannered as he was. But Nat was stubborn, a genius, and more famous now than Eddie. Without Eddie's help, Nat had marshaled a ragtag bunch of high school students into one of the hottest dance bands in Chicago. Almost from the beginning, Nathaniel was truly a bandleader, while his brother had never been much more than a sideman.

Jack Ellis's first mention of the merger in the *Defender* of October 19 puts it this way: "Eddie Cole, the bass player, formerly of Noble Sissle, has joined his brother Nat's band." But a week later it is clearly Ed "Jelly" Coles whose name is featured in a bold headline in the *Defender*: " 'Jelly' Coles and Brother Form a Band" above an article suggesting the band is not Nat Cole's Rogues of Rhythm anymore, but rather a group known as the Coles Brothers Band. "Coles left Sissle in Rochester, New York, and came here to join his brother who has already become nationally known as an orchestra leader. The Coles Brothers Band will start a tour early next week that will keep them on the road for several months. They will tour Oklahoma, Arkansas and other points in the southland and then set sail for the east. The band is booked to appear in New York early in December."

The prominence of this news story and the ambitious touring schedule look like the work of professional management. Whether it is Eddie's work or an agent's remains uncertain. We do know that when Eddie teamed with his brother he quickly relieved Malcolm Smith of his duties as the band's manager, taking control himself.

Returning from their tour in the winter of 1936, the Cole Brothers Band secured a nightly residency playing at the Panama Café on 58th Street.

Nat bought a new suit and shoes. He got mugged in his snazzy outfit, but the thief took only his shiny shoes. Nat bought better ones. The Coles were in demand, in the big time. Their affairs had become complicated. Accepting a gig at the Congress Hotel, a white venue on Chicago's Loop, they arrived to find Art Steward, the president of their musicians' union, Local 208. He had come to collect their money, to make sure there were no kickbacks for a black band playing a white club for less than union scale.

Now it is hard to know how grateful Nathaniel was for his brother's aggressive marketing of the combo formerly called the Rogues of Rhythm — hard to know how resentful he was that Eddie had taken over his band. The Panama display ads that appeared in the paper on January 18 and ran weekly until August 1936 bill the musicians as Eddie Cole's Band. In fine print underneath, almost as an afterthought, we find "with Nat Cole at Piano." In mid-March a reporter visited the Panama to catch the nightly show that Jimmie White was producing: tap dancer Nadine Robinson, torch singer Maxine Johnson, and the Cole Brothers. He writes: "Eddie Cole, the orchestra leader, assisted by his brother, Nat, completely stole the show with their own knockabout song and dance."

Though he may have needed Eddie's guidance, the boy wonder cannot have been entirely pleased with this turn of events.

The date at the Panama may have been Nathaniel's seventeenth birthday. Not too long before this Nathaniel had discovered women, which is a roundabout way of saying that women had discovered him. According to his sister Evelyn, he had been painfully shy in his early teen years. She used to go along with him to his gigs whenever she could, serving as a prop and a screen against the unwelcome advances of admiring girls. Sometime before his seventeenth birthday he must have dismissed the screen, so that women discovered him. Fact is, the boy was dangerously attractive to women, as the man would soon be — absolutely magnetic. He needed all the protection he could get.

Of all the women living on the South Side of Chicago, the one Nathaniel most wanted to be discovered by was Nadine Robinson. When she saw her own name in the paper, she spotted his a few inches away — his name or his picture. Nadine was a minor celebrity on the South Side, known for her beauty and her dancing. It is nearly certain he saw her dance at the Club De Lisa in 1934 and hard to believe he did not meet her on one of the spring nights in 1935 when Nat and Les Paul were jamming there.

Now Nat could hardly believe his good fortune, finding himself on the same bill with the gorgeous dancer. Dark-skinned, large-eyed, and petite, the twenty-six-year-old showgirl was a woman of great personal warmth and powerful sexual energy, an ebony Ruby Keeler, as one man described her. Her legs were a popular topic of conversation. Men were dazzled by her, pursued her. The fact that Miss Robinson was unmarried and highly respectable at age twenty-six had as much to do with her self-confidence as with her strict upbringing as a minister's daughter. This she had in common with Nathaniel, along with the guilt that comes of a career so far from the Church.

If she was not the prettiest woman the Cole brothers had ever seen, she was surely the best-looking woman they had ever worked with, night after night. Considering Eddie Cole's reputation as a lady's man (continually noted in the gossip columns) and the disintegration of his first marriage, we should not be surprised to learn that Eddie Cole, too, was smitten with the lithe figure of Nadine Robinson. We should be even less surprised to hear of his envy upon learning that the dancer had fallen in love with his kid brother.

NADINE

Sometime around Nathaniel's seventeenth birthday he fell in love with Nadine, and she with him, in what order only God knows. It may have started as the sort of teasing flirtation that seems the only suitable attitude of a twenty-six-year-old woman toward an admiring teenage boy. More likely, she had no idea how old he was (nobody else did) and did not care.

In love in the spring of 1936, Nathaniel did as love-struck youths have done since time began: he wrote songs and poems. While Eddie pranced and hustled, promoting the band he began calling the Coal Heavers, his artistic sibling began writing their material.

Inspired by his passion for Nadine he wrote a clever swing tune (based on a traditional song) called "Honey Hush," about a mythical charmer named Sadie Green. Sadie is so fine — such a class act — that the singer hardly dares to approach her:

> *All those girls are jealous of her*
> *Cause she dress so neat.*
> *All the boys are wild about her*
> *Cause she look so sweet.*

The subtext of the lyric is the poet's worry about differences in skin tone — he fears he might be too dark to appeal to her:

> *Steppin out with them high yellows,*
> *Snubbin all the other fellows,*
> *Boy that gal is really mellow*
> *With that "Honey hush."*

The obsession with skin color and the correlation of class with shade are evident from the advertisements in every issue of the *Chicago Defender* — display ads for creams and nostrums guaranteed to lighten the skin. The famous chorus girls at the Regal Theatre, the Regalettes, were exclusively "high yellow." And certain Negro bands refused to audition young Earl Hines because they thought him "too dark." Shy Nathaniel, whose rough skin was much darker than Earl's, may have wondered at first if Nadine would give him a second glance.

He composed a slow, sultry ballad full of yearning and twilight reflection called "Bedtime," subtitled "Sleep, Baby, Sleep." And he wrote two foot-stomping instrumentals, "Stomping at the Panama" and "Thunder."

Now Eddie felt it was time for them to have a record of their own. He had played on recordings with Noble Sissle as early as 1930 (in London) and then in 1934 (Chicago). Through Sissle, Eddie met Jack Kapp, the head of Decca in America, and convinced the record company executive to sign the brothers to a contract for Decca's race series.

Armed with Nathaniel's original tunes and calling themselves Eddie Cole's Solid Swingsters, the sextet entered the Decca studios in Chicago on July 28, 1936. Kenneth Roane, their trumpet player, had played with the Scott Brothers band in Harlem in 1927, and later with Sidney Bechet and Willie the Lion Smith. Almost nothing is known about the other sidemen, drummer Jimmy Adams and saxophonists Tommy Thompson and Bill Wright. Their playing is at best competent, un-memorable.

Full of high spirits, the men recorded four tunes that summer day, but these were not about to set the world on fire. Exuberance hardly makes up for uneven workmanship. The arrangements sound loose and clunky, and the sax solos and horn cho-ruses wander aimlessly, at times off-key. The best side is the "novelty" vocal number "Honey Hush," which Eddie sings in a husky, winning baritone. The up-tempo dance instrumentals are typical of the "jungle music" of the day as played by the Hines orchestra; in fact "Stomping at the Panama" sounds just like Hines's "Fat Babes" starved down for the sextet. The slow ballad "Bedtime" comes across as dreamy, more fune-real than romantic.

Yet these sessions are intriguing because they capture the piano technique of Nathaniel Cole a few months after he turned seventeen. As Tim Black notes: "He was no Earl Hines." But he does a very effective impersonation of Fatha Hines, for a teenager. Nat's solos dominate the songs. He is head and shoulders above the others in the group. Nat had mastered the "trumpet style" of piano, using octaves and tenths in the right hand to pro-claim his themes loud enough to hold his own against a horn. He skillfully sustains trills in both the left and right hands, and uses the whole length of the keyboard for rapid, if sometimes blurred, scale runs and arpeggios. During the solo in "Thunder," Nat maintains a complicated triplet figure in his right hand — high in the treble — for thirty-two dashing measures while his left hand sketches out the melody in the middle register. Then he launches into a second chorus, flying up and down the keyboard like a skylark trapped in a greenhouse, bumping into the bright boundaries of his youthful capability.

What is so exciting about Nat's soloing is its brazen aggression, his raw ambition. The young pianist is not content to play what he plays well; he constantly strives to play better than he can, to play what he cannot. While the effect of the plaintive "Bedtime" is not altogether satisfying, the piece is quite advanced, theoretically — highly chromatic and changing key with the frequency and ease of a Duke Ellington piece.

Nat's piano playing on this date provides us with a clear record of his musical lineage and a prophecy of what is to come. Even his brother's voice on "Honey Hush" sounds a prediction. Though Nat has not begun to discover his own singing talent, when he first tries to sing he will sound a lot like Eddie.

Then, as now, recording with a major record label was a key to fame and fortune. There was great excitement in the Cole household, neighborhood pride in the brothers, and hope for their bright future.

As Nathaniel showed the gold-on-black-labeled discs to Nadine Robinson, she knew her young man was bound for glory. But it was not going to happen in Eddie Cole's shadow. The release of the Decca records, which might have been a stepping-stone in the band's ascent, turned out to be the high point of its success, the beginning of the end. Some say this is because the records were not very good, others believe the boys began to quarrel, and some blame Nadine.

After finishing out the month of August at the Panama, Eddie booked the Solid Swingsters on a Southern tour, coinciding with the records' release in September. Road trips for unknown bands were risky business in those days, arranged without advances or guarantees. One started out with a stake of "case money," expecting the receipts from the first date at least to cover expenses to the second date, and so on, hoping to come home with a profit. But bands often got stranded.

Legend has it that two weeks into their schedule the Solid Swingsters ran out of luck in Jackson, Tennessee. With no money to continue, and no money to get home, the band members talked the bus driver into accepting horns and a bass fiddle as collateral for the fare back to Chicago. Who got their instruments out of hock is anybody's guess. Nat was just glad to see Nadine.

They were not out of work for long. In October the Cole brothers joined the cast of *Shuffle Along*, the revival of a Broadway comedy revue that had been a hit in the 1920s. Originally written and staged by Noble Sissle and Eubie Blake, *Shuffle Along* was the first all-black show to conquer

Broadway. It fueled the Harlem Renaissance. Now the dancer Flournoy Miller was organizing a revival in Chicago, with plans for a national tour and an eye on New York. Eddie Cole may have worked through Sissle to get jobs in *Shuffle Along* not only for his sextet but also for Nadine, Nat's dancing sweetheart.

Nat and Nadine had missed each other while he was on the road. Now their courtship heated up. That autumn he took her home to meet his family in the apartment on Prairie Avenue. She made a favorable impression despite her line of work. We wonder if anyone's age was mentioned.

On November 13, Nadine, Nathaniel, and the Solid Swingsters went on the road with *Shuffle Along* to Milwaukee, where opportunities for intimacy increased. Nat was straightforward by nature and still dear to his brother. If Nat and Nadine were considering marriage, and Eddie got wind of it, he would be furious at both of them. His own marriage was on the rocks, a public embarrassment. When Thelma broke her beer bottle over Eddie's head on the stage of the Panama, it made the gossip columns. Marriage was hard enough for consenting adults. It was no game for children, and Eddie knew — even if Nadine didn't — that she was robbing the cradle.

Being in love, Nathaniel of course had his own ideas. And almost everybody, including him, seemed to have forgotten how old he was. He had already learned that the mischievous spirit of Eros is no respecter of age, station, or skin tone. Given the prevailing morals of the decade and the strict upbringing of these two lovers, it is unlikely they would dabble in sex before marriage. Given the sex appeal of each and the wattage of the two together, it is easy to understand why they conspired to get married soon.

Sometime after Thanksgiving the tension between the brothers came to a head: a stew of jealousy, resentment, and struggle for control musically, personally, and financially. Nat's big brother was determined that the kid was not going to make a fool of himself and wreck his life, and Eddie's plans, by ruining what they had worked so hard to build. And the kid meant to throw his big brother off his back, be free of his meddling, and go his own way.

By the end of November, Eddie had had enough of traveling with the road show of *Shuffle Along*. Maybe he wanted more artistic freedom than he had found working for Flournoy Miller, and maybe he wanted to separate his brother from Nadine. Eddie said he was leaving the show and taking his band with him. Nat balked. Stiffnecked, he refused.

What began as a business disagreement about music and career strategy quickly became a quarrel over Nadine. Eddie said there was no reason for Nat to stay with *Shuffle Along* but Nadine Robinson — and a woman was not reason enough to break up the Solid Swingsters. Nat's temper flared. According to family members who witnessed the scene, the brothers' argument became so heated that Eddie looked ready to enforce his rights of seniority by use of his fists. Only Reverend Coles, stepping between them, kept the boys from coming to blows.

Eddie and Nathaniel did not speak to each other for a long time after that. A news article by Jack Ellis on December 5 makes light of the rift, reporting that Eddie "sent his band with his brother Nat Cole in charge to swing the *Shuffle Along* show and he went in the 5100 Club with a new band." It is clear where the musicians' loyalty lay — not a one of the Solid Swingsters went along with Eddie to the 5100.

Nadine and Nathaniel took to the road with the *Shuffle Along* troupe, after Christmas, playing cities and towns in the snowy northern Midwest and falling more deeply in love every day. On the 25th of January 1937, the lovers entered the courthouse in Kalamazoo, Michigan, where Judge of Probate John L. Hollander bound them in the ties of matrimony. In the presence of Charles and Marion Hughes, now known only as "witnesses" from Ypsilanti, Nat and Nadine recited the marriage vows. She gave her age as twenty-seven, which was true. He gave his age as twenty-one, which was a lie, a little white lie that allowed him to marry her without his parents' consent. The happy groom was only seventeen.

A few days later, according to Timmie Rogers, the lovers repeated their vows before a minister and friends in a private home in Kalamazoo. Details of the event are vague, but certainly this was not a family affair; we wonder when news of the wedding reached Reverend Coles and Perlina.

For the Coles family this was a time of transition. During the winter of 1936–37, Reverend Coles accepted a position to head the First Baptist

Church on Chicago's South Side. This was an important advance in his career. The Reverend and his wife and their sons moved from the apartment on Prairie Avenue to a gray frame house at 1412 Greenfield, in North Chicago.

Nathaniel and his bride celebrated their nuptials on the road with the company of *Shuffle Along*, a working honeymoon of one- and two-week stands in RKO houses from Duluth, Minnesota, to Los Angeles, California, where they arrived in mid-April.

Nat's band was booked to play the Golden Gate nightclub in Hollywood.

He would not be able to go home again for a long time.

PART TWO
Los Angeles

SUNSHINE AND SHADOW

California held a golden promise for the newly-weds arriving there in the spring of 1937. After the long train ride over deserts and mountains, they descended the Pacific slope and discovered a world different from any they had ever seen. Across the hills lay Los Angeles, blindingly white: miles of houses bright with stucco and hibiscus, concrete office buildings shining, gleaming viaducts over the stony bottom of the Los Angeles River. Rising above the sun-drenched scene was the chalk-white, tapering tower of City Hall.

The city of Angels made Chicago seem like a city of shadows.

Los Angeles spreads over a broad plain that descends gently from green and purple barrier ranges in the east to the azure of the Pacific. Palm and pepper trees brush the red tiles of rooftops. As Nathaniel and Nadine found it in 1937, this was a city of contrasts and curious excitements, where movie studios stood in the shadow of oil rigs and orange orchards bordered olive groves. It was a city of Chinese herb doctors, lady evangelists, nudism, and surfing. Along Wilshire Boulevard in the afternoon you might see a cowboy in his ten-gallon hat, a turbaned Hindu, or a kimonoed Japanese passing by the long-haired "Messiah" of a religious cult dressed in a robe of potato sacks. There was the liveliness of an outdoor circus, under the wide sky of Southern California.

The population was nearing a million and a half souls, including 100,000 Mexicans, 40,000 Japanese, and 50,000 African-Americans. Despite the city's reputation for freedom and tolerance, dark-skinned Angelinos of that time were not fully integrated into its social life. For instance, white patrons were welcome in black nightclubs, while a law (widely ignored) barred blacks from white clubs.

Fortunately, Nadine had an aunt who lived in Long Beach, a busy harbor and seaside resort on San Pedro Bay located twenty miles southeast of the city center. The newlyweds would stay there while Nat and the band played their two-week gig at the Golden Gate in Hollywood.

The *Shuffle Along* company arrived on May 7 to open at the Lincoln Theater on Central Avenue downtown. On May 15 a reporter wrote in the *Chicago Defender*: "With the 1937 edition of *Shuffle Along* arriving here [L.A.] last Friday morning, Central Avenue has been transformed into Seventh Avenue, and East Los Angeles to Harlem. Opening at the Lincoln here adds them to the list of eastern 'names' already here . . . Earl Hines' band, the Rhythm Pals, Buck and Bubbles, Art Tatum, Bill Robinson . . . and a number of others . . . who with a year's residence in California have become 'natives' and 'pioneers.' "

As the Golden Age of Jazz dissolved into the Swing Era, there was a migration from Chicago to Los Angeles. For some musicians this was as important as the move from New Orleans to Chicago had been fifteen years earlier. Benny Goodman's famous residency at the Palomar Ballroom ignited L.A. in the late summer of 1935. The scene heated up when Hines played Sebastian's Cotton Club in 1937, and would culminate in the music of saxophonists Benny Carter and Lester Young, drummer Buddy Rich, and the King Cole Trio in the legendary Philharmonic Jazz Concerts of the 1940s.

Los Angeles had been a goal of *Shuffle Along* since September 1936, when Flournoy Miller revived the show. Nat shared the excitement about California, and welcomed the chance to see the exotic City of Angels and play music there for a while. But pleased as he may have been to find the neighborhood friendly with Chicago faces, Cole had no idea he had come here to stay. The plan was to build up cash reserves in Los Angeles and then head back East, on to Broadway if possible.

In the same May 15 *Defender* column that applauded Earl Hines's band at the Cotton Club, critic Harry Levette gave the show a rave review, calling it "the best road show since Miller last came here."

But sometime in the next few weeks *Shuffle Along* stumbled and fell apart. Perhaps the company did not fill enough seats at the Lincoln, or at the New Strand Theater in Long Beach, where the show moved next. By several accounts, including Nat's, somebody in the troupe shuffled off with eight hundred dollars in receipts.

Without funds the show could not continue. Everybody but the thief was broke. The chorus went back to New York. In late June the principals, including Jesse Cryer, Evelyn Keyes, Jean

Calloway, and Nat Cole, were performing at a ritzy new nightclub, the Ubangi, on Atlantic Boulevard.

That summer the young bride and groom faced their first major decision — whether to return home broke or stay in Los Angeles and try to make a go of it in the sunshine. Most of Nat's band went back to Chicago. Nostalgia may have tempted him to follow, but he really could not go home yet, given the way he'd left. In a perceptive column written in 1943, Alyce Key would credit Nadine with persuading Nat to stay in California, noting that Nadine had fallen in love with the Golden State. Years later Nat claimed they stayed because of the climate. But that explains things only partly. Having eloped at seventeen, the musician did not want to face his stern father, his angry brother, or the cold winds of Chicago before showing some signs of success.

"I didn't want my dad to see me busted," he later admitted.

The appearance of success came quickly and fleetingly, long before the reality.

Nathaniel's family and friends were amazed to see the wanderer's face once more in the middle of the entertainment page of the July 10, 1937, *Defender*, beneath the headline "Hit on Coast." For the first time the pianist smiles broadly for the camera, his eyes twinkling wisely and with a touch of mischief. No longer the brooding adolescent, he has become a very handsome young man — the picture of success in a white necktie and dark button-down shirt under a pale double-breasted blazer. The caption reads: "NAT COLE: Youthful maestro and the pride of Bronzeville, with his young tunesmiths, are spreading white heat rhythms for dance patrons of the swanky Ubangi club in Los Angeles."

Someone in Chicago, some promoter or press agent, was beating the drum for "the pride of Bronzeville's" triumphant homecoming. Jack Ellis announces that "Nat Cole and his cats will hit Chicago for a few weeks, July 17," to join in a "Swing Parade" at the Savoy with Fletcher Henderson, Roy Eldridge, Erskine Tate, Jimmie Noone, and other stars. "These cats, twelve in all [Cole and Co.], will open in a night spot in Detroit, August 1."

The plan fell through. Nathaniel did not return to Chicago in July nor did he play his piano in Detroit in August. According to *Variety* cabaret bills, from July 28 through August 18, 1937, Cole was playing at the Café Century on Santa Monica Boulevard. He did not have the resources or the backing to tour the Midwest. For the next two and a half years the pride of Bronzeville would be fighting for survival in Southern California.

"It was a tough workout," he told a reporter years later. "I must have played every beer joint from San Diego to Bakersfield," never making more than five dollars a night.

He was entering a dark passage of his career, if not his life, a period of great interest — for it was during the years 1938–39 that he found his true "voice" as a pianist. Cole's late teens, years of grinding poverty and explosive artistic growth, are also a time when he worked in almost total obscu-

111

rity. The local papers had not yet noticed him. The *Chicago Defender*, which faithfully chronicled his career from the start, does not mention him for a year and half after July 1937. Then it gives him little notice for years. There is a virtual press blackout of the musician until *Down Beat* nods to his Trio in 1940. We must rely on the fading memories of a few friends who knew him then, and the vital recordings of the King Cole Trio that began in the autumn of 1938.

Soon after arriving in Los Angeles, Nat met a slender, light-skinned African-American drummer with gentle, merry blue eyes and delicate features. At the age of twenty Lee Young was, like Nat Cole, an "old soul," with wisdom beyond his years. In the clubs where Nat first performed, the Golden Gate and the Café Century, the two struck up a friendship that welcomed Nat to the West, a friendship that would last a lifetime.

Younger brother of the great sax player Lester Young, Leonidas Raymond Young was something of a musical blue blood. His father had studied at Tuskegee Institute, and his relatives included trombonist Austin Young and sax player Isaiah "Sports" Young. As a boy Lee played sax with the family band's sax trio. By the time he met Nat, Lee had worked as a singer in the Apex Club and played with Buck Clayton in 1936 and Eddie Barefield's big band in 1937. He knew the L.A. music scene as well as any man in the city, so he was the perfect friend to guide Nat into that world.

According to Young and others, life was hard for Nat and Nadine during those early years, but not without its pleasures and excitements. They were young, full of life, and very much in love. And they were part of a close-knit, supportive community of African-American musicians centered on Local 767, the musicians' union, located at 1708 South Central. Lee Young lived next door at 1706.

These musicians needed to stick together. The black population of Los Angeles was relatively small, unlike Chicago's. It could not support a lot of dances, concerts, or church socials requiring an orchestra. The white population generally hired white musicians. So Nat was not the only bandleader scrambling for work. After the brief run of his septet at the Ubangi Club, he had to give up the idea of leading a full band, and instead fight for jobs as a solo pianist.

In the late summer and autumn of 1937 he rambled from club to club, from piano to ruined piano, all over greater Los Angeles, playing for three or four dollars, playing for tips, playing for free. The saloon pianos, out of tune or missing keys, were an added challenge. Some say that Nat's style — its spareness, his unusual chord voicings — owes a good deal to his dodging sour keys on crippled pianos.

If there was no work for pay, then he would go wherever the music was, wherever good musicians were jamming: the Café Century, the Paradise Club, Ivie's Chicken Shack, Jim Otto's Steakhouse. Lee Young liked to go along. So did bass player Red Callender. Nat's distinctive piano style quickly earned him a following. Bandleader Bumps Blackwell heard Cole at the Century and later recalled: "All the musicians dug him. We went there just to listen to him because nobody was like him. That cat could play! He was unique."

Up half the night, Nat would come home to Nadine in a little house on 42nd Street near Avalon Avenue and Central Avenue. Nadine took what jobs she could get as a dancer or hostess in nightclubs. All agree the soft-voiced, kindly Nadine was then the most supportive and uncritical of wives. Saxophonist Buddy Banks knew them then. "She loved him very much," he recalls. "She was with him, right or wrong." James Haskins, who interviewed Nadine in 1981, describes the anxiety of Nat's situation: "He wasn't making any money . . . at times he longed to be at home where at least people knew him. Forced to go wherever someone would pay him, he was away from Nadine . . . and when he was with her he felt guilty about not being able to provide for her. At such times his dignity suffered." Yet she believed in him, never doubted his greatness. It was her dream that one day Nat would play Carnegie Hall.

Money was so tight it was often hard to put food on the table. They ate the green avocados from the tree in their backyard. They ate a lot of red beans and rice. Many people, including Mr. and Mrs. Buddy Banks, Lee Young, and the singer Nellie Lutcher, remember inviting the young couple to dinner repeatedly during the Coles' lean years in Los Angeles. When their luck turned they would return the favors.

Nellie Lutcher and others recall that during 1937 or 1938 Eddie Coles came through town and stayed with Nathaniel; so by then the brothers had been reconciled.

From Lee Young's recollections and the recordings that begin in late 1938, it is evident that Nathaniel Cole's waking hours, day and night, were consumed with making music. Though he did not confide his ambitions to Nadine or Lee or anyone else, Cole was obsessed with perfecting a keyboard technique that would put him in the same class as Earl Hines and Art Tatum, in terms of distinctive quality, if not quantity, of notes.

Lee Young would drive down to Nat Cole's house routinely at midday. Pretty Nadine would greet him at the door, and behind her he could hear the tinkling and slamming of Nat's upright piano in a back room. The house on Avalon Boulevard was small. Nat had to be alone to practice technique because it was a cruel noise he made breaking the boundaries of his skill with his bare hands, an ugly chaos out of which a beautiful order would emerge. Young waited patiently in the car outside, with his drums in the trunk, reading newspapers until Nat finished practicing. Every day Nathaniel drilled more than two hours at the piano, even on days when he planned to be performing or jamming from two in the afternoon until the early hours of the morning.

On weekdays they would drive up Central Avenue under palm trees to the union hall. The black Local 767 of the musicians' union had passed a rule against jamming in nightclubs. They did not want their members giving away music for free. This prohibition went against the grain of young artists like Lee Young, Nat Cole, and Red Callender, who had to play the way birds have to fly and dogs have to run. And paying jobs were scarce for black jazzmen in Los Angeles. Jamming was an opportunity to flex their muscles and hone their skills. Playing in public or at private after-hours clubs like Ivie's Chicken Shack or Brothers drew the attention of club owners with job offers — as well as admiring women with other kinds of offers to which few men are indifferent.

Cole and Young had gotten so many fines for jamming, fines suspended because they could not pay, that Lee thought of a scheme to change the union's rule. He got permission for the musicians to play in a room upstairs from the union hall. In the afternoon Lee would unpack his drums, and Nat would sit down at the piano and begin to riff. Callender soon arrived with his double bass. Twenty-one-year-old Charlie Christian, guitar virtuoso, tap dancer, and prizefighter, sat in, as did saxophonist Ben Webster from time to time. The music was so hot the office workers in neighboring buildings could not keep still; they took to jitterbugging around their desks, and the boss couldn't stop them. There were so many complaints that the union at last decided to let the boys go and play wherever they would, as long as they stayed away from the union hall.

At nightfall Nat headed off to the Century or any club he thought might pay him for six hours of playing on a wrecked piano for drunks. But after 2 a.m. he would meet Lee again. In his big blue Oldsmobile sedan, Lee picked Nat up and they drove through the balmy night air to a soul-food restaurant on Vernon and Central avenues called Ivie's Chicken Shack. Ivie had been a singer for Duke Ellington. She did not pay the musicians but kept her piano in tune and welcomed them to come and eat ribs and chicken and collard greens. And they came: Nat and Lee, Red Callender, clarinetist Barney Bigard, whoever happened to blow through town. Art Tatum would challenge pianist Eddie Beal, or play with Charlie Christian and Jimmy Blanton, two young geniuses marked for death.

They all came to jam until dawn.

If the Chicken Shack was too crowded, sometimes they went to Brothers, a club in a private home on Central Avenue. There was only room enough for a piano and ten or twelve people, and the place sold whiskey by the glass. That's where the pianists could go up against one another, mano a mano: Art Tatum, Eddie Beal, Gerald Wiggins, Nat Cole. They would challenge and learn from one another.

Sometimes Lee and Nat picked up their wives, both of whom worked at the Bal Tabarin, a club in Gardena about fifteen miles from the music district. The four of them would make the rounds of the after-hours clubs together. More often the men went alone, and when Nat returned in the gray morning light Nadine was sometimes worried about where he had been.

Nadine was devoted to her struggling husband and his blossoming talent. She worked as hard as she could to support them on the strength of her dancing feet. Every day she laundered and pressed his worn clothing, so if he was not in the height of fashion he was at least neat and clean. She was even known to appear backstage, unexpectedly, with a skillet and hot plate to cook him his only hot meal of the day.

The young men's schedule did not leave much time for rest and relaxation. Nat and Lee played baseball once in a while on the green lawn of Exposition Park near the union hall, where Nadine and Nat sometimes went for long walks. And in 1938 Nathaniel and Lee joined a lodge of the Masons founded by the African-American musicians of Local 767.

Nat's joining the Fraternal Order of Masons provides an insight into his spiritual and intellectual life during this time. The ancient Freemasons, builders in stone in the Middle Ages, handed down symbols and rites that preserve the form and spirit of a medieval guild. Custom is of supreme importance, along with belief in God, obedience to the law of the land, special obligations to brothers and their families, and charity without publicity.

While the order of Masons is not primarily religious, it provides a rigorous and imaginative spiritual life for its members through ritual and symbol. The symbolism of Freemasonry would have a strong impact upon a musician Nathaniel's age, a "builder" of musical architecture, a member of an ancient guild of players. Nat remained loyal to Masonic principles his whole life, though his active membership in the order ended during his twenties.

The Masons convey their ancient customs and

wisdom through catechism — oral questioning and memorization of answers. "Everybody got a ring and a pin," Lee Young explains. "When you met a brother you'd cover up your pin real fast, to get the jump on him, and then you would ask him a question about doctrine. If he couldn't answer the question, you got to take his pin. Then he would have to go home and study up, and come back to you with the right answer before you would give him his pin back." Young chuckles. "We use to love to snatch the guys' pins."

The lodge meant more to them than simple male bonding, more than camaraderie — it had a moral dimension. And for a young man who quit school at fifteen, whose calling was mostly non-verbal, Nat's study of Freemasonry provided the only scholarly discipline he would ever know as an adult.

THE TRIO

Like so many milestones in the history of the performing arts, the King Cole Trio sprang out of an artistic impulse as well as a practical need. In Los Angeles there was not enough work for full orchestras; yet some nightclub owners wanted more sound than a solo pianist could deliver on his own.

One night in the late summer of 1937, Nathaniel finished playing a set of piano tunes at the Century Club. A man in a pinstripe suit approached him and praised his style. He introduced himself as Bob Lewis, a music promoter who owned a nightclub in Hollywood on La Brea Avenue called the Swanee Inn. Lewis told Nat Cole that if he would organize a small group — say, a bass player, a guitarist, and a drummer — they could earn seventy-five dollars a week playing jazz in his nightclub.

Nat immediately thought of Lee Young. But Young took one look at the little bandstand at the cozy Swanee Inn, and said there was no room for a drummer.

Then Nat talked to Wesley Prince, a round-faced, balding bass player from Pasadena he had met soon after arriving on the scene. Prince was thirty. Nat had heard him playing behind Lionel Hampton at the Paradise Café on Main Street and liked his sound. A preacher's son, the bass man had a lot in common with the Chicago pianist, and had already expressed a desire to work with him.

Wesley told Nat he knew of a very good guitarist named Oscar Moore.

They called Oscar Moore "Jesus Boy" because he was born on Christmas Day in 1916, in Austin, Texas. His father was a blacksmith and the leader of a brass band in Phoenix, where Oscar grew up. As boys, he and his brother Johnny learned to strum the guitar from a wandering Mexican minstrel named Carl Gomez. Moore's father told him his hands were too small for him ever to be a guitarist. So little Oscar would sneak off to play in the closet. Like Nat and Eddie Coles, the Moore brothers had their own band in the early 1930s before moving to Los Angeles in 1936. Oscar found work in the movie studios, while jamming in clubs at night.

Oscar recalled the first night he met Nat Cole, at the Paradise Café in 1937, when he and Cole had both gone to hear Lionel Hampton play vibes. Oscar would never forget the effect of young Nathaniel's intensity, his concentration: "First time I laid eyes on Nat, he looked like a real mean guy — his eyes almost closed, glintin' out at you, diggin' what was goin' on. After I met him, I found out how wrong I was."

What Nat thought of the dapper guitarist that night has not been recorded. Oscar, with his merry tilted eyebrows over his dreamy eyes, and his neat mustache, had the charisma of a Latin Lothario out of central casting. He looked fit to cross swords with Errol Flynn. Yet one journalist describes him as singularly boyish and naive, with his passion for rings and fishing and flashy sport shirts.

The fact that Oscar was a jazz guitarist worthy of comparison with Charlie Christian did not escape Nat. Christian had jammed with Cole at the union hall. If Nat could not have Charlie for his trio, perhaps this Oscar would do. He was funny too; as a balance to the bass player's gravity, the guitarist had a sense of humor that matched Nat's whimsy.

The chemistry was right. No sooner did Oscar Moore unpack his sunburst acoustic guitar in the rehearsal room than Nathaniel discovered a musical soul mate. They had grown up listening to the same jazzmen: Louis Armstrong, Earl Hines, Jimmie Noone, Art Tatum. But who would have imagined they would think the same thoughts and feel the same things musically? "Those guys were joined at the hip," said Lee Young.

As the two played through the whole repertory of jazz classics, from New Orleans blues and Dixieland to high Chicago swing, steady Wesley Prince fell in behind them. Pausing only to light cigarettes, the trio played for hours on end.

Then they auditioned for Bob Lewis.

Lewis may have realized the Trio's potential before they did. Hiring the men for a two-week run sometime late in 1937, the promoter kept them on for six months.

Shadows fall on this period of Nat's history, and the facts and dates are hard to pin down. Memories of the Trio's schedule over the next year vary wildly. Though everyone agrees they opened at the Swanee Inn in 1937 and "stayed on six months," no one recalls when the six months began or ended. A contract has survived, from the American Federation of Musicians, between Nat Cole and the Swanee Inn. "Robert Lewis" signed his real surname, Lubitz. The agreement states that the three musicians will receive $110 weekly to play from 8:30 to 2:00 nightly, starting March 11, 1938, and is dated March 15. This confirms anecdotes that the Trio got a raise to $110 per week sometime early in 1938. But the contract shows no closing date, so there is no telling when they left the Swanee Inn. The next notice of a change in venue occurs in Variety, November 6, 1938, announcing that "King Cole and his Sepia Swingsters replaced Kay St. Germann & Co. at Jim Otto's in L.A." Johnny Mercer saw them there.

One thing is certain: During the year preceding September 1938, when the Trio made their first records for Standard Transcriptions in Hollywood, these musicians were busy night and day, forging and polishing a musical style that would capture the mood of a generation. In the life of a true artist there comes a time of inspiration so intense that the man becomes one with his creation. For Nat Cole the years 1938–42 were just such a time.

The recordings made in those years, about a hundred and twenty-five tunes, show a constant development of piano technique that is quite dazzling from the first. They also exhibit artistry in molding the small ensemble that ranks with the greatest achievements in jazz between the two World Wars. If there is a scarcity of data about

123

Nat's day-to-day life during this period, there is abundant evidence of his inner life in the shellac grooves of the recordings he made with dashing Oscar Moore and solid Wesley Prince.

The records tell a tale of struggle and unstinting labor, sheer delight in virtuosity and humor in the face of life's madness. They sing out the joys of friendship and romantic love, and loyalty to the great musical traditions.

Jazz began when the blues, spirituals, and field hollers of the rural South met the Negro marching bands and ragtime piano players of Storyville, New Orleans. The Dixieland music King Oliver brought with him from New Orleans to Chicago in 1919 was ensemble performance rooted in social rituals that had called it into being. This was dance music foremost. But it also echoed the sound of military marches, weddings and funerals, the track lining of gandy dancers and the call-and-response of revival meetings. The joy and exuberance of Dixieland comes from the liberty of its many musicians, sometimes verging on anarchy. But the ultimate success of a musical number comes from a balance of voices, so that no one dominates. This is a choral form, without a main soloist, without heroes. Dixieland is extroverted, made for action rather than reflection.

The blues was on its own course: A man with a guitar or a woman leaning against a piano could always draw the listener into a private world of thoughts and feelings, the world of lyric poetry. Guitar wizard Blind Lemon Jefferson and singer Ma Rainey, both working in relative obscurity, paved the way for the enormous popular success of Bessie Smith in the mid-1920s. With her sultry, romantic blues voice, Smith is the mother of all torch singers and "ballad" singers, from Billie Holiday and Frank Sinatra to Aretha Franklin. Bessie is the quintessential soloist, the voice that must be heard above all others for the urgency of its message.

Nat Cole and Oscar Moore learned to play during the so-called Golden Age of Jazz, roughly from 1924 to 1934. Explaining the richness of that musical era is beyond the scope of this book. But one reason the music flourished is that solo musicians, with their intense feelings and thoughts, their *personalities,* began to emerge from the symmetrical ranks of the Dixieland bands. The soloists were Jelly Roll Morton, Louis Armstrong, Earl Hines, Bix Beiderbecke, Jimmie Noone, Coleman Hawkins, and a dozen others less well known. Each stepped forward, tentatively at first. But as the crowd encouraged and identified with a player, he grew bolder until the goal was achieved: a full musical statement, anywhere from a few bars to a double chorus, that bore the artist's signature. This the jazzman managed to do without overwhelming, or even compromising, the ensemble and its larger purpose — to entertain the crowd, to make them dance, move them to tears and laughter. This was the glory of that decade, the Golden Mean, the perfect balance between the soloist's poetic ego and the social purpose of the jazz band.

By the 1940s the balance was gone. Benny Goodman's orchestra and the "sweet" dance bands of the Swing Era, Glenn Miller's and Artie Shaw's, had regulated the tempos and rhythms, squeezing the spontaneity out of jazz while making it more suitable for high school proms. Meanwhile at the other end of the spectrum stood the introspective Dizzy Gillespie, an avatar of bebop, in the cave of the after-hours club. He thought Louis Armstrong was sadly short of imagination, while Louis accused Dizzy of playing beyond the interests of the jazz audience. The precious balance was gone: between the ensemble and the soloist, between the choral and the lyric, between action and reflection. The age had been golden because it was precious, humanly fragile. And like all things human, it could not last.

Nathaniel Cole's childhood ambition was to be a big bandleader and soloist in the tradition of Jelly Roll Morton, Duke Ellington, and Earl Hines. After a moment of glory at the Ubangi Club in July 1937, the harsh realities of the music business made him give up that dream forever. But all of his musical instincts and his ambitions to shape the sound of an ensemble were then channeled into the vessels of three instruments: piano, guitar, and bass. Peculiar, because all three of these, technically, are rhythm instruments, or so they had been called in the context of the jazz orchestra. Without horns or reeds, the piano and guitar would maximize their potential for melody. Yet their percussive, rhythmic power made them irresistible to dancers. The Trio would largely define the term "swing" because, despite their modest number, no group on earth could swing like Nat Cole's Trio.

126

Nat and Oscar brought to the Trio the sum total of jazz wisdom they had learned from the music's Golden Age. This included the balance of soloist and ensemble, the balance of action and reflection, and the interplay of theme and improvisation. Nat and Oscar would play duets like no one since Louis Armstrong and Earl Hines. Less oppositional than Earl and Louis, Nat and Oscar could finish each other's lines with such seamless ease that at times you could not tell piano from guitar. They would sing or "scat-sing" tunes in unison (sometimes with Prince as a third voice) with astounding precision that must have taken long hours of practice, and with a lovely timbral blending that was simply a gift of the gods. They could play those same tunes in unison, creating a sound that was not quite guitar and not quite piano, but another tone richer than either, a voice greater than the sum of its parts.

At first most nightclub managers were skeptical: "You can't fill a club with a band of three. A stage or a dance floor just makes you look pathetic." They called them the Chamber Music Kids and the Trio from Hunger.

But wherever they played, they caught on.

In less than a year they had become a small sensation in Hollywood, a band with a cult following and the seeds of a legend. Some people say it was Bob Lewis who named them the King Cole Trio, but maybe it was Wesley Prince who thought of this after recalling the nursery rhyme "Old King Cole." The group knew their Mother Goose, as we shall see. Some say Bob Lewis tried to get Nathaniel to wear a cutout crown to suit the image; some say he never wore the cardboard because it was uncomfortable and undignified.

Some say Nat never sang until a drunk demanded it. But this is a whopper, made up to strengthen the myth that *all* of Nat's successes were somebody else's idea and not his. There was hardly ever a time the young man did not sing. He just got so much better at singing after "Sweet Loraine" (1939) that no one cares to recall the years of practice that led up to the triumph. This was all part of the legend, the "buzz" about the boys that started at once, as it will when a phenomenon appears on the scene. Folks try to account for it, to explain, creating a history or background if there is none. How can something so new be so ripe, so complex? The true answer is in the music, of course, in the jazz tradition. Nat Cole, Oscar Moore, and Wesley Prince were standing on the shoulders of giants, the master musicians of the Golden Age of Jazz.

After working and playing together for nearly a year at the Swanee Inn, then at Jim Otto's and Foxhill's Café, the Trio entered the studio for the first time in September of 1938. The recording company was Standard Transcriptions. They made sixteen-inch discs for radio, not for retail sale.

The performing style and subject matter of the tunes recorded that September give us a vivid idea of the group's appeal. The men's charm was youth, puppy love, playful innocence on the edge of the naive. The first cut on the album is Johnny Mercer's "Mutiny in the Nursery" ("Mother

Goose is on the loose, her kids are swingin' hot"), followed by "F.D.R. Jones," about the naming of a baby boy. Then there is "Button, Button" (Who's got the button?), a child's game, and "Jingle Bells."

These songs and others they sing — and scat-sing — stopping just short of dissolving into baby talk, while giving the impression, as did the early Beatles, of being so cute and cuddly and good that your daughter would be safe with them in the darkness of the Swanee Inn.

This childlike innocence, so appropriate to the Trio's formative years, stands in stark contrast to the players' musical virtuosity, the sophistication of their sound. Long hours of practice had given Nat the speed and agility on the keyboard he lacked in competition with Earl Hines, the sureness of touch and control that was wanting in the records he made with his brother Eddie in 1936. No longer was he reaching for unachievable effects. To borrow a sports phrase, he had started to play within himself — he had begun to find his own style. This is clear from the introductory section of "Mutiny" — the simple chords in the left hand, the spare, rippling one-note melody in the treble with only a single triplet for ornamentation. Here is the lightness of touch that would become the pianist's signature.

Other cuts from that date show Cole's technique in full flower. In "With Plenty of Money and You" (from the movie *Gold Diggers of 1937*), Moore and Cole exchange a machine-gun fire of notes for the first eight bars. From then on it is a race in triple time, slowing down only now and then to catch their breath, to clarify the theme, then hurtling on to another chorus at breakneck speed. After a few choruses Oscar surrenders to Nat because the guitar simply cannot play notes as quickly as the piano. Oscar "comps" chords as fast as he can while the piano plays three or four notes for every one of the guitar or bass. If it is possible to play faster than Earl Hines, Cole does it here, at one point playing a descending run of forty or more distinct notes in less than four seconds. This does not make for pleasant listening — it is rather nerve-wracking pyrotechnics. But it proves that Nat's obsessive practicing has paid off. He can do with the piano whatever he likes.

Fortunately what Cole liked to play was not the daredevil, exploratory style of Hines or the highly ornamental, baroque manner of Tatum. Instead, he preferred elegance and wit, chromatic richness and melodic invention. And above all he loved rhythm — nothing must interfere with the song's forward movement, the effect on the dancers, the swing.

Listen to what he does with Johann Strauss's "Blue Danube." His introductory measures are rapid arpeggios based on minor and diminished chords — dramatic, almost foreboding in mood. Suddenly the darkness gives way to Strauss's bright, cheerful, and utterly surprising theme — nothing in the chromatic introduction has prepared us for the old "Blue Danube." And when the theme at last arrives, it comes strutting on-stage like a buckdancer in a string tie — not in waltz time but in syncopated 4/4 rhythm (doo-*doo*-doo-doo) with a few guitar chords in the background. When they hit the bridge the musicians speed up into double time, then relax back into single time for the last eight bars. The mood is comic but the rhythm never loses its swing. From this rhythmic base the Trio breezes into a sunny field of freewheeling variations on the Strauss themes, a breadth of easy discourse where the piano and guitar can run and play joyously.

In October 1938 the Trio returned to the studio to record four final tunes. Perhaps by design, these four — "Don't Blame Me," "Lullaby in Rhythm," "Dark Rapture," and "By the River St. Marie" — are slightly more serious in tone, more grown-up. Anyone curious about Nat's singing voice at the time will find worthy solos on "Lullaby in Rhythm" and "By the River St. Marie," and the latter foreshadows his later ballad style — lisping and a bit husky, but the sweet tone and distinctive phrasing are there. He sounds somewhat like his brother Eddie, and a little like Louis Armstrong in his sharp, declarative delivery. But he sounds most like himself, ironically an *older* version of the singer we will hear ten years later.

The crowd at Jim Otto's Steak House in November 1938 included Lee Young, Red Callender, composer Johnny Mercer, Bing Crosby, Disney animator Marc Davis, every L.A. jazz musician and fanatic on the cutting edge of the art, and Carlos Gastel. Gastel was a stocky, streetwise kid on his way to becoming the finest agent in the music business. He had heard Nat on the radio and then met him at the Fox Hills cocktail lounge on Pico Boulevard. He brought his friends wherever

Nat played, including Jim Otto's.

What they saw through the iridescent smoke, on the little raised stage, was electrifying. A long-legged, slick-haired young man with a wide-mouth smile and a wicked twinkle in his eye sat sideways at the piano, facing the audience. To his left stood the dapper guitarist, handsome as Errol Flynn, fluttering his eyelashes, a peacock in his floral shirt. Behind them and behind his huge red bass stood Wesley Prince, a solid, paternal presence looking always amused, the faint smile on his face suggesting pride and wonder, as if to say, "I don't know what these guys might do next, but boys *will* be boys."

Oscar Moore strummed the introduction, and the Trio sang in unison:

> *Flea hop'll get you.*
> *Flea hop'll get you.*
> *Flea hop'll get you.*
> *Hop around like a kangaroo.*

It was nonsense, foolishness, kindergarten stuff Nat had made up. But in 1938 the world was all too serious, with ten million Americans out of work and a third of American families living below the poverty line. Woody Guthrie was moaning "Hard Traveling" somewhere in a union hall in the Dust Bowl. But here in sunny California these jazzmen sounded something like hope.

> *You do what you wanna.*
> *You do what you wanna.*
> *Hop around like a kangaroo.*

132

They were singing nursery rhymes, but with a beat that was adult, sophisticated, infectious; at once they were capturing the innocence — and the erotic energy — of youth.

The swinging beat was so contagious that, if there had been room to dance between the round tables at Jim Otto's, no one would be sitting there, smoking and drinking, while Oscar riffed and Nat backed up his chorus. But Nat would do the dancing for them all as he sat at the keyboard, stretching a leg out and tapping, snatching it back under him, shooting it out again, and rocking his shiny shoe on its heel. Meanwhile he was moving his shoulders in time to the beat, shifting them counter to his hips. The man was all rhythm, every lean inch of him. He never toed the piano pedals and hardly seemed, in fact, to touch the keyboard with his long fingers. That's just how smooth he was, looking out at you from the corners of his narrow eyes, grinning and then pursing his mouth in concentration while the piano seemed to be playing itself.

Suddenly they pulled long faces, and sang: "Nobody knows . . ." to the tune of the mournful spiritual "Nobody Knows the Trouble I've Seen," but then switched up on the audience and sang, with impish glee: "Nobody knows . . . the *fleas* I've seen . . . Rah dah, Rah dah, *Rah,* dah dah dah, *Rah* dah."

The Nat Cole Swingsters were tweaking the ears of despair, laughing in the face of the world's gloom.

A studio session later that month included "Flea Hop" and a number of other scat-singing

133

"novelty" tunes like "Chopsticks," "Patty Cake," and "Three Blind Mice." But the session also captured what must have been a grandstand solo at Otto's or the Foxhill Café, on Juan Tizol's exotic "Caravan." Nat plays most of the piece in octave trills, sometimes in the right hand, sometimes the left, sometimes in both, veering from the theme to create chromatic fantasies over a "pedal point" or sustained trill. At the climactic chorus he breaks into double time just as he changes from the minor key to the major. The second bar of the out-chorus is a scintillating descending run of triplet thirty-second notes that would have done credit to his old friend Art Tatum.

Disc jockeys liked the transcriptions. So did the radio audience. By the end of 1938, NBC radio wanted the King Cole Trio. On December 10, Nat's hometown newspaper the *Chicago Defender* rediscovered its lost son, reporting: "King Cole and his swing trio, a regular feature each Monday evening at 5 p.m. over the Blue network of NBC's new Hollywood Radio City, are causing as much consternation in the Movie City as the now formed Benny Goodman Trio. Their style of playing swing music has been accepted by Hollywood masters of swing."

They were no longer a well-kept secret.

The intense creative work — and play — of 1937 and 1938 yielded a more enduring music the next year, as Nat grew more confident and the combo began anchoring the style that would make them famous in the 1940s.

The schedule from New Year's Day until spring

left little time for Masonic meetings, pickup base-ball games, or swimming at the beach. From January 15 until April 23 the Trio appeared every night of the week at Jim Otto's except Monday. That day they took the guitar and bass to Hollywood Radio City, where they performed on NBC's *Swing Soiree* from 8:30 to 9:00.

On January 14 the combo did their first transcription session for Davis & Schwengler at Radio Recorder's Studio, waxing four of their own tunes. They returned to the studio twice more that month — as the King Cole Swingsters — to record, first with singer Bonnie Lake, then with Juanelda Carter, a gifted black vocalist, only seventeen years old at the time. Their collaborations with Lake, Carter, and later that April with Pauline Byrns (of the group Pauline and Her Perils) indicate that the Trio was still in flux, looking for their musical center of gravity.

The men had found their center of gravity as far as subject and theme were concerned. Having charmed and disarmed the nightclub audience and radio listeners with their innocent scat-singing of Mother Goose and jump-rope rhymes, now they were claiming a jazzman's dominion, the realm of jitterbug ecstasy and erotic love. They would return to the comic "novelty" tune in 1941, 1942, and 1943 for some of their greatest successes, including "Gone with the Draft" and "Straighten Up and Fly Right." But by then there would be nothing even remotely naive about the Trio's message. The later novelty tunes are the product of a sophisticated, ironic wit, more like Cole Porter than Mother Goose.

The first song they recorded in 1939 begins with a rhythmic rapping at a door. Wesley Prince is beating a tattoo on his bass. Soon Prince pipes up in a feminine falsetto:

"Who's dat knockin' at the doctor's door?"

"It's me, nurse, old Oscar Moore," says the guitarist.

"Whatta ya wanna see Dr. King Cole for?"

"It's about love, 'cause it's got me on the floor."

"I *am* the doctor!" says Nat. "What can I do you for?"

Oscar launches into the lover's complaint, the immemorial symptoms of lovesickness, to which Dr. Nat responds with the refrain "I'm sorry, there's no anesthetic for love."

Now these young musicians, with an audience increasing by leaps and bounds, and more and more attractive women attracted to them, were singing about something they understood. Moore's marriage would not survive the early, heady years of the Trio's success. And Nat and Nadine were soon feeling the stress of King Cole's appeal to women. From January to May the forty songs the Trio recorded, even Nat's duets with the white singer Bonnie Lake like "I Lost Control of Myself," display a growing romantic interest, unashamed of the erotic. The very song titles are revealing, seductive: "Some Like It Hot," "That Please Be Mineable Feeling," and "Don't Let That Moon Get Away." There were nights when her young husband would not come home, and Nadine sat on a park bench angry, worried, looking up at the moon, wondering where he could be. In the daylight she would find notes in girls' handwriting in his pockets as she took his shirts to the cleaners.

The music was progressing on two fronts, as popular music must. The dance tunes were becoming more irresistible, the love songs more intimate, reminding us of the old distinction between Dixieland-inspired ensemble jazz and the solo lyricism of the blues ballad. It was these two traditions, which the Trio had mastered, that were bearing fruit in the spare, elegant compositions for piano, guitar, and bass.

By May of 1939 it had all come together. Nearly two years of ceaseless creative work and practice had paid off. The musicians entered the Radio Recorder's Studio in Hollywood to wax eight songs that show the Trio in full maturity. It is not their greatest work (that is still to come), but it shows the form that will make them famous and one of them, eventually, a millionaire.

The May sessions include Nat's first recording of "Sweet Loraine," his instrumental tribute to Earl Hines's "Rosetta," and several stunning solos that prefigure the rhythmic leaps and harmonic surprises of bebop. In "Sweet Loraine" we discover the balladeer at last totally at ease, crooning his old friend Jimmie Noone's theme song. Though he has nearly conquered his lisp, Nathaniel's diction still has a way to go before it reaches the perfection that one day will make him the scourge of mediocre lyricists.

> *I just found joy.*
> *I'm as happy as a baby boy*
> *With another brand-new choo choo choy,*

The third line is not a typo. That is the way the young crooner sings it, twice, unable to pronounce the hard *t* in toy. But even the mistake has boyish charm, as the ballad reduces the audience to warm butter. After the bridge we hear, for the first time, Nat singing the famous *Wo-ho-ho* scat, mellow, honey-rich, a sound that will become a trademark — praised, mimicked, finally parodied, condemned in the 1940s as a mannerism.

"Rosetta" may be heard as Cole's ultimate tribute to his idol, Earl Hines, an homage and truce with the master pianist. Cole graciously accepts the lovely melody, and then smoothly takes it over, making it completely his own. He does not try to compete with Hines in quantity or velocity, although he plays a few runs and arpeggios at lightning speed. Cole's understanding of the theme has put him above such vulgar considerations. If Hines was the first jazz pianist to establish the independence of the left hand, the long-shackled bass, from the dominant right, then it was *this,* thought young Cole, that really counted. This duality the young genius carries to the realm of the sublime. In his left hand he carries the melody of "Rosetta," at once chaste and passionate. And in the right hand he plays the most imaginative, open descant, an obbligato of trills, triplets, and glissandos as natural as the singing of a wood thrush.

What sounds most remarkable about this solo, unparalleled, unexampled, is the complete independence of the two voices, the melody of the bass and the obbligato in the treble. It seems almost schizophrenic. Hard to believe it is not two people playing the piano, one ardent, the other carefree — on the one hand a seasoned master, on the other a boy wonder.

Despite the trio's growing popularity, money was still tight. When Nathaniel found the time, he made a little cash coaching singers and writing arrangements for musicians and dancers. Lee Young believes that Nat's own singing style was consciously forged in his efforts to explain the art of phrasing to aspiring vocalists. He also recalls that Cole was an uncommonly gifted arranger, so good he could get away with handing in his work in pencil; most arrangers had to pay a copyist to redo the score in ink.

Nadine and Nat, both working night and day, scraped together enough money to pay the rent on a small house, at 2910 South St. Andrews Place, a few miles west of Central Avenue. Maybe now they would have a child. At last they had a home, but it would be years before they would have the money to own one.

Disc jockeys were playing the Trio's transcription recordings as fast as they could get them, and the radio exposure attracted the attention of national jazz magazines. In September, *Down Beat* reported: "The King Cole Swingsters have moved back to the Swanee Inn. While Benny Goodman was in town, Lionel Hampton came every night to play two-finger piano with the King and his boys. Lionel plans to use the Trio on some records soon." In October a picture of Nat, Oscar, and

Wesley at the NBC microphone appeared in *Metronome.*

Their first out-of-town booking came in November when they got the call to go to New York City. Ralph Watkins, former bandleader and co-owner of Kelly's Stables on West 52nd Street, wanted them to play on a bill with Billie Holiday. Imagine the young men's excitement as they crossed the country for the first time in Nat's secondhand automobile, on the way to the Big Apple to play jazz with Lady Day! The gorgeous, appealingly vulnerable singer was only twenty-four, but already she had made great records with Buck Clayton as well as Lee Young's brother Lester. She wore a gardenia in her hair. Her sexy voice "rang like a bell and went a mile," according to one admirer.

Nathaniel had a lot to learn from the great ballad singer, heiress to Bessie Smith's legacy. He would hang on her every note.

A story has come down to us that Ralph Watkins had to coax Nat to sing at Kelly's. One day Watkins got a call from his bookkeeper, who could not do her work in the club because Nat was practicing his singing. "Singin' this one number over and over until I'm goin' nuts," said the poor woman.

"Nat doesn't sing," Watkins said, and hurried to the club. There he crept up on Nat as he practiced "Sweet Loraine." When Watkins heard how well Cole could sing, he insisted he share his gift with the patrons.

No doubt Billie Holiday was a hard act to follow. But certainly the younger man benefited from following Lady Day's example during that Yuletide season.

"They have done swell business at Kelly's Stables," *Down Beat* reported on New Year's Day 1940. They also printed a rumor that the Trio had signed with the William Morris Agency and would soon appear at the prestigious Offbeat Club in Chicago. But January found them back home in L.A., where their old friend Bob Lewis had booked them into the Radio Room. This club stood across the street from NBC in Hollywood, at the hub of the city's music life. Frank Sinatra would stop by and listen to the Trio, which was in residence there more than a year. That summer Johnny Mercer, a replacement artist on *The Bob Hope Show*, went again to hear Cole and his men; so did drummer Buddy Rich, and Mercer's friend bandleader Paul Weston.

They were such a draw that in July Glen Wallichs wanted them to play for the gala opening of his Music City at Sunset and Vine. This was a record store, where Wallichs soon began making his own records — 78 rpm wax cylinders — with a single microphone. In 1942, with Johnny Mercer and producer Buddy De Sylva, Glen Wallichs would found Capitol Records.

Lionel Hampton's flirtation with the Trio at last spawned two recording sessions for Victor, on May 10 and July 17. The eight sides waxed then are mostly a showcase for Hampton on vibes, piano, and drums, and for the memorable singer Helen Forest. But Nat Cole and Oscar Moore both play fine solos on the justly renowned "Jack the Bellboy," where Hampton practically remakes the drum kit as a solo instrument. The critic Hughes Panassie called "Bellboy" one of the most spectacular displays in the history of jazz, and not just for the drumming. The King Cole Trio was a flattering rhythm section for Hampton's little band. It is easy to see why he wanted to keep them.

On August 15, Leonard Feather reported in *Down Beat* that the King Cole Trio would form the basis for a new Hampton orchestra. But it did not happen. Lee Young, just returning from New York, had heard Clarence Profit's Trio, which was beginning to draw a crowd and make money. "You're much better than Profit," Lee told Nat. "Don't lose yourself in Hampton's orchestra." Nat took his friend's advice.

Already the Trio had made music that would long outlive them. And their fame was growing among the true jazz fans who understood their genius. But the men were working long, hard hours for little money. They had recorded more than a hundred tunes in two years, mostly for the transcription business, which paid little — a small hourly fee and no royalties. ("Transcriptions" were sixteen-inch discs made for radio broadcast and not retailed to the public.) The legend of Nat's facility in sight-reading and memorizing sheet music, his reputation as a "one take" recording artist, conceals the great labor that went into every song. They made it look easy, singing in unison faster than most people can sing solo, or playing arpeggios in unison so quickly you cannot tell piano from guitar. But this took long hours in a rehearsal room.

In a hot, sunny studio above Central Avenue, Nat King Cole sat at a battered piano smoking the last of his second pack of cigarettes of the day. He wore a loose-fitting beige short-sleeve shirt. Oscar Moore sat across from him, silently fingering his guitar fretboard, looking up at Nat, waiting for a sign. Oscar's shirt had a bright red floral print. Two rings on his left hand glittered in the sunlight. Wesley Prince leaned against the wall looking out the window at the traffic. The dark bass fiddle leaned against Wesley Prince.

World War II had been raging in Europe for nearly a year, and FDR had just started the first peacetime military draft in U.S. history. Any one of the musicians might be called away tomorrow. How did they handle the anxiety? Prince decided to write a funny song about it, taking off from the title of the recent movie sensation *Gone with the Wind*. The song was called "Gone with the Draft," and Nat was helping Wesley to write it.

By now their rehearsal procedure was well established. First they learned the melody. Then the group would sit around and improvise variations on the theme, discovering effective harmonies. Nat wrote down the notes. Then the leader-pianist would say to Wesley, "You take this," and to Oscar he would say, "You take that." Having established the voicing, having set the choruses and assigned the solos, they began to play.

Eight bars of piano and eight bars of bass intro and they started singing:

Gone, gone, gone with the Draft
Gone, gone, gone with the Draft . . .

143

Sometimes the boys could master a tune, particularly a standard, in an afternoon rehearsal. But this tune had taken days. The piece was original, the subject delicate, and if it did not have exactly the right tone, the perfect balance of wit, male camaraderie and self-parody, the effort would fall flat.

Nathaniel looked at his own body, and wrote these verses:

> *When skinny little me went out with my honey*
> *The boys who saw us all laughed.*
> *But now it's not so funny —*
> They're *all gone with the draft . . .*

The song describes a comic antihero, a skinny guy with flat feet who has always been the butt of jokes — that is, until the draft takes away all the men with "fine physiques," leaving him at home to make love to all the women.

If Nat, Wesley, and Oscar were nervous about the war and the draft, so were twenty million other men. It was a great relief to all of them to be able to laugh about it. The recording of this song for Standard Transcriptions in November 1940 was an important step for Cole in bonding with the men of his generation who would fight for their country in Europe and the Pacific in the coming years.

But he was still working for peanuts. His last transcription for Davis & Schwengler on July 22 was never paid for. The Trio recorded twelve songs on that date, and the company went bankrupt before they issued the records. The Trio sued, at considerable expense, and sometime that autumn they were awarded $7.47 for their pains.

At the end of the year, when Earl Hines came to Los Angeles with his band and singer Billy Eckstine, Nat went to visit his old Chicago friends at the Dunbar Hotel. Nadine was working as a waitress around the corner. According to Truck Parham, Hines's bass player, Earl and Billy found Nat in such dire financial straits they took up a collection for him among the band members, raising a couple of hundred dollars so Nat could pay his bills before Christmas.

A YEAR ON THE ROAD

Somebody at Decca Records spotted the commercial potential of "Gone with the Draft" and "Sweet Loraine." Perhaps the producer remembered the charismatic boy wonder pianist who had recorded four sides for the company in 1936. Major record labels were more or less subtly segregated for marketing purposes until after World War II, and Decca wanted Nat Cole's sound for their "Sepia" division. So on December 6, 1940, the Trio recorded the tunes on flip sides of "Honeysuckle Rose" and the blues number "This Side Up."

"A promising debut for this group," said *Down Beat*, when the platters were released in March of 1941. In a sense it *was* a debut for the Trio, their first commercial recording of 78s for a major label (they had waxed four sides for the obscure Ammor label in February of 1940). Nat's diction is more confident as he croons "Sweet Loraine," though the effort to conquer his lisp on the sibilants is evident in the thickness of the s's as he sings "When it's raining I don't miss the sun." His solo piano work shines on "Honeysuckle Rose," paying homage to Fats Waller while playing rings around him, with Hines runs and Tatum embellishments. And in the blues stomp "This Side Up" we begin to hear Nat "quote" from other melodies, notably Grieg's "Anitra's Dance," a witty allusion thematically and historically. Nat would become renowned for his wit in "quoting" passages of other music within an improvisation. His quotes were always resonant with meaning, never arbitrary or unfit, as Art Tatum's might be, never there simply to show off his technique.

The release of these records and the review of them in *Down Beat* mark a significant advance in the Trio's career. They were not finished with cheap radio transcription recordings, but the musicians were on their way to making their own highly marketable discs, for real money. The sixteen sides they waxed for Decca before November 1941 include the classics "This Will Make You Laugh," "I Like to Riff," "Call the Police," "That Ain't Right," and "Hit That Jive, Jack," catchy tunes that were soon on everyone's lips from Hollywood to New York. Al Jarvis, disc jockey and promoter in L.A., gave the records a big play on his show, and so did jockey Gene Norman.

The Decca records won them two influential fans in the business of booking talent: Tom Rockwell of L.A.'s General Artists Corporation, and his young Chicago associate Berle Adams. GAC (later renamed General Amusement) hired Adams, a boyish, energetic Chicagoan, to build the business in cocktail lounges. The mayor of Chicago wanted his city to be the U.S. military's capital of R & R.

When Rockwell approached Nat Cole early in 1941 with plans for a performance tour of Chicago, New York, Philadelphia, and Washington, D.C., Nat was eager, even though GAC could not promise much money. The Trio needed the exposure, especially in New York and Chicago. Companies like Decca considered L.A. a province, a backwater. They would even prefer having the artists record for them in a New York or Chicago studio.

Excited by the Trio's sound, Adams booked them into the Dome Room of the Sherman Hotel in Chicago, where they would open on March 7.

For Nathaniel and Nadine the homecoming must have been joyful though somewhat awkward. Nat had not seen his mother and father since he eloped with Nadine in the winter of 1937. The Reverend was a kind man but stern in his belief in old-fashioned proprieties. Now Nathaniel was driving a late-model Buick and in the trunk were presents for his brothers and sister. While the Reverend's brilliant son had a great deal to show for his years AWOL, he would also have a lot of explaining to do. His sister Evelyn, now a lovely woman of twenty-six, and his brothers Freddy and Ike, now nine and thirteen, were overjoyed to see him. So was Perlina, who had never doubted the authenticity of his calling, or his goodness.

But the Reverend Edward Coles, concerned about an older brother's example, would have a number of questions about the pianist's business in his hometown. It did not help matters that Adams had booked the Trio into the Dome Room, a notorious pickup joint and far from respectable.

On March 14 the Trio recorded "Babs," "Scotchin' with the Soda," "Slow Down," and "Early Morning Blues" in the Decca studios. A week later the manager of the Sherman Hotel, Er-nest Byfield, summoned Berle Adams into his office.

"Have you been in the Dome Room?" asked the kind manager.

"Yes," said the young promoter sheepishly.

"Well," said Mr. Byfield, raising his eyebrows, "Mr. Cole doesn't belong there, does he?" It was not so much a question as a statement of fact.

"No, sir, he doesn't," Adams admitted.

It was Byfield's observation that Nathaniel Cole was too refined for the vulgar revelry of the Dome Room. Reverend Coles would agree.

"Now you do have a contract, Mr. Adams. But everybody tells me you control a number of places in this city, and you can move people around. Mr. Cole is a very nice man, and I don't want him out of work . . . I would appreciate it . . . if you would find another job for Mr. Cole . . ."

At that time the Mills Brothers were working with Louis Jordan and Maurice Rocco at the Capitol Lounge. This was a real mecca for jazz fans, next to the Chicago Theater on State Street. It was a long room with a big bar to one side of the high stage and high-backed green booths across the back where people sat. Fans stood at the bar, ten or twelve deep, and drank and listened to music. The Mills Brothers were finishing their stint when Adams approached owners Milt Schwartz and Al Greenfield to convince them to hire the King Cole Trio for the bill. The owners resisted at first, saying they already had enough firepower to draw a crowd. But Adams would not take no for an answer.

So for a 35-cent glass of beer in late March

149

1941, if you happened to be in the Windy City, you could hear, any night at the Capitol Lounge: Louis Jordan and his Tympani Five singing "Choo, Choo, Ch'Boogie," Maurice Rocco playing stand-up piano, and the King Cole Trio. The Trio was a big hit there and stayed on into April. The Capitol paid little but the lounge was a perfect showcase for the jazz ensemble in Chicago.

Berle admired Nat's singing of Jimmie Noone's theme song, "Sweet Loraine." Nat had learned the tune from Jimmie and wanted Berle to meet the idol of his youth, his friend the master clarinetist. So one night Adams took the two of them to dinner.

Portly, dreamy Jimmie Noone could not be called old at age forty-six. But the years had not been kind to the clarinetist, though he was kindness itself. He played classic, small ensemble jazz of the Golden Age; swing music had practically put him out of business. His famous jollity was giving way to gloom. In the restaurant one noticed that, unlike other musicians, the clarinetist did not drink whiskey or smoke cigarettes. But Jimmie ate like he was going to jail. He ate rapidly and voraciously and for a long time. He had high blood pressure, and doctors warned that the food would kill him. But the jazzman did not seem to care.

Nathaniel was worried about Noone. He was out of work. Club owners would not hire him because of the way he looked. They wanted young, svelte hip cats like Nat King Cole. Could Berle find Jimmie a job somewhere? asked Nat Cole.

Adams looked at Cole in wonder, and he smiled. Here was a struggling pianist, a kid just

150

turned twenty-two. The promoter had just moved heaven and earth to get him the right gig in Chicago. And now what was the kid doing? He was asking a big favor, not for himself, but for this poor slob of a clarinetist who couldn't even get out of his own way.

Berle Adams found work for Jimmie Noone. More than once.

For almost a year, May 1941 until May 1942, the Trio lived in New York City, with side trips to play in Washington, D.C., Philadelphia, and a return engagement in Chicago at the Capitol Lounge in the autumn. They started out in a little club called Nick's on Seventh Avenue in Greenwich Village, a place known for Dixieland music. But by mid-June they were back at their old base on West 52nd Street, Kelly's Stables, as intermission band for Billie Holiday, "Hot Lips" Page and his orchestra, and Billy Daniels.

In New York's Decca studios, on July 16, they waxed four sides including the romantic ballad "This Will Make You Laugh." This plaintive record had such seductive appeal and created such a stir, it seemed sure to become a major hit. But Decca was using up its wartime ration of shellac to press Bing Crosby's discs; the company's failure to keep up with the demand for the Trio's "race" records would soon lead to a parting of the ways.

Singer Frankie "Mule Train" Laine recalls the first time he saw Nat Cole perform at Kelly's Stables. The joint had once been called O'Leary's Barn, and still had sawdust on the floor, and brass carriage lamps on either side of the stage. During

Billie Holiday's break, Nat led his group on to the small platform. Wearing a beige sport coat and a brown shirt, he sat at the keyboard in front of a wide mural depicting racehorses. Wesley Prince and Oscar Moore were in their shirtsleeves, ready to work. Someone offstage announced: "And now, ladies and gentlemen, the King Cole Trio!" Nat smiled and played with great joy and enthusiasm, but he seemed quite shy.

When Cole launched into an instrumental like "Sweet Georgia Brown" Oscar looked over Nat's shoulder at his hands, devouring the movement with his eyes. First Oscar's face was serious. Then the guitarist smiled slightly as he picked up the chord changes, filled in a phrase, played an obbligato. Nat knew that Oscar heard where the piano was headed in an improvisation before he did himself. Nat would show his appreciation with a glance at the guitarist out of the corners of his eyes or by biting his lower lip. The two men made up a single voice — joined at the hip, as Lee Young put it.

Nathaniel rarely spoke to the audience, even to introduce his sidemen. That's how it was in 1941, all music.

In the heat of July the Trio traveled to the nation's capital to play in Paul Young's Romany Room. This was where my father first heard Nat Cole. Young, a second-generation Russian Jew who became D.C.'s greatest restaurateur, was a family friend. So Don Epstein benefited from Paul Young's good taste in music, as the Trio first visited our hometown. My father then had a route of rainbow-lighted jukeboxes, which he kept well stocked with Cole records.

Back in New York for the autumn, Nat was happy to see one-eyed Art Tatum playing piano at Kelly's Stables. "Swing Street," as 52nd was called in those days, was swinging all that October, with Tatum on the same bill with the Trio and sax player Benny Carter and his sextet. Carter, thirty-four, had shaped a classic style on the alto sax, a perfect balance of urbane melody and improvisation. Cole and Carter had a natural musical affinity and for the next four years they would do a lot of performing together.

Just across the street from Kelly's was Hickory House, where you could hear the trumpet of Roy Eldridge or Chu Berry's tenor sax. Teddy Wilson or Benny Goodman would drop by after hours to jam or listen. All the pianists used to go to Jimmy Ryan's on Sunday: Nat Cole, Art Tatum, Fats Waller — even Earl Hines if he was in town. Nat was out late most nights jamming. Tatum loved to drink beer. He would finish a song and chug a sixteen-ounce mug of beer, grin, and attack the piano again. He was also "a hell of a pool player for a blind guy," Timmie Rogers recalls. Tatum would close his blind eye to sight down the shaft of the pool cue, which seemed silly, because the eye he was closing couldn't see anything anyway. All the musicians loved to shoot pool.

On a typical workday Nat would rise at noon, smoke, eat lunch, and start making the rounds of the publishers. He was looking for new songs, knowing good tunes were the key to success. Afternoons he devoted to rehearsals and composing, trying out songs and arrangements.

The Trio recorded four more songs for Decca on October 22: "Call the Police," a comic novelty tune Nat had penned; "Are You for It"; "Hit That Jive, Jack"; and "That Ain't Right," a low-down blues also written by Cole, one of his greatest compositions. The catchy lyrics of "Hit That Jive, Jack," written by Skeets Tolbert, became a hip litany, a new handshake routine for the younger generation.

> *Hit that jive, Jack, put it in your pocket*
> *Til I get back.*
> *I'm going downtown to see a man*
> *And I ain't got time to shake your hand.*

This was an early example of the "high fives," later to spread from the ghetto to the world via the athletic fields.

Soon after that session they took the train to Chicago, to play the Capitol Lounge for six weeks. Nat's old-fashioned blues "That Ain't Right" had become an immediate hit in certain local markets, including Chicago. When the Trio arrived in Nat's hometown in November, Sharon A. Pease was waiting to interview them for *Down Beat*. In August the magazine had reprinted a dramatic photo of Cole at the piano singing. Bill Gottlieb, jazz columnist of *The Washington Post*, took the photo, and its caption read: "Man, That's Groovy." Now *Down Beat* printed Gottlieb's photo again, with a full-length profile by Pease. The Trio was really hot, receiving praise from America's premier jazz journal. "Their jump into the national limelight was the result of a dozen good sides made for Decca and a successful tour through the East," wrote Pease. Then the writer focused on their leader: "Nat plays all styles well, slow blues, boogie and jump tunes."

Oscar Moore was also coming into his own, after switching from acoustic to electric guitar. His last note on "That Ain't Right" is a flatted fifth, which would become a standard bebop device. Moore had gone beyond his models Django Reinhardt and Charlie Christian to invent a style that paralleled Nat Cole's. Scholar Will Friedwald writes: "In tandem with Cole, Moore experimented extensively with chordal substitutions in a way that paralleled the developing music of Charlie Parker and Dizzy Gillespie . . . he constructed combinations of multiple tones that did not function as full-blown chords, and altered the placement of the traditional root, third and fifth of the chord with three adjacent notes separated by tiny secondary intervals." Also, Oscar had learned to "bend" notes in a new way, not merely finding the blue third between B and B flat in the key of G. Friedwald adds: "Moore had perfected a way to connect notes, striking one and bending it so it became a whole other note."

The King Cole Trio returned to New York two weeks before Christmas. On December 12 they joined an all-star revue at the Apollo Theater, the Fifth Annual Midnight Benefit Show for the African-American paper the *Amsterdam Star News*. The list of performers reads like a Who's Who of the jazz and movie world: Gene Krupa, Count Basie, Harry James, Benny Goodman, Lionel Hampton, Glenn Miller, Bill Bojangles Robinson,

155

Art Tatum, Fats Waller, Billie Holiday — even Nat's fellow alumnus from Phillips High, bandleader Lucky Millinder, and Nat's brother's old guru, Noble Sissle. Nat got to meet Ed Sullivan, as well as red-haired Lucille Ball and Desi Arnaz. What a thrill for a young performer, to see and be seen in such company!

But along with the heady excitement of having arrived, there came a certain anxiety and melancholy. Fame had not brought money. For a long while they had been playing for "scale" — $30 a week for Oscar and Wesley, and $45 for Nat. At the end Kelly's was paying them a total of $165 a week. The group bunked at the YMCA. And when the wives were in town they all stayed in a cheap hotel up in Harlem.

Nadine was not always with her husband to enjoy his new fame. She would go back to Chicago to stay with the Coles for weeks at a time while Nat was in New York. Or she would return to Los Angeles to take what jobs she could find as a dancer or waitress. A year of living out of suitcases in strange cities, in hotels acceptable only because they would accept blacks, had put a strain on the musicians' marriages — Oscar's especially. But Nathaniel and Nadine were beginning to have serious problems too.

FLY RIGHT

So Nat, Oscar, and Wesley were happy to go home to the California sunshine in June of 1942. And it was all the sweeter to return to a hero's welcome. Up-and-coming jazz impresario Norman Granz and radio disc jockey Al Jarvis led the cheering section.

Herb Rose made the Trio an attractive offer to be the house band at his 331 Club on Eighth Street in West Los Angeles. The small room was nearly always full when the Trio played, buzzing with musicians, songwriters, press agents, actors, and other show-business folk. Frank Sinatra and Judy Garland would drop in, and maybe sing a song or two with the group. Rose doubled the weekly salary the men had been making in New York, while providing them with a showcase at the hub of the L.A. music scene.

And Norman Granz got them another six dollars a night apiece for jamming at Billy Berg's dance hall. Granz organized the sessions on the musicians' night off that the union had just decreed. The jams at Billy's were a huge success. Jimmie Lunceford and Duke Ellington's bands performed there. So did Lee Young and his brother Lester.

The Trio's first months at the 331 Club were pleasantly uneventful. After the roller coaster ride of 1941–42 that landed them in the national limelight, it was time to lie back, consolidate, and regroup. That is literally what happened that summer, as Wesley Prince got his draft notice and Oscar Moore struggled with personal problems. His marriage was ending. His attendance at rehearsals became erratic, so that the guitarist missed out on one of the greatest jazz recording sessions of all time.

The session was Granz's idea. Two weeks before salary disputes caused the union to ban instrumentalists from recording, the impresario decided nothing would be finer than to record some sides with Nat Cole on piano, Lester Young on tenor sax, Oscar Moore on guitar, and Red Callender on bass.

At the appointed time on a Friday afternoon, in Glen Wallichs's studio, the musicians stood around waiting for Oscar Moore. After more than an hour Red Callender said, "Let's go ahead and do it."

The remaining trio of tenor sax, piano, and bass then "got a balance and played, having no notion it would be for posterity," Callender recalled. The four sides cut on that July 15, 1942, turned out to be a quintessential jazz statement. Granz later said the records "were cut one afternoon in about an hour with but one take for each tune . . . rare in a recording procedure . . . None of us had any idea these would ever be released . . . The session was done for our own private kicks."

This is swing music on a jag, delirious with harmonic possibilities and testing the limits of form. The musicians are so "cool" you never feel they are out of control, but the polyrhythms, stop-

time, and the liberal chromaticism in the piano solos keep the music on the edge. Bebop, as credited
to Charlie Parker, Dizzy Gillespie, and Thelonious Monk, loomed just around the corner, a
year and a half away. Yet in Nat's piano — percussive, spare, poetic — you can hear the roots of
Monk's technique — the same Monk who had
watched in wide-eyed wonder as Nat stroked the
keyboard at Kelly's Stables.

Many years later Oscar Peterson's students
would ask him, "How do you come up with this
thing you call improvisation, linear or harmonic?"
The great pianist would send them to study Nat
Cole and Lester Young, "Because of the simplicity of the lines."

Cole's first solo on the upbeat "Indiana" breaks
down into two choruses. The first is a spirited
romp in the manner of Earl Hines, except that
Cole makes more music out of pauses, notes
dropped, and chords deleted for stop-time than
most pianists make out of arpeggios. The second
chorus discovers a new world. In the first bars he
plays block chords that scarcely glance at the dia-
tonic scale or the melody; he finishes the first eight
measures, then begins the second eight with a
light show of treble figures and rising sixteenth-
note arpeggios against a simple walking bass ac-
companiment. But at the bridge he begins to shift
rhythms, playing now 4/4, now 2/4, now triplet
eighths (12/8), all the while creating a test pattern
of syncopations. Then comes a rippling descending run of sixteenth notes that starts a weird half
step above the dominant and ricochets off several
atonal notes on the way down. By the end of the

chorus he has returned to earth, playing solid stride like Fats Waller — except for his own trademark triplets, which give the moving impression of the piano playing single time and double time at once.

The better the players, the better you play. Red Callender was almost as good as Jimmy Blanton, who was a god on the bass. "The President," as Billie Holiday called Lester Young — "the Prez" for short — was thirty-three years old and at the top of his game. He was the finest tenor sax player before John Coltrane. Young's cool, romantic, and eloquent lead on "I Can't Get Started" gives weight to Nat's gossamer, flighty improvisations and ornaments. On "Body and Soul" the sax's deliberate, yearning chorus sets the stage for Cole's tour de force of improvisation. For eight bars the pianist echoes the sax's mood with rich block chords, then begins to play double-time variations starred with quotes, Grieg among others. Critic Gunther Schuller, praising Cole's later 1944 performance of this solo with Oscar Moore, calls it "the most memorable invention of his pianistic career." Oscar and Nat may have perfected it, but "the Prez" laid the foundation.

Also recorded that day was Nat's first take of "Tea for Two," a rip-roaring virtuoso piano piece. Young and Callender gave Cole the floor for this one, lending him a minimum of bass and obbligato whether he needed it or not. Twenty years later, when the old jazz fans in the audience beg for a little piano, Cole will give them a taste of this solo, one ounce of genius in ten ounces of water, and it will *still* bring down the house.

The trio would not celebrate a fifth anniversary. Wesley Prince's song had been prophetic. In August the bass player was "Gone with the Draft," employed in an aircraft factory.

That was the end of the original Trio, and all the trios that followed owe Prince a debt. Perhaps their greatest songs were still to come. But it was the first three players who cut the new wood, struggling for five years to create the jazz sound that defined the King Cole Trio.

Red Callender filled in on bass for a while, making some good sides with Nat and Oscar on October 11 for a small African-American–owned company called Excelsior: "Vom, Vim, Veedle" and "All for You." But Red had ambitions to start a trio of his own.

Nat telephoned a young bass player in San Diego named Johnny Miller soon after Prince was drafted. Prince had recommended him. Both bass players were born in Pasadena. Miller (born 1915) was much younger. Like Prince, Miller had played with Lionel Hampton's orchestra. Friends nicknamed him "Thrifty" because of his frugality. Handsome, urbane, and practical, the young married man had the skill, as well as the character, to make a solid third of the King Cole Trio. With two daughters, he was unlikely to be drafted. Miller had admired Cole since he first heard him, in 1937. When the bassist got the call to try out with the group, he was eager.

Jazz historians such as Will Friedwald note that Johnny Miller stands in relation to his instrument as Oscar Moore does to the guitar. The bass was converting from the "tuba-style timekeeping functions to the soloing front-line position it would later hold thanks to Jimmy Blanton," says Friedwald. Miller could do it all, providing sturdy support for the solo flights of Cole and Moore, and stepping up now and then to perform his own swinging solos. A youthful, round-cheeked twenty-seven-year-old, Johnny Miller replaced the paternal presence of Wesley Prince with more of what the Trio already had lots of — sex appeal. Now they were poised for stardom.

It was fortunate the original trio made so many fine records for Decca before the company let them down. The union, striking for higher pay for musicians, forbade the Trio to make new recordings in 1942. Their old discs got a lot of play, winning the Trio a high rank in the *Down Beat* reader's poll in December. Nat's tender rendition of the ballad "All for You" rose to #1 on the race charts. (Trade journals then had separate charts for African-American music.) By the end of the year the Trio was a favorite of soldiers, appearing on the first of many *Jubilee* and *Mail Call* broadcasts on the Armed Forces Radio Service, along with James Cagney, Clare Boothe Luce, and Hoagy Carmichael, who would become one of Nat's fans.

The Trio required three things to ascend to the next level in the cutthroat music business: a song that would break out of the race market and enter the popular mainstream, a record company that would market the tune aggressively, and a personal manager who would see to it the men got paid what they were worth. That all these blessings would come to them in a span of eight months in 1943 says something about fate, much about the whimsical ways of genius, and even more about the determination of these musicians to prevail, to make themselves heard in a world that needed to hear them.

The song would come first, of course, as any worthwhile feat in the entertainment world should flow from a genuine artistic discovery. "Straighten Up and Fly Right," the song about the monkey who takes a ride on a buzzard, is Nat's greatest composition. The song is so superior to his others that it stands apart, marking not only the peak of his own creative powers but also a certain moment in history and the mood of a nation, black and white, at war.

German U-boats were sinking ships off the Atlantic coast. Gasoline and other necessities were rationed. Germany had occupied France and U.S. airborne troops were poised to invade Sicily and bomb Rome. These historical circumstances did not *make* the song, nor was Cole writing about the war directly. Yet his song so fit the period that we cannot appreciate its perfections or wholly understand its appeal at the time without locating it in the historical moment.

But first we must correct a serious error in the record. Since the first recording of "Straighten Up" in 1943, all books and articles about Nat Cole have dated the writing of the song vaguely in the late 1930s, soon after Nat arrived in Los Angeles. (The single exception is May Okon's article of April 4, 1954, in the *Los Angeles Sunday News*.)

The often-told story is a sad one. Nat was poor, naive, and desperate for rent money. He had written this song. He showed it to Irving Mills, Duke Ellington's manager and the founder of two record companies, who happened to be in L.A. on business. Mills liked what he heard. According to who tells the story, he offered Nat $50, or $75, or a necktie, for the worldwide rights to the song in perpetuity. Nat signed on the dotted line, took his money (or his necktie), and never looked back until the mid-1940s, when the song became a cash cow for Mills Music, Inc.

That is how the story has come down to us. Nat never desired to correct the impression that he was a mere babe in the woods when he sold "Straighten Up and Fly Right," and eighteen years old when he wrote it. This is understandable. But it is unfortunate for anyone who wants to track the artist's development. Nat's masterpiece was not the freak effusion of a child prodigy — it was the climax of six years of labor as a songwriter.

The truth is that Nat King Cole wrote "Straighten Up and Fly Right" in a hotel room in Omaha, Nebraska, in the winter of early 1943.

Berle Adams had booked the Trio into the Lindsay Sky Bar in Cleveland. But when the group arrived there they found the joint padlocked. The previous attraction had been arrested on a charge of raping one of the customers. So the Sky Bar had terrible p.r. problems and was closed until further notice. Also its license had been revoked. Nat telephoned Adams in Chicago in a panic. Their road shows were still a hand-to-mouth operation. They needed work immediately.

"What do we do now?" asked Nathaniel. "We need bread . . ."

Berle started telephoning all over the country, and everybody was booked solid. At last he called a friend, Ralph Goldberg, a theater owner in Omaha. Goldberg had a restaurant. Adams explained to him that by bringing music into his restaurant he would sell more food and whiskey. Goldberg was hard to convince, but at last he agreed to take a chance on the King Cole Trio if they could arrive by the weekend.

"If they're not here by Friday, I don't want 'em," Goldberg told Adams.

That was on a Wednesday. The men drove in shifts, night and day, reaching Omaha just in time to play for the dinner crowd on Friday night. They were a smashing success and stayed there for several weeks.

"That was the biggest break in my life," Nat later told Adams. "Omaha, Nebraska. There was nothing to do there, I mean, *nothing* to do but think of songs. That's where I wrote 'Straighten Up and Fly Right.' "

The idea that Nat might have written such a tune in the 1930s and kept it out of the repertory for four years is absurd. The musicians were using up material as fast as they could write it or buy it. Nat wrote the song in the winter of 1943. While "Straighten Up" may not be about the perils of war, it was written under the chill of the military draft. Cole got his induction notice from the draft board in February 1943. *Down Beat* reports that he failed his physical due to "nervous hyperten-sion."

Irving Mills no doubt ran into Cole at Berg's nightclub when the author of "Straighten Up" re-turned to L.A. in May of that year. Mills was pro-moting Cole's friend Benny Carter. Nat King Cole, at twenty-four, as at eighteen, was short on cash. Mills bought the song. The tune first ap-pears in August on the soundtrack of a movie the King Cole Trio played in called Here Comes Elmer.

While there was no great hurry to register for copyright (nobody knew how valuable the song would be), Mills registered in May of 1944, sev-eral months after the first commercial recording of it in November of 1943. Mills would not have waited until 1944 to register a song he had pur-chased in 1938.

In November of 1944 Cole would file suit against Irving Mills to regain ownership of the precious song. His lawsuit went nowhere.

So much has been written, and so much more said, about this little song that we must avoid the temptation to dissect, overanalyze, or otherwise overburden it. It is a simple poem of no more than sixteen lines, a vivid narrative lyric, a fable, if you like.

A buzzard took a monkey for a ride in the air.
The monkey thought that everything
    was on the square.
The buzzard tried to throw the monkey
    off his back . . .

Quickly the dramatic situation grips us. Quickly the bold and jaunty monkey takes charge of the situation, reining in the false, turbulent buzzard, choking him, resisting the bird's treacherous pleas to "release your hold and I will set you free." The monkey commands his mount to "straighten up and fly right." And his is the last word.

The story appeals to us at a primitive, preconscious level, as do all effective works of symbolism. It elevates Cole to the ranks of storytellers, preachers, and poets whose images are so primal and rich in associations that they endure in the memory and become part of the living inventory of the collective unconscious.

In several interviews Cole explained that he had heard his father tell the story during a sermon. In another early interview he said it was his wife's uncle, also a minister, who told the story. But the little fable belongs to Nat King Cole for all his humble protestations. Whether or not he heard the story line in a sermon, he nonetheless made it his own, stamping it with his own personal brand of humor by adding the ingenious "payoff" line "Straighten up and fly right." Fine song lyrics often are based upon folk sayings, platitudes, clichés; great song lyrics *become* folk wisdom, platitudes, and clichés, so swiftly sometimes only the U.S. copyright office knows for sure.

The standard interpretation of the fable comes down to race relations. The buzzard is the white man who takes the black man, played by the brave monkey, for a ride into high and dangerous territory. Does the buzzard wish to carry the monkey to a perilous height, drop him to his death, and then eat him for dinner? The monkey thinks so, which is why he holds the bird's neck so tightly.

There are at least two morals to the tale: don't accept a free ride from someone you can't trust and don't underestimate the power of your victim. A third lesson to be learned is that the buzzard may have gotten them into this mess, but it will take the cooperation of both animals to get them safely down to earth.

It is appropriate to interpret "Straighten Up and Fly Right" as a parable about race relations in America so long as we see that the song has even broader meaning. The story applies to any use or abuse of power, wherein the evil party uses deceit to get an advantage — the rich over the poor, the clever over the simple, the strong over the weak. Perhaps a time will come when race will be no advantage or disadvantage; still the song will speak to the human condition. If nothing else, it expresses the private struggle *within* a person for self-mastery, the good impulses over the wicked ones. The phrase "a monkey on his back," referring to any sort of addiction (drugs, alcohol, ruinous sex), long predates this song. It is easy to imagine a hellfire-and-brimstone preacher building a sermon upon it.

Line officers in combat, who used Cole's words over and over in dressing down their weary and unruly infantry, were not thinking about race relations in America. They needed a catchphrase that would enforce discipline and inspire honor. Every man in military fatigues was a monkey on the back of a World War. Friends used the phrase "straighten up and fly right" if a buddy was drinking too much; wives used it to warn their straying husbands.

So now the Trio had a song with the poetic force to enter the mainstream. They still needed a record company to deliver the song to the market-place, and a good personal manager to beat the drum for them, to make the most of their opportunity.

CARLOS, AND CAPITOL RECORDS

Carlos Gastel had been following the Trio's progress since 1938, when he met Nat in the Fox Hills Café across from the Twentieth Century Fox movie lot. When Carlos heard Nat King Cole sing "Sweet Loraine" in the smoky spotlight of the 331 Club, the large, tenderhearted man got tears in his eyes.

He drank a cocktail of scotch and milk. Scotch for his soul, milk for his stomach lining.

Carlos had a high, broad forehead and dark, thick eyebrows over his wide-set eyes. Though his features were slightly heavy he had the well-shaped nose and mouth of an epicure, a man of refined if overzealous appetites.

He and his kid sister Chickie Gastel went to hear the Trio whenever they could. Carlos told Chickie the young pianist had a great future.

Carlos knew what he was talking about when it came to show business. In 1943 he was twenty-nine years old, married, with a daughter. He already had the life experience and bearing of a much older man — a premature paunch, a widow's peak, a double chin, and a jolly, man-about-town manner. Carlos's father, an intense, hard-drinking native of Honduras, had died in his fifties. Carlos, figuring that he too would not live long, resolved to cram seventy or eighty years of living, eating, drinking, working, and partying into the fifty-odd years fate had promised him. The strategy made him larger than life, which he was anyway, six feet two inches and 250 pounds, a great, warm, walruslike man full of passion, conversation, and good humor. Gene Norman said Carlos was like Smilin' Jack's assistant Fat Stuff, whose buttons were always popping off his shirt.

His very origins were the stuff of legends. His father, a Honduran diplomat, was on a mission in the Rhineland when he fell in love with a German girl named Maria. He convinced her to return to Central America with him and be his bride.

In her German accent Maria used to love to tell the story of Carlos's nativity, somewhere in the steamy jungle of Honduras. The young mother's water broke, and she had to drag herself over rough terrain to the nearest midwife, a mile away, with Carlos half in her womb and half out.

From the very beginning, it seems, Carlos Gastel could not wait to be out and about in the world. Half German, half Honduran, he had the passionate affections of a Latino and the logical powers we tend to associate with Mainz and Wittenberg. Born in San Pedro Sula on March 21, 1914, Carlos lived in Central America until his parents sent him at age ten to a California military academy. Summers and holidays in Europe made him fluent in Spanish, French, and German by the time he matriculated at UCLA in 1930. Residence in Paris, London, Berlin, and New York gave the boy an air of cosmopolitan sophistication.

But young Carlos was no stuffed shirt. He liked good-looking women, deep-sea fishing, football, jazz music, and the nightlife.

In the early 1930s Carlos heard the Casa Loma band at Glen Island Casino. Carlos, like other youngsters of his generation, was electrified by the tight, proto-swing arrangements of Spike Gray, the trombone of Pee Wee Hunt, and the high-note trumpet of Sonny Dunham. "I guess I was their greatest fan west of Denver," he said.

Casa Loma primed him for Benny Goodman. As the sixteen-year-old Nathaniel Coles was training to battle Earl Hines in Chicago in August 1935, plump Carlos Gastel, twenty-one, sat in the front row at the Palomar Ballroom in Los Angeles the night Goodman opened the engagement that launched the Swing Era. It was the greatest thrill of Gastel's life, before he met Nat King Cole.

Carlos did not go back to school that fall. He went to Agua Caliente and got a job as a radio announcer so that he "could sit up all night and play Goodman records." But the 150-mile drive to L.A. several times a week to hear Goodman, Louis Armstrong, and others live in nightclubs began to wear him out. Gastel decided to go to Los Angeles and set up shop as a band manager and promoter.

Strange as it sounds, his first client was Max Baer, the prizefighter who knocked out Primo Carnera in 1934 to become heavyweight champion of the world. Tired of dancing around the boxing ring getting his brains battered, Max decided to try his hand at leading a dance band. Somehow twenty-one-year-old Carlos Gastel persuaded the champ to let him handle bookings and musical personnel. Carlos had unlimited, un-

172

canny powers of persuasion, the ability to negotiate nearly anything between two parties, willing or unwilling.

But he could not make the prizefighter into a bandleader no matter how hard he tried. Max Baer got hungry and went back into the ring. Carlos Gastel took a job scraping the rust off the fenders of Greyhound buses for eighteen dollars a week. Then Al Jarvis of KFWB found him work promoting dances.

At last, in 1939, Carlos got back to artists' management. This time he had a real musician for a client, a trumpet player named Sonny Dunham who had played with Casa Loma. Carlos did nothing by halves. He borrowed $15,000 and sank every dollar of it, plus three years of his life, trying to make a headliner out of the talented but unmarketable trumpet player.

Meanwhile, hedging his bets, Gastel persuaded first Stan Kenton, then Benny Carter, to cast their lots with him. By 1943 nobody was getting rich, but together Carter and Kenton, mostly Carter, were beginning to make up the money Carlos was losing on the stalled career of Sonny Dunham.

And in those four years Carlos Gastel made a reputation for himself in L.A., New York, and beyond. He was known as a man of taste, business acumen, and keen loyalty to his artists. In short, he was an extremely desirable manager for an up-and-coming act like the King Cole Trio. Along with these strengths came the famous power of personality. Carlos had become renowned as a "big man," the big laughing man with the load of goodies for all, a green roll of cash in his pocket at all times to pay bar bills or restaurant tabs before anyone noticed. A hefty eater and hard drinker himself, Carlos inspired eating, drinking, and festivity in others. He was the life of the party, a one-man party in himself, a truly generous, charitable man — you could tell by looking at smiling Carlos Gastel that the charity began at home.

Nat had his eye on Carlos all the while Carlos and his sister Chickie were following the King Cole Trio from club to club in L.A., from record to record. Gene Andrews had been their manager until the spring of 1943, but Nat was not satisfied with the results. By the summer he was looking for someone else, someone like Gastel.

That summer Nat telephoned Carlos to come and hear him at the 331 Club. "And would you see if you can think of someone to manage the group?" Nat asked pointedly. Before this he had asked Carlos if he would consider the job. But Carlos declined. Big dance bands were his specialty and he was not sure how to sell a Trio. Besides he already had two acts that weren't earning him much money, Dunham and Kenton. What did he need with another one?

Riding in Carlos's Cadillac convertible to the 331 Club that night, Chickie Gastel discussed the Trio situation with her brother. She ran her hand through her hair. Chickie was pretty, with straight dark hair and big eyes and strong, chiseled features.

"You've got two headaches now," said Chickie. "So a third one will go right along with the other two." Somehow the logic appealed to Carlos. Chickie pointed out that Carlos was hanging out

174

with the Trio in much of his spare time anyway. "You feel they have such a good future, I just think you're crazy if you don't manage Nat."

That is how Carlos Gastel decided to take on the management of the King Cole Trio. It was not so much a business decision as an emotional commitment to the music and his friendship with the charming pianist.

There must have been much toasting of health and backslapping and rejoicing that night after hours at the 331 Club, as Nat got the manager he had hoped for and Carlos began pondering what he could do for the Trio.

Their first business disagreement (a rare thing in what became a twenty-one year association) was over Carlos's commission. He would not take any. Nat was stunned.

"Listen," said Carlos. "There's no sense in paying me anything now. You're not making enough money." The Trio was making about $225 a week. "It's better for you and me and everybody in the long run if you keep that money you would be paying me — to build something up."

Nat scratched his chin thoughtfully, brushing upward from beneath with the backs of his bitten fingernails. "No, I want to pay you right off the bat," he said. The logic was simple. "I'm not being overly *kind* to you. It's just that I want you to get paid so you'll do something. If you're not getting paid, chances are you won't pay as much attention as you should." Nat frowned, raising his thin eyebrows.

Carlos Gastel's good-natured laughter was one of his strongest lines of defense. He could negotiate anything, but was finding it most difficult to press his generosity on the streetwise pianist. At last they "compromised," agreeing that Carlos would take no percentage until the Trio was earning $800 per week. Nat thought the deal was unfair to Carlos and a little crazy. It seemed to Nat the Trio would not make $800 per week until snow buried Palm Springs.

Three weeks later the Trio hit the $800 a week mark as Carlos booked them into the Orpheum Theater in L.A.

"And if I had known what we were worth," said Carlos years later, "I would have gotten five thousand." Notice the use of the plural "we."

Carlos knew better than anyone just what Nat King Cole and the Trio were worth. At the Orpheum the gross was $30,000 a week. Within weeks of this success, Gastel secured them a seven-year exclusive recording contract with a promising new company. Capitol Records had been founded in 1942 in the back of Glen Wallichs's music shop on Sunset and Vine, by Wallichs, movie producer Buddy De Sylva, and gap-toothed Johnny Mercer, the brilliant song-writer, singer, and pianist.

Johnny Mercer looked like Huckleberry Finn. Already a legend at thirty-four, author of the sublime lyric "Blues in the Night," Mercer had made records with Benny Goodman, Jack Teagarden, and Eddie Condon. And he had become a radio star, singing and acting as master of ceremonies on the *Camel Caravan*. A black social club in Georgia voted the white Mercer their "favorite colored singer on radio." Everybody, black and white, loved him.

Wallichs had bright ideas for selling and distributing records, and Mercer had fresh artistic vision. The record business had fallen behind the times. While working at Paramount Pictures, Mercer convinced De Sylva to put up $10,000 in venture capital for a company that would compete with Victor and Decca.

April 1942 was a bad time to try to start a record company. Shellac for new discs came from India, and during the war the honey-colored resin was scarce. Wallichs got the idea to buy up old records at six cents a pound; by grinding them up they could harvest the shellac and make twenty thousand new records a week. But then there came the strike of the musicians' union for higher pay, barring all instrumentalists from making recordings. To keep the new company afloat, De Sylva came up with another $15,000.

Remembering the young pianist who had played at the opening of his shop years before, Wallichs purchased the masters to "Vom, Vim, Veedle" and "All for You," the recordings Nat made for the tiny Excelsior label in 1942. This way Capitol would have a record to sell during the musicians' strike. For his part, Mercer was a long-time Trio enthusiast; in fact he was one of the first fans to hail Nat's talent at Jim Otto's in 1938, and since then Mercer had been following his act from club to club.

"All for You," a smooth love song Nat rendered in a chaste, innocent manner, flatting many of the notes, did extremely well for the fledgling record company in its first year. *Billboard* ranked it #18

177

for 1943. So it is easy to understand why Capitol wished to sign up the Trio.

Carlos closed the deal in September. Wallichs returned then from a three-month trip to Atlanta and New York City to announce to the press that Nat Cole and Jack Teagarden would emerge as Capitol artists. Nat signed to a seven-year term, the maximum, as well as to the maximum royalty percentage, 5 percent.

There would be no dispute over the Trio's talent and potential — this was a clear "win-win" situation. Wallichs and Mercer were men of taste and integrity, as was Carlos Gastel. And there could be no disagreement about what the Trio lacked in the past, why they lacked it, or what they needed to assure a rich future.

Since Decca had recorded them in 1940, the Trio had suffered from the nearsighted provincialism of the recording industry. The old record companies, Victor, Decca, and Columbia, continued a segregation in marketing jazz records that amounted to musical apartheid. Black artists appeared under separate race labels. Except for the great jazz producer John Hammond, company executives simply assumed that a white musician would sell more units of a record than a black musician, and therefore should get more marketing and distribution muscle. This was not only unjust; it was stupid. Mercer and Wallichs could tell this from studying the sales of Louis Armstrong, Bessie Smith, and Lady Day. It made no business sense to refuse to invest time and money on a musician on the basis of skin color. Joe Glaser, Louis Armstrong's and Billie Holiday's manager, knew this. So did Carlos Gastel. And the plain truth would make these men rich.

The King Cole Trio's first recording session for Capitol took place on November 30, 1943, a Tuesday afternoon, from two until five, in the familiar MacGregor Studios on Melrose Avenue. Photographer Roland Shreves was on hand to capture the joy and excitement of that event, probably the most important recording session the group would ever do.

Behind Nat at the piano stands young Johnny Mercer grinning like the cat that swallowed the canary. Mercer wears a one-button-roll sport jacket over a sweater and white shirt open at the collar, his left hand jingling coins in his pocket. Oscar Moore, in a suit and necktie, strums his sunburst electric guitar earnestly as Johnny Miller, in shirtsleeves, looks over his shoulder, plucking the bass. Nat King Cole, in a white shirt and a pullover sweater, seems to have looked up from his playing just long enough to flash his million-dollar smile for the camera. His smooth hair shines like patent leather, and his face is beaming.

Microphone booms reach into the piano, and rise up into Nat's face. Bandleader Paul Weston sits in the control booth, balancing the guitar and bass; with him is recording engineer John Palladino. All around the cramped studio space, over the doors, over the clock, are signs that say "Positively No Smoking." On the piano in front of Nat and within reach is a square, clear-glass ashtray full of cigarette butts and one lighted cigarette — Philip Morris was his brand — balanced on the sharp corner. Other signs remind us of the war, such as "Serve in Silence: Do Not Reveal Military Information."

That afternoon produced the first commercial recording of "Straighten Up and Fly Right," a song that everyone in the studio by then must have known was a surefire breadwinner. Movie director Joe Santley had picked it for the Trio to play in his comedy *Here Comes Elmer* back in August, a film that would be released before Christmas. Then the Trio had recorded it in the NBC Studios for the Armed Forces Radio Services on August 11. The song was such a hit with the soldiers that it was rebroadcast again in October and early November.

The other three sides recorded before dinner were the great E-flat blues by Don Redman and Andy Razaf, "Gee Baby, Ain't I Good to You"; a new, bittersweet lovers' quarrel penned by Nat's friend Timmie Rogers, "If You Can't Smile and Say Yes (Please Don't Cry and Say No!)"; and an instrumental filler, the up-tempo "Jumpin' at Capitol." The steamy, loping "Gee Baby" has a stunning, note-bending solo by Oscar Moore in which he executes a perfect tremolo glissando, and another by Nat Cole displaying his mastery of quarter-note and eighth-note triplets to create a shuffling, syncopated blues rhythm.

That session set a high standard for the team of Johnny Mercer, Paul Weston, John Palladino, and the Trio at Capitol. Two sessions of equal quality followed, on December 15 and January 17 of the next year. The twelve tunes recorded on these dates are widely regarded as the pinnacle of the

King Cole Trio's artistry. Although Weston and others insist that Nat always chose the material for his sessions, we must see in these the guiding hand of Mercer. During the same period the Trio was recording extensively for MacGregor Transcriptions and others, some fifty sides, yet the Mercer-produced titles are clearly superior in song selection, arrangements, and sound quality.

The first session was a miscellany of treasures — ballads, a novelty tune, and a flag-waving instrumental. The next two meetings for Capitol each have a unified stylistic agenda. On December 15 the theme is love, and the star attraction is Cole's voice, which is now irresistible. Those long afternoons spent alone at the piano in Kelly's Stable singing "Sweet Loraine" over and over, until the poor bookkeeper upstairs thought she would go mad, have paid off. Nat sings on-key, mostly, and his lisp is gone. He now sings Jimmie Noone's theme song with assurance, slightly behind the beat, as Billie Holiday taught him, and with a piping warmth and ease natural as sunlight.

When it's raining I don't miss the sun
Because it's in my baby's eyes . . .

 To the Gershwins' classic "Embraceable You" the singer brings such conviction it seems less a performance than a real act of passion, graceful yet with an air of spontaneity.

Just one look at you, my heart goes tipsy in me,
You and you alone . . . bring out the gypsy in me . . .

At the last line the singer shifts his tone ever so subtly from grave to gay, delivering the gypsy phrase in double time, for relief, before continuing the crooning lover's appeal.

In these ballads, as well as in his up-tempo rendition of Billy Rose's "It's Only a Paper Moon," and in his own tune "I Can't See for Lookin'," we begin to see the lineaments of a giant, a singer who soon will rank with the greatest ballad interpreters of all time — Bessie Smith, Billie Holiday, Frank Sinatra. Nathaniel Cole had the perfect voice to sing love ballads, whispery, warm, and slightly hoarse. And he had the perfect temperament, a personal warmth and sincerity that is uncounterfeitable. If Nat himself was not sure of it, Johnny Mercer was, after seeing the success of "All for You." Mercer had a strong instinct for the marketplace. Love ballads were in demand, as the war upset marriages, engagements, and affairs.

Nat seemed hesitant, almost unwilling. Why was the man shy about singing love songs? Was it simple, charming modesty? He loved to sing, or he would not have worked so hard at it. Was he afraid of upsetting the Trio's delicate balance by dominating the spotlight?

The question leads us to a central paradox in Nat King Cole's career, a paradox that will appear and reappear in various guises throughout this story. The very thing for which Nat Cole was suited, by nature and temperament, was a thing that American society meant to deny him. Black men were not welcome to sing love songs to white women. Before the 1920s there was even a taboo against showing love *between* blacks onstage unless it was comic. Cole may have been cautioned by the fate of the strikingly handsome Billy Eckstine, who hit with several blues ballads, including the sexy "Jelly, Jelly," before his face appeared in a national magazine. The sudden recognition by the mainstream white audience that Eckstine was African-American nearly derailed the singer's career.

So we can understand the artist's shyness, or reluctance, his exasperating coyness about his vocation as a ballad singer. He was bound to do it, as he was fated to play the piano. But if he was going to get away with this role he had to make it look like an accident, an absurdity, or something forced upon him against his better judgment. Above all, the preacher's son from Bronzeville must not appear to have willfully and premeditatively pursued a course that would result in his crooning love ballads to white women. So he made up a story, several stories, that suited his image, easing his passage into the inevitable role.

However uneasy Nathaniel may have been about his role of balladeer, crooner of love songs, his partner Oscar Moore was even more uncomfortable with it. Remember, these young men had been nearly inseparable in friendship and creative spirit since 1938. It was a bond Nat never had with his brother. Nat and Oscar had worked, played, dreamed, and schemed together. They had eaten and gone hungry together, shared the spotlight and the applause. They had known the terror and weariness of the road, killing cockroaches in cheap hotels. Together they had known hardship, the ecstasy of improvisation, and some glory. Lee Young said they were "joined at the hip." He also has said that Oscar's devotion to Nat for years was unconditional, the sort that presumes "we will live and die together, as friends and collaborators."

But now Oscar was beginning to see that the thing that would make them rich, Nat's velvet voice, might upset the rare and delicate chemistry that was the Trio. Hearing Nat Cole sing, women of all kinds went out of their senses.

They recorded the love ballads on December 15. That evening they came home to the news that Fats Waller had died on the train from L.A. to New York. He was thirty-eight years of age. Waller, like the black vaudevillians, was able to sing about love only while laughing at himself.

If the December recording of love songs fed Oscar's anxiety, the Trio's session in January of 1944 would put him at ease for sure. That afternoon nobody sang a note. It was pure ensemble jazz of a quality so pure and inventive few "chamber" groups would ever equal it, and the Trio itself would never surpass it.

Under the byline "The Two Deuces," critics Barry Ulanov and Leonard Feather wrote a monthly review in *Metronome* in which they discussed and graded a dozen or more artists and their recordings, from A to D. A was artistically extraordinary, A– excellent, and so on, down to C mediocre and D horrible. The Deuces were tough — months would go by with nobody scoring better than a B+. For instance, they loved

"Straighten Up and Fly Right" but gave it only an A–.

But in November of 1944, reviewing the results of the latest Capitol sessions, professors Ulanov and Feather threw up their hands and gave the Trio straight A's. No other report card in the annals of *Metronome* looks like this one.

"As you might gather, we are not averse to this album," they write, tongue in cheek. "Such a large dose of the Cole Trio at one gulp has us gloriously giddy. If you have not yet been convinced that Cole's piano, Oscar Moore's guitar and Johnny Miller's bass can make the subtlest, finest jazz ever created by three men, this album should convert you . . . too many great moments here for us to list them all. Samples: Oscar Moore's best chorus ever, on 'Body and Soul'; the second eight bars of Nat's piano on the same side, which for sheer beauty of harmonic conception and phrasing has never been excelled. The tasteful transition into swing on the Rachmaninoff side ('Prelude in C Sharp Minor') . . . We could go on raving for hours . . . ."

Forty-five years later the American composer and jazz historian Gunther Schuller in his monumental work *The Swing Era* picks up raving where the Two Deuces left off. "Cole and Moore were already in the earliest forties . . . using advanced voicings and harmonic substitutions of a kind and quality that some of the early boppers, even Charlie Parker, were using only sporadically or tentatively at the time." Schuller says that it was more than a mere style the Trio created. He prefers the word "language." That is accurate. The Trio had created a musical language capable of expressing the finest shades of feeling and the most complex ideas.

I have discussed the technical features of this "language" at some length in the foregoing pages. But what, at last, does it all come down to? What was the Trio conveying, in this new language, that so deeply moved generations of listeners? The key is to be found here, in these recordings made on a Monday afternoon in January 1944. It is an intimate and passionate conversation between the guitar and the piano, sometimes playful, sometimes argumentative, but always utterly frank and clear. In "What Is This Thing Called Love?" it is a high-spirited dialogue between friends about the nature of love, in which the piano — more and more insistent and increasingly perplexed — asks the age-old question. And the calmer, bemused guitar offers the best answers it can. In the heart-rending "The Man I Love," the conversation is more collaborative, as if a woman were talking to herself, or to an intimate friend who was finishing her lines or repeating them in different words. The piano utters the first chorus almost casually, with light ornamentation of trills and triplets, only slightly plaintive. But when the guitar takes over at the bridge, it speaks with considerable gravity and yearning blue glissandos. The stakes have been raised. By the time Nat begins his second chorus the mood has changed entirely. The easy-going, optimistic lover of the first act has heard a little too much reality, and now moves into a realm of fantasy, floating chords, sostenuto, minor chords that rise into the clouds before returning to the earth to attend the guitar's sensible, reassuring counsel. And so it goes, back and forth, this great passionate conversation, never fully resolved — the way angels might talk of love in a universal tongue, if we could only hear them.

When was there ever a more urgent need to talk of love than in that war-tormented year of 1944? Think of Bogart in Casablanca, or Ingrid Bergman in *For Whom the Bell Tolls*. Think of the songs "Moonlight in Vermont" and "Sentimental Journey." Cole, Moore, and Miller addressed an urgent need to express profound emotions of love discovered, love thwarted, love lost and regained, and they did not shrink from it. Instrumental jazz had not been so emotionally articulate, so intimate, since Louis Armstrong played duets with Earl Hines in 1928. And the King Cole Trio had a richer vocabulary at its beck and call.

THE BIG MONEY

The Trio was not an overnight success, as anyone who has followed their story can see. Long ago they had grown accustomed to playing jazz for love and very little money. So for Nat, after a lifetime of toiling at the poverty line or near it, the dollars that began descending on him in 1944 must have seemed like a surreal blizzard of banknotes. He had no reference for it, no understanding — the wealth was like nothing he had ever known. As crazily as it appeared, it might vanish overnight. Or the money might continue pouring down on him forever.

"Straighten Up and Fly Right" sold half a million records as it moved from #8 to #3 on the pop charts in May of 1944. And the Trio, whom Carlos was booking far into the future, was commanding $2,000 per week in theaters and $1,000 in nightclubs. The money was apportioned as follows: expenses got paid first; Carlos got 10 percent of the net after expenses; of the rest Nat kept half, Oscar got 30 percent, and Johnny 20%. Nat got all of the record royalties after Carlos's commission. At first there were no complaints.

Soon the Trio was getting five-figure fees for three-minute musical vignettes in movies such as *Pistol Packing Mama*, *Under Western Skies*, and *The Mad Hatter*, and top dollar for frequent radio appearances on NBC, the AFRS *Mail Call*, and

Command Performance. And in the spring of 1944 they won a permanent spot on Orson Welles's new program on CBS, a weekly broadcast from Hollywood. A special room was designed for them at the Trocadero nightclub in Hollywood, where they continued to perform nightly.

After bonuses, Oscar Moore was making between $500 and $1,000 a week. Nat must have been earning at least three times that much.

Money is a strong and capricious agent. Studying the effects of sudden wealth, from surprise inheritances and lotteries, from unlikely inventions and freak best-sellers, psychologists all agree on one thing: No matter where the money comes from, no matter who you are — you will find your life and psyche profoundly affected by it, changed for a while if not forever. It is the greatest hazard to young athletes who become million-dollar bonus babies. Money presents a minefield to rock stars, lucky screenwriters, and whiz kid arbitrageurs.

Nat was twenty-five years of age when it happened to him, the overnight transformation from rags to riches. He was young enough to feel the full effect of money's random and amoral power, young enough to enjoy it. Nat was a clotheshorse. He bought a closetful of tailor-made suits and tweed sport jackets by designer Sy Devore, and colorful ties in floral and deco lightning-bolt motifs. He bought a new car. He sent money home to his family in Chicago. Nadine bought new clothes and took golf lessons, hoping they might ease her passage into society. She bought better marijuana.

Nadine liked reefer, though Nat couldn't stand it. Soon they would purchase a small home, a white stucco bungalow at 1977 West 21st Street.

Money and fame came at the same time, as they do in this business. They can consume a young man in a matter of months. Nat was born lucky in that he had — by nature and upbringing — the strength of character, the moral fiber to endure money and fame, to use them to make something more of himself and his world, beyond more money and more fame. He had a steely work ethic. This is not to say that he was a saint or a prude. Angered, he could swear mightily. He liked his J&B scotch and he liked to stay up half the night in rollicking jazz clubs jamming, smoking, and joking in the company of song pluggers and sharps and sharks and pretty women who were not his wife.

They had been married for seven years, and Nadine's loyal devotion to him and his music was one of the pillars that sustained him. But money and fame destroy marriages as relentlessly as they do individuals who lack the strength to resist the attendant temptations. Nat and Nadine had tried for years to have children, but in this they had been unlucky. Nadine had miscarried several times.

The marriage began to fray under the pressure of Nat's increased schedule of performances, in and out of town, and his greatly magnified visibility to the world's female population. There are many women in the world, and a dangerous percentage of these were so moved by Nat King Cole's perfections they would go to great lengths to get him alone in a room. He was a man of good character, certainly, but a man nonetheless who found himself under uncommon pressures. More on this in due course. For now suffice it to say that his manners with women of all ages were perfect, and he was never seen to pursue a woman inappropriately (excepting the one who would become his second wife). Women flocked to him, stalked him, besieged him from 1943 until he was practically on his deathbed.

At this point Cole's popular success as a performer went hand in hand with his rising stature as a jazz innovator. More and more fans wanted to hear him in concert.

Norman Granz, the young promoter and gifted producer who masterminded Cole's 1942 session with Lester Young, dreamed of staging jazz concerts in large, comfortable auditoriums where the new generation of jazz artists would get the serious attention they merited. This was not a new idea. In 1924, Paul Whiteman had staged such a concert in New York's Aeolian Hall during which George Gershwin premiered "Rhapsody in Blue." But twenty years later, presenting jazz in a forum reserved for classics was still a bold concept. It assumed the music deserved respect and that there was an audience to fill the seats. This was new to L.A.

Granz launched the concert series at Music Town, a southside auditorium, on February 6, 1944. Offering union-scale wages, eleven dollars per man for three hours, Granz put together a bill that included Nat King Cole, the "Texas tenor" saxophonist Illinois Jacquet, and a brilliant young white guitar player named Barney Kessel. Oscar Moore's absence from this concert, and from the Granz productions to follow, is significant — an early sign that the guitarist was distancing himself from his partner.

Down Beat reported that "the jazz really came on and never let down. The mixed audience, noticeably minus the drunken jitterbugs, enjoyed the music in ordinary chairs." Charging a dollar admission, Granz lost money. But he hoped, when word got around, that next time he would get better attendance. The impresario was not disappointed. The two concerts he staged in July at the Philharmonic Auditorium would make history as the first of the famous Jazz at the Philharmonic Series. Nat was featured in these concerts as a star attraction, a giant among giants.

America was steeling itself for that dread-ridden spring of 1944, when thousands of Allied troops perished at Monte Cassino, and General Eisenhower's forces prepared for D-Day. Cole read the paper daily with his morning coffee and cigarettes, the war news and the sports page. No one's good fortune was beyond reach of the bloodshed in Europe and the Philippines. Cole wrote a rousing song called "D-Day." In February, Oscar Moore passed his army physical, though he was not well. Inducted in March, he served only three weeks before drawing a medical discharge. While he was gone Nat replaced him with a clarinetist named Heinie Beau.

In the midst of America's dark passage came personal tragedies. On April 19, Nat learned that his old friend Jimmie Noone had died of heart failure. Partly because of Nat's presence, the clarinetist had come to Los Angeles, where he was working for Kid Ory in the Standard Oil broadcasts, and playing with pianist Eric Henry in the Streets of Paris club in Hollywood. Jimmie had very high blood pressure, and according to his son "he ate himself to death."

Sweet Jimmie Noone did not live to see fifty. Nat Cole had hardly gotten over the death of Fats Waller, whom he had visited in the company of Franz Jackson just before Christmas in Los Angeles. Fats was only thirty-eight when his life was over. Pianist Bob Zurke had dropped dead in February while playing a date at San Francisco's Hangover Club — fat, burnt out, a hopeless drunk at thirty-two. If Nathaniel was not having serious thoughts about a jazzman's mortality, his good friend Carlos Gastel would be quick to remind him that life is short and very hard on those who do not make the most of their opportunities.

Cole was blessed to be doing business with the likes of Gastel, Wallichs, and Mercer, who truly cared about him and would protect his interests. This was one of Cole's chief strengths, often overlooked, this instinct for choosing the right person for the right role at the right time. A poor businessman when it came to small details, Nat was more than capable when it came to the larger and more important matters of management and organization. A man of high character himself, with an unusual degree of self-knowledge and self-discipline (uncommon in any man, rare in performers), Nathaniel Cole chose to associate and do business with people of similar integrity, at least until the last years of his life. His exceptionally long dominance in the entertainment world — thirty years, twenty of them as a star — owes a great deal to Cole's instinct for management, his knack for getting the support he needed from friends and business associates.

Nat King Cole was making the most of his opportunities, which were looming large. Barry Ulanov knew him then, and said he was becoming a giant — his personality was growing, deepening in response to his increasing fame. He was coming out of his shell, becoming more poised, outgoing, articulate. Oscar Moore could not comprehend the change. Moore was troubled and sick from some internal illness which would require surgery in August a year later. Meanwhile his participation in the Trio's creative life in 1944–45 was erratic and strained. Ulanov says, "He was lightly hinged. You never knew when he was going to go off." Moore's ego was unsettled by Cole's stardom as well as his lion's share of the income.

The program for Jazz at the Philharmonic, July 2, 1944, features the King Cole Trio, Illinois Jacquet, Lee Young, Red Callender, Les Paul, Barney Bigard, James Johnson, Meade Lux Lewis, Buddy Rich, and other jazz notables. Oscar Moore's name appears as a Trio member, but Oscar failed to show up. Les Paul filled in for him that Sunday afternoon, playing brilliantly on several numbers, including a ten-minute "Blues," a six-minute "Rosetta," a twelve-minute "Tea for Two," and "Bugle Call Rag," a mere four and a half minutes.

A rare and amusing live recording captures the raucous exuberance of the event. Far from bestowing upon the musicians the compliment of serious attention, the cheering, shouting mob of 1,200 jazz fans sounds hell-bent on turning the concert into a three-ring circus. The musicians are happy to oblige in their grandstanding, double- and triple-chorus solos. Invited to stretch their wings, Illinois Jacquet and Jack McVea seem desperate to exhibit bebop virtuosity. The more the fans squeal at Jacquet's screeching high notes and honking low notes, the more he screeches and honks, until the theme becomes a shambles. Even Nathaniel loses his usual restraint in "Tea for Two," reviving a Hinesian "trumpet" style in his obbligato behind McVea; and when the time comes for his own solo Nat plays Hines-style rapid runs up and down the length of the keyboard. Applause for him grows nearly hysterical as Nat's playing grows more disjointed and begins to bop free of the original melody and rhythm. The spirit of the occasion is vividly captured in a passage of "Blues" when Les Paul and Nat Cole "chase" each other, imitating each other's runs, riffs, and phrases. The more they mock each other, the more the audience laughs, until the hilarity reaches a pitch near madness.

Proceeds of the concert went to the defense fund for a group of Mexican youths sent to San Quentin for a murder committed during the "zoot suit riots" in L.A. This concert and an equally successful one on July 30, with similarly integrated personnel, established Norman Granz as "local impresario for jazz and protagonist of racial unity," according to *Down Beat*.

Whatever their significance as musical statements, the Philharmonic shows made Los Angeles take its jazz musicians more seriously, especially the pianist Nat King Cole. Everyone was disappointed that Oscar Moore, whose name always appeared on the printed programs, never graced the stage of the Philharmonic. Oscar was nearly out of the picture.

At the peak of his powers as a pianist, Nat Cole entered the MacGregor Studios alone in August to record stunning solos of a dozen tunes, including "Poor Butterfly," "Rosetta," "The Man I Love," "Body and Soul," and "I Got Rhythm."

For depth of feeling and keyboard technique, one may search in vain throughout his vast discography for better examples. It was as if Cole knew he was peaking and seized this time alone in the studio to preserve the best of his solo art. This was rare for him. Unlike Art Tatum, Cole did not have the sort of ego that insisted upon regular solo recordings as updates of his artistic progress.

Quitting the Trocadero, the Trio went on the road again — to Milwaukee, Chicago, Washington, D.C., New York, Baltimore, back to the Regal Theatre in Chicago for the last week in September, then on to Detroit and St. Louis. Carlos Gastel had put together a package road show that included the King Cole Trio, Benny Carter and his band, Savannah Churchill, and Timmie Rogers.

Timmie always could make Nathaniel laugh, ever since they had been boys hanging out in the alley behind the Grand Terrace, listening to Earl Hines. After traveling the world in a comedy act with Freddie Gordon, singing, clowning, doing acrobatic dancing, Timmie had left Freddie in late 1943 to go it alone in Los Angeles, close to his old friend Nat Cole. Nat was happy to see him.

Timmie told Nat about a conversation he had with the comedian Tim (Kingfish) Moore a few years earlier. Rogers loved dancing. He meant to make his fortune as the next Bojangles. Moore liked Rogers, and he knew show business. Kingfish knew that Timmie had a better opportunity at hand.

"No, man," said the Kingfish. "You too ugly. You mouth so big you can whisper in you own ear."

Timmie Rogers patiently waited for the famous trouper's next words of wisdom.

"With a face like that," said the Kingfish, frowning, and then raising his eyebrows, "you *got* to be a comedian. Folks just look at you and laugh. Now, a dancer, he only good till his legs fail him. Then they take you out, shoot you like a horse. Ugliness don't never give out, it just blossom, and the clown can work forever. You got to be a comedian, son. Believe what I'm telling you."

Timmie took the great showman's advice and began to concentrate on the comedy monologues and popular song lyrics that would make his name. Nathaniel put him in touch with Johnny Mercer, who soon bought his song "If You Can't Smile and Say Yes" for the Trio's first Capitol session.

A few months later Timmie was in Nat's dressing room at the Orpheum. The Trio was on a bill with Ida James and June Richmond, and the emcee-comedian failed to show up. "No talent," Nat told Timmie, worried. "What am I gonna do?"

Nat looked around the room at no one in particular. He scratched his chin, flicking at it with the backs of his bitten fingernails, anxiously. Timmie gave Nat one of his jaw-breaking grins, the one that shows all of his white choppers from foreteeth to molars, and Nat told himself, What am I talking about? "Timmie, you're on, old man."

Timmie went onstage grinning. He sang a song about a newly drafted soldier called "Bring Enough Clothes for Three Days," strumming his five-string guitar. He did a routine satirizing the federal bureaucracy called "Alphabetical Jive." The audience went wild, laughing and cheering, calling out for Timmie to dance. "I danced, man, I just danced," he said later. Timmie danced like a man of rubber dodging arrows. The comedian "sang and talked and danced his way into the King Cole road show," wrote Barry Ulanov. And Nat took great comfort in Rogers's humor that autumn as they toured the East and Midwest.

In St. Louis the momentum of the Cole-Carter road show was broken by violence — an incident foreshadowing the infamous attack on the black balladeer a decade later in Alabama. "Hoods Attack Cole, Carter," shouts the *Down Beat* headline. A mobster in the Plantation Club took a fancy to Savannah Churchill. When Benny Carter and his trombonist J. J. Johnson stepped in to protect her from the hoodlum's unwelcome advances, other men appeared with drawn revolvers and threatened to shoot all the performers. They used racial epithets. In the ensuing melee in the ballroom a thug cracked J. J. Johnson's head with the butt of a pistol. They had to rush the trombonist to the hospital to put his skull back together.

When Plantation manager Tony Scarpelli told Nat and Benny he was sorry but he was powerless to control the racist gangsters, Carlos Gastel ordered his musicians to hurry on to their next engagement.

The troupe was happy to be back in New York City for the holidays. Critics raved about the show at the Apollo, "which broke all records for New York's eminent colored house . . . The pacing was perfect . . . From the opening Carter downbeat to the last scream elicited from the women in the audience by Nat Cole, both flash and substance characterized this show," wrote Barry Ulanov in November's *Metronome*. Another paper called Nat a "genius at improvisation."

Yes, the women had begun to scream for Nat King Cole as they screamed for Orpheus of Thrace and Frank Sinatra of Hoboken.

Gunther Schuller links their names, Sinatra and Cole, as the only two men since the 1920s to contribute new vocal conceptions to the language of popular music. "After decades of colorless, lightweight, expressionless male voices — mostly effeminate-sounding crooning tenors — Sinatra's virile, earthy baritone, with a rich bottom voice, was a startling departure from the popular norm . . . He also learned to stretch slow tempos almost

199

beyond the point of emotional endurance . . . For an abnormally slow tempo can be carried off only by a singer with perfect breath control and an exceptional sense of musical line." This was also true of Cole. The two singers developed their styles at about the same time, Sinatra a little earlier than Cole, who surely learned from his older friend's recordings.

They met in L.A. early in 1940, when Nat was playing the Radio Room across the street from NBC. Frank would drop by to dig the Trio when he was in Hollywood, and sometimes he would step up and sing with them. Then Nat saw more of Frank Sinatra on 52nd Street during that year the Trio spent in New York City, 1941–42. Sinatra had an instinct and respect for power in a man, and he sensed that this soft-spoken black pianist, with his natural dignity and a mischievous twinkle in his eye, had a rare power.

As Frank watched his friend's ascent in 1944 and listened to him sing that winter, "The Voice" himself found much to emulate in the younger singer's style. At the first opportunity, November 25, Frank would share the spotlight with Cole, on his CBS radio show.

All that winter of 1944–45 the Cole-Carter show continued to tour — Boston, Newark, Hartford, Philadelphia, and a half dozen other cities in the East and Midwest, breaking attendance records — before returning to Los Angeles in March. A joyful photo was taken on the stage of Loew's State Theater in Hollywood. The Trio was about to play with Benny Carter, who smiles as he presents a gilded *Down Beat* trophy to the threesome, all dressed in tuxedos.

This was to be a year of honors, trophies, and citations. *Metronome* magazine had thrown the Trio a bouquet of honors in January 1945. Readers voted them number one in the Small Bands category; the editors named them "Act of the Year," devoting an entire page to singing their praises under a photo of smiling Nathaniel at the keyboard. Seven of their tunes were cited as Records of the Year. (Other artists got one citation, except Duke Ellington, who received two.) The editors called the Trio's eight-side album (retailing for $2.50) "the finest jazz album ever," and the disc sold as fast as Capitol could press copies.

So it must have been the shortage of shellac that limited their recording sessions at Capitol that year. Between March 1944 and April 1945, only one session took place, yielding one negligible release. On April 13, the day after FDR's death, with the nation plunged into mourning, the Trio recorded "I'm a Shy Guy" and Frankie Laine's "It Only Happens Once."

As the war news brought hope and then joy in the victorious spring of 1945, the year went by in a whirlwind of activity — afternoons in the studio recording for radio programs and transcriptions, long nights in the spotlight of the Trocadero nightclub. The Trio were frequent guests on Armed Forces Radio and Bing Crosby's *Kraft Music Hall* on NBC. The Mutual Broadcast Network even taped radio shows in their space at the Trocadero, which was now called the King Cole Room. Finishing at the Trocadero on June 26, the Trio played the Golden Gate Theater in San

Francisco, then returned to L.A. to share the stage with Count Basie at the Casa Mañana.

Nat and Johnny were back on the stage of the sold-out Philharmonic Auditorium, to headline a program on July 30. The jazz extravaganza featured Buddy Rich, Charles Mingus, Jimmy Rushing, Georgie Auld, Barney Kessel, and half a dozen more, minus Oscar Moore — who again was mistakenly listed on the program.

Perhaps the guitarist was too ill to attend. On August 3 he entered a hospital in L.A. for an operation. This put him out of commission for weeks. During a time of intense pressure on the Trio to make the most of their new fame and booking momentum, Oscar's frailty was a burden. By the month's end he was just well enough to get on an airplane, an army B-17, with Nat and Johnny, to play military camps before the Trio launched another theater tour with saxophonist Andy Kirk's combo. According to one report, Oscar "turned green on the takeoff for Salt Lake City."

A quick stop in Chicago to play the Regal Theatre (August 31) gave Nat an opportunity to visit his family. He found time to play background music for a fashion-show benefit at his father's church. It was a rare opportunity for the Reverend to hear the Trio live. Nat's father still had never heard his son play in a nightclub or theater, for two reasons. First, the entertainment seemed inappropriate for a Baptist minister; second, as an older African-American, he did not feel comfortable in many of the white venues where his son performed.

On to New York then, with three weeks at the

swank Copacabana before returning to the Apollo Theater. In October the Trio performed "It's Only a Paper Moon" and "I've Found a New Baby" on Perry Como's NBC *Supper Club*.

And on November 25, the day before Thanksgiving, Nathaniel was a featured guest on his friend Frank Sinatra's program on CBS, sponsored by P. Lorillard, makers of Old Gold. Nat smoked Philip Morris, made by a rival company. They had placed an ad in the National Medical Journal that read: *"Don't smoke* is advice hard for patients to swallow. May we suggest smoking Philip Morris? Tests showed three out of four cases of smoker's cough clear on changing to Philip Morris. Why not observe the results for yourself?" Nat did not have a smoker's cough in 1945.

Young Sinatra of the hollow cheeks and cold blue eyes, rapier-thin, has finished crooning the last lovely phrases of "Nancy." The melting violins and harps have faded away. No sooner are they gone than we hear Nat King Cole's voice and piano, unannounced, launching into "Paper Moon," joyfully, irrepressibly. And Frank, the polite master of ceremonies, who has yet to take his bows for "Nancy," makes a comic business of chasing the whirlwind Trio, trying to overtake them — or at least keep up — as they ignore him.

"The King Cole Trio. Now there's an outfit that loves its work. Why, they don't even wait for their introduction! Say, Nat Cole . . . Hey, Nat, hey! [Nat keeps singing.] Hey, wait up! Nat

203

Cole!" Frankie yells. "Will you wait for the Go sign?"

Frankie whistles and the audience laughs. "Wait now, cut! Cut!"

At last Nathaniel stops. He looks up from his piano, like a man emerging from reverie, surprised he is being observed.

"Nat, honest, I hate to interrupt," says Sinatra. "I'd like the radio audience to know a bit more about your life story." At this Cole purses his lips, somewhat bashfully, looking to Oscar as if to ask, "Who? Me?"

"Tell me," says Frank, with easy intimacy, "when did you first realize that you were a great singer?"

At this the great pianist raises his eyebrows and shrugs, searching the air for an answer to this impossible question.

"I think it was . . . back in . . . uh . . ."

With superb comic timing he plays the moment of confusion, pointing behind him to the moment just past, with his thumb, like a hitchhiker, over his shoulder.

"Come again?" Frank prompts his shy guest, but already Nat King Cole has burst into a grin that says everything, and the audience dissolves in a mixture of laughter and feminine squeals.

"What I'm trying to say is this," the host continues, calming the crowd. "Nat Cole is a big man in the singing business — "

"That ain't what they say in the singing business," Nat snaps back.

"What do they say in the singing business?" Frank asks.

"They say Nat Cole ain't got no business sing-ing."

More laughter.

"Well, I guess they haven't heard about those phenomenal record sales of yours."

"Well, Frankie," Nat replies, dropping his bashful country boy air and communicating flu-ently with seasoned assurance, "I want to tell you something in strict confidence. I buy ninety-nine percent of those records myself."

"Now let me get this straight," Sinatra asks in-credulously. "You make records and then buy ninety-nine percent of them yourself? Nat, you can never make any loot that way!"

"Maybe not," says the pianist slyly. "But I can point to a ninety-nine percent increase in sales." Again the timing is perfect, a thing he learned singing and jive talking with Timmie Rogers. The audience cracks up.

"Now listen, Nathaniel, quit pulling my leg," the host advises. "Straighten up and fly right un-der that new record hit of yours. Ladies and gen-tlemen, the famous King Cole Trio, in 'Frim Fram Sauce.' "

The song was a scandal and a hit, a ribald blues in the vein of Bessie Smith's "Kitchen Man" with double entendres about food and sex. "Frim Fram Sauce" was a perfect vehicle for the Trio, with their knack for catchy nonsense and their pervasive, yet innocent, eroticism.

I don't want French-fried potatoes,
Red, ripe tomatoes.
I'm never satisfied . . .

I want the Frim Fram Sauce
With the Ausen fay
With chefafa on the side.

It wasn't so much what Nat sang as the way he sang it, so anyone who knew the first thing about sex or food knew he was thinking about both, or neither — and you could tell by the devil in his eye the man was thinking about *something*. CBS would ban it for a while, and Carlos Gastel added fuel to the fire of publicity by offering $5,000 to anyone who could "translate" the incendiary lyrics.

On Sinatra's show, Cole's swinging piano and clever "tag ending" ("Now if you don't have it just give me a check for the water") elicit cheers and shrieks of pleasure from the audience, and an invitation to return again soon.

So a few days before Nathaniel's twenty-seventh birthday, Frank Sinatra and Nat King Cole, this time in a Los Angeles CBS studio, resume their very public conversation: "You know, I sure don't see how you fellows do it, Nat, six nights a week at the Trocadero, picture dates, road trips. When do you get time to sleep?"

"Well, every now and then we play a dreamy little thing, and I sort of ooze and doze off," says Nat, miming the act of dozing off, and the audience laughs as Nat's smile lights up the theater.

"Nat, there's something I gotta say: A lot of us in Hollywood are awfully happy and proud about your success."

"Well, I ain't exactly *unhappy* about it myself," observes the kid from Chicago, and the crowd chuckles appreciatively.

206

"I see what you mean," Frank agrees, grinning. "Nine years ago, Nat, they tell me you had nothing. Now you've got everything. Isn't it amazing?"

"It sure is," says Nathaniel thoughtfully. "There's just one thing I can't figure out."

"What's that?"

"My income tax."

More laughter.

"Well, I got news for you, Nathaniel," says Frank like an older brother. "Don't try to figure it out. Just pay it."

In a few years Nat King Cole would wish he had taken his friend's advice to heart.

CHANGES

The frantic pace Sinatra has described was no exaggeration. Despite Oscar's ill health (he was back in the hospital on January 18) the Trio was constantly on the go. "Make hay while the sun shines" was Carlos Gastel's motto, and now the sun was shining on Nat King Cole day and night. No wonder he dozed at the piano.

Down Beat magazine honored him as an "All-Star Band Member" on January 28 in the Philharmonic Auditorium, where he played for a sold-out crowd of 2,300, along with Charlie Ventura, Mel Powell, Lester Young, Dizzy Gillespie, Charlie Parker, and friend Lee Young. Later that year Cole won two Esquire music awards: gold for piano, silver for singing. Oscar got the gold "Esky" for guitar.

In February the group made its fifth movie appearance. *Down Beat* applauded the film for one remarkable quality. "The chief interest in *Breakfast in Hollywood* is the fact that the Trio, which by the usual movie procedure might have been treated as a group of blackface comedians, gets excellent presentation in two unbroken sequences, each the length of a phonograph record. They do their own, original material, and provide a distinct lift for those who might find the rest of the picture pretty hard to take."

Nat and the Trio were beginning to cross over

from the jazz race market to the world of popular culture in a way that cigar-chewing Carlos Gastel might have planned, but which was beyond the Chicago kid's wildest dreams. Nat always said, "Carlos brings me luck." Now Carlos seemed a magician. Overnight Nat was on first-name terms with Frank Sinatra and Bing Crosby, not just in the small twilight world of jazz clubs, but on the national stage. This had something to do with the euphoria of V-J Day, the end of a war in which tens of thousands of soldiers, including many African-Americans, had died for their country. And it had a great deal to do with Cole's extraordinary charm, a charisma that made him irresistible to audiences regardless of color. White America was in a generous spirit, ready to accept the "otherness" that Nat Cole presented in such a lovable package.

Big money was the first consequence of the crossover, one that Louis Armstrong had experienced. Another eventuality was rather unprecedented, a sign of the times. This was the welcome Cole received in the mainly white society of show business. Most of his life he had moved in the close, familiar world of black musicians, from the rehearsal hall to the African-American union hall.

Beginning in 1944, Nat King Cole often found himself in white company: Carlos Gastel, Glen Wallichs, Norman Granz, Johnny Mercer — men who shared his goals and vision, who wished to be not only colleagues but friends. Easy for the cynic to say these men really desired to exploit the gifted performer, the golden goose, and that Nat was using them as they were using him. But such cynicism may blind us to an essential theme of this story.

Nathaniel Cole had a rare gift of friendship, born of natural sympathy and honesty. We shall see that his lifelong friends were men and women of diverse backgrounds, but all people of excellent character. It is evident from his teenage bond with red-haired Les Paul that Nat did not choose his friends according to race. He would form lasting bonds with Lee Young, Ivan Mogull, Charlotte Hawkins, a little later Eddie "Rochester" Anderson, Sarah Vaughan, Jack Benny, Edward G. Robinson, and Sidney Poitier, all individuals of extraordinary courage and probity. Where Nathaniel saw human virtues in a man or woman he was happily color-blind.

His growing social ease and mobility were not altogether shared by his wife, the chorus girl from St. Louis. First of all, she was not often a part of it. She stayed at home. All the money Nat was earning would not make up for his absence from the dinner table or the bedroom in the bungalow they now owned. And then, Nat's life was a constant, rigorous learning process. What had she learned? Nadine must have found Nat's new friends, stylish suits, new confidence, and fluency of diction as threatening as Oscar Moore found the balladeer's consuming fame. Barry Ulanov, who spent time with the couple, recalls that Nadine's good humor was not above some occasional sarcasm if she was provoked. "She had an edge." No doubt there were bitter words spoken and bitterer silences that passed between the twenty-seven-year-old star and his thirty-seven-year-old wife as they struggled to adjust to his success.

Busy as he was, every day Nat read the newspapers, as well as the trade magazines *Down Beat*, *Metronome*, and *Variety*. Seeing his name in print was still a thrill. The papers would pile up on the floor next to his bed in the Capitol Hotel on 51st Street and Eighth Avenue in New York.

In the November 1945 issue of *Metronome* his name appeared many times. There was a mixed review of his show at the Apollo with Andy Kirk and grinning Timmie Rogers. Turning pages, he saw a good photo of himself in a dapper suit at a table at the Turf restaurant in New York with Ray Nance, Monte Kay, and Mal Braverman, discussing a New Jazz Foundation.

And as an admirer of beauty in women, the reader noticed, a few pages deeper in the same magazine, a large photograph of a very beautiful young woman in a low-cut black dress, shoulders bare, arms crossed in an attitude that is too playful to be altogether defiant. Her smile is broad and warm, showing even teeth, and her large dark eyes, wide-set, slightly tilted like a cat's, her eyes smile also, her whole countenance simply beams. Her shiny black shoulder-length hair parted in the middle and pulled back from her shapely brow is flipped up in a permanent wave.

"Marie Ellington, known to Duke Ellington fans simply by her first name to avoid confusion, will further avoid confusion by working apart from the band hereafter. This month, she steps out under the management of Walter Bishop to sing and draw whistles as a single attraction."

She was about to change Nat's life.

He would not meet Marie until six months later, after each had seen troubles that would deepen their understanding of each other. In the meantime each would make the acquaintance of Ivan Mogull.

Mogull, a handsome, rock-jawed song plugger, worked for a music-publishing house. This streetwise, bantamweight Jew from New York's West Side met Marie Ellington that autumn. Two months out of the army, twenty-one years old, the song plugger was on an errand from Bergman, Vocco, and Conn, music publishers for Fox Pictures, to see Duke Ellington at the Zanzibar nightclub on Broadway, and sell him a song.

Duke told Mogull to show the song to Marie Ellington.

"Your daughter?" he asked.

The Duke shook his head.

"Your wife?"

"No," said the Duke. "We are not related. She sings for me."

Mogull went to find Marie in the nightclub, and introduced himself. She was a strikingly pretty young woman. He asked her if he could show her the song. She asked how he might demonstrate it, and he told her he had an office upstairs in the same building, the Brill Building which overlooked 50th Street. Between sets he would be glad to play it for her. Marie said that would be fine.

So Ivan Mogull met the young woman and led her upstairs. She had excellent posture and long legs. He played the tune for her: "Do ya love me? Do ya love me? Tell me, do ya?" When he was done he looked up and asked Marie what she thought. She said she was sorry but she did not like it.

This was the worst thing the song plugger could hear because it was his job to get Duke to do the song, and now this girl and not the Duke was telling him no.

In desperation, or seeking consolation, the army veteran made a subtle pass at the young singer.

Whatever it was she said to put him in his place put Ivan Mogull so firmly in it he would never forget the young woman's polite fury or his own embarrassment as long as he lived. And he would live a long time to become one of Marie's most loyal and devoted friends.

Soon after this, Mogull was in the Copacabana's upstairs lounge. He sat with his crew-cut drummer friend Buddy Rich and a pop singer named Eileen Barton listening to the King Cole Trio doing "Don't Blame Me" and Nat's jump tune "I'm an Errand Boy for Rhythm." Buddy Rich was a tough customer from Brooklyn with a wicked tongue, but he was good company. Buddy knew Nat Cole from playing Jazz at the Philharmonic in L.A., and on June 9 he had made a black-market recording of a bebop jam session with Nat, Charlie Shavers on trumpet, and Herbie Haymer on sax. Eileen Barton's father was a business associate of Sinatra's, so she knew Nat through Frank.

They sat drinking at a table near the small stage.

Nat King Cole looked up from the piano and smiled at Ivan Mogull. "You back again?"

"You're too good," Ivan shot back at him. When other lounge acts played, people drank, talked, came and went. When the Trio played a lounge, everybody got quiet as if they were at a concert. That November the Trio played the Copacabana for three weeks, and Buddy and Ivan were there almost every night. Sometimes Ivan would bring his older sister or entertainers he was persuading to perform his songs.

Eventually Cole came to sit with Buddy and Ivan. Mogull recalls that the young black artist was still very shy and reserved. The song plugger, with his gift for gab, was anything but shy. Before long he found himself in a wide-ranging conversation with Cole, despite the vast difference in their backgrounds. Mogull had played in a band in high school, and had met Louis Armstrong.

That night after Nat finished at the Copa, he and Ivan went out together for drinks. This became a regular thing, going out on the town after hours, sometimes with Buddy and Eileen and others, sometimes just themselves. Nat was "a pretty good drinker" in the days when people drank socially as a nightly ritual: J&B scotch on the rocks, a drink or so an hour, never to excess; nobody ever saw Nat Cole drunk except once, under extenuating circumstances that will be described in due course. Ivan could not keep up with Nat in the drinking, but his talking more than made up for it.

They were sitting in Lindy's, a mecca for show business people after hours, and one of the greatest deli restaurants in New York.

"So," Ivan began. "You want to be Jewish."

Nat's eyes widened in amazement. It was a crazy idea.

"Your name is Cohn, isn't it?"

"Cole."

"Cohn. Nat King Cohn?"

"Cole," said Cole, laughing. When he really got to laughing his whole body would shake.

"I thought you changed your name," said Ivan.

"It was Coles. I changed it from Coles to *Cole*."

"Whatever." Ivan pointed to the plates of food between them. There were golden brown bagels, sliced red onion, capers, and pink lox.

Nat looked around the room. He was not accustomed then to dining in restaurants with mostly white people. "I can't eat that," he said to Ivan, shifting in his seat.

"Go on, you'll like it."

"No," said the pianist, pointing delicately to the lox. "It's not cooked. It's raw." He looked at the lox out of the corners of his eyes.

"Nat," Ivan said patiently. "It's smoked."

Nathaniel smiled. "It smoked? Must have been what killed it. What kind of fish smokes? I don't want to eat *no* fish that —"

"No, I didn't say it *smoked*, I said it has been smoked."

"Say what you mean."

"Here, watch me." As the Jew picked up a bagel and sliced it, Nathaniel Cole of Bronzeville watched him very carefully. "You take this, and here you smear a little cream cheese, and you put a little onion, put some pepper . . ."

"I cannot," said Nat, looking hard at Ivan. Then Mogull noticed that Cole had remarkably beautiful eyes, narrow and set far apart and very dark — the eyes of a panther.

"Eat it! You're gonna love it!" said Ivan forcefully, and right then Nat bit into the bagel and lox, and he must have been very hungry, because the strangeness did not keep him from eating until the food was all gone.

And then there was the pastrami. He would not eat that either because he thought it was raw, until Mogull talked him into it. "You got to eat it if you want to be Jewish. Your name is Cohn, isn't it? You changed your name. Nat King Cohn."

And that is how Nat Cole became a lifelong convert to Jewish delicatessen.

In January the Trio left New York for L.A. With the full schedule of radio appearances, film cameos, and recording sessions for Capitol in Hollywood, they would not return to the Big Apple until May 1946.

In March of that year the soaring balloon of Nat's success was pricked, ever so lightly, from a quarter wholly unexpected: the jazz critics, his first advocates, started questioning his stylistic drift. *Metronome* critic Barry Ulanov dropped in to the Trocadero one night, and started the fuss: "Why are you playing so much pop music and neglecting the kind of jazz that made your reputation?" he asked. Cole got angry.

A few nights later at a party in Westwood, the writer Frank Stacy asked Nat the same question. Around them the noise of the phonograph and chattering crowd made conversation impossible. So the two men decided to meet the next day for brunch at the Radio Room on Hollywood and Vine.

The interview Cole gave Stacy is one of the most precise and significant on the record. Ulanov recalls how well Nat used words, how he would "construct" a conversation much the way he would develop variations on a piano melody — "soft-spoken, very careful, with a deliberate and sweet exactness, always with warm feeling for the listener, almost as if he were playing when he used a word, as if he were at the keyboard. There was so much of him, when one was privileged to spend time in a lengthy conversation, you carried away not just phrases but a whole longer sense of his ideas, about musicians, music, life."

This morning he spoke with unaccustomed heat, a touch of anger.

"I know that a lot of you critics think I've been fluffing off jazz. But I don't think you've been looking at the problem correctly. I'm even more interested in it now than I ever was."

If that was so, the critic wondered aloud, why was he singing so much romantic fluff?

Nat furrowed his brow, speaking grimly. "Frank, you know how long it took the Trio to reach a point where we started making a little money and found a little success? For years we did nothing but play for musicians and other 'hip' people. We practically starved to death. When we *did* click, it wasn't on the strength of the good jazz . . . we clicked with pop songs, pretty ballads and novelty stuff. You know that. Wouldn't we have been crazy if we'd turned right around after getting a break and started playing pure jazz again?

We would have lost the crowd right away."

The critic would not argue this point.

"We're only waiting," Nat continued, "until we've reached a firm enough point where we can mix the real stuff with the popular and still have an audience. And I think we're just about at that point now. I'm already planning to make more and more jazz records . . . and next year, at the very latest, I'm going to take the Trio on a concert tour of the U.S. playing a jazz program."

This marked the beginning of a controversy that followed the showman all over the world for the rest of his life. Was Nat King Cole a jazz artist or a popular entertainer, a serious musician or a sell-out? Hoping to end the fuss at once, Nat and Carlos cranked up the p.r. mill.

Even before Stacy's article came out in the monthly *Capitol* magazine, the March 25 issue of *Down Beat* released the details of Cole's high-minded plans for a jazz concert tour. "Concerts will feature more serious works than the current Trio fare, and will emphasize the unit's versatility and virtuosity." Nat's promises to soothe the jazz purists border on the grandiose. He announces he is composing a "concerto," and wants to perform the works of other serious composers. And in a subsequent article he declares: "The work will be modern music . . . experimentation . . . a little like Debussy or Gershwin's serious compositions."

"Maybe this is all a happy dream, and maybe it won't work," he notes, "but I'm going to try, and hard, and you can't blame me for trying, can you?" Try as he would, the happy dream remained just that. They never did the jazz tour. The real world of commerce and the entertainment business pressed in upon the Trio daily with increasing urgency. Cole's personal interest in jazz truly was as keen as ever. In April, Norman Granz produced one more astounding jazz session with Nat, Lester Young, and Buddy Rich, recording eight twelve-inch sides, including "I Cover the Waterfront," "Somebody Loves Me," and "Peg o' My Heart." And later that month Nat appeared on the AFRS *Jubilee* show playing with Rich, Benny Carter, and Charlie Parker. This is first-rate jazz music. But the public hardly noticed because it was drowned out by the jukebox and radio success of hits like "Route 66" and the love ballad "You Call It Madness." Time and thought spent on jazz got little response; effortless pop music won cash and acclaim.

The main reason Nat would never keep his promise to do an all-jazz tour was the Trio's phenomenal success on the radio. Their appearances on Bing Crosby's *Kraft Music Hall* on NBC brought such overwhelming applause that the network signed the Trio (with Eddy Duchin as MC) to substitute for Crosby during thirteen weeks beginning on May 16. This was the start of a fruitful two-year association with the network that, seven years later, would sponsor Nat King Cole's television show.

Yet he would keep trying to please the readers of *Down Beat,* even as he was charming the subscribers of Newsweek, where his picture was soon to appear. Nobody could blame him for trying.

MARIA

In New York for the spring and summer of 1946 to star on radio's *Kraft Music Hall*, the Trio worked nights at the Zanzibar nightclub on Broadway. They opened there on May 17, replacing the Mills Brothers vocal group. Also on the bill were comedian Eddie "Rochester" Anderson, pianist Maurice Rocco, a comedy duo, a chorus line called the Zanzibeauts, and the singer named Marie Ellington.

Nat King Cole was standing backstage at the Zanzibar when he first saw Marie Ellington in the flesh. He was talking to a buddy, a street hustler named Happy Robinson. Happy ran errands, drove cars, spread rumors — whatever needed to be done. Marie Ellington was singing Johnny Mercer's song "Personality." She was wearing a royal-blue gown glittering with sequins, tight-fitting and split up the front. And the way she moved made men forget about what she was singing. Nat craned his neck but he could not get the full view.

"*Who* is *that?*" whispered Nat King Cole.

"That," said Happy sadly, "is Marie Ellington." And he sighed. "She used to sing with Duke."

"Wow. If she looks as good from the front as she does behind . . ." He brushed beneath his chin with the back of his fingertips. He was struck by the grace of her carriage, the way she stood and moved. Marie Ellington looked good no matter where she turned. And at twenty-three she was already a "brilliant" woman, a woman with a story, several stories, and a name to go with each. Soon she would be called Maria.

She was born Marie Hawkins in the Roxbury section of Boston on August 1, 1922, and christened in an Episcopal church. Her father, blue-eyed Mingo Hawkins, was a mail carrier. It was a good middle-class job for an African-American in those days of sweatshops and seventy-hour workweeks.

She was the second of three sisters. Marie never knew her mother, who died giving birth to the youngest sister, Carol (called "Babe"), when Marie was a toddler. Charlotte, blue-eyed, blond-haired Charlotte, was the eldest of the girls. Only a couple of years older than Marie, she kindly assumed a nurturing, maternal role, one she would never really leave behind.

"We don't talk about it, but our father's father was white," says Charlotte. "So was a maternal grandfather, I believe." All the sisters were fair-skinned, Marie the least fair. And all were beautiful, like the sisters in a fairy tale. I have seen pictures of the three, Charlotte, Marie, and Babe, in the bloom of youth, and a man would be hard put to choose among them. Later it became the received opinion that Babe was the most beautiful but that was after she was dead and could not argue with Marie and Charlotte.

Postman Hawkins had every intention of raising his daughters himself in Roxbury. But in time it became evident that they were more than he could manage. Entering adolescence, the older girls needed a woman's guiding hand.

Fortunately Mingo Hawkins's sister Charlotte Hawkins Brown was one of the more distinguished and successful women in America. Granddaughter of a slave, Aunt Lottie founded the Palmer Memorial Institute in Sedalia, North Carolina, the nation's first black prep school, in 1902. She was only a teenager when she knocked on the doors of some rich white New Englanders — Charles Eliot, the Galen Stones, and Alice Freeman Palmer — and raised the money to start a school for girls. In an abandoned church Aunt Lottie opened the school and built it into a half-million-dollar institution.

Now in her late forties, Dr. Brown had honorary degrees from Wellesley and Mt. Holyoke, and a house in Sedalia they called Canary Cottage because Aunt Lottie kept canaries. Marie disliked the canaries, knowing her Blake: "A robin redbreast in a cage / Puts all Heaven in a rage," but liked the house in spite of the Blakean offense. It was a big white house of two stories with four bedrooms and two baths and a telephone, plenty of room for Marie and Charlotte. The gardens and lawns were well tended. When they were eight and ten the sisters began to winter in Sedalia under the watchful and exacting care of their famous aunt.

There they received a great deal in the way of creature comforts, education, and culture, and a lot was expected of them in return. They ate well and dressed tastefully and they had nurses to care for them. "We never plaited our own pigtails until I was thirteen," Maria recalls. At the Institute the girls got a first-class education, and at home they kept superb company. On a weekday evening or over a weekend the houseguests might include Eleanor Roosevelt, Langston Hughes, Roland Hayes, and W. E. B. Du Bois.

Aunt Lottie was often on the road, raising funds and lecturing, or abroad in Europe. Whether she was home or away she expected the girls to be models of scholarship and deportment. They rose at seven to get ready for school, and they kept busy all day with studies, formal teas in the afternoons, and church services on Sundays and Wednesday evenings. For fun they listened to the radio, read movie magazines, and went to the cinema on Friday nights. Once in a while there were dances at school, strictly chaperoned. Maria recalls, "You didn't dare dance too close to a boy." Aunt Lottie was the published author of a book of etiquette called *The Correct Thing*.

Christmas was special in Aunt Lottie's house, a time when she relaxed her customary discipline. Then she spoiled the girls with fancy dresses and gifts under the glittering tree, and a lavish roast beef dinner. All her life, wherever she lived, Maria would strive to re-create the mood of those holidays.

There was the sense, always, that a high price was to be paid for privilege, one way or another. Clearly the standard of living the Hawkins sisters enjoyed was well above the average for African-Americans. So was the respect they received. Poor whites in Sedalia, addressing Charlotte Hawkins Brown, said "Yes, ma'am, Dr. Brown," or "No, ma'am, Dr. Brown," the way a Southern cracker would scarcely talk to any other black person south of Philadelphia. Dr. Brown lived well and entertained well in her home. But when her nieces went shopping in nearby Greensboro the clerks had to sneak them into the dressing rooms, where black women were not permitted to try on clothing. Restaurants were out of bounds. And at the Carolina Theater they were forced to sit in a special balcony section until Aunt Lottie found out about it and declared an embargo. When the girls traveled with their aunt they motored in their own car or went by Pullman train. But Maria remembers how, when they ate in the dining car, sometimes a curtain would be pulled to spare them the view of white faces eyeing them with disdain.

Privilege of any sort came at a cost to yourself and others. The lucky girls had only to look around them, and at their family history, to see that. Marie was romantic. Sentimental Charlotte wrote publishable poetry, but she says that Marie was the true romantic of the family. Reading the movie magazines and dreaming in the theater's darkness, she longed to be rich, famous, to have a career in show business. But this was not idle conceit. She had the looks, the voice, and her Aunt Lottie's fiery determination to turn the dream into a reality.

Marie was twelve and living with her father in Cambridge one summer when she ran away from home for the first time. She hitchhiked with two friends bound for New York to compete in the Apollo Theater's amateur hour. They never made it. A minister picked them up in Rhode Island eight hours after they left and sent them home again. A few years later she got to the Apollo, where she sang at amateur hour, and won top honors.

Convinced that the stage was toxic to a young woman's character, her family did not encourage such ambitions. They insisted that Marie finish school, and then they wanted her to go to college. Aunt Lottie could have gotten the bright girl admitted almost anywhere. But Marie preferred to go back and live with her father, beyond the reach of her stern aunt, where she would attend Boston Clerical College. There she pursued her stage career at night, singing with Sabby Lewis's orchestra downtown. In her late teens Marie was offered a two-week gig in New York by bandleader Phil Edmond. Her father allowed her to accept if she would stay with an aunt and uncle. When the show was over she begged her father to let her stay on; instead he sent her down to Washington, D.C., where Aunt Lottie had secured Marie a good job at Howard University as secretary to the purchasing agent.

She would not toil long in the District of Columbia, for Marie Hawkins had put aside her destiny long enough. She went back to New York. And there, in 1941 under the name of Marie Winter, she commenced a brilliant if short-lived career as a jazz singer, often compared to Lena Horne. That year she sang at the Savoy with the great band of Benny Carter, who praised her for her versatility. She sang with Fletcher Henderson and others.

Then in 1943, following a wartime romance, she married Lieutenant Spurgeon Neal Ellington, a most romantic figure, a fighter pilot in the legendary black 332nd. She had met him while she was working in Washington, and in March they got married in Detroit. Lieutenant Ellington flew missions over Italy, for which he received the Distinguished Flying Cross, while Marie worked as a secretary at the Harlem YMCA and pursued her singing career at night. Sister Charlotte had come to New York. She gave a recording of Marie's voice to a friend, Freddie Guy, Duke Ellington's guitarist, who got it to Billy Strayhorn, Duke's arranger. Strayhorn hurried to Marie's office at the Y to offer her a job singing with Duke's orchestra.

She was performing with Duke Ellington late in 1945 when her husband finished his tour of duty. He took her by surprise, appearing backstage in his uniform. The next day he returned to his base in Tuskegee, Alabama.

The airman flew to see his wife in early December of that year. They were proud of each other, the handsome war hero and the Broadway singer, proud and happy. He had a dream: to become the first black commercial airline pilot. They were making plans for a Christmas together after he finished his military service in Alabama. But on December 10, after a routine training flight, he and his copilot were killed when their airplane crashed on the way back to the base. Charlotte handed Marie the telegram.

She cried for days. She wondered what she would do with his medals. It was illegal to sell them, though she could have used the money, and she was too sad to wear them on her suit coats, as so many war widows were doing. Charlotte says, "The war was over. I don't know how she ever got over the injustice of it."

It must have been not too long after this that the song plugger Ivan Mogull met the young widow of Lieutenant Spurgeon Ellington, and tried in vain to get her to like the song he was selling.

Toward the end of her own engagement at the Zanzibar in May 1946, Marie was rehearsing the song "Come Rain or Come Shine."

She noticed Nat King Cole sitting in the small, scattered audience watching her rehearsal. She could tell he did not like the way she sang the song. She thought he looked a bit sinister, studying her through his dark horn-rimmed glasses. The college kids started wearing glasses like this after the war, wanting to be hip like Nat King Cole.

Eddie Anderson introduced them all, Marie and Oscar and Johnny and Nat. She may have felt then how warmly he was regarding her, but she thought nothing of it, even after noticing that he always watched her perform from backstage. But then one night they passed as she was coming off her number and he was going on. And something about the way he looked at her and nodded could not be ignored. "Oh!" the lady exclaimed in mild indignation, tossing her head as she walked away from him into the wings. She was tired of men making passes at her.

The chorus girls dressed and undressed in a room just across from Marie's dressing room backstage at the Zanzibar. Marie walked into their dressing room and sat down in a chair next to Alice Bishop. Alice was powdering her face in the mirror. She had known Nat Cole for a long time. Alice liked Marie Ellington, and she began to tell young Marie all about Nat King Cole from Chicago, what a great talent he was and how kind, how generous, what a gentleman.

Marie sat and listened, brooding. Her husband had been dead only five months.

"You know," said Bishop, resting the powder puff long enough to look Marie in the eye, in the mirror wreathed with lightbulbs, "I think he really likes you."

Marie tried not to be impressed. But it seemed to her that everybody else she knew was falling in love with Nat King Cole and his music — the chorus girls, women in the audience, the critics, the general public, even her sister Charlotte.

Marie and Charlotte were living together in a fourth-floor flat in the Dunbar Apartments, an exclusive residence in Harlem. African diplomats resided there, prizefighters and entertainers. Bill Bojangles Robinson lived down the hall from them. "They had to know your whole family history before you could live there," Charlotte explains. She loved the King Cole Trio, swooned over Nat's love ballads. She was thrilled when she learned her sister Marie was on the bill with the King.

Marie was on her guard. Cole's valet, Otis Pollard, appeared at the door of her dressing room with a present of champagne. She politely waved it away, saying, "I don't drink." To her this was just one more musician making a play; it made her recall she was brought up in a family that never wanted her in show business in the first place. At that point she did not know enough about Cole to know he was married, or care.

Nat was constantly on the go that summer, in and out of rehearsal studios and radio theaters for his own NBC program, and as a guest on shows such as *Chesterfield Supper Club* and *Maggie's Private Wire*. Mel Tormé had come to him at the Trocadero in early May with a lovely new piece called "The Christmas Song" he had written with Robert Wells. Cole loved the song with its colorful imagery and haunting tune, and the Trio first recorded the holiday tribute, very simply, in the YMCA studios in New York on the unseasonable date of June 14, 1946.

But Nathaniel was not too busy to think about the lovely young singer, and he was determined to get Mrs. Ellington's attention. In Nat's heart it was Christmas already. He bought a $50 ticket to the heavyweight championship bout between Joe Louis and Billy Conn on June 19 at Yankee Stadium. Nat had heard through Rochester's wife, Mamie, who was going to the fight, that Marie wanted to go too. Unfortunately, Nat had to perform at the Zanzibar that night, but would she like to have his ticket and go along with Mamie and keep her company? She would indeed. And all at once Marie was struck by the star's kind consideration, his generosity toward a mere girl singer on the bill.

Dressed in their finest, Marie and Mamie had a wonderful time watching the Brown Bomber beat up Billy Conn in Yankee Stadium. The next day when Rochester had a horse running, he invited Nat and Marie to come along with him and

Mamie to the racetrack, and Marie could not say no.

So the young singers sat in the grandstand at Belmont Park and watched the horses leap out of the starting gate and gallop around the green curve of the track. She had bet two dollars on a colt named Grey Falcon, and got so excited as he broke into the lead that she held Cole's hand very tightly. And as the horse crossed the finish line a winner, the two of them were on their feet laughing and shouting together. The horse paid forty dollars. If Nat Cole and Marie Ellington did not know they were in love by that time, Rochester and Mamie did.

At four o'clock every morning Marie got off work and took the subway home to the Dunbar in Harlem. In those days it was not dangerous but the trip was a long one. The Trio was staying nearby at the Theresa Hotel on 125th Street. Nat asked if she wanted to ride uptown with them and of course she did. Soon it was just Nat driving her home in the dawn light. Oscar and Johnny joked with her that Nat had cut his old friends for *her*, not realizing how serious the joke was. She would be around when they were long gone.

The third or fourth time he drove her home he told her he was married, but by then it was too late to keep her from falling in love with him. One warm night in June when the moon was scarcely visible above the streetlights and skyscrapers, they were driving uptown together, both of them astonished and confused by what love was doing to them. They stopped in an all-night diner for a bite to eat and coffee but they were not much interested in food. When they got back in the car, dawn was tinting the sky pink above the buildings. On the radio was Gordon Jenkins's grand orchestral tribute to New York in music and words, the romantic "Manhattan Towers." Marie begged Nat not to go home just yet, but wait until the sentimental music was over. So they drove and drove, then parked somewhere on the Hudson and looked at the water and the city and the pink and gold sky over the river. They listened to the music until the sun came up.

And he told her he was in love with her, in a voice softer than any singing. He had never met anyone like her before, he said, gently, and he was in love with her even though he was married. "I know," she said, at once sad and happy and somewhat frightened. Not long after that he kissed her, and seemed only a little surprised that she did not reprimand him.

Soon after that Nat left town for a few days. She missed him so much she confided in her sister. Charlotte was appalled. "A married man *and* a musician?" She wondered which of the two descriptions would be more pleasing to Dr. Charlotte Hawkins Brown, author of *The Correct Thing*.

But when the married musician wired Marie that he was coming back and to please meet him at the airport, she was at La Guardia Field when the airplane touched down. They spent every minute together they could when they were not working, but it seemed hardly enough time before Nat had to go on the road again for two weeks.

The next time he came to New York only for a

day, July 19, to tape the *Kraft Music Hall* radio show. When he was planning to leave town again, to perform in Indianapolis, he asked her to go along with him, and she said yes.

Nat told Ivan Mogull, "I met this terrific girl."

Ivan nodded thoughtfully, knowing his friend was married.

"Who is it?" he asked.

"She's a singer. She was with Duke Ellington's band."

"You don't mean Marie, do you? Marie Ellington?" asked Ivan, remembering his encounter with the young woman.

"Yeah. How do you know?"

Ivan was afraid Marie would tell the embarrassing story about their meeting, so that Nat might then think less of him. But when they met again she smiled as if it had never happened. She really liked Ivan.

Mogull would be the one to put them on the train to Indianapolis, but before this Nat asked his friend to help Marie get ready to travel.

Ivan was surprised. "Are you really going with Nat?" he asked Marie, looking from her to Nat King Cole.

"Sure," she said, smiling.

"You don't have any clothes for the trip." Nat laughed.

"I don't care," she said.

Nat told Ivan to take the girl out and buy her a toothbrush, and they all laughed. And knowing this was scant apparel for daylight hours, when they got off the train in Indianapolis, Cole sent Marie out shopping. She bought suits and dresses and white shoes with a wedge heel and a plaid strap, the best she had ever worn. There was nothing to do but shop. Their hotel was old and run-down. The room was small and hot. She must not be seen with the married man in public. She waited up late for him to come back to her from work at the English Theater, so she could take him into her arms.

He was not so famous that they could not sit together on the train ride back from Indiana. But he would be, in about three weeks, when "Route 66" was #11 on the pop music charts, and the full-page spread and photo of him came out in *Newsweek*.

Everything was happening at once, in his public as well as his private life. He knew he was in real trouble now. It was one thing to sleep with women other than Nadine when he was on the road. It was quite another thing to fall in love with some-one else. And that is what had happened. He loved the sound of Maria's wise voice, low, clear, with a faint Boston accent. He called her Maria.

At the first opportunity, August 2, Nat King Cole got on an airplane and flew to Los Angeles to visit his wife. He hated airplanes. But now he was so busy he had no choice. Only four days before he had been onstage at the Savoy in Chicago between New York appearances. Three months had passed since he had been with Nadine, and now he had to see her. He had almost forgotten how she looked and why he loved her. It must have been difficult for both of them, no matter how hard he tried to assure her of his affection, no matter how hard she tried to conceal her awareness of the other woman.

When he left their bungalow in Los Angeles three days later, he may have known he would never go home again as her husband. But she did not.

Cole's sister Evelyn recalled, "Long before Nat asked Nadine for the divorce, he wrote me a letter telling me he had fallen in love with another woman. He asked me not to say anything to Mama and the rest of the family."

He returned to a grueling schedule in New York as he made ready for the watershed autumn of his career and the wild upheaval of his emotional life. Oscar Moore was ill again. Nat had to replace him with the drummer Jack "the Bear" Parker until late summer. Oscar did manage to get to the YMCA Studios on Monday, August 19, the afternoon the Trio rerecorded "The Christmas Song." The enchanting lyric cried out for strings; Nat had thought so from the first, and tried to persuade Wallichs and Mercer to hire an orchestra. But in the midst of all the furor over the Trio's "fluffing off" jazz, Capitol stood firmly against anything more than the straight Trio rendition they waxed in June. Under stubborn pressure from Nat and Carlos Gastel, Capitol at last put veteran Carl Kress in charge as producer for the session. He added four violins and a harp. And on that hot afternoon in late summer the group recorded what many believe to be the greatest American Christmas carol.

Nathaniel had never been inspired in just this way — he had never been so in love. He felt guilty. But his love for Maria overwhelmed his feelings of guilt about Nadine. Apparently he had made up his mind by the time he recorded his next hit, "For Sentimental Reasons," on August 22. Maria Cole recalls they were eating dinner in a Chinese restaurant when he looked up from his steak (he disliked Chinese food) and asked: "If I can get my divorce, will you marry me?" And she nodded in assent.

Yet there must have been real anguish on his part, if not ambivalence, about leaving Nadine. According to her account of it, he telephoned her while he was on tour in mid-October, performing in Philadelphia and Washington, D.C. He invited Nadine to come to New York and be with him while he was playing the Paramount Theater during the week of October 16. He said he had arranged for them to stay at the home of saxophonist Andy Kirk and his wife, Mary.

Although her husband was now earning well over $100,000 a year, Nadine wondered if she should travel the two thousand miles by the cheaper coach class or instead pay the expense of a Pullman.

Nathaniel did not go to the station to meet her train. He sent one of his valets. Perhaps his schedule made it impossible; certainly he dreaded the confrontation. It is hard to believe that he would make Nadine travel three thousand miles, first or second class, so he could tell his wife of ten years, in precise, virtually legalistic language, that he wanted a divorce, that he no longer loved her.

The minute Nadine was alone with him that is what he told her. He wanted a divorce. "It was a simple declaration of an apparently carefully studied decision," she later recalled. She returned to L.A., alone.

Carefully studied, but for how long? Was this the speech he planned to greet her with when he telephoned to invite her a week before? When he arranged with Mary Kirk to stay at their home? No, this is too cruel. More likely he had hoped to let her down gently, perhaps be with her once more as man and wife at least in friendship, perhaps even . . . to begin again. Whatever he felt when he called long-distance, by the time Nadine was on the train crossing the desert and prairie on her way to the estrangement, he had changed his mind. Some new pressure had come to bear on his affections, an insistence that he make a clean break with the past and embrace his future. Then it was too late to tell Nadine to turn back.

He lit a cigarette, and he sat down at the piano in Andy Kirk's apartment. The pianist Hank Jones remembers walking down the hallway to visit Kirk and hearing a piano, so rapidly and perfectly played he thought it must be a recording of Art Tatum. It was Nat King Cole, playing and smoking. He smoked for exhilaration and he smoked to calm down; he smoked upon waking, and snuffed his last cigarette in the ashtray next to his bed as he turned off the light to go to sleep. That year a tormented chemist at Lorillard wrote a letter to the manufacturing committee, saying that "the use of tobacco contributes to cancer development in susceptible people. Enough evidence has been presented to justify the possibility." The letter was not made public for fifty years.

ENGAGED

Big Carlos Gastel had his hands full. Carlos was a tremendous man with an abnormally large head. When he got serious he wrinkled his forehead and nodded like a Titan. He was flying and driving back and forth from New York to Los Angeles managing the King Cole Trio, Stan Kenton, Woody Herman, and Peggy Lee. Everybody was making money so fast they scarcely had time to count it.

Kenton, sharing the bill with Cole at the Paramount, was in the throes of a divorce. On one road trip to comfort Kenton in New York, Carlos turned over his heavy Cadillac convertible, and according to one account avoided death "by virtue of that astounding capacity for getting into and just as quickly out of trouble."

But the trouble with Nat and this girl Maria Ellington (she was now calling herself Maria) was a difficulty not quickly resolved. Called to New York by an associate (probably bandleader Woody Herman) who was alarmed by the threat to Cole's marriage, Carlos sat down with his friend and client in private and explained the facts of life.

They drank J&B scotch, on the rocks for Nat, for Carlos a cocktail of whiskey and milk.

The conversation went something like this: You love this woman? I do. Do you love her . . . sixty thousand dollars' worth? Yes, I do. Well, good, because that's what it's going to cost you, in the state of California, under the community property laws, to get rid of Nadine. Carlos had been through it all with Stan Kenton.

Gastel was not the only friend worried that Nat King Cole had lost his senses over the girl called Maria. His sister Evelyn recalled, "Our family loved Nadine. All marriages have rocky times, but none of us could accept that Nat wasn't willing to stick it out. Our dad was horrified at the cost of the divorce and felt his son was being frivolous. Mother didn't say much, but I know she was distressed. As far as she was concerned, Nat could do no wrong, but here he was, doing something which, at best, she didn't understand."

Most people who knew and liked Nadine, as well as everyone who had a stake in the status quo, felt threatened by the powerful presence of this young woman, a virtually unknown quantity. By now the King Cole Trio was big business, an industry that fed a lot of people. Running from city to city, the road show employed valets, press agents, secretaries, accountants, and a bodyguard, while attracting innumerable hangers-on and hustlers. Soon a road manager, a short bald man named Mort Ruby, would be hired to direct the traffic. Oscar Moore and Johnny Miller felt very vulnerable to the changes they saw coming when they realized Maria was more than a fling. If she could break up a marriage what would she break up next? Their humorous teasing turned to grave concern, and the sidemen advised Nat to forget her.

"If you don't like it," said the leader, "you can quit."

That was pretty much the end of the conversation, because Nat King Cole had made up his mind. As with other major decisions in his life, including marrying his first wife, he had made this one based on a gut feeling, knowing that the route was right for him before anyone else did.

The lovers had plenty to celebrate during that holiday season, as they pursued a romance that was now an open secret. Carlos had come around, accepting Maria. He was doing great things for Cole. He set up a publishing firm, Cole's King Music, Inc., to control song rights and avoid another fiasco like Irving Mills's purchase of "Straighten Up." And after weeks of wrangling and heroic negotiations with NBC and the Wildroot Cream Oil Company, Carlos landed the Trio its very own radio show, the *King Cole Trio Time*, in a prime spot, 5:45–6:00 p.m. on Saturdays.

The show premiered on October 19, with Jo Stafford (Paul Weston's wife) as guest. She asked the Trio to play certain favorites, and after they had obliged, Jo in turn sang Nat's request. The program opened and closed with a chorus of "Straighten Up and Fly Right." A few songs, a few commercial breaks (the Trio singing "Use Wildroot Cream Oil, Charlie!"), and some amusing banter between guest and host, and the quarter hour was gone in no time.

For nearly eighty shows over eighteen months that was the format. Guests included June Christy, Johnny Mercer, Mel Tormé, Pearl

Bailey, Sarah Vaughan, Earl Hines, Frankie Laine, Cab Calloway, Peggy Lee, and Duke Ellington. It was more than a little ironic that the man with the most famous "process" (artificially straightened hair) in America, the patent-leather-coiffed Nat King Cole, had become the chief spokesman for a cream oil hair tonic. NBC was already showing an admirable boldness in defying stereotypes the previous summer when it began using the black Trio not only for musical entertainment but for dialogue skits on *Kraft Music Hall*.

By early December "The Christmas Song" ("Chestnuts roasting on an open fire . . .") had risen to #3 on the popular music charts, where it could not go much higher because the Trio's "I Love You for Sentimental Reasons" was #1. Money was raining down so hard on them Carlos had to think of ways he could tie it up so Nadine wouldn't get it. On December 7, smiling Johnny Mercer was Nat's guest on the *King Cole Trio Time*. And after the songs and jokes, he presented them with an award for their awards: a special plaque in honor of the Trio's receiving four prestigious awards from *Metronome* magazine's poll of readers. The group was named best small combo and "the major influence of music for 1946." Nat Cole was named best pianist, and Oscar Moore was voted best guitarist. A week later J. Ward Maurer of the Wildroot Company appeared on the show to bestow on them *his* corporate compliments on their success. Not to be outdone, Nat surprised the executive with a parchment, a citation from *Metronome* naming Wildroot the "most musically progressive sponsor in radio." "Musically progressive" simply meant "progressive." NBC, Wildroot's network, was and would remain way ahead of its time in integrating the broadcast media.

That night, December 14, Nat got together with Frank Sinatra at a rehearsal session of the *Metronome* All Stars, that year's honorees. These included Charlie Shavers on trumpet, Johnny Hodges on alto, and Coleman Hawkins on tenor sax. Crazy Dave Tough from Chicago sat in for Buddy Rich, who got waylaid that night but would rattle the drum trap the next afternoon. At the rehearsal that night, and then on Sunday as they recorded the show, with Frank singing Nat's favorite "Sweet Loraine," the old friends enjoyed what time they could steal for conversation. They wanted to catch up on each other's stories, the pressures of stardom, the roller coaster of love. Nat felt guilty about leaving Nadine. Frank did not know her. He had no investment in Nat King Cole apart from a growing admiration, so he could listen without judging.

On the last day of the year, Nat performed in Hartford, where Maria joined him for the first of many New Year's celebrations together. Ivan Mogull, with a lady friend, made it a party of four.

Cole was living out of a suitcase during that hectic year, in and out of New York City, on the road, recording the Wildroot show in any city with an adequate studio — Hartford, Philadelphia, Detroit, Chicago. Maria's sister Charlotte Sullivan recalls that when Nat returned to New York he would drive up to Harlem to the Dunbar Apartments, where Maria was still living. He would stand under the window and whistle. The first time Charlotte heard it she was alarmed. "Who is that whistling?" she asked her sister. "Oh, it's Nat!" Maria cried joyfully, gathering her things and hurrying down the four flights of stairs. Charlotte added this to the list of behaviors unacceptable to Aunt Lottie.

"Nat had bad feet," Charlotte recalls. "Nat wasn't going to climb all those stairs. No, sir."

Maria would leap into his arms, and off they went. He nicknamed her Skeez, for the obvious reason (she was his main squeeze), and after the lovable, steady comic-strip character Skeezix from "Gasoline Alley." Skeezix, the foundling left on the doorstep on Valentine's Day, is a marvel of normalcy and optimism in a mad world.

They had much to learn from each other, and much to share. He knew the mysteries of music and the seamier side of existence, the compelling edges of urban life. She was a woman of proud sophistication, of ambitious refinement.

The couple found a lot to talk about but they rarely talked about the past. Nat knew something about Spurgeon Ellington, but he never asked a single question about Maria's first husband. And he never discussed Nadine until many months later when his new bride insisted upon it.

They went shopping. Maria had refined taste in clothing. She began to steer Nat toward suits and ties with less flash and more substance, more sartorial elegance. He was an eager pupil. Gently she began to influence his speech, mostly by example. He spoke well but not yet with the crystal clarity of diction that would soon make him a musical story-teller who could never be misunderstood. Cole still had the faintest remnant of a lisp and a bit more of the South Side transplanted Alabama hipster drawl than he needed to play the Radio City Music Hall or the Civic Opera House in Chicago. It was Maria of Boston and Sedalia who would put the final touches on Nathaniel's famous phrasing.

In the evening they would go to dinner with Mamie and Eddie Anderson, Carlos Gastel, or Ivan Mogull. Not all of their acquaintances could share their happiness. Women, particularly, could be rude.

One night they were sitting in a booth in Toots Shor's when Billy Strayhorn walked in with his friend Lena Horne. Lena knew Nat from the night they had been guests together on the Bing Crosby show. And in February they were together again, with Frank Sinatra, on AFRS *Jubilee*. She knew about Maria because everyone knew Maria and Lena were the most beautiful African-American singers alive, so they were often compared. Yet when Billy moved politely to introduce the two beauties, Lena tossed her head, ignoring Maria as if she were invisible. This hurt Maria. Evidently Lena knew Nadine and did not like what she had heard about how Nat had treated his wife. Like many women, she put the blame on Maria.

Nadine filed a divorce action in Los Angeles on January 6, 1947. The complaint states the "marriage defendant [Nathaniel Cole] has inflicted extreme cruelty upon plaintiff [Nadine]: a course of grievous suffering and anguish, and has been guilty of extreme cruelty towards plaintiff." Nat

243

was performing in Baltimore. On January 18 in New York he signed an agreement to pay Nadine $200 every week pending the divorce action, and to give her the $75,000 house in L.A. The balance owed on their home at that time was $8,357. The date for the trial was set for March 19. Her lawyers, Loeb & Loeb, estimated his income at $3,000–$5,000 a week, and this appears to be accurate.

Early in February, Nathaniel and Maria announced their engagement. This was only a few weeks before *Down Beat* broke the story of Nat and Nadine's "interlocutory divorce decree" being granted in January.

The public did not then know the details and "cause" of Nadine's divorce action. The general impression was that Nat had secured the divorce himself, and that it was amicable if regrettable. When the Associated Negro Press released the legal facts in late 1948, along with a news report of Cole's delinquency in paying $800 of alimony, a bitter battle ensued between the Coles and the ANP's head, Claude Barnett. Nadine was just as angry with Barnett as was Maria.

But for the time being the press showed little interest in the Cole domestic situation. An ANP release on May 22 praised the singer for a brave action in Kansas City. "The Trio lost thousands of dollars when Nat Cole refused to play a ballroom date when the segregation of white and Negro audiences was demanded." His career and his personal life progressed with minimal damage to his public image. This image, like everything else about Nat King Cole, had become a precious commodity upon which the livelihood of several dozen people, and the well-being of countless more, depended.

The trial for the divorce action on March 19 was a mere formality, as Cole did not contest. The conditions of the interlocutory decree were accepted as part of the settlement and the date set for the final divorce was March 22, 1948, a year in the future. After that date Nat and Maria were free to marry.

Nat was in Chicago with his fiancée, while Nadine was at the courthouse in Los Angeles, suing him. The lovers were in Nathaniel's hometown for two weeks, during which he broadcast three Wildroot shows, performed nightly at the Chicago Theater, and tried more or less successfully to get the Reverend and Perlina Coles used to the idea of Maria Hawkins Ellington as a daughter-in-law. They were unhappy about the divorce, and they were uncomfortable with Maria. Nadine had come to seem like one of their own, a preacher's kid who had strayed into show business, an East St. Louis girl without any airs. But this Maria of Boston was something else, a kind of princess with her way of talking and her all too refined manners.

And they could tell, or thought they could tell, what she thought of them, no matter how hard she tried to please them, to be sweet and considerate. And how she did try! She could see they were good-hearted and down-to-earth with their folksy wisdom, and stout Perlina was so funny she could see where Nat got his sense of humor. When she smiled her eyes were narrow like Nat's. But then Maria could not help but think, growing up as she had, being raised as she was raised, that they were somewhat, well, old-time, Southern, country. The way they lived, the way they talked and dressed, what they ate. Perlina and Edward thought Maria was thinking these things whether she was or not.

So the dinners and Sunday afternoons at the Coleses' house were tense, despite Evelyn's adoring attention and the boys' wide-eyed fascination with their older brother's success, his clothes, his car. Ike was nineteen and Freddy fifteen. If Nat's conscience was not troubled about the personal decisions he had made, then the Reverend would see to it his famous son felt a little guilt before he left home again. That was one of his ways of caring about him.

When the time came to leave Chicago after Easter, Nat was ready. They spent a week in Detroit, slipped into Chicago again on April 19 to tape the radio show, then went on to Missouri. On the 26th his idol Earl Hines followed him from Chicago to be his guest when Wildroot broadcast from St. Louis. If his flesh-and-blood father did not altogether appreciate what Nat had achieved, at least his artistic father Hines did, and Nat would do all he could to repay the man for his many kindnesses.

As "Fatha" Hines played a medley of tunes including "Rosetta," Nathaniel recalled his boyhood, standing under the el outside the Grand Terrace listening to the master's piano. He recalled the Battle of Bands at the Savoy, and remembered poignantly how Hines and Billy Eckstine passed the hat to help pay his debts in L.A. just five years ago.

The year Nat and Maria spent waiting and planning for their wedding passed in a whirl of coast-to-coast travel and performances almost nightly. It is difficult to convey how crammed their schedule was without mind-numbing repetition — cities, nightclubs, radio and recording dates. A new ban by union leader James Petrillo on recordings by union musicians (a strike for higher pay) was scheduled for 1948; this caused the Trio to squeeze the recording of eighty sides into a few months of sessions.

Long residencies — first in Los Angeles at the Bocage in the summer of 1947, then in New York at the Paramount during the fall and winter of 1947–48 — gave the Trio just enough stability to muster strength for road trips in September and October 1947, and then during the first three months of 1948. Nat and Maria had nowhere to set up housekeeping; wherever the lovers were together they called home — hotels, guesthouses, spare bedrooms of friends happy to welcome them to strange cities. If the room had twin beds they slept snuggled together in one.

Accommodations for black performers then, even the stars, were second-rate at best, especially in the South. It was the custom then for well-to-do African-Americans to offer their guest accommodations to musicians on tour, sparing them the indignity of shabby hotels.

"Maria is the one," says Ivan Mogull, "who got

him to straighten up and fly right. She was a proud lady. She had all the rights to be. She was educated and she simply would not take any more shit. This was her country as much as anybody else's. She saw to it he stayed in nicer hotels, like the Warwick in New York. Nat never complained about anything.

"Let me tell you a story about food. I went to visit Nat in Chicago, where he was doing four shows a day at the Regal. He says, 'Hey, Mo, I have an hour, hour and a half for dinner. There's a good place right near the theater. We can get in and get out and I will be in time for my show.'

"I said that was fine, and so we went to the steak house, Nat and this other song plugger Marvin Cane and me. And we sat down and Nat said, 'You all like steak?' I said sure I like it, and we all said we liked steak so we ordered three steaks.

"Well, the steaks came and we cut into the meat and started eating, chewing and chewing. And Marvin and I looked at each other. It was like eating wood. We were his guests. 'Is it good?' Nat asked us and he was smiling. We absolutely lied. When we were done eating and drinking we went back and hung out with Nat at the theater. And Marvin and I were not feeling too good.

"As we were going back into our hotel lobby, Marvin picks up the newspaper and shows me the headline: 'Horsemeat Sold Throughout Chicago.' We ate a horse with Nat King Cole. But he didn't complain. Nat never complained about anything."

Maria would eventually get him to cut down on the grease in his diet so his skin would begin to clear up. Friends recall that 1947 was the year when Maria had the greatest influence on her twenty-eight-year-old fiancé, his diet, his clothes, his accessibility, and to a lesser extent his business dealings. Like other young artists Nathaniel was highly developed in certain faculties at the expense of others.

For a man of the world he was remarkably unworldly in some ways, trusting to a fault, sometimes gullible if not quite naive. Basically honest and kind, he expected the best of everyone. And he was wonderfully philosophical about other people's failings. Maria found it astonishing.

"My father was a preacher, and he used to tell me a lot of stories," Nat told Gene Norman when the subject had turned to a man in the music business they did not like.

"A farmer walked out in a field on a cold winter's day and he found a snake. He didn't like snakes but he felt sorry for him because he looked half dead from the cold. So he took the snake into his house and kept it warm by the fireplace and fed it. And the first thing that snake did when he was feeling better was to bite the farmer.

"The farmer looked the snake in the eye and said, 'What have you done? I saved your life!'

" 'But you knew I was a snake,' " Nat concluded, his eyes twinkling, as he scratched his chin thoughtfully.

This tale was later immortalized in song by the soul singer Al Wilson in the 1960s. Show business was beset with snakes, and horsemeat, and all manner of hazards young Nathaniel had avoided mostly by instinct. But now he was really in a position where he needed the guidance of someone like Maria Ellington. Young as she was, she was shrewd. A great deal of money was changing hands.

Nat was notoriously casual about money. Soon after they fell in love Maria and Nat were getting out of a taxicab, and she watched in amazement as he fumbled with a roll of bills, peeling off nearly a thousand dollars in hundreds before he could find a fiver to pay the fare. He never knew how much money was in his pocket or in the bank. In 1946 he had no credit, paid cash for everything, and carried it in a tangle of bills in his left pants pocket. The pianist had gone from having nothing to having so much it was almost as meaningless as having nothing. Quietly Maria decided that if she ever married him she would handle the finances.

Every bum and hustler on 52nd Street knew Nat King Cole was a soft touch. They were always coming and going, clowning, jiving, running errands. Porters, bellboys, waiters, and drivers adored him. In this, he was like smiling Carlos Gastel.

One day Nat sent somebody off to Western Union with $750 in cash to be wired to another city. A little later he discovered the money never arrived where it was addressed; in fact the $750 never got to Western Union. Brought up for questioning, the man supposed to wire the money swore he had sent it. And though he could not produce a receipt or locate the money, Nat was sure his man was truthful and Western Union had blundered.

Slowly and surely, with the help of Carlos

Gastel and some gimlet-eyed bookkeepers, young Maria Cole would put a stop to this foolishness. Unfortunately she would not do it soon enough to avoid a financial disaster in the early 1950s. She had refined and sophisticated tastes and she was happy to make Nat happy by spending his money on beautiful things.

The greatest immediate change Maria effected in Nat's life was an inevitable result of the divorce: the reshaping of the entertainer's social life. Nadine had been a wife in absentia, allowing the musician rare liberty to move in a man's world, with access to loose women as well as protection from them whenever he desired it. Maria was determined to be on the scene, by his side, just as soon as the rule of etiquette would permit it, if not a little before. As she took her place in his dressing room, her reflection in the mirror transformed the male locker-room atmosphere the musicians had long enjoyed, the obscene banter, the camaraderie. The party, as Oscar, Johnny, and Nat had once known it, was over.

And of course a number of old friends, particularly women who had been close to Nadine, simply could not abide the young fiancée. They disliked her cleverness, her haughty accent and fine manners. Out of a sense of loyalty to Nadine, if nothing else, these dropped out of Nat's life, some temporarily, some forever.

Maria let it be known to Nat and Carlos and anyone else who cared to listen to her in 1947 that Nat King Cole was the star of the Trio, the reason for their spectacular success, and that Oscar and

Johnny were making too much money.

Johnny and Oscar were not happy with this, neither the fact of it nor hearing Nat's fiancée go on about it. But nobody could argue with her. It was true. Before Maria ever spoke up, Oscar knew it. He had been threatening to leave the Trio ever since Nat started crooning all those sappy ballads. It was not his kind of music, and the arrangements sidelined him. Oscar would go off in a pout, and Nat would give him more money to come back again.

All of this made the guitarist sick. Later Oscar claimed he quit the Trio because he was sick and tired of the road. He also said he was going to open a record shop, and that he wished to join his brother in his band, Johnny and the Blazers. This last excuse is the saddest, a story in itself. Lee Young recalls how pathetic it was that the great Oscar Moore got lost in a band named after his brother who was a nobody. By the 1950s Oscar was working in Las Vegas binding fishing rods.

The fact is that Nat King Cole had outgrown Oscar Moore, as brilliant as he was, just as he had outgrown his first wife. And it hurt Oscar almost as bad. No doubt Nat understood the extent of the guitarist's contribution to their achievement and their triumph. But now the scene had changed, and business was business.

Maria Ellington gave the leader the emotional support he needed to do what he was too tenderhearted to do on his own. He informed his sidemen they were welcome to continue to share his good fortune, but with a smaller slice of the pie. Judging from later contracts this amounted to cutting their salaries in half.

Oscar gave notice in the late summer of 1947. He was persuaded to stay on for a few months while his replacement, the gifted Irving Ashby, followed him around with a notepad, learning his role. After Oscar missed a concert in Pittsburgh, Nat wired Ashby: "Save me. Oscar Moore quitting." It was a good thing Oscar stayed through the summer. Union leader Petrillo threatened the AFM recording ban, to begin in 1948. So between August 6 and 29 in the studio, the Trio waxed forty brilliant sides for Capitol in a dozen sessions.

Again, it is hard to describe the labor involved in so much recording — songs ranging from "Rhumba Azul" (a Cole original) to the pop numbers "When I Take My Sugar to Tea" and "Makin' Whoopee" (which Mogull sold him), from ballads like "The Trouble with Me Is You" and Irving Berlin's "What'll I Do" to novelties, children's songs, and duets with Johnny Mercer.

And then there was the very strange song called "Nature Boy" recorded on August 22. The piece was so peculiar that Capitol did not think to release it until seven months had gone by.

Listen to the records to get an inkling of how much thought, emotion, and studio rehearsal went into each one of them. Look at the statistics. Between July 2 and December 21, 1947, the King Cole Trio recorded ninety sides for Capitol. Anyone who has had the experience of composing, learning, arranging, and performing music at this level can tell you the Trio's session work during the six months left them precious little time for anything else.

Yet a valet attending their nightclub act on Sunset Strip, as well as their radio and theater performances coast to coast during that period, would have said the same thing about the Trio's continuous, consuming live shows: That it was *impossible* that the boys were making records all day.

Cole seemed to be everywhere at once: Wednesday, a guest on Dinah Shore's radio show; Saturday, hosting Benny Carter on Wildroot; Monday, a celebrity guest of KFWB radio, honoring jockey Martin Block; Tuesday, a guest on NBC *Chesterfield Supper Club* with Jo Stafford — all this in one spring week in L.A. in 1947. Autumn finds the Wildroot show broadcasting from Salt Lake City, Louisville, Davenport, Iowa, and Cincinnati, en route to their New York residency. There they worked the Meadowbrook, the first African-American act to play there, and the Paramount Theater. They found time to join the testimonial concert for Billie Holiday, Jazz at the Philharmonic, at Carnegie Hall on November 29, to raise money for Lady Day's cure for heroin addiction.

The winter months took them back on the road — Hartford, Washington, D.C., Cleveland, Philadelphia, Baltimore, Chicago, Louisville, and back to Chicago, as Nat and Maria neared the date of their wedding. Only someone with prodigious stamina could maintain such a pace. No wonder Oscar dropped out in October. Johnny Miller would be gone nine months later, replaced by the light-skinned, pencil-mustached Joe Comfort on August 17.

Sometime around the end of 1947, at the suggestion of Carlos Gastel and Maria, Nat began to stand up from the piano bench in order to sing "The Christmas Song" more intimately to concert audiences. On September 16 he had sung the mystical ballad "Nature Boy" at the Civic Opera House in Chicago, totally mesmerizing the audience. The *Down Beat* critic Don C. Haynes, in a lengthy review of the show, called the vocal "the most impressive number of the entire concert." Like "The Christmas Song," "Nature Boy" had a certain poetic message that called for the whole man, from head to toe, to deliver it properly.

Much has been made of Nat Cole's reluctance to move away from the piano, take the microphone in his hands, and sing. He was too shy, some say. Others say he was petrified of facing the audience head-on, wondering what he would do with his hands. Finally and most significantly, there was the choreographic symbolism of the vocalist stepping in front of his colleagues, setting himself before them and above them as a prophet or hero. Perhaps he intuitively knew that the man who stands above the crowd at once becomes an idol and a target.

For almost a quarter of a century his art had been the art of the ensemble jazz musician. Now he was becoming, in spite of who he had been, and because of what he had gained, a lyric soloist and something of a hero.

By the time Oscar left in 1947, Nat King Cole had overcome his qualms about holding the microphone. When Johnny Miller gave notice in 1948, the King Cole Trio as an artistic entity was history. Soon even the name would be changed to reflect the alteration in the musical concept —

255

henceforth they would be billed as Nat King Cole and the Trio, as a drummer or conga player filled out the rhythm section.

And Nat King Cole was about to sing for America.

PART THREE
America

WEDDING BELLS

Nathaniel Cole and Maria Ellington were married in New York City on Easter Sunday in 1948.

It was a grand American wedding at the Abyssinian Baptist Church. The $17,500 price tag prompted the press to call this wedding the greatest Harlem had seen since the $45,000 nuptials of the granddaughter of Madam C. J. Walker, beauty products tycoon, in 1923.

As several hundred guests jammed the church, and several thousand more stood outside along 138th Street and Lenox Avenue, or leaned out of windows for a view, Nathaniel and Maria said their vows in front of Reverend Adam Clayton Powell, congressman from New York. Everyone in Harlem dressed in their finest on March 28, for the Easter Parade and the King's wedding.

Nathaniel dressed in a cutaway coat and striped trousers, a wing collar and dove-gray tie. The bride wore a pale blue satin gown, off the shoulder, with long sleeves ending in points over her hands, and a wide white lace shawl collar on the bodice of the gown. On her head shone a coronet of seed pearls and from it her bridal veil flowed down her back. She wore no jewelry but a string of pearls; and she held a bouquet of seven white orchids, and lilies of the valley, wound with white streamers.

Together they looked like a couple on a wedding cake.

Fragrance of orange blossoms and lilies filled the air. The altar, the chancel, and the aisles were banked with freesias, palms, and a host of Easter lilies and white orange blossoms artfully tied with yards of white ribbon.

These joyous occasions, wherein everyone smiles for the camera, usually transpire above a ground that seethes and rumbles with hidden rivers of sorrow, resentment, and spite. No doubt Maria and Nathaniel were very happy that day. But a wedding like this reminds us why famous lovers often elope. The planning and execution of the Easter bridal celebration was fraught with intrigue, logistical trouble, and family strife.

This is a good time to take stock of the members of the wedding, family, friends, and business associates, and review their interests and concerns, their hopes and fears.

At the groom's right hand stood Eddie Cole, the "best man," who found himself once again in a supporting role in his famous brother's life. Eddie looked uncomfortable, not just because of the morning dress and the wing collar. He was just getting over his rage at Nat and Maria for a painful offense to the dignity of the Coles clan. Sister Evelyn, Nat's dear sister, had not received the symbolic corsage of a bridesmaid. This made her cry, and made Eddie "raise hell," as Ike Cole later recalled. There were so many bridesmaids: Maria's younger sister Carol, friends Elaine Fein, Pauline Miller and Laveda Lewis, Elaine Robinson (Mrs. Bojangles), and Evelyn Ellington (Duke's daughter-in-law). But quickly a bridesmaid's corsage was produced for Nat's sister. So

Evelyn marched with the others to the altar, drying her eyes. Carol's little daughter Cookie was the flower girl. Beautiful Carol, recently widowed, was gravely ill but she had told no one.

Kind Charlotte stood at Maria's side as matron of honor, concerned for her father, father of the bride, white-haired, delicate Mingo Hawkins. The postman had found himself awkwardly squeezed between Harlem and Sedalia, where his sister Dr. Charlotte Hawkins Brown had threatened to spend Easter, in protest against the unseemly union. At last she relented. The newspapers said the bride's dress was a generous gift of Aunt Lottie, but it was a grand gesture covering a grand resentment. She had not raised her niece to marry a divorced minstrel in a Baptist temple in this wicked city.

Carlos Gastel, smiling, backslapping Carlos, with a breast pocket full of Havana cigars, had to consider what it was all going to cost. Not the festivities; they were nothing. He had to count Nat King Cole out of action for two weeks or more, fourteen days of honeymoon for an artist grossing three or four thousand dollars a day! Well, maybe Nat did need a breather. Besides, the new recording of "Nature Boy" had taken off like a rocket, and it would be working for them all night and day.

Proud Perlina Coles wore a voluminous dress and floral bonnet. The Reverend Coles was most conspicuous by his absence. He did not believe in divorce, and so he would not honor this unholy alliance by witnessing it. Besides, he was needed in his own church on this joyful day of the Lord's resurrection.

Johnny Miller, though his days with the Trio were numbered, was honored to see his wife, Pauline, among the bridesmaids; Oscar Moore was disgruntled to find his new wife had been left out.

Ivan Mogull and his friend from high school, the song plugger Marvin Cane, thought it was a beautiful wedding, and they were looking forward to the party in midtown at the Belmont Plaza. The two friends acted as Maria Cole's advance men in arranging the reception. She wanted a big wedding, though Nat did not care. He wanted her to be happy. She wanted to tie the knot at the Waldorf, which was *the* place to be married in those days. But when the Waldorf sales manager found out the groom was Nat King Cole, a black person, they turned Marvin and Ivan away. Ivan got furious at the manager, and lost his temper when he saw an Arab walk through the hotel lobby leading a goat on a leash. It was fine, screamed Ivan Mogull, for Arabs and goats to stay at the Waldorf, and do what Arabs and goats do. But you won't let the greatest entertainer in America get married here!

That is when they decided to get married in the Baptist Church in Harlem. Maria really would have preferred an Episcopalian service. Because Nat was divorced this would require special dispensation from the bishop, and they did not want to wait for it. The pianist Hazel Scott was a friend of Maria's, and her husband was the Reverend Adam Clayton Powell, who looked like a movie star. Maria was pleased to have this family friend officiate at the ceremony.

Marvin Cane went looking for a suitable ballroom to hold the reception. On Lexington Avenue in the East Forties was a fashionable new hotel, the Belmont Plaza. Cane liked the looks of their Moderne Room, and approached the sales manager on behalf of Nat King Cole and his betrothed. The manager did not say no outright, understanding the amount of money involved; he said it would be "hard to arrange." He mentioned a color line.

Marvin Cane made a forceful speech to the effect that Harlem would not overrun Manhattan. He went so far as to say that there wouldn't be all that many black people there. Whatever else Cane might have said or offered, he finally had his way with the reluctant manager. Cane persuaded him to step aside and let him, Marvin, take over the wedding reception in the Belmont Plaza Ballroom. Of course, by the time the limousines arrived Sunday in the late afternoon with the King and his Queen, the entire cast of *Stormy Weather*, and five blocks of the Harlem Easter parade, it was too late for the hotel management to do more than stare pop-eyed and fume. They thought the integrated affair would put them out of business.

Her last hours as Marie Ellington were spent in such a fury at Nathaniel Cole it is a wonder they got married that Sunday.

The twenty-nine-year-old bridegroom was probably under considerable stress from every quarter. His buddies, as buddies have done since the dawn of history, sought to distract Nathaniel from his cares in whatever way they might. They chose booze and exotic dancers. It worked.

On Friday evening at seven o'clock, Marie

Ellington and Elaine Fein, a bridesmaid, were waiting for Nat and his friend Hal Fein, an usher, to pick them up at the Taft Hotel for dinner. The guys never showed up. They were at a stag party upstairs at Al and Dick's Steakhouse on 54th Street and Seventh Avenue with all of Nat's musicians, Carlos Gastel, Bill Bojangles Robinson, "Rochester" Anderson, p.r. man Milton Karle, and a host of song pluggers including Mogull, Cane, and Marvin Fischer.

When the men had put aside their desire for eating and drinking, and were well oiled, they got in taxicabs and motored up to a private party in Harlem. There a live sex show was staged for their enjoyment, with kinks and embellishments that made it more comical than erotic.

Nat arrived back at the Taft at five in the morning in a state of intoxication that left him hung over the whole day. When Maria found out where he had been, she was so angry she would not speak to him or play her part in the wedding rehearsal that evening. Only at dinner later, at Hazel Scott Powell's home, were the lovers able to kiss and make up, just before the day of their wedding.

Nat Cole marched to the altar that cold, clear Sunday afternoon in a welter of emotions that would have reduced a lesser man to delirium tremens. Yet he looked as relaxed as ever. The ceremony was brief but it was a long time to go without smoking or singing. As the married couple left the church, three policemen on horseback restrained the crowd. Later the groom admitted that the flashbulbs going off in his face gave him the shakes. Surely it was the flashbulbs — but something more than lights flashing must have driven the usually temperate bridegroom to drink whiskey after whiskey at his reception, after he helped his happy bride cut the cake. His family surrounded him, and his friends, famous and unknown: those mentioned, plus Sarah Vaughan, Dizzy Gillespie, Andy Kirk, Canada Lee, Nellie Lutcher, Maxine Sullivan, and countless others; jazz writer Leonard Feather and a score of reporters from the *Times*, the *Herald Tribune*, *Life* magazine, seven from the *Afro-American* alone.

In this moment of intense personal emotion the shy man was on display for all of America to see. He lit a cigarette. If he drank to keep his hands from trembling it might have been in the premonition that his life was no longer his own, and that he might never again enjoy the leisure of a purely private moment. That night in the honeymoon suite, the bride dressed in a gossamer nightgown of silk and lace that had been sewn by hand for her trousseau. When they awakened the day after, she asked him how he had liked it, and was sad to hear he had no memory of it at all.

The newlyweds flew out of La Guardia on a Pan American flight with six suitcases, two of Maria's fur coats (she did not know the weather in Mexico), and a staff photographer from *Ebony* magazine named Griffith Davis. Davis was there to capture images of King Cole's honeymoon in Mexico City and the seaside resort of Acapulco.

Photos show them listening to a guide before the twin bell towers of the old Cathedral in the Zócalo, and frolicking on the beach like natives of some lost island — Maria smiling, riding piggy-back on Nathaniel — then the two of them hand in hand, running out of the surf.

For more than a minute the lovers felt the earth move, as a mild earthquake shook the capital. From the little airplane to the seaside they looked down on the brushfires burning. Other photos show them kissing, on the terrace of their Acapulco hotel suite, with a view of the staggered hills sweeping down to the sea; out shopping for leather goods and perfume; motorboating on the bay. High on a cliff overlooking the Pacific, Nat paid a daredevil ten pesos to dive eighty feet into a blue cove below. They went to the bullfights, of course, and saw four bulls killed. Maria did not like it, and got upset when a mad bull gored a horse, while Nat filmed the whole spectacle with his movie camera.

Despite the sometimes "posed" look of the magazine photographs, the newlyweds look genuinely relaxed and happy. Cole is enjoying a much-needed, long-overdue vacation. This is the first real break in his performing and practice schedule since he was fourteen years old. And it would be a long time before he would rest again.

On the way home, they touched down in Sedalia, North Carolina. Dr. Charlotte Hawkins Brown had invited them to a wedding reception in their honor at Canary Cottage, the home where Maria had grown up. Aunt Lottie invited the flower of North Carolina society to welcome her niece and her famous husband. Then the author of *The Correct Thing* left town without herself attending.

NATURE BOY

The day the newlyweds flew to Mexico City, March 29, 1948, the record "Nature Boy" was officially released. But some disc jockeys with advance copies had jumped the gun, so the song was already a sensation.

Everything about "Nature Boy," from its long-haired proto-hippie author to its mystical impact upon the public, was a publicist's dream come true. The details have a fairy-tale charm, so much the stuff of legend that soon the legends overwhelmed the facts. Half a century later almost nothing but the legend remains in the tangle of conflicting accounts.

According to an interview Cole gave in August 1948, he was performing at the Lincoln Theater in L.A. during the week of May 20, 1947, when he first received the disheveled pages of "Nature Boy." Cole was always on the lookout for material. He had a greater rapport with songwriters and song pluggers than any other singer. For a long time he had practiced an "open door" policy with regard to new material, reading everything. Maria Cole recalls how songwriters pestered him. No sooner would the Coles arrive in a city than the phone would start ringing — the songwriters had his number.

Everyone knew that Cole could make a hit of a song if anyone could. One time a reporter sent his card to Mort Ruby's table in a nightclub. Ruby, Nat's road manager, figured the newsman wanted an interview; but no, he wanted Nat to look at a song he had composed. Another time, Maria Cole recalls, "in Oklahoma, a deputy sheriff pulled the King Cole Trio's speeding bus over . . . and instead of handing out a traffic ticket, produced a song for Nat." He was defenseless in the lavatories of theaters and nightspots. Ivan Mogull remembers standing next to the star in adjacent urinals when one songwriter interrupted him, shoving a manuscript under his nose.

"Hey, man!" the singer groaned, in mid-micturation, waving his hands in the air. "I ain't got my piano!"

The lyricist of "Nature Boy," Eden Ahbez of Brooklyn, Tujunga Canyon, L.A., and parts unknown, was not so grossly aggressive. But he was very persistent. Ahbez, with his shoulder-length, strawberry-blond hair, his mustache and beard, and his nearly transparent eyelashes, looked for all the world like a hand puppet of Jesus of Nazareth. He had no shoulders and no neck, so his legs seemed to dangle irrelevantly from his large head and torso. Not much taller than five feet two, he dressed like an early beatnik: gray sweatshirt, loose-fitting culottes that came to mid-calf, and leather sandals. In his mid-thirties, Eden Ahbez, with his invented name, his ersatz Yoga philosophy, and his contempt for the details of modern life, had already created a mythic persona that forever obscured the real man that lay behind it.

Ahbez spent his early years in an orphanage. Like the hero of Somerset Maugham's 1944 best-seller, *The Razor's Edge*, Ahbez was on a spiritual quest. This led him to cross the continent on foot eight times before he was thirty-five. Then he wrote poetry and songs, stood on street corners lecturing on Oriental mysticism, and became known in the Hollywood Hills as "the Yogi" and "the Hermit." He slept in a sleeping bag under the stars with his wife, the former Anna Jacobsen. Maria Cole said she was exquisite and truly looked like Mary, the mother of Jesus. The two were married in an orchard by a black minister.

Ahbez's song, with its Hebraic minor chords and ancient wisdom, came to Cole's attention at the right time. In April 1947 the United Nations created a Committee on Palestine to settle the question of Jewish statehood in the Holy Land. The British had tried and failed to broker a plan to divide Palestine into Arab and Jewish zones. From spring until autumn the General Assembly debated the matter, with America siding with the Jews. In the wake of the Holocaust, and with an eye to Nat's popular audience, Mort Ruby had been urging Nat to record a Jewish song.

On a May morning in 1947, Eden Ahbez went to the stage door of the Lincoln Theater bearing the soiled, unsigned scroll of "Nature Boy." He may have had a note of introduction from Johnny Mercer. Ahbez asked to see Nat King Cole's manager. Mort Ruby sent word for the man to wait. When Ruby heard the visitor had a song for Cole, he told the doorman, "Tell the guy to get lost."

Ahbez stood his ground. When Ruby went out later that morning to get some fresh air, Ahbez stepped in front of him. The prophet wore a

269

sweatshirt, dungarees, and Nazarene sandals. The bald-headed manager recoiled.

The prophet said, "I have a song I want you to present to Nat for me."

Ruby did not stay to argue with him, but took his name and the sheet music and said he would do what he could.

After breakfast Ruby went to Nat's dressing room and tossed the pages of "Nature Boy" onto a makeup table. He had no idea the song was plugged into a socket of biblical history and was ready to light up the sky.

Cole had uncanny facility for reading sheet music. He took one look at "Nature Boy" and grasped its fundamental Jewishness in tone. Several days later, after the second show of the evening at the Lincoln, Cole told Ruby that "Nature Boy" might be just the Jewish song the road manager had hoped for. As Cole sang Ruby the lyrics, in waltz time, the manager expressed his skepticism.

The bearded Ahbez returned a few days later to see what had become of his song. Maria Cole recalls that he talked to Nat's valet, Otis Pollard, promising him a portion of the royalties if he could persuade Nat to record "Nature Boy." She goes on to add: "Ahbez gave fifty percent of the song to almost anybody with whom he came in contact." *Variety* reports: "Considerable rumors the tune is cut up six ways from the middle and Ahbez will wind up with a pittance. Actually he retains 75 percent of the tune: he gave 12.5 percent to Otis Pollard . . . and a like amount to Hy Cantor, Feist [sic] Coast Rep, for also helping him."

On June 3 the Trio opened at the Bocage night-club, a little room above a restaurant on Sunset Strip. That night, knowing the Jewish Irving Berlin was present, Cole decided to sing "Nature Boy," finishing his second set of the evening with the gentle, strange melody. Before Nat could reach his dressing room to light a cigarette, the singer was stopped in a backstage passageway by the composer of "Alexander's Ragtime Band" and "White Christmas." The sixty-year-old Irving Berlin was breathing heavily. He knew quality when he heard it; he wanted to buy all rights to "Nature Boy."

Nat King Cole could not do much for Irving Berlin, even if he had wanted to, because Cole did not know where the song had come from. But he wanted to find out immediately. He ordered Mort Ruby and Carlos Gastel to locate the author of "Nature Boy" without delay, so they could secure the rights to record and publish it.

Ruby had only the name Eden Ahbez to go on. Phone calls to the musicians' union and various song publishers turned up nothing. Nat continued to perform the song that summer at the Bocage and elsewhere. And he identified with the character of the song's title, the "strange enchanted boy" who comes from afar bearing the message that the greatest thing you'll ever learn is to love and be loved . . . Playing in a Jazz All-Stars Concert on June 23 with trumpeter Charlie Shavers, alto man Willie Smith, and the Trio, Nat assumed an alias to dodge his exclusive Capitol contract. He billed himself as Nature Boy.

With the planned recording ban hanging

heavily over the industry, there was enormous pressure to purchase songs and cut them before the New Year. Although he still had not found the author of "Nature Boy" or secured the song's rights, Cole had a conception of how the tune should sound — with strings. In August, Capitol producer Jim Conkling "finally let me try a session using Frank DeVol, and that was how we made 'Nature Boy,' " Cole told an interviewer.

DeVol, later a composer of film scores and an Oscar nominee, was then a "junior" orchestrator for Capitol. He was admired for his string arrangements as well as his artful use of flutes in jazz and pop music. In "Nature Boy" the flute would create the exotic mood of Asian mysticism. DeVol, interviewed forty years after the session, recalled going with Conkling to meet Cole at the Bocage. The producer and the arranger arrived between sets to discuss the key for "Nature Boy." When they played the tune in its original waltz time, it sounded like a Yiddish folk song. Nat said, "Why don't we do this out of tempo?" This was a stroke of genius. Cole sang the song rubato, free of rhythm, focusing attention upon the mystical lyric while allowing the singer perfect intimacy. Parlando, musicians call it, the style of Piaf that combines the powers of song and speech.

Though they still had not found the man behind "Nature Boy," Cole and DeVol recorded the song on August 22, 1947, with six violins, two violas, a cello, a harp, and two woodwinds. Edwin (Buddy) Cole played a piano solo that Nat composed. During the same session they waxed two titles for the *Cole for Kids* album, as well as "Wildroot Charlie," which was never officially issued.

DeVol thought "Nature Boy" sounded so weird he rather hoped the record would never be released; if people linked it to him, he might never work again. Others loved it, including a *Down Beat* reviewer who, in September, raved about Cole's concert performance of the song. Meanwhile Gastel and Ruby stepped up the search for Ahbez, and at last hit pay dirt. Ruby heard a rumor that the prophet and his pregnant wife were sleeping under the first L in the gigantic "HOLLYWOOD" sign that welcomes motorists to the Hollywood Hills. Maria Cole wrote that Mort Ruby "found his man under the first L," which is both picturesque and poetic, if you consider that the L stands for Love, the songwriter's theme.

Gastel and Ahbez got down to business. For the Yogi, business was simply to get Cole to sing his song (which he did not seem to know Nat was doing already). For Gastel it was to purchase all rights worldwide, until the end of time, as cheaply as possible. As yet nobody knew what the song was worth. But certainly Gastel had a better idea than the Yogi, who saw little value in anything in the world of the senses.

Variety reported: "King Cole and Carlos Gastel took the song from ahbez (who insists his name be spelled lowercase) before the disk deadline (ban) and did a perfect job of holding it exclusively for themselves." Soon every recording company in America wanted the sheet music. "Gastel and Cole are publishing it themselves under their own Crestview Music Co. label."

Eden Ahbez wanted his name printed on the record label in lowercase letters, believing that no mere mortal deserved capitals. But Capitol refused to make an exception for him, and printed his name like everybody else's.

"Nature Boy" was pressed on the flip side of a tune called "Lost April," a romantic ballad. The little song by Ahbez seemed an appropriate B side, unprepossessing, no threat to upstage "Lost April." Nat loved the ballad, from the movie *The Bishop's Wife* starring Loretta Young and Cary Grant, and was confident it would be a hit in the class of "Sentimental Reasons."

Now the miscalculation seems comical. The rumor mill started promoting the legend of "Nature Boy" weeks before Capitol released the record. It had a mystique that "Lost April" could not match. By the time the disc arrived at WNEW Radio in New York March 22, their music librarian, Al Trilling, couldn't wait to hear it. Trilling slapped "Nature Boy" onto the turntable and sat back. He went into a trance, a spiritual transport. Trilling had been in the business twenty-five years, and to his ears these eight lines of lyrics and sixteen bars of melody made "one of the most beautiful songs ever written . . . The words and music answer the longing in everyone's heart."

When he came to, Trilling carried the record into the control booth and handed it to disc jockey Jerry Marshall, whispering urgently to him to play it right away. And Marshall could tell from Trilling's tone of voice that something quite remarkable was in the grooves.

"Here's a winner," the jock declared, "a song

everybody is going to love." And he set the needle down on the spinning disc's B side.

That was at 2:16 p.m. The song was two minutes and thirty-eight seconds long, and by 2:20 the station's switchboard was entirely lit up with phone calls, people raving about "Nature Boy" and Nat King Cole, begging to hear the song again, wanting to know where it had come from. Trilling told Maria Cole that for the next few weeks the radio station played "Nature Boy" at least ten times a day, and each time it aired they would get twenty-five or thirty more telephone calls.

Nat and Maria returned from their honeymoon on April 9, after the disc jockeys had been flogging "Nature Boy" for three weeks, to find it was going to become the most popular song in America. Other artists had rushed to record it, a cappella, during the music ban: Frank Sinatra, Sarah Vaughan, and Dick Haymes. RCA Victor wanted Perry Como to record it too, but Como took a look at Cole's market lead and bowed out.

Three times since 1941, Nathaniel Cole had experienced this phenomenon, synchronicity, dancing a pas de deux with the spirit of his time. In each case he sang the song that exactly expressed the emotion of a popular majority of Americans, making him familiar to them, intimate. The first, "Gone with the Draft," bonded the singer with men, as they laughed together about what they most feared. The second, "Straighten Up and Fly Right," with its wide range of poetic meanings, touched everyone — men, women, and children

— by capturing the mood of a nation mobilized for war, with a moral lyric that so avoided direct treatment of the conflict that you could sing along while thinking of something else. The third, and most significant, "Nature Boy," delivers the good news of Rabbi Hillel and Jesus of Nazareth, the gospel of love. It is a love song, all but stripped of the flesh, transcending the erotic, the kind of song a black man could sing to white women, children, and men without menacing the status quo, without threatening "that Harlem would overrun Manhattan." It was, in short, the ultimate love song, the song that would seal Cole's place in the hearts of Americans.

The song's message is universal. It is hard to say just how much the Jews' struggle over their homeland enriched the passion for "Nature Boy." As the British began to withdraw from their peacekeeping role in Palestine in March 1948, the Jews and Arabs began making headlines battling along the Jerusalem-Tel Aviv road. On May 14, 1948, Zionists proclaimed the independence of the new State of Israel. President Truman recognized the Jewish homeland, whereupon Egypt bombed Tel Aviv. Given America's sympathy with the embattled Jews at this crucial moment in history, it is no mere coincidence that "Nature Boy," with its Hebraic-sounding minor chords, became the #1 song in the country (most played on jukeboxes) the same month Israel declared its independence. An Arab tune would not have fared so well.

"Nature Boy" was a triumph of the human heart. A writer in the African-American journal *The New York Age* wrote: "On 42nd Street, between Seventh and Eighth Avenues, record shops play this number constantly . . . Great crowds gather, some hearing it the umpteenth time, others just getting to know about it. Many of them head straight inside to buy it. We think it is an important artistic success and we couldn't help beaming with pride — inside — to hear some of the comments: 'That feller, King Cole, he's colored, isn't he?' "

Eden Ahbez, dressed in white, clambered out the back window of a house on 80th Street in Brooklyn and scampered away down the alley. He was in flight from the photographers who had camped out the night before June 1, hoping to get a picture of him and a statement. He had followed Nat Cole to New York to help him publicize "Nature Boy." But Ahbez did not like publicity, reporters, or cameramen. He claimed not to care for money either (he stood to earn $30,000 in royalties in 1948), though he bought a car with his first check. He needed little money. His diet consisted only of fruits and nuts, which cost three dollars a week. Ahbez said he would put the money away somewhere where he could not touch it.

He had to appear that evening with Nat King Cole on Fred Allen's radio show *We the People*. Ahbez did not want to talk to reporters about money or his diet or where he slept. And he particularly wished to avoid being quizzed about who wrote "Nature Boy." He did not want to hear the name Herman Yablakoff, the singer-comedian many called "the Payatz" (the Clown) of Yiddish theater, or the name of his publishers, J&J

Kammen Music, or of their lawyer, the plagiarism expert A. Edward Masters.

The Clown had written a tune called "Schweig Mein Hertz" in 1935, and Kammen Music published it. "Nature Boy" matched the Clown's melody note for note, and now his attorney was calling the Yogi to account for the amazing coincidence. Masters said that 100 percent of the song's royalties would account for the amazing coincidence just fine if Ahbez and his publisher would immediately pay the money to the real composer, Herman "the Clown" Yablakoff.

So it would come to pass that the Yogi would not be troubled with the royalty money from "Nature Boy" so much as he had feared. He would pay a tidy sum to lawyers to protect his interest in the song (the words were his). But when all was said and done he would not be left with so much money it would distract him from his spiritual pursuits. He kept reminding the bothersome reporters that "Nature Boy" was only one part of a suite of songs, and surely the others would be hits too. Nat King Cole had told him he was considering them all.

There are several publicity photos of Cole with Ahbez, taken in different places. In each case the two are scanning sheet music or a *Billboard* magazine. Nat's tuxedo contrasts with Eden's bohemian attire. What is unique about these photos is that Cole, who nearly always appears at ease whether he is posing with his wife, Frank Sinatra, or the Queen of England, looks pained to be breathing the same air with the unkempt Ahbez, as if the singer would be gone the instant the camera shutter clicked.

After Cole died, his thoughtful widow gave the publishing rights to "Nature Boy" (worth a small fortune) back to the Yogi. She recalls that her old friend Ivan Mogull, who had become a major music publisher, was furious with her.

While the new trio, with Irving Ashby, was on the road that spring of 1948 — Chicago, Omaha, Minneapolis, Springfield, and Detroit before a long June stint in New York — Nat's lawyers were negotiating a settlement with Oscar Moore. The guitarist always said there were no hard feelings between Nat and him, but his lawsuit belies it. After leaving the Trio, Moore sued Nat for 27 percent ($8,250) of the royalties he had earned from Capitol Records since Moore had left the combo. Plus, he demanded a cut of all future royalties from records on which he played. Contracts clearly showed Moore had no rights to record royalties, but accounts indicated that Cole had been generous in paying bonuses to the tune of $25,000 a year. The court might rule the bonuses were de facto evidence of a "royalty" payment pattern. So Nat settled out of court for a flat fee of $6,000. When Johnny Miller quit in August, Cole and Gastel would handle a similar lawsuit with similar results.

Perhaps it was the cost of the Moore lawsuit — more likely it was the hectic pace of the touring schedule in spring and summer — that caused Nathaniel to miss his alimony payments to Nadine the weeks of June 10, August 26, and September 2. The $200 per week was not much, but somehow having to pay it rankled him, stirring up guilt without assuaging it.

"It's like feeding oats to a dead horse," he told Maria, scratching his chin with the back of his fingers and frowning. Besides, his ex-wife had never returned his collection of Duke Ellington records, and some were irreplaceable.

Under Maria's influence, Nat began doing some charity benefit performances. On June 9, the Trio performed in New York on a bill with Thelonious Monk, Charlie Parker, Dean Martin and Jerry Lewis, Timmie Rogers, Miles Davis, and Jimmie Lunceford's band at the "Show for Sydenham Hospital," the only interracial hospital in the country. A week later Nat and Maria revisited the scene of their wedding, the Abyssinian Baptist Church in Harlem, to play a fund-raiser to send children to summer camp in Vermont. Though Cole was not yet thirty, he was beginning a lifelong pattern of leadership by example.

A HOME OF THEIR OWN

Nat and Maria returned to Los Angeles in mid-July for his important three-week engagement at Ciro's nightclub on Sunset Strip. Under the management of showman Herman Hover, Ciro's was already a legend, the swankest, most star-studded place in town. A big club, it seated 500 around a small dance floor in the two-tiered main room, and another 150 in a banquet room in the back. The banquettes were covered in green leather. There, if you could get in, you would see Judy Garland, Spencer Tracy, and Clark Gable at one table, and Marilyn Monroe and Walter Winchell huddled at another. Gene Kelly, Jack Benny, George Burns, Cary Grant, Rudy Vallee, all the biggest stars went there to drink and dance, to see and be seen. But in the 1940s no one there was black except Lena Horne. Nat Cole was about to change all that, and Ciro's became the site of many memorable events in his and Maria's life.

George Schlatter, who produced the shows, remembers "the most soulful ending of a Ciro's evening . . . was after all the customers were gone, we would get out a couple of bottles of champagne and put on the work lights. And Nat would sit down at the piano and, in the darkened room, play the soft jazz he could never play during the regular show, because people were talking."

The Trio packed the house with celebrities, including the Prince and Princess of Egypt, Louis Jourdan and his wife, and Ronald Reagan and Betty Blythe.

After a few weeks in L.A., the Coles were back on the road. When they did one-nighters, Nat and Maria traveled by Pullman.

"Sometimes we did thirty such shows in a stretch," recalls Maria. "On occasion I would get ill with all the riding, but I wouldn't tell Nat. I was so much in love with him and so determined to stay with him."

She was determined to stay with him because he was good company and because it was sound conjugal policy for a musician's wife. "I really was not quite sure about a lot of things that happened right after I married him — it disturbed me. Young as I was, I was naive to a certain extent. Some girl was running after Nat, and I said, 'Well, how did Nadine deal with this — how did she find out?'

" 'Oh,' he confessed, 'I had a habit of . . . some of them would write me notes. And I would leave the notes in my pocket. And she would be taking my clothes to the cleaners and find them.'

" 'And what did she do?'

" 'She would go out and sit in the park.' "

The only time Maria ever saw Nadine was by chance in a Los Angeles grocery, as Nadine was in the checkout line leaving and Maria was coming in. They recognized each other but did not speak and it was very awkward. Maria said she felt guilty.

At all events, Maria decided early on that she would not make the same mistakes Nadine had made. Old habits die hard. Nat was used to liberty. Maria would keep her glamorous husband in clear view whenever possible even if it meant living out of a suitcase and sleeping in train cars until the motion made her sick.

Nathaniel never complained about anything, not the food, not the drafty hotels, not the bouncing of the train cars. Nothing bothered him but the cloud of wet stockings his young wife strung up on the shower doors in the endless succession of hotels. And he didn't mind that very much.

He wanted them to have a child as soon as possible. She did not, knowing that a baby would keep her from being with him all the time.

That summer Maria turned twenty-six. Frank Sinatra's wife, Nancy, threw her a birthday party at their new home in Holmby Hills.

Maria and Nat wanted a home of their own. During their brief stays in Los Angeles, since they had been married, the couple had been living in an apartment in the Watkins Hotel.

Maria suggested they buy a house in Connecticut or elsewhere in New England. Nat had already been married and lived in Los Angeles, so Maria liked the idea of starting fresh someplace where she would not be haunted by Nadine and her friends. But the California weather and Cole's business dealings there won out over Maria's nostalgia for the New England autumns. "Are you kidding?" he asked. "I love Los Angeles."

So in mid-July they began looking at houses in Beverly Hills. Autograph seekers delayed them in the best neighborhoods. The most exclusive area in Los Angeles in those days, the place with the most beautiful homes, was Hancock Park. The governor lived there, and so did prominent doctors, lawyers, and oilmen. The Coles had looked at only a dozen dwellings before they drove down South Muirfield Road and saw the house of their dreams. It was a grand, twelve-room Tudor-style brick mansion, with twelve-foot ceilings, servants' quarters on the third story, and two chimneys.

Maria recalls that her husband walked through the great, wide oak door with its pointed arch, saw the sweeping staircase, and declared, "This is it!" before they had seen the bedrooms or the kitchen. The couple decided then and there to buy the house, and they informed their agent, of Smith and Canaday, a West Side realtor.

The Coles had no idea how much anguish their decision would cause the residents of this old, wealthy enclave. They never imagined their domestic plans would bring about a national controversy. Of course, the African-American real estate agent, Joe Bradfield, must have explained to them that a "restrictive covenant" had been in place since 1920, barring the sale of Hancock Park properties to Jews, Negroes, and other "undesirables." What the celebrity and his wife could not fathom is that such a snobbish rule would apply to them.

The cautious realtor Bradfield engaged a very light-skinned African-American named Camille Laflotte to act as the Coles' purchasing agent. At July's end, Laflotte walked into a white realtor's office in Beverly Hills and counted out $6,000 in thousand-dollar bills on the desk of Ann Winters, the seller's agent. The owner of the house, a Colonel Harry Gantz, had prepared a purchase agreement to sell for $85,000. Laflotte handed over the down payment, and the agreement was signed.

"Don't you check out the people you sell to?" the angry neighbors later asked Ann Winters.

"I sure do. Soon as they walk in the door I ask them, 'Have you got the down payment?' "

But it was no laughing matter. News of the deal spread, and people gathered in small groups on the lawn, pointing and muttering. Harry Gantz and Ann Winters soon were receiving anonymous phone threats. One warned Winters she was finished in the real estate business, and another predicted she would meet with a serious automobile accident. The Coles offered her legal assistance and bodyguards, but she accepted the protection of the Beverly Hills police when they offered the seller and his agent round-the-clock surveillance.

In a stately mansion somewhere in Hancock Park, the citizens gathered to express their anger and disgust, and to protest the outrageous violation of their rights, the flouting of their precious covenant. They formed the Hancock Park Property Owners Association, electing Andrew J. Copp, Jr., an attorney, as chairman. Copp appointed committees to "seek a solution to the problem." Reports at the time noted that "he was not at liberty to divulge their exact activities." Yet we trust these did not include threatening the lives of the seller and his agent, or firing bullets through the Coles' windows after the couple moved in. Somebody else must have done these things.

Copp pursued a course of diplomacy before he took legal action. On the night of July 30, the last

285

date of the Trio's gig at Ciro's, Copp went looking for Cole at the nightclub. It was not a convenient time. Nat's bassist Johnny Miller had just given two weeks' notice, saying he was "tired of the road." This is what musicians always say when their marriages are going to hell and the money they are making is not worth it. Nat had put in a call to bassist Joe Comfort. Like Miller and Wesley Prince, Comfort was a graduate of Hampton's orchestra.

So Nat was in no mood to talk to Copp, and the best the lawyer could do was convey an offer to the singer through Mort Ruby. "Tell Mr. Cole if he will rescind the sale of his house, we will give him his money back with a little profit," the lawyer ventured. Ruby raised his eyebrows.

A little later the bald-headed manager returned from backstage with this response from his boss: "If you give me a million dollars," said Nat King Cole, "I'll leave the country."

Copp may not have appreciated Cole's wit. "How would *you* like it," the lawyer hissed at Ruby, "if you had to come out of your home and see a Negro walking down the street wearing a big wide hat, a zoot suit, a long chain, and yellow shoes?"

And that was the end of the Property Owners Association's course of diplomacy. Nat held a small press conference at the Watkins Hotel a few days later to explain, as simply as he could, what should not need to be explained.

"This is not an act of defiance," said Cole. "My bride and I like this house. I can afford it. And we would like to make it our home. I have always been a good citizen. I would like to meet all my new neighbors face to face and explain these things to them."

According to Maria, Cole soon had a chance to talk with some of the neighbors at a gathering of the Hancock Park property owners. "There it was patiently explained to my husband that the good people of Hancock Park simply did not want any undesirables moving in."

"Neither do I," said Cole. "And if I see anybody undesirable coming in here, I'll be the first to complain."

On August 13, 1948, Camille Laflotte transferred her interest in the house to the Coles, and the closing was completed. Now the mansion in Hancock Park belonged to them, and the neighbors had no recourse left but legal devilry.

That same day the *Los Angeles Herald* reported that Cole faced the prospect of testing the Supreme Court's ruling against restrictive covenants, and that white residents had taken legal steps to prevent the Coles "from moving into their newly purchased home on fashionable Muirfield Road, which carries a restrictive covenant that forbids occupancy by other than Caucasians." The news article points out that the Court had already ruled against the covenants, yet "close to 100 individual lawsuits may be filed against Cole by residents of the Hancock Park area who object to having a colored family live in their vicinity."

"It is regrettable," Cole told the newsman. "I am an American citizen and I feel that I am entitled to the same rights as any other citizen. My wife and I like our home very much and we intend

287

to stay there the same as any other American citizens would." Maria wrote a letter to Eleanor Roosevelt, a friend of Aunt Lottie's. Roosevelt wired back her sympathies and support, saying she would do all she could.

Copp, president of the Property Owners Association, addressed an affidavit to the Coles. It stated in legalese that covenants restricted ownership of Hancock homes to Christian Caucasians. The house in question could not belong to a black man.

Nat and Maria knew that if they stood their ground, the law would stand behind them. Their attorney, Irving Hill, reassured them. Earlier that year the battle over housing had reached a climax in the case of *Shelley* v. *Kramer* when the Supreme Court ruled on May 3 that the government may not enforce private acts of discrimination such as restrictive covenants in deeds. In the 1940s a great outcry had arisen against these covenants in Hollywood, where blacks were getting more and better work. World War II heightened America's sensitivity to racism, as Jewish and African-American soldiers fought and died to uphold freedoms abroad that they did not have at home. Headliners like Benny Carter and June Richmond were not going to settle for the kind of housing that had been set aside for middle-class Negroes. They could afford the finer houses in white neighborhoods, and wanted them; both Richmond and Carter were willing to go to court to defend their right to live in the homes they purchased. So were a number of Jews. *Shelley* v. *Kramer* was the last legal nail in the coffin of restrictive covenants.

Yet the neighbors of Hancock Park would not give up without a struggle. And they found support in the business community, as the Cole case became a rallying point for segregation for white property owners and realtors. They hoped for a groundswell of sentiment to protect the restrictive covenants. Philip Rea, president of the Los Angeles Realty Board, called for a campaign to amend the Constitution, claiming it was necessary to "protect American life, stabilize home values . . ." He went on to say that blacks moving into white neighborhoods would "create racial tensions and antagonisms and do much harm to our national structure." Rea added that the amendment should be made retroactive, meaning the Coles would have to leave their home sooner or later.

Attack, and counterattack: On behalf of Cole, the Los Angeles Council of Industrial Organization issued a statement that "thousands of members of the CIO and other progressive-minded people in the community will stand behind your fight." The American Civil Liberties Union offered a $500 reward for information leading to the conviction of anyone guilty of a crime against a person of minority race taking possession of a home in Southern California. A year later the Anti-Defamation League of B'nai B'rith named the Hancock Park Property Owners Association and the Los Angeles Realty Board as organizations waging "a campaign of terrorism, vandalism, and discrimination . . . against Southern California families."

The campaign to amend the Constitution in favor of racism blustered, and sputtered, and petered out. Nat and Maria moved into the brick mansion soon after they bought it. On their front lawn a vandal drove in a sign that read "Nigger Heaven."

THE PRICE OF FAME

Asked how they managed to endure that difficult summer of 1948, Cole's widow sighs. "We were so young. Youth takes care of so many things." He was thirty, she was twenty-seven, and both were living their lives at an exhilarating pace. Momentum alone would carry them through a great deal of adversity.

While Maria set up housekeeping in Hancock Park in late August and September, Nat continued a brisk schedule of L.A. performances and tours in the West. On August 17, the Trio's new bassist, Joe Comfort, debuted with the group at the Coona Club in El Cerrito. In early October the Trio performed "The Trouble with Me Is You" for the Columbia Pictures film *Make Believe Ballroom*. And on the 14th they played a benefit for a bombed Hadassah hospital in Israel; on the same bill were Lucille Ball, Desi Arnaz, Danny Kaye, Chico Marx, John Garfield, and Carmen Miranda.

Then in mid-October the Coles of Hancock Park obliged their neighbors by going away for so long that they may have hoped the newcomers would never return. They would be gone ten months, with live-in caretaker Chauncey Shaw and his wife attending to the house. Unaware the Coles were gone, someone fired a shot through one of the windows on November 18, which Shaw dutifully reported to the police.

Beginning at the RKO Theater in Dayton on October 21, the Trio played eleven Midwestern theaters before arriving in New York for some Christmas shows. In the Big Apple on December 21, the Trio recorded four songs, including their next big hit, "Portrait of Jenny," but these takes were not quite good enough to be released. A few weeks later they would record "Jenny" with better orchestration.

Nathaniel's neglect of his alimony payments had prompted Nadine to serve him with a contempt order in October. When the Associated Negro Press got wind of it, their chief, Claude Barnett, prepared a November release, which partially revealed the heartache of the Coles' divorce. The publicity was upsetting to Nat; it was not widely known that Nadine had sued *him* and that he had let his obligations slide. On November 8, Barnett sent him a copy of the press release, at the Hollenden Hotel in Cleveland, where the Coles were staying.

Nat was perturbed. On the phone two days later he told Barnett there was no current action against him in the courts. This was literally true, because he had recently paid up. But Barnett was not about to kill the whole story because of this detail.

Those who insist that Nat Cole was a man without enemies must at least admit he had an adversary in Claude A. Barnett. He was a forceful man of conviction, with a long upper lip, a long neck, and little charm. Born in Sanford, Florida, in 1889, Barnett received an engineering degree from Tuskegee Institute in 1906. After three years of working in the Chicago Post Office, in 1909 he became an ad salesman for the *Chicago Defender*. Barnett founded the Associated Negro Press (ANP) in 1919, the year of Cole's birth, to supply news to black newspapers. Like the Associated Press, it worked on a subscription basis. During World War II, Barnett also advised the Secretary of Agriculture about the problems of black farmers. He was married to the singer-actress Etta Moten, and managed her career in his spare time; she was the lead in the Broadway premier of Gershwin's *Porgy and Bess*.

Perhaps it was personal jealousy, maybe it was unconscious fury about the disparity between Cole's fortunes and most people's, but something about Nat King Cole clearly got under the older man's skin. If they did not hate each other, there was certainly no love lost between them.

Barnett felt it was his duty to tell the alimony story, and it was too late for Cole to suppress the news. Robert Ratcliffe, editor of the *Pittsburgh Courier*, had printed the ANP story on November 6. When Cole saw it he was fit to be tied. His new lawyer, Leo Branton, Jr., threatened to sue everybody if the *Courier* did not print a front-page retraction. Ratcliffe wrote a blistering letter to Barnett saying, "I must think ten times before using ANP releases." All Barnett could do was explain to the angry editor the story was based on Court Records Case #D 329.238.

Barnett wrote a letter to Cole on November 24 that is eloquent testimony to the price of fame. After summing up the story of their misunderstanding, Barnett explains his motives and scolds the celebrity:

>We merely reported a matter we felt would be of interest to people generally. We had no wish to hurt you. Like all the rest of your fans, we are interested in anything newsworthy that concerns you. You are what you are because you have become famous. The price of fame is that you live in a glass bowl where your public can see you. Our business is to report anything newsworthy about you. All publicity is good, especially when it is true.
>
>It seems odd that a man who would stage the most spectacular marriage of the decade and who would petition a magazine to cover it, as I observed in the exchange which passed (LIFE magazine), would shrink from a little report on an alimony matter!

Barnett closes with a polite request that Nat report to any newspaper he has contacted that the ANP story is essentially correct. *"If not,"* he says, "we will be forced to send them copies of the court record."

Cole backed down. The complete court record with the "cause" of Nadine's action — the "extreme cruelty," etc. — was worse than what Barnett had released. As this part of the story never was published in the papers, you may marvel at the old-time journalist's code of honor as well as the young celebrity's willingness to learn from his mistakes. His guilt and embarrassment over Nadine had led him to the brink of a public relations nightmare.

On December 1, Cole wrote from Cincinnati to Barnett in Chicago, proposing a meeting there after the 9th when they might "clear up the matter in question." Relieved, Barnett wrote to Robert Ratcliffe on December 2: "He knew he was bluffing you." Barnett was proud to win this round against the King. It would not be the last.

Around the time they went house hunting, Nat and Maria dispensed with the birth control. He had wanted a child at once; she wanted to wait a while before she had to divide their time together with minding babies. But now several months had passed and Maria was not yet pregnant — around the holidays the couple began to wonder why.

Maria had reason to believe the fault did not lie with her. And Nat was confident in his own powers. He had seen Nadine pregnant. In any case it takes a physician only a few minutes to determine if the male is shooting blanks, while the female question is trickier to resolve. Gently Maria told him, "Nat, you know, things do happen to men too sometimes." She convinced him to see his doctor, James Scott in Chicago.

"He finally went to the doctor, and, of course, there were problems. He had had gonorrhea as a young guy," she recalls. "It hadn't been taken care of properly and his sperm was like eighty-five percent inactive. But I remember Dr. Scott saying right in front of him: 'We can do something about it.'"

At the thought of what they might do about it Nat winced and groaned, "Oh my God," before the doctor told him it was only medicine, a shot of hormones he would take every few days until his sperm count rose to where it could get things done. In a few months it would.

A specialist advises that Nat's gonorrhea had nothing to do with his sperm count. The treatment of choice for male infertility in 1949 was HCG, Human Chorionic Gonadotropin, injected several times a week, which would have had the desired effect on his sperm count. Maria remembers that soon after beginning the shots Nat needed to shave, which he had never done before. One wonders what effect it might have had on his famous voice.

They spent new year's in boston, Maria's hometown. The Trio had been booked into the RKO Theater for a New Year's Eve performance and Maria had a job a few days later at the Hi-Hat.

Nat sat in the audience for a change, watching his wife sing "Don't Blame Me for Falling in Love with You." She had missed singing. But any notion she may have entertained about resuming her career full-time got little encouragement from her husband. One performer in a family seemed more than enough. That January, Cole would have to work one-week gigs in Hartford, Philadelphia, and Pittsburgh before a long residence at the Blue Note on the Loop in Chicago, January 24 until Valentine's Day. Maria was content to travel with the Trio, supporting King Cole as his "better half," his Queen, sometimes wearing a light tiara when accompanying him to important engagements.

At the end of January 1949, Maria flew back to Los Angeles for ten days to redecorate the house while Nat opened his three-week engagement at the Blue Note. "Says he's having a heck of a time sleeping and eating while his beauteous bride is out on the coast," wrote Roy Topper of the Chicago *Herald-American*. "Up at the crack of dawn — even though he's working half the night at the Blue Note."

He was constantly on the go in Chicago, hiring key personnel and giving his time generously to newspaper columnists, plus charity and alumni causes. One Friday afternoon he showed up at the Altgeld Gardens Nursery School with a check for the March of Dimes, which he presented to a four-year-old polio victim. He was deeply moved by the devastation the disease was causing.

The Chicago visit yielded some rich newspaper interviews, notably one with Jimmy Savage of the *Tribune*. The newsman asked Nat "how the artist on a hit record ('Nature Boy') feels about his baby after the tumult dies down."

"Nature?" Nat groaned. "Don't even mention the word. I can't even look at a meadow anymore; I close my eyes when I fly over countrysides, hide under the seat when the train passes a woods. A song plugger comes into my dressing room and says, 'Got a great hit for you, it'll wow 'em. It's a sequel, see — 'Nature Girl.' I damn near hit him over the head with the piano."

For six months, journalists and music critics had been hounding the now-famous artist for his opinions on jazz, on bebop, on music criticism. Finding him knowledgeable and articulate, they stopped him on the street, called him on the phone, surprised him backstage.

Several Chicago columnists wanted Cole's opinion on bebop, the direction jazz had taken under the influence of Gillespie, Parker, and Cole himself. Bebop was a hot topic of debate among musicians, critics, and the public, with many finding the new sound ugly, antisocial, or downright degenerate. In his interview with Nat, Savage mentioned that New York disc jockey Martin Block had announced that "the rise of bebop portends another depression."

Nat shook his head, bemused. "Well, one thing is sure — the rise of television portends the decapitation of certain . . . blockheads," said the pianist, scratching his chin, savoring the pun on Block's name. "Trouble is, the people who know nothing about music are the ones always talking about it. Take this Block — he's supposed to be a record expert. But somebody else writes his script and somebody else even picks out his discs. A helluva way to make a million bucks."

Cole informed columnist Irv Kupcinet of the *Sun-Times*: "If bop has any social significance at all . . . it's a reflection of past trends . . . it was born among adolescent musicians in 1939 and 1940." Of course, he was thinking about himself, Oscar Moore, Red Callender, and Illinois Jacquet when they were youngsters jamming in L.A. But it is significant that Cole always saw musical trends in terms of the larger movements in jazz history.

Barbara Hodgkins of *Metronome* interviewed him backstage at the Apollo. "Musicians are losing their imaginations," he told her. "They say the public isn't wise, but it's much wiser than they think. People are beginning to get sick of the same old stereotyped stuff. That's the reason the box office has slumped." He was wearing a brilliant white dress shirt with French cuffs, a necktie with a pattern of whorls, and striped suspenders; in his black horn-rimmed glasses he looked like a dapper investment banker before lunch. Nat leaned back on the rear legs of a straight-backed chair. He flicked at his perfectly tailored trousers, brought the chair down foursquare on the floor with a thud, and went off looking for a cigarette, continuing all the while to discourse.

"For a while it was swooners. Anybody who could stand up and sing a little was in. But there got to be too many of them and they didn't excite anybody anymore. Then it was trios, but now all trios sound the same. Back in the old days every band had its own sound — Benny Goodman, Count Basie, Jimmie Lunceford, Duke Ellington. Now all bands sound practically the same except Dizzy and Kenton."

Nat waved his cigarette, indicating a rest in his oration, smiled broadly at the interviewer, and paced meditatively around the small dressing room.

"Everybody who has a creative mind should sit down and try something new. That's why I give Stan [Kenton] credit; he's going his own way. You can't cling to the past. Too many different things are coming into the world. I took a chance on 'Nature Boy,' though I think 'Lost April' is a much better song . . . the public liked 'Nature Boy' because it was something different."

Cole admitted he too must reinvent his sound. "I'm trying something different," he said. "The Trio has been successful commercially, but I think trios have gone about as far as trios can go, because they're all made up of 'cold' instruments." He mentions making more use of violins and cellos.

On the subject of critics and criticism: "Music can't be put into words, it can't be described on a typewriter. Music is emotional and you may catch a musician in a very unemotional mood or you may not be in the same frame of mind as the musician. And so a critic will often say a musician he used to like is slipping.

"People don't slip, time catches up with them."

Cole was not about to be left behind. "I'm going to keep pace with everything that happens," he promised.

That winter in Chicago, Nat made a musical choice so strange that few understood it. He decided to add a bongo player to the Trio and make it a quartet. As the interview above shows, Cole admired Kenton and Gillespie as groundbreakers. When Dizzy returned from Brazil with a conga player to flavor his bebop sound, Kenton (fellow client of Gastel) followed suit, hiring conga and bongo player Jack Costanzo in 1948. Nat liked Costanzo's work with Kenton's orchestra. So when Kenton dissolved his band for a year at the end of 1948, Costanzo was free to accept Cole's offer to play with the Trio.

Nat's hiring of a bongo player was more daring than Gillespie's or Kenton's. The Trio made a much more subtle and intimate music than those bands. In a trio every sound would be heard, each note and beat would change the shape of every other. And the King Cole Trio had become mainstream while Gillespie and Kenton appealed to the avant-garde. Before the Latin music craze of the 1950s, the bongos were so little known that reporters had to describe them. Costanzo was a challenge for Cole's popular audience. It was like a bluegrass band adding a drummer.

Irving Ashby and Joe Comfort were uneasy with the idea. "Jack was the beginning of the end of my happiness with the King Cole Trio," said Ashby. "A conga drum with a bass and guitar and piano? It's too lopey," added Joe Comfort, referring to the clomp-clomp sound of a loping horse.

Costanzo had once been a dancer. Now Cole welcomed the bright-eyed, sharp-featured, wiry white percussionist for a number of qualities, not least his sense of humor and generosity of spirit. "We had to broaden our scope," Nat told a reporter. "The change gives us that progressive feeling. Jack relaxes the guys. A lot of the tension the bass and I use to feel is gone now because the bongo and conga drums give the rhythm we were supposed to give. That leaves us free to do much more."

The demands of life on the road prompted two other personnel changes: Ashby's brother-in-law Baldwin ("Sparky") Tavares replaced Otis Pollard and Johnny Hopkins as Nat's personal valet; and Carl Carruthers of Chattanooga was hired to assist Mort Ruby with the tasks of road manager — lights, sound, and transportation. Carruthers, a rough-hewn joker, country-bred, had been a dining-car waiter on the Pennsylvania Railroad. He saw Nat late one night at the Persian Room, taking in the show after his own work was done at the Blue Note. Carl admired Nat's hat and coat. Flattery, to which Cole was famously susceptible, led him into a conversation with the drawling waiter. "Next thing I knew I was signed up to go on tour with him and Woody Herman," Carruthers recalled.

Sparky Tavares, a diminutive (less than five feet), slight, owlish man with the fabled owl's wisdom and a kind heart, showed an amazing range of abilities, from wardrobe details and road management to headshrinking. He spoke softly, concealing a mild lisp. He soon became an indispensable member of the Cole entourage, as confidant, doorkeeper, peacemaker, and family friend.

"Sparky was the best," Maria remembers. "He was like family." He was better than family in that he was selfless, moving through the complex drama of the Coles' business affairs and domestic life like a benevolent and unobtrusive genie. Cole's appointment of Tavares and his increasing reliance upon the valet's good judgment was one more proof of the entertainer's common sense in management.

Nathaniel wished to return to his high school, Wendell Phillips, to see old friends and share memories. Roy Topper of the *Herald-American* reported that "Nat King Cole, a local boy who made good, is trying to squeeze in a visit to the two high schools he attended here — Phillips and DuSable. He hasn't seen either of them since he was a youngster." If the record clerk's word can be trusted, Nat never saw the inside of DuSable at all. Two months after Cole quit school in November of 1934, a fire closed Phillips, and Nat's schoolmates all transferred to nearby DuSable, where they graduated in 1936.

According to classmate Tim Black, there was an alumni gathering at DuSable High School that February while Nat was in town. And the famous singer and pianist, the "boy who made good," joined his old friends and classmates for the festivities. He was quite gracious, remembering names and details about their lives. Some envied him. Nat was having a wonderful time in the warmth of sentiment and nostalgia until someone disappeared from the room and then reappeared, at which point the whispering started. Evidently somebody thought it important to uphold the dignity of the alumni by distinguishing the true graduates of Phillips and DuSable from the fly-by-nights and high school dropouts. Scuttling downstairs and into the file room this person diligently brought up Nathaniel Coles's records. You see, he did not graduate ever, the whisperers whispered, and eventually the cause of the commotion got back to the famous man. "He was embarrassed, humiliated," Tim Black recalls. "As he left you could see he was deeply hurt."

The group left Chicago in mid-February. As Nat King Cole and the Trio, they took to the road for a punishing month of one-night stands with Woody Herman's band in the Midwest and on the East Coast. Maria joined them. The musicians changed their outfits. For years the three had dressed the same; now that Nat was featured, he wore light gray if they wore blue, blue if they wore gray, always the odd man.

The trip got off to a bad start on Valentine's Day when the group's rented vehicle skidded on an icy highway going from Champaign, Illinois, into Ames, Iowa. The van bearing Nat and Maria, Irving Ashby, Joe Comfort, Jack Costanzo, Mort Ruby, and program manager Bill Kalman "turned turtle" into a ravine in the darkness and was demolished. Amazingly, no one was badly injured, though Nat sprained his ankle. A bakery truck gave them a ride, and the next evening they performed on schedule at the Iowa State College Armory.

After performances at Notre Dame University in South Bend, Indiana, and in Kalamazoo, Michigan, they drove day and night to do a concert at Carnegie Hall in New York on the 20th. Young Harry Belafonte, who would play an important role in Cole's life years later, sang during intermission. The "Gob with a Throb," as the moody crooner was then billed (English sailors were called "gobs"), had not yet discovered folk music. Dressed in a tuxedo and wearing a mustache, he sang pop tunes in a thin and high-pitched voice. The troupe continued on to one-nighters in Pittsburgh, Washington, D.C., and Philadelphia before arriving in Boston, where Nat was to sing at Symphony Hall on February 27.

That night Nat and Maria took her sister Carol Lane out to dinner. Maria had been worried about Babe since Christmas, when she had visited them in New York. Now she was thin and pale, and she coughed badly throughout the meal. Maria urged her sister to seek medical help in Boston.

Maria wanted Babe to see their new home. She had been on the phone several times with the interior decorator since her ten-day visit to Hancock Park. The work was coming along nicely, and in March Ebony ran a four-page article with ten photos of the Coles' new home.

There was plenty of money to pay for the best of everything. For the current tour, Carlos Gastel had demanded 70 percent of each night's gross, or a $3,000 per night guarantee against 50 percent. For example, in Champaign, Illinois, the musicians walked away with $6,800, 70 percent of the gross. Nat received the lion's share of it, night after night, in Boston, Syracuse, and Reading, before beginning a two-week gig at the Paramount Theater in New York. That day, March 16, *Variety* reported that Cole's share of the profits from their last fourteen concerts was about $25,000. And then there were the checks from record royalties, each one with a zero or two more than the last. The Coles must have thought they could afford anything. But Nat had not yet learned the true price of fame.

BOP CITY TO DIXIE

Bebop, the avant-garde jazz of Gillespie and Parker, was so hot in New York City that fans thought of it as Bop City (after a Broadway music hall of that name), and nobody talked about Swing Street anymore.

"Nat Nominates Himself Advance Man for Bop," says the headline in *Down Beat*. In a long interview with John S. Wilson that spring of 1949, Cole said he intended "to do the selling job the bop purists are neglecting because they're too engrossed in examining their own flatted fifths." He announced that the King Cole ensemble would be doing more bop, "but subtle bop, so the public will understand it." Of course, he assured Wilson, they would also continue to perform the familiar Cole ballads.

"Parents get upset about the alleged immoral influence of bop. They read these stories about musicians getting arrested . . . and the headlines always say 'Bop Musician.' Well, musicians are just like anybody else — some are worse than others. There are classical men who have some of the worst morals . . . I figure I can help by telling the public, 'Now I'm going to play bop, and we'll see if it changes my morals.'"

When Jack Costanzo and his bongos joined the Trio in mid-February, Nat devoted his creative energies to the new sounds, the polyrhythms and chordal extensions of bebop. The recordings Cole made in New York at WMGM Studios that March represent his last significant development as a jazz artist. He would continue to make fine records in both the popular and jazz idioms, notably the famous jazz album After Midnight (1956). But after 1950 he added little to the "language" that he and Oscar Moore had created.

At midnight on March 22, Cole and the Trio began a three-hour session that yielded a classic ballad and their two most sophisticated bebop recordings to date. Costanzo's bongos define the first two measures of "Laugh! Cool Clown" in moderate 4/4 tempo with a marked Latin syncopation that soon will be popularly called the "cha-cha-cha," then Comfort's bass enters on the second and fourth beats. When the piano joins in at the fourth bar, you immediately feel the new freedom Cole has gained from the Latin percussion. With no more responsibility for time-keeping, he can luxuriate in the melodic and harmonic possibilities of the right hand. He can play it like a flute or a saxophone if he likes. This number is a bop rendition of Ruggiero Leoncavallo's famous aria "Ridi, Pagliacci," as well known to opera lovers as to Marx Brothers' fans who recall Groucho's parody of it in *A Night at the Opera*. It is thrilling to hear Cole deconstruct the minor chords of Leoncavallo's verses, then — with the guitar's support — address the main theme with a casual, contemporary irony. Soon the fireworks begin. The bongos pick up speed in a more even eighth-note rhythm, and then the pianist uses his chorus as a stage on which to perform his own acrobatic opera, full of triplets and stop-time, double-time, and surprising blue-note arpeggios.

The up-tempo "Bop-Kick" sets off at such a furious pace, with the even eighth notes of the bongos ticking away like a watch gone mad, that you almost expect Cole and Ashby to play their parts in half time. They don't — they keep up the furious pace. Nat's solo work on this original composition reminds you that he is near the peak of his technical virtuosity as a pianist. For the first sixteen bars he plays at astonishing speed the same figures simultaneously in the right and left hands, which is stunning when he hits his trademark triplets. The tune is a collage of two blues riffs that play off the polyrhythms of the bongos and the well-placed heavy accents beboppers call kicks and bombs. Here melody is less important to the structure than the rhythm of the eight-bar blues riff Nat lays down, and repeatedly returns to, playing it and embellishing the theme in different keys. Nat's second solo, a double chorus, blends the bebop rhythm with a more joyful, openhearted swing sound; the music is wide open in every way — rhythmically, harmonically — yet it swings like bebop rarely does. Truly this is one of Cole's greatest improvisations, ranking with his best work with Lester Young, Oscar Moore, and Illinois Jacquet.

Cole's 1949 "bop" recordings are not so much a development of his stylistic virtues as they are a clarification, or even an exaggeration, of them. His influence on pianists such as Oscar Peterson, Thelonious Monk, and Bud Powell began years earlier. Cole's impact on the great bebop pianist

Powell, who played with Charlie Parker, has to do with Cole's "attack" and the brilliance of his up-tempo right-hand solos. While these strengths mark Cole's playing from the early forties, they are more obvious in 1949 and 1950, when Costanzo's percussion permits the pianist a lighter use of his left hand.

Before wrapping up the session, at three o'clock in the morning, Nat waved Jack Costanzo aside, with thanks. The bongos had no place in the last number, the soft, romantic ballad "For All We Know," ' written by Sam Lewis and Fred Coots in the early thirties.

For all we know, we may never meet again.
Before you go, make this moment sweet again . . .

It needed no more than the lightest touch on the piano or guitar, a soft bass note every other beat, and Nat's slow, caressing voice. That little couplet consumes thirty seconds of airtime. This was the tempo so slow that only he and Sinatra had the breath control to work it, the breath control and the sense of musical line. The vocal power he had displayed singing "Embraceable You" in December 1943 had reached a new level of richness and intimacy in the five years since. His mellow shaping of notes and the precision with which the vibrato diminishes and fades into silence at the line endings is absolutely mesmerizing. This is the form he will carry with him to the end of his singing career.

A week later they were back in the studio with a full orchestra, a vocal backup group, and a young

conductor named Pete Rugolo. A slender, bespectacled gentleman of thirty-four, the soft-spoken
Rugolo had the unworldly air of a scholar. "I was
pretty square in those days," he recalls with
amusement, his naiveté setting off Cole's premature ripeness. "I didn't smoke or drink." He was
associated with the singer for twenty years. Yet
now when I tell him Nat was considerably younger than he, the eighty-three-year-old musician
looks surprised.

Rugolo studied with the French composer Dar-
ius Milhaud when Milhaud taught at Mills College in Oakland. It was a girls' school until Rugolo
got special permission to take classes with Milhaud, the famous friend of Stravinsky and
Diaghilev, colleague of Eric Satie and Francis
Poulenc. Rugolo had a passion for jazz, combined
with the up-to-the-minute sophistication of the
modern classical composer. He first met Nat in
1944 at L.A.'s 331 Club, and the two men became
friends when the Trio shared the stage with Stan
Kenton, for whom Rugolo worked until 1948.
Carlos Gastel, of course, was the matchmaker
who drew all of these talents together.

The session started with a heavily produced
take of Eden Ahbez's "Land of Love," an ill-fated
sequel to "Nature Boy," resonant with harps,
mysterious oboes, and weird, quivering violins.
The day ended with two upbeat bongo-driven
love songs, "Yes Sir, That's My Baby" and "I
Used to Love You." But we prize the occasion
chiefly for the monumental Billy Strayhorn song
"Lush Life."

Strayhorn had written the dramatic recitative in

the late 1930s. Truly, its attitude of weltschmerz and atmosphere of anxiety belong more to the pre-war German cabaret scene than the boom-time American concert hall. But the vivid lyrics describe a world of cocktails and jazz dives alluring to hipsters of all eras. Strayhorn's boss Duke Ellington did not perform "Lush Life" until 1948. Cole got the sheet music then and started singing the torch song, as simply as he could, with the Trio in small clubs.

"It's too subtle for any real wide appeal," Nat told Don Freeman of *Down Beat*.

The song's protagonist tells the story of how his frivolous party life was promised meaning — and then nearly rescued — by love, how love failed and disappointed him ultimately. Beginning in carefree cynicism, the song descends into deeper cynicism before ending in pessimistic gloom:

> *Romance is mush, stifling those that strive.*
> *I'll live a lush life in some small dive.*
> *And there I'll be, where I'll rot with the rest*
> *Of those whose lives are lonely too.*

This is the perfect existential anthem for the jilted lover drowning his or her sorrows. And who has not felt this way? The song, in Nat's version, quickly became a cult classic, a favorite of movie stars like Lana Turner and Frank Sinatra's femme fatale, Ava Gardner. And all drunks loved it, especially drunks who had been unlucky in love.

Though others attempted to perform it, notably contralto Kay Davis, Cole got a monopoly on "Lush Life" because the piece was almost impossible to sing. It required a great vocalist who was also a convincing storyteller. And if you were drunk enough to understand the song, you were not sober enough to sing it. The melody is maddeningly complex, changing key more than a dozen times, often within a phrase. "Lush Life" has such potential to turn ugly you would not wish to hear Billie Holiday sing it, though you might admire her understanding of its theme. No, "Lush Life" required a lovely voice, but a voice wise in the world's ways — it called for Nat King Cole.

Cole longed to record "Lush Life" but doubted his producers would consider the song in its raw state. He handed Rugolo the sheet music, saying, "See what you think of this. It's pretty strange stuff, and I don't know if Capitol will really want me to record it. See what you can do with it."

Rugolo remembers, "I took the song and played around with it. I thought I would make a kind of tone poem out of it."

And that is what Milhaud's student did with "Lush Life," creating rich orchestration behind and between the lyrics, adding extra bars, highlighting the verses in a song that was largely rubato, out of tempo. By the time Rugolo was done, his version was nearly twice as long as the original. When Capitol released the record, a year later, Strayhorn was not pleased with the results and neither was Ellington. But Cole and Rugolo together had forged a masterpiece, an art song fit to be compared with the best of Hugo Wolf and Gustav Mahler. Rugolo would wax a total of forty-five sides with Nat King Cole, but none greater than "Lush Life."

In April, Nat and the Trio took to the road again, performing in half a dozen cities with long stays in Cleveland and Chicago. On April 25, 1949, a Monday morning, Nat, Maria, and their entourage arrived in Pittsburgh and went to the Roosevelt Hotel. The manager told them the hotel was filled up — he had not taken any reservations for five days. Wanting to be helpful, he suggested the Hotel Mayfair and offered to telephone there. Nat thanked the manager and watched as he rang up the Mayfair's desk clerk. Cole later recalled, "He told us that there were three double rooms over there. We went directly there. It probably took us only a few minutes."

They entered the Mayfair's lobby. While Nat and Maria stood chatting behind them, Mort Ruby and Jack Costanzo approached Al Stretiff, the desk clerk. Suddenly Nat heard the clerk say to Ruby, "Is he with you?" nodding toward the black Nat Cole. When Ruby confirmed that the African-American was indeed with the party, Stretiff turned his back on them and said, "I'm sorry. I can't take care of you then." Nat later recalled, "He muttered something about company policy as he walked away from us."

Nat may have been used to this sort of treatment, but Maria was quickly fed up with it. She had heard stories of Nat's shabby accommodations when he first played Las Vegas in May 1947. The Thunderbird Hotel was paying him $4,500 a week; while his road manager got a free suite at the hotel, Nat could not stay there. He had to stay in a dive in "Dustville" on the other side of the

313

tracks for $15 a day. The star of the show was shut out of the casino, too. If the guys in the Trio wanted to gamble, they had to go to a Chinese joint and play poker and shoot dice in the back room with the Native Americans.

And only two months before the Mayfair incident, when the group played Town Hall in Philadelphia, the management of the Ben Franklin Hotel made the Coles sleep on a foldout couch in the conference room. The Mayfair snub called for action. Nat hired two African-American attorneys, Paul F. Jones and Thomas Barton, who filed a $25,000 damage suit against the operators of the hotel. This was the first of two highly publicized lawsuits the Coles filed against hotels. While they received no more than an apology from the Mayfair and a public denial of any discriminatory policy, the publicity in *The New York Times* and elsewhere struck a blow for civil rights.

Returning to Bop City on May 4, Nat was about to settle in for a three-week run at the Royal Roost nightclub when he and Maria heard that her sister Babe had taken a turn for the worse. Maria and Charlotte hurried to Boston, where they found Carol "Babe" Lane in a hospital bed, wasted with consumption. "We had been in denial," Charlotte recalls. "We just could not believe how sick she was." The tuberculosis advanced with astonishing speed. The antibiotic streptomycin had just come on the market, says Maria, "but the young doctor attending Babe told us it was just like giving her water."

Babe's three-year-old daughter Carol, nicknamed Cookie, was not allowed in the hospital

314

room. Maria stood with her on a hill where her mother might wave to her from her bed, through a window. They realized Babe would not make it when Charlotte asked what was to be done with the little girl.

"That's up to you and Maria," whispered the dying woman.

Carol Lane passed away at 8 p.m. on May 7, the night before Mother's Day. Maria was in a state of stunned disbelief. From the hospital in Boston Maria had telephoned her husband in New York. "Nat, Babe's dying," she sobbed. "I don't know what's going to happen to Cookie. Could we take her?" He and Maria were of one mind: the right place for the orphan would be with them, in their new home. Charlotte, still unmarried, agreed.

The only family member who would not agree to this arrangement was Charlotte Hawkins Brown. Aunt Lottie, now in her sixties, arrived in Boston for the funeral at about the same time as Nat. The lonely woman looked upon little Cookie not only as a comfort in her sunset years but as a last chance to "get it right" in raising one of these girls to be a young lady in the Palmer Institute mold. Dr. Brown was used to having things her way. Maria and Nat were certain that Dr. Brown's home was not the best place for Babe's daughter, and that Cookie would be better off in Hancock Park. But Maria had never made much headway in confronting her dictatorial Aunt Lottie.

Years later Maria recalled the showdown between her stern aunt and her mild-mannered husband. It took place after the funeral, in Aunt Addie Willis's apartment on Townsend Street in

Roxbury, where the widow Babe had lived the last months of her life.

Everyone was in the kitchen. Aunt Lottie was wearing a dark suit, and she had not removed her narrow brimmed, veiled hat. She was speaking of her plans for Cookie as if there could be no doubt where the orphan was going, no doubt who was best fit to raise and care for her. So when Nat and the rest explained that other plans were in the offing, and they had made a place for Cookie in their Los Angeles home, Dr. Charlotte Hawkins Brown pulled herself up to her full height, hat and all. She issued a decree, as if the kitchen had been a class full of unruly youngsters, crushing protest under an iron heel.

When she had finished, there was a moment of silence.

Then Nat King Cole spoke a single sentence, in a voice that managed to be gentle while absolutely forbidding further argument: "You may run your family, but you won't run mine." The child's paternal grandfather, toothless, nearly blind, softly said to Maria, "You take her," gesturing to the orphan, who joined the Coles.

Dr. Brown returned to Sedalia. She hired lawyers to sue Nat and Maria for custody of the little girl.

For the time being Cookie stayed in Roxbury with Aunt Addie and the rest of the family while Maria followed Nat to New York. It was there in the month of May, while Nat finished his three-week engagement at the Royal Roost, that Maria conceived their first child.

They left New York on a road tour of the South — Louisiana, Texas, and Alabama — then wended their way through the rest of Dixie. Sometime in June, during a string of one-nighters in North Carolina, Maria told valet Sparky Tavares she wasn't feeling well.

"He was one of the family, and as such, he became the first to know," she recalls. When she told Sparky she thought she was pregnant, he begged her not to say anything unless she was sure. "We both knew how much Nat wanted a child, and we did not want to raise any false hopes."

She was so certain, she kissed her husband goodbye. Living conditions were hard for black musicians on the road in those days. In the South — for a woman in Maria's state — they were unacceptable. She returned to New York to have her own doctor confirm what she knew to be true.

"I telephoned Nat long-distance and told him in a singsong voice, 'You're going to be a Papa!' He was delirious with joy." He could hardly wait to see her again.

First he would have to survive one of the most grueling concert tours of his career, forty dates in thirty Southern cities and towns that concluded in mid-July. Many Southerners found it quite offensive enough that the King Cole Trio, rich and famous, was black. But now the addition of the white bongo player made matters worse, a gross affront to the proprieties of segregation.

Black entertainers in the South had never been allowed to perform in a white nightclub until the Monte Carlo in Miami hired the Ink Spots in 1948. Bill Bojangles Robinson was also a success there, and soon other nightclubs were calling agents to book acts like Cab Calloway, Lena Horne, and King Cole and the Trio. But their presence was highly controversial.

In most cities the black performers had to play for segregated audiences: blacks or whites, but never a mix. This was not mere custom — sometimes it was a municipal ban, as when the Censorship Board banned Costanzo from the W. C. Handy Theater in Memphis. In Little Rock, Shreveport, and Cole's hometown of Montgomery, the police enforced restrictions against integrated stage acts. So Costanzo had to cool his bongos in the alley outside when the Trio played in those cities. Sometimes the police would stop their bus outside the city limits. They would order the bongo player off the bus and take him to a white hotel. The next day they would bring the white man back to the bus as the combo was leaving town.

"The Cole group hung together in a pinch," says James Haskins, who interviewed Irving Ashby in 1982. "The whole idea was so repulsive," Ashby recalled. "We would have given up our salaries . . . and Nat would have paid Jack five times his salary just to have him, because he was part of us." They could not sleep in the same hotels, eat in the same diners, or use the same rest rooms. In many towns well-known black performers avoided these indignities by staying in private homes.

Joe Comfort recalled how they traveled in a red, white, and blue bus with "King Cole and his Trio" emblazoned on its side. And they had a white bus driver, a kind, portly fellow of more than three hundred pounds named Barney. Bassman Comfort was a heavy sleeper. One afternoon he woke up to find himself alone on the bus. They were at a truck stop, so he got down off the bus and went in the front door. Joe saw people sitting at the long counter, eating. And through the doorway at the back he could see Nat and Irving and some of the other men of color standing around. Joe thought they must be waiting to go to the toilet. He stood at the counter and ordered a ham sandwich and a Coke to go.

Back on the bus his friends accosted him. "Man, what are you doing? You're going to get us put in jail! You're supposed to go to the back!" That is what Joe had seen through the doorway: Nat King Cole and his black friends waiting patiently out of sight for their food to be packaged for carryout.

In June the men were unloading their gear from the bus outside the Lookout House, a bar-restaurant in Covington, Kentucky. Mort Ruby went to the office to meet the manager. No sooner had the club manager identified Ruby, handing him his mail from GAC, than he ordered him to take a seat, delivering this chilling speech, to be relayed to the musicians: "Under no circumstances are they to go anywhere but backstage. They are not allowed in the club, in the restaurant, in the gambling rooms, or in the bar, ever. And if I see you . . . you're a Jew, aren't you?"

"Yes."

"If I see *you* or any of those others in *any* of those places," the club manager said, his voice

trailing off as he opened a drawer to grab a .45 au-
tomatic, which he rested on the desk in front of
him, "then I'm going to shoot you."

FAMILY

Almost a year had passed since Nat had been home, a year since the purchase of the mansion in Hancock Park. He had hardly driven the shiny new black Cadillac he found parked in the driveway.

Maria and the decorators had been hard at work feathering the nest. That summer of 1949, as he entered his house through the paneled oak door, he could hardly believe his eyes. Months earlier, little Carol, arriving from the apartment in Roxbury where she had lived with her mother and aunt, thought the mansion looked like a castle. From the curving pathway it did look more like a New England house than a Californian, with its brick, its mullioned windows, the wooden beams, and ivy.

A crystal chandelier illuminated the main front hallway with its curving staircase. Under the stair a modern black lacquered mirror chest faced the door. On the chest stood two gunmetal "luster" lamps with silver-leaf shades, and in the curve of the balustrade sat a Tudor hall chair covered in deep rose velvet.

"Do you like it?" his wife asked. "Look, look!" she exclaimed, leading him to the left, into the living room. One wall of the huge room was nearly covered by a thirteen-foot-wide mirror that extended from the floor to the twelve-foot ceiling. A long custom-made sofa and four armchairs covered in white quilted silk with tropical patterns sat across from the fireplace. Six tall column lamps with white silk shades, pink-trimmed, stood upon marbleized pedestals of black lacquer. Coffee tables too were made of black lacquer, with gunmetal and glass tops; on either side of each table stood Regency chairs with button-tufted seats in butterfly-yellow satin.

How could he not like it? Had he ever dreamed of a home of his own so splendid? It was grand, yet the effect was of modern simplicity and comfort: "California Modern," the papers called it.

Beyond the foyer, on the dining-room wall, a tropical scene had been hand-painted. A long silver-leaf dining-room table, with twelve chairs covered in yellow antique satin, shone under a soft glow light in the center of the high ceiling. The wooden floor was stained green.

Upstairs the master bedroom was the same size as the living room, more than thirty feet long and half as wide. A king-sized bed lay under a five-by-eight-foot headboard quilted in pink satin with white trim. The walls were blue with a vine pattern. A chaise on one side of the bed and an armchair on the other were covered in pink-and-white-striped upholstery.

Across from the bed, over the fireplace, was a small painted portrait of Maria.

Nat was a funny sight to behold getting up in the morning. He slept in a mini-length nightshirt. He slept late, as most performers do, so often Maria would gently wake him after first freshening herself up and combing out her hair. "So nice to wake up and look at a beautiful woman," he once told her.

Sitting at the end of the bed, he would scratch the underside of his chin in that characteristic manner, with the backs of his fingers, flicking upward. He would reach for a cigarette before going into the bathroom.

Nat wore house shoes so old they were falling apart. He got attached to a pair and would not get new ones. Maria recalls, "For a full five minutes he would walk around as if still asleep, not saying anything." And she would tease him. "Honey, if I had seen your feet first, I never would have married you."

Nathaniel was truly delighted to be home, with a child in the nursery already and another on the way. Maria's due date was in February.

He made a priceless comment one morning as he emerged from the bathroom grinning. "I'm a man now, yessir. I knocked up my wife, and I just shaved for the first time," he announced, proud as a peacock. It would have made a great advertisement for Gillette. Whatever the hormone shots had done for his sperm count and his vocal cords, they sure had affected his body hair. Nat had always been what his wife called a "hairless wonder," from eyebrows to toes. This characteristic, taken with his smooth voice, earned him the whispered reputation among women without rights to such knowledge: Mr. Silk. "I suppose," says Maria in retrospect, with admirable humor, "that was all part of the mystique."

The couple had only two weeks in July to enjoy

their new home. At month's end the Trio, with Woody Herman's band, kicked off a West Coast tour with an appearance at the Shrine Auditorium in L.A. *Down Beat* reviewed the show zealously: "If progressive music . . . survives the attacks of the diehard dixiecats . . . the credit should go to Woody Herman, Nat Cole, and the concert promoter Gene Norman." This concert, which experts thought would be too avant-garde to please a large audience, was a huge success.

At the end of August the Trio flew to Honolulu to play at McKinley Auditorium, then performed at a private party for Doris Duke, heiress to a tobacco fortune. She gave Nat the text of "Nalani," a future hit song that a friend of hers had penned.

They appeared for two weeks at the Las Vegas Thunderbird Hotel where Nat was handsomely paid to suffer the same old indignities; then the group moved to greener pastures. Four-year-old Carol traveled with them on engagements in Minneapolis and Winnipeg, where *Down Beat* dubbed Nat an ambassador of goodwill and professionalism. "Ambassador": a title he would hear applied to him more often in the decade to come.

Autumn found them back in New York for two weeks. From there King Cole and Woody Herman began a meandering concert tour through the Midwest including a week in Chicago in mid-December. After this they flew home to play the Million Dollar Theater in Hollywood, the day before Christmas Eve.

This Christmas was the first in their new home. The Coles arrived in Hancock Park with little time to decorate the house or buy presents. He usually bought Maria a piece of antique jewelry; this year even that would have to be done at the last moment. "Now look here," he told Sparky, his little aide-de-camp, pointing to the ten-foot Christmas tree that had been delivercd. "We're going to put this up here," he said, pointing to the spot in the foyer. "And then we're going to put this out there," Nat went on, vaguely waving to a huge Santa Claus display with a sleigh and reindeer that would go on the lawn. In the sleigh was a music box that played carols when you turned a switch.

The phone rang. It was business for Nat, so he took the call, leaving Sparky to get started. By the time Nat returned, Sparky was on a ladder hanging tinsel and lights. And when Nat got tangled in the rigging, Sparky kindly told him to stand aside. This was not the musician's sort of task, and it made Sparky nervous to have him fumbling about. Cole was glad to leave the work to Sparky, who handled the Christmas decorations for the next fifteen years to everyone's satisfaction, including the exacting Mrs. Cole.

Watching Carol play under the Christmas tree, listening to "The Christmas Song" on the radio in their new house, the happy couple dreamed of the child that would be born to them in the new year. They hoped for a boy.

"Carol made a great difference in those early months," Nat recalled. "We had to learn the complex and tender art of being parents." Carol remembers that tenderness on her father's part when she was grieving over the loss of her mother, her home, and all that had been familiar, in a strange, faraway city. Cole stood with the beautiful child on the lawn under the clear night sky, holding her. Pointing up at the brightest star in the sky, he said to her, "Look, Cookie, see that big star shining there? That is your mother, there. If you miss her at night look up in the sky and there you will see her shining down on you." This was a comfort. And soon Carol would have a baby sister to keep her company.

Aunt Lottie's legal action to wrest away custody of Carol from Nat and Maria failed, and her anger at them expired with the lawsuit. Dr. Brown was the sort of woman who would pursue a course of action to its conclusion, for the principle of it, come hell or high water. Better to fight over the child than abandon her. It was as if the lawsuit had become sport, and when the game was done she accepted defeat as a good sportsman, without any hard feelings.

Maria's obstetrician, Dr. David Daniel, set her due date for February 15, so Nat scheduled all his early February bookings in the L.A. area in order to stay close to home.

Maria felt contractions early in the morning of February 6, 1950. Nat took her to Cedars of Lebanon Hospital. There, at 6:07 p.m., after an eleven-hour labor, Maria gave birth to a seven-pound-eleven-ounce girl. Maria cried when she saw the baby. "I thought Nat would be disappointed. We had anticipated a boy."

She need not have worried. The nurse held the baby up for her father to see. "I looked at that kid for a long time," he said. "I felt something impossible for me to explain . . . When they took her away, it hit me. I got scared all over again and began to feel giddy. Then it came to me — I was a father."

He reassured his trembling wife, "Girls stick closer to home." And later he recalled, "Truthfully, the moment I heard it was a girl, all the past feelings went away. I'm happy."

First they named her Stephanie Maria. Later they changed the name to Natalie, but everybody called her "Sweetie" until she was grown. Asked what plans they had for the child's future, Nat and Maria expressed one heartfelt wish: "We hope she won't go into show business. It just takes too, too much out of a human being."

Ever since the turn of the year the Internal Revenue Bureau had been breathing down King Cole's neck. Somehow he had neglected to pay — or his agents and accountants neglected to pay — more than $100,000 of income tax from 1947 through 1949. He was trying to negotiate with the agency. But he was not earning enough money to support his current lifestyle and pay the government the taxes and penalties he owed. The singer was making $200,000 a year, and decided he could pay $66,000 in current and back taxes over the twelve-month period beginning in March 1950.

He wondered what was the hurry. He put them off and worked harder, and worried about money. At the end of the day that Maria and Natalie came home from the hospital, February 11, someone took a photo of Nat lying on the striped chaise in the bedroom. The caption says "Exhausted," then explains the singer is grabbing a couple of hours' sleep before working his first show of the evening. But he does not look so much exhausted as worried, someone with the weight of the world on his shoulders. What man, during the first days of fatherhood, has not felt this seismic shift, this new sense of urgency to provide for the wife and baby? Why did the tax agents have to choose this year to pick on him?

Now, as the journalists asked him the same tiresome questions about selling out to popular music, in Nat's tone of voice we can begin to detect a change that either reflects a reshaping of his values or greater candor born of exasperation. "I'm in the music business for one purpose — to make money," he told Don Freeman of *Down Beat*. "I'm not playing for other musicians. We're trying to reach the guy who works all day and wants to spend a buck at night. We'll keep him happy.

"Jazz is pretty dead commercially anyway. We haven't had a new and fresh sound since [George] Shearing and he hasn't gone any further. He learned there's a limited number of rooms he can play. So now he tells jokes . . .

"We don't do much bop anymore. In fact, the Trio has gotten away from jazz."

In response the jazz critic admonishes: "A performer who sacrifices his art for the heavy money may reach a point of no return. The loss — even to himself — could mean more than wealth."

Mr. Cole was in no frame of mind to care much what Don Freeman had to say about his art or his money in 1950. He was biting his fingernails down to the quick. No wonder he jumped when the phone rang — Carlos Gastel with offers to sing all over America, in Canada, on television and radio.

Maria hired a nurse, a warmhearted Texas Baptist lady the children called Nana. Soon another nurse arrived, a tiny woman named Ida, a Pentecostal. Carol Cole remembers the black women were like Mutt and Jeff, their shapes so different. The nurses took the girls to church on Sundays, and Carol remembers it was a jolly experience, so different from the Episcopal church Maria and Nat attended.

Nurses, housekeepers, gardeners, and children soon were joined by two prize boxer dogs named Mr. Cole and Mr. Pep. The dogs were Nat's idea, and at first it may have been as much for security as for love of the species. But he soon talked to the dogs as if they were equals; there are funny movies of the young man romping and rolling on the lawn out back of the house with the boxers.

Two days after Natalie was born, Maria started on a regimen of exercise to restore her figure. When Nat left for New York in mid-March, his wife was on the airplane with him.

Maria was not about to be left behind. Not even motherhood could sway her resolve to be with Nat day and night, at home and on the road. She asked her doctor if it was all right, if there was something wrong with her: "I love my baby but I'd rather be with my husband." And the physician, with the wisdom of 1950, told the young mother what she wanted to hear: "Go back with your husband, that's where you belong, because when this child is sixteen it isn't going to make any difference to her whether you were there or not when she was five weeks old."

Now we know better, but we should not judge by Dr. Spock's standards a decision made a half century ago. Maria Cole was dealing with pressures few women ever know. The wonder is that she is so frank about it. "She had to watch her treasure," Geri Branton told James Haskins. The sentence is rich with meaning. Nat Cole was too loose with a buck — he could spend their money almost as fast as he was making it, while forgetting Uncle Sam's share. And then, the man himself, her lover and husband, father of her child, was a treasure she could not trust to the vagaries and temptations of the road. "She didn't want anybody else to get him the way she had," Branton added.

The out-of-tempo ballad "Mona Lisa," like the giant hit "Nature Boy," began as a B-side sleeper. No one expected it to do as well as the A side, "The Greatest Inventor of Them All," a rousing gospel tune with an old-time choir. Nat at first disliked "the Italian song," as he called it, put off by the title — he thought it was too highbrow. Carlos Gastel actually had to pressure Cole to record the number.

The song's genesis is a story in itself. Alan Ladd was starring in a war movie called *O.S.S.* when songwriter Jay Livingston was handed the following assignment from Paramount Pictures: Ladd's character was fighting alongside the Italian Partisans, operating a clandestine radio. In the scene that would feature the tune, a singer–accordion player was supposed to sing a code song to warn Ladd the Germans were coming.

Paramount needed the piece immediately. Livingston remembers he wrote most of the melody in his head in a half-hour drive to the studio, with the words "Prima donna, prima donna," instead of "Mona Lisa." Then he and co-author Ray Evans sat down and finished it, the music in one day, the words in two, still with the lead "Prima donna, prima donna." About the time they finished the song, Paramount rang them up to tell them the movie had a new name, *After Midnight*. Please rewrite "Prima donna" to fit the new title.

So Ray and Jay changed the words. Now the song began "After midnight, after midnight," and Paramount's music chief Louis Lipstone thought it was good enough, but evidently Ray Evans's wife did not. An art lover, Mrs. Evans thought the song should be about da Vinci's masterpiece, and on a lark the composers humored her, cooking up another set of lyrics.

The time came to do a demo of the soundtrack for *After Midnight* with a forty-four-piece orchestra. "When they finished, there was still a half hour of recording time left on the disc," Livingston recalls. "We asked the singer to do a take of the song with the 'Mona Lisa' lyrics, and so we had full production demos of both versions.

"A few days later I picked up *Variety*, where I read that *After Midnight* had been renamed *Captain Carey, U.S.A.* So now it was a fairly simple matter to convince Lipstone to use the more graceful 'Mona Lisa' lyrics for the Italian song. The studio sent it out to all the big-name Italian singers: Sinatra, Como, Damone. All of them turned it down." They sent "Mona Lisa" to Nat King Cole and he turned it down too. This was around the time he was expecting Natalie to be born, and the Internal Revenue Bureau was starting to bother him with notices about unpaid taxes and penalties — a bill in six figures. Nathaniel was getting edgy about recording risky material.

"What kind of a title is that for a song?" he asked.

Desperate for a top-notch performance, Lipstone appealed to his friend Carlos Gastel to get Cole to reconsider. Finally, according to Livingston, Nat agreed to let him come to the house and perform the song.

Songwriter Marvin Fischer happened to be visiting that day, and he and Maria were standing around the piano playing with the boxers, as Livingston began playing and singing. Maria made a face at Marvin and he made a face back at her, and they tried to keep from laughing. But when the composer finished performing his piece, Nat admitted that he liked it after all. He could not say no to the Italian song.

"Why do an Italian song?" Maria asked him. She hated it, and said so at the risk of offending the song's author. But Cole had made up his mind. And the dogs loved it.

Just before they left for their engagement at the Paramount Theater in New York in 1950, Nat and the Trio did a recording session with the Les Baxter Orchestra in Hollywood. Nat was happy to have his friend Lee Young join them on drums. On the afternoon of Saturday, March 11, they waxed five sides, several arranged by the brilliant young Nelson Riddle, including "Mona Lisa."

A few years later no one would remember anything about Alan Ladd's movie but "Mona Lisa," which won the Academy Award for best song and became a monster hit in 1950. By June it was #1 on the Billboard singles chart, selling more than a million copies before 1951. It became the biggest-selling record of Cole's career. As his first hit without the Trio featured, "Mona Lisa" is a turning point, sharply dividing his audience. The public was wild for it; jazz aficionados, Maria Cole, and many musicians (including Benny Carter) were indifferent at best.

Maria Cole did not want to be left behind when Nat went on the road. Yet parting from her five-week-old infant could not have been easy. Perhaps it was as a cure for those common feelings of anticlimax, the postpartum blues, that her husband agreed to a rebirth of Maria's singing career. Carol Cole believes that her mother's drive to perform professionally was never so easily sublimated as the proud wife pretended. The natural solution was for the husband and wife to sing together.

So in New York, in May of 1950, just after Nat's first appearance on Ed Sullivan's TV show, Nat and Maria began rehearsing together under the scholarly Pete Rugolo's direction. She would sing "A Woman's Got a Right to Change Her Mind." Rugolo recalls how "cute" the couple were, how deeply they were in love and how much fun they had — Nat at the piano, lovely Maria resting her hand on his shoulder. Her voice was warm, like his, a deep-throated alto that blended sweetly with Nat's as they sang duets in close harmony. If Nat had to coach her or give advice, he was gentle, even humble, given his greater experience, and she was his adoring pupil. Without ever playing down to Maria, he manages never to upstage or overpower her. The two generate a passionate heat, and the sparks fly, particularly in the comic dialogue of the Roy Alfred number "Hey, Not Now." Here they sing alternating phrases.

NAT: *When we take a walk at night,*
MARIA: *the stars are out,*
NAT: *and we find a place that's right,*
MARIA: *no one's about . . .*
NAT: *If I start to hold you tight, you always shout:*
MARIA: HEY! NOT NOW! NOT TONIGHT . . .

So it goes, for several choruses, Nat pursuing, Maria holding him up, teasing him, and then comes a chorus as the Alice King Vokettes sing the refrain, broadening the comedy as the roles reverse and the pursuer gets pursued:

NAT: *When we promise to be true, you'll be my own . . .*
MARIA: *You can call a preacher too, right on the phone!*
NAT: *When it's time to say "I do," you'll hear me moan, "Not now, I'll tell you when."*

Finally the lover and the beloved grow tired of playing hard to get; the singing breaks down into

334

whispering and sighing, and just as they are about to kiss, the chorus shouts: "Not now, *we'll* tell you when!"

This was all great fun, as Maria recalls, and so does Rugolo, who cannot figure out why one of these numbers was not a hit. Perhaps the records got lost in the shadow of giant successes like "Mona Lisa" and the Stan Kenton–King Cole Trio collaboration "Orange-Colored Sky" that rode high on the *Billboard* singles chart that autumn. At any rate, the duets are an eloquent souvenir, preserving the memory of a love that marriage had enriched, of a husband and wife who were still, undeniably, lovers.

Two weeks after the Coles made these recordings, the *Journal of the American Medical Association* published an alarming article by a scientist named Morton Levin. His was the first major study that linked smoking to lung cancer. The same issue also revealed that 96.5 percent of lung cancer patients were heavy smokers. Cole probably did not see the journal — few people did. And far fewer stopped smoking cigarettes because of Levin's claim.

Leaving New York in June, the couple flew to Duluth en route to Chicago. In 1950 a twenty-two-year-old ex-GI named Dick LaPalm lived there — a short, fiery-tempered Italian-American with street smarts and a passion for jazz. After serving in Japan during the occupation he worked in a record store; then for a while he managed a movie house. His life was destined to be entwined with Nat Cole's in significant and humorous ways. LaPalm was and is the ultimate jazz fanatic, a man who would turn his enthusiasm into a crusade for the music. He valued Nat King Cole above all other musicians, and truly, nobody ever loved Cole's music as did Dick LaPalm.

"I had heard 'I'm an Errand Boy for Rhythm' on the radio back in 1944, and I went absolutely crazy," he recalls.

He resolved to work for Cole, with or without pay. Hearing that the singer was on his way to play a week at the Regal Theatre, LaPalm laid his strategy. He left his movie theater and set about to waylay, lobby, and cajole the big Chicago disc jockeys — to get them to play Cole's music if they weren't already doing so, to play it more often if they already were.

Then he borrowed his aunt's little brown Zenith radio, tucked it under his arm, and hurried to the Regal. "A guy was nice enough to show me Nat's room," LaPalm remembers, his eyes shining.

Cole was in, and Dick LaPalm, with the self-confidence only madness or a sense of destiny can provide, entered and began talking in his bright, clipped Chicago accent. Cole, at first amused, found the little white man irresistible, like some sort of Windy City leprechaun, with his radio under his arm and his spiel. He was a live wire.

LaPalm searched for an outlet and plugged the radio in, all the while talking. "Now, you know you're very popular in Chicago and the jocks all know your name but it takes a little reminder now and then to get them to play you instead of Crosby or Sinatra or Eckstine but now listen," he said in a rush, as the radio tubes glowed warm and he adjusted the dial. "Listen and you'll hear one of your songs being played. No, not here," said the leprechaun, frowning, turning the dial to one station after another, while Nat joked with Sparky and Costanzo. Cole knew the odds of one of his songs coming up, even "Mona Lisa," on command were slight. Suddenly there it was. "You see, I told you!" LaPalm said, beaming, and, turning the dial to another station, found more Cole. "And there!" he said triumphantly.

"And Nat turns to Sparky and Mort Ruby and asks them what he should do," LaPalm recalls. "And I said, 'I want to get your records played all over the world.' So Nat called his manager, Carlos. And I was hired two weeks later. To do nothing but promote Nat's records in the Midwest. That's what I did originally." Later, LaPalm would go on the road with Cole as an advance man, publicist, factotum, and trusted friend.

After a week at the Regal Theatre, Nat and Maria headed for Rock Island, Illinois, where Ruby had booked rooms for the Coles and their entourage at the Hotel Fort Armstrong. When the desk clerk saw Nat King Cole and his wife, Irving Ashby and Joe Comfort — all black — he told them the hotel was full and that they had no reservations. Cole could hardly believe this was happening to him again after his highly publicized lawsuit against the Mayfair Hotel in Pittsburgh a year earlier.

Not a man to leave a job half done, Nat hired the prominent African-American attorney Aaron

337

Payne, who filed a $62,000 damage suit in federal court against the Hotel Fort Armstrong, $42,000 more than the Pittsburgh action. The price of denying the Coles a hotel room was going up. In court Nat testified he was treated "like a little fly that might be in the way" when he asked for the rooms he had reserved. The hotel maintained that the room was denied not because of any racial prejudice but only because the rooms were all taken. After six hours the jury in Peoria was deadlocked, so the Coles got no better results than they had achieved in Pittsburgh: a mountain of publicity for the cause, and the hotel's immediate adoption of an integration policy.

"Cole didn't bring the suit for the money," said Aaron Payne. "The suit was brought so that no other man should suffer what these men have suffered."

With gentle determination Cole became a civil rights activist before the "movement" even started.

Cole's ensemble and Lena Horne had been invited to tour the British Isles, Sweden, and Switzerland. General Artists, in association with Lew Grade, a British booking agent, had put the deal together; this would be the first American jazz group in twelve years to fulfill a peacetime engagement in England. But what would Nat and Maria do about the children while they were abroad?

That summer of 1950, Charlotte Hawkins Charity got the call from Maria and Nat, inviting her to come to Los Angeles and stay with the children while they went to Europe. "Maria called me in August," Charlotte recalls, "and she knew how to get to me."

"Why don't you come out here?" Maria pleaded with her sister. "After all, you haven't seen the baby, and I know you miss Cookie."

"Cookie was our heart," says Charlotte. "She had been our baby sister's baby . . . and, ah . . ." Charlotte sighs, reminiscing. "I guess that's all I needed was the encouragement." She was alone in New York, divorced from her first husband, whose name she had taken. "But I really thought when I came out that Nat and Maria were going to Europe and they'd be gone maybe a month or so. Then I didn't see them again until Christmas. So by that time I'm *in* here.

"They came back from Europe and telephoned from New York, and they were making other engagements and all . . . but they knew Baba was here. Baba, the children called me. I've been here ever since," she recalls, sitting in her small apartment in L.A., where she now lives with her dog.

Now that Baba was in residence to oversee the nursery — with the help of tall Nana and tiny Ida, Peter Dixon the butler and chauffeur, and the cook and the gardener — the household was complete.

"Someone had to be here. And that's why, I guess, I stayed, because I loved the children, and they did need, you know, children need parents. We were in a family where their dad, he had to go. And Maria certainly had to be with him.

"And so, it was so that they could have a sense of family that I stayed, and I did everything with them."

339

THE TAX MAN

The chance to tour the British Isles and perform with Lena Horne was a rich opportunity that would give Nat King Cole international stature and open up new markets. And he would be better prepared to deal with the tax man.

When the airplane arrived in London on September 3, the press was at the airport to greet them: the Coles, Jack Costanzo, Joe Comfort, and Irving Ashby. The British jazz journal *The Melody Maker* detailed their opening at the London Palladium, and later conducted a lengthy interview with all the band members. English jazz fans had been looking forward to this event for a long, long time. Nat King Cole was a hero, a legend the more mythic to English fans because he was American, a brother to Louis Armstrong, Billie Holiday, and Duke Ellington.

But what the Brits heard on the wide stage of the Palladium that week and the next left them roundly disappointed. They disliked the bongos, and complained about Nat's diction on "Yes Sir, That's My Baby," calling it "an overdone Kentish accent." For "Mona Lisa" and "Nature Boy," they had only grudging admiration. "Portrait of Jenny," which was a big hit Stateside, laid a big egg in England.

"Did he please them?" asks reviewer Mike Nevard of *The Melody Maker*. "Frankly, I think not. Not even when his programme had been tailored to what he described as 'his most commercial Variety offering ever.' The programme may have been commercial for the Paramount in New York, but for the Palladium in London — no! The performances were too sophisticated, too precise and lacking in the sparkle and ebullience necessary to make a group score here.

"Even the Trio's regular fans were disappointed . . . probably the result of expectations based on recorded specialties such as 'Lush Life.' Oh that we could have heard some of Nat's brilliant piano instead of his brilliantine voice!"

Down Beat's headline said: "Horne Scores, Not Nat, at London Palladium Shows," observing that many "elderly folk" left the theater while Nat was onstage, mostly during the bongo solo. "I don't see what some people see in his voice," said one woman fleeing the Palladium. "If an Englishman did the same he'd be thrown off the stage."

After one of the shows in London that received scattered applause, Maria recalls that Nat came off the stage with tears in his eyes. Later the theater manager told reporters, "Jazzmen don't pay." The truth is that *some* jazzmen pay in *some* situations. Horne and Armstrong made lots of money in England when they sang and played "traditional" jazz there. Cole would have done well there playing his Trio swing music from 1945, but the English audience was not eager for the half-baked mix of pop and bebop he was serving up in 1950.

The group had been bickering among themselves for a while, not so much onstage as off, and their journey increased the discord. "Can you imagine conga drums on 'Sweet Loraine'? That just turned my stomach — ker-plak, ker-plak, ker-plak," said Irving Ashby. And Joe Comfort felt the same. What began as a musical dispute eventually turned personal, as the conga player seemed less comfortable with the sidemen than he was with Maria. Jack did not smoke or drink, but he loved women, and not only as a "womanizer." He loved talking to Maria about fashions and perfumes in a way that neither she nor Nat found at all threatening. They were really good friends. Maria was aware that the married Costanzo sometimes had affairs on the road, and she asked him if he felt guilty. He told her no — that his wife had chosen to stay at home while he was gone for months at a time. Women besieged the musicians, and not one of the sidemen would survive the Trio experience with his marriage unscathed.

This is the way Maria and Jack would talk. And it got under Joe and Irving's skin, that Jack was closer to Nat and Maria than they were.

According to Ashby, an English tour manager insisted that the entourage observe "class distinctions." The Englishman informed them, "Over here we don't stay in the same hotel with our help." And while Nat objected, Maria persuaded him to accept the local custom. So they traveled to Scotland and Ireland in separate Rolls-Royces, the Coles in one, the sidemen in another, and slept in separate hotels. Maria Cole and Jack Costanzo both remember a lot of good times that autumn. But Costanzo also recalls that he and Ashby were not getting along, and once Jack almost punched the guitarist in the nose.

On the way home to America they sailed on the *Queen Mary*, Nat and Maria and Lena Horne and her husband, arranger Lennie Hayton, in luxury class, and everybody else in cabin class. This, of course, would have been a simple matter of economy — the tour had not done as well at the box office as they had hoped.

"That was where I learned to drink, just a little champagne," the temperate Maria recalls. Horne was very kind to her then, having put aside the judgment that made her snub Maria in Toots Shor's restaurant four years earlier. They became good friends.

And Nat King Cole strolled on the deck of the *Queen Mary*, taking the salt sea air and gazing at the wide horizon where the ocean meets the sky. He had lots of time to mull over his failure with the British public, time to consider how to succeed in America.

When they arrived in New York in early November, Maria was pregnant, but she would not carry the baby to term. Sometime during the intense schedule of touring that month, with shows in New York, Philadelphia, and Toronto, she miscarried.

It had been a hard year for all of them, and they arrived in Los Angeles before Christmas very weary and grateful to be home. The boxer Mr. Pep leapt on Nat and licked his face. Charlotte hugged Maria. Little Cookie had been looking forward to Christmas week like it was the Second Coming, as her glamorous parents had been away so long they seemed to her like gods. Maria was deeply moved to see the baby Natalie. She would never again leave the children for as long as she did in 1950.

The trip abroad had bombed, but Cole's records were making money. "Orange-Colored Sky" still ranked high on the charts, and for a week in January 1951, Nat's recording of "Frosty the Snowman" was the top-selling record in the country. Meanwhile "Mona Lisa" was still flying out of record stores. Twice in December, Cole appeared on Ed Sullivan's TV show, a convincing advertisement. So the singer trimmed his schedule during the early months of 1951.

In March Nat and Maria flew to Philadelphia for his brief engagement at the Click nightclub. Eddie Coles was living there with his second wife, Betty, and performing in nightclubs with his group, the Three Loose Nuts. The brothers enjoyed their reunion.

But on Wednesday, March 14, 1951, Charlotte called from Los Angeles with bad news. Tax agents from the Internal Revenue Bureau, dressed in pinstriped suits, loud ties, and fedoras, had knocked on the door. At first Baba refused to allow the four men to enter. They shouted through the window they were under orders from the government. The tax men had come to collect. Charlotte and a housemaid ran around hiding the jewelry and silverware, while Nana and Ida comforted the children.

At last Baba opened the door. The agents stated their business, invoking federal law. They had come to take Nat King Cole's house, his automobile, and everything of any value excluding $300 worth of food and "any livestock," looking warily at the teeth of a growling dog. When they went into the bedroom closets after Maria's mink coats, Charlotte told the vandals the wraps belonged to her. When they laid hands upon the mahogany Steinway grand, she grew ferocious: "You would not dare," said the blond guardian, "that is how he makes his living." And the thugs backed away.

Meanwhile a truck driver had attached a winch to the bumper of Nat's 1949 Cadillac and was towing it down Muirfield Road while another agent drove stakes into the lawn, posting notices of seizure that within hours made many a heart soar in Hancock Park.

Deputy collector Andrew Hagman told Charlotte that everybody had to be out of the house for good by March 28, and that they were not to take anything with them. Then he tipped his hat and went away to ruin someone else's afternoon.

The next day the story was in all the newspapers: "U.S. Seizes Singer's Home." "The Negro musician owed the government $146,000," the tax collector Robert A. Riddell informed *The New York Times*. In Philadelphia, Cole told the *Los Angeles Examiner* he had offered to pay the government his back income taxes if given more time to settle the entire amount, and said he would fly to Los Angeles on Monday. He "hoped to straighten out the matter after conferring with his attorney."

The performances that weekend in Philadelphia must have been strained. Saturday, March 17, was Nat's thirty-second birthday. Maria recalls that her husband, who never had trouble sleeping, lay awake all night, smoking and fretting, after hearing the news of the tax raid. This was one of several times she ever saw him weep. If they would just give him the time and peace of mind to do his work, he would pay them what he owed. He didn't want to cheat the government. As he told Frank Sinatra in 1946, he didn't know the first thing about income taxes. He had left that to his accountants, though he would not lay blame on anyone else.

On the airplane to Los Angeles, a gentleman approached the entertainer, a Phil Braunstein of New York. Braunstein was a tax lawyer. Like every CPA in America, Braunstein had read about Nat King Cole's tax difficulties. Braunstein and his West Coast partner, Harold Plant, kept the books for a number of show business people. While Cole was not much in the mood for making conversation, nevertheless he accepted the lawyer's card and agreed he would call if he wanted help.

Cole needed a great deal of help, and Braunstein, Plant & Chernin was one of the nation's sharpest accounting firms. Nat's tax liability was mounting by the day, with every check that came in the mail. And the government — for reasons the Coles could only wonder at — seemed peculiarly impatient and harsh. "Why didn't the Treasury Department agents move first to attach Cole's salary from his engagements and his royalties?" asked *Down Beat*. Some say their Hancock Park neighbors pressured the tax man; others suspect that prominent African-Americans and Jews, with their leftist leanings, fell under unfair scrutiny during the McCarthy era. Lena Horne was black-listed, so was Paul Robeson, whom Cole had visited in a clinic in England. His association with these people during the "Red scare" did him no credit with the government that levies our taxes.

Maria recalls that one of the government's chief investigators, who spoke with a Southern accent, "wanted to know why Nat lived in such a fine house, and why he had to carry so much life insurance. His implication was clear," she thought. "For black people, we were, in his opinion, living too high off the hog."

She never knew who might ask such a question. Dear Carlos, when he first saw the house, shook his head in admiration, exclaiming, "What do you need with so much house? Even *I* don't have a house like that." To which the shrewd wife replied, "You're not supposed to have a house like this. You're his manager. If your house looked like this, I'd begin to wonder what you were doing with his money."

It was a good thing Carlos had been honest and was loyal, because this was a time to try the best of friendships. The government wanted $146,000, and they wanted it in seven days or they would take everything. God had made the heavens and the earth and everything on it in six days, and it seemed no less a miracle that Nat King Cole should raise that amount of cash before March 28, 1951.

Carlos knew of Braunstein, Plant & Chernin by reputation and assured the Coles that the firm was top-notch. They arranged a meeting in Harold

Plant's office, a long meeting divided by lunch. Maria remembers that day, which was not only the beginning of the end of Cole's tax troubles but also the beginning of a friendship that would continue all of Nat's life. She recalls the four of them, Plant, Braunstein, and the Coles returning from lunch, when Nat's anxiety began to lift, and how he put his arm around Harold Plant's shoulder as they walked down the hallway, talking, "a small, innocent but warm gesture that Harold never forgot." Years later the accountant recalled it made him feel proud because he sensed that Nat Cole was accepting him not just as a business associate but as a friend.

After getting the whole story from Nat and Maria about their earnings and expenses for the past three years, plus Nat's prospects for the next several, Plant and Braunstein did what sharp tax lawyers do. They set about cutting a deal with the Internal Revenue Bureau.

This is truly like every other sort of horse trading or bargain and sale, complete with posturing, bluffing and blustering, dickering, threats and blackmail, melodrama and false exits. The only difference is that here the government pretends to have big chips not usually seen on the bargaining table — jail terms, forfeitures and fines, the rack and the screw. All these horrors and more the tax collectors must have arrayed on the table for Braunstein and Plant at their first meeting. And Nat's men had to remain cool and calm, knowing that after all the swaggering and thunder and baring of incisors it must all come down to this: How much money did Nat Cole have, and how much could the government take from him without cutting his earning power or engendering serious risk of some counteraction? How much could he pay now, and how much next year and the next? Braunstein and Plant's power was in their knowledge of the answers, which, of course, they would never share with the government.

While Plant and Braunstein were haggling with tax collector Riddell, Nat and Maria were fighting the battle in the newspapers. Vast news coverage of the affair was sympathetic to the Coles. "Nat Cole Hits Tax Action," noted *The New York Times*, "Suggests Pressure to Force Him Out." *The Mirror* went with "King Cole Maps Fight to Keep Home." The *Los Angeles Times* reported: "Cole said his attorney had offered to pay approximately one-third of the sum last Friday to gain time to obtain the remainder of the taxes due. The offer was refused." Riddell kept telling the press that the seizure had nothing to do with the neighbors' efforts to force Cole out of Hancock Park, but somehow the denial rang hollow. Riddell and his chief counsel, Eugene Harpole, agent Vernon Spaulding, and others at Internal Revenue involved in posting the distraint warrants on the Coles' lawn were soon feeling the heat of public opinion.

At last the tax collector caved in, agreeing to a plan that would permit the Coles to keep their house and other belongings. But it was not easy. Maria recalls "a cash payment of $50,000 was to be made to the government immediately." Nat did not have it. He felt an ache in the pit of his stomach. Since November he had not had enough money to pay Nadine her $200 a week alimony, and in March he was ordered to appear in court to answer her complaint. Nadine would have to get in line behind the tax man.

In 1951 Nat had a lot of friends. He had probably given away more money than many people make in a lifetime. And who do you think he called on to help him out of this jam? Aunt Lottie, Dr. Charlotte Hawkins Brown of North Carolina, the matron who went to his wedding under protest, gave the reception for him in Sedalia and then vanished, and had sued him and Maria for custody of Carol Lane. Maria called Aunt Lottie on the telephone and told her what the government had done. And Aunt Lottie wired Nat $20,000 immediately. That woman lived in the moment.

So they had a big chunk of the money. Gastel went to work on Glen Wallichs, Capitol Records president, to get the remaining $30,000. It was not difficult for Gastel to convince Wallichs the singer was worth it — Nat was grossing two million a year for the company. His contract was to expire at the end of 1951, so Carlos was able to negotiate from a position of strength. Wallichs was prepared to give Cole whatever he needed so as not to lose him. Capitol's president even accompanied Nat on a visit to the tax man. Though Wallichs told reporters then he would not make payments himself, he said on March 27, "The company is prepared to make a substantial payment of advance royalties to Cole." They would have been fools to do otherwise.

Under a new contract Capitol Records guaranteed advances to Cole of $120,000 over a four-year period, starting immediately. Cole, in turn, pledged to give that money to the government. As a safeguard for Capitol, any royalties Cole earned over his advance would be held in a deferred payment account. Nat could not have the money, and neither could the tax man, until Wallichs felt like handing it over. Nat and Carlos understood this, and so did Harold Plant, but the government did not.

On March 29, the *Los Angeles Examiner* reported that "after a 3½ hour conference with Cole, Collector of Internal Revenue Robert Riddell announced that the ivy-covered mansion at 401 South Muirfield Road is now released to the singer." Riddell said, "Cole made a cash payment in amount equal to what government appraisers determined could have been obtained through sale of his house . . . the balance [of his debt] will be paid over a period of time satisfactory to this office." Riddell "emphasized" for reporters that technically the "lien still is in effect and will remain so until Cole's taxes are paid in full." The tax man wanted the world to know that Nat King Cole still belonged to him.

"The sheriff is at the cash register," Nat told Duke Niles, a song plugger, "and if I don't get a hit soon, I don't know what I'll do." These were hard times for Cole, who had to change his lifestyle. For a while Maria put her husband on a weekly $200 allowance.

"I have no intention of being poor when we are old," she told him. "I don't want to look at anybody in our September years and envy them because they're living like I used to."

The love ballad "Too Young" hit the top of the charts a month later, the answer to a prayer. Nat kept working constantly that spring and summer — at the Tiffany Club in L.A., at Top's nightclub in San Diego — while Gastel negotiated with the Gale Agency to put together a big cross-country touring show with Cole, Duke Ellington, and Sarah Vaughan.

The King Cole Trio would not be featured, as such, in the forthcoming tour. The tax troubles of their leader had increased the tensions that had been growing in the Trio. The sidemen have bitter memories. Joe Comfort recalled, "Maria said to Nat right in front of us, 'You're paying them too much. Stan Kenton's men don't get that much money. You're the star.'" Costanzo had been earning $12,000 a year, Ashby and Comfort $15,000. Nat cut their salaries in half. Ashby remembers they were performing at Lake Tahoe when Nat broke the news to them. He had discovered roulette as a recreation that went well with a few drinks after work. Ashby remembers, "I'm watching him gamble . . . ten thousand dollars, fifteen thousand dollars a night — just having fun. He had a hell of a nerve to come out of the casino and call a meeting of the guys in the group and confront us with the fact that he's going to have to cut our salaries because of taxes." If this is to be believed, Nat had fallen into an old trap set for casino performers: he was taking his salary in gambling chips, and would go home with no more money than he had when he arrived.

In early June, *Billboard* published rumors that Cole was breaking up the Trio. On August 24, that magazine reported that "Cole will receive sole billing . . ." Bassist Comfort went on to do studio work with Nelson Riddle. Ashby, after driving a taxi for a while, worked with Oscar Peterson. Jack Costanzo stayed on long enough to wince at Leonard Feather's review of the group at L.A.'s Tiffany Club, published in February 1952, after guitarist John Collins and bassist Charlie Harris had come aboard.

"King Cole Trio isn't dead," wrote Feather, but "we'd prefer to forget that Jack Costanzo was there. On many items he seemed entirely superfluous and enough aware of it to keep pretty much in the background." Costanzo left to start his own group. But he remained on excellent terms with Cole, and continued to work for him freelance long afterward.

Guitarist Ashby, in an interview with *Down Beat*, remarked that "anyone who put in a year of study could play all the guitar Nat needs for the kind of music he's playing nowadays." Yet Cole hired two excellent musicians to take over the guitar and bass, men who could jam richly with the pianist when he asked. They would, at least once, contribute to a superb jazz album with Nat, the famous *After Midnight* sessions done in 1956.

Portly little John Collins was born in Cole's native city, Montgomery, in 1913. Originally a clarinetist, Collins moved to Chicago in the 1920s and by 1935 he was strumming guitar at the Three Deuces with Art Tatum. Collins joined trumpeter Roy Eldridge in 1936 and later worked with bandleaders Lester Young, Fletcher Henderson, and Benny Carter. The guitarist was playing with

Tatum again in August 1951 when Cole invited him to replace Ashby; Collins first played with the Trio at the Tiffany on September 5. For a few nights before Collins took over, Nat's original guitarist, the great Oscar Moore, joined them at the Tiffany, showing there were no more hard feelings between them. Each night an ailing Art Tatum would come to the club to hear Nat, and later they would jam if Tatum was up to it.

Charlie Harris, tall, elegantly slender, with his thin mustache and chiseled features, became the group's new "heartthrob," though he was also a devoted family man. Like Nat's other bassists, Baltimorean Harris came from Lionel Hampton's band. By now Hamp had made a joke of it — no sooner would he break in a bass fiddler than Nat would come and steal him away.

A raft of publicity generated by Cole's p.r. staff in the summer of 1951 was rehabilitating his image in time for the autumn tour with Ellington and Vaughan, to be called "The Biggest Show of 1951." Articles in *The Capitol News*, *Down Beat*, and *Time* magazine praised Cole's piano technique, his charm, versatility and endurance, as if his recent tax troubles and cynical career reflections might have called these into question. "You've got to change with the public's taste," he told *Time*. "Currently," the magazine reported, "the public's taste for a schmalzy ballad called 'Too Young' has put Crooner Cole's recording at the top of the bestselling heap." It tells the tale of young lovers who yearn to show a skeptical world that their devotion is real.

In this interview he comments perceptively on his style, explaining that "Too Young" is a success because he sings words rather than notes. "I'm an interpreter of stories. When I perform it's like I'm just sitting down at my piano and telling fairy stories." When another journalist asked him how he explained his success, he smiled and said, "Well, I guess I just get to the heart of people's feelings, that's all."

And when the reporter mentioned certain jazz critics who deplored his switch to commercial singing, Nat quipped: "Critics don't buy records — they get 'em free."

The First Trio: Oscar Moore, Nat King Cole, and Wesley Prince, 1938 (USC LIBRARY, COLE COLLECTION)

Nat King Cole,
publicity photo,
early 1940s

Nat King Cole in his dressing room, 1948
(USC LIBRARY, COLE COLLECTION)

Nat and Maria Cole in the backyard of their home in Hancock Park, Los Angeles, 1950
(ROBERT PERKINS, USC LIBRARY,

ABOVE: *The house in Hancock Park, undated*

BELOW: *Nat King Cole and Frank Sinatra,*
circa 1953
(USC LIBRARY, COLE COLLECTION)

Nat, Natalie, Louis Armstrong, Carlos Gastel, and Ella Fitzgerald in a Capitol Records studio, August 1955

(USC LIBRARY, COLE COLLECTION)

Maria, Natalie, Carol, and Nat, 1952
(USC LIBRARY, COLE COLLECTION)

This Is Your Life, *January 1960. From left to right, first row: emcee Ralph Edwards (with book), Glenn Wallichs, Nat, Maria, Natalie; second row: Oscar Moore, Reverend Edward Coles, Evelyn Coles, Eddie Cole, Carol Cole, Carlos Gastel; third row: Andrew Gardner, Henry Fort, Russell Shore, unidentified*
(NBC PHOTO BY PAUL BAILEY, COURTESY OF NBC)

Nat King Cole and Willie Mays, Los Angeles, 1961
(PHOTO BY GARRET-HOWARD, INC.
COURTESY OF USC LIBRARY,
COLE COLLECTION)

Nat King Cole, Ivan Mogull, and Vic Damone, Las Vegas, 1963
(COURTESY OF
IVAN MOGULL)

*Dick LaPalm and
Nat King Cole,
Chicago, undated*
(COURTESY OF
DICK LAPALM)

Nat King Cole winking at the piano

THE BIG SHOW

King Cole, Duke Ellington, Sarah Vaughan, Timmie Rogers, Peg Leg Bates, and the comedy hoofers Stump and Stumpy went on the road in September of 1951. Maria stayed home with the children.

Duke's band had fallen into a slump, partly due to the loss of Sonny Greer, Lawrence Brown, and Johnny Hodges. But Ellington was still a legend, a boyhood idol to Cole. As for twenty-seven-year-old Sarah Vaughan, her throaty voice was just acquiring the range of tone and authority that would put her in a class with Billie Holiday and Ella Fitzgerald.

Their show opened at Carnegie Hall on September 28 to sellout crowds. "Although the hepcats were out in force, this show bore no resemblance to any of the jazz sessions that have been housed in this auditorium in recent years," *Variety* reported. With its black hoofers and comedians as interludes to Ellington, Cole, and Vaughan, the show looked more like the vaudeville sessions at the old Harlem Apollo than a "longhair" jazz recital.

Duke was a suave emcee, a storyteller with flawless timing who wove the variety of acts into a seamless fabric of entertainment. He kicked it off with brassy housewarming numbers, "The Hawk Talks" and "Threesome," each showcasing the

365

solo skills of his various sidemen. After Duke played a few more tunes, he introduced grinning Timmie Rogers in his tuxedo, who, *Variety* noted, "scored solidly with his patter of gags," comic monologues, and satirical songs. After Rogers came the fresh-faced Vaughan, everybody's sweetheart, dressed like a valentine in a red-and-pink gown.

Stump and Stumpy, the dancer-comedians, warmed up the audience for the second act. Then out came Peg Leg Bates, the remarkable one-legged dancer, who pounded the stage, followed by the tonnage of Patterson and Jackson, tap-dancing, and tossing each other about.

Then came Nat King Cole and his Trio to close the show with "Route 66," "Straighten Up and Fly Right," "Too Young," and other hits. "Cole worked effortlessly," wrote the *Variety* reviewer, "exploiting his low-key voice with fine shadings . . . Unlike Miss Vaughan, however, Cole is less effective in larger halls, where he does not project with the intimacy he achieves on wax." English reviewers had made the same observation. He was not a born song belter like Bessie Smith. Like Holiday and Sinatra, Cole was a creature of the microphone. Nat's goal now was to overcome this limitation, by art if not by nature, and in the next few years he would.

The Big Show rolled on to Troy, New York, on October 2, then Worcester, Providence, and Boston on the way to a seventy-seven-day tour through the South and the Midwest.

Accommodations in the South were not much better for the black musicians than in 1949. Dick

LaPalm recalls a bizarre twist in the segregation theme that developed in Mississippi. They arrived in Biloxi and everybody checked into rooms at the hotel.

Early in the morning LaPalm's phone rang. "Is this Dick LaPalm? We'd like to talk to you," said the caller in a deep Southern drawl. The publicist figured the caller wanted an interview, but it was too early, so LaPalm told him so.

"No," said the voice. "We *have* to talk to you." LaPalm hung up on him. Two minutes later he heard a loud knocking. He jumped out of bed and looked at the door.

"Yes?" he said. "Can I help you?"

"Sir, we are with the White Citizens Council. You are in a black hotel. You've got to check out."

LaPalm explained that he would be checking out in the afternoon; his company was going to do their performance at the Keesler Air Force Base and then they would all be on their way.

"No, sir. You got to check out *right now*. Please open the door."

The white publicist opened the door, still dressed in his pajamas.

One man said, "We're sorry to have to do this but we have to take you out of this hotel. Got to check you out." Another man grabbed LaPalm's Val-pack, placed it on the unused twin bed, and started stuffing the publicist's clothing into it.

Walking in front of and behind LaPalm down the stairway, they reached the lobby. Several sleepy employees, the bellman, the cashier, and others, were standing and lounging around. And LaPalm started spinning around among them exclaiming, "It *is* a black hotel!" as if this were a wonder. "Look, everybody's black! They're all black!" The humorless White Councilmen guided the crazy man to the cashier, where he received his bill of $22. LaPalm handed the bill to one of his kidnappers. "Here. This was your idea. You can pay it." Without batting an eye the man put his hand in his pocket and paid the cashier. Then they led the prisoner to an old Plymouth parked outside.

They dropped LaPalm off at a white hotel. From his new room he telephoned Cole, who told LaPalm to come right over and have some breakfast.

"Well," said LaPalm, "it's not a matter of coming right over." When Nat asked why this was, LaPalm explained he was at a different hotel.

"All right, Dick!" said the boss, assuming an amorous conquest, and happy for the young man. "You scored! And so quick!"

"No," replied LaPalm. "No, not exactly."

"Well, what? Come on, man," Cole said, tenderly. "You can *tell* Nat . . . tell Nat." But LaPalm was speechless. Exasperated, Cole asked, "Well what the hell are you doing there?"

LaPalm said he would be right back. He took a taxi to Nat's hotel. He knocked on his door.

Nat was grinning, still assuming his friend had gotten lucky in love but was too shy to talk about it. "How was it?"

"Not too good," said LaPalm sadly.

"What do you mean not too good?" asked Cole, wrinkling his brow.

So LaPalm told him the whole story. Nat's eyes

widened in amazement as he realized how wrong he had been, and then he laughed. Cole laughed louder and louder until his whole body shook and there were tears in his eyes and LaPalm realized that he was not really laughing anymore but venting a deep rage that lay far beneath the black man's sense of humor.

"Well, shit," said Cole, sighing, drying his eyes, looking around him at the cheap furniture and the ceiling, and finally resting his wide-set eyes on his friend. "Don't tell anybody. Let me handle it." Cole understood how complicated it would be if certain members of the troupe got angry.

But by the time they got downstairs to the coffee shop everybody was talking about it. Ray Nance approached them, and then Duke Ellington. Duke was in a towering rage. He made LaPalm tell him the whole story.

Duke did not think it was at all funny. "Here we are, come all the way to Biloxi, Mississippi, to play Keesler Field, an American air force base, for God's sake, a *big* air force base! And what do they do? They come and take your guy," he said to Nat, "check him out of our hotel, and you don't think we should . . ." Duke was threatening to check out of Biloxi without performing, and letting the newspapers explain it.

LaPalm pleaded with the furious bandleader. "Duke, please, we gotta play this concert. These soldiers have been waiting for a month. We've got to do it." He felt like it was all his fault.

He could see Duke's fury was ebbing, he was listening carefully. But then the white man went too far. "Please, Duke," he said, "it happened to *me*."

Now this comment, made in all innocence, sent the bandleader into a new fit. "I *know* it happened to *you*," growled Ellington, "but you're missing the whole point of this" — the point being only a moment away from the young man's dawning comprehension. A lifetime of living with such insults had taught the black musician that the abuse of one man involves the whole community. It was a greater insult to the blacks than to LaPalm.

At this moment Nat stepped between LaPalm and the Duke, whispering to the young man. "I'll handle this. You get out of here."

Cole calmed Ellington with the logic that it was wrong to make thousands of innocent soldiers pay for the bigotry of a few idiots, and the show went on.

And then there was the time LaPalm and Sparky and Nat were sitting in the coffee shop of the Grayson Hotel in Indianapolis. LaPalm remembers: "It was late, we had stopped somewhere on our way back from our show at the State Fair. We're sitting there talking business when a guy walks in off the street, a stranger. And I lean over to Nat and say, 'Here comes Remember me?' Nat and I had this joke — I'd identify these guys who would say, *'Remember me?'* Sure enough, this guy comes up and says, 'Hi, Nat, remember me?'

"Well, the guy sat down. He told Nat how much he loved him and his music, and all these things . . ."

Some people behave curiously in the presence of a celebrity. Press agent Ben Irwin once observed that Cole "came with a strange kind of built-in dignity. He was never rude or sharp with people . . . a drunk would come up and say, 'Hey, Nat baby, you were hot tonight, kid!' And Nat would say very coldly, 'Thank you,' and stare at the guy for twenty seconds until the drunk would almost wither up and apologize and back away."

But the stranger in the Grayson coffee shop did not get the message. He was big and scary-looking. At length he put his hand in his pocket and gave Cole a scrap of paper; the singer signed his autograph, but the man stayed put.

Finally LaPalm said, "Look, no one invited you. We're talking some business here, so I'm going to have to ask you to leave."

Furious, the man got up and walked out. LaPalm paid the check while Sparky and Nat went out through the door to the hotel lobby. LaPalm recalls: "As I'm paying the check I can see through the window the stranger is going around and entering the hotel lobby through the main entrance. Just as I come into the lobby from the shop, this goon steps right in front of me, and he's got his hand in his pocket like this [a bulge in his coat pocket as if a pistol were there] and he says, 'You motherfucker. I'm gonna kill you.' And I looked at his pocket, and it looked to me like metal.

"Again the guy says, 'I'm gonna kill you.' And I said, 'Now just a minute.'

"Nat's at the desk checking messages. I don't know why, but suddenly Nat turns, sees the guy in front of me — he knows something's going on and he's across the lobby in a wink and puts himself right between me and this guy. He says to him, 'Look, Dick was doing his job, we were talking business, don't be fed up.' "

And something about Cole's voice, his presence, calmed the man. He turned away and walked out of the hotel.

"It's one of the most wonderful things anyone's ever done for me," LaPalm recalls, his eyes welling up with emotion.

On November 15 in Detroit, Nat, Duke, and Sarah slipped into a studio to record "I Love You Madly," Duke leading the band as Nat and Sarah sang their duet.

"Hi, Sweetheart," he wrote to Maria from St. Louis a few days later. "I sure will be glad to get home because I miss you and the kids like mad. I really enjoyed talking to you last night because you sounded a lot happier. I guess so, because you found someone to relieve you of the pressure . . . [Maria had been short of help.] Take care of yourself and kiss the kids for me. I love you. Nat. P.S. Forgive the pencil. I don't have a pen."

He was exhausted after the seventy-seven-night tour (mostly one-night stands) ended on December 5, and looked forward to a much-needed Christmas vacation. Now his stomach hurt him no matter what he ate. He smoked with such ferocity he burned his fingers. In 1952 Liggett and Myers publicized Arthur Little's test results showing that "smoking Chesterfields would have no adverse effects on the throat, sinuses or affected organs." Viewing the ads on Arthur Godfrey's TV show, Nat cheered for his unfiltered brand. He could have told them. The more he smoked, the better he sang. He celebrated by sending Sparky out for a dozen cartons.

The tour had been successful in every way, and the popularity of "Too Young," and "Unforgettable," recorded August 17 before he left, would help to pay his debt to the tax man. "Unforgettable" remained high on the charts for fifteen weeks that winter, and "Too Young" was the number one song of 1951, on the radio, on jukeboxes, and in record shops.

He relaxed by doing solo and trio work in nightclubs. In February, *Down Beat*'s Leonard Feather described Nat's show at the Tiffany. "The scene was an intimate L.A. bar . . . Perhaps because he has a home in L.A. and regarded this as a semi-vacation . . . Nat was his old wonderful self here. Nat is still one of the great pianists of jazz . . ." And Henry Whiston of *The Melody Maker*, recalling the performer's state of mind in the autumn, wrote: "Nat was pretty tired at that time and I began to wonder whether the traveling was catching up with him and he was feeling the loss of sleep. This month, however, he was in much better spirits."

The traveling *was* catching up with Nathaniel, yet no sooner did he feel "his old wonderful self" than he was on the train again. The Biggest Show of 1952 hit the road in April with different personnel: Frankie Laine, Patti Page, Billy May's orchestra, Illinois Jacquet, the Chocolateers vocal group, dancers, and comedians. Sparky and Maria went too. So did Timmie Rogers.

"How you doing, man?" Cole asked Rogers. The comic had been a smash during the first tour with Ellington. Timmie was the first black comedian to face the audience in a tuxedo. Nat loved him. Timmie told his friend he was doing all right. They were both clients of GAC. When Cole found out Rogers had been making only $500 a week during the first Big Show, he put pressure on GAC to double his salary for the second tour.

Home again in the early summer, Nat decided to cut down on his work schedule and spend more time with his family. Plans for the coming autumn included a "Fall Edition" of the Biggest Show, this time with Sarah Vaughan and Stan Kenton — eight weeks starting September 19 in Syracuse, seven evening performances and four matinees per week. But first Nat would make the most of his time at home, putting golf balls in the yard, playing with the kids and dogs, and entertaining the family.

Dr. Charlotte Hawkins Brown came to visit, and on July 17, 1952, the Coles hosted a formal luncheon for her, which was mentioned on the society pages. She had come to see the new baby and her darling Carol, and to take the eight-year-old girl back with her to Sedalia for a nice long stay, so that the child might have a taste of Palmer Institute civility.

That summer Nathaniel's parents came to stay with them, to see the new house and the two-year-old Natalie.

Nat wanted to breed Mr. Pep, so one day he asked his silver-haired father if he would like to go along for a drive to the farm where the boxer was to go a-courting. Nat and the Reverend got into the Cadillac with Mr. Pep in the back seat, and they drove away, leaving Maria with Perlina Coles.

"It was such a pleasure to have her," Maria recalls. "She was just a wonderful human being, funny like Nat, with that dry sense of humor." They sat in the colonnaded patio in back of the house, relaxing on green-upholstered white iron lounges, looking out through the tall brick arches onto the bright lawn and rose bushes. Maria was worried about her mother-in-law's health, especially the unsightly knot on her neck. She asked her, "Mom, what is that? Why don't you go to the doctor?"

"Oh, it's nothing," the older woman responded, wishing to change the subject, "a big mole or something."

"I am such a perfectionist," Maria says, "to a fault. None of us knew anything about cancer in those days. I just did not like the look of it."

When the men returned from their adventure, Nat was laughing on the verge of hysterics, laughing so hard you couldn't see his eyes and he could scarcely smoke his cigarette. Mr. Pep was skulking around Reverend Coles and looking guilty, as the Reverend disdainfully eyed the boxer.

"Skeez!" Nat cried to his wife, catching his breath. "You should have been there, you should have — "

"Man, I don't want to see any more dogs," said Maria.

"Well, *Dad* sure did! Mr. Pep, he didn't seem to know one end of the bitch from the other, so Dad meant to coach him. 'Go on, now, Mr. Pep,' he told him. 'Go on ahead, get up there and do what you supposed to do.' And Mr. Pep stalled and fooled around, and the more he stalled, the more

Dad egged him on. 'Go on, get up there! You know how to do it!'"

And Nat laughed in that way he did when something really struck him funny, his eyes narrowing, his whole body shaking at the thought of his straitlaced father cheering the sexual congress of the boxers. It was a great moment for father and son, a stepping-stone to friendship. And Mr. Pep did them proud. His offspring became Carol's dog, Princess. "They were two peas in a pod," says Natalie, laughing, "both of them wild."

His father was mellowing. A few months later the National University of Music in Chicago, a nonprofit music school, invited Nat to give a talk and receive a special citation "for his contribution to vocal music and by a scholarship named in his honor." Duke Ellington financed the scholarship. Nat happened to be in his hometown at the time, playing a week at the Chicago Theater after the autumn conclusion of the Biggest Show.

But the greatest honor of all that day came out of the blue. "In a surprise move arranged by the president of the school," the ANP reported, "the Reverend Edward James Coles presented the citation to the son."

"May God ever bless you, son," said the Reverend.

And Nathaniel responded. "I am glad to be home."

Charlie Harris, Cole's bass player, noticed the boss was losing weight. Nobody with a schedule like Nat Cole's could keep it going for long.

"The wear and tear on Negro entertainers with

these one-night stands," said the great gospel singer Mahalia Jackson, frowning and shaking her head sadly, "is unbelievable. Nat, all of us, has to hit places at night, fly by air, take his life in his hands . . . They simply do not have time to have themselves checked out medically . . . I know Nat must have kept going when he shouldn't."

Cole decided to develop his skills as an actor. Late in 1952 he tried to ease his touring schedule, putting out the word that he was available for more movie work. His appearances on TV with Ed Sullivan and Steve Allen had proved him to be a warm presence on the screen, photogenic and appealing. The *Los Angeles Examiner* reported on December 11 that Cole would receive $10,000 for a day's work in *Blue Gardenia* with Anne Baxter and Ann Sothern. Then he "jumped at a bid from the *Lux Video Theatre*" to co-star with Dick Haymes and Nancy Guild in a CBS television drama called "Song for a Banjo." Nat plays a pianist jailed for scrapping with his bandleader; learning that a fellow prisoner has been falsely accused, the pianist helps him to clear his name. For a week in Manhattan before Christmas, Cole attended five-hour rehearsals, eager to learn the technique of playacting. And he turned in a decent performance in a fairly easy role.

At night he was packing them in at La Vie en Rose nightclub, earning a salary of $7,500 a week. That made for a full day when you consider the TV appearances. "He almost needed roller skates to fill TV guest spot requests," reported *Our World* magazine. "So why not a program of his own? Good question, eh? It's being worked on now." This was in the early months of 1953. Carlos Gastel was trying to position his client so that he could make more money with fewer weeks of work. Soon Nat accepted a small role in the Jane Powell film *Small Town Girl*.

But for now, the winter of 1952–53, with the tax man still looking over his shoulder, Nat would have to stay on the nightclub and theater circuit to pay everybody's bills. The artist was on a treadmill, getting no creative time to himself. In January, Gastel booked Nat and the Trio into the Cal-Neva Lodge in Tahoe for three weeks, after failing to get his price at the El Rancho. Nat had a love-hate relationship with the city in the desert, the scene of so many triumphs, pleasures, and sorrows in his short life. It was Nat who broke the color line in Vegas after a series of offenses and indignities. Negotiating with Beldon Katleman, owner of the El Rancho Vegas in the early fifties, Gastel stipulated: "Nat and the boys can live, eat, gamble, drink, or whatever they want to do on the premises without any prejudice shown against them whatsoever."

But in that Mob-influenced town some bizarre rules could be invoked to keep the black performers in their place. In 1953 when Carlos asked for a big increase over the $4,500 a week the Trio had been getting, Katleman refused. He reminded him of "an agreement among the Las Vegas hotel owners that an entertainer couldn't play another place within a year after an engagement, and no owner could solicit an act within that time." So it was El Rancho or nothing. That is why Nat had gone up to Tahoe.

Jack Entratter had just come out to take over the Sands Hotel in Las Vegas. He was a sharp operator who had run the Copa in New York, and Carlos had known him well there. Entratter made his own rules. When Carlos explained what had happened, Jack told him, "Look, I came out here to get this place moving . . . I don't care about any Boy Scout rules they've got here." He made an offer, Carlos and Cole accepted it, and according to Maria: "That was the beginning of a lifelong deal between Nat and the Sands," though he would appear briefly at El Rancho once more in January of 1954.

Even after 1954 there were problems in Las Vegas. Charlie Harris remembers the time the stage manager at the Sands came running from the dining room, whining to Cole.

"Nat," said the nervous stage manager, "Charlie is in the dining room!" Cole's sidemen had been barred from the Sands dining room by the maître d' after the hotel had promised the musicians could sign for meals there and get a discount. But Harris was so light-skinned that the maître d' was not sure he was a black man, so Harris sat down and ordered a meal.

"Oh?" Nat replied, feigning astonishment. "Is he climbing any poles? Throwing food? Doing anything unusual?"

"He's eating, Nat."

"Get Jack Entratter on the phone," Nat told Sparky. Nat was lacing on a bow tie, a ritual he performed with great exactness, tying and untying it until it was perfect. A few people were standing around watching, looking at him in the lighted mirror. The stage manager, unaware of Nat's agreement with the Sands, tried to explain the difficulties involved in serving food to black persons in the hotel dining room.

"If you don't get Jack Entratter in five minutes," Cole thundered, "I'm packing up and getting the hell out of here."

There was a swift and orderly clearing of the room. In a few minutes Entratter arrived and asked what the trouble was.

"What about my fellows eating downstairs?" Cole demanded. The manager reassured him that they could. "Well then, call those bastards down there" — he pointed, jabbing his forefinger — "and tell *them*."

That was the end of the problem at the Sands. Entratter's hotel became an oasis of sanity in a desert of prejudice. Though Nat, personally, was welcome to go where he liked, to eat, drink, or gamble wherever he pleased, he made it a policy never to go where his friends were not as welcome as he.

Nat was pleased whenever Maria and the girls could travel with him, which they did in the summer, and during breaks in the school year. The Cal-Neva Lodge in Tahoe, Nevada, in January 1953, was where Nat was so distracted he lost three-year-old Natalie. He was rehearsing in the huge ballroom when Maria dropped the girls off to stay with him while she went shopping. He looked up from the piano, smiled, and said that was just fine. His stomach was hurting like crazy.

In a couple of hours Maria returned, laden with

shopping bags. She asked where the children were. Nat paused in his playing, and waved vaguely toward the back of the room. Maria could not find them there. None of the crew had noticed Cookie and Sweetie for a while. In a few minutes someone spotted eight-year-old Cookie outside, and she told Maria that Natalie was around somewhere, but they could not find her. The band stopped rehearsing, and the musicians set out over the landscape in search of Natalie Cole. Maria gazed at the great mounds of sand and soil that were being moved around to construct the resort town, terrified to think her child might be buried under one of them, or fallen into the lake. None of the construction workers had seen her.

Maria was furious with her husband. "You're a father and you can't even watch your children!" she yelled. But she could not make him feel worse than he felt already. They called the sheriff. He arrived with his posse, and the entire staff of the Cal-Neva fanned out across the countryside, all looking for the future star of records and screen.

Four hours later the hotel got a call from a woman who said, "I think I have Nat King Cole's little girl here at my house." There were not many black children abroad in western Nevada in 1953, so the woman had made a good calculated guess. It seems that Natalie had climbed on a tram near the hotel and gotten off with the mother and her little daughter, with whom she had struck up a friendship along the way. Natalie enjoyed a happy afternoon playing with her new friend, while the white child's mother puzzled over the foundling's origins and proper home. Now Sweetie was worn out from the day's adventures and fast asleep. The next time the Coles went on the road the children would stay home with their Aunt Charlotte.

Nat and Maria flew to Boston in March, as the Big Show of 1953 opened there, and swung through Springfield and Providence on the way to a highly publicized engagement at Carnegie Hall. Sarah Vaughan was back. Under the baton of the swinging bandleader Billy May, the troupe was booked to play dozens of cities before the summer break.

When the Coles arrived with the Big Show in New York City on April 3, Nat, from his suite at the Warwick Hotel, telephoned Ivan Mogull. Nat sounded uneasy, as Mogull recalls. Ivan had been looking forward to seeing his friend and he wanted to take the Coles out to dinner to celebrate their fifth anniversary, better late than never. Nat told Ivan to come right over, but the song plugger was working. Nat said he was doing Perry Como's television show the next day and asked his friend to go along, but Ivan's schedule would not permit it. He told Nat he would watch him on TV, and they would meet as soon as they could.

"I watched the show, and he looked white. There was no color television in those days. He was an ash-gray color," Mogull recalls.

From his office he called Cole, concerned. This was no time for a dinner party. Ivan said, "I'm gonna go home. You rest, and I'll see you tomorrow." The young man was depressed. He had just broken up with a girl, he had been looking forward to Cole's visit, but between his work schedule and

Nat's fatigue, they had not yet seen each other.

Leaving the TV studio and walking up Sixth Avenue at twilight, Nat suddenly felt very tired. He leaned on little Sparky Tavares, telling the valet he felt dizzy. That afternoon at a rehearsal break he had thrown up blood in the men's room. They walked a block, and at the corner he told Sparky his stomach was killing him.

Rain was beginning to fall. Sparky stepped to the curb to hail a taxi and soon one pulled over. Sparky opened the door. When the driver got a good look at Sparky's complexion he announced that he was "Off Duty." Sparky quickly explained that the man on the sidewalk was ill, but the cabbie reiterated, with vulgar emphasis, that he was "Off Duty."

Bessie Smith had died of such foolishness. Sparky grabbed Cole by the shoulders and shoved him into the cab first, climbed in behind the tall singer, and slammed the door. "I don't give a goddamn . . . I've got a sick man here," said the valet, and he ordered the driver to take them to the Warwick Hotel.

Looking in his rearview mirror, the disgruntled cabdriver suddenly recognized his famous passenger, squealed, and began to gush. "Oh! Nat King Cole!" said the cabbie, thrilled, forgetting the celebrity was African-American. "My family has *all* your records!"

By the time they arrived at the hotel Nat's pain had subsided. They decided to say nothing to Maria about it, and to hope with a good night's rest Nat would feel better in the morning. But the illness never left him altogether; it was a dull nagging pain when it was not like a knife turning in his abdomen. And he was afraid to move his bowels because of the blood that came then.

Ivan Mogull lived uptown in a flat on Central Park West. On Easter Sunday, he had the blues because it was all over with his girlfriend. So he went to visit his sister, who lived next door, and see his niece. Then he took his dog for a walk across Central Park in the spring light. Ivan had an English bulldog, the first of many he would own. In the green park he saw a blind boy who approached the bulldog, and the dog was gentle, so Ivan encouraged the child to feel the shape of the bulldog and pet him.

"I got so depressed over that kid with the dog," he remembers.

As he dressed that evening for the concert at Carnegie Hall, he was thinking about Nat Cole and how white he looked on the television. Ivan had a date with singer Georgia Gibbs that night. He told her he would pick her up at seven-thirty. First he wanted to stop by the Warwick and check up on his friend.

Ivan arrived at the Coles' suite around dinnertime. Nat answered the doorbell. "He looked horrible. He looked like he did on TV," Ivan recalls.

"Are you all right?" Ivan asked. Nat told him he was not all right, he was sick. Ivan asked him what was the matter with him.

"I don't know. I don't feel good, and I'm wheezing," Cole said, lighting a cigarette. Carlos, alarmed how much his client smoked, had given him a filtered holder, which he now used to elegant effect, smoking more than ever.

"I thought you had makeup on last night. You looked like you look now — ash color."

Nat admitted he did not feel good. But when Ivan said he was going to call his doctor and went to the phone, Nat stopped him. "No, no, no," he said, like a child who will not listen to reason.

"Nat," said Ivan firmly. "You don't feel good. You look lousy. You're doing a concert in a couple of hours at Carnegie Hall with Billy May. You've got shows at eight-thirty and midnight. You're going on a tour. Talk to a doctor."

"I'll wait. I'll do the show tonight," Cole bargained. "Monday I'll be in Washington, D.C., and I'll go see my doctor down there." Ivan looked at Maria, who threw up her hands, exasperated.

"Nat, do me a favor," Ivan began, drawing upon the sum of his emotions this sad Easter Day. "I'm depressed enough as it is. I just broke up with my girl. I went to see my sister and niece and that didn't help. I went for a walk in the park with my dog and this blind kid came up to us, and Nat it would break your heart to see how that blind kid petted the dog." Ivan began to cry. "Nat, I'm tortured like you would not fucking believe. Do me a favor! I'm going to call my doctor, talk to the doctor —"

Cole stood aside and let Mogull call his doctor, Jerry Lieberman, a childhood friend. Ivan explained to Jerry that the singer was ill and due at Carnegie Hall in an hour. He handed the phone to Nat. When Nat told the doctor he had blood in his stool and had been throwing up blood for days, Lieberman said this did not sound good. He said he would meet Cole backstage as soon as he could get there.

Evidently the physician did not get to Cole before eight-thirty that evening, because Nat King Cole, looking like the ghost of Christmas past, performed the first of the two shows at Carnegie Hall. He smiled and sang as sweetly as ever. When Dr. Lieberman saw the singer sometime before midnight, blood was pouring from both ends of him. The doctor explained to Cole that he was gravely ill and in danger of bleeding to death. The showman still would not leave for the hospital before the midnight curtain. He insisted on telling the audience in person that the doctor had forbidden him to perform. Then he got into the ambulance, complaining all the way to the hospital that he had never been to a hospital before, saying this over and over, as if his lack of experience in going to hospitals ought to disqualify him.

"Sidelight of the unhappy affair," *Down Beat* reported, "was that Sarah Vaughan had to sing an extra set, and, her pianist having already left, she sat at the piano and accompanied herself, and went off to a great hand."

Cole had bleeding ulcers. Had he waited until Monday to see the doctor, he would have died. They took him to New York Hospital–Cornell Medical Center at 68th and York Avenue. He stayed there for three weeks while Maria consulted with various specialists on the best course of treatment. At last she and the doctors decided the safest thing would be to section the injured part of the stomach, leaving him with about half of it. Dr. Nelson Cornell performed the surgery on April 28. Nat was forbidden to smoke cigarettes until three months after his operation.

So there would not be any Big Show for Nat King Cole in 1953, no touring, no airplanes, buses, or one-night stands. He would finally get the kind of vacation and rest he had not enjoyed since March 1948.

Aunt Charlotte, the children's Baba, remembers how Maria brought him home wan and thin, walking in the door in his long overcoat. He had lost seventeen pounds. "Hello, dear," he said to her in his warm, musical voice. He always greeted her thus, after a long absence. It made her heart soar. The boxers leapt around him as he hugged his daughters. Sparky took the bags upstairs and Nat began wandering around the house.

This time he was home to stay for a long while. The best thing about it was that he finally got to know his daughters. Carol was eight, a student at the Third Street Elementary School nearby, the first black child to enroll there. Bright-eyed, chirpy Natalie was three and a half. The girls loved their father's music, especially the romantic "Red Sails in the Sunset," with its plaintive theme of love's departure and the promise of homecoming. They put on little shows for Dad and Mom, with Natalie singing and both girls doing a dance that Carol choreographed. Natalie was already singing beautifully, and Carol had been taking dancing lessons in Hollywood. They played to their parents' delight, and applause as loud as Nat could manage from his sickbed.

"The trouble with Sweetie is that she yawns

when she sings," Nat commented wryly a few months later. "But she's only four. Maybe she's developing her own style of scat."

While Cole stayed off the road, a steady stream of royalty monies, from "Pretend" with Nelson Riddle, "Red Sails in the Sunset," and "Walkin' My Baby Back Home," paid the bills. At home Nat found time to watch the TV, with the boxers at his side, and worry along with other live entertainers about the invasion of television. He and Carlos were heatedly discussing how Cole could work his way into the new medium after his three months of rest were up.

If there was any consideration of a return to touring it was dismissed on May 28 when Nat was rushed to Beverly Glen Hospital in Hollywood. That night he had turned green suddenly and could not keep anything on his tiny stomach. Carlos, Maria, and Charlotte took him to the hospital. "This time we really thought he was going to die," Maria recalled. And Charlotte remembers Nat in the hospital bed. "They had a tube everywhere they could get a tube."

At first the newspapers reported he was "suffering a relapse" from the ulcer condition. But soon his physician, Dr. David Daniels, announced that he had "an intestinal infection." Food poisoning. Maria remembers a friend had given them some game to eat, pigeons that had been frozen, thawed, and frozen again.

Carlos canceled a booking planned for June 5 at the Tiffany Club. But by late July, Cole was performing at the Hotel Del Mar. A reviewer from *Variety* warmly welcomed him back from death's door. "Serious illness affects people in different ways. With Cole the change apparently brought greater warmth, a feeling of starting anew with a fresh, more expansive outlook. It's a re-realized and sincere *joie de vivre*," the writer says of Nat's show, with the Trio plus Jack Costanzo.

Soon Nat would get the break he was hoping for in television: a fifteen-week contract to appear with comedians Sid Caesar and Imogene Coca on Caesar's weekly variety program, *Your Show of Shows*. So, that Thanksgiving week as he flew to New York to play at his old haunt La Vie en Rose, Cole found himself fighting on both sides of the new war between TV and live entertainment. The English magazine *The Melody Maker* observed:

> The bubble of nightlife had burst. Well-known night spots were closing down, old-established bars were on the real estate market, and not one movie theater on Broadway was employing a house orchestra. And in two million rooms from Brooklyn Bridge to Harlem, the missing club clientele sat in the darkness, hushed and tongue-tied, hypnotized by the evil eye that put the hex on New York's famed night life . . . television!

Some of the missing clientele were watching Nat King Cole on Sid Caesar's *Your Show of Shows*. Many others wanted to see the performer in the flesh. On East 54th Street, La Vie en Rose was vibrant with optimism. The red carpet was unrolled to the curb. Taxis were jammed bumper to bumper for blocks up Park Avenue. In spite of bad weather the crowd started lining up at six. By nine, the "House Full" sign swung from the foyer curtains.

"What is this, New Year's Eve?" asked one woman who had been waiting in line for an hour. The club had been redecorated. The white roses on the dove-gray walls of La Vie en Rose shone anew, as if television had been only a bad dream. But the enlarged club was still too small for the "devotees of the King of Lush Life." Martinis and whiskeys spun on trays from the bar, champagnes and sparkling burgundies, lit by the soft houselights, bubbled on the tables.

"Nat stays on for an hour and a quarter, though it seems far less. He is superbly and unobtrusively accompanied by John Collins, guitar, Charlie Harris, bass, and Lee Young, Lester's brother, on drums," wrote young Nat Hentoff in *Down Beat*. Cole had wisely asked Lee Young to join the ensemble, for his steadiness of character and for his impeccable drumming. In the decade to come, Lee would be indispensable to his old friend. Hentoff praises "the sureness of Lee's rhythmic sense. Nat plays less piano in the act than he used to . . . he stands up before the mike and, on a reminiscing medley ("Mona Lisa" and "Too Young"), steps down on the floor for dramatic contrast. As for his singing, Nat's sound, placement, diction, phrasing and beat are the best in contemporary pop or jazz," writes Hentoff.

Celebrities swelled the crowd, but a young man Hentoff recognized as a former singer with Tex Beneke's band intrigued the writer. The now-forgotten vocalist was struggling to make it on his own. "He was standing near the door with no chance of a table . . . He'd been standing all night to hear Nat," studying the great jazzman in amazement and joy and a little envy. And during the second show, the writer could hear the fellow murmuring to himself, as if he were a witness to a natural wonder like Niagara Falls.

"When will it stop? The music just keeps pouring out of him."

Ten days before Nat arrived in New York City, Frank Sinatra had slit his wrists with a razor blade. He was lying on the floor of an elevator in Jimmy Van Heusen's apartment building when his friend Van Heusen found him.

Sinatra had just split up with his second wife, Ava Gardner, the love of his life, and he was beside himself with grief. As soon as he got out of Mount Sinai Hospital, the William Morris Agency assigned Frank a bodyguard to keep him from slashing his wrists again, and the heartbroken crooner started singing torch songs in the Royal Casino.

Ivan Mogull recalls going with Nat Cole to see Sinatra at the Royal Casino. "Frank was down the tubes. His voice was gone, he was drinking, he broke up with Ava, and he was distraught. We felt bad for Frank because the guy could not sing, his voice was gone." Sinatra did not even have a recording contract.

As Sinatra sang "My One and Only Love" and "There Will Never Be Another You," they could hear the anguish. Maybe the Voice wasn't pretty anymore, but it was about to be reborn with wisdom gained through suffering. After the show Ivan and Nat went backstage. They took Sinatra out for a night of drinking and conversation. Frank was glad to see Nat, was inspired by his example, how the black singer had survived his own ordeals of romantic turmoil and illness.

Cole called Alan Livingston and Glen Wallichs at Capitol and told his producers, "The man hasn't done his best work yet. Sign him and let him work with Nelson Riddle." In 1953, Frank signed a contract with Capitol, Nat's company, and his career was reborn. Soon Cole and Sinatra became the first and second performers to record "concept" albums, LPs with a theme, more than just a collection of singles.

Toward the end of 1953, on December 17, Capitol Records chief Glen Wallichs hosted an industry-wide cocktail party to celebrate the ten-year mark in Nat Cole's association with the company. He had sold 15 million singles and 5 million albums, and every year the musician had scored with a chart-busting hit. His gross sales for Capitol averaged $2.5 million a year. Cole's share of it was $250,000 a year. The new Capitol offices, the Tower, on Vine Street Hill, looked like a colossal stack of records — they called it "the house that Nat built."

Cole was still paying off his debt to the government. In interviews during these years, Nat said that Maria took over the family finances then, as well as many responsibilities of road management. On tour, she collected the money and sent it to Harold Plant. She now recalls that she assumed these tasks reluctantly and out of necessity — it did not come naturally to her. "Nat never took over in anything but his music, didn't want to. I was always forced to be a survivor, all my life. Don't think it's always that I wanted to be. I loved being feminine, and . . . helpless," she recalls, sighing, "but I didn't get much of a chance. I loved my husband. I did what I had to do because I loved him."

The only song she takes credit for is "Walkin' My Baby Back Home," which she urged Nat to record in 1951 after hearing it on her aunt's player piano. But he credited Maria with his financial salvation. "I make no claim to being a business genius," he said in 1953. "You can make so much money in this business that it loses value. I learned the hard way. I had my little follies. I was conned out of a lot of the money and I gave a lot of it away. But when I got in that trouble, I got the message. All of us get the message sooner or later. If you get it before it's too late or before you're too old . . .

"Maria created order out of chaos, made me conscious of expenditures and the need for efficient accounting . . . she is the chief reason why Nat Cole is solvent today," he concluded.

The day after his thirty-fifth birthday, March 17, 1954, she gave a big party for him in New York City. It was a grand ball at the Savoy Ballroom to benefit the Harlem YMCA, where Maria had once worked as a bookkeeper, where Billy Strayhorn had gone to hire her for Duke's band. A photo in *Jet* magazine shows Maria and Nat grinning alongside Vice President Richard Nixon, who purchased the first ticket to King Cole's party.

TOGETHER AND APART

The Coles celebrated their sixth wedding anniversary in London, where they flew on Saturday, March 20, 1954. A crowd of fans met them at the airport. Nat's return to the Palladium was crucial; his premiere there had been a disaster. Though the run was sold out before it started on March 22, Maria and Nat got down on their knees and prayed together backstage at the Palladium before the curtain went up on opening night. That's just how important it was to them.

The reviews were glowing. "Since he was last here Nat King Cole has completely changed his vocal style, and has switched from the more advanced forms to the purely melodious, with the result that the diffident-mannered dusky vocalist makes a far greater and more pleasing impact upon his audience. There is a soothing quality about his singing, a relaxed air with no gimmicks attached, and only infrequent brief visits to the piano." This from *The Performer* is representative. Nat did employ a sight gag that got big laughs. He came downstage to the audience, mouthing words to a song no one could hear, then casually returned upstage to the microphone and drawled, "I just thought you all would like to hear what we modern singers sound like without the microphone!" The great Henny Youngman, violin-playing comedian, was on the bill with Nat in

London — nothing Youngman said got warmer laughs than Nat's wisecrack.

The show toured the British Isles, and played the Palais du Chaillot in Paris, establishing Nat's international reputation. In Paris the Coles joined up with Lena Horne and her husband, Lennie Hayton, to see the sights and the nightlife. The American press called the tour "a second honeymoon," photographing the Coles strolling the bridge under Big Ben, admiring Buckingham Palace guards, feeding pigeons in Trafalgar Square, petting a sheep in the famous Parisian restaurant Au Mouton de Panurge. But Nat still looked fatigued and frail in his tweed greatcoat, overwhelmed by the mobs of teenagers that pursued him for autographs.

During the 15,000-mile tour, he grossed an estimated $125,000. He was truly astonished by the adulation of the foreigners and exclaimed, "Sometimes I would ask myself: *Am I worth all this?*" When a reporter once asked him if he rehearsed in front of a mirror, Nat was appalled. "I can't bear to see myself even in movies. The feeling is complex. I can't stand the sight of myself."

But when he got over the shock of being mobbed by foreign admirers, Cole found that he actually rather liked it. "Women chased him," Maria recalls. He loved women but never had the confidence to pursue them. "Nat was not that kind of man — he never had that kind of security because as a child he was not handsome, not at all; all of his grooming and appeal came with the years."

Now at age thirty-five maybe it was his fame and

maybe it was a new depth of personality and vulnerability that made him ever more attractive to his female fans. They were mobbing him in far-flung airports, and this struck a pleasing chord in him while the girls' dazzled eyes and eager fingers chilled his wife. Maybe Cole's illness had made him accept life's pleasures wherever they lay. He would enjoy it much more when he could be mobbed without his wife around to run interference.

The opportunity came soon enough. Back from England, after a few easy months of nightclub work in Chicago, Hollywood, and New York at the top clubs — Chez Paris, Ciro's, and the Copa — Cole was booked on a tour of New Zealand and Australia from mid-January to mid-February 1955. In New York before his departure, Nat visited the ailing composer W. C. Handy in Sydenham Hospital. The Father of the Blues was suffering from hardening of the arteries.

The decision for Nat to go alone to the other side of the world was difficult and divisive. His illness had put a strain on the marriage. Nat was suffering from the proverbial "seven-year itch." Photographs from 1954 and 1955 suggest that the convalescing singer, who had narrowly escaped death, felt that his wife, who had helped save him, was now crowding him. He told a reporter in Sydney his wife had had to abandon her plan to come to Australia with him: "Right up to the last minute she tried to make it . . . she couldn't take the idea of leaving the children. I sure wish she could be here." But Maria Cole says she wanted desperately to go along to Australia. Nat gently dissuaded her. That was the only way he could do it, gently, but it still hurt her feelings. She was worried he would fool around. That is what many musicians do on the road, as Maria knew.

When the fault lines begin to show in a high-visibility marriage, one of the first signs of it is an ostentatious display of conjugal harmony in their magazine coverage. While Nat was in the Southern Hemisphere, *Hue* magazine praised his "scandal free life," the fact that "he and his wife are inseparable," and how "Cole has steered clear of the romantic notions of scheming, swooning females . . ."

The crowds that mobbed Nat King Cole in New Zealand and Australia were like nothing that would be seen until Elvis hysteria and Beatlemania. The news coverage in Auckland, New Zealand, is colorful and amusing.

> Five thousand fans packed Whenuapai airport last night to see the triumphant arrival of Negro pianist and singer Nat King Cole. Poor Nat. He wasn't quite sure what had hit him when he finally walked down the steps to the tarmac and over to the airport lounge. For a quarter of an hour he had not been able to get off the plane as near-hysterical women, some with children, rushed onto the tarmac and closed on the plane.
>
> They broke the inadequate cordon of police and screamed "We want Nat!"
>
> Welcomers climbed onto the roof of the airport, sat on men's shoulders, and scrambled onto the fire truck.

A shouted threat by officials of 150-pound fines caused the rioters to move back enough so that the passengers could leave the plane. Blond singer June Christy got off, and so did the sidemen and the road crew. At last the King appeared. Wearing gray slacks, a dove-gray Western shirt with red-and-white beading, and a blue-and-white houndstooth-check sport coat, his black hair slicked back, he paused, and somewhat awkwardly blew kisses to the screaming girls. The throng surged forward, and he dashed back into the airplane. Eventually police cleared a path, and the celebrity squeezed through toward the customs shed.

When Cole reached the guarded reception lounge, he lit up a cigarette, thinking he was safe at last. But he was not. "His pursuers wrenched a window off the lounge, and put their heads through and called for Nat to shake their hands. They pushed against the front door, and three officials had to lean against it to stop it from caving in. When he had time to collect himself, Nat wandered over and shook the clutching hands, which by this time were waving at every window."

Once he had got through customs, the problem was: how to spirit the star away from the airport without his being trampled? Finally, police snuck him out a side door and pushed him into a waiting car before the crowd knew where he was. But a thousand cars had come to Whenuapai airport bearing Nat King Cole fans, and quite a few of these went off into the night, headlights beaming, in pursuit of him.

The crowds were the same in Australia. On February 15, Robert Ruark wrote from Sydney: "I haven't seen anything like the Cole reception since the kids went mad over Frank Sinatra. The moans and oohs and giggles and squeaks sound like a jungle full of tree frogs. It needs cops to get him in and cart him out." If Nat King Cole did not dally in Australia, it was not for any lack of an opportunity.

The homecoming was not easy. Maria said she could always tell when her husband had been unfaithful, not because of anything he said — he would never be so cruel as to tell her about it — she could tell by the weight of his guilt, which he bore with difficulty. Like most men of his generation, Nat never talked about these things. He would have to work through the shame on his own, and this took time. He would buy her jewelry.

But the wanderer was scarcely home before he took off again. Nat reported to the Sands Hotel in Las Vegas, and a dancing master. A photo spread in *Ebony* shows the singer high-stepping, leaping, and prancing on the stage of the Copa Room, in a chorus line, learning the steps in a production number, surrounded by a bevy of long-legged white showgirls. Maria was not amused. With a straw hat cocked on his head, a striped shirt, and a satin cummerbund he sang the humorous "Calypso Blues," then led the dancers "through a light-footed routine that proved a solid box office hit." With the grace of a natural athlete, "by show-time Nat was a confident, competent hoofer."

But his three-week booking in Vegas was cut short when Nat got the news his mother was gravely ill. She had cancer. The disease had spread to her kidneys and now she lay near death.

It had all happened quite suddenly. Nat and Maria flew to Chicago on a Monday. "I remember Nat kneeling at the bedside and his mother was fanning the covers she was so hot. I was standing over them," Maria recalls. On Wednesday, February 23, 1955, Perlina Coles breathed her last.

"Anyway, it just killed him. I did not go to the funeral, for some reason . . . I had the baby . . ."

Nat completely broke down at the funeral, weeping uncontrollably, and finally fainted dead away and had to be carried out of the church by his brothers.

He had wanted to include his mother more in his new life. "It was so sad," Cole's wife recalls. "He *really* missed her. Suddenly it is too late, and you can't do anything about it."

There is no grief for a young man like the grief over his mother's death. Men work through this sadness and heightened sense of mortality in a variety of ways. Religion is a solace, and friendship; booze, gambling, obsessive work, and erotic adventure all may provide relief for a moment or a day.

Many fortunate men take comfort in their wives and children during the mourning period, and Nat may have done this briefly between his mother's death and his thirty-sixth birthday on March 17. As for losing himself in his work, this is laughable, because he could never work any harder than he had been doing for twenty years. On March 19 he was in a New York City studio with Tommy Dorsey recording "Darling, Je Vous Aime Beaucoup," his next hit, and three other tunes.

And by summer he was back at the Chez Paris in Chicago. There the Reverend Coles at last agreed to watch one of his son's shows. Nat said, "I wanted to please him more than anyone I ever sang for." He sang "Faith Can Move Mountains," and later recalled, "He smiled and I breathed easier." From the stage, the star introduced his father. The minister stood, and bowed.

Cole had his singing as an outlet for his emotions — fortunate, because Maria says he rarely talked about his feelings. In a languid interview with *Look* magazine that month, there is no mention of his late mother, though the article is titled "The Melancholy Monarch" and the photos show him as "sad of eye," almost pitiful.

To ease his passage through the rest of that terrible year he chose the balm of erotic adventure, despite the fact that he may have seen his mother's death as a judgment on his behavior.

It made Maria uneasy before it made her furious. She was patient with him. She had a high tolerance for this sort of "bad boy behavior" in 1955, knowing it came with the territory — but her husband's philandering during this period sent her over the edge.

Avoiding the details, she states, emphatically, that she resumed her singing career that summer "because of Nat's fooling around with other women." She meant to defend herself. The press coverage of her debut at Ciro's explains her motivation in other ways, citing her husband's enthusiastic encouragement; but this was the cover story for a more painful drama.

Maria Cole's return to the stage was not a bored housewife's whim or the self-indulgence of the celebrity spouse. Only eight years earlier she was en route to stardom herself. Now, fueled by anger that the sacrifice she had made for Nat was ill appreciated, she threw herself into her work. She meant business. She hired Charles Henderson to coach and direct the act, Pete Rugolo to write scores, Marie Bryant to choreograph, and Bill Miller to accompany her on piano. Carol and Natalie watched their mother rehearse all summer long.

Maria's opening at Ciro's in October got as much press coverage as anything Nat had done since the IRS had taken his house. In a tight-fitting satin gown she faced the crowd, a full house at Ciro's that looked all the more crowded for the bouquets — the room looked like a florist's shop. At the front tables Dorothy Dandridge and Spike Jones were seated, Leo Durocher and Laraine Day, Mr. and Mrs. Milton Berle, Jimmy Van Heusen, and Pearl Bailey. Nat King Cole was there, having given up a week at Philadelphia's Latin Casino to be in L.A. for his wife's opening. He was nervous, as Maria stepped into the peach-colored spotlight to begin the show, singing "Sophisticated Lady." She was trembling as she began but "her qualms vanished when she felt the crowd warming up to her."

The Hollywood Reporter said: "She gathered up the tempo with Cole Porter's 'It's All Right with Me,' and smoothly introduced and chirped through what she termed 'The Ethel Waters Song Cavalcade.' The gal has all the physical equipment . . . she may rise to rank with some of the top vocalists in her field in a short time." Reviewers echoed the enthusiastic applause at Ciro's with praise only qualified by the footnote that Maria's "opening show was slightly hampered by her lack of self-assurance. It's an understandable hurdle for the wife of one of the nation's top singing stars to try and build a career of her own." And then, it had been a while since she had been in the spotlight.

"You moved 'em, girl," Pearl Bailey told Maria, in sincere admiration. She certainly moved her husband. In the midst of a song she caught sight of Nat, and tears were streaming down his face.

Maria Cole's modesty about her considerable talent and her ambivalence about following up on a promising debut tell us as much about her character as any action in her eventful life. She was a powerful woman, her daughter Carol tells us, strong-willed, highly energetic, and persuasive. Carol marvels over her mother's sublimation of ambition. Many women went much further on far less talent. Why wasn't Maria Cole herself a star? Quite simply, this was a woman whose ego did not demand the limelight. She was neither a narcissist nor an exhibitionist. Singing she found pleasant enough in itself but it was more of a means to an end — so it had been when she was a girl and so it was in the autumn of 1955. Now singing was to get her husband's attention; having done that, she surprised everyone by going back into "retirement." A few revealing sentences in her memoir sum up the episode: "I was a little annoyed at my husband, so I decided to take another fling at a career on my own. I put together my own act at Ciro's and I got a standing ovation and good reviews . . . It was not long, however, before Nat decided he had been right the first time: he would be the singer; I would be his wife . . . I had enjoyed the stage while I held it, but it was nice to have my man order me home again."

To understand the destiny of these lovers it is essential to see how profound was the marriage, the bond between them. Together they had forged an emotional connection and preserved an enterprise. What really occurred that autumn was a bargain, spoken or unspoken, that if Nat King Cole did not soon pay more allegiance to his vows, he was going to lose his wife to the same sort of career that had led him astray. She says that he ordered her home again, but the order cut both ways.

And now when she tells us how dearly she loved him, how Nat was her life and everything she did was for him, we better pay close attention, if we ever doubted her. Of course, she loved money and luxury and security, but who doesn't? She had choices, including a glamorous career of her own, though the rest of her life she would disclaim it. She could have done many things. Maria chose to work at the relationship because she loved her husband, and because she glimpsed in their partnership a potential to transcend the inconstant pleasures of youth and fortune.

MOBBED

Nat would not be mobbed in America in quite the same way as he had been in Australia. The hysterical teenagers of the United States were lusting after a different sort of idol: the rock-and-roll singer. Bill Haley's "Rock Around the Clock" and Chuck Berry's "Maybellene" hit hard in 1955, paving the way for Elvis Presley's "Hound Dog." Nat was only dimly aware then of the threat that rock would pose to his popularity.

It is good that Maria and Nat reached an understanding before the New Year. The coming year, 1956, held terrors and disappointments for Cole that no man should endure alone. He would need all the support he could get, particularly from his family.

After another argument over travel arrangements, Maria went with Nat when the group embarked for Australia in February. During a one-week visit, remarkably brief considering the distances, Nat gave a dynamic interview to Zelie McLeod of the Sydney *Telegraph*. Australia was strictly segregated. McLeod asked the black singer to discuss "the color bar in America."

"In the North I'm no different from any other guy. But when I play the Deep South, I'm never sure whether I get first-class treatment just because I'm Nat Cole . . ." He went on to explain the intricacies of anger and resentment in the South over the Supreme Court's ruling against segregation in schools, in the recent *Brown* v. *Board of Education of Topeka* case. "I'm proud of our court . . . it knocks back a lot of the propaganda the Communists put out about the way America treats her Negroes. But only time, education and plenty of good schooling will make anti-segregation work.

"I often wonder whether Negroes like myself who are pretty well known help out at all in breaking down barriers. Maybe in a way it's helping. I don't know." Lighting a cigarette, he fixed a steady gaze on the reporter. "You don't have anything like that here, do you?" And he began asking about the black Aborigines. "How many are there? Where are they? How do they live?" he asked pointedly. "Where could I go and meet some of those Aborigines?"

The interviewer was nonplussed, flustered.

Cole wondered aloud during the interview whether well-known Negroes like himself were helping to break down barriers. This was false modesty, because from the bottom of his heart he believed he was breaking barriers. He had come to believe so strongly in the role, the conviction was beginning to have more influence than his musical inspiration in shaping his explosive career. Not that civil rights would ever consume as much energy as his music. But his career choices, to sing rather than play piano, for instance, had not only a financial basis but also an impulse distinctly social and political. Money and power kept close company, in headlines, in the spotlight, on television, and in the movies. Whatever he could accomplish for himself, as a man of talent and character in the spotlight, would benefit his people too. But to advance the cause of integration, he must reach white audiences as well as African-Americans.

Nat King Cole was not a political philosopher schooled in rhetoric or the dialectics of history. He was a clear thinker with sound instincts and compassion, who had been nurtured in a caring black community before flourishing in the integrated mainstream. Where he had gone — to riches, fame, and honor — he hoped his brothers would soon follow. Like Armstrong and Ellington, he would go ahead and disarm the bigots with his charm and by example. Before long all others would be welcome as well.

So after Australia, he planned to launch another campaign through the Deep South, bigger than ever. The timing was dramatic. On March 1, 1956, the University of Alabama expelled its first black student, Autherine Lucy, in defiance of a court order. Martin Luther King was organizing the Montgomery bus boycott. Cole's integrated troupe — his black Trio, blond vocalist June Christy, English bandleader Ted Heath, the Four Freshmen, and white comedian Gary Morton — planned to entertain black and white audiences, challenging segregation policies wherever possible.

First Cole played a week in Havana, in early March. The dictator General Batista y Zaldívar was in power and nervous about the upstart Communist Fidel Castro. When Nat sang for the general and his men, fifty smiling guardsmen filled the front seats, with rifles resting across their laps. Cole, hearing they planned to come armed, had sent word their firearms were *not* welcome at his concert. But the rifles came anyway, and then there was not much the crooner could do but try to please the soldiers.

After the unsettling Cuban incident, Nat felt that he could handle any unpleasantness that might arise in the southern United States. But he did not reckon on the depth of hatred seething in the South that spring. Maria may have sensed it — once again she stayed home while Nat toured Dixie.

Everything went well in San Antonio, Texas, where they faced the town's first integrated audience, and in Fort Worth and Houston, where the show played to whites on one side of the auditorium and blacks on the other. Nobody fussed over the arrangement. That was just the way things were in Texas. Dick LaPalm recalls some amiable mixing, blacks sitting with whites, and vice versa, without tension.

But while Cole and Ted Heath and June Christy were touring Texas, a special surprise was being prepared for them by the White Citizens Council of Greater Birmingham. This was an Alabama chapter of the fraternity that once kidnapped Dick LaPalm from his hotel in Biloxi — the public branch of the faceless Ku Klux Klan.

The rustics who planned a homecoming for the state's most famous native were not Birmingham residents. They all hailed from Anniston, an Appalachian mining town sixty miles east. The citizens of Birmingham, that proud industrial center, would later take some small comfort in this.

On Saturday, April 7, while the Cole show was

en route to Mobile via New Orleans, a meeting of the White Citizens Council was called to order in Anniston. Kenneth Adams of the Board of Directors had summoned the Council to convene at his filling station. In his thirty-five years, Adams had logged a picturesque police record of assault and battery charges; he once served six months for attacking a baseball umpire with a bat. Adams greeted Mike Fox, a peer "belligerent," according to police, though in thirty-seven years brother Fox had been convicted of only two assaults. Lean Adams and fat, beady-eyed Fox hailed three younger citizens: Willis Vinson, twenty-three, and his brother Edgar, twenty-one, and an eighteen-year-old odd-jobs man named Orliss Clevenger. None of the Citizens had passed the seventh grade.

In the heady atmosphere of gasoline and crankcase oil, Adams lectured his compatriots on the evils of bebop, rhythm and blues, and Negro music in general. He snarled and railed. He called it an NAACP plot to mongrelize America. The music was meant to force "nigger culture" on the South. The blues contributed to the moral degradation of children. Word had come down from Ace Carter, head of the North Alabama Citizens Council: "Negro music appeals to the base in man, brings out animalism and vulgarity." Something had to be done. Get the music off the jukeboxes, talk to people who promote the music, talk them out of it.

Adams looked at the hangdog faces of his fellow citizens. He was not sure if they knew what the words degradation and animalism and vulgarity meant. But he knew they were angry and wanted to do something about the black folks and their infernal jungle music.

He had an idea. It shocked him like a snake's bite. Nat King Cole was coming to sing at the Municipal Auditorium in Birmingham on Tuesday the 10th. They would put out the word to every member of the Citizens Council they knew in Anniston, Piedmont, Bessemer, Tuscaloosa, and Birmingham. By telephone and by word of mouth they would plan to meet at the first show, and infiltrate the audience. At a signal, the Citizens would storm the stage and seize the black singer Nat King Cole and steal him away!

Adams's confederates howled their approval. They would lead the charge! Would not Ace Carter be proud of them? It was the best idea they had ever heard. In a matter of days they had received pledges of support from a hundred and fifty White Citizens.

What they meant to do with Nat King Cole once they caught him remains a mystery. Perhaps they would let him go after his promising never to sing anything but bluegrass music and Baptist hymns.

The day before Cole was to perform in Birmingham a brief article appeared in *The New York Times*, reporting on the White Citizens Councils in Alabama and their campaign against "bebop and Negro music." At that moment in history, it did not take a chief of detectives to see that Nat King Cole and his sidemen might be in some danger in Birmingham. Fortunately the local authorities had taken the precaution of assigning

410

Detectives C. B. Golden and Maurice House to keep their ears to the ground for any mischief that might be underfoot as the hour of the concert was approaching.

By Monday evening, April 9, when Cole and company finished a charity performance in Mobile, rumors reached them that trouble was brewing in Birmingham. Road assistant Carl Carruthers remembers he was nervous. "I told Nat something was going to happen. I tried to get him to cancel."

"We had played there before," says bassist Charlie Harris, "but you always felt that little bit of *envy* from folks you did not feel anywhere else. They were not friendly at all."

"We were warned before we went there," Lee Young recalls, "that there was going to be trouble. But most good musicians are very positive people." Nat did not have to ask his musicians twice to stay aboard. "I knew that there might be trouble, but I'm *with* him," says Young, "so I wasn't going to say I'm not going, you know, so we all went."

So while Nat Cole, Ted Heath, and their musicians and road crews were driving north to set up at the Municipal Auditorium in Birmingham, the white knights of Anniston — Kenneth Adams, Mike Fox, Orliss Clevenger, and the Vinson brothers — were driving west out of the foothills. They rode in a car with their homemade blackjacks and brass knuckles and .22 caliber squirrel-hunting rifles, to restore decency to the music world.

Two shows were planned for the evening: the

411

first for white fans, the second for blacks. Thirty-five hundred people, including the mayor of Birmingham, James W. Morgan, and a number of detectives and police officers, eagerly awaited the famous singer's entrance. They applauded when he came out on his side of the stage, separated from the white musicians by a light curtain intended to soften the impact of Caucasians and African-Americans appearing on the same platform. In this city, it had never happened before. The police, aware that a riot had been planned, were guarding the steps on either side of the high stage.

Nat crooned the sweet ballad "Autumn Leaves," and a peaceful calm descended upon the spectators — all but Kenneth Adams, Mike Fox, and the other hoodlums from Anniston. They were hopping mad. First, they were angry at Nat King Cole for being what he was and singing the way he was singing. Second, they were furious because the army of one hundred and fifty White Citizens who had sworn to join them in their noble mission were nowhere to be seen. More glory for us, the knights figured, and took their places.

Ted Heath and his eighteen-piece orchestra played the opening measures of "Little Girl," and Cole spread his arms wide — his narrow eyes half closed — then, opening that great smiling mouth, he sang. After one chorus the knights of Anniston just could not stand it anymore. One howled like a wolf, and at the sound of that prearranged signal, the men charged the spotlight, two down one aisle, three more down the other.

Someone screamed as the men dashed past the

rows of seated patrons. Someone else yelled, "Here they come!" Adams and the Vinson brothers crossed the space between the front row and the stage and climbed up the four-foot height to grab the singer. In the glare of the lights, Nathaniel saw a man leap for him out of the darkness. Willis Vinson swung at him, the microphone dropped to the stage with an echoing bang, and Nat was sent reeling back against the piano bench. The bench split as he fell over it.

Houselights came up. Cries filled the air. The police, having expected the attack to come from the steps on either side of the stage, ran in from the wings and fought the assailants. Willis Vinson was twisting Nat King Cole's left foot, trying to remove it, and a cop had to wrestle him loose. Adams hit a policeman, and in return got his skull whacked with a nightstick.

Men and women were rising from their seats, shouting, screaming, panicked. Drummer Lee Young saw it all — the men storming the stage, his friend struck down, the struggle with the police. Today, with the wisdom of eighty years in his calm, blue eyes he recalls: "I have never seen such hatred in a person's face. What baffles me — and does to this day — how can you just hate that much, and you don't even know the person, don't know anything *about* the person, and it's just hate, hate, hate?"

Lee Young called out to the Englishman Ted Heath, "Play the national anthem! Play the national anthem!" as the men tussled onstage and one policeman's glasses got smashed and another policeman's nose was broken, bleeding. Because

413

in those days if there was a barroom brawl or a riot and you played "The Star-Spangled Banner," everybody stopped whatever they were doing, stood tall, and saluted.

But Ted Heath, being an Englishman, struck up the band to play "God Save the Queen," which in America is "My Country, 'Tis of Thee," and of no particular use during a riot. "No, no!" yelled Dick LaPalm. "The American anthem, the *American* one! To hell with the Queen!" But in all the confusion Ted Heath and his band could not hear him.

Only a few seconds later Nat picked himself up off the floor. Eight policemen held five men in armlocks, some onstage and some down in front, and they were pushing the criminals out of the hall. "I was a little shaken up, but more stunned and amazed than anything else. If I'd expected anything like this I certainly wouldn't have been standing in the line of fire," he said.

Cole limped off the stage, touching his swollen lip. The curtain shut, and comedian Gary Morton explained to the stunned audience that the singer could not continue. Someone in the front called out, "Ask him to come back so we can apologize!" And the audience began applauding. They clapped for more than five minutes, until finally Cole came out in front of the curtain.

Later the singer told a reporter, "I knew they were trying to show me that they didn't sanction what had happened. So I thanked them for coming to the show and told them I knew they didn't hold with what had just occurred. I noticed some people were even crying."

"I was born here," he told the audience. "I just

414

came here to entertain you. That's what I thought you wanted."

"We do, we do! Sing! Sing!" they cried. But he would not do any more singing for this audience. "Those folks hurt my back. I cannot continue," he apologized, "because I have to go to a doctor."

Backstage, stunned, shaking, he smoked a cigarette and tried to regain his composure. "Man, I love show business, but I don't want to die for it."

A doctor examined the singer in his dressing room and determined that no bones had been broken when Cole was knocked over the piano bench. Mayor Morgan came backstage and apologized. And at ten o'clock Nat King Cole gave a brief performance for the African-American audience that had been waiting patiently and anxiously outside the Municipal Auditorium.

Some people just wished he would go home. The police, who already had sustained casualties, were torn by mixed emotions. One musician, who asks not to be quoted, recalls a policeman's angry comment, overheard after the late show, outside the dressing room. Cole used to take a lot of time getting changed and ready to leave after a concert, and this night was no different. The police could not quit the premises until Nat Cole was in his hotel room safe and sound. One went up into the dressing room to hurry the star along. But Cole would not be rushed. The cop stormed down the stairs and said to a valet, "If you don't get that fuckin' nigger out of this building, I can't be responsible for what might happen to him."

Maria had been dining out with friends in L.A.

and had just gotten home when she got the call. It was one of Sinatra's men.

"Maria Cole? Frank would like to talk to you." She sat down. However long it took for Frank to pick up the phone seemed to her like an eternity. Sinatra did not make casual phone calls to Maria Cole.

At last she heard Frank's weary voice on the line. After assuring her that Nathaniel was all right, he told her everything that had happened in Birmingham. She took a deep breath. Maria instinctively knew enough about Alabama to know that her husband was not safe until he was hundreds of miles away from there. She asked Frank Sinatra when, and how, her husband would ever get out of Birmingham.

"Don't you worry, honey," said Sinatra. "We'll get him out of there."

Now this is an intriguing statement. If anything could have comforted Maria in that terrible hour, it was these confident words from "the chairman of the board." There is a famous photo of Sinatra standing with Carlo and Joe Gambino, Jimmy Fratianno, and Salvatore Spatola, where the singer has his arms around two lesser persons of the nation's most powerful Mafia family. Frank knew Albert "the Executioner" Anastasia, Frank Costello, and Joe Bonanno. Frank was one of a community that thrived on danger, and knew how to get things done quickly, anywhere, even in Alabama.

Nathaniel and his musicians were not out of the woods yet.

Charlie Harris recalls this, and you can still see

the terror in his eyes. "It was a bad night for all of us. It happened so fast, and then the fright came and the fear never left us. We were up all night in that hotel because we were still in that 'thing,' not knowing what was going to happen. So even when they got us out in the morning — we could not get out during the night — we still had that worry that something awful might happen."

Whoever was calling the shots now — Carlos Gastel, Carlo Gambino, Frank Sinatra, or Vice President Nixon — wanted to see Nat King Cole flying to Chicago on the next plane leaving Birmingham. Wherever it had been scheduled to go, Chicago was where the plane was going now. The South needed no more black martyrs. Any heroic fantasies Cole may have had about soldiering on through the Carolinas were quickly dismissed.

The next morning, on the way to the airport, Cole announced to reporters that his shows for the rest of the week, in Greenville, Charlotte, and Raleigh, were canceled. He was going home to Chicago to rest and see a doctor.

Lee Young remembers: "That morning was really scary. You know, it was in the South, and I had never been there before. It was real foggy. And now the plane couldn't get out. And so many people came there, all white, came there to the airport in the fog, apologizing. And Nat said he wasn't mad, he knew it wasn't all of them. But they kept coming, a mob of them, more than fifty all around the plane, shouting that they didn't agree with the hoodlums, and apologizing, apologizing . . ."

Lee Young sits back, sighing deeply. "And so,

you know, that's what society is like." People in a fog, apologizing to some other people in a fog who are trying desperately to forgive them.

And at last the plane left Birmingham.

Willis Vinson and Kenneth Adams were charged with assault with intent to murder, while the rest of the Anniston hoodlums were jailed on charges of conspiracy to incite a riot, and disorderly conduct.

Nat King Cole stepped off the plane in Chicago to face a squad of clamorous and unusually excited reporters. He spoke to them and answered their questions with his usual friendliness and lack of guile, completely unaware his words would cause as much commotion as had the Anniston assassins.

"I was a guinea pig for some hoodlums who thought they could hurt me and frighten me and keep other Negro entertainers from the South. But what they did has backfired on them, because thousands of white people in the audience could see how terrible it is for an innocent man to be subjected to such barbaric treatment."

When Bernard Gavzer of the Associated Press asked Cole if he would continue performing before segregated audiences in the South, he said: "Sure I will. I'm not a political figure or some controversial person. I'm just an entertainer, and it's my job to perform for them. If I stop because of some state law, I'm deserting the people who are important to me. In my way I may be helping to bring harmony between people through my music."

In 1944, he had given up an engagement in Kansas City worth thousands because he refused to play for a segregated audience. But that was his choice, and it was Kansas City. Claude Barnett had run the story. Now no one remembered.

"As for challenging segregation, it's foolish to think a performer like me can go into a Southern city and demand that the audiences be integrated. The Supreme Court is having a hard time integrating schools. What chance do I have to integrate audiences?"

And the New York *Daily Worker* quoted him (or misquoted him, according to Cole) thus: "This was not a personal affront to me. It was part of that [integration] fuss over Autherine Lucy at the University of Alabama and the bus boycott in Montgomery . . . I didn't go there to be political. I'm not trying to prove anything. I leave that to the other guys."

But what had happened in Alabama was so dramatic, Cole had become a pivotal political figure like it or not, a target for frustrations on both sides of the segregation issue. The AP story hitting the metropolitan newspapers on April 13 spelled trouble for Cole, and the article in the *Daily Worker* on the 15th made the African-American public see red. Reactions were swift and fierce. In Harlem, tavern owners removed Nat King Cole's records from their jukeboxes. Outraged fans were seen trampling the discs underfoot, sailing them down Lenox Avenue. His old antagonist Claude Barnett, now almost seventy, pounced on the story, using the ANP's wire service to blast Nat King Cole in the words of others.

"To continue to have his records on our juke-boxes would be supporting his traitor ideas and narrow-minded way of thinking."

Thurgood Marshall, then the NAACP's chief counsel, quipped: "All Cole needs to complete his role as an Uncle Tom is a banjo." And the Baltimore *Afro-American* said the singer was "kneeling before the throne of Jim Crow." Noting that Cole was not a card-carrying member of the NAACP, executive secretary Roy Wilkins issued a public invitation for the singer to join "the crusade against racism." As of Monday the 16th Cole's only response was: "I shouldn't have to be asked my feelings about racism. I have children."

Nursing his injured back, right arm, and left leg, and taking comfort in Reverend Coles's company, Nathaniel was stunned by the criticism, flabbergasted, and deeply wounded. "It hurt him," Maria recalls. Though he reminded people, nobody seemed to care that "this was the first mixed show ever to appear in Birmingham." He meant to hold his ground in the controversy, which spread like wildfire from the taverns of Harlem and Bronzeville to the editorial pages of newspapers coast to coast. "I'm not mad at a soul," he told a reporter on the 17th. But a lot of people were mad at him. His hometown *Chicago Defender* wrote: "We wonder if Nat Cole shared the humiliation of the hundreds of his Negro fans who had to stand outdoors and wait while whites inside yelled 'Go home, nigger!' and attacked him as he performed. We hope Cole has learned a lesson."

He was definitely learning something, though it may not have been the lesson the *Defender* had in mind. Dr. George Cannon, African-American president of the Manhattan Medical Society, wrote "An Open Letter to Mr. Nat King Cole," in which he took the singer to task for his statement (which Cole denied he had made): "I leave that to the other guys."

Claude Barnett trumpeted Cannon's denunciation on his wire service: "Now there is where you showed your true colors and your total lack of real understanding. In these times . . . no Negro at all — especially one as prominent as you — can leave anything to the other guys. First of all you were dead wrong in having a concert to which Negroes were not allowed admission . . . It is a matter of pride, dignity and basic moral principle. Did you ever hear of those things, Mr. Cole? It seems you 'leave that to the other guys' also.

"Wake up, Mr. Cole, you're not that hungry. What do you want, more and more money even if it is any kind of money?"

Nat's own physician, James Scott, publicly answered Dr. Cannon: "Where and how a man makes his living is his own business. It's a personal matter and should be decided solely by the individual — not friends, fans or anyone else."

And more persuasive was a comment by the great Olympian Jesse Owens, who sprinted to Cole's defense. Noting that sports and entertainment are the two major fields in which Negroes have succeeded in breaking down the Jim Crow barriers, Owens declared, "If we are going to convince people of the job we can do, we certainly can't do it by staying away from them."

On Saturday, April 14, Cole rejoined the road

show in Norfolk, where Ivan Mogull and Marvin Cane met him and helped cheer him up. Cole went on to Richmond and Winston-Salem, where he sang for an integrated audience of 6,000. But he canceled his performance in Atlanta on the 17th, saying he would not appear in the Deep South at this time "for a million dollars."

In Detroit on April 23, Cole paid $500 for a life membership in the NAACP. He noted in a letter to *Down Beat* that he had long possessed canceled checks for donations to several NAACP chapters, as well as to the Montgomery bus boycott. He had contributed generously to the NAACP. "I forgot to bring along my press agent," he quipped.

"Should Any Negro Artist Perform Before a Segregated Audience at Any Time?" reads the headline in *The New York Age Defender*, above a lengthy treatment of the controversy that raged in papers well into the month of June. Old friends attacked Cole in the pages of black journals. Dinah Washington, Louis Jordan, and Cab Calloway all told *Jet* magazine Nat Cole had done wrong. On the same page singer Maxine Sullivan and sax great Earl Bostic rushed to Nat's defense. On Milton Berle's TV show, Sammy Davis, Jr., more beloved than ever after losing one eye in a car wreck, blasted his friend Cole, and Berle lustily defended him.

Amazed, indignant, wounded, Nat Cole would not be moved far from his original position, his responsibility as an artist to his fans white and black, wherever he found them. "Those people, segregated or not, are still record fans. They can't overpower the law of the South, and I can't come in on a one-night stand and overpower the law.

"The whites come to applaud a Negro performer like the colored do. When you've got the respect of white and colored, you can ease a lot of things. I can't settle the issue — if I was that good I should be President of the United States — but I can help to ease the tension by gaining the respect of both races all over the country."

"I still have many friends and fans down here despite this affair," he had told reporters as he left Birmingham. But he would never again set foot in the state where he was born.

HOME AGAIN

Home never seemed sweeter to the travel-weary musician than it did when he returned to his family in the spring of 1956. Roses were blooming in the garden, and larkspur, wisteria, and marigolds flowered in the yards all around Hancock Park. He embraced Maria. "Hello, dear," he said to Charlotte gently, affectionately as always but with a strange note of melancholy, as he embraced his sister-in-law, the children's Baba. The dogs leapt around him. Cookie and Sweetie hugged him, a little shyly; it had been five months since they had seen him. Charlotte had written a song she wanted to show him.

Cookie, almost twelve, and six-year-old Sweetie put on a musical show for Mom and Dad, singing and dancing. He was proud to hear how Natalie's singing had come along.

"Those two girls certainly keep the house humming," he told a visitor. "Cookie is the record collector — and like most teenagers, an avid Presley fan. Her mother and I gave her a miniature jukebox for her room so she can play her records when she wants. Once in a while she gets on a ballet kick and wants only that kind of music . . .

"Both Cookie and Sweetie give me their frank opinions of my records," he said, grinning. "They can hurt your feelings, so I don't often ask . . ."

Nat turned to television for relaxation. "I'm

also a golf student and I've been doing some motion picture photography . . . Also I'm a pretty fair record collector, from classical to jazz. I like all of Andrés Segovia's records." He described himself as a "short-order cook" who could throw together ham and eggs, and whose favorite home meals were steaks, Italian dishes, and anything highly seasoned. "Primarily I'm a meat man," he went on, "although once in a while I toy with a few vegetables."

Carol recalls that her father took a back seat to Maria in all things regarding rules and manners and discipline. "I try not to spoil them, but how can you avoid it? Maria is more exact with them. For one thing she insists that the TV goes off at a definite time each evening, and Cookie is allowed no personal calls after seven-thirty. On the whole, our girls are well-behaved youngsters," he said proudly.

They sure were proud of him. On May 24, 1956, he sang for the President of the United States, at a correspondents' dinner at the White House. Patti Page was there, and James Cagney, and Nat sang "Too Young to Go Steady." He showed the children the scroll President Eisenhower had sent him. Soon after Nat and Maria returned home from filming an Errol Flynn movie in Cuba in mid-June, the President was ill and had to go into the hospital. Nat called Ike in the hospital to wish him well, and on June 20 the President wrote to the singer thanking him for his thoughtfulness.

The consequences of the Alabama kidnapping

attempt were vast, profound, and surprising. In show business there is no such thing as bad publicity, and the Birmingham incident became a national media event, a windfall, a bonanza. No one in his right mind would ever wish such a disaster on a man like Nat Cole. But Carlos Gastel, the General Artists Corporation, and Capitol Records meant to get all the mileage they could get out of the publicity if only to compensate the star for what he had suffered.

Overnight Nat King Cole had become a public figure, like the President. No longer just a jazz pianist or a ballad singer, Cole took on the mantle of a secular saint. Nearly martyred in Alabama, he had been resurrected in the media as an apostle of peace, forgiveness, and charity. Despite the bitter criticism of the NAACP and the liberal black press — the Baltimore *Afro-American* and Claude Barnett's Associated Negro Press — Cole never stirred from his philosophical calm. Coached by his preacher father, Cole judged no man. He was not angry at anybody. This made a lot of people furious, including some of his friends. But eventually most Americans, black and white, were filled with admiration, having seen this sort of behavior only in the Scriptures. In a few months the negative criticism faded away, leaving the general impression that the black singer had acted nobly, even heroically, with courage and grace. "His quiet, dignified behavior after the attack made the hoodlums look that much more shameful," wrote Leonard Feather on May 30 in *Down Beat*.

There is no doubt that the plot to kidnap Cole backfired. Every newspaper in the South roundly condemned the attack, the White Citizens Council, and its mad ideas, so that afterward the racist organization was not able to gather enough members to hold a meeting. The Birmingham judge who imposed the maximum jail sentences on the hoodlums, 180 days and $100 fines, commended Cole for his conduct "at the scene of the disturbance and since then." Judge Ralph Parker added that the singer had respected Southern traditions in a way to "earn respect of his white friends." Again, though no sane person would have planned it, the ruined concert did more to integrate Birmingham than did Dinah Washington's refusal to perform in that tormented city.

In a spirited defense of Cole, critic Leonard Feather wrote: "Nat Cole has suffered enough . . . It is bad enough that, unlike Perry Como and so many others of his contemporaries, he cannot get his own television show, bad enough he is generally confined to minor singing parts in movies, bad enough obscene signs were placed on his lawn . . . and that vicious racists had to floor him in the middle of a song."

The Birmingham attack made the singer so eminent he could force the issue of the television show. "No Negro has a TV show. I'm breaking that down," he told *Ebony*. While Nat was resting in Los Angeles before his June 27 opening at the Sands in Las Vegas, Carlos Gastel was putting the screws to Tom Rockwell, president of Nat's booking agency, GAC. Gastel told Rockwell that he was tired of waiting — if GAC did not get a television deal for Nat soon, then they could forget about booking him for anything else.

Maria bitterly recalls: "In discussing it business-wise, nobody ever came right out and said, 'Well, the man is black and you can't get him on TV' . . . the excuses given were that they didn't have enough time, there wasn't enough money." Alan Livingston remembers when he was chief of programming at NBC and had the Dinah Shore show, Dinah wanted Nat as a guest. But she had a Southern image and "the sponsor Chevrolet said absolutely not, they did not want blond Dinah standing next to a black man."

Ad salesmen were hostile from the start. "There wasn't anybody going out and pitching a Negro on a show, because that wasn't the easiest thing to sell," says Maria. But Rockwell also handled Perry Como. NBC wanted Como on their show in New York, so the GAC president pressured the network to take the black star with the white one, all or nothing. It was still a tough sell, so Tom Rockwell had no good news for Cole for a while.

Meanwhile the artist did not sit on his hands waiting for the television networks and Madison Avenue to give him a break. He played the piano. For hours a day he played the mahogany grand piano in the living room, late at night after the children had gone to bed. He listened to the records of great pianists: Art Tatum, Teddy Wilson, Earl Hines, Vladimir Horowitz, and Arthur Rubinstein. The piano nourished him. The piano had made him, and in the last several years he had grown so far from the keyboard sometimes he felt guilty about it and would not practice because he was so out of practice. His illness and his trouble with Maria and then the horror of Birmingham had taken so much out of him, he had to reconstitute his spirit. He had to practice as he had done when he was a kid.

Cole kept practicing the piano through the month of June when Natalie was sick in bed with the measles and Carol graduated from grammar school. He fingered scales and trills and runs through the end of June, when he opened at the Sands Hotel on June 27. On the 29th the wire services reported that Cole had signed "the largest single contract for nightclub performances in the history of show business," half a million total for yearly appearances at the Sands through 1959. This eased his concerns about money, and would ratchet up pressure on GAC and the networks to crack him a television slot.

But at the moment, in July of 1956, Nat Cole was more excited by his renewed interest in jazz. After years of apologizing to his jazz fans (he recorded one lackluster album of piano music in 1952, adding four cuts in 1955) he wanted to return to his roots.

He thought about it that summer, walking the streets of Chicago's South Side, revisiting scenes of his youth like the Panama Club — now an abandoned store on Prairie Avenue — communing with the ghosts of Fats Waller, Johnny Dodds, and Jimmie Noone. Between engagements at the Chez Paris, Nat and Maria went to movies and baseball games, and visited Reverend Coles at home and at the church, where Nat played a tune on the organ.

In August, Cole was ready to record again. Producer Lee Gillette had talked to him about reviving the Trio, but Nat wanted something fresher and more spontaneous — like the jam sessions Billie Holiday was doing for Verve records. He called L.A. trumpeter Harry "Sweets" Edison, Frank Sinatra's accompanist, and asked Edison to meet the Trio and Lee Young at the new Capitol Tower Studios on August 15 and bring his horn.

They were there to have fun. Nat had a list of songs in his head, including "Route 66," "Sweet Loraine," and "It's Only a Paper Moon." Nothing had been written down; he would call out a title and the group would start playing. The cool declaration of Edison's muted trumpet over Young's steady brushwork in the opening measures of "Route 66" lets us know immediately we are on a newly paved superhighway, post-bebop, Cold War jazz that has heard rock and roll. Cole's spare chords, diminished, flatted fifths and occasional ninths, perfectly complement his voice, which works lazily, teasingly behind the beat — a little farther behind the beat than ever before. His one modest solo on "66" bounces playfully and bops around the chord progression — first emphasizing a single note melody in the right hand, developing a triplet figure, then building to a climax by playing the triplet against a bass pedal point until the hands join to play, again and again, the rich minor sixth chord. It is stunning rhythm and melody, spare and modern.

This was the first of four sessions employing various soloists that would yield the ten tunes on *After Midnight*, a jazz album classic. For many of us born after World War II, this "hi-fi" album was our first exposure to Nat King Cole's jazz talent —

excellent, though it was an introduction to the past rather than the future. Cole's idea was to capture the energy of an after-hours nightclub jam session, where the musicians drop in, play a number or two, and move on. On September 14 the great alto saxophonist Willie Smith took over Edison's spot; a week later the immortal Juan ("Caravan") Tizol on valve trombone replaced Smith; on September 24 the jazz fiddler Stuff Smith took center stage.

"Nothing was rehearsed," says Lee Young. "We sat down, and Nat would say how many choruses we were going to play, and 'you take this chorus, I'll take this, let's go,' and we would do it."

Cole's voice had matured into a highly polished, delicately nuanced instrument by 1956, as if he had taken voice lessons. He had not. Through practice he had developed the pinpoint accuracy of pitch, register (voice placement), and control of vibrato required to woo the pop audiences of the 1950s. Cole could croon pop music to beat Vic Damone. The remarkable thing about *After Midnight* is that Cole performs not as a crooner, but as a jazz *singer,* delightfully. On numbers like the upbeat Jesse Greer classic "Just You, Just Me," Cole's voice is actually more interesting than his sparkling piano chorus. He nails the high notes on the bridge line "Oh gee!" then slides down the phrases "What are your charms for? What are my arms for?" with the mellow ease of Willie Smith's silken sax, before climbing the steep hill of the climactic phrase, "Use your *ima*gination . . ." And no singer ever put more imagination into that five-syllable word than Cole does here. The second syllable is the top note; he mounts it in a bound, then trips lightly down the smooth far side, with a jeweled glissando at the penultimate syllable, and a dreamy low-toned labionasal ending. With his wide, closed mouth, Cole hums his way back to the refrain. The discourse takes all of three seconds.

The Nat King Cole we hear on the classic *After Midnight* album is a sadder, wiser man. "Sweet Loraine," which has become his theme song as it had once been Jimmie Noone's, Cole sings so slowly and soulfully it sounds almost like an elegy, or a melancholy farewell.

PART FOUR
This World and the Next

TELEVISION

At long last the call came from NBC. It was Harold Kemp, director of television programming on the West Coast. Kemp was an old vaudeville booker, a kind, bumbling sort of showbiz guy who had come up in the RKO circuit and still wore pinstriped black suits and a watch chain across his vest. In October, Carlos Gastel and GAC's Tom Rockwell, were in the agency's offices discussing Nat King Cole's TV ambitions, when Kemp called.

Kemp said, "We just had a cancellation — Frankie Carlyle. I'm going to try to sell the spot to New York for you guys. Come on over here and we'll talk about it." Singer Carlyle's TV spot had been fifteen minutes in the late afternoon, not exactly prime time, and NBC's financial package — salaries and production budget — was not a penny over union scale. But GAC leapt at the offer. Nat King Cole wanted a television show, and so now he would have it. Rockwell had done his job. Next, he and Gastel had to make sure that their franchise performer did not go broke while playing with television.

The problem was that Nat would have to spend a day a week in television studios in either New York or Hollywood, and Rockwell figured his time was worth at least $12,000 a week on the open road, $50,000 a week in Vegas. The TV show took a sizable bite out of Cole's income. According to Maria, what little he made in salary he plowed back into the show for sets and props. That is how determined he was to break down TV's race barrier. Of course, Nat believed the show would be so successful he soon would rival Perry Como in ratings and advertising dollars. "Nat'll get 'em," he used to tell Dick LaPalm, winking, punching his friend playfully on the arm before ambling onstage to face a crowd of thousands through the bright lights.

Cole saw his star rising. On October 13, he sang again for President Eisenhower, on his sixty-sixth birthday, on a coast-to-coast TV hookup, L.A. to D.C.

In New York the day before his TV premiere, Cole was modest but confident. He told *The New York Times*, "So many shows these days are big productions — they seem to stumble over themselves. I think something simple might be a good idea — for me, anyway." Gratified to be the first African-American star of network TV, he added, "I've been waging a personal campaign . . . I hit a few snags here and there but I didn't give up the fight. It could be a turning point . . ." The *Times* reporter notes that the "show will begin as a sustaining program [that is, network-supported]. Its star is confident that it soon will attract a sponsor."

Nat certainly looked the picture of confidence and graceful ease as he appeared on the TV screen that evening of November 5, singing "Nature Boy" and "Straighten Up and Fly Right," with his backup group of black vocalists, Charlie Harris on bass, and John Collins on guitar. Cole's wide smile and mild eyes were a delight to millions who loved his voice and had long awaited this moment to welcome him into their homes. To other viewers the black face in the living room came as a shock — some switched the channel immediately. Others, fascinated, lingered with the charming singer. There were arguments, as women watched Nat Cole and their men grumbled.

The show was simple as could be, similar to the old radio *King Cole Trio Time*: a few songs, a piano solo, a little patter, and before you knew it, the fifteen minutes were over. But it worked like magic. Cole was happily photogenic, and the ballad singer had a rare gift of balancing deep inward reflection with warm, intimate eye contact. "He would sing at the Hollywood Bowl," said Ivan Mogull, "and make you think he was singing to you alone, thirty rows back." Cole would close his eyes during a phrase of rising intimacy ("Are you warm, are you real, Mona Lisa?"), bringing his whole soul to bear upon the question before opening his gentle eyes again to take you into his world, his vision, his heart. This display was even more touching on television, with its magnifying power, than in the concert hall. For the rest, he was laid-back, casual as Perry Como, the perfect "cool" character for television.

The impact of Cole's show on the African-American community was immeasurable. In households from Bronzeville to East St. Louis, from Harlem and East Baltimore to Piedmont, West Virginia, everything stopped for fifteen minutes when Nat Cole came on the TV at 7:30. In his eloquent memoir *Colored People*, Henry Louis Gates, Jr., recalls the night Cole's show premiered, and how everyone came to his house to watch it. "His head looked like Rudolph Valentino's in the twenties . . ." And Gates stresses the importance of television in his black neighborhood of the Piedmont Valley. "The television . . . brought us together at night . . . brought in the world outside the Valley . . . In 1957, when I was in second grade, black children integrated Central High School in Little Rock, Arkansas . . . *All* the colored people in America watched it, together, with one set of eyes . . . The TV was the ritual arena for the drama of race."

And in 1957, Nat King Cole's television show became one of the most popular and closely watched shows in history — for its entertainment value, and as a social experiment in merchandising. The ad executives on Madison Avenue said, "Wonderful, wonderful, but we'll wait until you have public support."

Carlos Gastel was the executive producer, and Jim Johnson was the first writer-director. In February, after Johnson was arrested the fourth time for drunken driving, Hal Kemp summoned a bright thirty-seven-year-old director to his office. Robert Henry was a brown-haired, round-faced New Yorker whose dark eyes fairly danced with wit behind horn-rimmed glasses. He had majored in psychology at Tufts. Just under five and a half feet tall, Henry had the humorous calm of a man undergoing psychoanalysis not because he needs it but for the sheer excitement of the learning experience.

"Look," Kemp told the young director, "it's enough that NBC has a Negro on television. But now his white director is in the drunk tank. He goes to jail on the weekends and they let him out Monday so he can go to work. He could be drunk again by showtime. I'm taking Johnson off the project." Old Kemp had quit smoking and now chewed paper clips instead. He had a drawerful of paper clips and now he was straightening one out with his teeth.

"I want you to do the show," he told Robert Henry.

Nat's show had been on the air for four months, and while the reviews and ratings were excellent, the show was still "on sustaining." National sponsors would not risk offending the South. No one knows for sure how hard the sales force was trying. One Southern station master confided, "I like Nat Cole, but they told me if he came back on, they would bomb my house and my station." Nat remained hopeful the show's quality would soon garner the support it deserved. But he was beginning to feel an unmistakable chill from Madison Avenue. "The only racial prejudice I've found anywhere in TV is in some advertising agencies, and there it isn't so much prejudice as just fear of the unknown."

Bob Henry's vitality and creative vision made *The Nat King Cole Show* a landmark in the "variety comedy" format, and brought it within heartbreaking view of the success Cole desired. Henry had nothing to work with but the "talent" and the camera — small budget, little rehearsal time, and no technical or writing staff. He recalls: "I came

439

on in March. We had no budget, by the way, it was absolutely ridiculous. I was turned on by this challenge. The scenery budget, I'm not kidding, was $125, which even in those days was nothing.

"There was a show where we paid tribute to the record industry. And in the cellar of NBC, piled high, were these ETs, sixteen-inch electrical transcriptions, big records. These were made out of vinyl, and if you held one up to the light it was translucent. I hung these records all around and then flew the curtain. I lit them from the rear and they shone, all those circles hanging there, and it made it look as expensive as any one of the 'specials' in those days. Nat sang with the glowing records behind him, a curtain of shining records.

"One day I was desperate for a theme. My little boy had a mobile hanging over his crib, Little Bo-peep with the sheep. I unhooked that, brought it in, used the mobile as a foreground piece in front of the camera. And when I left the house I snapped off some tree branches. We could afford a stage doorframe, and the branches outside the door created the effect of home, Nat in an overcoat, arriving from the road, carrying his suitcase, happy to be home with his children. The theme was childhood — Nat had all these songs for kids. They made a wonderful program."

Union rules prohibited Henry from carrying props like the mobile into the studio. "The props had to be picked up by a union truck driver, delivered to the scenery dock at NBC by union men, etc., etc. You couldn't move a table without union help. Hell, we couldn't afford any of this. The prop men were some burly types who fought for the teamsters and things like that. But I was a nice guy and Nat was a nice guy and we weren't tough or demanding or full of ego. So I'd go to the guys and say, 'I need this, but you know we can't afford it. Hey! You know, this is a good time for you guys to take a break!' So I would haul in the props and the union guys looked the other way."

On April Fools' Day the great conductor Nelson Riddle was leading the orchestra. He alternated with bandleader Gordon Jenkins, but the handsome, charming Riddle was everybody's favorite. Henry recalls: "I went to the cameraman and I said, Put a camera on the right side of Nat Cole and behind him just some neutral scenery. On the other side of the stage put Riddle and the musicians, and focus another camera on them behind Nat. There. When I go from the first camera to the second, instantaneously it'll look like an orchestra appeared magically behind Nat. No problem. It was a trick, easy but impressive."

Cole, facing the rehearsal cameras announced, "Since it's April Fools' Day, there's no question but that what I should offer you is *Nelson Riddle and his Orchestra!*" He snapped his fingers like a magician and turned his body just slightly as Henry cut to the second camera — and suddenly the whole orchestra materialized behind the singer.

"He was synchronized beautifully," Henry recalls. "His timing was perfect." Everybody in the studio was excited about this when they saw the rehearsal. Hal Kemp, still nervous about the controversial show, called the director into his office and asked if the band was going to appear behind Nat.

"Yeah! Isn't it a great idea? It's not going to cost anything!"

"Well, you know, the musicians are white," said Kemp, huffing and puffing.

"Yeah?"

"Nat is black," said Hal Kemp.

"I noticed that," Henry replied agreeably.

Kemp reached into his drawer for a paper clip. "I don't know," he said, furrowing his brow, and attacking the paper clip with his teeth. "It's going to look like the white men are working for the black man. I don't know if it's going to work."

There was a long silence, in which Bob Henry considered the predicament. He recalls: "I took a moment, and I plotted. Is this really going to be my ass in the business? Whoa! And I thought, Hell, let me just try it once . . ."

And so he pleaded, and kind Hal Kemp was shaking with nerves so bad he could hardly hold the next paper clip, let alone unstring it like he had done the other four or five on his desk. At last he exploded, "All right, try it, but be careful!" and waved the director away.

"The reviewer for *Variety*, Jack Helman, gave that show a great review, Nat's timing was so good. And after that the show started being noticed."

Only a few days earlier, Nat Cole and Nelson Riddle had recorded the haunting "China Gate." This was the title song of Sam Fuller's movie, in production that spring, the drama in which Cole had his first significant movie role. (In 1955 Universal Films had made a twenty-minute melodrama called *The Nat King Cole Story*, in which Cole played himself.) In *China Gate* Nat and Gene Barry play soldiers who venture behind the lines in Indochina to find a secret munitions dump used by the Chinese Communists. The suspenseful film has a plot with a racial moral, as Barry's character has forsaken his Eurasian wife (young Angie Dickinson) because their child's features are too "oriental" for his liking. Cole plays Goldie, a brave and thoughtful warrior, and the reviewers were kind to him. The *Los Angeles Examiner* said, "He plays him with a sensitiveness and refinement that have the same warm effectiveness his singing possesses." Fuller was a savvy director. No doubt he told the beginning actor to "act naturally" in a role that suited him. Much was made of the moment when Cole steps into a booby trap and the camera close-up of his face displays real pain. Unfortunately this was the greatest scene of his short-lived acting career.

He was serious about his acting, for itself and as part of his many-fronted campaign to dissolve racial barriers in show business. But he discovered that it was hard work, "a lot more physical work than I'm used to. One day they had me clinging to a rock. Another day I had to leap into water waist-deep and then wade . . . The leaping wasn't so bad," he said, shivering, "but the ice-cold water sure was!"

Before Cole was done with *China Gate*, Paramount offered him the lead role in *St. Louis Blues*, the life story of composer W. C. Handy, a friend of

Cole's since 1943. On November 16, 1956, Nat had driven out to Handy's birthday party at his house in Yonkers, days after the TV show premiered. That day Cole had discussed with Handy making a movie of his life. Robert Smith produced and wrote the picture, which would be directed by Allen Reisner. The brilliant cast that included Cab Calloway, Pearl Bailey, Ruby Dee, Eartha Kitt, Ella Fitzgerald, and Billy Preston dissolved into a loose musical review chiefly because Nat Cole did not have the dramatic momentum to hold the story together. *Variety* called it a "disappointing biopic." Historian Donald Bogle, author of a definitive study of African-American entertainment, says of Cole's performance as W. C. Handy: "Thin and anemic and much too suave and courteous, Cole seemed out of place, and it was apparent that he lacked the strength and range to carry the picture." The movie bombed at the box office in 1958. And though he would have a few more minor roles, notably in the Julie London–John Drew Barrymore miscegenation drama *Night of the Quarter Moon*, Cole would never see another screen opportunity like *St. Louis Blues*.

There is little more to say about Nat Cole's acting. His artistic and human virtues, and weaknesses, evidently combined to make him a mediocre dramatic actor. He had great presence, but only in that single role he had forged during twenty years of struggling to put songs over to an audience. He lacked the shape-shifting gifts of Poitier, Belafonte, and Sammy Davis, Jr. Cole's timing was superb, but it was musician's timing that anticipates the beat rather than the actor's timing that responds to an emotional event. He was a master of the art of concealment. The face he had prepared to face the audience of millions he now commanded was a mask that concealed anger, fear, every kind of resentment, vexation, and bitterness. His face and bearing projected warmth, humor, shy vulnerability, and — in the transports of a ballad — introspective passion. His power lay in this strenuous refinement of self — he had become Nat King Cole to such a degree that he could never be anyone else, not even long enough to play a dramatic role convincingly.

To give Cole every benefit of the doubt, the man might have done better acting in *St. Louis Blues* that autumn had he not been fighting so hard to stay on television. Reporters following him from coast to coast marveled over his ability to juggle so many jobs at once — nightclub singer, TV star, movie actor.

"Before the end of the regular season, Cole had survived 34 early-evening shows," said *Newsweek* on July 15. "He was being carried by 77 stations (nearly half of them below the Mason-Dixon Line) and had shown such promise that last week NBC doubled the show's length, and shifted its summer time slot to Tuesday evenings opposite the competing *$64,000 Question* on CBS."

Cole said, "I know we have an audience. And it's not a teenage audience. Half are older women and a third are men. When you get men to look at a vocalist, you've really done something." With Robert Henry's staging, there was much more than a vocalist to look at. Henry was an ace com-

445

edy writer. They got 10,000 letters but still no sponsor. On July 2, the show went to a half hour, with its first white guest star, Frankie Laine.

And Nat King Cole went on the warpath. On July 9, columnist Hal Humphrey of the *Los Angeles Mirror News* published the quote that would be heard around the world — Nat's most famous epigram: "Madison Avenue is afraid of the dark." Humphrey wrote: "Cole is engaged in a battle every bit as significant as the one Jackie Robinson had in 1947 when he became the first Negro to play major league baseball in America . . . With a good audience rating, a star of Nat's stature and a prime evening time period, it became obvious why the ad agencies and their sponsors were staying away. To further eliminate any phony alibis, NBC expanded Nat's show to a half hour Tuesday nights." Within a week all the news magazines were echoing Hal Humphrey's column, and Cole's TV show became a crusade, what *Time* called television's "weightiest serving of social significance."

SAMMY AND HARRY
AND THE GENERAL

Nat King Cole and his director, Robert Henry, were ready for a battle, and the network stood squarely behind them. By summer's end the show was costing NBC $18,000 a week. Nat praised them: "Networks just don't go around putting shows on TV without sponsors, and I will always be grateful for this opportunity." In twenty years of show business he had made friends who were now stars. Frankie Laine, whose song "It Only Happens Once" Cole showcased in 1943 when Laine was unknown, was now getting $10,000 for TV appearances. But he was willing to visit Nat's show for "scale," then $155. Laine was the first of many headliners who would waive their fees, including Mel Tormé, Tony Martin, Betty Hutton, Peggy Lee, Ella Fitzgerald, Julius La Rosa, Tony Bennett, Sammy Davis, Jr., and Harry Belafonte. Nat had first seen Belafonte back in 1949 when the struggling singer sang between acts at Carnegie Hall. Now the Calypso King, the Jamaican folksinger turned matinee idol, was getting $20,000 to $30,000 to appear on TV. But Belafonte, like every other entertainer in America, would work Nat's show for scale. Out of his pocket, to show his appreciation, Nat bought gifts for the guests — Mahalia Jackson got a color TV set, and Sammy Davis got a Leica camera.

After Davis criticized Cole on Milton Berle's show, scolding Cole for entertaining a segregated audience in Alabama, the two men managed to patch up their differences. Sammy had an explosive personality, given to flights of fury and sentimentality. Thus he was an unlikely intimate of Cole, who tended to associate with steadier folk. Nevertheless, as the Rat Pack sought Nat's company in Vegas, the two would spend more and more time together in the 1960s. Sammy was a charter member.

Cole and Davis are a fascinating study in contrasts. Both men of prodigious natural talent and versatility, in background and character they were utterly dissimilar. Sammy was born in Harlem in 1925, child of a chorus girl and the lead dancer in a vaudeville revue called "Will Mastin's Holiday in Dixieland." One thing little Sammy did have in common with young Nathaniel was astonishing precocity. At ten Sammy was so accomplished as a dancer, singer, and mimic that Mastin created a trio to showcase the kid, the Will Mastin Trio, consisting of Will, Sam Sr., and Sammy Jr. They must have struggled to make ends meet — Oscar Moore remembered the kid shining shoes outside a Chicago nightclub in 1941.

Neglected by his mother, brought up in a tough world of crumbling vaudeville houses and nightclubs where his daily bread depended upon his pleasing an audience, Sammy had a need to be loved by them that was practical as well as emotional. He grew to be a man with a sketchy sense of self and a bottomless pit of need — for love, attention, and respect. Being black may have been the

448

least of Sammy's problems. He would do anything for attention, and then suffer pathetic remorse if he offended. Some who knew him say Davis never knew who he was. By one of those playful tricks of Providence, it was just those traits that made him a sublime actor and mimic.

I will never forget a television drama Davis made in the 1960s. He played an army private, a country bumpkin who somehow gets bunked as the only black in a company of unkind white soldiers. They make fun of his looks, his voice, and his manners. His even-tempered, good-natured response to their gibes just barely conceals his heartache, his need to be accepted. At last a demon among them devises the final torment: a dummy grenade he drops next to Sammy, the only soldier among them who thinks the bomb is real. Seeing the danger to all, the black man falls on the sputtering grenade, crying out, "Run, y'all, run, y'all!" His act of heroism moves everyone to tears. From beginning to end it is acting of enormous depth and fineness of detail. Davis has taken his own emotions and surrendered them to a character, making an enduring work of art.

Davis was an actor, a shape shifter, a chameleon. I dwell upon him here because Nat Cole's character emerges the more vividly in contrast to Sammy Davis's. Cole was a mediocre actor partly because he had so strongly refined his sense of self, his dignity and pride — he could not hide this under any other role. He had a strong emotional center, a fund of self-love, and he knew who he was. Humorous, he could not descend to the clown's role that black entertainers had played for generations. Sammy Davis remained a clown in that tradition (though he acted other parts), probably the greatest comic impersonator of his era.

Sammy Davis, Jr., was scheduled to be Nat's guest on July 30, 1957, in Chicago.

The show begins, as usual, with Cole the smiling host in his gray narrow-lapeled suit singing with Nelson Riddle's horns and strings the humble invitation: "In the evenings may I come and sing to you, all the songs that I would like to bring to you?" Then the camera cuts to three signs on spindles, old-fashioned vaudeville stage cards each with a crown on top, which together spell out *The Nat King Cole Show*, as a dignified voice-over proudly announces, "Ladies and gentlemen . . . *The Nat King Cole Show*!" to drums and fanfare. The signs spin one by one, with the guest stars' names, as the announcer intones: "With tonight's special guests . . . Sammy Davis, Jr., and . . . the Hi-Lo's!"

Riddle strikes up the band, and we see the Randy Van Horne Octet swaying, finger-popping, arms swinging side to side as tall Nat King Cole strides out in front of them singing "Here I go again . . . taking a chance on love," swinging his arms, snapping his fingers on the off beat.

When the song is done, Nat is beaming at the live audience's warm applause; his broad smile is dazzling as he thanks everyone for joining him again. "Well, tonight we'll have all sorts of things going on. We'll have the Hi-Lo's, one of the foremost vocal groups in the country, and our special guest, the dynamic Sammy Davis, Jr." Before he introduces Sammy, he stands alone before the closed curtain to sing the Irving Berlin ballad "Maybe I Love You Too Much," which he croons in his high style, intimate, smiling, but completely without irony, bowing his head for a moment at the end as if lost in thought, before being reawakened to this world and a million pairs of eyes by the audience's applause.

"You know, every so often the world of show business produces an extraordinary talent who can do just about everything — sing, dance, comedy, and do them all to perfection. In our time they call that combination Mr. Wonderful — and here he is, Sammy Davis, Jr.!"

Thunderous applause. And Sammy comes bounding onstage headfirst, that amazing head with the cobra neck on narrow shoulders, the rubber face with nerd's horn-rim glasses, grinning out of one side of his mouth. Sammy's head and neck are half as long as his torso, which looks longer than his rubber legs. Sammy comes charging, eager to be seen, eager to be loved, and slips affectionately under Nat's great arm. He's so short, his hairline is at the level of Nat's chin. Nat hugs him and the audience goes wild. Nat is father, big brother, and hero rolled into one.

For those of us who never knew Nat King Cole, the television shows are a precious record of his personality, the expressions, gestures, and mannerisms that are the emanation of character. Cole's face is mobile and expressive from the lift of his eyebrows to the point of his perfect chin; he "talks with his hands" eloquently and with economy of movement. The effect overall is one of dignified humor and affection, vulnerability and accessibility.

Bob Henry wrote the show and most of the gags are his, but a mere afternoon of rehearsal left a great deal of liberty to the improvisational skills of Cole and his guests. They are funny, spontaneous, and real.

Sammy asks the host if it's all right if he sends greetings to his father and his uncle Will Mastin of the Trio (free publicity). There is comic banter back and forth, as Nat lectures Sammy on the dos and don'ts of network television, greeting relatives being a major no-no. And Sammy grows more and more imploring and abashed, like a teenager asking Dad to borrow the car.

"Then what *can* I do?" the guest pleads. Nat says he can do imitations. And so Sammy stretches his face, points his fingers, plants his feet, and does a frightening impersonation of Jimmy Cagney, as Nat looks over Sammy's shoulder and smiles appreciatively. The audience roars approval. Nat steps up and does *his* impression of Cagney. It's not bad, actually, but after Sammy's it's charmingly lame. The crowd applauds Nat for his effort, and he leaves the stage to let Sammy sing a solo, "I'm Riding on the Moon," which he does with verve, but as a singer he's no King Cole. The two men's strengths complement each other.

As Sammy takes a bow, Nat enters applauding. Much of the excitement the two generate comes from Sammy's conspiratorial, second-story tone. He eyes the audience slyly, straightening his tie; he looks over his shoulder into the wings and stage-whispers to Nat as if they are *really* getting away with something, two African-Americans on network television and *wow*, if *they* find out about this, the jig is up. "Hey, Nat," he whispers, so that everybody in America can hear him, "I don't want this to get around, it's a big network and everything, but have you noticed that in television, sooner or later, the star of the show, if he's got a guest, he pulls up the stools, they sit down. Now, once in a while, this is all right. But lately it's getting to where it's *embarrassing!*"

He's making fun of Perry Como, Dinah Shore, the whole white television establishment. And Bob Henry does not shy away from this satire. He revels in it. As Nat admits, "Well, I'm embarrassed too," Henry pulls the curtain, and there are several dozen stools, in rows, in stacks, in pyramids. Sammy does a double take, screams in terror, and says, "I've got a phobia about stools, I'll have to get rid of them!" Nat says, "Be my guest!"

And as the drummer plays an up-tempo trap solo, Sammy does the Dance of the Destruction of the Stools. He kicks at them, tap-dances. He throws one at another and dances. He leapfrogs over several, knocks them down like dominoes, like so many ad reps; when he thinks he's conquered them all, he pauses to take a bow. Henry flies the rear curtain, and there are dozens of stools hanging in the air where Sammy can't reach them. Undaunted, the guest from Harlem strips off his coat and tie, and as Nelson Riddle rouses trumpets and trombones, Sammy does the wild dance of the entertainer whose spirit no number of stools or advertising executives can dampen.

It is great dancing and ingenious stagecraft.

When Sammy is done, Nat sits at the piano and plays "Paper Moon" while the dancer catches his breath. As the audience applauds the piano player, Sammy enters and lounges against the white Steinway.

"Nat, you're doing wonderful now," Sammy says, and then a tone of concern enters his voice. "But you need a *style* when you sing." Of course, this breaks up the house, because Cole is one of the greatest singing stylists since Louis Armstrong. As Billy Eckstine once said: "Nat took a style and made a voice of it."

"Style?" the host politely inquires. "Do you want to show me?"

"Well, there was a guy I remember, many years ago. He used to sing with a Trio, and he played the piano wonderful. King . . . something or other . . . he went like this . . ." And Sammy gestures to the keyboard for Nat to accompany him. All this is very natural, by the way, so we can scarcely detect they're putting us on.

What happens next is magical, and so gracefully developed that you nearly forget the technical virtuosity that makes it possible. Sammy Davis, Jr., black glasses and all, *becomes* Nat King Cole. Sammy stretches his rubber face to show Nat's wide mouth, high, delicate brows, his euphoric gaze, as he sings a soulful chorus of the ballad "Somewhere Along the Way." And the voice! The impression is so finely rendered that we can hear that this is not only Cole's voice but the Nat Cole of 1943, the singer who stretched his vowels with the South Side Chicago drawl, whose baritone had not yet been smoothed to perfection and refined beyond irony. As Sammy sings, Nat grins in wonder, frowns, and traces a square in the air with a free hand to show what he thinks of *that* style. In the middle of the chorus Sammy even imitates Cole's signature mannerism, flicking upward under his chin with the back of his fingers, something Nat would *never* do while performing, and even he cannot keep from laughing — it is hilarious.

Now Nat wants to try it. He takes the second chorus, and this is also funny, because Nat does a perfect comic impersonation of the voice he left behind sometime in the 1940s. He hasn't forgotten how he sounded fifteen years ago, but he exaggerates it to make us understand why he left the style behind as too crude, too raw, too Southern. He even flicks at his chin for us, heightening the comedy. Finally Sammy joins him for the last chorus, and the two voices and faces, heads together, almost become one — in a moment of clearly genuine affection.

As the audience applauds and cheers, Sammy tells his friend, "I been waitin' for years to do that."

"And I been waitin' for years to catch you at it," Nat snaps back at him fondly, in a flash of superbly timed wit. Cole really loved Sammy Davis, Jr. One of the moving things about this kinescope is that we can see in Nat's eyes and smile, in the way he puts his arm around Sammy, the emanation of that profound and sunny affection; we can imagine what it must have been like to know such attention. No theatrical fakery or showbiz sentiment here. Cole was not that good an actor.

So it is just as compelling to watch the host the following week with his guest Harry Belafonte. Their relationship was complex. The most we can say for their mutual feelings is that they sustained, over a period of years, a fund of enormous professional respect.

Belafonte was born in New York in 1927, but he spent much of his youth in Jamaica. His parents came from the West Indies; his maternal grandmother and paternal grandfather were white. As a poor boy in Harlem, he found himself in hostile competition with his younger, lighter-skinned brother. West Indians had strong notions of caste, and they prized "white" characteristics. Belafonte's sailor father coddled Harry's brother, and Harry never got over it, even long after his father left the family for a white woman.

His youth was troubled. Biographer Arnold Shaw wrote: "Color discrimination in his immediate family, prejudice and hostility in the world outside his home — all these conspired to create an insecure human being. The exterior of the man was marked by defiance, belligerence, and almost undirected hostility while the inner core was tender, gentle . . ." His intelligence, angry determination, and rare physical beauty saved him. Diahann Carroll said of him, "From the top of his head right down to his toes he's the most beautiful man I ever set eyes on." Few would quibble. But it would take him a lifetime to get over the sort of anger Nat Cole put behind him (to all appearances) by age eighteen.

Cole and Belafonte probably never got along

better than they did that evening on Cole's show. Ever the gracious host, Nat heralds his guest star, flatters him; they alternate in the spotlight, singing in their different styles; they tease each other in comic dialogues and ad-lib. But there is a real edge to their teasing, a competitive spirit throughout. On his show Nat always plays the role of the older, wiser, and more successful brother, and Belafonte clearly resents this, smiling through clenched teeth.

After singing the ballad "It's Not for Me to Say," Cole introduces his guest, with only a trace of condescension. "Now for our guest, motion picture star, recording favorite, concert artist — I don't know of anyone who's achieved so much in so short a time . . . and so deserving too. Here's . . . Harry Belafonte!"

The camera cuts to a deep spotlight, and Belafonte in silhouette. To the rhythmic strumming of a guitar, he comes strutting toward us, dramatically, the blousy-sleeved calypso shirt split to the sternum, frowning, hunching his shoulders, hands lightly clenched. "Did you hear about Jerry?" he sings, the angry folk song that made him famous, the one about the mule who takes revenge upon a tyrannical foreman.

As Belafonte sings, the round silver buckle on his belly accentuates the suggestive movement of his hips.

When he is done the lights dim as the applause rises, then the camera brings Belafonte and his guitarist into the same romantically lighted frame. The acoustic guitar in silhouette sounds its most beautiful major chord, the simple D chord, plucking it in slow waltz time, and Harry begins: "I peeked in to say goodnight / And then I saw my child in prayer / And for me, some scarlet ribbons, / Scarlet ribbons for my hair." He sings softly and simply and from the heart one of the greatest folk ballads in the language, the story of a man who cannot answer his child's prayers but finds by the grace of some miracle they are answered anyway. And when Belafonte has sung the last of his song there is not a dry eye in the audience or anywhere in earshot of an American television set tuned to *The Nat King Cole Show.*

It is a hard act to follow, but after the NBC commercial we see Nat, in a seersucker coat, relaxing on a comfortable living-room set. He picks up a picture of his beautiful wife, Maria, widely known as Cole's Queen, and sings the ballad "I Thought About Marie." It is just barely enough of a hook to win the audience back from Belafonte's sorcery.

Then at last the two men meet, as Belafonte enters in the clamor of applause for the host. Grinning, Harry tells Nat how well he sang, the two try to outdo each other in flattery, and they decide to review, together, the highlights of their careers. First Nat sings a medley of "Straighten Up and Fly Right," "Nature Boy," etc., but each song segues into a comedy routine. Harry had been to drama school and had a passion for comedy, so Bob Henry wrote him some clever bits. Black stars rarely got a chance to do anything but their specialty — in Harry's case, folk music — and he was eager to show his witty side.

So now Harry, wearing a white sailor's hat, is

swabbing the deck, elbows and knees making comic angles. Nat, his superior officer, comes to dress him down: "Seaman Belafonte, for your careless swabbing of the deck, I sentence you to three days in the brig, with nothing but bread and water and calypso records!" And Belafonte over-acts in horror, gasping, "Oh no! Not that! Please, sir, give a sailor his dignity!" Next we see Harry in a mortarboard, grinning in idiotic pride at his graduation from drama school as the chorus sings, "Hail to thee, O Belafonte / May your dreams come true / Don't call *us* we'll call *you* . . ." And his face drops. Still in his mortarboard he launches into a mock Shakespearean monologue, "To be or not to be," leading to the questions: What is he to do with a drama school degree? How shall he seek his fortune?

It's all in good fun, but all at the younger man's expense, as the dignified King plays straight man to Belafonte's clown. A format that delighted Sammy Davis, Jr., becomes somewhat of a strain for the proud and basically reserved Jamaican.

But the audience could scarcely detect the strain. They would never know what went on behind the scenes. They did not know the strings Gastel had to pull to get Belafonte to waive his fee and appear on the show in the first place: the appeal to their mutual interests, two African-Americans working for the cause, working to promote each other, and for the good of all. Few people knew what it was to go from the back of the bus to being millionaire stars; this forced them together regardless of their differences. And the audience did not know that during rehearsals that afternoon

459

a piece of scenery fell and hit Belafonte on the head, hurting him badly. The showman went on with the rehearsal, performing flawlessly that night, but the blow on the head was so violent he suffered a retinal detachment from it. Two weeks later he would be hospitalized, nearly blinded in his right eye from the injury sustained on Nat King Cole's set. Later he could not help but associate the injury with his host.

"What's it like working with Harry, Nat?" asked Bob Henry after it was over. Nat scratched his chin reflectively.

"Well . . . you know, he's not really a singer."

"Oh, jeez, what do you mean, not a singer? Hey, with those records?"

"He's a stylist. A song stylist. He gives a dramatic flavor, a kind of humorous, novelty kind of flavor . . ." and Cole's voice trailed off as he shrugged his shoulders.

And across town, says Henry, somebody was asking Belafonte about Cole. "When Harry left he was thinking to himself: Well, Nat's okay but he's a *record act*. A record act is someone like Smokey Robinson or the Beatles, whose true strengths are lost in live performance. Belafonte was saying, 'I don't have to worry about Nat upstaging me because he's a *record act*.' There was this competitive feeling between them."

But the audience did not know this. What they saw was two great entertainers working together at the top of their form, television at its best. One of the millions moved to tears and laughter by the show that night was General David Sarnoff, the owner of NBC, at home on Long Island.

The Davis and Belafonte episodes, aired back to back in the summer, were so good they created a sensation in the business and boosted the program's ratings. *The Nat King Cole Show* gained the critical mass that would have made any other show a slam dunk for ad salesmen. Letters poured in. "If he sells toothpaste, I'll buy it. If he sells beauty, I'll try it. If he sells a broomstick, I'll fly it," wrote one. And a white woman in a white neighborhood, struggling to raise "a child of mixed blood," wrote: "One of our most hostile neighbors stopped me and said he had seen *The Nat Cole Show*, and was terribly impressed by the warmth and sincerity he witnessed, and went on to say he hoped our little girl would have some of the talent Mr. Cole has . . . So one man has softened his heart just by seeing for himself that charm and talent are to be found under all colors of skin."

Robert Henry recalls: "After the Belafonte show I suddenly get a call from the NBC promotions department." They wanted to know what the next show was going to be, who was the next guest. They had never cared before. "And I asked why, and the p.r. people said they wanted to give us some publicity! So I went to my boss and asked, 'What's going on here?'

" 'Sit down,' said Hal Kemp. 'You know who was watching the show on Tuesday night? The General.'

" 'The General?' " Henry began to perspire. General David Sarnoff was head of RCA, founder of NBC, Mr. Broadcasting himself, the most powerful individual in the industry. He became a legend at age nineteen when as a wireless telegraph operator he picked up the *Titanic*'s SOS and stayed at the key for seventy-two hours directing ships to the sinking luxury liner. He perfected our first home radios and set up the nation's first television service. During World War II he was promoted to the rank of brigadier general in the Army Signal Corps, and ever after he liked to be called the General.

"He loved it," rasped Hal Kemp.

After watching Cole and Belafonte the General called in his vice president in charge of advertising and said to him, "I want that show to be sponsored, or heads will roll."

So Cole, Lee Young, John Collins, and Charlie Harris, heading down to Atlantic City on August 17 to play the 500 Club, had every reason to feel optimistic, even triumphant. Everyone was talking about how great the show was. Now that General Sarnoff was leading the charge, how could there be any question about their getting a national sponsor?

But the ad men had no good news for them in August, despite the fact that Bob Henry had lined up Peggy Lee and Ella Fitzgerald, Tony Martin and Tony Bennett. Home in L.A. that summer, Nat Cole and Lee Young kept waiting for the call that a sponsor was writing the big check. The call never came. When Young got a new dog, he named it "Sponsor Please." General Sarnoff and the network were doing all they could; this is evident from the blitz of Cole publicity NBC generated from mid-August until late September. Every word Cole's show received was publicity taken from somebody else. Sarnoff was declaring war upon the Lords of Madison Avenue, and Nat King Cole was his standard-bearer. When the show was canceled in Birmingham the week Pearl Bailey was on, Nat told Leonard Feather of *The Melody Maker*, "The show can be sold if the agency men look at it from a money point of view rather than at the race issue." That was clear. Nat's ratings were neck and neck with the *$64,000 Question* quiz show, which fetched top dollar for sponsors, playing opposite on Tuesday night on CBS.

This was war. On August 27 the governor of Georgia, Mavin Griffin, went out of his way during a speech at the Atlanta Masonic Lodge to criticize Nat Cole and Eartha Kitt for their suggestive lyrics, cautioning African-Americans not to aspire to be like these musicians. Many Southern stations refused to carry Cole's show, notably the NBC affiliate in New Orleans, which was bombarded by letters of protest from Nat's fans. The channel would soon relent.

In a frank interview with *Variety* on September 10, Cole lashed out against the ad representatives. "Madison Avenue is in the North, and that's where the resistance is . . . the South is used as a football to take some of the stain off of us in the North. Madison Avenue still runs television, and there is . . . reluctance on its part to sell my show.

"NBC and I are not doing this as a challenge, but as it should be done — as part of showbiz. Why shouldn't a Negro entertainer have a show of his own?

"It's not the people in the South who create racial problems — it's the people who are governing. Those who govern isolate the people by advocating a rigid policy of discrimination whether the people want it or not; they are not allowed to participate in mixed audiences because of their laws."

Angry, frustrated, Sarnoff hatched up a new tactic: cooperative sponsorship. If one company like Ford would not buy national network ads, then NBC would cobble together local deals, selling ads at a discount of fifty cents on a dollar of value. Before September 11 they had "full-sponsorship deals" in eight markets. Rheingold Beer came through first, buying up New York and Hartford. ("The fact that Cole is a Negro is of no importance to us," said Rheingold. "His show has quality.") Gunther Beer snapped up Washington, D.C.; Colgate and Gallo Wine took L.A. This was not enough to break even, but it was a beginning. Cole praised NBC's loyalty and courage. "I take my hat off to them. NBC is spending $17,500 a week on the show, taking that out of its own pocket . . . budget is being upped $2,500 when the new slot goes into effect." Sarnoff was giving them a good 7:30 slot, near prime time.

So there was hope, but it was beginning to dawn on Cole that all the talent in the world, all the network's support and effort he and his friends could muster, might not overcome the prejudices of the "smart boys" selling soap on Madison Avenue. While no one would call Nat temperamental, Bob Henry noted a couple of outbursts that autumn. On September 17 in Las Vegas their guest star was Tony Martin, a white crooner with a haughty manner. "The song Nat was rehearsing was 'Stardust.' I'll never forget it. Tony's hanging around, leaning on the piano. And if *anyone* could sing 'Stardust,' it was Nat Cole. Nelson Riddle sets the key, Nat starts to sing. And Tony Martin says, 'Uh, Nat! You know what you oughta do? You oughta . . .' and he told Nat how to sing this phrase. Nat turned and walked off the stage into his dressing room. Tony turned to me. 'What'd I say? What *did* I say? What's wrong?' Tony talked like Mae West. And Nelson's telling the band, 'All right, fellas, let's take out Tony's song . . .' The fact that *anyone* was trying to tell Nat Cole how to sing 'Stardust' was like teaching the Pope to speak Latin.

"The other time Nat blew up was when the music drowned him out. 'Bob?' he yelled at me. 'You gotta tell the piano player, where the hell does he get off playing the piano that loud? You could hardly hear me!' "

As the ratings improved with the show's quality, and the co-op deal attracted big companies in local markets, Nat was astounded he still could not get a national sponsor. He was growing bitter. One afternoon Carlos walked into Nat's dressing room. The manager told the star, "Max Factor's people say no Negro can sell lipstick for him."

"What do they think we use?" Nat asked. "Chalk? Congo paint? And what about the telephone company? A man sees a Negro on a television show. What's he going to do, call up the company and tell them to take out his telephone? In Houston, Texas, we were sponsored by Coca-Cola, a *Southern company!* Nobody

465

stopped drinking Coca-Cola!"

It was madness, and it was driving him mad. As *The Nat King Cole Show* sailed into late October with ratings that thrilled sponsors shrewd enough to buy the discounted ads, the star worked harder and harder to preserve its high-principled social agenda. At least he would have that. So there were more white guests — Gogi Grant, Tony Bennett, Hugh O'Brian, and blacks and whites mingling, which would culminate in a show where black Nat Cole *danced* with the white Betty Hutton.

And finally the *Nat King Cole Show* succumbed to pressures within the television network in addition to the contempt of the advertising agencies. Few people remember this part of the story. Robert Henry was there.

"Eight o'clock was prime time. We were on from seven-thirty till eight, kind of a ghetto time. Singer Eddie Fisher followed us at eight, and comedian George Gobel at eight the next week. They alternated. Gobel's was a crappy show and the ratings were terrible." Fisher's was worse. Berle Adams produced it for a while, and they had trouble booking guests. According to Adams: "None of them wanted to sing duets with Fisher because he sang off-key."

Henry remembers: "I went down to Fisher's set, and I've never seen anything like this: There was Eddie Fisher's piano player with a big cue card — a staff of music with notes. He had a pointer, and while Eddie was singing the pianist would point to the notes, up for this one, down for that one, up you sing, down you sing. Now, I have imagination but I'm not that good to make this up, that a nationally known singer, on network television, has to be told whether to sing the notes up or down."

In those days the two giants in the field of artists' representation were the General Amusement Corporation (GAC, originally General Artists) and the Music Corporation of America (MCA). These powers were in cutthroat competition. MCA controlled the Gobel and Fisher shows (their commission was huge), and GAC represented Nat King Cole.

Somebody from MCA went to the television network in mid-November, after Mahalia Jackson was on Cole's show, and at a moment when everybody's ratings were weak. And the agent blamed Eddie Fisher's poor ratings on the African-Americans. "Of course Eddie's ratings are bad, with that lousy Nat King Cole coming on just before us with sponsors like Rheingold Beer and Gallo Wine!"

The network had a huge investment in the hour-long Gobel and Fisher shows, and both had paying sponsors. After more than a year Cole was still "on sustaining," which means the co-op ads were not paying the bills. Harold Kemp saw that *The Nat King Cole Show* had cost the network nearly $400,000 — this could not go on forever. NBC was not a charity. Kemp and the General were about to pull the plug on Nat's show, and the pressure MCA put on them hastened the decision. Carlos Gastel and GAC had no leverage here to equal MCA's.

So on November 20, 1957, Hal Kemp telephoned Bob Henry to tell him *Treasure Hunt* was taking their spot, and the network would be moving Nat's show to Saturday at 7 p.m. "It was the graveyard," says Henry. "In those days anything before seven-thirty on a Saturday was garbage, sleaze. So I went to Nat and asked him what we should do."

Cole was concerned about Henry's job situation. So he asked the director what *he* thought they should do. After all, they had been partners in the show for most of a year. Henry had a wife and two children to support. Now it seems amazing to him that Cole would leave the decision to him. Maybe Nat knew what his answer would be.

With self-deprecating humor, Henry recalls: "I don't have *that* kind of guts. Yet this was one of those instances where I was a man of integrity."

He said to the star, "Nat, let's not go to that crappy time. If we do, this whole thing we've been trying to build takes a step backward."

"If we quit now, it's like Babe Ruth retiring in his prime, right?" Cole said.

Henry replied, "Exactly."

"So it's okay with you if we go off?"

Henry nodded and said, "I think we should."

That same day Cole issued this statement to the press: "Due to personal appearances previously contracted for, it becomes necessary for me to turn down a new series offered to me by NBC." And the next day he told *The New York Times* that when he started with NBC he knew "we would have a hard hill to climb, but I thought that after we'd been on the air a year or so the agencies would admit that myself and the show could be sold to a national sponsor." He said he felt from the beginning the advertising agencies were hostile.

"They offered me a new time . . . but I decided not to take it. I feel played out," Nat told the *Times*. "There won't be shows starring Negroes for a while," he added.

The next day he performed a Youth Benefit Concert for the Episcopal Diocese of L.A. and his own parish, the Church of the Advent, at the Shrine Auditorium. And on November 26 he flew to Australia again for a week of shows. Upon his return he did his last three TV shows, with Billy Eckstine as his final guest on December 17. Bob Henry went on to fame and glory in the 1960s, directing *The Flip Wilson Show* and other TV hits.

Maria Cole says, "It would be a long time before Nat Cole would lose his anger over the forces that caused him to abandon television."

He smoked more and more. In the mid-1950s, Gastel had given him a cigarette holder which he still used deftly, his only concession to the July 12, 1957, report of the Surgeon General that "prolonged cigarette smoking was a causative factor in the etiology of lung cancer." Sometimes he used a filter in the holder, sometimes not.

The Nat King Cole Show, the thirty segments that have been preserved on kinescope, often appears on PBS. Viewing these from the slag heap of forty years of TV history, it is small consolation to see, with certainty, that Nat Cole was too good for television. His gifts were out of place in a medium that — driven by Madison Avenue — has dependably nourished mediocrity, preferring *Hee Haw* to *The Jonathan Winters Show*, Jack Paar to Steve Al-

469

len, and George Gobel and Eddie Fisher to Nat Cole.

But Main Street is smarter than Madison Avenue knows. Steve Allen and Nat Cole live on in the affections of the public, while George Gobel and Eddie Fisher are all but forgotten.

GAMES AND CHILDREN

One of the best things that ever happened to Nat King Cole is that the Brooklyn Dodgers moved to Los Angeles in 1958. In a blue mood after the Birmingham attack, he had said, "If I ever get rich, I'm gonna buy me a plane and get a box in every ballpark in the country, then I'm gonna fly from city to city and do nothing but watch baseball games." And now he did not have to do that because one of the greatest baseball teams in history, the team of Gil Hodges and Duke Snider, Don Zimmer and Carl Furillo, had moved into Cole's backyard.

This was the team that had welcomed blacks to baseball, the team of Jackie Robinson, Roy Campanella, and the superb African-American pitcher Don Newcombe. That spring Nat could sit in his box at the Coliseum and watch the great left-handed pitcher Sandy Koufax pitch one day and right-hander Don Drysdale the next.

"I love sports. Baseball, soccer, boxing, golf, I love them all. The only sport I'm not interested in is horse racing." Cole grinned. "That's because I don't know the horses personally." The Coles were friends of the prizefighter Sugar Ray Robinson and his wife, and Mr. and Mrs. Joe Louis. Carol Cole recalls: "We used to spend weeks of the summer in Vegas with Joe Louis's son, Punchy. Can you imagine naming your child Punchy?"

Nat once owned the contract of a middleweight fighter, Gene Johns. Then one day Nat was in the gym with Dick LaPalm, who was punching the speedbag and working up a good rhythm, when Miles Davis started watching, dressed in sweats and sneakers. "Hey, Miles," said Dick. "Say, Dick," Miles replied. Then Nat walked over.

"Miles," said Nat brightly. "Have you seen my guy, my middleweight Gene Johns?"

"Yeah, I've seen him," said Miles Davis. "And I can beat the shit out of him." LaPalm was relieved that Miles had said it, because LaPalm was afraid to tell the boss he'd made a bad investment.

After giving up on the boxer, Cole said, "We parted nice and friendly. He wasn't hungry enough. Prizefighters are a special breed. I got him too late."

"Mom and Dad were real hard-core sports fans," says Carol Cole. "This was one of the things that really turned her on about Dad." One night in June the Coles were watching one of the famous heavyweight bouts between the big Swede Ingemar Johansson and the moody black Floyd Patterson on TV in the living room, the dogs at their feet. "This *thing* happened to both of them. I mean, they might as well have been at ringside. They were on their feet yelling at the television. And I was a kid wondering: What *is* this?

"And then you came to understand what it was, too — when we went to baseball games — this was a *serious* focus. Mother kept score with a pencil and her own box-score pad, and you would hear these people, your parents, talking like you have never heard them before, about players and statistics and everything under the sun. And it was contagious." This was a very intense couple, at work and play, and professional sports provided a diversion from work that was nearly as consuming as real life — another kind of theater, where Nat could sit in the audience for a change. Carol even recalls feeling some pressure on the children "to demonstrate how much we were into it. I loved it, up to a point."

"Nat Cole was the No. 1 Los Angeles Dodger fan," wrote Bud Furillo of the *Los Angeles Examiner*. When the team moved from the Coliseum (a converted football stadium) to their new park with gardens and palms in Chavez Ravine, the Coles purchased a box, five seats in the front row between home and first base. Many of his happiest hours were spent there with his family and friends eating popcorn and hot dogs, watching Sandy Koufax strike out a dozen batters in a game, watching Duke Snider and Tommy Davis belt home runs. In the 1960s Nat was player-manager of a baseball team called the Hollywood Celebrity All-Stars that challenged other amateur teams around the city in games raising money for charity. He sponsored one Little League team, and cut a record, "Good Night, Little Leaguer," the royalties from which he assigned to the L.A. Little League Organization. There is a publicity photo of a Little Leaguer standing between Willie Mays in his Giants uniform and Nat Cole in a plaid coat, narrow tie, and one of his beloved little tweed walking hats.

He needed the diversion, because after the TV show failed, his career, which had accelerated nonstop for twenty years, was losing momentum. Nat's film *St. Louis Blues*, finally released in April of 1958, two weeks after W. C. Handy's death, got bad reviews and flopped at the box office. Nat's was a gradual falling-off of popularity — he was still very successful by most standards. He made top dollar in Las Vegas and in the best nightclubs in New York, Chicago, and Miami, with raves in the trade journals, and now he was free to do more of it. "The audience took the versatile singer right into its collective arms, and he had to beg off after seven encores," *Variety* noted of his January 1958 performance at New York's Copa.

"Appearing in a smart, shiny tuxedo, Cole worked his infinite charm and humility on 45 minutes' worth of songs, including many of his disk hits," *Billboard* reported of his gig at Miami's Eden Roc Hotel. "He introduced one of his latest clicks, 'Send for Me,' with the wry comment on rock and rollers that 'If you can't beat 'em, join 'em,' to a stomping reception by the mink-clad and otherwise expensively clothed patrons."

His audience was aging.

Rock and roll was encroaching on Cole's market share. But "Send for Me" is as close as he would ever come to making a rock song, and though it sold a million copies then, now it sounds like a square Sam Cooke imitation. Cole could not beat *or* join the rock and rollers. He was a jazzman deep in his bones, and soon he would defiantly admit it. To the hilarity and applause of middle-aged nightclub patrons who disliked the harsh new music, he performed a long satirical piece by Noel and Joe Sherman called "Mr. Cole

474

Won't Rock and Roll." But when he recorded the piece in Las Vegas in January of 1960, the disc sold poorly to the general public.

Some of his new records were selling well, but not the way the old ones had. From mid-1955 until the success of "Ballerina" in mid-1957, none of Cole's singles hit the one million mark, though one of his sister-in-law's songs "With You on My Mind," did quite well. Charlotte's song "To Whom It May Concern" also enjoyed success, in 1958, and Nat sang it in the film *Night of the Quarter Moon*. Though his LPs continued to sell briskly, he would not see another hit single until "Ramblin' Rose" in 1962.

Early in 1958 Carlos Gastel had the bright idea of cultivating Nat's Latin American audience. That February in Havana, Cole recorded his first album in Spanish, under the direction of Armando Romeu, Jr. *Cole Español* became one of the biggest-selling albums in Capitol's history.

Carol Cole remembers the day her father telephoned Capitol and the receptionist answered brightly, "Capitol Records, Home of Elvis!" And Nat said, trying to hide his astonishment, "Excuse me?" He *had* built the tower, but at the moment Elvis was more important than Nat.

"People don't slip, time catches up with them," he had said in 1948.

In the spring of 1958, Nat and Maria celebrated their tenth anniversary, and he gave her a new diamond ring. They redecorated the huge brick garage that looked out on the swimming pool, converting it into Nat's own "playroom." Magnificent paneling was purchased from a house that Hearst had built years ago for his mistress, Marion Davies, mahogany with an egg-and-dart pattern in the moldings and trim. With a great stone fireplace, wide picture window, and a splendid bar and piano, the room became a haven for Cole, where he often retired after a long day to sit alone, play piano, or entertain friends. A lemon tree stood outside the window. Now that the children were more self-sufficient, Charlotte handled Nat's correspondence in an office above the playroom, and they had an intercom. She recalls: "Nat would play a new song to me on the intercom and say, 'Hey, listen to this!'"

Those years at the end of the decade were good family times, as Nat settled happily into the house in Hancock Park. And when he traveled abroad he took his wife and children along with him. His brother Eddie and his wife moved to L.A. that year. Betty remembered Nat as "the best brother-in-law in the world," and she and Maria got on well together. When Nat and his family traveled, Eddie got the Coles' baseball tickets.

Cookie, in her mid-teens, was struggling with the natural challenges of becoming a woman, a striking young woman no less, with high cheekbones, large wide-set brown eyes, and a perfect, joyful smile. She had inherited her mother Carol Lane's legendary beauty, and it was natural she would dream of becoming an actress. She was grateful for her father's warm attention and his advice, even in matters of love. Cookie would soon be falling in love and her father's voice would enchant her as he sang "When I fall in love / It will be forever" with such conviction. These lyrics among others led the girl to think her father must be expert in matters of the heart. So she would question him, and he always answered to the best of his knowledge.

First she had a crush on Johnny Mathis. It is not surprising that she should fall in love with the singer who sounded most like her father. In 1958 the crooner of "Chances Are" and "Twelfth of Never" released his *Greatest Hits* album, at the ripe age of twenty-three. And owing much to the style of Nat King Cole, the handsome singer was hugely popular. Half the girls in America were in love with soulful Johnny. Carol confided her secret passion to Cole, and he listened carefully and compassionately. Eventually she would mention certain rumors that would lead to a discussion of lifestyles and sexual preferences. Cole and Mathis were friends. Gently he explained to Carol that her affections were probably better directed toward someone more likely to appreciate them.

And then she must have had a crush on someone darker-skinned or lighter-skinned than she, or perhaps someone of a different background altogether. "I remember going to Dad when I was still very young and asking about interracial relationships and how he felt about that. And he just brought it down to this: *If you love someone then you love someone and all the rest really does not matter.*"

Carol had been a protective and affectionate big sister to Natalie. But now she wanted more time to herself, and she spent hours in the bathroom, in front of the mirror, and on the telephone. Sometimes she had to ask her parents to intervene, to get eight-year-old Sweetie out of her hair. Natalie — long-limbed, dark-skinned, athletic — had inherited her father's graceful proportions and many of his features and expressions, including his bright smile, and his laughing eyes, though her own dark eyes were larger, more like Maria's, with arched brows.

In 1999 in a hotel room in Baltimore, the Grammy award-winning singer Natalie Cole reminisces: "My mother used to always say, 'You're so much like your dad!' We're very much alike. That's probably why Dad and I got along so well. We had an unspoken bond, a camaraderie and communication. We had the best time. I liked to do all the things that nobody else liked to do with him. He was a horrible golfer but he loved the game. In the backyard he'd hit balls everywhere and I'd go and chase them. He loved baseball and boxing, and I got into boxing. Late at night he would eat sardine sandwiches and I'd sneak down and keep him company because Mom would not let him get back in the bed afterward unless he brushed his teeth again. Because it was so smelly. We loved the same kinds of foods — Southern foods, biscuits and syrup and grits. I got a lot of that Southern thing in me from my dad.

"When he was home it was like a holiday. I couldn't wait to get home from school. I couldn't wait till nighttime so we could watch TV together. He never had to beg me to do anything — when he was ready to go, bam, I was right there. He knew I'd just be there. I couldn't wait till he'd take a ride in his car so I could go with him. Mom had given him a sports car for Christmas. It was a Jaguar XKE, gray with a black convertible top and deep red leather interior and silver wire spoke wheels. I mean, I was the *only* one who would get in it! He liked to drive fast, and so do I."

The first time Natalie saw her father perform was in 1957 at the Hollywood Bowl. "My sister and I were sitting in the audience, and back then there was this pond between the stage and the seats. I was terrified Dad was going to fall into the water. I could hardly enjoy the show for thinking of that, because from our angle it looked like he was on the edge. I remember the effect he had on the crowd. After that I always sat out front, never wanted to be backstage. I wanted to sit out there and watch people respond."

A few months earlier in Tahoe, Natalie had stepped out in front of Nat while he was singing, walked out in her little skirt and knee socks and pigtails, and stole the show. So he preferred to have her in the audience where she would be less likely to upstage him.

"By the time I saw my dad perform, he was in his full glory; he was at his peak, so everything was right and perfect around him and it was just, I mean, it was my father, and it was a little surrealistic. You were just kind of caught up in the whole environment." She never got over it.

Her Aunt Charlotte says, "Sweetie was destined to be in show business. Soon as she was walking good she was always onstage, and Cookie was her director. Sweetie was into every kind of music. She could not have been more than nine when she heard about Elvis. And she told Nat all about Elvis, and when Hedda Hopper, the gossip columnist, the one with the big hat, came to visit us, Nat told Hedda that Sweetie liked Elvis. And Hedda said, 'Well, Nat, does she want to see him? He'll be at the Palladium.' So Nat got us tickets and I took Sweetie to see Elvis."

Natalie says, "We were some very lucky, fortunate children to have so much music around us, inside of us. We had access to it, you know, indefinitely."

On a typical evening during those years, Cole came home from the recording studio at around five o'clock, with a half dozen acetates (prototype records) representing the day's work. After greeting his wife and children and dogs at the door, he would change his clothes and begin mixing drinks for himself, Charlotte, and any visitors who happened to be on hand. Nat would make drinks for them, J&B scotch for himself, Canadian Club for Charlotte, and for Maria, a ginger ale.

Most nights it was just the family, and Carol and Natalie remember fondly the delight all of them took in listening to Nat's new recordings, made just that day, listening and singing along and applauding and criticizing. In the "library" through an arch at the far end of the living room, they had a state-of-the-art Seeburg Selectomatic record player, a magnificent machine that could handle a hundred demos or records at a time. It was there they heard for the first time Aunt Charlotte's song "To Whom It May Concern," under Nelson Riddle's baton, as well as Cole's album of spirituals arranged by Gordon Jenkins, and the Dave Cavanaugh-conducted "Sweet Bird of

Youth" and "The Happiest Christmas Tree," all destined to fall short of the hit parade. The girls recall that Dad welcomed their frank opinions but sometimes he was out of sorts when they did not like his new work.

So it was good that the Coles played a variety of music on the Seeburg Selectomatic in the evening, while folks sipped at their drinks and petted the boxers. "Dad was really wide open to all of the music," Carol says. "I was listening to rhythm and blues and rock and roll, and he was wanting to hear that too. Smokey Robinson, Motown stuff, Marvin Gaye. He was a very eclectic music lover. It was not just some egocentric Dad who was only going to play his stuff. He came home with Lambert, Hendricks, and Ross, and that just blew my mind — *Sing Along with Basie*, where these people sing the lines of the instruments — just extraordinary." And then of course he played classical music: Arthur Rubinstein, Jascha Heifetz, Andrés Segovia.

Exuberance sometimes inspires a couple to consider having more children — exuberance, and a feeling of abundant good fortune. Nat was happy with his daughters, but he wanted a son to share the excitements of baseball and boxing. Maria says, "With two girls in the family we naturally thought it was time to have a boy. There was only one absolute answer."

So in February of 1959 they approached the Children's Home Society of California to begin the application process for adoptive parents. Nat told a reporter, "I said frankly that I wanted a mischievous boy, one with a lot of spunk and fight in him. And I wouldn't mind too much if they could find one with an athletic background."

On July 20 the Coles were eating breakfast when they got the call. Nat dashed upstairs and started moving the furniture around to make way for the crib in the bedroom. Later he recalled that the girls "dressed in record time, and all of us piled in the car" to drive to the children's home. "There, in the reception room we met the young man of the hour . . . When I looked at Kelly for the first time I felt the same way I felt when I looked at Sweetie in the hospital." Well, not quite. "Although I knew the thought was premature, I could see the little fellow playing his first game of softball."

The boy was big, sturdy, dark-skinned, and quite handsome, with large eyes and a strong brow and fine chin, not unlike a darker version of Carol Cole. They named him Nat Kelly Cole ("since I was born on St. Patrick's Day, the name Kelly was a natural") and christened him in St. James Episcopal Church. His godparents were Nat's attorney Leo Branton, his wife, Geri, Maria's old friend, and the music publisher Sam Weiss. Mrs. Glen Wallichs gave Maria a baby shower. Nat was so crazy about Kelly, the first few months he insisted the baby travel with the Coles to New York and Chicago. "I took one look at him in his crib and told Maria that I couldn't leave him. He especially enjoyed New York and long walks in Central Park."

Nat told a reporter, "I have a model railroad set in the den. And I can't wait until he sees his first big league baseball game. Like every father, I want

482

to introduce my son to this world. Although I am getting on in age [he was forty], I have a lot of little boy left in me. It makes getting up in the morning an exciting adventure."

Natalie Cole says, "Dad taught me how to live heartily, you know. When he came home we would do things. He loved to eat. He loved to go to the movies. He loved to laugh. He didn't mind letting loose. He took my brother and me to see *It's a Mad Mad Mad Mad World*, and to this day I can't watch it without thinking of my dad. There's one part of the movie, I don't even remember the part it is. But my father laughed so hard he just fell out of his seat there in the theater. He just fell out! And I was so embarrassed. He was literally clutching himself on the floor and my brother and I didn't know whether to pick him up or what. Then, it was no big deal to him. If it was funny, it was funny, and he would scream."

And sometimes at bedtime he would sing to them the nonsensical children's song he had made famous: "Kee mo, ky mo, ma hi, ma ho, rumple stickle pumpernickel / soup bang nip cat pawla mitch kameo / We love you."

The whole family went on the Latin American tour in the spring of 1959. After the success of his *Cole Español* album, that is where the money was.

Just before leaving L.A., Cole broke from his usual policy of avoiding controversy by taking the government's side in the recent payola imbroglio. In a *Down Beat* interview he denounced the bribery of disc jockeys and supported the government investigation into racketeering in the jukebox business. "It doesn't take talent any more to become popular," he told the Associated Press. "It takes connections and push. Jukeboxes and record companies — they're the ones that are killing us off." He means old-fashioned balladeers like himself. "A guy with good songs, where's he going to take them?" Cole was taking them south of the border. Then he concluded: "Luckily I got my start at the right time — I don't think I could have made it today."

After Cole's six-week swing through six countries, Brazilian President Juscelino Kubitschek called the singer the U.S.A.'s best goodwill ambassador. When he returned home the U.S. ambassador in Caracas sent him a plaque. It was a token of thanks for his efforts on behalf of 160,000 homeless boys in Venezuela, a benefit performance the government staged in the Concha Acústica, an outdoor theater that seats 7,000. After that benefit Cole did charity shows in Montevideo and Buenos Aires for flood victims of Uruguay and Argentina. Carol and Natalie recall how upset their parents were by the poverty they witnessed during the South American tour.

They returned to baseball fever in Los Angeles. After a lackluster first season in their new home, the Dodgers were in a three-team pennant race with the Braves and the Giants by midsummer. The Dodgers' new left-handed slugger Wally Moon was driving his opposite field "Moon shots" over the left-field screen, and fleet-footed rookie Maury Wills had taken over at shortstop. On the last day of August, the Coles were in the Coliseum to see Sandy Koufax strike out eighteen

San Francisco Giants, including Willie McCovey, Orlando Cepeda, and Cole's hero Willie Mays. Cole and Mays posed for a picture before the game. A few weeks later the Dodgers won a critical series against the Giants in San Francisco. From then until the last week of the regular season Nat's Dodgers and the Milwaukee Braves were on a seesaw at the top of the standings, and no one in the Cole household or anywhere else in L.A. could think of much other than baseball. The teams finished in a dead heat, forcing them to settle the score in a best-of-three playoff. L.A. won the first game in Milwaukee, and when they returned home to play the second game the Coles were on hand to see the Dodgers win the pennant in extra innings, capping one of the most dramatic pennant races in baseball history.

And for Nathaniel the 1959 World Series was like a dream come true, a meeting of his past and future lives in an allegorical present — a Chicago and Los Angeles World Series. The last time the Chicago White Sox had won a pennant was in the year of Nat's birth, 1919, the year of the Black Sox scandal, when Shoeless Joe Jackson and other players "threw" the Series to Cincinnati. Now they were the Go-Go Sox, with speedsters Luis Aparicio at shortstop and Nellie Fox at second, and a team total of 113 stolen bases.

Nat arranged to work in Chicago that October, at the Chez Paris, knowing he could see half the World Series games there and fly home to see the series finale in L.A. — if it went to seven games. Journalists had fun with the match, calling L.A. "The City of Liquid Sunshine," "Smogland,"

"The Circus Without a Tent," and "Home of a Thousand Messiahs." They called Chicago "The Crime Capital," "Poor Man's New York," and "Hog Butcher for the World." Nat was a rare celebrity who hailed from both cities, though he made his loyalties known: he was for the Dodgers. When the owner of Chez Paris said, "Nat, your Dodgers don't have a prayer. Do you know how many bases the Sox have stolen this year?" Nat answered immediately, as he knew every player's position and every statistic, and then added, "But why do they keep stealing first base?"

So Nat King Cole was invited to sing the national anthem at the opening game at Comiskey Park on the afternoon of October 1. The song is notoriously difficult, especially for a singer with Cole's limited vocal range. Dick LaPalm remembers: "We all go to Comiskey Park, and we're having coffee before the game — Maria, Sparky, Nat, and me. And I ask him if he knows the words to 'The Star-Spangled Banner.' He says, 'Of course I know the words,' giving me this look. But I take out my pen anyway, and a scrap of paper, and I'm writing it out for him just in case. And he looks at it and says to me, 'I know the words,' as if he's irked at me, so I said, 'Okay, Nat.'"

In his sport coat and tie, on that crisp sunny day, Nat King Cole strolled to the pitcher's mound. In his best voice, before the crowd of 48,013, Nat sang our national anthem. People were moved. They were thrilled to hear the black musician, who had triumphed over so much, sing the song that for so many people captures the spirit of liberty and equality.

486

Then when he reached the climactic last verse, the one even Mahalia Jackson had trouble delivering, the crowd at the park and the TV and radio audience of millions coast to coast drew in their breath. Nat had changed the words. In "Oh, say, does that star-spangled banner yet wave / O'er the land of the free and the home of the brave?" the second line became "Over land and over sea, and the home of the brave?" as if the concept of freedom in our land at the moment was out of the question.

The audience was kind. No broadcasters mentioned the gaffe, though there was a great deal of whispering and tittering and eyebrow raising as the famous singer returned to his seat to join his wife and friends. Smiling, he shrugged it off as just a slip of the tongue.

But the foreign press attacked like sharks.

LaPalm recalls: "That evening these two reporters from Toronto came to interview Nat at the nightclub. One of them asks, 'Mr. Cole, is the reason you changed "land of the free" the way you did because of what's going on here, the segregation in Georgia and Alabama, the Ku Klux Klan, the bombing of Negro churches —' And Nat just freaked, man. I mean, when he got angry he really got angry. He stood up and said to this journalist, 'Absolutely not! What a dumb question! I just happened to forget the line.'"

Cole's Dodgers were trounced in that first game, 11 to 0, as old Early Wynn mystified the Dodger batters. But L.A. bounced back to win the series in six games when the teams returned to Chicago on October 8.

THE DAWN OF A NEW DECADE

For Nat Cole the 1960s got off to a strange start.

On January 6 his daughters begged to go along with him to the NBC Studios, where he had business. When they arrived the girls begged him to follow them into a room with a piano so he could hear them sing a duet. They started singing. Suddenly he heard the voice of the famous TV emcee Ralph Edwards talking about Cookie and Sweetie; lights flashed in Cole's face, and there he was, in front of television cameras, millions of people, and Edwards intoning those fateful words: *"Nat King Cole, This Is Your Life!"* He tried to run, but an aide restrained him.

Carol says, "We felt a little bad that we had tricked him. He was totally surprised. If he could have run off that stage, he would have been out of there." Edwards made him sit on a couch, shaking his head in wonder, holding his head in his hands. Then in the half hour that followed, he watched his life pass before him as Edwards told Nat Cole's story from the beginning.

One by one these figures appeared from his past, some ghostlike, more and less familiar: Henry Fort and Andrew Gardner, who had been in his high school band, Oscar Moore and Wesley Prince from the first Trio — each he embraced, shaking their hands. Then came the walruslike Carlos Gastel, who had probably engineered the whole stunt, Nat's brother Eddie, and his sister Evelyn. His proud wife entered, smartly dressed in a mink collar, her hair sleekly parted on the side. And the biggest surprise of all was his father, the Reverend Coles, white-haired, remarkably relaxed and charming, as he told the story of little Nathaniel and the limited power of the Lord, how the child had insisted God could not sit on a hot iron stove bare naked.

This is the sort of procession that generally is reserved for the dead. Cole handled the affair with his usual grace, but it was not his idea of a good time.

While Nathaniel still nourished the "little boy" that lived within him, in the new decade his fame and achievements had made him, at age forty, an ambassador and an *éminence gris,* a "gray eminence," if we may apply that venerable term to a man with hair the color of sable. Kings and queens sought Cole's company. Writers and politicians, candidates especially, solicited his opinions. One of these was the handsome young senator from Massachusetts, John F. Kennedy, whom Cole had befriended in October 1958. Back then the Coles had attended a dinner in support of Kennedy's reelection to the Senate, and the grateful JFK sent a letter that was hand-delivered to them at the Copacabana in New York. "I am aware of the difficulties which surround your attending such affairs and so I am doubly appreciative . . . I look forward to other occasions on which we may meet to renew such a pleasant acquaintance and to advance the causes in which we share mutual interest." There would be many such occasions on the road to Camelot. In the late winter of 1960, JFK wired Cole: "I would hope that in one of the primaries that is to follow Wisconsin that you would be willing to assist me. I am most grateful to you." The presidential candidate wanted the singer to appear with him on the stump in Wisconsin, but their schedules did not permit it. Cole would attend the Democratic National Convention at the L.A. Sports Arena that summer in support of Jack Kennedy.

And the singer had been invited to perform for the Queen of England during his upcoming tour of Europe.

So how could it happen, in this new decade, that Cole's booking at San Francisco's 3,200-seat Masonic Auditorium on March 5 got canceled? The auditorium's manager told reporters: "No assumption [sic] on the man's color. We just don't want the class of people Cole attracts." Carlos Gastel "replied ironically that the singer himself is a 32nd degree Mason," which was news to the public. Secretary of the Lodge Lloyd Wilson insisted it was not a racial matter, and said that Sarah Vaughan had performed there with Dave Brubeck. But "we don't want people who jump on the seats," Wilson added, and then noted that if Cole really was a 32nd degree Mason, "he then of necessity is a member of a Negro Lodge. Therefore he is not recognized."

A booking agent promptly scheduled Cole into the 7,800-seat Civic Auditorium, wisecracking that the Masons must have gotten Cole confused with Fats Domino. Cole, performing in Puerto Rico when he got the news, was so angry he refused to go to San Francisco altogether. "Nat Cole Gives Frisco the Brushoff," read the headlines.

At the beginning of that year Nat Cole and Harry Belafonte started discussing ways of pooling resources to produce movies, television, and radio shows in order to have more control over their destinies. In February, *Down Beat* reported that the two giants were starting "a production firm" designed to open opportunities to Negroes and that the signing of papers was imminent. "Cole has been offered another television show . . . starting in the spring." He told the magazine, "If I accept this series, it will be included in the corporation Harry and I are forming . . . and we will select our own writers and directors wherever possible." He and Belafonte hoped to show African-Americans in more "progressive" roles, more progressive than what they had seen recently in *Porgy and Bess*. And Nat purchased the rights to a novel based on the life of abolitionist Frederick Douglass, hoping to make it into a movie.

Asked whether the company would be called Cole-Belafonte or Belafonte-Cole, the older man (Cole) smiled and said their agents would flip a coin. Of course, things were never so simple between these two showmen. A grip-and-grin photograph of them in *Jet* magazine on March 10, 1960, proves they have signed the papers for Cole-Belafonte Enterprises, Inc., and the caption notes they will produce movies and TV shows. But this would never happen; the papers would be torn up not long after the ink had dried.

There were too many differences bred in the

bone between these men for them to remain partners. Maria recalls that Belafonte was everything Cole was *not* as a businessman — Harry was shrewd and calculating, whereas Nat was instinctive, impulsive, and disorganized. Harry was an ideologue and social activist, whereas Nat preferred to create change either behind the scenes or by example. That year the men got into a row about Miriam Makeba, the folksinger exiled from South Africa for her political views. Belafonte loved Makeba, and meant to go on an American tour with her. Nat did not care much about Makeba or folk music one way or the other. But when Harry asked Nat to go with him to the airport in New York to meet the African folksinger's plane, Nat begged off, pleading more important matters to attend to. "What am I, some sort of taxi service?" he asked his insistent partner. Belafonte was furious with him.

A few weeks later in Miami, Maria Cole remembers, the two men were drinking in a bar late one night. Harry liked to give advice. He was explaining to his partner how Nat really was not being presented to advantage in his nightclub act. Harry announced, "I'm going to sit down and write an act for you." He went on like this for quite some time, while Nat patiently listened and sipped at his J&B scotch and smoked five or six Philip Morrises. Harry talked and talked in his husky Jamaican accent, and finally Nat said, "I tell you what, Harry. You take care of Harry, and I'll take care of Nat."

Now that seems fair enough on the face of it, but Belafonte felt the wind full in his jib, and meant to sail onward whatever the weather. So he began describing Nat's new wardrobe, new style, and new sound, which would be a pale reflection of Harry's own glory. And at last Cole could not take any more. "Look, I don't have to bare my chest and sing calypso! I was singing calypso before you! I'm a musician first, a singer second. You leave my act alone and I'll leave your act alone. I don't think I'm at the point where I need 'Harry Belafonte presents Nat King Cole.' "

His anger at Belafonte was fueled by suspicion that the younger man might have a point. Nat King Cole did not need Harry Belafonte to present him, but in the spring of 1960 he needed something to take his idling career to a new level. Television was probably not the answer, even if the network did meet his conditions. Since the demise of his TV show, Nat had taken solace in the fact that over the long haul TV is not a singer's medium. "A singing variety show can give you exposure trouble," he said. "That overexposure bit has to get everybody who sings on TV. A non-performing star emcee like Ed Sullivan can last forever." But even singers like Dinah Shore and Perry Como had burned out on TV.

At this moment in Cole's career, the dapper, aggressive African-American attorney Leo Branton, who had been hovering at the fringes of Cole's business life since 1948, wormed his way to the center of things. The balding young lawyer was a man of unsettling charm. Leo and his wife, Geri Branton, had been friends of Maria's for a long time, and they had stood as godparents to Kelly Cole. Now Leo Branton organized a new production company to handle Nat's artistic projects, and he began to offer suggestions about the Coles' investments — a prizefighter here, a paper cup factory there. It made Carlos Gastel very nervous; Carlos drank more scotch.

The July 7 issue of *Jet* magazine announced "the formation of a new company, Kell-Cole" (named for Nat's son), which would do everything that Cole-Belafonte had planned to do in March. Young actor-director Ike Jones headed Kell-Cole. Harry and Nat later cited "artistic differences" for their parting of the ways, but that was only the tip of the iceberg.

Cole admired musical theater. So he looked to Broadway for the future of his career. The 1950s had been the golden age of the American musical, with *Can-Can*, *The Pajama Game*, *Oklahoma!*, and *Damn Yankees* drawing crowds, culminating in *My Fair Lady*, which packed New York's Hellinger Theater from March 1956 until long after JFK was elected. Cole had taken his daughters to see *Damn Yankees* and to see Mary Martin in *Peter Pan*. Afterward the girls went home to act the roles themselves. There was plenty of money to be made on the Broadway stage. Cole's friend Sammy Davis, Jr., had done it in 1956 with his show *Mr. Wonderful*, which ran on Broadway for a year. And Lena Horne, too. In 1957–58 she had made it big at the Imperial Theatre with Ossie Davis and Ricardo Montalban in *Jamaica*; this kept her name in lights for 558 performances on the Great White Way.

So why not Nat King Cole?

On the way to London to sing for the Queen in

early May, with his wife and daughters by his side, Cole granted an interview to AP reporter William Glover in New York. The headline read "Broadway Musical for Nat Cole." "I'm kind of stepping out of my realm, but I think I can handle it." He described his show as "a kind of *Our Town* in reverse," in which he, as the stage manager, narrates the connections between songs, dances, and characters. He explained that a dozen tunes written by the young team of Dotty Wayne and Ray Rasch had inspired Cole and "some people in regular Broadway theater" to bring the music to life on the stage.

The Coles' three-week tour of europe was successful in every way, an adventure the children would never forget. On May 16 Cole performed for the Queen of England at the Victoria Palace, along with Sammy Davis, Jr., Liberace, and a number of British acts. Afterward the Queen came backstage, where an alert photographer snapped a picture of Queen Elizabeth and King Cole beaming at each other, the King in white tie and tails, the Queen in a full white gown and crown.

"We stayed at the Savoy," Natalie recalls. She was ten. "You can just imagine then, being in London, the combination of being black and being in London where there were no black people then that we could see. But then we were with my father, so that made us special in another way. I remember we saw everything, the palace, the changing of the guards, the museum. Dad liked seeing the sights. Madame Tussaud's — which was a novelty then — it scared me to death! And then I remember we went to visit Charles Dickens's home."

Carol recalls the magic of Monte Carlo, where her father was scheduled to sing for Princess Grace of Monaco. "We were staying in the Hotel de Capri with the casino, and seeing people from all over the world in this one place. In the lobby of the hotel here is some sheik in his turban, and Natalie and I are just going crazy! It was so different from anything we had experienced and there was something about the blue of the water and the beauty of the village that was self-contained, and a feeling of romance and mystery. I fell in love with some guy in the hotel — he might have been the elevator operator," she recalls, laughing. She was fifteen.

Young Quincy Jones was in Europe and needed work. So Norman Granz put him in touch with Nat King Cole, who hired Jones and his band to back the show in Sweden, Denmark, Germany, Switzerland, and Italy. In Frankfurt, Germany, on May 24, Cole gave an interview that appeared the next day in *Variety* magazine, angering jazz fans in general and his old friend Granz in particular. Cole blasted record companies for their payola support of rock and roll. "Let's face it," he said. "The record business is open to make money . . . Jazz in the U.S. is at the bottom of the commercial barrel. It doesn't draw enough business and that's why rock and roll came into being." Granz published a letter in *Variety* arguing, "Nat should know better, because jazz in every conceivable form is bigger than ever . . . Let him check the sales of Brubeck and Garner on Columbia and Ella Fitzgerald on Verve." After correcting a few of Nat's misstatements about jazz in Europe, Granz concludes: "By the way, if anyone is curious about my authority in writing this letter, I was the man who brought Nat Cole to Europe and paid the fare."

Granz had a point. Though jazz was *not* bigger than ever in terms of market share, certain artists such as Brubeck and Fitzgerald were making millions playing a kind of music Cole had left behind to play music that made even more money. Of course, it is arguable that Cole playing jazz in 1942 was operating at a level of pure art way beyond the commercial fare that made millions for Miss Ella and Mr. Dave; it is apples and oranges. *Cole* had never made any big money playing jazz, though others might have. At any rate, he was not about to try again, at age forty-one, not with a wife, three children, and several dozen employees. Cole would never add his name to the list of jazz martyrs ruined by the boom-and-bust cycle of the marketplace.

As much as Nat Cole honored the past, it was never his way to go back to an old idea for inspiration or livelihood. This showman had thrived on the cutting edge of popular culture for most of his life, often anticipating the public's tastes and moods. "I'm a great one for nostalgia — but music must have a chance to develop," he told the press when he announced his plans to tackle Broadway. He hoped his show would make people "forget all the 'Mona Lisa' and 'Nature Boy' tunes . . . I think

I'm old enough now to try a new audience . . . They'd probably stone me if I tried something like this in a nightclub. But Broadway, on the legitimate stage, is where you can take your liberties." Cole said he meant to capture New York by "showing Broadway a new kind of musical show."

Veterans of that lunatic casino sprawled at Broadway and 42nd Street which calls itself the "legitimate stage" must have been sniggering and guffawing, or else cluck-clucking in pity over Nat's naiveté. Others less kind were licking their chops. Here was a chicken ripe to be plucked by a sharp general manager or co-producer who could get a piece of the bankroll that would follow Nat King Cole wherever whimsy took him.

And then, who knows? After all, he *was* Nat King Cole, and nearly everything he touched had turned to gold. A legitimate theater operative might even get involved in such a folly, with a good conscience. So Nat would not lack encouragement, not for a minute, no; he would have backers and yes-men and "artistic consultants" as he dreamed and schemed his way to the stage — the last frontier for him in American entertainment.

The Broadway dream consumed so much of Cole's time, money, and creative energy from 1960 until 1963, we need to know something about the show itself and the hero's role in it in order to understand Nathaniel's life during these years.

That spring, when Ike Jones was approached to take charge of Cole's production company, Jones's first task was to find a musical vehicle that would deliver the star to Broadway. Jones found a producer, Paul Gregory, who was only too happy to lend a hand. The men did not look long or far. Composers Ray Rasch and Dotty Wayne had written a dozen songs at the turn of the year, titles such as "Wild Is Love," "Hundreds and Thousands of Girls," "Pick-Up," "Tell Her in the Morning," and "Are You Disenchanted?" The lyrics tell the story of man's search for romantic love — its excitements and frustrations, joys and sorrows — with a forward, blunt emphasis on carnal lust, and an edge of cynicism that would have been wholly offensive only a few years earlier. Rasch and Wayne convinced Cole to record the songs as a "concept album" on March 1, 1960. With Nelson Riddle's most ingenious and mannered arrangements, by turns brassy, deafening, enchanting, and discordant, the album now sounds like Las Vegas high camp. But in 1960 it was daring and seductive, the choice soundtrack for a penthouse orgy.

The expensive album cover of *Wild Is Love*, with a full-size, four-color pictorial insert on laid paper, looks like a wide-format section of *Playboy* magazine, boys and girls together, girls mostly, flirting, teasing, undressing, making love. And not a black face to be seen among them, except on the back cover — Nat Cole in his best golfer's outfit and his little narrow-brimmed tweed hat, smoking a cigarette in its elegant holder — the cool, calm master of the revels, the black Dionysus himself. There can be no question now about what he is selling.

With his usual uncanny sense of timing and a

keen instinct for popular trends, Nat King Cole had stumbled upon the libretto to usher in the sexual revolution of the sixties. In 1959 Grove Press freed *Lady Chatterley's Lover* from the censors, and in a few years *Oh! Calcutta!* would be the rage of Broadway; in 1960 the first birth control pill, Enovid 10, was made commercially available for $11 a month. And sex was about to replace baseball as America's number one sport and pastime. Who was better suited to lead the bacchanal than the greatest singer of love ballads, Nature Boy himself, Nat King Cole?

This role may or may not have been Cole's own idea. I like to think it was not. But however the idea came to him, he was a businessman, and had to weigh it as such. Broadway was his idea, and if becoming chief pitchman for sex, singing love songs onstage to women of all colors, would take him to Broadway, then so be it. Some of his trusted associates were not wild about *Wild Is Love*; they began to distance themselves from the star as others crowded in upon him. Carlos Gastel and Lee Young were both gone by 1963. The musical alone did not drive them away, but something in the manner of Cole's dealings made them uncomfortable. Art and business had long been dual expressions of the Nat King Cole personality. He was too honest, fundamentally, to conceal himself for long.

Under several titles and in many shapes the musical lumbered and tilted toward Broadway between the autumn of 1960 and the winter of 1960–61, before it crashed and burned; eventually a new musical without the tawdry Rasch-

Wayne songs would arise from its ashes. But first Cole would suffer a torment reserved for stage-struck showmen who make the mistake of producing or financing their own plays. No one should ever do this. But who was to tell him? Gastel was drinking more and more heavily, and one bad marriage followed another for him; he was beginning to lose his magic and his influence. Jones and Gregory were figuring Cole had succeeded at everything except television, and maybe movies. Their thinking was: Just get Madison Avenue out of the picture, and take the man straight to his audience. Then there should be little more to do than count the box office receipts.

Capitol Records and Cole put up the front money, $150,000 according to some accounts. After Capitol invested their $75,000, Nat was probably on his own. It is not known what cash, if any, the producer Paul Gregory brought to the table.

Soon after *Wild Is Love* went into production, the name was changed to *I'm With You*. If talent alone could conquer Broadway, this show had it. Nat's female co-star was the stunning beauty Barbara McNair, an African-American singer and actress who at age twenty-one was already making headlines. Maria Cole saw her on Ed Sullivan and practically insisted that Nat hire her to play his leading lady.

"The one thing he had never done," McNair recalls wistfully, "was go to Broadway. He very much wanted to do that." The interracial cast of thirty singers and dancers, backed by a full orchestra, opened in Denver on October 17. After the

501

hysterical brass and screaming chorus of the overture, Nat King Cole entered the spotlight to pro-
claim the musical's theme: "As a rule, man is a
fool / When it's hot he wants it cool / When it's
cool he wants it hot / Always wanting what is not."
Spoken in his most sultry, worldly-wise tone,
these feeble lines of doggerel at least have the ring
of truth. They are, sadly, the apex from which the
show plunges to its death. It is a series of skits
based on the Rasch-Wayne songs, connected by
vapid, cliché-ridden, or leering speeches. After a
number called "Girls, Girls, Girls," which illustrates a man's dilemma — being surrounded by
attractive women — Cole at last frees himself
from the clutches of the long-legged chorus girls,
stands alone in the spotlight, and declares, "And
so it begins . . . but you can't have them all . . .
your heart has to settle down somewhere . . . And
sure enough, one night it happens . . . the crickets,
the mockingbirds, the perfume in the air, it's all
there, you get the feeling Mother Nature's working overtime." And Nat sings "It's a Beautiful
Evening for Falling in Love."

The Denver critics were working overtime that
night to make sure people stayed away from *I'm
With You*. The reviews were bad. But no one in
the troupe was discouraged yet, especially Nat,
who remained confident — he thought the show
just needed fine-tuning before opening in San
Francisco on October 30.

McNair says, "His idea was to go to Broadway,
but obviously we never got there. We opened in
San Francisco and we got terrible reviews." Dotty
Wayne and Sparky Tavares felt that the audience

502

was uncomfortable with Cole's seductive inter-play with the white chorus girls. McNair does not mention this, but says that the connecting dia-logue was bad and most of the songs were just not good enough.

Everyone marveled at Cole's composure and good humor during this time. After the bad re-views in San Francisco, the artistic staff fell apart, and the show's "backers" ran for cover. In a room full of cigarette smoke at the Fairmont Hotel, Cole and McNair tried to rewrite the stilted dia-logue. Maria flew up from L.A. with the children. Kelly Cole, twenty months old, ran around the room wanting to play with ashtrays, table lamps, scripts. Nat would be scribbling with his right hand while his left was pulling Kelly away from an electrical socket. McNair took Cookie and Sweetie to an ice-cream parlor so that Nat and Maria could have some time alone together.

Cole was the perfect ship's captain, giving most people the impression he had no intention of leav-ing his sinking musical. Without anger he took the blame for the show's shortcomings. Wayne said, "With all the turmoil of changing directors, chore-ographers, and writers, Nat only voiced his opin-ions. He never blew up. I even blew up and left my own show but Nat . . . had stick-to-itiveness." Sometimes she wished he would have a temper tantrum.

Only McNair knew how depressed he was. Cole would sit slumped in his seat in the theater, which was uncharacteristic, she remembers, because "he was always so very up, upright, erect." But now he was sitting slumped, and smoking until the butts burned his fingers. "Oh, he was depressed. He was like crushed, you know. This was a challenge that was not working. It might have been one of the first times in his career things were not going the way he wanted. The review, I mean, it was not just bad, it was horrible. Nat almost wanted to stop the show there in San Francisco."

He should have stopped it then and there, because after that he was virtually on his own as producer, writer, and financier. Not only did he have to endure flop-sweat on the stage night after night, he had to keep the cast and musicians and crew alive with transfusions from his own savings as *I'm With You* hemorrhaged money. "We took the show to Minneapolis for a week trying to improve it," McNair recalls. "Then we took it to Detroit and it wasn't getting better or receiving any better reviews. So he finally gave up on it. He said it wasn't going to work — we're not going to make it to Broadway."

The day after Thanksgiving, Cole announced to the press that *I'm With You* was closing, and a reorganized version, under the title *The Wandering Man*, would begin in New York on January 10, with an eye to a Broadway premiere in February 1961. The title alone says something about Cole's state of mind at the end of that hard year. By the time he pulled the plug on rehearsals for *The Wandering Man* in the first days of the new year, Cole had spent $200,000 of his own money not getting to Broadway. He had lost his sense of direction.

While Nat was doctoring his musical in San Francisco, on November 8, his friend John F.

Kennedy defeated Richard Nixon by a narrow margin to become President of the United States. Maria had worked on the campaign as one of the Wives for Kennedy group that included Mrs. Milton Berle and Mrs. Jack Benny, Janet Leigh, and Nancy Sinatra. JFK had fallen in with the Rat Pack — Frank Sinatra, Dean Martin, Sammy Davis, Jr., Peter Lawford, and Joey Bishop — in Las Vegas on the eve of the 1959 New Hampshire primary. Later Kennedy spent so much time in L.A. with the entertainers that Sinatra renamed the group the Jack Pack in his honor. Sinatra's friends, including certain mobsters, may have made the difference in Kennedy's winning the very close election. In any case, the President was extremely grateful, and rewarded Sinatra by putting him in charge of entertainment for the Inaugural Gala to take place the night before the President-elect's swearing-in on January 20. Ethel Merman, Anthony Quinn, Laurence Olivier, Shirley MacLaine, Gene Kelly, and Ella Fitzgerald were leaving their engagements and flying from the four corners of the earth to be in D.C. Leonard Bernstein would conduct "Stars and Stripes Forever." Harry Belafonte would perform, and so would Milton Berle, Juliet Prowse, Mahalia Jackson, Jimmy Durante, Bette Davis, and Nelson Riddle and his orchestra. Sammy Davis, Jr., would not be there because his recent scandalous marriage to the blond Swedish actress May Britt might distract the crowd from its major purpose, fund-raising to cover the Democrats' campaign deficit. Belafonte had also married a white woman, but that had happened a long time

505

ago, and she was not blond.

And, of course, the gala would not be complete without Frank's old friend Nat King Cole singing "Mona Lisa." Cole had sung for President Eisenhower, but Kennedy had an aura of magic. For Nat and Maria the inauguration was one of the highlights of their lives. She recalls: "At dinner I sat next to the President. He remembered seeing the spread on our wedding in *Ebony*, and said how wonderful it was; I had never liked those pictures but I didn't tell him. Frank was sitting near me, too. And Frank said out loud, 'Doesn't she have the most gorgeous eyes!' which made me blush. Later Frank was escorting me up the stairs — I don't know where Nat was — and the next day there was this crack in the papers about *Who* was the lovely woman with Frank Sinatra last night? Frank was angry that I wasn't identified."

Maria had flown to the inaugural from the funeral of her Aunt Charlotte Hawkins Brown on January 15. Aunt Lottie suffered from senile dementia and had been staying in a Boston nursing home. She died on January 11. Her grandniece Carol Cole inherited a fourth of Dr. Brown's estate, and $5,000 in life insurance. The judge put Maria under bond as legal guardian of Carol's inheritance.

Maria was astonished in February to discover that she was pregnant. She was thirty-eight. "I wasn't particularly thrilled," she recalls. She had probably conceived during Christmas week. When Maria got the news from her doctor, Robert Kositchek, Nat was performing at the Sands in

Las Vegas, where the Rat Pack was still celebrating JFK's election. She decided to fly out to see her husband on March 6 and tell him in person. The next day this item appeared in Louella Parsons's column: "Nat King Cole and his pretty wife Maria are expecting a baby, and a happier man is not to be found than Nat, who comes right out and says he hopes they have a little Prince Cole. 'We are surprised and happy, because Maria never expected to have another child.' "

Of course, the papers do not explain why the news took them by surprise; they do not mention the hormone Nat had injected in order to bring Natalie about. Presumably the Coles thought they were "safe" without the HCG injections. But nature works in strange ways. The couple was startled and confused.

They spent much of that month and the next happily in New York in their suite at the Taft Hotel on West 51st Street. They went to dinner with Ivan Mogull (the two men always celebrated their birthdays together, Nat's on the 17th and Ivan's on the 21st of March); they went to movies; and they went to Sunday brunch with Steve Lawrence and Eydie Gormé, the songwriters Joe and Noel Sherman, and others at the Stage Delicatessen. Nat opened at the Copa on the 16th and sang there every night, while spending most of his days in the Capitol studios. Between March 22 and April 7, under the batons of Ralph Carmichael, Richard Wess, and Dave Cavanaugh, Cole recorded fifty songs. Most were revised, updated performances of his greatest hits. In mid-May the Coles flew to Tokyo, where Nat played a dozen concerts in two weeks "to less than capacity halls," according to *Variety*. Gastel had miscalculated and overbooked him — not a disaster, by any means, as the reviews were good and the tour made money. But Carlos was slipping.

In Tokyo, Cole confessed to a Variety correspondent the failure of *The Wandering Man*. "It never reached New York," Cole sighed. "We had a bad start and had to change writers and producers. Each time it cost money until we had spent $300,000. By the time it would have gotten to Broadway it would have cost almost $500,000. That's too much when you still have to wait for the critics. And since I'm not unknown, it could resound harder for me."

Back in Los Angeles he promised Maria he would not leave town until the baby was born. The summer of 1961 was a good family time, as they looked forward to the new baby and Nat worked on a new musical that might take him to Broadway. There was lively discussion of these prospects at the Coles' July 4th party. Over the last several years this annual gathering had become a major Hollywood event. You could see Loretta Young, Danny Kaye, Frankie Laine, Mr. and Mrs. Milton Berle, Ricardo Montalban, Walter Winchell, Billy Daniels, Danny Thomas, Jose Ferrer, Hedda Hopper, the Gene Barrys, Peggy Lee, the Eddie Andersons, the Sugar Ray Robinsons, the Jack Bennys, the Joe Louises, the Edward G. Robinsons, all of them gathered in the Coles' backyard to eat charcoal-grilled hot dogs and hamburgers and drink champagne. Children and dogs were welcome. Dodgers owner Walter

O'Malley was a regular guest, and so was the team's manager Walt Alston.

The Dodgers were delighted with Cole's leadership in organizing the Hollywood Celebrity All-Stars as their player-manager. On August 5, Nat Cole, Johnny Mathis, Phil Silvers, Dean Martin, and Vince (Ben Casey) Edwards, dressed in baseball uniforms, played a game against the L.A. Sportscasters, journalists and broadcast personalities, at Dodger Stadium to raise money for charity. A photo shows bald Phil Silvers clowning for Cole and Mathis, Nat with his arm around little Johnny, all of them laughing hysterically. Mathis, who was the heir to Nat's vocal legacy, had become a dear friend.

The musical that Cole was refining to supersede *The Wandering Man* was taking no risks. While keeping Barbara McNair and the main concept of the balladeer as the pitchman for love and leader of an interracial band of merrymakers, *The Nat Cole Show*, as it was briefly titled, scrapped the songs that had framed *Wild Is Love*. Nat sang old favorites, show tunes and a medley of his hits, backed by his trio, a trumpet player, and a few dancers.

Natalie Cole recalls she wanted to get into the act. "I said, 'Dad, I want to be in this show.' He said, 'Well, what makes you think that *you* can be in this show?' "

She told him she knew one of the songs, and could sing it as well as anybody. He told her she would have to audition just like anybody else.

"And he did make me audition, in front of ev-

509

erybody. I was ten and I had braces." She got the job, singing a song from *Gigi*. "I don't know how I convinced my mom to let me be in the show."

Although Natalie was in the musical for only two weekends during the summer (Maria would not allow her to miss school), she made quite an impression. "I sang 'It's a Bore,' the song Louis Jourdan sang with Maurice Chevalier, and I had to be very bored and unmoved, while Dad sings to me. The curtain opens, the lights come up, and I'm sitting there on a stool looking bored. And I have to look that way till the end of the song. I was scared. And when I get nervous I laugh. So in rehearsals I would be cracking up, I couldn't help it. And then on opening night, he says to me, 'If you laugh, I'll kill you.' I said, 'Okay, Dad.' I was more scared of him than of the audience. But anyway we had the best time!" So did the crowd in the outdoor Greek Theater on Franklin Boulevard.

The show opened on August 28, 1961. *Down Beat* said, "The most appealing bit in the first half was 'It's a Bore,' which Papa Cole shared with his daughter, 11-year-old Natalie. The child came across with poise and aplomb in singing and spoken lines and with every mark of a professional."

Natalie was fascinated by her father's effect on the showgirls. "These ladies, these singers, they were *gaga* over my dad. It was really something being around these beautiful women first of all, who had this big crush on my father. I mean, even as a little girl I knew *that* much. They would be backstage just in a tizzy, running around in their little, you know, getting ready, in their gowns. And I felt like an observer, not like his daughter —

not that that was a bad thing. He was very aware and conscious of my presence; it's not like he ever ignored us. But I was a little intimidated to be just . . . right in the *middle* of it all."

On September 19, Maria Cole, nine months pregnant in the summer heat, learned that she was carrying twins. "She said it was quite a shock," wrote Louella Parsons. Maria told Parsons that she was happy and hoped the twins would be boys. Like most parents receiving such news, the Coles had mixed feelings they could not share with a columnist.

Nat was so stunned and obsessed with this development, he might not have noticed a news report that went out two days later on the Associated Negro Press wire: "Nat King Cole has been named a defendant in a lawsuit filed in Superior Court Wednesday asking $158,000 damages for alleged 'fraud' in connection with a West Side real estate transaction involving John T. Graves." Cole's old adversary Claude Barnett was firing his last shot at the Chicago boy who made good. This time Cole should have paid attention. The lawsuit accuses one of Cole's attorneys of persuading Graves to convey the title of a building to him temporarily, upon the assurance Cole would invest a lot of money in it. Then the lawyer kept the building. It is not known what came of the lawsuit, but this should have red-flagged the Coles that their business affairs had fallen into the hands of unreliable counsel.

But there were more pressing concerns. Maria was upset over the prospect of having twins. She recalled: "Nat was scheduled to leave for Canada. I was sure he would be gone before I went to the hospital. He insisted he would not, and as it turned out he was right.

"Complications developed," Maria remembers. Her life was in danger, and so were the lives of the twins. On September 26, Geri Branton was on hand when her friend Maria was admitted to the labor and delivery ward of St. John's Hospital. Branton told Nat she was concerned that, in the Catholic hospital, if it came to a choice between saving the mother or the child, Maria's life would not be spared. "Mrs. Cole is not a Catholic," the lawyer's wife told the nurse on duty. And Nat said, "I don't know anything about those babies, just save my wife."

Dr. Alexander Glyn-Davies was equal to the task. The first girl was born at eleven, and her identical twin a few minutes later. No one could tell them apart. One was named Casey, after Casey Stengel of the Yankees; the other got the Celtic name Timolin. Maria once again told Nat she had meant to have a boy, and again he assured her he did not care. "You gave me two beautiful girls, and I love you so much," he said tearfully. She would always cherish the memory of that moment, a time "when Nat became completely uninhibited in his expression of love for me."

Within hours the showman was gone on an airplane to Canada, where he had a date to sing on television. And Maria soon fell prey to a postpartum depression. The woman who had always looked like a picture out of *Vogue*, associating slenderness with health and happiness, now was matronly, twenty-five pounds heavier than she had ever been. She had two infants, a three-year-old boy, and daughters in the throes of adolescence.

Carol Cole was in the bloom of young womanhood. As prominent African-Americans, the Coles would see to it that their daughter, at age seventeen, had a proper debut. In the autumn she must attend the Links Cotillion debutantes' ball to be presented to society.

Links is an African-American civic organization. Since the early 1950s the Links Cotillion at the Beverly Hills Hilton had been the debut of choice for black girls. Carol would not only be welcome; she would be expected.

Carol and Maria both had ironic feelings about this business. Carol, being an enlightened child, thought that this debutante parade was silly, especially for black people, heedlessly mimicking upper-class whites. Maria agreed, and said so. *But,* and this was decisive, the Coles had a huge responsibility to the black community to play by the rules, and in 1961 the rules were that a Cole daughter made the scene of the Links Cotillion. Carol was not a revolutionary. She was a dutiful daughter. So she went along with the program, attending debutant rehearsals that autumn.

"I went to rehearsals for this thing, something I never really wanted to do," Carol recalls. "I had just been given a car, and I went off. I was supposed to come back right after this rehearsal, and I just could not come home. I decided to take a drive to the beach. As time went on I realized I had really blown it. I should have been home, should have called, but I couldn't. I didn't know how I was going to face the music.

"So I drove home, but I parked the car around the corner, rolled up the windows, locked the doors, and went to sleep."

A while later someone tapped on the car window. "It was a friend of the family who also happened to be a juvenile police officer. He told me to unlock the door and go with him, he would take me home.

"When I got there the lights were on and I could almost feel rays of heat coming out the door. My father is standing there, at two in the morning, and he's sort of smiling but he's furious. He gave me a hug to show he was glad I was okay, but he was angry. My mother was inside waiting, and she really gave it to me. From the time we were small we were told that if we did wrong it would reflect badly on our family, on our father's name, and on our race. We were carrying it all. Mother was saying you did not just 'mess up,' you did not just 'blow it,' you came close to jeopardizing your father's whole career. It was always that. I said I was sorry many times. I was terrified. The hardest part for me was when they asked why, why, why, and I could not tell them why. I cried. First Mother said, 'You're not going to be in this Cotillion,' which of course would have been fine with me. But as you know, a few days later we went."

Everybody in America would know about it. Nat had been invited to sing at a $100-a-plate fund-raising dinner at the Palladium for JFK and the Democrats on the same night as Carol's debut. Cole had kept in touch with Kennedy. In September he had written to the President praising a speech to the United Nations and Kennedy responded with thanks and wrote, "I tried to reflect my deepest convictions. I hope this administration will contribute toward the basic objective we so earnestly seek — a world in which the strong are just, the weak secure, and the peace preserved."

So in the early evening of November 18, 1962, Cole sang for the President at the Palladium. After performing, Nat stayed just long enough to exchange a few words with JFK. He needed a light for his cigar, and Nat, of course, had fire; they joked about that, as Nat lit the cigar, but then the President grew serious as he urged his friend to give up cigarettes. In June the American Cancer Society, the American Heart Association, and other groups together had approached JFK to sound the alarm about cigarettes, and the President had invited a commission to study the problem. But already he knew enough to tell his friends to quit smoking cigarettes.

Nat hurried from the Palladium to the Hilton, so as not to keep his wife and daughter waiting, and joined them at the dinner table. The women looked lovely: Carol so grown-up in her silk faille gown with its scooped neckline, wearing long, buttoned French kid gloves; Maria in lace, so youthful-looking she might have been mistaken for Carol's sister. They had not yet got over the tension caused by Carol's beach escapade, but the family was putting on their most cheerful faces. Maria probably would have preferred not having to compete with the President of the United States for Nat's attention on this important night.

A stranger in a suit approached the table. "Excuse me, Mr. Cole?" Maria had always thought he was too generous when people approached him, for autographs, for a word. This night he was not, and politely told the man not to disturb him.

"No, Mr. Cole, the President wants to see you."

"The President of what?" Cole said with some irritation.

"The President of the United States," said the Secret Service man. So Cole went with the agent to a room at the Hilton where Kennedy was staying. JFK wanted to know if it would be all right if he visited the Links Cotillion. He mentioned his fear of movement in strange crowds, and Cole assured the President he had nothing to worry about at the Links Cotillion.

From the lobby of the Hilton, President John F. Kennedy and Nat King Cole entered the ballroom where five hundred African-Americans had gathered. The President told the crowd: "Nat was at our dinner tonight, so I thought I would reciprocate. I congratulate you girls and your families, and I am grateful that you let an itinerant President come to your party."

King Cole presented his daughter to the President. A reporter wrote, "Carol's bow was most regal." The President stayed as the twenty-eight debutantes formed an aisle; he strode down the aisle, and then shook each girl's hand.

The event made headlines and social history. It could never have happened before the 1960s and JFK's Camelot.

JACKPOT ATTRACTION

At the Sands Hotel in Las Vegas during the month of January 1962, Nat King Cole was one of Jack Entratter's "jackpot attractions." Cole was the past master of the smooth, highly produced nightclub stage show, with full orchestra and chorus line, which delighted middle-age swingers and high rollers. *Variety* reported: "Opening and closing with 'This Is a Lovely Way to Spend an Evening,' the meat of Cole's session includes such numbers as 'Unforgettable,' 'Avalon,' and a dramatically effective 'Where Did Everyone Go?' He revives his amusing 'Mr. Cole Won't Rock 'n' Roll' with a neat segue into 'I Won't Twist.' " He had become set in his ways musically. At sixteen he had been a precocious disciple of the Golden Age of Jazz. Now at forty-two Cole's deep roots in the musical tradition of Hines, Armstrong, and Lunceford made him a precocious old fogy, no less beloved for that, but no longer in the popular mainstream where Elvis Presley, Chubby Checker, and Paul Anka ruled the charts.

In Vegas he was still a King. The singer and movie actor Vic Damone, a friend of Cole's for more than a decade, got to know Nat in the sauna of the Sands Hotel health club. "We used to go every afternoon to get a rubdown and a sauna, Jerry Lewis, myself, and Jack Entratter, who ran the Sands. We would hang out there because everybody was there: Don Rickles, Joey Bishop, the singers Bobby Darin and Buddy Greco. Nat played the Sands, I played the Flamingo. Nat was a star and of course he was treated royally. He'd get his rubdown, we'd all take a sauna. Sometimes Sinatra was there, and Dean Martin — the whole Rat Pack. Sometimes Nat would even fly into town for fun, when Sammy Davis was there. A lot of us would fly in and hang out and have some fun with them because it was always party time. We would have so much fun when Sinatra was there. We all played golf at the Desert Inn, then we'd go to the health club. And after work we'd go and hang out. It was like a club, a bunch of guys we admired and liked hanging out with, kidding each other. Nat was just one of the guys."

Now, anyone who was sexually active in the 1960s could tell you that the sexual free-for-all was well underway by 1962; anyone at all curious was quickly swept up in it. Las Vegas had always been a wide-open, swinging town where lively citizens went to escape small-town morals. In the 1960s it was Sodom and Gomorrah west of the Gallinas. If you had a husband, you prayed he would not go there without you. If you had a daughter who moved there unmarried, you gave her up for lost. In those days after the discovery of the pill and before the spread of AIDS, no one could tell the "working girls" from the amateur adventuresses who prowled the casinos looking to score. And star entertainers were big game.

What JFK, Frank Sinatra, Dean Martin, and Nat Cole did to pass the hours between midnight and 9 a.m. in Las Vegas in 1962 may be found in

518

some other book. Certainly when their wives were not there the men did whatever they pleased, and such liberty has not been seen since the revels of Imperial Rome described by Petronius Arbiter. These ballad singers were the prophets and heralds of the sexual revolution. Las Vegas was their Mecca, the Sands their temple. Frank Sinatra owned 9 percent of the Sands Hotel's stock, and mobsters Meyer Lansky and Joseph "Doc" Stacher held the rest. When Nat Cole played there he stayed in a luxury suite and the management catered to him like a sultan. He loved it. Maria hated the place, and as he made it clear he would rather enjoy the facilities without her, she finally let him. It was a big boys' club. Boys will be boys. She had five children to take care of.

As the chief spokesman for romantic love in the early 1960s, it was inevitable that Cole would sample some of what he was selling. "You know," said Lee Young, "the world loves a lover. He sang love songs and they were positive songs. Did women pursue him? Ah, sure. They call them groupies now, and they follow musicians. But these women were a little more sophisticated than groupies. I've lived long enough to know how women will chase men, as men will chase women. But women are a little different. A man will give up. But these women won't give up, they'll follow you from town to town, especially women of means. Maria knew that. You had to know this about him."

Said one press agent that traveled with Cole, who asked not to be named, "Nat was very discreet. He was not the sort of guy who would say,

519

arriving in a city, 'Hey, let's go get some girls and have a party!' But then we'd get off the plane and there they would be, two or three of them, absolutely gorgeous, foxes." Others in the business, including Alan Livingston, say that song pluggers often would employ beautiful women to get the singer's attention when nothing else would work.

Something passed between Lee Young and Nat Cole in early March of 1962, a disagreement over some matter of principle while they were performing in Mexico City. "Something had happened and I left," Young explains. "I'm overprincipled, you know, in some situations. All my life, principle comes first — integrity, principle, and your word. When any of that is broken, then I never feel comfortable." Had he been in the wrong, Young would not be sharing this story. Pressed for details, he maintains a dignified silence, as loyal to his friend's memory as he was to the living man. He will admit only that the argument was not over money. "I'd made up my mind I was gone. He asked me not to leave. We were in the dressing room. It was very personal, what happened between us. But it didn't break our feeling for one another. Never did. I was leaving. He embraced me."

That was the last time Nathaniel saw Lee, who soon became a successful producer at Motown Records. Losing such a friend, a man of integrity one has known for twenty-five years, more than half of one's life, over a "matter of principle" is a frightening thing and the stuff of tragedy. Lee Young was gone and Carlos Gastel was on his way out, making way for shysters and investment counselors who could be trusted only by a man who was beginning to lose his instinctive powers of judgment.

Maria was not with her husband during his three-week engagement at the Palmer House in Chicago that began on March 26. So she missed the testimonial feast in April honoring the Reverend Coles for his quarter century of service to the First Baptist Church. The Reverend was remarried. In his sunset years he indulged his passion for learning by acquiring a doctor of divinity degree in 1954 and a doctor of law degree in 1957. He had founded the Baptist Pastors' Conference in Chicago and was president of the Baptist Ministers' Conference.

Nat sat on his father's right between the Reverend and sister Evelyn, proud to hear a host of clergy and community leaders praising his seventy-six-year-old father. Would Nathaniel ever measure up to his father's expectations? "It is possible to live an exemplary life regardless of your profession," the Reverend grudgingly conceded. "It is my boy's *finest* quality that success didn't go to his head. With me, he has the same sense of obedience and respect." These words would echo in Nathaniel's memory ever after, for he would not see his father again in this world.

A few months later it was Nat's turn to sit in the place of honor on the dais, as Capitol Records and the Urban League of L.A. co-sponsored the Silver Anniversary of Cole's career in show business. Twenty-five years had passed since the debut of the King Cole Trio. On August 5, 1962, Edie Adams organized a testimonial dinner at the Ambassador Hotel. Nine hundred civic and industry leaders and show business celebrities crowded the Embassy Room to praise and applaud Nat King Cole. Who was in the audience, nearest the dais? Mickey Rooney, Groucho Marx, Ricardo Montalban, Ed Wynn, Robert Stack, Art Linkletter, Andre Previn, Tony Bennett, Doris Day, Jerry Lewis, Joe Louis, Eartha Kitt, Jonathan Winters, Colleen Gray, and Sarah Vaughan, to mention only a few.

Steve Allen, whom Nat had known as a struggling songwriter, now a TV personality, author, and comedian, was master of ceremonies for the black-tie gala. "These days, you just walk right in the front door of that hotel, if you're on the dais or entertaining — it's very simple. The point I'm about to raise," says Allen, recalling the event, "might have something to do with the number of black entertainers and guests involved that night. I'm not sure. But they were taking us through what seemed like an interminable and dumb route to get to the ballroom, about twelve of us in formal dress. So we're going through kitchens, and walking over spilled soup and ducking under steam pipes — looked like a submarine sketch in some old Sid Caesar show. And I was walking next to Nat and somebody was leading us. So I muttered to myself, to myself as much as to him, 'Boy, this is a really stupid way to get into a hotel.' And I've never forgotten his answer. He said to me, very softly, 'This is the way I *always* have to go into hotels.' " It was no longer true, but the bitter memory remained.

The program of speeches and entertainment would move the crowd to laughter and tears. "Gaiety and grief — the twin masks of show business — covered the faces of Hollywood as Marilyn Monroe lay masked only in death in the county morgue," the *Los Angeles Herald* reported. Marilyn had been found dead in her room from an overdose of barbiturates. "Within hours after news of the death of the blonde beauty, the film greats gathered for a testimonial dinner honoring musician Nat King Cole."

Marilyn Monroe's ghost hovered over the dais and tables of the Embassy Room as people took their places. Maria Cole remembered a night recently when she and Nat had gone to a party at Peter and Pat Lawford's house and Marilyn was there. Maria's back was troubling her, so she went home early, leaving Nat at the party. It got late, and Marilyn had to go home; Jimmy Van Heusen and Nat took Marilyn home from the party, at least that's what Maria heard, and Nat was out very late and did not call. Maria waited up for him, as she always did. And when he finally got home at 2 a.m. with this story about him and Van Heusen taking Marilyn Monroe home, Maria got so mad she threw a shoe at her husband.

Nat told the *Herald* reporter, "It's tragic. I really don't know what to say. I was shocked when I heard the news as I left Salt Lake City to come here. She seemed so full of life when I saw her just a few weeks ago." Rumors floated through the room. "I have been awake long enough to know what has happened," said Gary Crosby, "and I would rather reserve comment." Others whispered about the Kennedys and the Mob.

But as the genial Steve Allen called the meeting to order, "and the applause for Nat Cole swept through the hall, attention returned to the honors at hand and the spectre of Marilyn disappeared," reported the *Herald*. Not entirely. Emotions ran high. Earl Hines stood up to recall the Chicago days when Nat played a battle of the bands against him at the Savoy. Mahalia Jackson, who had known young Cole when he played at the Panama, sang out a rousing chorus of "Joshua," and the crowd rose to its feet to applaud, relieved by the emotion the spiritual released. Songwriters Sammy Cahn and Jimmy Van Heusen had written new lyrics to songs rendered by Patti Page ("I Love Nat King Cole") and Rosemary Clooney ("You're the Tops"), comic Dick Gregory delivered a satire on bigotry, and Rowan and Martin offered some lighthearted comic testimony. Messages arrived from President Kennedy and Richard Nixon, plus a tribute from Governor Pat Brown. With great verve and humor, Maria Cole sang a parody of "The Man I Married," segueing into the tender ballad "But Beautiful."

Toward the end of the barrage of encomiums the thoughtful Steve Allen delicately mentioned Marilyn Monroe's death that morning, "and remarked that the tribute to Cole was a heartwarming contrast in which people did not wait until it was too late to demonstrate their affection," Variety noted. Cole himself was overcome with emotion. Events like this, and the spectacle of *This Is Your Life*, would rattle any man but the most attention-starved. After all, he was only forty-three, and it was like attending his own funeral, with young Marilyn's ghost fluttering in the smoky light, batting her eyelashes, with that come-hither smile.

When it came his turn to express his gratitude, the guest of honor spoke a few words and decided that singing "Unforgettable" would be more appropriate. But he got so choked up he could not finish. As applause thundered around him, the embarrassed singer sat down and, trembling, lit a cigarette.

Glen Wallichs presented him with a solid-gold microphone for his profitable years with Capitol. His album sales had exceeded 75 million.

Carol Cole graduated from Immaculate Heart High School on June 12. Her proud father, sitting with his wife and children, watching his eldest cross the stage to get her diploma, was still worried about money. If you are tempted to count the Coles' money and wonder *why* he was worried, consider the following: Cole never forgot what it was like to be poor, or the roll call of great African-American musicians who died with nothing. In the mid-fifties he was still paying off his debts to the tax man. The musical *I'm With You* had depleted his savings, and while developing it he gave up lucrative nightclub engagements. Performing artists, like athletes, usually have a few years of peak earning power in which they must provide for retirement. They never know when the income stream will cease. Add to these circumstances five children, a wife with refined tastes, Cole's generous nature and his naiveté about finances, and you have the makings of a great anxiety about money.

He was concerned he might never again see his name at the top of a singles chart. Five years had passed since the success of "Ballerina." But on June 19, Cole recorded an upbeat ballad with a Country-Western flavor called "Ramblin' Rose." By autumn of 1962, Cole had a hit single on his hands, another surprise million-seller as unlikely as "Nature Boy." "Ramblin' Rose" gave him confidence.

The musical he had opened so successfully at the Greek Theater with Natalie had developed into a revue called *Sights and Sounds*. With an interracial chorus line of sixteen dancers known as "The Merry Young Souls" and a full orchestra, the stage show was marketed in August as a celebration of Cole's twenty-five years in show business. In amphitheaters from Salt Lake City to Buffalo and Framingham, Massachusetts, the show was a hit as "family entertainment." Nat sang and joked his way through two hours of Western music like "Skip to My Lou" and "Don't Fence Me In," donned a straw hat to sing "Calypso Blues," and chased the dancers around the stage as they sang "Anything You Can Do I Can Do Better." Cole sang blues and spirituals, and at last entranced the crowd with a medley of his greatest hits. Of course he belted out "Ramblin' Rose" too, reminding his fans he was a hit-maker.

His wide smile still could light up the night under the stars. *Billboard* reported: "The show, Broadway bound, is full of tried and true music . . . There is more sound than sight. The sight part is the young people who sing, do simple dance movements, and act out bits from Western medleys or pop tunes. But the sight is also Cole. He sits serenely onstage singing sentimental songs in his quiet catlike way and it seems as if the audience could go on like this forever, so compelling is his mastery, until suddenly, with a glint of a wicked grin, he whoops into comedy."

"For tent impresarios," *Variety* advised, "this is a handsome package which should spell money in the till. For Cole aficionados . . . it is a jackpot." The show toured for six weeks in August and September 1962 through 1964, but it would never get to Broadway.

Sparky Tavares still served as Cole's personal valet and doorkeeper, with a monk's devotion and the dignified composure of a man who has seen everything and learned to keep his own counsel. Though he had fathered a daughter of his own, Sparky seems to have accepted the Coles as a surrogate family. Orphaned in childhood, he was African-Portuguese, raised in Massachusetts, Maria's home state. He called Maria, whom he dearly loved, "Lady C." They talked astrology — it seemed natural to him that Maria, a Leo, would take charge of the dreamy Nathaniel, a Pisces.

The scene in Cole's dressing room before a show had the combined air of a pre-prizefight locker room, a Broadway greenroom, and a royal levee. Everybody loved Cole. Many people were desperate for his attention and some people wanted a piece of him — song pluggers, journalists, old friends and casual acquaintances, movie stars, politicians. Every person who has been mentioned in this book plus several hundred more might have the impulse and feel entitled to join Nat backstage when he played the Copa, the Chez Paris, or the Cocoanut Grove. "There were always a lot of people around Nat," Charlie Harris recalls, people smoking, pouring champagne from the iced silver bucket on the table, drinking, and joking while Nat dressed. Women were not allowed; Sparky had firm orders from Lady C. The star might say hello to women as they stood briefly at the door. Sparky would ask one to meet Cole later at the bar if it was a lady friend or relative of importance. And thus the company avoided gossip. It was Sparky's job to keep the cheerful party in the dressing room from turning into a mob scene, and in the major cities this was a challenge.

Before the singer appeared onstage he sat down at the makeup mirror, put on his ruffled dress shirt, and tied his bow tie. He was the first to wear lace tuxedo shirts — Maria's idea. She had them handmade of Italian lace. He smelled faintly of English Leather cologne. The bow tie he worked at lacing for ten minutes or more until it was perfect. Sparky handed him his knee-length black socks with garters, and his file-top shoes. He sat around smoking and conversing in that attire until the stage manager rapped for showtime, at which point Sparky would hand him the trousers of his mohair tuxedo. Old Sy Devore had custom-made the tuxedo to Maria's specifications. When Nat walked onstage, all six feet one and 170 pounds of him, there was not a wrinkle from his black satin hair and bow tie to the stylish break in his cuffless pants at the top of his shiny shoes.

In the singer's last years Tavares knew Cole

528

better than anyone except his wife. After Lee Young's departure and just before Carlos Gastel's, Tavares sensed that Cole was losing the support of trusted friends and business associates and that neither of the Coles was in command of the lawyers and entrepreneurs who had taken over the management of Kell-Cole Productions. Perhaps it was this intuitive sense that Cole needed help that prompted Tavares to open the stage door one night to a total stranger named Domenith C. (Bud) Basolo, Jr.

The stocky, square-jawed rancher, dark-haired, hazel-eyed, with his string tie and ten-gallon hat, was a power in California's Democratic Party. At thirty-nine years of age, Basolo had a beautiful home in Hillsborough and a hundred square miles of ranch in Wyoming with the largest herd of privately owned buffalo in the world. He would later be known as the first breeder of the "beefalo," the cross between bison and beef cattle. Basolo was organizing a hundred-dollar-a-plate dinner at the Pioneer Hotel in Woodside for Pat Brown's gubernatorial race, and wondering how he would sell five hundred tickets. Bud and his blond wife, Georgia, were taking in Nat Cole's performance at the Fairmont Hotel in San Francisco when Bud leaned over to his wife and told her that this singer could easily pack the Pioneer Hotel, so he was going to get Cole to come to the fund-raiser. She laughed and said it was impossible.

After the show Bud Basolo knocked at the stage door. Sparky opened it, and Basolo looked him in the eye, stating his business. Sparky sized him up and decided this was a man worth knowing. He

529

told the rancher to come up to Cole's hotel room in an hour.

"Sometimes you meet someone in this life and you just hit it off," the millionaire recalls. Cole agreed to sing for Pat Brown's fund-raiser. And the success of that event held on May 19, 1962, cemented a friendship between the couples, and between Nat and Bud especially, that would be precious to the entire Cole family. The couples vacationed together in Carmel in November, and attended the World Series together in L.A. in the autumn of 1963, and both Kelly and Natalie spent summers on the Wyoming ranch. During a period of painful difficulty in the Coles' marriage and increasing confusion of their finances, Bud Basolo was a steady voice of reason. A master of finance as Cole was a master of jazz music, Basolo was a welcome presence because he had no show business connections and he was so rich he wanted nothing from Nathaniel but his friendship.

Sparky was wise to let this extraordinary spirit into Nat's life. Much of what is known about the singer's mysterious last years comes from this clear source. But not even a friend like the tycoon rancher could save Cole from the impending disaster.

Like many vital men in their forties, Nat Cole was taking his time making his last will and testament. Some superstition persuades a man that by ignoring his mortality he might overcome it. Cole never went to a doctor either, "unless he was dying," said his wife with grim humor. But more and more lawyers and investment counselors were telling him he had more and more money (always a danger sign, if you don't know more about it than they do). And so in 1963, with plans to journey again to Japan in March and the British Isles in the summer, he admitted he could no longer postpone the responsibility of his will. On February 7 he sat down and signed it, with Sparky Tavares as witness.

His brothers Isaac, Fred, and Eddie each would get a thousand dollars. His sister Evelyn would share five thousand with her daughter Janice. Nat's father was bequeathed five thousand, and the three sons of Isaac Cole would share five thousand equally. Kelly got his father's jewelry. The rest of Cole's estate was left to Maria and the children, with Mr. and Mrs. Leo Branton and Charlotte Sullivan named as trustees. The will points out that everything is "community property" except two trusts.

One of the Cole trusts was the brainchild of a clever attorney whom Leo Branton and Harold Plant brought into the Kell-Cole production company. Harry Margolis was a hotshot tax lawyer in his late forties, always carefully dressed in gray or dark blue suits, balding, gaunt, tall, and preternaturally pale. Soft-spoken and unctuous, Margolis had the eyes of a hawk. But what everyone remembers about him was his deathlike pallor.

Margolis made his name with a couple of high-profile cases in which he defended private fortunes from the rapacious agents of the Internal Revenue Bureau. Naturally this would make him welcome to the Coles' business organization. And the lawyer inspired confidence, as all confidence men do. Certain of Nat's attorneys were very grateful for Margolis's cutting-edge schemes for creating tax shelters for the Coles' royalty income because all stood to gain from the government's loss. Soon the Coles were happy to guarantee the lawyers a third of whatever they kept from the government. Accountant Harold Plant, who had saved the Coles from ruin during the 1951 tax war, confessed to Maria on his deathbed forty years later that "the worst thing I ever did was to trust Harry Margolis."

In brief, Margolis established an "offshore trust" that became the holding company to "shelter" Cole's royalty income during a period when the tax laws tolerated such activity. Margolis promised that the foreign trust would avoid taxes. The Coles received a fraction of their gross income in monthly checks which more than met their needs. And they were assured that "the rest of the money" was brilliantly invested in the trust, from whence it would go forth and multiply, and become a fortress and mountain of gold that would support the Coles and their children and grandchildren unto eternity.

Bud Basolo was alarmed. "I had this ranch in Wyoming. I paid eighteen dollars an acre, about a million dollars, and it was a steal. I could see what was going to happen with land investments in Wyoming — the oil activity and the coal. Another ranch came up for sale, and I told Nat to buy it. He said it sounded good to him and I should talk to his business manager.

"So I flew down to Hollywood and went to Margolis's office. I explained everything to him.

There was potential oil. Big coal deposits. And even if you never get oil or coal, it's real fine grassland. Margolis said, 'I'll let you know.' I flew back to Wyoming, and he turned it down. I couldn't pressure Nat because of our friendship.

"Four years later they struck a big oil field on the land. And the coal rights sold out for four hundred an acre. All that could have been picked up for a lousy twenty dollars an acre! The oil field is still pumping oil today. That property would have made the Coles all multimillionaires.

"And you know why Margolis turned it down? You see, you can squander any kind of paper — money, stocks, bonds — a lot of things you can pick up and take away. But you can't pick up a piece of land and take it. It's pretty well set there by God. And Margolis didn't want Nat to have anything he couldn't get his hands on. He took a lot of Nat's wealth."

Margolis lied to the Coles about the trust, about what was going into it, and about how the money was being invested and spent. Much of the money that went into that trust was never seen again by its owners. But of course the tax agents had little difficulty determining what had been paid *into* the trust. And like the angel of Death himself, the tax man would not be denied. Eventually he would come to collect what was his, and by then the trust did not have the cash to pay it. This would not be Nat's problem, but Maria's. Nat would not live long enough to know his error.

Cole's case is a cautionary tale of how a man who does not balance his checkbook (or even write his own checks) will sooner or later be parted from his money by wizards who can write checks simultaneously in different bankbooks. But it is much more than that. It is the story of how such wizards find their fortune in the lives of entertainers. The Coles had fallen into the hands of a master. Now the ingenious strategies of Harry Margolis are studied in law schools as shining examples of how a smiling tax lawyer can separate an enormous fortune from its rightful owners.

Careful planning of Cole's second Japan tour in mid-March — fewer shows at lower prices — made his act a smash hit in Tokyo, and also in Seoul. On the same trip he performed in Australia and Honolulu.

That was Carlos Gastel's last trip with Cole. Leo Branton, Harry Margolis, Ike Jones, and others shouldered Gastel out of the Kell-Cole organization. Some say Carlos was drinking too heavily to pull his great weight; many others, including Sparky Tavares and Gene Norman, say Carlos was drinking no more or less than ever, but that he did not get along well with the new regime.

On the eve of his next British tour, in the summer 1963, the star informed Leonard Feather of *The Melody Maker* on July 6 that "he no longer needs Carlos Gastel, his personal manager of more than 20 years." Tavares told writer Leslie Gourse in 1990, "That was the only bad thing that Nat Cole ever did, firing Carlos." Gastel may have been a drunk, but he was honest. The trade papers, describing the "End of a Long Business Association" (*Down Beat*, August 1), make the parting sound amicable. Nat and Carlos may still have been friends, but no love was lost between the ex-manager and the staff at Kell-Cole.

Nat was on a roll again, as the success of "Ramblin' Rose" was followed by the million-selling "Those Lazy, Hazy, Crazy Days of Summer." He recorded the Hoagy Carmichael tune on April 11 in L.A., and that summer the cheerful anthem could be heard blaring from car radios on their way to beaches from coast to coast. "Cheerfully unabashed sing-along corn," English writer David Griffiths called it. Money was pouring in. Who would imagine that such simple-hearted, sentimental fare would thrive in the American marketplace in the year the Beatles were rocking out of Liverpool and Bob Dylan was honing his ironic wit to shake the world with "The Times They Are a-Changin'" and "It Ain't Me, Babe"? That summer there seemed to be no stopping Nat King Cole.

And that same year, the agony over race in the South came to a head. After Martin Luther King's famous speech at the Lincoln Memorial — "I have a dream that one day on the red hills of Georgia sons of former slaves and sons of former slaveowners will be able to sit down together at the table of brotherhood" — events seemed to conspire to deny Dr. King's dream. President Kennedy had to call the National Guard to force Governor George Wallace to admit black students to the University of Alabama on June 12. And the very next day, NAACP leader Medgar Evers was shot to death in his doorway in Jackson, Mississippi.

Harry Belafonte and Lena Horne met with Attorney General Robert Kennedy to demand justice. Mahalia Jackson held a benefit in Chicago for Dr. King, where Dinah Washington and Eartha Kitt donated their services. Comedian Dick Gregory went to Birmingham and got arrested for his part in anti-segregation demonstrations. When Claude Barnett found out Nat King Cole was not going along to demonstrate in Alabama, he heated up the wires at the Associated Negro Press, eager for another chance to take a shot at the King. Barnett scolded Cole for "refusing to follow Dick Gregory's example." Cole's response: "What good, except for his own publicity, has it done for Dick Gregory to go down there? Harry Belafonte is a professional integrationist. We don't see eye to eye."

In a *Down Beat* interview, Cole criticized the "idea that Negro entertainers should lead the way." The singer said, "They spend their lives weaving dreams. What kind of effect would I have if each of my songs was a 'cause' song? Nobody would want to listen to me. I am a singer of songs, I am not a public speaker." But then he made a powerful statement supporting Dr. King and the civil rights movement: "With money I earn from my songs, I do and will continue to help their fight, which is also my fight." Before leaving for England, Cole planned a benefit at the Shrine Auditorium for August 8, the proceeds to be divided among the NAACP, CORE, and Dr. King's Conference. He pledged at least $50,000.

Nat and Maria, with Kelly and Natalie, flew to London on July 12 for a joyful ten days. Carol, eighteen, stayed home to work that summer as a camp counselor; the twins, age twenty-one months, were too young for the trip. Performances in London, Glasgow, Birmingham, Manchester, Leeds, and Liverpool were sold out and wildly successful. "What is the secret?" an English reporter wonders. "Possibly that throaty huskiness that can get into the soul of a tender ballad . . . that huskiness . . . Never have I seen him off-stage without a cigarette." The writer mentions this to the singer, who shrugs. "I know, I just can't keep away from 'em." By now he would have quit if he had been able.

The English press was fixated upon Cole's image as a moneymaker and tycoon, as if the music now were incidental. His new managers' obsession with wealth had begun to speak through him, unmistakably. "Listen, I'm a businessman. I work with business people. The kind of thing they say is, 'Now we've sold a lot of records, let's sell some more.'" Articles referred to the "millionaire singer" or the "tycoon mentality." The British journalist David Griffiths even prophesied, "Nat will milk the market as much as he can in the next year or two, and then concentrate more on business than on singing. Nat Cole, the millionaire businessman, will take over."

Now it is eerie to see just how close to the truth the journalist came in his prediction.

LOVE AND DEATH

In early August, the 1963 edition of Nat's stage show *Sights and Sounds* opened in Los Angeles. The late summer tour included weeklong engagements in Washington, D.C., Pittsburgh, and Philadelphia. In Washington, Cole performed at the Carter Baron Amphitheater most nights, while during the day he and Maria enjoyed the sights of the capital. One evening Nat accompanied Robert F. Kennedy to Eastern High School to encourage the students to finish their education.

And the next day the White House called. The President would like to see him there at one o'clock. Of course they talked about the crises in the South, and JFK's new civil rights legislation, and the forthcoming March on Washington on August 28th. But they also reminisced about the inauguration, and the time JFK thrilled the debutantes at the Links Cotillion. Before leaving the Oval Office, Nat received five autographed pens for his children and a handful of PT-109 tie clasps. And President Kennedy, smiling warmly, reflecting Nat Cole's smile, said he looked forward to seeing Nat again soon.

Cole would not attend the civil rights march because he had a singing engagement in Pittsburgh shortly before driving his daughter Natalie to Northfield, Massachusetts, for her freshman year at boarding school. Maria drove Carol to

Cazenovia College in upstate New York while Nat took Natalie to enroll at Northfield. Having her father alone was a thrill for the girl, and he made quite a scene when he appeared at registration and went to get her settled in her dorm room.

A week later a bomb exploded at a Birmingham Baptist church on a Sunday, killing four black children and injuring nineteen other people. The deaths provoked racial riots in which police turned their dogs on civil rights demonstrators. Dr. King and JFK were doing all they could do to desegregate the public schools, but the harder they worked, the harder Governor Wallace and his kind worked against them. Cole looked forward to seeing JFK again and discussing these things, but it would not happen in this world.

President Kennedy, riding in his open Lincoln Continental through the Dallas streets, was killed by an assassin's bullet on November 22. When he died, many young people who were not driven crazy by the tragedy were driven to despair by it. Their hopes died with the beautiful young President. Natalie Cole says this was the only time she can remember seeing her father cry. The Coles were in Hancock Park for Thanksgiving week and mourned the President together. Cole was heart-broken.

It is my opinion that soon after this time the cells of the upper lobe of Nathaniel Cole's left lung, after the continuous insult and injury of thirty years of cigarette smoke, began to grow the tiny epithelial pearl of the carcinoma. No physician will either confirm or deny this, but all will agree that this timing is neatly in accord with the known facts of the cancer's progress and the patient's death. Probably by the turn of the year 1964, and certainly by the spring of that year, the great musician was dying.

And about this time, Nathaniel fell in love. We are no more certain about the moment of the onset of love than we are about the onset of his illness — only that it was well underway before the spring of 1964, so consuming he could not hide it from his wife. And the man was so unpracticed at lying and deceit, he could not have concealed a full-blown love affair from Maria for very long, as close as the two of them had been.

In the chorus line of *Sights and Sounds*, in late 1963, was a young woman named Gunilla Hutton. She was born in Göteborg, Sweden, on May 15, 1944. And like other blond beauties from Scandinavia, Hutton came to America to seek her fortune in modeling and show business. She was likely to succeed — a tall, ravishing girl who could sing and dance, with a lively wit that would one day make her a good living as a TV comedian, not a star but an enduring minor character.

The program for *Sights and Sounds* 1963 includes a group portrait of "The Merry Young Souls," sixteen singers and dancers selected from hundreds of applicants, eight young women seated, eight men standing behind them, a mix of Caucasians, African-Americans, and Asian-Americans. The tall blond Gunilla Hutton sits at the center of the portrait, a diamond surrounded by lesser gems, hands folded, legs crossed at the ankle. She is wearing a silk suit jacket, unbuttoned and collarless, to accentuate her long swan's neck. Her shiny blond hair combed back from her wide brow falls in waves framing the round curve of her cheeks and the strong, perfect chin. She has the high cheekbones of a beauty that will improve with age. Her blue eyes are wide-set, the brows arch high above, and the mouth, delicately drawn, is a wide flower not yet fully in bloom. The overall effect is of dreamy delight, the spiritual looks of a dreamer in the twilight between sleep and waking. Ms. Hutton was not yet twenty.

This is the woman, not yet fully a woman, Nathaniel fell in love with when he was dying. Given what is already known about Cole's manners, and what transpired in 1964, it is nearly certain the chorus girl pursued the star of *Sights and Sounds*. Most men, seeing such an opportunity, would find the nineteen-year-old Swedish charmer irresistible, and Nat Cole was not exceptional in his powers to resist a beautiful woman. And we are not talking here about your garden-variety chorus girl petunia; this was a woman so gorgeous her comic stock-in-trade for twenty years would be reducing men to pop-eyed, weak-kneed idiots. There are degrees in this as in most things.

Anyway, there were plenty of opportunities for Ms. Hutton to get Cole alone in a room as the show toured the country late in 1963. And by early spring of 1964, what started as a diversion for Cole, the reliable balm of erotic adventure, had begun to spin out of control and become an obsession. He really loved this girl, who was so different from his wife in every way, so gentle, so simple, so *undemanding*. Gunilla was funny and she had quiet courage; she had made the great crossover from culture to culture, language to language. And who knows what other changes and challenges she might have the strength of character to endure? In the unreal erotic world of their hours alone together Cole was able to imagine a future free of all that weighed him down — the expectations of children, parents, the press, his public, his people, who looked to him for leadership, wanted him to be a saint; above all he imagined freedom from his wife, who seemed to him, in his befuddlement, to be the warden of this prison, his life. These thoughts are familiar to any man who has passed through a "midlife crisis." Such giddy, ecstatic thoughts are endemic to an illicit love affair; and so is the guilt that shadows them.

"He was consumed with guilt," says his friend Ivan Mogull. Mogull was married in February of 1964. At Cole's invitation Ivan and his wife, Marcia, flew to Las Vegas for a belated honeymoon, and so that the friends could celebrate the marriage as well as the men's birthdays. "I can't believe it!" Nat said as Ivan introduced his bride at the Sands restaurant. "He finally got married! Before forty! I never thought it would happen," he said, flattering Marcia as the beauty who had charmed the old bachelor. Nat had a birthday surprise. Pulling a pipe out of his pocket, he told Ivan he had given up cigarettes. Ivan had been nagging him to quit for years. When they were alone Nat confided to Ivan that he had fallen in love. Well, a girl who could get him to stop smoking cigarettes must be something. But Ivan was deeply concerned, and told him so. Mogull never met Hutton.

Cole began to distance himself from his wife, seeking more chances to perform and travel without Maria. At first, watching his curious behavior — elation one minute, irritation the next — she attributed it to depression, anger, and sadness over Kennedy's death, and career pressures. And perhaps she worried that she had grown less attractive to him since the difficult birth of the twins. Knowing that sometimes it was best not to crowd him, for a while she gave her husband the space he desired.

But the more Nat was away, the less he wanted to come home. She needed him and so did the children. One weekend he was performing in San Diego, and she thought he might be pleased if she brought the twin girls down with her to see him. "Like all women, I thought if I take my babies to see him, that will bring us together. So I took them down there with me, and I brought their nurse. And I don't remember his remarks now but it was something like: Well, what are you here for? Remarks that hurt me. He was never mean to me before; that's the only time I can remember. He wasn't that kind of man. But that time he was mean, for him. And I knew then that something was going on."

And not long after this he came home from touring with *Sights and Sounds* and Maria was upstairs in the bedroom unpacking his suitcase. She usually unpacked his bags when he came home from a trip. This time when Maria opened the suitcase, amid the socks and undergarments she found some unfamiliar "things," implements she had heard about but never actually seen, let alone held in her hands, accessories to the act of love. She declines to be more specific. It was a message from the other woman. "She was *Swedish,*" says Maria Cole, rolling her eyes, as if that word encoded the wild maze of Eros. "I have heard about these Swedish women . . . Gunilla Hutton, that was her name . . . anyway, these things were in the bag. I found them. I was so ashamed of myself! I remember I took them and wrapped them in a newspaper. He did not know they were in there. Can you imagine him bringing them home to me? So I never told him, never said a word.

"Well, she was smart. She knew I was going to unpack his bags. It's obvious she wanted me to find out he was doing these things. He'd never, never admitted anything to me before this — only in the telegram, much later. When I first realized what was going on it was a terrible shock. I lost weight. I looked like a beanpole."

Though they could not discuss his love affair straightforwardly, there were harsh words that passed between them that summer as he hardened his heart against Maria — harsh words after long, stony silences. "I have to be honest," she says. "I probably would have left him. I had three little children, and morally, I couldn't handle it. I never would have left him ill, but I had made up my mind that if . . ."

In June of 1964 Carol graduated from Cazenovia, then she went to work with the Kenley Players, a summer stock company in Warren, Ohio. Nat went to her graduation but Maria did not. In August, Carol received letters from Maria confessing that there was trouble in the marriage and that she was considering a trip to Europe, alone.

Nat was driving Maria home one night from a party that summer when she broke the silence with the angry sentence "I don't know what's going on, but you're not getting this house, you know." And wearily he replied, "Oh well, you can have the house." And it hurt her badly because then she was certain he had been thinking about it.

That was the closest the two of them ever came to an open discussion of divorce. But things went from bad to worse.

In September, Nat drove Natalie back to school in Northfield as he had done the year before. To her, he seemed just fine.

In October, Cole went to New York to perform at the Copa, and Maria was not made welcome to go with him. And what did Maria do? She did what any proud, furious wife with five children and some cash does when her husband is thinking of leaving her for another woman — any shrewd wife who is looking divorce in the eye — she hired a private investigator to prove what she most feared. The detective came away from Gunilla Hutton's flat in L.A. with enough billets-doux and mementos to fry King Cole in the divorce courts, if Maria took a fancy to do it. In California, she and the kids would get everything he had.

While Nat was in New York, Carol visited the small apartment he and Maria had recently purchased on West End Avenue near Lincoln Center. She had become involved in a relationship of which her mother was particularly critical. Carol was grateful for her father's understanding. He was, as always, a great comfort, which stood in contrast to her mother's practical stoicism.

By this time he was in considerable physical and psychic pain, as the growth of the tumor had started to affect the nerves of his spine and his guilt about Gunilla Hutton was beginning to take some of the joy out of the secret time he spent with her. Friends who visited the Manhattan apartment recall how he complained of back pain and how he was losing weight. He spent a lot of time lying on a chaise longue watching baseball and football games. Sparky, his valet, punched a new hole in the belt Nat wore with his suit, then another, and another. He told Nat he ought to eat more, but Cole paid no attention.

In September, Cole was with *Sights and Sounds* in Lake Tahoe, commuting by plane to Hollywood at dawn every day to film the music for the movie *Cat Ballou*, in which he and Stubby Kaye played the wandering minstrels. The schedule was grueling, Nat's back was killing him, and he was still losing weight. Buckling on his trousers one night and finding them too loose, he complained to Sparky, "You didn't fix these pants!" The little valet explained that he had taken them in only two days before. When Sparky told Cole to see a doctor, he got angry and said there was nothing wrong with him but the movie and when it was done he would get some rest.

Back in L.A., Maria was biding her time. In her

anguish and fury, her mood swung from pole to pole, as one minute she wanted to leave her husband and the next she envisioned a tearful reconciliation. And she was sure in her heart that he had not let go of her, yet, for this other woman; she felt that the affair that had burned brightly in the spring and summer was beginning to cool by the autumn.

So in mid-October she flew to see him in Tahoe. "Sparky met me at the airport. They knew I was coming, because Sparky was sent to meet me. We drove to Harrah's. I remember walking into the big room where they were rehearsing. Ms. Hutton was sitting in a chair and he was leaning over her, telling her something — very intense. Then someone said, 'There's Maria!' Another of the girls passed between us, and I remember Nat walking up to me. And I just looked at him and knew he was still carrying on with her. I slapped him across the face, and I walked out. Left him standing there."

Still she did not give up hope. "I knew he didn't want a divorce. I always knew it. He never asked for one."

At the end of October he came home briefly to see Kelly and the twins before flying to Vegas to do his annual stint at the Sands Hotel. In the house that for years had rung with laughter, welcoming him home from his hard travels, the air was heavy with rage and melancholy. Charlotte was angry at him. He hardly knew the little twin girls. And Kelly had missed him so much.

Maria remembers: "Just before he went to play Vegas the last time, we were standing in my dressing room. And I don't even know why he was in there, but he was hugging me and kissing me. I was crying and he, you know, he still didn't want to admit to the affair, he said, 'It's all right, Skeez, it's all right. Please come down to Vegas for two or three days.' Of course, I knew this might hurt me all the more, because I knew Vegas — he wouldn't let me stay but so long. And now he was leaving and he wouldn't let me take him to the airport. He got in a cab and I stood there in the dining room, crying, and looked out the window."

So in November she flew to Las Vegas as he had asked her to do, to try once again to regain her place in his affections. But she did not let him know exactly when she would be arriving. The following story is either French farce or Italian opera depending upon who tells it, and several people tell it. The balladeers of the Rat Pack paid the luggage porters at the airport to be on the lookout for wives. Somehow Maria slipped by the scouts unnoticed. By the time the warning call went up to Nat's hotel room that evening, he was so deeply engaged he did not answer the phone.

Maria went directly to the door of his suite, heard his voice, heard the unmistakable voice of the Swedish mistress. Maria knocked and knocked, called out, and there was a great scuffling and commotion inside the suite, which was a den of connecting rooms. Ms. Hutton was hustled out a back door, and by the time the front door opened there were several men in the room, Nat among them, men laughing, joking, trying to act as if nothing were amiss. As her husband tried to escape from the mess he was in, Maria grabbed him, spun him around, and, eyes blind with tears, lashed out at his face with her fingernails.

"I caught myself and recoiled. I thought: How terrible for me to do something like this. This is not me. I am not like this. I ran out of the hotel. I got on the next plane that was going to L.A."

Ivan Mogull, who had known Cole since 1946, and knew the couple as well as anyone, believes that by that time Nathaniel was no longer himself. "I think that by then he was so sick he didn't know what he was doing."

Maria called her husband from home a few days later, when he had gone to San Francisco with *Sights and Sounds* to play a theater in San Carlos. She wanted to tell him she was leaving for Paris. He sent her this telegram at 8:51 p.m. on November 23: "Thanks for calling me. I can't forgive myself, but I hope someday you will forgive me. Love, Nat."

"My husband did not know how to get me back," she recalls.

Nat did not come home for Thanksgiving, so Charlotte took the twins and Kelly and the maids to Palm Springs. Charlotte was furious at Nat, and perplexed. "I loved him dearly, as if he were my brother, the brother I never had. I always felt he was one of the chosen, an extra-special man. He was wonderful, wonderful. But he wasn't Jesus. And all of us are faced, at some time or other, with some kind of temptation. People had built this idea of him, making him more saint than man because they adored him so."

While he was home for a brief visit after Maria had gone to Europe, Charlotte got him alone at the breakfast table.

"What are you doing?" she pleaded, as the light of late morning poured into the dining room and Nat stared at his cup of coffee and his burning cigarette in the ashtray. "My God, man, you are loved by so many people! You are so blessed. You have a beautiful wife, you have great kids. All over the world you're loved. Not too many people get that kind of blessing. What *are* you doing?"

As he listened to the anguished words of his wife's sister, Cole's eyes filled with tears. And he answered her with a cry from the depths of his soul, and a gesture more meaningful than any words; making a light fist with his right hand, he tapped his left breast, softly, where he knew his heart to be, and where he sensed a disease was growing. And he said, "It has something to do with this, it's something *here*," indicating the place within him where love was fighting a losing battle against death.

Nat had been onstage performing when a drawn-out, burning pain seized his chest so violently he could hardly finish singing. Back in his hotel suite at the Sands the pain struck him so hard he fell to the floor. He called Carl Carruthers, who had been rehired since the advent of Hutton so that Maria's friend Sparky would never have to deal with the nineteen- year-old mistress; Sparky could honestly say he knew nothing about her. Carruthers called a local doctor, who came to Cole's hotel room with a portable EKG machine. Cole refused to go to the hospital, saying it was bad publicity. Ascertaining that the singer had not suffered a heart attack, the physician advised him to take a few days off. It never occurred to the doctor to X-ray Cole's lungs.

By the time he was working in San Francisco, after Thanksgiving, Nat had a bad cough and constant back pain. The show had to be rewritten so he came on first and could leave early.

He was staying at the Hotel Fairmont when finally, on December 1, Tavares and Carruthers insisted he see the hotel's doctor. Later this physician told Maria, "From the minute I walked into his room I knew he was a very sick man." Wheezing and coughing, Cole went with the doctor to his office to get a chest X ray. When the doctor saw the X ray of Nat's lungs he drew in his breath. The tumor on the left upper lobe of Cole's left lung was unmistakable and far advanced. Later the doctor told Maria, "We were all broken up. It was obvious he only had a couple of months." Maybe so, but this is not what he told Nat Cole. The word "cancer" was not spoken, though the word "tumor" was. The doctor put Cole on penicillin and advised the singer to cancel his performances and go home to his own doctor.

Cole did not follow the doctor's orders. He remained in San Francisco to finish his two-week engagement there. In the City by the Bay he held his last recording sessions, December 1, 2, and 3. With Ralph Carmichael conducting he recorded "More," "My Kind of Girl," "The Girl from Ipanema," and nine other tunes. But he was short-tempered and gruff, unlike his usual relaxed self in the studio, as he struggled to suppress his cough. Sparky recalled Nat being so weak at times he had to help the star up the stairs of the theater in the round where *Sights and Sounds* was playing.

Cole summoned his friend Bud Basolo from the ranch and poured out his heart to him. "After the show we got together. He said, 'Bud, this is my last time around.' I didn't get it at first. It could have meant retirement. 'No, Bud. I have cancer. I do not want you to tell the family, you're the only one who knows.'"

Months earlier at Tahoe, Nat had confided in Basolo that he was in love with Hutton, and Basolo cautioned his friend about jeopardizing the marriage. According to Basolo, Cole had been tempted to leave his wife for the girl, but could not bring himself to do it, "because of the hurt he would bring on his family."

Basolo always believed that Nat drew him into his life so that when he was gone there would be a man Cole trusted to look out for Kelly, his little boy. "I will always believe it," Basolo says. "He loved that little Kelly. The good Lord was driving it, so that when he was gone, someone would take care of the boy for him. I believe it was all designed." Basolo assured Cole that he would do all he could do for the family, bade his friend adios, and went back to his ranch, where Kelly one day would spend the happiest days of his youth. In the 1990s, when Cole's son was terminally ill, Bud and Georgia Basolo worked tirelessly to find a cure for his disease.

And around this time Cole introduced his bass player Charlie Harris to the wealthy Baltimore furniture dealer Stanley Fradkin. Fradkin came backstage after a show, and Nat said to him,

"Hey! I got a fellow working with me from Baltimore," and sat the millionaire down beside the elegant bassist, who had once played with Hampton.

"Nat was very ill," Harris recalls. And the bassist had grown weary of life on the road. "I knew it was time for me to stop doing what I was doing. Stanley Fradkin and I hit up a friendship. I came back home and went with the Fradkin Brothers in the furniture business. And I started to make a beautiful living in Baltimore." Cole was pleased. He would not be needing any more of Lionel Hampton's bass players.

In early December, Cole may have known he was dying, but he was not going to let that ruin his last days in the beautiful city of San Francisco. He kept the bad news from his young paramour. Hutton had become his dream of the future, his fountain of youth, his breath of life. No talk of death would spoil their stolen hours of joy. If he was ill and had to go into the hospital soon, she would be waiting for him when he got out, to breathe new life into him again.

Finally he left San Francisco, on Monday, December 7, the same day that his wife arrived in New York from her ten days in Paris. Maria knew nothing about his illness. She was making the most of the time and distance she had placed between herself and the humiliations and heartaches of the autumn, gathering strength for the Christmas season, when perhaps Cole would be ready to come home to her. The marriage was in serious trouble, but she had not given up hope.

The evening of the day she arrived from Paris, Maria went with friends to see Sammy Davis, Jr., in *Golden Boy* on Broadway. After the show, actor Anthony Quinn, actor Paul Burke, and other friends came back to Maria's apartment. And that is when she received the phone call from her sister Charlotte.

It was early evening in Los Angeles and near midnight in New York when Maria's phone rang. Charlotte told her sister that Nat was going into the hospital and that it was serious. She gave Maria the number of Dr. Robert Kositchek, the fifty-one-year-old doctor who would be supervising Nat's care at St. John's. Maria called him. He explained that Cole had a tumor on his lung, and when she asked if she should come home immediately, Kositchek said, "I think you should." Stunned, she asked the doctor if her husband had lung cancer, and he told her that he thought so and it looked pretty bad. She told Kositchek she would be on the next plane, hung up the phone, and asked Paul Burke to take her to the airport.

Nat had been to the doctor's office in Los Angeles that Monday. Consulting his notes from thirty-five years ago, Dr. Kositchek recalls: "He had a cough, chest pain, and weight loss — which he complained of having for five weeks. Severe low back pain. Been smoking one and a half packs of cigarettes daily. [He had cut way back.] His temperature was normal, his pulse was 88 and his respirations were 22. His blood pressure 136/84. His chest wheezed above the left upper lobe. During the examination he felt a great deal of pain over the lumbosacral spine. My diagnosis at that time [from X ray] was carcinoma of the left upper lobe of the left lung."

Sparky Tavares was with Nat and Charlotte at home in Hancock Park when Charlotte summoned Maria the evening of December 7. Sparky took Nat to the hospital. While they were driving to St. John's in Santa Monica, Nat asked Sparky for a cigarette. "Man, what's *wrong* with you?" Sparky exclaimed. And Nat replied, "I said give me a cigarette." Sparky was furious but he gave him one of his Salems. Cole had been trying to quit, and was not carrying his own brand. Sparky watched him light a cigarette with trembling fingers. "He took two puffs of it, put it out on the dashboard ashtray, and said he would never smoke again."

Until then the two friends had not spoken the word "cancer" though both of them knew what the doctor had said. Sparky insisted that Nat tell him, in plain English, what his illness was. "I want to hear it from you," said the little man, in his kind, stern voice. And Cole said to him, "I've got cancer." Sparky accompanied Cole up the white steps of St. John's and waited while he was admitted. The patient deposited five thousand dollars in cash in the safe. The men said goodbye, and that was the last Sparky ever saw of Cole alive. A few days later Leo Branton, "cutting costs," gave Sparky his walking papers, and the veteran went to work immediately as Nancy Wilson's road manager.

The day Cole entered the hospital he had a bronchoscopy, a biopsy of the lung tissue. Kositchek recalls: "The impression was the neoplasm of the left apical and anterior segment of the left upper lobe. A pearly raised mass was found in the bronchus. Typical of carcinoma. It was fixed and not removable. Dr. Elmer Rigby [a prominent "test specialist and surgeon"] suggested radiation and then surgery later. It was not a difficult diagnosis. He was far advanced. Cobalt was to be started. His main complaints were chronic cough and severe backache and hip pain, which required a great deal of medication. Demerol. We started at 50 milligrams and took it up slowly to 100."

After the bronchoscopy he lay in his room on the sixth floor of the North Wing of St. John's, West Side. From up there in good weather you could see the ocean and the mountains, but now it was raining and misty and the sun would not shine for weeks. He fell asleep with tubes in his nose and throat.

Glen Wallichs was waiting for Maria Cole when her plane touched down at Los Angeles airport that afternoon. She was jet-lagged and in a mild state of shock. The president of Capitol was one of her dearest friends but even he could not begin to fathom the turmoil in the woman's mind and heart. Her silences were as terrible as her words.

As magnificent as she had been in love, in devotion, in fighting for her husband's career and their rights to happiness, now she was no less magnificent in her rage. She was furious at Nathaniel Cole, his weakness, his folly, no more than she was furious at the folly of men in general and vain ballad singers in particular. She was furious at show business and Las Vegas, which catered to men's lowest instincts. She was angry at teenage chorus girls, and blond ones especially, and everyone who pretended to look the other way while they spoiled good marriages, families with little children, and the pride of honest wives. She was angry at cigarettes, specifically Philip Morris, and this nightmare sneaking disease, cancer of the lung. And in all the hurricane of her fury, Maria never ceased for a minute to love her husband — though if he ever got well again she might just kill him.

Boys will be boys, will they? He had acted like a child, and gotten himself into this mess, gotten them, *all* of them, into this mess. Did he know what a mess they were in? Did he have any notion what was at stake? Everyone's future, his, hers, the children's, a fortune of millions. All over a nineteen-year-old girl? Look what had happened to Belafonte when he left his black wife for a white woman! Look what happened to Sammy Davis when he married May Britt, the Swedish beauty! Now what would Nat Cole's stock be worth, his legacy, if the press found out how the singer had spent his last year?

She had gone through a period of grieving over the damaged marriage. Now that she had put that grief aside for a while her raw anger would give Maria the strength to face the challenges ahead — to preserve their pride, their dignity, the fortune they had fought so hard to earn and defend. The women of the Hawkins family had been lionesses and so was she. Now, however weak he was, she would have to be strong enough for both of them.

When she arrived at the hospital she found him

asleep with the tubes in his nose and throat. St. John's Hospital is a unique institution, clinically excellent, and used to meeting the extraordinary demands of celebrity patients, famous Hollywood actors and actresses. Maria Cole approached certain key personnel and explained as little of the Coles' marital problem as was necessary to enlist their support, knowing she could depend upon their strict confidentiality, both within the hospital and in dealing with the media. "Under no circumstances was anybody allowed to come and see the patient without Mrs. Cole's permission. The phones were to be blocked," a member of the staff recalls. Maria had the power to do this and she did it. Now was the time for damage control, whether he was to live or die. His wife would see to it he did no more damage to his image, the family franchise. He had acted like a child. Now on his sickbed or his deathbed, whichever it proved to be, he would be treated like a child until, if ever, he regained a man's strength, the strength of the man she knew and loved.

She was making a list, consciously and unconsciously, of everyone she knew and everyone that Nat knew who might have aided the Hutton romance or simply made it possible by directly encouraging the star in his erotic adventure or by looking the other way. It was a long list that included everyone under the slightest suspicion, and if you were on the list you would never see Nat Cole again. He was so sick and so weak he would have precious little time for company. When she had him all to herself, the two of them would see what they might do about a reconciliation; at the very least, they would appear to the world as a loving couple united in their battle against the cancer.

Their first hours together in the hospital room were awful. She was angry. He was so frightened and so wracked with pain and guilt he could not speak. And so they remained frozen in a murderous silence as the rain poured down outside the window on the streets of Santa Monica. Their words when they came were cruel and the silences were no better. And both of them must have wondered if death might be the kindest thing of all. It was like that on Wednesday and Thursday as Nat's pain increased and Maria got over her jet lag and some of the shock of realizing he might really die.

On Friday morning she sent him a white rose, a single rose. It was in a vase on the table beside him when he opened his eyes, and a note beside it reminded him how much she loved him. During the next two months he would receive flowers enough to fill a cathedral, but none so meaningful as the single white rose, symbol of purity, she sent him every morning without fail. It would be there whatever hateful things might pass between them.

Cole was scheduled to perform on December 12 at a special show to dedicate Los Angeles's new music center. Frank Sinatra sang in his place. Cobalt treatment started on the 10th and so did radiation. Newspapers broke the story of Cole's lung cancer on December 17. The hospital's statement was that, based on his response to treatment, "and without minimizing the seriousness of his condition, the medical prognosis is optimistic." They also said he would be released in ten days, but would cancel all bookings for several months. The truth is that the doctors were pretty sure he was going to die, and the "optimistic" prognosis was hope for a miracle. Maria eventually pushed that hope for a miracle so far beyond reason no honest discussion of his illness would ever be possible. Cole knew he was dying but did not want her and the world to know he knew. She knew he was dying but was afraid an honest press release would kill him when he heard — on the radio, or on the TV — that his case was terminal. And so it went, until the last day of his life, Nathaniel Cole playing the role he had perfected, the calm, brave, smiling fellow whose demeanor even Death cannot ruffle.

"On December 18 he started to run a temperature," Dr. Kositchek recalls. "He had fever, chills, and esophagitis as the result of the cobalt therapy. Two days later his temperature was 103, and he was getting a bad reaction to the cobalt and radiation, with the esophagitis. He could eat, but most of it was liquids. He was one sick cookie." He was rapidly losing weight.

Sick as Cole was in December he could still get out of bed, and when he was up to it, he would go for a stroll. His nurse Naida Barnes recalls: "We just joked around and walked the halls. We even went into the coffee shop. And he was so darn friendly that anyone could stop him, any of the patients, and he would talk with them. The personnel at St. John's was simply wonderful. They acted like he was any other patient. They didn't rush him or ask for autographs or anything. Visitors would, and he would sign them. Finally I told him, 'Nat you really have to stop doing that because of your blood count. Your immune system is in jeopardy because you're on cobalt.' Once he went to the auditorium and played the piano for some patients. For the holidays he gave the hospital staff a complete collection of his records and a phonograph to play them on.

"He gave me *My Fair Lady*, his album of those songs, and signed his whole name, and wrote: 'To the fairest lady of them all.' He was one of the most delightful people, and I have had a lot of good patients, a lot of celebrities," Barnes recalls. Everyone says he was a model patient, an inspiration. As we know, he never complained, about the terrible hospital food (except once) or the rain or the fact he was going to die. He only complained about the awful back pain. The nurse rubbed his back. She held his hand when the pain was unendurable. She helped him to wash his hair. She sprayed his back with ethyl chloride to help with the pain, but nothing worked.

His best hours were in the morning. Then the nurse would drive him a few blocks away in Santa Monica to get his cobalt treatments, and sometimes Maria went too. Usually by the time Maria arrived in the early afternoon, he was fading, sullen. She recalls: "Although Nat and I communicated, I just couldn't seem to reach him. The back pains came so strong that Nat could not hide his discomfort. 'I can't stand this!' he cried out at one point. 'Let me die.'"

She wanted him to come home for Christmas,

and when she mentioned it to the doctor he said, "I don't see why not," and then, "It might be the last Christmas he'll ever spend at home." This was harsh, but, she recalls, "he was simply telling me like it was, and frankly I wanted to know the truth."

But Nat was in no condition to go home for Christmas. He was still running a high fever. So the family celebrated Christmas at the hospital. "The Sisters at St. John's fixed up a room for us and prepared food. But Nat was so ill he could not help but be a bit irritable, and Casey and Timolin, our three-year-old twins, seemed to be a little frightened of him." With his sunken cheeks and hair gone white, he was hardly recognizable to Kelly and the little girls They unwrapped a gift or two and picked at the food. "We decided not to stay too long, and went back to friends and relations at home where it seemed like a wake."

Dr. Kositchek recalls: "On the 30th of December the patient's temperature resolved. His only complaint was his back and his weakness. I got him out of the hospital to go home for New Year's." His nurse Naida Barnes took him to Hancock Park on the 30th. He really did not need any nursing care at home — he was that well then — but she would be there just in case. "On the way to his home he took my hand, this guy was as nervous as could be, he was very, very emotional. I could tell it was difficult for him, going home after not being there for so long, not seeing his children. But then we got there and the house was just lovely and Maria was very nice. And I saw his

562

beautiful bedroom, all done in pink."

He spent most of those two days sitting in his rocking chair in the bedroom. One afternoon he got up and hobbled downstairs and through the backyard to the "play house." There Maria and Charlotte and some friends were sitting on the parquet floor sorting through some of the hundreds of thousands of letters the postmen had been delivering in great canvas bags. John Wayne and Arthur Godfrey, who had both won battles with cancer, sent their best wishes. So did the cast of the Broadway show *Fiddler on the Roof*. Mr. and Mrs. Robert Kennedy sent a message in which he promised "I will not sing publicly again unless it is with you." Governor Pat Brown wrote, "Get well. I need you." Letters came from senators, congressmen, diplomats, baseball teams, police departments; but the most moving thing was the sheer bulk of envelopes from strangers sending their love and good wishes. The postmaster said no individual in California's history had ever received so much mail.

Cole watched them shovel mail for about five minutes, but he was so weak he kept nodding. He whispered, "Is all this for me?" And Charlotte, his secretary, replied, "Yes, dear . . . Everyone loves you . . . just like we do." And then they helped him back to the bedroom.

The last time Natalie ever saw him was in that room, the New Year's before she went back to boarding school. "He had aged easily twenty, thirty years. I almost didn't recognize him. His hair was all gray and cut very close to his head. He was very, very thin, and the color of his skin was

. . . it had lost its glow, it was ashen. He was in a rocking chair, and I was so angry, so sad. I thought: Who is this? What happened? But his mood was actually quite good, in spite of the way he looked." He did his best to put on a good face for his daughter as he looked upon Natalie for the last time. "I knew that was the look of someone getting ready to die. And they had all of us believing he was going to be okay. I went back to school in January."

Cole returned to the hospital on January 2. Dr. Elmer Rigby, the surgeon who had done Nat's biopsy, was an authority on chest tumors, and he was called in, to work alongside Dr. Kositchek. On January 7, Cole's X rays showed myotasis (violent muscle spasms) in his lower back. "Pain was so severe that he was given Xylocaine and Benadryl injections at least every two or three hours." They knew that the cancer had spread and the doctors were looking for telltale changes in the architecture of the vertebrae.

When he awoke every morning from the drug-induced sleep, it was pain that reminded him he was still alive, pain and the dim light of another rainy day. The last time he could remember being happy was in a sun-drenched room of the Fairmont Hotel with a beautiful girl, and outside their window shone the golden stairs of San Francisco that led to the sea. She had thoughts only of life, more and more life for both of them, and his fantasy of the future lay with her. He had not told her he was dying and she did not know it. And maybe as long as Gunilla Hutton believed he would live so that the two of them might share the future, then perhaps there was a chance for him, there was some hope.

From such thoughts he gathered what strength he could. On January 9, rising up, he tied his robe tightly around him. He stepped into his slippers and made his way down to the front desk on the ground floor. He asked the cashier to give him the envelope he had deposited in the safe. The cashier cheerfully handed it over.

With the five thousand dollars in fifty hundred-dollar bills in the envelope in his robe pocket, he returned to his hospital bed. He asked a nurse for some stationery and stamps. She wasn't supposed to give it to him, but she did. He wrote a letter to Gunilla Hutton, enclosing the five thousand dollars in cash. He gave the letter to the nurse and asked her to mail it. She wasn't supposed to mail it, but she did. Then he asked her for a dime so he could call Hutton on the pay phone near the desk.

Three days later Maria Cole got a phone call from Gunilla Hutton. To the wife the young woman bravely explained she was in love with Nat and he was in love with her. And then she asked Maria why she did not give the man a divorce so he might follow his heart's desire? That was her straightforward proposal. Maria remembers that the girl seems to have had no inkling that the man they loved was dying. Maria's brief response was: "He never asked for a divorce but if he does you can have him. Just don't do *anything* to hurt my children." As the widow recalls, it was not a lengthy conversation but it was excruciating. Thirty-five years later she harbors no bitterness toward Hutton. She regards her with a mixture of pity for her devastated innocence and admiration for the woman she became, one who, among other strengths, had the character to keep a valuable secret.

But at the time, January 12, 1965, Hutton's early morning phone call was a call to arms. Maria had thought Nat was beyond such foolishness. He nearly was, but now she had to make sure of it. She telephoned a nurse in whom she had placed her confidence and poured out the whole painful story. She told the nurse she was on her way down to Santa Monica, and the witness recollects that Maria's phone call was to prepare the patient for a hard confrontation concerning the "other woman."

Now for the first time in nearly a month the sun broke through the clouds and the sky cleared. The nurse took Nathaniel up to the solarium on the seventh floor, where there was a view of the sea. She told him about her conversation with Maria, and he became silent, lost in thought. Later she led him back to his room, where he lay on a heating pad, and she held his hand. He did not speak another word until his wife arrived. The nurse left the room. Cole knew what was going to happen and he was prepared.

Maria came marching down the corridor of the North Wing on the sixth floor of St. John's Hospital, burst into her husband's room, and lit into him as if the two of them were in their twenties. Her voice could be heard by anyone in the North Wing who was curious, and by some who were not, until she got control of her fury. Behind closed doors she told him of Hutton's call. He gave her Hutton's phone number and she dialed it and handed him the phone. In his faint voice he asked the girl, "What do you mean by calling my wife on the phone?" And then he went on to say the things he could not say to the girl in the dream world that they had enjoyed together — that he was dying, that he had to be with his family, that it was over between them. Then she said some things to him and he nodded silently as she said them; he bade her goodbye and hung up the phone. This probably was the last time he ever communicated with Gunilla Hutton. Now he would have to turn his attention to the profound mysteries of illness and death.

The pain in his back was unrelenting. While the physicians continued cobalt therapy they kept X-raying Cole's back looking for changes in the bone that would prove a distant metastasis of the cancer. Says Kositchek, "On January 16, he had repeated lumbosacral films [X rays of the spine]. They showed deformity evidence of pedicle changes over the first lumbar vertebrae. We continued radiation therapy to the spine and pelvis. He developed pain on the sixteenth for the first time over the right rib, posteriorly. The seventh rib. X rays showed the changes in architecture. We talked about surgery."

The doctor explains that when a patient is this ill, "without any question, family only is permitted to visit." But there were exceptions made on days when Cole was up to it, for the friends Maria approved. The following people were okay and had limited visiting privileges: Glen Wallichs,

Dick LaPalm, Leo Branton, Alan Livingston, Jack Benny, and Danny Thomas. Frank Sinatra, inhabiting a parallel universe with its own rules, came and went in the guarded corridors of St. John's as he pleased, his coat slung over his shoulder. He stood at the foot of Cole's bed and talked about himself — how he meant to give up his smoking and drinking and other bad habits so he might live forever. Over the holidays Frank had fallen in love with nineteen-year-old Mia Farrow. Lawyer Leo Branton came slithering in and out of Nat's room with documents for Nat to sign without reading — he was too sick to read them — powers of attorney for this and that, assuring that Kell-Cole and the trusts could continue in their wondrous work while Nat was indisposed. So at one point the patient looked up at his wife and the lawyer and quipped, "You would think I was dying," and they all chuckled, but at least two of them knew it was gallows humor.

Carol Cole flew to Los Angeles as soon as she could leave New York. She wished to provide what support she could to her parents in their agony but was afraid she might only be an added burden. Maria picked her up at the airport and tried to explain all that had come to pass — it seemed overwhelming to the young woman, incomprehensible, her mother's fury, her father's guilt and dismay. But Carol would do all she could in the weeks that followed to be a source of strength to the family, while taking comfort in the magnanimous presence of her Aunt Charlotte.

Maria summoned Dick LaPalm from Chicago because Nat kept asking for him. "I remember

Charlotte picking me up at the airport and as we were driving to St. John's I remembered how much he loved cream puffs. So I saw a bakery on Wilshire and bought a dozen. I went into the hospital and he was so happy to see me and the cream puffs, he ate one of them, the first thing he had been able to eat that day. Then I went out another day and spent time with him, and as I was leaving, Maria stopped me in the corridor and said, 'Dick, go back. He hasn't been eating. Please go back and tell him he's got to eat for his strength.'

"Because I'd spent so much time with him I knew his favorite dish was pan-fried pork chops. So I walked into his room and he was happy to see me back, and I said, 'Nat you've got to eat.' He started complaining about the hospital food. And I said, 'We'll have 'em make you some pan-fried pork chops.' He laughed and said, 'Dick, this is St. John's Hospital, they're not gonna make any pork chops just for me!' So I called the nurse in, and told her to ask the cook if he would make Nat King Cole some pan-fried pork chops. And she said certainly — all he had to do was ask.

"Now the thing I remember so well about that particular visit, it was the last, when I bent down to shake his hand, he grabbed my hand and with his left hand covering it he squeezed like this — and as thin as he was he was actually hurting me. I had to tell him. He just said, 'I'm sorry.' And in later years I thought he must have been holding on for life."

His physician recalls: "One of my most vivid memories of him was that he kept saying, 'Bob, get me well so I can get on television and tell people to stop smoking.' He said this again and again. All during this time, he wanted to live, to be able to tell people to quit smoking." According to Maria, he had other reasons to fight for life. The glacier of anger, guilt, and resentment between husband and wife had begun to melt, slowly, slowly, as death loomed and the warm memories of their seventeen years together began to crowd out the awful events of the more recent past. And they were bonded in their love of the children. They decided that if and when he got out of the hospital they would buy a summer house at the beach nearby where he could regain his health. At one point he got out of bed to go into the bathroom, and he was crying, and as he turned from her she saw him strike the palm of his left hand with the fist of his right as he said, "I've got to get well again so I can make you happy." They wept, and after that they would both struggle to forgive and be kind to each other, to make the most of whatever time together they had left.

"She was a tremendously devoted wife and mother," says Kositchek. "I have the highest regard for her."

On January 24 he was wheeled into surgery. "We did a left exploration at the left upper lobe because we were uncertain of the bone changes being a distant metastasis. We wanted to be sure. Biopsies were all found to be malignant." (All pathology records were destroyed in 1985.)

On January 25 the surgeon, Elmer Rigby, removed Cole's cancerous left lung. On the 27th they thought he was responding favorably. But on the 28th his heartbeat was racing because the cancer was pushing against the mediastinum (the septum that divides the thoracic cavity) and pinching the heart. He was also developing extreme anemia. On the 29th he was feeling more comfortable but the back pain was still severe.

"We had him walking in the hall on January 31," Kositchek recalls, "but he was developing muscle atrophy in his legs." After surgery he was on morphine and Miltown, but he could not stay on the morphine long because they did not want to depress his respiration. By early February he was back on heavy doses of Demerol. He was developing pleurisy in the remaining lung due to the shift in his mediastinum.

Press releases from the hospital remained optimistic. Knowing Cole's vocal cords were not damaged, Dr. Kositchek, when asked, said Cole might sing again. Publicist Ben Irwin even stated that Cole planned to tour Japan in April. Of course this was all nonsense, an illusion kept up for the benefit of — well, who benefited from it? Maria says, "The problem was in trying to prepare the public for the inevitable, since many of his fans expected him soon to be leaving the hospital." This included his daughter Natalie, away at school, and other family and friends.

The Reverend Coles, who had been ill for months with complications of diabetes, entered a Chicago hospital with a heart ailment the day Nat's lung was removed. The family had tried to keep news of Nat's illness from his sick father. But according to sister Evelyn, the Reverend had a premonition that Nat would follow him into the next world, and among his last words was an expression of profound sympathy to Evelyn for her brother's passing. Edward Coles died on February 1.

Maria says that Nat received the news of his father's death "without uttering a word." By now he could only move about the hospital in a wheelchair. He visited the chapel daily to pray for his father, himself, and his family. One day when he was alone in the sanctuary and had finished his devotions, he could not find the strength to move his chair. Sister Madelon Burns, passing by, noticed the old man's difficulty and asked if she might help him. They had never met, and the unworldly nun in her habit knew neither the old gentleman nor his famous name. "I'm Nat King Cole," he whispered to her, smiling, to which the kind Sister of Charity replied, not wishing to shatter the lunatic's harmless fantasy:

"That's all right, Your Majesty. I'll take you anywhere you'd like to go."

Carlos Gastel, Alan Livingston, and Ben Irwin came to visit on the 9th. They said Nat sounded optimistic. "Jack Benny had just been in to see him, and told him about twenty minutes of jokes," said Irwin. The anecdote proves Jack Benny's genius. Cole had no reason for optimism other than the comedian's patter. Dr. Kositchek sadly recalls: "On the 11th my notes show the cancer had invaded the liver. The liver was enlarged. I said that day the general condition was of rapid deterioration. Coughing up huge amounts of sputum, some blood flakes. Course of treatment now is making the patient as comfortable as possible. On the 14th my only note says the patient is terminal."

St. John's publicist John Kelly held a phone conference with Maria, her lawyer, and Nat's press agent Ben Irwin after getting the news about Nat's liver. Kelly would not be made to look like a fool. On Friday the 12th Cole was placed on the hospital's critical list. Later, journalist Louie Robinson wrote: "In view of the public's optimism, the question was how to begin to prepare his legion of fans for the inevitable." They decided first to issue a statement that Nat's recovery had slowed, and gradually admit he was dying. But there would not be time enough.

The next day Nat woke up feeling better. He sat up and had a little breakfast. Maria halted the news release that was about to admit the gravity of his condition. The next day, Sunday, was Valentine's Day. He said he wanted to go for a drive with Maria and Charlotte to the seashore, where they had planned to buy the cottage. So they got into the car, the sisters and Nat and nurse Viviane McKenzie and their old friend Dr. James Scott from Chicago, with the oxygen equipment. Charlotte drove the car to the beach.

The sun was shining on the sand and gentle surf when they arrived. But they stayed only long enough to glimpse the sea from the car, because Nat was losing his strength and the nurse said, "No, I think we're overdoing it. We better get back to the hospital."

Charlotte remembers that as they were getting out of the car at the hospital, "a doctor approached and asked, 'Mr. Cole, can I help you?'

And Nat was in the wheelchair, and he said, 'No, no, thank you,' just so polite and sweet."

While Maria and Dr. Scott and the nurse went upstairs to prepare the hospital room, Charlotte accompanied Nat up the ramp and through the doors of St. John's. He told Charlotte everything was going to be all right. She was crying. He told her again. She recalls: "Nat had a lot of faith. He was brought up as a preacher's son and all. While I felt it was sad for him to go, he believed that this was what he needed to do now. He had faced everything. He was answering to God, as if God had said to him, 'I'm not going to let you destroy what I have done for you here — you're too good, and you're just going to leave your good behind.'

"Finally we went up, and walked to the end of the hall where there was that beautiful view of Santa Monica, and the mountains and sea and the blue sky. I remember he kept gazing and gazing, and I had my arm around his shoulder. And I'll never forget his reaching up and taking my hand in his and saying, 'Turn me away from the window.' It was like he was saying goodbye."

Nathaniel Adams Cole was pronounced dead at 5:30 a.m., the morning of February 15, 1965. Dr. Kositchek and the nurses were with him then, nurse Casey Bower having detected that he was slipping into a coma a little earlier. He was discharged to the morgue.

Charlotte remembers: "Maria called and told me he was gone. And I jumped up — I still don't know how I drove to that hospital. All I know is, when I got there, of all things, I arrived at the time they were bringing his body out. I could not believe it. And I couldn't even cry then, I just repeated, 'How dare they? How dare they?' Then I sat thinking I've got to be practical-minded about his things, his personal things and all that. So I went to the main desk downstairs and said to a nurse, 'I want to get Mr. Cole's belongings.' She looked me up and down and said, 'I can't give Mr. Cole's belongings to anyone but him.' And I said, 'Well, you can't,' just like that, and she said, 'What's wrong with you?' And I said angrily, 'You can't because he's dead!' And she screamed. She hadn't known it. I apologized. To this day I'm sorry. It must have been horrible the way it came out. I just couldn't believe it myself."

Shock, disbelief, horror — these were the first reactions to the news that spread in a matter of hours from the halls of St. John's to the reporters and to family and friends and strangers around the world. CBS radio interrupted scheduled morning programs at 7:57 with a bulletin that the beloved singer had died. L.A. newspapers published extras with bold headlines and black borders. One nurse at St. John's said, "When he died we all felt as if a member of our family, someone we had known and loved dearly, was gone."

Maria telephoned Northfield, where Natalie was in school, and spoke to the headmaster. Only days earlier Natalie had received a telegram saying the surgery was successful and that they had removed all the cancer. This morning she was in biology class when someone entered with the message that her housemother wanted to see her back in the dormitory. Natalie remembers: "It happened so quickly none of us had time to pre-pare. My birthday is the sixth and my best friend at school's birthday was the fifteenth. We were sitting in class together. As soon as Mrs. Trask called for me, I felt this dread. I walked so slow to that dormitory. It was a bright winter day. It was a beautiful old building where we lived, and as I walked down the hallway the sunlight was streaming in the windows. And the first person I saw was the housemother's assistant, one of those cheerful women with a plump, Mrs. Smith's Cookies type of face. And she looked so sad. And I thought, oh, this is only going to get worse. Mrs. Trask was a fragile little elf, the sweetest lady. And I mean, she didn't have to say anything because I knew, I knew, and I just thought her heart was broken.

"She helped me pack and the headmaster and his wife took me to the airport. It was such a surreal thing. My sister Carol met my plane in L.A. I didn't cry until I saw my mom. It was one of those rare moments we went to the front door, Carol and I, and she opened the door to us. My mother never opened the door. Now, just to see her there, all dressed in black, opening the door for us, and she was just so broken. I mean, she was in little pieces. We all were, and we just didn't have a clue as to how to deal with it. My mom and my sister and I, we just clung to each other during that time."

The day after Cole died, the L.A. City Council adjourned in respect, flags at the New Music Center and the musicians' union flew at half-staff. Capitol Records received orders for more than a million of his discs. Carol had gotten Sparky on the phone in Florida, where he was on the road with Nancy Wilson, and he spoke to Maria, promising to fly home at once. Nat's dear friend and valet would see to it the boss was dressed right for his last engagement.

Sparky arrived to find Cole laid out at the Angelus Funeral Home that sad day, the 16th, and he was so wasted from disease Maria requested that the casket remain closed after it left the funeral home. Sparky noticed Nat's gold ID bracelet, which he always wore on his right hand, had been fastened on his left. So he put the bracelet back where it belonged.

On Wednesday, the 17th, from 3 to 10 p.m. in St. James Episcopal Church on Wilshire Boulevard, Cole's body lay in the sealed bronze coffin covered with velvet cloth, a green cross upon a purple ground. The church, built in 1926, is a grand architectural variation on the English perpendicular Gothic style, with a vaulted wooden roof and tall graceful columns separating the nave from the darker side aisles. Colorful Judson Studio stained glass shines in the pointed arch window over the choir, and more stained-glass windows light the side aisles.

In niches on either side of the altar the stone figures of St. James and St. Barnabas stood watch over Cole's dark coffin. It lay before the altar under two candelabra as hundreds of friends and strangers filed by to pay their respects. A reporter noted: "There were Boy Scouts and bankers, maids and musicians, judges and janitors. The sick, the well; the aged and the young; blondes, brunettes; Caucasians, Negroes, Mexicans,

Orientals." Some wept, some were dry-eyed, and "some emerged with a faraway stare, remembering some secret moment, some private memory . . ." One old woman sat near the church door, her tears falling on the Nat King Cole album she held in her arms.

Journalist Louie Robinson said, "Most could not believe him dead. Statesmen die, athletes wither and are gone; old heroes fade away. But dreams never die, and Nat Cole was the symbol of men's dreams. Millions fell in love to Nat Cole, proposed marriage to Nat Cole, celebrated anniversaries to Nat Cole and made love to Nat Cole."

The weather had been beautiful since Valentine's Day, and the day of the funeral, Thursday, the 18th, dawned sunny and warm. At 10:50 the white-robed altar boys lit the eighteen candles on the altar as the organ played the hymn "Answer Me." At 11:00 more than sixty active and honorary pallbearers, black-suited, wearing white carnations on their lapels, entered the brass doors of the church: Robert Kennedy, Count Basie, Frank Sinatra, Sammy Davis, Jr., Billy Daniels, Peter Lawford, Eddie Anderson, George Burns, Johnny Mathis, Ricardo Montalban, Danny Thomas, Gordon Jenkins, Nelson Riddle, Billy May, Jimmy Durante, Steve Allen, Jack Entratter, Ivan Mogull, Charlie Harris, Frankie Laine, Governor Pat Brown, Alan Livingston, John Collins, accountant Harold Plant, Capitol executives Lee Gillette and Glen Wallichs, booking agent Henry Miller, Nat's old manager Carlos Gastel, writer Leonard Feather, Nat's tailor Sy Devore, and others.

Publisher Marvin Fisher, one of the active pall-bearers, said to the others as he prepared to lift the coffin covered with white roses, "He's been carrying us all our lives; now it's our turn to carry him." And they bore the casket to the altar.

Maria, in a black calf-length dress with a long black veil and black gloves, entered the church with the twins in checkered capes, Carol, twenty, holding five-year-old Kelly's hand, and fifteen-year-old Natalie in a dark suit over a plaid blouse. Brothers Edward and Freddy followed with their sister Evelyn and Maria's sister Charlotte. When the family had taken their seats, the service began. There were four hundred people in the church and another thousand gathered quietly outside, where a dozen policemen were directing traffic in the 80-degree heat.

The dignified, bespectacled Jack Benny delivered the first eulogy, and for once the comedian was guilelessly solemn as he spoke. "In accepting the belief 'Thy will be done,' many times we are prompted to question the justice of events such as the one that brings us here today. Nat Cole was a man who gave so much and still had so much to give. He gave it in song, in friendship to his fellow man, devotion to his family. He was a star, a tremendous success as an entertainer, an institution. But he was even a greater success as a man, as a husband, as a father, as a friend."

Many wept, but there were no outcries, no displays. "It was heartrending," said a bystander, "a pathetic thing to see a young man like this, with all the future ahead of him."

Jack Benny continued: "Sometimes death isn't

as tragic as not knowing how to live. This nice man knew how to live and how to make others glad they were living."

After the Reverend Samuel D'Amico conducted the Episcopal Order of the Burial of the Dead, the pallbearers carried the coffin out the door. Maria followed with little Kelly walking beside her, reminding many of Kennedy's boy, trying to comfort his mother, at the President's recent funeral. But Kelly was taking it hard. The child was frightened and mystified, wondering if this was all some cruel game or nightmare from which he or Dad might suddenly awaken. He was fortunate in having two devoted surrogate fathers: Bud Basolo and Edward G. Robinson. "Once during the services," Maria recalls, "Kelly turned to me and said, 'Let me just touch the casket.' Later that magnificent little boy sat with me in the mausoleum at Forest Lawn and shook everyone's hand."

The honorary pallbearers formed an honor guard of two columns as the rose-covered coffin was carried between them to the door of the hearse that would carry Nat King Cole to the Freedom Mausoleum in Forest Lawn Cemetery. Outside the church Dick LaPalm fainted and Vic Damone helped to lift him up and revive him. Lee Young says that no one was more grief-stricken than the great guitarist Oscar Moore, who had virtually given up playing his instrument after parting with Cole in 1947.

At Forest Lawn, Cole was entombed in a crypt in the top row center of the "Sanctuary of Heritage," also called the "Court of Freedom." To his left lie the remains of the comedienne Gracie Allen and to his right is the actor Alan Ladd.

Near the entrance to the hall that leads to Cole's crypt, a Bible sculpted in marble lies open to these lines of the 37th Psalm:

The Lord knows each day of the good man's life
And his inheritance shall last forever.

EPILOGUE

Two weeks after Cole's death the American Medical Association backed the tobacco industry's refusal to label cigarettes a health hazard. Nevertheless, later in 1965 Congress passed the Federal Cigarette Labeling and Advertising Act, which required that cigarette packs display the Surgeon General's warnings.

Jack Benny died of lung cancer in 1974 and so did Duke Ellington.

The inevitable illusion of a full-length biography is that it includes the most important events and personalities of the subject's life. But much is hidden, more is lost, and many things cannot be said. Finally, a life such as Cole's is too large to be pressed within the covers of a companionable book.

I met and talked with everyone I could who knew Cole well, or worked with him, and those I met sometimes figure more prominently in the story than other important persons who have passed on. Jack Benny, Sparky Tavares, Eddie Anderson, Oscar Moore, and Glen Wallichs all played larger roles in Nat's life than I could accurately depict, because I did not know them. And then, for every musician, song plugger, publicist, and friend I have mentioned there are others nearly as important; it would not be possible to describe even half of the people in Nat King

Cole's life without turning the story into a shapeless pageant. I have written what I know. So Ivan Mogull has come to stand for many song pluggers, and Dick LaPalm has been generous enough to represent several publicists.

Now I face the task of sharing my knowledge of the fates, fortunes, and whereabouts of people with whom the reader has become acquainted (those not already accounted for). Having spent so many pages upon my subject, Nat Cole, trying to do justice to his life, I have so few words to spare for his friends and family that the greatest justice I can do them is to be as succinct as possible.

Carlos Gastel died of a heart seizure in San Jose in 1970 at age fifty-six. After a lifetime of getting and spending 10 percent of the gross income of Nat Cole, Peggy Lee, Mel Tormé, Stan Kenton, Benny Carter, Nelson Riddle, June Christy, and others, he died with next to nothing.

Oscar Moore, during his last decades, lived a quiet life devoted to his second family, raising two sons while his wife went off daily to work as a hospital administrator. He had a small business binding fishing rods. He could not be lured back to performing. He died in Las Vegas in 1981 of a heart attack, at age sixty-four. After Moore's death, his son Kenneth discovered, buried in a pile of rummage in the garage, the dusty, tarnished plaques and trophies from *Esquire* and *Down Beat* his father had won for his guitar playing in the 1940s.

Nadine Coles never remarried. She once told Kelly Cole, in the early 1980s, that after Nat "I never even thought of falling in love again." They stayed in touch until his death and he left her an insurance policy. She lived for a while near Los Angeles, where she worked with the handicapped, then eventually moved back to St. Louis, where she lived her last years.

In 1963 *Ebony* magazine ranked Claude Barnett among the one hundred most influential black Americans. He retired in 1964 and the ANP closed its doors. He suffered paralysis from a stroke and died in 1967.

Gunilla Hutton delighted television audiences for more than twenty years in various comic roles. She is probably best known for her antics as Nurse Goodbody on the long-running show *Hee Haw*.

Ivan Mogull has had success in several fields, notably as a music publisher and record producer with clients as various as Curtis Mayfield and Judy Collins. He lives in Manhattan, Palm Beach, and Remsenburg, New York, with Marcia, his wife of thirty years. They have two sons, Peter and David.

Dick LaPalm lives in L.A., where he represents songwriters such as Robbie Robertson and Donald Fagan, and enjoys his four sons and five grandchildren. LaPalm is still America's number one jazz lobbyist.

Eddie Coles died of a heart attack in 1970. His brothers Ike and Freddy are still living, and Freddy, a singer, still performs widely.

In 1965 Carole Cole (she has changed the spelling of her first name) became the first African-American actress to be signed by Columbia Pictures as a contract player. The dearth of roles available to black women in Hollywood led her to the theater. She was highly lauded for her performance in the West Coast premiere of *The Owl and the Pussycat* and later for her Broadway debut in Gore Vidal's play *Weekend*. In addition to many Off-Broadway credits Carole has had roles in the movies *The Mad Room* and *The Taking of Pelham One Two Three* and in the NBC television series *Grady*. After *Grady*, she decided to focus on raising her children and managing the company that oversees Natalie Cole's music publishing concerns. In 1976, Carole and her sons, Sage and Harleigh, met artist John Ensdorf and his son, Seth, and they became a family. Since 1991, Carole and her siblings have been overseeing the licensing and marketing of their father's catalogue of recordings via the family-owned companies of King Cole Productions, Inc., and King Cole Partners, LP.

Natalie Cole, after graduating from the University of Massachusetts in 1972 with a psychology degree, became a singer. Writer Louie Robinson has described her "dazzling flourish of versatility: ballads, torch-rock, rhythm and blues." In 1976 she won her first Grammy, as best new artist, for her work on the 1975 albums *Inseparable* and *Dangerous*. Critic John Storm Roberts says, "In a period of decadence, fatigue and gimmicks, she returns to the central issues of voice, tune and spirit." Her 1991 album *Unforgettable with Love* has sold fifteen million copies and won seven Grammy Awards, including Album of the Year. Her son, Robert Yancey, will attend the Berklee College of Music in Boston, and plans to become a professional drummer.

Kelly Cole was a serious scholar with special interests in gnostic mysticism, mythology and epic poetry, and the writings of Carl Jung. With writer Nicholas Xatzis, Kelly was working on a book about his father in 1995 when he died of complications related to AIDS.

Timolin Cole Augustus graduated in 1983 from Amherst College, where she majored in English before studying at the University of Texas School of Journalism. She worked for NBC Network News and for public relations firms and then opened her own Cole Public Relations firm in 1990. She closed the company in 1997. Presently she lives in Boca Raton with her husband, songwriter Gary Augustus, and their two sons, Julian and Justin.

Casey Cole Ray graduated from Brown University in 1983 with a B.A. in French. Then she returned to L.A. to pursue a career in public relations, working for two years with BMI before joining forces with her sister Timolin to become co-president of Cole Public Relations from 1992 to 1997. She presently resides in the Hancock Park section of L.A. with her two-year-old son, Wyatt.

Charlotte Sullivan lives in Los Angeles, where she writes poetry and songs, and takes great pleasure in the company of her nieces and their children.

After the death of her husband, Maria Cole put her energy into sorting out his estate, raising her children, and setting up the Nat King Cole Cancer Foundation. It would be years before Maria could rescue Cole's estate from the depredations of Margolis and the Kell-Cole organization, but meanwhile the income stream from Nat's records was so great that she and her children would want for nothing. Maria raised $50,000 for the Foundation, which was used to build a room in the Wilson Pavilion of the UCLA Medical Center.

She did some singing in the late 1960s, and co-hosted a television talk show in L.A., but she preferred family life to show business. In 1971 she remarried, to writer Gary Devore, and they moved to a large house in Tyringham, Massachusetts. They were divorced in 1976, and when Kelly, Casey, and Timolin were grown, Maria moved to a condominium at the Ritz Hotel in Boston. She lives there still. She is active in philanthropic work, and enjoys spending time with her children and grandchildren.

I sat with Maria Cole in her apartment overlooking the swan lake and leafless trees of Boston Common, on a cold day in February. Finding us at the end of a long conversation that was the last of many conversations about her life with the great man, I had only two more questions.

"What do you miss most about Nat Cole?"

"His attention," said Maria. "I was spoiled, really spoiled. I didn't have to ask for it, it just came. He had a way of being with you, that's the way he was with people, but especially with me. I miss that attention."

It was a wonderful thing, Cole's attention. He paid attention to his parents, to Earl Hines, Louis Armstrong, Jimmie Noone, and the other giants of the Golden Age of Jazz; he paid attention to his friends, his children, his sidemen, his audiences, and most of all to his music. In paying attention to his music he paid attention to all of us. He was full of love.

And the last question: "What would you say to him if you could speak to him once more?"

"I would tell him how much I love him. That's all."

ACKNOWLEDGMENTS

I am most grateful to Maria Cole for encouraging me to write this book and for her patience and courage in answering countless difficult questions during many hours of interviews. Through Mrs. Cole's kindness I was able to interview Nat Cole's friends and relatives, and his attending physician, Dr. Robert Kositchek, about the details of his last months. I owe a debt of gratitude to Carole Cole and Natalie Cole, who were so generous with their time and detailed memories of their life growing up in the Cole household; and to Charlotte Sullivan, their dear aunt, who witnessed and understood so much.

I am indebted to all previous biographers of Nat King Cole — James Haskins, Leslie Gourse, Louie Robinson, and Maria Cole herself — all of whom are quoted in this book. Each interviewed subjects who were no longer living when I began my work. The finest writers on Cole's music are Will Friedwald and Gunther Schuller, also quoted. Without their work my appreciation of the music would be the poorer. For background concerning Cole's early Chicago years and the jazz scene then, I am deeply indebted to Dempsey Travis for his books, *An Autobiography of Black Jazz* and *The Louis Armstrong Odyssey*, his kind hospitality in Chicago, and his patience in answering so many questions in interviews, in person, and on the telephone. Pianist Hank Jones described to me Cole's playing in 1935. My knowledge of Hines's life comes largely from Stanley Dance's biography, *The World of Earl Hines*. Klaus Teubig's book *Straighten Up and Fly Right*, a chronology and discography of Cole's career focusing on 1936–50, is a masterwork of scholarship, upon which I based much of my own chronology.

Many individuals and institutions have contributed to the research on this book. These include my research assistants Susan Gray, Dennis Greenia, and Anny Turbyville, and transcriptionist Tammy Everly; for medical matters Dr. Robert Liner and Dr. William Bell. I am grateful to Dan Morgenstern and the staff of the Jazz Institute at Rutgers University; Ned Comstock, the curator of the University of Southern California Cinema-Television Library, which houses the Cole Collection; Ellen Luchinsky and Eva Slezak of the Enoch Pratt Library; Linda Evans of the Chicago Historical Society; the Vivien Harsh Collection at the Woodson Library in Chicago; Roxie Powell and Neil Grauer, friends who secured important documents and facts when I needed them. Rosemarie Gawelko of Warner-Chappell music helped secure permission to quote from songs. Michael Cuscuna of Mosaic Records kindly provided *The Complete Capitol Recordings of the Nat King Cole Trio*, and Ann Douglas of HG Associates supplied the tapes of *The Nat King Cole Show*. Nick Xatzis sent me the pages and notes for Kelly Cole's unpublished book on his father. Marc and Alice Davis provided hospitality in Los Angeles. Jazzman Franz Jackson gave me an eyeful and an earful of Chicago jazz history. Zelma Stennis gave me a tour of the Coles' house in L.A.

I want to thank my narrative coach, Rosemary Knower, for helping to straighten out one more of my tangled tales, and Michael Yockel, whose comments upon style improved so many paragraphs. I am grateful to my editor Elisabeth Kallick Dyssegaard at FSG and my agent Neil Olson of Donadio & Olson for their support of this project from the beginning — likewise to Harry Crews and David Bergman. Thanks also to Jack Lynch for his careful copyediting, and Elaine Blair for her editorial assistance. The book might never have been written had it not been suggested by my friend Murray Horwitz of NPR and encouraged by my mother-in-law, Katharine McLennan, who introduced me to her friend Maria Cole.

I am grateful to dozens of people who gave generously of their time, sharing their memories of Nat King Cole in interviews, on and off the record, for background and for attribution. A list of these appears in the bibliography. Special thanks go to Dick LaPalm, Lee Young, Ivan Mogull, Berle Adams, Harold Jovien, and Barry Ulanov, who not only submitted to repeated interviews in person and on the telephone but also put me in touch with others of Cole's friends and business associates.

Finally I want to thank my wife, Jennifer Bishop, for her insight into several mysteries of character I encountered in telling this story.

NOTES

THE KID — CHICAGO, 1935

11 **The kid was wearing** Dempsey Travis, Interview, March 20, 1998.

11 **rain-filled clouds** "The Weather," *Chicago Tribune*, September 9, 1935.

11 **They came to hear him play** Tim Black, Interview, May 29, 1998.

12 **It was 30 cents a head** "Ad," *Chicago Defender*, September 7, 1935, p. 4.

13 **Last night the show had gone** "Election Ball," *Chicago Defender*, August 31, 1935.

13 **Battle of Rhythm** "Ad," *Chicago Defender*, September 7, 1935, p. 4.

14 **Almost a year earlier** "Plenty Hot," *Chicago Defender*, October 6, 1934.

14 **battling every Sunday afternoon** Jack Ellis, "The Orchestras," *Chicago Defender*, November 17, 1934.

14 **They called Tony "Little Duke"** "Chicago Has Own Duke Ellington," *Chicago Defender*, September 15, 1934.

15 **On December 15** "Nat to Play," *Chicago Defender*, December 15, 1934.

15 **This was the seventh annual** David Kellum, "Season's Largest Crowd," *Chicago Defender*, December 22, 1934.

15 **"You are sure to like his playing"** "Nat

to Play," *Chicago Defender*, December 15, 1934.

GATEMOUTH

16 **Sometimes he smiled so hard** Stanley Dance, *The World of Earl Hines* (New York: Charles Scribner's Sons, 1977), p. 88.

17 **Hines, too, had been a prodigy** Dance, *The World of Earl Hines*, pp. 15–16.

17 **Mr. Deppe the jazz singer** Ibid., p. 18.

17 **Deppe took him** Ibid., p. 26.

18 **By the time Earl Hines arrived** Ibid.

19 **He would pound the keyboard** Dempsey Travis, *An Autobiography of Black Jazz* (Chicago: Urban Research Institute, 1983), pp. 52–53.

21 **On his birthday** Dance, *The World of Earl Hines*, pp. 57–61.

21 **"I have a hundred thousand dollars"** Ibid., p. 57.

22 **In 1932, when business** Ibid., p. 58.

22 **"We're going to take twenty-five percent"** Ibid.

22 **Capone began to think** Ibid., p. 61.

23 **The jazz slave masters** Travis, *Autobiography of Black Jazz*, p. 41.

23 **But while Fox** Ibid., p. 45.

24 **"Everybody standing around"** Dempsey Travis, Interview, March 20, 1998.

25 **It was almost nine o'clock** Tim Black, Interview, May 29, 1998.

25 **At the sound of Cole's name** Dempsey Travis, Interview.

25 **The Schoolboy had the home-court ad-**

vantage Tim Black, Interview.

26 **The kid jerked his left hand** Ibid.

26 **"No gal made has *got a shade*"** Descriptions of the music are necessarily impressionistic, based on the Hines recordings of the period. Nat was roughly imitating the Hines arrangements of these songs, according to eyewitnesses Tim Black and Dempsey Travis. Hank Jones has contributed details of Cole's keyboard technique.

26 **Then the crowd** See the preceding note.

26 **The next chorus** Hank Jones, Interview, January 26, 1999. The great Detroit pianist Hank Jones heard Cole play this solo in 1936 and remembers this particular "release" as I have described it.

27 **all the kids in the ballroom** Tim Black, Interview.

FLIGHT OUT OF EGYPT

29 **The authorities in Alabama** Maria Cole, Interview, August 12, 1997.

29 **We might still** Department of Commerce, Bureau of the Census, Fourteenth Census of the U.S., 1920 Population, State: Alabama, County: Montgomery, Enumeration District #188, sheet #4698 A.

30 **Reverend Dan Adams** Leslie Gourse, *Unforgettable* (New York: St. Martin's Press, 1991), p. 3.

31 **They were joining the Great Migration** William Kenny, *Chicago Jazz* (New York: Oxford University Press, 1993), p. 11.

32 **By the mid-twenties** Ibid., p. 12.

32 **"to organize the Second Progressive Baptist Church"** *Chicago Tribune*, February 1, 1965, p. 1.

33 **1925** Klaus Teubig, *Straighten Up and Fly Right* (Westport, CT: Greenwood Press, 1994), p. 18.

34 **got pneumonia** Gourse, *Unforgettable*, p. 7.

SCHOOLBOYS

35 **"The Lord," the Reverend Coles announced** Maria Cole, *Nat King Cole: An Intimate Biography* (New York: William Morrow, 1971), p. 37.

36 **He would send Nathaniel** Maria Cole, Interview, August 12, 1997.

36 **As a boy Eddie** Dayle J. Carr, *Pittsburgh Courier*, magazine section, "Have You Ever Heard of Nat King Cole's Brother?" (n.d.), p. 6.

37 **All the Coles children** Milt Hinton, Interview, February 4, 1998.

37 **The autumn after** Ike Coles, Interview, April 30, 1998.

38 **Music inspired the children** Ibid.

38 **That man was Major N. Clark Smith** Travis, *Autobiography of Black Jazz*, p. 489.

39 **In that neighborhood** Ibid.

40 **Bass player Milt Hinton and band leader Lionel Hampton would recall** Milt Hinton, Interview, February 4, 1998.

41 **Hinton tells** Ibid.

41 **Entering his teens, Eddie** James Haskins

with Kathleen Benson, *Nat King Cole* (New York: Stein & Day, 1984), p. 16.

41 **"Who took the straps?"** Ibid.

42 **Eddie was no more than thirteen** Gourse, *Unforgettable*, p. 6.

44 **A short five-block walk** Travis, *Autobiography of Black Jazz*, p. 30.

44 **It was dangerous, erotic** Kenny, *Chicago Jazz*, p. 25.

44 **"the embodiment of culture" . . . "immoral entertainment"** Ibid., p. 21.

44 **"the white plague"** Ibid., p. 23.

45 **white women were not safe** Ibid., p. 22.

45 **On Christmas night** Travis, *Autobiography of Black Jazz*, p. 33.

45 **"particularly vicious"** Ibid.

46 **When Louis first came to Chicago** Dempsey Travis, *The Louis Armstrong Odyssey* (Chicago: Urban Research Institute, 1977), p. 33.

47 **Armstrong was incredibly kind** Franz Jackson, Interview, March 21, 1998.

48 **"I want you kids to listen"** Travis, *Louis Armstrong Odyssey*, p. 196.

48 **If Eddie Coles was lucky** Ibid.

49 **And on that day** Teubig, *Straighten Up and Fly Right*, p. 18.

49 **According to his own account** Doyle Carr, "Have You Ever Heard."

50 **According to Eddie Coles** Ibid.

BUD BILLIKEN DAYS

52 **the band broke up in** Lisbon Ibid.

52 **On a rainy Saturday** "Kids Have Merry Time," *Chicago Defender*, November 24, 1928.

53 **The next division** Ibid.

54 **"We are planning a picnic"** Ibid.

54 **As Milt Hinton says** Milt Hinton, Interview.

54 **Back in 1923** Roi Ohley, *The Lonely Warrior: The Life and Times of R. Abbot* (Chicago: Henry Regnery, 1955), p. 351.

55 **When young Motley** Ibid.

55 **Dempsey Travis, who grew up with Nat** Dempsey Travis, Interview.

56 **From the sirens** "Crowd of 35,000 Attends Bud Billiken Big Picnic," *Chicago Defender*, August 22, 1931.

57 **The crowd of 35,000** Ibid.

59 **"too much on the hot side"** Haskins, *Nat King Cole*, p. 17.

60 **Built in 1928** Travis, *Autobiography of Black Jazz*, pp. 146–48.

61 **The Regal auditorium** Ibid.

61 **On Saturday morning** "Billiken Party Attracts 12,000," *Chicago Defender*, November 28, 1931.

62 **Hines and his men** Tim Black, Interview, May 29, 1998.

63 **What did Nat play** Ibid.

ON THE TOWN

66 **So in good weather** Dempsey Travis, Interview.

66 **bronze figures of Negro soldiers** John

Ashenhurst, *All About Chicago* (Boston: Houghton Mifflin, 1933), p. 161.

66 **Down the small side streets** Henry Horner, *Illinois* (Chicago: A. C. McClurg & Co., 1939), p. 296.

66 **a schoolmate recalls** Dempsey Travis, Interview, May 29, 1998.

67 **According to one account** Timmie Rogers, Interview, February 21, 1998.

67 **A review of his high school record** Louie Robinson, *Jet*, March 4, 1965, pp. 44–45.

67 **Tim Black sat in the seat** Tim Black, Interview.

67 **Byron Minor is very specific** Anecdotal evidence of Coles remaining in high school at either DuSable or Wendell Phillips after November 28, 1934, is vague and contradictory. There is no reliable evidence he attended school after 1934.

68 **Captain Walter Dyett** Gwendolyn Dyett Burks (Mrs. Walter Dyett), Interview, March 23, 1998.

69 **Sad-eyed, slender** Ibid.

69 **"His ear was so sensitive"** Dorothy Donegan, Telephone Interview, March 10, 1998; Travis, *Autobiography of Black Jazz*, p. 30.

70 **Nat could hang out** Franz Jackson, Interview.

70 **"His sound was so beautiful"** Ibid.

71 **"sinuous Nadine Robinson"** Bob Hayes, "Here and There," *Chicago Defender*, August 18, 1934.

71 **"a standout tap dancer"** "Cabarets," *Chicago Defender*, September 21, 1934.

71 **"Eddie Coles is playing"** Jack Ellis, *Chi-*

599

cago Defender, January 27, 1935.

71 **Bassist Henry Fort recalls getting a phone call** Travis, *Autobiography of Black Jazz*, p. 179.

72 **We hear stories** Harold Jovien, Interview, February 21, 1998.

72 **For on October 6** "Plenty Hot," *Chicago Defender*, October 6, 1934.

73 **Nathaniel and his family** "Back Stage," *Chicago Defender*, October 6, 1934.

73 **Malcolm Smith had something** Julius J. Adams, "Pal Who Discovered Nat Cole," *New York Age*, March 20, 1954, p. 22.

74 **Tony "Little Duke" Fambro and his band** "Chicago Has Own Duke Ellington," *Chicago Defender*, September 15, 1934.

74 **Smith hired Cole** Jack Ellis, "The Orchestra," *Chicago Defender*, November 17, 1934.

74 **Nathaniel met a youngster from Detroit** Timmie Rogers, Interview, February 21, 1998.

75 **"I love that tune"** Ibid.

75 **"They were rogues"** Dempsey Travis, Interview.

75 **Eddie was home** "Going Backstage," *Chicago Defender*, December 8, 1934.

76 **On December 15** Photo of Nat Cole and caption, *Chicago Defender*, December 15, 1934.

76 **"well-known young pianist"** Ibid.

77 **"It is a pleasure"** David Kellum, "Season's Largest Crowd Sees Midnight Show Hit," *Chicago Defender*, December 22, 1934.

77 **"in every joint on the South Side"** Gourse, *Unforgettable*, pp. 16–17.

78 **Louis Armstrong was back** Travis, *Louis*

Armstrong Odyssey, p. 106.

78 **Tatum allowed himself** Gourse, *Unforgettable*, p. 17.

79 **On Easter Sunday** Adams, *New York Age*.

79 **"when he turns that five-part brass loose"** Jack Ellis, "The Orchestras," *Chicago Defender*, September 14, 1935, p. 9.

79 **"Nat seemed much older"** Travis, *Autobiography of Black Jazz*, p. 179.

80 **"Nat could sit down"** Ibid., p. 180.

80 **Malcolm Smith was able to book them** Al Monroe, "Everybody Goes When the Wagon Comes," *Chicago Defender*, June 15, 1935.

80 **"Nate (schoolboy bandleader)"** Ibid.

80 **Armstrong was also going on tour** Jack Ellis, "The Orchestras," *Chicago Defender*, June 22, 1935, p. 7.

81 **According to Henry Fort** Travis, *Autobiography of Black Jazz*, p. 180.

THE SAVOY BALLROOM —
SEPTEMBER 8, 1935

82 **It wasn't yet midnight** Tim Black, Interview, May 29, 1998.

83 **But the kid** Dempsey Travis, Interview, March 20, 1998.

84 **The King of the Ivories set the glowing coal** Franz Jackson, Interview, March 20, 1998.

85 **Hines would play two solo choruses** "Angry," recorded in Chicago in 1934 (September 13, 1934), Decca Records.

88 **Now the kid lightly played** Tim Black, Interview.

BROTHERS

90 **"Earl Father Hines and Nat Cole's cats"** Jack Ellis, "The Orchestra," *Chicago Defender*, September 14, 1935, p. 9.

90 **"Nat was no Earl Hines"** Tim Black, Interview.

92 **"Eddie Cole, the bass player"** Jack Ellis, "The Orchestra," *Chicago Defender*, October 19, 1935, p. 9.

92 **" 'Jelly' Coles and Brother Form a Band"** *Chicago Defender*, October 26, 1935.

92 **We do know** Al Monroe, "Everybody Goes," *Chicago Defender*, November 16, 1935, p. 12.

93 **The Coles were in demand . . . Accepting a gig** Jack Ellis, "The Orchestra," *Chicago Defender*, February 22, 1936, p. 8.

93 **"Eddie Cole, the orchestra leader** Bob Hayes, "Cabaret," *Chicago Defender*, March 21, 1936.

94 **an ebony Ruby Keeler** Marc Davis, Interview, February 15, 1998.

NADINE

98 **Kenneth Roane, their trumpet player** Leonard Feather, liner notes, *Nat King Cole — From the Very Beginning*, MCA Records, CA 1973.

100 **Legend has it** Haskins, *Nat King Cole*, p. 21.

101 **When Thelma broke her beer bottle** Jack Ellis, "The Orchestras," *Chicago Defender*, August 8, 1936.

102 **What began as** Haskins, *Nat King Cole*, p. 22.

103 **A news article** Jack Ellis, "The Orchestras," *Chicago Defender*, December 15, 1936.

103 **the lovers entered the courthouse** Marriage License No. 30075, Kalamazoo, MI; Certificate of Marriage, 396038, 1937.

103 **A few days later** Timmie Rogers, Interview, February 21, 1998.

104 **Nathaniel and his bride** Jack Ellis, "The Orchestras," *Chicago Defender*, February 27, 1937.

SUNSHINE AND SHADOW

107 **Across the hills** *Los Angeles*, USWPA, 1941, pp. 3–6.

107 **Los Angeles spreads** Ibid.

108 **The population** Ibid.

108 **"With the 1937 edition of *Shuffle Along*"** Harry Levette, "Thru Hollywood," *Chicago Defender*, May 15, 1937.

109 **"the best road show"** Ibid., p. 21.

109 **By several accounts** Richard Hubler, "$12,000-a-week Preacher's Boy," Saturday Evening Post, July 17, 1954, p. 106.

109 **In late June the principals** *Chicago Defender*, June 27, 1937, p. 12.

110 **"I didn't want my dad to see"** Hubler, op cit., p. 106.

110 **Nathaniel's family and friends** "Hit on Coast," *Chicago Defender*, July 10, 1937, p. 10.

111 **Jack Ellis announces** Jack Ellis, "Musicians," *Chicago Defender*, July 24, 1937, p. 12.

111 **According to *Variety*** Teubig, *Straighten Up and Fly Right*, p. 25.

111 **"It was a tough workout"** Hubler, op cit., p. 106.

112 **Soon after arriving** Lee Young, Interview, February 17, 1998.

112 **According to Young** Ibid.

113 **The saloon pianos** Haskins, *Nat King Cole*, p. 24.

113 **If there was no work** Lee Young, Interview.

114 **"All the musicians dug him"** Haskins, *Nat King Cole*, p. 25.

114 **"She loved him"** Gourse, *Unforgettable*, p. 22.

114 **"He wasn't making"** Haskins, *Nat King Cole*, p. 25.

114 **It was her dream** "King Cole's Forgotten Love," *Tan*, September 1954, p. 25.

115 **From Lee Young's recollections** Lee Young, Interview.

115 **On weekdays** Ibid.

116 **Cole and Young** Ibid.

117 **Nadine was devoted** *Tan*, op. cit.

118 **The young men's schedule** Lee Young, Interview.

118 **Nat's joining the Fraternal Order of Masons** Ibid.

119 **"Everybody got a ring"** Ibid.

THE TRIO

120 **One night in the late summer** Hubler, op. cit., p. 106.

120 **But Young took one look** Lee Young, Interview.

120 **Then Nat talked** Ralph Gleason, "Just Can't See for Lookin'," *Esquire*, January 1947, p. 107.

121 **They called Oscar Moore "Jesus Boy"** Ibid.

121 **"First time I laid eyes on Nat"** John Tynan, "Nat Cole," *Down Beat*, May 16, 1957, p. 15.

121 **singularly boyish and naive** "Harlem's Apple," unidentified newspaper clipping, November 18, 1944, USC Library, Cole Collection.

122 **"Those guys were joined"** Lee Young, Interview.

122 **Lewis may have** Alyce Key, *Keynotes* USC Library, Cole Collection, *LA News*, April 1944.

123 **A contract has survived** Contract blank of the American Federation of Musicians, Local #767, 1710 South Central Ave., L.A., March 15, 1938, USC Library, Cole Collection.

123 **"King Cole and his Sepia Swingsters"** *Variety*, November 6, 1938.

127 **"You can't fill a club with a band of three"** Hubler, op. cit., p. 106.

131 **The crowd at Jim Otto's** Marc Davis, Interview, February 15, 1998.

134 **On December 10** *Chicago Defender*, December 10, 1938.

134 **The schedule from New Year's** Teubig, *Straighten Up and Fly Right*, pp. 29–34.

137 **By May 1939** Ibid., pp. 34–35.

139 **Lee Young believes** Lee Young, Interview.

139 **"The King Cole Swingsters have moved"** *Down Beat*, September 1939.

140 **One day Watkins** Arnold Shaw, *52nd St. — The Street of Jazz* (New York: Da Capo Press, 1977), p. 202.

141 **"They have done swell business"** *Down Beat*, January 1, 1940.

141 **Glen Wallichs wanted them** "New Music Center," *Down Beat*, July 15, 1940.

141 **Lionel Hampton's flirtation** Teubig, *Straighten Up and Fly Right*, pp. 41–43.

142 **The critic Hughes Panassie** Eric Townley, "Tell Your Story," *A Dictionary of Jazz and Blues Recordings* 1917–1950 (Essex, England: Storyville Publications, 1976).

142 **On August 15** Leonard Feather, "King Cole Trio Will Form Basis for New Hampton Ork," *Down Beat*, August 15, 1940.

142 **Lee Young, just returning from New York** Lee Young, Interview.

143 **By now their rehearsal** Barry Ulanov, "Fly Right," *Metronome*, 1943.

144 **His last transcription** Gord Grieveson, "A Disco-Bio-Chronology for The Complete Early Transcriptions of the King Cole Trio 1938–1941" (Vintage Jazz Classics, Ltd., 1991).

145 **At the end of the year** Charles "Truck" Parham, Interview, March 21, 1998.

146 **"A promising debut"** *Down Beat*, April, 1941.

147 **Al Jarvis, disc jockey** Gene Norman, Interview, February 20, 1998.

147 **The Decca records won them** Berle Adams, Interview, February 19, 1998.

149 **"Have you been in the Dome Room?"** Ibid.

150 **Nathaniel was worried** Ibid.

151 **Singer Frankie "Mule Train" Laine** Frankie Laine, Interview, July 7, 1998.

152 **Oscar looked over Nat's shoulder** Gord Grieveson, "Here Comes Charlie," liner notes from *Crazy Rhythm* (Vintage Jazz Classics, 1991), p. 5.

152 **In the heat** "Man, That's Groovy," *Down Beat*, August 1, 1941, p. 23.

153 **Back in New York** "Ad," *New York Times*, October 29, 1941.

154 **When the Trio arrived** Sharon Pease, "Swing Piano Styles," *Down Beat*, December 1941.

155 **Scholar Will Friedwald writes** Will Friedwald, "All the King's Men" (Mosaic Records, Stamford, 1991), p. 15.

155 **they joined an all-star review** *New York Amsterdam Star News*, December 12, 1942, p. 4.

FLY RIGHT

157 **So Nat, Oscar, and Wesley** Teubig,

Straighten Up and Fly Right, pp. 60–62.

158 **The session was Granz's** "Norman Granz," *Down Beat*, August 15, 1942.

158 **"Let's go ahead"** Red Callender, "Unfinished Dream" (London and Melbourne: Quartette Books, 1985), p. 50.

158 **"were cut one afternoon"** Teubig, *Straighten Up and Fly Right*, p. 61.

160 **"the most memorable invention"** Schuller, *The Swing Era*, p. 820.

161 **Both bass players** Gourse, *Unforgettable*, p. 46.

162 **"tuba-style timekeeping functions"** Will Friedwald, liner notes to The Complete Capitol Recordings of the Nat King Cole Trio, p. 15.

163 **all books and articles** Excepting May Akon's interview in *The Sunday News*, April 4, 1954, and the English newspaper *Balham News*, "His Song Made Publisher a Fortune," April 9, 1954.

164 **a necktie** Dick LaPalm, Interview, February 23, 1998.

164 **The truth is** Berle Adams, Interview, February 19, 1998.

165 **"That was the biggest break"** Ibid.

166 **"nervous hypertension"** *Down Beat*, March 15, 1943.

166 **Mills registered in May 1944** Letter from Audrey J. Ashby, senior director of EMI Publishing to Ivan Mogull of 11 East Corporation, April 23, 1998.

167 **In several interviews** Buster Sherwood, "Ole King Cole," *Orchestra World*, April 1945, p. 5.

170 **He drank a cocktail of scotch and milk** Barry Ulanov, Interview, April 8, 1998.

171 **larger than life** Harold Jovien, Interview, August 20, 1998.

171 **Gene Norman said** Gene Norman, Interview, February 20, 1998.

171 **the story of Carlos's nativity** Barry Ulanov, Interview.

171 **Born in San Pedro Sula** Billy May, Interview, August 20, 1998.

171 **Summers and holidays in Europe** Milton Benny, "Character," *Metronome*, September 1944.

172 **"I guess I was their greatest fan"** Ibid.

172 **the Palomar Ballroom** Ibid.

172 **Carlos did not go back to school** Ibid.

172 **his first client was Max Baer** Ibid.

174 **Gene Andrews had been their manager** *Down Beat*, April 15, 1943, p. 6.

174 **"And would you see"** Maria Cole, *Nat King Cole*, pp. 42–44.

174 **"You've got two headaches"** Ibid., p. 43.

175 **"Listen," said Carlos** Ibid.

175 **"No, I want to pay you"** Ibid., p. 44.

178 **Wallichs returned** *Metronome*, October 1943.

179 **The King Cole Trio's first recording session** Teubig, *Straighten Up and Fly Right*, pp. 70–71.

185 **"As you might gather"** Feather and Ulanov, *Metronome*, November 1944.

185 **"Cole and Moore"** Gunther Schuller, *The Swing Era* (New York: Oxford University Press, 1989), p. 817. For an extended discussion of "Body and Soul," which Schuller calls "sublime," the reader is advised to read his essay on the Trio in *The Swing Era*.

THE BIG MONEY

188 **The money was apportioned as follows** Maria Cole, *Nat King Cole*, p. 45.

189 **spot on Orson Welles's** "Orson Horsin with Jazz," *Metronome*, May 1944, p. 3.

190 **Nadine liked reefer** Maria Cole, Interview, January 10, 1998.

190 **Nadine had miscarried several times** Haskins, *Nat King Cole*, p. 23.

192 **"the jazz really came on"** *Down Beat*, March 1, 1944.

192 **In February, Oscar Moore** Ibid.

192 **Inducted in March** *Down Beat*, April 15, 1944.

193 **working for Kid Ory** Carr, Fairweather, *Jazz: The Rough Guide* (London: Penguin Books, 1995), p. 477.

193 **in the company of Franz Jackson** Franz Jackson, Interview, March 21, 1999.

194 **he was becoming a giant** Barry Ulanov, Interview, April 8, 1998.

194 **"He was lightly hinged"** Ibid.

195 **"local impresario for jazz"** "Los Angeles," *Down Beat*, July 1, 1944, p. 11.

196 **Quitting the Trocadero** "Ad," *Metro-*

nome, September 1944.

197 **Timmie told Nat** Timmie Rogers, Interview, February 21, 1998.

197 **"With a face like that"** Ibid.

198 **"No talent"** Barry Ulanov, "Timmie Rogers," *Metronome*, n.d., approx. 1945, Cole Collection, USC Library.

198 **Timmie went onstage** Barry Ulanov, Interview, April 8, 1998.

198 **"Hoods Attack Cole"** "Hoods Attack Cole, Carter," *Metronome*, November 1944.

199 **"which broke all records"** Barry Ulanov, *Metronome*, January 1945.

199 **"genius at improvisation"** Unidentified clipping, USC Library, Cole Collection.

199 **"After decades of colorless"** Schuller, *The Swing Era*, p. 818.

200 **A joyful photo** *Down Beat*, April 1, 1945.

201 **"the finest jazz album"** "Record of the Year," *Metronome*, January 1945.

202 **share the stage with Count Basie** Barry Ulanov, "California," *Metronome*, September, 1945, p. 19.

202 **The jazz extravaganza** Barry Ulanov, "The Trio Con Brio," *Metronome*, September 1945, p. 19.

202 **Perhaps the guitarist was** "Los Angeles," *Down Beat*, August 15, 1945.

202 **an army B-17** *Metronome*, September 1945.

202 **A quick stop in Chicago** Teubig, *Straighten Up and Fly Right*, p. 120.

202 **On to New York** "King Cole Trio," *Metronome*, November 1945, p. 34.

203 **In October the Trio performed** Teubig, *Straighten Up and Fly Right*, p. 121.

203 **Young Sinatra** "Frank Sinatra Show," CBS Broadcast, November 28, 1945, *CBS Playhouse* No. 3, New York LP, Songs by Sinatra, Canada P.J. 004.

206 **CBS would ban it** Dixon Gayer, "Jazz in Small Packages," *Collier's*, Drawing by Hirschfield, Jazz Institute, Rutgers.

206 **So, a few days before Nat's twenty-seventh** "Songs by Sinatra," March 13, 1946, Hollywood, CA.

CHANGES

208 **Down Beat magazine** *Down Beat*, February 11, 1946.

208 **"All-Star Band Member"** Gleason, *Esquire*, January 1947, p. 107.

208 **"The chief interest"** "The King Cole Trio, Breakfast in Hollywood," *Down Beat*, April 8, 1946.

210 **Nadine's good humor** Barry Ulanov, Interview, April 8, 1998.

211 **"Marie Ellington, known to Duke Ellington fans"** *Metronome*, November 1945.

212 **The streetwise, bantamweight** Jew Ivan Mogull, Interview, February 5, 1998. The following pages, 149, 150, 151, are all based on the Mogull interview.

217 **The interview Cole gave Stacy** Frank Stacy, "Nat Cole Talks Back to Critics," *The Capitol*, April 1946.

217 **Ulanov recalls** Barry Ulanov, Interview.

217 **"I know that a lot of you critics"** Stacy, op. cit.

218 **"We're only waiting"** Ibid.

218 **"Concerts will feature"** *Down Beat*, March 25, 1946.

218 **"The work will be modern"** *Down Beat*, July 1, 1946, p. 2.

218 **"Maybe this is all"** *Down Beat*, March 25, 1946.

219 **In April, Norman Granz** Teubig, *Straighten Up and Fly Right*, pp. 133–37.

219 **the network signed the Trio** *Down Beat*, May 6, 1946.

MARIA

220 **Trio worked nights** *Variety*, May 15, 1946; "Zanzibar Has Signed King Cole Trio," *Variety*, May 29, 1946, p. 56.

220 **Happy ran errands** Maria Cole, Interview, August 12, 1998.

220 **She was wearing a royal-blue gown** Cole, *Intimate Biography*, p. 16.

221 **"We don't talk about it"** Charlotte Sullivan, Interview, November 28, 1998.

221 **All the sisters** Charlotte Sullivan, Interview, February 19, 1998.

222 **Charlotte Hawkins Brown** Maria Cole, Interview, August 12, 1997.

222 **Dr. Brown had honorary degrees** Cole, *Intimate Biography*, p. 59.

222 **"We never plaited"** Ibid., p. 58.

223 **"You didn't dare dance"** Ibid., p. 60.

224 **Maria remembers** Ibid., p. 61.

224 **Sentimental Charlotte** Charlotte Sullivan, Interview, February 19, 1998.

224 **Marie was twelve** Cole, *Intimate Biography*, p. 12.

225 **her stage career** Ibid., pp. 12–13.

225 **band of Benny Carter** Gourse, *Unforgettable*, p. 77.

225 **Then in 1943** Kelly Cole, *A Celebration of the American Dream*, unpublished biography, pp. 57–65.

226 **She gave a recording** Cole, *Intimate Biography*, p. 13.

226 **his tour of duty** Kelly Cole, op. cit.

226 **his medals** Maria Cole, Interview, August 12, 1997.

226 **"The war was over"** Kelly Cole, op. cit.

227 **She noticed Nat** Cole, *Intimate Biography*, p.15.

227 **The chorus girls dressed** Maria Cole, Interview, August 12, 1997.

228 **"You know"** Ibid.

228 **the Dunbar Apartments** Charlotte Sullivan, Interview, February 19, 1998.

228 **Cole's valet, Otis Pollard** Maria Cole, Interview, August 12, 1997.

229 **Mel Tormé had come** Leonard Feather 1961, quoted by Friedwald.

229 **He bought a $50 ticket** Cole, *Intimate Biography*, p. 16–17.

230 **She had bet** Ibid., p. 17.

230 **At four o'clock** Maria Cole, Interview, August 12, 1997.

230 **he told her he was married** Ibid.

231 **"I know," she said** Ibid.

231 **"A married man *and* a musician?"** Cole, *Intimate Biography*, p. 19.

232 **"I met this terrific girl"** Ivan Mogull, Interview, February 5, 1998.

232 **Ivan was afraid** Ibid.

232 **She bought suits** Maria Cole, Interview, August 12, 1997.

233 **At the first opportunity** "Fiddler's Three," *Newsweek*, August 12, 1946, p. 97; *Metronome*, August 1946.

234 **"Long before Nat asked Nadine"** Kelly Cole, op. cit.

235 **"If I can get my divorce"** Cole, *Intimate Biography*, p. 20.

235 **According to her account** "King Cole's Forgotten Love," *Tan*, September 1954.

235 **Nadine wondered** Ibid., p. 77.

235 **Nathaniel did not go** Gourse, *Unforgettable*, p. 84.

235 **"It was a simple declaration"** *Tan*, p. 77.

236 **The pianist Hank Jones** Hank Jones, Interview, January 26, 1999.

ENGAGED

237 **"by virtue"** "Carlos Gastel," *Metronome*, October 1945.

237 **You love this woman?** Cole, *Intimate Biography*, p. 21.

238 **"Our family loved Nadine"** Kelly Cole, op. cit.

239 **"If you don't like it"** Gourse, Interview with Ike Coles, *Unforgettable*, p. 83.

239 **The show premiered** "The King Cole Trio with Jo Stafford," *Variety Radio Reviews*, October 23, 1946, p. 30.

240 **On December 7** Teubig, *Straighten Up and Fly Right*, p. 154.

240 **"the major influence"** Ibid.

241 **That night, December 14** Ibid.

241 **when Nat returned to New York** Charlotte Sullivan, Interview, February 19, 1998.

242 **"Who is that whistling?"** Ibid.

243 **One night they were sitting** Maria Cole, Interview, August 12, 1997.

243 **The complaint states** Superior Court Case D 329, 238, Hall of Records, Los Angeles, California, Chicago Historical Society, Copy in Claude Barnett Collection.

244 **"interlocutory divorce decree"** "Nat Coles Get Their Decree," *Down Beat*, February 26, 1947.

244 **"The Trio lost thousands"** Harold Jovien, "Let's Listen," Associated Negro Press, May 22, 1947.

245 **And they could tell** Maria Cole, Interviews.

246 **his idol Earl Hines** Teubig, *Straighten Up and Fly Right*, p. 167.

247 **"Maria is the one"** Ivan Mogull, Interview, February 5, 1998.

248 **"Let me tell you"** Ibid.

249 **"My father was a preacher"** Gene Norman, Interview, February 20, 1998.

250 **Nat was notoriously casual** Cole, *Intimate Biography*, p. 68.

250 **Nat sent somebody off to Western Union** Ibid., pp. 69–70.

251 **And of course** Maria Cole, Interview, August 12, 1997.

251 **Maria let it be known** Ibid.

252 **Lee Young recalls** Lee Young, Interview, February 17, 1998.

252 **binding fishing rods** Kenneth Moore, Interview, January 8, 1999.

252 **Judging from later contracts** Ashby's letter of agreement quoted in Haskins, *Nat King Cole*, p. 58.

253 **"Save me. Oscar Moore quitting"** Will Friedwald, "All the Kings Men," Mosaic Records, Stamford, 1991, p. 16.

253 **between August 6 and 29** Teubig, *Straighten Up and Fly Right*, pp. 180–99.

253 **Look at the statistics** Teubig, *Straighten Up and Fly Right*, p. 175–212.

254 **Cole seemed to be everywhere** Teubig, *Straighten Up and Fly Right*, p. 169.

255 **"the most impressive number"** Don C. Haynes, "Trio Concert at Civic Opera House," *Down Beat*, October 8, 1947, p. 2.

WEDDING BELLS

259 **Nathaniel Cole and Maria** ANP, ; "King Coles $17,500 wedding," *Los Angeles Sentinel*, April 1, 1948.

259 **As several hundred guests** Lydia Brown, "King Cole Married," *Providence Chronicle*, April 5, 1948.

259 **The bride wore** Ibid.

260 **made Eddie "raise hell"** Gourse, *Unforgettable*, p. 98.

260 **There were so many bridesmaids** Cole, *Intimate Biography*, p. 23.

261 **The newspapers said the bride's dress** Brown, op. cit.

262 **Ivan Mogull and his friend** Ivan Mogull, Interview, February 5, 1998.

262 **Marvin Cane went** Gourse, *Unforgettable*, p. 99.

263 **They chose booze** Ivan Mogull, Interview, February 5, 1998.

264 **stag party upstairs** Ibid.

264 **When Maria found out** Cole, *Intimate Biography*, pp. 24–25.

265 **Sarah Vaughan, Dizzy Gillespie** Brown, op. cit.

265 **That night in the honeymoon suite** Cole, *Intimate Biography*, p. 25.

265 **The newlyweds flew out** *Ebony*, August 1948, pp. 24–28.

266 **On the way home** Maria Cole, Interview, August 12, 1997.

NATURE BOY

267 **According to an interview** Marie Mesmer, "King Cole Remembers L.A. for First Big Break," *Los Angeles California News*, August 10, 1948. Note: Maria Cole writes that it was the *Million Dollar Theater*, but this is impossible. He did not perform there during this time.

267 **One time a reporter** Cole, *Intimate Biography*, p. 28.

268 **"in Oklahoma"** Ibid., p. 29.

268 **Ivan Mogull remembers** Ivan Mogull, Interview, February 5, 1998.

268 **Ahbez spent** Haskins, *Nat King Cole*, p. 66.

269 **Maria Cole said she was exquisite** Maria Cole, Interview, August 12, 1997.

269 **Mort Ruby had been urging** Cole, *Intimate Biography*, p. 30.

270 **"I have a song"** Ibid.

270 **"Ahbez gave fifty percent"** Cole, *Intimate Biography*, p. 31.

270 **"Considerable rumors"** "Nature Boy Rolls Natural," *Variety*, April 14, 1948.

271 **That night, knowing** Cole, *Intimate Biography*, p. 32.

271 **Playing in a Jazz All-Stars Concert** Gene Norman, Interview, February 20, 1998.

272 **"finally let me try"** Friedwald, quoting Leonard Feather, p. 36.

273 **DeVol, interviewed** Ibid.

273 **DeVol thought** Gourse, *Unforgettable*, p. 110.

273 **Ruby heard a rumor** Cole, *Intimate Biography*, p. 33.

273 **"found his man"** Ibid.

273 **"King Cole and Carlos"** *Variety*, April 14, 1948.

274 **"Nature Boy"** Cole, *Intimate Biography*, p. 34.

274 **By the time the disc** Ibid., p. 35.

274 **"Here's a winner"** Ibid.

275 **Trilling told Maria** Ibid.

275 **Other artists had rushed** *Variety*, April 14, 1948.

276 **"On 42nd Street"** Haskins, *Nat King Cole*, p. 70, quoting *The New York Age*, April 23 (?), 1948.

277 **Eden Ahbez, dressed in white** "Nature Boy Draws Strings on His Tenet Flap," *New York Times*, June 1, 1948.

279 **After Cole died** Maria Cole, Interview, August 12, 1997.

279 **Moore sued Nat** *Down Beat*, June 2, 1948, p. 2.

280 **"It's like feeding oats"** Maria Cole, Interview, August 12, 1997.

280 **On June 9, the Trio performed** *New York Amsterdam News*, June 5, 1945, p. 24.

A HOME OF THEIR OWN

281 **Ciro's** Sheila Weller, "Life Begins at 8:30," *Vanity Fair*, April 1998, pp. 260–87.

281 **The Trio packed the house** Haskins, *Nat King Cole*, p. 74.

282 **"Sometimes we did thirty"** Cole, *Intimate Biography*, p. 62.

282 **"I really was not quite sure"** Maria Cole, Interview, August 12, 1997.

283 **Frank Sinatra's wife, Nancy** Maria Cole, Interview, June 10, 1998.

283 **Autograph seekers** "King Cole Faces Covenant Battle," *Oakland California Herald*, August 13, 1948, p. 75.

284 **"This is it!"** Cole, *Intimate Biography*, p. 76.

284 **Of course, the African-American** "Hancock Park Home Purchase Stirs Quandary," *Los Angeles Times*, August 6, 1948.

284 **Camille Laflotte** Maria Cole, Interview, August 12, 1997.

284 **The owner of the house** "King Cole Faces Covenant Battle," *Oakland California Herald*, August 13, 1948.

285 **"Don't you check"** Cole, *Intimate Biography*, p. 78.

285 **News of the deal** "New King Cole Home Opposed," *Los Angeles Examiner*, August 3, 1948.

285 **In a stately mansion** *Los Angeles Times*, August 3, 1948.

285 **"seek a solution"** *Los Angeles Examiner*, August 3, 1948.

286 **"Tell Mr. Cole"** Cole, *Intimate Biography*, p. 77.

286 **"How would *you* like it"** Haskins, *Nat King Cole*, p. 78.

286 **"This is not an act"** *Los Angeles Times*, August 3, 1948.

287 **"There it was patiently explained"** Cole, *Intimate Biography*, p. 78.

287 **"Neither do I"** Ibid.

287 **"It is regrettable"** Ibid.

288 **Copp, president of** "Protest Sale of L.A. House to King Cole," Associated Press release, approx. August 17, 1948, USC Library, Cole Collection.

288 ***Shelly* v. *Kramer*** James Trager, *The Peo-*

ple's Chronology (New York: Henry Holt, 1992), p. 911.

288 **World War II heightened** Haskins, *Nat King Cole*, p. 80.

289 **Yet the neighbors** Ibid., p. 81.

289 **"to protect American life"** Ibid.

289 **"thousands of members"** Ibid.

THE PRICE OF FAME

291 **"We were so young"** Maria Cole, Interview, February 15, 1999.

292 **Nathaniel's neglect of his alimony** "King Cole Forced to Appear in Court," *Pittsburgh Courier*, November 6, 1948.

292 **On November 8** Letter from Claude Barnett of Associated Negro Press to Nat King Cole, November 8, 1948, Chicago Historical Society, Claude A. Barnett Archive.

293 **"I must think ten times"** Letter from Robert Ratcliffe, Pittsburgh Courier, to Claude Barnett, ANP, November 23, 1948, Claude A. Barnett Archive.

294 **"We merely reported"** Letter from Claude A. Barnett to Nat King Cole, November 24, 1948, Barnett Archive.

295 **"clear up the matter"** Letter from Nat Cole to Claude Barnett, December 1, 1948, Barnett Archive.

295 **"He knew he was bluffing"** Letter from Claude A. Barnett to Robert Ratcliffe, December 2, 1948, Chicago Historical Society.

295 **Around the time** Maria Cole, Interview,

January 10, 1998.

295 **"He finally went"** Ibid.

296 **A specialist advises** Dr. Robert Liner, letter, December 7, 1998.

296 **Maria had a job** Haskins, *Nat King Cole*, p. 93.

297 **"Says he's having a heck"** Roy Topper, *Herald American*, January 30, 1949.

297 **One Friday afternoon** Colleen Hoefer, unpublished release, January 24, 1949, Jazz Institute at Rutgers.

297 **"Nature?"** Jimmy Savage's column, *Chicago Tribune*, February 7, 1949.

298 **"Well, one thing is sure"** Ibid.

298 **"Musicians are losing"** Barbara Hodgkins, "Backstage with Nat," *Metronome*, August 1948.

299 **"For a while it was swooners"** Ibid.

299 **"Everybody who has a creative mind"** Ibid., p. 10.

300 **"People don't slip"** Ibid.

300 **When Dizzy returned** "Cole's Costanzo," *Metronome*, May 1949, pp. 18–25.

301 **"Jack was the beginning"** Haskins, *Nat King Cole*, p. 97.

301 **"We had to broaden"** *Metronome*, May 1949, p. 18.

301 **Carl Carruthers** Haskins, *Nat King Cole*, pp. 97–98.

302 **"Sparky was the best"** Maria Cole, Interview, August 12, 1997.

302 **"Nat King Cole, a local boy"** Roy Topper, *Herald American*, February 7, 1949.

303 **If the record clerk's word** "Mystery

Shrouds Nat Cole's School Dropout Record," *Jet*, March 4, 1965, pp. 44–45.

303 **According to classmate** Tim Black, Interview, May 29, 1998.

303 **"He was embarrassed"** Ibid.

304 **The trip got off** United Press, "Auto Mishap for King Cole," *Iowa Tribune*, February 15, 1949.

304 **"turned turtle"** *Variety*, February 16, 1949.

304 **A bakery truck** *Iowa State Daily*, February 16, 1949.

304 **That night Nat** Cole, *Intimate Biography*, p. 64.

305 **There was plenty** Haskins, *Nat King Cole*, p. 98.

305 **That day, March 16** *Variety*, March 16, 1949, p. 44.

BOP CITY TO DIXIE

306 **"to do the selling"** "Nat Nominates Himself Advance Man for Bop," *Down Beat*, April 22, 1949.

306 **"Parents get upset"** Ibid.

310 **"I was pretty square"** Pete Rugolo, Interview, February 20, 1998.

311 **"It's too subtle"** "Critics to Blame for Confusion," *Down Beat*, October 5, 1951.

312 **He handed Rugolo** Pete Rugolo, Interview, February 20, 1998.

312 **"I took the song"** Ibid.

313 **On April 25** "Noted Singer Sues Hotel in

Pittsburgh," *Pittsburgh Courier*, approx. May 2, 1949, USC Library, Cole Collection.

313 **While Nat and Maria** Cole, *Intimate Biography*, p. 105.

314 **And only two months before** Ibid., p. 111.

314 **Nat hired two** "Nat Cole Sues Hotel," *New York Times*, April 29, 1949.

314 **"We had been in denial"** Charlotte Sullivan, Interview, February 19, 1998.

314 **"but the young doctor"** Cole, *Intimate Biography*, p. 64.

315 **"That's up to you"** Charlotte Sullivan, Interview, February 19, 1998.

315 **Years later** Maria Cole, Interview, July 10, 1997.

316 **"You may run"** Ibid.

317 **"He was one"** Cole, *Intimate Biography*, p. 63.

317 **"I telephoned Nat"** Ibid., p. 64.

317 **Black entertainers in** Haskins, *Nat King Cole*, p. 102.

318 **police enforced restrictions** Ibid.

318 **"The Cole group"** Ibid.

318 **Joe Comfort recalled** Haskins, *Nat King Cole*, p. 103.

319 **"Man, what are you"** Ibid.

319 **"Under no circumstances"** Cole, *Intimate Biography*, p. 110.

FAMILY

321 **A crystal chandelier** "King Cole Decorates

His New $65,000 Home," *Ebony*, March 1949, pp. 26–29.

322 **"So nice to wake"** Maria Cole, Interview, August 12, 1997.

323 **He would reach** Ibid.

323 **"For a full five"** Cole, *Intimate Biography*, p. 62.

323 **"I'm a man now, yessir"** Maria Cole, Interview, January 10, 1998.

323 **"I suppose," says Maria** Ibid.

324 **"If progressive music"** Charles Emge, "Cole-Woody Concerts to Revitalize Coast Music?" *Down Beat*, September 9, 1949, p. 2.

324 ***Down Beat* dubbed Nat** *Down Beat*, December 30, 1949.

325 **"Now look here"** Maria Cole, Interview, July 10, 1998.

325 **"Carol made a great difference"** Nat King Cole, "Are Second Marriages Better?" *Ebony*, March 1953, p. 86.

326 **"Look, Cookie"** Carol Cole, Interview, February 17, 1998.

326 **Maria felt contractions** "King Cole Baby," *Ebony*, June 1950, p. 31.

326 **"I thought Nat"** Ibid., p. 33.

326 **"I looked at that kid"** Ibid., p. 31.

327 **"We hope she won't"** Ibid., p. 33.

327 **someone took a photo** Ibid., p. 31.

328 **"I'm in the music business"** Don Freeman, "I Want to Make Money," *Down Beat*, October 6, 1950.

328 **"A performer who sacrifices"** Ibid.

329 **Maria hired a nurse** Carol Cole, Interview, February 17, 1998.

329 **Two days after** "King Cole Baby," *Ebony*, June 1950.

329 **"I love my baby"** Cole, *Intimate Biography*, pp. 66–67.

330 **"She had to watch"** Haskins, *Nat King Cole*, p. 111.

330 **"She didn't want"** Ibid.

330 **Alan Ladd was starring** Jay Livingston, Interview, February 22, 1998.

331 **"When they finished"** Ibid.

331 **"A few days later"** Ibid.

332 **"What kind of a title"** Gourse, *Unforgettable*, p. 146.

332 **Songwriter Marvin Fischer** Maria Cole, Interview, January 10, 1998.

333 **Carol Cole believes** Carol Cole, Interview, February 17, 1998.

333 **Rugolo recalls** Pete Rugolo, Interview, February 22, 1998.

335 **This was all great fun** Maria Cole, Interview, January 10, 1998.

335 **Two weeks after** Gene Borio, Tobacco Timeline, http://www.tobacco.org/, 1998.

335 **In 1950 a twenty-two-year-old** Dick LaPalm, Interview, February 23, 1998.

337 **After a week** Maria Cole, Interview, January 10, 1998.

338 **"like a little fly"** "Jury Weighs Cole Suit," *New York Times*, September 20, 1951; "King Cole's Suit Is Dismissed," *New York Times*, September 21, 1951.

338 **"Cole didn't bring"** John H. Britton, "What Will History Say About Nat Cole and Civil Rights?" *Jet*, March 4, 1965, pp. 18–19.

338 **"Maria called me in August"** Charlotte Sullivan, Interview, February 19, 1998.

THE TAX MAN

340 **tour of the British Isles** "Concerts, Variety for 'King' Cole and Trio," *Melody Maker*, September 16, 1950, p. 4.

340 **"Did he please them"** Mike Nevard, "Palladium Postscript," *Melody Maker*, September 23, 1950, p. 3.

341 **"Horne Scores, Not Nat"** *Down Beat*, October 20, 1950.

342 **"Can you imagine"** Haskins, *Nat King Cole*, p. 97.

342 **Women besieged the musicians** Gourse, *Unforgettable*, p. 142.

342 **"class distinctions"** Haskins, *Nat King Cole*, p. 117.

342 **But Costanzo also** Gourse, *Unforgettable*, p. 139.

343 **"That was where"** Maria Cole, Interview, August 12, 1997.

344 **Tax agents** "U.S. Seizes Singer's Home," *New York Times*, March 15, 1951.

345 **"any livestock"** A. C. (Doc) Young, "King Cole's House, Car Taken for Taxes," *Baltimore Afro-American*, March 20, 1951, pp. 1–2.

345 **"The Negro musician owed"** *New York Times*, March 15, 1951.

345 **he had offered to pay** *Los Angeles Examiner*, March 15, 1951.

345 **Maria recalls** Maria Cole, Interview,

August 12, 1997.

346 **On the airplane** Ibid., p. 82.

346 **"Why didn't the Treasury"** *Down Beat*, April 20, 1951.

346 **others suspect** Haskins, *Nat King Cole*, p. 112.

347 **"wanted to know"** Cole, *Intimate Biography*, p. 81.

347 **"You're not supposed"** Cole, *Intimate Biography*, p. 70.

348 **"a small, innocent"** Cole, *Intimate Biography*, p. 82.

349 **"Nat Cole Hits"** "Nat Cole Hits Tax Action," *New York Times*, March 20, 1951.

349 **"King Cole Maps"** "King Cole Maps Fight to Keep Home," *The Mirror*, Los Angeles, March 20, 1951.

349 **"Cole said his attorney"** "King Cole Hits U.S. Seizure of Home," *Los Angeles Times*, March 20, 1951.

349 **"a cash payment of $50,000"** Cole, *Intimate Biography*, p. 83.

349 **Since November** "King Cole to Court!" AP, March 1951, unidentified clipping, USC Library, Cole Collection.

350 **Aunt Lottie** Cole, *Intimate Biography*, p. 83.

350 **Aunt Lottie wired** Maria Cole, Interview, August 12, 1997.

350 **"The company is prepared"** "King Cole May Save Home by Records Deal," *Los Angeles Times*, March 28, 1951.

351 **"after a 3½ hour conference"** "Singer Cole Regains Home," *Los Angeles Examiner*,

March 29, 1951.

351 **Riddell "emphasized"** Ibid.

351 **"The sheriff"** Gourse, *Unforgettable*, p. 155.

351 **"I have no intention"** Cole, *Intimate Biography*, p. 69.

352 **"Maria said to Nat"** Haskins, *Nat King Cole*, p. 119.

352 **"I'm watching him gamble"** Haskins, *Nat King Cole*, pp. 119–20.

353 **"King Cole Trio isn't dead"** "King Cole Trio Isn't Dead Beams Feather," *Down Beat*, February 22, 1952.

353 **"anyone who put in a year"** *Down Beat*, October 5, 1951.

354 **Like Nat's other bassists** Charlie Harris, Interview, March 9, 1998.

354 **"You've got to change"** *Time*, July 30, 1951.

355 **"I'm an interpreter"** Ibid.

THE BIG SHOW

365 **Their show opened** *Variety*, October 3, 1951.

365 **"Although the hepcats"** Ibid.

366 **"Cole worked effortlessly"** Ibid.

366 **Dick LaPalm recalls** Dick LaPalm, Interview, February 23, 1998.

368 **"All right, Dick!"** Ibid.

370 **"I *know* it happened to *you*"** Ibid.

370 **And then there was the time** Ibid.

370 **Some people behave** Norman Poirier

and Lael Scott, "Nat King Cole," *Pittsburgh Post Daily Magazine*, February 17, 1965.

370 **"came with a strange"** Ibid.

371 **But the stranger** Dick LaPalm, Interview, February 23, 1998.

371 **"Look, no one invited"** Ibid.

372 **"Hi, Sweetheart"** Cole, *Intimate Biography*, p. 98.

372 **He was exhausted** Henry F. Whiston, "You Can Go a Little Commercial," *Melody Maker*, February 23, 1952, p. 3.

372 **"smoking Chesterfields"** Borio, op. cit.

373 **"The scene was"** Feather, *Down Beat*, February 22, 1952.

373 **"Nat was pretty tired"** Whiston, op. cit.

373 **"How you doing"** Timmie Rogers, Interview.

374 **Dr. Charlotte Hawkins Brown** *Los Angeles Times*, July 18, 1952.

374 **Nat wanted to breed** Maria Cole, Interview, August 12, 1997.

375 **"It was such a pleasure"** Ibid.

375 **"Man, I don't want to see"** Ibid.

376 **"They were two peas"** Natalie Cole, Interview, January 24, 1999.

376 **"for his contribution"** Charles Livingstone, "Music School in Chicago Honors Nat King Cole," ANP Wire Service, December 3, 1952.

376 **Charlie Harris, Cole's bass** Charlie Harris, Interview, March 9, 1998.

376 **"The wear and tear"** Chester Higgins, "Nat Must Have Kept Going," *Jet*, March 4, 1965, pp. 22–23.

377 **The *Los Angeles Examiner* reported** *Los Angeles Examiner*, December 11, 1952.

377 **"Song for a Banjo"** *Our World*, April 1953, pp. 45–47.

377 **"He almost needed roller skates"** Ibid.

377 **"So why not"** Ibid.

378 **"Nat and the boys"** Cole, *Intimate Biography*, p. 106.

378 **"an agreement among"** Ibid.

379 **"Look, I came out"** Ibid.

379 **"Charlie is in the dining room"** Charlie Harris, Interview, March 9, 1998.

379 **"Get Jack Entratter"** Cole, *Intimate Biography*, p. 107.

380 **"If you don't"** Ibid., p. 108.

380 **The Cal-Neva Lodge** Ibid., p. 93–95.

381 **Maria was furious** Ibid., p. 94.

382 **"I watched the show"** Ivan Mogull, Interview, February 5, 1998.

383 **walking up Sixth Avenue** Cole, *Intimate Biography*, p. 101.

383 **"I don't give"** Ibid., p. 102.

384 **Ivan Mogull lived** Ivan Mogull, Interview, February 5, 1998.

385 **"No, no, no"** Ibid.

385 **shows at eight-thirty** "Nat Cole Hospitalized," *Down Beat*, May 6, 1953.

385 **"Nat, do me a favor"** Ivan Mogull Interview, February 5, 1998.

385 **Cole stood aside** Ibid.

386 **"Sidelight"** *Down Beat*, May 6, 1953.

386 **They took him** Ibid.

387 **Nat was forbidden** Cole, *Intimate Biography*, pp. 103–4.

387 **"Red Sails in the Sunset"** Carol Cole, Interview, February 17, 1998.

387 **"The trouble with Sweetie"** Hubler, op. cit., p. 106.

388 **"This time we really"** Cole, *Intimate Biography*, p. 104.

388 **"suffering a relapse"** *Los Angeles Examiner*, May 29, 1953; *Los Angeles Examiner*, May 30, 1953.

388 **Maria remembers** Maria Cole, Interview, January 10, 1998.

389 **"Serious illness affects"** "Hotel Del Mar, Cal," *Variety*, July 22, 1953.

389 ***Your Show of Shows*** *Ebony*, October 1953, p. 88.

389 **"The bubble"** William Lovelock, "The Singer Who Beat the Evil Eye," *Melody Maker*, March 20, 1954.

390 **"What is this"** Nat Hentoff, "Nat Cole, La Vie," *Down Beat*, December 30, 1953, p. 4.

390 **"devotees of the King"** Lovelock, op. cit.

390 **"Nat stays on"** Hentoff, op. cit.

391 **"When will it stop?"** Ibid.

391 **Sinatra had just split** Ivan Mogull, Interview, February 5, 1998.

391 **"Frank was down"** Ibid.

392 **"The man hasn't done"** Kelly Cole, op. cit.

392 **Toward the end of 1953** *Billboard*, December 26, 1953.

392 **His gross sales** Hubler, op. cit., p. 106.

393 **"Nat never took over"** Maria Cole, Interview, August 12, 1997.

393 **"Walkin' My Baby"** Maria Cole, Inter-

view, July 10, 1997.

393 **"I make no claim"** Nat King Cole, "Are Second Marriages Better?" *Ebony*, March 1953, p. 83.

393 **"You can make so much money"** "The Nat King Cole Nobody Knows," *Ebony*, October 1956, p. 45.

393 **"Maria created order"** "Are Second Marriages Better?"

393 **A photo in *Jet*** *Jet*, March 25, 1954.

TOGETHER AND APART

394 **Maria and Nat got down** Maria Cole, Interview, August 12, 1997.

394 **"Since he was last here"** "London Palladium," *The Performer*, March 25, 1954.

394 **"I just thought"** Ibid.

395 **The American press** "Nat King Cole's Second Honeymoon," *Ebony*, August 1954.

395 **"Sometimes I would ask"** Ibid., p. 24.

395 **"I can't bear to see"** Betty Best, "Charm," *Australian Women's Weekly*, January 19, 1955.

395 **"Women chased him"** Maria Cole, Interview, January 10, 1998.

396 **The Father of the Blues** *Jazz Magazine*, December 1954, p. 10.

396 **Photographs** "The Melancholy Monarch," *Look*, April 1955.

396 **He told a reporter** Best, "Charm," p. 17.

396 **But Maria Cole says** Maria Cole, Interview, August 12, 1997.

397 **"scandal free life"** "King Cole's Success Secrets," *Hue*, January 1955.

397 **"Cole has steered clear"** Ibid.

397 **"Five thousand fans"** "Airport Furor for Nat Cole," *Auckland Star*, January 17, 1955.

398 **A shouted threat** Ibid.

398 **"His pursuers wrenched"** Ibid.

398 **"I haven't seen"** Robert C. Ruark, "Cole Cash," February 15, 1955, USC Library, Cole Collection.

399 **Maria said she** Maria Cole, Interview, August 12, 1997.

399 **a dancing master** "Nat King Cole Learns to Dance," *Ebony*, May 1955.

399 **"through a light-footed"** Ibid.

400 **"I remember Nat kneeling"** Maria Cole, Interview, August 12, 1997.

400 **"It was so sad"** Ibid.

401 **"I wanted to please"** Normand Poirier, "Nat King Cole, His Rise to Fame," *Post Daily Magazine*, February 17, 1965.

401 **a languid interview** "The Melancholy Monarch," *Look*, April 1955.

401 **"because of Nat's fooling"** Maria Cole, Interview, August 12, 1997.

402 **Maria's opening at Ciro's** "King Cole's Wife Goes Back to Work," *Ebony*, December 15, 1955, p. 132.

402 **"her qualms vanished"** Ibid.

402 **"She gathered up"** Hal Landers, "Ciro's," Hollywood Reporter, October 7, 1955.

403 **"opening show was"** Paul Coates, "Confidential File," *Los Angeles Mirror News*, October 7, 1955.

403 **"You moved 'em"** *Ebony*, December 15, 1955, p. 135.

403 **She was a powerful** Carol Cole, Interview, February 17, 1998.

404 **"I was a little annoyed"** Cole, *Intimate Biography*, p. 62.

MOBBED

405 **"In the North"** Zelie McLeod, "Parson's Son," *Sydney Daily Telegraph*, February 11, 1956.

406 **"I'm proud"** Ibid.

407 **First Cole played** Dick LaPalm, Interview, February 23, 1998.

408 **Everything went well** "Nat Cole–Ted Heath Package," *Variety*, April 11, 1956.

408 **The rustics who planned** "Nat Cole Kidnap Plot," *New York Post*, April 12, 1956.

409 **a picturesque police record** "Alabama," *Newsweek*, April 23, 1956, p. 32.

409 **Word had come down from Ace Carter** Ibid.

410 **They would put out the word** *New York Post*, April 12, 1956.

410 **The day before Cole** *New York Times*, April 10, 1956.

411 **Detective C. B. Golden** *New York Post*, April 12, 1956.

411 **"I told Nat something"** Haskins, *Nat King Cole*, p. 138.

411 **"We had played there before"** Charlie Harris, Interview.

411 **"We were warned"** Lee Young, Interview.

411 **Two shows were planned** "Alabamans Attack King Cole," *New York Times*, April 11, 1956.

412 **Nat crooned the sweet ballad** "Unscheduled Appearances," *Time*, April 23, 1956, p. 31.

413 **In the glare of the lights** "Nat King Cole Tells a Story," as told to Edward Newman, *New York Journal-American*, April 11, 1956.

413 **Houselights came up** *Time*, April 23, 1956.

413 **"I have never seen such hatred"** Lee Young, Interview.

413 **"Play the national"** Ibid.

414 **"No, no!" yelled Dick** Dick LaPalm, Interview, February 23, 1998.

414 **"I was a little shaken"** "Nat King Cole Tells a Story"

414 **"Ask him to come back"** *Time*, April 23, 1956.

414 **"I was born here"** *New York Times*, April 11, 1956.

415 **"Man, I love show business"** *Time*, April 23, 1956.

415 **Maria had been dining** Maria Cole, Interview, August 12, 1997.

416 **"Don't you worry, honey"** Ibid.

417 **"It was a bad night"** Charlie Harris, Interview, March 9, 1998.

417 **on the way to the airport** "Nat King Cole Cancels Dixie," *New York Journal-American*, April 11, 1956.

417 **Lee Young remembers** Lee Young, Interview.

418 **Willis Vinson and Kenneth Adams** "4 White Men Sentenced," *Chicago Daily Tribune*, April 19, 1956, p. 10.

418 **"I was a guinea pig"** Bernard Gavser, Associated Press, *Chicago Dateline*, April 12, 1956.

419 **"This was not a personal"** "The Week in Negro Affairs," *Daily Worker*, April 15, 1956.

420 **"To continue to have his records"** ANP, "Deadline Release," April 16, 1956, from Chicago Historical Society, Claude Barnett Archives.

420 **"All Cole needs"** Cole, *Intimate Biography*, p. 125.

420 **"kneeling before the throne"** Leonard Feather, "Feather's Nest," *Down Beat*, May 30, 1956, p. 33.

420 **"I shouldn't have to be asked"** ANP, April 16, 1956.

420 **"I'm not mad"** *Los Angeles Examiner*, April 17, 1956, USC Library, Cole Collection.

420 **"We wonder if Nat"** "Editorial," *Chicago Defender*, April 12, 1956.

421 **"An Open Letter"** "Nat Cole Ignores Critics," ANP Release, *Chicago Dateline*, April 18, 1956, Chicago Historical Society, Claude Barnett Archives.

421 **"Now there is where"** Ibid.

421 **"Where and how a man makes his living"** Ibid.

421 **Olympian Jesse Owens** Ibid.

422 **"for a million"** *Los Angeles Examiner*, April 18, 1956.

422 **Cole paid $500** *New York Times*, April 24, 1956.

422 **"I forgot to bring"** *Jet*, April 26, 1956, p. 20.

422 **"Should Any Negro Artist"** *New York Age Defender*, April 28, 1956, p. 4.

422 **Old friends attacked Cole** "Nat Cole Attacked," *Jet*, April 26, 1956, pp. 58–59.

422 **"Those people, segregated"** Ibid., pp. 60–61.

423 **"I still have many"** AP, April 11, 1956.

HOME AGAIN

424 **"Hello, dear"** Charlotte Sullivan, Interview.

424 **"Those two girls"** "The Very Private Life of Nat King Cole," unidentified clipping, March 16, 1957, USC Library, Cole Collection.

425 **"a golf student"** Ibid.

425 **"I try not to spoil"** Ibid.

425 **he sang for the President** *Los Angeles Examiner*, May 19, 1956.

425 **He showed the children** *Los Angeles Examiner*, May 30, 1956.

425 **on June 20** Letter from Dwight D. Eisenhower to Nat Cole, June 20, 1956. USC Library, Cole Collection.

426 **"His quiet, dignified"** Leonard Feather, "Feather's Nest," *Down Beat*, May 30, 1956.

427 **"at the scene"** "Four White Men Sentenced in Attack on Cole," *Chicago Daily Tribune*, April 19, 1956.

427 **"Nat Cole has suffered"** Leonard Feather, "Feather's Nest," *Down Beat*, May 30, 1956, p. 33.

427 **"No Negro has"** "The Nat King Cole Nobody Knows," *Ebony*, October 1956, p. 48.

427 **"In discussing it"** Cole, *Intimate Biography*, p. 114.

427 **Alan Livingston remembers** Alan Livingston, Interview, February 20, 1998.

429 **Natalie was sick** Tyrone Power, unidentified clipping, June 14, 1956, USC Library, Cole Collection.

429 **"the largest single"** "Cole Signs $500,000 Contract," *New York Times*, June 29, 1956.

429 **He thought about it** *Ebony*, October 1956, p. 46.

429 **Producer Lee Gillette** Will Friedwald, *The Complete Capitol Recordings*, p. 47.

430 **They were there** Charlie Harris, Interview.

431 **"Nothing was rehearsed"** Lee Young, Interview.

TELEVISION

435 **Kemp was** Robert Henry, Interview, March 31, 1998.

435 **"We just had a cancellation"** Cole, *Intimate Biography*, p. 114.

436 **According to Maria** Ibid., p. 115.

436 **"Nat'll get 'em"** Dick LaPalm, Interview, February 23, 1998.

436 **"So many shows"** J. P. Shanley, "People on TV," *New York Times*, November 4, 1956.

437 **"He would sing"** Ivan Mogull, Interview,

February 5, 1998.

438 **"His head looked like"** Henry Louis Gates, Jr., *Colored People* (New York: Alfred A. Knopf, 1994), p. 48.

438 **"television . . . brought us together"** Ibid., p. 20.

438 **"In 1957"** Ibid., p. 25.

438 **"the ritual arena"** Ibid., p. 27.

438 **In February, after** Robert Henry, Interview, March 31, 1998.

439 **"Look," Kemp told** Ibid.

439 **"I want you to do"** Ibid.

439 **"I like Nat Cole"** Ibid.

439 **"The only racial"** "The King's Own Show," *Newsweek*, July 15, 1957.

439 **"I came on in March"** Robert Henry, Interview.

441 **"I went to the cameraman"** Ibid.

441 **"Since it's April Fools' "** Ibid.

441 **"He was synchronized"** Ibid.

443 **In *China Gate*** "China Gate," *Variety*, May 22, 1957.

443 **"He plays him"** Ruth Waterbury, "Cole Tops in China Gate," *Los Angeles Examiner*, May 10, 1957.

443 **"a lot more physical"** "Crooner Nat King Cole Turns Actor," *Ebony*, June 1957.

444 **"Thin and anemic"** Donald Bogle, *Toms, Coons, Mulattoes, Mammies and Bucks* (New York: Continuum, 1989), p.188.

445 **"Before the end"** "The King's Own Show," *Newsweek*, July 15, 1957.

445 **"I know we have"** Ibid.

446 **"Madison Avenue is afraid"** Hal

641

Humphrey, *Los Angeles Mirror News*, July 9, 1957.

SAMMY AND HARRY
AND THE GENERAL

447 **"Networks just don't"** Hal Humphrey, *Los Angeles Mirror News*, July 9, 1957.

447 **Out of his pocket** Nat King Cole, "Why I Quit My TV Show," *Ebony*, February 5, 1957, p. 31.

448 **Sammy was born** James Thorburn, "Bio: Sammy Davis Jr.," Wad Entertainment Group, www.interlog.com.

456 **Belafonte was born** Arnold Shaw, *Belafonte* (Philadelphia: Chilton Book Co., 1960), pp. 19–21.

456 **"Color discrimination"** Ibid., p. 3.

458 **Black stars rarely** Robert Henry, Interview, March 31, 1998.

459 **They did not know** Ibid.

460 **scenery fell** Shaw, *Belafonte*, p. 257.

460 **"What's it like"** Robert Henry, Interview.

461 **"If he sells toothpaste"** Nat King Cole, "Why I Quit TV," *Ebony*, February 1958, pp. 30–34.

461 **"a child of mixed"** Ibid.

461 **"After the Belafonte"** Robert Henry, Interview.

462 **"He loved it"** Ibid.

462 **"Sponsor Please"** Lee Young, Interview, February 17, 1998.

463 **"The show can be"** Leonard Feather,

"King Cole vs. Jim Crow," *Melody Maker*, August 17, 1957.

463 **On August 27** "Governor Griffin of Georgia Sounds Off," unidentified clipping, Atlanta, August 1957, Jazz Institute at Rutgers.

463 **"Madison Avenue is in"** Dave Kauffman, "Nat Cole Hits Madison Avenue," *Variety*, September 11, 1957, p. 2.

464 **"It's not the people"** Ibid.

464 **"The fact that Cole"** "Host with the Most," *Time*, September 23, 1957, p. 56.

464 **"I take my hat"** *Variety*, September 11, 1957, p. 22.

464 **Bob Henry noted** Robert Henry, Interview.

465 **"tell the piano player"** Ibid.

465 **"What do they think"** Cole, *Intimate Biography*, p. 119.

465 **"In Houston, Texas"** "Why I Quit My TV Show," p. 30.

466 **"Eight o'clock was prime"** Robert Henry, Interview.

466 **"None of them wanted"** Berle Adams, *A Sucker for Talent* (Los Angeles: Self-published, 1995), p. 178.

467 **In those days** Robert Henry, Interview.

467 **"Of course Eddie's"** Ibid.

468 **"It was the graveyard"** Ibid.

468 **"Due to personal"** "Nat Cole Leaves NBC," *Los Angeles Examiner*, November 21, 1957.

468 **he told *The New York Times*** Oscar Godbout, "Nat Cole Scores Ad Men," *New York Times*, November 22, 1957.

643

469 **"It would be a long time"** Cole, *Intimate Biography*, p. 118.

469 **July 12, 1957, report** Gene Borio, *Tobacco Timeline*, http://www.tobacco.org/, 1998.

GAMES AND CHILDREN

471 **"If I ever"** "The Nat King Cole Nobody Knows," *Ebony*, October 1956, p. 48.

471 **"I love sports"** *Jet*, March 4, 1965.

471 **"We used to spend"** Carol Cole, Interview, February 17, 1998.

472 **Nat once owned** Dick LaPalm, Interview, February 23, 1998.

472 **"Miles," said Nat** Ibid.

472 **"Mom and Dad"** Carol Cole, Interview.

473 **"Nat Cole was the No. 1** "Nat Cole's Last Honor," *Jet*, March 4, 1965, p. 52.

473 **"Good Night, Little Leaguer"** Ibid., p. 54.

474 **"The audience took"** "Copacabana, N.Y.," *Variety*, January 15, 1958, p. 66.

474 **"Appearing in a smart"** "King Again Sells Charm," *Billboard*, March 3, 1958, p. 9.

475 **Carol Cole remembers** Carol Cole, Interview, February 17, 1998.

475 **"People don't slip"** Barbara Hodgkins, "Backstage with Nat," *Metronome*, August 1948, p. 25.

476 **"Nat would play"** Charlotte Sullivan, Interview, February 19, 1998.

476 **"the best brother-in-law"** Gourse, *Unforgettable*, p. 233.

477 **First she had a crush** Carol Cole, Interview, February 17, 1998.

477 **"I remember going to Dad"** Ibid.

477 *"If you love someone"* Ibid.

478 **"My mother used to always say"** Natalie Cole, Interview, January 24, 1999.

478 **"When he was home"** Ibid.

479 **"My sister and I"** Ibid.

479 **"By the time"** Ibid.

479 **"Sweetie was destined"** Charlotte Sullivan, Interview.

480 **"We were some"** Natalie Cole, Interview.

481 **"Dad was really"** Carol Cole, Interview.

481 **"With two girls"** Cole, *Intimate Biography*, p. 95.

482 **On July 20** "Why We Adopted Kelly," *Ebony*, April 1960, pp. 35–41.

482 **"There, in the reception"** Ibid.

482 **His godparents** Ibid.

482 **"I have a model"** Ibid.

483 **"Although I am getting"** Ibid.

483 **"Dad taught me"** Natalie Cole, Interview, January 24, 1999.

483 **And sometimes at bedtime** Ibid.

483 **"It doesn't take talent"** AP, San Francisco, March 13, 1959.

484 **"Luckily I got"** "Music News," *Down Beat*, May 28, 1959.

484 **Brazilian President** "Ambassador Cole Returns," unidentified clipping, July 9, 1959, USC Library, Cole Collection.

484 **thanks for his efforts** News Release, GAC (?), USC Library, Cole Collection.

484 **Dodgers were in a three-team pennant race** Stanley Cohen, *Dodgers! The First One Hundred Years* (New York: Carol Publishing Group, 1990), p. 130.

485 **From then until** Ibid.

485 **Dodgers win the pennant** Ibid., p. 131.

485 **Now they were** Ibid., p. 132.

486 **"Nat, your Dodgers"** Dick LaPalm, Interview, February 23, 1998.

486 **So Nat King Cole was invited** Dick LaPalm, Interview, February 23, 1998.

481 **"That evening these two"** Dick LaPalm, Interview, February 23, 1998.

487 **Cole's Dodgers** *New York Times*, October 2, 1959, p. 1; *New York Times*, October 9, 1959, p. 1.

THE DAWN OF A NEW DECADE

489 **"I am aware of the difficulties"** Letter from John F. Kennedy, U.S . Senate, to Mr. and Mrs. Nat Cole, Copacabana, 10 East 60th St., New York NY, USC Library Archives, Cole Collection.

490 **"I would hope"** John F. Kennedy, Western Union telegram to Nat King Cole, March 11, 1960, USC Archives, Cole Collection.

490 **"No assumption"** UPI, San Francisco, February 17, 1960.

490 **Secretary of the Lodge** Bill Steif, "Frisco Masonic Temple's Cryptic Nix," *Variety*, February 17, 1960.

490 **"we don't want people who"** "Nat Cole

Gives Frisco the Brushoff," *Variety*, December 24, 1960.

491 **"production firm"** "Cole-Belafonte Start Production Firm," *Down Beat*, February 4, 1960.

491 **A grip-and-grin** "Signed and Sealed," *Jet*, March 10, 1960, p. 59.

492 **"What am I"** Ivan Mogull, Interview, February 5, 1998.

492 **Maria Cole remembers** Maria Cole, Interview, January 10, 1998.

492 **"I'm going to sit down"** Cole, *Intimate Biography*, p. 91.

493 **"A singing variety show"** Ibid., p. 120.

495 **"I'm kind of stepping out"** "Broadway Musical for Nat Cole," AP, New York May 6, 1960.

495 **On May 16 Cole performed** Norman Heath, "This Royal Was Certainly a Dish," *Melody Maker*, May 21, 1960.

495 **"We stayed at the Savoy"** Natalie Cole, Interview, January 24, 1999.

496 **Carol recalls** Carol Cole, Interview, February 17, 1998.

496 **"Let's face it"** Hazel Guild, "Nat Cole Hits Diskeries Yen," *Variety*, May 25, 1960.

496 **"Nat should know better"** "Norman Granz Rebuts Nat Cole," *Variety*, June 8, 1960.

497 **"I'm a great one"** "Broadway Musical for Nat Cole," AP, May 6, 1960.

497 **to tackle Broadway** "NKC to Try Broadway Show in the Fall," *Jet*, May 19, 1960, p. 58.

501 **according to some accounts** Haskins, *Nat King Cole*, p. 147.

501 **"The one thing"** Barbara McNair, Interview, February 21, 1999.

502 **"As a rule"** *Wild Is Love*, Columbia Records LP, 1960.

502 **"His idea"** Barbara McNair, Interview.

502 **Dotty Wayne and Sparky** Gourse, *Unforgettable*, p. 205.

503 **"With all the turmoil"** Ibid., p. 207.

503 **"he was always"** Barbara McNair, Interview.

504 **"We took the show"** Ibid.

504 **The day after Thanksgiving** Gourse, *Unforgettable*, p. 207.

504 **Cole had spent** Maria Cole, Interview, February 20, 1999; Maria Cole's estimate.

505 **Inaugural Gala** *Washington Post*, January 20, 1961.

506 **"At dinner I sat"** Maria Cole, Interview, February 20, 1999.

506 **Her grandniece Carol** "King Cole's Wife Heiress' Guardian," *Los Angeles Examiner*, April 20, 1961.

506 **"I wasn't particularly thrilled"** Cole, *Intimate Biography*, p. 98.

507 **"Nat King Cole and his pretty wife"** Louella Parsons, "Tiny Prince Expected," *Los Angeles Examiner*, March 7, 1961.

508 **"to less than capacity"** "Cole Raps Fast-Buck Diskers," *Variety*, May 31, 1961, p. 47.

508 **"It never reached New York"** Ibid.

508 **the Coles' July 4th party** Maria Cole, Interview, January 10, 1998.

509 **The musical that Cole** Herbert

Donaldson, "King Cole's Show," *Los Angeles Examiner*, August 29, 1961.

509 **Natalie Cole recalls** Natalie Cole, Interview, January 24, 1999.

510 **"The most appealing"** "Caught in the Act," *Down Beat*, October 12, 1961, p. 38.

510 **Natalie was fascinated** Natalie Cole, Interview.

511 **"She said it was quite a shock"** "Snapshots of Hollywood," *Los Angeles Examiner* (?), September 20, 1961, USC Library, Cole Collection.

511 **"Nat King Cole has been named a defendant"** "King Cole Named in Lawsuit," ANP Wire, Dateline September 22, 1961, Chicago Historical Society, Claude Barnett Archive.

512 **"Nat was scheduled"** Cole, *Intimate Biography*, pp. 98–99.

512 **"Complications developed"** Ibid.

512 **"Mrs. Cole is not a Catholic"** Ibid., p. 99.

513 **"I went to rehearsals"** Carol Cole, Interview, February 17, 1998.

515 **"I tried to reflect"** Letter from John F. Kennedy to Nat King Cole, October 6, 1961, USC Library, Cole Collection.

515 **He needed a light** *Jet*, March 4, 1965, p. 27.

516 **"Excuse me, Mr. Cole"** Carol Cole, Interview, February 11, 1998.

516 **"Nat was at our dinner"** Jessie Mae Brown, "President Kennedy Visits Nat King Cole," *Sepia*, February 1962, p. 56.

516 **"Carol's bow"** Ibid.

517 "jackpot attractions" "Sands, Las Vegas," *Variety*, January 17, 1962.

517 "We used to go" Vic Damone, Interview, April 4, 1998.

519 "the world loves a lover" Lee Young, Interview, February 17, 1998.

520 Something passed Ibid.

521 feast in April "Night to Remember," *The Guardian*, February 6, 1965, USC Library, Cole collection.

521 In his sunset years "Reverend Coles Dies," *Chicago Defender*, February 5, 1965.

521 "It is possible" Norman Poirier, "Where He Stood," *Post Daily Magazine*, February 17, 1965.

522 Steve Allen, whom Nat Steve Allen, Interview, February 18, 1998.

522 "These days, you just walk" Ibid.

523 "Gaiety and grief" Jim Denyer, *Los Angeles Herald*, August 6, 1962, p. 1.

523 Maria Cole remembered Maria Cole, Interview, February 20, 1999.

523 "It's tragic" Denyer, op. cit.

524 "and remarked that the tribute" "Show Biz, Civic Notables Salute Nat King Cole," *Variety*, August 8, 1962.

525 When it came his turn Ibid.

526 "The show, Broadway bound" Cameron Dewar, "Nat Cole's Royal Gifts," *Billboard*, September 22, 1962.

527 "For tent impresarios" Nat King Cole, "Sights and Sounds," *Variety*, August 29, 1962, p. 43.

527 **Sparky Tavares still served** Lee Young, Interview, February 17, 1998.

528 **"There were always a lot of people"** Charlie Harris, Interview, March 9, 1998.

528 **Sparky had firm orders** Gourse, *Unforgettable*, p. 139.

528 **lace tuxedo shirts . . . file-top shoes** Ibid., p. 93.

529 **The stocky, square-jawed rancher** Bud and Georgia Basolo, Interview, February 27, 1998.

529 **After the show** Ibid.

530 **"Sometimes you meet someone"** Ibid.

530 **last will and testament** "Bulk of Cole's Estate Bequeathed to Widow," *Variety*, March 3, 1965.

531 **Harry Margolis was a hotshot** Berle Adams, Interview, February 19, 1998; Maria Cole, Interview, February 20, 1999; Ivan Mogull, Interview, March 11, 1999; Bud and Georgia Basolo, Interview, February 27, 1998.

532 **"the worst thing"** Maria Cole, Interview, February 20, 1999.

532 **"offshore trust"** Ibid.; also Interviews with Mogull, Basolo, and Adams.

532 **"I had this ranch"** Bud and Georgia Basolo, Interview.

534 **Now the ingenious strategies** Berle Adams, Interview, February 19, 1998.

534 **smash hit** "Nat Cole SRO in 2nd Japan Tour," *Variety*, March 13, 1963.

534 **many others, including Sparky** Gene Norman, Interview, February 20, 1998.

534 **"he no longer needs Carlos"** Leonard

Feather, "Nat Cole — The Man Behind the Image," *Melody Maker*, July 6, 1963.

534 **"That was the only bad thing"** Gourse, *Unforgettable*, p. 219.

535 **"End of a Long"** *Down Beat*, August 1, 1963, p. 13.

535 **"Cheerfully unabashed sing-along corn"** David Griffiths, "Great Jazzman to Great Businessman," unidentified British newspaper, USC Library, Cole Collection.

535 **Harry Belafonte and Lena Horne** "Cole on Color Crisis," *Melody Maker*, June 22, 1963, p. 5.

536 **Barnett scolded Cole** *Down Beat*, July 4, 1963, p. 11.

536 **"idea that Negro entertainers"** Ibid., p. 12.

537 **"What is the secret"** "At 44, Nat Is Still a King Spin," *London Standard*, July 13, 1963.

537 **"Nat will milk the market"** Griffiths, "Great Jazzman to Great Businessman."

LOVE AND DEATH

538 **Nat accompanied Robert F. Kennedy** Winzola McLendon, "She Likes to Travel," *Washington Post*, approx. August 18, 1963, USC Library, Cole Collection.

538 **the White House called** Ibid.

538 **driving his daughter Natalie** Natalie Cole, Interview, January 24, 1999.

539 **Natalie Cole says** Ibid.

540 **born in Göteborg, Sweden** AFTRA

(American Federation of Television and Radio Artists), Membership Roster 1988.

540 **ravishing girl . . . a lively wit** Sam Lovullo, *Life in the Kornfield* (New York: Boulevard Books, 1996), p. 34.

540 **The program for *Sights and Sounds*** Nat King Cole in *Sights and Sounds* (program).

542 **"He was consumed"** Ivan Mogull, Interview, February 5, 1998.

542 **Mogull was married in February** Ivan Mogull, Interview, March 11, 1999.

543 **"Like all women, I thought"** Maria Cole, Interview, January 10, 1998.

543 **unpacking the suitcase** Maria Cole, Interview, August 12, 1997.

544 **"She was *Swedish* . . . Gunilla Hutton"** Maria Cole, Interview, January 10, 1998.

544 **"wrapped them in a newspaper"** Maria Cole, Interview, August 12, 1997.

544 **"Well, she was smart"** Maria Cole, Interview, February 20, 1999.

544 **"I lost weight. I looked like a beanpole"** Maria Cole, Interview, August 12, 1997.

544 **"I have to be honest, I probably would have left him"** Ibid.

545 **"I don't know what's going on"** Ibid.

545 **"Oh well, you can have the house"** Ibid.

545 **In September** Natalie Cole, Interview, January 24, 1999.

545 **she hired a private investigator** Maria Cole, Interview, February 20, 1999.

546 **Sparky, his valet** Cole, *Intimate Biography*, pp. 134–35.

546 **When Sparky told Cole** Ibid., p. 135.

547 **In her anguish and fury** Maria Cole, Interview, January 10, 1998.

547 **"Sparky met me"** Ibid.

547 **"Just before he went to play Vegas"** Maria Cole, Interview, February 20, 1999.

548 **Maria went directly** Maria Cole, Interview, August 12, 1997.

549 **"I caught myself and recoiled"** Ibid.

549 **"I think that by then he was so sick"** Ivan Mogull, Interview, February 5, 1998.

549 **"Thanks for calling me"** Western Union telegram from Nat King Cole to Mrs. Maria Cole, LA264 OF617 PD, San Francisco, CA, November, 23, 1964.

549 **"My husband did not know how to get me back"** Maria Cole, Interview, February 20, 1999.

549 **"I loved him dearly"** Charlotte Sullivan, Interview, February 19, 1998.

550 **"What are you doing?"** Ibid.

550 **"It has something to do with this"** Ibid.

550 **Nat had been onstage** Cole, *Intimate Biography*, p. 135.

550 **Cole had refused to go** Haskins, *Nat King Cole*, p. 165.

551 **He was staying at the Hotel Fairmont** Robert Kositchek, Interview, July 16, 1998.

551 **"From the minute"** Cole, *Intimate Biography*, p. 137.

551 **his last recording sessions** Roy Holmes, *The Nat King Cole Discography* (Surrey, England: Self-published, n.d.), p. 114.

551 **Sparky recalled Nat** Gourse, *Unforgettable*, p. 221.

552 **"After the show we got together"** Bud and Georgia Basolo, Interview, February 27, 1998.

552 **"No, Bud, I have cancer"** Ibid.

553 **"Hey! I got a fellow working"** Charlie Harris, Interview, March 9, 1998.

553 **"Nat was very ill"** Ibid.

554 **Maria went with friends** Maria Cole, Interview, August 12, 1997.

554 **It was early evening** Cole, *Intimate Biography*, pp. 137–38.

554 **"I think you should"** Ibid.

554 **"He had a cough"** Robert Kositchek, Interview.

555 **"Man, what's *wrong* with you"** Maria Cole, Interview, August 12, 1997.

555 **"I said give me a cigarette"** Ibid.

555 **"The impression was the neoplasm"** Robert Kositchek, Interview. The pathology records (cell analyses) were destroyed in 1985.

556 **Glen Wallichs was waiting** Maria Cole, Interview, August 12, 1997.

556 **She was furious** Maria Cole, Interview, February 20, 1999.

558 **St. John's Hospital is a unique institution** Sister Maureen Craig, Interview, February 23, 1998.

558 **"Under no circumstances"** Naida Barnes, Interview, March 12, 1998.

559 **Their first hours together** Maria Cole, Interviews.

559 **she sent him a white rose** Naida Barnes, Interview.

559 **Cole was scheduled** Gene Grove, "Cobalt Treatment for Cole's Tumor," *New York Post*, February 17, 1964.

559 **"and without minimizing"** "Nat Cole Has Lung Tumor," *New York Times*, December 17, 1964.

560 **"On December 18"** Robert Kositchek, Interview.

560 **"We just joked"** Naida Barnes, Interview.

561 **"He gave me *My Fair Lady*"** Ibid.

561 **"Although Nat and I communicated"** Cole, *Intimate Biography*, p. 139.

562 **"I don't see why not"** Ibid., p. 140.

562 **"The Sisters at St. John's"** Ibid., p. 141.

562 **"On the 30th of December"** Robert Kositchek, Interview.

562 **He really did not need** Naida Barnes, Interview.

563 **hundreds of thousands of letters** Cole, *Intimate Biography*, pp. 141–42.

563 **"Is all this for me"** Ibid., 142.

563 **"He had aged"** Natalie Cole, Interview, January 24, 1999.

564 **Cole returned to the hospital** Robert Kositchek, Interview.

564 **"Pain was so severe"** Ibid.

565 **On January 9** Naida Barnes, Interview.

565 **He asked a nurse** Ibid.

565 **Maria Cole got a phone call from Gunilla Hutton** Maria Cole, Interview, August 12, 1997.

565 **"don't you do *anything* to hurt my children"** Ibid.

566 **She telephoned a nurse** Naida Barnes, Interview.

567 **"What do you mean by calling my wife"** Maria Cole, Interview, January 10, 1998.

567 **"On January 16"** Robert Kositchek, Interview.

567 **"without any question"** Ibid.

568 **Frank Sinatra, inhabiting** Naida Barnes, Interview.

568 **He stood at the foot of Cole's bed** Ibid.

568 **Leo Branton came** Maria Cole, Interview, February 20, 1999.

568 **"You would think I was dying"** Ibid.

568 **Carol Cole flew** Carol Cole, Interview, February 17, 1998.

568 **"I remember Charlotte"** Dick LaPalm, Interview, February 23, 1998.

569 **"Because I'd spent so much"** Ibid.

569 **"One of my most vivid memories"** Robert Kositchek, Interview.

570 **"I've got to get well"** Maria Cole, Interview, August 12, 1997.

570 **"She was a tremendously devoted"** Robert Kositchek, Interview.

570 **On January 24** Ibid.

571 **"We had him walking"** Ibid.

571 **The Reverend Coles** *New York Times*, February 2, 1965.

571 **according to sister Evelyn** Kelly Cole, unpublished memoir.

572 **One day when he was alone** Sister Maureen Craig, Interview.

572 **"I'm Nat King Cole"** Ibid.

572 **Carlos Gastel, Alan Livingston** Nor-

man Poirier, "His Rise to Fame," *Post Daily Magazine*, February 17, 1965.

572 **"On the 11th"** Robert Kositchek, Interview.

573 **"In view of the public's"** Louie Robinson, *Jet*, March 4, 1965, p. 16.

573 **The next day Nat** Charlotte Sullivan, Interview.

574 **"Nat had a lot of faith"** Ibid.

574 **"Finally we went up"** Ibid.

574 **pronounced dead** *Jet*, March 4, 1965, p. 17.

574 **"Maria called and told me"** Charlotte Sullivan, Interview.

575 **"When he died"** *Sepia*, April 1965, p. 14.

576 **"It happened so quickly"** Natalie Cole, Interview, January 24, 1999.

576 **The day after** "The King," *Time*, February 26, 1965.

577 **"There were Boy Scouts and bankers"** Louie Robinson, "Nation Says 'Sweet Dreams,' " *Jet*, March 4, 1965, p. 4.

578 **"Most could not believe"** "Many Fell in Love," *Jet*, March 4, 1965, p. 6.

578 **the white-robed altar boys** Ibid., p. 8.

579 **"He's been carrying us"** Cole, *Intimate Biography*, p. 157.

579 **"In accepting the belief"** Brad Pye, Jr., "Funeralized in Simple Dignity," *Sepia*, April 1965.

580 **"Once during the services"** Cole, *Intimate Biography*, p. 158.

580 **Cole was entombed** *Sepia*, April 1965.

581 **Near the entrance** Ibid.

582 **Two weeks after** Borio, op. cit.

583 **Carlos Gastel** "Obituaries," *Variety*, November 18, 1970.

583 **Oscar Moore** Kenneth Moore, Interview, January 8, 1999. Also *Variety*, October 21, 1981.

583 **Nadine Coles** Kelly Cole, op. cit.

584 **Claude Barnett** Linda J. Evans, "Claude A. Barnett and the Associated Negro Press, *Chicago History*, Spring 1983, p. 56.

584 **Ivan Mogull** Ivan Mogull, Interviews.

584 **Dick LaPalm** Dick Lapalm, Interviews.

584 **Eddie Coles** Gourse, *Unforgettable*, p. 232.

584 **Carole Cole** Fax letter to Daniel Mark Epstein, May 1, 1999.

585 **Natalie Cole** Anne Janette Johnson, Contemporary Musicians, June 1989; fax letter to Daniel Mark Epstein, May 6, 1999.

586 **Kelly Cole** Nicholas Xatzis, letter to Daniel Mark Epstein, February 8, 1999.

586 **Timolin Cole Augustus** Fax letter to Daniel Mark Epstein, March 19, 1999.

586 **Casey Cole Ray** Ibid.

586 **After the death** Maria Cole, Interview, February 20, 1999.

587 **"His attention"** Ibid.

588 **"I would tell him"** Ibid.

BIBLIOGRAPHY

BOOKS ABOUT NAT KING COLE

Cole, Kelly. *Nat King Cole: A Celebration of the American Dream.* Notes, unpublished.

Cole, Maria, with Louie Robinson. *Nat King Cole: An Intimate Biography.* New York: William Morrow, 1971.

Gourse, Leslie. *Unforgettable: The Life and Mystique of Nat King Cole.* New York: St. Martin's Press, 1991.

Haskins, James, with Kathleen Benson. *Nat King Cole.* New York: Stein & Day, 1984.

Holmes, Roy. *The Nat King Cole Discography, 1936–64.* Surrey, England, n.d.

Teubig, Klaus. *Straighten Up and Fly Right: A Chronology and Discography of Nat King Cole.* Westport, CT: Greenwood Press, 1994.

BOOKS ON RELATED TOPICS

Adams, Berle. *A Sucker for Talent.* Los Angeles: Self-published, 1995.

Ashenhurst, John and Ruth L. *All About Chicago.* Boston: Houghton Mifflin, 1933.

Carlson Publishing, Inc. *The Kaiser Index to Black Resources, 1948–1986.* Brooklyn, NY: Carlson Publishing, Inc., 1992.

Carr, Ian, Digby Fairweather, and Brian

Priestley. *Jazz*. London: Rough Guides, 1995.

Chadwick, Bruce, and David M. Spindel. *The Dodgers*. New York: Abbeville Press, 1993.

Chilton, John. *Who's Who of Jazz*. Philadelphia: Chilton Book Co., 1972.

Cohen, Stanley. *Dodgers! The First Hundred Years*. New York: Carol Publishing Group, 1990.

Cuney-Hare, Maud. *Negro Musicians and Their Music*. Washington, D.C.: Associated Publishers, 1936.

Dance, Stanley. *The World of Earl Hines*. New York: Charles Scribner's Sons, 1977.

Feather, Leonard. *The Book of Jazz*. New York: Bonanza, 1957.

————. *The New Edition of the Encyclopedia of Jazz*. New York: Bonanza, 1960.

Gates, Henry Louis, Jr. *Colored People*. New York: Alfred A. Knopf, 1994.

Hampton, Lionel, and James Haskins. *Hamp: An Autobiography*. New York: Warner Books, 1989.

Hennessey, Thomas J. *From Jazz to Swing*. Detroit: Wayne State University Press, 1994.

Henry, Robert. *The Jazz Ensemble*. Englewood Cliffs, NJ: Prentice Hall, 1981.

Hentoff, Nat, and Albert J. McCarthy. *The Roots of Jazz*. New York: Da Capo Press, 1974.

Honig, Donald. *The Los Angeles Dodgers*. New York: St. Martin's Press, 1983.

Horner, Henry. *Illinois: A Descriptive and Historical Guide*. Chicago: A. C. McClurg & Co., 1939.

Laine, Frankie, with Joseph Laredo. *"That Lucky Old Son": The Autobiography of Frankie Laine*. Ventura: Pathfinder, 1993.

Lovullo, Sam. *Life in the Kornfield*. New York: Boulevard Books, 1996.

Lyons, Ken. *The Great Jazz Pianists*. New York: William Morrow, 1983.

Russell, Ross. *Jazz Style in Kansas City and the Southwest*. Berkeley: University of California Press, 1971.

Schuller, Gunther. *Early Jazz*. New York: Oxford University Press, 1968.

———. *The Swing Era* (Vol. 2 of *The History of Jazz*). New York: Oxford University Press, 1989.

Shaughnessy, Mary Alice. *Les Paul: An American Original*. New York: William Morrow, 1993.

Shaw, Arnold. *Belafonte*. Philadelphia: Chilton Book Co., 1960.

Southern, Eileen. *The Music of Black Americans: A History*. New York, W. W. Norton, 1984.

Stearns, Marshall W. *The Story of Jazz*. New York: Oxford University Press, 1956.

Stokes, W. Royal. *The Jazz Scene*. New York: Oxford University Press, 1991.

Taylor, Billy. *Jazz Piano*. Dubuque: William C. Brown Co., 1983.

Travis, Dempsey. *An Autobiography of Black Jazz*. Chicago: Urban Research Institute, 1983.

———. *The Louis Armstrong Odyssey*. Chicago: Urban Research Institute, 1977.

Ulanov, Barry. *A History of Jazz in America*. New York: Viking, 1952.

Williams, Martin, ed. *The Art of Jazz*. New York: Grove Press, 1960.

"Accident." *St. Louis Star Times*, February 16, 1949.

Ackerman, P. "Cole Sheer Class at Copa." *Billboard*, March 20, 1961, p. 11.

"Act of the Year: King Cole Trio." *Metronome*, January 1945, p. 15.

Adams, Julius J. "Pal Who Discovered Nat Would Be Happiest over Harlem's Tribute." *New York Age*, March 20, 1954, p. 22.

"Airport Furor for Nat Cole." *Auckland Star*, January 17, 1955.

"Alabamans Attack 'King' Cole on Stage." *New York Times*, April 11, 1956, p. 1.

"Ambassador, L.A." *Variety*, July 24, 1957, p. 68.

"Ambassador, L.A." *Variety*, April 30, 1958, p. 83.

Arneel, G. "Negro Pix on Do-It-Yourself." *Variety*, November 1, 1961, p. 5.

"Around the Hot Spots," *Chicago Defender*, April 25, 1936.

Atlas, Ben. "Nat Cole Hits 10-Year Mark." *Billboard*, December 26, 1953, p. 1.

"Auto Mishap for King Cole." *Des Moines Tribune*, February 15, 1949.

"Back to America and Bronzeville." *Chicago Defender*, January 2, 1937.

"Backstage with Nat." *Metronome*, June 18, 1948.

Bailer, Don. "Nat King Cole's Dynasty Is Stronger Than Ever." *Los Angeles Herald*, May 9, 1958.

"Battle of Rhythm, Earl Hines vs. Nat Cole." *Chicago Defender*, September 7, 1935, p. 4.

Benny, Milton. "Character." *Metronome*, September 1944.

Bernstein, Harry. "Singer Nat (King) Cole Will Join Other Members of the AFL-CIO . . ." *Los Angeles Examiner*, May 22, 1957.

Best, Betty. "Charm — Both On and Off the Stage." *Australian Women's Weekly*, January 19, 1955, p. 17.

"Billie Holiday — King Cole Trio — Billy Daniels — 'Hot Lips' Page and His Orchestra — 'Taps' Miller M.C. at Kelly's Stables." *New York Times*, June 19, 1941.

"Billy Eckstine Reaches the Finale." *Melody Maker*, September 11, 1954, p. 9.

"The Blue Gardenia." *Variety*, March 18, 1953.

Boulton, Derek. "Horne Scores, Not Nat, at London Palladium Shows." *Down Beat*, October 20, 1950, p. 15.

Britton, John. "What Will History Say About Nat Cole and Civil Rights?" *Jet*, March 4, 1965, pp. 18–20.

Brown, G. "Nat (King) Cole's Daughter Follows in His Footsteps." *Jet*, September 4, 1968, pp. 58–61.

Brown, Jessie Mae. "President Kennedy Visits Nat King Cole." *Sepia*, February 1962, p. 56.

Brown, Lydia T. "King Cole Married in Gala Ceremony." *Providence Chronicle*, April 4, 1958.

"Bulk of Cole Estate Bequeathed to Widow." *Variety*, March 3, 1965, p. 55.

Burckel, Christian E. *Who's Who in Colored America*, 1950.

"Cabarets." *Chicago Defender*, September 21, 1934, and July 11, 1936, p. 9.

"Cancer Strikes Nat Cole." *Sepia*, March 1965, p. 8.

"Cat Ballou." *Variety*, May 12, 1965.

"Carlos Gastel." *Metronome*, October, 1945.

"Caught in the Act." *Down Beat*, July 14, 1954, p. 24.

"Chez Paree, Chi." *Variety*, June 2, 1954, p. 52.

"Chez Paree, Chi." *Variety*, May 29, 1957, p. 64.

"Chez Paree, Chi." *Variety*, October 1, 1958, p. 61.

"Chicago Has Own Duke Ellington." *Chicago Defender*, September 15, 1934.

"China Gate." *Variety*, May 22, 1957.

"Ciro's, Hollywood." *Variety*, September 1, 1954, p. 78.

"Clambake." *Metronome*, August 1943, p. 22.

Coates, Paul V. "Confidential File." *Los Angeles Mirror*, October 7, 1955, p. 8.

Cocks, J. "Off on a Cashmere Cloud." *Time*, December 16, 1991, p. 78.

"Cocoanut Grove, L.A." *Variety*, November 29, 1961, p. 63.

"Cocoanut Grove, L.A." *Variety*, May 8, 1963, p. 213.

Cole, Marie. "King and I." *Our World*, July 1954, pp. 22–27.

———. "My Husband Is a King." *Tan*, February 1954, pp. 30–52.

Cole, Nat. "Are Second Marriages Best?" *Ebony*, March 1953, pp. 82–84.

———. "Chords and Discords." *Down Beat*,

May 30, 1956, p. 4.

————. "Go Out and Get an Act." *Hollywood Reporter*, November 16, 1959.

————. "King Cole's Honeymoon Diary." *Ebony*, August 1948, pp. 24–28.

————. "Music — The Universal Language." *Hollywood Reporter*, November 24, 1958, sec. 2.

————. "True Is the Word." *Hollywood Reporter*, November 19, 1963.

————. "Why I Decided to Learn Spanish." *Melody Maker*, April 18, 1959, p. 7.

————. "Why I Made the Trio a Quartet." *Melody Maker*, September 23, 1950, p. 3.

———— and L. Bennett. "Why I Quit My TV Show." *Ebony*, February 1958, pp. 29–34.

———— and ————. "Why We Adopted Kelly." *Ebony*, April 1960, pp. 35–38.

"Cole-Belafonte Start Production Firm." *Down Beat*, February 4, 1960, p. 13.

"Cole Blasts Music Graft." *Down Beat*, May 28, 1959, p. 9.

"Cole Breaks Up Trio for Sole Billing." *Billboard*, September 1, 1951, p. 18.

"Cole-Carter." *Metronome*, January 1945.

"Cole, Carter for Troc." *Metronome*, March 1945.

"Cole, Carter Together." *Metronome*, August 1944.

"Cole on Colour Crisis." *Melody Maker*, June 22, 1963, p. 5.

"Cole's Costanzo." *Metronome*, May 1949, p. 18.

"Cole Disclaims Entertainers' Role in Integration Fight." *Down Beat*, July 4, 1963, pp. 11–12.

"Cole Estate & Cap Sue over 'Poor' LP." *Variety*, March 16, 1966, p. 55.

"Cole Gets 55 G Guarantee for Southern Tour." *Billboard*, May 14, 1961, p. 20.

"Cole Incident Starts Debate on Jim Crow Shows, Stars Take Sides." *Jet*, May 3, 1956, pp. 58–59.

"Cole Joins N.A.A.C.P." *New York Times*, April 24, 1956, p. 11.

"Cole, Kirk Team Up." *Metronome*, June 1945, p. 7.

"Cole Memorial Ball May Raise 100 G." *Billboard*, March 18, 1967, p. 3.

"Cole Raps Fast-Buck Diskers, Agencies for Disintegrating Show Biz Standards." *Variety*, May 31, 1961, p. 47.

"Cole Says No, to Atlanta." *Los Angeles Examiner*, April 18, 1956.

"Cole Signs $500,000 Contract." *New York Times*, June 29, 1956, p. 16.

"Cole-Sullivan Rift." *New York Times*, January 28, 1961, p. 3.

"Cole to Copa; Makes Movie." *Metronome*, September 1945.

"Cole to Fight Home Seizure." *Los Angeles Examiner*, March 20, 1951, sec. 1, p. 3.

"Cole Trio Added to Herman Tour." *Billboard*, February 5, 1949, p. 21.

"Cole Trio Performs Despite Accident." *Ames [IA] State Daily*, February 16, 1949.

"Cole Trio Receive Their 'Oscar.' " *Down Beat*, April 1, 1945.

"Cole Wary of Disk Juve 'Exclusivity': Need Adult Fans." *Variety*, December 30, 1953, p. 43.

Coleman, Ray. "An Irreplaceable Vocal Giant." *Melody Maker*, February 20, 1965, p. 3.

"Concerts, Variety for 'King' Cole and Trio." *Melody Maker*, September 16, 1950, p. 4.

"Congratulations to King Cole." *Down Beat*, December 2, 1946, p. 9.

"Copacabana, N.Y." *Variety*, October 26, 1955, p. 51.

"Copacabana, N.Y." *Variety*, January 15, 1958, p. 66.

"Copacabana, N.Y." *Variety*, October 29, 1958, p. 55.

"Copacabana, N.Y." *Variety*, October 28, 1959, p. 61.

"Copacabana, N.Y." *Variety*, November 1, 1961, p. 76.

"Copacabana, N.Y." *Variety*, October 24, 1962, p. 70.

"Copacabana, N.Y." *Variety*, February 5, 1964, p. 52.

"Costanzo Due with Cole in Los Angeles." Capitol News, July 1949, p. 6.

"'Counterspy' at 6:30." Des Moines Tribune, February 15, 1949.

"Cozy Cole." *Metronome*, October 1944.

"Crooner Nat King Cole Turns Actor." *Ebony*, June 1957, p. 74.

Dawburn, Bob. "He Could Have Been a Jazz Great." *Melody Maker*, February 20, 1965, p. 3.

"A Day with Nat (King) Cole." *Record Whirl*, August 1955.

Denyer, Jim. "Nat Cole Honored at Dinner." *Los Angeles Herald Examiner*, August 6, 1962.

"Dernier Bilan de l'Affaire King Cole." *Jazz

Magazine, June 1956, p. 9.

Dewar, C. "Nat Cole's Royal Gifts." *Billboard*, September 22, 1962, p. 10.

Dexter, D. "Rare Cole Trio Transcriptions Issued." *Billboard*, December 11, 1968, p. 46.

Donaldson, Herbert. "King Cole's Show Warm, Friendly." *Los Angeles Examiner*, August 29, 1961.

Down Beat, June 2, 1948.

"Dream Fulfilled for Maria Cole." *Capitol Record News*, February 20, 1956.

"Earl Hines, Don Redman and Noble Sissle to Fete Kiddies," *Chicago Defender*, August 11, 1934.

"Eddie Albert Will Head Nat Cole Foundation." *Billboard*, June 26, 1965, p. 4.

"Eden Roc, Miami Beach." *Variety*, February 20, 1957, p. 55.

"Eden Roc, Miami Beach." *Variety*, February 15, 1961, p. 66.

"Eden Roc, Miami Beach." *Variety*, February 28, 1962, p. 57.

"18,000 Merry Souls Cheer for 'King' Cole." *Los Angeles Examiner*, July 15, 1957.

"El Rancho, Las Vegas." *Variety*, January 13, 1954, p. 64.

"Ellington-Vaughan-Cole in Sock $4.80 — Top Show at N.Y.'s Carnegie Hall." *Variety*, October 3, 1951, p. 52.

Ellis, Jack. "Musicians." *Chicago Defender*, July 24, 1937, p. 12.

———. "Orchestras." *Chicago Defender*, September 21, November 17, 1934.

———. "Orchestras." *Chicago Defender*, January 25, February 22, August 8, September 12, November 21, December 5, 1936.

————. "Orchestras." *Chicago Defender*, January 30, February 27, 1937.

Emge, Charles. "Cole-Woody Concerts to Revitalize Coast Music?" *Down Beat*, September 9, 1949, p. 2.

————. "Los Angeles Band Briefs." *Down Beat*, March 1, 1941, p. 5.

"End of a Long Business Association." *Down Beat*, August 1, 1963, p. 13.

"L'Esprit de Famille." *Jazz Magazine*, January 1955, p. 13.

"Europeans Struggle to Play Jazz Music." *Cleveland Call & Post*, February 8, 1958.

Evans, Linda. "Claude A. Barnett and the Associated Negro Press." *Chicago History: The Magazine of the Chicago Historical Society*, Spring 1983.

"Fairmont, San Francisco." *Variety*, September 7, 1960, p. 53.

"Fairmont, San Francisco." *Variety*, February 14, 1962, p. 55.

"The Famous King Cole Trio." *Santa Barbara News-Press*, August 15, 1948.

"Famous Stars to Appear at N.A.A.C.P. Midnight Show." *Chicago Defender*, August 4, 1934.

Feather, Leonard. "Again, Stars to Appear at Jazz Foundation Concert." *Metronome*, July 1945, p. 27.

————. "The Blindfold Test." *Metronome*, March 1948, p. 19.

————. "Cole Raps Ad Men." *Melody Maker*, November 30, 1957, p. 2.

———. "Feather's Nest." *Down Beat*, May 30, 1956, p. 33.

———. "Feather's Nest." *Down Beat*, May 6, 1965, p. 39.

———. " 'My Heart Is Still with Jazz' — Nat." *Down Beat*, July 30, 1952, p. 12.

———. "Now Comes the Tribute to Nat King Cole." *Melody Maker*, February 26, 1966, p. 9.

"Fete Nat Cole for 25 Years' Entertaining." *Billboard*, August 18, 1962, p. 5.

"Fiddlers Three." *Newsweek*, August 12, 1946, p. 97.

"$50,000 a Day; Nat Cole May Gross Amount from Singing Just One Song." *Ebony*, October 1953, pp. 85–88.

"Final Bar." *International Musician*, April 1965, p. 17.

"Fine 2 Whites in Alabama Attack on Nat Cole." *Jet*, December 20, 1956, p. 60.

"500 Club, A.C." *Variety*, August 21, 1957, p. 55.

"5,000 Fight to See Nat 'King' Cole." *New Zealand Herald*, January 17, 1955.

"Flags Fly Half-Staff for Pastor." *News-Sun*, February 5, 1965.

Fol, R., and D. Filipacchi. "33 Tours." *Jazz Magazine*, December 1955, p. 24.

"Forgiving Spirit." *Los Angeles Examiner*, April 17, 1956.

"Form Nat Cole Cancer Foundation as a 'Living Memorial' to Late Singer." *Variety*, March 24, 1965, p. 72.

"400 at Funeral Services for Cole"; "Cole Cancer Fund Formed on W. Coast." *Billboard*, February 27, 1965, p. 1.

"4 Jailed in Cole Assault." *Los Angeles Examiner*, April 19, 1956.

"Four White Men Sentenced in Attack on Cole." *Chicago Daily Tribune*, April 19, 1956.

Francis, B. "Cole Restored to Copa's Throne." Billboard, October 29, 1955, p. 11.

———. "Nat Cole' s Indeed King of Song at the Copa." *Billboard*, November 6, 1954, p. 19.

Freeman, Don. "Critics to Blame for Confusion in Music: Cole." *Down Beat*, October 5, 1951, p. 3.

———. "I Want to Make Money, Not Play Jazz: Nat Cole." *Down Beat*, October 6, 1950, p. 1.

———. "Nat Cole Cuts Piano Set: 'It's One I'm Happy About.' " *Down Beat*, November 2, 1955, p. 16.

———. "The Real Reason Nat Cole Cut His Piano-Only Album." *Down Beat*, January 28, 1953, p. 3.

"Friars' Luncheon for Nat King Cole a Not Too Ribald Ribfest." *Variety*, January 29, 1964, p. 62.

Gardner, M. "Record Reviews." *Jazz Journal*, June 1968, p. 34.

Gardner, Paul. "Nat Cole Praises New TV Attitude." *New York Times*, February 17, 1964, p. 53.

"George and Ralph Present Benny Carter." *New York Times*, October 29, 1941, p. 17.

"Giants of Jazz." *International Musician*, January 1966, p. 5.

Gleason, Ralph. "Just Can't See for Lookin'." *Esquire*, January 1947, p. 107.

———. "Nat 'Always Comes Through Bigger Than Ever.' " *Down Beat*, July 13, 1951, p. 2.

———. "Perspectives." *Down Beat*, August 11, 1954, p. 4.

Glover, William. "Broadway Musical for Nat Cole." *Los Angeles Examiner*, May 6, 1960.

Godbout, Oscar. "Nat Cole Scores Ad Men on Ouster." *New York Times*, November 22, 1957, p. 51.

"Going Backstage." *Chicago Defender*, December 8, December 29, 1934.

Goldie, Syd. "Around the Town at Night." *San Francisco Ingleside Progress*, August 13, 1955.

Gottlieb, Bill. "Posin'." *Down Beat*, May 21, 1947, p. 7.

Granz, N. "Norman Granz Rebuts Nat Cole on State of Jazz Here and Abroad." *Variety*, June 8, 1960, pp. 51–52.

Greene, Patterson. "Nat Came West — and Became King." *Los Angeles Examiner*, August 27, 1961.

Grevatt, R. " 'King' Again Sells Charm & Good Taste." *Billboard*, March 3, 1958, p. 9.

———. "Nat Keeps Topping That Cole." *Billboard*, October 27, 1962, p. 10.

Griffiths, David. "Great Jazzman to Great Businessman." Unidentified British newspaper, USC Library, Cole Collection.

Grove, Gene. "Cobalt Treatments for Cole's Tumor." *New York Post*, December 17, 1964.

Guild, H. "Nat King Cole Hits Diskeries' Yen for Rock 'n' Roll, But Sez TV Will Kill It." *Variety*, May 25, 1960, p. 57.

Hamilton, Sara. " 'Kiss Me' Tough Tale." *Los*

Angeles Examiner, May 19, 1955.

———. " 'Small Town Girl' Tops." *Los Angeles Examiner*, May 2, 1953.

———. " 'St. Louis Blues' Tribute to Handy." *Los Angeles Examiner*, April 24, 1958.

"Hancock Park Home Purchase Stirs Quandary." *Los Angeles Times*, August 6, 1948.

Hanes, Harold C. "Trio Concert at Civic Opera House." *Down Beat*, October 8, 1947.

"Harlem 'King' Marries Singer." *Decatur* [IL] *Herald*, March 29, 1948.

"Harlem Wedding Is Best Easter Parade." *La Salle* [IL] *Post-Tribune*, March 29, 1948.

"Harrah's Lake Tahoe." *Variety*, January 30, 1963, p. 59.

"Harrah's Lake Tahoe." *Variety*, May 20, 1964, p. 53.

"Harrah's Lake Tahoe." *Variety*, October 21, 1964, p. 69.

Harris, Bud. "Bud Harris Buzzes." *Chicago Defender*, March 6, March 20, 1937.

"Harry' s Upbeat." *New York Mirror*, February 16, 1949.

Hayes, Bob. "Cabarets." *Chicago Defender*, March 21, April 4, 1936.

———. "Here and There." *Chicago Defender*, August 18, September 1, 1934.

"Hearings Held on Cap vs. Cole Estate Dispute." *Billboard*, July 27, 1968, p. 3.

Henshaw, L. "Cole Play." *Melody Maker*, December 25, 1968, p. 30.

Higgins, Chester. " 'Nat Must Have Kept Going When He Shouldn't' — Mahalia." *Jet*, March 4, 1965, pp. 22–25.

"His Song Made Publishers a Fortune." *Balham News*, April 9, 1954.

"Hit on Coast." *Chicago Defender*, July 10, 1937, p. 10.

"The Hits and the Artists Who Made Them." *Billboard*, August 2, 1952, p. 68.

Hodgkins, Barbara. "Backstage with Nat." *Metronome*, August 1948, p. 9–25.

———. "King Cole Trio." *Metronome*, December 1946.

———. "King Cole Trio." *Metronome*, November 1954, p. 34.

"Holdup Robs 'King' Cole Wife." *Los Angeles Examiner*, September 20, 1948.

"Hollywood Stars Jam Nitery for Big Premiere." *Chicago Defender*, May 1, 1937.

"Home of 'King' Cole Seized in Tax Break." *Los Angeles Examiner*, March 15, 1951, sec. 1, p. 3.

"Hoodlums vs. Decency." *Billboard*, April 21, 1956, p. 29.

"Hoods Attack Cole, Carter." *Metronome*, November 1944.

"Hooligan Attack on Nat Cole Ricochets vs. Racists; Even Dixie Press Irate." *Variety*, April 18, 1956, p. 1.

"Host With the Most." *Time*, September 23, 1957, p. 56.

"Hotel Del Mar, Cal." *Variety*, July 22, 1953, p. 54.

"How to Make and Lose Money." *Down Beat*, April 20, 1951, p. 10.

Hubler, Richard G. "$12,000-a-Week Preacher's Boy." *Saturday Evening Post*, July 17, 1954, p. 30.

Humphrey, Hal. "Madison Ave. Is Afraid of the Dark." *Los Angeles Mirror*, July 9, 1957, p. 6.

"Hundreds Attend Nat Cole Funeral." *New York Times*, February 19, 1965, p. 35.

Hutton, Jack. "Nat 'King' Cole — His Voice Was an Accident." *Melody Maker*, September 4, 1954, p. 15.

"I Thoroughly Enjoyed . . ." *Los Angeles Examiner*, September 5, 1960.

"I Thought You Ought to Know." *Metronome*, September 1945.

"I Was Very Pleased When Nat 'King' Cole Made Me a Visit . . ." *Los Angeles Examiner*, December 24, 1955.

"Illness Strikes Nat King Cole." *Melody Maker*, January 2, 1965, p. 11.

"I'm Proud of This Picture." *Melody Maker*, May 24, 1958, p. 3.

"An Incredible $20,000 a Day . . ." *Los Angeles Examiner*, February 4, 1957.

"Istanbul." *Variety*, January 16, 1957.

" 'Itinerant' JFK Visits Links Ball." *Los Angeles Examiner*, November 19, 1961.

"It's No News . . ." *Los Angeles Examiner*, September 9, 1957.

Jackson, George. "Nat 'King' Cole Takes Over at Sands Tonight." *Los Angeles Herald*, March 1, 1961.

"Jazz Albums: Jazz at the Philharmonic 1944–46." *Melody Maker*, July 10, 1968, p. 24.

"Jazz at the Philharmonic ou L'Apothéose de la Jam-session." *Jazz Magazine*, February 1954, p. 30.

"Jazz Photos." *Down Beat*, March 21, 1956, p. 42.

Jovien, Harold. "Let's Listen." *Associated Negro Press*, May 22, 1947.

"Jury Weighs Cole Suit." *New York Times*, September 20, 1951, p. 21.

"Just Heard from Nat 'King' Cole . . ." *Los Angeles* Examiner, May 19, 1956.

Kaufman, D. "Nat Cole Hits Madison Ave. Resistance to Negroes on TV." *Variety*, September 11, 1957, p. 2.

Kellum, David W. "Season's Largest Crowd Sees Midnight Show Hit." *Chicago Defender*, December 22, 1934.

————. "Spectacular Event to Culminate at Savoy Ballroom." *Chicago Defender*, September 15, 1934.

Kelly, Fran. "This King Cole Is a Wise Old Soul." *Metronome*, April 1957, p. 6.

Kelly, John. "A Baltimorean Remembers the King." *Baltimore Sun*, August 21, 1983, sec. D, p. 13.

"The King." *Time*, February 26, 1965, p. 60.

"King Cole." *Metronome*, February 1944, p. 11.

"King Cole." *Metronome*, March 1944.

"King Cole." *Metronome*, April, 1944, p. 24.

"King Cole." *Metronome*, December 1944.

"King Cole Album." *Metronome*, November 1944.

"King Cole Baby; Bringing First Born Home from Hospital Is Big Moment for Popular Trio Leader and Singer-Wife." *Ebony*, June 1950, pp. 31–34.

"'King Cole' Cancels Show in Atlanta, Fears Attack." *New York Times*, April 1956, p. 29.

"King Cole Faces Covenant Battle on $85,000

Home." *Oakland Herald*, August 13, 1948.

"King Cole Farewell Fine." March 1943, p. 18.

"King Cole Forced to Appear in Court." *Pittsburgh Courier*, November 6, 1948.

"King Cole's Forgotten Love." *Tan*, September 1954, pp. 22–27.

"King Cole Gravely Ill: Wife & Manager at Bedside." *Melody Maker*, June 6, 1953, p. 1.

"King Cole Hits U.S. Seizure of Home for Taxes." Los Angeles Examiner, March 20, 1957, p. 3.

"King Cole Hospitalisé." *Jazz Magazine*, January 1965, p. 16.

"The King Cole Incident." *World-Telegram and Sun*, April 12, 1956.

" 'King' Cole in Episcopal Benefit." *Los Angeles Examiner*, October 19, 1957.

" 'King' Cole Maps Fight to Keep Home." *The Mirror*, March 20, 1951, p. 5.

"King Cole May Save Home by Records Deal." *Los Angeles Examiner*, March 28, 1951.

"King Cole of Jukeboxes Has $17,500 Wedding." *Los Angeles Times*, March 29, 1948.

"King Cole's $17,500 Wedding Largest in Harlem Since '23." *Los Angeles Sentinel*, April 1, 1948.

"King Cole Still Reigns As a Top Seller at Cap." *Billboard*, November 11, 1967, p. 8.

"King Cole's Success Secrets." *Hue*, January 1955, p. 41.

" 'King' Cole's Suit Is Dismissed." *New York Times*, September 21, 1951, p. 13.

"King Cole Takes a Queen." *Baltimore Afro-American*, April 3, 1948, p. 3.

" 'King' Cole to Get Dinner." *Los Angeles Her-*

ald-*Examiner*, July 28, 1962.

"King Cole Tour Plans Feature Serious Stuff." *Down Beat*, March 25, 1946, p. 3.

"King Cole Trio." *Jazz Magazine*, February 1956, p. 25.

"King Cole Trio." *Metronome*, January 1944, p. 32.

"King Cole Trio." *Metronome*, September 1945.

"The King Cole Trio." *Opportunity*, January 1947, p. 28.

"King Cole Trio — Breakfast in Hollywood." *Down Beat*, April 8, 1946.

"King Cole Trio Escape When Car Turns Over." *Hollywood Variety*, February 16, 1949.

"King Cole Trio, 4 Others in Crash." *Omaha Morning World Herald*, February 16, 1949.

"King Cole Trio in Automobile Accident." *Cedar Rapids Gazette*, February 15, 1949.

"King Cole Trio Isn't Dead, Beams Feather." *Down Beat*, February 22, 1952, p. 2.

"King Cole Trio with Jo Stafford." *Variety Radio Reviews*, October 23, 1946.

"King Cole Turns Actor." *Our World*, April 1953, pp. 45–47.

"King Cole versus Jim Crow." *Metronome*, August 1957, p. 6.

"King Cole's Wife Goes Back to Work." *Ebony*, December 1955, pp. 132–38.

" 'King' Cole's Wife Heiress' Guardian." *Los Angeles Examiner*, April 20, 1961.

"The 'King's' Own Show." *Newsweek*, July 15, 1957, p. 90.

"King Wins High Favor." *Lansing State Journal*, April 24, 1956.

"Kiss Me Deadly." *Variety*, April 20, 1955.

"Ladies An' Gents, This Is the Back Door Run-around." *Chicago Defender*, June 20, 1936, p. 10.

Land, Richard. "Small Bands." *Metronome*, March 1944, p. 18.

"Launch Cole Cancer Drive." *Billboard*, December 25, 1965, p. 3.

Laverdure, Michel. "Il y a Dix Ans King Cole." *Jazz Magazine*, February 1975, pp. 24–26.

"La Vie en Rose, N.Y." *Variety*, December 10, 1952, p. 59.

Lee, Marilyn. "'Be Yourself: Nat Cole Discusses Racial Problems with Teens." *Los Angeles Examiner*, September 22, 1956.

" 'Let's Forget Alabama'; Cole Is King to 7,000 at Columbus." *Indianapolis News*, April 20, 1956.

Levette, Harry. "Thru Hollywood." *Chicago Defender*, May 15, July 24, 1937, pp. 21, 12.

Lewis, Vic. "Ray, Laine, Cole — The Men As They Really Are." *Melody Maker*, June 25, 1955, p. 11.

"Life Is Gr-a-a-nd for Nat (King) Cole These Days." *Los Angeles Examiner*, July 13, 1957.

"Life Members." *The Crisis*, June–July 1956, p. 359.

"London Palladium." *The Performer*, March 25, 1954.

"Long Live the King." *Billboard*, February 27, 1965, p. 4.

"Los Angeles." *Down Beat*, July 1, 1944.

"Los Angeles." *Down Beat*, August 15, 1945.

"The Lucky King." Erie [PA] *Times*, December 20, 1964.

"Make Believe Ballroom." *Variety*, April 20, 1949.

"Makes Acting Debut." *Jet*, January 8, 1953, p. 62.

" 'Man, That's Groovy.' " *Down Beat*, August 1, 1941, p. 23.

Manners, Dorothy. " 'Breakfast' Exploited." *Los Angeles Examiner*, March 15, 1946.

———. " 'Elmer' Film on Screen at Two Theaters." *Los Angeles Examiner*, December 18, 1943.

———. "Nat Cole; He Deserved It." *Los Angeles Examiner*.

———. " 'Pin Up Girl' Light on Plot, Heavy with Lavishness." *Los Angeles Examiner*, May 26, 1944.

"Mary-like." *Metronome*, December 1945, p. 22.

McAndrew, John. "Star-Studded Shellac." *Record Research*, August 1960, p. 24.

McLendon, Winzola. "She Likes to Travel Along Rather Than Sing Along." *Washington Post*, n.d. USC Library, Cole Collection.

McLeod, Zelie. "Parson's Son to a King of Jazz." *Sydney Daily Telegraph*, February 11, 1956, *Saturday Magazine*, p. 13.

"Melancholy Monarch." *Look*, April 19, 1955, pp. 119–21.

Mesmer, Marie. "King Cole Trio Remembers L.A. for First Big Break." *Los Angeles News*, August 10, 1948.

Monroe, Al. "Everybody Goes — When the Wagon Comes." *Chicago Defender*, March 14, 1936.

"Mrs. Nat Cole Will Have Twins . . ." *Los An-*

geles Examiner, September 20, 1961.

"Mrs. Nat King Cole Joins Peggy Lee in Suit on Disks." New York Times, May 18, 1965, p. 35.

"'Music City' Opens in Los Angeles." Down Beat, July 15, 1940, p. 7.

"Music City Stores Aid Cole Fund." Billboard, March 20, 1965, p. 3.

"Nat's Back." Melody Maker, July 13, 1963, p. 6.

"Nat Cole." Melody Maker, June 19, 1971, p. 47.

"Nat Cole." Metronome, March 1948.

"Nat Cole." Metronome, January 1949, p. 20.

"Nat Cole." Metronome, July 1949.

"Nat Cole." Metronome, October 1952, p. 13.

"Nat Cole." Metronome, July 1953.

"Nat Cole's Adoption of Boy OK'd." Los Angeles Examiner, March 30, 1960.

"Nat Cole Attacked in Alabama: Kidnap Plot Is Uncovered." Jet, April 26, 1956, pp. 60–62.

"Nat Cole's Father Dies." New York Times, February 2, 1965, p. 33.

"Nat Cole Forms Pop Label; Artist to Stay with Capitol." Billboard, October 16, 1961, p. 1.

"Nat Cole Foundation Hits Heavy Returns at $100 Top in L.A. Benefit." Variety, December 15, 1965, p. 62.

"Nat Cole Gets His Trio Set for Concerts." Down Beat, July 1, 1946, p. 2.

"Nat Cole Gives Frisco the Brushoff; Masons Claim Nix Not Race-Based." Variety, February 24, 1960, p. 2.

"Nat Cole Has Lung Tumor; Undergoing Cobalt Therapy." New York Times, December 17, 1964, p. 17.

"Nat Cole Hits Tax Action." *New York Times*, March 20, 1951, p. 23.

"Nat Cole Ill, Hospitalized." *Los Angeles Examiner*, May 29, 1953.

"Nat Cole's Illness Cancels All Appearances." *Down Beat*, January 28, 1965, p. 10.

"Nat Cole Kidnap Plot Hinted As Cops Reveal Mob Planned to Storm Theater." *New York Post*, April 12, 1956.

"Nat Cole Knocks No-Talent Singers in U.S. Disk Biz." *Variety*, May 4, 1960, p. 1.

"Nat Cole, La Vie en Rose, New York." *Down Beat*, December 30, 1953, p. 4.

"Nat Cole Leaves NBC." *Los Angeles Examiner*, November 21, 1957.

"Nat Cole's Lung Removed in Battle Against Cancer." *New York Times*, January 26, 1965, p. 42.

"Nat Cole Marries in Harlem." *New York Times*, March 29, 1948, p. 18.

"Nat Cole's New, 10-Yr. Deal with Cap But Leaves Door Open for Own Prod. Set." *Variety*, June 14, 1961, p. 43.

"Nat Cole on Ed Sullivan's Toast of the Town." *Metronome*, January 1951, p. 32.

"Nat Cole's Sparkling Sessions." *Melody Maker*, July 13, 1974, p. 48.

"Nat Cole SRO in 2d Japan Tour." *Variety*, March 13, 1963, p. 64.

"Nat Cole Stands on Artist's Right to Plug New Disk in Sullivan Row." *Variety*, February 1, 1961, p. 57.

"Nat Cole Sues Hotel." *New York Times*, April 29, 1949, p. 13.

"Nat Cole — Ted Heath Package Draws Solid $83,000 in Tour's First Week." *Variety*, April 11, 1956, p. 45.

"Nat Cole to Continue in South Despite Attack." *Daily Worker*, April 12, 1956.

"Nat Cole — The Man Behind the Image." *Melody Maker*, July 6, 1963, p. 8.

"Nat Cole Visits Johnson." *New York Times*, January 10, 1964, p. 19.

"Nat Cole Was to Get an Honorary Degree." *New York Times*, February 17, 1965, p. 43.

"Nat Cole's Wife Has Twins." *New York Times*, September 27, 1961, p. 30.

"Nat Cole, Wife on Honeymoon in Old Mexico." *Capitol News*, April 1948, p. 11.

"Nat Cole's Will Probated; Cancer Fund Begun in His Name." *Down Beat*, April 8, 1965, p. 12.

"Nat Coles Get Their Decree." *Down Beat*, February 26, 1947.

"Nat's Family Growing by Leaps." *Down Beat*, March 1950.

"Nat (King) Cole." *Army Times Weekend Magazine*, July 9, 1959, p. 15.

"Nat King Cole." *International Musician*, March 1965, p. 41.

"Nat King Cole." *Jazz Magazine*, May 1972, pp. 44–45.

"Nat (King) Cole." *Metronome*, November 1943.

"Nat King Cole." *Metronome*, June 1946.

"Nat King Cole and Wife Adopt Baby." *Los Angeles Herald*, March 30, 1960.

"Nat 'King' Cole at the Palladium." *New Musi-*

cal Express, March 26, 1954.

"Nat 'King' Cole at the Royal Has Little Time for Clowning." *Irish Times*, April 9, 1954.

"Nat King Cole Fans Jam Astoria, London, As Singer Opens Brit. Concert Tour." *Variety*, July 24, 1963, p. 53.

"Nat King Cole Forms Theatrical Film Company." *Jet*, July 7, 1960, p. 44.

"Nat King Cole, 45, Is Dead of Cancer." *New York Times*, February 16, 1965, p. 1.

"Nat King Cole's Gift to Maria . . ." *Los Angeles Examiner*, July 22, 1958.

"Nat (King) Cole, Hit by Lung Tumor, Cancels His Bookings Thru March." *Variety*, December 23, 1964, p. 39.

"Nat 'King' Cole Learns to Dance." *Ebony*, May 1955, p. 24.

"Nat 'King' Cole Memorial Issue." *Sepia*, April 1965, p. 8.

"Nat 'King' Cole Merry; He's to Be New Papa." *Los Angeles Herald*, March 7, 1961.

"Nat 'King' Cole Much Improved." *Los Angeles Examiner*, May 30, 1953.

"Nat 'King' Cole, 1917–1965." *Down Beat*, March 25, 1965, p. 14.

"Nat 'King' Cole; No. 1 Hitmaker." *Our World*, April 1952, pp. 28–31.

"The Nat King Cole Nobody Knows." *Ebony*, October 1956, pp. 42–48.

"Nat King Cole, on Scot-Nightet Tour, Would Ride That 'Freedom Bus.' " *Variety*, July 31, 1963, p. 95.

"Nat King Cole Praised by Council for Benefits." *Los Angeles Examiner*, August 18, 1959.

"Nat 'King' Cole Says Europeans Are Hungry for American Jazz." *Miami News*, February 16, 1958.

"Nat 'King' Cole's Second Honeymoon." *Ebony*, August 1954, pp. 17–22.

"Nat King Cole Sends Me Word." *Los Angeles Examiner*, May 30, 1956.

"Nat King Cole Sings a Sad Song of Songs." *New York Post*, March 13, 1959, p. 22.

"Nat King Cole Still Plays a Mean Piano." *Detroit Free Press*, April 16, 1958.

"Nat King Cole Still Rules Record Roost." *Down Beat*, January 11, 1968, p. 13.

"Nat King Cole to Try a Broadway Show in Fall of 1960." *Jet*, May 19, 1960, p. 58.

"Nat King Cole Twins." *Ebony*, August 1963, pp. 106–12.

"Nat 'King' Cole Will Be Off the Air As of December 17." *Los Angeles Examiner*, November 21, 1957.

"Nat King Cole Will Make a Fine Good-Will Ambassador . . ." *Los Angeles Examiner*, January 24, 1959.

"Nat to Be Billed as Soloist From Now On." *Down Beat*, October 15, 1951, p. 1.

" 'Nat' to Play." *Chicago Defender*, December 15, 1934.

"Nation's Stations Pay Tribute: Air His Songs." *Billboard*, February 27, 1965, p. 1.

" 'Nature Boy' Ahbez Flying to New York." *Capitol News*, June 1948.

" 'Nature Boy' Draws Strings on His Tenet Flap." *New York Times*, 1948, USC Library, Cole Collection.

"Nature Boy Rolls Natural with 'Nature Boy' Before Copies Printed." *New York Variety*, April 14, 1948.

"'Negro' Music Protested." *New York Times*, April 10, 1956, p. 20.

"New Arena, Pittsburgh." *Variety*, December 16, 1959, p. 55.

"New Domain for King." *Metronome*, May 1944, p. 13.

"New Jazz Gets Foundation." *Metronome*, November 1945.

"New King Cole Home Opposed." *Los Angeles Examiner*, August 3, 1948.

"Newly-hitched." *Metronome*, February 1949.

New York Amsterdam News, June 5, 1945.

New York Times, October 2, 1959.

New York Times, October 9, 1959.

"Night Club Reviews." *Variety*, July 28, 1948.

"Night of the Quarter Moon." *Variety*, February 11, 1959.

"Night to Remember." *Guardian*, February 6, 1965.

"Nixon Joins Cole Bandwagon." *Jet*, March 25, 1954.

"No More Gimmicks to Invent — So Let's Play Music Again." *Melody Maker*, July 26, 1952, p. 3.

"Nob Hill Won't Let 'King' Cole Play Auditorium." *Los Angeles Examiner*, February 18, 1960.

"Norman Granz." *Down Beat*, August 15, 1942.

"Les Obséques du Roi." *Jazz Magazine*, April 1965, p. 9.

"Organizes Cole-Belafonte Enterprises, Inc.; Company Will Produce Movies and TV Shows."

Jet, March 10, 1960, p. 59.

"Palmer House, Chi." *Variety*, April 4, 1962, p. 77.

"Papee, Famous Cafe . . ." *Chicago Defender*, June 26, 1937.

Parsons, Louella. " 'King' Coles Welcome Twin Girls." *Los Angeles Examiner*, September 27, 1961.

————. "Nat Cole Adopts 5-Mos. Boy." *Los Angeles Examiner*, July 22, 1959.

Pearson, Howard. "Nat King Cole's Music Captures Near-Capacity Crowd at Lagoon." *Desert News and Telegram*, August 3, 1962.

"Petit Dictionnaire du Jazz." *Jazz Magazine*, May 1954, p. 18.

"Petit Dictionnaire du Jazz." *Jazz Magazine*, February 1955, p. 18.

"Pioneer." *Time*, July 15, 1957, p. 66.

"Plenty Hot: Nat Cole." *Chicago Defender*, October 6, 1934.

"Plot on Cole by Mob Told." *Los Angeles Examiner*, April 12, 1956.

Power, Tyrone. "Nat 'King' Cole and Maria Are Back Home . . ." *Los Angeles Examiner*, June 14, 1956.

Proctor, Kay. " 'Quarter Moon' Provoking." *Los Angeles Examiner*, April 2, 1959, sec. 3, p. 2.

"Promoters Holding to Southern Bookings, Despite Cole Incident." *Billboard*, April 21, 1956, p. 29.

Pryor, T. "Show Biz, Civic Notables' Salute to Nat King Cole." *Variety*, August 8, 1962, p. 2.

"The Question of the Week" and "Ace High King." *Melody Maker*, March 27, 1954, p. 3.

"Questions." *Jazz Magazine*, October 1956, p. 34.

"Reaping the Whirlwind." *Christian Science Monitor*, April 13, 1956.

"Record Reviews." *Metronome*, April 1946.

"Recording Artists' Roster." *Down Beat*, June 30, 1954, p. 93.

"Records of the Year." *Metronome*, January 1945.

"Remember the Public." *Time*, July 30, 1951, pp. 63–64.

"Reviews." *Sunday Pictorial*, March 28, 1954.

Robinson. Louie. "The Life and Death of Nat King Cole." *Ebony*, April 1965, pp. 123–34.

————. "Nation Says 'Sweet Dreams, Good Man' in Last Tribute to Nat Cole" and "Jet's West Coast Editor Recalls Personal Meetings with Nat Cole." *Jet*, March 4, 1965, pp. 4–17, 26–29.

"Le Roi Est Mort." *Jazz Magazine*, March 1965, pp. 13–14.

Roy, Rob. "Miller Heads Latest Crew of Stars Who Took Broadway." *Chicago Defender*, September 12, 1936, p. 20.

Ruark, Robert. "Cole Cash," USC Library, Cole Collection, February 1955.

"Sally Rand, Famous Fan Dancer." *Chicago Defender*, June 28, 1934.

"Sands, Las Vegas." *Variety*, March 19, 1958, p. 86.

"Sands, Las Vegas." *Variety*, March 4, 1959, p. 55.

"Sands, Las Vegas." *Variety*, January 17, 1962, p. 66.

"The Scarlet Hour." Variety, April 18, 1956.

Schumach, Murray. "TV Called 'Timid' on Negro Talent." *New York Times*, October 24, 1961, p. 41.

"Scintillating Nat Cole Is Still the King." *Melody Maker*, May 21, 1960, p. 12.

Shanley, J. P. "People on TV." *New York Times*, November 4, 1956, sec. 2, p. 13.

Sherwood, Buster. " 'Ole King Cole.' " *Orchestra World*, April 1945, p. 5.

"Should ANY Negro Artist Perform Before a Segregated Audience??" *New York Age Defender*, April 28, 1956, p. 4.

" 'Shuffle Along' Coming to Regal." *Chicago Defender*, December 22, 1934.

Simon, George. "Kenton-Cole." *Metronome*, December 1946.

"Singer Cole Regains Home." *Los Angeles Examiner*, March 29, 1951, sec. 1, p. 3.

"Singer Cole Says Attack to Aid Integration." *Los Angeles Examiner*, April 13, 1956.

"Singer Unhurt Given Ovation by Audience." *Los Angeles Examiner*, April 11, 1956.

"The Singer Who Beat the Evil Eye." *Melody Maker*, March 20, 1954, p. 3.

"Singers Pledge Money for Civil-Rights Struggle." *Down Beat*, August 15, 1963, p. 11.

"66th Birthday Fete Planned for President; He Will Thank Nation over TV Saturday." *New York Times*, October 7, 1956, p. 3.

Skolsky, S. "Tintypes . . . Nat King Cole." *New York Post*, December 13, 1964, p. 52.

"Snapshots of Hollywood Collected at Random." *Los Angeles Examiner*, March 17, 1951.

"Soft Answers." *Newsweek*, March 1, 1965, p. 81.

"Some Background." *Down Beat*, January 9, 1958, p. 13.

"St. Louis Blues." *Variety*, April 9, 1958.

Stacy, Frank. "Nat Cole Talks Back to Critics." *The Capitol*, April 1946, p. 7.

"Stars Flock to Nat Cole Funeral." *Melody Maker*, February 27, 1965, p. 19.

"Stars Pay Tribute to Nat Cole." *Melody Maker*, February 20, 1965, p. 3.

Steif, B. "Frisco Masonic Temple's Cryptic Nix of Cole, Who Shifts to Civic Aud." *Variety*, February 17, 1960, pp. 49–50.

Stone, Chuck. "A Chat with Nat 'King' Cole — A True 'Philosopher-King.' " *Baltimore Afro-American*, March 18, 1961, p. 20.

Strayhorn, Billy. "Billy Strayhorn on Pianists." *Metronome*, October 1943, p. 29.

"Swift Justice." *Time*, April 30, 1956, p. 23.

Tanner, P. "Oh Didn't They RRRRRamble." *Jazz Journal*, July 1966, p. 4.

"Telephoned to Thank Nat King Cole for His Album . . ." *Los Angeles Examiner*, July 30, 1958.

"$10,000 for One Day's Work . . ." *Los Angeles Examiner*, December 11, 1952.

"That's Nat." *Metronome*, June 1945.

"There's a Very Proud Young Girl at the Immaculate Heart High School . . ." *Los Angeles Examiner*, September 22, 1960.

Thompson, T. "A King of Song Dies, and a Friend Remembers Him." *Life*, February 26, 1965, p. 36.

"Three Onto One." *Indianapolis Times*, April 13, 1956.

Tiegel, E. "Brothers & Daughters Keep Nat Cole Tradition Alive." *Billboard*, July 26, 1968, p. 37.

"Times and Clerics Lose in Libel Suit." *New York Times*, February 2, 1961, p. 17.

"Tiny 'Prince' Expected by Nat Cole." *Los Angeles Examiner*, March 7, 1961.

Travis, Dempsey J. "Chicago's Jazz Trail: 1893–1950." *Black Music Research Newsletter*, Columbia College, Chicago, Fall 1987, pp. 1–3.

"Two Colleges Planned for Cole; L.A. to Build Memorial"; "Form Cole Cancer Fund for Research"; "400 Attend L.A. Rites for Nat Cole." *Variety*, February 24, 1965, p. 58.

"Two Fined for Attacking Cole." *Los Angeles Examiner*, December 8, 1956.

"Two Indicted in Cole Attack." New York *Times*, May 12, 1956, p. 38.

Tynan, J. "Caught in the Act." *Down Beat*, October 12, 1961, p. 38.

———. "Nat Cole." *Down Beat*, May 2, 1957, pp. 13, 24, May 16, 1957, p. 15.

Ulanov, Barry. "Esquire Concert." *Metronome*, February 1946.

———. "Hollywood Periscope." *Metronome*, March 1946.

———. "3's No Crowd." *Metronome*, November, n.d., Jazz Institute, Rutgers.

———. "The Trio Con Brio." *Metronome*, September 1945, p. 19.

" 'Unforgettable' Nat Cole Truly a King to the Last." *Billboard*, February 27, 1965, p. 4.

"Unit Reviews." *Variety*, August 29, 1962, p. 45.

"Unscheduled Appearance." *Time*, April 23, 1956, p. 31.

"U.S. Seizes Singer's Home." *New York Times*, March 15, 1951, p. 22.

"Variety." *The People*, March 28, 1954.

Walker, D. "Broadway." *New York Daily News*, April 5, n.d.

Wallichs, G. "A Personal Statement." *Billboard*, February 27, 1965, p. 3.

Waterbury, Ruth. " 'Blue Gardenia' Relaxing Film." *Los Angeles Examiner*, March 28, 1953.

————. "Cole Tops in 'China Gate.' " *Los Angeles Examiner*, May 10, 1957, sec. 1, p. 12.

"The Weather." *Chicago Defender*, September 7–9, 1935.

"The Week in Negro Affairs." *Daily Worker*, April 15, 1956.

Weller, Sheila. "Ciro's: Life Begins at 8:30." *Vanity Fair*, April 1998.

"What Men Notice About Women." *Ebony*, January 1950.

Whiston, Henry F. "You Can Go a Little Commercial and Still Play Good Jazz." *Melody Maker*, February 23, 1952, p. 3.

"Who the Hoodlums Are." *Newsweek*, April 23, 1956, pp. 31–32.

"A Wicked Rumor Is Being Circulated About Nat 'King' Cole . . ." *Los Angeles Examiner*, January 2, 1958.

Wilson, John S. "Nat Nominates Himself Advance Man for Bop." *Down Beat*, April 22, 1949, p. 1.

Wilson, Russ. "King Cole Kids Rock 'n' Roll, Sings Smooth Stuff in S.F." *Oakland Tribune*,

September 2, 1960.

"You Can Bet the Umpires . . ." *Los Angeles Examiner*, July 27, 1961.

Young, A. C. "King Cole's House, Car Taken for Taxes." *Baltimore Afro-American*, March 20, 1951, p. 1.

Zaccagnino, Mike. "Nat Is Gone." *Record Research*, April 1965, p. 12.

ARTICLES ON RELATED TOPICS

"Black Concert Music in Chicago, 1890 to the 1930s." *Black Music Research Newsletter*, Columbia College, Chicago, Fall 1987, pp. 3–7.

Dixon, George. "Earl Hines and Band Leave Sebastian Club." *Chicago Defender*, June 12, 1937.

————. " 'Father' Hines and Band Are Breaking Records on Coast." *Chicago Defender*, July 3, 1937.

"Earl Hines and Band to Play Hi-Low Jazz for Us." *Chicago Defender*, November 1932.

"Earl Hines at His Best As Grand Terrace Opens." *Chicago Defender*, September 28, 1935.

" 'Father' Hines Bing Crosby's Dinner Guest." *Chicago Defender*, May 29, 1937.

Floyd, Samuel A., ed. *Black Music Research Journal*, Fall 1988.

"Fraternity Swimming." *Ames State Daily*, February 15, 1949.

"Here's Chance to Get One of Those Turkeys." *Chicago Defender*, November 5, 1932.

Hyltone, David. "L.A. Local Will Elect Wallace

Aides." *Down Beat*, February 1, 1940, p. 19.

—————. "Les Hite Gets Break; Goes Out on MCA Tour." *Down Beat*, January 1, 1940, p. 21.

"June Christy Set for Bocage." *Down Beat*, May 7, 1947, p. 1.

"Marie Ellington." *Metronome*, November 1945, p. 45.

"Miami Union Bars Fletcher Henderson Band Because of Its Three White Musicians." *Metronome*, January 1944.

"Night Life in Detroit." *Chicago Defender*, November 7, 1936.

" 'Nothing Like It,' Say 5,000 As They Hear Bud's Proteges." *Chicago Defender*, April 22, 1932.

INTERVIEWS

Adams, Berle, 10 a.m., February 19, 1998, in Los Angeles.

Allen, Steve, 11 a.m., February 18, 1998, in Los Angeles.

Barnes, Naida, 8 a.m., March 12, 1998, in Los Angeles by telephone.

Basolo, Bud and Georgia, 11 a.m., February 27, 1998, in Tracy, CA.

Black, Tim, May 29, 1998, in Chicago.

Burks, Gwendolyn Dyett (Mrs. Walter Dyett), 4 p.m., March 23, 1998, in Chicago.

Cole, Carol, 2 p.m., February 17, 1998, in Los Angeles, also by telephone on numerous dates including March 7, 1999.

Cole, Isaac (Ike), 7 p.m., April 30, 1998, in Phoenix by telephone.

Cole, Maria, 11 a.m., July 10, 1997; 10 a.m., August 12, 1997; 12 noon, January 10, 1998; 11 a.m., February 20, 1999; all in Boston.

Cole, Natalie, 2:30 p.m., January 24, 1999, in Baltimore.

Sister Maureen Craig (of St. John's Hospital), 12 noon, February 23, 1998, in Los Angeles.

Damone, Vic, 11:30 a.m., April 4, 1998, in Palm Beach.

Davis, Marc, 5 p.m., February 15, 1998, in Los Angeles.

Donegan, Dorothy, 11 a.m., March 10, 1998, in Los Angeles by telephone.

Edison, Harry "Sweets," 3 p.m., February 16, 1998, in Los Angeles.

Harris, Charlie, 2 p.m., March 9, 1998, in Baltimore.

Henry, Robert, 5 p.m., March 31, 1998, in Los Angeles by telephone.

Hinton, Milt, 4 p.m., February 4, 1998, in New York.

Jackson, Franz, 9 p.m., March 20, and 1 p.m., March 21, 1998, in Chicago.

Jones, Hank, 4 p.m., January 26, 1999, in Detroit by telephone.

Jovien, Harold, 12:30 p.m., February 21, 1998, in Los Angeles.

Kositchek, Robert, 5 p.m., July 16, 1998, in Los Angeles by telephone.

Laine, Frankie, 10:30 a.m., July 7, 1998, in Los Angeles by telephone.

LaPalm, Dick, 4 p.m., February 23, 1998, in

Los Angeles, then numerous conversations by telephone.

Livingston, Alan, 11 a.m., February 20, 1998, in Los Angeles.

Livingston, Jay, 3 p.m., February 22, 1998, in Los Angeles.

May, Billy, 1:30 p.m., September 10, 1998, in Los Angeles.

McNair, Barbara, 11 a.m., February 21, 1998, in Los Angeles.

Miller, Henry, 3 p.m., April 1, 1998, in Los Angeles by telephone.

Mogull, Ivan, 5:30 p.m., February 5, 1998, in New York, and 5:30 p.m., March 11, 1999, in New York, and numerous telephone interviews.

Moore, Kenneth, 8 a.m., January 8, 1999, Bakersfield, CA, by telephone.

Norman, Gene, 4 p.m., February 20, 1998, in Los Angeles.

Parham, Charles "Truck," 5 p.m., March 21, 1998, in Chicago.

Rogers, Timmie, 3 p.m., February 21, 1998, in Los Angeles.

Rugolo, Pete, 11 a.m., February 22, 1998, in Los Angeles.

Sullivan, Charlotte, 2 p.m., February 19, 1998, in Los Angeles, and by telephone on November 28, 1998.

Travis, Dempsey, 2:15 p.m., March 20, 1998, in Chicago.

Ulanov, Barry, 4 p.m., April 8, 1998, in New York, by telephone.

Young, Lee, 10 a.m., February 17, 1998, in Los Angeles, then numerous telephone interviews.

FROM THE CLAUDE BARNETT
ARCHIVE AT THE
CHICAGO HISTORICAL SOCIETY

Associated Negro Press Release, December 3, 1952.

Associated Negro Press Release, April 16, 1956.

Associated Negro Press Release, April 18, 1956.

" 'King' Cole Named in Lawsuit," September 22, 1961, p. 1.

"The King Cole Trio," Gene Howard Public Relations, Inc.

Letter from Charles D. Wherry to C. Barnett, October 28, 1948.

Letter from C. Barnett to Nat Cole, November 8, 1948.

Letter from C. Barnett to R. Ratcliffe, November 24, 1948.

Letter from C. Barnett to Harry Levette, November 24, 1948.

Letter from C. Barnett to Nat Cole, November 24, 1948.

Letter from C. Barnett to R. Ratcliffe, December 2, 1948.

Letter from C. Barnett to C. Wherry, December 4, 1948.

Letter from C. Barnett to Nat Cole, August 3, 1949.

Letter from H. Levette to C. Barnett, November 26, 1948.

Letter from H. Levette to C. Barnett, November 28, 1948.

Letter from Robert M. Ratcliffe to C. Barnett, November 23, 1948.

Scott, Vernon. " 'King' Cole Says Latins' View of U.S. Race Problems Distorted." *Nashville Banner*, May 22, 1959, p. 10.

Summary of Los Angeles Superior Court Case D 329, 238: *Idell Nadine Coles* v. *Nathaniel Coles*.

Telegram from Nat Cole to C. Barnett, December 1, 1948, 2:17 p.m.

OTHER SOURCES

Borio, Gene. *Tobacco Timeline. http://www.tobacco.org/*, 1998.

Contract of American Federation of Musicians Local 767, Los Angeles California, March 15, 1938, between Nat Cole and Robert Lubitz of Swanee Inn.

Letter from John F. Kennedy to Nat and Maria Cole: October 28, 1958. USC Cinema Library, Cole Collection.

Letter from Audrey Ashby of EMI Publishing to Ivan Mogull, April 23, 1998.

Letter from Maria Cole to Daniel Mark Epstein, February 26, 1999.

Letter from Maria Cole to Daniel Mark Epstein, June 9, 1999.

Letter from Maria Cole to Daniel Mark Epstein, June 11, 1999.

Fax letter from Natalie Cole to Daniel Mark Epstein, May 6, 1999.

Letter from Nicholas Xatzis to Daniel Mark Epstein, February 8, 1999.

Fax letter from Timolin Cole Augustus to Daniel Mark Epstein, March 19, 1999.

Letter from Robert Liner to Daniel Mark Epstein, December 7, 1998.

Walter Henry Dyett, "Services of Memory" (Funeral Program Notes), November 19, 1969.

Telegram from John F. Kennedy to Nat Cole: March 11, 1960, 5:57 p.m. USC Cinema Library, Cole Collection.

Telegram from Nat Cole to Maria Cole, November 23, 1964.

Fourteenth Census of the U.S. 1920 Population. State: Alabama; County: Montgomery; Enumeration District #188; Sheet #4698A.

Marriage License #30075 for Kalamazoo County, Michigan, January 25, 1937.

The Complete Capitol Recordings of the Nat King Cole Trio. With notes by Michael Cascuna, Will Friedwald, and Dick Katz; produced by Michael Cascuna for Mosaic Records, Inc., 1991.

The Complete Early Transcriptions of the NKC Trio 1938–41. With notes by Gord Grieveson and Ken Crawford, 1991. Vintage Jazz Classics.

The King Cole Trio: The MacGregor Years, 1941–1945. Music and Arts Programs of America, 1995.

Nat King Cole Trio. Live 1947–48 (radio programs). With notes by Gord Grieveson. Vintage Jazz Classics, 1991.

ACKNOWLEDGMENTS

Every effort has been made to secure the right to reprint previously published material in this book. Grateful acknowledgment is made for permission to reprint excerpts from:

"Embraceable You," by George Gershwin, © EMI Mills. Used by permission.

"For All We Know," words by Sam M. Lewis, music by J. Fred Coots, © 1934 (renewed), 1956 (renewed) Cromwell Music Inc., New York and Toy Town Tunes, Inc. Boca Raton, Florida. Used by permission.

"The Frim Fram Sauce," by Redd Evans and Joe Ricardel, © 1943 (renewed) by Music Sales Corporation (ASCAP). International copyright secured. All rights reserved. Reprinted by permission.

"Gone with the Draft," by Nat Cole and Wesley Prince, © 1940 EMI Mills. Used by permission.

"Hey Not Now," by Roy Alfred, © Jonroy Music Co. International copyright secured. All rights reserved. Reprinted by permission.

"Hit That Jive, Jack," Skeets Tolbert and Johnny Alston, © MCA Music Publishing/A Div. Used by permission.

"Just You, Just Me," by Jesse Greer and Raymond Klages, © EMI Mills. Used by permission.

"Lush Life," by Billy Strayhorn, © 1949 (renewed) by Music Sales Corporation (ASCAP) and Tempo Music, Inc. All rights administered by Music Sales Corporation. International copyright secured. All rights reserved. Reprinted by permission.

"Rosetta," words and music by Earl Hines and Henri Wood, © 1933, 1935 (renewed) Morley Music Co. All rights reserved.

"Straighten Up and Fly Right," by Nat Cole, © 1944 (renewed) EMI Mills. Used by permission.

"Sweet Loraine," by Cliff Burwell and Mitch Paris, © EMI Mills. Used by permission.

The employees of G.K. Hall hope you have enjoyed this Large Print book. All our Large Print titles are designed for easy reading, and all our books are made to last. Other G.K. Hall books are available at your library, through selected bookstores, or directly from us.

For information about titles, please call:

(800) 223-2336

To share your comments, please write:

Publisher
G.K. Hall & Co.
P.O. Box 159
Thorndike, ME 04986

MHc   SP
 6   9
 26   25
 00   60

Quadratic Formula

If $ax^2 + bx + c = 0$, where $a \neq 0$, then

$$x = \frac{-b \pm \sqrt{b^2 - 4ac}}{2a}$$

Straight Lines

$$m = \frac{y_2 - y_1}{x_2 - x_1} \quad \text{(slope formula)}$$

$$y - y_1 = m(x - x_1) \quad \text{(point-slope form)}$$

$$y = mx + b \quad \text{(slope-intercept form)}$$

$$x = \text{constant} \quad \text{(vertical line)}$$

$$y = \text{constant} \quad \text{(horizontal line)}$$

Logarithms

$$\log_b x = y \text{ where } x = b^y$$

$$\log_b (mn) = \log_b m + \log_b n$$

$$\log_b \frac{m}{n} = \log_b m - \log_b n$$

$$\log_b m^n = n \log_b m$$

$$\log_b N = \frac{\log_a N}{\log_a b}$$

Variation

$$y = kx^n \quad \text{(direct variation)}$$

$$y = \frac{k}{x^n} \quad \text{(inverse variation)}$$

Binomial Theorem

$$(a + b)^n = a^n + \frac{n}{1!} a^{n-1} b + \frac{n(n-1)}{2!} a^{n-2} b^2$$

$$+ \frac{n(n-1)(n-2)}{3!} a^{n-3} b^3 + \cdots + b^n$$

Geometric Formulas

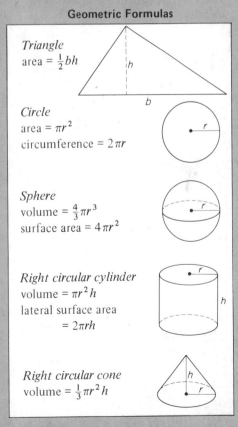

Triangle
area $= \frac{1}{2} bh$

Circle
area $= \pi r^2$
circumference $= 2\pi r$

Sphere
volume $= \frac{4}{3} \pi r^3$
surface area $= 4\pi r^2$

Right circular cylinder
volume $= \pi r^2 h$
lateral surface area
$\quad = 2\pi rh$

Right circular cone
volume $= \frac{1}{3} \pi r^2 h$

Greek Alphabet

alpha	A	α		nu	N	ν
beta	B	β		xi	Ξ	ξ
gamma	Γ	γ		omicron	O	o
delta	Δ	δ		pi	Π	π
epsilon	E	ϵ		rho	P	ρ
zeta	Z	ζ		sigma	Σ	σ
eta	H	η		tau	T	τ
theta	Θ	θ		upsilon	Υ	υ
iota	I	ι		phi	Φ	ϕ, φ
kappa	K	κ		chi	X	χ
lambda	Λ	λ		psi	Ψ	ψ
mu	M	μ		omega	Ω	ω

essentials
of technical
mathematics

**PRENTICE-HALL SERIES
IN TECHNICAL MATHEMATICS**

Frank L. Juszli, Editor

SECOND EDITION

essentials of technical mathematics

RICHARD S. PAUL

Department of Mathematics
The Pennsylvania State University

M. LEONARD SHAEVEL

Department of Physics
The Pennsylvania State University

Prentice-Hall, Inc., Englewood Cliffs, New Jersey 07632

Library of Congress Cataloging in Publication Data

PAUL, RICHARD S. (date)
   Essentials of technical mathematics.

   Includes index.
   1. Mathematics—1961—   . I. Shaevel,
M. Leonard. II. Title.
QA39.2.P39 1982   512′.1   81-10597
ISBN 0-13-288050-4   AACR2

Printed in the United States of America

10   9

Editorial/production supervision
and interior design by Ellen W. Caughey
Cover art: "Squared Rectangle and Euler Line," a painting by Crockett Johnson
(Smithsonian Institution Photo No. 80-3241)
Cover design by Maureen Olsen
Manufacturing buyer: Gordon Osbourne

ISBN 0-13-288050-4

Prentice-Hall International, Inc., *London*
Prentice-Hall of Australia Pty. Limited, *Sydney*
Prentice-Hall of Canada, Ltd., *Toronto*
Prentice-Hall of India Private Limited, *New Delhi*
Prentice-Hall of Japan, Inc., *Tokyo*
Prentice-Hall of Southeast Asia Pte. Ltd., *Singapore*
Whitehall Books Limited, *Wellington, New Zealand*

contents

2   introduction to exponents and radicals

49

3   fundamental operations with algebraic expressions

73

4   fractions

110

5   equations

142

6   functions, graphs, and straight lines

178

7 trigonometric functions and vectors
222

8 systems of equations
283

9 exponents and radicals
315

14 trigonometric graphs and polar coordinates

461

15 trigonometric formulas and equations

501

16 oblique triangles and applications
of angular measurement

529

17 inequalities

547

preface

The second edition of *Essentials of Technical Mathematics* is an outgrowth of extensive class testing and numerous comments and suggestions from users of the first edition. The text is designed to meet the mathematical needs of students in the various engineering technologies. Special care has been taken to retain the character and spirit of the first edition. Throughout this edition we continue to include not only the "how," but also the "why."

The developments in the text present a balance between mathematical concepts, manipulations, and applications. Our aim has been to make the material understandable and meaningful and the language and writing style appropriate to students having limited mathematical backgrounds.

In this edition, the exposition has been improved and reorganized where needed. There are over 1000 examples, which are given in step-by-step detail. These include a large increase in the number of illustrative technical applications. These applications show the student many of the relevant ways in which the mathematics being studied is applied to the engineering technologies. However, the text is virtually self-contained in that *it assumes no prior exposure to the concepts on which the applications are based.* We point out that these applications simply pose a technical framework for the mathematics problems. We are not concerned with teaching the nonmathematical aspects of the applications.

The exercise sets, which have been greatly expanded, now contain over 5000 problems. They include a large number of drill problems that the student should be able to do rather easily. This will allow students to gain confidence, develop manipulative skills, and understand fully the basic concepts being studied.

New topics in this edition include evaluating formulas, a comprehensive treatment of SI units, properties of determinants, simple harmonic motion, polar coordinates, and linear interpolation in a technical context. Appendix A covers the most important uses of the scientific calculator in technical mathematics and includes exercises (with answers) for practice.

Chapter 0 covers selected arithmetic and geometric concepts. Although it is not necessarily intended to be part of a formal course, it can provide a needed review for many students. With the exception of Chapter 0, each chapter contains a review section. This consists of programmed-type questions that relate to the mathematical concepts of the chapter as well as numerous review problems.

Answers to odd-numbered problems appear at the end of the text. An extensive solutions manual is available upon adoption from the publisher. It includes answers to all problems as well as detailed solutions to a great many of them, including all verbal problems and all problems involving a technical application. The manual should be an aid for teachers in planning assignments.

We express our appreciation to the following colleagues who contributed comments and suggestions that were invaluable in developing the manuscript:

Harry C. Adams (Gulf Coast Community College), Norman J. Finizio (University of Rhode Island), Bruce H. Hoelter (Somerset County College), George E. Lyons (Washington Technical College), N. Maulding (Somerset County College), Laurence C. Miller (Gulf Coast Community College), David Petrie (Cypress College), Laurence Rubin (Nashville State Technical Institute), Don Sibrel (Nashville State Technical Institute), Ann Tiber (Washington Technical College), John S. Vonhold (Genesee Community College), and Arthur Ward (Nashville State Technical Institute).

We especially wish to express our most grateful appreciation to George E. Lyons (Washington Technical College) and Donald Reichman (Mercer County Community College) who reviewed the manuscript and provided criticisms and suggestions for its improvement.

Finally, a special word of thanks is due to Ellen Caughey, our production editor, for her efficiency, competent assistance, and enthusiastic cooperation.

RICHARD S. PAUL

M. LEONARD SHAEVEL

essentials
of technical
mathematics

0

preliminary topics

0-1 Introduction

This chapter gives a brief review of selected topics in arithmetic and geometry. Even though you have probably seen much of this material before, an immediate second exposure to these topics may be beneficial. You should devote whatever time is necessary to those topics in which you need review.

0-2 Operations with Whole Numbers

Whole numbers are numbers used in counting, such as 0, 1, 2, 13, 44, and 610. Whole numbers are either **even** or **odd,** depending, respectively, on whether or not they are divisible by 2. For example, 2, 10, and 64 are even, and 1, 3, and 29 are odd.

Whole numbers are represented by combinations of the ten **digits** 0, 1, 2, 3, 4, 5, 6, 7, 8, and 9. An analysis of the numeral 234 shows that the digit 4 occupies the units place and represents four 1's (4), the digit 3 occupies the tens place and represents three groups of 10 (30), and the digit 2 occupies the hundreds place and represents two groups of 100 (200). Note that the value of each group is ten times that of the group to its immediate right. This system of writing numbers is called the **decimal system.**

We shall assume that you are totally familiar with the fundamental operations of addition, subtraction, multiplication, and division of whole numbers, and so we

1

dispense with any further discussion of these operations. It is appropriate, however, to state four important rules that apply to all types of numbers. We give two rules first:

---
1.   Numbers can be added in any order.

2.   Numbers can be multiplied in any order.

For example, by Rule 1 we have $2 + 3 + 4 = 4 + 2 + 3 = 4 + 3 + 2 = 9$. We can show a multiplication such as 3 times 2 by 3×2, $3 \cdot 2$, $(3)(2)$, $(3)2$, and $3(2)$. Thus, by Rule 2, $(3)(2)(4) = (2)(3)(4) = (4)(3)(2) = 24$. Because the numbers 2, 3, and 4 give 24 when multiplied together, 2, 3, and 4 are called **factors** of 24, and 24 is called the **product** of 2, 3, and 4. The next rules are for subtraction and division:

---
3.   Subtraction must be performed in the given order.

4.   Division must be performed in the given order.

For example, $5 - 2$ is *not* the same as $2 - 5$, and $6 \div 3$ is *not* the same as $3 \div 6$. In the statement $6 \div 3 = 2$, 6 is called the **dividend,** 3 is the **divisor,** and 2 is the **quotient.**

In computations involving more than one operation, first perform any multiplications and divisions. Then do any additions and subtractions, as Example 1 shows.

example 1

---

a. $6 + (6)(2) = 6 + 12 = 18$.

b. $12 - (2)(2) = 12 - 4 = 8$.

c. $(12)(2) + 6 \div 3 = 24 + 2 = 26$.

When any operations are inside parentheses, do those first, as Example 2 shows.

example 2

---

a. $12 + (2 + 3) - (4)(6 - 3)$

$= 12 + 5 - (4)(3) = 12 + 5 - 12$

$= 17 - 12 = 5$.

b. $16 + (12 \div 3)(4 - 3)$

   $= 16 + (4)(1) = 16 + 4$

   $= 20.$

c. $(2 - 2)(5) = (0)(5) = 0.$ *Remember*: Zero times any number is zero.

Exercise 0-2

In Problems 1–32, compute the numbers.

1. $5 + (2)(8).$ **2.** $17 - (3)(4).$ **3.** $(2)(4) - 7.$

4. $(3)(2) - (2)(2).$ **5.** $(8 - 3)(4).$ **6.** $2(5 + 1).$

7. $15 - 3(4).$ **8.** $(6 - 4) + 3.$ **9.** $3(4 + 6).$

10. $(6 - 6)8.$ **11.** $(7 - 2)(3 + 1).$ **12.** $(4 + 5)(2 - 0).$

13. $0(8 - 5).$ **14.** $(3 - 3)(4 - 4).$ **15.** $(6 - 1) - (10 - 7).$

16. $(6 + 7) - (8 - 4).$ **17.** $(8 \div 4) + 3.$ **18.** $(7 - 2)(3) + 2(3 + 1).$

19. $10 + (9 \div 3).$ **20.** $(3 \div 3) + (2)(3 - 1).$

21. $18 \div (6 + 3).$ **22.** $55 \div (17 - 6).$

23. $(6 + 2 - 3) \div (7 - 2).$ **24.** $(8 - 4)(7 - 3) + (16 \div 4).$

25. $13 - 2(5 - 2) + (2 + 3).$ **26.** $8 + (15 \div 3)(3 - 1).$

27. $(36 \div 6)(6 \div 2) - 6.$ **28.** $16 + (12 \div 3)(4 - 3).$

29. $4(4 - 1) - 5(4 \div 2) + 9.$ **30.** $2(3 + 4) + 5 - (2 - 1)(2 + 1).$

31. $3(6 \div 3) + 2 - 4(2 \div 2).$ **32.** $(4 + 3)(3) + 5(5 - 2)(2 - 2).$

33. In $8 \div 2 = 4$, what is the dividend? What is the divisor?

34. In $16 \div 8 = 2$, what is the quotient?

35. In $30 \div (3 + 2) = 6$, what is the divisor?

36. The product of three factors is 30. Two of the factors are 2 and 3. What is the other factor?

37. The product of five factors is 32. Three of the factors are each 2. What is the *product* of the other factors?

38. The numbers 2 and 3 are factors of 6. Find two other whole numbers that are also factors of 6.

39. The tens and units digits of the number 862 are reversed and the new number is subtracted from 862. What is the result?

40. What digit must be changed in 6257 to make it an even number?

41. In the number 62,417, what place does the 6 occupy?

0-3   Common Fractions

The division $6 \div 3$ can be written as the fraction $\frac{6}{3}$, where 6 is the **numerator** and 3 is the **denominator.** The fraction is also called the **quotient** of 6 divided by 3, or simply the quotient $\frac{6}{3}$. You may recall that $\frac{6}{3}$ means the number which when multiplied by 3 gives 6. Because $(3)(2) = 6$, then $\frac{6}{3} = 2$.

Let us quickly do away with one point of confusion—*division by zero is not defined.* For example, $\frac{1}{0}$ means a number which when multiplied by 0 gives 1. But there is no such number, since any number times 0 is 0. Thus $\frac{1}{0}$ has no meaning. Sometimes students write $\frac{1}{0} = 0$, which is *false.* However, it *is* true that $\frac{0}{1} = 0$, because $\frac{0}{1}$ is the number which when multiplied by 1 gives 0: That number is 0. Similarly, $\frac{0}{5} = 0$ because $(5)(0) = 0$.

Fractions are of two types, depending on the relationship between the numerator and denominator. If the numerator is *less* than the denominator, as in $\frac{3}{8}$, the fraction is called a **proper fraction** and its value is less than 1. If the numerator is *equal to or greater than* the denominator, as in $\frac{3}{3}$ and $\frac{3}{2}$, the fraction has a value of at least 1 and is called an **improper fraction.**

Any improper fraction can be written either as a whole number or as the sum of a whole number and a proper fraction. This last form is called a **mixed number.** For example, because $23 \div 6$ gives 3 with a remainder of 5, then

$$\frac{23}{6} = 3 + \frac{5}{6} = 3\frac{5}{6}.$$

The improper fraction $\frac{23}{6}$ has the same value as the mixed number $3\frac{5}{6}$, which means 3 *plus* $\frac{5}{6}$.

example 1

a. $\dfrac{16}{13} = 1 + \dfrac{3}{13} = 1\dfrac{3}{13}.$

b. $\dfrac{14}{3} = 4 + \dfrac{2}{3} = 4\dfrac{2}{3}.$

c. $\dfrac{27}{4} = 6 + \dfrac{3}{4} = 6\dfrac{3}{4}.$

Fractions that have the same value (or represent the same number) are called **equivalent fractions.** The basic rule used in obtaining equivalent fractions is called the **fundamental principle of fractions:**

> Multiplying or dividing the numerator and denominator of a fraction by the same number, except zero, results in a fraction that is equivalent to the original fraction.

For example,

$$\frac{2}{5} = \frac{(2)(4)}{(5)(4)} = \frac{8}{20} \quad \text{and} \quad \frac{14}{21} = \frac{14 \div 7}{21 \div 7} = \frac{2}{3}.$$

By using the fundamental principle, we can write a fraction as an equivalent fraction with a specified numerator or denominator. For example, suppose we write $\frac{5}{8}$ as an equivalent fraction with denominator 24. Because the original denominator 8 must be multiplied by 3, so must the numerator:

$$\frac{5}{8} = \frac{(5)(3)}{(8)(3)} = \frac{15}{24}.$$

example 2

a. Write $\frac{3}{8}$ as an equivalent fraction with denominator 32.

$$\frac{3}{8} = \frac{(3)(4)}{(8)(4)} = \frac{12}{32}.$$

b. Write 12 as an equivalent fraction with denominator 2.

$$12 = \frac{12}{1} = \frac{(12)(2)}{(1)(2)} = \frac{24}{2}.$$

c. Write $\frac{12}{20}$ as an equivalent fraction with numerator 3.

$$\frac{12}{20} = \frac{12 \div 4}{20 \div 4} = \frac{3}{5}.$$

A fraction is in **lowest terms,** or is (completely) **reduced,** when its numerator and denominator have no whole-number factors in common except 1. For example, $\frac{18}{12}$ is not in lowest terms because 18 and 12 have a common factor of 6:

$$18 = (6)(3) \quad \text{and} \quad 12 = (6)(2).$$

To reduce $\frac{18}{12}$, we use the fundamental principle by dividing the numerator and denominator by the common factor 6.

$$\frac{18}{12} = \frac{\frac{18}{6}}{\frac{12}{6}} = \frac{3}{2}.$$

Because 3 and 2 have no factors in common except 1, then $\frac{3}{2}$ is the reduced form of $\frac{18}{12}$. More simply, to reduce $\frac{18}{12}$ we usually write

$$\frac{\overset{3}{\cancel{18}}}{\underset{2}{\cancel{12}}} = \frac{3}{2},$$

where the slashes indicate the division by a common factor. Sometimes this division is called **cancellation.** You can think of this problem in another way by showing the common factor 6:

$$\frac{18}{12} = \frac{\overset{1}{\cancel{(6)}}(3)}{\underset{1}{\cancel{(6)}}(2)} = \frac{3}{2}.$$

The fraction $\frac{18}{12}$ can also be reduced by repeated cancellation. Watch how we cancel a factor of 2 and then 3:

$$\frac{\overset{9}{\cancel{18}}}{\underset{6}{\cancel{12}}} = \frac{\overset{3}{\cancel{9}}}{\underset{2}{\cancel{6}}} = \frac{3}{2}.$$

In the next example we reduce a more complicated fraction in a similar manner.

example 3

$$\frac{(12)(6)\overset{1}{\cancel{(3)}}(14)}{(22)(14)\underset{7}{\cancel{(21)}}(18)} = \frac{(12)(6)\overset{2}{\cancel{(14)}}}{(22)(14)\underset{1}{\cancel{(7)}}(18)} = \frac{(12)(6)\overset{1}{\cancel{(2)}}}{\underset{11}{\cancel{(22)}}(14)(18)}$$

$$= \frac{(12)\overset{1}{\cancel{(6)}}}{(11)(14)\underset{3}{\cancel{(18)}}} = \frac{\overset{4}{\cancel{(12)}}}{(11)(14)\underset{1}{\cancel{(3)}}}$$

$$= \frac{\overset{2}{\cancel{(4)}}}{(11)\underset{7}{\cancel{(14)}}} = \frac{2}{77}.$$

This can be written more compactly as

$$\frac{\overset{\overset{2}{\cancel{4}}}{\cancel{(12)}}\overset{1}{\cancel{(6)}}\overset{1}{\cancel{(3)}}\overset{\overset{1}{\cancel{2}}}{\cancel{(14)}}}{\underset{11}{\cancel{(22)}}\underset{7}{\cancel{(14)}}\underset{\underset{1}{7}}{\cancel{(21)}}\underset{\underset{1}{\cancel{3}}}{\cancel{(18)}}} = \frac{2}{77}.$$

In Example 3, we used cancelling of common factors to reduce a fraction in which the numerator and denominator were written as a *product* of numbers. In a fraction where the numerator or the denominator is a *sum* or *difference* of numbers, this type of cancellation *cannot* be done. For example, $\frac{6}{2}$, which is 3, can be written $(4 + 2)/2$. But

$$\frac{4 + \overset{1}{\cancel{2}}}{\underset{1}{\cancel{2}}} = \frac{5}{1} \qquad \text{is } false.$$

Exercise 0-3

1. Fill in the blank: $\frac{24}{8}$ is the number which when multiplied by ____ gives 24.
2. In the fraction $\frac{6}{11}$, what is the numerator?
3. In the fraction $\frac{5}{6}$, what is the denominator?
4. Which of the following are proper fractions?

$$\frac{3}{5}, \quad \frac{8}{7}, \quad \frac{2}{9}, \quad \frac{7}{11}, \quad \frac{8}{8}.$$

5. Which of the following are improper fractions?

$$\frac{8}{7}, \quad \frac{12}{13}, \quad \frac{7}{7}, \quad \frac{8}{1}.$$

6. Which of the following fractions are in lowest terms?

$$\frac{9}{27}, \quad \frac{4}{7}, \quad \frac{13}{3}, \quad \frac{14}{21}.$$

In Problems **7–14,** *write the fractions as mixed numbers.*

7. $\frac{23}{3}$.　　　　**8.** $\frac{37}{6}$.　　　　**9.** $\frac{18}{5}$.　　　　**10.** $\frac{74}{9}$.

11. $\frac{3}{2}$.　　　　**12.** $\frac{251}{24}$.　　　　**13.** $\frac{13}{4}$.　　　　**14.** $\frac{5003}{1000}$.

15. Write $\frac{2}{3}$ as an equivalent fraction with denominator 18.

16. Write $\frac{3}{7}$ as an equivalent fraction with numerator 21.

In Problems **17–28,** *fill in the missing numbers.*

17. $\frac{4}{5} = \frac{?}{25}$.　　　　**18.** $\frac{15}{24} = \frac{5}{?}$.　　　　**19.** $\frac{2}{3} = \frac{22}{?}$.

20. $\frac{12}{32} = \frac{?}{8}$.　　　　**21.** $\frac{8}{24} = \frac{1}{?}$.　　　　**22.** $\frac{100}{5} = \frac{?}{1}$.

23. $\frac{18}{12} = \frac{?}{2}$.　　　　**24.** $7 = \frac{?}{3}$.　　　　**25.** $5 = \frac{?}{3}$.

26. $3 = \frac{?}{12}$.　　　　**27.** $\frac{1}{7} = \frac{7}{?}$.　　　　**28.** $\frac{6}{6} = \frac{?}{12}$.

In Problems **29–50,** *completely reduce the fractions.*

29. $\frac{28}{12}$.　　　　**30.** $\frac{210}{26}$.　　　　**31.** $\frac{60}{45}$.

32. $\frac{18}{99}$.　　　　**33.** $\frac{24}{30}$.　　　　**34.** $\frac{275}{1000}$.

35. $\frac{66}{144}$.　　　　**36.** $\frac{7+9}{2}$.　　　　**37.** $\frac{4}{8+8}$.

38. $\frac{(10)(3)}{5}$.　　　　**39.** $\frac{6}{(12)(5)}$.　　　　**40.** $\frac{(9)(10)}{(6)(8)}$.

41. $\frac{(3)(16)}{(4)(9)}$.　　　　**42.** $\frac{(4)(14)}{(21)(2)}$.　　　　**43.** $\frac{(21)(15)}{(5)(14)}$.

44. $\frac{(4)(9)(6)}{(6)(18)}$.　　　　**45.** $\frac{(8)(12)(15)}{(3)(4)(6)}$.　　　　**46.** $\frac{(100)(12)(5)}{(6)(15)(25)}$.

47. $\frac{(12)(6)(3)(14)}{(22)(14)(21)(18)}$.　　　　**48.** $\frac{(4)(12)(10)(7)}{(14)(8)(5)(6)}$.

49. $\frac{(81)(5)(3)(7)}{(27)(18)(4)}$.　　　　**50.** $\frac{(24)(50)(3)}{(75)(6)(16)(5)}$.

The sum (or difference) of two fractions with the *same* denominator is a fraction which has the same (common) denominator and a numerator which is the sum (or difference) of the numerators of the original fractions.

example 1

a. $\dfrac{2}{3} + \dfrac{5}{3} = \dfrac{2+5}{3} = \dfrac{7}{3}$.

b. $\dfrac{8}{9} - \dfrac{6}{9} = \dfrac{8-6}{9} = \dfrac{2}{9}$.

c. $\dfrac{7}{18} + \dfrac{3}{18} - \dfrac{5}{18} = \dfrac{7+3-5}{18} = \dfrac{5}{18}$.

d. $\dfrac{12}{27} - \dfrac{6}{27} + \dfrac{4}{27} - \dfrac{1}{27} = \dfrac{12-6+4-1}{27} = \dfrac{9}{27} = \dfrac{1}{3}$. *Always reduce your answer, if possible.*

We point out that when adding fractions, we *do not* add the denominators. For example,

$$\frac{1}{2} + \frac{1}{2} = \frac{1+1}{2+2} \text{ is } false:$$

$$\frac{1}{2} + \frac{1}{2} = \frac{1+1}{2} = \frac{2}{2} = 1, \quad \text{but} \quad \frac{1+1}{2+2} = \frac{2}{4} = \frac{1}{2}.$$

To add or subtract fractions with denominators that are not the same, the fractions must first be rewritten as equivalent fractions that *do* have a common denominator. The simplest common denominator to use is the least whole number such that each of the given denominators is a factor of it. This is called the **least common denominator,** or L.C.D., of the fractions. For example, the denominators of $\frac{1}{3}$, $\frac{5}{8}$, and $\frac{7}{12}$ are 3, 8, and 12. These denominators divide 24, and 24 is the *least* such number that has 3, 8, and 12 as factors. Thus 24 is the L.C.D.

Basically, finding an L.C.D. involves using *prime numbers*. A **prime number** is a whole number greater than 1 that has only two whole-number factors: itself and 1. Thus 2, 3, 5, 7, 11, 13, and 17 are prime numbers. However, 15 is *not* a prime, because 15 has 3 and 5, as well as 15 and 1, as factors. In Example 2 we illustrate the following fact:

> Every whole number greater than 1 can be written as a product of primes.

example 2

Write each number as a product of primes.

a. $20 = (2)(10) = (2)(2)(5)$.   (Because $10 = (2)(5)$.)

b. $35 = (5)(7)$.

c. $42 = (2)(21) = (2)(3)(7)$.

d. $24 = (2)(12) = (2)(2)(6) = (2)(2)(2)(3)$.

How to Find an L.C.D.

In general, to find the L.C.D. of a group of fractions, first write each denominator as a product of prime factors. Next, from the different prime factors that occur, form a product in which the number of times each different prime appears is the greatest number of times that it appears in any *single* denominator. This product is the L.C.D. For example, to determine the L.C.D. of $\frac{1}{3}$, $\frac{5}{12}$, and $\frac{7}{10}$, we first write each denominator as a product of primes:

$$3 = 3,$$
$$12 = (2)(6) = (2)(2)(3),$$
$$10 = (5)(2).$$

There are three different prime factors involved: 3, 2, and 5. The greatest number of times that 3 appears in any *single* denominator is once. For 2, it is twice. For 5, it is once. Thus

$$\text{L.C.D.} = (3)(2)(2)(5) = 60.$$

Similarly, the L.C.D. of $\frac{1}{6}$, $\frac{2}{9}$, and $\frac{5}{12}$ is determined as follows:

$$6 = (3)(2),$$
$$9 = (3)(3),$$
$$12 = (2)(2)(3).$$

There are two different prime factors involved: 3 and 2. In any single denominator, the most often that 3 occurs is twice. The most often that 2 occurs is also twice. Thus

$$\text{L.C.D.} = (3)(3)(2)(2) = 36.$$

To show how to add (or subtract) fractions with different denominators, we shall find

$$\frac{1}{6} + \frac{2}{9} + \frac{5}{12}.$$

First we find the L.C.D. As shown before, it is 36. Next we write each fraction as an equivalent fraction with a denominator of 36.

$$\frac{1}{6} = \frac{(1)(6)}{(6)(6)} = \frac{6}{36}, \qquad \frac{2}{9} = \frac{(2)(4)}{(9)(4)} = \frac{8}{36}, \qquad \frac{5}{12} = \frac{(5)(3)}{(12)(3)} = \frac{15}{36}.$$

Now that all denominators are the same, we add the fractions directly as in Example 1.

$$\frac{1}{6} + \frac{2}{9} + \frac{5}{12} = \frac{6}{36} + \frac{8}{36} + \frac{15}{36} = \frac{6 + 8 + 15}{36} = \frac{29}{36}.$$

example 3

Find $\frac{2}{3} + \frac{7}{8} + \frac{3}{16}$.

Because $3 = 3$, $8 = (2)(2)(2)$, and $16 = (2)(2)(2)(2)$, then

$$\text{L.C.D.} = (3)(2)(2)(2)(2) = 48.$$

Thus

$$\frac{2}{3} + \frac{7}{8} + \frac{3}{16} = \frac{(2)(16)}{(3)(16)} + \frac{(7)(6)}{(8)(6)} + \frac{(3)(3)}{(16)(3)}$$

$$= \frac{32}{48} + \frac{42}{48} + \frac{9}{48} = \frac{32 + 42 + 9}{48} = \frac{83}{48}.$$

example 4

Perform the operations and simplify.

a. $\dfrac{3}{5} - \dfrac{1}{2} + \dfrac{1}{4} = \dfrac{12}{20} - \dfrac{10}{20} + \dfrac{5}{20} = \dfrac{12 - 10 + 5}{20} = \dfrac{7}{20}.$

b. $2 + \dfrac{1}{6} + \dfrac{1}{3} = \dfrac{2}{1} + \dfrac{1}{6} + \dfrac{1}{3} = \dfrac{12}{6} + \dfrac{1}{6} + \dfrac{2}{6} = \dfrac{15}{6} = \dfrac{5}{2}.$

Just as we can write an improper fraction as a mixed number, we can also write a mixed number as an improper fraction. To do this, we write the whole-number part as a fraction and add it to the fractional part.

example 5

a. $3\dfrac{3}{4} = 3 + \dfrac{3}{4} = \dfrac{3}{1} + \dfrac{3}{4} = \dfrac{12}{4} + \dfrac{3}{4} = \dfrac{15}{4}.$

b. $5\dfrac{2}{7} = \dfrac{5}{1} + \dfrac{2}{7} = \dfrac{35}{7} + \dfrac{2}{7} = \dfrac{37}{7}.$

To add mixed numbers, we can add the whole-number parts first and treat the fractional parts as before. For example,

$$1\frac{3}{4} + 2\frac{2}{3} = (1 + 2) + \left(\frac{3}{4} + \frac{2}{3}\right)$$

$$= 3 + \left(\frac{9}{12} + \frac{8}{12}\right)$$

$$= 3 + \frac{17}{12} = 3 + 1\frac{5}{12}$$

$$= 4\frac{5}{12}.$$

To subtract one mixed number from another, a slight modification in the above procedure may be necessary, as shown in the following example:

$$6\frac{1}{3} - 2\frac{2}{3}.$$

We cannot subtract $\frac{2}{3}$ from $\frac{1}{3}$ (without introducing negative numbers). However, we can express $6\frac{1}{3}$ as $5 + 1 + \frac{1}{3} = 5 + \frac{3}{3} + \frac{1}{3} = 5\frac{4}{3}$. Thus we can rewrite the problem as

$$6\frac{1}{3} - 2\frac{2}{3} = 5\frac{4}{3} - 2\frac{2}{3} = 3\frac{2}{3}.$$

Alternatively, we can express the given fractions as improper fractions and subtract. (This method also applies to addition.)

$$6\frac{1}{3} - 2\frac{2}{3} = \frac{19}{3} - \frac{8}{3} = \frac{11}{3} = 3\frac{2}{3}.$$

example 6

a. $3\frac{3}{4} + 4\frac{2}{3} = 3\frac{9}{12} + 4\frac{8}{12} = 7\frac{17}{12} = 8\frac{5}{12}.$

b. $4\frac{3}{4} - 2\frac{7}{8} = 4\frac{6}{8} - 2\frac{7}{8} = 3\frac{14}{8} - 2\frac{7}{8} = 1\frac{7}{8}.$

Exercise 0-4

In Problems 1–8, perform the operations and simplify.

1. $\dfrac{7}{8} + \dfrac{17}{8}.$

2. $\dfrac{8}{9} - \dfrac{6}{9}.$

3. $\dfrac{7}{12} - \dfrac{5}{12}.$

4. $\dfrac{7}{18} + \dfrac{3}{18} - \dfrac{5}{18}.$

5. $\dfrac{5}{13} + \dfrac{11}{13} - \dfrac{4}{13}.$

6. $\dfrac{12}{27} - \dfrac{6}{27} + \dfrac{4}{27} - \dfrac{1}{27}.$

7. $\dfrac{2}{8 + 8}.$

8. $\dfrac{6 + 6}{3 + 3}.$

In Problems 9–16, find the L.C.D. of the fractions.

9. $\dfrac{5}{6}, \dfrac{2}{9}$.

10. $\dfrac{4}{21}, \dfrac{3}{14}$.

11. $\dfrac{7}{4}, \dfrac{3}{2}, \dfrac{1}{5}$.

12. $\dfrac{1}{15}, \dfrac{3}{8}, \dfrac{7}{10}$.

13. $\dfrac{1}{3}, \dfrac{7}{18}, \dfrac{5}{12}$.

14. $\dfrac{5}{6}, \dfrac{9}{20}, \dfrac{2}{15}$.

15. $\dfrac{7}{30}, \dfrac{5}{12}, \dfrac{11}{20}$.

16. $\dfrac{3}{20}, \dfrac{14}{25}, \dfrac{27}{50}$.

In Problems 17–20, write the mixed numbers as fractions.

17. $4\dfrac{3}{5}$.

18. $3\dfrac{2}{3}$.

19. $7\dfrac{2}{7}$.

20. $10\dfrac{1}{10}$.

In Problems 21–38, perform the operations and simplify.

21. $\dfrac{3}{4} + \dfrac{5}{6}$.

22. $\dfrac{3}{5} + \dfrac{2}{3}$.

23. $\dfrac{3}{8} - \dfrac{5}{14}$.

24. $\dfrac{5}{6} - \dfrac{2}{21}$.

25. $\dfrac{1}{3} + \dfrac{8}{9} + \dfrac{5}{12}$.

26. $\dfrac{2}{3} + \dfrac{3}{4} + \dfrac{5}{8}$.

27. $\dfrac{7}{4} - \dfrac{3}{2} + \dfrac{1}{5}$.

28. $\dfrac{1}{5} + \dfrac{1}{8} + \dfrac{1}{12}$.

29. $\dfrac{5}{6} + \dfrac{2}{15} - \dfrac{1}{3}$.

30. $\dfrac{7}{12} - \dfrac{5}{18} + \dfrac{3}{8}$.

31. $7\dfrac{2}{3} - 4\dfrac{3}{4}$.

32. $2\dfrac{1}{12} - 1\dfrac{7}{8}$.

33. $3\dfrac{2}{3} + 4\dfrac{1}{8} - 6\dfrac{1}{4}$.

34. $4\dfrac{2}{7} - 2\dfrac{2}{5} + 1\dfrac{2}{35}$.

35. $3 - \dfrac{7}{15} + \dfrac{3}{10}$.

36. $2 + \dfrac{3}{8} - \dfrac{1}{6}$.

37. $\dfrac{2}{5} + 2 - \dfrac{3}{8}$.

38. $\dfrac{5}{12} + \dfrac{11}{18} - 1$.

0-5 Multiplication and Division of Fractions

The product of two or more fractions is a fraction with numerator and denominator that are obtained by multiplying the numerators and denominators of the fractions, respectively. For example,

$$\frac{2}{3} \cdot \frac{5}{7} = \frac{(2)(5)}{(3)(7)} = \frac{10}{21}.$$

example 1

a. $\dfrac{3}{5} \cdot \dfrac{8}{4} \cdot \dfrac{2}{9} = \dfrac{(3)(8)(2)}{(5)(4)(9)} = \dfrac{\overset{1}{\cancel{(3)}}\,\overset{2}{\cancel{(8)}}\,(2)}{(5)\,\underset{1}{\cancel{(4)}}\,\underset{3}{\cancel{(9)}}} = \dfrac{4}{15}$.

We could have cancelled immediately, as the following shows:

$$\frac{\overset{1}{\cancel{3}}}{5} \cdot \frac{\overset{2}{\cancel{8}}}{\underset{1}{\cancel{4}}} \cdot \frac{2}{\underset{3}{\cancel{9}}} = \frac{4}{15}.$$

b. $\dfrac{17}{3} \cdot \dfrac{11}{4} \cdot \dfrac{2}{17} = \dfrac{\overset{1}{\cancel{17}}}{3} \cdot \dfrac{11}{\underset{2}{\cancel{4}}} \cdot \dfrac{\overset{1}{\cancel{2}}}{\underset{1}{\cancel{17}}} = \dfrac{11}{6}.$

c. $3\left(\dfrac{1}{2}\right) = \left(\dfrac{3}{1}\right)\left(\dfrac{1}{2}\right) = \dfrac{3}{2}.$

d. $5 \cdot \dfrac{2}{5} = \dfrac{\overset{1}{\cancel{5}}}{1} \cdot \dfrac{2}{\underset{1}{\cancel{5}}} = \dfrac{2}{1} = 2.$

Usually we simply write

$$\cancel{5} \cdot \dfrac{2}{\cancel{5}} = 2.$$

e. $\dfrac{4}{9} \cdot 18 = \dfrac{4}{\underset{1}{\cancel{9}}} \cdot \overset{2}{\cancel{18}} = 8.$

f. $\left(2\dfrac{1}{2}\right)\left(\dfrac{4}{5}\right) = \dfrac{\overset{1}{\cancel{5}}}{\underset{1}{\cancel{2}}} \cdot \dfrac{\overset{2}{\cancel{4}}}{\underset{1}{\cancel{5}}} = \dfrac{2}{1} = 2.$

Note that we first wrote the mixed number $2\frac{1}{2}$ as the improper fraction $\frac{5}{2}$.

Turning to division of fractions, we consider $\frac{2}{3} \div \frac{3}{4}$ or

$$\dfrac{\dfrac{2}{3}}{\dfrac{3}{4}}.$$

If we use the fundamental principle and multiply both $\frac{2}{3}$ and $\frac{3}{4}$ by $\frac{4}{3}$, we obtain

$$\dfrac{\dfrac{2}{3}}{\dfrac{3}{4}} = \dfrac{\dfrac{2}{3} \cdot \dfrac{4}{3}}{\cancel{\dfrac{3}{4}} \cdot \cancel{\dfrac{4}{3}}} = \dfrac{\dfrac{2}{3} \cdot \dfrac{4}{3}}{1} = \dfrac{2}{3} \cdot \dfrac{4}{3} = \dfrac{8}{9}.$$

Notice that to *divide* $\frac{2}{3}$ by $\frac{3}{4}$, we can simply interchange the numerator and denominator of the divisor, $\frac{3}{4}$, and *multiply* $\frac{2}{3}$ by the result (look above at the next-to-last step). That is,

$$\dfrac{2}{3} \div \dfrac{3}{4} = \dfrac{2}{3} \cdot \dfrac{4}{3} = \dfrac{8}{9}.$$

The interchanging of numerator and denominator is called **inverting.** Thus to divide one fraction by another, we *invert the divisor and multiply.*

Division of fractions can be described in terms of the *reciprocal* of a number. The **reciprocal** of a number, *other than zero*, is 1 divided by that number. For example, the reciprocal of 2 is $\frac{1}{2}$ and the reciprocal of $\frac{3}{4}$ is

$$\frac{1}{\frac{3}{4}} = 1 \div \frac{3}{4} = 1 \cdot \frac{4}{3} = \frac{4}{3}.$$

From this last example it is clear that *the reciprocal of a fraction can be found by interchanging its numerator with its denominator.* Thus we can say that $\frac{2}{3}$ divided by $\frac{3}{4}$ is equal to $\frac{2}{3}$ multiplied by the reciprocal of $\frac{3}{4}$, or $\frac{4}{3}$.

example 2

a. $\dfrac{7}{8} \div \dfrac{5}{4} = \dfrac{7}{\overset{}{\underset{2}{\cancel{8}}}} \cdot \dfrac{\overset{1}{\cancel{4}}}{5} = \dfrac{7}{10}.$

b. $\dfrac{\frac{3}{5}}{\frac{9}{10}} = \dfrac{3}{5} \div \dfrac{9}{10} = \dfrac{\overset{1}{\cancel{3}}}{\underset{1}{\cancel{5}}} \cdot \dfrac{\overset{2}{\cancel{10}}}{\underset{3}{\cancel{9}}} = \dfrac{2}{3}.$

c. $\dfrac{\frac{4}{3}}{\frac{3}{2}} = 4 \div \dfrac{3}{2} = 4 \cdot \dfrac{2}{3} = \dfrac{4}{1} \cdot \dfrac{2}{3} = \dfrac{8}{3}.$

d. $\dfrac{\frac{3}{8}}{4} = \dfrac{3}{8} \div 4 = \dfrac{3}{8} \div \dfrac{4}{1} = \dfrac{3}{8} \cdot \dfrac{1}{4} = \dfrac{3}{32}.$

e. $4\dfrac{1}{3} \div \dfrac{5}{3} = \dfrac{13}{\underset{1}{\cancel{3}}} \cdot \dfrac{\overset{1}{\cancel{3}}}{5} = \dfrac{13}{5}.$

example 3

Simplify.

a. $\dfrac{2 - \frac{3}{4}}{3 + \frac{1}{8}}.$

We first separately simplify the numerator $2 - \frac{3}{4}$ and the denominator $3 + \frac{1}{8}$.

$$\dfrac{2 - \frac{3}{4}}{3 + \frac{1}{8}} = \dfrac{\frac{8}{4} - \frac{3}{4}}{\frac{24}{8} + \frac{1}{8}} = \dfrac{\frac{5}{4}}{\frac{25}{8}} = \dfrac{\overset{1}{\cancel{5}}}{\underset{1}{\cancel{4}}} \cdot \dfrac{\overset{2}{\cancel{8}}}{\underset{5}{\cancel{25}}} = \dfrac{2}{5}.$$

b. $\dfrac{\frac{1}{5} + \frac{3}{4}}{\frac{1}{8}} = \dfrac{\frac{4}{20} + \frac{15}{20}}{\frac{1}{8}} = \dfrac{\frac{19}{20}}{\frac{1}{8}} = \dfrac{19}{\underset{5}{\cancel{20}}} \cdot \dfrac{\overset{2}{\cancel{8}}}{1} = \dfrac{38}{5}.$

c. $\dfrac{\left(\frac{3}{5}\right)\left(\frac{4}{7}\right)}{\frac{6}{11}} = \dfrac{\cancel{3}^{1}}{5} \cdot \dfrac{\cancel{4}^{2}}{7} \cdot \dfrac{11}{\cancel{6}_{1}^{2}} = \dfrac{22}{35}.$

Exercise 0-5

*In Problems **1–42**, compute and give answers in reduced form.*

1. $\left(\frac{3}{5}\right)\left(\frac{25}{9}\right).$

2. $\left(\frac{8}{3}\right)\left(\frac{15}{4}\right).$

3. $\frac{14}{15} \cdot \frac{25}{24}.$

4. $\frac{7}{12} \cdot 9.$

5. $\frac{6}{7} \cdot \frac{0}{3}.$

6. $0 \cdot \frac{2}{15}.$

7. $(7)\left(\frac{6}{21}\right).$

8. $\left(\frac{2}{3}\right)(5).$

9. $\frac{1}{9} \cdot \frac{10}{3}.$

10. $\frac{1}{4} \cdot \frac{3}{1}.$

11. $\frac{3}{4} \cdot \frac{8}{5} \cdot \frac{4}{9}.$

12. $\frac{2}{5} \cdot \frac{3}{6} \cdot \frac{7}{5}.$

13. $\frac{3}{5} \cdot \frac{4}{11} \cdot \frac{7}{3} \cdot \frac{25}{4}.$

14. $7 \cdot \frac{8}{5} \cdot \frac{6}{12} \cdot \frac{10}{49}.$

15. $\left(2\frac{2}{5}\right)\left(1\frac{1}{8}\right).$

16. $(8)\left(3\frac{1}{8}\right).$

17. $\left(5\frac{2}{3}\right)\left(2\frac{3}{4}\right)\left(\frac{2}{17}\right).$

18. $\left(2\frac{2}{3}\right)\left(3\frac{1}{2}\right)(4).$

19. $\frac{8}{3} \div \frac{5}{4}.$

20. $\frac{7}{5} \div \frac{3}{10}.$

21. $16 \div \frac{12}{5}.$

22. $0 \div \frac{8}{4}.$

23. $\dfrac{\frac{7}{10}}{\frac{21}{5}}.$

24. $\dfrac{\frac{14}{3}}{\frac{6}{15}}.$

25. $\dfrac{\frac{18}{11}}{\frac{8}{33}}.$

26. $\dfrac{\frac{2}{5}}{\frac{2}{5}}.$

27. $\dfrac{\frac{3}{5}}{2}.$

28. $\dfrac{7}{\frac{1}{4}}.$

29. $\dfrac{4}{\frac{1}{5}}.$

30. $\dfrac{\frac{3}{5}}{6}.$

31. $\dfrac{4}{\frac{8}{9}}.$

32. $\dfrac{1}{\frac{2}{3}}.$

33. $\dfrac{\frac{12}{25} \cdot \frac{15}{7}}{20}.$

34. $\dfrac{\frac{4}{9}}{\frac{2}{3} \cdot 8}.$

35. $\dfrac{6 + \frac{1}{3}}{7}.$

36. $\dfrac{\frac{3}{4} - \frac{3}{16}}{\frac{1}{3}}.$

37. $\dfrac{7 - \frac{2}{3}}{15 - \frac{1}{3}}.$

38. $\dfrac{1 + \frac{1}{2}}{1 - \frac{1}{2}}.$

39. $\dfrac{\frac{8}{5} + \frac{2}{3}}{2 + \frac{4}{7}}.$

40. $\dfrac{\dfrac{6}{7} - \dfrac{6}{7}}{\dfrac{4}{3} + \dfrac{5}{3}}.$

41. $\dfrac{\dfrac{1}{2} - \dfrac{1}{3}}{\dfrac{1}{4} + \dfrac{1}{5}}.$

42. $\dfrac{\left(\dfrac{2}{3}\right)\left(\dfrac{4}{5}\right) + 1}{2 + \dfrac{1}{15}}.$

*In Problems **43–48**, find the reciprocals.*

43. 6.

44. $\dfrac{3}{2}.$

45. $\dfrac{3}{5}.$

46. 1.

47. $\dfrac{1}{9}.$

48. $\dfrac{1}{2}.$

0-6 Operations with Decimals

A **decimal fraction** is a fraction having a denominator that is a power of 10, that is, 10, 100, 1000, and so on. A decimal fraction, such as $\frac{6}{10}$, $\frac{15}{100}$, $\frac{121}{1000}$, or $\frac{62}{1000}$, can be written as an equivalent *decimal* number if we remove the denominator and place a *decimal point* in the numerator. We position the decimal point so that the number of digits to its right is equal to the number of zeros in the denominator of the original fraction. This means that to the right of the decimal point are units of tenths, hundredths, thousandths, and so on. For example, we shall convert the following fractions to decimal form:

$$\tfrac{6}{10} = 0.6 \qquad \text{one digit to the right,}$$

$$\tfrac{15}{100} = 0.15 \qquad \text{two digits to the right,}$$

$$\tfrac{121}{1000} = 0.121 \qquad \text{three digits to the right,}$$

$$\tfrac{1624}{100} = 16.24 \qquad \text{two digits to the right,}$$

$$\tfrac{62}{1000} = 0.062 \qquad \text{three digits to the right.}$$

Because $\frac{6}{10} = 0.6$ and $\frac{6}{10} = \frac{60}{100} = 0.60$, you can see that inserting zeros to the right of the decimal point after the last digit of a decimal does not change its *value*.

To add or subtract decimals, we place each number so that the decimal points are aligned, one under another, and then add or subtract the numbers as if there were no decimal points. In the result, we insert a decimal point that is aligned with the others.

example 1

a. Find $0.123 + 1.624 + 0.0621 + 0.1$.

$$
\begin{array}{r}
0.1230 \\
1.6240 \\
0.0621 \\
0.1000 \\
\hline
1.9091
\end{array}
$$

b. Find 0.726 − 0.0246.

$$\begin{array}{r} 0.7260 \\ -0.0246 \\ \hline 0.7014 \end{array}$$

In multiplying decimals, the decimal point can, as usual, be disregarded as far as the calculation is concerned. After obtaining the product, however, we insert a decimal point in it at such a position so that the number of digits to its right is the sum of the number of digits to the right of the decimal point in each of the numbers to be multiplied. If the number of digits in the product is not sufficient, additional zeros can be inserted to the left of the leftmost digit. For example:

$$\begin{array}{r} 62.4 \\ \times\ 1.23 \\ \hline 1872 \\ 1248 \\ 624 \\ \hline 76.752 \end{array}$$

The factor 62.4 has one digit to the right of the decimal point and the factor 1.23 has two digits to the right. Their sum, 3, is the number of digits to the right of the decimal point in the product. As an additional example, we have:

$$\begin{array}{r} 0.123 \\ \times\ 0.012 \\ \hline 246 \\ 123 \\ \hline 0.001476 \end{array}$$

Here, two zeros were properly inserted in the answer to agree with the requirement that there be six digits to the right of the decimal point. The additional zeros are necessary to determine the correct value of the decimal.

It should not be difficult for you to realize that to multiply any decimal by 10, we need only to move the decimal point one position to the right. Similarly, we move the decimal point two, three, and four places to the right to multiply by 100, 1000, and 10,000, respectively. For example:

$$(12.12)(10) = 121.2,$$

$$(12.12)(100) = 1212. = 1212,$$

$$(12.12)(10,000) = 121,200.$$

To divide a decimal by a power of 10, we move the decimal point to the left the same number of places as there are zeros in the power of ten. For example:

$$\frac{26.24}{10} = 2.624,$$

$$\frac{0.08624}{100} = 0.0008624,$$

$$\frac{1183.421}{1000} = 1.183421.$$

We can write a decimal as a common fraction by replacing the decimal point by the appropriate power of 10 in the denominator. For example,

$$62.5 = \frac{625}{10} = \frac{125}{2},$$

$$2.432 = \frac{2432}{1000} = \frac{304}{125}.$$

When using long division to divide a decimal by a decimal, we first multiply both the numerator and denominator by the power of 10 that will make the denominator a whole number. That is, the decimal points in the numerator and denominator are shifted. For example,

$$\frac{62.314}{72.62} \quad \text{becomes} \quad \frac{6231.4}{7262.}$$

or

$$72.62 \overline{)62.314} \quad \text{becomes} \quad 7262 \overline{)6231.4}.$$

The division is then performed without regard to the decimal point. However, a decimal point must be inserted in the quotient in such a manner that it is aligned with the decimal point in the dividend. For example:

```
              0.8 5 8 0 8
    7 2 6 2)6 2 3 1.4 0 0 0 0
            5 8 0 9 6
            ─────────
              4 2 1 8 0
              3 6 3 1 0
              ─────────
                5 8 7 0 0
                5 8 0 9 6
                ─────────
                  6 0 4 0 0
                  5 8 0 9 6
                  ─────────
                    2 3 0 4
```

In this case the answer is not an exact quotient; to approximate it, we round the quotient by disregarding all digits beyond a desired place. If the first digit to the right of the last retained digit is less than five, the last retained digit remains unchanged. If the first digit to the right of the last retained digit is five or more, the last retained digit is increased by one. For example, rounding 0.85808 to four, three, two, and one decimal places gives 0.8581, 0.858, 0.86, and 0.9, respectively. Similarly, to one decimal place:

$$48.329 \quad \text{becomes} \quad 48.3;$$

$$48.392 \quad \text{becomes} \quad 48.4;$$

$$48.076 \quad \text{becomes} \quad 48.1;$$

$$48.95 \quad \text{becomes} \quad 49.0.$$

The digits used to represent the accuracy of an approximate number, such as a number obtained in a physical measurement, are said to be **significant figures**, or **significant digits.** If an approximate number is not a whole number, the digits beginning with the leftmost nonzero digit and ending with the rightmost digit are significant.

Number	Significant figures
0.023	2
0.00062141	5
0.00010	2
2.43	3
2.430	4
2.04300	6
89.620	5
18.0	3

Unless stated otherwise, if an approximate number is a whole number, the digits beginning with the leftmost nonzero digit and ending with the rightmost nonzero digit are significant.

Number	Significant figures
35,000	2
8,020	3
7,890	3
284,000,000	3
284,001,000	6

In problems involving multiplication or division of approximate numbers, the result usually should not have more significant figures than the number of significant figures in the least accurate number in the problem. To see why this is reasonable, suppose that the length and width of a rectangle are estimated to be 8.32 and 5.27 centimeters, respectively. Here the 8.32 actually signifies a number between 8.315 and 8.325. The 5.27 signifies a number between 5.265 and 5.275. You might be tempted to say that the area of the rectangle is $8.32 \times 5.27 = 43.8464$ square centimeters. However, since the length and width are measured only to an accuracy of three significant figures, we cannot expect to compute the area to an accuracy of six significant figures. Since both numbers have three-figure accuracy, so will our result, which we give as 43.8 square centimeters. If the given numbers were exact, then we could use the value 43.8464.

example 2

Assume all numbers are approximate and compute.

a. $22.3 \times 13.65 = 304$, not 304.4, because the least accurate number has three significant figures.

b. $\dfrac{85.32}{37.624} = 2.268$, not 2.2677.

c. $\dfrac{0.00349}{0.051} = 0.068$, not 0.0684, because the least accurate number has two significant figures.

In addition or subtraction of approximate numbers, the result should be no more accurate than the least precise of the numbers involved. For example, $21.31 + 100.6 = 121.91$ would be rounded off to 121.9 because 100.6 is measured to the nearest tenth and thus is less precise than 21.31, which is measured to the nearest hundredth.

Finally, we observe that sometimes we can express a common fraction as an equivalent decimal by placing a decimal point in the numerator and then dividing. For example:

$$\frac{5}{8} = \frac{5.}{8} = 0.625,$$

$$\frac{43}{64} = 0.671875.$$

Exercise 0-6

*In Problems **1–8**, compute the given sums and differences. Assume all numbers are exact.*

1. $0.021 + 0.1206 + 12.6 + 123.$
2. $1.006 + 1.0 + 0.629 + 0.4.$
3. $71.62 + 0.01 + 0.0006 + 4.1.$
4. $84.0264 + 0.621 + 0.006 + 71.$
5. $0.6241 - 0.5968.$
6. $0.0026 - 0.00094.$
7. $1.006 - 0.99.$
8. $71.6241 - 12.345.$

*In Problems **9–14**, state the number of significant digits in each number.*

9. 0.0023.
10. 8.620.
11. 92,500.
12. 23.00.
13. 14.620.
14. 5000.

In Problems **15–20**, *round each number to three significant figures.*

15. 0.3256.   **16.** 84162.   **17.** 0.0026514.

18. 72.6001.   **19.** 983.7.   **20.** 7.698.

In Problems **21–28**, *compute the given approximate numbers.*

21. (72.64)(0.023).   **22.** (861.4)(0.6241).

23. (0.00601)(1.005)(0.04).   **24.** (0.621)(0.101)(0.8)(1000).

25. 24.530688 ÷ 0.310.   **26.** 246.21 ÷ 8.60.

27. 0.00241 ÷ 1.6.   **28.** 0.624 ÷ 1.002.

In Problems **29–34**, *change each of the given decimals to fractions.*

29. 0.6241.   **30.** 1.0241.   **31.** 0.006.

32. 22.01.   **33.** 0.62415.   **34.** 11.6.

In Problems **35–38**, *change each of the given fractions to decimals.*

35. $\frac{1}{8}$.   **36.** $\frac{63}{64}$.   **37.** $\frac{3}{32}$.   **38.** $\frac{160.7}{2500}$.

0-7 Geometrical Concepts and Formulas

At times we shall refer to basic results of plane geometry, some of which are now listed for you:

1. A **right angle** is an angle of 90°. See Fig. 0-1.

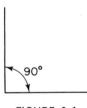

FIGURE 0-1

2. Two lines are **perpendicular** to each other if they intersect at right angles. The lines in Fig. 0-2 are (mutually) perpendicular, as indicated by the right-angle symbol.

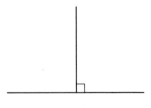

FIGURE 0-2

3. Two angles are **complementary** if their sum is 90°. Two angles are **supplementary** if their sum is 180°. In Fig. 0-3(a), *A* and *B* are complementary angles; in (b), angles *A* and *B* are supplementary.

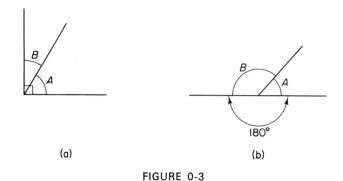

(a)   (b)

FIGURE 0-3

4. The **bisector** of an angle is the line that divides the angle into two equal angles. In Fig. 0-4, line *L* bisects angle *A*.

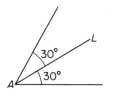

FIGURE 0-4

5. The **perpendicular bisector** of a line segment is the line that is perpendicular to the segment at its midpoint. In Fig. 0-5, *L* is the perpendicular bisector of segment *AB*.

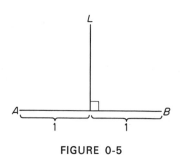

FIGURE 0-5

6. If two parallel lines are cut by a **transversal**, any pair of **alternate interior angles** formed are equal. In Fig. 0-6, angle *A* equals angle *D* and angle *B* equals angle *C*.

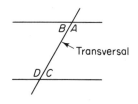

FIGURE 0-6

7. The sum of the angles of a triangle is 180°. See Fig. 0-7.

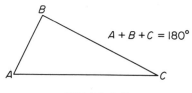

FIGURE 0-7

8. In an **isosceles** triangle (one in which at least two sides are equal), the angles opposite the equal sides are equal. In Fig. 0-8, if $a = b$, then $A = B$.

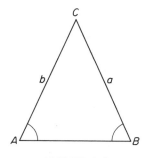

FIGURE 0-8

9. An **equilateral** triangle is one with three equal sides and, therefore, with three equal angles of 60°. The triangle in Fig. 0-9 is equilateral.

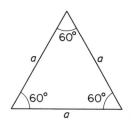

FIGURE 0-9

10. Two triangles are **similar** if their corresponding angles are equal. The triangles in Fig. 0-10 are similar: $A = A'$, $B = B'$, and $C = C'$. If two triangles are

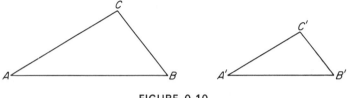

FIGURE 0-10

similar, then the lengths of their corresponding sides are proportional. That is, for example,

$$\frac{\overline{AB}}{\overline{A'B'}} = \frac{\overline{CB}}{\overline{C'B'}},$$

where the *length* of the line segment from A to B is denoted $\overline{AB}$ and similarly for the other sides.

11. Two triangles are **congruent** if they can be made to coincide, that is, if they have equal corresponding angles and sides. Two triangles are congruent if any of the following conditions holds.

   (a) Two sides and the included angle of one are equal, respectively, to two sides and the included angle of the other.
   (b) Two angles and the included side of one are equal, respectively, to two angles and the included side of the other.
   (c) Three sides of one are equal, respectively, to three sides of the other.

12. The **Pythagorean theorem** states that the square of the hypotenuse of a right triangle is equal to the sum of the squares of the legs of the triangle. Symbolically (Fig. 0-11),

$$c^2 = a^2 + b^2$$

and

$$c = \sqrt{a^2 + b^2}.$$

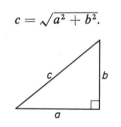

FIGURE 0-11

13. The **area of a triangle** is equal to one-half the product of the base and height. In Fig. 0-12, the area is $\frac{1}{2}bh$.

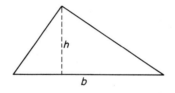

FIGURE 0-12

14. **A central angle** of a circle is an angle formed by two radii of the circle. In Fig. 0-13, angle A is a central angle.

FIGURE 0-13

15. In the following useful formulas, r denotes a radius and h denotes an altitude. Refer to Fig. 0-14.

(a) Circle:

$$\text{Area} = \pi r^2;$$
$$\text{Circumference} = 2\pi r.$$

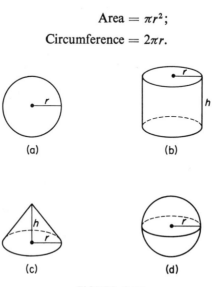

FIGURE 0-14

(b) Right circular cylinder:

$$\text{Volume} = \pi r^2 h;$$

$$\text{Lateral surface area} = 2\pi rh;$$

$$\text{Total surface area} = 2\pi rh + 2\pi r^2.$$

(c) Right circular cone:

$$\text{Volume} = \tfrac{1}{3}\pi r^2 h.$$

(d) Sphere:

$$\text{Volume} = \tfrac{4}{3}\pi r^3,$$

$$\text{Surface area} = 4\pi r^2.$$

16. The **perimeter** of a geometric figure is the measure of the boundary of the figure. In Fig. 0-11, the perimeter is $a + b + c$.

Exercise 0-7

1. Find the area of the shaded region in Fig. 0-15 if the radius of the inner circle is 8.72 centimeters and the radius of the outer circle is 9.88 centimeters. Use $\pi = 3.1416$ and give your answer to two decimal places.

FIGURE 0-15

2. Find the area of the region in Fig. 0-16. Assume that all units are in centimeters.

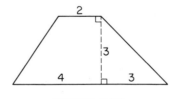

FIGURE 0-16

3. Find the hypotenuse of a right triangle if its other sides have lengths 6 and 8 units.

4. In Fig. 0-17, find angle E if $A = 20°$, $C = 90°$, and AB and CD are parallel.

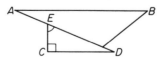

FIGURE 0-17

5. Find the length of the belt around the pulleys in Fig. 0-18 if the centers of the pulleys are 28 centimeters apart and the radius of each pulley is 5 centimeters. Use $\pi = 3.14$.

FIGURE 0-18

6. Find the area and perimeter of the metal plate in Fig. 0-19. Assume that all units are centimeters.

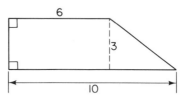

FIGURE 0-19

7. A crate is at rest on the inclined plane shown in Fig. 0-20. Find the angle A between the weight **W** and the perpendicular to the incline.

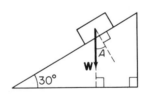

FIGURE 0-20

8. A cylindrical concrete pipe, which is 100 centimeters long, has an inner radius of 4 centimeters and an outer radius of 5 centimeters. Find the volume of concrete that was used to make the pipe. Use $\pi = 3.1416$.

9. Given a circle of radius 3 units, show that if the radius is doubled, then the area is four times as great.

10. Given a sphere of radius 3 units, show that if the radius is doubled, then the volume is eight times as great.

operations
with real numbers

1-1 Real Numbers and the Real Number Line

In some ways, beginning the study of mathematics is like beginning the study of a language. There are words, phrases, concepts, and symbols with meanings to be learned. As a first step, you must become acquainted with the types of numbers that we will be using.

The **positive integers** are the numbers 1, 2, 3, . . . (the three dots mean *and so on*). The **negative integers** are $-1, -2, -3, \ldots$. The positive integers, the negative integers, and zero (0) are collectively referred to as the **integers.**

A **rational number** is a number that can be written as an integer divided by an integer, that is, as the ratio of two integers. (Think of the word *rational* as *ratio*-nal.) For example, some rational numbers are $\frac{1}{2}, \frac{5}{3}, \frac{-3}{7}$, and 4 (or $\frac{4}{1}$). In fact, all integers are rational. We point out that although $\frac{3}{0}$ appears to be a ratio of two integers, *division by zero has no meaning*. Thus $\frac{3}{0}$ does not represent a number.

Any rational number can be represented by either a *terminating decimal*, such as $\frac{3}{4} = 0.75$ and $\frac{3}{2} = 1.5$, or a *repeating decimal* (one in which a block of one or more digits repeats itself without end), such as $\frac{1}{9} = 0.111 \ldots$. Another example is $\frac{61}{495} = 0.12323 \ldots$, where the repeating block consists of the digits 2 and 3. It is also a fact that every terminating or repeating decimal represents a rational number.

A *nonterminating, nonrepeating decimal* does not represent a rational number and is called an **irrational number.** The number π (the lowercase Greek letter pi), which represents the ratio of the circumference of a circle to the diameter of the circle, is known to be irrational. It is approximately 3.14159 . . . , where no block of digits repeats. Although π is often approximated by the rational numbers $\frac{22}{7}$ and 3.14, it is really a nonterminating, nonrepeating decimal and cannot be represented as an integer divided by an integer. The number $\sqrt{2}$, which is approximately 1.4142, also is irrational.

The **real numbers** consist of the rational numbers and irrational numbers, that is, all decimals. Thus 4, -2, π, $\frac{2}{3}$, and $\sqrt{2}$ are real numbers. For the time being, whenever we use the word *number*, we shall mean *real number*.*

We can represent real numbers by points on a line, like the markings on a thermometer. First we choose a point, called the **origin**, to represent 0 (Fig. 1-1).

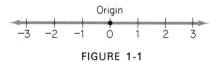

FIGURE 1-1

Then a standard measure of distance, called a *unit distance*, is chosen and is successively marked off both to the right and to the left of the origin. These points represent the positive and negative integers, as shown. The remaining points on the line correspond to all other real numbers. In Fig. 1-2, various points and their associated real numbers are identified. To each real number there corresponds exactly one

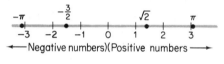

FIGURE 1-2

point on the line, and to each point on the line there corresponds exactly one real number. To describe this, we say that there is a **one-to-one correspondence** between real numbers and points on the line. In fact, we sometimes refer to points on the line as numbers. For example, we can speak of the *number* 7 and the *point* 7 interchangeably. It should be obvious to you why we refer to this line as the **(real) number line.**

Numbers to the right of zero on the number line are called **positive numbers;** those to the left of zero are **negative numbers.** Thus real numbers can be thought of as being **signed numbers:** either positive $(+)$, negative $(-)$, or zero. As a result we shall feel free, for example, to write 7 as $+7$ when the sign is to be emphasized.

In technical work we often represent unspecified numbers (or quantities) by letters, such as a, b, x, y, and so on. Letters used in this way are called **literal numbers.** A symbol that represents a fixed number throughout a discussion is called a **constant.** The numbers 2 and π are constants. On the other hand, a symbol that can represent more than one number is called a **variable.** For example, in the formula $A = \pi r^2$ for the area A of a given circle, r represents the radius of the given circle and is a

*Numbers that are not real numbers are discussed in Chapter 11.

constant. However, if we consider *all* possible circles, r is a variable and can assume infinitely many values. Thus in one case, r denotes a constant and in the other case, a variable. It is customary to use letters at the beginning of the alphabet, such as a, b, and c, to represent constants, and letters at the latter part, such as x, y, and z, to represent variables. Remember, however, that there are exceptions.

Suppose a and b are numbers on the number line. Then either a and b are the same, or a lies to the left of b, or a lies to the right of b (Fig. 1-3). If a and b are the

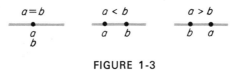

FIGURE 1-3

same, then $a = b$. If a lies to the left of b, we say that a is **less than** b and write $a < b$, where the **inequality symbol** $<$ is read *is less than*. For example, $1 < 3$, because 1 is to the left of 3. On the other hand, if a lies to the right of b, we say that a is **greater than** b, written $a > b$, where the inequality symbol $>$ is read *is greater than*. Thus $3 > 1$. To write $a > b$ is equivalent to writing $b < a$. The statements *a is positive* and $a > 0$ have the same meaning. Similarly, *a is negative* and $a < 0$ mean the same.

There are two other inequality symbols. Each has a double meaning. The symbol $\leq$ is read *is less than or equal to*. Thus $a \leq b$ means that *either $a < b$ or $a = b$*. For example, $3 \leq 6$ and $3 \leq 3$. Similarly, $a \geq b$, which is read *a is greater than or equal to b*, means that *either $a > b$ or $a = b$*. For example, $7 \geq 6$ and $7 \geq 7$.

example 1

From Fig. 1-4 it should be clear that $3 < 7, 7 > 3, -5 < -2, -2 < 1, -5 < 0$, $0 > -2, 7 \leq 7$, and $3 \geq 0$.

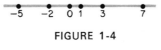

FIGURE 1-4

If $a < b$ and x is between a and b, then not only is $a < x$, but $x < b$ also. We indicate this by writing $a < x < b$. For example, $0 < 7 < 9$. Similarly, the statement $-1 \leq x < 3$ means that $-1 \leq x$ and $x < 3$, *simultaneously*.

The distance between a number x and the origin, regardless of direction, is called the **absolute value** of x and is written as $|x|$. For example, because 5 and -5 are both five units from the origin (Fig. 1-5), we can write $|5| = 5$ and $|-5| = 5$. Similarly, $|3| = 3, |-8| = 8, |+\frac{1}{2}| = \frac{1}{2}, |-\pi| = \pi$, and $|0| = 0$. Note that $|x|$ is *never* negative; it is always *positive or zero*, that is, *nonnegative*. Symbolically, we

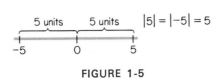

FIGURE 1-5

have $|x| \geq 0$. Numbers that have equal absolute values, such as 5 and -5, are said to be **numerically equal** or **equal in magnitude**.

example 2

a. $|5 - 3| = |2| = 2$.

b. $|-2| > -4$, because $|-2| = 2$ and $2 > -4$.

c. $-4 < 2$, but $|-4| > |2|$, because $|-4| = 4$, $|2| = 2$, and $4 > 2$.

From time to time we shall find it convenient to make use of the concept of a *set*. A **set** is a collection of objects. Every object in a set is called a **member** or **element** of that set. For example, the set of even numbers between 5 and 11 has as its elements the numbers 6, 8, and 10.

One common way to specify a set is by listing its members inside braces. For the above set, we can write

$$\{6, 8, 10\}.$$

The order in which the elements are listed is not important. Instead of $\{6, 8, 10\}$ we could have written $\{10, 6, 8\}$. There are four other ways to write that set—can you list them?

Exercise 1-1

*In Problems **1–10**, classify the statement as either true or false.*

1. 12 is a positive number.

2. $\frac{2}{3}$ is an integer.

3. 0 is not rational.

4. π is a real number.

5. $\frac{5}{2}$ is a rational number.

6. -421 is an integer.

7. $\frac{4}{2}$ is not a positive integer.

8. Every integer is positive or negative.

9. The sets $\{1, 3, 5\}$ and $\{3, 5, 1\}$ are not the same.

10. On the number line, -9 is to the left of -8.

*In each of Problems **11–14**, determine the number that is farther from zero on the number line.*

11. 3, 4.   **12.** 7, -8.   **13.** -3, 1.   **14.** -5, -8.

In each of Problems **15–18**, *determine the number that is to the right of the other number on the number line.*

15. 6, −5.   **16.** −3, −4.   **17.** −13, −12.   **18.** 0, −2.

In Problems **19–24**, *put* < *or* > *in the blank so that the statement is true.*

19. 7 ____ 16.   **20.** 8 ____ 0.   **21.** −5 ____ −7.

22. −3 ____ 2.   **23.** 0 ____ −2.   **24.** −4 ____ −1.

In Problems **25–30**, *find the value of the number.*

25. $|-4|$.   **26.** $|319|$.   **27.** $\left|-\dfrac{2}{3}\right|$.

28. $|0|$.   **29.** $\left|7 \cdot \dfrac{1}{7}\right|$.   **30.** $|15 - 13|$.

In Problems **31–33**, *you are given a pair of numbers. Determine which number has the greater absolute value.*

31. 5, 3.   **32.** −5, −3.   **33.** −4, 2.

34. Arrange the numbers −6, −3, 0, 4, 5 in a list so that each number has a smaller absolute value than the numbers that follow it in the list.

35. Determine whether the statements are true or false.
   (a) $|-2| > |-1|$.   (b) $|-1| \le 0$.   (c) $|-9| < -8$.   (d) $-4 < -1 < 2$.

1-2   Basic Properties of Real Numbers

The sum of the numbers a and b is written $a + b$; a and b are called **terms** of the sum. The product of a and b is written $a \cdot b$; a and b are called **factors** of the product. Other ways to write the product $a \cdot b$ are ab, $a(b)$, $(a)b$, and $(a)(b)$. Thus we may write the product of 4 and x as $4x$. The subtraction of b from a is written $a - b$. The division of a by b, or the *quotient* of a by b, is written $a \div b$ or a/b.

Many operations with real numbers are based on three important properties: the *commutative, associative,* and *distributive laws*. These are powerful laws, and it is important that you understand them and make effective use of them.

The **commutative laws** state that numbers can be added or can be multiplied in any order.

$$\begin{array}{ll} a + b = b + a & \text{commutative law of addition.} \\ a \cdot b = b \cdot a & \text{commutative law of multiplication.} \end{array}$$

example 1

a. $3 + x = x + 3$.   b. $yx = xy$.   c. $x \cdot \tfrac{2}{3} = \tfrac{2}{3}x$.

The **associative laws** state that in addition or in multiplication, numbers can be grouped in any order.

$$a + (b + c) = (a + b) + c \quad \text{associative law of addition.}$$
$$a(bc) = (ab)c \quad \text{associative law of multiplication.}$$

example 2

Perform the indicated operations by using the associative laws.

a. $(x + 5) + 9 = x + (5 + 9) = x + 14.$

b. $2(4y) = (2 \cdot 4)y = 8y.$

c. $\frac{1}{2}(\frac{2}{3}p) = (\frac{1}{2} \cdot \frac{2}{3})p = \frac{1}{3}p.$

d. $x(2y) = (x \cdot 2)y = (2x)y = 2xy.$ Here we used the fact that $x \cdot 2 = 2x$ by the commutative law.

The **distributive laws** involve *both* addition and multiplication.

DISTRIBUTIVE LAWS
$$a(b + c) = ab + ac.$$
$$(a + b)c = ac + bc.$$

For example, to find $7(2 + 3)$ we can multiply 7 by 5, or we can multiply the first factor 7 by *each* term in the second factor $(2 + 3)$ and add the results:

$$7(2 + 3) = 7 \cdot 2 + 7 \cdot 3 = 14 + 21 = 35.$$

example 3

Perform the indicated operations by using the distributive laws.

a. $2(x + 5) = 2 \cdot x + 2 \cdot 5 = 2x + 10.$ Note that $2(x + 5) = 2x + 5$ is **false**, because each term within the parentheses must be multiplied by 2.

b. $(7 + x)y = 7 \cdot y + x \cdot y = 7y + xy.$

There are two other useful properties related to the distributive laws:

$$a(b - c) = ab - ac.$$
$$(a - b)c = ac - bc.$$

We also refer to these as distributive laws.

example 4

Perform the indicated operations.

a. $(2 - x)y = 2y - xy$.

b. $x(y - 3) = xy - x(3) = xy - 3x$. The last step follows from the commutative law.

The distributive laws can be extended to sums and differences involving any number of terms. For example,

$$x(y - z + w) = xy - xz + xw.$$

Exercise 1-2

In Problems 1–8, determine whether the given statement is true or false.

1. $(x + y) + z = (y + x) + z$.　　　　　**2.** $7 + (4 + y) = (7 + 4) + y$.

3. $4(x + 4) = 4x + 4$.　　　　　　　　　**4.** $(x - 2)y = y(x - 2)$.

5. $3(x - 4) = 3x - 4$.　　　　　　　　　**6.** $x + 3y = 3y + x$.

7. $2(3 \cdot 6) = 2 \cdot 3 + 2 \cdot 6$.　　　　　　　**8.** $(3 + x) + 2 = 3 + (x + 2)$.

In Problems 9–30, perform the indicated operations.

9. $(x + 3) + 5$.　　　　**10.** $4 + (7 + y)$.　　　　**11.** $7 + (4 + y)$.

12. $(t + 1) + 1$.　　　　**13.** $4(3x)$.　　　　　　　**14.** $4\left(\dfrac{3}{4}w\right)$.

15. $5\left(\dfrac{2}{5}x\right)$.　　　　**16.** $6\left(\dfrac{3}{8}x\right)$.　　　　**17.** $\dfrac{1}{5}(5a)$.

18. $\left(\dfrac{6}{5}\right)\left(\dfrac{10}{9}x\right)$.　　　**19.** $4(2 + t)$.　　　　**20.** $(x + 2)y$.

21. $(5 - y)z$.　　　　**22.** $6(7 + t)$.　　　　**23.** $x(7 - y)$.

24. $(a - 3)2$.　　　　**25.** $x(y + z - w)$.　　　　**26.** $4(x - z + y - w)$.

27. $a(3c)$.　　　　**28.** $a\left(\dfrac{2}{3}y\right)$.　　　　**29.** $p\left(\dfrac{3}{4}rs\right)$.　　　　**30.** $ab\left(\dfrac{3}{4}\right)$.

1-3   The Arithmetic of Real Numbers

Recall that real numbers can be thought of as signed numbers: either positive (+), negative (−), or zero. We now consider the rules that govern how the operations of arithmetic apply to signed numbers. There are two rules for addition. The first is as follows:

> The sum of two numbers of like signs is obtained by adding their absolute values and prefixing their common sign to the result.

Thus the sum of two positive numbers is positive, and the sum of two negative numbers is negative.

example 1

a. $(+2) + (+7) = +(2 + 7) = +9 = 9$.

b. $(-3) + (-5) = -(3 + 5) = -8$.

c. $(-7) + (-\pi) = -(7 + \pi)$.

d. $(-12) + (-10) + (-2) = (-22) + (-2) = -24$.   Here we used the associative law to first add -12 and -10.

The second rule for addition is:

> The sum of two numbers of unlike signs is obtained by subtracting the smaller absolute value *from* the larger absolute value and prefixing to the result the sign of the number with the larger absolute value. When two numbers with unlike signs have the same absolute value, their sum is zero.

example 2

a. $(+3) + (-11) = -(11 - 3) = -8$.

b. $(-4) + 9 = +(9 - 4) = 5$.

c. $3 + (-3) = 0$, because 3 and -3 have unlike signs but have the same absolute value.

d. $(-4) + (2) = -2.$

e. $7 + (-3) = 4.$

Subtraction involves the fact that every number has an *opposite*. The **opposite** (or **negative**) **of** a, written $-a$, is that number which when added to a gives zero. Thus $a + (-a) = 0$. For example, the opposite of 4 is -4, as $4 + (-4) = 0$. Similarly, the opposite of -6, which is represented by $-(-6)$, is 6 because $-6 + (6) = 0$. Thus $-(-6) = 6$. In general, we have this rule:

$$-(-a) = a.$$

That is, the opposite of the opposite of a number is that number. The opposite of 0 is 0, because $0 + 0 = 0$. Thus $-0 = 0$. From our examples, it should be clear that the negative of a number need not be negative.

Subtraction is defined in terms of addition and an opposite:

SUBTRACTION
$$a - b = a + (-b).$$

That is, *to subtract b from a, we **add** the opposite of b to a*. Note that the first minus sign in the above box refers to subtraction, but the second one refers to the opposite of b.

example 3

a. $8 - (5) = 8 + (-5) = 3.$

b. $2 - 7 = 2 + (-7) = -5.$

c. $-12 - 10 = -12 + (-10) = -22.$

d. $2 - (-7) = 2 + (7) = 9.$

e. $-6 - (-10) = -6 + 10 = 4.$

Parts (d) and (e) of Example 3 illustrate an important rule:

$$a - (-b) = a + b.$$

Now let us consider how to simplify the following:

$$11 - 5 + 4 - 9,$$

which is actually the *sum*

$$11 + (-5) + 4 + (-9).$$

Using the commutative law, we can "shuffle" the terms so that positive numbers are together and negative numbers are together:

$$11 + 4 + (-5) + (-9).$$

By proper grouping (associative law), the positive and negative numbers can be added separately:

$$15 + (-14) = 1.$$

More simply, we write

$$11 - 5 + 4 - 9 = 15 - 14 = 1.$$

Similarly, $-12 + 4 - 6 + 3 = 7 - 18 = -11.$

Division involves the notion of the *reciprocal* of a number. If $a \neq 0$ (the symbol $\neq$ is read "is not equal to"), then the **reciprocal** of a, written $1/a$, is that number which, when multiplied by a, gives 1. Thus, $a \cdot (1/a) = 1$. For example, the reciprocal of 2 is $\frac{1}{2}$ (because $2 \cdot \frac{1}{2} = 1$), and the reciprocal of $\frac{2}{3}$ is $\frac{3}{2}$ (recall that $\frac{1}{2/3}$ and $\frac{3}{2}$ are equivalent). Note that the reciprocal of zero is not defined, because there is no number which when multiplied by zero gives 1.

Division is defined in terms of multiplication and a reciprocal. If $b \neq 0$, then a divided by b, or the *quotient* of a by b, is denoted by $a \div b$ or a/b and is given by the following.

> **DIVISION**
>
> $$\frac{a}{b} = a \cdot \frac{1}{b}.$$

The number a is called the **dividend**, and b is the **divisor**. The rule above states that *to divide a by b, we **multiply** a by the reciprocal of b.* This is sometimes referred to as *inverting the divisor and multiplying.* For example,

$$\frac{3}{4} = 3 \cdot \frac{1}{4}, \qquad \frac{\frac{1}{2}}{8} = \frac{1}{2} \cdot \frac{1}{8} = \frac{1}{16},$$

$$\frac{x}{3} = x \cdot \frac{1}{3} = \frac{1}{3}x, \qquad 8 \cdot \frac{1}{12} = \frac{8}{12} = \frac{2}{3}.$$

An alternative definition of division is:

$$\frac{a}{b} = c \quad \text{means} \quad a = bc.$$

Thus $\frac{6}{2} = 3$ because $6 = 2 \cdot 3$, and $\frac{0}{7} = 0$ because $0 = 7 \cdot 0$.

Because division is defined in terms of multiplication, the rules for handling signs are the same for both operations.

> The product (or quotient) of two numbers of like signs is obtained by multiplying (or dividing) their absolute values. The product (or quotient) of two numbers of unlike signs is obtained by prefixing the product (or quotient) of their absolute values with a negative $(-)$ sign.

Thus the product (or quotient) of two positive numbers or two negative numbers is positive. The product of a positive number and a negative number is negative.

example 4

a. $(+2)(+6) = +12 = 12.$

b. $(-3)(-5) = +15 = 15.$

c. $\dfrac{+14}{+2} = +7 = 7.$

d. $\dfrac{-6}{-3} = +\dfrac{6}{3} = +2 = 2.$

e. $(-2)(4) = -8.$

f. $3\left(-\dfrac{1}{3}\right) = -\left(3 \cdot \dfrac{1}{3}\right) = -1.$

g. $\dfrac{-4}{5} = -\dfrac{4}{5}.$

h. $\dfrac{18}{-6} = -\dfrac{18}{6} = -3.$

i. $(-2)\left(\dfrac{1}{-4}\right) = (-2)\left(-\dfrac{1}{4}\right) = +\left(2 \cdot \dfrac{1}{4}\right) = \dfrac{2}{4} = \dfrac{1}{2}.$

j. $(-1)(3) = -(1 \cdot 3) = -3.$

We can generalize the result of Example 4(j):

> $(-1)(a) = -a.$

Thus $(-1)x = -x$ and $-4 = (-1)(4).$

example 5

a. $\dfrac{7(-4)}{3} = \dfrac{-28}{3} = -\dfrac{28}{3}.$

b. $\dfrac{6(-2)}{-3} = \dfrac{-12}{-3} = \dfrac{12}{3} = 4.$

c. $\dfrac{6(-7)}{9} = \dfrac{\overset{2}{\cancel{6}}(-7)}{\underset{3}{\cancel{9}}} = \dfrac{2(-7)}{3} = \dfrac{-14}{3} = -\dfrac{14}{3}.$

d. $\dfrac{2}{3(-5)} = \dfrac{2}{-15} = -\dfrac{2}{15}$.

e. $\dfrac{-6}{(-5)(-7)} = \dfrac{-6}{35} = -\dfrac{6}{35}$.

f. $(-6)(-2)(-1) = (12)(-1) = -12$. This illustrates that *the product of an odd number of negative numbers is negative.* Similarly, $(-2)(-3)(-4) = -(2\cdot3\cdot4) = -24$.

g. $(-2)(-5)(-3)(-4) = (10)(12) = 120$. *The product of an even number of negative numbers is positive.*

h. $\left(-\dfrac{4}{9}\right)(18) = -\left(\dfrac{4}{\cancel{9}} \cdot \overset{2}{\cancel{18}}\right) = -(4\cdot2) = -8$.

i. $\dfrac{-6-2}{-4} = \dfrac{-8}{-4} = \dfrac{8}{4} = 2$.

j. $\dfrac{-3-6}{-2-1} = \dfrac{-9}{-3} = \dfrac{9}{3} = 3$.

k. $\dfrac{-\frac{7}{2}}{4} = -\dfrac{\frac{7}{2}}{4} = -\left(\dfrac{7}{2}\cdot\dfrac{1}{4}\right) = -\dfrac{7}{8}$.

l. $-\dfrac{-3}{-8} = -\left(\dfrac{-3}{-8}\right) = -\left(\dfrac{3}{8}\right) = -\dfrac{3}{8}$.

Symbolically, the previous laws of signed numbers for multiplication and division can be stated as follows.

MULTIPLICATION	DIVISION
$(a)(b) = (-a)(-b) = ab$.	$\dfrac{-a}{-b} = \dfrac{a}{b}$.
$(a)(-b) = (-a)(b) = -ab$.	$\dfrac{-a}{b} = -\dfrac{a}{b} = \dfrac{a}{-b}$.

For example, $\dfrac{-4}{5} = -\dfrac{4}{5}$ matches $\dfrac{-a}{b} = -\dfrac{a}{b}$.

example 6

---

a. $(-2)(-x) = 2\cdot x = 2x$.

b. $\dfrac{(-x)y}{z} = \dfrac{-(xy)}{z} = -\dfrac{xy}{z}$.

example 7

---

a. To simplify $-(-xy)$, we match it with the previously given form $-(-a) = a$. Here xy plays the role of a. Thus $-(-xy) = xy$.

b. $-\dfrac{x}{y(-z)} = -\dfrac{x}{-(yz)} = -\left(-\dfrac{x}{yz}\right) = \dfrac{x}{yz}$.

c. $2(-4x) = -(2\cdot4x) = -8x$.

When the order of doing operations is not clear to you, do the multiplications and divisions first. Then do the additions and subtractions. For example,

$$-4 + 2(6) = -4 + 12 = 8,$$
$$-3 - (4)(-2) = -3 - (-8) = -3 + 8 = 5.$$

Note above that $-4 + 2(6) \neq -2(6)$: You must perform the multiplication first. Similarly, $-3 - 4(-2) \neq -7(-2)$. Any operations within parentheses should be done first, as Example 8 shows.

example 8

a. $(-2)(-7 + 4) = (-2)(-3) = 6.$

b. $7 - (4 - 9) = 7 - (-5) = 7 + 5 = 12.$

c. $-2(1 - 5) = -2(-4) = 8.$

d. $\dfrac{8(4 + 3)}{-3} = \dfrac{8(7)}{-3} = \dfrac{56}{-3} = -\dfrac{56}{3}.$

The following properties concerning fractions and operations with zero and 1 are important. Lack of understanding and improper use of these properties often lead to errors. Check them carefully.

	Property	*Example*
1.	$0 + a = a.$	$0 + (-4) = -4.$
2.	$0 - a = -a.$	$0 - 6 = -6; \quad 0 - (-4) = -(-4) = 4.$
3.	$a - 0 = a.$	$xy - 0 = xy.$
4.	$a \cdot 0 = 0.$	$(-3)(0) = 0.$
5.	$\dfrac{0}{a} = 0 \quad$ if $a \neq 0.$	$\dfrac{0}{7} = 0.$
6.	$1 \cdot a = a.$	$xy = 1 \cdot xy.$
7.	$\dfrac{a}{1} = a.$	$\dfrac{4x}{1} = 4x; \quad 12y = \dfrac{12y}{1}.$
8.	$a\left(\dfrac{b}{a}\right) = b.$	$2\left(\dfrac{7}{2}\right) = 7.$
9.	$\dfrac{ab}{c} = \left(\dfrac{a}{c}\right)(b) = a\left(\dfrac{b}{c}\right).$	$\dfrac{2 \cdot 7}{3} = \dfrac{2}{3} \cdot 7 = 2 \cdot \dfrac{7}{3}.$
10.	$\dfrac{a}{bc} = \left(\dfrac{a}{b}\right)\left(\dfrac{1}{c}\right) = \left(\dfrac{1}{b}\right)\left(\dfrac{a}{c}\right).$	$\dfrac{2}{3 \cdot 7} = \dfrac{2}{3} \cdot \dfrac{1}{7} = \dfrac{1}{3} \cdot \dfrac{2}{7}.$

11. $\dfrac{a}{b} \cdot \dfrac{c}{d} = \dfrac{ac}{bd}.$

$$\dfrac{2}{3} \cdot \dfrac{4}{5} = \dfrac{2 \cdot 4}{3 \cdot 5} = \dfrac{8}{15};$$

$$\dfrac{2}{3} \cdot \dfrac{1}{x} = \dfrac{2 \cdot 1}{3 \cdot x} = \dfrac{2}{3x}.$$

example 9

a. $\dfrac{4x}{y} = 4\left(\dfrac{x}{y}\right).$ Property 9 was used here.

b. $\dfrac{\frac{2}{3}a}{b} = \dfrac{2}{3}\left(\dfrac{a}{b}\right) = \dfrac{2a}{3b}.$ Properties 9 and 11 were used here.

Exercise 1-3

In Problems **1–4,** *find the reciprocal of the given number.*

1. $\dfrac{1}{3}$ **2.** $\dfrac{4}{y}$ **3.** $\dfrac{x}{10}$ **4.** $w.$

In Problems **5–89,** *simplify.*

5. $(+4) + (+8).$ **6.** $(-2) + (-3).$ **7.** $(-7) + (-2).$

8. $-5 + 0.$ **9.** $6 + (-4).$ **10.** $-2 + 4.$

11. $5 - 7.$ **12.** $6 - 9.$ **13.** $-5 + 2.$

14. $8 + (-9).$ **15.** $-2 - 8.$ **16.** $3 - (-4).$

17. $-6 - (-5).$ **18.** $(-8) - 7.$ **19.** $-14 - (-14).$

20. $(+3)(+4).$ **21.** $(-3)(-4).$ **22.** $(-5)(-2).$

23. $7\left(-\dfrac{2}{7}\right).$ **24.** $(-3)(7).$ **25.** $\left(-\dfrac{4}{9}\right)(-18).$

26. $-2 - 5 + 9 - 1.$ **27.** $(-2) + (-1) - 5.$ **28.** $5 - 6 + 1.$

29. $3 - 5 + 6 - 4.$ **30.** $(-2)(4)(-3) + 6(-2).$ **31.** $4 - 8 + 6(-2).$

32. $\dfrac{+4}{+2}.$ **33.** $\dfrac{-6}{-3}.$ **34.** $\dfrac{10}{-2}.$

35. $\dfrac{-\frac{1}{2}}{4}.$ **36.** $\dfrac{-5}{25}.$ **37.** $\dfrac{10}{-1}.$

38. $\dfrac{-4}{-2}.$ **39.** $(-2)\left(\dfrac{3}{-2}\right).$ **40.** $-(-4).$

41. $(-1)a.$ **42.** $\dfrac{2}{3}(-6).$ **43.** $3(-4w).$

44. $\left(-\dfrac{4}{5}\right)\left(\dfrac{-25}{8}\right).$ **45.** $(5)\left(\dfrac{-3}{5}\right).$ **46.** $(-6 - 7) + 8.$

47. $\dfrac{-3}{6(-2)}.$ **48.** $(-1)(-abc).$ **49.** $\dfrac{6 - 6}{3}.$

50. $(-6)(-7) - 8.$

51. $-2(-2 + 3).$

52. $\dfrac{12}{-6 + 7}.$

53. $\dfrac{3 - 5}{4 - 6}.$

54. $3(5 + 1).$

55. $(8 + 1) \cdot 7.$

56. $\dfrac{-7 - 5}{4}.$

57. $-8 + (-2 - 5).$

58. $-7 - (-3 - 2).$

59. $\dfrac{(-3)(3 - 5)}{(2 - 5) - 6}.$

60. $\dfrac{7 - 12}{-3}.$

61. $\dfrac{2(-2 + 1)(3 - 4)}{12}.$

62. $(-2)(-3) - (-4)(2).$

63. $\dfrac{(-3)(2) - (-2)(4)}{-4 - (2 - 2)}.$

64. $16 - \dfrac{4(-2)}{2} - \dfrac{(32)(-4)}{-(-1)}.$

65. $\dfrac{16(-3) - 7(-2)(-3)}{(-4) - (-4)}.$

66. $(-1)(-x).$

67. $-\dfrac{-6}{-8}.$

68. $-\dfrac{7}{-14}.$

69. $-\dfrac{-8}{24}.$

70. $-\dfrac{-10}{-2}.$

71. $\dfrac{\frac{8}{3}}{-2}.$

72. $\dfrac{-\frac{7}{3}}{7}.$

73. $-(-5xy).$

74. $-\dfrac{x}{(-y)z}.$

75. $-\dfrac{-x}{(-y)(-z)}.$

76. $(-7)(x).$

77. $(-6)(-y).$

78. $0 - xy.$

79. $\dfrac{x}{(-y)(z)}.$

80. $\dfrac{(-x)(-y)}{(-w)(-z)}.$

81. $|7| - |23|.$

82. $-|-2| - 3.$

83. $\dfrac{0}{3 - 2}.$

84. $-(-|-4| + 3)(-6) - |-4 - 2|.$

85. $|921 - (-1032)| + 6.$

86. $\dfrac{16(-3 - 5 + 6)(0 - 4)}{3}.$

87. $\dfrac{(-4) - (-9)(2) + 6(-1)}{-[-8 + 4 - (-2)]}.$

88. $\dfrac{\frac{4}{5}x}{y}.$

89. $\dfrac{\frac{3}{5}xy}{z}.$

90. The power of a lens (in diopters) is the reciprocal of the focal length of the lens (in meters). If a lens has a focal length of 0.2 meter, find its power.

In Problems 91–94, evaluate. Assume that all numbers are approximate. (See Sec. 0-6 for a discussion of approximate numbers.)

91. $\dfrac{3.21}{5.02} \left(\dfrac{3.62 - 4.73}{8.31} \right).$

92. $\dfrac{(-7.62)(5.13) - (-5.62)(6.69)}{-4.11 - (6.21 - 4.45)}.$

93. $\dfrac{-\dfrac{6.42}{-1.12}}{8.73 - 4.14}.$

94. $\dfrac{8.62}{\dfrac{-4.10(7.21 + 2.91)}{6.84}}.$

1-4   Evaluating Formulas

A knowledge of the arithmetic of signed numbers is essential to the evaluation of formulas, as the following examples show.

example 1

In the study of straight lines, the following formula (called the *slope formula*) occurs:

$$m = \frac{y_2 - y_1}{x_2 - x_1}.$$

The small numbers to the right and just below the letters are called **subscripts***. We read x_1 as *x sub one*, and so on. Find m when $x_1 = 5$, $x_2 = 3$, $y_1 = -5$, and $y_2 = 7$.

$$m = \frac{y_2 - y_1}{x_2 - x_1} = \frac{7 - (-5)}{3 - 5} = \frac{12}{-2} = -6.$$

example 2

To describe statistical data, the terms **average value**, or **(arithmetic) mean**, are used. Given the set of n values $x_1, x_2, x_3, \ldots, x_n$, the mean $\bar{x}$ (read *x bar*) is their sum divided by n, the number of values. That is,

$$\bar{x} = \frac{x_1 + x_2 + x_3 + \cdots + x_n}{n}. \tag{1}$$

Suppose that the Celsius temperature of methyl alcohol used in a manufacturing process was measured at different times. The readings are given in Table 1-1.

Table 1-1

Reading	Temperature (°C)
1	4.2
2	−3.0
3	−2.6
4	1.7
5	2.2

Find the mean temperature, denoted by $\bar{T}$ (read *T bar*).

Because there are five readings here, $n = 5$. Replacing the x's in Eq. 1 by T's, we have

$$\bar{T} = \frac{T_1 + T_2 + T_3 + T_4 + T_5}{5}.$$

Setting $T_1 = 4.2$, $T_2 = -3.0$, and so on, gives

$$\bar{T} = \frac{4.2 + (-3.0) + (-2.6) + 1.7 + 2.2}{5} = \frac{2.5}{5} = 0.5°C.$$

*Subscripts are commonly used in science and technical work to name variables in a convenient manner.

example 3

The relationships between the Celsius, Fahrenheit, and Kelvin (absolute) temperature scales are familiar to scientists and engineers:

$$T_C = \frac{5}{9}(T_F - 32);$$

$$T_F = \frac{9}{5}T_C + 32;$$

$$T_K = T_C + 273.$$

Here T_C, T_F, and T_K represent the respective temperatures on the three scales. As before, the small letters to the right of and just below the T's are subscripts. For example, T_C is read T *sub* C and represents a temperature on the Celsius scale. On the Celsius temperature scale, the normal melting point of mercury is $-39°C$. What is the normal melting point of mercury when expressed on the Kelvin (absolute) and Fahrenheit temperature scales?

The melting point of mercury on the Kelvin* scale is

$$T_K = T_C + 273 = -39 + 273 = 234 \text{ K}.$$

On the Fahrenheit scale the corresponding temperature is

$$T_F = \frac{9}{5}T_C + 32 = \frac{9}{5}(-39) + 32 = -70.2 + 32 = -38.2°F.$$

example 4

The **percentage error** is an indication of the accuracy of a measurement and is given by

$$\% \text{ ERR} = \frac{|\text{ Standard value} - \text{Measured value}|}{\text{Standard value}} \times 100.$$

To determine the accuracy of a frequency meter, a frequency *standard* of 60 hertz is measured. If the measured value is 58.5 hertz, find the percentage error.

In this case,

$$\% \text{ ERR} = \frac{|60 - 58.5|}{60} \times 100 = \frac{1.5}{60} \times 100 = 2.5\%.$$

Exercise 1-4

In Problems 1 and 2, use the slope formula in Example 1 to find m from the given information.

1. $x_1 = 5, x_2 = -8, y_1 = -1, y_2 = -2.$
2. $x_1 = 3, x_2 = 5, y_1 = 4, y_2 = 1.$

*In modern notation, an absolute (or Kelvin) temperature is indicated by using the symbol K without any degree symbol.

3. A calculus student must compute y' (y prime), where

$$y' = \frac{(x)(1) - (x - 5)(1)}{(x)(x)}$$

and $x = -2$. What is this value?

4. Repeat Problem 3 if $x = 3$.

The formula

$$d = |a - b|$$

gives the distance d between the numbers a and b on the number line. In Problems 5 and 6, find d for the given numbers.

5. $a = -3, b = 5$.   6. $a = -4, b = -9$.

7. During an experiment with mercury, both its volume, in cubic centimeters (cm^3), and Celsius temperature were measured. The data are given in Table 1-2.

Table 1-2

Reading	Temperature (°C)	Volume (cm³)
1	3.6	460.0
2	2.8	450.0
3	1.3	448.0
4	−0.8	435.0
5	−1.4	419.0
6	−1.6	415.0

(a) Find the mean temperature $\bar{T}$. (Refer to Example 2.)

(b) Find the mean volume $\bar{V}$.

8. At room temperature the horizontal velocities of five oxygen molecules are −475, 478, −472, 482, and 483 meters per second. Find the mean velocity, $\bar{V}$. (Refer to Example 2.)

9. In technical situations, room temperature is often taken to be 20°C. Express this temperature on the Fahrenheit and Kelvin temperature scales. (Refer to Example 3.)

10. The normal melting point of nitrogen is about −210°C. Express this temperature on the Fahrenheit and Kelvin temperature scales. (Refer to Example 3.)

For an arrangement of three particles on a number line, the location $\bar{x}$ of the center of mass is given by the formula

$$\bar{x} = \frac{m_1 x_1 + m_2 x_2 + m_3 x_3}{m_1 + m_2 + m_3}.$$

Here m_1, m_2, and m_3 are the masses of the particles, and x_1, x_2, and x_3 are their locations, respectively. In Problems 11 and 12, find $\bar{x}$ from the given information.

11. $m_1 = 2, m_2 = 3, m_3 = 4, x_1 = -2, x_2 = -3, x_3 = 8$.

12. $x_1 = -4, x_2 = 4, x_3 = -4, m_1 = 2, m_2 = 2, m_3 = 2$.

13. If **speed** is defined to be the absolute value of velocity, find the mean speed of the molecules in Problem 8.

14. A 2000-ohm resistor is found to have a measured value of 2050 ohms. Find the percentage error. (Refer to Example 4.)

15. A voltage standard of 50 volts is measured with two different instruments. One gives a reading of 49 volts and the other a reading of 51 volts. Find the percentage error in each case. (Refer to Example 4.)

16. The ends of a certain copper rod are kept at different temperatures. The rate H at which heat is conducted through the rod, in calories per second, is given by

$$H = 0.14(T_h - T_l),$$

where T_h is the higher temperature and T_l is the lower temperature. Find the rate at which heat is conducted through the rod in each case.
(a) $T_h = 820°C, T_l = 200°C.$ (b) $T_h = 50°C, T_l = -50°C.$
(c) $T_h = 0°C, T_l = -10°C.$ (d) $T_h = -10°C, T_l = -20°C.$

1-5 Review

Review Questions

1. A real number that cannot be expressed as a ratio of two integers is called a(n) _____ number.

2. The number 7 is _(rational) (irrational)_ .

3. True or false: If $x = -4$, then $|x| = -x$. _____

4. The statement $a < b$ means that b lies to the _____ of a on the real number line.

5. The product of an odd number of negative number is _(positive) (negative)_ , and
$$\qquad\qquad\qquad\qquad\qquad\qquad\qquad\text{(a)}$$
the product of an even number of negative numbers is _(positive) (negative)_ .
$$\qquad\qquad\qquad\qquad\qquad\qquad\qquad\qquad\text{(b)}$$

6. By the definition of division, $a/b = c$ if $a =$ _(a)_ , or a/b means a times _(b)_ .

7. The _____ law of addition states that $a + b = b + a$.

8. The result of subtracting -7 from 0 is _____.

9. The distributive law states that $a(b + c) =$ _____.

10. $|-6| =$ _(a)_ , $|0| =$ _(b)_ , and $|6| =$ _(c)_ .

11. The associative law states that $a(bc) =$ _____.

12. The sets $A = \{1, 2, 3, 4\}$ and $B = \{1, 3, 2, 4\}$ _(are) (are not)_ equal.

13. True or false: $|x| > 0$ for any real number x. _____

14. The sum of four negative numbers is a _____ number.

15. $\dfrac{8}{5}$ means _____ times $\dfrac{1}{5}$.

16. If -6 is subtracted from 6, the result is _____.

17. $\dfrac{-7}{1}$ in a simpler form is just _____.

18. The opposite of 5 is __(a)__ , and the reciprocal of 5 is __(b)__ .

19. The sum of a number and its opposite is _____ .

20. The product of a nonzero number and its reciprocal is _____ .

21. The reciprocal of $\dfrac{3}{5}$ is _____ .

22. The opposite of -4 is _____ .

23. All numbers have a reciprocal except _____ .

24. The product of $\dfrac{x}{2}$ and _____ equals 1.

25. $\dfrac{7}{0}$ has no meaning, but $\dfrac{0}{7} =$ _____ .

26. $8 - 5$ means $8 +$ _____ .

27. $5 +$ _____ $= 0$.

Answers to Review Questions

1. Irrational.   **2.** Rational.   **3.** True.   **4.** Right.   **5.** (a) Negative,   (b) Positive.
6. (a) bc,   (b) $1/b$.   **7.** Commutative.   **8.** 7.   **9.** $ab + ac$.
10. (a) 6,   (b) 0,   (c) 6.   **11.** $(ab)c$.   **12.** Are.   **13.** False.   **14.** Negative.   **15.** 8.
16. 12.   **17.** -7.   **18.** (a) -5, (b) $\tfrac{1}{5}$.   **19.** 0.   **20.** 1.   **21.** $\tfrac{5}{3}$.   **22.** 4.   **23.** 0.
24. $2/x$.   **25.** 0.   **26.** -5.   **27.** -5.

Review Problems

*In Problems **1–8**, name the law used in the given statement.*

1. $8 + y = y + 8$.

2. $2(x + 3y) = 2x + 6y$.

3. $2x + (x + y) = (2x + x) + y$.

4. $2(4x) = (2 \cdot 4)x$.

5. $5(x + 4) = (x + 4)5$.

6. $5(x + 4) = 5(4 + x)$.

7. $(a - 3)b = ab - 3b$.

8. $(3x)(y) = 3(xy)$.

*In Problems **9–16**, determine whether each statement is true or false.*

9. $-3 < -2$.

10. $3 > 0$.

11. $|-6| = 6$.

12. $-5 > 1$.

13. $|-3| < |-2|$.

14. $-|-4| = 4$.

15. $2(3 \cdot 7) = (2 \cdot 3)(2 \cdot 7)$.

16. $(3 - x)2 = 3 - 2x$.

*In Problems **17–52**, simplify.*

17. $\dfrac{(-2)(-4)}{-16}$.

18. $(-3)(-4 + 7)$.

19. $5(3x)$.

20. $2(x - y)$.

21. $2(-5y)$.

22. $\dfrac{7}{2 - 2}$.

23. $-6 - (-5)$.

24. $\dfrac{-2}{6}$.

25. $3(-8 + 4)$.

26. $(-2)(-4)(-1)$.

27. $\dfrac{14}{(-2)(-7)}$.

28. $\dfrac{6(-3)}{-2}$.

29. $4(5x - 3)$.

30. $8\left(\frac{5}{12}x\right)$.

31. $(7 + x) - 8$.

32. $\frac{6 - 8}{-4}$.

33. $2(-6) + (-4)(-1)$.

34. $\frac{8 - 9}{7 - 6}$.

35. $-(-3xz)$.

36. $-6 + 4 - 9(2)$.

37. $\left(-\frac{3}{4}\right)(-20)$.

38. $-9(-12 - 8)$.

39. $(-8)\left(\frac{-5}{8}\right)$.

40. $(a + b)c$.

41. $(4x)7$.

42. $-\frac{-8}{-64}$.

43. $\frac{7 - 9}{(7)(-9)}$.

44. $(8 - 8)(8x)$.

45. $\frac{6(-4)}{-2}$.

46. $\frac{(-2)(4)(-6)}{0 - 3}$.

47. $\frac{(-2) - (-1)(0)}{-2}$.

48. $\frac{8(-2) - (-2)(-8)}{3(-2) - 2}$.

49. $-4(3x)$.

50. $x(1 - y + z)$.

51. $(8 - x)y$.

52. $(x + 7) - (7 - 4)$.

53. Compute $\dfrac{a - 2b + c}{ad}$ in each case.

  (a) $a = 2, b = -3, c = 4, d = -1$.   (b) $a = -3, b = 4, c = -2, d = -2$.

*In Problems **54** and **55**, for the given values of x and y, find* (a) $|x + y|$, (b) $|x - y|$, (c) $|x| + |y|$, *and* (d) $|x| - |y|$.

54. $x = 2, y = 5$.   **55.** $x = -3, y = -8$.

56. Convert a temperature of $-40°F$ to degrees Celsius. (Refer to Example 3 of Sec. 1-4.)

introduction
to exponents
and radicals

2-1 Exponents

Recall that when numbers are multiplied to form a product, each number is called a *factor* of the product. Thus, for the product $2ab$, we can say that 2, a, and b are factors. The product

$$a \cdot a \cdot a \cdot a$$

is abbreviated a^4, which is read *the fourth power of a* or *a (raised) to the fourth*. The number a is called the **base** and 4 is the **exponent**. In general, if a is used as a factor n times, we have

> The nth power of a:
> $$a^n = \underbrace{a \cdot a \cdots a.}_{n \text{ factors of } a}$$

example 1

a. $6^2 = 6 \cdot 6 = 36$ (the *second power* of 6, or 6 *squared*).

b. $2^3 = 2 \cdot 2 \cdot 2 = 8$ (2 to the third, or 2 *cubed*).

c. $(-1)^4 = (-1)(-1)(-1)(-1) = 1$. In general, *an even power of a negative number is positive*.

49

d. $(-6)^3 = (-6)(-6)(-6) = -216$. *An odd power of a negative number is negative.*

e. $4^2 x^3 = 4 \cdot 4 \cdot x \cdot x \cdot x$.

f. $3(x + 2)^2 = 3(x + 2)(x + 2)$.

If an exponent is not written, it is understood to be 1; that is, $x^1 = x$. Keep in mind that *an exponent applies only to the quantity immediately to the left and below it.* Thus in $(-3)^2$ the base is -3, but in -3^2 the base is 3. That is,

$$(-3)^2 = (-3)(-3) = 9, \quad \text{but} \quad -3^2 = -(3)(3) = -9.$$

Similarly,

$$(3x)^2 = (3x)(3x), \quad \text{but} \quad 3x^2 = 3 \cdot x \cdot x.$$

Also, do not confuse 3^2 with $3 + 3$:

$$3^2 \neq 3 + 3.$$

We turn now to the basic rules of exponents. Observe that

$$a^2 \cdot a^3 = (a \cdot a)(a \cdot a \cdot a) = a \cdot a \cdot a \cdot a \cdot a$$
$$= a^5 = a^{2+3}.$$

In general, *to multiply numbers with the **same base**, add the exponents and keep the base the same*:

$$\boxed{\textbf{1.} \quad a^m a^n = a^{m+n}.}$$

example 2

---

a. $3^5 \cdot 3^9 = 3^{5+9} = 3^{14}$.

b. $2^2 \cdot 2 = 2^2 \cdot 2^1 = 2^{2+1} = 2^3 = 8$.

c. $y^6 \cdot y^6 = y^{12}$.

d. $x^2(x^n) = x^{2+n} = x^{n+2}$.

e. $(-1)(-1)^2 = (-1)^3 = -1$.

f. $(x - 2)^5(x - 2)^9 = (x - 2)^{14}$.

g. $\dfrac{x^2 x^3}{y^3 y^4} = \dfrac{x^5}{y^7}$.

h. $(3x^5)(9x^2) = 3 \cdot x^5 \cdot 9 \cdot x^2 = 3 \cdot 9 \cdot x^5 x^2 = 27x^7$.

Rule 1 can be extended to products of more than two factors. Thus

$$x^2x^5x^4 = x^{2+5+4} = x^{11}.$$

Keep in mind that Rule 1 requires that the bases *must* be the same. For example,

$$(-2)^4(-2^2) \neq (-2)^6 \quad \text{but} \quad (-2)^4(-2^2) = 16(-4) = -64.$$

Another rule of exponents concerns raising a power of a number to a power. Observe that

$$(a^3)^2 = a^3 \cdot a^3 = a^6 = a^{3 \cdot 2}.$$

In general, *to find a power of a power, multiply the exponents and keep the base the same*:

$$\boxed{\textbf{2.} \quad (a^m)^n = a^{mn}.}$$

example 3

a. $(10^2)^6 = 10^{2 \cdot 6} = 10^{12}.$ b. $(x^2)^3 = x^{2 \cdot 3} = x^6.$

c. $(y^8)^5 = y^{40}.$ d. $[(-2)^2]^3 = (-2)^6 = 64.$

e. $[(x+7)^2]^{10} = (x+7)^{20}.$ f. $(r^n)^p = r^{np}.$

g. Do not confuse $(2^3)^4$ with 2^32^4. That is, $(2^3)^4 \neq 2^7$, but $(2^3)^4 = 2^{12}.$

Consider the quotient

$$\frac{4^5}{4^3},$$

which has more factors of 4 in the numerator than in the denominator. By the familiar process of cancellation,

$$\frac{4^5}{4^3} = \frac{\cancel{4} \cdot \cancel{4} \cdot \cancel{4} \cdot 4 \cdot 4}{\cancel{4} \cdot \cancel{4} \cdot \cancel{4}} = 4^2.$$

The same result is obtained by raising 4 to that power found by subtracting the smaller exponent 3 in the denominator from the larger exponent 5 in the numerator. That is,

$$\frac{4^5}{4^3} = 4^{5-3} = 4^2.$$

Similarly,

$$\frac{4^3}{4^5} = \frac{\cancel{4} \cdot \cancel{4} \cdot \cancel{4}}{\cancel{4} \cdot \cancel{4} \cdot \cancel{4} \cdot 4 \cdot 4} = \frac{1}{4^2} = \frac{1}{4^{5-3}}.$$

More generally we have Rules 3–5. Here, as elsewhere in this book, we assume that *no denominators are zero*.

$$3. \quad \frac{a^m}{a^n} = a^{m-n} \qquad \text{for } m > n,$$

$$4. \quad \frac{a^m}{a^n} = \frac{1}{a^{n-m}} \qquad \text{for } n > m,$$

$$5. \quad \frac{a^n}{a^n} = 1.$$

example 4

a. $\dfrac{2^6}{2^4} = 2^{6-4} = 2^2 = 4.$

b. $\dfrac{x^3}{x^2} = x^{3-2} = x^1 = x.$

c. $\dfrac{x^7}{x^{10}} = \dfrac{1}{x^{10-7}} = \dfrac{1}{x^3}.$

d. $\dfrac{2^8}{2^{12}} = \dfrac{1}{2^{12-8}} = \dfrac{1}{2^4} = \dfrac{1}{16}.$

e. $\dfrac{y^{10}}{y^{10}} = 1.$

f. $\dfrac{-y^6}{y^4} = -\dfrac{y^6}{y^4} = -y^2.$

g. $\dfrac{(x^2 + 1)^4}{(x^2 + 1)^{12}} = \dfrac{1}{(x^2 + 1)^{12-4}} = \dfrac{1}{(x^2 + 1)^8}.$

h. $\dfrac{(-2)^3}{(-2)^4} = \dfrac{1}{(-2)^{4-3}} = \dfrac{1}{(-2)^1} = \dfrac{1}{-2} = -\dfrac{1}{2}.$

i. $\dfrac{x^{1+n}}{x^n} = x^{1+n-n} = x^1 = x.$

The next rules of exponents involve powers of products and quotients. Notice that by the commutative and associative laws, we have

$$(2 \cdot 3)^2 = (2 \cdot 3)(2 \cdot 3) = 2 \cdot 2 \cdot 3 \cdot 3 = 2^2 3^2$$

and

$$\left(\frac{2}{3}\right)^2 = \frac{2}{3} \cdot \frac{2}{3} = \frac{2 \cdot 2}{3 \cdot 3} = \frac{2^2}{3^2}.$$

More generally, *to raise a product to a power, each factor is raised to that power. To raise a quotient to a power, both the numerator and denominator are raised to that power.*

$$6. \quad (ab)^n = a^n b^n.$$

$$7. \quad \left(\frac{a}{b}\right)^n = \frac{a^n}{b^n}.$$

example 5

a. $(xy)^4 = x^4y^4$.

b. $\left(\dfrac{x}{y}\right)^{12} = \dfrac{x^{12}}{y^{12}}$.

c. $(ab)^{2n} = a^{2n}b^{2n}$.

d. $\left(\dfrac{2}{x}\right)^4 = \dfrac{2^4}{x^4} = \dfrac{16}{x^4}$.

e. $(3x)^3 = 3^3x^3 = 27x^3$. *Do not write* $(3x)^3 = 3x^3$, which is *false* except when x is 0. Students often make this error.

f. $2^4 \cdot 3^4 = (2 \cdot 3)^4 = 6^4$.

g. Rule 6 can be extended to more than two factors. For example, $(xyz)^3 = x^3y^3z^3$.

h. $(-x)^9 = [(-1)x]^9 = (-1)^9x^9 = (-1)x^9 = -x^9$. Similarly, we have $(-x)^{10} = (-1)^{10}x^{10} = 1 \cdot x^{10} = x^{10}$.

The next example shows various ways in which Rules 1–7 can be used. These rules are now summarized:

1. $a^m a^n = a^{m+n}$.

2. $(a^m)^n = a^{mn}$.

3. $\dfrac{a^m}{a^n} = a^{m-n}$ for $m > n$.

4. $\dfrac{a^m}{a^n} = \dfrac{1}{a^{n-m}}$ for $n > m$.

5. $\dfrac{a^n}{a^n} = 1$.

6. $(ab)^n = a^n b^n$.

7. $\left(\dfrac{a}{b}\right)^n = \dfrac{a^n}{b^n}$.

example 6

In each of the following, the numbers to the right refer to the rules used.

a. $\dfrac{(x^6)^3}{(x^3)^4} = \dfrac{x^{18}}{x^{12}} = x^6$.   (2) and (3)

b. $\dfrac{(x^2)(x^4)^3}{x^{90}} = \dfrac{(x^2)(x^{12})}{x^{90}} = \dfrac{x^{14}}{x^{90}} = \dfrac{1}{x^{76}}$.   (2), (1), and (4)

c. $(w^2r^4)^3 = (w^2)^3(r^4)^3$ (6)

     $= w^6 r^{12}$.   (2)

d. $(2x^2y^3)^3 = 2^3(x^2)^3(y^3)^3 = 8x^6y^9.$ (6) and (2)

e. $\left(\dfrac{2z}{3}\right)^2 = \dfrac{(2z)^2}{3^2}$ (7)

    $= \dfrac{2^2z^2}{9} = \dfrac{4z^2}{9}.$ (6)

f. $\left(\dfrac{a^2b^3}{c^4}\right)^5 = \dfrac{(a^2b^3)^5}{(c^4)^5}$ (7)

    $= \dfrac{(a^2)^5(b^3)^5}{(c^4)^5}$ (6)

    $= \dfrac{a^{10}b^{15}}{c^{20}}.$ (2)

g. $\left(\dfrac{ab^2}{c^2d}\right)^6 = \dfrac{(ab^2)^6}{(c^2d)^6} = \dfrac{a^6(b^2)^6}{(c^2)^6d^6} = \dfrac{a^6b^{12}}{c^{12}d^6}.$ (7), (6), and (2)

h. $\dfrac{(20)^3}{5^3} = \left(\dfrac{20}{5}\right)^3 = 4^3 = 64.$ (7)

example 7

The energy $\mathcal{E}$ stored in the electric field of a charged capacitor is given by $\mathcal{E} = \frac{1}{2}CV^2$, where C is the capacitance and V is the voltage across the terminals of the capacitor. What is the effect of doubling the voltage?

Let $\mathcal{E}_0$ be the energy when the voltage is doubled, that is, after the voltage is changed from V to $2V$. Then

$$\mathcal{E}_0 = \tfrac{1}{2}C(2V)^2 = \tfrac{1}{2}C(4V^2) = 4(\tfrac{1}{2}CV^2) = 4\mathcal{E}.$$

Thus the energy is increased by a factor of four; that is, it increased to four times its original value.

Exercise 2-1

In Problems 1–12, evaluate the given numbers.

1. $2^3.$ **2.** $(-3)^2.$ **3.** $2^4 - 2^5.$

4. $(-7)^1.$ **5.** $-(-2)^4.$ **6.** $\dfrac{-2^2}{(-2)^3}.$

7. $(-2^3)(-3)^2.$ **8.** $(3 - 5)^2.$ **9.** $\dfrac{-(-3)^2}{(-3)^3}.$

10. $2^3 \cdot 3^2 - 6^2.$ **11.** $(-2^2)^3.$ **12.** $(-2 + 3^2)^2.$

In Problems 13–80, simplify.

13. $x^3x^8.$ **14.** $x^4x^4.$ **15.** $y^5y^4.$

16. $t^2t.$ **17.** $x^2x^4x.$ **18.** $x^ax^b.$

19. $(x - 2)^5(x - 2)^3$.

20. $y^9 y^{91} y^2$.

21. $\dfrac{x^5 x^2}{y^2 y^3 y^4}$.

22. $\dfrac{x(x^2)}{y^2 y^3}$.

23. $(2x^2)(7x^6)$.

24. $x^4(3x^2)$.

25. $(-3x)(4x^3)$.

26. $(-2x^5)(-3x^4)$.

27. $(x^8)^2$.

28. $(x^4)^3$.

29. $(x^3)^3$.

30. $(x^5)^7$.

31. $(t^2)^n$.

32. $(x^b)^c$.

33. $(x^4)^2(x^3)^7$.

34. $x^6(x^4)^2$.

35. $\dfrac{x^7}{x^3}$.

36. $\dfrac{x^8}{x^{12}}$.

37. $\dfrac{x^{21}}{x^{22}}$.

38. $\dfrac{(a + b)^{16}}{(a + b)^{12}}$.

39. $\dfrac{y^{14}}{-y^8}$.

40. $\dfrac{-y^2}{-y^5}$.

41. $\dfrac{x^2 x^8}{x^{16}}$.

42. $\dfrac{x^{18}}{x^{10} x^{10}}$

43. $\dfrac{(x^5)^3}{x^2}$.

44. $\dfrac{(x^4)^2}{(x^5)^3}$.

45. $\dfrac{(x^4)^2}{x(x^6)}$

46. $\dfrac{t^{12}(t^6)}{(w^5)^3}$.

47. $\dfrac{(x^2)^4(x^4)^2}{(x^3)^7}$.

48. $\dfrac{1}{(x^4)^5}(x^4)^5$.

49. $(ab)^6$.

50. $(xy)^4$.

51. $(2x)^4$.

52. $(3x)^3$.

53. $(2x^4 y^2)^4$.

54. $(x^2 yz^3)^2$.

55. $\left(\dfrac{a}{b}\right)^3$.

56. $\left(\dfrac{x}{2}\right)^4$.

57. $\left(\dfrac{3}{x}\right)^4$.

58. $\left(\dfrac{x}{y}\right)^2$.

59. $(xy^2)^4$.

60. $(3x^2)^3$.

61. $\left(\dfrac{2y}{z}\right)^3$.

62. $\left(\dfrac{1}{x^2 y^3}\right)^5$.

63. $\left(\dfrac{2}{3} a^2 b^3 c^6\right)^2$.

64. $(-4)(2x^2)^2$.

65. $\left(\dfrac{x^2}{y^5}\right)^3$.

66. $\left(\dfrac{2x^2}{y^2}\right)^4$.

67. $\left(\dfrac{x^2 y^3}{2z^4}\right)^4$.

68. $\left(\dfrac{2x^4}{5y^2}\right)^3$.

69. $(-x)^{13}$.

70. $(-3x)^4$.

71. $(-2x^2 y)^4$.

72. $(-3)^2(-x)^3$.

73. $\dfrac{(-xy)^5}{(-t)^4}$.

74. $\dfrac{-y^3}{(-z)^2}$.

75. $(-x)^2(-x^2)$.

76. $\dfrac{5^{100}}{5^{99}}$.

77. $\dfrac{2^6 2^{11}}{(2^5)^3}$.

78. $\dfrac{(80)^6}{(40)^6}$.

79. $(x^a y^b)^c$.

80. $\left(\dfrac{x^a}{y^b}\right)^a$.

In Problems **81** *and* **82,** *evaluate. Assume that all numbers are approximate.*

81. $\dfrac{-(4.61)^3(-3.12)^2}{(5.77)^2}$.

82. $\dfrac{(2.41)^3 - (1.73)^2}{(1.82)^2}$.

83. The power P (in watts) dissipated in a resistance R (in ohms) is given by $P = I^2R$, where I is the current (in amperes). Find the power in each of the following cases.
    (a) $I = 3$ amperes and $R = 2$ ohms.
    (b) $I = -2$ amperes and $R = 2$ ohms.
    (c) $I = 0.1$ ampere and $R = 5$ ohms.

84. Under certain conditions, the pressure p of a vacuum system is given by the formula

$$p = \frac{ah^2}{V_0}.$$

    Find p if (a) $h = 3d$, and (b) $h = \frac{2}{3}d$.

85. In addition to the formula in Problem 83, another formula for the power P dissipated in a resistance R is $P = V^2/R$, where V is the voltage across the resistor terminals. What happens to the power if the voltage is (a) doubled, (b) tripled, and (c) halved.

86. Compute the value of

$$\frac{(x_1 - \bar{x})^2 + (x_2 - \bar{x})^2 + (x_3 - \bar{x})^2 + (x_4 - \bar{x})^2 + (x_5 - \bar{x})^2}{4}$$

    if $x_1 = 6$, $x_2 = 8$, $x_3 = 5$, $x_4 = 3$, $x_5 = 3$, and $\bar{x} = 5$.

87. Repeat Problem 86 if $x_1 = 3.45$, $x_2 = 4.81$, $x_3 = 9.84$, $x_4 = 7.11$, $x_5 = 3.84$, and $\bar{x} = 5.81$. Give your answer to two decimal places.

2-2   Zero and Negative Exponents

Until now we have worked only with exponents that were positive integers. We shall now attach a meaning to a zero exponent, as in a^0, so that Rules 1–7 hold. For example, we want Rule 1 ($a^m a^n = a^{m+n}$) to be true if either m or n is zero. Thus we must have

$$a^m a^0 = a^{m+0} = a^m; \quad \text{that is,} \quad a^m a^0 = a^m.$$

But we also know that multiplying a^m by 1 gives a^m:

$$a^m \cdot 1 = a^m.$$

Because a^0 plays the same role in multiplication as 1 does, it seems reasonable to define a^0 to be 1. But suppose a were zero. If $0^0 \cdot 0 = 0^{0+1} = 0^1 = 0$, then 0^0 could be any number. For this reason, 0^0 has no meaning in mathematics. Thus we make the following definition:

$a^0 = 1$ if $a \neq 0$.   The symbol 0^0 is undefined.

It can be shown that the other rules of exponents also hold true for this definition.

example 1

a. $2^0 = 1.$

b. $100^0 = 1.$

c. $(x^2 + 3)^0 = 1.$

d. $2(\frac{3}{4})^0 = 2(1) = 2.$

Now let us attach a meaning to a negative exponent, as in a^{-n}, so that Rules 1–7 hold. From Rule 1, we must have

$$a^n \cdot a^{-n} = a^{n+(-n)} = a^0 = 1; \quad \text{that is,} \quad a^n a^{-n} = 1.$$

But we also know that multiplying a^n by its reciprocal gives 1:

$$a^n\left(\frac{1}{a^n}\right) = 1.$$

Because we want a^{-n} to play the same role in multiplication as $1/a^n$ does, it is natural that we make the following definition.

$$a^{-n} = \frac{1}{a^n}.$$

For example, $4^{-2} = 1/4^2 = 1/16$. Do not confuse negative exponents with negative numbers. That is, $4^{-2} \neq -4^2$, since $\frac{1}{16} \neq -16$.
     Because

$$\frac{1}{a^{-n}} = \frac{1}{\frac{1}{a^n}} = a^n,$$

we also have the following rule:

$$\frac{1}{a^{-n}} = a^n.$$

example 2

a. $3^{-4} = \frac{1}{3^4} = \frac{1}{81}.$

b. $-x^{-6} = -(x^{-6}) = -\frac{1}{x^6}.$

c. $\frac{1}{3^{-2}} = 3^2 = 9.$

d. $\frac{1}{x^2} = x^{-2}.$

e. $\frac{1}{(x+2)^{-2}} = (x+2)^2.$

f. $2^{-3} \cdot 4^0 = \frac{1}{2^3} \cdot 1 = \frac{1}{8}.$

example 3

a. $2x^{-3} = 2\left(\dfrac{1}{x^3}\right) = \dfrac{2}{x^3}$, but $(2x)^{-3} = \dfrac{1}{(2x)^3} = \dfrac{1}{2^3x^3} = \dfrac{1}{8x^3}$.

b. $\dfrac{1}{(-2)^{-3}} = (-2)^3 = -8$.   We change the sign of the exponent only, not the sign

of the base. That is, $\dfrac{1}{(-2)^{-3}} \neq (2)^3$.

c. $3^{-1} + 4^{-1} = \dfrac{1}{3} + \dfrac{1}{4}$.   *Note:* $3^{-1} + 4^{-1} \neq \dfrac{1}{3+4}$.

Observe that from our previous results we can write

$$\frac{x^3}{x^5} = \frac{1}{x^{5-3}} = \frac{1}{x^2} = x^{-2} = x^{3-5}.$$

In general,

$$\boxed{\dfrac{a^m}{a^n} = a^{m-n}}$$

regardless of the values of m and n. This rule replaces Rules 3–5.

Also notice how we can manipulate factors in a fraction.

$$\frac{x^2y^{-3}}{z^{-4}} = x^2 \cdot y^{-3} \cdot \frac{1}{z^{-4}} = x^2 \cdot \frac{1}{y^3} \cdot z^4 = \frac{x^2z^4}{y^3}.$$

That is, a nonzero *factor* of the numerator (or denominator) of a fraction may be equivalently expressed as a factor of the denominator (or numerator) if the sign of its exponent is *changed*. For example,

$$\frac{x^{-2}y^3}{2z^{-2}} = \frac{y^3z^2}{2x^2}.$$

The word *factor* above is crucial! For example,

$$\frac{1}{2^2 + 3^2} \neq 2^{-2} + 3^{-2} \quad \text{but} \quad \frac{1}{2^23^2} = 2^{-2}3^{-2}.$$

example 4

a. $x^{-4}y^{-4} = \dfrac{1}{x^4y^4}$.

b. $\dfrac{4x^{-7}}{x^2} = \dfrac{4}{x^2x^7} = \dfrac{4}{x^9}$.

c. $-\dfrac{x^{-2}}{y^{-3}z^2} = -\dfrac{y^3}{x^2z^2}$.

d. $\dfrac{x^{-7}y^6}{x^9y^{-2}} = \dfrac{y^6y^2}{x^9x^7} = \dfrac{y^8}{x^{16}}$.

e. $\dfrac{2+x}{y^{-2}} = (2+x)y^2 = 2y^2 + xy^2$ by the distributive law, but in general*

$$\frac{2+x}{y^{-2}} \neq 2 + xy^2.$$

That is, the parentheses originally placed around the $2+x$ are crucial because the entire numerator is considered to be a single factor.

Although the rules of exponents stated in this chapter assumed the exponents to be positive integers, *the rules of exponents are equally true for any exponents.* Henceforth, we assume this fact, as Example 5 shows.

example 5

---

a. $x^5 x^{-2} = x^{5+(-2)} = x^3$.

b. $2x^{-2}x^{-3} = 2x^{-2-3} = 2x^{-5} = \dfrac{2}{x^5}$.

c. $(2x^3y^{-6})^2 = 2^2(x^3)^2(y^{-6})^2 = 4x^6y^{-12} = \dfrac{4x^6}{y^{12}}$.

d. $(x^2y^{-4})^{-3} = (x^2)^{-3}(y^{-4})^{-3} = x^{-6}y^{12} = \dfrac{y^{12}}{x^6}$.

Alternatively,

$$(x^2y^{-4})^{-3} = \frac{1}{(x^2y^{-4})^3} = \frac{1}{x^6 y^{-12}} = \frac{y^{12}}{x^6}.$$

e. $\left(\dfrac{x^{-2}y^3}{z^{-4}}\right)^{-6} = \dfrac{(x^{-2}y^3)^{-6}}{(z^{-4})^{-6}} = \dfrac{x^{12}y^{-18}}{z^{24}} = \dfrac{x^{12}}{y^{18}z^{24}}$.

f. $\left(\dfrac{3}{2}\right)^{-2} = \dfrac{3^{-2}}{2^{-2}} = \dfrac{2^2}{3^2} = \dfrac{4}{9}$.

Exercise 2-2

In Problems 1–15, find the values of the numbers.

1. 2^0.

2. $\left(\dfrac{3}{4}\right)^0$.

3. 2^{-3}.

4. 3^{-2}.

5. $\dfrac{2}{3^{-3}}$.

6. $\dfrac{4}{4^{-2}}$.

7. $2x^0 + (2x)^0$.

8. $2(-3)^0$.

9. $\dfrac{-1^0}{4^{-1}}$.

*Here, by the phrase *in general*, we mean *for all allowable values of x and y.* The statement $(2+x)/y^{-2} = 2 + xy^2$ may be true or false, depending on the values of x and y. For example, it is false if $x = 0$ and $y = 2$.

10. $-5^{-2}(25)$.

11. $\dfrac{1}{(-3)^{-3}}$.

12. $2^{-1} + 3^{-1}$.

13. $\dfrac{6^{-4}}{6^{-2}}$.

14. $\dfrac{2^{-1} \cdot 2^0}{3^0 \cdot 4^{-1}}$.

15. $\dfrac{(3^{-2})^0}{1^{-1}}$.

*In Problems **16–30**, write the expression by using positive exponents only. Simplify.*

16. x^{-2}.

17. x^{-6}.

18. $2^{-1}x$.

19. $\dfrac{1}{x^{-3}}$.

20. $\dfrac{1}{3x^{-2}}$.

21. $3y^{-4}$.

22. $2^{-2}x^{-4}$.

23. $\dfrac{x}{4^{-2}}$.

24. $\dfrac{7^0}{x^{-1}yz^{-2}}$.

25. $x^{-5}y^{-7}$.

26. $x^{-1}y^{-2}z^4$.

27. $\dfrac{2a^2b^{-4}}{c^{-5}}$.

28. $\dfrac{a^5b^{-4}}{c^{-3}d}$.

29. $\dfrac{x^9y^{-12}}{w^2z^{-4}}$.

30. $\dfrac{(x^2 + 4x^4)^0}{x^{-2}}$.

*In Problems **31–62**, perform the operations and simplify. Give all answers with positive exponents only.*

31. x^8x^{-7}.

32. $x^{-7}x$.

33. $x^{-2}x^{-3}$.

34. $x^2x^{-4}x^9$.

35. $(xy^{-5})^{-4}$.

36. $(2x^2y^{-1})^2$.

37. $2(x^{-1}y^2)^2$.

38. $(x^{-5}y^6)^{-1}$.

39. $(3t)^{-2}$.

40. $(x^{-4}y^{-4})^4$.

41. $(x^{-5}y^5z)^{-3}$.

42. $\dfrac{10x^6}{x^{-2}}$.

43. $\dfrac{t^{-8}}{t^{-12}}$.

44. $\dfrac{-2b^{-30}}{b^{-5}}$.

45. $\dfrac{x^{-2}y^4}{x^6y^{-1}}$.

46. $\dfrac{(x^{-6}y^2)xy^{-2}}{xy}$.

47. $\dfrac{x^{-2}(yz)^2w}{x^{-3}y^5}$.

48. $\dfrac{x^6}{(x^{-4}y^8)y^{-8}}$.

49. $\dfrac{2(2x^2y)^2}{3y^{-13}z^{-2}}$.

50. $\dfrac{x^2y^{-5}}{(x^{-8}y^6)^{-3}}$.

51. $\dfrac{2^0}{(xy)^{-4}(x^2y)}$.

52. $\left(\dfrac{y}{z^{-1}}\right)^{-1}$.

53. $\left(\dfrac{3}{4}\right)^{-3}$.

54. $\left(\dfrac{2}{5}\right)^{-2}$.

55. $\left(\dfrac{8x^2}{5y^2}\right)^{-1}$.

56. $\dfrac{1}{(3x^{-1})^{-1}}$.

57. $\left(-\dfrac{z^{-1}}{x}\right)^{-1}$.

58. $\dfrac{xyz^{-1}}{(x^2)^{-4}}$.

59. $\left(\dfrac{x^{-3}y^{-6}z^2}{2xy^{-1}}\right)^{-2}$.

60. $\left[\left(\dfrac{x}{y}\right)^{-2}\right]^{-4}$.

61. $\left[\dfrac{x^{-1}y^4}{(z^2)^{-2}}\right]^{-5}$.

62. $\dfrac{[(xy)^{-2}]^3}{[(x^2y^{-2})^3]^{-2}}$.

*In Problems **63–66**, evaluate. Assume that all numbers are approximate.*

63. $\dfrac{(4.75)^{-1}}{(8.21)^{-2}}$.

64. $\left(\dfrac{4.62}{8.14}\right)^{-3}$.

65. $\dfrac{(3.24)^{-2}(1.11)^2}{(3.13 - 1.24)^4}$.

66. $\dfrac{(2.67 + 6.04)^{-3}}{(1.73)^2}$.

2-3   Scientific Notation

In science and technology, we often have to deal with numbers that are either very small or very large. Writing such numbers in our usual notation may be inconvenient. For example, the longest wavelength of visible red light is about 0.00000076 meter. The speed at which that light travels through air is about 300,000,000 meters per second, and the frequency of the light is 390,000,000,000,000 hertz. To avoid having to write so many zeros to locate the decimal point in such numbers, we may express the numbers in a compact form called *scientific notation*.

Scientific notation is based on powers of 10, some of which are as follows:

$$10 = 10^1 \qquad 0.1 = \frac{1}{10} \quad = 10^{-1}$$

$$100 = 10^2 \qquad 0.01 = \frac{1}{100} \quad = 10^{-2}$$

$$1000 = 10^3 \qquad 0.001 = \frac{1}{1000} \quad = 10^{-3}$$

$$10,000 = 10^4 \qquad 0.0001 = \frac{1}{10,000} = 10^{-4}.$$

We describe scientific notation as follows.

A number N is in **scientific notation** when it is expressed as the product of a decimal number between 1 and 10 and some integer power of 10. That is, $N = a \times 10^n$ where $1 \le a < 10$ and n is an integer.

example 1

Write the following numbers in scientific notation.

a. 0.063. Here we want to move the decimal point two places to the right to get 0.063 to be 6.3. To do this, we multiply by $10^2 \times 10^{-2}$ (which is 1):

$$0.063 = (0.063 \times 10^2) \times 10^{-2}$$
$$= 6.3 \times 10^{-2}.$$

b. 2575. Here we want to move the decimal point three places to the left to get 2575 to be 2.575. To do this, we multiply by $10^{-3} \times 10^3$:

$$2575 = (2575 \times 10^{-3}) \times 10^3 = 2.575 \times 10^3.$$

In each answer of Example 1, notice that the exponent of the power of 10 corresponds to the number of places the decimal point must be moved from its original position. If the decimal point is moved to the *right*, the exponent is *negative*; if it is moved to the *left*, the exponent is *positive*. Use this technique to verify the results in Example 2.

example 2

a. $0.000624 = 6.24 \times 10^{-4}$.

b. $21,000,000 = 2.1 \times 10^{7}$.

c. $0.000000000000409 = 4.09 \times 10^{-13}$.

d. $6170 = 6.17 \times 10^{3}$.

e. $16.2 = 1.62 \times 10$.

f. $0.005930 = 5.930 \times 10^{-3}$.

g. The wavelength and frequency given at the beginning of this section can be written 7.6×10^{-7} meter and 3.9×10^{14} hertz, respectively.

To change a number from scientific notation to ordinary decimal notation, we use the exponent of the power of 10 to help us locate the decimal point. If the exponent is *positive*, the decimal point is moved to the *right*; if it is *negative*, the decimal point is moved to the *left*. This is illustrated in Example 3.

example 3

a. To change 6.23×10^{5} to decimal notation, we must move the decimal point five places to the right. So $6.23 \times 10^{5} = 623,000$.

b. To change 4.53×10^{-4} to decimal notation, we must move the decimal point four places to the left. So $4.53 \times 10^{-4} = 0.000453$.

c. $6.24 \times 10^{-3} = 0.00624$.

d. $2.613 \times 10^{8} = 261,300,000$.

e. $7.0030 \times 10^{-5} = 0.000070030$.

example 4

a. $(0.0003)^{3} = (3 \times 10^{-4})^{3} = 3^{3} \times 10^{-12} = 27 \times 10^{-12} = 2.7 \times 10^{-11}$.

b. $(3 \times 10^{4})(5 \times 10^{4}) = (3 \times 5)(10^{4} \times 10^{4}) = 15 \times 10^{8} = 1.5 \times 10^{9}$.

example 5

Coulomb's law states that the force F (in newtons) acting between two small objects having electric charges q_1 and q_2 (in coulombs) is given by

$$F = \frac{(9 \times 10^9)q_1 q_2}{r^2},$$

where r is the distance between the objects (in meters). Given that in the hydrogen atom the electron and proton each have a charge of 1.6×10^{-19} coulomb and are separated by a distance of 5.3×10^{-11} meter, compute the force between them. Give the answer in scientific notation.

Here we treat the powers of 10 and the other factors separately:

$$F = \frac{(9 \times 10^9)(1.6 \times 10^{-19})(1.6 \times 10^{-19})}{(5.3 \times 10^{-11})^2}$$

$$= \frac{(9 \times 1.6 \times 1.6)(10^9 \times 10^{-19} \times 10^{-19})}{(5.3)^2(10^{-22})}$$

$$= \left[\frac{9 \times 1.6 \times 1.6}{(5.3)^2}\right]10^{9-19-19+22}.$$

The first factor is approximately 0.82, and the second factor is 10^{-7}. Thus

$$F = 0.82 \times 10^{-7} = 8.2 \times 10^{-8} \quad \text{newton.}$$

The use of the equals sign in $F = 0.82 \times 10^{-7}$ is a convenience that we shall adopt throughout the text. More precisely, we should write $F \approx 0.82 \times 10^{-7}$, where $\approx$ is read *is approximately equal to.*

In Example 5, the separation of powers of 10 and the other factors illustrates the mathematics of the computation. When calculators are used, such a separation may or may not be necessary. For example, a calculator that allows us to enter numbers which are no more than 8 to 10 digits long could not directly handle this calculation without a scientific-notation capability. This is a good time for you to see if your calculator allows entry of a number in scientific notation and how such a number is displayed.

Exercise 2-3

*In Problems **1–10**, express the given number in scientific notation.*

1. 0.0000060214.

2. 213,146,100,000,000.

3. 10.4.

4. 0.006241001.

5. 26,245.1001.

6. 2,600,000.

7. 142.

8. 0.0071.

9. 0.76.

10. 0.1.

Write the numbers in Problems 11–18 in decimal notation.

11. 2.62×10^8. **12.** 1.234×10^{-8}.

13. 6.24×10^{-10}. **14.** 1.006×10^4.

15. 2.020×10^{-1}. **16.** 6.0411×10^{12}.

17. 7.611×10^5. **18.** 2.0×10.

19. The mass of the earth, in kilograms, is usually taken to be

$$5,983,000,000,000,000,000,000,000.$$

Express this mass in scientific notation.

20. The speed of light in a vacuum is taken to be 300,000,000 meters per second. Express this speed in scientific notation.

21. A numerical value of the gravitational constant is

$$0.0000000000667.$$

Express this constant in scientific notation.

22. The Milky Way galaxy is estimated to contain about one hundred billion stars. Express this number in scientific notation.

23. A current I of 10^4 amperes is produced in a conductor, with length L of 4 meters, at a point where the earth's magnetic field B is 5×10^{-5} teslas at right angles to the conductor. The force F, in newtons, on the conductor is given by

$$F = IBL$$
$$= (10^4)(5 \times 10^{-5})(4).$$

Evaluate F.

24. While the universe is about 10^{10} years old, humans have existed only for about 10^6 years. Determine the number of years the universe existed before humans, and express that number in scientific notation.

25. If the mass of an electron is 9.11×10^{-31} kilogram, how many electrons would it take to make 1 kilogram?

26. The electric potential at a distance of 1.73×10^{-4} meter from a point charge of 4.62×10^{-2} coulomb is

$$\frac{(9 \times 10^6)(4.62 \times 10^{-2})}{1.73 \times 10^{-4}} \quad \text{volts.}$$

Evaluate this potential.

In Problems 27–32, perform the indicated operations and give your answer in scientific notation.

27. $(1.3 \times 10^{-4})(2.0 \times 10^6)$. **28.** $\dfrac{9.3 \times 10^{-1}}{3.1 \times 10^5}$.

29. $\dfrac{(3.0 \times 10^{11})(4.2 \times 10^{-4})}{2 \times 10^{13}}$. **30.** $\dfrac{(4.8 \times 10^{-1})(5.0 \times 10^{-2})}{(3.2 \times 10^{-3})(3.0 \times 10^{-4})}$.

31. $\dfrac{(1.0 \times 10^4)^3}{2.5 \times 10^5}$. **32.** $\dfrac{(1.2 \times 10^{-2})^2}{2.88 \times 10}$.

33. The volume V of a sphere is given by $V = \frac{4}{3}\pi r^3$, where r is the radius. Find the volume of the earth (in cubic meters) if the earth's radius is 6.37×10^6 meters.

37. An equilibrium constant, K, that relates to the solubility of lead iodide is given by

$$K = [Pb^{++}][I^-]^2.$$

Calculate K if $[Pb^{++}]$ is 1×10^{-2} and $[I^-]$ is 1.2×10^{-3}.

35. Two small objects have electric charges of 3.3×10^{-6} and 4×10^{-6} coulomb. Find the force between the objects when they are placed 2 meters apart. (Refer to Example 5.)

36. In calibrating the scale of a voltmeter, the following formula is used.

$$R_x = R_T\left(\frac{I_M - I_x}{I_x}\right).$$

Find the value of R_x (in ohms) if $R_T = 2000$ ohms, $I_M = 10^{-3}$ ampere, and $I_x = 7.5 \times 10^{-4}$ ampere.

37. The resistance R (in ohms) of a wire of length L (in meters) and cross-sectional area A (in square meters) is given by $R = \rho L/A$, where ρ (the Greek letter rho) is the resistivity of the material (in ohm·meters). Find the resistance of a copper wire 5 meters long with a cross-sectional area of 0.0000003 square meter. The resistivity of copper is 0.000000017 ohm·meter.

2-4 Radicals

If $b^n = a$, where n is a positive integer, then b is called an **nth root of a**. For example, because $2^3 = 8$, we call 2 a **cube root** (or third root) of 8. Similarly, 3 is a **square root** (or second root) of 9 because $3^2 = 9$. Since $(-3)^2 = 9$, -3 is also a square root of 9. Even though 3 and -3 are both square roots of 9, there is a way to distinguish between these two roots. Whenever a number has a *positive* nth root, it is called the **principal nth root**. Thus the principal square root of 9 is 3. For convenience, we shall omit the word *principal* and simply say that 3 is *the* square root of 9. If a number has only a negative nth root, that root is considered the principal nth root. For example, *the* cube root of -8 is -2 because $(-2)^3 = -8$ and there are no positive cube roots of -8.

We denote the principal nth root of a by the symbol $\sqrt[n]{a}$, where n is called the **index**, a is the **radicand**, and $\sqrt{}$ is the **radical sign**. For example, $\sqrt[3]{-8} = -2$. The symbol $\sqrt[n]{a}$ is itself called a **radical**. The index 2 is usually omitted for principal square roots. Thus $\sqrt{9} = 3$ (not -3). We define $\sqrt[n]{0}$ to be 0.

example 1

a. $\sqrt{25} = 5$ (and 5 is *the* square root of 25), because $5^2 = 25$.

b. $\sqrt[4]{16} = 2$ (and 2 is *the* fourth root of 16), because $2^4 = 16$. In the radical $\sqrt[4]{16}$, the index is 4 and the radicand is 16.

c. $\sqrt[3]{-1} = -1$ (and -1 is *the* cube root of -1), because $(-1)^3 = -1$ and no positive number has its cube equal to -1.

d. $\sqrt[5]{0} = 0$, because any root of 0 is 0.

e. $\sqrt[3]{\dfrac{1}{125}} = \dfrac{1}{5}$, because $\left(\dfrac{1}{5}\right)^3 = \dfrac{1}{125}$.

f. $\sqrt{0.01} = 0.1$, because $(0.1)^2 = .01$.

g. $-\sqrt{81} = -(\sqrt{81}) = -(9) = -9$.

h. $-\sqrt[3]{-8} = -(-2) = 2$.

We wish to point out two things. First, difficulties arise with even roots of negative numbers because such roots are not real numbers. For example, $\sqrt{-4}$ does not represent a real number, as there is no real number with a square that is negative. Such roots are called *imaginary numbers* and will be discussed in Chapter 11. Therefore, for the present we shall avoid any questions concerning even roots of negative numbers.

Second, some roots of numbers are irrational. For example, $\sqrt{2}$ is irrational but is often approximated by 1.414. In some calculations we shall find it convenient to leave an answer in radical form instead of using a decimal approximation obtained with a calculator.

example 2

Given the formula

$$d = \sqrt{(x_2 - x_1)^2 + (y_2 - y_1)^2},$$

find d if $x_1 = 1$, $x_2 = -7$, $y_1 = 2$, and $y_2 = 8$.

$$d = \sqrt{(x_2 - x_1)^2 + (y_2 - y_1)^2} = \sqrt{(-7 - 1)^2 + (8 - 2)^2}$$

$$= \sqrt{(-8)^2 + (6)^2} = \sqrt{64 + 36} = \sqrt{100}$$

$$= 10.$$

This formula, called the **distance formula,** is used in analytic geometry. Notice that $\sqrt{64 + 36} \neq \sqrt{64} + \sqrt{36}$. In general, $\sqrt{a + b} \neq \sqrt{a} + \sqrt{b}$. Also, we point out that $\sqrt{a^2 + b^2} \neq a + b$, which is clear by letting $a = 8$ and $b = 6$.

example 3

The impedance Z of a series R-L circuit is given by

$$Z = \sqrt{X_L^2 + R^2},$$

where X_L is the inductive reactance, R is the resistance, and all quantities are measured in ohms. Find the impedance of a circuit in which $X_L = 10$ ohms and $R = 12$ ohms.

$$Z = \sqrt{(10)^2 + (12)^2} = \sqrt{100 + 144} = \sqrt{244} = 15.6 \text{ ohms.}$$

example 4

The current I (in amperes) in a resistance R (in ohms) in which the power dissipation is P (in watts) is given by

$$I = \sqrt{\frac{P}{R}}.$$

Find the current if the resistance is 3×10^3 ohms and the power dissipation is 3×10^{-3} watts.

$$I = \sqrt{\frac{3 \times 10^{-3}}{3 \times 10^3}} = \sqrt{10^{-3}(10^{-3})} = \sqrt{10^{-6}} = 10^{-3} \text{ ampere.}$$

There are three properties of radicals that will be useful in our future work. To begin with, note that since $\sqrt{5}$ is a number which has a square of 5, we have $\sqrt{5} \cdot \sqrt{5} = 5$. More generally, we have this rule:

$$\boxed{\textbf{1.} \quad (\sqrt[n]{a})^n = a.}$$

Thus $\sqrt[3]{2} \cdot \sqrt[3]{2} \cdot \sqrt[3]{2} = (\sqrt[3]{2})^3 = 2$. There are two additional properties that allow us to simplify radicals:

$$\boxed{\begin{aligned} \textbf{2.} \quad & \sqrt[n]{ab} = \sqrt[n]{a}\,\sqrt[n]{b}. \\ \textbf{3.} \quad & \sqrt[n]{\frac{a}{b}} = \frac{\sqrt[n]{a}}{\sqrt[n]{b}}. \end{aligned}}$$

For example, by Rule 2 we have $\sqrt{24} = \sqrt{4 \cdot 6} = \sqrt{4}\sqrt{6} = 2\sqrt{6}$. Here 24 was written as a product of factors so that we could easily compute the square root of one of them. We say that the factor 4 has been "removed" from the radicand, and $2\sqrt{6}$ is considered to be a *simplified form* of $\sqrt{24}$. Writing $\sqrt{24} = \sqrt{8 \cdot 3}$ would not have helped in the simplification.

example 5

Simplify the numbers.

a. $\sqrt{18} = \sqrt{9 \cdot 2} = \sqrt{9}\sqrt{2} = 3\sqrt{2}$.

b. $\sqrt[3]{-16} = \sqrt[3]{(-8)(2)} = \sqrt[3]{-8}\sqrt[3]{2} = -2\sqrt[3]{2}$.

example 6

a. Write $\sqrt{\frac{11}{25}}$ in a simpler form that does not contain a fractional radicand.

By Rule 3 we have

$$\sqrt{\frac{11}{25}} = \frac{\sqrt{11}}{\sqrt{25}} = \frac{\sqrt{11}}{5}.$$

b. Write $\frac{\sqrt{20}}{\sqrt{5}}$ in a simpler form that is free of radicals.

By Rule 3,

$$\frac{\sqrt{20}}{\sqrt{5}} = \sqrt{\frac{20}{5}} = \sqrt{4} = 2.$$

When a fraction has a square root in its denominator, such as $\frac{2}{\sqrt{3}}$, it is possible to express the fraction so that no radical appears in the denominator. For example,

$$\frac{2}{\sqrt{3}} = \frac{2}{\sqrt{3}} \cdot 1 = \frac{2}{\sqrt{3}} \cdot \frac{\sqrt{3}}{\sqrt{3}} = \frac{2\sqrt{3}}{(\sqrt{3})^2} = \frac{2\sqrt{3}}{3}.$$

Similarly,

$$\frac{4}{\sqrt{5}} = \frac{4}{\sqrt{5}} \cdot \frac{\sqrt{5}}{\sqrt{5}} = \frac{4\sqrt{5}}{5}.$$

This procedure is called *rationalizing the denominator* and will be discussed more fully in Chapter 9.

Exercise 2-4

In Problems 1–38, compute the numbers without the aid of a calculator.

1. $\sqrt{49}$.
2. $\sqrt[3]{125}$.
3. $\sqrt[3]{8}$.
4. $\sqrt{81}$.
5. $\sqrt{36}$.
6. $\sqrt{100}$.
7. $\sqrt[3]{-27}$.
8. $\sqrt[3]{-8}$.
9. $-\sqrt[3]{-64}$.
10. $\sqrt[4]{1}$.
11. $\sqrt[4]{16}$.
12. $\sqrt[5]{-1}$.
13. $\sqrt[5]{0}$.
14. $\sqrt[3]{64}$.
15. $\sqrt[3]{-125}$.
16. $\sqrt[5]{32}$.
17. $\sqrt[6]{64}$.
18. $\sqrt{12 \cdot 3}$.
19. $\sqrt{0.04}$.
20. $\sqrt{0.25}$.
21. $\sqrt{\frac{1}{16}}$.
22. $\sqrt{\frac{1}{100}}$.
23. $-\sqrt{25}$.
24. $-\sqrt[3]{-1}$.

25. $\sqrt{81} - \sqrt[3]{-8}.$

26. $\sqrt{64} - \sqrt[3]{-8}.$

27. $\dfrac{\sqrt{64} + \sqrt[3]{-64}}{\sqrt{81} + \sqrt[4]{81}}.$

28. $\sqrt[3]{|-8|}.$

29. $\sqrt{5} \cdot \sqrt{5}.$

30. $\sqrt[3]{7} \cdot \sqrt[3]{7} \cdot \sqrt[3]{7}.$

31. $(\sqrt[4]{4})^4.$

32. $(\sqrt{3})^2.$

33. $\sqrt{(-3)^2} - \sqrt{3^2}.$

34. $\dfrac{\sqrt{49} - \sqrt{36}}{\sqrt{100} - \sqrt[3]{1}}.$

35. $\dfrac{(-1)^2 - (3\sqrt{9})}{|-4| + \sqrt{16}}.$

36. $\dfrac{(-2)^2 + (-3)^4}{\sqrt[5]{1} + |2 - 3|}.$

37. $\sqrt{0.01} + \sqrt{0.0025}.$

38. $2(\sqrt[3]{.008}) - (0.01)^2.$

In Problems **39–65,** *simplify the numbers by using properties of radicals, as in Examples 5 and 6.*

39. $\sqrt{50}.$

40. $\sqrt{75}.$

41. $\sqrt{12}.$

42. $\sqrt{32}.$

43. $\sqrt{8}.$

44. $\sqrt{18}.$

45. $\sqrt{54}.$

46. $\sqrt[3]{24}.$

47. $\sqrt[4]{48}.$

48. $\sqrt[4]{162}.$

49. $\sqrt[5]{64}.$

50. $\sqrt[3]{-54}.$

51. $\sqrt[3]{-500}.$

52. $\sqrt{\dfrac{3}{2}} \cdot \sqrt{6}.$

53. $\sqrt{\dfrac{3}{5}} \cdot \sqrt{\dfrac{1}{15}}.$

54. $\sqrt{\dfrac{5}{4}}.$

55. $\sqrt{\dfrac{14}{9}}.$

56. $\sqrt{\dfrac{2}{25}}.$

57. $\sqrt[3]{\dfrac{10}{27}}.$

58. $\dfrac{\sqrt{90}}{\sqrt{10}}.$

59. $\dfrac{\sqrt{50}}{\sqrt{2}}.$

60. $\dfrac{\sqrt[4]{64}}{\sqrt[4]{4}}.$

61. $\dfrac{\sqrt[3]{-2}}{\sqrt[3]{16}}.$

62. $\dfrac{\sqrt[5]{-4}}{\sqrt[5]{-128}}.$

63. $\sqrt{8} \cdot \sqrt{2}.$

64. $\sqrt{27} \cdot \sqrt{3}.$

65. $\sqrt[3]{4} \cdot \sqrt[3]{16}.$

In Problems **66–71,** *rationalize the denominators.*

66. $\dfrac{5}{\sqrt{6}}.$

67. $\dfrac{3}{\sqrt{2}}.$

68. $\dfrac{2.4}{\sqrt{6}}.$

69. $\dfrac{1}{\sqrt{7}}.$

70. $\dfrac{3}{2\sqrt{5}}.$

71. $\dfrac{4}{3\sqrt{2}}.$

In Problems **72** *and* **73,** *use the distance formula in Example 2 to find d with the given information.*

72. $x_1 = 10, y_1 = 2, x_2 = 7, y_2 = -2.$

73. $x_1 = -1, y_1 = 1, x_2 = -6, y_2 = 13.$

74. Compute y' where

$$y' = \frac{\dfrac{x + 5}{2\sqrt{x + 1}} - \sqrt{x + 1}}{(x + 5)^2}$$

and $x = 3.$

75. In statistics, the standard deviation of the numbers x_1 and x_2 is given by

$$\sqrt{\frac{(\bar{x} - x_1)^2 + (\bar{x} - x_2)^2}{2}},$$

where $\bar{x} = (x_1 + x_2)/2$. Find the standard deviation of $x_1 = 0$ and $x_2 = 4$.

76. The relationship between the molecular velocity (v) and molecular weight (M) of two gases A and B at the same temperature is given by Graham's diffusion law:

$$\frac{v_A}{v_B} = \sqrt{\frac{M_B}{M_A}}.$$

Given that the molecular weight of hydrogen (H_2) is 2 and the molecular weight of oxygen (O_2) is 32, find the value of

$$\frac{v_{H_2}}{v_{O_2}}.$$

77. In an R-L series circuit, $X_L = 5$ ohms and $R = 12$ ohms. Find the circuit impedance. (Refer to Example 3.)

78. The filament of a 100-watt light bulb has a resistance of 144 ohms. Find the current through the filament. (Refer to Example 4.)

79. The radius of a circle with area A is given by

$$r = \sqrt{\frac{A}{\pi}}.$$

Find the radius of a circle if the area is (a) 4π square meters, and (b) 15 square centimeters.

80. The Pythagorean theorem allows one side of a right triangle to be found when the other two sides are known. The relationships to be used are given in Fig. 2-1. Find the value of the indicated variable in each case.

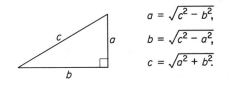

$$a = \sqrt{c^2 - b^2},$$
$$b = \sqrt{c^2 - a^2},$$
$$c = \sqrt{a^2 + b^2}.$$

FIGURE 2-1

(a) a if $c = 5$ meters and $b = 4$ meters.
(b) a if $c = 25$ centimeters and $b = 24$ centimeters.
(c) b if $c = 5 \times 10^{-2}$ meter and $a = 4 \times 10^{-2}$ meter.
(d) b if $c = 7.2 \times 10^{-2}$ meter and $a = 3.1 \times 10^{-2}$ meter.

2-5 Review

Review Questions

1. In $(3x)^2$ the base is __(a)__, but in $3x^2$ it is __(b)__.

2. The cube of $2x$ is equal to _____.

3. Although $2^2 = 4$ and $(-2)^2 = 4$, by the symbol $\sqrt{4}$ we mean __(2)(−2)__.

4. The principal square root of 16 is _____ .

5. In scientific notation, the number 0.026 is written as _____ .

6. $x^2(x^3) = $ __(a)__ and $(x^3)^2 = $ __(b)__ .

7. The expression x^2/x^3 may be written as x raised to what negative power? _____

8. $7^0 = $ _____(a)_____ but 0^0 is _____(b)_____ .

Answers to Review Questions

1. (a) $3x$, (b) x.   **2.** $8x^3$.   **3.** 2.   **4.** 4.   **5.** 2.6×10^{-2}.   **6.** (a) x^5, (b) x^6.
7. -1.   **8.** (a) 1, (b) Not defined.

Review Problems

In Problems **1–24,** *determine whether each statement is, in general, true or false.*

1. $a^3a^2 = a^6$.

2. $\left(\dfrac{1}{x}\right)^3 = \dfrac{1}{x^3}$.

3. $2^2 + 3^2 = 5^2$.

4. $(-a)^4 = a^4$.

5. $3 + 3 + 3 = 3^3$.

6. $(x^2y)^2 = x^4y$.

7. $(2x^2)^3 = 2^3x^5$.

8. $\dfrac{x^5}{x^3} = x^2$.

9. $(-y)^3 = -y^3$.

10. $2^2 \cdot 2^4 = 4^8$.

11. $3x = xxx$.

12. $(-3)^3 = -3^3$.

13. $(-2)^2 = -2^2$.

14. $(2 + 5)^2 = 2^2 + 5^2$.

15. $a^3a^7 = a^7a^3$.

16. $(x^2)^y = x^{2y}$.

17. $(2x)^2 = 2x^2$.

18. $\sqrt{16} = -4$.

19. $\sqrt{5}\sqrt{5} = \sqrt{25}$.

20. $\sqrt{4 \cdot 2} = 4\sqrt{2}$.

21. $\sqrt[3]{-\dfrac{1}{8}} = -\dfrac{1}{2}$.

22. $\sqrt[3]{0} = 0$.

23. $\sqrt{1} + \sqrt{1} = \sqrt{2}$.

24. $(\sqrt[3]{-1})^2 = 1$.

In Problems **25–62,** *simplify.*

25. $x^6x^4x^3$.

26. $\dfrac{x^2x^{20}}{y^5y^2}$.

27. $\dfrac{(x^2)^5}{(y^5)^{10}}$.

28. $(5x^2)(2x^3)$.

29. $(-2xy^4)^5$.

30. $\left(\dfrac{2xy^3}{z^2}\right)^2$.

31. $\dfrac{(x^3)^6}{x(x^3)}$.

32. $\dfrac{(xy^2)^2}{(t^2w)^3}$.

33. $(-x)^2(-x)^3$.

34. $\dfrac{(x^2)^3(x^4)^5}{(x^3)^8}$.

35. $\dfrac{(5^7)^2}{(5^4)^4}$.

36. $\dfrac{2^62^{11}}{(2^5)^3}$.

37. $(x^2y^{-3}z^{12})^4$.

38. $\dfrac{x^2x^{-5}x^{10}}{x^{12}}$.

39. $(4t^2)^{-2}$.

40. $(x^{-2}y^2)^3$.

41. $\dfrac{x^{-2}y^{-6}z^2}{xy^{-1}}$.

42. $(-2z)^{-3}$.

43. $-\sqrt{36} + \sqrt{81}$.

44. $\dfrac{-\sqrt{144}}{|-12|}$.

45. $|-2| - \sqrt[4]{16}$.

46. $(\sqrt[3]{2})^3$.

47. $\sqrt{13} \cdot \sqrt{13}$.

48. $\dfrac{(-1)^3 - 3\sqrt{49}}{|-5| + \sqrt{81}}$.

49. $\dfrac{1}{3}\sqrt[3]{\dfrac{1}{27}}$.

50. $\dfrac{\sqrt[5]{-32}}{\sqrt{9}}$.

51. $\sqrt[3]{0.001} + \sqrt{0.0025}$.

52. $\dfrac{\sqrt{4} - \sqrt[3]{8}}{\sqrt{6}}$.

53. $\sqrt{45}$.

54. $\sqrt{72}$.

55. $\sqrt[4]{810}$.

56. $\sqrt[3]{40}$.

57. $\sqrt{\dfrac{7}{16}}$.

58. $\sqrt{\dfrac{10}{9}}$.

59. $\dfrac{\sqrt[3]{24}}{\sqrt[3]{3}}$.

60. $\dfrac{\sqrt{72}}{\sqrt{2}}$.

61. $\sqrt{18} \cdot \sqrt{2}$.

62. $\sqrt[3]{8} \cdot \sqrt[3]{16}$.

*In Problems **63** and **64**, rationalize the denominator.*

63. $\dfrac{6}{\sqrt{3}}$.

64. $\dfrac{2}{\sqrt{8}}$.

*In Problems **65–68**, write the numbers in scientific notation.*

65. 0.0000564.

66. 45,030,000,000.

67. 28,000,000.

68. 0.007007.

69. The elastic potential energy PE (in joules) of a spring is given by

$$PE = \tfrac{1}{2}kx^2,$$

where k is the spring constant (in newtons per meter) and x is the displacement of the spring (in meters) from the equilibrium position ($x = 0$). Find the potential energy of a spring in each of the following cases.
(a) $k = 3.2$, $x = 0.2$.
(b) $k = 4$, $x = -0.2$.
(c) $k = 2$, $x = -1.2$.

70. The resistivity of silver is 0.000000016 ohm·meter. A coil is to be made by using 2500 meters of wire. If the wire has a circular cross section of radius 5×10^{-2} meter, find the resistance of the coil. (Refer to Problem 37 in Sec. 2-3.)

3

fundamental operations with algebraic expressions

3-1 Algebraic Expressions

If numbers, including literal numbers, are combined by the operations of addition, subtraction, multiplication, division, or extraction of roots, then the resulting expression is called an **algebraic expression**. A constant or variable by itself is also considered to be an algebraic expression. For example, some algebraic expressions are 7, $2x^2$, $3 + 4\sqrt{y}$, and x/y.

If an algebraic expression consists of parts that are connected by plus or minus signs, then each part, together with the sign preceding it, is called a **term** of the expression. For example, the expression $5ax^3 - 2bx + 3$ has three terms: The first is $+5ax^3$, the second is $-2bx$, and the third is $+3$. The expression $4x^2$ is considered to consist of one term, $+4x^2$.

If a term can be written as the product of two or more expressions, then each expression is called a **factor** of that term. For example, because $5ax^3$ can be written as $(5a)(x)(x^2)$, we can say that $5a$, x, and x^2 are factors of $5ax^3$. These are not the *only* factors of $5ax^3$. We can write $5ax^3 = (5a)(x^3)$. Thus $5a$ and x^3 are also factors of $5ax^3$. In fact, since $5ax^3 = (1)(5ax^3)$, certainly $5ax^3$ can be considered a factor of $5ax^3$. In general, any term is a factor of itself.

When a term is considered as the product of two factors, each factor is called the **coefficient** of the other factor. For example, in the term $6xy^2$ the factor $6x$ is the coefficient of y^2, and $6y^2$ is the coefficient of x. If a term is a constant or is the product of a constant factor and a literal factor, then the constant is called the **(numerical) coefficient** of the *term*. Thus the coefficient of the term $6xy^2$ is 6 (the literal factor is xy^2).

example 1

Consider the four terms of $x^3 - 2x^2 + \frac{x}{3} + 7$. Because $x^3 = 1 \cdot x^3$ and $-2x^2 = -2 \cdot x^2$, the coefficients of the terms x^3 and $-2x^2$ are 1 and -2, respectively. Similarly, the coefficient of the term $x/3$ is $\frac{1}{3}$, because $x/3 = \frac{1}{3} \cdot x$. Finally, the coefficient of the constant term 7 is 7.

Algebraic expressions having exactly one term, such as $4x^2$, are called **monomials**. Those having more than one term, such as $x^2 + 2x + 3$, are called **multinomials**. Two special cases of multinomials, namely those containing exactly two and exactly three terms, are called **binomials** and **trinomials**, respectively. Thus, $3x^2 - 2$ is a binomial, and $2x^2 + \sqrt{x} + 2$ is a trinomial.

example 2

a. $6 - x^2 + 5x^4$ is a multinomial and a trinomial.

b. $\frac{6}{7}y$ is a monomial.

c. $\frac{2}{x^4} + 6$ is a multinomial and a binomial.

The word *polynomial* refers to an algebraic expression with a special form. A **polynomial** in one variable, such as x, is an expression in which *each term is either a constant or of the form* ax^n, where a is a constant and n is a *positive* integer. For example, $2x^4 + 6x - 7$ is a polynomial in x. The exponent of the greatest power of x that occurs in a polynomial is called the **degree** of the polynomial, and the coefficient of the corresponding term is called the **leading coefficient**. Thus $2x^4 + 6x - 7$ has degree 4 and leading coefficient 2. Similarly, $8y^5 - 6y^4 - \sqrt{2}y + 3$ is a polynomial in y of degree 5 and has leading coefficient 8. A *nonzero* constant is considered to be a polynomial of degree zero; thus 7 is a polynomial of degree zero. The constant zero is also a polynomial, but no degree is attached to it.

example 3

a. $6 - x^2 - x^5$ is a polynomial in x. The term with the greatest power of x is $-x^5$. Thus the polynomial has degree 5 and leading coefficient -1. This polynomial is also a multinomial.

b. $\frac{6}{7}y$ is a polynomial in y with degree 1 and leading coefficient $\frac{6}{7}$. This polynomial is also a monomial.

c. $\frac{2}{x^2} + 6$ is *not* a polynomial, because the term $\frac{2}{x^2}$, which can be written $2x^{-2}$, is not a constant or of the form ax^n where n is a *positive* integer.

Exercise 3-1

1. Given the term $3x^2y$, state (a) the coefficient of y, and (b) the coefficient of $3y$.
2. Given the term $-4a^2b^3c$, state (a) the coefficient of b^3, and (b) the coefficient of $-4c$.

In Problems **3–10**, *give the (numerical) coefficient of each term.*

3. $2x^3 + 3x^2 - 4x$.   4. $3x^2 - x$.   5. $2x^2y - 2x + 1$.

6. $4x - 6x^2y^2$.   7. $4wx^2 + x - 2$.   8. x^2.

9. $2 + \frac{7x}{3}$.   10. $-\frac{x}{2} + \sqrt{2}\,x^2$.

In Problems **11–28**, *classify each expression as (a) a monomial, (b) a multinomial, (c) a binomial, or (d) a trinomial. More than one classification may apply. For those that are polynomials in x or y, give the degree.*

11. $2x^2$.   12. $2x^3 + 6$.   13. $y^2 - 2y + 3$.

14. $4z$.   15. $3x^4 - \sqrt{3}$.   16. $2 - x^2 - x$.

17. $3x$.   18. $2y^4 + \frac{2}{y^4}$.   19. $\frac{1}{x} + 3x - 4$.

20. $x - x^9$.   21. $\frac{4}{5}x - x^4$.   22. $x - 2$.

23. $2 + \frac{1}{x^3} + x - x^2$.   24. 7.

25. $x^5 - x^4 - x^3 + x^2 - x + 1$.   26. $x^2(x^3)$.

27. 5.   28. x^4.

3-2 Addition and Subtraction of Algebraic Expressions

The addition or subtraction of algebraic expressions involves the notion of *similar terms*. **Similar terms**, or **like terms**, are terms that differ at most only in their numerical coefficients. That is, similar terms have the same literal parts. For example, the terms $3x^2y$ and $-42x^2y$ are similar, as well as the pairs $-2x$ and $6x$, and 2 and 7. However, the terms $2x^2y^3$ and $2x^3y^2$ are not similar, because x^2y^3 is not the same as x^3y^2.

Similar terms are added or subtracted by using the basic laws we already know. For example, to simplify

$$-4x^2 + 5x + 2 + 9x^2 - x - 3,$$

we first gather similar terms together by using the commutative law:

$$-4x^2 + 9x^2 + 5x - x + 2 - 3.$$

Using the distributive law, we now combine similar terms:

$$-4x^2 + 9x^2 = (-4 + 9)x^2 = 5x^2,$$
$$5x - x = 5x - 1 \cdot x = (5 - 1)x = 4x,$$

and

$$2 - 3 = -1.$$

Thus

$$-4x^2 + 5x + 2 + 9x^2 - x - 3 = 5x^2 + 4x - 1.$$

Sometimes a number of terms in an algebraic expression are grouped together to indicate that they are to be treated as a single number or quantity. The most common symbols of grouping are **parentheses** ( ), **brackets** [ ], and **braces** { }. These symbols can be removed from an expression by using the distributive law, as Example 1 shows.

example 1

Remove symbols of grouping and simplify.

a. $2a + 3(b - c) = 2a + 3b - 3c$. *Each* term within the parentheses was multiplied by 3 as required by the distributive law. That is,

$$2a + 3(b - c) \neq 2a + 3b - c.$$

b. $-4[-2 + 3x] - y = (-4)(-2) + (-4)(3x) - y$
$$= 8 - 12x - y.$$
Here we multiplied each *enclosed* term by -4.

c. $x^2 + 3[-6x + x^2] = x^2 - 18x + 3x^2$ (removing brackets)
$$= x^2 + 3x^2 - 18x$$ (gathering similar terms)
$$= (1 + 3)x^2 - 18x$$ (distributive law)
$$= 4x^2 - 18x.$$

We can develop rules for conveniently removing grouping symbols immediately preceded by a plus or minus sign. For the case of a plus sign, consider the following.

$$2 + (x - 3y) = 2 + (1)(x - 3y)$$
$$= 2 + x - 3y \qquad \text{(distributive law)}.$$

We would arrive at the same result by merely removing the parentheses that appear in the original expression. On the other hand, consider

$$2 - (x - 3y)$$
$$= 2 + (-1)(x - 3y)$$
$$= 2 + (-1)(x) - (-1)(3y) \qquad \text{(distributive law)}$$
$$= 2 - x + 3y.$$

The same result would be obtained from the original expression by removing the minus sign in front of the parentheses, changing the sign of each term within the parentheses, and removing the parentheses. Generalizing our observations, we have these rules:

RULE 1

If symbols of grouping immediately preceded by a plus sign are to be removed, the sign of *each* term within the grouping symbols must remain the same.

RULE 2

If symbols of grouping immediately preceded by a minus sign are to be removed, then the minus sign should be removed and the sign of *each* term within the grouping symbols must be changed.

---

example 2

Remove symbols of grouping.

a. $3x + (2y + 3z) = 3x + 2y + 3z.$

b. $(2b - 3c - 4d) + 6 = 2b - 3c - 4d + 6.$ Here a plus sign is understood to be in front of the parentheses.

c. $2x - (3y - z) = 2x - 3y + z.$ Note that, in general,

$$2x - (3y - z) \neq 2x - 3y - z.$$

*The sign of **each** enclosed term must be changed.*

d. $(3a + b) - (-x^4 + 3x^2 - 1) = 3a + b + x^4 - 3x^2 + 1.$

e. $-(x - y) - (a + b) = -x + y - a - b.$

example 3

Simplify $-(3x + y^2 - 2) + (y^2 - 2x + 1).$

$$-(3x + y^2 - 2) + (y^2 - 2x + 1)$$

$= -3x - y^2 + 2 + y^2 - 2x + 1$ (removing parentheses)

$= -3x - 2x - y^2 + y^2 + 2 + 1$ (gathering similar terms)

$= -5x + 3$ (combining similar terms).

Sometimes grouping symbols appear within other grouping symbols, as in

$$-2[x - (5y - 3)].$$

When you remove grouping symbols, mistakes are less likely to occur if you remove the *innermost* grouping symbols first, then the next innermost, and so on, with the outermost grouping symbols being removed last. For example,

$$-2[x - (5y - 3)]$$

$= -2[x - 5y + 3]$ (removing parentheses)

$= -2x + 10y - 6$ (removing brackets).

example 4

Simplify.

$$-[3w^2x^2y - (2xy^2 - 3w^2) - 3(w^2x^2y + w^2)]$$

$= -[3w^2x^2y - 2xy^2 + 3w^2 - 3w^2x^2y - 3w^2]$

$= -[-2xy^2] = 2xy^2.$

example 5

Simplify.

$$-2\{2 - 3[-(x + 1)]\} - x$$

$= -2\{2 - 3[-x - 1]\} - x$ (removing parentheses)

$$= -2\{2 + 3x + 3\} - x \qquad \text{(removing brackets)}$$
$$= -2\{3x + 5\} - x \qquad \text{(combining within braces)}$$
$$= -6x - 10 - x \qquad \text{(removing braces)}$$
$$= -7x - 10 \qquad \text{(combining).}$$

Exercise 3-2

*In Problems **1–46**, simplify each expression by removing all symbols of grouping and combining similar terms.*

1. $3x - 6 + 8x + 4$.

2. $9x^2 - 3x - 4x^2 - 5x$.

3. $(3x + 2y - 5) + (8x - 4y + 2)$.

4. $(6x^2 - 10xy + 7) + (2z - xy + 4)$.

5. $(3x + 2y - 5) - (8x - 4y + 2)$.

6. $(6x^2 - 10xy + 7) - (2z - xy + 4)$.

7. $4y + (4y - 8)$.

8. $2 - (6x + 7) - 2x^2$.

9. $3x + 5y - (8y - x)$.

10. $2(x^2 + 5) - 8x$.

11. $3a - 2b + (4a - 6b + c)$.

12. $6x + 5 - (8x + 3)$.

13. $a - b - (c - d)$.

14. $8x - y + 2(y^2 - x^2)$.

15. $-(a - b - c) - (-a - b)$.

16. $-(-a + b - c) + (-a + b)$.

17. $4(9x + 3y + x)$.

18. $3(a - 5b) - a$.

19. $-2(7x - 8y + 2y)$.

20. $5(a - 5b - a)$.

21. $a + 2(b + c)$.

22. $2x + 3(1 - x^2)$.

23. $2(x^2 - 3) + 3(x^2 + 7)$.

24. $4(3 - a) - 2(a - 1)$.

25. $5(xy + z) - (3xy + 7)$.

26. $2[x + 3z] - 4(z + x) + 3\{x - 4z\}$.

27. $6(x^2 - 2x) + (3x - 5) - 4(x^2 + 2)$.

28. $2[(3x - 5) + 4]$.

29. $2[-(5 - x) + x]$.

30. $3[4x + (2 + 5x)]$.

31. $5[3x + 2(5 - x)]$.

32. $7[4 - (y + 8)]$.

33. $-\{4a - (6 + 3a)\}$.

34. $-2\{9(z^2 - 1)\}$.

35. $5x^2 + 3[8(x^2 - 1)] + 2$.

36. $[2a + 3(b - a)] + 7a$.

37. $\{9a - (3b + a + c)\} - 4\{2b + 3c\}$.

38. $4x^2 - [8x + 2(x + x^2)]$.

39. $[3x + 2y - (5x + 6y - 1)] - 3xy$.

40. $3(x + 2) - [5x - 6y - (x + y - w)]$.

41. $3\{4x - 2[5 - (x + 1)]\}$.

42. $-\{2[3(2x + 5) + 6x]\}$.

43. $3x - 3[2 - 2\{x^2 - 2y\}] - x^3$.

44. $2a^2b - [ab + 3(a - \{b + c\})]$.

45. $9 - 2\{8x - 3[4(y - 2x) - 6(x - y)]\}$.

46. $3\{5 - [xy - 2(xy + x)]\} - 4x$.

In Problems 47–50, write each expression in an equivalent form in which no symbols of grouping appear and then enclose all terms that contain x to any power within one set of grouping symbols preceded by a minus sign. For example,

$$3x^2 - (x - 5) = 3x^2 - x + 5 = -(-3x^2 + x) + 5.$$

47. $x + 2(x^2 + b) - 3x^3 + 1.$ **48.** $3(x^2y + b - x) - 4(x^2 + 2).$

49. $[-2x^2 + 3x^2y - (5x + 6y + 1)] - 3xy.$

50. $3(x - y) - 4(w - x^2 + xy).$

51. In a discussion of the oscillations of a circular disc, the expression

$$10[(10 - 100\theta) - (10 + 100\theta)]$$

occurs, where θ is the Greek letter theta. Simplify the expression.

52. The moment M for a particular loaded beam is given by

$$M = 1970x - 1200(x - 3) - 1000(x - 9).$$

Find a simplified expression for M.

53. The emf of a standard cell is found to be

$$1.0187[1 - 0.0004(T - 20)] \text{ volts,}$$

where T is the surrounding temperature of the cell in °C.
(a) Simplify the expression.
(b) Find the emf of a standard cell at 22°C.

54. A rectangle has dimensions $2a$ and $3(b + c)$, while a smaller rectangle has dimensions a and $b + c$. Write an expression for the difference in the perimeters of the rectangles, the larger minus the smaller perimeter; perform all indicated operations and simplify.

3-3   Multiplication of Algebraic Expressions

We now examine three situations that arise in the multiplication of algebraic expressions.

A.   Product of Two Monomials

Consider $(4x^2)(2xy)$, which is the product of two monomials. By the associative law of multiplication, the order of grouping is unimportant and we can remove the parentheses:

$$(4x^2)(2xy) = 4 \cdot x^2 \cdot 2 \cdot x \cdot y.$$

By the commutative law of multiplication, we can rearrange the factors so that those involving the same letters are adjacent. This gives

$$4 \cdot 2 \cdot x^2 \cdot x \cdot y.$$

Finally, by the rules of exponents we obtain

$$(4x^2)(2xy) = 8x^3y.$$

Thus we have the following rule:

> To multiply monomials, multiply their coefficients and multiply their literal factors.

example 1

Determine the following products.

a. $2x^2y(-4xy^3) = (2)(-4)(x^2x)(yy^3) = -8x^3y^4.$

b. $3x^2y^2(-2xyz^2)(-3xz) = (3)(-2)(-3)(x^2xx)(y^2y)(z^2z)$

$$= 18x^4y^3z^3.$$

Another way to find the product is to begin by multiplying the first two factors.

$$(3x^2y^2)(-2xyz^2)(-3xz) = (-6x^3y^3z^2)(-3xz)$$

$$= 18x^4y^3z^3.$$

Be careful about exponents when you multiply monomials. For example, to find $a(ac)^2$ we *do not* multiply a by ac and obtain $(a^2c)^2$. Rather, we must multiply a by $(ac)^2$ or a^2c^2. Thus $a(ac)^2 = a(a^2c^2) = a^3c^2.$

example 2

Determine the following products.

a. $(8ab^2)(4a^2b^3)^3.$

We *first* apply the rules of exponents to $(4a^2b^3)^3$:

$$(8ab^2)(4a^2b^3)^3 = 8ab^2(64a^6b^9) = 512a^7b^{11}.$$

b. $(-2x^2yz)^4(-2xy)^3 = (16x^8y^4z^4)(-8x^3y^3) = -128x^{11}y^7z^4.$

B. Product of a Monomial and a Multinomial

The distributive law is the key tool that is used in multiplying a monomial and a multinomial. Consider

$$2x(x + 4).$$

Here $2x$ is a monomial and $x + 4$ is a multinomial. By considering $2x$ as a single number and using the distributive law $a(b + c) = ab + ac$, we reduce the problem to that of multiplying monomials.

$$\underline{(2x)}(x + 4) = \underline{(2x)}(x) + \underline{(2x)}(4) = 2x^2 + 8x.$$

$$a \quad (b + c) = \quad a \quad b \quad + \quad a \quad c$$

More generally, we have the rule:

> To multiply a monomial and a multinomial, multiply the monomial by each term of the multinomial.

example 3

Perform the indicated operations and simplify.

a. $2xy(x^2 + 2x - y) = (2xy)(x^2) + (2xy)(2x) - (2xy)(y)$
$$= 2x^3y + 4x^2y - 2xy^2.$$

b. $-7x(-2 - y) = (-7x)(-2) - (-7x)(y)$
$$= 14x - (-7xy) = 14x + 7xy.$$

c. $(ab)^2(2aby - 8ab + 2) = (ab)^2(2aby) - (ab)^2(8ab) + (ab)^2(2)$
$$= (a^2b^2)(2aby) - (a^2b^2)(8ab) + (a^2b^2)(2)$$
$$= 2a^3b^3y - 8a^3b^3 + 2a^2b^2.$$

d. $2(2x^3 + 3x) - 3x(x^2 - 2x) = 4x^3 + 6x - 3x^3 + 6x^2$
$$= x^3 + 6x^2 + 6x.$$

e. $3x[2 - 4x(x - y)] = 3x[2 - 4x^2 + 4xy] = 6x - 12x^3 + 12x^2y.$

C.   Product of Two Multinomials

To find $(x + 2)(x + 3)$, which is the product of two multinomials, we use the distributive law $(a + b)c = ac + bc$, where $x + 2$ matches $a + b$ and $x + 3$ plays the role of c. That is, we take the first term in the left factor times the right factor, plus the second term in the left factor times the right factor:

$$(x + 2)\underline{(x + 3)} = x\underline{(x + 3)} + 2\underline{(x + 3)} = x^2 + 3x + 2x + 6 = x^2 + 5x + 6.$$

$$(a + b) \quad c \quad = a \quad c \quad + b \quad c$$

More generally, we have the rule:

> To multiply two multinomials, multiply each term of the first multinomial by the second multinomial.

example 4

Find the product $(2x - 3)(5x^2 + 3x - 1)$ and simplify.

$$
\begin{aligned}
(2x - 3)(5x^2 + 3x - 1) &= 2x(5x^2 + 3x - 1) - 3(5x^2 + 3x - 1) \\
&= 10x^3 + 6x^2 - 2x - 15x^2 - 9x + 3 \\
&= 10x^3 - 9x^2 - 11x + 3.
\end{aligned}
$$

example 5

Find the product $3x(2x + 1)(x - 2)$ and simplify.

$$
\begin{aligned}
3x(2x + 1)(x - 2) &= (6x^2 + 3x)(x - 2) \\
&= 6x^2(x - 2) + 3x(x - 2) \\
&= 6x^3 - 12x^2 + 3x^2 - 6x \\
&= 6x^3 - 9x^2 - 6x.
\end{aligned}
$$

example 6

Find the product $(2a + b - 1)(3a - 2b + c)$ and simplify.

$$
\begin{aligned}
&(2a + b - 1)(3a - 2b + c) \\
&= 2a(3a - 2b + c) + b(3a - 2b + c) - 1(3a - 2b + c) \\
&= 6a^2 - 4ab + 2ac + 3ab - 2b^2 + bc - 3a + 2b - c \\
&= 6a^2 - ab + 2ac - 2b^2 + bc - 3a + 2b - c.
\end{aligned}
$$

example 7

When finding $x - (x + 1)(x - 2)$, keep in mind that the first minus sign applies to the *product* of the binomials and must be kept until *after* that product is found.

$$
\begin{aligned}
x - (x + 1)(x - 2) &= x - [x(x - 2) + 1(x - 2)] \\
&= x - [x^2 - 2x + x - 2]
\end{aligned}
$$

$$= x - [x^2 - x - 2]$$
$$= x - x^2 + x + 2$$
$$= -x^2 + 2x + 2.$$

Before concluding this section, we leave you with some important notes. Do not confuse

$$a + 2(a + 3) \quad \text{with} \quad (a + 2)(a + 3).$$

We have

$$a + 2(a + 3) = a + 2a + 6 = 3a + 6,$$

but

$$(a + 2)(a + 3) = a(a + 3) + 2(a + 3)$$
$$= a^2 + 3a + 2a + 6$$
$$= a^2 + 5a + 6.$$

Similarly, do not confuse

$$(a + 2)a + 3 \quad \text{with} \quad (a + 2)(a + 3),$$

because

$$(a + 2)a + 3 = a^2 + 2a + 3,$$

but

$$(a + 2)(a + 3) = a^2 + 5a + 6,$$

as shown above.

Exercise 3-3

In Problems 1–64, perform the indicated operations and simplify.

1. $(3x)(5x^2)$.　　　　2. $(-4z)(10z)$.　　　　3. $(2x)(3xy)$.

4. $-a(ac)$.　　　　5. $3ab(a^2b)$.　　　　6. $xy(xz)(xw)$.

7. $2xy^2(-4x^3y^2)$.　　　　8. $-a^2b(-ac)$.　　　　9. $ab(a^2b)(bc^2)$.

10. $x(xy^2)(y^2z)$.　　　　11. $2x^2yz^2\left(\frac{1}{2}xz^2\right)$.　　　　12. $(2xy^2)^3(2y)^2$.

13. $(-3x)(4xy^2)(-2x^2y^3)$.　　　　14. $x(x^3y^2)^2(-2xy^2)^3$.

15. $(10x^4)(3x^3)^2$.　　　　16. $(3y^3)^2(-y)^3$.

17. $a(-bc)^2(cd)^2$.　　　　18. $(-xy)^3(-x)^2$.

19. $x(x^2 - 4x + 7)$.　　　　20. $-2(x - 2y^2 + 7xy)$.

21. $a^2b(-3 + ab - a)$.　　　　22. $2x(-x + 2y + 1)$.

23. $-5xy(x^2 - y^2 + xy)$.　　　　24. $a(b - a)(ac)$.

25. $(2x^2y)^2(x + 2y^2 - 3x^2)$.

26. $x^2yz(xy - yz - xz)$.

27. $-2xy(7 - 4x - 2y + x^2)$.

28. $(ab)^2(a^2 - b^2c + ac^2)$.

29. $(x + 2)(x + 5)$.

30. $(x + 4)(x + 5)$.

31. $(y - 2)(3y + 2)$.

32. $(y - 2)(y + 2)$.

33. $(3x - 1)(3x - 1)$.

34. $(2x + 3)(3x + 2)$.

35. $(4x + y)^2$.

36. $(x^2 + 4)(x^4 + 4)$.

37. $(3x^2)(2xy)(x + y)$.

38. $(x + 3)(5x^2)$.

39. $(t - 2)(t^2 + 2t + 4)$.

40. $(x + 5)(x^2 - x - 1)$.

41. $(x^2 - 2)(x^2 - 5x + 1)$.

42. $(2 + x - y)(x - y)$.

43. $(y^3 + 3y)(y^2 - y + 2)$.

44. $(2ab + b^2)^2$.

45. $(x + y + 1)(x + y - 1)$.

46. $(2x - 1)(2x^3 - 3x + 1)$.

47. $4x(2x - 1)(2x + 1)$.

48. $-3x^2(x - 2)(x - 1)$.

49. $(2ab + rt)^2$.

50. $3x^2(x + 2)(x^2 - 2)$.

51. $xy + y(y + x)$.

52. $(x - 3)x - 4$.

53. $(x^2 + 1)(2x) - (x^2 - 2)(2x)$.

54. $x^2y - 2x - x^2y(1 + x)$.

55. $x(x - 1) - 2(3 - x)$.

56. $2xy(x^2y) - y^2(2x^3 - 2xy)$.

57. $3x(x^2y - xy^2) - 3y(x^3 + 4x^2y)$.

58. $2(x^3y - 2x^2) - 2x^2(x^2 - 2xy)$.

59. $3(x - x^2) + (x + 1)(x - 1)$.

60. $(x + 1)(x^2 - x + 1) - 1 - x^3$.

61. $x^3 + y^3 - (x + y)(x^2 - xy + y^2)$.

62. $(-x - 2)(x + 2) - (-1 + x)x$.

63. $(1.4x + 3.2)(2.6x - 4.1)$.

64. $x + 4.54(2.32x - 1.41)$.

65. One rectangle has dimensions $2a$ and $3(b + c)$, while a smaller rectangle has dimensions $a - 1$ and $b + c$. Write an expression for the difference in the areas of the rectangles, namely, the larger area minus the smaller; perform all indicated operations and simplify.

66. In a mathematical development of the relativity of time, the following expression was encountered:

$$K\left\{(t_1 - t_2) - \frac{v}{c^2}(x_1 - x_2)\right\}.$$

Remove all symbols of grouping.

67. The condition necessary for a battery to deliver maximum power to a resistive load involves the expression

$$(R + r)^2(1) - R(2)(R + r).$$

Perform the indicated operations and simplify.

68. The approximate length of a suspension bridge cable is given by

$$a\left[1 + \frac{8}{3}\left(\frac{d}{a}\right)^3\right],$$

where a is the span and d is the sag. Perform the indicated operations.

69. The electrical resistance of a wire at temperature T is given by

$$R_0[1 + \alpha(T - T_0)],$$

where T_0 is a reference temperature and R_0 is the resistance of the wire at that temperature. The constant α (alpha) is called the *temperature coefficient of resistance*. Perform the indicated operations.

3-4 Division of Algebraic Expressions

A. Division of Monomials

To divide a monomial by a monomial, the rules of exponents are used. For example,

$$\frac{6x^2y^5}{18x^3y^3} = \frac{6}{18} \cdot \frac{x^2}{x^3} \cdot \frac{y^5}{y^3} = \frac{1}{3} \cdot \frac{1}{x} \cdot y^2 = \frac{y^2}{3x}.$$

In actual practice, some intermediate steps may be done mentally. For example, convince yourself that

$$\frac{-35x^3y^2}{7xy^2} = -5x^2.$$

example 1

Simplify.

a. $\dfrac{(2a^3b^2d)(3a^5b^2c)}{-3a^4b^2cd} = \dfrac{6a^8b^4cd}{-3a^4b^2cd}$

$$= \frac{6}{-3} \cdot \frac{a^8}{a^4} \cdot \frac{b^4}{b^2} \cdot \frac{c}{c} \cdot \frac{d}{d} = -2a^4b^2.$$

b. $\left(\dfrac{x^2y^3}{2xy^2}\right)^3 = \left(\dfrac{xy}{2}\right)^3 = \dfrac{x^3y^3}{8}.$ Here we simplified *before* cubing. It is a general practice that you should follow.

c. $\dfrac{(2a^2x)^3(-2a^4y)}{(2xy^2)^2} = \dfrac{(8a^6x^3)(-2a^4y)}{4x^2y^4} = \dfrac{-16a^{10}x^3y}{4x^2y^4} = -\dfrac{4a^{10}x}{y^3}.$

In general,

$$\frac{(a^2x)^2}{ay} \neq \frac{(ax)^2}{y} \qquad \text{(you must not divide } a^2 \text{ by } a),$$

but

$$\frac{(a^2x)^2}{ay} = \frac{a^4x^2}{ay} = \frac{a^3x^2}{y}.$$

B. Division of a Multinomial by a Monomial

When the numerator of a fraction is a multinomial, the fraction can be broken up into simpler fractions. This is based on the definition of division and the distributive law:

$$\frac{a+b+c}{d} = (a+b+c)\left(\frac{1}{d}\right) = a \cdot \frac{1}{d} + b \cdot \frac{1}{d} + c \cdot \frac{1}{d}.$$

But

$$a \cdot \frac{1}{d} + b \cdot \frac{1}{d} + c \cdot \frac{1}{d} = \frac{a}{d} + \frac{b}{d} + \frac{c}{d}.$$

Thus,

$$\boxed{\frac{a+b+c}{d} = \frac{a}{d} + \frac{b}{d} + \frac{c}{d}.}$$

More generally,

To divide a multinomial by a monomial, divide *each* term of the multinomial by the monomial.

For example,

$$\frac{3x^6 + x^3}{x} = \frac{3x^6}{x} + \frac{x^3}{x} = 3x^5 + x^2,$$

and

$$\frac{20x^2y^2 + 5xy^2 - 2x}{2xy} = \frac{20x^2y^2}{2xy} + \frac{5xy^2}{2xy} - \frac{2x}{2xy}$$

$$= 10xy + \frac{5y}{2} - \frac{1}{y}.$$

Students often make errors by applying the previous rule to a monomial divided by a multinomial. In such cases the rule *does not* apply. In general,

$$\frac{a}{b+c} \neq \frac{a}{b} + \frac{a}{c}.$$

For example,

$$\frac{8}{6+2} \neq \frac{8}{6} + \frac{8}{2},$$

because $1 \neq \frac{16}{3}$. However, by the rule we have

$$\frac{6+2}{8} = \frac{6}{8} + \frac{2}{8}.$$

example 2

Perform the divisions and simplify.

a. $\dfrac{6a^4b^2c^3 + 3a^5b^2c - 12a^6bc}{-6a^4b^2c^2} = \dfrac{6a^4b^2c^3}{-6a^4b^2c^2} + \dfrac{3a^5b^2c}{-6a^4b^2c^2} - \dfrac{12a^6bc}{-6a^4b^2c^2}$

$$= -c - \dfrac{a}{2c} + \dfrac{2a^2}{bc}.$$

b. $\dfrac{3x - (2x^2y)^2 - 7x^2(x^2y^2)}{3x(2y^2)} = \dfrac{3x - 4x^4y^2 - 7x^4y^2}{6xy^2}$

$$= \dfrac{3x - 11x^4y^2}{6xy^2} = \dfrac{3x}{6xy^2} - \dfrac{11x^4y^2}{6xy^2}$$

$$= \dfrac{1}{2y^2} - \dfrac{11x^3}{6}.$$

example 3

The reciprocal of the total resistance of three resistors, R_1, R_2, and R_3, connected in parallel in an electric circuit is

$$\dfrac{R_2R_3 + R_1R_3 + R_1R_2}{R_1R_2R_3}.$$

Simplify this expression.

$$\dfrac{R_2R_3 + R_1R_3 + R_1R_2}{R_1R_2R_3} = \dfrac{R_2R_3}{R_1R_2R_3} + \dfrac{R_1R_3}{R_1R_2R_3} + \dfrac{R_1R_2}{R_1R_2R_3}$$

$$= \dfrac{1}{R_1} + \dfrac{1}{R_2} + \dfrac{1}{R_3}.$$

C. Division of a Polynomial by a Polynomial

To divide a polynomial by a polynomial, we use so-called long division. But before we show you how, let us review long division with numbers:

$$
\begin{array}{r}
14 \\
16\,\overline{)\,239} \\
\underline{16} \\
79 \\
\underline{64} \\
15
\end{array}
$$

Here, 239 is the **dividend**, 16 is the **divisor**, the **quotient** is 14, and the **remainder** is 15. A method of checking a division is to verify that

$$(\text{quotient})(\text{divisor}) + \text{remainder} = \text{dividend}.$$

In our case

$$(14)(16) + 15 = 239,$$

which checks. The answer may be expressed as $14\frac{15}{16}$ or $14 + \frac{15}{16}$. Thus

$$\frac{239}{16} = 14 + \frac{15}{16} = \text{quotient} + \frac{\text{remainder}}{\text{divisor}}.$$

We now turn to dividing a polynomial by a polynomial when the degree of the divisor is less than or equal to the degree of the dividend. For example, consider

$$\frac{2x^3 - 5x^2 + 3x + 4}{x - 2}.$$

The polynomial $2x^3 - 5x^2 + 3x + 4$ is the dividend and the polynomial $x - 2$ is the divisor. Note that the powers of x in the dividend and divisor are written in decreasing order. First we divide $2x^3$, the first term of the dividend, by x, the first term of the divisor. This gives $2x^2$, the first term of the quotient.

$$
\begin{array}{r}
2x^2 - x + 1 \longleftarrow \text{quotient} \\
x - 2 \overline{\smash{)}\, 2x^3 - 5x^2 + 3x + 4} \\
\underline{2x^3 - 4x^2} \\
-x^2 + 3x \\
\underline{-x^2 + 2x} \\
x + 4 \\
\underline{x - 2} \\
6 \longleftarrow \text{remainder}
\end{array}
$$

Next, we multiply this quotient term $(2x^2)$ by the divisor $(x - 2)$, obtaining $2x^3 - 4x^2$, which is written below the corresponding similar terms of the dividend and *subtracted* from them. We obtain $-x^2$ and "bring down" $3x$, the next term of the dividend. Now we divide $-x^2$ by x (the first term of the divisor). This gives $-x$, the second term of the quotient, which we multiply by the divisor $(x - 2)$. This gives $-x^2 + 2x$, which we write below $-x^2 + 3x$ and *subtract*. We obtain x and bring down 4, the last term of the dividend. Repeating the division process, we arrive at 6, the remainder here. In general, *we end the division process when the remainder is zero or has degree less than the degree of the divisor.* Our answer may be written as

$$2x^2 - x + 1 + \frac{6}{x - 2}.$$

The division can be checked by verifying that

$$(\text{quotient})(\text{divisor}) + (\text{remainder}) = \text{dividend}.$$

Doing this we have

$$(2x^2 - x + 1)(x - 2) + (6) = 2x^2(x - 2) - x(x - 2) + 1(x - 2) + 6$$
$$= 2x^3 - 4x^2 - x^2 + 2x + x - 2 + 6$$
$$= 2x^3 - 5x^2 + 3x + 4,$$

which is equal to the dividend.

example 4

Divide $x^3 + 8$ by $x + 2$.

When a dividend is arranged in order of decreasing powers of the variable, there are times when certain powers do not appear. In $x^3 + 8$ there is no term containing x^2 and no term containing x. Because division of polynomials involves subtraction of similar terms, you will find it less confusing and possibly avoid error if each of the missing terms is inserted with a coefficient of 0. To do this in our case, we write the dividend as $x^3 + 0x^2 + 0x + 8$.

$$
\begin{array}{r}
x^2 - 2x\ + 4 \\
x + 2 \overline{\smash{\big)}\ x^3 + 0x^2 + 0x + 8.} \\
\underline{x^3 + 2x^2} \\
-2x^2 + 0x \\
\underline{-2x^2 - 4x} \\
4x + 8 \\
\underline{4x + 8} \\
0
\end{array}
$$

The answer is $x^2 - 2x + 4$.
Check: $(x^2 - 2x + 4)(x + 2) + 0 = x^3 + 2x^2 - 2x^2 - 4x + 4x + 8 = x^3 + 8$.

example 5

Divide $-2x^3 + 3x^4 - 3x^2 + 7$ by $3x^2 + x - 1$.

Remember to write the dividend in order of decreasing powers of x.

$$
\begin{array}{r}
x^2 - x\ - \tfrac{1}{3} \\
3x^2 + x - 1 \overline{\smash{\big)}\ 3x^4 - 2x^3 - 3x^2 + 0x + 7.} \\
\underline{3x^4 + x^3 - x^2} \\
-3x^3 - 2x^2 + 0x \\
\underline{-3x^3 - x^2 + x} \\
-x^2 - x + 7 \\
\underline{-x^2 - \tfrac{1}{3}x + \tfrac{1}{3}} \\
-\tfrac{2}{3}x + \tfrac{20}{3}
\end{array}
$$

Note that here the remainder has an x-term. The division should not be continued because the remainder has a lower degree (1) than the divisor (2). You should perform the necessary operations to check the work of this example. The answer is

$$x^2 - x - \frac{1}{3} + \frac{-\frac{2}{3}x + \frac{20}{3}}{3x^2 + x - 1}.$$

Exercise 3-4

In Problems **1–38**, *perform the divisions.*

1. $\dfrac{2ab}{4a}.$

2. $\dfrac{-14ab^2}{7a^2}.$

3. $\dfrac{35x^3y^2}{-7xy}.$

4. $\dfrac{-ax^2y^5}{-x^3y^3}.$

5. $\dfrac{-16x^2yz}{-32xy^2z^3}.$

6. $\dfrac{15xy^6z^2}{10x^2y^3z}.$

7. $\dfrac{2x^4yw^2}{4x^3yw}.$

8. $\dfrac{25ab^3c^2}{-5ab^2}.$

9. $\dfrac{-9x^2y^3w}{3x^2w}.$

10. $\dfrac{6x^2y^2z^3}{2xy^3z^2}.$

11. $\dfrac{(3xy)^2}{y}.$

12. $\left(\dfrac{3xy}{6y}\right)^2.$

13. $\dfrac{(abc^2)^2(ab)}{2(ab)^2}.$

14. $\dfrac{(3x^2y^2z)^2}{x^4y^8z}.$

15. $\dfrac{x^3y^2}{(x^2y)^2}.$

16. $\dfrac{(a^2bc^2)(ab^2c^2)}{a^2b^4c}.$

17. $\dfrac{(-2xy)^2(x^2y)}{(xyz)^3}.$

18. $\dfrac{abc(ab)^2}{a^2b^2}.$

19. $\dfrac{(2a^2b^2)^4(2abc)}{8ab^2c}.$

20. $\dfrac{(5u^2v^2w)(-3u^4v^2w^5)^2}{2v^3u^2w^2}.$

21. $\dfrac{(-2x)^2(-xy^2)^3}{(-2x^2y)^2}.$

22. $\dfrac{(-x)(-y)^2(xy)^3(y^4x)}{-xy^2}.$

23. $\dfrac{5 - x^2 + 2x}{x}.$

24. $\dfrac{10x^3 - 15x + 2}{5x}.$

25. $\dfrac{4x + 2y}{-2x}.$

26. $\dfrac{xy + x^2}{xy}.$

27. $\dfrac{3x^2y - x^3y^2 + 1}{x^2y^2}.$

28. $\dfrac{2x^2y^2 - 6xz^2 + 4x}{2xy^2z}.$

29. $\dfrac{(x^3y^2)^2 + 3x^2y^3 - x}{xy^3}.$

30. $\dfrac{p(pr) + p(pr)^2 + r(pr)^2}{pr^2}.$

31. $\dfrac{(4xy^2z)^2 + 8x^5y^4z^3 - 4x^6y^3z^2}{4x^2y^2z^2}.$

32. $\dfrac{(3p^2qr)^2(-p)^{15}}{3pqr}.$

33. $\dfrac{6x^2y - 2y^2 + 7x - 4}{-3x}.$

34. $\dfrac{2x^2 - 6y^2 + 5z^2 + 3w^2}{-30xyz^2}.$

35. $\dfrac{2xy - (2xy^2)^2 - 3x^3y^3}{(xy)^2}.$

36. $\dfrac{x(xy) + y(-x^2) + x^3y^3}{-x(xy)}.$

37. $\dfrac{2x(x^3y^2)^2 + 3x^2(2y^2) - x}{-xy^4}.$

38. $\dfrac{x(x - y) - y(2x)}{xy}.$

In Problems **39–56**, *perform the long divisions.*

39. $\dfrac{2x^2 + 3x - 4}{x - 2}.$

40. $\dfrac{9x^2 - 6x - 6}{3x - 1}.$

41. $\dfrac{x + 3}{x + 2}.$

42. $\dfrac{x}{x + 1}.$

43. $\dfrac{4x^2 - 7x - 5}{4x + 1}.$

44. $\dfrac{5x^2 + 26x + 8}{x + 5}.$

45. $\dfrac{x^3 + 2x^2 - 5x + 2}{x - 1}$.

46. $\dfrac{3x^3 + 2x^2 + 3x + 1}{3x + 2}$.

47. $\dfrac{1 + 2x - x^2 - 2x^3 - 3x^4}{3x + 5}$.

48. $\dfrac{8x^4 - 4x^2 + x}{2x + 1}$.

49. $\dfrac{8x^3 - 2x^2 + 4x - 3}{4x - 1}$.

50. $\dfrac{3x^3 + x^2 - 6x + 1}{3x + 1}$.

51. $\dfrac{x^4 - 2x^2 + 1}{x - 1}$.

52. $\dfrac{x^4 - 8x^2 + 16}{x + 2}$.

53. $\dfrac{x^4 - y^4}{x + y}$.

54. $\dfrac{x^5 + y^5}{x + y}$.

55. $\dfrac{5x^4 - 18x^3 + 7x^2 - 3x + 4}{x^2 - x + 6}$.

56. $\dfrac{x^3 + x^2 + x + 3}{x^2 - x - 1}$.

57. The efficiency ε of a reversible heat engine operating between a high-temperature reservoir at an absolute temperature T_1 and a low-temperature reservoir at temperature T_2 is given by

$$\varepsilon = \frac{T_1 - T_2}{T_1}.$$

Find another form for ε. The absolute temperature scale has a range from zero degrees through all positive values. From purely mathematical considerations, is there any restriction imposed on the value of T_1?

58. The equivalent resistance of two resistors R_1 and R_2 connected in parallel is

$$\frac{R_1 R_2}{R_1 + R_2}.$$

(a) Simplify this expression, if possible.
(b) Simplify the reciprocal of this expression, if possible.

59. When three capacitors C_1, C_2, and C_3 are connected in series, the total capacitance of the combination, C_t, is given by

$$C_t = \frac{C_1 C_2 C_3}{C_2 C_3 + C_1 C_3 + C_1 C_2}.$$

Find the reciprocal of C_t and perform the indicated division.

60. When a weight W is suspended from a system of three springs having elastic constants k_1, k_2, and k_3, respectively, the displacement of the weight is found to be

$$W\left(\frac{4k_1 k_2 + k_1 k_3 + k_2 k_3}{4k_1 k_2 k_3}\right).$$

Perform the indicated operations.

61. The average speed $\bar{v}$ of a certain particle, in meters per second, is given by

$$\bar{v} = \frac{2t^2 + 7t + 3}{t + 3},$$

where t is in seconds.
(a) Perform the indicated division to find a simplified expression for $\bar{v}$.
(b) Show that the given expression and the simplified expression give the same value for $\bar{v}$ when $t = 2$.

3-5   Special Products

In mathematics, certain products occur so often that we find it worthwhile to memorize their patterns. But just "knowing" these so-called *special products* is not enough. You have to be so familiar with them that you can easily recognize them in any form. Each special product can be obtained by the use of the distributive law. This will be shown for the first special product, and you may verify the others for yourself.

We begin with the square of a binomial:

$$(a + b)^2 = (a + b)(a + b)$$
$$= a(a + b) + b(a + b) = a^2 + ab + ba + b^2$$
$$= a^2 + 2ab + b^2.$$

That is, *the square of a binomial is equal to the square of the first term, plus twice the product of the terms, plus the square of the second term.* This implies that $(a - b)^2 = a^2 + 2a(-b) + (-b)^2 = a^2 - 2ab + b^2$, and we have our first two special products:

SQUARE OF A BINOMIAL

$$(a + b)^2 = a^2 + 2ab + b^2.$$
$$(a - b)^2 = a^2 - 2ab + b^2.$$

Note that the square of a binomial is a trinomial. Thus the patterns above *do not* mean that $(a + b)^2 = a^2 + b^2$ or that $(a - b)^2 = a^2 - b^2$. For example,

$$(1 + 2)^2 \neq 1^2 + 2^2 \quad \text{because} \quad 9 \neq 5.$$

We point out that letters, such as a and b, that appear in the statements of special products are understood to denote any expression representing a number.

example 1

Find the given products.

a. $(x + 3)^2$.

Here x plays the role of a in $(a + b)^2$ and 3 plays the role of b.

$$(x + 3)^2 = x^2 + 2(x)(3) + 3^2 = x^2 + 6x + 9.$$

b. $(y - 4)^2 = y^2 - 2(y)(4) + 4^2 = y^2 - 8y + 16.$

c. $(2x + 4)^2$.

Here $2x$ plays the role of a in $(a + b)^2$.

$$(2x + 4)^2 = (2x)^2 + 2(2x)(4) + 4^2$$
$$= 4x^2 + 16x + 16.$$

d. $(x^2 - 3y^3)^2$.

Here x^2 is a and $3y^3$ is b in $(a - b)^2$.

$$(x^2 - 3y^3)^2 = (x^2)^2 - 2(x^2)(3y^3) + (3y^3)^2$$
$$= x^4 - 6x^2y^3 + 9y^6.$$

e. $-3a(-4a + b)^2$.

You may be tempted to use the distributive law immediately. However, because of the exponent 2, the distributive law does not directly apply. It can be used *after* the binomial $-4a + b$ is squared.

$$-3a(-4a + b)^2 = -3a[(-4a)^2 + 2(-4a)b + b^2]$$
$$= -3a[16a^2 - 8ab + b^2]$$
$$= -48a^3 + 24a^2b - 3ab^2.$$

The next special product is used for multiplying the sum and difference of two terms.

PRODUCT OF THE SUM AND DIFFERENCE
$$(a + b)(a - b) = a^2 - b^2.$$

That is, *the product of the sum and difference of two terms is equal to the square of the first term, minus the square of the second term.*

example 2

Find the given products.

a. $(x + 4)(x - 4) = x^2 - 4^2 = x^2 - 16$.

b. $(4x - 3y)(4x + 3y)$.

Here $4x$ plays the role of a and $3y$ plays the role of b.

$$(4x - 3y)(4x + 3y) = (4x)^2 - (3y)^2 = 16x^2 - 9y^2.$$

c. $(a^2 + 1)(a^2 - 1) = (a^2)^2 - 1^2 = a^4 - 1$.

d. $(y - \sqrt{2})(y + \sqrt{2}) = y^2 - (\sqrt{2})^2 = y^2 - 2$.

e. $(3x - 4)(-4 - 3x)$.

This will have the form $(a + b)(a - b)$ if we write $3x - 4$ as $-4 + 3x$.

$$(3x - 4)(-4 - 3x) = (-4 + 3x)(-4 - 3x)$$
$$= (-4)^2 - (3x)^2 = 16 - 9x^2.$$

The next special product of binomials gives rise to a trinomial.

$$(x + a)(x + b) = x^2 + (a + b)x + ab.$$

example 3

a. $(x + 7)(x + 4) = x^2 + (7 + 4)x + (7)(4) = x^2 + 11x + 28.$

b. $(x - 2)(x + 6).$

   Here -2 is a because $x - 2 = x + (-2).$

   $$(x - 2)(x + 6) = x^2 + (-2 + 6)x + (-2)(6)$$
   $$= x^2 + 4x - 12.$$

c. $(z - 1)(z - 2).$

   Here -1 is a and -2 is $b.$

   $$(z - 1)(z - 2) = z^2 + (-1 - 2)z + (-1)(-2)$$
   $$= z^2 - 3z + 2.$$

The previous special product $(x + a)(x + b)$ can also be conveniently obtained by following a schematic three-step method. To illustrate, we shall redo Example 3(b). Refer to Fig. 3-1.

Step 1.   Multiply the *first* terms in the binomials, ①, to obtain the first term of the result: $(x)(x) = x^2.$

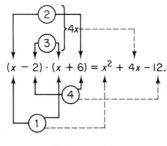

$$(x - 2) \cdot (x + 6) = x^2 + 4x - 12.$$

FIGURE 3-1

Step 2.   The middle term of the result is the product of the *outer* terms of the binomials ②, *plus* the product of the *inner* terms ③: $6x + (-2x) = 4x.$

Step 3.   Multiply the *last* terms in the binomials, ④, to obtain the last term of the result: $(-2)(6) = -12.$

The computations in Steps 1–3 are usually done mentally. This method is also useful for multiplying binomials of the general form $(ax + b)(cx + d)$, as Example 4 shows.

example 4

Find $(x + 2)(3x - 7)$ by using the three-step method. (See Fig. 3-2.)

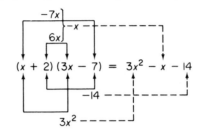

FIGURE 3-2

example 5

Find each of the following by using the three-step method.

a. $(x + 2)(x - 3) = x^2 - x - 6.$

b. $(2x - 1)(x - 3) = 2x^2 - 7x + 3.$

c. $(3y - 4)(2y + 3) = 6y^2 + y - 12.$

example 6

Find each of the following by using special products.

a. $(x + 1)(x - 1) + (x + 2)^2 = [x^2 - 1] + [x^2 + 4x + 4]$
$$= 2x^2 + 4x + 3.$$

b. $(x^2 + 4)(x + 2)(x - 2) = (x^2 + 4)[(x + 2)(x - 2)]$
$$= (x^2 + 4)(x^2 - 4) = x^4 - 16.$$

c. $(x - 2)^2 - (3 - x)^2 = x^2 - 4x + 4 - (9 - 6x + x^2)$
$$= x^2 - 4x + 4 - 9 + 6x - x^2$$
$$= 2x - 5.$$

Note that parentheses were used to enclose the square of $3 - x$ because the minus sign in front of $(3 - x)^2$ applies to the entire square. *Do not write*
$$(x - 2)^2 - (3 - x)^2 = x^2 - 4x + 4 - 9 - 6x + x^2.$$

d. $(x + 1)(x - 1)^2 = (x + 1)(x^2 - 2x + 1)$
$$= x(x^2 - 2x + 1) + 1(x^2 - 2x + 1)$$
$$= x^3 - 2x^2 + x + x^2 - 2x + 1$$
$$= x^3 - x^2 - x + 1.$$

Exercise 3-5

*In Problems **1–50**, find the indicated products by direct use of the special product relationships. It should not be necessary to refer to the relationships.*

1. $(x + 5)^2$.　　　　**2.** $(x - 2)^2$.　　　　**3.** $(x - 4)^2$.　　　　**4.** $(x + 12)^2$.

5. $(t + \frac{1}{2})^2$.　　　　**6.** $(x - \frac{7}{3})^2$.　　　　**7.** $(x + 2y)^2$.　　　　**8.** $(t - 3s)^2$.

9. $(2x + 3)^2$.　　　　**10.** $(3 - 4x)^2$.　　　　**11.** $(3x - 4y)^2$.　　　　**12.** $(3x + \frac{1}{3}y)^2$.

13. $(-8x - 2y)^2$.　　　　**14.** $(-2x + y)^2$.　　　　**15.** $(3abc - 4ef)^2$.

16. $\left(\dfrac{x}{y} + 3\right)^2$.　　　　**17.** $(-6x + 5y)^2$.　　　　**18.** $(-x - 3y)^2$.

19. $(x + 8)(x + 3)$.　　　　**20.** $(x - 6)(x - 1)$.　　　　**21.** $(x - 2)(x + 1)$.

22. $(s + 5)(s + 4)$.　　　　**23.** $(y + 7)(y - 5)$.　　　　**24.** $(x + 14)(x - 2)$.

25. $(x - 2)(x - 3)$.　　　　**26.** $(x + 4y)(x - 2y)$.　　　　**27.** $(x - 3)(x + 3)$.

28. $(y - 8)(y + 8)$.　　　　**29.** $(3s + 4)(3s - 4)$.　　　　**30.** $(x - 2y)(x + 2y)$.

31. $(\frac{1}{2}x + 2)(\frac{1}{2}x - 2)$.　　　　**32.** $(3x - 4y)(3x + 4y)$.　　　　**33.** $(2x + 3)(5x + 2)$.

34. $(y^2 - 4)(y^2 + 4)$.　　　　**35.** $(4x - 3)(3x - 4)$.　　　　**36.** $(3x - 2)(-x + 7)$.

37. $(x^2 - 3)(x^2 + 3)$.　　　　**38.** $(3x^2 - 4)(3 - 4x^2)$.　　　　**39.** $(\frac{2}{3}a + 1)(\frac{1}{3}a - 2)$.

40. $\left(\dfrac{ab}{c} + d\right)\left(\dfrac{ab}{c} - d\right)$.　　　　**41.** $(2t - 1)(t + 3)$.

42. $(6x + b)(-b + 6x)$.　　　　**43.** $(xyz + a)(xyz - a)$.

44. $(-x + 7)(7 + x)$.　　　　**45.** $(x + \sqrt{3})(x - \sqrt{3})$.

46. $(\sqrt{6} - \sqrt{7})(\sqrt{6} + \sqrt{7})$.　　　　**47.** $(xy^2 + a)^2$.

48. $(x^3 - 1)(x^3 - 1)$.　　　　**49.** $(x^2 - 2)^2$.　　　　**50.** $(x^2 - y^2)(x^2 + y^2)$.

*In Problems **51–72**, perform the operations.*

51. $4(x + 3)^2$.　　　　**52.** $x(x - 2)^2$.　　　　**53.** $2x(y - 3)(y + 3)$.

54. $-2a(a + 4)^2$.　　　　**55.** $(a^2b - 2m^2n)^2$.　　　　**56.** $(x - 1)(x + 1)(x)$.

57. $(x + 2)(x - 2)(x^2 + 4)$.　　　　**58.** $(x + 1)(x + 1)(x + 2)$.

59. $(a - b)^2 - (b - a)^2$.　　　　**60.** $(x + y)^2 - (y - x)^2$.

61. $(2x - 3)^2 + (x + 1)(x + 2)$.　　　　**62.** $(t + 3)(t - 3) - (t + 3)^2$.

63. $(x + 2)(x - 2)^2$.　　　　**64.** $a(a - b)^2 - b(b - a)^2$.

65. $[4x(x - 3)]^2$.

66. $[2x^2(x - y)]^2$.

67. $3x(x + 2) - (\sqrt{3}\,x - 1)(\sqrt{3}\,x + 1)$.

68. $(5x^2 + 1)(\sqrt{5}\,x + 1)(\sqrt{5}\,x - 1)$.

69. $[(x - y) + 2][(x - y) - 2]$.

70. $[(x + y) - (a + b)]^2$.

71. $(a + b + c)(a + b - c)$.

72. $(x + 1)(x - 1)(x - 3)$.

73. Use the formula
$$(a + b)^3 = a^3 + 3a^2b + 3ab^2 + b^3$$
to find $(x + 2)^3$.

74. Use the formula
$$(a - b)^3 = a^3 - 3a^2b + 3ab^2 - b^3$$
to find $(x - 1)^3$.

75. In the study of X-ray spectroscopy, it is shown that the frequency of the K_α line of any element is given by
$$\frac{3}{4} Rc(Z - 1)^2,$$
where c is the speed of light, Z is the atomic number of the element, and R is a constant called the Rydberg constant. Perform the indicated multiplication.

76. When a flexible chain l units long and of linear density w is released with a length c overhanging a smooth table, energy considerations result in the following expression for the square of the velocity of the chain as it leaves the table:
$$\frac{2g}{wl}\left[wc(l - c) + \frac{1}{2} w(l - c)^2 \right].$$
Perform all indicated operations and simplify.

77. The kinetic energy (KE) of an object of mass m moving with a speed v is given by
$$\text{KE} = \frac{1}{2} mv^2.$$
If the speed of an object at time t is $v = 2t + 1$, find an expression for the kinetic energy in terms of t and m and expand your result.

78. The speed v of a model rocket at time t is given by $v = t + 2$. The mass m of the rocket decreases as fuel is burned. If $m = 12 - 0.1t$, find the kinetic energy of the rocket in terms of t and expand your result. Refer to Problem 77.

79. For a body moving in a straight line with constant acceleration, it is shown in mechanics that
$$s = v_{\text{ave}} \cdot t, \tag{1}$$
$$v_{\text{ave}} = \frac{v_f + v_0}{2}, \tag{2}$$
and
$$t = \frac{v_f - v_0}{a}, \tag{3}$$

where s = displacement of the body, v_{ave} = average velocity, t = time, v_0 = initial velocity, v_f = final velocity, and a = acceleration. Show by substituting (2) and (3) into (1) that

$$s = \frac{v_f^2 - v_0^2}{2a}.$$

3-6 Factoring

The process of writing an expression as a product of its factors is called **factoring**. For example, because $(x + 1)(x - 1) = x^2 - 1$, then $x + 1$ and $x - 1$ are factors of $x^2 - 1$ and a *factored form* of $x^2 - 1$ is $(x + 1)(x - 1)$. In later chapters, factoring will play an important role when we are working with fractions, solving equations, and investigating the behavior of certain expressions.

When factoring a polynomial, we shall choose only those factors that are polynomials themselves. Thus we shall not write $x - 1$ as $(\sqrt{x} + 1)(\sqrt{x} - 1)$, even though it may be mathematically correct. Furthermore, we usually factor a polynomial so that no factor can be written as a product of other factors except itself and 1 or -1. When this is done, we consider the polynomial to be **completely factored**. For example, $x^2 - 1 = (x + 1)(x - 1)$ is completely factored, because $x + 1$ and $x - 1$ cannot be factored any further. To describe this, we say that $x + 1$ and $x - 1$ are **prime polynomials**.

The simplest type of factoring is called **removing a common factor**. If a particular factor is common to *each* term in an expression, this factor can be *removed* by the distributive law:

> **COMMON FACTOR**
> $ab + ac = a(b + c).$

Here, as with other factoring formulas, the letters a, b, and c can be replaced by any expression. For example, given $6x + 9y$, note that 3 is a factor of both $6x$ and $9y$ because $6x = 3 \cdot 2x$ and $9y = 3 \cdot 3y$. Thus

$$6x + 9y = 3(2x + 3y).$$

Similarly, given $2xy^2 + 8xy^4$, note that $2x$ is a factor of both terms: $2xy^2 = 2x(y^2)$ and $8xy^4 = 2x(4y^4)$. Thus

$$2xy^2 + 8xy^4 = 2x(y^2 + 4y^4).$$

But the last expression is not completely factored. Because $y^2 = y^2 \cdot 1$ and $4y^4 = y^2(4y^2)$, then y^2 can be removed from the factor $y^2 + 4y^4$. So we have

$$2xy^2 + 8xy^4 = 2xy^2(1 + 4y^2).$$

Although we must always factor *completely*, it does not necessarily involve more than one step, as in the last case. If we had originally removed the factor $2xy^2$, then we would have the desired form in one step. In short, when removing a common factor, you should attempt to remove the *largest* common factor.

example 1

For each of the following, factor completely.

a. $x^5 - 2x^3 + x^2 = x^2(x^3 - 2x + 1)$.   *Do not forget the 1.*

b. $8a^5y^3 - 6a^2y^5z + 2a^2y^4 = 2a^2y^3(4a^3 - 3y^2z + y)$.

c. $3y(x + 2) - 2z(x + 2)$.

Here the factor $x + 2$ is common to both terms and can be factored out.

$$3y(x + 2) - 2z(x + 2) = (x + 2)(3y - 2z).$$

In removing a common factor that has more than one term, the use of parentheses is essential! *Do not write*

$$3y(x + 2) - 2z(x + 2) = x + 2(3y - 2z).$$

d. $(x + 2)^2(x - 3) + (x + 2)(x - 3)^2$.

Here the factors $x + 2$ and $x - 3$ are common to both terms and can be factored out.

$$(x + 2)^2(x - 3) + (x + 2)(x - 3)^2$$
$$= (x + 2)(x - 3)[(x + 2) + (x - 3)]$$
$$= (x + 2)(x - 3)(2x - 1).$$

e. $6ac - 6bc + a - b$.

Here, appropriate grouping will allow us to factor.

$$6ac - 6bc + a - b = (6ac - 6bc) + (a - b)$$
$$= 6c(a - b) + (a - b)(1)$$
$$= (a - b)(6c + 1).$$

In the last step we removed the common factor $a - b$.

The special-product relationships given in the previous section form the basis of our remaining techniques of factoring. For example, because $(a + b)(a - b) = a^2 - b^2$, a difference of two squares can be factored into a sum and difference:

> **DIFFERENCE OF TWO SQUARES**
>
> $a^2 - b^2 = (a + b)(a - b).$

example 2

a. $x^2 - 4 = x^2 - 2^2 = (x + 2)(x - 2).$

b. $4y^2 - 1 = (2y)^2 - 1^2 = (2y + 1)(2y - 1).$

c. $9x^2 - 16y^2 = (3x)^2 - (4y)^2 = (3x + 4y)(3x - 4y).$

d. $x^4 - y^4 = (x^2)^2 - (y^2)^2 = (x^2 + y^2)(x^2 - y^2).$

Although $x^2 + y^2$ cannot be factored (it is prime), $x^2 - y^2$ can be factored into $(x + y)(x - y)$. Thus

$$x^4 - y^4 = (x^2 + y^2)(x + y)(x - y).$$

e. $x^2 - 5 = x^2 - (\sqrt{5})^2 = (x + \sqrt{5})(x - \sqrt{5}).*$

Because $(x + a)(x + b) = x^2 + (a + b)x + ab$, trinomials with a leading coefficient of 1, such as $x^2 + 3x - 18$, can sometimes be factored into the product of two binomials of the form $(x + a)(x + b)$. Suppose

$$x^2 + 3x - 18 = (x + a)(x + b)$$
$$= x^2 + (a + b)x + ab.$$

By matching corresponding coefficients, we must have

$$a + b = 3 \quad \text{and} \quad ab = -18.$$

There are several choices of a and b such that their product is -18:

$$-18 \quad \text{and} \quad 1, \qquad 18 \quad \text{and} \quad -1,$$
$$-6 \quad \text{and} \quad 3, \qquad 6 \quad \text{and} \quad -3,$$
$$-9 \quad \text{and} \quad 2, \qquad 9 \quad \text{and} \quad -2.$$

However, because the sum of a and b must be 3, we choose $a = 6$ and $b = -3$ (or vice versa). Thus

$$x^2 + 3x - 18 = (x + 6)(x - 3).$$

This can easily be checked by using the three-step method on $(x + 6)(x - 3)$.

---

*If only rational numbers are to be considered, then $x^2 - 5$ is prime.

example 3

Completely factor the following.

a. $x^2 - 7x + 12$.

We must find two numbers with product 12 and sum of -7. The numbers -3 and -4 work. Thus
$$x^2 - 7x + 12 = (x - 3)(x - 4).$$

b. $y^2 + 4y + 4 = (y + 2)(y + 2) = (y + 2)^2$, which is the square of a binomial.

c. $z^2 + 4z - 32 = (z - 4)(z + 8)$.

d. $z^2 - 4z - 32 = (z + 4)(z - 8)$. Compare this with part (c), where we chose -4 and $+8$ because we wanted the middle term to have a positive coefficient.

If a trinomial with a leading coefficient which is not 1 factors into a product of two binomials, the method of factoring involves reversing the three-step method and using trial and error. For example, to factor $6x^2 - 5x - 6$, we must have

$$6x^2 - 5x - 6 = (\_ + \_)(\_ + \_).$$

That is, the product of the first terms of the binomials must be $6x^2$, and the product of the last terms must be -6. One combination of binomials for which that is true is $(x + 3)(6x - 2)$. But here the sum of the products of the outer terms and inner terms, which is $16x$, is not equal to the middle term of $6x^2 - 5x - 6$, namely $-5x$. By trial and error we try other combinations, such as:

$$(3x - 1)(2x + 6),$$
$$(x + 3)(6x - 2),$$
$$(3x - 2)(2x + 3).$$

You should verify that although each of these gives the correct first and last terms of the given trinomial, the middle term is wrong in each case. Trying other combinations, we find that $3x + 2$ and $2x - 3$ work. Thus

$$6x^2 - 5x - 6 = (3x + 2)(2x - 3).$$

example 4

Completely factor the following.

a. $2x^2 + 5x + 2 = (2x + 1)(x + 2)$.

b. $8y^2 - 6y - 9 = (2y - 3)(4y + 3)$.

c. $9y^2 - 12y + 4 = (3y - 2)(3y - 2) = (3y - 2)^2$, which is the square of a binomial.

d. $x^4 - 5x^2 + 4 = (x^2 - 1)(x^2 - 4)$
$$= (x + 1)(x - 1)(x + 2)(x - 2).$$

When factoring, you should *first remove any common factors*, as Example 5 shows.

example 5

Completely factor the following.

a. $4x^3 - 36x = 4x(x^2 - 9) = 4x(x + 3)(x - 3)$.

b. $8ay^2 + 8ay + 2a = 2a(4y^2 + 4y + 1)$
$$= 2a(2y + 1)(2y + 1) = 2a(2y + 1)^2.$$

c. $6x^5 - 4x^3 - 2x = 2x(3x^4 - 2x^2 - 1)$
$$= 2x(3x^2 + 1)(x^2 - 1)$$
$$= 2x(3x^2 + 1)(x + 1)(x - 1).$$

d. $ax^2 - ay^2 + bx^2 - by^2 = (ax^2 - ay^2) + (bx^2 - by^2)$
$$= a(x^2 - y^2) + b(x^2 - y^2)$$
$$= (x^2 - y^2)(a + b)$$
$$= (x + y)(x - y)(a + b).$$

Here factoring was achieved by making use of appropriate grouping.

example 6

The total work done on a body of mass m is given by
$$\tfrac{1}{2}mv_f^2 - \tfrac{1}{2}mv_0^2,$$
where v_0 and v_f are the initial and final speeds of the body, respectively. Completely factor this expression.

$$\tfrac{1}{2}mv_f^2 - \tfrac{1}{2}mv_0^2 = \tfrac{1}{2}m(v_f^2 - v_0^2) = \tfrac{1}{2}m(v_f + v_0)(v_f - v_0).$$

Exercise 3-6

Completely factor the expressions in Problems **1–92.** *If prime, so indicate.*

1. $8x + 8$.

2. $9x - 9$.

3. $14y - 8$.

4. $9 - 21x$.

5. $10x - 5y + 25$.

6. $12x^2 + 24y - 4$.

7. $5cx + 9x$.

8. $16mx + 4m$.

9. $4y - 16y^2$.

10. $8a - 4ab$.

11. $6xy + 3xz$.

12. $4xyz - 5yz$.

13. $2x^3 - x^2$.

14. $5x^8 - 4x^7$.

15. $2x^3y^3 + x^5y^5$.

16. $m^2y - y^2m$.

17. $4m^2x^3 - 8mx^4$.

18. $25a^5x^9 - 15a^4x^{10}$.

19. $9a^4y^3 + 3a^2y^5 - 6a^3y^4z$.

20. $by^5 - 2b^3y^4 - 8b^2y^2$.

21. $21z^2y + 7zyw^2 + 14z^3y^3w^3$.

22. $-2x^2y - 4x^3y^2w + 6x^5y^5w$.

23. $x^2 - 16$.

24. $x^2 - 25$.

25. $x^2 + 6x + 8$.

26. $x^2 - 3x + 2$.

27. $x^2 + 2x - 15$.

28. $x^2 + 4x - 21$.

29. $x^2 - 9x + 20$.

30. $x^2 + 3x - 10$.

31. $y^2 + 2y - 24$.

32. $y^2 - 12y + 35$.

33. $y^2 + 3$.

34. $4 + y^2$.

35. $x^2 + 12x + 36$.

36. $x^2 - 3x - 28$.

37. $x^2 - 4x - 32$.

38. $x^2 - 8x + 12$.

39. $y^2 - 10y + 25$.

40. $y^2 + 8y + 16$.

41. $25x^2 - 16$.

42. $4x^2 - 49y^2$.

43. $y^2 - \dfrac{4}{9}$.

44. $x^2y^2 - \dfrac{1}{4}$.

45. $3x^2 + 7x + 2$.

46. $5x^2 - 12x + 4$.

47. $2y^2 - 7y + 3$.

48. $7y^2 + 9y + 2$.

49. $16x^2 + 8x + 1$.

50. $4x^2 - 4x + 1$.

51. $9 - 4x^2y^2$.

52. $a^2b^2 - c^2d^2$.

53. $4y^2 + 7y - 2$.

54. $8y^2 + 2y - 3$.

55. $6x^2 - 11x - 10$.

56. $5x^2 + 14x - 3$.

57. $12x^2 + x - 6$.

58. $10x^2 - 19x + 6$.

59. $2x^2 + 4x - 6$.

60. $a^2x^2 + a^2x - 20a^2$.

61. $3x^3 + 18x^2 + 27x$.

62. $3x^4 - 15x^3 + 18x^2$.

63. $16s^2t^3 - 4s^2t$.

64. $a^2b^2 - a^4b^4$.

65. $4y^2 - 6y - 18$.

66. $30y^2 + 55y + 15$.

67. $x^4 - x^2$.

68. $x^4 - 16$.

69. $81x^4 - y^4$.

70. $y^8 - 1$.

71. $t^4 - 4$.

72. $x^4 + x^2 - 2$.

73. $x^4 - 5x^2 + 4$.

74. $x^5 - 2x^3 + x$.

75. $4x^3 - 6x^2 - 4x$.

76. $y^2 - 3$.

77. $(x + 3)^3(x - 1) + (x + 3)^2(x - 1)^2$.

78. $(x + 5)^2(x + 1)^3 + (x + 5)^3(x + 1)^2$.

79. $(x + 4)(2x + 1) + (x + 4)$.   **80.** $(x - 3)(2x + 3) - (2x + 3)(x + 5)$.

81. $(m + n)^2(m - n) - (m + n)(m - n)^2$.

82. $(y^2 - x^2)(n - m) + (m + n)(m - n)(x + y)$.

*Problems **83–92** require a bit more thought than the preceding problems. In some cases appropriate grouping is helpful.*

83. $x^2 - y^2 + x + y$.

84. $x^8 - y^8$.

85. $9z^2 - 4x^2 + 4x - 1$.

86. $x^3 - x^2 + x - 1$.

87. $x^3 + x^2 + x + 1$.

88. $x^2 - 6x + 9 - 4z^2 - 4z - 1$.

89. $a^2 - b^2 - c^2 + 2bc$.

90. $16x^2 - z^2 - 8x + 1$.

91. $x^2 + x - y^2 - y$.

92. $4x^2 + 4x + 1 - a^2$.

93. Use the formula

$$a^3 + b^3 = (a + b)(a^2 - ab + b^2)$$

to factor $x^3 + 8$.

94. Use the formula

$$a^3 - b^3 = (a - b)(a^2 + ab + b^2)$$

to factor $8x^3 - 27$.

95. The total surface area of a closed cylinder of radius r and altitude h is given by

$$2\pi r^2 + 2\pi rh.$$

Completely factor this expression.

96. The moment of inertia of a right circular cone of base radius r and altitude h about a certain axis is

$$\tfrac{1}{20}(\pi \rho r^4 h) + \tfrac{1}{5}(\pi \rho r^2 h^3),$$

where ρ (rho) is mass density. Completely factor this expression.

97. The effective emf (electromotive force) of a thermocouple is given by

$$c(T_1 - T_2) + k(T_1^2 - T_2^2),$$

where c and k are constants that depend on the metals used, and T_1 and T_2 are the temperatures of the hot and cold junctions, respectively. Completely factor this expression.

98. The power P supplied to a motor by a battery of emf V was found to be given by

$$P = \frac{mg}{BL}\left(V - \frac{Rmg}{BL}\right) + R\left(\frac{mg}{BL}\right)^2.$$

Completely factor and simplify this expression.

99. The moment of inertia of a right circular cylinder about a certain axis is found to be

$$\tfrac{1}{4}mR^2 + \tfrac{1}{12}mh^2.$$

Show that by factoring this expression properly, you can arrive at

$$\tfrac{1}{12}m(3R^2 + h^2),$$

which was found in a reference table.

100. When two bodies at different temperatures face each other, the net rate at which energy is radiated from the warmer body is given by

$$kT_2^4 - kT_1^4,$$

where k is a constant and T_1 and T_2 are the temperatures of the bodies. Completely factor this expression.

Review Questions

1. An algebraic expression composed of more than one term can *always* be called a _____(a)_____ ; however, expressions containing exactly two and three terms are usually referred to as _____(b)_____ and _____(c)_____ , respectively.

2. An algebraic expression in which every term is either a constant or the product of a constant and a positive integral power of x is called a _____ .

3. For the polynomial $3x^2 - 4x + 7$, the degree is equal to __(a)__ , the coefficient of the second term is __(b)__ , and the constant term is __(c)__ .

4. In the division of one polynomial by another, the process is ended when the degree of the _____(a)_____ is less than the degree of the _____(b)_____ .

5. The coefficient of $4x^2$ is __(a)__ ; the coefficient of $-x$ is __(b)__ ; the coefficient of x is __(c)__ .

6. Two terms are similar terms if they have the same _____ part.

7. The product $(x + 3)(y - 5)$ is equal to $x(y - 5) +$ _____ .

In Problems 8–10, insert T (true) or F (false).

8. $(2x)(3y)(4z) = 8xz(3y)$. _____

9. $a(ac)^2 = a^3c^2$. _____

10. $x(yx) = x^2y$. _____

11. In the division $2x + 5 \overline{)\ -8x^2 + x + 1}$, the first term of the quotient is _____ .

In Problems 12 and 13, fill in either $+$ or $-$.

12. $4(x - 3y + 5) = 4x$ _____ $12y$ _____ 20.

13. $-3(1 + 4x - 6y) = -3$ _____ $12x$ _____ $18y$.

14. The expression $-\{1 - [(-1)^2(-1)] - 1\}$ is equal to _____ .

15. $x^2 + 6x + 9$ _(is)(is not)_ the square of a binomial.

16. To factor $2x^3 + 10x^2 + 12x$, you should first remove the common factor _____ .

17. If $x^4 - y^4$ is written as $(x^2 + y^2)(x^2 - y^2)$, is it completely factored? _____

18. $(53)(47) = (50 + 3)(50 - 3) = 2500 -$ _____ .

19. $(22)^2 = (20 + 2)^2 = 400 +$ _____ $+ 4$.

20. Because $x^2 + 36$ cannot be factored, it is said to be _____ .

Answers to Review Questions

1. (a) Multinomial, (b) Binomials, (c) Trinomials. 2. Polynomial (in x).
3. (a) 2, (b) -4, (c) 7. 4. (a) Remainder, (b) Divisor. 5. (a) 4, (b) -1, (c) 1.
6. Literal. 7. $3(y - 5)$. 8. T. 9. T. 10. T. 11. $-4x$. 12. $-$, $+$. 13. $-$, $+$.
14. -1. 15. Is. 16. $2x$. 17. No. 18. 9. 19. 80. 20. Prime.

Review Problems

In Problems 1–10, simplify.

1. $(3x + 2y - 5) + (8x - 4y + 2)$.
2. $7x + 5(4x + 3)$.
3. $6(a + 3b) - (8a - b - 4)$.
4. $2(a + 4b) - 3(3b - 2a)$.
5. $2[3(xy - 5) + 7(4 - xy)]$.
6. $(4xy + 7) - 5[xy - (4 - 3xy)]$.
7. $4x + [-5(2 - x) - 8]$.
8. $\{1 - 2[x - (x - 1)]\} + 1$.
9. $-3\{x^2 - [3(2x - 4) + 2x^2]\}$.
10. $2\{x^2 + 3[x - (x^2 + 4)]\} + 7$.

In Problems 11–48, perform the indicated operations and simplify.

11. $(2x^2yz)(xy^3z^6)$.
12. $3xy(-2xy^2)$.
13. $8ab^2(3a^2b)^2$.
14. $-xy^3(-3xz)$.
15. $(2x^2y)^2(xy)^3(xy^2)$.
16. $(xy)^2(xz)^2(yz)^2$.
17. $x(x^2 - 2x + 4)$.
18. $x^2y(xy - xz + yz)$.
19. $a^2b(-2a^2b + 2ab - 3)$.
20. $(2xy)^2(x - y + 2xy)$.
21. $(x + 3)(x - 4)$.
22. $(y - 4)(y^2 - 3y + 5)$.
23. $(x + 4)(x - 4)$.
24. $(3 - x)(3 + x)$.
25. $(x - 3)(x - 2)$.
26. $(x - 3)^2$.
27. $(x + 2y)^2$.
28. $(x^2 + 1)(x^2 - 2)$.
29. $(x^2 + 3)(x - 4)$.
30. $(x - 3y)^2$.
31. $(3x - 1)(2x^3 - 3x^2 + 5)$.
32. $(y - 4)(y^2 - 3y + 5)$.
33. $(x + y + 2)(2x - 3y + 1)$.
34. $(1 + x + y)(1 - x - y)$.
35. $3x(x - 4) - 2(x^2 - 9)$.
36. $2x^2(x^2 - xy) + 2(x^4 - x^3y)$.
37. $\dfrac{ax^2y^5}{x^3y^3}$.
38. $\dfrac{2xy^2}{4y^3}$.
39. $\dfrac{(2ab)(a^2b)}{10a^2}$.
40. $\dfrac{(ab)^2(2ab^2)}{2ab^3}$.
41. $\dfrac{(-3x^2y)(2xy)}{(4x^2y)^2}$.
42. $\dfrac{(xy^2)^2(-3x)^3}{9x(xy)}$.
43. $\dfrac{x^2 - 5x + 7}{x}$.
44. $\dfrac{-3x^3 - 5x^2 + 6}{30x}$.
45. $\dfrac{x^2y - 5xy^3 + 7xy}{xy^2}$.
46. $\dfrac{6x^2y - 3y^2 + 2x - 2}{-4x}$.
47. $\dfrac{2x^2y + (2xy^2w)^2 - 4x^3y^3w}{-2xy}$.
48. $\dfrac{3xy^2 - xy^2 + 3}{xy^2}$.

In Problems 39–44, perform the long divisions.

49. $\dfrac{6x^3 + 3x^2 - 5x - 1}{2x - 1}$.
50. $\dfrac{3x^3 - 5x^2 + x + 1}{3x + 1}$.
51. $\dfrac{x^4 + x^3 + 8x - 30}{x + 3}$.
52. $\dfrac{5 - x + 4x^2 - 3x^3 - 4x^4}{4x + 3}$.

53. $\dfrac{3x + 3x^3 - 2x^4}{2x + 1}$.

54. $\dfrac{9 - x^3}{x - 2}$.

In Problems 55–74, find the special products.

55. $(x + 6)^2$.

56. $(x - 7)^2$.

57. $(x - 5)^2$.

58. $(x + 3y)^2$.

59. $(2x + 4y)^2$.

60. $(3x - 6)^2$.

61. $(x - 8)(x + 8)$.

62. $(9 - 2x)(9 + 2x)$.

63. $(3x + 2)(3x - 2)$.

64. $(1 - 3x)(3x + 1)$.

65. $(2x - 4y)(2x + 4y)$.

66. $(a - 2b)(a + 2b)$.

67. $(x - 6)(x + 4)$.

68. $(x + 3)(x - 2)$.

69. $(x - 6)(x - 7)$.

70. $(x + 5)(x + 8)$.

71. $(2x - 3)(2x - 4)$.

72. $(3x - 2)(2x + 3)$.

73. $(y^2 + 4)(y^2 - 4)$.

74. $(y^3 + 1)(y^3 - 1)$.

In Problems 75–80, perform the indicated operations.

75. $2x^2(x - 3)(x + 4)$.

76. $-3x(x + 3)^2$.

77. $(y - \sqrt{2})(y + \sqrt{2}) - (y - 4)^2$.

78. $5y(1 + 2y)^2$.

79. $(4x + 3)(4x - 3)(x + 2)$.

80. $3(3x - 1)^2 + 5x(x + 2)^2$.

In Problems 81–98, factor completely.

81. $6x^3y^4 + 4xy^6$.

82. $10abc^8 - 15ab^2c$.

83. $x^2 - 11x + 30$.

84. $x^2 + 6x + 8$.

85. $16 - y^2$.

86. $y^2 - 7$.

87. $x^3 - x^2 - 56x$.

88. $2x^2 + 4x - 96$.

89. $3x^2 + 10x - 8$.

90. $2x^2 + 9x - 35$.

91. $8x^2 - 50$.

92. $x^2 - \dfrac{1}{16}$.

93. $15y^2 + 2y - 8$.

94. $8y^2 + 6y + 1$.

95. $x^4 - 2x^2 - 8$.

96. $x^4 + 10x^2 + 25$.

97. $x^3(x - 6)^2 + x^4(x - 6)$.

98. $(x + 4)^3(x + 6)^4 + (x + 4)^4(x + 6)^3$.

99. The image distance for a simple lens is given by

$$\frac{fp}{p - f},$$

where p is the object distance and f is the focal length.
(a) Simplify this expression, if possible.
(b) Simplify the reciprocal of this expression, if possible.

100. When a flexible chain l units long and of linear density w is released with a length c overhanging a smooth table, energy considerations result in the following expression for the square of the velocity of the chain as it leaves the table:

$$\frac{2g}{wl}\left[wc(l - c) + \frac{1}{2}w(l - c)^2\right].$$

Show that this can be expressed in completely factored from as

$$\frac{g}{l}(l + c)(l - c).$$

101. According to the Bohr theory of the hydrogen atom, the frequency of the energy radiated when an electron goes from orbit n_1 to orbit n_2 is given by

$$\frac{2\pi^2 m e^4}{h^3 n_2^2} - \frac{2\pi^2 m e^4}{h^3 n_1^2},$$

where m is the mass of the electron, e is the charge of the electron, and h is Planck's constant. Express this in completely factored form.

102. Under certain conditions, the force that the rear wheels of an automobile of weight W must exert on the ground to cause an acceleration a is given by

$$\frac{\mu W d}{c + d} + \frac{\mu W h a}{g c + g d},$$

where μ (mu) is the coefficient of friction, g is the acceleration due to gravity, and c, d, and h are constants that specify the location of the center of gravity of the automobile. Express this force in factored form.

fractions

4-1 Simplifying Fractions

The basic property that is used to change the form of a fraction is known as the *fundamental principle of fractions:*

FUNDAMENTAL PRINCIPLE OF FRACTIONS

Multiplying or dividing both the numerator and denominator of a fraction by the same number, except zero, results in a fraction that is equivalent to the original fraction.

For example,

$$\frac{2}{3} = \frac{2 \cdot 4}{3 \cdot 4} = \frac{8}{12} \quad \text{and} \quad \frac{4}{10} = \frac{\frac{4}{2}}{\frac{10}{2}} = \frac{2}{5}.$$

Thus, $\frac{2}{3}$ and $\frac{8}{12}$ are equivalent (they represent the same number).

Similarly, the fundamental principle allows us to manipulate signs in a fraction:

$$\frac{-a}{b} = \frac{(-a)(-1)}{b(-1)} = \frac{a}{-b}.$$

Indeed, the laws of signed numbers in Chapter 1 stated that

$$\frac{-a}{b} = \frac{a}{-b} = -\frac{a}{b},$$

which can be written as

$$+\frac{-a}{+b} = +\frac{+a}{-b} = -\frac{+a}{+b}. \tag{1}$$

Our insertion of plus signs in (1) makes it clear that with each fraction we can associate three signs: the sign in front of the fraction, the sign of the numerator, and the sign of the denominator. From an observation of (1), you can see that changing any two of these three signs results in a fraction that is equivalent to the original fraction. For example, by successively changing two signs we have

$$\frac{-2}{7} = \frac{2}{-7} = -\frac{2}{7} = -\frac{-2}{-7}$$

and

$$\frac{3}{5} = \frac{-3}{-5} = -\frac{3}{-5} = -\frac{-3}{5}.$$

example 1

a. $-\dfrac{x(-y)}{z} = -\dfrac{-(xy)}{z} = \dfrac{xy}{z}.$ b. $\dfrac{w(-x)}{(-y)(-z)} = \dfrac{-(wx)}{yz} = -\dfrac{wx}{yz}.$

c. $\dfrac{y}{(-1)ab} = \dfrac{y}{-(ab)} = -\dfrac{y}{ab}.$

The next example makes use of the following fact.

$$\boxed{a - b = -(b - a) = (-1)(b - a).}$$

This follows from results in Chapters 1 and 2.

example 2

a. $-\dfrac{8}{x - y} = -\dfrac{8}{-(y - x)} = \dfrac{8}{y - x}.$

b. $\dfrac{4 - x}{3 - x} = \dfrac{-(x - 4)}{-(x - 3)} = \dfrac{x - 4}{x - 3}.$

c. $\dfrac{(a - b)(c - d)}{(e - f)(g - h)} = \dfrac{(a - b)(-1)(d - c)}{(-1)(f - e)(g - h)} = \dfrac{(b - a)(d - c)}{-(f - e)(g - h)}$

$$= -\frac{(b - a)(d - c)}{(f - e)(g - h)}.$$

Care must be taken when you are using the previous boxed rule. In general,

$$\frac{x-1}{x+1} \neq \frac{-(x+1)}{x+1}, \qquad \frac{1-x}{x+1} \neq \frac{-(x+1)}{x+1},$$

and

$$\frac{1+x}{x+1} \neq \frac{-(x+1)}{x+1}.$$

A fraction is said to be in **simplest form**, or to be **reduced**, when its numerator and denominator have no factors in common other than 1. For example, suppose we simplify the fraction

$$\frac{(x+2)(x+3)}{(x+2)(x+1)}.$$

Noting that the numerator and denominator have the *common factor* $x+2$, we multiply *both* the numerator and denominator by the reciprocal of $x+2$, namely $1/(x+2)$. Because any number times its reciprocal is 1, we have

$$\frac{(x+2)(x+3)}{(x+2)(x+1)} = \frac{\dfrac{1}{x+2}(x+2)(x+3)}{\dfrac{1}{x+2}(x+2)(x+1)} = \frac{1(x+3)}{1(x+1)} = \frac{x+3}{x+1}.$$

The last fraction is in simplest form. (Here, as elsewhere in this book, in a fraction we exclude all values of the variables that make the denominator zero.) The procedure we used to replace the common factors by 1's is called *cancelling common factors*, or *cancellation*. Keep in mind that it is actually an application of the fundamental principle. For convenience, the procedure can be shown more simply by writing

$$\frac{\cancel{(x+2)}^{1}(x+3)}{\cancel{(x+2)}_{1}(x+1)} = \frac{x+3}{x+1}.$$

In fact, that step is often done mentally and we write

$$\frac{(x+2)(x+3)}{(x+2)(x+1)} = \frac{x+3}{x+1}.$$

More generally, we have the following property.

CANCELLATION PROPERTY

$$\frac{ab}{ac} = \frac{b}{c},$$

---

where a, b, and c can be replaced by other expressions.

Before the cancellation property can be applied to a fraction, the numerator and denominator may have to be factored so that common factors are found. For example,

$$\frac{3ab - 3b^2}{a^2 - b^2} = \frac{3b\overset{1}{\cancel{(a - b)}}}{(a + b)\underset{1}{\cancel{(a - b)}}} = \frac{3b}{a + b}.$$

Keep in mind that you can cancel only **factors** that are common to the entire numerator and entire denominator. *Common terms* **cannot** *be cancelled.* Here are some examples of incorrect cancelling. In each case the error can be seen by replacing x by 2.

$$\frac{\overset{1}{\cancel{4}} + 3x}{\underset{1}{\cancel{4}}} \neq 1 + 3x \qquad (4 \text{ is } \textbf{not} \text{ a factor of the entire numerator}),$$

$$\frac{\overset{1}{\cancel{x}}}{3 + 4\underset{1}{\cancel{x}}} \neq \frac{1}{3 + 4} \qquad (x \text{ is } \textbf{not} \text{ a factor of the entire denominator}),$$

$$\frac{\overset{1}{\cancel{x}} + 3}{\underset{1}{\cancel{x}} + 5} \neq \frac{1 + 5}{1 + 3} \qquad (x \text{ is } \textbf{not} \text{ a factor}).$$

example 3

Reduce the following fractions.

a. $\dfrac{x^2 + 7x + 10}{x^2 + 4x - 5} = \dfrac{(x + 2)\overset{1}{\cancel{(x + 5)}}}{\underset{1}{\cancel{(x + 5)}}(x - 1)} = \dfrac{x + 2}{x - 1}.$

b. $\dfrac{4x^2}{8x^2 - 4x^3} = \dfrac{\overset{1\ 1}{\cancel{4x^2}}}{\underset{1\ 1}{\cancel{4x^2}}(2 - x)} = \dfrac{1}{2 - x}.$

c. $\dfrac{2x + 6}{12 + 4x} = \dfrac{\overset{1}{\cancel{2}}(x + 3)}{\underset{2}{\cancel{4}}(3 + x)} = \dfrac{\overset{1}{\cancel{x + 3}}}{2\underset{1}{\cancel{(x + 3)}}} = \dfrac{1}{2}.$ Here the commutative law allowed us to replace $3 + x$ by $x + 3$.

d. $\dfrac{x^2 - 1}{x^2 + 2x + 1} = \dfrac{(x - 1)\overset{1}{\cancel{(x + 1)}}}{\underset{x + 1}{\cancel{(x + 1)^2}}} = \dfrac{x - 1}{x + 1}.$

e. $\dfrac{2x^2 - 2x - 12}{4x^2 - 8x - 12} = \dfrac{\overset{1}{\cancel{2}}(x^2 - x - 6)}{\underset{2}{\cancel{4}}(x^2 - 2x - 3)} = \dfrac{(x + 2)\overset{1}{\cancel{(x - 3)}}}{2(x + 1)\underset{1}{\cancel{(x - 3)}}} = \dfrac{x + 2}{2(x + 1)}.$

The next example shows how to simplify fractions containing factors with terms that differ in sign.

example 4

Simplify the following.

a. $\dfrac{3-x}{x-3} = \dfrac{-(x-3)}{x-3} = \dfrac{(-1)\overset{1}{\cancel{(x-3)}}}{\underset{1}{\cancel{x-3}}} = -1.$

b. $\dfrac{a^2-b^2}{b-a} = \dfrac{(a+b)(a-b)}{b-a} = \dfrac{(a+b)\overset{1}{\cancel{(a-b)}}}{(-1)\underset{1}{\cancel{(a-b)}}} = -(a+b).$

c. $\dfrac{3x^2+9x-12}{8-4x-4x^2} = \dfrac{3(x^2+3x-4)}{4(2-x-x^2)} = \dfrac{3(x-1)(x+4)}{4(1-x)(2+x)}$

$\qquad = \dfrac{3\overset{1}{\cancel{(x-1)}}(x+4)}{4(-1)\underset{1}{\cancel{(x-1)}}(2+x)} = \dfrac{3(x+4)}{-4(2+x)}$

$\qquad = -\dfrac{3(x+4)}{4(2+x)}.$

Exercise 4-1

In Problems 1–6, write each fraction so that minus signs do not appear in the numerator and in the denominator. For example, write $\dfrac{ab}{-c}$ as $-\dfrac{ab}{c}$.

1. $\dfrac{-x}{-y}.$

2. $-\dfrac{-wx}{-z}.$

3. $-\dfrac{a}{b(-c)}.$

4. $-\dfrac{ab}{(-c)(-d)}.$

5. $\dfrac{x}{-y-z}.$

6. $\dfrac{-x(y+z)}{(-a)(b)(-c)}.$

Determine whether the statements in Problems 7–16 are, in general, true or false.

7. $-\dfrac{x}{x-y} = \dfrac{x}{y-x}.$

8. $\dfrac{(x+y)(y-z)}{z-x} = \dfrac{(y+x)(z-y)}{x-z}.$

9. $\dfrac{(a-b)(b-c)}{c-a} = \dfrac{(c-b)(b-a)}{c-a}.$

10. $\dfrac{x-y}{z} = \dfrac{y-x}{z}.$

11. $-\dfrac{a-b}{c} = \dfrac{-(b-a)}{c}.$

12. $-\dfrac{x-y}{w-z} = \dfrac{x-y}{z-w}.$

13. $\dfrac{x}{y} = -\dfrac{-x}{y} = \dfrac{-x}{-y}.$

14. $\dfrac{a-b}{-x} = -\dfrac{b-a}{x}.$

15. $\dfrac{(x-a)(x-b)}{(x-c)(x-d)} = -\dfrac{(x-a)(b-x)}{(x-c)(d-x)}.$

16. $\dfrac{(x-a)(x-b)(x-c)}{(x-d)(x-e)} = \dfrac{(x-a)(b-x)(c-x)}{(e-x)(d-x)}.$

*In Problems **17–42**, reduce the fractions.*

17. $\dfrac{(x + 2)(x - 1)}{(x - 1)(3x + 5)}.$

18. $\dfrac{(x - 3)(x + 4)(x + 6)}{3x^2(x - 3)}.$

19. $\dfrac{3y + 12}{y + 4}.$

20. $\dfrac{x^2 - y^2}{x + y}.$

21. $\dfrac{2x + 2y}{6ax + 6ay}.$

22. $\dfrac{3x^2 - 12}{3x - 6}.$

23. $\dfrac{x^2 - 81}{x^2 + 9x}.$

24. $\dfrac{x^2y - 4xy}{x^3y^2 - 2x^2y^2}.$

25. $\dfrac{6m + 2m^2}{8m - 8m^2}.$

26. $\dfrac{y^4 + y^2}{y^6 - 4y^5}.$

27. $\dfrac{x + 1}{x^2 + 7x + 6}.$

28. $\dfrac{z^2 - 9}{z^2 - 6z + 9}.$

29. $\dfrac{2x^2 + 11x + 12}{2x^2 + 8x}.$

30. $\dfrac{3z^2 + z - 2}{6z^2 - z - 2}.$

31. $\dfrac{25 - t^2}{t^2 - 2t - 15}.$

32. $\dfrac{x^2 + 3x - 4}{2 - x - x^2}.$

33. $\dfrac{(x + 3)(x^2 - 144)}{(x^2 - 9)(x + 12)}.$

34. $\dfrac{6a^2b^2 + 6ab^3y + 6a^2b^2c^2}{3abc}.$

35. $\dfrac{x^2 + 5x + 6}{x^2 - 2x - 8}.$

36. $\dfrac{x^2 + x - 12}{x^2 - 6x + 9}.$

37. $\dfrac{c - d}{d - c}.$

38. $\dfrac{(x - 2)(4 - x)}{(x - 4)(2 - x)}.$

39. $\dfrac{(x + 5)(2 - x)(x + 7)(6 - x)}{(x - 6)(7 - x)(x - 2)(x + 5)}.$

40. $\dfrac{(x + a)(-x - b)(c - x)(x + d)}{(-x - d)(x - c)(x + b)(x - a)}.$

41. $\dfrac{x^2 + x - 12}{-x - 4}.$

42. $\dfrac{16x^4 - 4b^4}{4x^2 - 2b^2}.$

*Reducing the fractions in Problems **43–50** is somewhat more challenging than the preceding problems.*

43. $\dfrac{(x - 2y)^2}{(2y - x)^3}.$

44. $\dfrac{(y - x)^2y}{(x^2 - xy)(x + y)}.$

45. $\dfrac{a^4 - b^4}{a + b}.$

46. $\dfrac{3(x + y) - 6x - 6y}{-3(x - y)}.$

47. $\dfrac{(2x^2 - x - 3)(4x^2 - 1)}{(2x^2 + 3x + 1)(6x^2 - 13x + 6)}.$

48. $\dfrac{(x^2 - xy)(x^2 - y^2)(xy - 2y^2)}{(x - y)^2(x^2 - 3xy + 2y^2)(x^2 + xy)}.$

49. $\dfrac{9w^2 - 4x^2 + 4x - 1}{3w + 2x - 1}.$

50. $\dfrac{(x + y)(y - x)(x + 1)}{x^3 - xy^2 + x^2 - y^2}.$

51. For the arrangement of particles shown in Fig. 4-1, it is shown in mechanics that

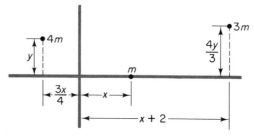

FIGURE 4-1

the coordinates $\bar{x}$ and $\bar{y}$ of the center of mass of the particles are given by

$$\bar{x} = \frac{m(x) + 3m(x + 2) + 4m\left(-\frac{3x}{4}\right)}{m + 3m + 4m}$$

and

$$\bar{y} = \frac{m(0) + 3m\left(\frac{4y}{3}\right) + 4m(y)}{m + 3m + 4m}.$$

Simplify the expressions for $\bar{x}$ and $\bar{y}$.

4-2 Multiplication and Division of Fractions

To multiply fractions, we multiply their numerators, multiply their denominators, and simplify.

MULTIPLICATION OF FRACTIONS

$$\frac{a}{b} \cdot \frac{c}{d} = \frac{ac}{bd}.$$

Here a, b, c, and d can be replaced by other expressions, and the rule also applies to more than two fractions.

example 1

Perform the indicated operations and simplify.

a. $\dfrac{2}{x} \cdot \dfrac{3}{y} = \dfrac{2 \cdot 3}{x \cdot y} = \dfrac{6}{xy}$.

b. $\dfrac{2x^2y}{z^2} \cdot \dfrac{3z^2}{7} = \dfrac{6x^2yz^2}{7z^2} = \dfrac{6x^2y}{7}$.

c. $\dfrac{x}{x+2} \cdot \dfrac{x+3}{x-5} = \dfrac{x(x+3)}{(x+2)(x-5)}.$ *We usually keep such answers in factored form.*

d. $\dfrac{3}{-x} \cdot \dfrac{x^2+4}{x} = \dfrac{3(x^2+4)}{-x^2} = -\dfrac{3(x^2+4)}{x^2}.$

e. $z^3 \cdot \dfrac{z+2}{z-7} \cdot \dfrac{z-7}{4} = \dfrac{z^3}{1} \cdot \dfrac{z+2}{z-7} \cdot \dfrac{z-7}{4} = \dfrac{z^3(z+2)\overset{1}{\cancel{(z-7)}}}{4\underset{1}{\cancel{(z-7)}}} = \dfrac{z^3(z+2)}{4}.$

Before multiplying fractions, you should completely factor all numerators and denominators. This may simplify the final reducing process, as Example 2 shows.

example 2

Perform the indicated operations and simplify.

a. $\dfrac{5}{x} \cdot \dfrac{3x-3}{x^2-1} = \dfrac{5}{x} \cdot \dfrac{3\overset{1}{\cancel{(x-1)}}}{(x+1)\underset{1}{\cancel{(x-1)}}} = \dfrac{15}{x(x+1)}.$

b. $\dfrac{x^3}{4x^2-9} \cdot \dfrac{2x+3}{x^2+x} = \dfrac{x^3}{(2x+3)(2x-3)} \cdot \dfrac{2x+3}{x(x+1)}$

$= \dfrac{\overset{x^2}{\cancel{x^3}}\,\overset{1}{\cancel{(2x+3)}}}{\underset{1}{\cancel{(2x+3)}}(2x-3)\underset{1}{\cancel{x}}(x+1)}$

$= \dfrac{x^2}{(2x-3)(x+1)}.$

c. $\dfrac{x^2+8x+16}{x^2+5x+6} \cdot \dfrac{x^2+3x+2}{x^2+2x-8} = \dfrac{(x+4)^2}{(x+3)(x+2)} \cdot \dfrac{(x+1)(x+2)}{(x+4)(x-2)}$

$= \dfrac{\overset{(x+4)}{\cancel{(x+4)^2}}(x+1)\overset{1}{\cancel{(x+2)}}}{(x+3)\underset{1}{\cancel{(x+2)}}\underset{1}{\cancel{(x+4)}}(x-2)}$

$= \dfrac{(x+4)(x+1)}{(x+3)(x-2)}.$

d. $\dfrac{6}{x^2-3x+2} \cdot \dfrac{2-x}{x+3} = \dfrac{6}{(x-1)(x-2)} \cdot \dfrac{2-x}{x+3}$

$= \dfrac{6(-1)\overset{1}{\cancel{(x-2)}}}{(x-1)\underset{1}{\cancel{(x-2)}}(x+3)} = \dfrac{-6}{(x-1)(x+3)}$

$= -\dfrac{6}{(x-1)(x+3)}.$

Here we wrote $2-x$ as $(-1)(x-2)$ so that we could reduce the fraction.

By the definition of division in Chapter 1, to divide a/b by c/d, we *multiply a/b* by the reciprocal of c/d, namely d/c. This is commonly referred to as *inverting c/d and multiplying.*

DIVISION OF FRACTIONS

$$\dfrac{\dfrac{a}{b}}{\dfrac{c}{d}} = \frac{a}{b} \div \frac{c}{d} = \frac{a}{b} \cdot \frac{d}{c} = \frac{ad}{bc}.$$

example 3

Perform the indicated operations and simplify.

a. $\dfrac{4y}{3z} \div \dfrac{z}{9} = \dfrac{4y}{3z} \cdot \dfrac{9}{z} = \dfrac{4y(9)}{(3z)z} = \dfrac{4y(3)}{z^2} = \dfrac{12y}{z^2}.$

b. $\dfrac{x}{x+2} \div \dfrac{x+3}{x-5} = \dfrac{x}{x+2} \cdot \dfrac{x-5}{x+3} = \dfrac{x(x-5)}{(x+2)(x+3)}.$

c. $\dfrac{\dfrac{4x}{x^2-1}}{\dfrac{2x^2+8x}{x-1}} = \dfrac{4x}{(x+1)(x-1)} \cdot \dfrac{x-1}{2x(x+4)}$

$\qquad = \dfrac{4x(x-1)}{(x+1)(x-1)(2x)(x+4)} = \dfrac{2}{(x+1)(x+4)}.$

d. $\dfrac{\dfrac{x}{7}}{3y} = \dfrac{x}{7} \div 3y = \dfrac{x}{7} \cdot \dfrac{1}{3y} = \dfrac{x}{21y}.$

e. $\dfrac{4}{\dfrac{y}{x}} = 4 \div \dfrac{y}{x} = \dfrac{4}{1} \cdot \dfrac{x}{y} = \dfrac{4x}{y}.$

Exercise 4-2

In Problems 1–52, perform the indicated operations and simplify.

1. $\dfrac{7}{y} \cdot \dfrac{1}{x}.$

2. $\dfrac{2}{x} \cdot \dfrac{y}{5}.$

3. $\dfrac{2x^2}{3} \cdot \dfrac{6}{x^5}.$

4. $\dfrac{1}{x} \cdot \dfrac{3xy^2z^3}{x^2y} \cdot \dfrac{x^2}{3yz^3}.$

5. $\dfrac{x^2y^2z}{abc} \cdot \dfrac{b^2c}{y^3z} \cdot \dfrac{a^2b}{x^3y}.$

6. $\dfrac{3x^2y}{a^4} \cdot \dfrac{2ab^2x}{y} \cdot \dfrac{a^2x^3}{6} \cdot \dfrac{a^2}{b^2x^6}.$

7. $\dfrac{y^2}{y-3} \cdot \dfrac{-1}{y+2}.$

8. $\dfrac{x-3}{x+4} \cdot \dfrac{x-5}{x-3}.$

9. $\dfrac{x-3}{x^2} \cdot \dfrac{x-3}{x^4}.$

10. $\dfrac{-x}{x+2} \cdot \dfrac{x+2}{x^2}$.

11. $\dfrac{2x-3}{x-2} \cdot \dfrac{2-x}{2x+3}$.

12. $\dfrac{x^2-3x+2}{x^2-7x+12} \cdot \dfrac{(x-3)(x+2)}{x^2+x-2}$.

13. $\dfrac{x^2-y^2}{x+y} \cdot \dfrac{x^2+2xy+y^2}{y-x}$.

14. $\dfrac{b(6a-6b)}{a^2+ab} \cdot \dfrac{a^3-ab^2}{2b^2}$.

15. $\dfrac{5x-10}{5(x+3)} \cdot \dfrac{x}{2x-4}$.

16. $\dfrac{4}{6x^2} \cdot \dfrac{3x+9}{x^2+3x}$.

17. $(x^2-9) \cdot \dfrac{x-3}{4x+12}$.

18. $\dfrac{5}{(x+1)^2} \cdot (x^2+2x+1)$.

19. $\dfrac{x^2-5x+6}{x-1} \cdot \dfrac{x-1}{x-3} \cdot \dfrac{x+3}{(x-2)^2}$.

20. $\dfrac{(x-2)^2}{x+4} \cdot \dfrac{(x+4)^2}{x-2} \cdot \dfrac{(x-1)^2}{(x+4)^2}$.

21. $\dfrac{x^2+6x+8}{x^2-5x+6} \cdot \dfrac{x-2}{x^2+5x+4}$.

22. $\dfrac{2x^2+3x+1}{x^2-4x-5} \cdot \dfrac{x^2-25}{4x^2-1}$.

23. $\dfrac{8x^2+32}{x^2+2x} \cdot \dfrac{x^2+4x+4}{8x^2-32}$.

24. $\dfrac{x^3+8x^2+15x}{x^2+4x+3} \cdot \dfrac{x-1}{x^2+5x}$.

25. $\dfrac{x^2-8x+7}{(x+2)^2} \cdot \dfrac{x^2+x-2}{49-x^2}$.

26. $\dfrac{8-4x}{6x^3} \cdot \dfrac{4-x}{x^2-6x+8}$.

27. $\dfrac{2x^2y^3}{5w^2} \div \dfrac{2xy^2}{3wz^2}$.

28. $\dfrac{3xy}{2w^2z} \div \dfrac{4xyz}{5w}$.

29. $\dfrac{x+3}{x-4} \div \dfrac{x+3}{x+2}$.

30. $\dfrac{x+5}{x-3} \div \dfrac{x-5}{x-3}$.

31. $\dfrac{2x-2y}{3z} \div \dfrac{x-y}{6z^3}$.

32. $\dfrac{x^2-y^2}{xy} \div \dfrac{x+y}{xy}$.

33. $\dfrac{x-1}{x(x^2-y^2)} \div \dfrac{1-x}{x+y}$.

34. $\dfrac{3xz-15z}{2x^2y} \div \dfrac{5-x}{2(x+1)}$.

35. $6 \div \dfrac{x}{y}$.

36. $\dfrac{x}{6} \div y$.

37. $\dfrac{2}{9x} \div x$.

38. $\dfrac{\dfrac{x^2}{6}}{\dfrac{x}{3}}$.

39. $\dfrac{\dfrac{4x^3}{9x}}{\dfrac{x}{18}}$.

40. $\dfrac{\dfrac{2m}{n^3}}{\dfrac{4m}{n^2}}$.

41. $\dfrac{\dfrac{c+d}{c}}{\dfrac{c-d}{2c}}$.

42. $\dfrac{\dfrac{4x}{3}}{2x}$.

43. $\dfrac{-9x^3}{\dfrac{x}{3}}$.

44. $\dfrac{x-5}{\dfrac{x^2-7x+10}{x-2}}$.

45. $\dfrac{\dfrac{x^2+6x+9}{x}}{x+3}$.

46. $\dfrac{\dfrac{2x-4}{-6x}}{\dfrac{x-2}{3x^2}}$.

47. $\dfrac{\dfrac{x^2-4}{x^2+2x-3}}{\dfrac{x^2-x-6}{x^2-9}}$.

48. $\dfrac{\dfrac{x^2+7x+10}{x^2-2x-8}}{\dfrac{x^2+6x+5}{x^2-3x-4}}$.

49. $\dfrac{\dfrac{2x^2+5x-3}{4x^2-1}}{\dfrac{x^2+4x+3}{6x^2+x-1}}$.

50. $\dfrac{\dfrac{(x+2)^2}{3x-2}}{\dfrac{9x+18}{4-9x^2}}$.

51. $\dfrac{\dfrac{3}{5}(x^2+4x+4)}{\dfrac{9}{8}(x^2-4)}$.

52. $\dfrac{\dfrac{8}{3}(x^2+x-20)}{\dfrac{3x+15}{4}}$.

53. For a stretched steel wire, stress $= F/A$ and strain $= e/L$, where F is the tension in the wire, A is its cross-sectional area, e is its elongation, and L is its original length. Young's modulus for the material is stress/strain. Find an expression for this modulus and simplify.

54. Dimensional analysis of a fluid flow equation leads to the expression

$$L^3\left[L\left(\frac{M}{L^3}\right)\left(\frac{L}{T^2}\right)\right]\left(\frac{T}{L^2}\right).$$

Simplify the expression.

55. The power P dissipated in a resistance R is given by $P = V^2/R$, where V is the voltage across the resistor terminals. What happens to the power if the voltage is halved?

56. Under certain conditions, the pressure p of a vacuum system is given by the formula

$$p = \frac{ah^2}{V_0}.$$

Find p if $h = \frac{2}{3}d$.

57. In determining the moment of inertia of a flywheel, the expression for the ratio of natural frequencies of vibration of the flywheel with and without added loads is

$$\frac{\dfrac{JG}{IL}}{\dfrac{JG}{(I + 2mr^2)L}}.$$

Simplify the expression.

58. When a certain yo-yo is allowed to fall, the tension in the supporting string is found to be

$$\frac{\dfrac{1}{2}\left(\dfrac{W}{g}\right)\left(\dfrac{1}{6}\right)^2(6a)}{\left(\dfrac{1}{6}\right)},$$

where W is the weight and g and a are accelerations. Simplify this expression.

59. The power P dissipated in a resistor is given by $P = i^2R$, where i is current and R is resistance. In terms of time t, the current and resistance are given by

$$i = \frac{2t + 1}{3t^2} \quad \text{and} \quad R = \frac{3t}{2t + 1}.$$

Find an expression for P in terms of t and simplify.

4-3   Addition and Subtraction of Fractions

We now turn to adding fractions that have a *common denominator*. By the definition of division and the distributive law, it follows that

$$\frac{a}{c} + \frac{b}{c} = a \cdot \frac{1}{c} + b \cdot \frac{1}{c} = (a + b)\frac{1}{c} = \frac{a + b}{c}.$$

Thus

$$\frac{a}{c} + \frac{b}{c} = \frac{a+b}{c}.$$

That is, the sum of two fractions with a common denominator is a fraction with a denominator that is the common denominator and a numerator that is the sum of the numerators of the fractions. There are similar rules for handling sums and differences involving any number of fractions having a common denominator. For example,

$$\frac{a}{d} - \frac{b}{d} + \frac{c}{d} = \frac{a-b+c}{d}.$$

example 1

Perform the indicated operations and simplify.

a. $\dfrac{x}{y} + \dfrac{3x^2}{y} = \dfrac{x + 3x^2}{y}.$

b. $\dfrac{x^2}{5w} - \dfrac{x-2}{5w} = \dfrac{x^2 - (x-2)}{5w} = \dfrac{x^2 - x + 2}{5w}.$

c. $\dfrac{x^2 - 5}{x - 2} + \dfrac{2x - 3}{x - 2} = \dfrac{(x^2 - 5) + (2x - 3)}{x - 2}$

$$= \frac{x^2 + 2x - 8}{x - 2}$$

$$= \frac{\cancel{(x-2)}(x+4)}{\cancel{x-2}}$$

$$= x + 4.$$

We emphasize that *only fractions with the **same** denominator can be directly combined under addition or subtraction.* In general,

$$\frac{a}{b} + \frac{a}{c} \neq \frac{a}{b+c} \quad \text{and} \quad \frac{a}{b} + \frac{c}{d} \neq \frac{a+c}{b+d}.$$

example 2

In each of the following, note that the numerators are added when and only when the denominators are the same.

a. $\dfrac{x^2 - 5x + 4}{x^2 + 2x - 3} - \dfrac{x^2 + 2x}{x^2 + 5x + 6}$

$$= \frac{\cancel{(x-1)}(x-4)}{\cancel{(x-1)}(x+3)} - \frac{x\cancel{(x+2)}}{\cancel{(x+2)}(x+3)} \qquad \text{(factoring and cancelling)}$$

$$= \frac{x-4}{x+3} - \frac{x}{x+3} \qquad \text{(denominators now the same)}$$

$$= \frac{x-4-x}{x+3} = \frac{-4}{x+3} = -\frac{4}{x+3}.$$

b. $$\frac{x^2+x-5}{x-7} - \frac{x^2-2}{x-7} + \frac{8-4x}{x^2-9x+14}$$

$$= \frac{x^2+x-5}{x-7} - \frac{x^2-2}{x-7} + \frac{-4\cancel{(x-2)}}{\cancel{(x-2)}(x-7)} \qquad \text{(denominators now the same)}$$

$$= \frac{(x^2+x-5)-(x^2-2)+(-4)}{x-7}$$

$$= \frac{x^2+x-5-x^2+2-4}{x-7}$$

$$= \frac{x-7}{x-7} = 1.$$

To add or subtract fractions with different denominators, we first use the fundamental principle of fractions to rewrite the fractions as equivalent fractions that do have the same denominator. Then we add or subtract as we did before. For example, to find

$$\frac{2}{x} + \frac{3}{x+4},$$

we can begin by rewriting the first fraction as

$$\frac{2(x+4)}{x(x+4)} \qquad \text{(multiplying numerator and denominator by } x+4)$$

and rewriting the second one as

$$\frac{3x}{(x+4)x} \qquad \text{(multiplying numerator and denominator by } x).$$

Because these fractions have the same denominator, we can combine them.

$$\frac{2}{x} + \frac{3}{x+4} = \frac{2(x+4)}{x(x+4)} + \frac{3x}{(x+4)x}$$

$$= \frac{2(x+4)+3x}{x(x+4)}$$

$$= \frac{2x+8+3x}{x(x+4)}$$

$$= \frac{5x+8}{x(x+4)}.$$

We could have rewritten the original fractions with other common denominators. But we chose to rewrite them as fractions with the denominator $x(x + 4)$, which is called the **least common denominator** (L.C.D.) of the fractions $2/x$ and $3/(x + 4)$.* It can be shown that if any other common denominator were chosen, it must have the L.C.D. as a factor. In this sense the L.C.D. is the *least* such common denominator. For this reason, our work may be simplified by using the L.C.D. In general, we have the following.

> To find the L.C.D. of two or more fractions, multiply all the different factors that occur in the denominators of the fractions, each raised to the highest power to which that factor occurs in any one denominator.

example 3

Find the L.C.D. of the fractions

$$\frac{2x}{(x + 1)(x - 2)}, \quad \frac{x - 3}{x^2(x + 1)}, \quad \text{and} \quad \frac{x^2 + x}{x(x - 2)^2}.$$

There are three different factors in the denominators:

$$x + 1, \quad x - 2, \quad \text{and} \quad x.$$

The factor $x + 1$ occurs at most one time in any denominator. The factor $x - 2$ occurs at most two times (in the third fraction). The factor x occurs at most two times (in the second fraction). The L.C.D. is the product of these factors, each raised to the highest power to which it occurs in any one denominator. Thus the L.C.D. is

$$(x + 1)(x - 2)^2 x^2.$$

example 4

Find the L.C.D. of the fractions

$$\frac{2}{x^2}, \quad \frac{x}{x + 1}, \quad \frac{3x}{x^3(x - 1)}, \quad \text{and} \quad \frac{5}{\underbrace{x^2 + 2x + 1}_{(x + 1)^2}}.$$

The factor x occurs at most three times, the factor $x + 1$ occurs at most twice, and the factor $x - 1$ occurs at most once. Thus the L.C.D. is

$$x^3(x + 1)^2(x - 1).$$

*Section 0-4 discussed finding the L.C.D. of numerical fractions. A review of that section may be helpful.

To add or subtract fractions with different denominators, use the following rule.

> For each fraction, multiply both its numerator and denominator by a quantity that makes its denominator equal to the L.C.D. of the fractions. Then combine the fractions and, if possible, simplify.

example 5

Find $\dfrac{3}{x+2} + \dfrac{x-1}{x-6}$.

The L.C.D. is $(x+2)(x-6)$. To change the first fraction to an equivalent fraction with the L.C.D., we multiply the numerator and denominator by $x-6$. In the second fraction we multiply numerator and denominator by $x+2$.

$$\frac{3}{x+2} + \frac{x-1}{x-6}$$

$$= \frac{3(x-6)}{(x+2)(x-6)} + \frac{(x-1)(x+2)}{(x-6)(x+2)} \qquad \text{(putting the L.C.D. in each fraction)}$$

$$= \frac{3(x-6)+(x-1)(x+2)}{(x+2)(x-6)} \qquad \text{(combining fractions with common denominators)}$$

$$= \frac{3x-18+x^2+x-2}{(x+2)(x-6)}$$

$$= \frac{x^2+4x-20}{(x+2)(x-6)}.$$

example 6

Find $\dfrac{2}{x} - \dfrac{3}{xy} + \dfrac{4}{xz^2}$.

The L.C.D. is xyz^2.

$$\frac{2}{x} - \frac{3}{xy} + \frac{4}{xz^2} = \frac{2(yz^2)}{xyz^2} - \frac{3(z^2)}{xyz^2} + \frac{4(y)}{xz^2y}$$

$$= \frac{2yz^2 - 3z^2 + 4y}{xyz^2}.$$

example 7

When two springs are connected in series as shown in Fig. 4-2, the reciprocal of the effective spring constant k is given by

$$\frac{1}{k} = \frac{1}{k_1} + \frac{1}{k_2},$$

where k_1 and k_2 are the spring constants for each spring. Find a single fraction that gives the value of $1/k$.

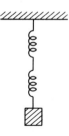

FIGURE 4-2

$$\frac{1}{k} = \frac{1}{k_1} + \frac{1}{k_2} = \frac{k_2}{k_1 k_2} + \frac{k_1}{k_1 k_2} = \frac{k_2 + k_1}{k_1 k_2}.$$

example 8

Find $\dfrac{6x - 17}{x^2 - 5x + 6} - \dfrac{1}{x - 3} + 3.$

The first denominator factors into $(x - 3)(x - 2)$. Thus the denominators of the three terms are $(x - 3)(x - 2)$, $x - 3$, and 1. The L.C.D. is $(x - 3)(x - 2)$.

$$\underbrace{\frac{6x - 17}{x^2 - 5x + 6}}_{(x-3)(x-2)} - \frac{1}{x - 3} + 3 = \frac{6x - 17}{(x - 3)(x - 2)} - \frac{x - 2}{(x - 3)(x - 2)} + \frac{3(x - 3)(x - 2)}{(x - 3)(x - 2)}$$

$$= \frac{6x - 17 - (x - 2) + \overbrace{3(x - 3)(x - 2)}^{x^2 - 5x + 6}}{(x - 3)(x - 2)}$$

$$= \frac{6x - 17 - x + 2 + 3x^2 - 15x + 18}{(x - 3)(x - 2)}$$

$$= \frac{3x^2 - 10x + 3}{(x - 3)(x - 2)} = \frac{(3x - 1)(x - 3)}{(x - 3)(x - 2)}$$

$$= \frac{3x - 1}{x - 2}.$$

example 9

Find $\dfrac{6}{x - 2} + \dfrac{7}{2 - x}.$

You might be tempted to use $(x - 2)(2 - x)$ as the L.C.D. However, we can simplify our work by rewriting the second fraction so that its denominator is $x - 2$:

$$\frac{6}{x-2} + \frac{7}{2-x} = \frac{6}{x-2} + \frac{7}{-(x-2)}$$

$$= \frac{6}{x-2} - \frac{7}{x-2} = \frac{6-7}{x-2} = \frac{-1}{x-2}$$

$$= -\frac{1}{x-2}.$$

example 10

Find $\dfrac{x-2}{x^2+6x+9} - \dfrac{x+2}{2(x^2-9)}$.

Because $x^2 + 6x + 9 = (x+3)^2$ and $2(x^2 - 9) = 2(x+3)(x-3)$, the L.C.D. is $2(x+3)^2(x-3)$.

$$\frac{x-2}{(x+3)^2} - \frac{x+2}{2(x+3)(x-3)} = \frac{(x-2)(2)(x-3)}{(x+3)^2(2)(x-3)} - \frac{(x+2)(x+3)}{2(x+3)(x-3)(x+3)}$$

$$= \frac{(x-2)(2)(x-3) - (x+2)(x+3)}{2(x+3)^2(x-3)}$$

$$= \frac{2(x^2 - 5x + 6) - [x^2 + 5x + 6]}{2(x+3)^2(x-3)}$$

$$= \frac{2x^2 - 10x + 12 - x^2 - 5x - 6}{2(x+3)^2(x-3)}$$

$$= \frac{x^2 - 15x + 6}{2(x+3)^2(x-3)}.$$

Exercise 4-3

In Problems 1–8, find the L.C.D. of the fractions.

1. $\dfrac{6}{(x-4)^2}, \dfrac{7}{(x-4)^5}$.

2. $\dfrac{x}{x+1}, \dfrac{2}{x-3}$.

3. $\dfrac{4}{x^2y}, \dfrac{5}{xy^3}$.

4. $\dfrac{x+1}{x^2y^3z}, \dfrac{y-1}{xyz^4}$.

5. $\dfrac{3x}{x^2+6x+9}, \dfrac{x^2}{x^2-9}$.

6. $\dfrac{2}{x^2+3x-4}, \dfrac{1}{x-1}$.

7. $\dfrac{1}{2x+2}, \dfrac{x}{x^2+x}, \dfrac{2}{x+1}$.

8. $\dfrac{x}{4x+2}, \dfrac{4}{4x^2-1}, \dfrac{x}{3}$.

In Problems 9–51, perform the indicated operations and simplify.

9. $\dfrac{x+1}{x-3} + \dfrac{4}{x-3}$.

10. $\dfrac{x^2}{x-2} + \dfrac{x-6}{x-2}$.

11. $\dfrac{3x}{x+1} + \dfrac{4}{x+1} - \dfrac{x+2}{x+1}.$

12. $\dfrac{2x}{x^2-1} - \dfrac{2}{x^2-1}.$

13. $\dfrac{3x^2+6x}{x^2+x-2} - \dfrac{x^2+2x+1}{x^2-1}.$

14. $\dfrac{3x+4}{x+2} + \dfrac{x^2-9}{x^2+5x+6}.$

15. $\dfrac{2}{x} + \dfrac{3}{y}.$

16. $3 + \dfrac{x}{y}.$

17. $\dfrac{x-4}{6} - \dfrac{x-2}{9}.$

18. $\dfrac{x-2}{3} + 1.$

19. $\dfrac{3}{2x} - \dfrac{2}{xy}.$

20. $\dfrac{4}{x} + \dfrac{2}{y} - \dfrac{x+1}{xy}.$

21. $\dfrac{x}{2} + \dfrac{2}{x}.$

22. $\dfrac{1}{x} - \dfrac{2}{3x} + \dfrac{4}{3}.$

23. $\dfrac{5}{x-2} + \dfrac{3}{x-3}.$

24. $\dfrac{y}{y-2} - \dfrac{3}{y}.$

25. $\dfrac{5y}{x^2} - \dfrac{2}{xy} + \dfrac{3}{y}.$

26. $\dfrac{x}{a^2} + \dfrac{y}{ab}.$

27. $\dfrac{x+3}{x-1} + 4.$

28. $\dfrac{a}{b} + \dfrac{c}{d}.$

29. $\dfrac{x}{x-y} + \dfrac{y}{x+y}.$

30. $\dfrac{2}{x+1} - \dfrac{3}{x-1}.$

31. $\dfrac{x+3}{x-3} - \dfrac{x-3}{2(x+3)}.$

32. $\dfrac{4}{2x-1} + \dfrac{x}{x+2}.$

33. $\dfrac{6x+12}{x^2+5x+4} + \dfrac{x}{x+4}.$

34. $\dfrac{5}{x^2+3x-4} + \dfrac{1}{x+4}.$

35. $\dfrac{1}{x^2-1} - \dfrac{1}{x-1} + \dfrac{1}{x+1}.$

36. $\dfrac{x}{x+1} - \dfrac{2x}{x^2+3x+2}.$

37. $\dfrac{x-1}{x^2+6x+9} + \dfrac{2}{x^2-9}.$

38. $x^2 + 2 - \dfrac{x^4}{x^2-2}.$

39. $\dfrac{x+1}{x^2+7x+10} - \dfrac{2x}{x^2+6x+5}.$

40. $\dfrac{y}{3y^2-5y-2} - \dfrac{2}{3y^2-7y+2}.$

41. $\dfrac{2x-6}{x^2-5x+6} + \dfrac{x^2+8x+16}{x^2+6x+8}.$

42. $\dfrac{2}{x^3(x-3)} + \dfrac{3}{x(x-3)^2}.$

43. $2x + 3 + \dfrac{2}{x-1}.$

44. $\dfrac{3}{x-1} - \dfrac{4}{1-x}.$

45. $\dfrac{x-2}{x^2+x} + \dfrac{3}{x^3+2x^2} - \dfrac{2x-3}{x^2+3x+2}.$

46. $\dfrac{2}{x^2-5x+6} - \dfrac{1}{x^2-3x+2} + \dfrac{4}{x^2-4x+3}.$

47. $\dfrac{y}{2y^2+7y+3} - \dfrac{2}{4y^2+4y+1}.$

48. $\dfrac{3}{x+3} + \dfrac{1}{x-3} - \dfrac{4}{x+2}.$

49. $\dfrac{y}{x^2+2xy+y^2} + \dfrac{3x}{x^2-y^2} - \dfrac{2}{x+y}.$

50. $1 - \dfrac{2y^2}{x^2-y^2} + \dfrac{2xy}{x^2+y^2}.$

51. $\dfrac{1}{x+y} - \dfrac{1}{y-x} + \dfrac{3}{x^2-y^2}.$

Problems 52–56 are more challenging than the previous ones. Again, perform the indicated operations and simplify.

52. $\dfrac{3m+n}{m-n} + \dfrac{m+3n}{n-m}.$

53. $\left(2x - \dfrac{x+3}{2} - 2a\right) + \dfrac{a-4}{3} - a.$

54. $\dfrac{ay}{a-y} + \dfrac{a^2}{y-a} + a.$

55. $\dfrac{2y+3}{2-y} - \dfrac{2-3y}{y+2} + \dfrac{16y - y^2}{(y+2)(y-2)}.$

56. $\dfrac{1}{8 - 6x + x^2} - \dfrac{x+2}{(x-3)(4-x)} + \dfrac{x+2}{x^2 - 5x + 6}.$

57. For the arrangement in Fig. 4-3, it is shown in physics that the potential at point O due to the point charges q_1, q_2, and q_3 is given by

$$\frac{kq_1}{x} + \frac{kq_2}{x+2} + \frac{kq_3}{x+3}.$$

Express the potential as a single fraction. Do not simplify your answer.

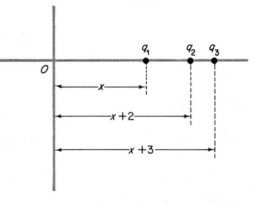

FIGURE 4-3

58. For the arrangement in Fig. 4-3, if the distance of charge q_2 from point O were doubled, theory shows that the potential at point O would be

$$\frac{kq_1}{x} + \frac{kq_2}{2(x+2)} + \frac{kq_3}{x+3}.$$

Express the potential as a single fraction. Do not simplify your answer.

59. In studies of electric potential, the expression

$$\frac{1}{4\pi\epsilon_0}\left(\frac{q_1}{r_1} - \frac{q_2}{r_2}\right)$$

was encountered. Write this expression as a single fraction.

60. When three springs with spring constants of k_1, k_2, k_3 are connected in series (see Example 7), the reciprocal of the effective spring constant k is given by

$$\frac{1}{k} = \frac{1}{k_1} + \frac{1}{k_2} + \frac{1}{k_3}.$$

Find a single fraction that gives the value for $1/k$.

61. The expression for the viscosity of a liquid has the form

$$\frac{a}{kR_1^2} - \frac{a}{kR_2^2}.$$

Combine these fractions and give your answer in factored form.

62. The formula for the stress factor f of a particular coil spring is

$$f = \frac{4k - 1}{4k - 4} + \frac{0.5}{k}.$$

Express f as a single fraction and simplify.

63. When two batteries with emf and internal resistance $\mathcal{E}_1, r_1$ and $\mathcal{E}_2, r_2$, respectively, are connected in parallel, the effective emf $\mathcal{E}$ of the combination is given by

$$\mathcal{E} = \left(\frac{1}{r_1} + \frac{1}{r_2}\right)\left(\frac{\mathcal{E}_1}{r_1} + \frac{\mathcal{E}_2}{r_2}\right).$$

Express $\mathcal{E}$ as a single fraction. Do not simplify your answer.

64. The reciprocal of the square of the impedance of an ac circuit containing a resistor, capacitor, and inductor connected in parallel is given by

$$\frac{1}{R^2} + \left(\frac{1}{X_L^2} - \frac{1}{X_C^2}\right)^2.$$

Express this quantity as a single fraction.

4-4 Complex Fractions

A **complex fraction** is one in which the numerator or denominator (or both) contains a fraction. There are two methods commonly used to simplify a complex fraction:

Method 1. Perform any indicated operations in the numerator and in the denominator. Then divide the numerator by the denominator.

Method 2. Multiply the numerator and denominator of the given fraction by the L.C.D. of the fractions that appear in the numerator or denominator. This gives an equivalent fraction.

In Example 1, both methods will be shown.

example 1

Simplify $\dfrac{1 + \dfrac{1}{x}}{2 - \dfrac{1}{y}}$.

Method 1.
We separately combine the terms in the numerator and denominator and then divide.

$$\frac{1 + \dfrac{1}{x}}{2 - \dfrac{1}{y}} = \frac{\dfrac{x}{x} + \dfrac{1}{x}}{\dfrac{2y}{y} - \dfrac{1}{y}} = \frac{\dfrac{x+1}{x}}{\dfrac{2y-1}{y}}$$

$$= \frac{x+1}{x} \div \frac{2y-1}{y} = \frac{x+1}{x} \cdot \frac{y}{2y-1}$$

$$= \frac{y(x+1)}{x(2y-1)}.$$

Method 2.
We multiply the numerator and denominator by the L.C.D. of the fractions that appear. The L.C.D. of $\dfrac{1}{x}$ and $\dfrac{1}{y}$ is xy. Note the use of the distributive law below.

$$\frac{1 + \dfrac{1}{x}}{2 - \dfrac{1}{y}} = \frac{xy\left(1 + \dfrac{1}{x}\right)}{xy\left(2 - \dfrac{1}{y}\right)} = \frac{xy(1) + xy\left(\dfrac{1}{x}\right)}{xy(2) - xy\left(\dfrac{1}{y}\right)}$$

$$= \frac{xy + y}{2xy - x} = \frac{y(x+1)}{x(2y-1)}.$$

example 2

Simplify $\dfrac{3 - \dfrac{1}{2x}}{6x + \dfrac{11x}{x-2}}$.

Using Method 1, we have

$$\frac{3 - \dfrac{1}{2x}}{6x + \dfrac{11x}{x-2}} = \frac{\dfrac{3(2x) - 1}{2x}}{\dfrac{6x(x-2) + 11x}{x-2}} = \frac{\dfrac{6x-1}{2x}}{\dfrac{6x^2 - x}{x-2}}$$

$$= \frac{\cancel{6x-1}}{2x} \cdot \frac{x-2}{x\cancel{(6x-1)}} = \frac{x-2}{2x^2}.$$

example 3

Simplify $\dfrac{\dfrac{x}{x-1}}{\dfrac{1}{x-1}+\dfrac{1}{x+1}}$.

Using Method 2, we multiply the numerator and denominator by the L.C.D. of the fractions that appear. The L.C.D. is $(x-1)(x+1)$.

$$\frac{\dfrac{x}{x-1}}{\dfrac{1}{x-1}+\dfrac{1}{x+1}} = \frac{(x-1)(x+1)\left[\dfrac{x}{x-1}\right]}{(x-1)(x+1)\left[\dfrac{1}{x-1}+\dfrac{1}{x+1}\right]}$$

$$= \frac{(x+1)(x)}{(x-1)(x+1)\left(\dfrac{1}{x-1}\right)+(x-1)(x+1)\left(\dfrac{1}{x+1}\right)}$$

$$= \frac{(x+1)(x)}{(x+1)+(x-1)} = \frac{(x+1)(x)}{2x} = \frac{x+1}{2}.$$

Exercise 4-4

*In Problems **1–20**, simplify.*

1. $\dfrac{\dfrac{1}{2}+\dfrac{1}{3}}{\dfrac{1}{2}}.$

2. $\dfrac{2^{-2}+3^{-2}}{13}.$

3. $\dfrac{\dfrac{1}{x}+\dfrac{3}{x}}{4}.$

4. $\dfrac{\dfrac{x}{x-1}-\dfrac{1}{x-1}}{x-1}.$

5. $\dfrac{4-\dfrac{6}{x}}{2}.$

6. $\dfrac{x-1}{1-\dfrac{1}{x}}.$

7. $\dfrac{7}{3x-\dfrac{1}{2}}.$

8. $\dfrac{x-\dfrac{1}{x}}{x+1}.$

9. $\dfrac{3-\dfrac{1}{y}}{2+\dfrac{1}{x}}.$

10. $\dfrac{\dfrac{a}{b}+2}{\dfrac{b}{a}-2}.$

11. $\dfrac{\dfrac{1}{x}+\dfrac{x}{2x-3}}{\dfrac{x-1}{x}}.$

12. $\dfrac{a-\dfrac{b^2}{a}}{b-\dfrac{a^2}{b}}.$

13. $\dfrac{\dfrac{x}{y}-\dfrac{y}{x}}{\dfrac{x+y}{xy}}.$

14. $\dfrac{\dfrac{x^2-9}{4}}{\dfrac{1}{x}-\dfrac{1}{3}}.$

15. $\dfrac{\dfrac{x}{y}+\dfrac{y}{x}}{\dfrac{x}{y}-\dfrac{y}{x}}.$

16. $\dfrac{\dfrac{x}{x^2 + 4x + 3}}{\dfrac{1}{x^2 - 1} + 1}.$

17. $\dfrac{x + 1 + \dfrac{1}{x + 3}}{\dfrac{x + 2}{3}}.$

18. $\dfrac{3x + \dfrac{x}{x - 3}}{3x - \dfrac{x}{x - 3}}.$

19. $\dfrac{\dfrac{1}{x^4} + \dfrac{1}{x^2} + 1}{\dfrac{1}{x^3} + \dfrac{1}{x} + x}.$

20. $\dfrac{\dfrac{a + b}{a - b} - \dfrac{a - b}{a + b}}{1 - \dfrac{a^2 + b^2}{(a + b)^2}}.$

21. $\dfrac{a}{1 + \dfrac{c}{d + \dfrac{1}{2}}}.$

22. $\dfrac{\dfrac{x}{y} + x}{y - \dfrac{1}{y}} - 1.$

23. The effective spring constant k of three springs connected in series is given by

$$k = \frac{1}{\dfrac{1}{k_1} + \dfrac{1}{k_2} + \dfrac{1}{k_3}}.$$

Simplify the expression for k.

24. The equivalent spring constant k for a certain spring system is given by

$$k = \frac{1}{4\left(\dfrac{1}{k_1} + \dfrac{1}{k_2}\right)}.$$

Simplify the expression for k.

25. The theory of relativity shows that the mass m of an object varies with its speed v according to the equation

$$m^2 = \frac{m_0^2}{1 - \left(\dfrac{v}{c}\right)^2},$$

where m_0 is the rest mass of the object and c is the speed of light. Simplify the expression for m^2.

26. When the system of masses shown in Fig. 4-4 is released from rest, the acceleration a of the masses is found to be given by

$$a = \frac{g}{1 + \dfrac{m_1}{m_2}}.$$

Simplify the expression for a.

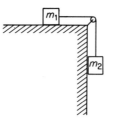

FIGURE 4-4

27. The lensmaker's equation gives the focal length f of a lens with spherical surfaces of radii R_1 and R_2. The equation is

$$f = \frac{1}{\left(\frac{n_1}{n_2} - 1\right)\left(\frac{1}{R_1} + \frac{1}{R_2}\right)},$$

where n_1 and n_2 are the indices of refraction of the lens material and surrounding medium, respectively. Simplify the expression for f.

4-5 Ratio—SI Units

Throughout the engineering technologies we find physical quantities that are expressed as quotients. For example, pressure (p) is equal to force (F) divided by area (A), and we can write $p = F/A$. In general terms, the quotient a/b is also called the **ratio of a to b**.* Thus pressure is the ratio of force to area. Similarly, average power ($\bar{P}$) is the ratio of work to time ($\bar{P} = W/t$) and acceleration (a) is the ratio of force to mass ($a = F/m$).

In all aspects of science and technology, we must be able to measure physical quantities. The concept of ratio is basic to the process of measurement. In fact, to measure a quantity *means* to determine the ratio of that quantity to some chosen unit. For example, to measure the length of a cable with a meter stick, we determine how many times the length of the meter stick is contained in the length of the cable. If the meter stick can be fitted along the length of the cable six times, the measurement is $6/1 = 6$ meters. In this example the **unit of measurement** is the *meter*.

By selecting units for some fundamental physical quantities, we form a *system* of units. In science, technology, and industry, the universally accepted system of units is a metric system called the **International System of Units**, abbreviated SI. The seven SI basic units are listed in Table 4-1.

Table 4-1 SI basic units

Quantity	Unit	Symbol
Length	meter	m
Mass	kilogram	kg
Time	second	s
Electric current	ampere	A
Thermodynamic temperature	kelvin	K
Amount of substance	mole	mol
Luminous intensity	candela	cd

To express large multiples or small submultiples of basic units (or other units), we can use the prefixes listed in Table 4-2. The symbol μ is the Greek letter *mu*.

*The ratio of a to b is sometimes denoted by $a : b$.

Table 4-2 SI prefixes

Factor	Prefix	Symbol	Factor	Prefix	Symbol
10^{18}	exa-	E	10^{-1}	deci-	d
10^{15}	peta-	P	10^{-2}	centi-	c
10^{12}	tera-	T	10^{-3}	milli-	m
10^{9}	giga-	G	10^{-6}	micro-	μ
10^{6}	mega-	M	10^{-9}	nano-	n
10^{3}	kilo-	k	10^{-12}	pico-	p
10^{2}	hecto-	h	10^{-15}	femto-	f
10^{1}	deka-	da	10^{-18}	atto-	a

The use of prefixes makes this metric system especially convenient because it is essentially a *decimal* or *power-of-ten* system. You must understand how the prefixes are used. To illustrate, note that the factors represented by the prefixes *centi, milli,* and *kilo* are

$$\text{centi} \longrightarrow 10^{-2} = \frac{1}{100},$$

$$\text{milli} \longrightarrow 10^{-3} = \frac{1}{1000},$$

$$\text{kilo} \longrightarrow 10^{3} = 1000.$$

Using the meter as our basic unit (we could use *any* unit whatever), we have

$$1 \text{ centimeter} = \frac{1}{100}(1 \text{ meter}) \quad \text{or} \quad 1 \text{ cm} = \frac{1}{100} \text{ m},$$

$$1 \text{ millimeter} = \frac{1}{1000}(1 \text{ meter}) \quad \text{or} \quad 1 \text{ mm} = \frac{1}{1000} \text{ m},$$

$$1 \text{ kilometer} = 1000(1 \text{ meter}) \quad \text{or} \quad 1 \text{ km} = 1000 \text{ m}.$$

Similarly, a thousandth of an ampere is a milliampere (mA). The other prefixes are used in a similar manner. From the discussion above it should be clear to you that

$$1 \text{ m} = 100 \text{ cm} = 1000 \text{ mm} = \frac{1}{1000} \text{ km}.$$

Most physical quantities require both a *number* and a *unit* if they are to be completely specified or measured. It is meaningless to say that the length of a wire is 5. We must state whether we mean 5 m, 5 cm, 5 mm, or 5 km, for example. That is, the unit must be given. It often happens, though, that the given unit is not the desired unit. When units are treated as algebraic quantities, we can use ratios to obtain a method of converting from one unit to another unit.

example 1

Convert 5 kilometers to millimeters.

First we shall convert kilometers to meters. Because 1 km = 1000 m, the ratio (1000 m)/(1 km) is equal to 1. We can now write

$$5 \text{ km} = (5 \text{ km})(1) = (5 \text{ km}) \cdot \frac{1000 \text{ m}}{1 \text{ km}} = 5000 \text{ m}.$$

Cancelling the unit, km, is just like cancelling x in

$$5x \cdot \frac{1000y}{1x} = 5000y.$$

That is, the units are treated like algebraic quantities. We point out, however, that the ratio was set up so that the units would cancel. Now we convert meters to millimeters. Because 1 m = 1000 mm, the ratio (1000 mm)/(1 m) is also equal to 1. So,

$$(5000 \text{ m})(1) = (5000 \text{ m})\left(\frac{1000 \text{ mm}}{1 \text{ m}}\right) = 5 \times 10^6 \text{ mm}.$$

Conversions like this are not usually written as separate steps. We write

$$5 \text{ km} = (5 \text{ km})\left(\frac{1000 \text{ m}}{1 \text{ km}} \cdot \frac{1000 \text{ mm}}{1 \text{ m}}\right) = 5 \times 10^6 \text{ mm}.$$

example 2

Convert 2 A to microamperes.

$$2 \text{ A} = (2 \text{ A})\left(\frac{1 \text{ } \mu\text{A}}{10^{-6} \text{ A}}\right) = \frac{2}{10^{-6}} \text{ } \mu\text{A} = 2 \times 10^6 \text{ } \mu\text{A}.$$

example 3

Convert 5 square centimeters (cm²) to square meters (m²).

$$5 \text{ cm}^2 = (5 \text{ cm}^2)\left(\frac{1 \text{ m}}{100 \text{ cm}}\right)^2 = (5 \text{ cm}^2)\left(\frac{1^2 \text{ m}^2}{100^2 \text{ cm}^2}\right)$$

$$= (5 \text{ cm}^2)\left(\frac{1 \text{ m}^2}{10^4 \text{ cm}^2}\right) = 5 \times 10^{-4} \text{ m}^2.$$

Notice here that we had to *square* the ratio (1 m)/(100 cm) so that the unit cm² could be cancelled. Students often make mistakes in doing this, so you should be careful! As the next example shows, we must *cube* the basic ratios when converting units of volume.

example 4

The density (mass per unit volume) of copper is 8.93×10^3 kg/m³. Express this density in grams per cubic centimeter.

The gram, g, is a submultiple of the kilogram, the basic SI unit of mass. Clearly 1 kg = 1000 g, so

$$8.93 \times 10^3 \, \frac{\text{kg}}{\text{m}^3} = \left[\left(8.93 \times 10^3 \frac{\text{kg}}{\text{m}^3} \right) \left(\frac{1000 \text{ g}}{1 \text{ kg}} \right) \right] \left(\frac{1 \text{ m}}{100 \text{ cm}} \right)^3$$

$$= \left[8.93 \times 10^6 \, \frac{\text{g}}{\text{m}^3} \right] \left(\frac{1 \text{ m}^3}{10^6 \text{ cm}^3} \right)$$

$$= 8.93 \text{ g/cm}^3.$$

In many technical areas, we find examples of SI **derived units**, which are units that are combinations of the seven basic units given in Table 4-1. For example, *velocity* is the rate at which position changes. The SI unit of velocity, meters per second (m/s), is derived from the SI units of length and time. *Acceleration* is the rate at which velocity changes, so its unit is the ratio of units of velocity to time. Thus the SI unit of acceleration is

$$\frac{\text{m/s}}{\text{s}} = \frac{\text{m}}{\text{s}} \left(\frac{1}{\text{s}} \right) = \frac{\text{m}}{\text{s}^2},$$

where the last fraction is read *meters per second squared*.

Many SI derived units are so common that they have been given special names. For example, the unit of force is the product of the units of mass and acceleration. Thus

$$\text{unit of force} = \text{kg} \left(\frac{\text{m}}{\text{s}^2} \right) = \frac{\text{kg m}}{\text{s}^2},$$

which is called a **newton**, N. Some of the derived units that you will encounter in your technical studies are shown in Table 4-3, where Ω is the Greek letter omega.

example 5

As shown in Table 4-3, the farad is a unit of capacitance, the property of a device often found in electrical circuits. When capacitors are connected in parallel, the total capacitance of the combination is the sum of the individual capacitances. If three capacitors with capacitances of 0.5 μF, 1.0 μF, and 2.0 μF are connected in parallel, what is the capacitance of the combination, in farads?

Let C_t be the total capacitance. We have

$$C_t = C_1 + C_2 + C_3$$
$$= 0.5 \, \mu\text{F} + 1.0 \, \mu\text{F} + 2.0 \, \mu\text{F} = 3.5 \, \mu\text{F}.$$

Then

$$3.5 \ \mu F = (3.5 \ \mu F)\left(\frac{10^{-6} \ F}{1 \ \mu F}\right) = 3.5 \times 10^{-6} \ F.$$

Table 4-3 Some SI derived units

Quantity	Name	Symbol	In terms of other units	In terms of SI base units
Force	newton	N		$m \cdot kg/s^2$
Pressure	pascal	Pa	N/m^2	$kg/(m \cdot s^2)$
Energy	joule	J	$N \cdot m$	$kg \cdot m^2/s^2$
Power	watt	W	J/s	$kg \cdot m^2/s^3$
Electric charge	coulomb	C		$A \cdot s$
Electric potential	volt	V	W/A	$kg \cdot m^2/(A \cdot s^3)$
Capacitance	farad	F	C/V	$A^2 \cdot s^4/(kg \cdot m^2)$
Resistance	ohm	Ω	V/A	$kg \cdot m^2/(A^2 \cdot s^3)$

example 6

Astronomers deal with such large distances that they find it convenient to use the *light year* as a unit of distance. One **light year** is the distance traveled by light in a vacuum in 1 year. Given that the speed of light is 3×10^8 m/s in a vacuum, determine the number of meters in a light year to three significant figures.

$$distance = [rate][time]$$

$$= \left[\frac{3 \times 10^8 \ m}{s}\right][1 \ yr]\left(\frac{365 \ d}{1 \ yr}\right)\left(\frac{24 \ h}{1 \ d}\right)\left(\frac{60 \ min}{1 \ h}\right)\left(\frac{60 \ s}{1 \ min}\right)$$

$$= 9.46 \times 10^{15} \ m.$$

Note the abbreviations for day (d), hour (h), minute (min), and second (s).

Exercise 4-5

In Problems 1–29, use the prefixes and the factors given in Table 4-2 to make the required conversion.

1. 2.5 m to millimeters.

2. 4 m to centimeters.

3. 8.2 m to kilometers.

4. 12 cm to kilometers.

5. 15 cm to meters.

6. 100 cm to millimeters.

7. 50 mm to centimeters.

8. 10 mm to kilometers.

9. 25 mm to meters.

10. 1 μm to centimeters.

11. 6.0 μF to farads.

12. 8.2 F to microfarads.

13. 2.1 pF to microfarads.

14. 1.0 μm to centimeters.

15. 700 nm to millimeters.

16. 0.005 A to milliamperes.

17. 6.2 μA to milliamperes.

18. 10 mA to microamperes.

19. 40 kg to grams.

20. 350 g to kilograms.

21. 300 kW to watts.

22. 0.2 W to microwatts.

23. 0.2 W to milliwatts.

24. 12,000,000 Ω to megohms.

25. 22,000 Ω to megohms.

26. 0.016 mV to volts.

27. 0.2 mV to microvolts.

28. 2 kV to millivolts.

29. 1.6×10^{-19} C to microcoulombs.

30. Convert 6 m² to square centimeters.

31. Convert 2.4 cm² to square millimeters.

32. Convert 800 mm² to square meters.

33. Convert 5.1 m³ to cubic centimeters.

34. Convert 60 mm³ to cubic centimeters.

35. Convert 500 cm³ to cubic meters.

36. Near the earth's surface, the acceleration due to gravity is about 9.80 m/s². Convert this acceleration to centimeters per second squared.

37. Five 1.5-μF capacitors are connected in parallel. Find the total capacitance in farads. (Refer to Example 5.)

38. A light pulse would take about 100,000 years to travel from one edge of the Milky Way to the other. What is the distance across the Milky Way in kilometers? (Refer to Example 6.)

39. At 0°C, the speed of sound in air is about 331 m/s. Convert this speed to kilometers per hour.

40. The density of gold is 1.93×10^4 kg/m³. Find the density of gold in grams per cubic centimeter. (Refer to Example 4.)

41. Aluminum has a density of 2.70 g/cm³. Find the density of aluminum in kilograms per cubic meter. (Refer to Example 4.)

42. The heat of fusion of water is 3.33×10^5 J/kg. Given that 4.186 J = 1 calorie, find the heat of fusion of water in calories per gram.

43. Einstein's famous mass-energy equivalance formula is $E = mc^2$, where m is a mass and c is the speed of light. Given that $c = 3 \times 10^8$ m/s and that 1 kg·m²/s² = 1 J, find the energy in joules associated with a mass of 1 g.

44. The green line of the mercury spectrum has a wavelength of 0.00005461 cm. Given that 1 Angstrom (Å) equals 10^{-7} mm, find this wavelength in Angstrom units.

45. Assuming there are 365 days in each year, determine the number of seconds there are in a century.

46. The charge to mass ratio of an electron is 1.76×10^{11} C/kg. Express this ratio in microcoulombs per gram.

47. The length of each edge of a cubical block is 8 cm. Find the surface area of the block in square meters.

48. The liter (ℓ) is a commonly used unit for volume; $1\ \ell = 10^3\ \text{cm}^3$. If a cylindrical container has a radius of 2.0 m and a height of 3.0 m, find the volume of the tank in liters.

49. Find the volume of the block in Problem 47 in liters. (See Problem 48.)

50. In making one revolution around the earth, the moon travels about 2.4×10^6 km in 28 days. Find the speed of the moon in meters per second.

51. In addition to the pascal (Pa), other units used to measure pressure are the atmosphere (atm) and the torr. The relationships between these units are

$$1\ \text{atm} = 1.01 \times 10^5\ \text{Pa},$$
$$1\ \text{torr} = 133.3\ \text{Pa}.$$

If a gas is compressed in a tank until its pressure is 5.2 atm, find the pressure of the gas in torrs.

4-6 Review

Review Questions

1. What rule allows you to multiply the numerator and denominator of a fraction by the same nonzero number? _____

2. Insert $+$ or $-$ in the parentheses to make the equalities true in the following.
$$\frac{a-b}{c-d} = (\quad)\ \frac{-(a-b)}{c-d} = (\quad)\ \frac{b-a}{d-c} = (\quad)\ \frac{b-a}{-(c-d)}. \quad\underline{\hspace{3cm}}$$

Write true *if the following are, in general, true and write* false *if otherwise.*

$$\frac{a+bx}{a+cy} = \frac{bx}{cy}. \qquad\qquad \underline{\hspace{2cm}} \quad (3)$$

$$\frac{1}{x} + \frac{1}{y} = \frac{xy}{x+y}. \qquad\qquad \underline{\hspace{2cm}} \quad (4)$$

$$\frac{abx}{acy} = \frac{bx}{cy}. \qquad\qquad \underline{\hspace{2cm}} \quad (5)$$

$$\frac{1}{x} - \frac{x-y}{x^2} = \frac{x-x-y}{x^2}. \qquad\qquad \underline{\hspace{2cm}} \quad (6)$$

$$\frac{1}{a} + \frac{1}{b} = \frac{2}{ab}. \qquad\qquad \underline{\hspace{2cm}} \quad (7)$$

$$\frac{a^2-b^2}{a-b} = a-b. \qquad\qquad \underline{\hspace{2cm}} \quad (8)$$

$$\frac{\dfrac{1}{x}}{y} = \frac{1}{xy}. \qquad\qquad \underline{\hspace{2cm}} \quad (9)$$

$$\frac{1}{x} - \frac{1}{y} = \frac{x-y}{xy}. \qquad\qquad \underline{\hspace{2cm}} \quad (10)$$

$$\frac{x-y}{y+x} + \frac{y-x}{x+y} = 0. \hspace{2cm} \underline{\hspace{3cm}} \quad \textbf{(11)}$$

$$\frac{1}{x} + \frac{1}{y} = \frac{1}{x+y}. \hspace{2cm} \underline{\hspace{3cm}} \quad \textbf{(12)}$$

$$\frac{1}{x} \cdot \frac{1}{y} = \frac{1}{xy}. \hspace{2cm} \underline{\hspace{3cm}} \quad \textbf{(13)}$$

14. The L.C.D. of the fractions

$$\frac{6}{x^2-1} \cdot \frac{8}{x+1}, \quad \text{and} \quad \frac{7}{2(x+1)}$$

is \underline{\hspace{3cm}} .

Answers to Review Questions

1. Fundamental principle of fractions. **2.** $-, +, +$. **3.** False. **4.** False. **5.** True.
6. False. **7.** False. **8.** False. **9.** True. **10.** False. **11.** True. **12.** False.
13. True. **14.** $2(x+1)(x-1)$.

Review Problems

In Problems **1–26**, *perform the indicated operations and simplify your answers.*

1. $\dfrac{2}{x} + \dfrac{4}{x-6}$.

2. $\dfrac{x-7}{x+4} - \dfrac{6}{2x+8}$.

3. $\dfrac{x^2-64}{x^3} \cdot \dfrac{x^2}{2x+16}$.

4. $\dfrac{x-2}{4} \cdot \dfrac{8x+4}{x^2+2x-8}$.

5. $\dfrac{x+2}{\dfrac{2x+4}{3}}$.

6. $\dfrac{\dfrac{x^3}{x-1}}{x^5}$.

7. $\dfrac{3}{x-2} - \dfrac{x+2}{x-3}$.

8. $\dfrac{2}{3x} + \dfrac{3}{x} - \dfrac{4}{5x}$.

9. $\dfrac{9x}{x^2+2x+1} \cdot \dfrac{(x+1)^3}{-3}$.

10. $\dfrac{-(x+3)}{x^2+x} \cdot \dfrac{x}{-(x^2-9)}$.

11. $2 + \dfrac{x}{x-1} - \dfrac{x-1}{x^2-1}$.

12. $\dfrac{2}{x-y} + \dfrac{2}{y-x}$.

13. $\dfrac{x^2+5x+6}{x^2-2x-8} \cdot \dfrac{x^2-16}{x^2+7x+12}$.

14. $\dfrac{4x^2+4x+1}{x^2-2x-3} \cdot \dfrac{x^2+2x+1}{2x^2+3x+1}$.

15. $\dfrac{\dfrac{8-4x}{2x}}{\dfrac{x^2-4x+4}{x^2-2x}}$.

16. $\dfrac{\dfrac{4x^2-9}{(x+1)^3}}{\dfrac{4x+6}{(x+1)^2}}$.

17. $\dfrac{x+2}{x^2+4x+4} + \dfrac{x-3}{x+2}$.

18. $\dfrac{6}{y+3} - \dfrac{2y}{y-3} + \dfrac{3}{y^2-9}$.

19. $\dfrac{\dfrac{2x+2}{x^3-x}}{\dfrac{x-1}{x^2}}$.

20. $\dfrac{\dfrac{3x^2-12x-15}{x^2+5x+4}}{\dfrac{30-6x}{x+4}}$.

21. $\dfrac{x+1}{x^2+x-12} \cdot \dfrac{9-x^2}{x^2+3x+2}.$

22. $\dfrac{4-x^2}{25-x^2} \cdot \dfrac{x-5}{x-2}.$

23. $\dfrac{x+2}{\dfrac{x}{x+1}+\dfrac{4}{x}}.$

24. $\dfrac{\dfrac{1}{x+2}-\dfrac{1}{x-2}}{\dfrac{2}{x-2}}.$

25. $\dfrac{1-\dfrac{7}{x^2-9}}{\dfrac{x-4}{3-x}}.$

26. $\dfrac{\dfrac{2}{x+3}+1}{1-\dfrac{2}{x+4}}.$

27. An expression for the energy stored in the magnetic field of an inductor is

$$\left(\frac{it}{2}\right)\left(\frac{Li}{t}\right).$$

Simplify this expression.

28. The static displacement of an object connected to a certain complex system of springs is given by

$$\frac{W}{k}+\frac{1}{2}\left(\frac{W}{2k}+\frac{W}{3k}\right).$$

Simplify this expression.

29. The equivalent resistance R of three resistances R_1, R_2, and R_3 connected in series is given by

$$R=\frac{1}{\dfrac{1}{R_1}+\dfrac{1}{R_2}+\dfrac{1}{R_3}}.$$

Simplify this complex fraction.

30. The Doppler effect for light can be used to determine the speeds of heavenly bodies that are moving toward or receding from the earth. The frequency f' received from such a body is given by

$$f'=f-\frac{fv}{c}+\frac{f}{2}\left(\frac{v}{c}\right)^2,$$

where f is the emitted frequency, v is the speed of the body, and c is the speed of light. Write the expression for f' as a single fraction.

31. The threshold of hearing corresponds to a sound intensity of about 10^{-12} W/m^2. Express this intensity in microwatts per square centimeter.

32. Convert 2.31×10^{-5} A to microamperes.

equations

5-1 Types of Equations

Even a beginning student in engineering technology is faced with solving elementary equations. The purpose of this chapter is to develop techniques to accomplish this task and to apply these methods to practical situations.

An **equation** is a statement that two algebraic expressions are equal. The two expressions that make up an equation are called its **sides** or **members.** They are separated by the equality sign, $=$.

example 1

The following statements are equations.

a. $3x + 1 = 16$.

b. $x^2 + 2x - 8 = 0$.

c. $\dfrac{y}{y - 4} = 6$.

d. $s = 7 - t$.

Conditions imposed by an equation can be expressed verbally (that is, in words). For example, the equation $3x + 1 = 16$ states that when three times a number x is added to 1, the result is 16.

In Example 1, each equation contains at least one variable. Recall that a **variable** is a symbol, such as x, that can be replaced by any one of a set of different numbers. The most popular symbols for variables are letters from the latter part of the alphabet, such as x, y, z, s, and t. For example, the equations in (a) and (c) of Example 1 are said to be in the variables x and y, respectively. The equation in (d) is in the variables s and t.

We *never* allow a variable in an equation to have a value for which any expression in that equation is undefined. For example, if $y/(y - 4) = 6$, then y cannot be 4, because this would make the denominator zero (we cannot divide by zero). In some equations the allowable values of a variable are restricted for physical reasons. For example, if the variable t represents time, negative values of t may not make sense. Hence we should assume that $t \geq 0$.

Equations in which some of the constants are not specified but are represented by letters, such as a, b, c, or d, are called **literal equations**, and the letters are called **literal constants** or **arbitrary constants**. For example, in the literal equation $x + a = b$, we may consider a and b to be arbitrary constants. Equations with more than one variable, such as the formula $C = 2\pi r$ for the circumference C of a circle of radius r, are also considered literal equations.

In the equation $3x + 1 = 16$, if x takes on a specific value, then the resulting equation may be either a true or a false statement. For example, if x is 5, then the equation becomes $3(5) + 1 = 16$, or simply $16 = 16$, which is true. On the other hand, if x is zero, the equation becomes $3(0) + 1 = 16$, or $1 = 16$, which is false. The given equation is called a *conditional equation* in the following sense:

> A **conditional equation** is an equation that is true for at least one, but not all, of the allowable values of its variables.

Consider the equation

$$2(x + 1) = 2x + 2.$$

By applying the distributive law to the left side, $2(x + 1)$, we observe that it is identically equal to the right side $2x + 2$. Thus the equation is always a true statement, regardless of the value of x. We call this equation an *identity* in the following sense:

> An **identity** is an equation that is true for all allowable values of its variables.

To **solve** an equation means to find *all* values of its variables for which the equation is true. These values are called **solutions** of the equation and are said to **satisfy** the equation. When only one variable is involved, a solution is also called a **root**. The set of all solutions of an equation is called the **solution set** of that equation.

Often a letter representing an unknown quantity in an equation is called an **unknown**. Example 2 illustrates the terminology that we have introduced.

example 2

a. In the equation $x + 3 = 4$, the variable or unknown is x. The only value of x that satisfies the equation is obviously 1. Hence 1 is a root and the solution set is $\{1\}$.

b. Suppose the equation $W_1 + W_2 = 7$ newtons indicates that the sum of the weights of two bodies, namely the variables W_1 and W_2, is equal to 7 newtons (N). One solution is the *pair* of values $W_1 = 1$ N and $W_2 = 6$ N. However, there are obviously infinitely many solutions.

c. One root of the equation $x^2 + 2x - 8 = 0$ is -4, because substituting -4 for x gives $(-4)^2 + 2(-4) - 8 = 0$, or $0 = 0$. Thus -4 satisfies the equation.

d. The equation $2 + 2x^2 = x^2 + 2 + x^2$ is an identity, because both sides are identically equal to $2x^2 + 2$.

Some equations are false regardless of the value of the variable involved. For example, in the equation $x + 2 = x$, there is no number x which when added to 2 is equal to the original number x. Such an equation is called an **impossible equation**. Since there is no solution, the solution set is a set with no elements in it, $\{\ \}$. It is called the **empty set** (or **null set**) and is denoted by $\varnothing$. Do not confuse the set $\varnothing$ with $\{0\}$, which is not empty; $\{0\}$ has the number zero in it.

We conclude this section with an example of translating a verbal statement into an algebraic one.

example 3

When a battery of emf $\mathcal{E}$ (in volts) is connected to a group of resistors in parallel, the current I (in amperes) in the battery is equal to the product of the emf and the sum of the reciprocals of the resistances. Write an equation for the current I in a battery that is connected to two parallel resistors R_1 and R_2. Evaluate the current if $\mathcal{E} = 12$ V, $R_1 = 6\ \Omega$, and $R_2 = 3\ \Omega$.

Because I is the product of $\mathcal{E}$ and $1/R_1 + 1/R_2$, the equation is

$$I = \mathcal{E}\left(\frac{1}{R_1} + \frac{1}{R_2}\right).$$

By substituting 12 for $\mathcal{E}$, 6 for R_1, and 3 for R_2, we obtain

$$I = 12\left(\frac{1}{6} + \frac{1}{3}\right) = 12\left(\frac{1+2}{6}\right) = 12\left(\frac{3}{6}\right) = 6 \text{ A}.$$

Exercise 5-1

In Problems **1–6**, *use substitution to determine which of the given numbers, if any, satisfy the given equation.*

1. $9x - x^2 = 0$; 1, 0.

2. $20 - 9x = -x^2$; 5, 4.

3. $y + 2(y - 3) = 4$; $\frac{10}{3}$, 1.

4. $2x + x^2 - 8 = 0$; 2, −4.

5. $x(7 + x) - 2(x + 1) = -7$; −1, −7.

6. $x(x + 1)^2(x + 2) = 0$; 0, −1, 2.

In Problems **7–10**, *determine which of the given equations are identities. See Example 2(d).*

7. $x - 5 = 2(x - 10) - x + 15$.

8. $x - 3(x + 2) + 4x - 7 = -13 + 2x$.

9. $3x(7) - 5 + x = 21x$.

10. $2\left(\dfrac{x}{2} + 3\right) - x = 6$.

In Problems **11–24**, *translate the verbal statements into algebraic equations.*

11. When 10 is subtracted from a number n, the result is zero.

12. When five times a number n is decreased by 3, the result is 14.

13. The product of x and the sum of a and b is equal to the sum of b times x and a times x. Show that the resulting equation is an identity.

14. If 3 is decreased by 15 times a number x, the result is 3, plus 4 times the number.

15. Twice the sum of x and 3 is equal to five times the result of subtracting 9 from x.

16. The sum of a number n and 2 is multiplied by the value of the number decreased by 2. The result is equal to -4 plus the square of the number. Show that the resulting equation is an identity.

17. The reciprocal of t_1 plus the reciprocal of t_2 is equal to the reciprocal of T.

18. The sum of three consecutive integers is 36. Assume that the first integer is x.

19. The distance s traveled by a particle along a path is equal to the product of its velocity v and the time t it travels.

20. The number z exceeds $y - 4z$ by $5(z - \frac{1}{3}y)$.

21. Fahrenheit temperature F is equal to $\frac{9}{5}$ Celsius temperature C, plus 32.

22. If a mass were converted into energy, the amount E of energy liberated is equal to the product of the mass m and the square of the speed of light c.

23. An interpretation of Newton's second law leads to the result that W, the weight of an object, is equal to the mass m of the object times the acceleration g due to gravity.

24. The product of the pressure P of a gas and the volume V of the gas is equal to a constant k.

25. A spring stretches 5.3 cm for each newton of weight that is suspended from it. If the initial length of the spring is 20 cm, write an equation that relates the length L (in centimeters) of the stretched spring to the load W (in newtons) suspended from it. From this equation, find the length of the spring when 2.0 N are suspended from it.

26. The weight of a large lump of clay decreases by 9.8 N for each kilogram of clay that is removed from it.
    (a) If the initial weight is 45 N, write an equation that gives the weight W (in newtons) of the clay after a mass of m kg of clay is removed from it.
    (b) Find the weight of clay after a mass of 2 kg has been removed.

27. A 12-volt battery is connected to three resistors in parallel. If $R_1 = 12\,\Omega$, $R_2 = 4\,\Omega$, and $R_3 = 3\,\Omega$, find the current in the battery. (See Example 3.)

5-2   Equivalent Equations

When solving an equation, we want any operation performed on it to result in another equation with exactly the same solutions as the given equation. Equations with the same solutions are said to be **equivalent**. For example, you can easily see by inspection that the equations

$$2x = 4 \quad \text{and} \quad 3x = 6$$

have exactly the same solution, namely, $x = 2$. Thus these equations are equivalent.
    An equation will be transformed into an equivalent equation by any of the following two operations.

1. **Adding (subtracting) the same expression to (from) both sides of an equation.**
   For example, if $-3x = 3 - 4x$, then adding $4x$ to both sides gives the equivalent equation $-3x + 4x = 3 - 4x + 4x$, or simply $x = 3$.

2. **Multiplying or dividing both sides of an equation by the same constant, except zero.**
   For example, if $8x = 4$, then dividing both sides by 8 gives the equivalent equation $\dfrac{8x}{8} = \dfrac{4}{8}$, or simply $x = \dfrac{1}{2}$.

Performing Operations 1 and 2 on an equation will *guarantee* that the result is equivalent to the original equation.
    Sometimes in solving an equation we have to perform operations other than 1 and 2. These operations do not always result in equivalent equations. They include the following.

3. **Multiplying both sides of an equation by an expression involving the variable.**
   For example, by inspection the only root of $x - 1 = 0$ is 1. Multiplying each

side by x gives $x^2 - x = 0$, which is satisfied if x is zero or 1 (you should check this by substitution). But zero *does not* satisfy the *original* equation. Thus the equations are not equivalent. The "root" zero, which was introduced in $x^2 - x = 0$, is sometimes referred to as an **extraneous root**.

4. **Dividing both sides of an equation by an expression involving the variable.**
   For example, you may easily check that the equation $(x - 4)(x - 3) = 0$ is satisfied when x is 4 or 3. Dividing both sides by $x - 4$ gives $x - 3 = 0$, which has 3 as its only root. Again we do not have equivalence because, in this case, a root has been "lost." In fact, when x is 4, which is a root of the given equation, division by $x - 4$ (which is 0) is not defined.

5. **Raising both sides of an equation to equal powers.**
   For example, squaring each side of the equation $x = 2$ gives $x^2 = 4$, which is true if x is 2 or -2. But -2 does not satisfy the *original* equation. Thus, the equations are not equivalent.

From our discussion it is clear that when Operations 3–5 are performed, we must be careful about drawing conclusions concerning the roots of a given equation. Operations 3 and 5 *can* produce an equation with more roots. Thus you should check whether or not each "solution" obtained by these operations satisfies the *original* equation. Operation 4 *can* produce an equation with fewer roots. In this case, any "lost" roots may never be determined. Avoid Operation 4 whenever possible.

Exercise 5-2

*For each of the following, determine what operations were applied to the first equation to obtain the second equation. State whether or not the operations **guarantee** that the equations are equivalent.*

1. $x - 5 = 4x + 10$; $x = 4x + 15$.

2. $8x - 4 = 16$; $x - \frac{1}{2} = 2$.

3. $x = 4$; $x^2 = 16$.

4. $\frac{1}{2}x^2 + 3 = x - 9$; $x^2 + 6 = 2x - 18$.

5. $x^2 - 2x = 0$; $x - 2 = 0$.

6. $\dfrac{2}{x - 2} + x = x^2$; $2 + x(x - 2) = x^2(x - 2)$.

7. $\dfrac{x^2 - 1}{x - 1} = 3$; $x^2 - 1 = 3(x - 1)$.

8. $x(x + 5)(x + 9) = x(x + 1)$; $(x + 5)(x + 9) = x + 1$.

9. $\dfrac{x(x + 1)}{x - 5} = x(x + 9)$; $x + 1 = (x + 9)(x - 5)$.

10. $x^2 = 6x$; $x = 6$.

5-3 Linear Equations

The principles presented thus far will now be demonstrated in the solution of a *linear equation.*

> A **linear equation** in the variable x is an equation that can be written in the form
> $$ax + b = 0, \tag{1}$$
> where a and b are constants and $a \neq 0$.

A linear equation is also called a **first-degree equation** or an *equation of degree* 1, because the highest power of the variable that occurs in Eq. 1 is the first.

To solve a linear equation, we perform Operations 1 and 2 of the previous section until the solution is obvious. More specifically, our goal is to isolate the variable on one side of the equation. To achieve our goal, we make use of opposites and reciprocals. For example, we shall solve

$$3x + 2 = 17.$$

The only term involving x is $3x$, which we first isolate. To remove the 2 that is *added* to $3x$, we *subtract* 2 from *both* sides (Operation 1) and simplify. This is equivalent to adding the opposite of 2, which is -2, to both sides.

$$3x + 2 - 2 = 17 - 2$$
$$3x = 15. \tag{2}$$

Now, because x is *multiplied* by 3, we *divide both* sides of Eq. 2 by 3 (Operation 2) and simplify. This is equivalent to multiplying both sides by the reciprocal of 3, which is $\frac{1}{3}$.

$$\frac{3x}{3} = \frac{15}{3}$$
$$x = 5.$$

Clearly 5 is the only root of the last equation. Because each equation is equivalent to the one before it, we conclude that 5 must be the only root of $3x + 2 = 17$. We can check our answer by substitution: If $x = 5$, the left side of the original equation is $3(5) + 2$ or 17, which agrees with the right side. Thus the solution set is $\{5\}$. We emphasize that *you must perform the **same** operation on **both** sides of an equation.* Given Eq. 2, *do not write* $x = 15 - 3$. Here the left side was *divided* by 3, but 3 was *subtracted* from 15 on the right side. You should divide *both* sides of $3x = 15$ by 3.

Observe that the original equation can be written as $3x - 15 = 0$, which is Eq. 1 with $a = 3$ and $b = -15$. Thus it is a linear equation. *Every linear equation in one variable has one and only one root.*

example 1

Solve the following equations.

a. $-10x - 9 = 0$.

$$-10x - 9 = 0$$
$$-10x - 9 + 9 = 0 + 9 \quad \text{(adding 9 to both sides)}$$
$$-10x = 9$$
$$\frac{(-10)x}{-10} = \frac{9}{-10} \quad \text{(dividing both sides by } -10)$$
$$x = -\frac{9}{10}.$$

Check: $\quad -10\left(-\frac{9}{10}\right) - 9 \overset{?}{=} 0$

$$9 - 9 \overset{?}{=} 0$$
$$0 = 0.$$

b. $3.264 = -8.124 + 5.74t$.

Here the unknown is t.

$$3.264 = -8.124 + 5.74t$$
$$3.264 + 8.124 = 5.74t \quad \text{(adding 8.124 to both sides)}$$
$$11.388 = 5.74\,t$$
$$\frac{11.388}{5.74} = \frac{5.74\,t}{5.74} \quad \text{(dividing both sides by 5.74)}$$
$$1.984 = t \quad \text{(approximately)}.$$

Check: $\quad 3.264 \overset{?}{=} -8.124 + 5.74(1.984)$

$$3.264 \overset{?}{=} -8.124 + 11.388$$
$$3.264 = 3.264.$$

c. $2(x + 4) = 7x + 2$.

Here we get the terms involving x on one side of the equation and get the constant terms on the other side.

$$2(x + 4) = 7x + 2$$
$$2x + 8 = 7x + 2 \quad \text{(distributive law)}$$
$$2x = 7x - 6 \quad \text{(subtracting 8 from both sides)}$$
$$2x - 7x = 7x - 6 - 7x \quad \text{(subtracting } 7x \text{ from both sides)}$$
$$-5x = -6$$

$$x = \frac{-6}{-5} \qquad \text{(dividing both sides by } -5)$$

$$x = \frac{6}{5}.$$

$$\text{Check:} \quad 2\left(\frac{6}{5} + 4\right) \overset{?}{=} 7\left(\frac{6}{5}\right) + 2$$

$$2\left(\frac{26}{5}\right) \overset{?}{=} \frac{42}{5} + 2$$

$$\frac{52}{5} = \frac{52}{5}.$$

The next examples involve equations in which fractions appear. You may check each root to see that it does satisfy the given equation.

example 2

Solve $-\dfrac{3}{8}u + 1 = -2$.

$$-\frac{3}{8}u + 1 = -2$$

$$-\frac{3}{8}u = -3 \qquad \text{(subtracting 1 from both sides)}$$

$$8\left(-\frac{3}{8}u\right) = 8(-3) \qquad \text{(multiplying both sides by 8)}$$

$$-3u = -24 \qquad \text{(because } 8(-\tfrac{3}{8}u) = -(8 \cdot \tfrac{3}{8})u = -3u)$$

$$\frac{(-3)u}{-3} = \frac{-24}{-3} \qquad \text{(dividing both sides by } -3)$$

$$u = 8.$$

example 3

Solve $3\left(\dfrac{7}{5}x - 1\right) = 2x$.

$$3\left(\frac{7}{5}x\right) - 3(1) = 2x \qquad \text{(distributive law)}$$

$$\frac{21}{5}x - 3 = 2x$$

$$5\left(\frac{21}{5}x - 3\right) = 5(2x) \qquad \text{(multiplying both sides by 5)}$$

$$21x - 15 = 10x \qquad \text{(distributive law)}$$
$$11x - 15 = 0 \qquad \text{(subtracting } 10x \text{ from both sides)}$$
$$11x = 15 \qquad \text{(adding 15 to both sides)}$$
$$x = \frac{15}{11} \qquad \text{(dividing both sides by 11).}$$

example 4

Solve $\dfrac{8y}{3} = \dfrac{7y + 5}{6} + 8$.

When two or more terms in an equation are fractions, you may clear the equation of fractions by multiplying *both* sides by the L.C.D. Here the L.C.D. is 6.

$$6\left(\frac{8y}{3}\right) = 6\left(\frac{7y + 5}{6} + 8\right) \qquad \text{(multiplying both sides by L.C.D.)}$$
$$6\left(\frac{8y}{3}\right) = 6\left(\frac{7y + 5}{6}\right) + 6(8) \qquad \text{(distributive law)}$$
$$2(8y) = (7y + 5) + 6(8)$$
$$16y = 7y + 5 + 48$$
$$16y = 7y + 53$$
$$9y = 53 \qquad \text{(subtracting } 7y \text{ from both sides)}$$
$$y = \frac{53}{9} \qquad \text{(dividing both sides by 9).}$$

Now let us solve some literal equations. If we want to express a particular letter in a formula in terms of the remaining letters, that particular letter is considered to be the unknown. The procedures used are the same as those in the previous examples.

example 5

a. The equation $P_1 V_1 = P_2 V_2$ is a statement of Boyle's law of gases, where P_1 and P_2 are variables denoting pressures and the variables V_1 and V_2 denote volumes. Express V_1 in terms of P_1, P_2, and V_2.

Here V_1 is considered to be the unknown.

$$P_1 V_1 = P_2 V_2$$
$$\frac{P_1 V_1}{P_1} = \frac{P_2 V_2}{P_1} \qquad \text{(dividing both sides by } P_1\text{)}$$
$$V_1 = \frac{P_2 V_2}{P_1} \qquad \text{(cancellation).}$$

b. The relationship between Fahrenheit and Celsius temperature readings can be expressed by the equation

$$\frac{F - 32}{180} = \frac{C}{100},$$

where F and C represent the corresponding temperatures. Solve for F.

Multiplying both sides by 180 (this is more efficient than clearing fractions), we have

$$180\left(\frac{F - 32}{180}\right) = 180\left(\frac{C}{100}\right)$$

$$F - 32 = \frac{9}{5}C$$

$$F = \frac{9}{5}C + 32.$$

You should be able to give the justification for each step in Examples 6 and 7.

example 6

If $(a + c)x + x^2 = (x + a)^2$, solve for x.

Here a and c are assumed to be literal constants.

$$(a + c)x + x^2 = (x + a)^2$$
$$ax + cx + x^2 = x^2 + 2ax + a^2$$
$$ax + cx = 2ax + a^2$$
$$ax + cx - 2ax = a^2$$
$$cx - ax = a^2$$
$$x(c - a) = a^2 \quad \text{(factoring)}.$$

Assuming that $c - a \neq 0$, we divide both sides by $c - a$:

$$x = \frac{a^2}{c - a}.$$

example 7

In a heat-measurement experiment, a mass m_1 of water at a high temperature T_h is added to a mass m_2 of water at a lower temperature T_l. At thermal equilibrium, the final temperature T_f of the mixture satisfies the equation

$$m_1(1000)(T_h - T_f) = m_2(1000)(T_f - T_l).$$

If 4 kg of water at 60°C are mixed with 3 kg of water at 30°C, find the final temperature of the mixture.

Here we have $T_h = 60°C$ and $T_l = 30°C$. The mass of water at the higher temperature is $m_1 = 4$ kg, and at the lower temperature it is $m_2 = 3$ kg. Substituting these values into the given equation and solving for T_f, we have

$$(4)(1000)(60 - T_f) = 3(1000)(T_f - 30)$$

$$4(60 - T_f) = 3(T_f - 30) \qquad \text{(dividing both sides by 1000)}$$

$$240 - 4T_f = 3T_f - 90$$

$$240 = 7T_f - 90$$

$$330 = 7T_f$$

$$T_f = \frac{330}{7} = 47.1°C.$$

Exercise 5-3

In Problems 1–64, solve the equations.

1. $x + 3 = 0.$

2. $x - 6 = 0.$

3. $4 - x = 0.$

4. $8 = y + 6.$

5. $8x = 36.$

6. $0.2x = 7.$

7. $\frac{x}{8} = 3.$

8. $\frac{x}{7} = 0.$

9. $8y = 0.$

10. $2x - 3 = 4.$

11. $3 - 5x = 9.$

12. $9x - 12x = 0.$

13. $6x + 4x = 20.$

14. $6y + 5y - 3 = 41.$

15. $\frac{x}{-7} = 2.$

16. $-2x - 3 = -4.$

17. $1 - 3y = -8.$

18. $-1 = 4 + 2u.$

19. $-5 = 7 - 8u.$

20. $5x - 10x = 15.$

21. $-x = -15.$

22. $-4x = 8.$

23. $3x - 8 = 7.$

24. $6x + 7 = 7.$

25. $\frac{2x}{5} = -\frac{3}{2}.$

26. $\frac{9}{8}x = \frac{3}{2}.$

27. $-\frac{2y}{3} = \frac{5}{2}.$

28. $\frac{z}{2} = \frac{z}{3}.$

29. $3x - \frac{1}{5} = 4.$

30. $3x - \frac{9}{4} = 2.$

31. $2(y - 5) = y + 1.$

32. $-3(y - 1) = 4y + 17.$

33. $7(3 - 2z) = 3 - 5z.$

34. $8 - 6z = 4(3z + 5).$

35. $(4x + 3) - (7 - x) = 7x.$

36. $2(x - 1) - (3x + 7) = x.$

37. $2(x - 1) - 3(x - 4) = 4x.$

38. $x = 2 - 2[2x - 3(1 - x)].$

39. $\frac{x}{5} = 2x - 6.$

40. $\frac{5y}{7} - \frac{6}{7} = 2 - 4y.$

41. $5 + \frac{4x}{9} = \frac{x}{2}.$

42. $\frac{x}{3} - 4 = \frac{x}{5}.$

43. $y = \frac{3}{2}y - 4.$

44. $\frac{x}{2} + \frac{x}{3} = 7.$

45. $-\frac{1}{12} = -2 - \frac{3}{4}x.$

46. $\frac{x - 3}{4} = 5.$

47. $\dfrac{3}{4} = \dfrac{2-x}{3}.$

48. $\dfrac{3}{8} = \dfrac{2x-2}{6}.$

49. $\dfrac{1}{2}\left(x + \dfrac{4}{3}\right) = 3 - (x+1).$

50. $\dfrac{7}{2} - (x+5) = \dfrac{x}{4}.$

51. $3x + \dfrac{x}{5} - 5 = \dfrac{1}{5} + 5x.$

52. $y - \dfrac{y}{2} + \dfrac{y}{3} - \dfrac{y}{4} = \dfrac{y}{5}.$

53. $w + \dfrac{w}{2} - \dfrac{w}{3} + \dfrac{w}{4} = 5.$

54. $\dfrac{z}{3} + \dfrac{3}{4}z = \dfrac{9}{2}(z-1).$

55. $\dfrac{x+2}{3} - \dfrac{2-x}{6} = x - 2.$

56. $\dfrac{x}{5} + \dfrac{2(x-4)}{10} = 7.$

57. $\dfrac{3}{4}(z-3) = \dfrac{9}{5}(3-z).$

58. $\dfrac{2y-7}{3} + \dfrac{8y-9}{14} = \dfrac{3y-5}{21}.$

59. $\dfrac{2}{3}(x-5) = 4x + \dfrac{1}{2}.$

60. $\dfrac{x}{3} + 1 = 4\left(x - \dfrac{1}{2}\right).$

61. $2[x + 3(x-4) - 2] + 4(x+1) = 5.$

62. $\dfrac{3}{2}(4x - 3) = 2[x - (4x - 3)].$

63. $2y + \{-y - 6[2 - 3(y - 4)]\} = -8.$

64. $(3x - 1)^2 - (5x - 3)^2 = -(4x - 2)^2.$

The relationships in Problems 65–90 occur in physics, chemistry, and various branches of engineering technology. Express the indicated symbol(s) in terms of the remaining symbols.

65. $P_1 V_1 = P_2 V_2;\quad V_2.$

66. $PV = nRT;\quad R.$

67. $v = v_0 - at;\quad a.$

68. $E = mc^2;\quad m.$

69. $K = \frac{1}{2}mv^2;\quad m.$

70. $mgh + \frac{1}{2}mv^2 = c;\quad m.$

71. $V = \pi r^2 h;\quad h.$

72. $S = v_0 t + \frac{1}{2}at^2;\quad v_0.$

73. $P = i^2 R;\quad R.$

74. $I = \dfrac{n\mathcal{E}}{r + nR};\quad \mathcal{E}.$

75. $2R_1 i + 3R_2 i - 4R_4 i = -(E_1 - E_2);\quad i.$

76. $T^2 = 4\pi^2\left(\dfrac{L}{g}\right);\quad L.$

77. $F = k\dfrac{QQ'}{r^2};\quad Q'.$

78. $P = \dfrac{E^2}{R + r} - \dfrac{E^2 r}{(R + r)^2};\quad E^2.$

79. $V = V_0\left(\dfrac{P_1}{P_2}\right)\left(\dfrac{T_2}{T_1}\right);\quad T_2.$

80. $F = \dfrac{1}{2\pi}\left(\dfrac{e}{m}\right)b;\quad b.$

81. $I = \dfrac{E}{R}(1 - e^{-Rt/L});\quad E.$

82. $F = \dfrac{9}{5}C + 32;\quad C.$

83. $Q = mc(t_2 - t_1) + mL;\quad t_2, t_1, c.$

84. $Q = kA\left(\dfrac{t_2 - t_1}{d}\right)\tau;\quad t_1, t_2.$

85. $mgh = \frac{1}{2}mv^2 + \frac{1}{2}I\omega^2;\quad m, I.$

86. $y = mx + b;\quad x, m.$

87. $V = 2\pi r^2 + 2\pi rh;\quad h.$

88. $y = \dfrac{(B + D)\lambda}{2B(N - 1)\alpha};\quad \lambda, B.$

89. $U = \left(\dfrac{f - f_0}{f_0}\right)\dfrac{\epsilon}{v_0}; \quad f.$

90. $\sigma = \dfrac{n_0 - n_e}{\lambda}L; \quad n_0, n_e.$

91. If a ball of mass m is tied to a string and whirled around in a vertical circle, at the ball's lowest point Newton's second law indicates that

$$T - mg = m\frac{v^2}{r},$$

where T is the tension in the string, g is the acceleration due to gravity, v is the speed of the ball, and r is the radius of the circle. Solve the equation for m.

92. Applying the conservation of energy principle to analyze the motion of a cylinder 'rolling down an incline of height h results in the equation

$$mgh = \frac{1}{2}mv^2 + \frac{1}{2}\left(\frac{1}{2}mR^2\right)\left(\frac{v}{R}\right)^2.$$

Here m and R are the mass and radius of the cylinder, g is the acceleration due to gravity, and v is the speed of the cylinder at the bottom of the incline. Solve for v^2.

93. Find the final temperature when 2 kg of water at 79°C is mixed with 4 kg of water at 40°C. (See Example 7.)

94. When 3 kg of water at temperature T_h is mixed with 2 kg of water at 10°C, the final temperature of the water is 15°C. Find T_h to one decimal place. (See Example 7.)

95. When 5 kg of water at 80°C is mixed with a certain mass of water at 10°C, the final temperature is 40°C. Find, to one decimal place, the mass of the water that was initially at 10°C. (See Example 7.)

96. In analyzing a circuit by nodal analysis, the following equation occurs:

$$\frac{V - 100}{40} + \frac{V}{80} + \frac{V - 150}{60} = 0.$$

Solve for V (to one decimal place).

5-4 Fractional Equations

Some equations that are not linear may lead to linear equations. Of this type is a **fractional equation**, which is an equation in which a variable occurs in the denominator of a fraction. A method of solving a fractional equation is to first write it in a form that is free of such fractions. To do this, we multiply each side by the L.C.D. of the fractions involved. In each case *we must exclude from our considerations those values of the variable for which any denominators are zero.*

example 1

Solve the following equations.

a. $\dfrac{6}{x - 3} = \dfrac{5}{x - 4}.$

Here we assume that $x \neq 3$ and $x \neq 4$ so that both sides are defined. Multiplying both sides by the L.C.D., which is $(x - 3)(x - 4)$, and cancelling, we have

$$(x - 3)(x - 4)\left(\frac{6}{x - 3}\right) = (x - 3)(x - 4)\left(\frac{5}{x - 4}\right)$$

$$6(x - 4) = 5(x - 3)$$

$$6x - 24 = 5x - 15$$

$$x = 9.$$

In the first step we multiplied each side by an expression involving the variable x. As mentioned in Sec. 5-2, this means that we must check whether or not 9 satisfies the original equation. If 9 is substituted for x in that equation, the left side is

$$\frac{6}{9 - 3} = \frac{6}{6} = 1$$

and the right side is

$$\frac{5}{9 - 4} = \frac{5}{5} = 1.$$

Because both sides are equal, 9 is a root.

b. $\dfrac{4}{x - 1} = \dfrac{7}{x - 1} - 2.$

Assuming that $x \neq 1$, we multiply both sides by the L.C.D., which is $(x - 1)$. This gives

$$(x - 1)\left(\frac{4}{x - 1}\right) = (x - 1)\left(\frac{7}{x - 1} - 2\right)$$

$$(x - 1)\left(\frac{4}{x - 1}\right) = (x - 1)\left(\frac{7}{x - 1}\right) - (x - 1)(2)$$

$$4 = 7 - 2x + 2$$

$$2x = 5$$

$$x = \frac{5}{2}.$$

You may verify by substitution that $\frac{5}{2}$ is indeed a root.

example 2

Solve the following equations.

a. $\dfrac{9}{x - 3} = 0.$

Assuming that $x \neq 3$, we multiply both sides by the L.C.D., which is $x - 3$. This gives

$$9 = 0.$$

Because it is never true that $9 = 0$, we conclude that there are no roots. The solution set has no elements in it. Recall that we denote this set by $\varnothing$, the empty set. There is another way of handling the given equation that is useful. The *only* way a fraction can equal zero is if the numerator is zero and the denominator is different from zero. Because the numerator, 9, is never zero, the solution set is $\varnothing$.

b. $\dfrac{3x+4}{x+2} - \dfrac{3x-5}{x-4} = \dfrac{12}{x^2-2x-8}$.

Notice that $x^2 - 2x - 8$ factors into $(x+2)(x-4)$. We conclude that the L.C.D. of the fractions is $(x+2)(x-4)$. Multiplying both sides by the L.C.D. and cancelling gives

$$(3x+4)(x-4) - (3x-5)(x+2) = 12$$
$$(3x^2 - 8x - 16) - (3x^2 + x - 10) = 12$$
$$3x^2 - 8x - 16 - 3x^2 - x + 10 = 12$$
$$-9x - 6 = 12$$
$$-9x = 18$$
$$x = -2.$$

However, the *original* equation is not defined when x is -2 (we cannot divide by zero), and so there is no solution. That is, the solution set is $\varnothing$.

example 3

Solve $\dfrac{1}{a} + \dfrac{1}{x} = \dfrac{1}{b}$ for x.

Multiplying both sides by the L.C.D., which is abx, we have

$$abx\left(\frac{1}{a} + \frac{1}{x}\right) = abx\left(\frac{1}{b}\right)$$
$$abx\left(\frac{1}{a}\right) + abx\left(\frac{1}{x}\right) = abx\left(\frac{1}{b}\right)$$
$$bx + ab = ax$$
$$bx - ax = -ab$$
$$x(b - a) = -ab$$
$$x = \frac{-ab}{b-a} = \frac{ab}{a-b}$$

assuming $b - a \neq 0$.

example 4

If n cells, each having an internal resistance r and electromotive force ε, are connected in series to a load resistance R, the current i in the circuit is given by

$$i = \frac{n\varepsilon}{R + nr}.$$

Solve for r.

$$i = \frac{n\mathscr{E}}{R + nr}$$

$$i(R + nr) = n\mathscr{E} \qquad \text{(multiplying both sides by } R + nr)$$

$$iR + nir = n\mathscr{E}$$

$$nir = n\mathscr{E} - iR$$

$$r = \frac{n\mathscr{E} - iR}{ni}.$$

example 5

An important equation for lenses is

$$\frac{1}{f} = \frac{1}{p} + \frac{1}{q},$$

where f is focal length, p is object distance, and q is image distance. Suppose that for a converging lens the focal length is 12 cm and the object distance is 24 cm. Find the image distance.

$$\frac{1}{f} = \frac{1}{p} + \frac{1}{q}$$

$$\frac{1}{12} = \frac{1}{24} + \frac{1}{q}$$

$$24q\left(\frac{1}{12}\right) = 24q\left(\frac{1}{24} + \frac{1}{q}\right)$$

$$2q = q + 24$$

$$q = 24 \text{ cm.}$$

Exercise 5-4

Solve the equations in Problems 1–22.

1. $\dfrac{3}{x} = 12.$

2. $\dfrac{4}{x-1} = 2.$

3. $\dfrac{3}{7-x} = 0.$

4. $\dfrac{5x-2}{x+1} = 0.$

5. $\dfrac{4}{8-x} = \dfrac{3}{4}.$

6. $\dfrac{x+3}{x} = \dfrac{2}{5}.$

7. $\dfrac{q}{3q-4} = 3.$

8. $\dfrac{4p}{7-p} = 1.$

9. $\dfrac{1}{p-1} = \dfrac{2}{p-2}.$

10. $\dfrac{2x-3}{4x-5} = 6.$

11. $\dfrac{1}{10} + \dfrac{1}{x} = \dfrac{4}{5}.$

12. $\dfrac{1}{2} - \dfrac{3}{x} = \dfrac{2}{3}.$

13. $\dfrac{3x-2}{2x+3} = \dfrac{3x-1}{2x+1}$.

14. $\dfrac{x+2}{x-1} + \dfrac{x+1}{2-x} = 0$.

15. $\dfrac{y-6}{y} - \dfrac{6}{y} = \dfrac{y+6}{y-6}$.

16. $\dfrac{y-1}{y+3} = 4 + \dfrac{2}{y+3}$.

17. $\dfrac{-4}{x-1} = \dfrac{7}{2-x} + \dfrac{3}{x+1}$.

18. $\dfrac{1}{x-3} - \dfrac{3}{x-2} = \dfrac{4}{1-2x}$.

19. $\dfrac{9}{x-3} = \dfrac{3x}{x-3}$.

20. $\dfrac{x}{x+3} - \dfrac{x}{x-3} = \dfrac{3x-4}{x^2-9}$.

21. $\dfrac{2x}{x-1} - \dfrac{3}{x+2} = \dfrac{4x}{(x+2)(x-1)} + 2$.

22. $\dfrac{2}{x} + \dfrac{3}{x+1} = \dfrac{x}{x+1} - \dfrac{x+1}{x}$.

In Problems 23–26, express the indicated letter(s) in terms of the remaining letters.

23. $2 + \dfrac{b}{abx} = \dfrac{4}{x} - \dfrac{a}{b}$; x.

24. $\dfrac{x-a}{b-x} = \dfrac{x-b}{a-x}$; x.

25. $\dfrac{P_1 V_1}{T_1} = \dfrac{P_2 V_2}{T_2}$; T_1.

26. $h = kat\left(\dfrac{T}{L}\right)$; L.

27. $V = V_0 \left(\dfrac{P_1}{P_2}\right)\left(\dfrac{T_2}{T_1}\right)$; P_2.

28. $F = \dfrac{1}{2\pi}\left(\dfrac{e}{m}\right)b$; m.

29. $\dfrac{1}{p} + \dfrac{1}{q} = \dfrac{1}{f}$; q, f.

30. $\dfrac{1}{C_t} = \dfrac{1}{C_1} + \dfrac{1}{C_2} + \dfrac{1}{C_3}$; C_t.

31. $R_t = \dfrac{R_1 R_2}{R_1 + R_2}$; R_1.

32. $\dfrac{x}{a} + \dfrac{y}{b} = 1$; a.

33. $\dfrac{1}{2}mv^2 - \dfrac{p^2}{2m} = 0$; m^2.

34. $S = \dfrac{\dfrac{W_s}{V}}{\dfrac{W_w}{V}}$; W_w, W_s.

35. $\dfrac{1}{f} = (n-1)\left(\dfrac{1}{R_1} + \dfrac{1}{R_2}\right)$; R_1.

36. $V = \dfrac{1}{4\pi\epsilon_0}\left(\dfrac{q_1}{r_1} + \dfrac{q_2}{r_2}\right)$; r_1.

37. When three cells, each having an internal resistance of 0.2 Ω and emf $\varepsilon = 5$ V, are connected in series with a load resistance R, the current in the circuit is 0.1 A. Find the load resistance R, in ohms. (See Example 4.)

38. When an object is placed in front of a converging lens with a focal length of 20 cm, the image distance is 40 cm. Find the object distance. (See Example 5.)

39. The combined resistance R of two resistors R_1 and R_2 connected in parallel is given by

$$R = \dfrac{1}{\dfrac{1}{R_1} + \dfrac{1}{R_2}}.$$

(a) If the combined resistance is 10 ohms and one resistor has a resistance of 60 ohms, find the resistance of the other resistor.

(b) Show that $R = \dfrac{R_1 R_2}{R_1 + R_2}$.

40. The total capacitance C_T of a circuit network containing two capacitors C_1 and C_2 in series is given by

$$\frac{1}{C_T} = \frac{1}{C_1} + \frac{1}{C_2}.$$

If $C_1 = 2\ \mu F$ and $C_T = \frac{2}{3}\ \mu F$, find C_2.

41. The reciprocal of the focal length f of a thin lens with spherical surfaces is

$$\frac{1}{f} = (n - 1)\left(\frac{1}{R_1} + \frac{1}{R_2}\right)$$

(called the lensmaker's equation), where n is the index of refraction of the lens material and R_1 and R_2 are radii of curvature of the surfaces. For a certain double-convex lens, $n = 1.5$, $R_1 = 10$ cm, and $R_2 = 20$ cm. Find f to one decimal place.

42. If a space capsule of mass m were launched from the surface of the earth with speed v, it would rise, neglecting the effects of air resistance, to a height h such that

$$\frac{1}{2}mv^2 = \frac{mghR}{R + h},$$

where R is the radius of the earth and g is the acceleration due to gravity at the earth's surface. Solve for h.

5-5 Proportion

In physics and chemistry, a type of equation that occurs frequently is that of a *proportion*.

A **proportion** is a statement that two ratios are equal. That is, it is an equation of the form

$$\frac{a}{b} = \frac{c}{d} \quad \text{or} \quad a : b = c : d.$$

The numbers a and d above are called the **extremes** of the proportion, while b and c are called the **means**. Either of the proportions above can be read *a is to b as c is to d*. To say that the three numbers a, b, and c are in the ratio $2 : 3 : 5$ means that $a/b = 2/3$, $b/c = 3/5$, and $a/c = 2/5$. Thus 8, 12, and 20 are in the ratio $2 : 3 : 5$.

example 1

Solve the following proportions for x.

a. $\dfrac{7}{5} = \dfrac{2}{x}$.

Multiplying both sides by $5x$, the L.C.D., we have

$$5x\left(\frac{7}{5}\right) = 5x\left(\frac{2}{x}\right)$$

$$7x = 10 \tag{1}$$

$$x = \frac{10}{7}.$$

The solution is $x = \frac{10}{7}$, as you may verify. Note that Eq. 1 illustrates that the product of the means is equal to the product of the extremes.

b. $(3 - x):4 = (x + 2):5.$

$$\frac{3 - x}{4} = \frac{x + 2}{5}$$

$$5(3 - x) = 4(x + 2)$$

$$15 - 5x = 4x + 8$$

$$7 = 9x$$

$$\frac{7}{9} = x.$$

example 2

A triangle whose shortest side has a length of 14 units (see Fig. 5-1) is similar to a triangle having sides of lengths $10, 15,$ and 20 units. Find the lengths of the other two sides of the triangle.

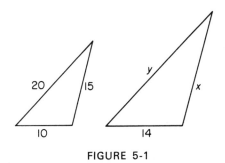

FIGURE 5-1

From geometry, recall that if two triangles are similar, the lengths of their corresponding sides are proportional. Let x be the side corresponding to the side 15. Then

$$\frac{x}{15} = \frac{14}{10}.$$

Multiplying both sides by 15 gives

$$x = 15\left(\frac{14}{10}\right) = 21.$$

Let y be the side corresponding to the side 20. Then

$$\frac{y}{20} = \frac{14}{10}$$

$$y = 20\left(\frac{14}{10}\right) = 28.$$

Hence, the other two sides of the triangle have lengths of 21 and 28 units.

example 3

In an architect's drawing, the scale used is $\frac{1}{4}$ cm $=$ 2 m. Find the scale length of an object if its true length is 56 m.

Let x be the scale length of the object in centimeters. Then

$$\frac{x}{56} = \frac{\frac{1}{4}}{2}$$

$$\frac{x}{56} = \frac{1}{8}$$

$$x = 56\left(\frac{1}{8}\right) = 7 \text{ cm.}$$

example 4

Find the ratio of a to b given the proportion

$$\frac{a+b}{a-b} = \frac{5}{2}.$$

Clearing fractions and solving for a/b, we have

$$2(a + b) = 5(a - b)$$

$$2a + 2b = 5a - 5b$$

$$7b = 3a$$

$$7 = \frac{3a}{b}$$

$$\frac{7}{3} = \frac{a}{b}.$$

Thus, the ratio of a to b is $\frac{7}{3}$. This does *not* mean that a must be 7 and b must be 3. Why?*

*Because $\frac{7}{3}$ might be the reduced form of the ratio a/b. For instance, we could have $a = 14$ and $b = 6$.

example 5

On the Celsius temperature scale, the normal freezing point of water is 0°C and the normal boiling point is 100°C. On the Fahrenheit scale, the corresponding temperatures are 32°F and 212°F. By using a proportion, determine the temperature on the Celsius scale that corresponds to 100°F.

The temperature scales are shown in Fig. 5-2, where t is the Celsius temperature that we want to find. Because these temperature scales each have uniform divisions and use

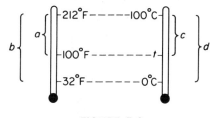

FIGURE 5-2

the same fixed points (the freezing and boiling points of water), the proportion

$$\frac{a}{b} = \frac{c}{d}$$

holds, where a, b, c, and d are the lengths of the temperature intervals shown. Thus

$$\frac{212 - 100}{212 - 32} = \frac{100 - t}{100 - 0}$$

$$\frac{112}{180} = \frac{100 - t}{100}$$

$$100(112) = 180(100 - t)$$

$$11{,}200 = 18{,}000 - 180t$$

$$180t = 6800$$

$$t = \frac{6800}{180} = 37.8°C.$$

Exercise 5-5

In Problems **1–10,** *solve the given proportion.*

1. $\dfrac{x + 1}{5} = \dfrac{3}{7}.$

2. $\dfrac{x - 3}{6} = \dfrac{x}{5}.$

3. $\dfrac{4}{8 - x} = \dfrac{3}{4}.$

4. $\dfrac{2y - 3}{4} = \dfrac{6y + 7}{3}.$

5. $x : \frac{3}{2} = 2\frac{1}{3} : 3\frac{1}{6}.$

6. $3\frac{1}{2} : 2\frac{1}{2} = 6 : x.$

7. $\dfrac{2(x+3)^2}{4} = \dfrac{x^2+1}{2}.$

8. $\dfrac{7+2(x+1)}{3} = \dfrac{8x}{5}.$

9. $\dfrac{\frac{1}{3}}{2} = \dfrac{\frac{1}{4}}{x}.$

10. $\dfrac{\frac{1}{2}}{x} = \dfrac{8}{\frac{2}{3}}.$

In Problems **11–14,** *find the ratio of a to b.*

11. $\dfrac{a-b}{a+b} = \dfrac{4}{13}.$

12. $\dfrac{a+2b}{b-a} = \dfrac{7}{2}.$

13. $\dfrac{2(a+2b)}{13b-a} = \dfrac{1}{2}.$

14. $\dfrac{2(2b-a)}{3(a-b)} = \dfrac{1}{3}.$

15. A triangle in which the longest side has a length of 14 m is similar to a triangle with sides of lengths 3, 5, and 6 m. Find the lengths of the other two sides of the triangle.

16. The length and width of a sheet metal plate must be in the ratio of 7:5, respectively. If the length of plate is to be 56 cm, what must its width be?

17. A Wheatstone bridge is a device that can be used to measure an unknown resistance. In a balanced condition it is governed by the proportion

$$\frac{R_1}{R_2} = \frac{R_3}{R_4},$$

where the R's are the resistances in ohms in each arm of the bridge. If $R_1 = 3$ ohms, $R_2 = 5$ ohms, $R_3 = 7$ ohms, and $R_4 = 1 + x$ ohms, find x.

18. If a block is on a frictionless inclined plane as shown in Fig. 5-3, the following proportion applies:

$$\frac{F}{W} = \frac{h}{l},$$

where F is the force to just start the block moving up the inclined plane, W is the weight of the block, and h and l are the height and length, respectively, of the inclined plane. Find l if $W = 50$ N, $F = 5$ N, and $h = 2$ m.

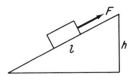

FIGURE 5-3

19. Graham's law of diffusion of two gases is given by the proportion

$$\frac{\text{Rate of diffusion of gas A}}{\text{Rate of diffusion of gas B}} = \frac{\sqrt{\text{Density of B}}}{\sqrt{\text{Density of A}}}.$$

Suppose gas A is nine times as dense as B (that is, take the density of B to be x and that of A to be $9x$). In a certain diffusion apparatus, and under constant temperature and pressure, gas A diffuses 8 cm/s. Under the same conditions, what is the rate of diffusion of B?

20. For the proportion in Problem 19, suppose gas A is 25 times as dense as gas B. How do their rates of diffusion compare?

21. Under conditions of constant pressure, Charles's law of gases is given by the proportion

$$\frac{V_1}{V_2} = \frac{T_1}{T_2},$$

where V_1 and V_2 are the volumes of the gas at temperatures T_1 and T_2, respectively. Suppose that at a particular pressure gas A has a volume of 200 cm³ at a temperature of 273 K (the Kelvin scale). What volume will it occupy at 373 K? Give your answer to the nearest cubic centimeter.

22. Under conditions of constant temperature, Boyle's law for gases is given by the proportion

$$\frac{P_1}{V_2} = \frac{P_2}{V_1},$$

where P_1 and P_2 are the pressures of the gas at volumes V_1 and V_2, respectively. If 10 liters of hydrogen gas at a pressure of 1 atm is allowed to expand at constant temperature to a new volume of 18 ℓ, find the resulting pressure of the gas.

23. A step-up transformer having 100 turns on the input winding is connected to a 10-volt generator. The desired output voltage is to be 40 volts. To find the number of turns, N_2, that the output winding must have, it is necessary to solve the proportion

$$\frac{V_1}{V_2} = \frac{N_1}{N_2},$$

where $V_1 = 10$, $V_2 = 40$, and $N_1 = 100$. Find N_2.

24. Two circles have radii of r_1 and r_2 and corresponding areas of A_1 and A_2. Show that $A_1 : A_2 = r_1^2 : r_2^2$.

25. Use a proportion to find (to one decimal place) the temperature on the Celsius temperature scale that corresponds to 200°F. (See Example 5.)

26. Use a proportion to find the temperature on the Fahrenheit scale that corresponds to 50°C. (See Example 5.)

27. Suppose we define a new temperature scale on which the normal freezing and boiling points of water are −20° and 200°, respectively. What temperature on this scale corresponds to (a) 50°C, (b) 50°F? (See Example 5.)

28. On the Kelvin temperature scale, the freezing and boiling points of water are 273 K and 373 K, respectively. What temperature on the Kelvin scale corresponds to 50°C? (See Example 5.)

29. When a galvanometer of resistance R_G (in ohms) is used as an ammeter (Fig. 5-4), a shunt resistance R_S is used. The relationship between the currents I_G (through the galvanometer) and I_S (through the shunt resistance) is given by

$$\frac{I_G}{I_S} = \frac{R_S}{R_G}.$$

Given that $I_G = 0.005$ A, $I_S = 4.995$ A, and $R_G = 50\ \Omega$, find R_S to two decimal places.

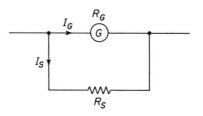

FIGURE 5-4

30. In an analysis of a negative feedback amplifier, the following equation was obtained:

$$V_0 = \alpha(V_s - \beta V_0),$$

where V_0 and V_s are output and input voltages, respectively. Find the ratio of V_0 to V_s.

31. At a temperature of 0°C, the frequency f_s emitted by a source and the frequency f_0 heard by a stationary observer are related by the proportion

$$\frac{f_0}{f_s} = \frac{331}{331 \pm v_s}.$$

In this special case of the Doppler effect, v_s is the speed of the source in meters per second. The plus sign is used if the source recedes from the observer, and the minus sign if it approaches the observer. What frequency would you hear in a laboratory if a tuning fork with a frequency of 256 hertz were moved *toward* you at a speed of 4 m/s? Give your answer to the nearest hertz.

32. In Problem 31, what frequency would you hear if the same tuning fork were moved *away* from you at 4 m/s?

33. For the frequencies in Problem 31, if the *source* is stationary and the observer is moving, then under the same conditions the Doppler effect gives

$$\frac{f_0}{f_s} = \frac{331 \pm v_0}{331},$$

where v_0 is the speed of the observer in meters per second. Here the plus sign is used if the observer moves toward the source. If you were approaching a stationary fire siren emitting a frequency of 512 hertz at a speed of 20 m/s, what frequency would you hear?

34. In Problem 33, if you were moving *away* from the given source at the given speed, what frequency would you hear?

5-6   Word Problems

We now turn to verbal, or word, problems. With a word problem, the equation to be solved is not given to you. You have to set it up by first expressing, in terms of mathematical symbols, the relationships that the problem states in words. The following suggestions may be used as a guide in solving word problems.

1. Read the problem more than once so that all of the given facts and relationships are clearly understood.

2. Choose a variable to represent an unknown quantity that you want to find.

3. Use mathematical symbols to express the given relationships and facts in terms of an equation involving the variable. Drawing a diagram often is useful.

4. Solve the equation and check your solution to see if it answers the question that the problem posed. Sometimes the solution to an equation will not be a direct answer to the question asked, but it can be of use in obtaining the required answer. In some cases a solution may have to be rejected for physical reasons.

The following model problems illustrate these basic techniques and concepts. Study them carefully before you proceed to the exercises. We begin with mixture problems.

example 1

a. How many liters of antifreeze that is 70 percent alcohol (70 percent by volume is alcohol) must be added to 10 liters of a 35 percent solution to yield a 50 percent solution?

Drawings like Fig. 5-5 are very helpful in problems like this. Refer to that drawing as you follow the discussion. Let x be the number of liters of the 70 percent solution to be added to the 10 liters of the 35 percent solution. Then we end up with $x + 10$ liters, of which 50 percent must be alcohol. That is, $0.50(x + 10)$ is alcohol. This

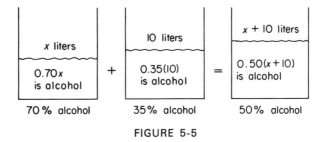

FIGURE 5-5

alcohol comes from two sources: $0.70x$ comes from the 70 percent solution and $0.35(10)$ comes from the 35 percent solution. Thus

$$0.70x + 0.35(10) = 0.50(x + 10)$$
$$0.70x + 3.5 = 0.50x + 5$$
$$0.20x = 1.5$$
$$x = \frac{1.5}{0.20} = 7.5.$$

Thus 7.5 liters of the 70 percent solution must be added.

b. A chemical manufacturer mixes a 30 percent acid solution (30 percent by volume is acid) with an 18 percent acid solution. How much of each solution should be used to obtain 500 liters of a 25 percent acid solution?

Let x be the number of liters of the 30 percent solution to be used. To get a total of 500 liters, there must be $500 - x$ liters of the 18 percent solution (Fig. 5-6).

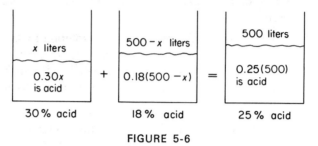

FIGURE 5-6

The total amount of acid in the 500 liters of the 25 percent solution is 0.25(500). This acid comes from two sources: $0.30x$ comes from the 30 percent solution and $0.18(500 - x)$ comes from the 18 percent solution. Thus

$$0.30x + 0.18(500 - x) = 125$$
$$0.30x + 90 - 0.18x = 125$$
$$0.12x = 35$$
$$x = \frac{35}{0.12} = \frac{3500}{12}$$
$$= 291\tfrac{2}{3}.$$

Thus $500 - x = 500 - 291\tfrac{2}{3} = 208\tfrac{1}{3}$. The manufacturer should mix $291\tfrac{2}{3}$ liters of the 30 percent solution and $208\tfrac{1}{3}$ liters of the 18 percent solution.

example 2

In order to produce 350 kg of a certain compound, chemicals A and B must be combined in the ratio of 2 : 3, respectively (by mass). Find the amount of each chemical that must be used.

The ratio of 2 : 3 means that the compound consists of two parts A and three parts B. Let m be the mass of each part, in kilograms.

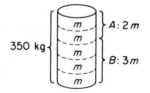

FIGURE 5-7

From Fig. 5-7, we have

$$2m + 3m = 350$$

$$5m = 350$$

$$m = \frac{350}{5} = 70.$$

But $m = 70$ is *not* the answer to the original problem. The mass of A is $2m = 2(70) = 140$, and the mass of B is $3m = 3(70) = 210$. Thus 140 kg of chemical A and 210 kg of chemical B must be used.

We now turn to rate problems. You may recall that

$$\text{distance} = (\text{rate})(\text{time}).$$

Two other forms of this are

$$\text{time} = \frac{\text{distance}}{\text{rate}}, \quad \text{rate} = \frac{\text{distance}}{\text{time}}.$$

example 3

If a man can row 11 km/h in still water and the rate of a stream is 3 km/h, how far upstream can he row if he is to be back at his starting point in 2 h?

Upstream the rate of the boat is $11 - 3 = 8$ km/h; downstream, it is $11 + 3 = 14$ km/h. Let d be the distance, in kilometers, that the man can row upstream (Fig. 5-8). Then the time, in hours, to row upstream at 8 km/h is $\dfrac{\text{distance}}{\text{rate}}$ or $\dfrac{d}{8}$. Downstream the distance is also d, but the time, at 14 km/h, is $\dfrac{\text{distance}}{\text{rate}}$ or $\dfrac{d}{14}$. Thus

$$\left(\begin{array}{c}\text{time} \\ \text{upstream}\end{array}\right) + \left(\begin{array}{c}\text{time} \\ \text{downstream}\end{array}\right) = \text{total time},$$

$$\frac{d}{8} + \frac{d}{14} = 2$$

$$56\left(\frac{d}{8} + \frac{d}{14}\right) = 56(2) \qquad \text{(multiplying both sides by 56, the L.C.D.)}$$

$$7d + 4d = 112$$

$$11d = 112$$

$$d = \frac{112}{11} = 10\frac{2}{11}.$$

Thus he can row upstream a distance of $10\frac{2}{11}$ km.

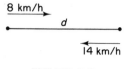

FIGURE 5-8

Another way of arriving at the answer is to first find the *time* he can row upstream. Let t be the time, in hours, he rows upstream at 8 km/h. Because the total time traveled is 2 h, then $2 - t$ is the time he rows downstream at 14 km/h. See Fig. 5-9.

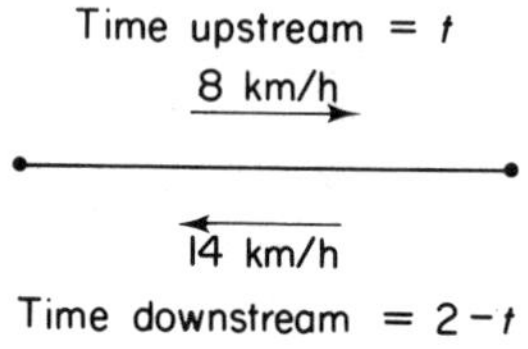

Time upstream = t

8 km/h

14 km/h

Time downstream = $2 - t$

FIGURE 5-9

Now, distance = (rate)(time) and distance upstream = distance downstream. Thus we have

$$(\text{rate})(\text{time}) = (\text{rate})(\text{time})$$

$$8t = 14(2 - t)$$

$$8t = 28 - 14t$$

$$22t = 28$$

$$t = \frac{28}{22} = \frac{14}{11} \text{ h.}$$

Thus the distance upstream is (rate)(time) = $(8)(\frac{14}{11}) = \frac{112}{11} = 10\frac{2}{11}$ km.

example 4

Entering a certain storage tank are three pipes: A, B, and C. Pipe A can fill the tank in 2 h, pipe B in 3 h, and pipe C in 4 h. How long will it take to fill the tank if all three pipes are used?

In 1 h, pipe A fills $\frac{1}{2}$ of the tank, pipe B fills $\frac{1}{3}$ of the tank, and pipe C fills $\frac{1}{4}$ of the tank. When all three pipes are used, a total of $\frac{1}{2} + \frac{1}{3} + \frac{1}{4}$ of the tank is filled in 1 h. Let n be the number of hours it takes when the three pipes are used together. Then $\frac{1}{2} + \frac{1}{3} + \frac{1}{4}$ would be $1/n$ of the tank. Thus

$$\frac{1}{2} + \frac{1}{3} + \frac{1}{4} = \frac{1}{n}$$

$$12n\left(\frac{1}{2} + \frac{1}{3} + \frac{1}{4}\right) = 12n\left(\frac{1}{n}\right)$$

$$6n + 4n + 3n = 12$$
$$13n = 12$$
$$n = \frac{12}{13}.$$

The time required is $\frac{12}{13}$ h.

Our last example deals with forces acting on a beam. This topic is typically found in technical physics courses.

example 5

If two downward forces F_1 and F_2 act on a very light beam (Fig. 5-10), the beam will balance on the pivot when $F_1 d_1 = F_2 d_2$. Here d_1 and d_2 are the distances of F_1 and

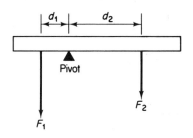

FIGURE 5-10

F_2, respectively, from the pivot. The distances d_1 and d_2 are called **lever arms,** and the product of a force and its lever arm is called a **torque.**

a. If $F_1 = 20$ N, $F_2 = 13$ N, and $d_1 = 0.5$ m, find d_2 so that the beam balances.

$$F_1 d_1 = F_2 d_2$$
$$(20)(0.5) = (13)d_2$$
$$\frac{20(0.5)}{13} = d_2$$
$$d_2 = \frac{10}{13} \text{ m.}$$

Thus the force of 13 N should be applied $\frac{10}{13}$ m to the right of the pivot.

b. If the beam in Fig. 5-11 is in balance on the pivot shown, how large is the force F?

For the beam to balance, the sum of the clockwise torques—that is, the torques associated with forces tending to cause clockwise rotation about the pivot—must equal the sum of the counterclockwise torques.

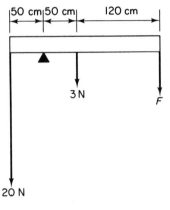

FIGURE 5-11

sum of clockwise torques = sum of counterclockwise torques.

$$3(50) + F(120 + 50) = 20(50)$$

$$150 + 170F = 1000$$

$$170F = 850$$

$$F = \frac{850}{170} = 5 \text{ N}.$$

Exercise 5-6

1. How many kiloliters of a 60 percent acid solution (60 percent is acid by volume) must be added to 12 kiloliters of a 35 percent acid solution so that the resulting solution is 50 percent acid?

2. A 6-liter car radiator is two-thirds full of water. How much of a 90 percent antifreeze solution (90 percent is alcohol by volume) must be added to it to make a 10 percent antifreeze solution in the radiator?

3. A chemical manufacturer mixes a 20 percent acid solution (20 percent is acid by volume) with a 30 percent acid solution to get 700 liters of a 24 percent acid solution. How many liters of each must be used?

4. To produce iron for miscellaneous castings, how many kilograms of ferrosilicon (86 percent silicon) should be added to 2000 kg of the base iron (2.17 percent silicon) to give the iron a 2.25 percent silicon content, making it easier to machine?

5. How many milliliters of water must be evaporated from 80 ml of a 12 percent salt solution (12 percent is salt by volume) so that what remains is a 20 percent salt solution?

6. A company manufactures a drain cleaner, which consists of a chemical compound and metal shavings. The chemical compound loosens grease and, when dissolved in water, gives off heat which speeds up the reaction. It also reacts with the metal to generate hydrogen, which loosens dirt and grease. The company markets two forms of the cleaner: industrial strength, of which 9 percent is metal shavings (by mass); and household strength, of which 6 percent is metal shavings. A motel chain has placed an order with the company to supply them with 12,000 kilograms of new motel strength, which is 8 percent metal shavings. To fill the order, the company will mix the industrial and household forms. How many kilograms of each should go into the mixture?

7. In order to produce a certain compound, chemicals A and B must be combined, by mass, in the ratio of 3 : 11, respectively. If 175 grams of the compound are needed, how many grams of each of A and B must be used?

8. A lab assistant is to prepare 84 milliliters of a chemical solution. It is to be made up of 2 parts alcohol and 3 parts acid. How much of each should be used?

9. A certain alloy is made up of 8 parts of metal A, 3 parts of metal B, and 1 part of metal C by mass. How much of each metal is needed to make 168 kg of the alloy?

10. How many kilograms each of chemicals A, B, and C must be combined to obtain 93 kg of a compound that consists of A, B, and C in the ratio 1 : 2 : 3, respectively, by mass?

11. On the moon, a lunar rover traveled from point A to point B at the rate of 5 km/h and returned to A along the same path at the rate of 15 km/h. The *total* traveling time was 2 h. Find the distance from A to B.

12. Suppose that the lunar rover in Problem 11 traveled from A to B at 6 km/h and returned at 10 km/h. If the total traveling time was 3 h, find the distance from A to B.

13. A pilot, flying against a headwind, traveled from A to B at 250 km/h. She flew back, with the wind, at 300 km/h. Her trip from B to A took one hour less than the trip from A to B. Find the distance from A to B.

14. From two airports that are 300 km apart, two airplanes leave at the same time and fly toward each other. One flies at 275 km/h and the other at 325 km/h. How long will it take for the planes to pass each other? *Hint*: When they pass, the sum of the distances traveled by the planes is 300 km.

15. A chemical company can fill a tank car with an industrial solvent with a regular pump in 20 min. Another pump, one that the company keeps in reserve, can fill the tank car in 30 min. How many minutes would it take to fill the tank car if both pumps were used together?

16. Water is flowing into a tank by means of pipes A and B. Pipes A and B can fill the tank, individually, in 2 h and 5 h, respectively. However, water is also flowing out of the tank into another tank by pipe C, which can completely empty the original tank in 4 h. How long would it take to fill the original tank if it were initially empty and pipes A, B, and C were all opened?

17. If the beam shown in Fig. 5-12 is balanced on the pivot, how large is the force *F*? (See Example 5.)

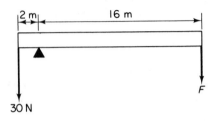

FIGURE 5-12

18. If the beam shown in Fig. 5-13 is balanced on the pivot, how large is the force *F*? (See Example 5.)

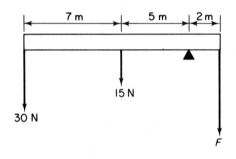

FIGURE 5-13

19. If the beam shown in Fig. 5-14 balances on the pivot, determine *d*. (See Example 5.)

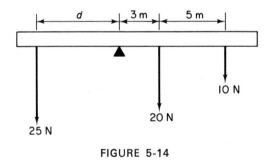

FIGURE 5-14

20. A space shuttle orbits the earth in a circular path of radius 6600 km at constant speed. If the period of its motion, the time to complete one orbit, is 98 min, what is the speed of the shuttle to the nearest kilometer per hour? (Approximate π by 3.1416.)

21. A sharpshooter hears his bullet strike a target 3 s after the report of his rifle. If the bullet travels 580 m/s and sound travels 331 m/s, find the distance to the target and the time the bullet was in the air.

22. If you travel 120 km from A to B at an average speed of 60 km/h and then you return to A at an average speed of 40 km/h, what is your average speed for the entire trip? *Note*: The answer is not 50 km/h.

23. On a certain day, the temperature rose 2° hourly from 3 A.M. until noon. If the average hourly temperature reading for this period was 26°C, what was the temperature at 8 A.M.?

24. Assuming that the velocity of sound in air increases 60 cm/s for each degree Celsius of increase in temperature, estimate the velocity of sound in meters per second at 0°C from the following data. When the temperature is −3°C, a sound produced at A is heard at B after an interval of $5\frac{1}{3}$ s; when the temperature is 19°C, the interval is 5 s.

25. The water level in a certain reservoir is 6 m deep, but the level is sinking at the rate of 4 cm a day. The water in another reservoir is 4.92 m deep and is rising 5 cm a day. After how many days will the depths of the two reservoirs be the same, and what will this depth be?

26. A man rowed downstream for 10 km and then rowed upstream for the same period of time. However, he covered only 5 km going back. If the rate of the stream was $1\frac{1}{4}$ km/h, find how fast the man can row in still water.

27. The top section of a transmitting antenna tower was blown over by the wind. This top section, still attached to the bottom section, touched the ground at a point 20 m from the base of the tower. If the top section was 5 m longer than the bottom section, how high was the original tower?

28. Two airplanes leave two airports that are 300 km apart at the same instant and fly toward each other. One plane flies 50 km/h faster than the other and the planes pass each other in 30 min. Find the speed of each plane.

29. A beam has weights of 50 N and 100 N attached to its ends. A pivot is located 10 cm from the center of the beam in the direction of the 100-N weight. If the beam balances on the pivot, how long is the beam?

5-7 Review

Review Questions

1. An equation that can be written in the form $ax + b = 0$, where $a \neq 0$, is called a(n) _____ equation.

2. In the equation $x + 3 = 3(x - 5)$, we call $x + 3$ the _____(a)_____ side and $3(x - 5)$ the _____(b)_____ side.

3. The equation $x + 4 = 5$ $\underset{(a)}{\text{(is) (is not)}}$ equivalent to $x + 6 = 7$. The equation $x + 5 = 7$ $\underset{(b)}{\text{(is) (is not)}}$ equivalent to $2x + 10 = 9$.

4. The equation $7 - 4x = 9$ is of the _____(a)_____ degree and its solution set is _(b)_ .

5. With regard to being an identity or a conditional equation, we would classify $2(x + 3) + 1 = 7 + 2x$ as a(n) _____.

6. If $p_1/p_2 = t_1/t_2$, then $t_2 = $ _____.

7. The number of roots of a linear equation is _____.

8. If the solution of $ax + b = 0$ is $x = -a$, then b must be equal to _____.

9. If the solution of $ax + b = 0$ is $x = 1/a$, then b must be equal to _____.

10. The statement "2 is to x as 3 is to 4" can be written algebraically as _____.

11. The statement $a : b = c : d$ is referred to as a(n) _____.

Answers to Review Questions

1. Linear or first-degree.   **2.** (a) Left,   (b) Right.   **3.** (a) Is,   (b) Is not.

4. (a) First,   (b) $\{-\frac{1}{2}\}$.   **5.** Identity.   **6.** $\frac{t_1 p_2}{p_1}$.   **7.** One.   **8.** a^2.   **9.** -1.

10. $\frac{2}{x} = \frac{3}{4}$, or $2 : x = 3 : 4$.   **11.** Proportion.

Review Problems

In Problems **1–18**, solve the equations.

1. $4x + 1 = 3$.

2. $9x - 7 = 11$.

3. $5 = 8 - 2y$.

4. $6y = 3y$.

5. $8 - \dfrac{4x}{3} = 10$.

6. $6x - \dfrac{1}{3} = 5$.

7. $\dfrac{3}{4}z + 2 = \dfrac{1}{3}$.

8. $\dfrac{1}{10} - \dfrac{2z}{5} = 4$.

9. $9(3u + 2) = 3 - (u + 7)$.

10. $4\left(u - \dfrac{5}{7}\right) = -3u$.

11. $\dfrac{3}{2}(x - 8) = 2x + 4$.

12. $3\{2x + 4[(7 - 2x) - 5x]\} = 0$.

13. $5[3 - 2(3x - 4)] = 18 - 9x$.

14. $7x - [8x + 4(x + 2)] = -(1 + x)$.

15. $\dfrac{2}{x + 5} = \dfrac{4}{x - 5}$.

16. $\dfrac{2x}{x - 3} - \dfrac{x + 1}{x + 2} = 1$.

17. $\dfrac{x + 2}{x - 5} - \dfrac{7}{x - 5} = 0$.

18. $\dfrac{5}{p} - \dfrac{2}{3p} = 6$.

In Problems **19** and **20**, use the given formulas to express the given symbols in terms of the remaining symbols.

19. $n - 1 = C + \dfrac{C'}{\lambda^2}$; C, C'.

20. $\sigma = \dfrac{n_0 - n_e}{\lambda} L$; n_0, n_e.

21. If 2 is to $x + 5$ as 4 is to $x - 5$, find x.

22. Into a graduated container two-thirds full, 10 liters of fluid were poured and it was found to be five-sixths full. How many liters does the storage tank hold?

23. A new insect spray is in the experimental stages. It contains the remarkable new "killer" ingredient K-57. A lab assistant has two spray formulas available: Formula A, of which 10 percent is K-57; and Formula B, of which 16 percent is K-57. So far, Formula A has proved to be too weak. On the other hand, Formula B seems too strong to be used near house pets. The lab assistant is told to mix Formula A with 400 ml of Formula B so that the result is 14 percent K-57. How many milliliters of Formula A should be used?

24. Suppose that the lab assistant in Problem 23 had needed exactly 500 ml of a 14 percent K-57 solution. How much of each formula would be used?

25. A construction firm has a government contract to build a swimming pool for the use of certain public officials. According to the contract, the pool must be completed within the next 21 days. The construction supervisor knows that the regular crew would take 45 days to build it. To meet the deadline, the supervisor decides to use a second crew, who can build the pool by themselves in 30 days. How long will it take both crews to construct the pool if they work together?

26. Suppose that a lunar rover traveled from point A to point B at 8 km/h and returned along the same path at 12 km/h. If the total time were 4 h, find the distance from A to B.

27. Suppose that 108 kg of a certain chemical compound must be made up, by mass, of one part chemical A, three parts chemical B, and five parts chemical C. How many kilograms of each chemical must be used?

28. When the temperature of a rod of length l_0 is increased from T_0 to T, its length l is given by

$$l = l_0\{1 + \alpha(T - T_0)\},$$

where α is a constant. Solve for T_0.

functions, graphs, and straight lines

6-1 Functions

In 1694 the word *function* was first introduced into the mathematical vocabulary. Today the concept of a function is one of the most basic in all of mathematics. As you will soon see, a function is a special type of input-output relation.

Let us begin by considering the data obtained in a study of the elongation of a vertical coil spring. The data are shown in the table in Fig. 6-1. Here F is a load, in newtons, that is suspended on the spring and S is the elongation, in centimeters, that it produces. We can think of the table as defining a rule, namely, to each load F assign the corresponding elongation S. If we think of the F's as input numbers and the S's as output numbers, then the rule assigns to each input number F *exactly one* output number S. This is symbolized by the arrow notation below.

$$F \longrightarrow S.$$

| input | output |
| number | number |

We call this rule a *function* in the following sense.

> A **function** is a rule that assigns to each input number exactly one output number. The set of all input numbers to which the rule applies is called the **domain** of the function. The set of all output numbers is called the **range**.

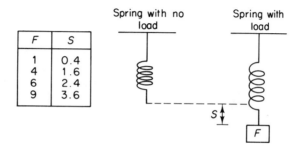

F	S
1	0.4
4	1.6
6	2.4
9	3.6

FIGURE 6-1

For the spring function above, the domain consists of the numbers 1, 4, 6, and 9; the range consists of the numbers 0.4, 1.6, 2.4, and 3.6.

Actually, we are using the word *function* in a restricted sense, because in general the inputs or outputs need not necessarily be numbers. For example, a table of chemical elements and their abbreviations assigns to each element (not a number) exactly one abbreviation (not a number). Thus a function is implied.

Usually, letters such as f, g, h, F, and G are used to name functions. Suppose we give the function defined in Fig. 6-1 the name f. Then to indicate that f assigns to the input 1 the output 0.4, we write $f(1) = 0.4$, which is read f *of* 1 *equals* 0.4. Similarly, $f(4) = 1.6$, $f(6) = 2.4$, and $f(9) = 3.6$. More generally,

	input
$f(x)$, which is read f *of* x, means the output number in the range of f that corresponds to the input number x in the domain.	$\downarrow$
	$\underline{f(x)}$
	$\uparrow$
	output

Output numbers, such as $f(1)$ and $f(4)$, are often called **functional values**. We emphasize that $f(x)$ *does not mean f times x.*

As another example, suppose f is the function that assigns to an input number x the output number x^2. That is, f squares an input number. Then $f(2) = 2^2 = 4$. Other functional values are $f(-3) = (-3)^2 = 9$ and $f(0) = 0^2 = 0$. In fact, if x is *any* input, then $f(x) = x^2$. Actually, f can be defined by the equation $f(x) = x^2$, which is called *functional notation*. For brevity we shall speak of "the function $f(x) = x^2$," although it is understood that we mean the function f defined by that equation.

example 1

Let $f(x) = x^2$.

a. To find $f(\frac{3}{4})$, we replace x in $f(x) = x^2$ by the input $\frac{3}{4}$:

$$f\left(\frac{3}{4}\right) = \left(\frac{3}{4}\right)^2 = \frac{9}{4}.$$

179

b. To find $f(x + h)$, we square the input number $x + h$:

$$f(x + h) = (x + h)^2 = x^2 + 2xh + h^2.$$

Note that $f(x + h) \neq x^2 + h$. That is, $f(x + h) \neq f(x) + h$; we do not write $f(x)$ and add h. Also, because $f(x)$ does not mean f times x, *do not* use the distributive law on $f(x + h)$:

$$f(x + h) \neq f(x) + f(h).$$

c. $f(3z) = (3z)^2 = 9z^2$.   Here the input is $3z$.

example 2

Let $g(x) = x^3 - 2x + 1$. Some functional values are:

$$g(-1) = (-1)^3 - 2(-1) + 1 = -1 + 2 + 1 = 2,$$

$$g\left(\frac{x}{2}\right) = \left(\frac{x}{2}\right)^3 - 2\left(\frac{x}{2}\right) + 1 = \frac{x^3}{8} - x + 1.$$

Note that $g(x/2)$ was found by replacing each x in $x^3 - 2x + 1$ by the input $x/2$. That is, the function g cubes an input number, subtracts twice the input, and adds 1.

The equation $y = x + 2$ also defines a function, because it gives the rule: Add 2 to x. This rule assigns to each input x exactly one output $x + 2$, which is y. For example, if $x = 1$, then $y = 1 + 2 = 3$. If we denote this function by f, then the output $f(x)$ is the same as y. Thus $y = f(x) = x + 2$. For example, if $x = 1$, then $y = f(1) = 3$. Here we can speak of "the function $y = x + 2$."

Unless otherwise stated, the domain of a function consists of all real numbers for which that function has meaning. For example, the function $f(x) = x^2$ has meaning for every input x. That is, if x is any real number, then x^2 is also a real number. Thus the domain of f consists of all real numbers. However, for the function $y = 1/(x - 6)$, the domain is understood to consist of all real numbers except 6, because the equation has no meaning if $x = 6$ (we cannot divide by zero).

In some cases the domain of a function is restricted for physical reasons. For example, the formula $C = 2\pi r$ for the circumference of a circle defines a function, where the radius r is the input and the circumference C is the output. Because the radius is positive, the domain consists of all positive numbers; that is, all $r > 0$.

A variable that represents input numbers for a function is called an **independent variable**. One that represents output numbers is called a **dependent variable**, because its value *depends* on the value of the independent variable. We also speak of the dependent variable as being a *function of* the independent variable. For example, given the function $y = x^2$, the independent variable is x, the dependent variable is y, and y is a function of x. In the circumference formula $C = 2\pi r$, C is a function of r.

There are three important points. First, not all equations in x and y define y as a function of x. For example, let $y^2 = x$. If x is 4, then $y^2 = 4$; thus y can be 2 or -2. That is, to the input 4 there are assigned *two* output numbers, 2 and -2. This violates the definition of a function, so y is **not** a function of x. In short, x and y are related by $y^2 = x$, but this relation is not a function of x.

The second point is that the letters used to define a function are not important. For example, the equation $w = f(z) = z^2$ defines the same function as $y = g(x) = x^2$. In both cases the output number is obtained by squaring an input number, and the domain in each case is all real numbers.

Third, some equations in two variables may define either variable as a function of the other. For example, if $s = 2t$, then s is a function of t. However, because $t = s/2$, then t is a function of s.

Functions with particular forms are given special names, as Example 3 shows.

example 3

a. The equation $g(x) = 2$ defines a *constant function*. For any input, the output is 2. The domain is all real numbers and the range consists only of 2. For example,

$$g(4.1) = 2,$$
$$g(-420) = 2.$$

In general, a **constant function** is one of the form $g(x) = c$, where c is a fixed real number.

b. The function $f(x) = 2x + 3$ is an example of a **linear function**. It has the form $f(x) = ax + b$, where a and b are constants and $a \neq 0$. The domain is all real numbers. For example,

$$f(-5) = 2(-5) + 3 = -7,$$
$$f(t + 7) = 2(t + 7) + 3 = 2t + 14 + 3$$
$$= 2t + 17,$$
$$f[f(x)] = f[2x + 3] = 2(2x + 3) + 3$$
$$= 4x + 6 + 3 = 4x + 9.$$

c. The function $y = h(x) = -3x^2 + x - 5$ is a **quadratic function**, one of the form $h(x) = ax^2 + bx + c$, where a, b, and c are constants and $a \neq 0$. The domain of h is all real numbers, and y is a function of x. For example,

$$h(2) = -3(2)^2 + 2 - 5 = -15,$$
$$h\left(\frac{1}{t}\right) = -3\left(\frac{1}{t}\right)^2 + \left(\frac{1}{t}\right) - 5 = -\frac{3}{t^2} + \frac{1}{t} - 5,$$
$$h(r^2) = -3(r^2)^2 + r^2 - 5 = -3r^4 + r^2 - 5,$$
$$h(x + t) - h(x) = [-3(x + t)^2 + (x + t) - 5] - (-3x^2 + x - 5)$$
$$= -3(x^2 + 2xt + t^2) + x + t - 5 + 3x^2 - x + 5$$
$$= -3x^2 - 6xt - 3t^2 + t + 3x^2$$
$$= -6xt - 3t^2 + t.$$

d. The function $f(x) = |x|$ is called the **absolute value function**. Its domain is all real numbers. For example,

$$f(6) = |6| = 6,$$
$$f(-2) = |-2| = 2,$$
$$f(2x + 1) = |2x + 1|.$$

example 4

a. For the function

$$f(t) = \frac{2t}{(t - 1)(t + 1)}.$$

the independent variable is t. The right side is defined, provided the denominator is not zero. Thus the domain consists of all real numbers except 1 and -1, that is, all $t \neq 1, -1$.

b. If $g(w) = \sqrt{w}$, then for $\sqrt{w}$ to be a real number, w cannot be negative. Thus the domain is all $w \geq 0$.

example 5

The voltage pulse V (in volts) produced by a signal generator is a function of time t (in seconds) and is given by

$$V = f(t) = \begin{cases} 2.4t, & \text{for } 0 \leq t \leq 1, \\ -4, & \text{for } 1 < t \leq 2, \\ 2t + 6, & \text{for } 2 < t \leq 4. \end{cases}$$

Find $f(\frac{1}{2})$, $f(2)$, and $f(3)$.

This is an example of a **compound function**, so called because it is defined by more than one equation. The value of an input number t determines which equation to use. The required functional values are found as follows.

$$\text{Because} \quad 0 \leq \tfrac{1}{2} \leq 1, \quad f(\tfrac{1}{2}) = 2.4(\tfrac{1}{2}) = 1.2.$$
$$\text{Because} \quad 1 < 2 \leq 2, \quad f(2) = -4.$$
$$\text{Because} \quad 2 < 3 \leq 4, \quad f(3) = 2(3) + 6 = 12.$$

Observe that the function is defined for all values of t between 0 and 4, inclusive, so the domain is all t where $0 \leq t \leq 4$.

example 6

In a laboratory experiment, a potential difference of 10 V is applied across an initially uncharged capacitor in series with a resistor, as shown in Fig. 6-2. The readings obtained for the potential difference V, in volts, across the capacitor at various times t, in seconds, are given in the indicated table. For each time there corresponds exactly

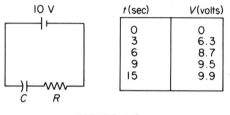

FIGURE 6-2

one potential difference. Thus this table defines V as a function of t, $V = f(t)$, and $f(0) = 0$, $f(3) = 6.3$, and so on.

If f is a function, any value of x for which $f(x) = 0$ is called a **zero** of the function. For example, we obtain zeros of $f(x) = 2x - 3$ by substituting 0 for $f(x)$ and solving for x.

$$2x - 3 = 0$$
$$2x = 3$$
$$x = \frac{3}{2}$$

Thus the only zero of f is $\frac{3}{2}$. That is, $f(\frac{3}{2}) = 0$.

Exercise 6-1

For each function in Problems 1–22, determine the independent variable and domain. Also find the indicated functional expressions.

1. $f(x) = 4x$; $f(0)$, $f(3)$, $f(-\frac{1}{4})$, $f(t)$, $f(xy)$.

2. $F(x) = x + 8$; $F(4)$, $F(-\frac{1}{2})$, $F(12)$, $F(-3)$, $F(x_1)$.

3. $g(x) = 1 - 2x$; $g(0)$, $g(-u)$, $g(7)$, $g(-2x)$, $g(x + h)$, $g(xy)$.

4. $h(x) = -\frac{9}{2}$; $h(0)$, $h[(13)^2]$, $h(t)$, $h(x + 1)$.

5. $G(t) = 1.02$; $G(5)$, $G(-107.3)$, $G(x^2)$, $G(2 + x)$, $G(x^2) - [G(x)]^2$.

6. $F(s) = 2(4 - s)$; $F(0)$, $F\left(\frac{1}{s}\right)$, $F(1 + \frac{1}{3})$, $F\left(\frac{s}{2}\right)$.

7. $q = h(p) = \dfrac{3(4p + 1)}{2}$; $h(1)$, $h\left(\frac{p}{2}\right)$, $h\left(\frac{1}{p}\right)$.

8. $g(x) = 3x^2$; $g(-4)$, $g(-3u)$, $g(x^3)$, $g\left(\frac{2}{x}\right)$, $g[g(x)]$.

9. $f(p) = p^2 + 2p + 1$; $f(0)$, $f(2)$, $f(x_1)$, $f(w)$, $f(p + h)$, $f\left(\frac{x}{y}\right)$,
   $f(2x) - 2f(x)$.

10. $x = H(y) = 2y^2 - 3y + 1$; $H(1)$, $H(-\frac{1}{2})$, $H(z)$, $H(z + 1)$.

11. $y = G(t) = (t + 4)^2$; $G(0)$, $G(2)$, $G(2 + h)$, $\dfrac{G(2 + h) - G(2)}{h}$.

12. $F(x) = |x - 3|$; $F(10)$, $F(3)$, $F(-3)$, $F(4t + 2)$.

13. $f(q) = |2q - 7|$; $f(6)$, $f(2)$, $f(7/2)$, $f(x^2 + 5)$.

14. $s = h(t) = \sqrt{6t}$; $h(0)$, $h(6)$, $h(\frac{2}{3})$, $h(6t)$.

15. $H(x) = \sqrt{4 + x}$; $H(0)$, $H(-4)$, $H(-3)$, $H(x + 1) - H(x)$.

16. $y = F(t) = \dfrac{t}{t - 3}$; $F(0)$, $F(4)$, $F(-1)$, $F(t + 2)$.

17. $h(z) = \left(\dfrac{z + 1}{z - 1}\right)^2$; $h(0)$, $h(1)$, $h(-\frac{1}{2})$, $h(z - 1)$.

18. $f(x) = \begin{cases} 4, & \text{if } x \geq 0 \\ 3, & \text{if } x < 0 \end{cases}$; $f(3)$, $f(-4)$, $f(\frac{17}{3})$, $f(-7.3)$.

19. $H(x) = \begin{cases} 1, & \text{if } x > 1 \\ x + 1, & \text{if } -1 \leq x \leq 1 \\ 1, & \text{if } x < -1 \end{cases}$; $H(7)$, $H(-7)$, $H(0.5)$, $H(-\frac{1}{2})$.

20. $h(r) = \begin{cases} 3r - 1, & \text{if } r > 2 \\ r^2 - 4r + 7, & \text{if } r < -2 \end{cases}$; $h(3)$, $h(-3)$, $h(5)$, $h(-5)$.

21. $y = g(x) = \dfrac{1}{x - 2} + \dfrac{1}{x + 3}$; $g(-2)$, $g(3)$, $g(0)$.

22. $y = f(x) = \dfrac{1}{\sqrt{x}}$; $f(1)$, $f(\sqrt{16})$.

23. If $z = 4x^2$, can z be considered a function of x? Can x be considered a function of z?

24. If $2p = 3q - 2$, can p be considered a function of q? Can q be considered a function of p?

25. Suppose $f(x) = 2.41x^2 - 3.12x + 8.14$. (a) Find $f(2.3)$. (b) Find $2f(2.3)$. (c) Find $f[2(2.3)]$.

26. Suppose $f(x) = 0.4ax^2 + 0.3a^2x + 2.31$. (a) Find $f(3)$. (b) Find $f(3)$ if $a = -4.1$.

27. The distance s, in meters, that an object will fall from rest in a vacuum in t seconds is given by $s = f(t) = 4.9t^2$. Find $f(0)$, $f(1)$, and $f(2)$. From a practical standpoint, what would you define the domain of f to be?

28. Express the perimeter P of a square as a function of the length of a side, l.

29. Express the area A of a square as a function of the length of a side, l.

30. Express the area A of a circle as a function of (a) its radius r; (b) its diameter d.

31. Suppose a ball is thrown up from the ground and the equation $s = 14.7t - 4.9t^2$ gives the height s (in meters) of the ball after t seconds. Find the heights when $t = 1$ and $t = 2$. Is t a function of s? Is s a function of t?

32. A solid cylinder has a radius of 2 cm and a height h, in centimeters. Express the total surface area A of the cylinder as a function of h.

33. An automobile averages 12.7 kilometers per liter of gasoline used. Express the number of liters n of gasoline used as a function of distance d traveled, in kilometers.

34. In Problem 33, express the number of liters n as a function of the distance d traveled, in *meters*.

35. A cylindrical storage tank with a radius of 2 m and a height of 6 m is filled with an industrial solvent. As liquid is drained from the tank, the height of the liquid decreases at the rate of 1 meter per hour. Express the volume V of liquid in the tank as a function of the time t, in hours, that the liquid is drained.

36. The period T (in seconds) of a simple pendulum is given by

$$T = f(l) = 2\pi \sqrt{\frac{l}{g}},$$

where l is the length of the pendulum in meters and g is the acceleration due to gravity, which is taken to be 9.8 m/s². Find $f(2)$ to two decimal places.

37. A metal plate which is to be used in the construction of an electromechanical device is shown in Fig. 6-3. Express the area A of the metal surface as a function of a. Give your answer in simplest form.

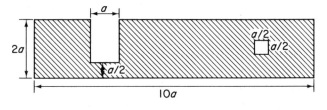

FIGURE 6-3

38. An open-top box is to be made from a rectangular piece of sheet metal, 12 cm by 16 cm, by cutting out equal squares from each corner and folding up the sides. Express the volume V of the box as a function of the length x of a side of the squares cut out. Give your answer in factored form.

39. The acceleration g due to gravity, in meters per second squared, at an altitude h meters above the earth's surface is given, approximately, by

$$g = f(h) = \frac{3.98 \times 10^{14}}{[(6.37 \times 10^6) + h]^2}.$$

(a) What is the approximate value of g at the earth's surface?

(b) What is the approximate value of g at a distance of 3.7×10^8 m from the earth's surface? (That would be near the moon!)

(c) Consider the values of g as h gets large. Based on your observation, would you ever expect a spaceship to *entirely* escape from the earth's influence?

6-2   Graphs in Rectangular Coordinates

A **rectangular** (or *Cartesian*) **coordinate system** allows us to specify and locate points in a plane. It also provides a geometrical way to represent equations in two variables and to represent functions. Such a system is obtained as follows. In a plane two real number lines, called **coordinate axes**, are constructed perpendicular to each other so that their origins coincide, as in Fig. 6-4. Their point of intersection is called the

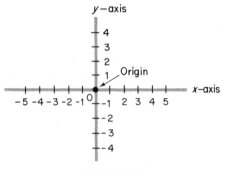

FIGURE 6-4

origin of the coordinate system. The positive numbers on the horizontal axis, or *x-axis*, are to the right of the origin, and the positive numbers on the vertical axis, or *y-axis*, lie above the origin. The unit distance on the *x*-axis does not necessarily have to be the same as that on the *y*-axis, and convenience should dictate an appropriate choice.

The plane on which the coordinate axes are placed is called a **rectangular coordinate plane** or, more simply, an **xy-plane**. Every point in the *xy*-plane can be assigned a pair of numbers to indicate its position. For example, from point *P* in Fig. 6-5(a), we draw perpendiculars to the *x*- and *y*-axes. They meet these axes at *x* and *y*, respectively. Thus *P* determines two numbers, *x* and *y*, and with *P* we associate the **ordered pair** (x, y). Here *x* is called the **abscissa** or *x*-coordinate of *P*, and *y* is the

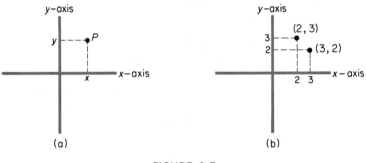

FIGURE 6-5

ordinate or *y*-**coordinate** of *P*. The abscissa is *always* written before the ordinate. Thus the word *ordered* is important. For example, in Fig. 6-5(b) the point corresponding to $(2, 3)$ is not the same as that for $(3, 2)$. That is, $(2, 3) \neq (3, 2)$. Together, *x* and *y* are called the **rectangular coordinates** of *P*.

Thus with each point in a given rectangular coordinate plane, we can associate exactly one ordered pair (x, y) of real numbers. On the other hand, it should be clear that with each ordered pair (x, y) of real numbers, we can associate exactly one point in that plane. Since there is a *one-to-one correspondence* between the points in the plane and all ordered pairs of real numbers, we shall refer to a point P with abscissa x and ordinate y simply as the point (x, y), or as $P(x, y)$. Moreover, we shall use the words *point* (in a plane) and *ordered pair* interchangeably.

In Fig. 6-6 various points in the xy-plane are located, or **plotted**. For example, $(2, -3)$ is located two units to the right of the y-axis and three units below the x-axis. Notice that the origin has coordinates $(0, 0)$. Any point on the x-axis has a y-coordinate of zero, and any point on the y-axis has an x-coordinate of zero.

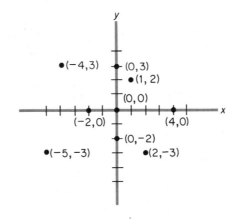

FIGURE 6-6

The coordinate axes divide the plane into four regions called **quadrants**, which are numbered in a counterclockwise direction as in Fig. 6-7. Quadrant I consists of all points (x_1, y_1) such that $x_1 > 0$ and $y_1 > 0$; that is, both coordinates are positive.

Quadrant II
(x_2, y_2) •
$x_2 < 0, y_2 > 0$

Quadrant I
• (x_1, y_1)
$x_1 > 0, y_1 > 0$

Quadrant III
(x_3, y_3) •
$x_3 < 0, y_3 < 0$

Quadrant IV
• (x_4, y_4)
$x_4 > 0, y_4 < 0$

FIGURE 6-7

The other quadrants can be characterized as indicated. A point on an axis does not lie in any quadrant.

By using a rectangular coordinate system, we can geometrically represent the solutions of an equation in two variables. For example, let us consider the equation

$$y = 2x + 1.$$

A solution is a value of x and a value of y that make the equation true. If $x = 1$, then $y = 2(1) + 1 = 3$. Thus one solution is $x = 1$, $y = 3$. We represent this solution geometrically by the point $(1, 3)$ in a coordinate plane [Fig. 6-8(a)]. Similarly, if we choose $x = -1$, then $y = 2(-1) + 1 = -1$. This solution is represented by the point $(-1, -1)$ in Fig. 6-8(a).

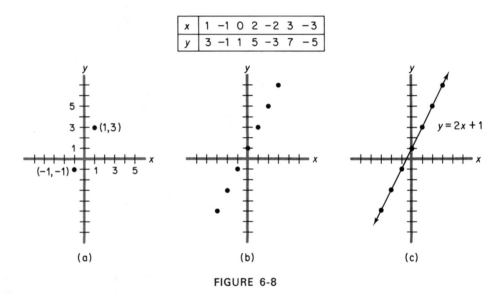

x	1	−1	0	2	−2	3	−3
y	3	−1	1	5	−3	7	−5

FIGURE 6-8

Figure 6-8(b) shows a table listing other solutions, together with the corresponding points in the plane. If we could plot all such solutions, we would have the *graph* of the equation.

> The **graph of an equation** in two variables is the geometric representation of all its solutions.

Thus the points in Fig. 6-8(b) lie on the graph of $y = 2x + 1$, because their coordinates satisfy that equation.

Since the equation has infinitely many solutions, it seems impossible to determine its graph precisely. However, our interest is only in the general shape of the graph. For this reason, we only have to locate enough points so that we can make an intelligent guess about its general behavior. Then we join those points by a *smooth curve* wherever conditions permit. This process is called *sketching the graph of the equation*. It is apparent in our case that the points seem to lie on a straight line. A sketch of a portion of the graph appears in Fig. 6-8(c). Here we assume that the graph extends indefinitely, which may be indicated by arrows. At times we may refer to the graph of an equation in two variables simply as a *curve;* thus we speak of the curve $y = 2x + 1$.

Because the equation $y = 2x + 1$ determines one and only one value of y for each value of x, it defines a function of x, call it f, and we can say that

$$y = f(x) = 2x + 1.$$

Figure 6-8(c) is then the graph of the function $y = f(x) = 2x + 1$. More generally:

> The **graph of a function** f with independent variable x is the set of all points $(x, f(x))$, where x is in the domain of f.

Let us now consider the graph of $y = x^2 + 2x - 3$. By setting $x = 1$ and then $x = -2$, we obtain the points $(1, 0)$ and $(-2, -3)$, shown in Fig. 6-9(a). At this stage, you should not hastily conclude that the graph is a straight line. Without

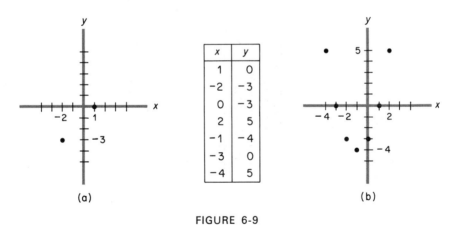

x	y
1	0
-2	-3
0	-3
2	5
-1	-4
-3	0
-4	5

(a)   (b)

FIGURE 6-9

a guarantee that the graph is a straight line, two points are *never* sufficient for a graph. We must plot as many points as necessary to make the general behavior of the graph reasonably apparent. Figure 6-9(b) gives a table of x- and y-values, together with the corresponding points in the plane. Although the more points we plot, the better our graph will be, these points give us a good idea of the graph's general shape. A sketch of (a portion of) the graph appears in Fig. 6-10:

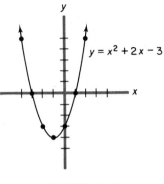

FIGURE 6-10

example 1

a. Sketch the graph of the equation $z = w^3 + 1$.

Using w for the horizontal axis and z for the vertical axis, we obtain Fig. 6-11. Although the points $(-\frac{1}{4}, \frac{63}{64})$ and $(\frac{1}{4}, \frac{65}{64})$ in the table in Fig. 6-11 are difficult to

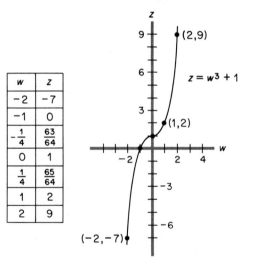

w	z
-2	-7
-1	0
$-\frac{1}{4}$	$\frac{63}{64}$
0	1
$\frac{1}{4}$	$\frac{65}{64}$
1	2
2	9

FIGURE 6-11

show in the graph, their location serves to reassure us about the behavior of the curve.

b. Sketch the graph of the equation $x = 2$.

Because there is no restriction on y, the graph consists of all points with abscissa 2. In other words, we can think of this as an equation in x and y if we write it as $x = 2 + 0y$. Here y can be any value, but x must be 2. See Fig. 6-12. The graph is a vertical line, that is, a line parallel to the y-axis.

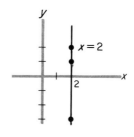

FIGURE 6-12

example 2

a. Sketch the graph of the absolute value function $f(x) = |x|$.

See Fig. 6-13. We label the vertical axis as $f(x)$. This axis is sometimes called the *function-value axis*.

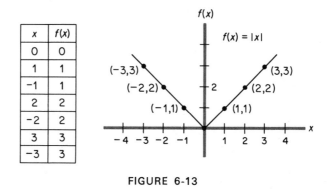

x	f(x)
0	0
1	1
−1	1
2	2
−2	2
3	3
−3	3

FIGURE 6-13

b. Sketch the graph of $z = f(r) = \dfrac{100}{r}$.

It is customary to *use the independent variable* (r) *to label the horizontal axis*. See Fig. 6-14. The vertical axis can be labeled either z or $f(r)$. This function is not defined when $r = 0$, so there is no corresponding point in the plane. Notice that our choice of the unit distance on each axis makes the graphing easy to handle.

c. The electric potential V, in volts, at a distance r, in meters, from a small object with an electric charge of $\frac{1}{9} \times 10^{-7}$ C is given by

$$V = V(r) = \frac{100}{r}.$$

Sketch the graph of this function.

Observe that this function is identical in form to that of (b). Here, however, the variable r has a physical meaning—it represents a measurable distance. For this reason the values of r must be restricted to positive values. The graph of this electric

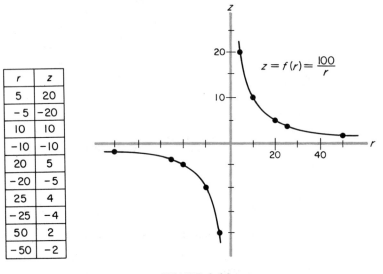

r	z
5	20
-5	-20
10	10
-10	-10
20	5
-20	-5
25	4
-25	-4
50	2
-50	-2

FIGURE 6-14

potential function is identical to the portion of the graph of part (b) that lies in the first quadrant.

example 3

The current i in a 1-Ω resistor as a function of the power P developed in the resistor is given by

$$i = f(P) = \sqrt{P}.$$

Sketch the graph of this function.

Because P is the independent variable, the horizontal axis is labeled as the P-axis. The vertical axis is labeled with the dependent variable, i. Here the domain is all $P \geq 0$, since the square root of a negative number is *not* a real number. See Fig. 6-15.

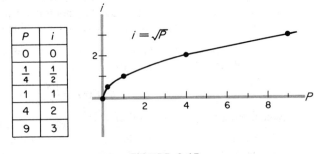

P	i
0	0
$\frac{1}{4}$	$\frac{1}{2}$
1	1
4	2
9	3

FIGURE 6-15

example 4

One automobile in a 5-second drag race is given a handicap by being allowed to start at a point ahead of the starting line. Its distance d, in meters, from the starting line is given by $d = f(t) = 3t^2 + 5$, where t is elapsed time in seconds. Sketch the graph of this function.

See Fig. 6-16. Notice that we have used only nonnegative values for time, because negative time has no meaning.

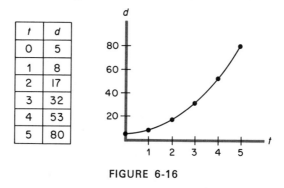

t	d
0	5
1	8
2	17
3	32
4	53
5	80

FIGURE 6-16

example 5

a. For the spring in Fig. 6-1, the elongation S is a function of load F and is given by $S = 0.4F$. The graph of this function is given in Fig. 6-17. The independent variable F represents the load on the spring and must be positive or zero. Thus we restrict the graph to nonnegative values of F.

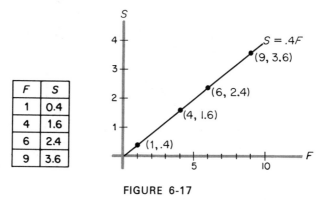

F	S
1	0.4
4	1.6
6	2.4
9	3.6

FIGURE 6-17

b. In Fig. 6-2 a table was given in which the potential difference V across a capacitor was a function of time t. That table, repeated on page 194, gives the following time-volt pairs: (0, 0), (3, 6.3), (6, 8.7), (9, 9.5), and (15, 9.9). In Fig. 6-18 we have plotted each pair. We can approximate points in between the data by connecting the data

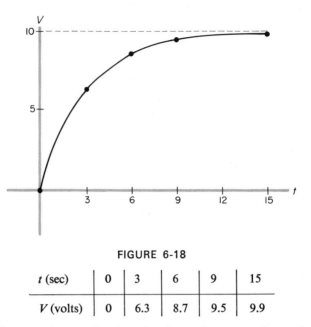

FIGURE 6-18

t (sec)	0	3	6	9	15
V (volts)	0	6.3	8.7	9.5	9.9

points with a smooth curve. By observing the graph, we note that as time increases, the voltage increases, getting closer and closer to 10. That is, as t gets large the curve "settles down" near the broken line. Such a line is called a **horizontal asymptote** of the curve. It is *not* part of the graph.

example 6

Sketch the graph of the compound function

$$f(x) = \begin{cases} x, & \text{if } 0 \leq x < 3, \\ x - 1, & \text{if } 3 \leq x \leq 5, \\ 4, & \text{if } 5 < x \leq 7. \end{cases}$$

The domain of f is $0 \leq x \leq 7$. The graph is given in Fig. 6-19. The *hollow dot* means that the point is *not* included in the graph.

x	$f(x)$
0	0
1	1
2	2
3	2
4	3
5	4
6	4
7	4

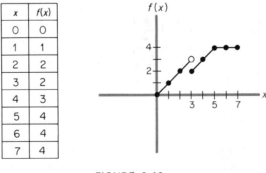

FIGURE 6-19

There is a simple graphic technique, the *vertical-line test*, to determine whether the graph of an equation is indeed that of a function. If a *vertical* line L can be drawn that intersects the graph of an equation in the variables x and y in at least two points, then the equation *does not* define y as a function of x. Such a condition implies the existence of two different points with the same x-coordinate, and this would pair an input number x with more than one output number y. However, if no such vertical line can be drawn, then the graph is that of a function of x. Thus the graphs in Fig. 6-20 do not represent functions of x, but those in Fig. 6-21 do.

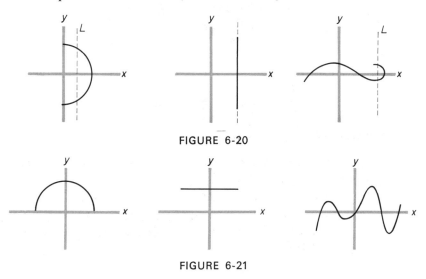

FIGURE 6-20

FIGURE 6-21

example 7

Sketch the graph of $x = 2y^2$.

Here it is convenient to choose values of y and then find the corresponding values of x. See Fig. 6-22. Using the vertical-line test, you can see that the equation does *not* define a function of x.

x	y
0	0
2	1
2	-1
8	2
8	-2
18	3
18	-3

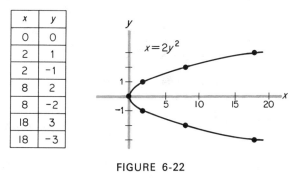

FIGURE 6-22

There is a connection between the zeros and the graph of a function f. The x-coordinates of the points where the graph of f touches the x-axis are zeros of f. For example, Fig. 6-23 shows that 3 and -1 are zeros of $f(x) = x^2 - 2x - 3$.

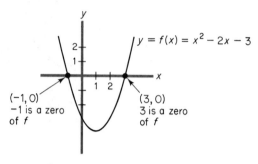

FIGURE 6-23

Exercise 6-2

In Problems **1** *and* **2**, *locate and label each of the given points and state, if possible, the quadrant in which each point lies.*

1. $(2, 7)$, $(8, -3)$, $(-\frac{1}{2}, -2)$, $(0, 0)$.   **2.** $(-4, 5)$, $(3, 0)$, $(1, 1)$, $(0, -6)$.

3. The following results were obtained in an experiment to measure the current i (in amperes) as a function of time t (in seconds) in an electrical circuit containing a resistor and an inductor:

t	0	2	4	6	8	10	12
i	0	6.3	8.7	9.5	9.8	9.9	10.0

Represent these data graphically and connect the points by a smooth curve.

4. In a certain experiment, a mass m was suspended from a vertical spring and allowed to come to rest. It was then pulled down 10 cm below its equilibrium position and released. The position s (in centimeters) of the mass as a function of time t (in seconds) was found to be as follows:

t	0	0.5	1	1.5	2	2.5	3	3.5	4
s	-10	-8	0	8	10	8	0	-8	-10

Represent these data graphically and connect the points by a smooth curve. Based on the data, can we say that t is a function of s?

In Problems **5–38**, *sketch the graph of the given equation or function. For any equations in* x *and* y, *indicate those for which* y *is not a function of* x.

5. $y = x$.   **6.** $y = 3x$.

7. $y = -2x + 1$.   **8.** $y = 3x - 5$.

9. $s = f(t) = t^2$.

10. $z = f(x) = 3x^2 - 1$.

11. $f(x) = -x^2 + 2$.

12. $f(x) = \frac{1}{2}x^2 + 4$.

13. $f(x) = |x| + 1$.

14. $f(x) = x^2 + x + 1$.

15. $h(w) = 2w^2 + 2w + 1$.

16. $g(t) = 2\sqrt{t}$.

17. $y = x^3$.

18. $y = x^3 - 2x^2 + x$.

19. $g(x) = x^3 - 3x$.

20. $x = -4$.

21. $f(z) = \dfrac{1}{z}$.

22. $f(t) = t(2 - t)$.

23. $y = \sqrt{4 - x^2}$.

24. $y = -8$.

25. $F(w) = 1 + w$, where $1 \le w \le 5$.

26. $f(x) = \dfrac{2}{x - 4}$.

27. $y = g(x) = 2$.

28. $y = |x - 3|$.

29. $x = 0$.

30. $x + y = 1$.

31. $x = -3y^2$.

32. $s = f(t) = \sqrt{t - 5}$.

33. $2x + y - 2 = 0$.

34. $f(x) = -2.1x^2 + 4.2x + 3.5$.

35. $F(x) = \begin{cases} x^2, & \text{if } 0 \le x \le 2, \\ 2x, & \text{if } 2 < x \le 3, \\ 6, & \text{if } x > 3. \end{cases}$

36. $f(x) = \begin{cases} 2x, & \text{if } x \le 2, \\ 4, & \text{if } x > 2. \end{cases}$

37. An automobile is moving in a straight line at a speed of 20 m/s. The brakes are applied and the vehicle is brought uniformly to rest. The speed v of the automobile is given by

$$v = f(t) = 20 - 2t,$$

where t is the time elapsed, in seconds, after the brakes are applied. Sketch the graph of this function for $0 \le t \le 10$.

38. In Problem 37, the distance d moved by the automobile, in meters, after t seconds is given by

$$d = d(t) = 20t - t^2$$

Sketch the graph of this function for $0 \le t \le 10$.

39. For a tuned electronic circuit, the output voltage V (in volts) as a function of frequency f (in kilohertz) was observed to be as follows:

f	1300	1325	1375	1400	1425	1475	1500
V	0.01	0.03	0.25	0.95	0.35	0.10	0.05

Represent the given data graphically and connect the points by a smooth curve.

40. While monitoring a radioactive sample with a detection instrument, a technician observed the disintegration rate R (in counts per minute) as a function of time t (in hours) to be as follows:

t	R	t	R
0.5	9535	6.0	1800
1.0	8190	7.0	1330
1.5	7040	8.0	980
2.0	6050	9.0	720
3.0	4465	10.0	535
4.0	3300	11.0	395
5.0	2430	12.0	290

Represent the given data graphically and connect the points by a smooth curve.

41. If a horizontal force F acts on a 20-N block resting on a horizontal surface and if the coefficients of static and kinetic friction are 0.3 and 0.1, respectively, then the frictional force f (in newtons) acting on the block can be written as a function of F defined by

$$f = g(F) = \begin{cases} F, & \text{if } 0 \leq F \leq 6, \\ 2, & \text{if } F > 6. \end{cases}$$

Sketch the graph of g for values of F from 0 to 10 N.

42. The speed v of sound in air as a function of the temperature T (in °C) of the air is given by

$$v = f(T) = 331\sqrt{\frac{T + 273}{273}},$$

where v is in meters per second. Sketch the graph of this function for $0 \leq T \leq 100$.

43. The branch voltage V in a circuit as a function of time t is given by the function

$$V = V(t) = \begin{cases} 2t, & \text{if } 0 \leq t \leq 1, \\ 4 - 2t, & \text{if } 1 \leq t \leq 2, \\ 0, & \text{if } t > 2. \end{cases}$$

Sketch the graph of this function. Based on the graph, can we say that t is a function of V?

44. The stopping distance d of an automobile as a function of its initial speed v is given by

$$d = f(v) = \frac{v^2}{2.5},$$

where v is in meters per second and d is in meters.
(a) Sketch the graph of this function.
(b) What happens to the stopping distance if the initial speed is doubled? *Hint*: Express $f(2v)$ in terms of $f(v)$. (The result should be a caution for all drivers!)

*In Problems **45** and **46**, find zeros of the given functions by graphical means.*

45. $f(x) \doteq x^2 + 2x$.   **46.** $f(x) = x^2 - x - 2$.

47. A signal generator produces a square-wave pulse V, in volts, given by

$$V = f(t) = \begin{cases} 2.3, & \text{for } 0 \leq t < 1, \\ -2.3, & \text{for } 1 \leq t < 2, \\ 0, & \text{for } t \geq 2. \end{cases}$$

Sketch the graph of this function.

6-3   Slope of a Straight Line

Many physical relationships in science and engineering can be represented by straight lines. One feature of a straight line is its "steepness." For example, in Fig. 6-24, line L_1 rises faster as it goes from left to right than line L_2. In this sense L_1 is steeper than L_2.

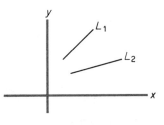

FIGURE 6-24

To measure the steepness of a line, we examine two points on the line to see how the y-values change as the x-values change. For example, consider the line through the points (2, 1) and (4, 5) in Fig. 6-25. As x increases from 2 to 4 (an in-

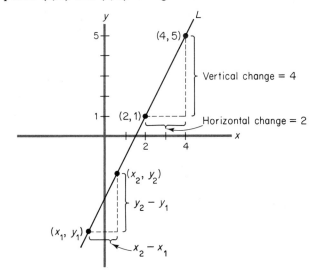

FIGURE 6-25

crease of two units), notice that y changes from 1 to 5 (an increase of four units). To determine how y changes for each one-unit increase in x, we divide the change in y (vertical change) by the change in x (horizontal change). This gives the **average rate of change** of y with respect to x. Denoting the change in x by the symbol Δx (read *delta x*) and the change in y by Δy, we have

$$\frac{\Delta y}{\Delta x} = \frac{\text{change in } y}{\text{change in } x} = \frac{5-1}{4-2} = \frac{4}{2} = \frac{2}{1} = 2.$$

This means that for each one-unit increase in x, there is a two-unit *increase* in y. Thus the line must *rise* from left to right. Choosing two other different points on this line would give the same rate of change. For if (x_1, y_1) and (x_2, y_2) were such points, then the right triangles shown in Fig. 6-25 are similar. Thus the ratios of the lengths of their corresponding sides are equal. Therefore

$$\frac{4}{2} = \frac{y_2 - y_1}{x_2 - x_1},$$

so the rate of change is always equal to 2. We call 2 the *slope* of the line.

SLOPE OF A STRAIGHT LINE

If (x_1, y_1) and (x_2, y_2) are two different points on a nonvertical line, the **slope** m of the line is the number given by

$$m = \frac{y_2 - y_1}{x_2 - x_1}.$$

In the slope formula, the order of the subscripts in the denominator *must* be the same as in the numerator. It is *incorrect* to write $m = (y_2 - y_1)/(x_1 - x_2)$, but correct to write $m = (y_1 - y_2)/(x_1 - x_2)$, which is obtained by multiplying the fraction in the box by $(-1)/(-1)$.

For a vertical line the number $x_2 - x_1$ is zero, because any two points on the line have the same abscissa (Fig. 6-26). Hence the ratio $(y_2 - y_1)/(x_2 - x_1)$ has no meaning (we cannot divide by zero). For this reason, *the slope of a vertical line is not defined.*

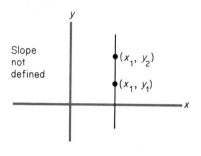

FIGURE 6-26

example 1

a. Determine the slope of the line passing through $(3, 4)$ and $(5, 1)$ [Fig. 6-27(a)].

If we choose $(3, 4)$ as (x_1, y_1) and $(5, 1)$ as (x_2, y_2), then

$$m = \frac{y_2 - y_1}{x_2 - x_1} = \frac{1 - 4}{5 - 3} = \frac{-3}{2} = -\frac{3}{2}.$$

Here the slope is negative, $-\frac{3}{2}$. This means that for each one-unit increase in x, there corresponds a *decrease* in y of $\frac{3}{2}$. Due to this decrease, the line *falls* from left to right. If we choose $(5, 1)$ as (x_1, y_1) and $(3, 4)$ as (x_2, y_2), then

$$m = \frac{y_2 - y_1}{x_2 - x_1} = \frac{4 - 1}{3 - 5} = \frac{3}{-2} = -\frac{3}{2},$$

as before.

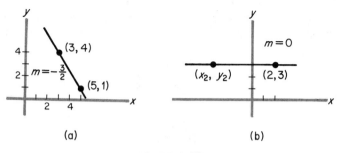

(a)   (b)

FIGURE 6-27

b. Determine the slope of the horizontal line passing through $(2, 3)$ [Fig. 6-27(b)].

Let $(x_1, y_1) = (2, 3)$. If (x_2, y_2) is any other point on the line, then y_2 must be 3 and

$$m = \frac{y_2 - y_1}{x_2 - x_1} = \frac{3 - 3}{x_2 - 2} = 0.$$

In fact, *the slope of every horizontal line is zero.*

In summary, we have the following.

Zero slope:	horizontal line.
No slope:	vertical line.
Positive slope:	line rises from left to right.
Negative slope:	line falls from left to right.

Now you can see why the slope is a measure of the steepness of a line. If two lines have slopes of 4 and 2, respectively, then in the first case we go up four units for a one-unit change in x to the right, while in the second case we would go up two units for the same change in x (Fig. 6-28). In this sense, the first line is steeper than

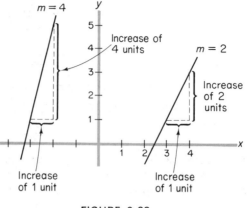

FIGURE 6-28

the second. Similarly, if two lines had slopes of -3 and $-\frac{2}{3}$, respectively, then in the first case we would go down three units while moving one unit to the right, while in the second case we would go down two-thirds unit (Fig. 6-29). Thus there is a

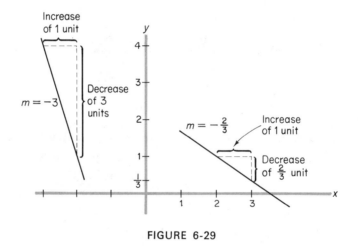

FIGURE 6-29

much sharper decline in the first line than in the second. In short, *the closer the slope is to zero, the more nearly horizontal is the line. The greater the absolute value of the slope, the more nearly vertical is the line.*

When the graph of a relationship between physical quantities is a straight line, its slope may have special physical significance, as Example 2 shows.

example 2

Under the condition of constant acceleration, the graph of the velocity v of an object as a function of time t will always be a straight line. The acceleration of the object is the rate of change of velocity with respect to time. That is, it is the slope of the line.

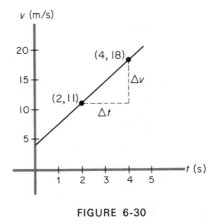

FIGURE 6-30

Suppose $v = 11$ m/s when $t = 2$ s, and $v = 18$ m/s when $t = 4$. Find and interpret the slope.

A graph of the relationship appears in Fig. 6-30. In the slope formula we replace the y's by v's and the x's by t's. Letting $(2, 11) = (v_1, t_1)$ and $(4, 18) = (v_2, t_2)$, we have

$$m = \frac{\Delta v}{\Delta t} = \frac{v_2 - v_1}{t_2 - t_1} = \frac{18 \text{ m/s} - 11 \text{ m/s}}{4 \text{ s} - 2 \text{ s}} = \frac{7 \text{ m/s}}{2 \text{ s}}$$

$$= 3.5 \text{ m/s}^2.$$

Notice that the slope has units attached to it, namely, m/s², which are the units of an acceleration. The positive slope of 3.5 m/s² means that for each increase in time of 1 s, there corresponds an *increase* in velocity of 3.5 m/s.

In summary, keep these points in mind:

1. Slope is a measure of steepness.

2. Slope indicates a rate of change.

3. Slope may have units attached to it.

Exercise 6-3

In Problems 1–8, find the slope of the straight line that passes through the given points.

1. $(1, 2)$, $(4, 8)$.

2. $(-1, 9)$, $(1, 5)$.

3. $(6, -3)$, $(-7, 5)$.

4. $(2, -4)$, $(3, -4)$.

5. $(-2, 4)$, $(-2, 8)$.

6. $(0, -6)$, $(3, 0)$.

7. $(5, -2)$, $(4, -2)$.

8. $(1, -6)$, $(1, 0)$.

9. When a small ball is thrown straight downward from the roof of a building, it falls with constant acceleration. If the ball has a velocity of 24.6 m/s after 2 seconds

of motion, and a velocity of 54.0 m/s after 5 seconds of motion, find the acceleration of the object. (See Example 2.)

10. The velocity of an object as a function of time is given by $v = 3t + 6$, where t is in seconds and v is in meters per second. The graph of this equation is a straight line. Find the acceleration of the object. (See Example 2.) *Hint*: First find two points on the line.

11. For a metallic conductor, the graph of the voltage V, in volts, as a function of current i, in amperes, is a straight line. The slope of this line gives the resistance R of the conductor. If $i = 4$ A, then $V = 2$ V; if $i = 12$ A, then $V = 6$ V. Determine the resistance (in ohms).

12. For an object moving in a straight line without accelerating, the graph of the displacement s, in meters, as a function of time t, in seconds, is a straight line. The slope of this line gives the velocity of the object, in meters per second. Find the velocity if $s = 13$ m when $t = 2$ s, and $s = 65$ m when $t = 10$ s.

13. In an experiment, a steel rod is found to have an initial length of 1.0000 m at a temperature of 0°C and a length of 1.0012 m at a temperature of 100°C. The graph of the length L as a function of temperature T is a straight line. The slope m of this line is related to α, the coefficient of linear expansion of steel. Specifically, $m = L_0\alpha$, where L_0 is the original length of the rod, in meters. From the given data, determine α.

14. One form of a capacitor, a device commonly used in electronics, consists of two parallel metal plates. When these plates are given equal and opposite electric charges, the graph of the potential difference V, in volts, as a function of the separation s of the plates, in meters, is a straight line. The slope of this line gives the strength of the electric field (in volts per meter) between the plates. For a particular capacitor, it is found that $V = 0.09$ V when $s = 0.001$ m, and $V = 0.45$ V when $s = 0.005$ m. Find the electric field strength between the plates of this capacitor.

15. An object has a constant acceleration of -6 m/s². Its velocity at time $t = 2$ s is 4 m/s. Find the velocity at $t = 5$ s. (See Example 2.)

6-4 Equations of Straight Lines

If we know the slope of a line and the coordinates of one point on the line, we can find an equation having that line as its graph. Suppose that a line L has slope m and passes through a given point (x_1, y_1). If (x, y) is *any* other point on L (see Fig. 6-31), then by the slope formula we obtain

$$\frac{y - y_1}{x - x_1} = m,$$

from which

$$y - y_1 = m(x - x_1). \tag{1}$$

That is, the coordinates of every point on L satisfy Eq. 1. It can also be shown that every point with coordinates that satisfy Eq. 1 must lie on L. Thus we say that Eq. 1

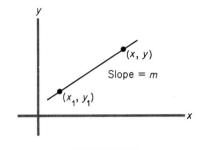

FIGURE 6-31

is an equation for L. More specifically,

$$y - y_1 = m(x - x_1)$$

is the **point-slope form** of an equation of the line passing through (x_1, y_1) and having slope m.

example 1

Determine and sketch an equation of the line that has slope 2 and passes through $(2, -3)$.

Using a point-slope form, we set $m = 2$ and $(x_1, y_1) = (2, -3)$.

$$y - y_1 = m(x - x_1)$$
$$y - (-3) = 2(x - 2)$$
$$y + 3 = 2x - 4.$$

This can be written as

$$y = 2x - 7.$$

To sketch the line, only two points need be plotted, because two points determine a straight line. See Fig. 6-32.

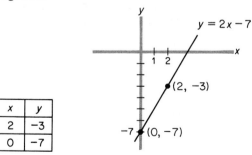

x	y
2	-3
0	-7

FIGURE 6-32

An equation of the line passing through two points can be found by first determining the slope of the line and then using a point-slope form with either point as (x_1, y_1).

example 2

Determine an equation of the line passing through $(4, 1)$ and $(-5, 4)$.

We first find the slope. Let $(4, 1) = (x_1, y_1)$ and $(-5, 4) = (x_2, y_2)$. Then

$$m = \frac{y_2 - y_1}{x_2 - x_1} = \frac{4 - 1}{-5 - 4} = \frac{3}{-9} = -\frac{1}{3}.$$

Now we shall use a point-slope form with $(4, 1)$.

$$y - y_1 = m(x - x_1)$$
$$y - 1 = -\frac{1}{3}(x - 4)$$
$$y - 1 = -\frac{1}{3}x + \frac{4}{3}.$$

This can be written

$$y = -\frac{1}{3}x + \frac{7}{3}.$$

Choosing $(-5, 4)$ as (x_1, y_1) gives the same result:

$$y - 4 = -\frac{1}{3}[x - (-5)]$$
$$y - 4 = -\frac{1}{3}x - \frac{5}{3}$$
$$y = -\frac{1}{3}x + \frac{7}{3}.$$

If a line L with slope m intersects the y-axis at some point $(0, b)$ (Fig. 6-33), the y-coordinate b is called the **y-intercept** of L. The point $(0, b)$ is on the line and, using a point-slope form for L, we obtain

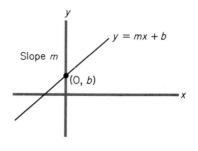

FIGURE 6-33

$$y - y_1 = m(x - x_1)$$
$$y - b = m(x - 0)$$
$$y = mx + b.$$

We say that

$$y = mx + b$$

is the **slope-intercept** form of an equation of
the line with slope m and y-intercept b.

example 3

a. An equation of the line with slope -2 and y-intercept -3 is as follows (Fig. 6-34).

$$y = mx + b$$
$$y = -2x + (-3)$$
$$y = -2x - 3.$$

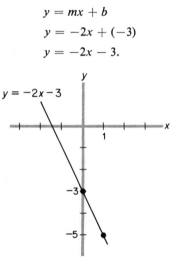

$y = -2x - 3$

FIGURE 6-34

b. The equation $y - \frac{8}{9}x + 7 = 0$ can be written $y = \frac{8}{9}x - 7$, which has the form
$y = mx + b$, where $m = \frac{8}{9}$ and $b = -7$ (not 7). Thus its graph is a line with slope
$\frac{8}{9}$ and y-intercept -7.

One point is worthy of emphasis. The function $f(x) = ax + b$, where $a \neq 0$,
is called a **linear function**. If we replace $f(x)$ by y, then $y = ax + b$, which is an equation of a line with slope a and y-intercept b. Thus *the graph of a linear function is a
straight line*. For example, the graph of the linear function $f(x) = 3x + 5$ is a straight
line with slope 3 and y-intercept 5. We point out that the y-intercept of the graph of a

linear function is the value of the dependent variable when the independent variable is zero.

example 4

When an object moves in a straight line with constant acceleration, its velocity v is a linear function of time t. The slope of this function is the acceleration of the object. Suppose $v = 3$ m/s when $t = 2$ s, and the acceleration is $\frac{1}{4}$ m/s².

a. Determine v as a linear function of t.

Because v is a linear function of t, it has the form $v = at + b$. The slope is $\frac{1}{4}$ and so $a = \frac{1}{4}$. Thus

$$v = \frac{1}{4}t + b.$$

To determine b in the above equation, we use the fact that $v = 3$ when $t = 2$.

$$3 = \frac{1}{4}(2) + b$$

$$\frac{5}{2} = b.$$

Thus $v = \frac{1}{4}t + \frac{5}{2}$.

b. Find the initial velocity of the object (the velocity when $t = 0$).

The v-intercept $\frac{5}{2}$ m/s gives the initial velocity of the object.

If a *vertical* line L passes through the point (a, b) [see Fig. 6-35(a)], then any other point (x, y) lies on L if and only if $x = a$. There is no restriction on y. Hence an equation for L is $x = a$. Similarly, an equation for the *horizontal* line passing through (a, b) is $y = b$ [Fig. 6-35(b)].

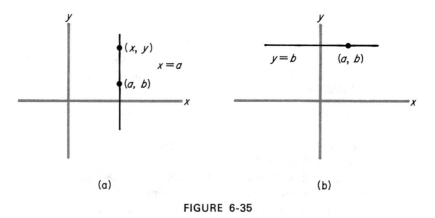

(a)   (b)

FIGURE 6-35

example 5

An equation of the vertical line passing through (5, 3) is $x = 5$ (Fig. 6-36). An equation of the horizontal line passing through (5, 3) is $y = 3$ (Fig. 6-37). An equation of the x-axis is $y = 0$, and an equation of the y-axis is $x = 0$.

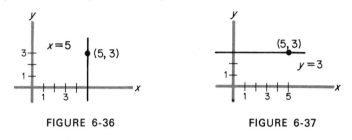

FIGURE 6-36   FIGURE 6-37

Based on our discussions, it can be shown that every straight line is the graph of an equation of the form $Ax + By + C = 0$, where A, B, and C are constants and A and B are not both zero. We call this form a **general linear equation** (or an *equation of the first degree*) **in the variables x and y**, and x and y are said to be **linearly related**. For example, a general linear equation for the line $y = 3x - 4$ is $(-3)x + (1)y + (4) = 0$. Conversely, the graph of every general linear equation is a straight line. For example, $3x + 4y + 5 = 0$ is equivalent to $y = (-\frac{3}{4})x + (-\frac{5}{4})$, so its graph is a straight line with slope $-\frac{3}{4}$ and y-intercept $-\frac{5}{4}$.

example 6

Sketch the graph of $3x - 4y + 12 = 0$.

Because this is a general linear equation, its graph is a straight line. Thus to sketch the graph, we need only to determine two different points on it. If $x = 0$, then $y = 3$, and if $y = 0$, then $x = -4$. We therefore draw the line passing through (0, 3) and (−4, 0) (Fig. 6-38). The x-coordinate of the point (−4, 0) is called the **x-intercept** of the line.

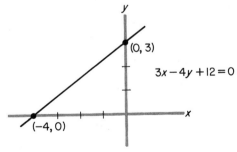

FIGURE 6-38

example 7

Fahrenheit temperature F and Celsius temperature C are linearly related. Use the facts that $32°F = 0°C$ and $212°F = 100°C$ to find an equation that relates F and C. Also, find C when $F = 50$.

Because F and C are linearly related, the graph of the equation is a straight line. In Fig. 6-39, we used F for the horizontal axis and C for the vertical. (We could just as well have used C for the independent variable.) When $F = 32$, then $C = 0$, and so (32, 0) is on the line. Likewise, (212, 100) is on it.

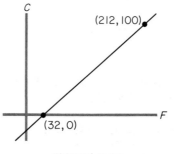

FIGURE 6-39

The slope of the line is

$$\frac{C_2 - C_1}{F_2 - F_1} = \frac{100 - 0}{212 - 32} = \frac{100}{180} = \frac{5}{9}.$$

Using a point-slope form with the point (32, 0), we get

$$C - C_1 = m(F - F_1)$$

$$C - 0 = \frac{5}{9}(F - 32)$$

$$C = \frac{5}{9}(F - 32).$$

We can use this equation to find C when $F = 50$:

$$C = \frac{5}{9}(F - 32) = \frac{5}{9}(50 - 32) = \frac{5}{9}(18) = 10.$$

Thus $50°F = 10°C$.

For your convenience, we summarize the various forms of equations of straight lines in the following table.

> **FORMS OF EQUATIONS OF STRAIGHT LINES**
>
> Point-slope form $y - y_1 = m(x - x_1)$
> Slope-intercept form $y = mx + b$
> Vertical line $x = a$
> Horizontal line $y = b$
> General linear form $Ax + By + C = 0$

Finally, we point out that if L_1 and L_2 are straight lines, then L_1 is parallel to L_2 if and only if L_1 and L_2 are vertical lines or if they have the same slope. Thus, the line $y = 3x + 5$ is parallel to the line $y = 3x - 7$, since they both have a slope of 3. Moreover, it can be shown that if L_1 and L_2 have slopes of m_1 and m_2, respectively, and $m_1 = -1/m_2$, then L_1 and L_2 are perpendicular to each other.* Thus, the line $y = -\frac{1}{3}x - 9$ is perpendicular to $y = 3x + 5$, because the slope of the first line $(m_1 = -\frac{1}{3})$ is the negative reciprocal of the slope of the second line $(m_2 = 3)$. Of course, a vertical line and a horizontal line are mutually perpendicular.

Exercise 6-4

*In Problems **1–14**, find an equation of the line satisfying the given conditions. Give your answer in slope-intercept form if possible. Sketch each line.*

1. Passes through $(1, 2)$ and has slope 6.

2. Passes through $(5, -2)$ and has slope $-\frac{1}{5}$.

3. Passes through the origin and has slope -5.

4. Passes through $(0, 2)$ and has slope $\frac{3}{5}$.

5. Passes through $(2, -5)$ and $(3, 4)$.

6. Passes through $(0, 0)$ and $(2, 3)$.

7. Passes through $(-2, 5)$ and $(3, 5)$.

8. Passes through $(2, 3)$ and $(2, 4)$.

9. Passes through $(2, 4)$ and has y-intercept 3. $\rightarrow$ $4 = m(2) + 3$

10. Passes through $(-3, 2)$ and has x-intercept -3.

11. Passes through $(7, 5)$ and is vertical.

12. Passes through $(2, 4)$ and is horizontal.

13. Passes through $(2, 1)$ and is parallel to the line $y = 2x + 3$.

14. Passes through $(-5, 4)$ and is perpendicular to the line $2y = 6x + 1$.

*This will be shown in Sec. 15-2.

In Problems 15–24, determine, if possible, the slope and y-intercept of the straight line determined by the equation and sketch the graph.

15. $y = 2x - 1$.

16. $(x - 1) + (y - 2) = 0$.

17. $3x - 8y = 8$.

18. $2y - 3 = 1$.

19. $x = -5$.

20. $x = y$.

21. $y = 1$.

22. $x - 1 = 5y + 3$.

23. $x + 2y - 3 = 0$.

24. $y - 7 = 3(x - 4)$.

In Problems 25–34, determine a general linear form $(Ax + By + C = 0)$ and the slope-intercept form of the given equation.

25. $x = -2y + 4$.

26. $3x + 2y = 6$.

27. $4x + 9y - 5 = 0$.

28. $2(x - 3) - 4(y + 2) = 8$.

29. $\frac{3}{4}x = \frac{7}{3}y + \frac{1}{4}$.

30. $\frac{y}{-2} + \frac{x}{3} = 1$.

31. $\frac{x}{2} - \frac{y}{3} = -4$.

32. $y = \frac{1}{300}x + 8$.

33. $3x + 4y - 7 = 2x + 3y - 6$.

34. $3x - 4y = 13$.

In Problems 35–38, determine the slope of the graph of the given linear function.

35. $f(x) = x + 2$.

36. $f(x) = 2x + 3$.

37. $f(x) = -3x$.

38. $f(x) = x$.

In Problems 39–48, determine if the lines are parallel, perpendicular, or neither.

39. $y = 7x + 2$, $y = 7x - 3$.

40. $y = 4x + 3$, $y = 5 + 4x$.

41. $y = 5x + 2$, $-5x + y - 3 = 0$.

42. $y = x$, $y = -x$.

43. $x + 2y + 1 = 0$, $y = 2x$.

44. $x + 2y = 0$, $x + y - 4 = 0$.

45. $y = 3$, $y = -\frac{1}{3}$.

46. $x = 3$, $x = -4$.

47. $3x + y = 4$, $3x - y + 1 = 0$.

48. $x - 1 = 0$, $y = 0$.

49. If a straight line passes through $(1, 2)$ and $(-3, 8)$, find the coordinates of the point on the line that has an abscissa of 5.

50. If a straight line has slope -3 and passes through $(4, -1)$, find the coordinates of the point on the line that has an ordinate of -2.

51. Determine whether the point $(0, -7)$ lies on the graph of the straight line passing through $(1, -3)$ and $(4, 9)$.

52. The slope of the line joining $(2, 5)$ and $(3, k)$ is 4. Find k.

53. Suppose that s and t are linearly related such that $s = 40$ when $t = 12$, and $s = 25$ when $t = 18$. Find an equation that relates s and t. Also find s when $t = 24$.

54. The force F exerted on a spring and the stretch S of the spring that the force produces are linearly related. When $F = 1$ N, then $S = 0.4$ cm. When $F = 4$ N, then $S = 1.6$ cm. Find an equation relating F and S. Also find the stretch when a force of 2 N is exerted.

55. In a circuit, the voltage V (in volts) and current i (in amperes) are linearly related. When $i = 4$, then $V = 2$; when $i = 12$, then $V = 6$. Find an equation relating V and i. Also find the voltage when the current is 10.

56. If a ball is thrown straight up in the air with an initial velocity of 50 m/s, the velocity at the end of t seconds is given by $v(t) = 50 - 9.8t$. Sketch this linear function for $0 \leq t \leq 5$.

57. The pressure P of a fixed volume of gas, in centimeters of mercury, is linearly related to temperature T, in degrees Celsius. In an experiment with dry air, it was found that $P = 90$ when $T = 40$, and that $P = 100$ when $T = 80$. Express P as a function of T.

58. When a graph of the terminal potential difference V, in volts, of a Daniell cell is plotted as a function of the current i, in amperes, delivered to an external resistor, a straight line is obtained. The slope of this line is the negative of the internal resistance of the cell. For a particular cell with an internal resistance of 0.06 ohm, it was found that $V = 0.6$ V when $i = 0.12$ A. Express V as a function of i.

59. A formula used in hydraulics is

$$Q = 3.340b^3 + 1.8704b^2x,$$

where b is a constant. (a) Is the graph of this equation a straight line? (b) If so, what is its slope when $b = 1$?

60. A coordinate map of a college campus gives the coordinates of three major buildings as follows: Computation Center $(3.5, -1)$, Engineering Lab $(0.5, 0)$, and Library $(-1, -4.5)$. Find the equations of the straight-line paths connecting (a) the Engineering Lab with the Computation Center, and (b) the Engineering Lab with the Library. (c) Show that these two paths are perpendicular.

61. When the acceleration is constant, the velocity of an object varies linearly with time. Under this condition the velocity v of a certain object is 20 m/s at $t = 1$ s, and 2 s *later* its velocity is 24 m/s. (a) Express the velocity of the object as a function of time. (b) Did the object start from rest at $t = 0$?

62. The graph in Fig. 6-40 was constructed by observing the first 10 seconds of motion of a racing car.

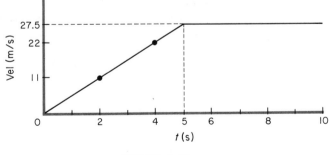

FIGURE 6-40

(a) Given that the slope of each part of the graph is the acceleration, determine the acceleration of the racing car for the intervals $0 < t < 5$ and $5 < t < 10$.

(b) Find equations for the velocity v of the car as functions of time t for these same intervals.

63. Small oscillations of a simple pendulum can be used to determine a local value of g, the acceleration due to gravity. When the *square* of the period T, the time in seconds for one complete oscillation, is plotted as a function of the length l in meters, a straight line is obtained. The slope of the line gives the value of $4\pi^2/g$. Given that $T = 1.418$ when $l = 0.5$ and $T = 1.553$ when $l = 0.6$, (a) determine the slope, and (b) find the value of g (to one decimal place).

6-5 Linear Interpolation

For a laboratory experiment in optics, suppose that you need the value of the index of refraction (n) of pure water at 31°C. In a standard reference table, you find the information shown in Table 6-1.

Table 6-1

T (°C)	n	T (°C)	n
20	1.33299	30	1.33192
22	1.33281	32	1.33164
24	1.33262	34	1.33136
26	1.33241	36	1.33107
28	1.33219	38	1.33079

Here you want an n-value for a T-value of 31, which is between two T-values in the table. This type of situation occurs often in scientific and technological work. A useful method of estimating the value of n is called **linear interpolation**. As its name implies, linear interpolation assumes that for a small change in T, the variable n is linearly related to T. In other words, we assume that for small changes in T, the graph of n as a function of T is a straight line and, therefore, n changes *uniformly*. Although this assumption is not necessarily true, the method of linear interpolation usually gives good estimates. The method is described in the following examples.

example 1

Estimate the index of refraction of water at 31°C.

The value $T = 31$°C lies between the consecutive entries 30°C and 32°C in Table 6-1. Since 31°C is half of the way from 30°C to 32°C, we assume that the value of n at

31°C is also half of the way from the *n*-value for 30°C to that for 32°. These are 1.33192 and 1.33164, respectively, which differ by 0.00028. Note that *n decreases* in value. Thus, one-half of the decrease, or $\frac{1}{2}$(0.00028) = 0.00014, must be *subtracted* from 1.33192. Therefore, at 31°C, we estimate that $n = 1.33192 - 0.00014 = 1.33178$. These results can be shown in a tabular arrangement:

$$T(°C) \qquad n$$

$$2\left[1\begin{bmatrix}30 & 1.33192 \\ 31 & ? \end{bmatrix}d \atop 32 \quad 1.33164\right]0.00028 \text{ decrease}$$

$$d = \frac{1}{2}(0.00028) = 0.00014,$$

$$n = 1.33192 - 0.00014 = 1.33178.$$

We point out that the difference *d* can also be obtained by solving the proportion

$$\frac{1}{2} = \frac{d}{0.00028}.$$

example 2

Use Table 6-1 and linear interpolation to estimate the index of refraction of water at 24.3°C.

Following the procedure used in Example 1, we write the needed information below.

$$T(°C) \qquad n$$

$$2\left[0.3\begin{bmatrix}24 & 1.33262 \\ 24.3 & ? \end{bmatrix}d \atop 26 \quad 1.33241\right]0.00021 \text{ decrease}$$

Assuming that *n* for $T = 24.3°C$ is $\frac{0.3}{2}$ of the way from 1.33262 to 1.33241, we compute $\frac{0.3}{2}$ of the decrease.

$$d = \frac{0.3}{2}(0.00021) = 0.00003,$$

where we have rounded to five decimal places. Thus, at 24.3°C,

$$n = 1.33262 - 0.00003 = 1.33259.$$

Our final example of linear interpolation will deal with the total pressure (in millimeters of mercury) of saturated steam at various temperatures, as given in Table 6-2.

Table 6-2

T (°C)	P (mm Hg)	T (°C)	P (mm Hg)	T (°C)	P (mm Hg)
0	4.579	5	6.541	10	9.205
1	4.924	6	7.011	11	9.840
2	5.290	7	7.511	12	10.513
3	5.681	8	8.042	13	11.226
4	6.097	9	8.606	14	11.980

example 3

The total pressure of saturated steam is found to be 7.821 millimeters of mercury. Estimate the temperature of the steam by using linear interpolation. Give your answer to one decimal place.

The given value of pressure, 7.821, is between the consecutive entries 7.511 and 8.042, which correspond to 7°C and 8°C, respectively. Following the same basic technique used in Examples 1 and 2, we tabulate the needed information.

$$T\,(°C) \qquad P\,(\text{mm Hg})$$

$$1\ \text{increase}\left[d\begin{bmatrix}7 \\ ? \\ 8\end{bmatrix}\begin{matrix}7.511 \\ 7.821 \\ 8.042\end{matrix}\left.0.310\right] 0.531\right.$$

The given pressure is $\dfrac{0.310}{0.531}$ of the way from the pressure for 7°C to that for 8°C.

So the desired temperature is assumed to be $\dfrac{0.310}{0.531}$ of the way from 7°C to 8°C, which differ by 1°C:

$$d = \left(\frac{0.310}{0.531}\right)(1) = 0.6,$$

when rounded to one decimal place. Because the temperature *increases* as P changes from 7.511 to 8.042, the temperature of the saturated steam is estimated to be 7°C + 0.6°C = 7.6°C.

Exercise 6-5

In Problems 1–8, use Table 6-1 and the method of linear interpolation.

1. Find *n* at 20.4°C.

2. Find *n* at 24.7°C.

3. Find *n* at 37.3°C.

4. Find n at 31.8°C.

5. If $n = 1.33253$, find T to one decimal place.

6. If $n = 1.33147$, find T to one decimal place.

7. If $n = 1.33114$, find T to one decimal place.

8. If $n = 1.33210$, find T to one decimal place.

In Problems 9–12, use Table 6-2 and the method of linear interpolation.

9. Find P at 7.3°C. 　　　　　　　　　　**10.** Find P at 11.4°C.

11. If $P = 5.436$, find T to one decimal place.

12. If $P = 9.962$, find T to one decimal place.

13. The table below gives some numbers (N) and the square of each number (N^2). Use linear interpolation to find an approximate value of the square of 90.3. By how much is your estimate in error?

N	90	91	92	93
N^2	8100	8281	8464	8649

14. Use the table in Problem 13 and linear interpolation to estimate the number having a square of 8300. Express your answer to one decimal place. Use a calculator to check the accuracy of this interpolation method.

15. When x milliliters of a 0.2-molar HCl solution are added to 25 ml of a 0.2-molar KCl solution, the pH of the resulting solution is as given in the table below.

x	33.6	26.6	20.7	16.2
pH	1.30	1.40	1.50	1.60

Using linear interpolation, estimate how many milliliters of the HCl solution are needed to give a pH of 1.43.

16. In Problem 15, if 23.2 ml of the HCl solution are used, what is the approximate pH of the resulting solution?

17. The surface tension γ (the Greek lowercase letter *gamma*) of a 34-percent solution (by volume) of alcohol in water varies with temperature as follows:

T (°C)	20	40	50
γ (10^{-2} N/m)	3.324	3.158	3.070

Use linear interpolation to estimate the temperature at which the surface tension is 3.094×10^{-2} N/m.

6-6 Review

Review Questions

1. If f is a function, the set of all input numbers is called the ____(a)____ of f. The set of all output numbers is the ____(b)____ of f.

2. The domain of the function $f(x) = x + 1/x$ consists of all real numbers except _____.

3. The sign of the abscissa of a point in the third quadrant is _____.

4. The point three units to the right of the y-axis and two units below the x-axis as coordinates _____.

5. A linear equation in x and y is one that can be written in the general form _____.

6. The line in Fig. 6-41 has a _(positive) (negative)_ slope.

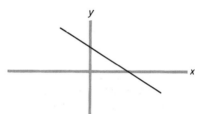

FIGURE 6-41

7. If $f(x) = -x^2 - 1$, then $f(-1) = $ __(a)__ . If $g(x) = 2$, then $g(3) = $ __(b)__ .

8. The graph of $x = 7$ is a line parallel to the _____ axis.

9. If the points $(4, 5)$ and $(2, 1)$ lie on the graph of a straight line, then the line has a slope of _____.

10. The y-intercepts of the lines $y = x$ and $y = 2x$ are __(a)__ and __(b)__, respectively.

11. A point-slope form of an equation of the line through $(2, -3)$ with slope 5 is _____.

12. The point $(2, -6)$ lies in quadrant __(a)__, while the point $(-2, 6)$ lies in quadrant __(b)__.

13. The abscissa of the point $(2, 3)$ is __(a)__ and its ordinate is __(b)__.

14. The slope of the line $y = 2x - 1$ is _____.

15. An equation of the vertical line passing through $(5, -3)$ is _____.

16. A variable representing input numbers of a function is called a(n) _(dependent)(independent)_ variable.

17. Which of the graphs in Fig. 6-42 represent functions of x? _____

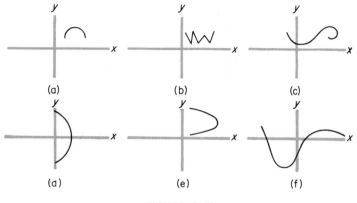

FIGURE 6-42

18. A straight line for which the slope is not defined has an equation of the form __(x = c)(y = c)__ .

19. The slope of the line $2y = 3x + 2$ is ____.

20. True or false: The value obtained for the slope of a straight line depends on which two points on the line are used for its computation. _____

21. A line for which the slope is zero is __(parallel)(perpendicular)__ to the y-axis.

22. If the line $y = kx + 4$ is parallel to the line $y = 7x + 16$, then $k = $ ____.

23. The graph of a linear function is a _____.

Answers to Review Questions

1. (a) Domain,   (b) Range.   **2.** Zero.   **3.** Negative.   **4.** $(3, -2)$.
5. $Ax + By + C = 0$, where A and B are not both zero.   **6.** Negative.
7. (a) -2,   (b) 2.   **8.** y.   **9.** 2.   **10.** (a) Zero,   (b) Zero.   **11.** $y + 3 = 5(x - 2)$.
12. (a) IV,   (b) II.   **13.** (a) 2,   (b) 3.   **14.** 2.   **15.** $x = 5$.   **16.** Independent.
17. a, b, and f.   **18.** $x = c$.   **19.** $\frac{3}{2}$.   **20.** False.   **21.** Perpendicular.   **22.** 7.
23. Straight line.

Review Problems

*In Problems **1–6**, give the domains of the functions.*

1. $f(x) = x^2 + x$.   **2.** $g(x) = 7 - x$.

3. $F(t) = \dfrac{t}{(t - 1)(t - 2)}$.   **4.** $G(x) = \dfrac{\sqrt{x}}{x - 1}$.

5. $h(x) = 4$.   **6.** $f(s) = \dfrac{\sqrt{s - 1}}{2}$.

*In Problems **7–14**, find the functional values for the given functions.*

7. $f(x) = 3x^2 - 4x + 7$; $f(0), f(-3), f(5), f(t)$.

8. $g(x) = 4$; $g(4), g(\frac{1}{100}), g(-156), g(x + 4)$.

9. $G(x) = \sqrt{x - 1}$; $G(1), G(10), G(t + 1), G(x^2)$.

10. $F(x) = \dfrac{x - 3}{x + 4}$; $F(-1), F(0), F(5), F(x + 3)$.

11. $h(u) = \dfrac{\sqrt{u + 4}}{u}$; $h(5), h(-4), h(x), h(u - 4)$.

12. $H(s) = \dfrac{(s - 4)^2}{3}$; $H(-2), H(7), H(\frac{1}{2}), H(x^2)$.

13. $f(x) = \begin{cases} 4, & \text{if } x < 2 \\ 8 - x^2, & \text{if } x > 2 \end{cases}$; $f(4), f(-2), f(0), f(10)$.

14. $h(q) = \begin{cases} q, & \text{if } -1 \leq q < 0 \\ 3 - q, & \text{if } 0 \leq q < 3; \\ 2q^2, & \text{if } 3 \leq q \leq 5 \end{cases}$ $h(0), h(4), h(-\frac{1}{2}), h(\frac{1}{2})$.

In Problems 15 and 16, for the given function find $f(x + h)$ and simplify your answer.

15. $f(x) = 3 - 7x$.

16. $f(x) = x^2 + 4$.

In Problems 17–30, graph the given equation or function.

17. $y = -3x + 4$.

18. $x = y^2$.

19. $f(t) = 5t - 4$.

20. $y = f(x) = -1 - x$.

21. $f(x) = 5$.

22. $x = 4$.

23. $2x = -y + 3$.

24. $3x + 2y - 6 = 0$.

25. $z = F(w) = \dfrac{1}{2w}$.

26. $f(p) = \sqrt{p + 3}$.

27. $y = x^2 - 2$.

28. $y = -x^2 + 2x - 1$.

29. $f(x) = \begin{cases} 1 - x, & \text{if } x \leq 0, \\ 1, & \text{if } x > 0. \end{cases}$

30. $f(x) = \frac{1}{2}|x|$.

In Problems 31–34, find the slope of the line passing through the given points.

31. $(2, 3), (-1, 4)$.

32. $(1, -1), (2, 3)$.

33. $(2, 1), (5, 1)$.

34. $(-2, 3), (3, -2)$.

In Problems 35–40, determine, if possible, the slope-intercept form and a general linear form of an equation of the straight line that has the indicated properties.

35. Passes through $(-2, 3)$ and $(4, 5)$.

36. Passes through $(-6, 2)$ and has slope 3.

37. Passes through $(3, 5)$ and is parallel to the line $9x - 3y + 14 = 0$.

38. Passes through $(2, 4)$ and is vertical.

39. Passes through $(-3, 1)$ and is horizontal.

40. Passes through $(1, 2)$ and is perpendicular to the line $-3y + 5x = 7$.

In Problems **41–46**, *determine if the lines are parallel, perpendicular, or neither.*

41. $x + 4y + 2 = 0, 8x - 2y - 2 = 0.$

42. $y - 2 = 2(x - 1), 2x + 4y - 3 = 0.$

43. $x - 3 = 2(y + 4), y = 4x + 2.$ **44.** $3x + 5y + 4 = 0, 6x + 10y = 0.$

45. $y = \frac{1}{2}x + 5, 2x = 4y - 3.$ **46.** $y = 7x, y = 7.$

In Problems **47–52**, *find the slope and y-intercept of each line.*

47. $y = 2x - 1.$ **48.** $y = -3x + 2.$ **49.** $2y = -6x + 4.$

50. $y = x.$ **51.** $y - 4x = 0.$ **52.** $x = 2y + 1.$

53. Suppose f is a linear function such that $f(1) = 5$, and $f(x)$ decreases by 4 units for every 3-unit increase in x. Find $f(x)$.

54. A line has slope 2 and y-intercept 1. Does the point $(-1, -1)$ lie on the line?

55. Suppose s and t are linearly related so that $s = 1$ when $t = 2$, and $s = 2$ when $t = 1$. Find a general linear form of an equation that relates s and t. Find s when $t = 3$.

Given the corresponding values of D, S, and C in Table 6-3, use linear interpolation in Problems **56–61**.

56. Find S and C for $D = 23.02$.   **57.** Find S and C for $D = 23.36$.

58. Find D if $S = 0.3912$.   **59.** Find D if $S = 0.3969$.

60. Find D if $C = 0.9187$.   **61.** Find D if $C = 0.9200$.

Table 6-3

D	S	C
23.0	0.3907	0.9205
23.1	0.3923	0.9198
23.2	0.3939	0.9191
23.3	0.3955	0.9184
23.4	0.3971	0.9178

62. A small aircraft weighs 17,800 N at takeoff. If the plane burns 1200 N of fuel each hour, express the weight of the plane W as a function of the time of flight t, in hours.

63. The hydrostatic pressure at a point 2 m below the surface of a body of water is 19,600 N/m². The pressure is 49,000 N/m² at a depth of 5 m. The graph of the pressure p as a function of depth d is a straight line. Find the slope of this line, which is the weight density of the water.

7

trigonometric functions and vectors

7-1 Introduction

Trigonometry is concerned in part with the relations between the angles and sides of triangles and in part with functions based on these relations. It is an indispensable mathematical tool in many of the areas of science and engineering. For example, it is used in surveying, electricity, vibrations, statics, and optics. You may already be familiar with the advantages of the indirectness of trigonometric measurement. For instance, using trigonometry we can measure the height of a cliff without ever climbing it, and we can measure the width of a river without ever crossing it.

Our study of trigonometry begins with descriptions of angles and angular measurement. Then we shall define six special functions, called trigonometric functions, for which the inputs are angles.

7-2 Angles and Angular Measurement

To begin, we consider the *half-line OA* shown in Fig. 7-1(a). The term **half-line** refers to that part of a straight line which extends indefinitely to one side of a point O on the line. If, in a plane, this half-line is rotated about its *endpoint O* to the new position OB, then an **angle** is said to be generated. We call OA the **initial side** of the angle, OB the **terminal side**, and point O the **vertex**. Greek letters, such as θ (theta), α (alpha), β (beta), and γ (gamma), are commonly used to name angles. When the rotation is

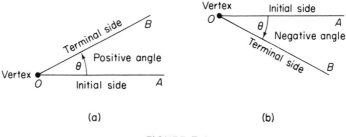

FIGURE 7-1

counterclockwise, the generated angle θ is called a **positive angle** [Fig. 7-1(a)]; when the rotation is clockwise, θ is called a **negative angle** [Fig. 7-1(b)]. In both cases note the use of arrows to indicate the direction of rotation.

When an angle θ has its vertex at the origin of a rectangular coordinate system and its initial side lies on the positive x-axis, we say that the angle is in **standard position**. Examples of angles in standard position are given in Fig. 7-2. If the terminal

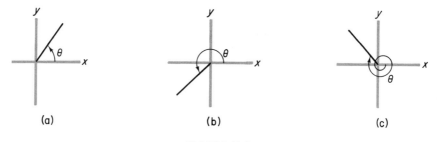

FIGURE 7-2

side of θ lies in the first quadrant, θ is called a *first-quadrant angle*, and similar names are used when terminal sides lie in the other quadrants. Figure 7-2 shows a first-quadrant angle in (a), a third-quadrant angle in (b), and a second-quadrant (negative) angle in (c). An angle with terminal side lying on an axis is called a **quadrantal angle**. The angles in Fig. 7-3 are quadrantal angles. Notice that for the first angle, the initial and terminal sides coincide.

FIGURE 7-3

When no confusion results, an angle may be referred to by the letter associated with its vertex. In Fig. 7-4(a) the angle can be called angle A, which is sometimes written with the *angle symbol* $\sphericalangle$ as $\sphericalangle A$. Similarly, in Fig. 7-4(b) the three angles of

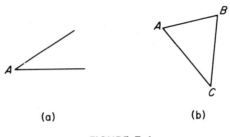

(a)   (b)

FIGURE 7-4

the triangle are angle A, angle B, and angle C. We can also name an angle by three letters, where the letter associated with the vertex is the middle letter. For example, in Fig. 7-4(b) angle A can also be called angle BAC or angle CAB. In Fig. 7-5 we can identify three angles: angle ABC, angle ABD, and angle CBD. The three-letter designation completely eliminates any confusion in identifying a particular angle. Angle ABC has also been labeled α, angle ABD has been labeled β, and angle CBD has been labeled γ.

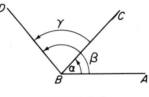

FIGURE 7-5

There are two commonly accepted units for measuring angles—*degrees* and *radians*. If a circle is divided into 360 equal arcs, then the central angle subtended by each such arc is said to have a measure of *one degree*.* Equivalently, **one degree**, written 1°, is the measure of an angle generated by $\frac{1}{360}$ of a counterclockwise revolution. Thus one counterclockwise revolution has a measure of 360°. Figure 7-6 gives the degree measure of some angles in standard position. Notice in (b) and (e) that the measure of a negative angle is preceded by a minus sign. In (b) we simply say that the angle is −45°, although we mean that the angle has a *measure* of −45°.

An angle α greater than 0° but less than 90° (that is, $0° < \alpha < 90°$) is called an **acute angle**. One between 90° and 180° (that is, $90° < \alpha < 180°$) is an **obtuse angle**. A 90° angle is called a **right angle**. See Fig. 7-7.

Because it is often necessary to measure an angle with a more precise unit than a degree, a degree is subdivided into 60 equal parts called **minutes**, and each minute is further subdivided into 60 equal parts called **seconds**. The symbol ′ is used to denote

---

*Recall that a central angle of a circle is an angle formed by two radii; that is, its vertex is at the center of the circle.

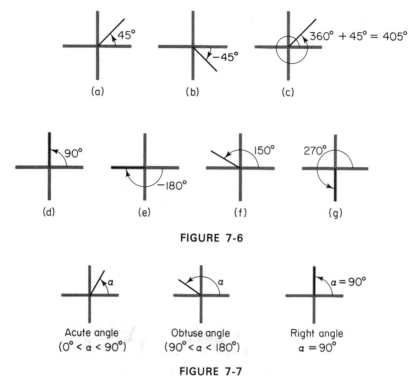

FIGURE 7-6

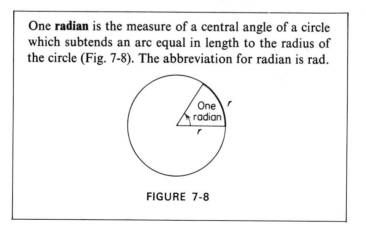

FIGURE 7-7

minutes, and the symbol '' denotes seconds. Thus $60' = 1°$ and $60'' = 1'$. We can also use decimal form. For example, $30' = (\frac{30}{60})° = 0.5°$.

The second commonly used unit for measuring an angle is the *radian*.

One **radian** is the measure of a central angle of a circle which subtends an arc equal in length to the radius of the circle (Fig. 7-8). The abbreviation for radian is rad.

One radian

r

r

FIGURE 7-8

For a circle of radius r, a central angle of 1 radian subtends an arc of length r. Thus a central angle of 2π radians subtends an arc of length $2\pi \cdot r$. But $2\pi r$ is the length of arc subtended by a central angle of 360° (that is, $2\pi r$ is the circumference). Thus

$$2\pi \text{ rad} = 360°.$$

Dividing both sides by 2, we have

$$\boxed{\pi \text{ rad} = 180°,} \tag{1}$$

which is the basic relationship between degree measure and radian measure. Dividing both sides of Eq. 1 by π gives

$$1 \text{ rad} = \frac{180°}{\pi} = 57.296° \quad \text{(approximately)}.$$

By dividing both sides of Eq. 1 by 180, we have

$$1° = \frac{\pi}{180} \text{ rad} = 0.01745 \text{ rad} \quad \text{(approximately)}.$$

When an angle is measured in radians, the word *radian* can be omitted. That is, measuring an angle in radians can be thought of as measuring the angle in terms of a number. Thus an angle of π is understood to mean π rad; similarly, $\theta = 1$ means that $\theta = 1$ rad. You must, however, always include the degree symbol if that unit of measure is used. We point out that the SI preferred unit for measuring angles is the radian, although degree measure is acceptable. When degrees are used, however, the use of calculators makes it convenient to give any parts of degrees in decimal form. We shall adopt that convention. For example, we shall write 23.15° rather than 23° 9'.

By using Eq. 1, we can convert degree measure to radian measure, and vice versa, as the following examples show.

example 1

a. Convert 30° to radians.

Because π rad $= 180°$, dividing both sides by 180° gives $\frac{\pi \text{ rad}}{180°} = 1$. Thus

$$30° = 30°(1) = 30°\left(\frac{\pi \text{ rad}}{180°}\right).$$

On the right side, the degree units cancel and we are left with radians:

$$30° = 30°\left(\frac{\pi \text{ rad}}{180°}\right) = \frac{30\pi}{180} \text{ rad} = \frac{\pi}{6} \text{ rad} \approx 0.5236 \text{ rad}.$$

Note that $\pi/6$ rad is an exact answer, while 0.5236 rad is an approximation. The decimal result was obtained by using the approximation $\pi \approx 3.14159$. The π key found on many calculators is useful when a decimal answer is required. In many instances an answer in terms of π is not only acceptable, it is preferred.

b. Convert $-240°$ to radians.

$$-240° = -240°\left(\frac{\pi}{180°}\right) = -\frac{4\pi}{3}.$$

example 2

a. Convert $\frac{\pi}{4}$ rad to degrees.

Because π rad $= 180°$, dividing both sides by π rad gives $1 = \frac{180°}{\pi\,\text{rad}}$. Thus

$$\frac{\pi}{4}\,\text{rad} = \frac{\pi}{4}\,\text{rad} \cdot (1) = \frac{\pi}{4}\,\text{rad} \cdot \frac{180°}{\pi\,\text{rad}}.$$

On the right side, the radian units cancel and we are left with degrees:

$$\frac{\pi}{4}\,\text{rad} = \frac{\pi}{4}\,\text{rad} \cdot \frac{180°}{\pi\,\text{rad}} = 45°.$$

b. Convert $-\frac{5\pi}{6}$ rad to degrees.

$$-\frac{5\pi}{6} = -\frac{5\pi}{6}\left(\frac{180°}{\pi}\right) = -150°.$$

c. Convert an angle of 10 to degrees.

$$10 = 10\left(\frac{180°}{\pi}\right) = \left(\frac{1800}{\pi}\right)°.$$

In decimal form we have 10 rad $\approx 572.96°$, which you should verify.

Using radian measure, we can derive a formula for the length of a circular arc. Figure 7-9 shows a circle of radius r on which an arc of length s is subtended by the central angle θ, where θ is in radians. Recall that each angle of 1 rad subtends an

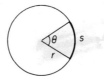

FIGURE 7-9

arc of length r. Thus an angle of θ rad subtends an arc of length θr. But in Fig. 7-9 that length is s. Thus $s = \theta r$.

> The length s of the arc subtended on a circle of radius r by a central angle θ is given by
> $$s = r\theta,$$
> where θ is in radians.

example 3

a. Find the length of the arc subtended by a central angle of 60° on a circle of radius 10 m.

To use the formula for arc length, we must first convert 60° to radians.

$$60° = 60° \cdot \frac{\pi}{180°} = \frac{\pi}{3}.$$

The arc length is given by

$$s = r\theta = (10 \text{ m})\left(\frac{\pi}{3}\right) = \frac{10\pi}{3} \text{ m} = 10.47 \text{ m}.$$

In the last line you can see that writing the value of θ as the number $\frac{\pi}{3}$ rather than $\frac{\pi}{3}$ rad results in a unit that is meaningful.

b. On a circle of radius 6 m, the arc subtended by a central angle θ has length 24 m. Find θ.

Because $s = r\theta$,

$$24 \text{ m} = (6 \text{ m})\theta$$

$$\theta = \frac{24 \text{ m}}{6 \text{ m}} = 4.$$

When the terminal sides of two or more angles in standard position coincide, the angles are said to be **coterminal angles**. For example, some pairs of coterminal angles are 30° and 390° [Fig. 7-10(a)], 30° and −330° [Fig. 7-10(b)], 0° and 360°, and 270° and −90°. Although the coterminal angles 30° and 390° in Fig. 7-10(a) may *look*

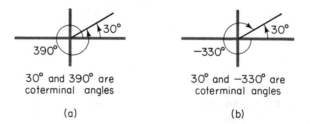

30° and 390° are coterminal angles

(a)

30° and −330° are coterminal angles

(b)

FIGURE 7-10

the same, they are not equal angles; 390° is one revolution more than 30°. For a given angle θ, there are infinitely many positive angles and infinitely many negative angles that are coterminal with θ. These angles can be obtained by adding or subtracting a multiple of 360° (or 2π) to or from θ.

example 4

a. Find two positive and two negative angles that are coterminal with 10°.

One counterclockwise revolution beyond 10° yields an angle of $10° + 360° = 370°$. An additional revolution yields $10° + 2(360°) = 730°$ (Fig. 7-11). One clockwise revolution from a position of 10° gives an angle of $10° - 360° = -350°$. A second clockwise revolution gives $10° - 2(360°) = -710°$ (Fig. 7-12).

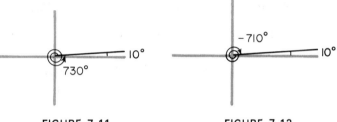

FIGURE 7-11   FIGURE 7-12

b. Find the angle θ that is coterminal with $16\pi/3$, such that $0 \le \theta < 2\pi$.

Because $16\pi/3 \ge 2\pi$, we shall keep subtracting 2π from $16\pi/3$ until we reach an angle between 0 and 2π.

$$\frac{16\pi}{3} - 2\pi = \frac{16\pi}{3} - \frac{6\pi}{3} = \frac{10\pi}{3}.$$

Because $10\pi/3 \ge 2\pi$, we continue.

$$\frac{10\pi}{3} - 2\pi = \frac{10\pi}{3} - \frac{6\pi}{3} = \frac{4\pi}{3}.$$

Now, $0 \le \frac{4\pi}{3} < 2\pi$ and $\frac{4\pi}{3}$ is coterminal with $\frac{16\pi}{3}$. Thus $\theta = \frac{4\pi}{3}$.

Exercise 7-2

*In Problems **1–20**, convert each degree measure to radians and each radian measure to degrees. Give an exact answer. Draw each angle in standard position.*

1. 60°.

2. 135°.

3. $\dfrac{3\pi}{4}$.

4. $\dfrac{2\pi}{3}$.

5. $\dfrac{\pi}{2}$.

6. $-\dfrac{3\pi}{4}$.

7. 45°.

8. 210°.

9. $-330°$.   **10.** $-270°$.   **11.** $\dfrac{7\pi}{6}$.   **12.** $15°$.

13. $-\dfrac{\pi}{8}$.   **14.** $\dfrac{5\pi}{6}$.   **15.** $720°$.   **16.** $\dfrac{3\pi}{2}$.

17. 6π.   **18.** $\dfrac{7\pi}{8}$.   **19.** 4.   **20.** $\dfrac{1}{2}$.

*In Problems **21–36**, determine whether the angle is quadrantal, or a first-, second-, third-, or fourth-quadrant angle.*

21. $130°$.   **22.** $\dfrac{\pi}{3}$.   **23.** $-45°$.   **24.** $90°$.

25. $\dfrac{5\pi}{6}$.   **26.** $250°$.   **27.** $-\pi$.   **28.** $-\dfrac{\pi}{4}$.

29. $370°$.   **30.** 0.   **31.** $210°$.   **32.** $\dfrac{2\pi}{3}$.

33. 4π.   **34.** $\pi°$.   **35.** $-\dfrac{\pi}{6}$.   **36.** $270°$.

*In Problems **37–40**, determine θ in the given figure.*

37.
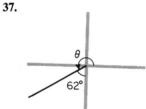

FIGURE 7-13

38.
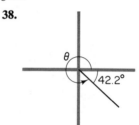

FIGURE 7-14

39.

FIGURE 7-15

40.
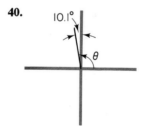

FIGURE 7-16

*In Problems **41–48**, find two positive angles and two negative angles that are coterminal with the given angle.*

41. $\theta = 35°$.   **42.** $\theta = 480°$.   **43.** $\theta = 221.4°$.   **44.** $\theta = 90°$.

45. $\theta = -70°$.   **46.** $\theta = -115°$.   **47.** $\theta = \dfrac{\pi}{6}$.   **48.** $\theta = \dfrac{2\pi}{3}$.

*In Problems **49–54**, find the angle θ that is coterminal with the given angle and meets the given condition.*

49. 420°; 0° ≤ θ < 360°.   **50.** 1080°; 0° ≤ θ < 360°.

51. $\frac{13\pi}{4}$; 0 ≤ θ < 2π.   **52.** $\frac{15\pi}{3}$; 0 ≤ θ < 2π.

53. $\frac{17\pi}{2}$; 0 ≤ θ < 2π.   **54.** $-\frac{5\pi}{6}$; 0 ≤ θ < 2π.

*In Problems **55–62**, give all answers to three decimal places. Assume that π = 3.14159 or use the π key on your calculator.*

55. Convert 35° to radians.   **56.** Convert 212° to radians.

57. Convert 84.23° to radians.   **58.** Convert 19.601° to radians.

59. Convert 2.36 rad to degrees.   **60.** Convert −5.23 rad to degrees.

61. Convert −3.742 rad to degrees.   **62.** Convert 17.031 rad to degrees.

*In Problems **63–66**, determine the length of the arc subtended by the central angle θ of a circle of radius r. Give your answers to two decimal places.*

63. $\theta = \frac{\pi}{6}$, r = 13 km.   **64.** $\theta = \frac{\pi}{3}$, r = 25 m.

65. θ = 45°, r = 18 cm.   **66.** θ = 225°, r = 5 km.

*In Problems **67** and **68**, determine θ in the given figure.*

67.

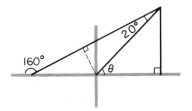

FIGURE 7-17

68.

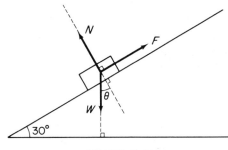

FIGURE 7-18

69. Convert 7.26 radians per second to revolutions per minute.

70. Through how many radians does the minute hand of a clock rotate in 40 minutes? In 40 hours?

71. When a spectrometer is used to view the spectral lines of a light source, a doublet (two spectral lines representing light of nearly equal wavelengths) is observed at angular positions 121.99° and 122.04°. What is the angular separation of the two lines in radians?

72. A certain telescope is designed so that it can distinguish two points 1.0 cm apart at a distance of 1.6 km. The angular separation of the two points at that distance is 6.25×10^{-6} rad. What is the angular separation in degrees?

73. The angle θ (in radians) through which the rotor of a motor has turned is given by $\theta = \omega t$, where t is elapsed time in seconds and ω (omega) is the angular speed in radians per second. If a motor makes 600 revolutions per minute, find the angle through which the rotor turns in 2.0 s.

74. The sensitivity of a certain measuring instrument is given as 10 μA per degree deflection. What is the sensitivity in amperes per radian?

75. Suppose that a pendulum of length 20 cm swings through an arc of length 12 cm. Through how many degrees does the pendulum swing?

76. The minute hand of a clock is 6 cm long. In a time period of 50 min, through what distance does the tip of the minute hand move?

77. An engineer is to design a cloverleaf for an exit on an interstate road. A part of the cloverleaf can be thought of as an arc of a circle of radius 300 m. The central angle of this arc is 120°. Find the length of this part of the cloverleaf.

7-3   Trigonometric Functions of Acute Angles

The entire realm of trigonometry is based on six special functions, called the *trigonometric functions,* for which the inputs are angles and the outputs are numbers. We shall first consider these functions for an acute angle; later in this chapter we shall give a complete treatment for any angle.

Suppose we have an acute angle θ in standard position, as shown in Fig. 7-19. On the terminal side we choose *any* point $P(x, y)$ except the origin. The distance from the origin to P is denoted by r, where $r > 0$, and is called the **radius vector**. By constructing a perpendicular from P to the x-axis, we see that r is the length of the hypotenuse of a right triangle in which the other sides have lengths x and y. This triangle is called the **reference triangle** for θ. By the Pythagorean theorem,

$$r^2 = x^2 + y^2,$$

from which

$$r = \sqrt{x^2 + y^2}.$$

Thus with point P there are associated three numbers—its abscissa x, its ordinate y, and the radius vector r—and from these numbers six ratios can be formed. It

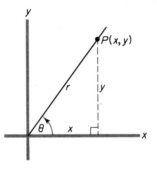

FIGURE 7-19

is these ratios that define the trigonometric functions of θ. Their names (and abbreviations) are **sine** function (**sin**), **cosine** function (**cos**), **tangent** function (**tan**), **cotangent** function (**cot**), **secant** function (**sec**), and **cosecant** function (**csc**). Just as the output of a function f is written $f(x)$, the output of the sine function is written $\sin(\theta)$, or simply $\sin \theta$. The functions are defined as follows.

TRIGONOMETRIC FUNCTIONS

Suppose θ is in standard position. Let (x, y) be any point on the terminal side except $(0, 0)$, and let $r = \sqrt{x^2 + y^2}$. Then

$$\sin \theta = \frac{y}{r},$$

$$\cos \theta = \frac{x}{r},$$

$$\tan \theta = \frac{y}{x},$$

$$\cot \theta = \frac{x}{y},$$

$$\sec \theta = \frac{r}{x},$$

$$\csc \theta = \frac{r}{y}.$$

Notice that the inputs are angles and the outputs are numbers (provided the denominators are not zero).

The value of each trigonometric function depends only on the angle θ and not upon the choice of the point $P(x, y)$ on the terminal side of θ. To see why, let $P_1(x_1, y_1)$ be any other point (except the origin) on the terminal side of θ. In Fig. 7-20 the triangles OAP and OBP_1 are similar triangles, because their corresponding angles

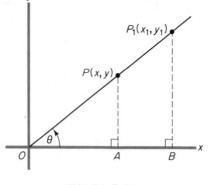

FIGURE 7-20

are equal. From geometry, the lengths of corresponding sides of similar triangles are proportional. It follows that for any ratio formed by the sides of triangle OAP, the corresponding ratio from triangle OBP_1 will be equal to it. For example,

$$\frac{y}{x} = \frac{y_1}{x_1}.$$

Thus, for a given angle θ, the ratios are independent of the choice of (x, y). As a result, the definition in the previous box associates the unique number $\tan\theta$ with a given angle θ and in this sense defines a function $f(\theta) = \tan\theta$. A similar statement could be made for each of the other trigonometric functions.

example 1

If the terminal side of an acute angle θ in standard position passes through the point $(6, 8)$, find the values of the six trigonometric functions of θ (Fig. 7-21).

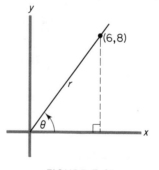

FIGURE 7-21

We use the point $(6, 8)$ as the point (x, y) on the terminal side of θ. Thus $x = 6$, $y = 8$, and

$$r = \sqrt{x^2 + y^2} = \sqrt{6^2 + 8^2} = \sqrt{100} = 10.$$

Applying the definitions of the trigonometric functions of θ, we have

$$\sin \theta = \frac{y}{r} = \frac{8}{10} = \frac{4}{5},$$

$$\cos \theta = \frac{x}{r} = \frac{6}{10} = \frac{3}{5},$$

$$\tan \theta = \frac{y}{x} = \frac{8}{6} = \frac{4}{3},$$

$$\cot \theta = \frac{x}{y} = \frac{6}{8} = \frac{3}{4},$$

$$\sec \theta = \frac{r}{x} = \frac{10}{6} = \frac{5}{3},$$

$$\csc \theta = \frac{r}{y} = \frac{10}{8} = \frac{5}{4}.$$

Many important relationships exist between the trigonometric functions. From their definitions and our knowledge of reciprocals, it follows that

$$\sin \theta = \frac{y}{r} = \frac{1}{\frac{r}{y}} = \frac{1}{\csc \theta}.$$

Similarly, we can obtain the following reciprocal relations.

RECIPROCAL RELATIONS

$$\sin \theta = \frac{1}{\csc \theta} \quad \text{and} \quad \csc \theta = \frac{1}{\sin \theta}.$$

$$\cos \theta = \frac{1}{\sec \theta} \quad \text{and} \quad \sec \theta = \frac{1}{\cos \theta}.$$

$$\tan \theta = \frac{1}{\cot \theta} \quad \text{and} \quad \cot \theta = \frac{1}{\tan \theta}.$$

To describe these results we say that the sine and cosecant, the cosine and secant, and the tangent and cotangent functions are pairs of **reciprocal functions**. This means, for example, that if $\sin \theta = 0.5$, then $\csc \theta = 1/0.5 = 2$. Similarly, if $\cos \theta = 2/3$, then $\sec \theta = 3/2$. We encourage you to verify the reciprocal relations for the results of Example 1.

We can obtain two more important relationships. Because $\sin \theta = y/r$ and $\cos \theta = x/r$, then

$$\frac{\sin \theta}{\cos \theta} = \frac{\frac{y}{r}}{\frac{x}{r}} = \frac{y}{r} \cdot \frac{r}{x} = \frac{y}{x} = \tan \theta.$$

Similarly, $(\cos \theta)/(\sin \theta) = \cot \theta.$

$$\tan \theta = \frac{\sin \theta}{\cos \theta} \quad \text{and} \quad \cot \theta = \frac{\cos \theta}{\sin \theta}.$$

Thus if $\sin \theta = 0.3420$ and $\cos \theta = 0.9397$, then $\tan \theta = 0.3420/0.9397 = 0.3639$.

Trigonometric function values for an acute angle θ of a right triangle can be conveniently interpreted in terms of the sides of the right triangle. Suppose that we wish to find these values for θ in Fig. 7-22(a). By appropriate positioning of the

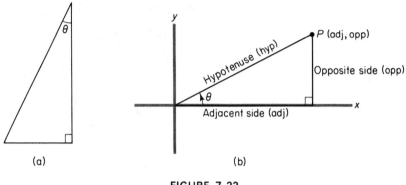

(a)   (b)

FIGURE 7-22

triangle, we can place θ in standard position as shown in Fig. 7-22(b). Observe that the abscissa of point P on the terminal side of θ is equal to the length of the side that is *adjacent* to θ, and the ordinate is equal to the length of the side that is *opposite* θ. The length of the *hypotenuse* is r. Thus the trigonometric values of θ can be given in term of these sides.

$$\sin \theta = \frac{\text{opposite side}}{\text{hypotenuse}} \qquad \csc \theta = \frac{\text{hypotenuse}}{\text{opposite side}}$$

$$\cos \theta = \frac{\text{adjacent side}}{\text{hypotenuse}} \qquad \sec \theta = \frac{\text{hypotenuse}}{\text{adjacent side}}$$

$$\tan \theta = \frac{\text{opposite side}}{\text{adjacent side}} \qquad \cot \theta = \frac{\text{adjacent side}}{\text{opposite side}}$$

With these relations we can determine the values of the trigonometric functions of an acute angle θ of a right triangle without directly considering θ in standard position.

example 2

Find the values of the six trigonometric functions of angles A and B in Fig. 7-23.

The hypotenuse has length r, where

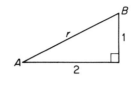

FIGURE 7-23

$$r = \sqrt{1^2 + 2^2} = \sqrt{5}.$$

For angle A, the opposite side has length 1 (unit) and the adjacent side has length 2. We shall find sin A, cos A, and tan A, and then use the reciprocal relations for cot A, sec A, and csc A. We have:

$$\sin A = \frac{\text{opp}}{\text{hyp}} = \frac{1}{\sqrt{5}}, \qquad \csc A = \frac{1}{\sin A} = \frac{1}{1/\sqrt{5}} = \sqrt{5},$$

$$\cos A = \frac{\text{adj}}{\text{hyp}} = \frac{2}{\sqrt{5}}, \qquad \sec A = \frac{1}{\cos A} = \frac{1}{2/\sqrt{5}} = \frac{\sqrt{5}}{2},$$

$$\tan A = \frac{\text{opp}}{\text{adj}} = \frac{1}{2}, \qquad \cot A = \frac{1}{\tan A} = \frac{1}{1/2} = 2.$$

For angle B, the opposite side has length 2 and the adjacent side has length 1.

$$\sin B = \frac{\text{opp}}{\text{hyp}} = \frac{2}{\sqrt{5}}. \qquad \csc B = \frac{1}{\sin B} = \frac{1}{2/\sqrt{5}} = \frac{\sqrt{5}}{2},$$

$$\cos B = \frac{\text{adj}}{\text{hyp}} = \frac{1}{\sqrt{5}}, \qquad \sec B = \frac{1}{\cos B} = \frac{1}{1/\sqrt{5}} = \sqrt{5},$$

$$\tan B = \frac{\text{opp}}{\text{adj}} = \frac{2}{1} = 2, \qquad \cot B = \frac{1}{\tan B} = \frac{1}{2}.$$

For any right triangle, the sum of the acute angles is 90°; that is, the acute angles are **complementary**. In Fig. 7-23, angles A and B are complementary. Notice in Fig. 7-23 that the side opposite A is adjacent to B; the side adjacent to A is opposite B. Thus sin A = cos B, tan A = cot B, sec A = csc B, and so on. The pairs of functions sine and cosine, tangent and cotangent, and secant and cosecant are called **cofunctions**. We draw the following conclusion.

> A trigonometric function of an acute angle θ is equal to the corresponding cofunction of the complementary angle, $90° - \theta$.

For example, sin 10° = cos 80° and sec 30° = csc 60°. Do not confuse cofunction relationships with reciprocal relationships. For example, sin 30° = cos 60° and sin 30° = 1/csc 30°.

example 3

Find the values of the six trigonometric functions of the acute angle θ if $\cos \theta = \frac{5}{7}$.

A right triangle containing an angle θ which has cosine of $\frac{5}{7}$ is shown in Fig. 7-24. The adjacent side of θ has length 5 and the hypotenuse has length 7. The opposite side of θ has length y, where

$$5^2 + y^2 = 7^2$$
$$y^2 = 49 - 25 = 24$$
$$y = \sqrt{24} = \sqrt{4}\sqrt{6} = 2\sqrt{6}.$$

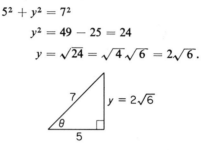

FIGURE 7-24

Thus

$$\sin \theta = \frac{2\sqrt{6}}{7}, \qquad \csc \theta = \frac{7}{2\sqrt{6}} = \frac{7\sqrt{6}}{12},$$

$$\cos \theta = \frac{5}{7}, \qquad \sec \theta = \frac{7}{5},$$

$$\tan \theta = \frac{2\sqrt{6}}{5}, \qquad \cot \theta = \frac{5}{2\sqrt{6}} = \frac{5\sqrt{6}}{12}.$$

Note that $\csc \theta$ and $\cot \theta$ are given with rationalized denominators.

Exercise 7-3

In Problems 1–14, determine the values of the six trigonometric functions of an angle θ in standard position if the terminal side of θ passes through the given point. Give all answers in rationalized form.

1. $(8, 6)$.
2. $(12, 5)$.
3. $(3, 4)$.
4. $(4, 3)$.
5. $(1, \sqrt{3})$.
6. $(\sqrt{3}, 1)$.
7. $(\sqrt{5}, 2)$.
8. $(2, 3)$.
9. $(3, \sqrt{3})$.
10. $(1, 7)$.
11. $(1, 1)$.
12. $(5, 12)$.
13. $(\sqrt{2}, 1)$.
14. $(\sqrt{15}, 1)$.

In Problems 15–18, the value of a trigonometric function of an acute angle θ is given. Find the values of the remaining trigonometric functions of θ.

15. $\sin \theta = \frac{2}{5}$.

16. $\cos \theta = \frac{2}{3}$.

17. $\tan \theta = 4 = \dfrac{4}{1}$.

18. $\sec \theta = \dfrac{5}{4}$.

19. If $\sin \theta = 0.6$ and $\cos \theta = 0.8$, find $\tan \theta$ and $\sec \theta$ in an easy way.

20. If $\sin \theta = \sqrt{2}/2$ and $\cos \theta = \sqrt{2}/2$, find $\cot \theta$ in an easy way.

In Problems 21 and 22, find values of the six trigonometric functions of angles A and B in the given figure.

21. See Fig. 7-25(a).

22. See Fig. 7-25(b).

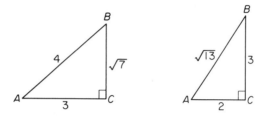

FIGURE 7-25

In Problems 23–28, give a reason why the given statement is true.

23. $\sin 35° = \cos 55°$.

24. $\sin \dfrac{\pi}{4} = \cos \dfrac{\pi}{4}$.

25. $\tan 2° = \dfrac{1}{\cot 2°}$.

26. $\sin \dfrac{\pi}{4} = \dfrac{1}{\csc (\pi/4)}$.

27. $\tan 0.32 = \dfrac{\sin 0.32}{\cos 0.32}$.

28. $\sec 1 = \dfrac{1}{\cos 1}$.

29. If $\sin \theta = 0.9659$ and $\cos \theta = 0.2588$, find the value of $\tan \theta$.

7-4 Values of the Trigonometric Functions

By using geometry we can find the exact values of the trigonometric functions of 30°, 45°, and 60°, which are called **special angles**.

Figure 7-26(a) shows an equilateral triangle, in which each side has a length of two units. Each angle must be 60°. The bisector of any of these angles will also be the perpendicular bisector of the side opposite the angle, and Fig. 7-26(b) shows the result of constructing such a bisector. The length b of the bisector is found by

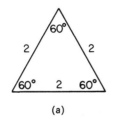

(a)

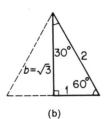

(b)

FIGURE 7-26

the Pythagorean theorem:

$$2^2 = 1^2 + b^2 \quad \text{and thus} \quad b = \sqrt{4-1} = \sqrt{3}.$$

By considering the right triangles in Fig. 7-27, which were obtained from Fig. 7-26(b), we can immediately find values for the trigonometric functions of 30° and 60°. For example,

$$\sin 30° = \frac{\text{opp}}{\text{hyp}} = \frac{1}{2}, \quad \cos 30° = \frac{\text{adj}}{\text{hyp}} = \frac{\sqrt{3}}{2}, \quad \text{and so on,}$$

and

$$\sin 60° = \frac{\text{opp}}{\text{hyp}} = \frac{\sqrt{3}}{2}, \quad \cos 60° = \frac{\text{adj}}{\text{hyp}} = \frac{1}{2}, \quad \text{and so on.}$$

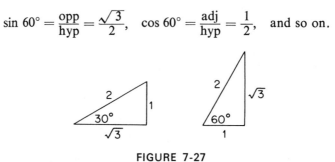

FIGURE 7-27

We can do the same type of thing for 45°. Figure 7-28(a) is a square, in which each side has a length of one unit. From geometry, the diagonal of a square forms angles of 45° with the sides of the square. By the Pythagorean theorem, the length d

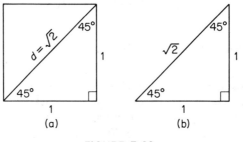

(a)   (b)

FIGURE 7-28

of the diagonal is given by

$$d^2 = 1^2 + 1^2$$
$$d = \sqrt{2}.$$

From Fig. 7-28(b) we obtain, for example,

$$\sin 45° = \frac{\text{opp}}{\text{hyp}} = \frac{1}{\sqrt{2}} = \frac{\sqrt{2}}{2}.$$

The results of the preceding discussion of special angles are summarized in Table 7-1. These angles occur so frequently that you should become totally familiar with these results. Rather than memorize the table, however, we suggest that you memorize the triangles from which the results were obtained and use them in conjunction with the definitions of the trigonometric functions. The important triangles are repeated for your convenience in Fig. 7-29. Because 30° and 60° are complementary and the values of cofunctions of complementary angles are equal, we have sin 30° = cos 60°, and so on.

Table 7-1

		$30° \left(or \ \frac{\pi}{6} \right)$	$45° \left(or \ \frac{\pi}{4} \right)$	$60° \left(or \ \frac{\pi}{3} \right)$
sin	$\dfrac{opp}{hyp}$	$\dfrac{1}{2}$	$\dfrac{1}{\sqrt{2}} = \dfrac{\sqrt{2}}{2}$	$\dfrac{\sqrt{3}}{2}$
cos	$\dfrac{adj}{hyp}$	$\dfrac{\sqrt{3}}{2}$	$\dfrac{1}{\sqrt{2}} = \dfrac{\sqrt{2}}{2}$	$\dfrac{1}{2}$
tan	$\dfrac{opp}{adj}$	$\dfrac{1}{\sqrt{3}} = \dfrac{\sqrt{3}}{3}$	$\dfrac{1}{1} = 1$	$\dfrac{\sqrt{3}}{1} = \sqrt{3}$
cot	$\dfrac{adj}{opp}$	$\dfrac{\sqrt{3}}{1} = \sqrt{3}$	$\dfrac{1}{1} = 1$	$\dfrac{1}{\sqrt{3}} = \dfrac{\sqrt{3}}{3}$
sec	$\dfrac{hyp}{adj}$	$\dfrac{2}{\sqrt{3}} = \dfrac{2\sqrt{3}}{3}$	$\dfrac{\sqrt{2}}{1} = \sqrt{2}$	$\dfrac{2}{1} = 2$
csc	$\dfrac{hyp}{opp}$	$\dfrac{2}{1} = 2$	$\dfrac{\sqrt{2}}{1} = \sqrt{2}$	$\dfrac{2}{\sqrt{3}} = \dfrac{2\sqrt{3}}{3}$

FIGURE 7-29

Trigonometric Functions on a Calculator

We will obtain the values of the trigonometric functions of most angles by using a calculator.* Some calculators have only a decimal-degree mode; others can be set either for decimal-degree measure or for radian measure. If yours accepts degree measure only and an angle is given in radians, it will be necessary for you first to convert from radians to degrees. Now is a good time to determine exactly what

*Trigonometric tables are discussed in Sec. 7-9 and are found in Appendix B.

modes your calculator can handle and to learn how to use them. The information in Appendix A may be a helpful supplement to the manual that came with your calculator.

Assuming that the calculator is in decimal-degree mode, with some calculators we would find the trigonometric values of 28.4° by keying in 28.4 and then pressing the key for the desired trigonometric function. For example, to four decimal places we have

$$\sin 28.4° = 0.4756.$$

(For mathematical exactness the statement should be $\sin 28.4° \approx 0.4756$.) Similarly,

$$\cos 28.4° = 0.8796 \quad \text{and} \quad \tan 28.4° = 0.5407,$$

which you should verify. Most calculators do not have keys for cotangent, secant, and cosecant. Instead, you must use the reciprocal relations $\cot \theta = 1/(\tan \theta)$, and so on. A reciprocal key $(1/x)$ is useful here. You should verify that

$$\cot 28.4° = \frac{1}{\tan 28.4°} = 1.8495,$$

$$\sec 28.4° = \frac{1}{\cos 28.4°} = 1.1368,$$

$$\csc 28.4° = \frac{1}{\sin 28.4°} = 2.1025.$$

To find the value of a trigonometric function of an angle in radians, either place the calculator in radian mode (if possible) and proceed as above, or multiply the angle by $180/\pi$ and proceed as above. You should verify that

$$\sin 0.3053 = 0.3006 \quad \text{and} \quad \tan 1.1694 = 2.3560.$$

To find an acute angle when you are given the value of one of its trigonometric functions, use the keys marked $\sin^{-1}$, $\cos^{-1}$, $\tan^{-1}$, which are read *arc sine*, *arc cosine*, and *arc tangent*, respectively.* For example, if $\sin \theta = 0.5209$, enter 0.5209 and use the $\sin^{-1}$ key. This gives $\theta = 31.4°$ (to one decimal place) or $\theta = 0.55$ rad (to two decimal places). Similarly, if $\cot \theta = 1.419$, then $\tan \theta = 1/1.419$ from which $\theta = 35.2°$.

example 1

Figure 7-30 shows the reflected and refracted rays when light strikes (or is *incident on*) a glass plate of refractive index n. Snell's law states that $\sin \theta_1 = n \sin \theta_2$, where θ_1 and θ_2 are measured from the line perpendicular to the glass surface as indicated. If $\theta_1 = 53.4°$ and $\theta_2 = 32.3°$, find the refractive index of the glass.

*These functions will be discussed more fully in Chapter 14. With some calculators having no $\sin^{-1}$ key, for example, an INV key is used with the sin key. We also speak of $\sin^{-1}$ as the "inverse sine."

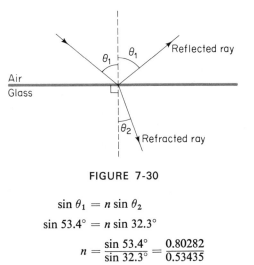

FIGURE 7-30

$$\sin \theta_1 = n \sin \theta_2$$
$$\sin 53.4° = n \sin 32.3°$$
$$n = \frac{\sin 53.4°}{\sin 32.3°} = \frac{0.80282}{0.53435}$$
$$= 1.50.$$

example 2

When a beam of electrons moving in a transparent medium travels at a speed that is greater than the speed of light in that medium, visible radiation, called Cerenkov radiation, is emitted at an angle θ to the direction of motion of the electrons, where

$$\cos \theta = \frac{c}{nv}.$$

Here c is the speed of light in vacuum, n is the index of refraction of the medium, and v is the speed of the electrons. For a particular crystal, suppose that $n = 1.785$ and $v = 0.5711c$. Find θ.

$$\cos \theta = \frac{c}{nv} = \frac{c}{(1.785)(0.5711c)} = 0.9810$$
$$\theta = 11.2°.$$

Finally, we point out that we abbreviate $(\sin \theta)^2$ by writing $\sin^2 \theta$ (read *sine squared theta*). Similar abbreviations are used with the other trigonometric functions.

Exercise 7-4

In Problems 1–18, find the the values of the given trigonometric functions. Give all answers to four decimal places.

1. $\sin 32°$.   **2.** $\cos 75°$.   **3.** $\cos 14.3°$.

4. $\sin 32.4°$.   **5.** $\tan 53.04°$.   **6.** $\tan 0.66°$.

7. cot 12.4°.   **8.** sec 79.16°.   **9.** sec 45.11°.

10. csc 80.25°.   **11.** csc 33.01°.   **12.** cot 74.129°.

13. sin 0.6109.   **14.** csc 0.6109.   **15.** cos 1.1606.

16. sec 1.1606.   **17.** tan 0.8901.   **18.** cot 0.8901.

In each of Problems 19–22, find the acute angle θ, in degrees, subject to the given condition. Give your answer to one decimal place.

19. $\sin \theta = 0.7269$.   **20.** $\csc \theta = 8.206$.   **21.** $\cos \theta = 0.1249$.

22. $\sec \theta = 1.054$.   **23.** $\cot \theta = 1.6247$.   **24.** $\tan \theta = 0.8847$.

In each of Problems 25–28, find the acute angle θ, in radians, subject to the given condition. Give your answer to two decimal places.

25. $\sin \theta = 0.2979$.   **26.** $\cos \theta = 0.6648$.

27. $\tan \theta = 2.723$.   **28.** $\cot \theta = 0.3346$.

29. Find the exact value of $\cos^2 \dfrac{\pi}{4}$.

30. Find the exact value of $\left(\sin \dfrac{\pi}{3}\right)\left(\cos \dfrac{\pi}{3}\right)$.

31. Find the exact value of $(\sin 30°)(\cos 60°) + (\cos 30°)(\sin 60°)$.

32. Find the exact value of $\sin^2 \dfrac{\pi}{4} + \cos^2 \dfrac{\pi}{4}$.

33. If light is incident on glass of refractive index $n = 1.60$ at an angle $\theta_1 = 30.3°$, find the angle θ_2 that the refracted ray makes with the perpendicular to the glass surface. (See Example 1.)

34. When a beam of electrons moves at a speed of $0.6c$ in a crystal whose index of refraction is 1.75, at what angle to the electron beam is the Cerenkov radiation emitted? (See Example 2.)

35. When vertically polarized light of intensity I_0 is incident on a polarizing filter that has its polarizing axis at an angle θ with the vertical, the intensity of the transmitted light, I_t, and θ are related by

$$\cos \theta = \sqrt{\frac{I_t}{I_0}}.$$

If $I_t = \frac{1}{4}I_0$, find θ by using your knowledge of special angles instead of a calculator.

36. For what value of θ will the intensity of the incident light in Problem 35 be reduced by one-half in passing through a polarizing filter? Use your knowledge of special angles instead of a calculator.

37. In an ac circuit, the potential difference V_R across a resistor as a function of time t, in seconds, is given by

$$V_R = 12 \sin \theta = 12 \sin (40\pi t),$$

where V_R is in volts and θ is in radians. Find the exact value of V_R when $t = \frac{1}{120}$.

38. When a plane flies with a speed v_p that is greater than the speed v of sound in air, the envelope of the waves created is a cone, the surface of which makes an angle θ

with the direction of motion of the plane. It can be shown that

$$\sin \theta = \frac{v}{v_p},$$

where the ratio v_p/v is called the *Mach number*. Find θ if the speed of a plane is Mach 1.3.

39. The range R of a projectile having an initial speed v_0 and an angle of projection θ is given by

$$R = \frac{v_0^2}{9.8} \sin (2\theta),$$

where v_0 is in meters per second and R is in meters. (a) Find the range of a projectile fired with an initial speed of 40 m/s at an angle of 45°. (b) Find the range of the same projectile if the angle of projection is lowered by 10°.

40. When a ball is thrown with an initial velocity of v_0 at an acute angle θ with the horizontal, the upward component of the velocity is given by the expression $v_0 \sin \theta$. If the initial velocity of the ball is 20 m/s, what value of θ will result in an upward component of 10 m/s?

41. The angle of deviation θ for which maxima occur in the diffraction pattern produced by a plane grating can be found from the equation

$$\sin \theta = \frac{m\lambda}{d},$$

where m is the order of the observed spectrum, λ is the wavelength of light, and d is the grating spacing. If a particular grating has a spacing of $d = 1.69 \times 10^{-6}$ m, what is the angular deviation of violet light of wavelength $\lambda = 4 \times 10^{-7}$ m in the first-order ($m = 1$) visible spectrum?

42. In 1812, Brewster showed that when the refracted and reflected rays are perpendicular (see Example 1), the reflected light is completely polarized. Show that for this condition, Snell's law can be written $\tan \theta_1 = n$. *Hint:* First show that θ_1 and θ_2 are complementary.

43. When light is incident on glass with a refractive index $n = 1.57$, the reflected ray is found to be completely polarized; that is, the reflected and refracted rays are perpendicular. (a) Find the angle (of incidence) θ_1. (b) Find the angle that the refracted ray makes with the perpendicular to the glass surface. (See Example 1 and Problem 42.)

44. If θ is an angle near zero, then $\sin \theta \approx \tan \theta \approx \theta$, where θ is in radians. Confirm this by computing $\sin \theta$ and $\tan \theta$ if θ is (a) 0.4, (b) 0.1, (c) 0.01, (d) 0.001, and (e) 0.00034. Give your answers to five decimal places. The statement $\sin \theta \approx \tan \theta \approx \theta$ for θ near zero is often called the **small-angle approximation.**

7-5   Solution of a Right Triangle

Six parts are associated with a right triangle: three sides and three angles. The angles are commonly called A, B, and C, where C is the right angle (Fig. 7-31), and the sides opposite these angles are a, b, and c, respectively. **To solve a right triangle**

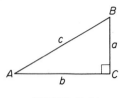

FIGURE 7-31

means to find all unknown parts when we know either the lengths of any two sides or the length of one side and the measure of any acute angle.

Certain facts are useful when we are solving a right triangle. Recall that the sum of the two acute angles is 90°; that is, the acute angles of a right triangle are *complementary angles*. Also, when two sides are known, the third side can be found by applying the Pythagorean theorem. The examples that follow illustrate basic techniques in solving a right triangle. We shall omit units of length for convenience.

example 1

Given two sides.

Solve right triangle *ABC* given that $c = 13$ and $b = 5$ (Fig. 7-32).

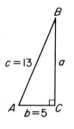

FIGURE 7-32

First we shall use the Pythagorean theorem to find *a*.

$$a^2 + 5^2 = 13^2$$

$$a = \sqrt{13^2 - 5^2} = \sqrt{144} = 12.$$

To find angle *A*, we have

$$\cos A = \frac{\text{adj}}{\text{hyp}} = \frac{5}{13} = 0.38462$$

$$A = 67.4°.$$

Because $A + B = 90°$,

$$B = 90° - A = 90° - 67.4° = 22.6°.$$

Thus the missing parts are $a = 12$, $A = 67.4°$, and $B = 22.6°$.

With efficient use of a calculator, in Example 1 it is unnecessary to show (or write down) the rounded number 0.38462. In actual practice, the displayed value of 5/13 may be 0.38461538 from which (by the use of the $\cos^{-1}$ key) we have $A = 67.4°$ (approximately). For the time being, we shall continue to show such intermediate values because of the mental pictures they convey.

example 2

Given one side and an acute angle.

Solve right triangle ABC given that $A = 32.2°$ and $b = 16.4$ (Fig. 7-33).

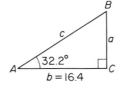

FIGURE 7-33

The remaining angle is found easily:

$$B = 90° - 32.2° = 57.8°.$$

To find a we use the relation $\tan 32.2° = $ opp/adj:

$$\tan 32.2° = \frac{a}{16.4}.$$

Multiplying both sides by 16.4 gives

$$a = 16.4(\tan 32.2°) = 16.4(0.62973) = 10.3.$$

We can find c with the cosine function.

$$\cos 32.2° = \frac{\text{adj}}{\text{hyp}} = \frac{16.4}{c}$$

$$c \cos 32.2° = 16.4$$

$$c = \frac{16.4}{\cos 32.2°} = \frac{16.4}{0.84619} = 19.4.$$

Thus the missing parts are $a = 10.3$, $c = 19.4$, and $B = 57.8°$. We chose not to use the Pythagorean theorem to find c because that would have required us to use a calculated value of a. If we had made an error in finding a, we would not get a correct value for c. Whenever practical, use the *given* parts to find the missing parts of a right triangle.

example 3

The right triangle shown in Fig. 7-34(a) is called a **power triangle** and is used in solving ac circuit problems. The hypotenuse represents the **apparent power** P_A, measured in volt-amperes (VA). The other sides represent the **real power** P, measured in watts (W),

FIGURE 7-34

and the **reactive power** P_R, measured in vars. The angle θ is called the **phase angle**. In a particular circuit, the real power is $P = 23$ W and the reactive power is $P_R = 5.1$ vars. Find the apparent power P_A and the phase angle.

Figure 7-34(b) shows the values for our particular problem. We have

$$\tan \theta = \frac{5.1}{23} = 0.22174$$

$$\theta = 12.5°.$$

Also

$$P_A = \sqrt{23^2 + 5.1^2} = 23.6 \text{ VA}.$$

example 4

An ac circuit has an inductive reactance $X_L = 10.1$ Ω and a resistance $R = 22.3$ Ω. In such a circuit the **impedance** Z, in ohms, can be represented by the hypotenuse of a right triangle with X_L and R as its other sides, as shown in Fig. 7-35. The angle θ is called the **phase angle**. Find the phase angle and the impedance.

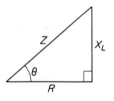

FIGURE 7-35

From Fig. 7-35, we have

$$\tan \theta = \frac{X_L}{R} = \frac{10.1}{22.3} = 0.45291.$$

Thus

$$\theta = 24.4°.$$

Also

$$Z = \sqrt{22.3^2 + 10.1^2} = 24.5 \ \Omega.$$

example 5

A plane flying at an altitude of 1.6 km begins to climb at a constant angle of 28°. To the nearest second, how long will it take the plane to reach an altitude of 2.8 km if its constant speed throughout the climb is 320 km/h?

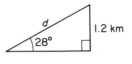

FIGURE 7-36

The plane must increase its altitude by 1.2 km (Fig. 7-36). We first find the distance d of the climb.

$$\sin 28° = \frac{1.2}{d}$$

$$d \sin 28° = 1.2$$

$$d = \frac{1.2}{\sin 28°} = \frac{1.2}{0.46947} = 2.556 \text{ km.}$$

The time to travel 2.556 km is given by

$$\text{time} = \frac{\text{distance}}{\text{rate}} = \frac{2.556 \text{ km}}{320 \text{ km/h}} = 0.008 \text{ h.}$$

We must now express 0.008 h in terms of seconds. Because 1 h = 3600 s,

$$0.008 \text{ h} = (0.008 \text{ h})\left(\frac{3600 \text{ s}}{1 \text{ h}}\right) = 29 \text{ s.}$$

In Fig. 7-37(a), if an observer at point P looks up at a point Q, then the angle that the line PQ makes with the horizontal line containing P is called the **angle of elevation of Q from P**. If an observer at Q looks down at P, then the angle that PQ

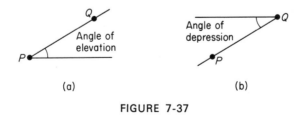

(a)   (b)

FIGURE 7-37

makes with the horizontal line containing Q is called the **angle of depression of P from Q** [Fig. 7-37(b)]. The angle of elevation of Q from P is equal to the angle of depression of P from Q, because these are alternate interior angles formed by two parallel lines cut by a transversal.

example 6

The length of a kite string is 76 m and the angle of elevation of the kite is 60°. Find the height of the kite (Fig. 7-38).

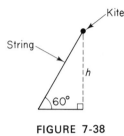

FIGURE 7-38

If *h* is the height, then

$$\sin 60° = \frac{h}{76}$$

$$h = 76 \sin 60° = 65.8 \text{ m.}$$

Exercise 7-5

In Problems 1–6, ABC is a right triangle with right angle C. Solve for the remaining parts of the triangle. Do not use a calculator.

1. $B = 60°, a = 3$. **2.** $A = 30°, b = 3$. **3.** $A = 45°, c = 6$.

4. $B = 60°, c = 1$. **5.** $b = 4, c = 8$. **6.** $a = 2, b = 2$.

In Problems 7–16, solve the right triangle ABC for the remaining parts.

7. $c = 12.4, A = 33.5°$. **8.** $a = 12, A = 12°$. **9.** $a = 23.4, b = 18.1$.

10. $a = 4, c = 15$. **11.** $b = 24.6, B = 27.4°$. **12.** $a = 3.5, b = 2.8$.

13. $b = 24.7, c = 60.3$. **14.** $c = 80.4, B = 86.5°$. **15.** $a = 23.1, B = 12.6°$.

16. $a = 82.5, B = 65.7°$.

17. An ac circuit has an impedance $Z = 36\ \Omega$. If the phase angle $\theta = 32.6°$, find the resistance R and the inductive reactance X_L. (See Example 4.)

18. An ac circuit has an impedance $Z = 22\ \Omega$. If the circuit has a resistance $R = 18.9\ \Omega$, find the inductive reactance X_L and the phase angle θ. (See Example 4.)

19. The apparent power in a circuit is 1.65 VA and the phase angle is 59°. Find the real power and the reactive power. (See Example 3.)

20. If the real power in a circuit is 1.73 W and the phase angle θ is 66.5°, find the apparent power and the reactive power. (See Example 3.)

21. From the top of a 50-meter cliff that overlooks a bay, the angle of depression of a buoy is 14°. To the nearest meter, what is the distance along the water of the buoy from the cliff?

22. The length of a kite string is 200 m and the angle of elevation of the kite is 34°. How high is the kite?

23. A tree casts a shadow 17 m long when the angle of elevation of the sun is 50°. Find the height of the tree.

24. From the top of a 100-m tower, the angle of depression of a man on the ground is 39°. How far from the base of the tower is the man?

25. An airplane pilot needs to increase his altitude by 5 km. He plans to climb at a constant angle of 10° and a constant rate of 300 km/h. To the nearest minute, how long will it take to reach that altitude?

26. A wire that braces an antenna is 15 m long. One end is attached to the top of the antenna, and the other end is attached to the ground at a distance of 12 m from the base of the antenna. Find the angle that the wire makes with the ground.

27. A bridge will be constructed at a certain point along a river. To gather engineering data, a surveyor is sent out to find the width w of the river (Fig. 7-39). With her

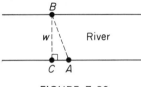

FIGURE 7-39

transit at C, the surveyor determines the right angle C. She measures the distance from point C to point A and finds it to be 33 m. Then, with her transit at point A, she determines that angle A is 69.6°. What is the width of the river?

28. An escalator inclined at an angle of 42.6° moves at a constant speed of 0.6 m/s. A person steps on the escalator and reaches the top in 42 s. Through what vertical height has the person been lifted?

29. To determine the height of a building, a surveyor determines that the angle of elevation to the top is 53.5°. If the sighting instrument was 30.3 m from the building and 1.5 m above the ground, find the height of the building.

30. The leaning tower of Pisa was designed to be 56 m high and its top is now 5.2 m out of plumb. Find the angle that the axis of the tower makes with the vertical.

31. A handrail is to be installed along a stairway that rises 6.1 m vertically in its horizontal distance of 9.1 m. How long must the handrail be and at what angle with the horizontal should it be mounted?

32. After passing a toll gate, a car travels on a road that rises until it reaches a bridge. If the angle of elevation of the road is 3.5° and the length of the road is 170 meters, how high above the toll gate is the bridge?

33. The Arctic Circle is approximately at latitude 66.5° N (Fig. 7-40). Given that the radius of the earth is 6370 km, find the radius of the Arctic Circle.

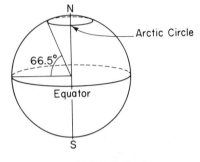

FIGURE 7-40

34. An airplane, flying at 90 km/h, travels for 1.5 h on a straight-line course heading 15.8° west of north. How far west and how far north of its starting point is it?

35. An antenna is situated on the edge of a cliff. From a point 480 m from the base of the cliff, the angle of elevation of the top of the antenna is 15°; the angle of elevation of the bottom of the antenna is 13°. How tall is the antenna?

36. The floor of a wedge-shaped storage shed is a square that is 5.0 m on a side. If the roof contacts the back edge of the floor at an angle of 16°, find the dimensions of the roof.

7-6 Trigonometric Functions of Any Angle

Thus far, we have considered the values of the trigonometric functions for acute angles only. For any angle θ, we use the same definition as before:

1. Place θ in standard position.
2. Let (x, y) be any point on the terminal side of θ (except the origin).
3. If $r = \sqrt{x^2 + y^2}$, then

$$\sin \theta = \frac{y}{r}, \qquad \csc \theta = \frac{r}{y},$$

$$\cos \theta = \frac{x}{r}, \qquad \sec \theta = \frac{r}{x},$$

$$\tan \theta = \frac{y}{x}, \qquad \cot \theta = \frac{x}{y}.$$

example 1

Find the values of the trigonometric functions of θ given that θ is in standard position and the point $(-3, 2)$ lies on its terminal side (Fig. 7-41).

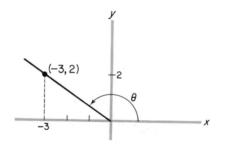

FIGURE 7-41

Letting $-3 = x$ and $2 = y$, we have

$$r = \sqrt{(-3)^2 + 2^2} = \sqrt{13}.$$

Thus

$$\sin \theta = \frac{y}{r} = \frac{2}{\sqrt{13}} = \frac{2\sqrt{13}}{13},$$

$$\cos \theta = \frac{x}{r} = \frac{-3}{\sqrt{13}} = -\frac{3\sqrt{13}}{13},$$

$$\tan \theta = \frac{y}{x} = \frac{2}{-3} = -\frac{2}{3},$$

$$\cot \theta = \frac{x}{y} = \frac{-3}{2} = -\frac{3}{2},$$

$$\sec \theta = \frac{r}{x} = \frac{\sqrt{13}}{-3} = -\frac{\sqrt{13}}{3},$$

$$\csc \theta = \frac{r}{y} = \frac{\sqrt{13}}{2}.$$

You should realize that *the reciprocal relations of Sec. 7-3 are true for any angle θ for which they are defined.* As a result, we could have used them here to find cot θ, sec θ, and csc θ from tan θ, cos θ, and sin θ, respectively.

We now consider the values of the trigonometric functions of some quadrantal angles. You will see that such values are not always defined.

example 2

a. Find the six trigonometric values of $0°$.

Figure 7-42(a) shows the angle $0°$. For a point (x, y) on the terminal side, we shall choose $(1, 0)$. Then $r = 1$ and we have

$$\sin 0° = \frac{y}{r} = \frac{0}{1} = 0,$$

$$\cos 0° = \frac{x}{r} = \frac{1}{1} = 1,$$

$$\tan 0° = \frac{y}{x} = \frac{0}{1} = 0,$$

$$\cot 0° = \frac{x}{y} = \frac{1}{0}, \quad \text{which is } \textit{not defined,}$$

$$\sec 0° = \frac{r}{x} = \frac{1}{1} = 1,$$

$$\csc 0° = \frac{r}{y} = \frac{1}{0}, \quad \text{which is } \textit{not defined.}$$

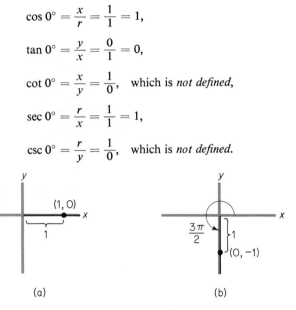

(a)   (b)

FIGURE 7-42

b. Find the six trigonometric values of $\frac{3\pi}{2}$.

See Fig. 7-42(b). We shall choose $(0, -1)$ as (x, y). Then $r = 1$ and we have

$$\sin\left(\frac{3\pi}{2}\right) = \frac{y}{r} = \frac{-1}{1} = -1,$$

$$\cos\left(\frac{3\pi}{2}\right) = \frac{x}{r} = \frac{0}{1} = 0,$$

$$\tan\left(\frac{3\pi}{2}\right) = \frac{y}{x} = \frac{-1}{0}, \quad \text{which is } \textit{not defined,}$$

$$\cot\left(\frac{3\pi}{2}\right) = \frac{x}{y} = \frac{0}{-1} = 0,$$

$$\sec\left(\frac{3\pi}{2}\right) = \frac{r}{x} = \frac{1}{0}, \quad \text{which is } \textit{not defined,}$$

$$\csc\left(\frac{3\pi}{2}\right) = \frac{r}{y} = \frac{1}{-1} = -1.$$

The trigonometric values for 90° and 180° can be found as in Example 2 by using the points $(0, 1)$ and $(-1, 0)$, respectively. Table 7-2 summarizes the values of the trigonometric functions for quadrantal angles. A dash means that the value is not defined.

Table 7-2

	0° *(or 0)*	90° $\left(or\ \dfrac{\pi}{2}\right)$	180° *(or π)*	270° $\left(or\ \dfrac{3\pi}{2}\right)$
sin	0	1	0	−1
cos	1	0	−1	0
tan	0	—	0	—
cot	—	0	—	0
sec	1	—	−1	—
csc	—	1	—	−1

If α and β are coterminal angles, then we can choose a point (x, y) on the terminal sides of *both* α and β [Fig. 7-43(a)]. It follows from the definitions of the

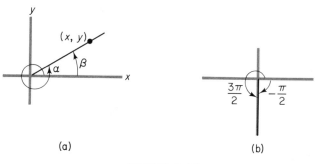

(a)   (b)

FIGURE 7-43

trigonometric functions that **the values of the trigonometric functions of coterminal angles are equal.** For example, $-\pi/2$ and $3\pi/2$ are coterminal [Fig. 7-43(b)]. Thus $\sin(-\pi/2) = \sin 3\pi/2 = -1$ (from Example 2).

In Example 1, some trigonometric values of the second-quadrant angle θ are positive and others are negative. Suppose we consider the signs of the trigonometric functions of angles in the various quadrants. Let (x, y) be a point on the terminal side of θ. In the first quadrant, both x and y are positive. Because r is *always* positive, we conclude that all trigonometric functions of a first-quadrant angle are positive. For a second-quadrant angle, x is negative, while y and r are positive; hence, only the sine and cosecant functions have positive values. Using similar reasoning you should determine the signs of the functions for third- and fourth-quadrant angles. Figure 7-44 gives the functions that have positive values for angles in the various quadrants. For example, $\tan 200°$ is positive, because $200°$ is a third-quadrant angle. Similarly, $-\pi/6$ is a fourth-quadrant angle; thus $\cos(-\pi/6)$ and $\sec(-\pi/6)$ are positive, but $\sin(-\pi/6)$ and $\tan(-\pi/6)$, for example, are negative.

Positive trigonometric functions

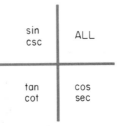

FIGURE 7-44

With each angle θ that is not quadrantal, we can associate another angle, called the **reference angle** of θ. It is the *acute* angle between the terminal side of θ *and the x-axis* (not the *y*-axis). Figure 7-45 shows different situations. We can find the trigo-

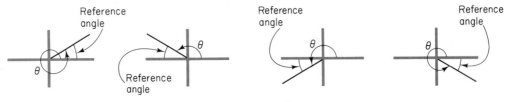

FIGURE 7-45

nometric values of a given θ from its reference angle. For example, consider 150° [Fig. 7-46(a)]. Its reference angle is $180° - 150° = 30°$. To locate a point on the

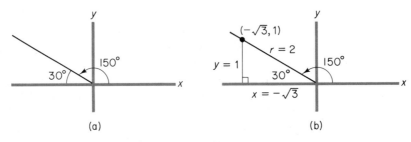

FIGURE 7-46

terminal side of 150°, we shall make use of a 30°-60°-90° triangle. From Fig. 7-46(b), $(-\sqrt{3}, 1)$ lies on the terminal side and $r = 2$. Thus

$$\sin 150° = \frac{y}{r} = \frac{1}{2},$$

$$\cos 150° = \frac{x}{r} = \frac{-\sqrt{3}}{2} = -\frac{\sqrt{3}}{2},$$

and so on. We can obtain these values in a simpler way. From a 30°-60°-90° triangle, we know that, for example,

$$\sin 30° = \frac{1}{2} \quad \text{and} \quad \cos 30° = \frac{\sqrt{3}}{2}.$$

Notice that the trigonometric values of 150° are the same as those of its reference angle 30° except, perhaps, for sign. Thus, to find cos 150° we can find cos 30° and put a minus sign in front of it. The minus sign is needed because the cosine of a second-quadrant angle (150°) is negative. Similarly, tan 150° must be negative, so tan 150° = −(tan 30°) = −1/√3 = −√3/3. In general, we have the following.

> To find a trigonometric value of an angle θ that is not quadrantal, find the same trigonometric value of its reference angle and attach the proper sign. This sign depends on the function involved and the quadrant that contains the terminal side of θ.

example 3

a. Find sin 135°.

Because 135° is a second-quadrant angle [Fig. 7-47(a)], sin 135° is positive. The reference angle is 180° − 135° = 45°. Thus

$$\sin 135° = +\sin 45° = \frac{1}{\sqrt{2}} = \frac{\sqrt{2}}{2}.$$

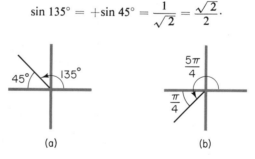

(a)   (b)

FIGURE 7-47

b. Find $\cos \frac{5\pi}{4}$.

Because $\frac{5\pi}{4}$ is a third-quadrant angle [Fig. 7-47(b)], $\cos \frac{5\pi}{4}$ is negative. The reference angle is $\frac{5\pi}{4} - \pi = \frac{\pi}{4}$ (or 45°). Thus

$$\cos \frac{5\pi}{4} = -\cos \frac{\pi}{4} = -\frac{1}{\sqrt{2}} = -\frac{\sqrt{2}}{2}.$$

example 4

a. Find $\cot\left(-\dfrac{\pi}{6}\right)$.

Because $-\pi/6$ is a fourth-quadrant angle [Fig. 7-48(a)], $\cot(-\pi/6)$ is negative. The reference angle is $\pi/6$ (or $30°$). Thus

$$\cot\left(-\frac{\pi}{6}\right) = -\cot\frac{\pi}{6} = -\frac{\sqrt{3}}{1} = -\sqrt{3}.$$

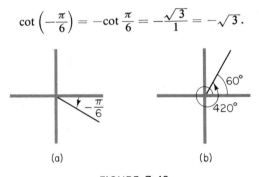

(a)   (b)

FIGURE 7-48

b. Find $\sec 420°$.

Because $420°$ is a first-quadrant angle [Fig. 7-48(b)], $\sec 420°$ is positive. The reference angle is $420° - 360° = 60°$. Thus

$$\sec 420° = +\sec 60° = \frac{2}{1} = 2.$$

example 5

Find $\tan 164.6°$.

Because $164.6°$ is a second-quadrant angle (Fig. 7-49), $\tan 164.6°$ is negative.

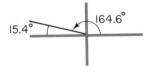

FIGURE 7-49

The reference angle is $180° - 164.6° = 15.4°$. Thus

$$\tan 164.6° = -\tan 15.4° = -0.2754.$$

You should verify the result by finding $\tan 164.6°$ directly with a calculator without using a reference angle.

example 6

Find all angles θ, where $0° \leq \theta < 360°$, such that $\tan \theta = -0.3640$.

We ignore the minus sign for now. Using the $\tan^{-1}$ key on a calculator, we find that the acute angle with tangent of 0.3640 is 20°. Thus the reference angle of θ is 20°. The tangent function is negative for second- and fourth-quadrant angles. Thus there must be two values of θ that meet the given conditions (Fig. 7-50). We have $\theta = 180° - 20° = 160°$ and $\theta = 360° - 20° = 340°$, which both meet the condition that $\tan \theta = -0.3640$.

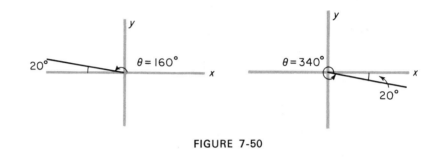

FIGURE 7-50

In Example 6, the condition that $\tan \theta = -0.3640$ was given and the *acute* reference angle with tangent of 0.3640 was initially found with the use of the $\tan^{-1}$ key. If, instead, this key is used after entering the given value, -0.3640, a typical calculator result is $-20°$. You should try it on your calculator before you read on. The calculator result is not incorrect, because $\tan(-20°) = -0.3640$, but it does have to be interpreted in the context of the problem. Calculators usually give values of an angle that are within a defined range of values. For $\tan^{-1}$, these **principal values** are between $-90°$ and $90°$.* You can see that the calculator result is within that range. However, the problem requires that $0° \leq \theta < 360°$, so $\theta = -20°$ is unacceptable. The coterminal angle $360° - 20° = 340°$ is appropriate, as is the second-quadrant angle 160°.

example 7

Find θ if $\cos \theta = -0.8360$ and $0° \leq \theta < 360°$.

The cosine function is negative for second- and third-quadrant angles. The acute angle with cosine of 0.8360 is 33.3°. Thus (Fig. 7-51)

$$\theta = 180° - 33.3° = 146.7°,$$

*We shall have more to say about principal values in Chapter 14.

FIGURE 7-51

and

$$\theta = 180° + 33.3° = 213.3°.$$

Exercise 7-6

In Problems 1–8, find the reference angle of the given angle.

1. 115°.   **2.** 310°.   **3.** 227°.   **4.** 405°.

5. −22.6°.   **6.** $\dfrac{5\pi}{6}$.   **7.** $\dfrac{13\pi}{6}$.   **8.** $-\dfrac{3\pi}{4}$.

In Problems 9–28, find the values of the trigonometric functions without using a calculator.

9. sin 150°.   **10.** sin 120°.   **11.** cos 240°.   **12.** cos 225°.

13. tan (−225°).   **14.** tan 300°.   **15.** cot 315°.   **16.** cot (−210°).

17. sec 210°.   **18.** sec 330°.   **19.** csc (−90°).   **20.** csc 150°.

21. sin 450°.   **22.** cos 720°.   **23.** sin $\dfrac{5\pi}{4}$.   **24.** cos $\dfrac{2\pi}{3}$.

25. tan $\dfrac{4\pi}{3}$.   **26.** sin $\dfrac{7\pi}{4}$.   **27.** cos $\dfrac{11\pi}{6}$.   **28.** cos $\left(-\dfrac{11\pi}{6}\right)$.

In Problems 29–48, find the values of the trigonometric functions.

29. tan 337°.   **30.** sin 190.5°.   **31.** csc 534°.   **32.** cot 295°.

33. sin 100.3°.   **34.** cos 349.2°.   **35.** cot (−158.4°).   **36.** sec (−255°).

37. sec (−84°).   **38.** tan 500°.   **39.** cos (−170°).   **40.** cos 140.2°

41. tan 570°.   **42.** csc 450°.   **43.** tan 161.6°.   **44.** cos 187.4°.

45. sin (−740°).   **46.** tan (−98°).   **47.** sin (−3.3).   **48.** cos 3.2.

In Problems 49–66, determine all values of θ, where 0° ≤ θ < 360°, such that the given conditions are met.

49. tan θ = −1.   **50.** cos θ = −0.8616.   **51.** sin θ = −0.3907.

52. csc θ = −1.390.   **53.** cos θ = $\dfrac{1}{2}$.   **54.** sin θ = 0.4512.

55. sin θ = $\dfrac{\sqrt{2}}{2}$.   **56.** tan θ = 0.4245.   **57.** sec θ = −1.122.

58. sec θ = 1.122.   **59.** sin θ = 0.6428.   **60.** cos θ = 0.8192.

61. tan θ = 7.953.   **62.** cot θ = −1.799.

63. $\cos\theta = 0.2345$ and $\sin\theta$ is positive.

64. $\cos\theta = -0.9877$ and $\sin\theta$ is negative.

65. $\tan\theta = -0.7813$ and $\sin\theta$ is negative.

66. $\sin\theta = 0.4566$ and $\cos\theta$ is positive.

67. The index of refraction n of a prism with apex angle A is given by

$$n = \frac{\sin\left(\dfrac{A+\delta}{2}\right)}{\sin\left(\dfrac{A}{2}\right)},$$

where δ (delta) is called the angle of minimum deviation. If a prism has an angle of minimum deviation of 27° and an apex angle of 55°, determine its index of refraction.

7-7 Vectors

If you were presented with a rectangular box and a measuring stick and were asked to determine the length and area of a specified side of the box, you would probably be able to supply the answers in short order. You might find the length of the side to be 1.2 m and the area to be 2.4 m². However, you might overlook the fact that these quantities have a common property. Each is completely specified by a *number* and a *unit*. Such physical quantities—others are mass, speed, distance, and temperature—are called **scalar quantities**.

In science and engineering, however, there are other physical quantities that cannot be completely specified that simply. These quantities have associated with them not only a number and a unit, which indicate magnitude, but also a characteristic *direction*. Such quantities are called **vector quantities**. Examples are displacement, force, velocity, acceleration, and torque. For example, we speak of a displacement (or change in position) of 10 m *south*.

To represent a vector quantity, we can use a directed line segment or arrow, which is called a **vector**. The length of the arrow represents, to some suitable scale, the magnitude of the quantity. The direction of the arrow gives the direction of the quantity. For example, with a scale of 1 cm = 4 m/s, a velocity of 20 m/s south can be represented by a 5-cm arrow pointing south. Similarly, the arrow in Fig. 7-52 is a vector. Its **initial point**, or **tail**, is at A and its **terminal point**, or **head**, is at B. The

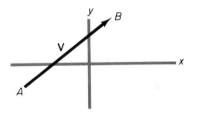

FIGURE 7-52

head of the arrow indicates direction, and we refer to this vector as the vector from A to B.

To denote a vector, we may use boldface letters or use letters with arrows. For example, the vector in Fig. 7-52 may be denoted by **AB**, **V**, $\overrightarrow{AB}$, or $\vec{V}$. The magnitude of a vector **V** can be denoted by $|\mathbf{V}|$ or by ordinary type, V. Thus if $\mathbf{A} = 3$ m/s northward, then $|\mathbf{A}| = A = 3$ m/s. The magnitude of a vector is always nonnegative. We shall feel free to use any of the above notations to indicate a vector or its magnitude, as convenient.

Let us be specific about when two vectors are *equal*.

> Two vectors are **equivalent** or **equal** if and only if they have the same magnitude (length) and the same direction.

The vectors **A**, **B**, and **C** in Fig. 7-53 are equivalent; they have the same length and direction. They differ, however, in their initial and terminal points. The notion of

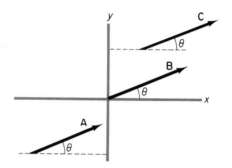

FIGURE 7-53

equivalent vectors is similar to the notion of equivalent rational numbers. That is, just as we can replace the number $\frac{2}{3}$ by $\frac{4}{6}$ without affecting a calculation, so can we represent a vector by any equivalent vector. More specifically, at times we shall find it convenient to represent a vector by an equivalent vector with initial point at the origin of a rectangular coordinate system. This type of vector is said to be in **standard position**. Vector **B** in Fig. 7-53 is in standard position.

Given a vector **A**, then the product $n\mathbf{A}$, where n is a number, is a vector with magnitude $|n|$ times that of **A** and with the following direction:

1. The same as **A** if $n > 0$.

2. Opposite that of **A** if $n < 0$.

3. Anywhere if $n = 0$. In this case the product is called the **zero vector**.

The product $(-1)\mathbf{A}$ is simply written $-\mathbf{A}$ and is called the **negative** of **A**; it has the same magnitude as **A** but points in the opposite direction.

example 1

Given the vector **F** with magnitude 1 N in the direction due northeast, Fig. 7-54 shows **F**, 2**F**, −**F**, and −3**F**.

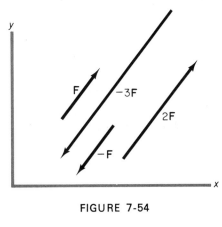

FIGURE 7-54

In Fig. 7-55(a), two successive displacements from A to B and then from B to C are represented by the vectors $\mathbf{d_1}$ and $\mathbf{d_2}$, respectively. The resulting effect, or net

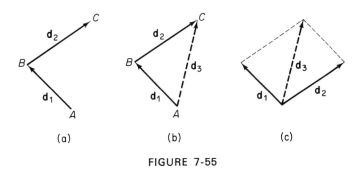

(a)   (b)   (c)

FIGURE 7-55

displacement, is the same as the displacement from A to C. This is represented in Fig. 7-55(b) by the vector $\mathbf{d_3}$ from the tail of $\mathbf{d_1}$ to the head of $\mathbf{d_2}$. We call $\mathbf{d_3}$ the **vector sum** or **resultant** of $\mathbf{d_1}$ and $\mathbf{d_2}$. Symbolically, we write

$$\mathbf{d_1} + \mathbf{d_2} = \mathbf{d_3}. \tag{1}$$

We point out that the plus sign in Eq. 1 does not imply ordinary addition of numbers. The vector addition in Eq. 1 implies all the geometric considerations necessary to account for the directions of the quantities involved.

The previous sum $\mathbf{d_1} + \mathbf{d_2}$ can be expressed another way. If we place $\mathbf{d_1}$ and $\mathbf{d_2}$ so that their tails are at a common point, then [Fig. 7-55(c)] you can see that the

resultant $\mathbf{d}_3$ is the vector from the common point to the opposite corner of the parallelogram having adjacent sides of $\mathbf{d}_1$ and $\mathbf{d}_2$. That is, the resultant is the directed
diagonal of this parallelogram. This is a common interpretation for the sum of two
vectors.

Two fundamental properties of vector addition are given by the commutative
and associative laws:

Commutative law: $\mathbf{A} + \mathbf{B} = \mathbf{B} + \mathbf{A}.$

Associative law: $\mathbf{A} + (\mathbf{B} + \mathbf{C}) = (\mathbf{A} + \mathbf{B}) + \mathbf{C}.$

These laws imply that regardless of the order in which vectors are added and regardless of how they are grouped, their vector sum is the same. Given the vectors **A**, **B**,
and **C** in Fig. 7-56(a), the commutative law is illustrated in Fig. 7-56(b) and the
associative law in Fig. 7-56(c).

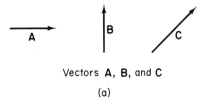

Vectors **A**, **B**, and **C**

(a)

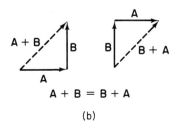

$\mathbf{A} + \mathbf{B} = \mathbf{B} + \mathbf{A}$

(b)

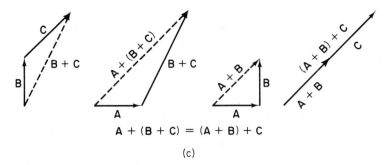

$\mathbf{A} + (\mathbf{B} + \mathbf{C}) = (\mathbf{A} + \mathbf{B}) + \mathbf{C}$

(c)

FIGURE 7-56

To geometrically add vectors **A, B, C, D, ... , N**, we may follow these steps:

1. Draw **A** to scale on a diagram.

2. Draw **B** with its tail at the head of **A**.

3. Draw **C** with its tail at the head of **B**.

4. Continue in this manner until **N** has been drawn.

5. The resultant is the vector from the tail of **A** to the head of **N**.

example 2

A boy delivering newspapers covers his route by traveling 3 blocks west, 3 blocks north, and then 7 blocks east. Determine the displacement of the boy at the end of his route.

The displacement of the boy in moving from one point to another is the directed straight-line distance from the first point to the second point. The boy undergoes three separate displacements:

$$\mathbf{d}_1 = 3 \text{ blocks, west;}$$

$$\mathbf{d}_2 = 3 \text{ blocks, north;}$$

$$\mathbf{d}_3 = 7 \text{ blocks, east.}$$

The displacement of the boy at the end of his route is the resultant displacement **d**, where

$$\mathbf{d} = \mathbf{d}_1 + \mathbf{d}_2 + \mathbf{d}_3.$$

Following the procedure given above for adding vectors, we chose a scale of 1 unit = 1 block and constructed the diagram shown in Fig. 7-57. Note that $\mathbf{d}_1$ is placed in standard position.

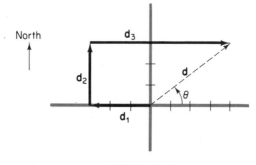

FIGURE 7-57

The resultant displacement is represented by the vector drawn from the tail of $\mathbf{d}_1$ to the head of $\mathbf{d}_3$ and is shown by the broken arrow. Measuring its length, we find that it is 5 units long, which represents a distance of 5 blocks according to our scale. The angle θ is measured with a protractor and is found to be approximately 36.9°. Thus the displacement of the boy at the end of his route is 5 blocks, 36.9° north of east.

As illustrated by the answer in Example 2, a nonzero vector **V** in standard position can be specified by giving its magnitude V and the angle θ that **V** makes with the positive x-axis (Fig. 7-58). That is, θ specifies the direction of **V**. We say that V and θ are **polar coordinates** of **V**. *We shall usually choose θ between 0° and 360°.*

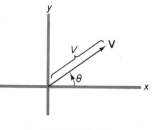

FIGURE 7-58

Another way of specifying a vector **V** in standard position is by giving the rectangular coordinates V_x and V_y of the head of **V**, as shown in Fig. 7-59. That is, **V** is specified by the point (V_x, V_y). The numbers V_x and V_y are called the **horizontal**

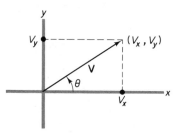

FIGURE 7-59

and **vertical** (scalar) **components** of **V**, respectively. Observe that if θ is measured as in Fig. 7-59, then $\cos \theta = V_x/V$ from which

$$V_x = V \cos \theta,$$

and $\sin \theta = V_y/V$ from which

$$V_y = V \sin \theta.$$

We also have

$$V = \sqrt{V_x^2 + V_y^2}$$

and

$$\tan \theta = \frac{V_y}{V_x}.$$

Note that V_x and V_y can be positive or negative, depending on the quadrant in which **V** lies. If **V** is horizontal, then $V_y = 0$ and θ is either $0°$ or $180°$. For a vertical vector, $V_x = 0$ and θ is either $90°$ or $270°$.

example 3

Find the components of **V** given that $V = 20$ and $\theta = 140°$.

An appropriate diagram is given in Fig. 7-60. The components are
$$V_x = V \cos 140° = 20(-0.7660) = -15.32,$$
$$V_y = V \sin 140° = 20(0.6428) = 12.86.$$

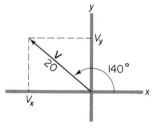

FIGURE 7-60

example 4

Find the magnitude V and direction θ of **V** if $V_x = -4$ and $V_y = -3$.

We have
$$V = \sqrt{V_x^2 + V_y^2} = \sqrt{(-4)^2 + (-3)^2} = \sqrt{25} = 5.$$

Because V_x and V_y are negative, the head of **V** is in the third quadrant (Fig. 7-61). Also,
$$\tan \theta = \frac{V_y}{V_x} = \frac{-3}{-4} = 0.75.$$

We find the reference angle for θ to be $36.9°$, so
$$\theta = 180° + 36.9° = 216.9°.$$

Therefore $V = 5$ and $\theta = 216.9°$.

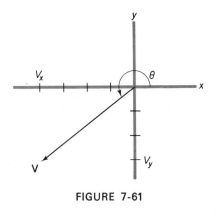

FIGURE 7-61

Whenever a given vector **V** is the resultant of two vectors, the two vectors are called **vector components** of **V**, and **V** is said to be *resolved* into these two components. This notion is especially useful when the components are mutually perpendicular. For example, in Fig. 7-62 the vector **V** is resolved into a horizontal vector component **V**$_h$ and a vertical vector component **V**$_v$. Because **V** = **V**$_h$ + **V**$_v$, **V** can be replaced by its vector components. Figure 7-63 shows other vectors **V** resolved into horizontal and vertical vector components. We point out that any vector can be replaced by its vector components, because their sum is the given vector.

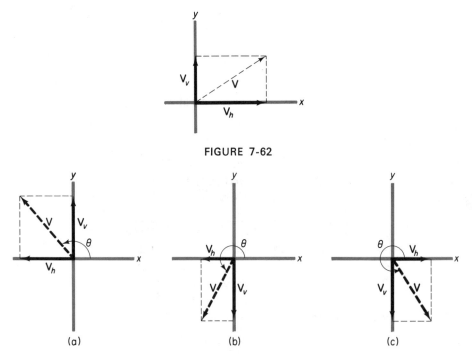

FIGURE 7-62

(a)   (b)   (c)

FIGURE 7-63

example 5

A straight portion of a hill is inclined at an angle of 38° with the horizontal. If the speed of a sled down this hill is 18.3 m/s, find the magnitudes of the horizontal and vertical vector components of the sled's velocity. See Fig. 7-64(a).

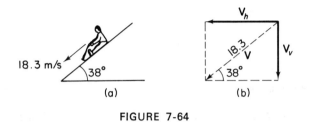

(a)   (b)

FIGURE 7-64

The velocity vector **V** is shown in Fig. 7-64(b). The magnitudes of the vector components V_v and V_h can easily be found from the right triangle shown.

$$\sin 38° = \frac{\text{opp}}{\text{hyp}} = \frac{V_v}{18.3}$$

$$V_v = 18.3 \sin 38° = 18.3(0.6157)$$

$$= 11.3 \text{ m/s.}$$

$$\cos 38° = \frac{V_h}{18.3}$$

$$V_h = 18.3 \cos 38° = 18.3(0.7880)$$

$$= 14.4 \text{ m/s.}$$

example 6

The weight **W** of an object on an inclined plane can be resolved into two vector components: one, W_1, parallel to the plane, and one, W_2, perpendicular to the plane (Fig. 7-65). Suppose a 150-N weight rests on an incline that rises 4 m vertically to every 3 m horizontally (Fig. 7-66). Find the magnitudes of the vector components of the weight.

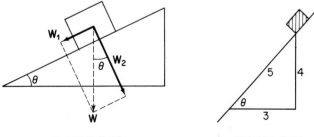

FIGURE 7-65   FIGURE 7-66

From the right triangle in Fig. 7-65, we have

$$\sin \theta = \frac{\text{opp}}{\text{hyp}} = \frac{W_1}{W}.$$

Thus

$$W_1 = W \sin \theta = 150 \left(\frac{4}{5}\right) = 120 \text{ N}.$$

Similarly,

$$W_2 = W \cos \theta = 150 \left(\frac{3}{5}\right) = 90 \text{ N}.$$

Exercise 7-7

1. A car travels 5.0 km east, 3.0 km south, and then 2.0 km west. Graphically estimate the resultant displacement of the car. (See Example 2.)

2. A helicopter flies 240 km, 45° north of east, and then flies 100 km due south. Graphically estimate the displacement of the helicopter. (See Example 2.)

*In Problems **3–12**, find the horizontal and vertical components of the vector with the given polar coordinates.*

3. $V = 150$, $\theta = 35°$.   4. $V = 10$, $\theta = 15.2°$ 5. $V = 10.1$, $\theta = 273°$.

6. $V = 0.100$, $\theta = 226°$.   7. $V = 32$, $\theta = 184°$.   8. $V = 50$, $\theta = 316°$.

9. $V = 200$, $\theta = 101°$.   10. $V = 3000$, $\theta = 137°$.

11. $V = 150$, $\theta = 306°$.   12. $V = 720$, $\theta = 67°$.

*In Problems **13–20**, the components of a vector **V** in standard position are given. Find V and θ.*

13. $V_x = 5$, $V_y = 7$.   14. $V_x = -3.4$, $V_y = 7.9$.

15. $V_x = 6.1$, $V_y = -3.2$.   16. $V_x = 23.5$, $V_y = 15.8$.

17. $V_x = -2.1$, $V_y = -4.8$.   18. $V_x = 0$, $V_y = 17$.

19. $V_x = -3$, $V_y = 0$.   20. $V_x = 0$, $V_y = -4$.

21. A baseball is thrown into the air with a speed of 32 m/s directed at an angle of 32° with the horizontal. Find the magnitudes of the horizontal and vertical vector components of the ball's initial velocity. (See Example 5.)

22. An airplane flies 168 km in the direction 26° south of west. How far south and how far west has it traveled?

23. An automobile travels down a hill with an acceleration of 5 m/s². The hill makes an angle of 40° with the horizontal. Find the magnitudes of the horizontal and vertical vector components of the acceleration.

24. A home-run ball moving at 42.6 m/s is caught by a fan in the bleachers. At the instant the ball was caught, it was moving at an angle of 27.5° below the horizontal. Find the magnitudes of the horizontal and vertical vector components of the ball's velocity as it was caught.

25. A child pulls a wagon by exerting a 30-N force at an angle of 20° above the horizontal. Find (a) the magnitude of the horizontal vector component of the force which tends to move the sled along the ground, and (b) the magnitude of the vertical vector component of the force that tends to lift the sled.

26. A woman *pushes* a lawn mower by applying a force of 10 N along its handle. If the handle is inclined at an angle of 42° with the horizontal, find (a) the magnitude of the horizontal vector component of the applied force that tends to move the lawn mower along the ground, and (b) the magnitude of the downward vertical vector component of the applied force.

27. A block weighing 65 N is placed on a 55° inclined plane. Find the magnitudes of the vector components of the weight that are (a) parallel and (b) perpendicular to the inclined surface. (See Example 6.)

28. Consider two displacements: one of magnitude 3 m and one of magnitude 4 m. Show geometrically how these displacement vectors can give a resultant displacement of magnitude (a) 7 m, (b) 1 m, and (c) 5 m.

7-8 Addition of Vectors—Analytical Method

The geometric method of vector addition that was given in the previous section is useful in only the simplest cases. In more complicated situations, we use an analytic method involving the use of components.

If **R** is the resultant (or vector sum) of two or more vectors in standard position, then the following can be shown geometrically:

1. R_x, the horizontal component of **R**, is the sum of the horizontal components of the vectors in the sum.

2. R_y, the vertical component of **R**, is the sum of the vertical components of the vectors in the sum.

These facts are illustrated in Fig. 7-67, where the horizontal component of $\mathbf{A} + \mathbf{B}$ is $A_x + B_x$ and the vertical component of $\mathbf{A} + \mathbf{B}$ is $A_y + B_y$.

As a result of the previous facts, we can perform the following steps to determine the resultant of two or more vectors.

1. Find the horizontal and vertical components of each of the given vectors.

2. Determine the sum R_x of the horizontal components.

3. Determine the sum R_y of the vertical components.

4. Use the Pythagorean theorem and basic trigonometric relations to find the magnitude and direction of the resultant vector **R**. That is,

$$R = \sqrt{R_x^2 + R_y^2},$$

$$\tan \theta = \frac{R_y}{R_x}, \qquad 0° \leq \theta < 360°.$$

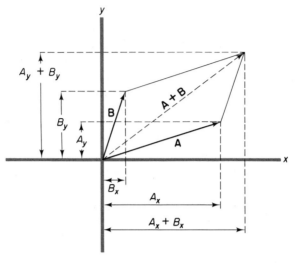

FIGURE 7-67

If $R_x = 0$, then $\theta = 90°$ if $R_y > 0$ and $\theta = 270°$ if $R_y < \theta$. If $R_y = 0$, then $\theta = 0°$ if $R_x > 0$ and $\theta = 180°$ if $R_x < 0$.

example 1

Find the resultant of **A, B,** and **C** if their polar coordinates are:

$$A = 30 \text{ N}, \qquad \theta_A = 30°;$$
$$B = 10 \text{ N}, \qquad \theta_B = 270°;$$
$$C = 10 \text{ N}, \qquad \theta_C = 135°.$$

These vectors are shown in Fig. 7-68.

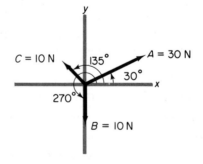

FIGURE 7-68

The components of **A** are

$$A_x = A \cos 30° = (30)(0.8660) = 25.98 \text{ N},$$
$$A_y = A \sin 30° = (30)(0.5000) = 15 \text{ N}.$$

The components of **B** are

$$B_x = B \cos 270° = (10)(0) = 0 \text{ N},$$
$$B_y = B \sin 270° = (10)(-1) = -10 \text{ N}.$$

For vector **C**, the reference angle is 45°:

$$C_x = C \cos 135° = C(-\cos 45°) = (10)(-0.7071) = -7.071 \text{ N},$$
$$C_y = C \sin 135° = C \sin 45° = (10)(0.7071) = 7.071 \text{ N}.$$

The components R_x and R_y of the resultant **R** are

$$R_x = A_x + B_x + C_x = 25.98 + 0 - 7.071 = 18.91 \text{ N},$$
$$R_y = A_y + B_y + C_y = 15 - 10 + 7.071 = 12.07 \text{ N}.$$

Because these components are positive, they correspond to points on the positive x- and y-axes. Thus **R** lies in the first quadrant (Fig. 7-69). By the Pythagorean theorem,

$$R = \sqrt{R_x^2 + R_y^2}$$
$$R = \sqrt{(18.91)^2 + (12.07)^2} = 22.4 \text{ N}.$$

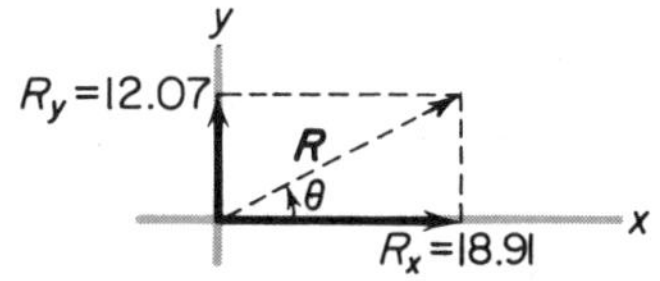

FIGURE 7-69

To determine the direction of θ, we have

$$\tan \theta = \frac{R_y}{R_x} = \frac{12.07}{18.91} = 0.6383$$
$$\theta = 32.6°.$$

Thus the resultant force **R**, which can replace **A**, **B**, and **C**, has magnitude $R = 22.4$ N and direction $\theta = 32.6°$.

example 2

A boat in still water leaves a dock and travels 200 km at an angle of 23° east of north. It then travels 100 km due east. How far is the boat from the dock?

The displacements of the boat are shown in Fig. 7-70(a). Putting the displacement vectors in standard position gives Fig. 7-70(b). For the resultant displacement **d**, we have

$$d_x = A_x + B_x = 200 \cos 67° + 100 \cos 0°$$
$$= 200(0.39073) + 100(1) = 178.15 \text{ km},$$
$$d_y = A_y + B_y = 200 \sin 67° + 100 \sin 0°$$
$$= 200(0.92050) + 100(0) = 184.10 \text{ km}.$$

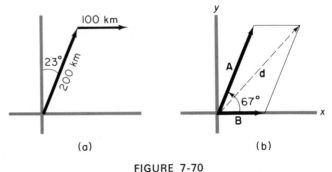

(a)   (b)

FIGURE 7-70

The distance of the boat from the dock is given by the magnitude of **d**:

$$d = \sqrt{d_x^2 + d_y^2} = \sqrt{178.15^2 + 184.10^2}$$
$$= 256.2 \text{ km}.$$

example 3

A plane is traveling due east at an airspeed of 400 km/h. If a wind of 100 km/h is blowing due southeast, find the magnitude and direction of the plane's resultant velocity.

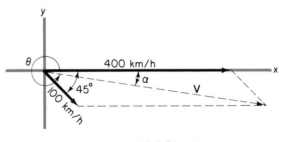

FIGURE 7-71

The resultant velocity **V** of the plane is the sum of the velocities 400 km/h east and 100 km/h southeast. The vector sum is shown in Fig. 7-71. The components of the wind velocity (**W**) are

$$W_x = 100 \cos 315° = 70.711 \text{ km/h},$$
$$W_y = 100 \sin 315° = -70.711 \text{ km/h}.$$

(Note the use of 315°, not 45°.) The components of the air velocity (**A**) of the plane are $A_x = 400$ km/h and $A_y = 0$ km/h. Thus the components of **V** are

$$V_x = W_x + A_x = 70.711 + 400 = 470.711 \text{ km/h},$$
$$V_y = W_y + A_y = -70.711 + 0 = -70.711 \text{ km/h},$$

so

$$V = \sqrt{V_x^2 + V_y^2} = \sqrt{470.711^2 + (-70.711)^2}$$
$$= 476.0 \text{ km/h}.$$

Also,

$$\tan \theta = \frac{V_y}{V_x} = \frac{-70.711}{470.711} = -0.15022.$$

Because $V_x > 0$ and $V_y < 0$, θ is a fourth-quadrant angle. The reference angle α is 8.5°, so the direction of **V** is

$$\theta = 351.5°.$$

Thus the plane's velocity is 476.0 km/h at 351.5°, which can be given as 8.5° south of east.

example 4

A block of weight W newtons rests on a plane inclined at an angle of 30° with the horizontal (Fig. 7-72). If the frictional force is 3 N and the block remains at rest, find the weight of the block. Assume all forces act at the center of the block.

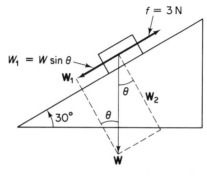

FIGURE 7-72

The weight **W** of the block is the force due to gravity and is directed vertically downward. The frictional force **f**, which always opposes motion or impending motion, is directed up the plane. Because the block does not move, *the net force up the plane must equal the net force down the plane*. The frictional force **f** is the only force upward, and the vector component **W₁** of the weight is the only force downward. Using geometry we can show that $\theta = 30°$. Hence $\sin 30° = W_1/W$ or $W_1 = W \sin 30°$. Thus

$$W_1 = f$$
$$W \sin 30° = f$$
$$W = \frac{f}{\sin 30°} = \frac{3}{\frac{1}{2}} = 6 \text{ N}.$$

example 5

An object is dropped from an airplane flying horizontally at a speed of 78 m/s (Fig. 7-73). The vertical component of its velocity as a function of time t (in seconds) is given by $V_y = -9.8t$ m/s. What is the magnitude of the velocity of the object after 5 s, and at what angle with the horizontal is the object moving at that time?

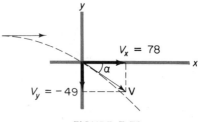

FIGURE 7-73

It is shown in physics that when air resistance is negligible, the horizontal component of the velocity **V** of such a free-falling object is constant. At every point along the object's flight path, V_x is the same as its initial value, namely, 78 m/s. At $t = 5$ s, the vertical component of **V** is $V_y = -9.8(5) = -49$ m/s. Thus the magnitude of the velocity is

$$V = \sqrt{78^2 + (-49)^2} = 92.1.$$

To find the angle α, which is measured below the horizontal, we have

$$\tan \alpha = \frac{|V_y|}{V_x} = \frac{49}{78} = 0.62821$$

$$\alpha = 32.1°.$$

Thus, at $t = 5$ s, the object's velocity is 92.1 m/s directed at an angle of 32.1° below the horizontal.

Exercise 7-8

In Problems 1–10, determine the magnitude R and direction θ of the resultant of the given vectors.

1. $A = 220, \quad \theta_A = 225°$
  $B = 100, \quad \theta_B = 16°.$

2. $A = 50, \quad \theta_A = 30°$
  $B = 120, \quad \theta_B = 30°$
  $C = 100, \quad \theta_C = 90°.$

3. $A = 200, \quad \theta_A = 210°$
  $B = 300, \quad \theta_B = 45°$
  $C = 400, \quad \theta_C = 120°.$

4. $A = 500, \quad \theta_A = 0°$
  $B = 300, \quad \theta_B = 180°$
  $C = 200, \quad \theta_C = 315°.$

5. $A = 300, \quad \theta_A = 80°$
  $B = 10, \quad \theta_B = 270°$
  $C = 100, \quad \theta_C = 30°.$

6. $A = 200, \quad \theta_A = 200°$
  $B = 50, \quad \theta_B = 50°$
  $C = 400, \quad \theta_C = 400°.$

7. $A = 310, \quad \theta_A = 330°$
  $B = 260, \quad \theta_B = 150°$
  $C = 550, \quad \theta_C = 120°.$

8. $A = 10, \quad \theta_A = 0°$
  $B = 5, \quad \theta_B = 226°$
  $C = 10, \quad \theta_C = 180°.$

9. $A = 80, \quad \theta_A = 30°$
  $B = 50, \quad \theta_B = 50°$
  $C = 60, \quad \theta_C = 60°$
  $D = 30, \quad \theta_D = 80°.$

10. $A = 10, \quad \theta_A = 10°$
  $B = 20, \quad \theta_B = 20°$
  $C = 30, \quad \theta_C = 30°$
  $D = 40, \quad \theta_D = 40°$
  $E = 50, \quad \theta_E = 50°.$

In Problems **11** *and* **12,** *find the resultant of the forces shown.*

11. See Fig. 7-74(a).

12. See Fig. 7-74(b).

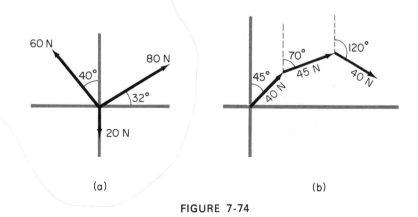

(a)

(b)

FIGURE 7-74

13. A plane in calm air leaves an airport and flies 300 km at an angle of 32° west of north. It then flies 200 km due west. How far from the airport is the plane? (See Example 2.)

14. Given a displacement of 300 m, 30° north of east, followed by a displacement of 400 m due north, find the magnitude and direction of the resultant displacement.

15. A plane is traveling eastward at an airspeed of 480 km/h. If a wind of 90 km/h is blowing northward, find the magnitude and direction of the plane's resultant velocity. (See Example 3.)

16. Find the magnitude and direction of the plane's resultant velocity in Problem 15 if the wind is blowing due northwest.

17. In still water a boat has an average speed of 41.3 km/h. If the boat heads due west in a river that flows due south at 14.1 km/h, find the resultant velocity of the boat. (See Example 3.)

18. Find the magnitude and direction of the resultant velocity in Problem 17 if the boat heads 22.3° south of west.

19. The angle between two displacements having magnitudes 20 km and 30 km is 42°. Find the magnitude of the resultant displacement. *Hint:* Place one of the displacements along the *x*-axis.

20. Two vectors **A** and **B** are added. Suppose $A = 10$ m, $B = 14$ m, and the magnitude of the resultant is 10 m. If the resultant **R** is perpendicular to **A**, determine the angle between **A** and **B**. *Hint:* Place **A** along the *x*-axis and **R** along the *y*-axis.

21. A block having a weight of 15 N rests on a 35.7° inclined plane. If the block does not move, determine the frictional force. (See Example 4.)

22. The resultant of two mutually perpendicular forces has magnitude 20 N. If one of the forces makes an angle of 28° with the resultant, what is the magnitude of that force?

23. An object is dropped from a plane that is traveling at a speed of 100 m/s at a direction of 30° above the horizontal. The vertical component of the object's velocity is given by $V_y = 50 - 9.8t$, where t is time in seconds. In the absence of air resistance, what is the speed of the object after 2 s, and in what direction with respect to the horizontal is the object moving at that time. (See Example 5.)

24. An object is dropped from a plane flying horizontally at a speed of 110 m/s.
    (a) After 6 s, what is the magnitude and direction of the object's velocity if its vertical component is given by $V_y = -9.8t$, where t is in seconds? (See Example 5.)
    (b) How long after being released will the object have a velocity that is directed at an angle of 45° below the horizontal?

25. In calm air the speed of a plane is 200 m/s. If a wind is blowing due east at 20 m/s, in what direction should the plane head if it is to fly due south?

7-9   A Comment on Trigonometric Tables

Although calculators have made it easy to obtain values of trigonometric functions, tables of such values are commonly available. A brief table is given in Appendix B, and a portion of it appears in Table 7-3.

Table 7-3

Degrees	Radians	Sin	Cos	Tan	Cot		
0	0.0000	0.0000	1.0000	0.0000	......	1.5708	90
1	0.0175	0.0175	0.9998	0.0175	57.290	1.5533	89
2	0.0349	0.0349	0.9994	0.0349	28.636	1.5359	88
3	0.0524	0.0523	0.9986	0.0524	19.081	1.5184	87
4	0.0698	0.0698	0.9976	0.0699	14.301	1.5010	86
5	0.0873	0.0872	0.9962	0.0875	11.430	1.4835	85
6	0.1047	0.1045	0.9945	0.1051	9.5144	1.4661	84
7	0.1222	0.1219	0.9925	0.1228	8.1443	1.4486	83
8	0.1396	0.1392	0.9903	0.1405	7.1154	1.4312	82
9	0.1571	0.1564	0.9877	0.1584	6.3138	1.4137	81
		Cos	Sin	Cot	Tan	Radians	Degrees

For an angle between 0° and 45° that is listed in the left-hand column, we use the column headings at the *top* and read *down* the columns. For an angle between 45° and 90° that is listed in the right-hand column, we use the column headings at the *bottom* and read *up* the columns. For example, referring to Table 7-3, we see that sin 6° = 0.1045 and tan 84° = 9.5144. These are approximate values, as is the case with most entries. Trigonometric values for an angle that is between two angles in the table can be estimated by the method of linear interpolation that was discussed in Sec. 6-5. The following examples will illustrate.

example 1

Find sin 8.4°.

Referring to Table 7-3, we have the following setup.

$$
1 \left[0.4 \left[\begin{array}{l} \sin 8.0° = 0.1392 \\ \sin 8.4° = \quad ? \end{array} \right] d \\ \quad\quad \sin 9.0° = 0.1564 \right] 0.0172 \text{ increase}
$$

We assume that sin 8.4° is $\dfrac{0.4}{1}$ or 0.4 of the way from sin 8° to sin 9°. Thus

$$d = 0.4(0.0172) = 0.0069.$$

Because the values of the sine function *increase* as an angle goes from 8° to 9°, we *add* d to sin 8°.

$$\sin 8.4° = 0.1392 + 0.0069 = 0.1461.$$

example 2

Find the acute angle θ such that cos $\theta = 0.1100$.

Referring to Table 7-3, we read *up* the column with *Cos* at the bottom.

$$
1 \left[d \left[\begin{array}{l} \cos 83.0° = 0.1219 \\ \cos \quad \theta \;\; = 0.1100 \end{array} \right] 0.0119 \\ \quad\quad \cos 84.0° = 0.1045 \right] 0.0174
$$

$$d = \frac{0.0119}{0.0174}(1) = 0.7,$$

$$\theta = 83.0° + 0.7° = 83.7°.$$

Exercise 7-9

In Problems 1–10, use Appendix B and linear interpolation to estimate the given trigonometric values.

1. sin 23.2°.   **2.** tan 12.6°.   **3.** cos 43.4°.   **4.** tan 53.1°.

5. cos 84.7°.   **6.** cos 79.3°.   **7.** tan 45.6°.   **8.** sin 46.8°.

9. cos 49.4°.   **10.** sin 12.4°.

In Problems 11–20, find the acute angle θ that has the given trigonometric value. Use Appendix B and linear interpolation.

11. cos $\theta = 0.7470$.   **12.** sin $\theta = 0.3199$.   **13.** sin $\theta = 0.9628$.

14. tan $\theta = 2.6280$.   **15.** sin $\theta = 0.2120$.   **16.** sin $\theta = 0.8350$.

17. tan $\theta = 2.0000$.   **18.** sin $\theta = 1.5900$.   **19.** cos $\theta = 0.4741$.

20. tan $\theta = 1.1800$.

7-10 Review

Review Questions

1. Which is larger, cos 0° or cos 90°? _____

2. Which of the following statements is (are) true? _____.
   (a) sin 21° = 1/sec 69°.
   (b) sin (−20°) = −sin 20°.
   (c) sin 100° = −sin 80°.
   (d) tan 60° = cot 30°.
   (e) sin 90° = sin 270°.
   (f) sin 20° = sin 380°.

3. In three minutes the second hand of a clock rotates through _____ radians.

4. The only trigonometric functions that have positive values for an angle in Quadrant III are the _____ functions.

5. The value of sin 280° is equal to the negative of the sine of what acute angle? _____

6. If 0° ≤ θ < 360°, then sin θ = 0 for what two values of θ? _____

7. The angles 10°, 370°, and −350° are _____ with one another.

8. In Fig. 7-75, a = _____ .

FIGURE 7-75

9. In Fig. 7-76, θ = _____ .

FIGURE 7-76

10. A vector quantity has both magnitude and _____.

11. In Fig. 7-77, what angle does the resultant of the given vectors make with the positive x-axis?

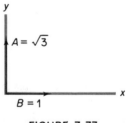

FIGURE 7-77

12. True or false: If sin A = sin B, then A must be equal to B. _____ (a) _____
    If A and B are coterminal angles, then sin A = sin B. _____ (b) _____

13. If $\sin \theta$ is negative and $\tan \theta$ is positive, then θ lies in the _____ quadrant.

14. 720° equals how many radians? _____.

15. To convert x radians to degrees, we multiply x by _____.

Answers to Review Questions

1. $\cos 0°$.   **2.** a, b, d, and f.   **3.** 6π.   **4.** Tangent and cotangent.   **5.** 80°.
6. 0°, 180°.   **7.** Coterminal.   **8.** 2.   **9.** 45°.   **10.** Direction.   **11.** 60°.
12. (a) False,   (b) True.   **13.** Third.   **14.** 4π.   **15.** $180°/\pi$.

Review Problems

In Problems 1–8, convert each degree measurement to radians, and each radian measurement to degrees.

1. 300°.   **2.** 750°.   **3.** $\dfrac{5\pi}{6}$.   **4.** $-\dfrac{9\pi}{4}$.

5. −50°.   **6.** 36°.   **7.** $\dfrac{\pi}{18}$.   **8.** $\dfrac{3\pi}{10}$.

In Problems 9–12, find the quadrants of the angles.

9. 224°.   **10.** −370°.   **11.** $\dfrac{7\pi}{3}$.   **12.** $\dfrac{9\pi}{10}$.

In Problems 13–16, find the exact arc length cut off by the given central angle θ on a circle with the given radius r.

13. $\theta = \dfrac{7\pi}{6}, r = 12$.   **14.** $\theta = \dfrac{5\pi}{4}, r = 10$.

15. $\theta = 135°, r = 2$.   **16.** $\theta = 60°, r = 3$.

17. Find an angle θ that is coterminal with 500°, such that $0° \le \theta < 360°$.

18. Find an angle θ that is coterminal with $-5\pi/4$, such that $0 \le \theta < 2\pi$.

In Problems 19–22, the given point lies on the terminal side of an angle θ in standard position. Find the values of the six trigonometric functions of θ.

19. $(1, -6)$.   **20.** $(-2, 0)$.   **21.** $(-2, -3\sqrt{5})$.   **22.** $(\sqrt{11}, -5)$.

23. If $\sin \theta = \dfrac{1}{5}$ and $\cos \theta = -\dfrac{2\sqrt{6}}{5}$, find the other trigonometric values of θ.

24. If $\tan \theta = -\dfrac{3}{5}$ and $\sec \theta = -\dfrac{\sqrt{34}}{5}$, find the other trigonometric values of θ.

25. If $\cos \theta = \dfrac{3}{7}$ and $\tan \theta$ is negative, find the other trigonometric values of θ.

26. If $\tan \theta = -\dfrac{\sqrt{51}}{7}$ and $\sin \theta$ is positive, find the other trigonometric values of θ.

In Problems 27–38, find the given values without the use of a calculator.

27. $\cos \dfrac{2\pi}{3}$.   **28.** $\tan \dfrac{5\pi}{6}$.   **29.** $\sec \pi$.   **30.** $\sin(-120°)$.

31. $\csc 135°$.   **32.** $\cot 270°$.   **33.** $\tan 210°$.   **34.** $\sec 405°$.

35. $\sin(-180°)$.   **36.** $\cos \dfrac{11\pi}{6}$.   **37.** $\csc \dfrac{4\pi}{3}$.   **38.** $\cot\left(-\dfrac{3\pi}{2}\right)$.

In Problems 39–46, solve the right triangle ABC for the remaining parts.

39. $a = 4$, $b = 10$.   **40.** $a = 5$, $c = 21$.   **41.** $a = 6$, $B = 15°$.

42. $b = 9$, $A = 24°$.   **43.** $b = 7$, $A = 46°$.   **44.** $c = 12$, $B = 35.2°$.

45. $c = 20$, $A = 32.6°$.   **46.** $a = 45$, $A = 60°$.

In Problems 47 and 48, find the magnitude and direction of the resultant of the given vectors.

47. $A = 100$, $\theta_A = 320°$ **48.** $A = 20$, $\theta_A = 220°$
$B = 120$, $\theta_B = 40°$ $B = 30$, $\theta_B = 310°$
$C = 50$, $\theta_C = 55°$. $C = 10$, $\theta_C = 50°$.

49. An alternating emf $\mathcal{E}$ is produced by rotating a coil in a magnetic field. For a particular coil, the emf (in volts) is given by $\mathcal{E} = 110 \sin \theta$, where θ is the angle through which the coil has turned. Find $\mathcal{E}$ when θ is (a) 120°, (b) 598°, and (c) 8.5 rad.

50. A wrecking company needs to know the height of a smokestack, which is to be demolished. At a point 34 m from the base of the stack, the wreckers find that the angle of elevation of its top is 32°. What is the height of the smokestack?

51. An antenna mast, which had its top section blown over by the wind, forms a right triangle with the ground. The broken part makes an angle of 57° with the ground. The top of the antenna touches the ground at a point 30 m from the base of the antenna. Find the original height of the antenna.

52. A man 2 m tall stands 4 m from the base of a street light. He can observe the light when his line of sight makes an angle of 42° with the horizontal. Find the length of the shadow cast by the man.

53. An airplane flies 400 km in the direction 30° west of south. Find the horizontal and vertical components of the displacement **d** of the airplane.

54. A balloon, which rises 10 m/s, is released when there is a wind of 4 m/s blowing due east. Find the magnitude and direction of the resultant velocity of the balloon.

systems
of equations

8-1 Systems of Linear Equations in Two Variables

When a physical situation must be described in mathematical terms, it is not unusual for a set of equations to arise. For example, suppose an airplane travels 1440 km in 3 hours with the aid of a tail wind, but takes 3 hours and 36 minutes for the return trip in which the pilot flies against the same wind. What is the average speed of the airplane in still air, and what is the speed of the wind?

Suppose we let x denote the (average) speed of the airplane in still air and y denote the speed of the wind, where both speeds are in kilometers per hour. Then, with the wind the speed of the airplane is $x + y$, and against the wind its speed is $x - y$. Because (rate)(time) = distance, the conditions imposed by the situation are

$$(x + y)(3) = 1440$$

and (because 3 hours 36 minutes $= 3\frac{3}{5}$ hours)

$$(x - y)(3\tfrac{3}{5}) = 1440.$$

Equivalently, we have the following two linear equations in x and y:

$$3x + 3y = 1440$$
$$\tfrac{18}{5}x - \tfrac{18}{5}y = 1440.$$

The final step is to find values of x and y for which *both* equations above are true.

283

Let us first consider such a situation on a more general level. We shall return to our particular problem shortly.

The set of linear equations

$$\begin{cases} a_1x + b_1y = c_1 & (1) \\ a_2x + b_2y = c_2 & (2) \end{cases}$$

is called a **system** of two linear equations in the variables (or unknowns) x and y. The brace indicates that each equation is to be considered in conjunction with the other. A **solution of the system** consists of values of x and y that satisfy *both* equations *simultaneously*.

Because Eqs. 1 and 2 are linear, their graphs are straight lines, call them L_1 and L_2. The coordinates of any point on a line satisfy the equation of that line, so the coordinates of any point of intersection of L_1 and L_2 will satisfy *both* equations. This means that a point of intersection gives a solution of the system, and vice versa. If L_1 and L_2 are drawn on the same plane, they will appear in one of three ways:

1. L_1 and L_2 may intersect at exactly one point, (x_0, y_0) (Fig. 8-1). Thus the system has the solution $x = x_0$ and $y = y_0$.

2. L_1 and L_2 may be parallel and have no points in common (Fig. 8-2). Thus there is no solution.

3. L_1 and L_2 may be the same line (Fig. 8-3). Thus the coordinates of *any* point on the line is a solution of the system, so there are infinitely many solutions. In this case the equations for L_1 and L_2 must be equivalent.

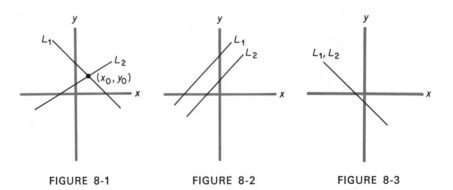

FIGURE 8-1   FIGURE 8-2   FIGURE 8-3

If a solution to a system exists, the system is said to be **consistent**. Otherwise, the system is **inconsistent**. For example, Figs. 8-1 and 8-3 represent consistent systems, but Fig. 8-2 represents an inconsistent system. A system of linear equations with exactly one solution is said to be **independent**. If more than one solution exists, the system is **dependent**. The system represented in Fig. 8-1 is independent, but that in Fig. 8-3 is dependent.

Returning to our original system concerning the airplane, we shall graphically solve

$$\begin{cases} 3x + 3y = 1440 \\ \frac{18}{5}x - \frac{18}{5}y = 1440. \end{cases}$$

To sketch the first equation (or line), we note that if $x = 0$, then $3y = 1440$ and so $y = 480$. If $y = 0$, then $x = 480$. Thus the x- and y-intercepts are both 480. Using these points we graph the line in Fig. 8-4. For the second line, the x- and y-intercepts are found to be 400 and -400, respectively; these intercepts are then used to sketch the graph. Figure 8-4 shows the result of sketching the system. Because x and y are

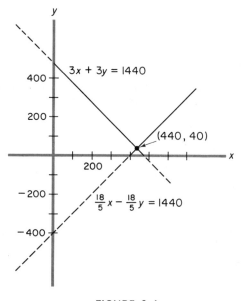

FIGURE 8-4

speeds, the lines have no physical meaning for $x < 0$ or $y < 0$. We estimate the point of intersection to be $x = 440$, $y = 40$. By substituting these values into *both* of the given equations, we find that the system is satisfied. For example, the first equation becomes $3(440) + 3(40) = 1440$, which is true. Thus the speed of the airplane in still air is 440 km/h and the speed of the wind is 40 km/h.

example 1

Graphically solve the linear system

$$\begin{cases} 4T_1 + 2T_2 = 8 \\ 2T_1 + T_2 = -3. \end{cases}$$

Choosing T_1 for the horizontal axis and T_2 for the vertical axis, we obtain Fig. 8-5. Note that the lines are different but seem to be parallel, which implies that the system

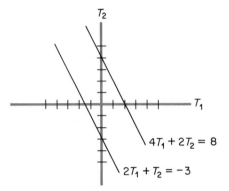

FIGURE 8-5

has no solution. To confirm this, we can analyze an equivalent system (that is, one with identical solutions) in which both lines are written in slope-intercept form:

$$\begin{cases} T_2 = -2T_1 + 4 \\ T_2 = -2T_1 - 3. \end{cases}$$

Because the lines have the same slope ($m = -2$) but different T_2-intercepts (4 and -3), the system is indeed represented by different parallel lines. Thus no solution exists and the system is inconsistent.

example 2

Graphically solve the system

$$\begin{cases} 2y = 4x + 2 & \text{(3)} \\ y = 2x + 1. & \text{(4)} \end{cases}$$

Graphing both equations gives the same line, shown in Fig. 8-6. Observe that if both sides of Eq. 4 are multiplied by 2, the result is Eq. 3. Thus, the equations are equivalent.

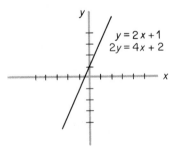

FIGURE 8-6

Therefore the coordinates of any point on the line $y = 2x + 1$ is a solution, so there are infinitely many solutions. For example, one solution is $x = 0$, $y = 1$. The system is consistent and dependent.

In the next section we shall focus our attention on algebraic methods of solving a system of equations. The graphical approach is not precise and should be used only when other methods are not practical.

Exercise 8-1

Solve the following systems by graphing.

1. $\begin{cases} x - 2y = -3 \\ 3x + y = -2. \end{cases}$ **2.** $\begin{cases} y = x - \frac{1}{2} \\ 2y = -1 + x. \end{cases}$ **3.** $\begin{cases} y + 2x = 2 \\ y - 5 = -2x. \end{cases}$

4. $\begin{cases} 2x - y = -11 \\ y + 5x = -7. \end{cases}$ **5.** $\begin{cases} 2x + y = 4 \\ 10y - 41 = -21x. \end{cases}$ **6.** $\begin{cases} \frac{3}{2}y = 2x - 1 \\ y + \frac{2}{3} = \frac{4}{3}x. \end{cases}$

7. $\begin{cases} y = 6x - 3 \\ 18x = 9 + 3y. \end{cases}$ **8.** $\begin{cases} 3F_1 - 2F_2 = 1 \\ 2F_1 - 3F_2 = -6. \end{cases}$ **9.** $\begin{cases} 2i_2 = -i_1 + 4 \\ i_2 + 5 = 2i_1. \end{cases}$

10. $\begin{cases} 3(x + y) = 4(x - y) + 3 \\ 2(x - y) = 2y + 1. \end{cases}$

8-2 Methods of Elimination

We now turn to algebraic methods of solving a system of two linear equations. These methods involve performing algebraic operations to obtain an equation in which only one of the variables appears. The other variable is *eliminated*. After solving that equation, we can easily find the value of the eliminated variable.

To illustrate, we shall solve the system

$$\begin{cases} 2x - 3y = -12 & (1) \\ 3x + y = -7 & (2) \end{cases}$$

by obtaining an equation in which y does not appear. That is, we shall eliminate y. First, we find an equivalent system in which the coefficients of y differ only in sign. To do this we multiply Eq. 2 by 3 (that is, we multiply both sides of Eq. 2 by 3).

$$\begin{cases} 2x - 3y = -12 & (3) \\ 9x + 3y = -21. & (4) \end{cases}$$

Because the left and right sides of Eq. 3 are equal, each side can be *added* to the corresponding side of Eq. 4. Equation 4 becomes $11x = -33$ or, more simply,

$x = -3$. Thus we have the equivalent system

$$\begin{cases} 2x - 3y = -12 & \quad (5) \\ x = -3. & \quad (6) \end{cases}$$

Note that y does not appear in Eq. 6. Replacing x in Eq. 5 by -3 gives

$$2(-3) - 3y = -12$$
$$-6 - 3y = -12$$
$$-3y = -6$$
$$y = 2.$$

The solution is $x = -3$ and $y = 2$. We check our solution by substituting these values into *both* Eqs. 1 and 2. In Eq. 1, we have $2(-3) - 3(2) = -12$, or $-12 = -12$. In Eq. 2, we have $3(-3) + 2 = -7$, which is true.

The procedure we used to solve the system is referred to as **elimination by addition**. Although we chose to eliminate y, we could have eliminated x instead. If we multiply Eq. 1 by 3 and multiply Eq. 2 by -2, the coefficients of x in the resulting equivalent system will differ only in sign:

$$\begin{cases} 6x - 9y = -36 & \quad (7) \\ -6x - 2y = 14. & \quad (8) \end{cases}$$

Adding Eq. 7 to Eq. 8 (that is, adding corresponding sides of Eq. 7 to Eq. 8), we obtain

$$-11y = -22$$

or

$$y = 2.$$

By replacing y in Eq. 7 by 2, we find that $x = -3$, as expected. Figure 8-7 shows the graph of the system.

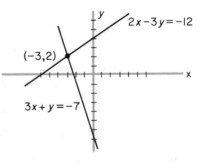

FIGURE 8-7

example 1

By using elimination by addition, solve the system

$$\begin{cases} y - 2x = 4 \\ 4x - 2y = -5. \end{cases}$$

Aligning the x- and y-terms, we have

$$\begin{cases} -2x + y = 4 & (9) \\ 4x - 2y = -5. & (10) \end{cases}$$

Multiplying Eq. 9 by 2 gives

$$\begin{cases} -4x + 2y = 8 & (11) \\ 4x - 2y = -5. & (12) \end{cases}$$

Adding Eq. 11 to Eq. 12 gives $0 = 3$, and we therefore have the equivalent system

$$\begin{cases} -4x + 2y = 8 & (13) \\ 0 = 3. & (14) \end{cases}$$

Because Eq. 14 is *never* true, there is no solution to the original system. Observe that by using the slope-intercept form, we can write the original system as

$$\begin{cases} y = 2x + 4 \\ y = 2x + \frac{5}{2}. \end{cases}$$

These equations represent straight lines with slopes of 2 but different y-intercepts, 4 and $\frac{5}{2}$; that is, they determine different parallel lines (Fig. 8-8). The system is inconsistent.

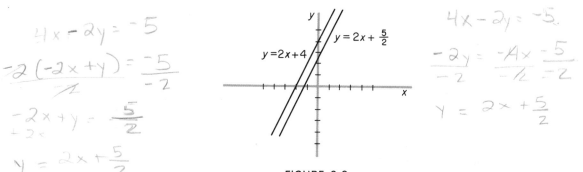

FIGURE 8-8

example 2

By using elimination by addition, solve the system

$$\begin{cases} 2x + y = 1 & (15) \\ 4x + 2y = 2. & (16) \end{cases}$$

Multiplying Eq. 15 by -2 gives

$$\begin{cases} -4x - 2y = -2 & \text{(17)} \\ 4x + 2y = 2. & \text{(18)} \end{cases}$$

Adding Eq. 18 to Eq. 17, we have

$$\begin{cases} 0 = 0 & \text{(19)} \\ 4x + 2y = 2. & \text{(20)} \end{cases}$$

Any solution of Eq. 20 is a solution of the system because Eq. 19 is always true. Looking at it another way, by writing Eqs. 15 and 16 in their slope-intercept forms, we obtain

$$\begin{cases} y = -2x + 1 \\ y = -2x + 1, \end{cases}$$

in which both equations represent the same line. Thus Eqs. 15 and 16 are equivalent (Fig. 8-9). The coordinates of any point on the line $y = -2x + 1$ is a solution, so there are infinitely many solutions. The given system is consistent and dependent. Some solutions are $x = 0, y = 1$; $x = 1, y = -1$; and $x = -3, y = 7$.

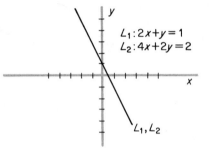

FIGURE 8-9

To solve the system

$$\begin{cases} 2i_1 + 3i_2 = -10 & \text{(21)} \\ 3i_1 - 2i_2 = -2 & \text{(22)} \end{cases}$$

by a method that is an alternative to elimination by addition, we first choose either equation and solve it for one unknown in terms of the other. For example, solving Eq. 22 for i_2 gives

$$i_2 = \frac{3i_1 + 2}{2}. \qquad (23)$$

By *substitution*, we eliminate i_2 in Eq. 21:

$$2i_1 + 3\left(\frac{3i_1 + 2}{2}\right) = -10.$$

(We did not substitute for i_1 in Eq. 22 because it is the same equation from which i_2 was obtained. We must substitute into the other equation.) Clearing of fractions and solving for i_1 gives

$$4i_1 + 9i_1 + 6 = -20$$
$$13i_1 = -26$$
$$i_1 = -2.$$

Replacing i_1 in Eq. 23 by -2 gives

$$i_2 = \frac{3(-2) + 2}{2} = \frac{-4}{2} = -2.$$

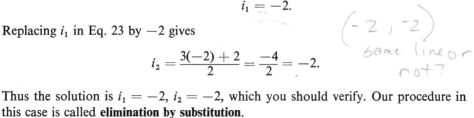

$\left(-2, -2\right)$
same linear
not?

Thus the solution is $i_1 = -2$, $i_2 = -2$, which you should verify. Our procedure in this case is called **elimination by substitution**.

Exercise 8-2

In Problems 1–4, use elimination by addition to solve the systems.

1. $\begin{cases} x + 2y = 1 \\ 3x + y = -2. \end{cases}$ **2.** $\begin{cases} 2x + 3y = -10 \\ 3x - 2y = -2. \end{cases}$

3. $\begin{cases} 4T_1 - 3T_2 = 6 \\ 3T_1 + 2T_2 = 13. \end{cases}$ **4.** $\begin{cases} 5i_1 + 3i_2 = 10 \\ 3i_2 + 4i_2 = 6. \end{cases}$

In Problems 5–8, use elimination by substitution to solve the systems.

5. $\begin{cases} 4x + y = 6 \\ 3x + 2y = 2. \end{cases}$ **6.** $\begin{cases} x + 5y = -14 \\ -2x - 7y = 16. \end{cases}$

7. $\begin{cases} 5x + 7y = 13 \\ -x + 5y = 7. \end{cases}$ **8.** $\begin{cases} 4x - 3y = 13 \\ 3x + y = 0. \end{cases}$

In Problems 9–20, solve the systems by addition or substitution.

9. $\begin{cases} 3F_1 + F_2 = 7 \\ 2F_1 + 2F_2 = -2. \end{cases}$ **10.** $\begin{cases} 2x - y = -11 \\ y + 5x = -7. \end{cases}$

11. $\begin{cases} 3x - 4y - 13 = 0 \\ 2x + 3y - 3 = 0. \end{cases}$ **12.** $\begin{cases} 5x - 3y = 2 \\ -10x + 6y = 4. \end{cases}$

13. $\begin{cases} 2i_2 = 36 - 5i_1 \\ 8i_1 = 3i_2 - 54. \end{cases}$ **14.** $\begin{cases} T_1 = 3 - T_2 \\ 3T_1 + 2T_2 = 19. \end{cases}$

15. $\begin{cases} 4x + 12y = 6 \\ 2x + 6y = 3. \end{cases}$ **16.** $\begin{cases} 2u - v - 1 = 0 \\ -u + 2v - 7 = 0. \end{cases}$

17. $\begin{cases} 2x + y = 4 \\ 10y - 41 = -20x. \end{cases}$ **18.** $\begin{cases} 3y = 4x - 2 \\ y + \frac{2}{3} = \frac{4}{3}x. \end{cases}$

19. $\begin{cases} \frac{2}{3}x + \frac{1}{2}y = 2 \\ \frac{3}{8}x + \frac{5}{6}y = -\frac{11}{2}. \end{cases}$ **20.** $\begin{cases} 3(x + y) = 4(x - y) + 3 \\ 2(x - y) = 2y + 1. \end{cases}$

21. A 49-N block is to be moved without acceleration along a horizontal surface by means of a force F parallel to the surface. The coefficient of kinetic friction between the block and the surface is 0.3. For this situation, Newton's laws lead to the system

$$\begin{cases} F - 0.3N = 0 \\ N - 49 = 0, \end{cases}$$

where N is the normal force exerted on the block by the surface, and F and N are in newtons. Find F and N.

22. If the block in Problem 21 is to accelerate at 2 m/s², the appropriate system of equations is

$$\begin{cases} F - 0.3N = \dfrac{49}{9.8}(2) \\ N - 49 = 0. \end{cases}$$

Find F and N.

23. In a given electrical circuit, two currents i_1 and i_2, in amperes, can be found by solving the system

$$\begin{cases} 3i_1 + 5i_2 = -3 \\ 4i_1 + 2i_2 = 4. \end{cases}$$

Find i_1 and i_2.

24. Masses of 7 kg and 9 kg are attached to a cord passing over a light frictionless pulley. When the masses are released, the acceleration a of each mass (in meters per second squared) and the tension T in the cord (in newtons) are related by the system

$$\begin{cases} T - 68.6 = 7a \\ 88.2 - T = 9a. \end{cases}$$

Find T and a.

25. A 1-kg ball moving at 12 m/s has a head-on collision with a 2-kg ball moving in the opposite direction at 24 m/s. If the coefficient of restitution for the collision is $\frac{2}{3}$, then the velocities v_1 and v_2 of the balls after the collision are related by the system

$$\begin{cases} v_1 + 2v_2 = -36 \\ v_2 - v_1 = 24, \end{cases}$$

where v_1 and v_2 are measured in meters per second. Find v_1 and v_2.

26. If the collision described in Problem 25 were perfectly elastic, then the system of equations would be

$$\begin{cases} v_1 + 2v_2 = -36 \\ v_2 - v_1 = 36. \end{cases}$$

Solve for v_1 and v_2.

27. A child pulls a 5-kg sled across the snow with constant velocity. The rope used to pull the sled makes an angle of 36.9° with the horizontal. The relationship between

the force F exerted by the rope and the normal force N exerted by the ground, both measured in newtons, is given by the system

$$\begin{cases} F \sin 36.9° + N - 49 = 0 \\ F \cos 36.9° - 0.3N \quad = 0. \end{cases}$$

Find F and N.

8-3 Systems of Linear Equations in Three Variables

An equation of the form $Ax + By + Cz = D$, where A, B, C, and D are constants and A, B, and C are not all zero, is called a general **linear equation in the variables x, y, and z.** To solve a system of three such equations, we use the methods of elimination discussed in the last section.

One approach is to select two *pairs* of the given equations and eliminate the *same* variable from each pair. The resulting two equations, being in the same two variables, can then be solved by elimination. Substitution of these two values in any of the original equations will yield the value of the third variable. This technique can be extended to a system of n linear equations in n variables by reducing the system to $n - 1$ equations in $n - 1$ variables, which is then reduced, and so on. An alternative method will be given in Example 2.

example 1

Solve the system

$$\begin{cases} 4x - y - 3z = 1 & \text{(1)} \\ 2x + y + 2z = 5 & \text{(2)} \\ 8x + y - \quad z = 5. & \text{(3)} \end{cases}$$

Here we have a system of three linear equations in three variables. Selecting Eqs. 1 and 2, we have

$$\begin{cases} 4x - y - 3z = 1 \\ 2x + y + 2z = 5. \end{cases}$$

Adding these to eliminate y gives

$$6x - z = 6. \qquad \text{(4)}$$

Repeating this procedure, we select Eqs. 2 and 3:

$$\begin{cases} 2x + y + 2z = 5 \\ 8x + y - \quad z = 5. \end{cases}$$

We must also eliminate y from these. Multiplying the bottom equation by -1 gives

$$\begin{cases} 2x + y + 2z = 5 \\ -8x - y + z = -5. \end{cases}$$

Adding these, we have

$$-6x + 3z = 0. \tag{5}$$

A new system is formed by Eqs. 4 and 5:

$$\begin{cases} 6x - z = 6 & (6) \\ -6x + 3z = 0. & (7) \end{cases}$$

Adding Eq. 6 to Eq. 7 and solving for z gives

$$2z = 6$$
$$z = 3.$$

Substituting $z = 3$ in Eq. 6 gives $6x - 3 = 6$, or simply $x = \frac{3}{2}$. Substituting $x = \frac{3}{2}$ and $z = 3$ in Eq. 1 gives $4(\frac{3}{2}) - y - 3(3) = 1$, from which $y = -4$. The solution is $x = \frac{3}{2}$, $y = -4$, $z = 3$, which you should verify.

example 2

Solve the system

$$\begin{cases} 2x + y - z = -2 & (8) \\ x - 2y = \dfrac{13}{2} & (9) \\ 3x + 2y - 2z = -\dfrac{9}{2}. & (10) \end{cases}$$

Since Eq. 9 can be written $x - 2y + 0z = \frac{13}{2}$, we can view Eqs. 8, 9, and 10 as a system of three linear equations in the variables x, y, and z. We shall solve this system by a different approach than that of the previous example. From Eq. 9, $x = 2y + \frac{13}{2}$. By substituting for x in Eqs. 8 and 10, we obtain

$$\begin{cases} 2\left(2y + \dfrac{13}{2}\right) + y - z = -2 \\ 3\left(2y + \dfrac{13}{2}\right) + 2y - 2z = -\dfrac{9}{2}, \end{cases}$$

or, more simply,

$$\begin{cases} 5y - z = -15 & (11) \\ 4y - z = -12. & (12) \end{cases}$$

We now solve the system formed by Eqs. 11 and 12. Multiplying Eq. 11 by -1 and adding the result to Eq. 12 gives $-y = 3$, or $y = -3$. Substituting -3 for y in Eq. 11 gives $5(-3) - z = -15$, from which $z = 0$. Substituting these values into Eq. 9 gives $x - 2(-3) = \frac{13}{2}$, from which $x = \frac{1}{2}$. Thus the solution of the original system is $x = \frac{1}{2}$, $y = -3$, $z = 0$.

Exercise 8-3

In Problems **1–10**, *solve the systems.*

1. $\begin{cases} x + y + z = 6 \\ x - y + z = 2 \\ 2x - y + 3z = 6. \end{cases}$

2. $\begin{cases} 2x - y + 3z = 12 \\ x + 2y - 3z = -10 \\ x + y - z = -3. \end{cases}$

3. $\begin{cases} x - z = 14 \\ y + z = 21 \\ x - y + z = -10. \end{cases}$

4. $\begin{cases} x + y = -6 \\ z = 4 \\ -x + y + 2z = 16. \end{cases}$

5. $\begin{cases} 2x + y + 6z = 3 \\ x - y + 4z = 1 \\ 3x + 2y - 2z = 2. \end{cases}$

6. $\begin{cases} 5x - 7y + 4z = 2 \\ 3x + 2y - 2z = 3 \\ 2x - y + 3z = 4. \end{cases}$

7. $\begin{cases} 2x - 3y + z = -2 \\ 3x + 3y - z = 2 \\ x - 6y + 3z = -2. \end{cases}$

8. $\begin{cases} x + y + z = -1 \\ 3x + y + z = 1 \\ 4x - 2y + 2z = 0. \end{cases}$

9. $\begin{cases} x + y + 5z = 6 \\ x + 2y + w = 4 \\ 2y + z + w = 6 \\ 3x - 4z = 2. \end{cases}$

10. $\begin{cases} x - y + 3z + w = -14 \\ x + 2y - 3w = 12 \\ 2x + 3y + 6z + w = 1 \\ x + y + z + w = 6. \end{cases}$

11. The boom in Fig. 8-10 has weight **W** and is acted upon by the forces shown, in newtons. The force exerted by the string is **T**, and **V** and **H** are forces exerted by the

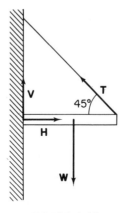

FIGURE 8-10

wall. In mechanics it is shown that for the boom to be in equilibrium,

$$\begin{cases} H - T\cos 45° = 0 \\ V + T\sin 45° - W = 0 \\ W(\tfrac{1}{2}) - T\sin 45° = 0. \end{cases}$$

If $W = 100$ N, find the exact values for H, T, and V.

12. If the weight of the boom in Problem 11 is doubled, what are the exact values for H, T, and V?

13. In the analysis of direct-current circuits, Kirchhoff's laws are often used. Application of these laws to the circuit of Fig. 8-11 gives the following system:

$$\begin{cases} R_1 i_1 + R_2 i_1 + R_3 i_3 + \mathcal{E}_1 = 0 \\ \qquad\qquad R_3 i_3 + R_4 i_2 + \mathcal{E}_2 = 0 \\ \qquad\qquad\qquad\qquad i_1 + i_2 = i_3, \end{cases}$$

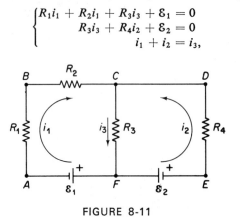

FIGURE 8-11

where the R's are resistances, the i's are currents, and the $\mathcal{E}$'s are potential differences. Given that $R_1 = 2$, $R_2 = 3$, $R_3 = 5$, and $R_4 = 3$ ohms and $\mathcal{E}_1 = 15$ volts and $\mathcal{E}_2 = 2$ volts, solve the system of equations for i_1, i_2, and i_3. This gives the current, in amperes, in each branch of the circuit.

14. In the circuit of Problem 13, if $R_1 = 1$, $R_2 = 1$, $R_3 = 4$, and $R_4 = 6$ ohms and $\mathcal{E}_1 = 2$ volts and $\mathcal{E}_2 = 60$ volts, find i_1, i_2, and i_3.

15. In the circuit of Problem 13, with $\mathcal{E}_1 = \mathcal{E}_2$ a student measured and found that $i_1 = i_2$. Show that, as a consequence,

$$R_1 + R_2 - R_4 = 0.$$

You may assume that $i_1 \neq 0$.

8-4 Determinants of Order 2

Consider a system of two linear equations in two variables of the general form $ax + by = c$, namely

$$\begin{cases} a_1 x + b_1 y = c_1 & \text{(1)} \\ a_2 x + b_2 y = c_2. & \text{(2)} \end{cases}$$

To solve for x, we can eliminate y by first multiplying Eq. 1 by b_2 and Eq. 2 by $-b_1$:

$$\begin{cases} a_1 b_2 x + b_1 b_2 y = b_2 c_1 \\ -a_2 b_1 x - b_1 b_2 y = -b_1 c_2. \end{cases}$$

Adding these equations, we have

$$a_1 b_2 x - a_2 b_1 x = b_2 c_1 - b_1 c_2.$$

Factoring and solving for x gives

$$x(a_1 b_2 - a_2 b_1) = b_2 c_1 - b_1 c_2$$

$$x = \frac{b_2 c_1 - b_1 c_2}{a_1 b_2 - a_2 b_1}, \tag{3}$$

provided $a_1 b_2 - a_2 b_1 \neq 0$. Similarly, we can show that

$$y = \frac{a_1 c_2 - a_2 c_1}{a_1 b_2 - a_2 b_1}. \tag{4}$$

Note that the denominators in Eqs. 3 and 4 are the same number, $a_1 b_2 - a_2 b_1$. This number will be denoted by a *square array of numbers* enclosed by vertical bars:

$$\begin{vmatrix} a_1 & b_1 \\ a_2 & b_2 \end{vmatrix} = a_1 b_2 - a_2 b_1.$$

In this form the number $a_1 b_2 - a_2 b_1$ is called a **determinant**. More precisely, it is called a **second-order determinant** since there are two entries in each row and column. The rows and columns are identified in the more general array:

$$\begin{array}{c} \text{row 1} \longrightarrow \\ \text{row 2} \longrightarrow \end{array} \begin{vmatrix} a & b \\ c & d \end{vmatrix} = ad - bc.$$

$$\begin{array}{cc} \uparrow & \uparrow \\ \text{col. 1} & \text{col. 2} \end{array}$$

In the future we shall find it convenient to simply call the above array a determinant, although what is meant is the *number* represented by the array. With this in mind, the value of a second-order determinant is simply the difference of the products of its diagonal entries. For example,

$$\begin{vmatrix} 2 & 1 \\ 3 & -4 \end{vmatrix} = (2)(-4) - (1)(3) = -8 - 3 = -11,$$

$$\begin{vmatrix} -3 & -2 \\ 0 & 1 \end{vmatrix} = (-3)(1) - (-2)(0) = -3 - 0 = -3,$$

and

$$\begin{vmatrix} 2 & 0 \\ 0 & 2 \end{vmatrix} = (2)(2) - (0)(0) = 4.$$

Returning to the given system of equations, we can now write Eqs. 3 and 4, which form the solution of the system, as

$$x = \dfrac{\begin{vmatrix} c_1 & b_1 \\ c_2 & b_2 \end{vmatrix}}{\begin{vmatrix} a_1 & b_1 \\ a_2 & b_2 \end{vmatrix}}, \qquad y = \dfrac{\begin{vmatrix} a_1 & c_1 \\ a_2 & c_2 \end{vmatrix}}{\begin{vmatrix} a_1 & b_1 \\ a_2 & b_2 \end{vmatrix}}, \qquad (a_1 b_2 - a_2 b_1 \neq 0).$$

In these expressions for x and y, we form the determinant in the denominator from the coefficients of the variables in the given system, keeping in mind the proper order necessary. In the expression for x, the determinant in the numerator is that obtained by replacing the first column (or x-*column*) of the determinant in the denominator by the column of constants appearing to the right of the equality signs in the equations of the system. Similarly, the second column in the numerator for y consists of the constant terms. This method of using determinants for obtaining x and y is referred to as **Cramer's rule**.

example 1

Solve the following system by using Cramer's rule:

$$\begin{cases} 2x + y + 5 = 0 \\ \quad\ 3y + x = 6. \end{cases}$$

We first write the system in an appropriate form. That is, the x- and y-terms are aligned on one side and constant terms are on the other side.

$$\begin{cases} 2x + \ y = -5 \\ \ \ x + 3y = 6. \end{cases}$$

Using Cramer's rule, we form the determinants for x and y according to the instructions given above. Thus

$$x = \dfrac{\begin{vmatrix} -5 & 1 \\ 6 & 3 \end{vmatrix}}{\begin{vmatrix} 2 & 1 \\ 1 & 3 \end{vmatrix}} = \dfrac{(-5)(3) - (1)(6)}{(2)(3) - (1)(1)} = \dfrac{-15 - 6}{6 - 1} = -\dfrac{21}{5}$$

and

$$y = \dfrac{\begin{vmatrix} 2 & -5 \\ 1 & 6 \end{vmatrix}}{\begin{vmatrix} 2 & 1 \\ 1 & 3 \end{vmatrix}} = \dfrac{(2)(6) - (-5)(1)}{5} = \dfrac{12 + 5}{5} = \dfrac{17}{5}.$$

The solution is $x = -\dfrac{21}{5}, y = \dfrac{17}{5}.$

example 2

Solve the following system by using Cramer's rule.

$$\begin{cases} 0.24i_1 - 0.34i_2 = 0.28 \\ 0.11i_1 + 0.21i_2 = 0.86. \end{cases}$$

We have

$$i_1 = \frac{\begin{vmatrix} 0.28 & -0.34 \\ 0.86 & 0.21 \end{vmatrix}}{\begin{vmatrix} 0.24 & -0.34 \\ 0.11 & 0.21 \end{vmatrix}} = \frac{(0.28)(0.21) - (-0.34)(0.86)}{(0.24)(0.21) - (-0.34)(0.11)}$$

$$= \frac{0.3512}{0.0878} = 4,$$

and

$$i_2 = \frac{\begin{vmatrix} 0.24 & 0.28 \\ 0.11 & 0.86 \end{vmatrix}}{0.0878} = \frac{(0.24)(0.86) - (0.28)(0.11)}{0.0878}$$

$$= \frac{0.1756}{0.0878} = 2.$$

The solution is $i_1 = 4$, $i_2 = 2$.

Exercise 8-4

1. Evaluate the following:

(a) $\begin{vmatrix} 2 & 1 \\ 3 & 2 \end{vmatrix}$

(b) $\begin{vmatrix} 3 & 2 \\ -5 & -4 \end{vmatrix}$

(c) $\begin{vmatrix} -2 & -1 \\ -2 & -1 \end{vmatrix}$

(d) $\begin{vmatrix} -3 & 1 \\ a & b \end{vmatrix}$

(e) $\begin{vmatrix} a & e \\ h & z \end{vmatrix}$

(f) $\begin{vmatrix} -2 & -a \\ -a & 2 \end{vmatrix}$

(g) $\begin{vmatrix} 1 & 2 \\ 3 & 4 \end{vmatrix} \begin{vmatrix} 2 & 1 \\ 5 & 6 \end{vmatrix}$

(h) $\begin{vmatrix} 6 & 2 \\ 1 & 5 \end{vmatrix} \begin{vmatrix} 2 & -6 \\ 5 & 3 \end{vmatrix}$

2. Solve for k if

$$\begin{vmatrix} 2 & 3 \\ 4 & k \end{vmatrix} = 12.$$

*Solve Problems **3–14** by using Cramer's rule.*

3. $\begin{cases} 2x - y = 4 \\ 3x + y = 5. \end{cases}$

4. $\begin{cases} 3x + y = 6 \\ 7x - 2y = 5. \end{cases}$

5. $\begin{cases} \frac{3}{2}x - \frac{1}{4}z = 1 \\ \frac{1}{3}x + \frac{1}{2}z = 2. \end{cases}$

6. $\begin{cases} s - \frac{1}{4}t = 1 \\ s + t = -4. \end{cases}$

7. $\begin{cases} 0.14i_1 - 0.31i_2 = 1.97 \\ 0.34i_1 + 0.52i_2 = -1.58. \end{cases}$

8. $\begin{cases} 0.6x - 0.7y = 0.33 \\ 2.1x - 0.9y = 0.69. \end{cases}$

9. $\begin{cases} x - 2y = 4 \\ x - 6 = -y. \end{cases}$

10. $\begin{cases} x + 4 = 3x \\ 3x + 2y = 8. \end{cases}$

11. $\begin{cases} -2x = 4 - 3y \\ y = 6x - 1. \end{cases}$

12. $\begin{cases} x + 2y - 6 = 0 \\ y - 1 = 3x. \end{cases}$

13. $\begin{cases} 2 - u = t \\ 3 + t = -u. \end{cases}$

14. $\begin{cases} \frac{3}{2}w + \frac{1}{4}z = 1 \\ \frac{1}{3}w = 2 - \frac{1}{2}z. \end{cases}$

8-5 Determinants of Order 3

The value of the **third-order determinant**

$$
\begin{array}{c}
 \text{col. 1} \quad \text{col. 2} \quad \text{col. 3} \\
 \downarrow \qquad \downarrow \qquad \downarrow \\
\begin{array}{l}
\text{row 1} \longrightarrow \\
\text{row 2} \longrightarrow \\
\text{row 3} \longrightarrow
\end{array}
\begin{vmatrix}
a_1 & b_1 & c_1 \\
a_2 & b_2 & c_2 \\
a_3 & b_3 & c_3
\end{vmatrix}
\end{array}
$$

is defined in the following manner. With a given entry in the array, we associate the second-order determinant obtained by crossing out the row and column in which the entry lies. Hence, for a_2 we cross out the second row, which consists of the entries a_2, b_2, c_2, and the first column, which consists of the entries a_1, a_2, a_3:

$$
\begin{vmatrix}
a_1 & b_1 & c_1 \\
a_2 & b_2 & c_2 \\
a_3 & b_3 & c_3
\end{vmatrix}.
$$

This leaves the determinant

$$
\begin{vmatrix}
b_1 & c_1 \\
b_3 & c_3
\end{vmatrix},
$$

which is called the **minor** of the entry a_2. With each entry is also associated the number

$$(-1)^{i+j},$$

where i is the number of the row and j is the number of the column in which the entry lies. Because a_2 lies in row 2 and column 1, we associate $(-1)^{2+1} = (-1)^3 = -1$. The **cofactor** of a_2 is the product of this number and the minor of a_2:

$$
-1 \cdot \begin{vmatrix}
b_1 & c_1 \\
b_3 & c_3
\end{vmatrix}.
$$

To evaluate any third-order determinant, select **any** row (or column) and multiply each entry in the row (column) by its cofactor. The sum of these numbers is defined to be the value of the determinant.

To illustrate, we shall evaluate

$$\begin{vmatrix} 2 & -1 & 3 \\ 3 & 0 & -5 \\ 2 & 1 & 1 \end{vmatrix}$$

by applying the above rule to the first row (sometimes referred to as *expanding along the first row*). For

2   we obtain $(2)(-1)^{1+1}\begin{vmatrix} 0 & -5 \\ 1 & 1 \end{vmatrix} = (2)(1)(5) = 10,$

−1   we obtain $(-1)(-1)^{1+2}\begin{vmatrix} 3 & -5 \\ 2 & 1 \end{vmatrix} = (-1)(-1)(13) = 13,$

3   we obtain $(3)(-1)^{1+3}\begin{vmatrix} 3 & 0 \\ 2 & 1 \end{vmatrix} = 3(1)(3) = 9.$

Hence

$$\begin{vmatrix} 2 & -1 & 3 \\ 3 & 0 & -5 \\ 2 & 1 & 1 \end{vmatrix} = 10 + 13 + 9 = 32.$$

If we had expanded along the second column, then

$$\begin{vmatrix} 2 & -1 & 3 \\ 3 & 0 & -5 \\ 2 & 1 & 1 \end{vmatrix} = (-1)(-1)^{1+2}\begin{vmatrix} 3 & -5 \\ 2 & 1 \end{vmatrix} + 0 + (1)(-1)^{3+2}\begin{vmatrix} 2 & 3 \\ 3 & -5 \end{vmatrix}$$

$$= 13 + 0 + 19 = 32,$$

as before.

It can be shown that the value of a determinant is unique and does not depend on the row or column chosen for its evaluation. In the above problem the second expansion is preferable, since the 0 in column 2 contributed nothing to the sum, thus simplifying the calculation.

example 1

a. Evaluate

$$\begin{vmatrix} 12 & -1 & 3 \\ -3 & 1 & -1 \\ -10 & 2 & -3 \end{vmatrix}.$$

Expanding along the first row gives

$$12(-1)^{1+1}\begin{vmatrix}1 & -1 \\ 2 & -3\end{vmatrix} + (-1)(-1)^{1+2}\begin{vmatrix}-3 & -1 \\ -10 & -3\end{vmatrix} + 3(-1)^{1+3}\begin{vmatrix}-3 & 1 \\ -10 & 2\end{vmatrix}$$

$$= 12(1)(-1) + (-1)(-1)(-1) + 3(1)(4) = -1.$$

b. Evaluate

$$\begin{vmatrix}0 & 1 & 1 \\ 2 & 3 & 2 \\ 0 & -1 & 3\end{vmatrix}.$$

Expanding along column 1 for convenience, we have

$$0 + 2(-1)^{2+1}\begin{vmatrix}1 & 1 \\ -1 & 3\end{vmatrix} + 0 = 2(-1)(4) = -8.$$

Cramer's rule for solving a system of three linear equations in three variables follows the same method as that for two equations in two variables, as Example 2 shows.

example 2

Solve by using Cramer's rule:

$$\begin{cases}2x + y + z = 0 \\ 4x + 3y + 2z = 2 \\ 2x - y - 3z = 0.\end{cases}$$

We have

$$x = \frac{\begin{vmatrix}0 & 1 & 1 \\ 2 & 3 & 2 \\ 0 & -1 & -3\end{vmatrix}}{\begin{vmatrix}2 & 1 & 1 \\ 4 & 3 & 2 \\ 2 & -1 & -3\end{vmatrix}}.$$

The value of the denominator, expanded along the first row, is

$$2(-1)^{1+1}\begin{vmatrix}3 & 2 \\ -1 & -3\end{vmatrix} + 1(-1)^{1+2}\begin{vmatrix}4 & 2 \\ 2 & -3\end{vmatrix} + 1(-1)^{1+3}\begin{vmatrix}4 & 3 \\ 2 & -1\end{vmatrix}$$

$$= 2(1)(-7) + 1(-1)(-16) + 1(1)(-10)$$

$$= -8.$$

The numerator, expanded along the first column for convenience, is

$$0 + 2(-1)^{2+1}\begin{vmatrix}1 & 1 \\ -1 & -3\end{vmatrix} + 0 = 2(-1)(-2) = 4.$$

Thus $x = 4/(-8) = -\frac{1}{2}$. Similarly,

$$y = \frac{\begin{vmatrix} 2 & 0 & 1 \\ 4 & 2 & 2 \\ 2 & 0 & -3 \end{vmatrix}}{-8} = \frac{2(-1)^{2+2}\begin{vmatrix} 2 & 1 \\ 2 & -3 \end{vmatrix}}{-8} = \frac{2(1)(-8)}{-8} = 2,$$

and

$$z = \frac{\begin{vmatrix} 2 & 1 & 0 \\ 4 & 3 & 2 \\ 2 & -1 & 0 \end{vmatrix}}{-8} = \frac{2(-1)^{2+3}\begin{vmatrix} 2 & 1 \\ 2 & -1 \end{vmatrix}}{-8} = \frac{2(-1)(-4)}{-8} = -1.$$

The solution is $x = \frac{1}{2}$, $y = 2$, $z = -1$.

Finally, we remark that a determinant of order n, where $n > 3$, can also be evaluated by the method of minors and cofactors.

Exercise 8-5

In Problems 1–5, evaluate the determinants.

1. $\begin{vmatrix} 2 & 1 & 3 \\ 2 & 0 & 1 \\ -4 & 0 & 6 \end{vmatrix}$

2. $\begin{vmatrix} 3 & 2 & 1 \\ 1 & -2 & 3 \\ -1 & 3 & 2 \end{vmatrix}$

3. $\begin{vmatrix} 1 & 2 & -3 \\ 4 & 5 & 4 \\ 3 & -2 & 1 \end{vmatrix}$

4. $\begin{vmatrix} 1 & 0 & -1 \\ 0 & 1 & 0 \\ 1 & -1 & 1 \end{vmatrix}$

5. $\begin{vmatrix} 2 & 1 & 5 \\ -3 & 4 & -1 \\ 0 & 6 & -1 \end{vmatrix}$

6. A *nomogram* is one type of graphical process that can be used to solve certain types of equations. One nomogram yields the basic (determinant) equation

$$\begin{vmatrix} \frac{1}{2}f_1 & \frac{1}{2} & 1 \\ -f_2 & 1 & 1 \\ -3f_1 & 0 & 1 \end{vmatrix} = 0.$$

What is the relation between f_1 and f_2?

In Problems 7–16, solve the systems by using Cramer's rule.

7. $\begin{cases} x + y + z = 6 \\ x - y + z = 2 \\ 2x - y + 3z = 6. \end{cases}$

8. $\begin{cases} 2x - y + 3z = 12 \\ x + y - z = -3 \\ x + 2y - 3z = -10. \end{cases}$

9. $\begin{cases} 2i_1 - 3i_2 + 4i_3 = 0 \\ i_1 + i_2 - 3i_3 = 4 \\ 3i_1 + 2i_2 - i_3 = 0. \end{cases}$

10. $\begin{cases} 3r - t = 7 \\ 4r - s + 3t = 9 \\ 3s + 2t = 15. \end{cases}$

11. $\begin{cases} 2x - 3y + z = -2 \\ x - 6y + 3z = -2 \\ 3x + 3y - 2z = 2. \end{cases}$

12. $\begin{cases} T_1 - T_3 = 14 \\ T_2 + T_3 = 21 \\ T_1 - T_2 + T_3 = -10. \end{cases}$

13. $\begin{cases} 2a + b + 6c = 3 \\ a - b + 4c = 1 \\ 3a + 2b - 2c = 2. \end{cases}$

14. $\begin{cases} x + y + z = -1 \\ 3x + y + z = 1 \\ 4x - 2y + 2z = 0. \end{cases}$

15. Solve for y:

$\begin{cases} 5x - 7y + 4z = 2 \\ 3x + 2y - 2z = 3 \\ 2x - y + 3z = 4. \end{cases}$

16. Solve for z:

$\begin{cases} 3x - 2y + z = 0 \\ -2x + y - 2z = 5 \\ \frac{3}{2}x + \frac{4}{5}y + 4z = 10. \end{cases}$

17. Loads weighing 200 N and 300 N are suspended from the pulley system shown in Fig. 8-12. One pulley is fixed in position and the other is free to move up and down.

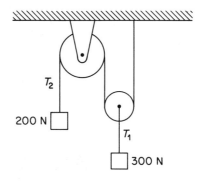

FIGURE 8-12

If the pulleys are frictionless and without mass, the tensions T_1 and T_2 in the cords and the acceleration a of the 200-N load are found by solving the system

$$\begin{cases} T_1 = 2T_2 \\ T_1 - 300 = 15.3a \\ 200 - T_2 = 20.4a, \end{cases}$$

where T_1 and T_2 are in newtons and a is in meters per second squared. Find the approximate values of T_1, T_2, and a.

8-6   Properties of Determinants   (Optional)

The evaluation of determinants is often simplified by the use of various properties, some of which we now list.

1. **If each of the entries in a row (or column) of a determinant is zero, then the value of the determinant is zero.**

   Thus

$$\begin{vmatrix} 6 & 2 & 5 \\ 7 & 1 & 4 \\ 0 & 0 & 0 \end{vmatrix} = 0.$$

2. **If two rows (or columns) of a determinant are identical or proportional, then the value of the determinant is zero.**

   Thus

   $$\begin{vmatrix} 2 & 5 & 2 & 1 \\ 2 & 6 & 2 & 3 \\ 2 & 4 & 2 & 1 \\ 6 & 5 & 6 & 1 \end{vmatrix} = 0, \qquad \text{(because column 1 = column 3)}.$$

   and

   $$\begin{vmatrix} 1 & 2 & 3 \\ 7 & 4 & 2 \\ 2 & 4 & 6 \end{vmatrix} = 0, \qquad \text{(because row 3 is 2 times row 1)}.$$

3. **If all the entries below (or above) the main diagonal entries (from the upper left corner to the lower right corner) of a determinant are zero, then the value of the determinant is equal to the product of the main diagonal entries.**

   Thus

   $$\begin{vmatrix} 2 & 6 & 1 & 0 \\ 0 & 5 & 7 & 6 \\ 0 & 0 & -2 & 5 \\ 0 & 0 & 0 & 1 \end{vmatrix} = (2)(5)(-2)(1) = -20.$$

4. **The value of a determinant is unchanged if a multiple of one row (or column) is added to another row (or column).**

   Thus if we add -4 times row 2 to row 3 below, then

   $$\begin{vmatrix} 1 & 3 & 5 \\ 0 & 2 & 3 \\ 0 & 8 & -1 \end{vmatrix} = \begin{vmatrix} 1 & 3 & 5 \\ 0 & 2 & 3 \\ 0 & 0 & -13 \end{vmatrix} = -26 \qquad \text{(Property 3)}.$$

5. **If two rows (or two columns) of a determinant are interchanged, then the value of the determinant is multiplied by -1.**

   Thus by interchanging rows 2 and 4 below and using Property (3), we have

   $$\begin{vmatrix} 2 & 2 & 1 & 6 \\ 0 & 0 & 0 & 1 \\ 0 & 0 & 2 & 0 \\ 0 & 1 & -3 & 4 \end{vmatrix} = -\begin{vmatrix} 2 & 2 & 1 & 6 \\ 0 & 1 & -3 & 4 \\ 0 & 0 & 2 & 0 \\ 0 & 0 & 0 & 1 \end{vmatrix} = -(4) = -4.$$

6. **If each entry of a row (or column) of a determinant is multiplied by the same constant k, then the value of the determinant is multiplied by k.**

Thus

$$\begin{vmatrix} 2 \cdot 3 & 2 \cdot 5 & 2 \cdot 7 \\ 5 & 2 & 1 \\ 6 & 4 & 3 \end{vmatrix} = 2 \begin{vmatrix} 3 & 5 & 7 \\ 5 & 2 & 1 \\ 6 & 4 & 3 \end{vmatrix}.$$

Essentially, a number can be "factored out" of one row or column.

example 1

Evaluate

$$\begin{vmatrix} 1 & 1 & 0 & 5 \\ 1 & 2 & 1 & 0 \\ 0 & 2 & 1 & 1 \\ 3 & 0 & 0 & -4 \end{vmatrix}.$$

We shall express the determinant in a form in which all entries below the main diagonal are zero. Then, by Property 3, we shall take the product of the entries of the main diagonal.

$$\begin{vmatrix} 1 & 1 & 0 & 5 \\ 1 & 2 & 1 & 0 \\ 0 & 2 & 1 & 1 \\ 3 & 0 & 0 & -4 \end{vmatrix} = \begin{vmatrix} 1 & 1 & 0 & 5 \\ 0 & 1 & 1 & -5 \\ 0 & 2 & 1 & 1 \\ 0 & -3 & 0 & -19 \end{vmatrix}$$

(by adding -1 times row 1 to row 2; adding -3 times row 1 to row 4)

$$= \begin{vmatrix} 1 & 1 & 0 & 5 \\ 0 & 1 & 1 & -5 \\ 0 & 0 & -1 & 11 \\ 0 & 0 & 3 & -34 \end{vmatrix}$$

(by adding -2 times row 2 to row 3; adding 3 times row 2 to row 4)

$$= \begin{vmatrix} 1 & 1 & 0 & 5 \\ 0 & 1 & 1 & -5 \\ 0 & 0 & -1 & 11 \\ 0 & 0 & 0 & -1 \end{vmatrix}$$

(by adding 3 times row 3 to row 4)

$$= (1)(1)(-1)(-1) = 1.$$

Exercise 8-6

*Evaluate the determinants in Problems **1–9** by using properties of determinants.*

1. $\begin{vmatrix} -2 & 5 & 7 \\ 0 & 0 & 0 \\ 5 & 9 & 4 \end{vmatrix}.$

2. $\begin{vmatrix} -3 & -5 & 6 \\ 0 & 4 & 6 \\ 0 & 0 & 2 \end{vmatrix}$

3. $\begin{vmatrix} 2 & 1 & -6 \\ -1 & 7 & 3 \\ 3 & 2 & -9 \end{vmatrix}.$

4. $\begin{vmatrix} 4 & 2 & -4 \\ 2 & 4 & 6 \\ 4 & 2 & -4 \end{vmatrix}.$

5. $\begin{vmatrix} 1 & 7 & -3 & 8 \\ 0 & 1 & -5 & 4 \\ 0 & 0 & 1 & 7 \\ 0 & 0 & 0 & 1 \end{vmatrix}.$

6. $\begin{vmatrix} 1 & 2 & -3 & 4 \\ 3 & -1 & 2 & 4 \\ -2 & -4 & 6 & -8 \\ 0 & 3 & -1 & 2 \end{vmatrix}.$

7. $\begin{vmatrix} 1 & 0 & 0 & 0 \\ 0 & -2 & 0 & 0 \\ 0 & 0 & 4 & 0 \\ 0 & 0 & 0 & -3 \end{vmatrix}.$

8. $\begin{vmatrix} 7 & 6 & 0 & 5 \\ -3 & 2 & 0 & 1 \\ 4 & -3 & 0 & 2 \\ 1 & 0 & 0 & 6 \end{vmatrix}.$

9. $\begin{vmatrix} 1 & 0 & 3 & 2 \\ 4 & -1 & 0 & 1 \\ 2 & 1 & 0 & 3 \\ -1 & 2 & 3 & -1 \end{vmatrix}.$

10. Suppose the value of a determinant of order 4 is 12. What is the value of the determinant obtained by multiplying every entry in the given determinant by 2?

8-7 Word Problems

Each word problem in this section gives rise to a system of linear equations. After an appropriate system has been determined, you may use any method to solve it. The following examples illustrate some basic techniques.

example 1

In a laboratory, a student is to combine a 25-percent hydrogen peroxide solution (25 percent by volume is hydrogen peroxide) with a 40-percent hydrogen peroxide solution to obtain 2 liters of a 30-percent solution. How many liters of each solution should the student mix?

Let x be the number of liters of the 25 percent solution, and y be the number of liters of the 40 percent solution that should be mixed. Then

$$x + y = 2. \tag{1}$$

See Fig. 8-13. In 2 liters of a 30-percent solution there is $0.30(2) = 0.6$ liters of hydrogen peroxide. This hydrogen peroxide comes from two sources: $0.25x$ liters of it come from the 25-percent solution, and $0.40y$ liters come from the 40-percent solution. Thus

$$0.25x + 0.40y = 0.6. \tag{2}$$

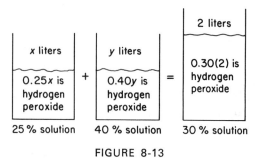

FIGURE 8-13

Equations 1 and 2 form a system. Solving Eq. 1 for x gives $x = 2 - y$. Substituting $2 - y$ for x in Eq. 2 gives

$$0.25(2 - y) + 0.40y = 0.6$$
$$0.5 - 0.25y + 0.40y = 0.6$$
$$0.15y = 0.1$$
$$y = \frac{0.1}{0.15} = \frac{10}{15} = \frac{2}{3}.$$

From Eq. 1, $x = 2 - y = 2 - \frac{2}{3} = \frac{4}{3}$. Thus $\frac{4}{3}$ liters of the 25-percent solution and $\frac{2}{3}$ liter of the 40-percent solution must be mixed.

example 2

Suppose it is known that quantities x and y are linearly related by an equation of the form

$$y = mx + b.$$

If measurements are made and it is found that $y = 4$ when $x = 3$, and $y = 13$ when $x = 6$, find m and b.

Substituting the data into the given equation, we obtain the system

$$\begin{cases} 4 = 3m + b \\ 13 = 6m + b. \end{cases}$$

Multiplying the first equation by -1 and adding the result to the second equation gives $9 = 3\,m$, from which $m = 3$. Substituting 3 for m in the first equation gives $4 = 9 + b$, from which $b = -5$. Thus $m = 3$ and $b = -5$.

example 3

To determine the height h of the top of an antenna situated on a cliff (Fig. 8-14), the angle of elevation of the top from a point on level ground is measured to be 35°. From a point 95 m farther away, the angle of elevation is 25°. Find h.

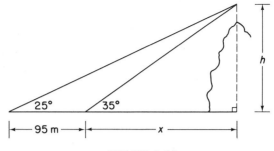

FIGURE 8-14

From the smaller right triangle in Fig. 8-14, we have

$$\tan 35° = \frac{h}{x}$$

$$x = \frac{h}{\tan 35°}. \tag{3}$$

From the larger right triangle,

$$\tan 25° = \frac{h}{95 + x}$$

$$h = (\tan 25°)(95 + x). \tag{4}$$

Equations 3 and 4 form a system of two linear equations in the unknowns h and x. Substituting x in Eq. 3 into Eq. 4 gives

$$h = (\tan 25°)\left(95 + \frac{h}{\tan 35°}\right)$$

$$h = 95 \tan 25° + \frac{h \tan 25°}{\tan 35°}$$

$$h = 44.299 + 0.66596h.$$

$$0.33404h = 44.299$$

$$h = \frac{44.299}{0.33404} = 132.6 \text{ m.}$$

example 4

In Fig. 8-15(a), a weight of 20 N is supported by two cables. Find the tensions T_1 and T_2 in the cables.

Because the system is in equilibrium (the weight is at rest), it is shown in physics that the sum of the forces acting at point O must be zero. As a result, at that point the sum of all horizontal components is zero and the sum of all vertical components is zero. In Fig. 8-15(b), this means that

$$\begin{array}{ll} \text{Hor.} & \begin{cases} T_1 \cos 55° - T_2 \cos 70° + 20 \cos 270° = 0 \\ T_1 \sin 55° + T_2 \sin 70° + 20 \sin 270° = 0. \end{cases} \end{array}$$

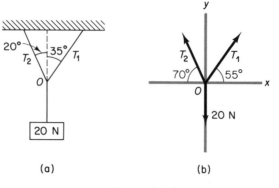

(a)   (b)

FIGURE 8-15

In setting up the first equation, for $T_2 \cos \theta$ we used the fact that $\cos 110° = -\cos 70°$. Thus we have

$$\begin{cases} 0.5736T_1 - 0.3420T_2 = 0 \\ 0.8192T_1 + 0.9397T_2 = 20. \end{cases}$$

By Cramer's rule,

$$T_1 = \frac{\begin{vmatrix} 0 & -0.3420 \\ 20 & 0.9397 \end{vmatrix}}{\begin{vmatrix} 0.5736 & -0.3420 \\ 0.8192 & 0.9397 \end{vmatrix}} = \frac{6.840}{0.8192} = 8.4 \text{ N}$$

and

$$T_2 = \frac{\begin{vmatrix} 0.5736 & 0 \\ 0.8192 & 20 \end{vmatrix}}{0.8192} = \frac{11.47}{0.8192} = 14.0 \text{ N}.$$

Exercise 8-7

1. The perimeter of a rectangle is 26 m. The length exceeds the width by 3 m. Find the dimensions of the rectangle.

2. The length of a rectangle is twice the width. The perimeter is 60 m. Find the dimensions of the rectangle.

3. One of two complementary angles is three-fifths of the other one. Find the angles.

4. One of two supplementary angles is three-fifths of the other one. Find the angles.

5. A chemical manufacturer needs to fill an order for 700 liters of a 24-percent acid solution (24 percent by volume is acid). Solutions of 20 percent and 30 percent are in stock. How many liters of each must be mixed to fill the order? (See Example 1.)

6. A chemical manufacturer needs to obtain 500 liters of a 25-percent acid solution by mixing a 30-percent solution with an 18-percent solution. How many liters of each must be mixed?

7. A 10,000-liter tank is to be filled with solvent from storage tanks A and B. Solvent from A is pumped at the rate of 20 ℓ/min, and solvent from B is pumped at the

rate of 30 ℓ/min. Usually, both pumps operate at the same time. However, because of a blown fuse, the pump on A is delayed 10 min. How many liters from each storage tank will be used to fill the tank?

8. On a trip on a raft it took $\frac{3}{4}$ h to travel 20 km downstream. The return trip took $1\frac{1}{2}$ h. Find the speed of the raft in still water and the speed of the current.

9. Table 8-1 shows how alloys A, B, and C are composed (by mass). How much of A, B, and C must be mixed to produce 100 kg of an alloy that is 53 percent copper and 19 percent zinc?

Table 8-1

	A	B	C
Copper	50%	60%	40%
Zinc	30%	20%	
Nickel	20%	20%	60%

10. A company manufactures industrial control units. Their new models are the Argon I and the Argon II. Each Argon I unit requires 6 transistors and 3 integrated circuits. Each Argon II unit requires 10 transistors and 8 integrated circuits. The company receives a total of 760 transistors and 500 integrated circuits each day from its supplier. How many units of each model of the Argon can the company make each day? Assume that all the parts are used.

11. The graph of $y = ax^2 + bx + c$ passes through the points $(2, 0)$, $(0, 0)$, and $(-1, 3)$. Find a, b, and c. (See Example 2.)

12. Repeat Problem 11 if the graph passes through the points $(2, 5)$, $(-3, 5)$, and $(1, 1)$.

13. From a point on the ground, the angle of elevation of the top of a building is $35°$. From a point 50 m farther away, the angle of elevation is $30°$. Find the height of the building. (See Example 3.)

14. From a point on level ground, the angle of elevation of the top of a mountain is $58°$. From a point 340 m farther away, the angle of elevation is $46°$. Find the height of the mountain.

15. In Fig. 8-16, a weight of 15 N is supported by two cables. Find the tensions T_1 and T_2 in the cables. (See Example 4.)

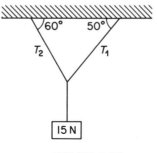

FIGURE 8-16

16. A very light boom is shown in Fig. 8-17. A 100-N load is suspended from its end. The forces acting at point O are the tension **T** in the horizontal cable, the 100-N force due to the load, and the force **F** due to the boom. Find T and F. (See Example 4.)

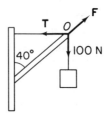

FIGURE 8-17

17. A 440-N weight is supported by three cables, as shown in Fig. 8-18. The tension in the vertical cable is 440 N and is due to the weight. Find the tensions T_1 and T_2 in the other two cables. (See Example 4.)

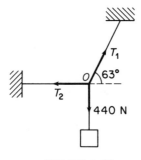

FIGURE 8-18

8-8 Review

Review Questions

1. Two methods by which a system of two linear equations in two variables can be solved are by elimination by _____(a)_____ and elimination by _____(b)_____.

2. If a system of two linear equations is graphically represented by two different parallel lines, then what can be said about the solution of the system? _____

3. A system of two linear equations that has at least one solution is said to be _____.

4. The equations in the system

$$\begin{cases} y = 2x - 4 \\ y = 3x - 4 \end{cases}$$

represent lines with different (slopes)(y-intercepts) and hence must have exactly one solution.

5. To solve the system

$$\begin{cases} 3x - 4y = 10 \\ 8x + 5y = -40 \end{cases}$$

by eliminating y by addition, we can first multiply the top equation by 5 and the bottom equation by _____.

6. The minor of the entry 3 in

$$\begin{vmatrix} 0 & 1 & 3 \\ 2 & 4 & 0 \\ 1 & 5 & 2 \end{vmatrix}$$

is equal to ___(a)___ and its cofactor is equal to ___(b)___.

7. Expanding

$$\begin{vmatrix} 1 & 0 & 0 \\ 1 & 1 & 1 \\ 2 & 1 & 2 \end{vmatrix}$$

along the first row gives a value of _____.

Answers to Review Questions

1. (a) Addition, (b) Substitution. **2.** No solution. **3.** Consistent. **4.** Slopes.
5. 4. **6.** (a) 6, (b) 6. **7.** 1.

Review Problems

In Problems **1–16**, *solve the system by any method.*

1. $\begin{cases} 2x - y = 6 \\ 3x + 2y = 5. \end{cases}$

2. $\begin{cases} 3x + 5y = -6 \\ 2x - 5y = 6. \end{cases}$

3. $\begin{cases} 5x + 2y = 36 \\ 8x - 3y = -54. \end{cases}$

4. $\begin{cases} x + y = 3 \\ 3x + 2y = 19. \end{cases}$

5. $\begin{cases} 3s + t - 4 = 0 \\ 12s + 4t - 2 = 0. \end{cases}$

6. $\begin{cases} u - 3v + 11 = 0 \\ 4u + 3v - 9 = 0. \end{cases}$

7. $\begin{cases} 3x + \frac{1}{2}y = 2 \\ \frac{1}{2}x - \frac{1}{4}y = 0. \end{cases}$

8. $\begin{cases} \frac{1}{3}x - \frac{1}{2}y = 4 \\ \frac{1}{4}x - \frac{3}{8}y = 3. \end{cases}$

9. $\begin{cases} 6x = 3 - 9y \\ 12y = 4 - 8x. \end{cases}$

10. $\begin{cases} 4x = 7 + 12y \\ 5x = 15y - 2. \end{cases}$

11. $\begin{cases} 2(x - y) + 6(x + y) = 13 \\ 3(x + y) - 4(x - y) = 10. \end{cases}$

12. $\begin{cases} x + \dfrac{2y + x}{6} = 14 \\ y + \dfrac{3x + y}{4} = 20. \end{cases}$

13. $\begin{cases} x - y = 2 \\ x + z = 1 \\ y - z = 3. \end{cases}$

14. $\begin{cases} 2x - 4z = 8 \\ x - 2y - 2z = 14 \\ 3x + y + z = 0. \end{cases}$

15. $\begin{cases} 4r - s + 2t = 2 \\ 8r - 3s + 4t = 1 \\ r + 2s + 2t = 8. \end{cases}$

16. $\begin{cases} 3u - 2v + w = -2 \\ 2u + v + w = 1 \\ u + 3v - w = 3. \end{cases}$

*In Problems **17–20**, evaluate the given determinants.*

17. $\begin{vmatrix} 2 & -1 \\ 4 & 7 \end{vmatrix}$

18. $\begin{vmatrix} 5 & 8 \\ 3 & 0 \end{vmatrix}$

19. $\begin{vmatrix} 1 & 2 & -1 \\ 0 & 1 & 4 \\ 1 & 2 & 2 \end{vmatrix}$

20. $\begin{vmatrix} 2 & 0 & 3 \\ 1 & 4 & 6 \\ -1 & 2 & -1 \end{vmatrix}$

*Solve Problems **21** and **22** by Cramer's rule.*

21. $\begin{cases} 3x - y = 1 \\ 2x + 3y = 8. \end{cases}$

22. $\begin{cases} x + 2y - z = 0 \\ y + 4z = 0 \\ x + 2y + 2z = 0. \end{cases}$

23. Two alloys of copper are to be mixed so that the result is 15 kg of a 45-percent alloy (by mass). One alloy is 20 percent copper, and the other is 50 percent copper. How many kilograms of each should be used?

24. A 30-N weight is supported by two cables, as shown in Fig. 8-19. Find the tensions T_1 and T_2 in the cables.

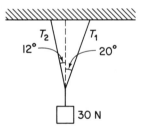

FIGURE 8-19

exponents and radicals

9-1 Fractional Exponents

The basic rules of exponents are given in Chapter 2. They are repeated here for your convenience (we assume that all denominators are different from zero).

1. $a^m a^n = a^{m+n}$.	**2.** $(a^m)^n = a^{mn}$.
3. $\dfrac{a^m}{a^n} = a^{m-n}$.	**4.** $\dfrac{a^n}{a^n} = 1$.
5. $(ab)^n = a^n b^n$.	**6.** $\left(\dfrac{a}{b}\right)^n = \dfrac{a^n}{b^n}$.
7. $a^{-n} = \dfrac{1}{a^n}$.	**8.** $\dfrac{1}{a^{-n}} = a^n$.
9. $a^0 = 1$, for $a \neq 0$.	

Our purpose in this section is to give a meaning to a *fractional* exponent, such as in $5^{1/3}$, that is consistent with the rules of exponents. For example, by Rule 2 the cube of $5^{1/3}$ must be

$$(5^{1/3})^3 = 5^{(1/3)(3)} = 5^1 = 5.$$

But recall that, by definition, $\sqrt[3]{5}$ is a number which has a cube of 5:

$$(\sqrt[3]{5})^3 = 5.$$

Thus the cube of $5^{1/3}$, namely 5, must be the same as the cube of $\sqrt[3]{5}$. For this reason we define $5^{1/3}$ to be $\sqrt[3]{5}$. More generally, we define $a^{1/n}$ to be the principal nth root of a (where n is a positive integer)*:

$$\boxed{\textbf{10. }\ a^{1/n} = \sqrt[n]{a}.}$$

It can be shown that Rules 1 to 9 hold for this definition of $a^{1/n}$.

example 1

a. $27^{1/3} = \sqrt[3]{27} = 3.$

b. $(-32)^{1/5} = \sqrt[5]{-32} = -2.$

c. $16^{-(1/2)} = \dfrac{1}{16^{1/2}} = \dfrac{1}{\sqrt{16}} = \dfrac{1}{4}.$

d. $xy^{1/2} + (xy)^{1/2} = x\sqrt{y} + \sqrt{xy}.$

e. $\sqrt[4]{7} = 7^{1/4}.$

f. $\sqrt[5]{y - z} = (y - z)^{1/5}.$ *Do not write* $\sqrt[5]{y - z} = \sqrt[5]{y} - \sqrt[5]{z}.$

Definition 10 can be made more general to include other rational exponents. We define $a^{m/n}$, where m and n are integers and n is positive, by the following:

$$\boxed{\textbf{11. }\ a^{m/n} = (\sqrt[n]{a})^m = \sqrt[n]{a^m}.}$$

That is, $a^{m/n} = (a^{1/n})^m = (a^m)^{1/n}$. By our definition, $x^{4/3}$ can be looked at in two ways: first, as the fourth power of the cube root of x, $(\sqrt[3]{x})^4$; and second, as the cube root of the fourth power of x, $\sqrt[3]{x^4}$.

example 2

Find the value of each of the following.

a. $8^{2/3} = (\sqrt[3]{8})^2 = 2^2 = 4.$ Alternatively, we have $8^{2/3} = \sqrt[3]{8^2} = \sqrt[3]{64} = 4.$

b. $\left(\dfrac{1}{4}\right)^{3/2} = \left(\sqrt{\dfrac{1}{4}}\right)^3 = \left(\dfrac{1}{2}\right)^3 = \dfrac{1}{8}.$

*In Definition 10 we exclude the case where a is negative and n is even. For example, $\sqrt{-4}$ is not a real number.

c. $(-27)^{4/3} = (\sqrt[3]{-27})^4 = (-3)^4 = 81.$

d. $27^{-2/3} = \dfrac{1}{27^{2/3}} = \dfrac{1}{(\sqrt[3]{27})^2} = \dfrac{1}{(3)^2} = \dfrac{1}{9}.$

In definition 11 we must require that $a \geq 0$ if n is even. Otherwise, the statement $\sqrt{x^2} = x^{2/2} = x$ is not always true. To see why, let $x = 6$. Then $\sqrt{x^2} = \sqrt{36} = 6 = x$. But if $x = -6$, then $\sqrt{x^2} = \sqrt{36} = 6 = -(-6) = -x$. Thus $\sqrt{x^2}$ is x if x is positive, and is $-x$ if x is negative. (Remember that if x is negative, then $-x$ is positive.) More simply, for the general case we can say that

$$\sqrt{x^2} = |x|.$$

Thus

$$\sqrt{6^2} = |6| = 6 \quad \text{and} \quad \sqrt{(-6)^2} = |-6| = 6.$$

Unless otherwise stated, we shall assume that all literal numbers appearing under radical signs are positive. As a result we are free to write, for example, $\sqrt{y^2} = y$.

In Examples 3 and 4, you should be able to understand how the rules of exponents are applied in each step.

example 3

Write each of the following with fractional exponents and simplify if possible.

a. $\sqrt[5]{x^4} = x^{4/5}.$

b. $x\sqrt[6]{y^5} = xy^{5/6}.$

c. $(\sqrt{3})^4 = (3^{1/2})^4 = 3^{4/2} = 3^2 = 9.$

d. $\sqrt[4]{a^4b^8} = (a^4b^8)^{1/4} = (a^4)^{1/4}(b^8)^{1/4} = ab^2.$

example 4

Perform the indicated operations and give the answer with positive exponents only.

a. $x^{1/2}x^{1/3} = x^{(1/2)+(1/3)} = x^{5/6}.$

b. $\dfrac{2x}{x^{1/4}} = \dfrac{2x^1}{x^{1/4}} = 2x^{1-(1/4)} = 2x^{3/4}.$

c. $\dfrac{y^{2/3}}{x^{2/3}y^{1/3}} = \dfrac{y^{1/3}}{x^{2/3}}.$

d. $(8a^3)^{2/3} = 8^{2/3}(a^3)^{2/3} = (\sqrt[3]{8})^2a^2 = 2^2a^2 = 4a^2.$

e. $(15^{-1/2})^4 = 15^{-4/2} = 15^{-2} = \dfrac{1}{15^2} = \dfrac{1}{225}$.

f. $(x^{2/9}y^{-4/3})^{1/2} = (x^{2/9})^{1/2}(y^{-4/3})^{1/2} = x^{1/9}y^{-2/3} = \dfrac{x^{1/9}}{y^{2/3}}$.

g. $\left(\dfrac{x^{12}}{y^6}\right)^{-1/3} = \dfrac{(x^{12})^{-1/3}}{(y^6)^{-1/3}} = \dfrac{x^{-4}}{y^{-2}} = \dfrac{y^2}{x^4}$.

h. $\left(\dfrac{x^{1/5}y^{6/5}}{z^{2/5}}\right)^{15} = \dfrac{(x^{1/5}y^{6/5})^{15}}{(z^{2/5})^{15}} = \dfrac{(x^{1/5})^{15}(y^{6/5})^{15}}{z^6} = \dfrac{x^3y^{18}}{z^6}$.

i. $\dfrac{(4x^4y)^{-1/2}(y^4)^{-1/8}}{3xy^{-3}} = \dfrac{y^3}{3x(4x^4y)^{1/2}(y^4)^{1/8}} = \dfrac{y^3}{3x(2x^2y^{1/2})(y^{1/2})}$

$\qquad = \dfrac{y^3}{6x^3y} = \dfrac{y^2}{6x^3}$.

Exercise 9-1

In Problems 1–15, find the value of each expression without the use of a calculator.

1. $25^{1/2}$.
2. $125^{1/3}$.
3. $81^{-1/2}$.
4. $4^{-1/2}$.
5. $27^{2/3}$.
6. $(\tfrac{1}{9})^{3/2}$.
7. $27^{-2/3}$.
8. $9^{3/2}$.
9. $(-8)^{4/3}$.
10. $(-8)^{-1/3}$.
11. $16^{3/4}$.
12. $(64^{1/2})^{1/3}$.
13. $(-\tfrac{1}{32})^{-1/5}$.
14. $(\tfrac{1}{27})^{-2/3}$.
15. $(4^3)^{2/3}$.

In Problems 16–30, rewrite each expression by using positive fractional exponents.

16. $\sqrt[3]{y}$.
17. $\sqrt{x}$.
18. $\sqrt[4]{x^9}$.
19. $\sqrt[3]{x^2}$.
20. $\dfrac{\sqrt{y}}{\sqrt[4]{x}}$.
21. $\sqrt[4]{x^3y^5}$.
22. $\sqrt[4]{x}\,\sqrt[5]{y}$.
23. $\sqrt[6]{x^5y^{12}}$.
24. $\dfrac{1}{\sqrt{2}}$.
25. $x^2\sqrt[4]{x}$.
26. $\dfrac{2}{\sqrt[3]{x-5}}$.
27. $\dfrac{3}{\sqrt{x}}$.
28. $\sqrt[3]{7-x}$.
29. $\sqrt[3]{(x^2-5x)^2}$.
30. $\dfrac{1}{\sqrt[6]{(x^2-2x)^5}}$.

In Problems 31–68, perform the operations and simplify. Write your answers with positive exponents only.

31. $x^{1/2}x^{3/2}$.
32. $x^{2/3}x^{4/3}$.
33. $x^{4/3}x^{-1/3}$.
34. $x^{-1/2}x^{3/2}$.
35. $x^{-2}x^{7/2}x^{5/2}$.
36. $x^3x^{-3/8}x^{-5/8}$.
37. $x^{1/2}x^{1/4}$.
38. $x^{3/5}x^{1/3}$.
39. $x^{1/2}(3x^{1/2}y)$.
40. $(xy^{-1/2})y^{5/2}$.
41. $(x^{1/2})^3$.
42. $(y^{-1/3})^6$.

43. $(y^6)^{1/3}$.

44. $(t^{10})^{4/5}$.

45. $2(x^{-2/3})^6$.

46. $(-y^{1/3})^6$.

47. $(2x^{-2}y^{1/3})^3$.

48. $(3x^3y^{1/2})^4$.

49. $(ab^2c^3)^{3/4}(a^{1/4}b^{3/4})^5$.

50. $(x^{1/2}y^{2/3})(x^2y)^{1/3}$.

51. $(27x^{15})^{-1/3}$.

52. $(8x^{-6})^{1/3}$.

53. $(-8x^{-6})^{1/3}$.

54. $(27^{-1}x^{15})^{-1/3}$.

55. $\left(\dfrac{x^{-4/3}}{y^{-2/3}}\right)^{-3}$.

56. $\left(\dfrac{3^{1/4}x^{3/4}}{y^{1/2}}\right)^4$.

57. $\left(\dfrac{x^{-1}}{x^{1/3}}\right)^2$.

58. $\left(\dfrac{y^{2/3}}{x^{3/4}}\right)^{2/3}$.

59. $\left(\dfrac{2^{1/3}x^{2/3}}{x^{1/3}}\right)^6$.

60. $\left(\dfrac{x^{3/2}}{x^{-1}}\right)^{-4}$.

61. $\dfrac{x^{4/9}y^{2/5}}{x^{1/9}y^{7/5}}$.

62. $\dfrac{x^{4/7}y^{3/20}}{x^{3/7}y^{17/20}}$.

63. $\dfrac{x^{2/3}y^{-9/4}}{x^{-4/3}y^{-1/4}}$.

64. $\dfrac{xy^{2/5}}{x^{1/2}y^{2/5}z^{-1/3}}$.

65. $\dfrac{(2x^{1/2}y)^3(4x)^{-1/2}}{x}$.

66. $\dfrac{(x^{1/3}y^{1/6})^3(2x^{-2})}{xy^{1/2}}$.

67. $\dfrac{(3x^{-2}yw^{1/2})^2(2xy)}{(xyw)^{-1}}$.

68. $\dfrac{(2xy)^{-2}(x^{1/2}w^2)(-x)^3}{x^{1/2}y^{-2}}$.

In Problems **69** *and* **70**, *use a calculator to find the given functional values*.

69. $f(x) = x^{2/3}$; $f(2), f(14), f(22.3)$.

70. $g(x) = \sqrt[8]{x-3}$; $g(5), g(20), g(85.3)$.

71. Experimental data indicate that the radius R of a nucleus of an isotope of mass number A is given by

$$R = r_0 A^{1/3}.$$

The value of r_0, the radius parameter, can be taken to be 1.5×10^{-13} cm. Determine the radius of a naturally occurring isotope of zinc whose mass number is 64.

72. In studies of the effect of an electrical current in a ferromagnetic material, the equation $W = KB^{8/5}$ occurs. If $B = 0.60$, express W in terms of K.

73. The rate R (in m³/s) at which water discharges over a 90° V-notch wier is given by $R = 1.37h^{5/2}$, where h is the height (in meters) of the water above the wier crest. Find R if $h = 2.4$ m.

74. When 20 m³ of oxygen at a temperature of 285 K and a pressure of 10^5 N/m² is adiabatically compressed to 0.5 m³, its new pressure p and temperature T are given by

$$p = (10)^5 \left(\frac{20}{0.5}\right)^{7/5}$$

and

$$T = (285)\left(\frac{20}{0.5}\right)^{7/5}.$$

Find p and T.

75. If the gas in Problem 74 is helium, the expressions for p and T have a fractional exponent of $\frac{5}{3}$ instead of $\frac{7}{5}$. Find the values of p and T if the gas is helium.

*Section A-5 may be helpful.

9-2 Further Operations with Exponents

From the title of this section, you may think that we are about to introduce "new" operations with exponents. Actually, we shall introduce nothing new at all. In earlier chapters we performed operations involving algebraic expressions with positive integral exponents. Now we shall perform the same operations with expressions involving negative and fractional exponents.

example 1

Simplify each of the following expressions.

a. $2x^{1/2} + (x^{1/6})^3$.
$$2x^{1/2} + (x^{1/6})^3 = 2x^{1/2} + x^{3/6} = 2x^{1/2} + x^{1/2} = 3x^{1/2}.$$

In the last step we combined similar terms.

b. $(27x)^{1/3} - (2x^{1/3} - 4x^{1/3})$.
$$(27x)^{1/3} - (2x^{1/3} - 4x^{1/3}) = \sqrt[3]{27}\, x^{1/3} - (-2x^{1/3})$$
$$= 3x^{1/3} + 2x^{1/3} = 5x^{1/3}.$$

example 2

Perform the indicated operations and write the answer with positive exponents only.

a. $2x^{-2} + y^{-1}$.
$$2x^{-2} + y^{-1} = \frac{2}{x^2} + \frac{1}{y} = \frac{2y + x^2}{x^2 y}.$$

In the last step, the fractions were added in the usual manner.

b. $x^{-2}(x^{-2} + y^3)$.

By the distributive law, we have
$$x^{-2}(x^{-2} + y^3) = x^{-4} + x^{-2}y^3$$
$$= \frac{1}{x^4} + \frac{y^3}{x^2} = \frac{1 + x^2 y^3}{x^4}.$$

c. $x^{1/2}(2 - x^{3/2}) = 2x^{1/2} - x^{1/2}x^{3/2} = 2x^{1/2} - x^2$.

d. $(x^{1/2} + y^{1/2})^2$.

This is the square of a binomial:
$$(x^{1/2} + y^{1/2})^2 = (x^{1/2})^2 + 2(x^{1/2}y^{1/2}) + (y^{1/2})^2$$
$$= x + 2x^{1/2}y^{1/2} + y.$$

e. $(x^{-1} - y^{-1})^2 = \left(\dfrac{1}{x} - \dfrac{1}{y}\right)^2 = \left(\dfrac{y - x}{xy}\right)^2 = \dfrac{(y - x)^2}{(xy)^2} = \dfrac{y^2 - 2xy + x^2}{x^2 y^2}.$

f. $\dfrac{3x^4 - 2x^2}{x^{1/3}}.$

Here we divide each term of the numerator by the denominator.

$$\frac{3x^4 - 2x^2}{x^{1/3}} = \frac{3x^4}{x^{1/3}} - \frac{2x^2}{x^{1/3}} = 3x^{4-(1/3)} - 2x^{2-(1/3)}$$

$$= 3x^{11/3} - 2x^{5/3}.$$

example 3

a. Simplify $\dfrac{1}{x^{-1} + y^{-1}}.$

$$\frac{1}{x^{-1} + y^{-1}} = \frac{1}{\dfrac{1}{x} + \dfrac{1}{y}} = \frac{1}{\dfrac{y + x}{xy}}$$

$$= 1 \cdot \frac{xy}{y + x} = \frac{xy}{x + y}.$$

b. Simplify $\dfrac{1 + x^{-2}}{y^{-2} + 1}.$

$$\frac{1 + x^{-2}}{y^{-2} + 1} = \frac{1 + \dfrac{1}{x^2}}{\dfrac{1}{y^2} + 1} = \frac{\dfrac{x^2 + 1}{x^2}}{\dfrac{1 + y^2}{y^2}}$$

$$= \frac{x^2 + 1}{x^2} \cdot \frac{y^2}{1 + y^2} = \frac{y^2(x^2 + 1)}{x^2(1 + y^2)}.$$

Exercise 9-2

In each of the following, perform the indicated operations and simplify. Express your answers with positive exponents only. Combine any resulting sum or difference of fractions into a single fraction.

1. $2x^{1/2} - 5x^{1/2}.$

2. $7x^{3/2} + 2x^{3/2} - 5x^{3/2}.$

3. $4x^{-1/3} - 2(x^2)^{-1/6}.$

4. $3x^{1/4} - (x^{-1/2})^{-1/2}.$

5. $x^{1/3}(x^{2/3} + 3).$

6. $x^{3/2}(1 - x^{1/2}).$

7. $3x^{-2}(x^{-1} + y).$

8. $2x^{-3}(x^{-2} + y).$

9. $x^{-1} + y^{-1}.$

10. $x^{-2} - y^{-2}.$

11. $2 + 2x^{-1}.$

12. $3 - y^{-1}.$

13. $3x^{-1} + y.$

14. $(x^{-1} + y^{-1})(4).$

15. $(x + y^{-1})^2$.

16. $(x - y)^{-2}$.

17. $(x^{3/2} + 2)^2$.

18. $(x^{1/3} - 1)^2$.

19. $(x^{1/2} + 1)(x^{3/2} - 2)$.

20. $(x^{2/3} + 3)(x^{1/3} - 1)$.

21. $(x^{1/2} + x^{3/2})^2$.

22. $(x^{1/3} - x^{2/3})^2$.

23. $(x^{1/2} + y^{1/2})^2$.

24. $(x^{1/3} + y^{1/3})^2$.

25. $\dfrac{x^{4/3} + x^2 - x^4}{x}$.

26. $\dfrac{x^2 + x - 2}{x^{1/2}}$.

27. $\dfrac{x^{4/3} + x^2 - x^4}{x^{1/3}}$.

28. $\dfrac{y^{5/4} - y^3 - y^{1/4}}{y^{1/4}}$.

29. $\dfrac{x^{1/2} - 3x^{1/3}}{x^{1/4}}$.

30. $\dfrac{2x^{1/3} + 3x^{1/5}}{x^{1/5}}$.

31. $\dfrac{1^{-1} + 2^{-1} + 3^{-1}}{4^{-1}}$.

32. $\dfrac{x^{-1} - 4^{-1}}{x^{-1} + 4^{-1}}$.

33. $\dfrac{x^{-1} + y^{-1}}{y^{-1}}$.

34. $\dfrac{y^{-1}}{x^{-1} + y^{-1}}$.

35. $(x^{-1} + b^{-1})(x^{-1} - b^{-1})$.

36. $(2x^{3/4} + 1)(2x^{3/4} - 1)(4x^{3/2} + 1)$.

37. $(y^{2/3} + 2)(y^{4/3} - 2y^{2/3} + 4)$.

9-3 Changing the Form of a Radical

The basic rules for radicals,* which are given in Chapter 2, are:

$$\boxed{\begin{aligned} &\textbf{12.}\ \sqrt[n]{ab} = \sqrt[n]{a}\,\sqrt[n]{b}. \\ &\textbf{13.}\ \sqrt[n]{\dfrac{a}{b}} = \dfrac{\sqrt[n]{a}}{\sqrt[n]{b}}. \\ &\textbf{14.}\ (\sqrt[n]{a})^n = a. \end{aligned}}$$

Rule 14 may also be written as

$$\boxed{\sqrt[n]{a^n} = a.}$$

Using this form, we can replace a radical having index n by an equal expression that does not have a radical, provided the radicand is a perfect nth power of an expression. For example, just as $\sqrt[3]{x^3} = x$, we have

$$\sqrt[3]{x^6 y^9} = \sqrt[3]{(x^2 y^3)^3} = x^2 y^3.$$

Note that the exponents 6 and 9 in $x^6 y^9$ are multiples of the index 3. This guarantees

*In Rules 12–14, we assume that if n is even, then a and b are not negative. Otherwise, these rules may not hold true.

that x^6y^9 is a perfect cube. Other examples of the use of Rule 14 are shown in Example 1.

example 1

a. $\sqrt{x^6y^8} = \sqrt{(x^3y^4)^2} = x^3y^4$. Alternatively, by Rule 12,
$$\sqrt{x^6y^8} = \sqrt{x^6}\sqrt{y^8} = x^3y^4.$$

b. $\sqrt[4]{\dfrac{x^{16}}{y^8}} = \sqrt[4]{\left(\dfrac{x^4}{y^2}\right)^4} = \dfrac{x^4}{y^2}$. Alternatively, by Rule 13, $\sqrt[4]{\dfrac{x^{16}}{y^8}} = \dfrac{\sqrt[4]{x^{16}}}{\sqrt[4]{y^8}} = \dfrac{x^4}{y^2}$.

c. $\sqrt[5]{32x^5y^{15}} = \sqrt[5]{(2xy^3)^5} = 2xy^3$.

One way to change the form of a radical with index n is to "*remove*" from the radicand all factors whose nth roots can easily be found. The rule $\sqrt[n]{ab} = \sqrt[n]{a}\,\sqrt[n]{b}$ is used. For example,
$$\sqrt{50} = \sqrt{25\cdot2} = \sqrt{25}\,\sqrt{2} = 5\sqrt{2}.$$

In general, radicals should be expressed in a form such that the exponent of any factor in the radicand is less than the index of the radical. For example,
$$\sqrt[3]{x^7y^5} = \sqrt[3]{(x^6y^3)(xy^2)} = \sqrt[3]{x^6y^3}\,\sqrt[3]{xy^2} = x^2y\sqrt[3]{xy^2}.$$

example 2

Remove as many factors as possible from the radicand.

a. $\sqrt{8} = \sqrt{4\cdot2} = \sqrt{4}\,\sqrt{2} = 2\sqrt{2}$.

b. $\sqrt[4]{48} = \sqrt[4]{16\cdot3} = \sqrt[4]{16}\,\sqrt[4]{3} = 2\sqrt[4]{3}$.

c. $\sqrt[3]{x^3y} = \sqrt[3]{x^3}\,\sqrt[3]{y} = x\sqrt[3]{y}$.

d. $\sqrt{25x^7} = \sqrt{(25x^6)(x)} = \sqrt{25x^6}\,\sqrt{x} = 5x^3\sqrt{x}$.

e. $\sqrt[5]{64x^6y^{14}z^2} = \sqrt[5]{(32x^5y^{10})(2xy^4z^2)} = 2xy^2\sqrt[5]{2xy^4z^2}$, because $\sqrt[5]{32x^5y^{10}}$ is $2xy^2$.

f. $\sqrt{x^2 + 2x + 1} = \sqrt{(x+1)^2} = x + 1$, provided $x + 1 \geq 0$. Otherwise we must write $\sqrt{(x+1)^2} = |x + 1|$.

example 3

The frequency of vibration of a string of length L, fixed at both ends and vibrating in its fundamental mode, is given by
$$f = \frac{1}{2L}\sqrt{\frac{T}{\mu}},$$

where f is frequency, μ (mu) is mass per unit length, and T is the tension in the string. If the tension in the string is quadrupled, what happens to the frequency?

Let f_0 denote the frequency when the tension is quadrupled, that is, when it is $4T$. Then

$$f_0 = \frac{1}{2L}\sqrt{\frac{4T}{\mu}} = \frac{1}{2L}(2)\sqrt{\frac{T}{\mu}} = 2\left(\frac{1}{2L}\sqrt{\frac{T}{\mu}}\right) = 2f.$$

Thus the frequency is doubled.

When a radicand is a fraction, sometimes the rule $\sqrt[n]{\dfrac{a}{b}} = \dfrac{\sqrt[n]{a}}{\sqrt[n]{b}}$ can be used to obtain an equal expression in which the radicand is not a fraction. This process is called **rationalizing the denominator**. For example,

$$\sqrt{\frac{7}{16}} = \frac{\sqrt{7}}{\sqrt{16}} = \frac{\sqrt{7}}{4}.$$

Often the radicand must be written in a different form before the rule is used to rationalize a denominator. This is the case for

$$\sqrt{\frac{3}{7}}.$$

Because the index is 2, we want the denominator to be a perfect square of a number. We can make the denominator 7^2 if we multiply numerator and denominator by 7. This gives

$$\sqrt{\frac{3}{7}} = \sqrt{\frac{3}{7} \cdot \frac{7}{7}} = \sqrt{\frac{21}{7^2}} = \frac{\sqrt{21}}{\sqrt{7^2}} = \frac{\sqrt{21}}{7}.$$

It is sometimes preferred that an answer to a problem be expressed in rationalized form.

example 4

Rationalize the denominator of each expression.

a. $\sqrt[4]{\dfrac{y}{x^8}} = \dfrac{\sqrt[4]{y}}{\sqrt[4]{x^8}} = \dfrac{\sqrt[4]{y}}{x^2}.$

b. $\sqrt{\dfrac{21}{x}} = \sqrt{\dfrac{21}{x} \cdot \dfrac{x}{x}} = \dfrac{\sqrt{21x}}{\sqrt{x^2}} = \dfrac{\sqrt{21x}}{x}.$

c. $\sqrt[5]{\dfrac{x}{y^2}}.$

Because the index is 5, we shall make the denominator a perfect fifth power of y by multiplying numerator and denominator by y^3.

$$\sqrt[5]{\frac{x}{y^2}} = \sqrt[5]{\frac{x}{y^2} \cdot \frac{y^3}{y^3}} = \sqrt[5]{\frac{xy^3}{y^5}} = \frac{\sqrt[5]{xy^3}}{\sqrt[5]{y^5}} = \frac{\sqrt[5]{xy^3}}{y}.$$

d. $\sqrt[3]{\dfrac{2}{3x^4y^2}}$.

Because the index is 3, we want each factor in the denominator to be a perfect cube of a number. That is, the exponent of each such factor must be a 3 or a multiple of 3. This will be the case if we multiply the 3 by 3^2, the x^4 by x^2, and the y^2 by y. Thus we multiply both numerator and denominator by 3^2x^2y.

$$\sqrt[3]{\frac{2}{3x^4y^2}} = \sqrt[3]{\frac{2}{3x^4y^2} \cdot \frac{3^2x^2y}{3^2x^2y}} = \sqrt[3]{\frac{2 \cdot 3^2x^2y}{3^3x^6y^3}} = \frac{\sqrt[3]{18x^2y}}{\sqrt[3]{(3x^2y)^3}} = \frac{\sqrt[3]{18x^2y}}{3x^2y}.$$

You may recall from Chapter 2 that the phrase *rationalizing the denominator* is also used when a fraction with a radical in its denominator is rewritten in a form in which the denominator contains no radical. For example, to rationalize the denominator of $2/\sqrt[3]{5}$, we want the radicand to be a perfect cube. This will be the case if we multiply the numerator and denominator by $\sqrt[3]{5^2}$, because $\sqrt[3]{5}\,\sqrt[3]{5^2} = \sqrt[3]{5^3} = 5$. Thus

$$\frac{2}{\sqrt[3]{5}} = \frac{2}{\sqrt[3]{5}} \cdot \frac{\sqrt[3]{5^2}}{\sqrt[3]{5^2}} = \frac{2\sqrt[3]{5^2}}{\sqrt[3]{5^3}} = \frac{2\sqrt[3]{25}}{5}.$$

Similarly

$$\frac{4}{\sqrt{3}} = \frac{4}{\sqrt{3}} \cdot \frac{\sqrt{3}}{\sqrt{3}} = \frac{4\sqrt{3}}{\sqrt{3^2}} = \frac{4\sqrt{3}}{3}.$$

example 5

Rationalize the denominator of the following.

a. $\dfrac{3}{\sqrt{2x}} = \dfrac{3}{\sqrt{2x}} \cdot \dfrac{\sqrt{2x}}{\sqrt{2x}} = \dfrac{3\sqrt{2x}}{\sqrt{2^2x^2}} = \dfrac{3\sqrt{2x}}{2x}.$

b. $\dfrac{6}{\sqrt[4]{2}} = \dfrac{6}{\sqrt[4]{2}} \cdot \dfrac{\sqrt[4]{2^3}}{\sqrt[4]{2^3}} = \dfrac{6\sqrt[4]{8}}{\sqrt[4]{2^4}} = \dfrac{6\sqrt[4]{8}}{2} = 3\sqrt[4]{8}.$

c. $\dfrac{7xy^2}{2\sqrt[5]{3x^3}} = \dfrac{7xy^2}{2\sqrt[5]{3x^3}} \cdot \dfrac{\sqrt[5]{3^4x^2}}{\sqrt[5]{3^4x^2}} = \dfrac{7xy^2\sqrt[5]{81x^2}}{2\sqrt[5]{3^5x^5}} = \dfrac{7xy^2\sqrt[5]{81x^2}}{2(3x)} = \dfrac{7y^2\sqrt[5]{81x^2}}{6}.$

We can obtain another rule for radicals that involves a root of a root of a number. Because $\sqrt[m]{\sqrt[n]{a}} = (a^{1/n})^{1/m} = a^{1/(mn)} = \sqrt[mn]{a}$, we have:

$$15. \ \sqrt[m]{\sqrt[n]{a}} = \sqrt[mn]{a}.$$

For example

$$\sqrt[3]{\sqrt{64}} = \sqrt[6]{64} = 2.$$

Alternatively,

$$\sqrt[3]{\sqrt{64}} = \sqrt[3]{8} = 2.$$

example 6

a. $\sqrt[3]{\sqrt[4]{2}} = \sqrt[12]{2}.$

b. $\sqrt{\sqrt[4]{x}} = \sqrt[8]{x}.$

c. $\sqrt[4]{81} = \sqrt{\sqrt{81}} = \sqrt{9} = 3.$

Sometimes it is possible to **reduce the index** of a radical, as the following shows.

$$\sqrt[6]{x^3} = x^{3/6} = x^{1/2} = \sqrt{x}.$$

Here the index 6 was reduced to 2. The rule $\sqrt[mn]{a} = \sqrt[m]{\sqrt[n]{a}}$ can also be used for such a problem.

$$\sqrt[6]{x^3} = \sqrt{\sqrt[3]{x^3}} = \sqrt{x}.$$

example 7

Reduce the index of the following radicals.

a. $\sqrt[4]{25} = \sqrt[4]{5^2} = 5^{2/4} = 5^{1/2} = \sqrt{5}$ or, alternatively,
$$\sqrt[4]{25} = \sqrt{\sqrt{25}} = \sqrt{5}.$$

b. $\sqrt[6]{16x^2}.$

We cannot conveniently take the sixth root of the radicand, but we can take the square root. Since $6 = 3 \cdot 2$, we have
$$\sqrt[6]{16x^2} = \sqrt[3]{\sqrt{16x^2}} = \sqrt[3]{4x},$$

or, alternatively, we have

$$\sqrt[6]{16x^2} = \sqrt[6]{(4x)^2} = (4x)^{2/6} = (4x)^{1/3} = \sqrt[3]{4x}.$$

c. $\sqrt[12]{8x^6y^9} = \sqrt[4]{\sqrt[3]{8x^6y^9}} = \sqrt[4]{2x^2y^3}.$

We shall consider a radical to be **simplified** when all of the following are true:

1. *As many factors as possible are removed from the radicand (Example 2).*
2. *The denominator is rationalized (Example 4).*
3. *The index cannot be reduced (Example 7).*

example 8

Simplify the following.

a. $\sqrt{\dfrac{x^5}{z}} = \sqrt{\dfrac{x^5}{z} \cdot \dfrac{z}{z}} = \dfrac{\sqrt{x^5 z}}{\sqrt{z^2}} = \dfrac{\sqrt{x^5 z}}{z} = \dfrac{\sqrt{x^4(xz)}}{z} = \dfrac{x^2 \sqrt{xz}}{z}.$

b. $\sqrt[4]{x^6 y^{10}} = \sqrt[4]{x^4 y^8 (x^2 y^2)} = xy^2 \sqrt[4]{x^2 y^2} = xy^2 \sqrt[4]{(xy)^2}$

$\qquad\qquad\qquad\qquad = xy^2 (xy)^{2/4} = xy^2 (xy)^{1/2}$

$\qquad\qquad\qquad\qquad = xy^2 \sqrt{xy}.$

c. $\sqrt[6]{\dfrac{x^3}{y^9}} = \sqrt[6]{\dfrac{x^3}{y^9} \cdot \dfrac{y^3}{y^3}} = \sqrt[6]{\dfrac{x^3 y^3}{y^{12}}} = \dfrac{\sqrt[6]{x^3 y^3}}{\sqrt[6]{(y^2)^6}} = \dfrac{\sqrt[6]{(xy)^3}}{y^2} = \dfrac{\sqrt{xy}}{y^2}.$

d. $\sqrt[3]{x^{-6} y^6} = \sqrt[3]{\dfrac{y^6}{x^6}} = \sqrt[3]{\left(\dfrac{y^2}{x^2}\right)^3} = \dfrac{y^2}{x^2}.$

Exercise 9-3

In Problems 1–14, find the root.

1. $\sqrt[4]{x^8}.$ 2. $\sqrt[3]{x^9}.$ 3. $\sqrt[3]{8x^{12}}.$

4. $\sqrt[6]{9^{12}}.$ 5. $\sqrt{9x^{16} y^{18}}.$ 6. $\sqrt[3]{x^3 y^3 z^6}.$

7. $\sqrt[3]{x^3 y^6 z^9}.$ 8. $\sqrt{(x^3 y^7)(x^7 y^{13})}.$ 9. $\sqrt[5]{\dfrac{x^{15}}{y^{20}}}.$

10. $\sqrt[4]{\dfrac{16x^8}{y^{16}}}.$ 11. $\sqrt{\sqrt{x^8}}.$ 12. $\sqrt[3]{\sqrt{x^{18}}}.$

13. $\sqrt[4]{\sqrt[3]{x^{12}}}.$ 14. $\sqrt{\sqrt[6]{x^{24}}}.$

In Problems 15–72, simplify the radicals.

15. $\sqrt{12}.$ 16. $\sqrt{18}.$ 17. $\sqrt{32}.$

18. $\sqrt{20}.$ 19. $\sqrt[3]{16}.$ 20. $\sqrt[3]{54}.$

21. $\sqrt{x^7}.$ 22. $\sqrt[3]{x^7}.$ 23. $\sqrt[3]{24x^6}.$

24. $\sqrt{8x^3}.$ 25. $\sqrt[4]{x^9 y^2}.$ 26. $\sqrt[5]{x^{17} y^{20}}.$

27. $\sqrt[3]{x^6 y z^4}.$ 28. $\sqrt{x^5 y^4 z}.$ 29. $\sqrt[3]{8a^3 y^5}.$

30. $\sqrt[3]{24(a+b)^7}$.

31. $\sqrt[5]{x^{23}y^{10}z^6}$.

32. $\sqrt[4]{x^3y^3z^7}$.

33. $\sqrt{81xy^2z^3w^4}$.

34. $\sqrt[4]{32x^{17}}$.

35. $\sqrt{\dfrac{1}{2}}$.

36. $\sqrt{\dfrac{1}{5}}$.

37. $\sqrt[3]{\dfrac{2}{5}}$.

38. $\sqrt[3]{\dfrac{1}{3}}$.

39. $\sqrt[3]{\dfrac{x^2}{y^3}}$.

40. $\sqrt[4]{\dfrac{3}{x^4}}$.

41. $\sqrt{\dfrac{x}{y^4}}$.

42. $\sqrt[3]{\dfrac{y^2}{x^{12}}}$.

43. $\sqrt{\dfrac{2x}{y}}$.

44. $\sqrt{\dfrac{y}{x^9}}$.

45. $\sqrt[3]{\dfrac{2}{xy^2}}$.

46. $\sqrt[3]{\dfrac{2y}{xz}}$.

47. $\sqrt[4]{\dfrac{3}{2x^7yz^2}}$.

48. $\sqrt[4]{\dfrac{1}{x^3yz^5}}$.

49. $\sqrt[6]{x^2}$.

50. $\sqrt[8]{(xy)^4}$.

51. $\sqrt[4]{9}$.

52. $\sqrt[6]{8}$.

53. $\sqrt[4]{16x^4y^2}$.

54. $\sqrt[6]{27x^3y^3z^3}$.

55. $\sqrt[8]{\dfrac{x^4}{y^4}}$.

56. $\sqrt[6]{\dfrac{16x^2}{y^2}}$.

57. $\sqrt[12]{x^2y^2z^{10}}$.

58. $\sqrt[15]{x^3y^{15}z^6}$.

59. $\sqrt[4]{x^{10}y^2}$.

60. $\sqrt[12]{x^{15}y^{27}}$.

61. $\sqrt[6]{x^{20}x^{26}}$.

62. $\sqrt[8]{x^2z^{10}}$.

63. $\sqrt[3]{\sqrt{x^{12}y^5w^{25}}}$.

64. $\sqrt{\sqrt[3]{64x^{12}y^{11}w^7}}$.

65. $\sqrt[4]{\dfrac{16x^5}{y^8}}$.

66. $\sqrt[3]{\dfrac{x^6}{y^{-3}}}$.

67. $\sqrt[4]{\dfrac{1}{4}}$.

68. $\sqrt[6]{\dfrac{x^9}{y^{15}}}$.

69. $\sqrt[8]{\dfrac{x^4}{y^{12}}}$.

70. $\sqrt{x^4(2+x)}$.

71. $\sqrt[3]{\sqrt{x^3}}$.

72. $\sqrt[4]{\sqrt[3]{\sqrt{x^{48}}}}$.

*In Problems **73–84**, rationalize the denominators and simplify.*

73. $\dfrac{3}{\sqrt{7}}$.

74. $\dfrac{5}{\sqrt{11}}$.

75. $\dfrac{4}{\sqrt{2x}}$.

76. $\dfrac{y}{\sqrt{2y}}$.

77. $\dfrac{1}{\sqrt[3]{2}}$.

78. $\dfrac{3}{\sqrt[4]{2}}$.

79. $\dfrac{1}{\sqrt[3]{3x}}$.

80. $\dfrac{4}{3\sqrt[3]{x^2}}$.

81. $\dfrac{2xy}{3\sqrt[5]{xy^3z^6}}$.

82. $\dfrac{-3y}{x\sqrt{x^3y}}$.

83. $\dfrac{4ab^2}{\sqrt[4]{2ab^3}}$.

84. $\dfrac{3a^2b^2c}{\sqrt[3]{9abc^2}}$.

85. When a solid sphere of radius r and mass m is released from the top of an inclined plane of vertical height h, its speed v at the bottom, if the sphere rolls without slipping, can be shown to be

$$v = \sqrt{\dfrac{10gh}{7}}.$$

Express v in rationalized form.

86. When the mass m shown in Fig. 9-1 is released from rest and falls through a distance h, the wheel can be shown to have an angular speed ω, given by

$$\omega = \sqrt{\frac{2mgh}{mr^2 + I}},$$

where I is the moment of inertia of the wheel and g is the acceleration due to gravity. Express ω with a rationalized denominator.

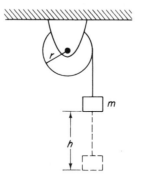

FIGURE 9-1

87. In the formula of Example 3, if the mass per unit length is quadrupled, what happens to the frequency?

88. The grating spacing, the distance between ions, of a sodium chloride crystal can be shown to be given by the expression

$$\sqrt[3]{\frac{M}{2\rho N_0}}.$$

Express this distance in rationalized form.

89. If a circular ring of radius r has a charge per unit length of λ, it can be shown that the electric field intensity E at a point a distance y from the center of the ring on an axis perpendicular to the plane of the ring (Fig. 9-2), is given by

$$E = \frac{\lambda r y}{2\epsilon_0 \sqrt{(r^2 + y^2)^3}},$$

where ϵ_0 is a constant. Express E in rationalized form.

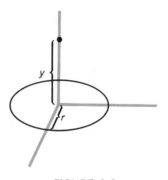

FIGURE 9-2

9-4 Addition and Subtraction of Radicals

Radicals that have the *same radicand* and the *same index* are said to be **similar**. We can add or subtract similar radicals by using the distributive law. For example,

$$8\sqrt{xy} - 4\sqrt{xy} + 7\sqrt{xy} = (8 - 4 + 7)\sqrt{xy} = 11\sqrt{xy}.$$

Radicals that are not similar can sometimes be combined after they are first simplified. For example, in $\sqrt[3]{81} - \sqrt[3]{24}$ the indices (plural of *index*) are the same but the radicands are different. However, we have

$$\sqrt[3]{81} - \sqrt[3]{24} = \sqrt[3]{27 \cdot 3} - \sqrt[3]{8 \cdot 3}$$
$$= 3\sqrt[3]{3} - 2\sqrt[3]{3} = \sqrt[3]{3}.$$

example 1

Perform the indicated operations.

a. $(16\sqrt[3]{x} + 15) - (12 - 2\sqrt[3]{x}) = 16\sqrt[3]{x} + 15 - 12 + 2\sqrt[3]{x}$
$$= 18\sqrt[3]{x} + 3.$$

b. $3\sqrt{75} - 2\sqrt{12} + \sqrt{7} = 3\sqrt{25 \cdot 3} - 2\sqrt{4 \cdot 3} + \sqrt{7}$
$$= 3(5\sqrt{3}) - 2(2\sqrt{3}) + \sqrt{7}$$
$$= 15\sqrt{3} - 4\sqrt{3} + \sqrt{7} = 11\sqrt{3} + \sqrt{7}.$$

c. $\sqrt[3]{\dfrac{3}{4}} + \sqrt[3]{\dfrac{2}{9}} - \sqrt[3]{\dfrac{1}{36}} = \sqrt[3]{\dfrac{3}{4} \cdot \dfrac{2}{2}} + \sqrt[3]{\dfrac{2}{9} \cdot \dfrac{3}{3}} - \sqrt[3]{\dfrac{1}{6^2} \cdot \dfrac{6}{6}}$

$$= \dfrac{\sqrt[3]{6}}{2} + \dfrac{\sqrt[3]{6}}{3} - \dfrac{\sqrt[3]{6}}{6}$$

$$= \left(\dfrac{1}{2} + \dfrac{1}{3} - \dfrac{1}{6}\right)\sqrt[3]{6} = \dfrac{2}{3}\sqrt[3]{6}.$$

d. $\sqrt{16} + \sqrt{9} \neq \sqrt{16 + 9} = \sqrt{25} = 5$, but $\sqrt{16} + \sqrt{9} = 4 + 3 = 7.$

Exercise 9-4

In Problems 1–20, perform the indicated operations and simplify.

1. $4\sqrt[3]{3} - 2\sqrt[3]{3} + \sqrt[3]{3}.$

2. $6\sqrt{7} - (2\sqrt{7} + 3\sqrt{7}).$

3. $x^2\sqrt{2x} - 3x^2\sqrt{2x} + 4x^2\sqrt{2x}.$

4. $xy\sqrt{x} + 4xy\sqrt{x} - 2xy\sqrt{x}.$

5. $3\sqrt{75} - 2\sqrt{12}.$

6. $5\sqrt{18} - (\sqrt{2} + 1).$

7. $5\sqrt{8} - (2\sqrt{18} - 4\sqrt{32}).$

8. $\sqrt{75} - (\sqrt{27} - 2\sqrt{3}).$

9. $2y\sqrt{16x} - 3y\sqrt{9x}.$

10. $3\sqrt[3]{16} - \sqrt[3]{54}.$

11. $\sqrt[3]{128} - 6\sqrt[3]{16}$.

12. $2(\sqrt[3]{54} - 2\sqrt[3]{128}) - 2\sqrt[3]{16}$.

13. $30\sqrt{\dfrac{1}{15}} - 72\sqrt{\dfrac{5}{12}} + 50\sqrt{\dfrac{3}{5}}$.

14. $20\sqrt{\dfrac{2}{5}} - 3\sqrt{40} - 4\sqrt{\dfrac{5}{2}}$.

15. $4\sqrt[3]{\dfrac{1}{2}} + \sqrt[3]{32} - 3\sqrt[3]{4}$.

16. $\sqrt{\dfrac{1}{6}} + \sqrt{\dfrac{2}{3}} + \sqrt{\dfrac{3}{2}}$.

17. $\sqrt{98x^2} + \sqrt[4]{4x^4} - 3\sqrt[6]{8x^6}$.

18. $\sqrt{98x} + \sqrt[4]{4x^2} - 3\sqrt[6]{8x^3}$.

19. $5x\sqrt[3]{3000y} - 2x\sqrt[3]{81y} - \sqrt[3]{24x^3y}$.

20. $4x^2\sqrt{27y} - (\sqrt{75x^4y} - 2x^2\sqrt{3y}) + 3x^2\sqrt{12}$.

9-5 Multiplication of Radicals

Radicals having the *same index* can be multiplied by means of the previous rule $\sqrt[n]{a} \cdot \sqrt[n]{b} = \sqrt[n]{ab}$. For example,

$$\sqrt{2x^3} \cdot \sqrt{8x} = \sqrt{(2x^3)(8x)} = \sqrt{16x^4} = 4x^2.$$

example 1

Determine the given products and simplify.

a. $\sqrt{yz} \cdot \sqrt{3z} = \sqrt{3yz^2} = z\sqrt{3y}$.

b. $\sqrt[4]{\dfrac{3}{2}} \cdot \sqrt[4]{6} = \sqrt[4]{\dfrac{3}{2} \cdot 6} = \sqrt[4]{9} = \sqrt[4]{3^2} = 3^{2/4} = 3^{1/2} = \sqrt{3}$.

c. $\sqrt{3}(\sqrt{3} - \sqrt{6}) = \sqrt{3}(\sqrt{3}) - \sqrt{3}(\sqrt{6})$

$$= 3 - \sqrt{18} = 3 - \sqrt{9 \cdot 2} = 3 - 3\sqrt{2}.$$

d. $(a\sqrt[3]{a^2b^3})^4 = a^4(\sqrt[3]{a^2b^3})^4$ \qquad (Rule 2)

$$= a^4\sqrt[3]{(a^2b^3)^4} \qquad \text{(Definition 11)}$$

$$= a^4\sqrt[3]{a^8b^{12}} \qquad \text{(Rules 5 and 2)}$$

$$= a^4(a^2b^4\sqrt[3]{a^2}) \qquad \text{(simplifying)}$$

$$= a^6b^4\sqrt[3]{a^2}.$$

example 2

Determine the given products and simplify.

a. $(\sqrt{8} - \sqrt{3})(\sqrt{18} - \sqrt{48})$.

Simplifying the radicals and multiplying, we have

$$(2\sqrt{2} - \sqrt{3})(3\sqrt{2} - 4\sqrt{3})$$

$$= 2\sqrt{2}(3\sqrt{2} - 4\sqrt{3}) - \sqrt{3}(3\sqrt{2} - 4\sqrt{3})$$

$$= 2\sqrt{2} \cdot 3\sqrt{2} - 2\sqrt{2} \cdot 4\sqrt{3} - \sqrt{3} \cdot 3\sqrt{2} + \sqrt{3} \cdot 4\sqrt{3}$$

$$= 6(\sqrt{2})^2 - 8\sqrt{6} - 3\sqrt{6} + 4(\sqrt{3})^2$$
$$= 12 - 11\sqrt{6} + 12$$
$$= 24 - 11\sqrt{6}.$$

b. $(\sqrt{5} - 2\sqrt{7})(\sqrt{5} + 2\sqrt{7})$.

This has the form $(a - b)(a + b)$. Thus

$$(\sqrt{5} - 2\sqrt{7})(\sqrt{5} + 2\sqrt{7}) = (\sqrt{5})^2 - (2\sqrt{7})^2$$
$$= 5 - 4(7) = 5 - 28 = -23.$$

c. $(\sqrt{x} - \sqrt{y})^2$.

This is the square of a binomial.

$$(\sqrt{x} - \sqrt{y})^2 = (\sqrt{x})^2 - 2\sqrt{x}\,\sqrt{y} + (\sqrt{y})^2$$
$$= x - 2\sqrt{xy} + y.$$

Radicals with different indices can be multiplied if they are first rewritten so that they do have the same index. To do this we use fractional exponents, as Example 3 shows.

example 3

Determine the given products and simplify.

a. $\sqrt{2} \cdot \sqrt[3]{3}$.

We first express each factor in terms of fractional exponents.

$$\sqrt{2} \cdot \sqrt[3]{3} = 2^{1/2} \cdot 3^{1/3}.$$

Next we rewrite the exponents so that their denominators are the same. Because $\frac{1}{2} = \frac{3}{6}$ and $\frac{1}{3} = \frac{2}{6}$, we have

$$2^{1/2} \cdot 3^{1/3} = 2^{3/6} \cdot 3^{2/6}.$$

Going back to radical form and multiplying gives

$$2^{3/6} \cdot 3^{2/6} = \sqrt[6]{2^3}\,\sqrt[6]{3^2} = \sqrt[6]{2^3 \cdot 3^2} = \sqrt[6]{8 \cdot 9} = \sqrt[6]{72}.$$

Summarizing, we can write

$$\sqrt{2} \cdot \sqrt[3]{3} = 2^{1/2} \cdot 3^{1/3} = 2^{3/6} \cdot 3^{2/6} = \sqrt[6]{2^3 \cdot 3^2} = \sqrt[6]{72}.$$

b. $\sqrt[4]{3x^2}\,\sqrt[3]{2x^2} = (3x^2)^{1/4}(2x^2)^{1/3}$

$$= (3x^2)^{3/12}(2x^2)^{4/12} = \sqrt[12]{(3x^2)^3} \cdot \sqrt[12]{(2x^2)^4}$$
$$= \sqrt[12]{(3x^2)^3(2x^2)^4} = \sqrt[12]{3^3 x^6 \cdot 2^4 x^8}$$
$$= \sqrt[12]{432x^{14}} = x\,\sqrt[12]{432x^2}.$$

Exercise 9-5

In Problems **1–34**, *perform the operations and simplify.*

1. $\sqrt{3}\,\sqrt{4}$. $\qquad$ 2. $\sqrt{9}\,\sqrt{2}$. $\qquad$ 3. $(2\sqrt{6})(3\sqrt{3})$.

4. $(5\sqrt{27})(2\sqrt{3})$. $\qquad$ 5. $\sqrt[3]{3}\,\sqrt[3]{9}\,\sqrt[3]{12}$. $\qquad$ 6. $\sqrt[3]{4}\,\sqrt[3]{16}\,\sqrt[3]{-1}$.

7. $\sqrt{2x}\,\sqrt{x}\,\sqrt{3x}$. $\qquad$ 8. $\sqrt{5y}\,\sqrt{2y}\,\sqrt{y}$. $\qquad$ 9. $(-\sqrt{3})^2$.

10. $(-\sqrt{5})^3$. $\qquad$ 11. $(2\sqrt[3]{x})^4$. $\qquad$ 12. $(\frac{1}{3}\sqrt{x})^3$.

13. $\sqrt{30}\,\sqrt{\dfrac{2}{3}}$. $\qquad\qquad\qquad$ 14. $\sqrt{\dfrac{5}{8}}\,\sqrt{\dfrac{16}{3}}$.

15. $\sqrt{3}(2\sqrt{6}-4\sqrt{3})$. $\qquad$ 16. $\sqrt{2}(\sqrt{2}+2\sqrt{18})$.

17. $(\sqrt{6}+\sqrt{2})(\sqrt{2}-2\sqrt{6})$. $\qquad$ 18. $(\sqrt{3}-1)(\sqrt{3}+2)$.

19. $(2+\sqrt{7})(2-\sqrt{7})$. $\qquad$ 20. $(\sqrt{7}-\sqrt{2})(\sqrt{7}+\sqrt{2})$.

21. $(\sqrt{5}+2)^2$. $\qquad$ 22. $(1-\sqrt{5})^2$.

23. $(\sqrt{x}-1)(2\sqrt{x}+5)$. $\qquad$ 24. $\sqrt{ab}\,\sqrt{a^2bc^2}\,\sqrt{abc^2}$.

25. $\sqrt{3xy^2}\,\sqrt{2xy}\,\sqrt{3xy^3}$. $\qquad$ 26. $5\sqrt[4]{ab}(1-2\sqrt[4]{ab})$.

27. $(\sqrt{6}-5)^2$. $\qquad$ 28. $(\sqrt{3}+4)^2$.

29. $(3\sqrt{8}+\sqrt{3})(8\sqrt{3}-\sqrt{8})$. $\qquad$ 30. $(5\sqrt{2}+\sqrt{5})(2\sqrt{5}-\sqrt{2})$.

31. $(\sqrt{2y}+3)^2$. $\qquad$ 32. $(\sqrt{xy}-\sqrt{z})(2\sqrt{x}+\sqrt{y})$.

33. $(\sqrt{2x^2y})^5$. $\qquad$ 34. $(\sqrt[4]{2x^3y^2z})^5$.

In Problems **35–46**, *perform the operations and simplify.*

35. $\sqrt{5}\cdot\sqrt[4]{5}$. $\qquad$ 36. $\sqrt[3]{2}\cdot\sqrt[6]{3}$. $\qquad$ 37. $\sqrt{3x}\cdot\sqrt[3]{x^2}$.

38. $\sqrt[4]{x}\cdot\sqrt[3]{x^2}$. $\qquad$ 39. $\sqrt[3]{9x}\cdot\sqrt{3x}$. $\qquad$ 40. $\sqrt{8x^2}\cdot\sqrt[3]{4x^3}$.

41. $(3\sqrt[3]{x^2y})(2\sqrt{2x})$. $\qquad$ 42. $5\sqrt{ab^2}\cdot\sqrt[3]{ab}$. $\qquad$ 43. $\sqrt[5]{x^2y^3}\cdot\sqrt[4]{xy^2}$.

44. $\sqrt[6]{xy^5}\cdot\sqrt[3]{x^2y}$. $\qquad$ 45. $\sqrt{x}\cdot\sqrt[3]{x^2y}\cdot\sqrt[4]{x^4y^2}$. $\qquad$ 46. $\sqrt{x}\cdot\sqrt[4]{y}\cdot\sqrt[8]{xy}$.

9-6 Division of Radicals

Division of radicals with the same index can be performed by using the rule $\dfrac{\sqrt[n]{a}}{\sqrt[n]{b}}=\sqrt[n]{\dfrac{a}{b}}$ and simplifying the result. For example,

$$\frac{\sqrt{7}}{\sqrt{3}}=\sqrt{\frac{7}{3}}=\sqrt{\frac{7}{3}\cdot\frac{3}{3}}=\frac{\sqrt{21}}{3}.$$

Alternatively,

$$\frac{\sqrt{7}}{\sqrt{3}}=\frac{\sqrt{7}}{\sqrt{3}}\cdot\frac{\sqrt{3}}{\sqrt{3}}=\frac{\sqrt{21}}{3}.$$

example 1

Perform the indicated operations and simplify.

a. $\dfrac{\sqrt[3]{3x}}{\sqrt[3]{2x}} = \sqrt[3]{\dfrac{3x}{2x}} = \sqrt[3]{\dfrac{3}{2}} = \sqrt[3]{\dfrac{3}{2} \cdot \dfrac{2^2}{2^2}} = \dfrac{\sqrt[3]{12}}{2}.$

b. $\dfrac{\sqrt[4]{x^2y}}{\sqrt[4]{z}} = \sqrt[4]{\dfrac{x^2y}{z}} = \sqrt[4]{\dfrac{x^2y}{z} \cdot \dfrac{z^3}{z^3}} = \dfrac{\sqrt[4]{x^2yz^3}}{z}.$

c. $\dfrac{\sqrt{5xy}}{\sqrt{18xy^3}} = \dfrac{\sqrt{5xy}}{3y\sqrt{2xy}} = \dfrac{1}{3y}\sqrt{\dfrac{5xy}{2xy}} = \dfrac{1}{3y}\sqrt{\dfrac{5}{2}} = \dfrac{1}{3y}\sqrt{\dfrac{5}{2} \cdot \dfrac{2}{2}} = \dfrac{\sqrt{10}}{6y}.$

Sometimes the denominator of a fraction is the sum or difference of two terms involving square roots, such as $\sqrt{5} + \sqrt{2}$. In such cases the denominator can be rationalized by multiplying the numerator and denominator of the fraction by an expression that makes the denominator a difference of two squares. For example, if the denominator is $\sqrt{a} + \sqrt{b}$, the expression we use is $\sqrt{a} - \sqrt{b}$ (and vice versa), because

$$(\sqrt{a} + \sqrt{b})(\sqrt{a} - \sqrt{b}) = (\sqrt{a})^2 - (\sqrt{b})^2 = a - b.$$

To illustrate, we have

$$\frac{4}{\sqrt{5} + \sqrt{2}} = \frac{4}{\sqrt{5} + \sqrt{2}} \cdot \frac{\sqrt{5} - \sqrt{2}}{\sqrt{5} - \sqrt{2}}$$

$$= \frac{4(\sqrt{5} - \sqrt{2})}{(\sqrt{5})^2 - (\sqrt{2})^2} = \frac{4(\sqrt{5} - \sqrt{2})}{5 - 2}$$

$$= \frac{4(\sqrt{5} - \sqrt{2})}{3}.$$

example 2

Rationalize the denominators.

a. $\dfrac{2}{x - \sqrt{3}} = \dfrac{2}{x - \sqrt{3}} \cdot \dfrac{x + \sqrt{3}}{x + \sqrt{3}} = \dfrac{2(x + \sqrt{3})}{x^2 - (\sqrt{3})^2} = \dfrac{2(x + \sqrt{3})}{x^2 - 3}.$

b. $\dfrac{\sqrt{2}}{\sqrt{2} - \sqrt{3}} = \dfrac{\sqrt{2}}{\sqrt{2} - \sqrt{3}} \cdot \dfrac{\sqrt{2} + \sqrt{3}}{\sqrt{2} + \sqrt{3}} = \dfrac{\sqrt{2}(\sqrt{2} + \sqrt{3})}{2 - 3}$

$$= \dfrac{2 + \sqrt{6}}{-1} = -2 - \sqrt{6}.$$

c. $\dfrac{\sqrt{5} - \sqrt{2}}{\sqrt{5} + \sqrt{2}} = \dfrac{\sqrt{5} - \sqrt{2}}{\sqrt{5} + \sqrt{2}} \cdot \dfrac{\sqrt{5} - \sqrt{2}}{\sqrt{5} - \sqrt{2}}$

$= \dfrac{(\sqrt{5} - \sqrt{2})^2}{5 - 2} = \dfrac{5 - 2\sqrt{5}\sqrt{2} + 2}{3}$

$= \dfrac{7 - 2\sqrt{10}}{3}.$

To find the quotient of two radicals with different indices, we first use fractional exponents to rewrite each radical so that the indices are the same.

example 3

Perform the indicated operations and simplify.

a. $\dfrac{\sqrt[3]{10}}{\sqrt{10}} = \dfrac{10^{1/3}}{10^{1/2}} = \dfrac{10^{2/6}}{10^{3/6}} = \dfrac{\sqrt[6]{10^2}}{\sqrt[6]{10^3}} = \sqrt[6]{\dfrac{10^2}{10^3}} = \sqrt[6]{\dfrac{10^2}{10^3} \cdot \dfrac{10^3}{10^3}} = \dfrac{\sqrt[6]{10^5}}{10}.$

b. $\dfrac{\sqrt{2}}{\sqrt[3]{3}} = \dfrac{2^{1/2}}{3^{1/3}} = \dfrac{2^{3/6}}{3^{2/6}} = \dfrac{\sqrt[6]{2^3}}{\sqrt[6]{3^2}} = \sqrt[6]{\dfrac{2^3}{3^2} \cdot \dfrac{3^4}{3^4}} = \dfrac{\sqrt[6]{8 \cdot 81}}{3} = \dfrac{\sqrt[6]{648}}{3}.$

c. $\dfrac{\sqrt[4]{2}}{\sqrt[3]{xy^2}} = \dfrac{2^{1/4}}{x^{1/3}y^{2/3}} = \dfrac{2^{3/12}}{x^{4/12}y^{8/12}} = \sqrt[12]{\dfrac{2^3}{x^4y^8} \cdot \dfrac{x^8y^4}{x^8y^4}} = \dfrac{\sqrt[12]{8x^8y^4}}{xy}.$

Exercise 9-6

In Problems 1–28, perform the indicated operations and simplify.

1. $\dfrac{\sqrt{32}}{\sqrt{2}}.$ 2. $\dfrac{\sqrt{18}}{\sqrt{2}}.$ 3. $\dfrac{\sqrt{3}}{\sqrt{7}}.$

4. $\dfrac{\sqrt{8}}{\sqrt{3}}.$ 5. $\dfrac{\sqrt{18}}{\sqrt{3}}.$ 6. $\dfrac{\sqrt{15}}{\sqrt{5}}.$

7. $\dfrac{\sqrt{2a^3}}{\sqrt{a}}.$ 8. $\dfrac{\sqrt{3x^5}}{\sqrt{x}}.$ 9. $\dfrac{2x\sqrt[4]{x^7}}{\sqrt[4]{x^{12}}}.$

10. $\dfrac{3a^2b\sqrt[5]{a^3}}{\sqrt[5]{a^5}}.$ 11. $\dfrac{\sqrt[3]{6}}{\sqrt[3]{4x}}.$ 12. $\dfrac{\sqrt[3]{3y}}{\sqrt[3]{x}}.$

13. $\dfrac{\sqrt[3]{2x}}{\sqrt[3]{5xy^2}}.$ 14. $\dfrac{\sqrt{7xy}}{\sqrt{14xy^3}}.$ 15. $\dfrac{1}{2 + \sqrt{3}}.$

16. $\dfrac{1}{1 - \sqrt{2}}.$ 17. $\dfrac{2}{\sqrt{3} - \sqrt{2}}.$ 18. $\dfrac{5}{\sqrt{6} - \sqrt{3}}.$

19. $\dfrac{2\sqrt{2}}{\sqrt{2} - \sqrt{3}}.$ 20. $\dfrac{2\sqrt{3}}{\sqrt{5} - \sqrt{2}}.$ 21. $\dfrac{1 + \sqrt{2}}{\sqrt{3} + \sqrt{6}}.$

22. $\dfrac{3 - \sqrt{5}}{\sqrt{2} + \sqrt{4}}$.

23. $\dfrac{\sqrt{6} - \sqrt{3}}{\sqrt{6} + \sqrt{3}}$.

24. $\dfrac{\sqrt{3} - 5\sqrt{2}}{\sqrt{3} + \sqrt{2}}$.

25. $\dfrac{1}{x + \sqrt{5}}$.

26. $\dfrac{x - 3}{\sqrt{x - 1}} + \dfrac{4}{\sqrt{x - 1}}$.

27. $\dfrac{5}{1 + \sqrt{3}} - \dfrac{4}{2 - \sqrt{2}}$.

28. $\dfrac{4}{\sqrt{x + 2}} \cdot \dfrac{x^2}{3}$.

*In Problems **29–38**, perform the indicated operations and simplify.*

29. $\dfrac{\sqrt{6}}{\sqrt[4]{6}}$.

30. $\dfrac{\sqrt[3]{5}}{\sqrt[6]{5}}$.

31. $\dfrac{\sqrt[3]{3}}{\sqrt{2}}$.

32. $\dfrac{\sqrt[8]{3}}{\sqrt[4]{2}}$.

33. $\dfrac{\sqrt{2x}}{\sqrt[3]{x}}$.

34. $\dfrac{\sqrt{2x}}{\sqrt[3]{y}}$.

35. $\dfrac{\sqrt[9]{2y}}{\sqrt[3]{y}}$.

36. $\dfrac{\sqrt[3]{3y}}{\sqrt[9]{x}}$.

37. $\dfrac{\sqrt{xy}}{\sqrt[4]{xy}}$.

38. $\dfrac{2x\sqrt{x}}{\sqrt[3]{2xy}}$.

39. If a block of mass m were released at the top of a frictionless inclined plane with the same vertical height h as in Problem 85 of Sec. 9-3, its speed v at the bottom of the incline is $\sqrt{2gh}$. Find the ratio of the speed of the block to the speed of the sphere in Problem 85 and simplify.

9-7 Radical Equations

An equation in which the unknown occurs under a radical sign or has a fractional exponent is called a **radical equation**. A common method of solving a radical equation is to raise both sides to the same appropriate power to eliminate the radical. This operation, you may recall from Chapter 5, does not guarantee that the resulting equation is equivalent to the original one. The resulting equation may have more roots. For that reason it is essential that all "solutions" be checked so that any extraneous roots that may have been introduced can be rejected.

example 1

Solve the following radical equations.

a. $\sqrt{x - 7} - 4 = 0$.

When a radical equation has only one radical term, you should first rewrite the equation so that the radical is isolated on one side. Doing this, we have

$$\sqrt{x - 7} = 4$$

$$(\sqrt{x - 7})^2 = 4^2 \qquad \text{(squaring both sides)}$$

$$x - 7 = 16$$
$$x = 23.$$

Substituting 23 for x in the original equation gives $\sqrt{23 - 7} - 4 = 0$ or $4 - 4 = 0$, which is true. Thus 23 is a solution.

b. $\sqrt{y - 3} - \sqrt{y} = -3.$

When an equation has two terms involving radicals, you should first rewrite the equation so that a radical is on each side.

$$\sqrt{y - 3} = \sqrt{y} - 3$$
$$(\sqrt{y - 3})^2 = (\sqrt{y} - 3)^2 \qquad \text{(squaring both sides)}$$
$$y - 3 = y - 6\sqrt{y} + 9$$
$$6\sqrt{y} = 12$$
$$\sqrt{y} = 2$$
$$y = 4. \qquad \text{(squaring both sides)}$$

Replacing y by 4 in the left side of the original equation gives $\sqrt{1} - \sqrt{4}$, which is -1. Since this does not equal the right side, -3, there is *no solution*.

c. $\sqrt[3]{x - 4} = 3.$

$$\sqrt[3]{x - 4} = 3$$
$$x - 4 = 27 \qquad (\textit{cubing} \text{ both sides})$$
$$x = 31.$$

You may check that 31 is indeed a solution.

d. $\sqrt{(x - 3)^3} - 64 = 0.$

This equation can be rewritten as

$$(x - 3)^{3/2} = 64.$$

Raising both sides to the two-thirds power gives

$$[(x - 3)^{3/2}]^{2/3} = (64)^{2/3}$$
$$x - 3 = (\sqrt[3]{64})^2 = 4^2 = 16$$
$$x = 19.$$

You should verify that 19 is a solution.

Exercise 9-7

In Problems 1–18, solve the radical equations.

1. $\sqrt{x - 2} = 5.$

2. $\sqrt{x + 7} = 9.$

3. $\sqrt{2y - 5} - 6 = 0.$

4. $\sqrt{2x - 6} - 16 = 0.$

5. $(x^2 + 33)^{1/2} = x + 3$.

6. $(y + 6)^{1/2} = 7$.

7. $\left(\dfrac{x}{2} + 1\right)^{1/4} = \dfrac{1}{2}$.

8. $\sqrt[4]{2x + 1} = 3$.

9. $(z - 3)^{3/2} = 8$.

10. $\sqrt{x - 3} + 4 = 1$.

11. $2\sqrt{2x + 1} = 3\sqrt{3x - 8}$.

12. $\sqrt{4x - 6} - \sqrt{x} = 0$.

13. $\sqrt{x} - \sqrt{x + 1} = 1$.

14. $4\sqrt{8y + 1} = 5\sqrt{5y + 1}$.

15. $\sqrt{x + 1} = \sqrt{x} + 1$.

16. $\sqrt{7 - 2x} - \sqrt{x - 1} = 0$.

17. $\sqrt{y} + \sqrt{y + 2} = 3$.

18. $\sqrt{\dfrac{1}{x}} - \sqrt{\dfrac{2}{5x - 2}} = 0$.

19. The time T, in seconds, for one complete oscillation of a simple pendulum is given by

$$T = 2\pi\sqrt{\dfrac{L}{g}},$$

where L is the length of the pendulum and g is the acceleration due to gravity. Solve the equation for g.

20. The formula $f_r = \dfrac{1}{2\pi\sqrt{LC}}$ occurs in the study of alternating current. Here f_r is resonant frequency, L is inductance, and C is capacitance. Solve for C.

21. Two sources, A and B, are 8 m apart as shown in Fig. 9-3. The sources emit waves of wavelength $\lambda = 5$ m. *Constructive* interference of the waves from A and B

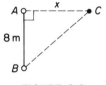

FIGURE 9-3

will occur at point C, located a distance x to the right of A, when

$$\overline{BC} - \overline{AC} = \lambda.$$

How far is point C from A when constructive interference of the waves from A and B occurs at C?

22. In Problem 21, *destructive* interference of the waves from A and B occurs at C when

$$\overline{BC} - \overline{AC} = \dfrac{\lambda}{2}.$$

How far is point C from source A when such destructive interference occurs?

23. In the study of the flow of water through a sloped rectangular channel, the equation $AR^{2/3} = 0.892$ occurs. For a certain channel, $A = b^2/2$ and $R = b/4$, where b is the width of the channel in meters. Find b.

24. An analysis of the structure of the hydrogen atom involves expressions for the angular momentum L and the total energy E. These can be written

$$L = \frac{nh}{2\pi} = \sqrt{\frac{me^2r}{4\pi\epsilon_0}}$$

and

$$E = -\frac{e^2}{8\pi\epsilon_0 r}.$$

Solve the first equation for r and, by substituting into the second equation, show that

$$E = -\frac{me^4}{8\epsilon_0^2 h^2 n^2}.$$

9-8 Review

Review Questions

1. $64^{1/3} = \sqrt[n]{64}$, where $n = $ _____.

2. $x^{5/4} = \sqrt[n]{x^m}$, where $m = $ _____ and $n = $ _____.

3. $x^{2/3} = (\sqrt[n]{x})^m$, where $m = $ _____ and $n = $ _____.

4. $\sqrt[7]{x^5} = x^{m/n}$, where $m = $ _____ and $n = $ _____.

5. $(\sqrt[4]{x})^9 = x^{m/n}$, where $m = $ _____ and $n = $ _____.

6. $\sqrt[4]{x^4} = $ _____; $\sqrt[3]{z^6} = \sqrt[3]{(z^2)^3} = $ _____.

7. $\sqrt[5]{x^{10}y^{15}} = \sqrt[5]{(\underline{})^5} = $ _____.

8. $\sqrt{32} = \sqrt{(\underline{})\cdot 2} = \sqrt{\underline{}}\cdot\sqrt{2} = $ _____ $\sqrt{2}$.

9. $\sqrt[3]{x^5y^4} = \sqrt[3]{(\underline{})x^2y} = \sqrt[3]{\underline{}}\cdot\sqrt[3]{x^2y} = $ _____ $\sqrt[3]{x^2y}$.

10. $\sqrt{\dfrac{5}{36}} = \dfrac{\sqrt{5}}{\sqrt{\underline{}}} = \dfrac{\sqrt{5}}{(\underline{})}$.

11. $\sqrt[5]{\dfrac{x^3}{y^2}} = \sqrt[5]{\dfrac{x^3(\underline{})}{y^5}} = \dfrac{\sqrt[5]{x^3(\underline{})}}{\sqrt[5]{y^5}} = \dfrac{\sqrt[5]{x^3(\underline{})}}{y}$.

12. $6\sqrt[4]{3x} + 2\sqrt[4]{3x} - 3\sqrt[4]{3x} = $ _____ $\sqrt[4]{3x}$.

13. $\sqrt{x^3} + 2x\sqrt{x} = \sqrt{x^2\cdot x} + 2x\sqrt{x} = $ _____ $\sqrt{x} + 2x\sqrt{x} = $ _____ $\sqrt{x}$.

14. $\sqrt[3]{y^2}\cdot\sqrt[3]{y} = \sqrt[3]{(\underline{})} = $ _____.

15. $\dfrac{1}{\sqrt[3]{x}} = \dfrac{1}{x^{1/3}}\cdot\dfrac{(\underline{})}{x^{2/3}} = \dfrac{\sqrt[3]{(\underline{})}}{x}$.

16. $\dfrac{\sqrt{10xy}}{\sqrt{5x}} = \sqrt{\dfrac{10xy}{5x}} = \sqrt{(\underline{})}$.

17. $\dfrac{1}{3 + \sqrt{2}} = \dfrac{1}{3 + \sqrt{2}}\cdot\dfrac{3 - \sqrt{2}}{3 - \sqrt{2}} = \dfrac{3 - \sqrt{2}}{(\underline{})}$.

Answers to Review Questions

1. 3.   **2.** 5, 4.   **3.** 2, 3.   **4.** 5, 7.   **5.** 9, 4.   **6.** x, z^2.   **7.** x^2y^3, x^2y^3.   **8.** 16, 16, 4.
9. x^3y^3, x^3y^3, xy.   **10.** 36, 6.   **11.** y^3, y^3, y^3.   **12.** 5.   **13.** $x, 3x$.   **14.** y^3, y.
15. $x^{2/3}, x^2$.   **16.** $2y$.   **17.** 7.

Review Problems

In Problems 1–14, evaluate the expressions without the use of a calculator.

1. 3^0.

2. $2\left(-\dfrac{2}{3}\right)^0$.

3. 5^{-1}.

4. $(-3)^{-1}$.

5. $4\left(-\dfrac{2}{3}\right)^{-2}$.

6. $\dfrac{2^{-1}}{4^{-2}}$.

7. $100^{1/2}$.

8. $64^{1/3}$.

9. $4^{3/2}$.

10. $(25)^{-3/2}$.

11. $(32)^{-2/5}$

12. $\left(\dfrac{9}{100}\right)^{3/2}$.

13. $\left(\dfrac{1}{16}\right)^{5/4}$.

14. $\left(-\dfrac{27}{64}\right)^{2/3}$.

In Problems 15–74, perform the operations and simplify. Write all answers in terms of positive exponents only. Rationalize all denominators. Avoid fractional exponents in the final form. For example, $y^{-1}x^{1/2} = \dfrac{\sqrt{x}}{y}$.

15. $\sqrt{32}$.

16. $\sqrt[3]{24}$.

17. $\sqrt[3]{2x^3}$.

18. $\sqrt{4x}$.

19. $\sqrt{16x^4}$.

20. $\sqrt[4]{\dfrac{x}{16}}$.

21. $(9z^6)^{1/2}$.

22. $(16y^8)^{3/4}$.

23. $\left(\dfrac{27t^3}{8}\right)^{2/3}$.

24. $\left(\dfrac{1000}{a^9}\right)^{-2/3}$.

25. $\dfrac{x^3y^{-2}}{x^5z^2}$.

26. $\sqrt[5]{x^2y^3z^{-10}}$.

27. $2x^{-1}x^{-3}$.

28. xy^{-1}.

29. $(4t^2)^{-2}$.

30. $(-2z)^{-3}$.

31. $(x^{-2}y^2)^3$.

32. $(ab^2c^3)^{3/4}$.

33. $\dfrac{x^{-2}y^{-6}z^2}{xy^{-1}}$.

34. $(2x^{-1}y)^{-2}$.

35. $(2x^{3/4}y^{1/2})(xy^{3/2})$.

36. $(xy^{-2}\sqrt{z})^4$.

37. $x^{-3}(2x^4y^{-2})$.

38. $(x^{1/2} + y^{1/2})(x^{1/2} - y^{1/2})$.

39. $(-3x^{1/2}y^{2/3})^3$.

40. $[(x-4)^{1/5}]^{10}$.

41. $2x^{1/2}y^{-3}x^{1/3}$.

42. $(4xy^3)^{1/2}(-2x^{3/2}y)^4$.

43. $\sqrt{7}\sqrt{4}\sqrt{14}$.

44. $\dfrac{2}{\sqrt{x^3}}$.

45. $\sqrt{\sqrt[3]{t^4}}$.

46. $\dfrac{\sqrt{3}\sqrt{6}}{\sqrt{2}}$.

47. $\dfrac{2^0}{(2^{-2}x^{1/2}y^{-2})^3}$.

48. $\dfrac{\sqrt[3]{t^5}}{\sqrt[3]{t^2}}.$

49. $\dfrac{(x^2y^{-1}z)^{-2}}{(xy^{1/2})^{-4}}.$

50. $\left(\dfrac{2x^2y}{8y^3z^{-2}}\right)^{1/2}.$

51. $2\sqrt{8} - (5\sqrt{2} - \sqrt{18}).$

52. $(\sqrt{3} - \sqrt{2})(\sqrt{3} + 2\sqrt{2}).$

53. $\sqrt{2}(1 - \sqrt{6}).$

54. $\sqrt{75k^4}.$

55. $(\sqrt[5]{2})^{10}.$

56. $\sqrt{x}\,\sqrt{x^2y^3}\,\sqrt{xy^2}.$

57. $\dfrac{2}{\sqrt{7}}.$

58. $\dfrac{8}{\sqrt[3]{4}}.$

59. $\dfrac{3}{\sqrt[4]{x}}.$

60. $\sqrt[5]{\sqrt[3]{x^{10}}}.$

61. $\sqrt[4]{81x^6}.$

62. $(\sqrt[5]{x^2y})^{10}.$

63. $\sqrt[3]{\sqrt{\sqrt[3]{x^{36}}}}.$

64. $\sqrt[4]{2}\,\sqrt[4]{24}.$

65. $\sqrt{x}\,\sqrt{3x}.$

66. $\sqrt[6]{x^7y^{13}z^{12}}.$

67. $\sqrt[6]{\dfrac{x^6}{y^9}}.$

68. $\sqrt[9]{x^3y^6}.$

69. $\dfrac{3}{\sqrt[3]{xy^2}}.$

70. $\dfrac{1}{\sqrt{x}\,\sqrt{y}}.$

71. $\dfrac{\sqrt[3]{3x^2}}{\sqrt[3]{2x}}.$

72. $\sqrt[5]{\dfrac{xy^2}{x^2y}}.$

73. $\dfrac{1}{\sqrt{6} - 2}.$

74. $\dfrac{4\sqrt{6}}{\sqrt{6} + \sqrt{4}}.$

In Problems 75–82, solve the equations.

75. $\sqrt{2x + 5} = 5.$

76. $\sqrt{3x - 4} = \sqrt{2x + 5}.$

77. $\sqrt[3]{11x + 9} = 4.$

78. $\sqrt{x^2 + 5x + 25} = x + 4.$

79. $\sqrt{y} + 6 = 5.$

80. $2\sqrt{x - 2} = \sqrt{3}(\sqrt{x - 2}).$

81. $\sqrt{x - 1} + \sqrt{x + 6} = 7.$

82. $\sqrt{z^2 + 2z} = 3 + z.$

83. In Fig. 9-4 an arrangement of two charges q_1 and q_2 is indicated. Theory shows

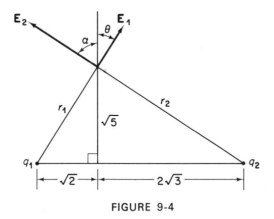

FIGURE 9-4

that the magnitudes of the electric field vectors $\mathbf{E}_1$ and $\mathbf{E}_2$ due to the charges q_1 and q_2, respectively, are given by

$$E_1 = \frac{kq_1}{r_1^2} \quad \text{and} \quad E_2 = \frac{kq_2}{r_2^2}.$$

Find expressions for the magnitudes of the *vertical components* of $\mathbf{E}_1$ and $\mathbf{E}_2$ and simplify each. *Hint*: For $\mathbf{E}_1$ it is given by $E_1 \cos \theta$.

84. For the arrangement in Problem 83, find an expression for the magnitude of the *horizontal component* of $\mathbf{E}_1$ and simplify.

variation

10-1 Direct Variation

Many physical laws encountered in science and engineering express a functional relationship called *direct variation*. For example, consider the area A of a circle as a function of its radius r (in centimeters):

$$A = \pi r^2.$$

Observe that the ratio of A to r^2 is constant for $r > 0$:

$$\frac{A}{r^2} = \pi.$$

Such a constant ratio of variable quantities characterizes the notion of direct variation.

> A variable y is said to **vary directly** as, or be **directly proportional** to, the nth power of the variable x (for $n > 0$) if $y = kx^n$, where k is a nonzero constant called the **constant of variation** or **constant of proportionality**.

In view of that definition, we can say that the area of a circle is directly proportional to the *square* of the radius. The constant of proportionality is π. Figure 10-1

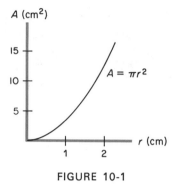

FIGURE 10-1

shows the graph of $A = \pi r^2$. Clearly, the greater the radius, the greater is the area. More generally, with direct variation the absolute value of the dependent variable increases as the independent variable increases through positive values. For the particular case that y is directly proportional to x, then $n = 1$ and $y = kx$, the graph of which is a straight line.

example 1

If y varies directly as x^3, and $y = 4$ when $x = 2$, then (a) find the function that relates y and x, and (b) find y when $x = 10$.

a. Because y varies directly as x^3, by definition we have

$$y = kx^3. \tag{1}$$

From the given data, $y = 4$ when $x = 2$. Substituting into Eq. 1, we can find the constant of variation.

$$4 = k(2)^3$$

$$k = \frac{4}{8} = \frac{1}{2}.$$

Replacing k in Eq. 1 by its value, we have the function that relates y and x:

$$y = \frac{1}{2}x^3. \tag{2}$$

b. When $x = 10$, from Eq. 2 we have

$$y = \frac{1}{2}(10)^3 = 500.$$

example 2

Hooke's law states that if the elastic limit is not exceeded, the force F exerted by a spring on an attached body is directly proportional to the displacement x of the end of the spring from its unstretched position. If a 40-N force results from a displacement of 5 cm, what displacement corresponds to a 10-N force?

Because F is directly proportional to x, we have $F = kx$. From the given data, if $x = 5$ cm, then $F = 40$ N. Thus

$$F = kx \tag{3}$$

$$40\text{ N} = k(5\text{ cm})$$

$$k = \frac{40\text{ N}}{5\text{ cm}} = 8\,\frac{\text{N}}{\text{cm}}.$$

Therefore, from Eq. 3, the equation that relates F and x is

$$F = \left(8\,\frac{\text{N}}{\text{cm}}\right)x.$$

If $F = 10$ N, then

$$10\text{ N} = \left(8\,\frac{\text{N}}{\text{cm}}\right)x$$

$$x = \frac{10\text{ N}}{8\text{ N/cm}} = \frac{5}{4}\text{ cm}.$$

Note the algebraic treatment of the units involved. You should also realize that k can be determined if *any* pair of corresponding values of x and F are known (except $F = 0$ when $x = 0$).

The basic definition of direct variation can be extended to the case where one variable varies directly as the *product* of powers of other variables. We call this *joint variation.*

> A variable y is said to **vary jointly** as, or be **directly proportional to the product of**, x^m and z^n if $y = kx^m z^n$ where $m, n > 0$ and k is a nonzero constant.

example 3

If y is directly proportional to the product of the square of x and the cube root of z, find y when $x = 2$ and $z = 16$ given that $y = 1$ when $x = 1$ and $z = 2$.

From the statement of the problem,

$$y = kx^2\sqrt[3]{z}.$$

Substituting the given values ($y = 1$ when $x = 1$ and $z = 2$), we have

$$1 = k(1)^2\sqrt[3]{2}$$

$$k = \frac{1}{\sqrt[3]{2}}.$$

Thus

$$y = kx^2\sqrt[3]{z} = \frac{1}{\sqrt[3]{2}}x^2\sqrt[3]{z}.$$

When $x = 2$ and $z = 16$,

$$y = \frac{1}{\sqrt[3]{2}}(2)^2\sqrt[3]{16} = 4\sqrt[3]{\frac{16}{2}} = 4\sqrt[3]{8} = 8.$$

example 4

The kinetic energy K of a particle varies jointly as the mass m of the particle and the square of the particle's speed v. When a particle of mass 0.1 kg has a speed of 20 m/s, its kinetic energy is 20 kg m²/s². What is the kinetic energy of the same particle when its speed is 10 m/s?

$$K = kmv^2$$

$$20\,\frac{\text{kg m}^2}{\text{s}^2} = k(0.1\text{ kg})\left(20\,\frac{\text{m}}{\text{s}}\right)^2$$

$$20\,\frac{\text{kg m}^2}{\text{s}^2} = 40k\,\frac{\text{kg m}^2}{\text{s}^2}$$

$$k = \frac{1}{2}.$$

Note that here the constant of proportionality has no units associated with it. Now, when $v = 10$ m/s,

$$K = \frac{1}{2}mv^2$$

$$= \frac{1}{2}(0.1\text{ kg})\left(10\,\frac{\text{m}}{\text{s}}\right)^2$$

$$= 5\,\frac{\text{kg}\cdot\text{m}^2}{\text{s}^2}.$$

You may recall from Chapter 4 that this basic SI unit of energy, kg·m²/s², is called a joule (J). Thus $K = 5$ J.

example 5

If y varies jointly as x and w^2, how is y affected if x is increased by 20 percent and w is decreased by 10 percent?

We have

$$y = kxw^2. \tag{4}$$

Let the initial values of y, x, and w be y_0, x_0, and w_0, respectively. Then

$$y_0 = kx_0w_0^2. \tag{5}$$

Rather than solve for k, we proceed as follows. Let the new values of x and w be $1.2x_0$ and $0.9w_0$. Then from Eq. 4, the corresponding value of y is given by

$$y = k(1.2x_0)(0.9w_0)^2$$
$$= (1.2)(0.81)(kx_0w_0^2)$$
$$= (1.2)(0.81)(y_0) \qquad \text{(from Eq. 5)}$$
$$= 0.972y_0.$$

Thus y is decreased by 2.8 percent.

Exercise 10-1

1. If y varies directly as x, and $y = 8$ when $x = 2$, (a) find the function that relates y and x, and (b) find y when $x = 6$.

2. If y is directly proportional to x^3, and $y = 16$ when $x = 2$, find y when $x = 3$.

3. If y is directly proportional to x^2, and $y = 2$ when $x = 4$, find y when $x = 6$.

4. If y is directly proportional to $\sqrt{x}$, and $y = 4$ when $x = 25$, find y when $x = 16$.

5. If y varies jointly as x and z^2, and $y = 6$ when $x = 2$ and $z = \frac{1}{2}$, find y when $x = 4$ and $z = \sqrt{2}$.

6. If y varies jointly as $\sqrt{x}$ and $\sqrt{z}$, find y when $x = 4$ and $z = 8$, if $y = 11$ when $x = 2$ and $z = 1$.

7. The elongation of a supporting cable varies directly as the load if the elastic limit is not exceeded. Find the elongation (in centimeters) when the load is 1000 N, if a load of 300 N causes an elongation of 0.6 cm.

8. In the equation $f = \dfrac{1}{2L}\sqrt{\dfrac{T}{m}}$, where m is a constant, the frequency f of a vibrating string of fixed length L is directly proportional to the square root of the tension T in the string, since

$$f = \frac{1}{2L\sqrt{m}}\sqrt{T} = k\sqrt{T}.$$

Show that T is directly proportional to the square of the frequency.

9. The weight W of an object is directly proportional to the product of the mass m of the object and the acceleration g due to gravity. If a mass of 2 kg weighs 19.6 N on the earth's surface, where $g = 9.80$ m/s^2, then (a) find a formula for W and simplify by using the fact that $1\ \mathrm{N} = 1\ \mathrm{kg \cdot m/s^2}$, and (b) find what the same mass would weigh on the moon where $g = 1.67$ m/s^2.

10. Experiments indicate that thin rods, when heated, expand principally in one dimension along their lengths. The change in length of a rod, ΔL, varies jointly as the original length of the rod, L_0, and the change in temperature, Δt. If a rod is initially 20 cm long at 50°C and then 20.0072 cm at 80°C, find its length at 110°C.

11. When a substance is heated without changing its state, the amount of heat Q added to the substance is directly proportional to the product of the mass m of the substance and the change in temperature, Δt. If it requires 60 calories of heat to

raise the temperature of 100 g of lead from 50° to 70°C, how many more calories are necessary to raise the temperature of the same mass an additional 10 Celsius degrees?

12. Total internal reflection of a light ray takes place at the boundary of two surfaces if the angle of incidence is greater than the critical angle for those surfaces. The sine of the critical angle θ_c varies directly as the ratio n_2/n_1 of the indices of refraction of the two surfaces. If the index of refraction of air is $n_2 = 1.00$ and that of of glass is $n_1 = 1.50$ and the critical angle for an air-glass boundary is 42°, find the critical angle for an air-water boundary if the index of refraction of water is $n_1 = 1.33$. Give your answer to the nearest degree.

13. Experiments indicate that the potential difference V across an ohmic conductor varies jointly as the current i and the resistance R. This is known as Ohm's law. If a conductor having a fixed resistance of x ohms has a potential difference of 30 V across it when it carries a current of 2 A, what is the potential difference across the same conductor when $i = 6$ A?

14. The angular deflection θ of a galvanometer varies jointly as the current i through the coil and the number n of turns in the coil. If a galvanometer deflects 60° for a current of 6 A, what would be the deflection, in radians, if the current is reduced to two-thirds of its original value?

15. When a space capsule is launched from a planet (or satellite), it can be shown, under simplifying assumptions, that the capsule must be given an initial speed (or escape velocity) v if it is to escape the planet's gravitational field and that v varies jointly as the square root of the radius r of the planet and the square root of the acceleration g due to gravity. The escape velocity on the earth is about 11.2 km/s. The radius of the earth is (approximately) four times that of the moon and the acceleration due to gravity on the earth is six times that of the moon. Find the escape velocity on the moon.

16. The potential V at a given point due to a number of distinct point charges varies directly as the algebraic sum of the ratios of the charges to the distances of the charges from the given point. Consider three point charges, two positive and one negative, all having magnitude q and equidistant from a given point. How is the potential at the given point affected if the negative charge is doubled in magnitude and one of the positive charges is moved three times as far away from the given point?

10-2 Inverse and Combined Variation

Another type of functional relationship between variables is known as *inverse variation*.

> A variable y is said to **vary inversely** as, or be **inversely proportional** to, the nth power of the variable x if $y = \dfrac{k}{x^n}$, where $n > 0$ and k is a nonzero constant.

For example, if y is inversely proportional to x^2, then $y = k/x^2$, the graph of which is shown in Fig. 10-2 for $x, k > 0$. With inverse variation, the absolute value of the dependent variable *decreases* as the independent variable increases through positive values.

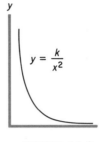

FIGURE 10-2

example 1

If y varies inversely as the cube root of z, and $y = 2$ when $z = 2$, find y when $z = 8$.

Since y varies inversely as $\sqrt[3]{z}$,

$$y = \frac{k}{\sqrt[3]{z}}.$$

When $z = 2$, then $y = 2$:

$$2 = \frac{k}{\sqrt[3]{2}}$$

$$k = 2\sqrt[3]{2}.$$

Thus the function that relates y and z is

$$y = \frac{2\sqrt[3]{2}}{\sqrt[3]{z}}.$$

When $z = 8$,

$$y = \frac{2\sqrt[3]{2}}{\sqrt[3]{8}} = \frac{2\sqrt[3]{2}}{2} = \sqrt[3]{2}.$$

example 2

The weight W of an object on or above the earth's surface is inversely proportional to the square of the distance r of the object from the center of the earth. Take the radius of the earth to be 6.37×10^6 m. If an astronaut weighs 800 N on the earth, what does he weigh at an altitude of 5.63×10^6 m above the earth's surface?

Because W is inversely proportional to r^2,

$$W = \frac{k}{r^2}.$$

On the earth's surface, we have $W = 800$ N when $r = 6.37 \times 10^6$ m. Thus

$$800 \text{ N} = \frac{k}{(6.37 \times 10^6 \text{ m})^2}$$

$$k = 3.25 \times 10^{16} \text{ N·m}^2.$$

At an altitude of 5.63×10^6 m, we have

$$r = (6.37 \times 10^6) + (5.63 \times 10^6)$$
$$= 1.2 \times 10^7 \text{ m}$$

and

$$W = \frac{k}{r^2} = \frac{3.25 \times 10^{16} \text{ N·m}^2}{(1.2 \times 10^7 \text{ m})^2} = 226 \text{ N}.$$

example 3

The resonant frequency f_r of a series ac circuit containing an inductance L and a capacitance C varies inversely as the square root of the product of L and C. If $f_r = 10,000/\pi$ hertz (Hz) when $L = 5 \times 10^{-3}$ henries (H) and $C = 5 \times 10^{-7}$ farads (F), find f_r in terms of π when $L = 4 \times 10^{-3}$ H and $C = 9 \times 10^{-7}$ F.

Here

$$f_r = \frac{k}{\sqrt{LC}}$$

$$\frac{10,000}{\pi} = \frac{k}{\sqrt{(5 \times 10^{-3})(5 \times 10^{-7})}}$$

$$k = \frac{10,000}{\pi}\sqrt{(5 \times 10^{-3})(5 \times 10^{-7})}$$

$$= \frac{10,000}{\pi}\sqrt{25 \times 10^{-10}}$$

$$= \frac{10,000}{\pi}(5)(10^{-5}) = \frac{0.5}{\pi} = \frac{1}{2\pi}.$$

Thus

$$f_r = \frac{1}{2\pi\sqrt{LC}}.$$

For the given data we have

$$f_r = \frac{1}{2\pi\sqrt{(4 \times 10^{-3})(9 \times 10^{-7})}} = \frac{1}{2\pi(6 \times 10^{-5})}$$

$$= \frac{10^5}{12\pi} \text{ Hz}.$$

Sometimes a variable simultaneously varies directly as one quantity and inversely as another quantity. We speak of this situation as **combined variation**, which Example 4 illustrates.

example 4

If y varies directly as x and inversely as z, find y when $x = 6$ and $z = 2$, if $y = 4$ when $x = 5$ and $z = 4$.

We express the fact that y varies directly as x and inversely as z by writing

$$y = \frac{kx}{z}.$$

Now, $y = 4$ when $x = 5$ and $z = 4$; therefore

$$4 = \frac{k \cdot 5}{4}$$

$$k = \frac{16}{5}.$$

Thus

$$y = \frac{\frac{16}{5}x}{z} = \frac{16x}{5z}.$$

When $x = 6$ and $z = 2$ we have

$$y = \frac{16(6)}{5(2)} = \frac{48}{5}.$$

Exercise 10-2

1. If y is inversely proportional to x, and $y = 12$ when $x = 3$, (a) find the function that relates y and x, and (b) find y when $x = 4$.

2. If p is inversely proportional to t^3, and $p = \frac{1}{36}$ when $t = 3$, find p when $t = 2$.

3. If r varies directly as s and inversely as t^2, and $r = 10$ when $s = 1$ and $t = 2$, (a) find the function that relates r to s and t, and (b) find r when $s = 4$ and $t = 9$.

4. If Q varies directly as $\sqrt{u}$ and inversely as v, and $Q = 1$ when $u = 4$ and $v = 4$, find Q when $u = 9$ and $v = 2$.

5. If y varies directly as x^2 and inversely as z, and $y = 8$ when $x = 2$ and $z = 2$, find y when $x = 3$ and $z = 4$.

6. If y varies jointly as x^2 and z and inversely as $\sqrt{w}$, and if $y = 12$ when $x = 1$, $z = 3$, and $w = 4$, find y when $x = 4$, $z = 2$, and $w = \pi^2$. Give your answer in terms of π.

7. If a varies jointly as b^2 and c^3 and inversely as d^2, and if $a = 25$ when $b = 2$, $c = 2$, and $d = 2$, find a when $b = 3$, $c = 2$ and $d = 1$.

8. If y varies directly as x and inversely as $\sin z$, and $y = 7$ when $x = 4$ and $z = \pi/2$, find y when $x = \sqrt{2}$ and $z = \pi/4$.

9. Newton's second law of motion states that when a mass m is acted upon by a force F, the acceleration a of the mass is directly proportional to F and inversely

proportional to m. If a mass of 50 kg initially at rest on a horizontal surface is acted upon by a force of 500 N, the acceleration is 10 m/s². What force would give a mass of 30 kg an acceleration of 75 m/s²?

10. The resistance of a copper wire varies directly as its length and inversely as its cross-sectional area. If a copper wire of length 500 cm and radius 0.2 cm has a resistance of 0.025 ohms, what will the resistance be for the same copper wire of length 1000 cm and radius 0.1 cm?

11. Under certain conditions, the illumination E of a surface varies directly as the intensity I of the light source and inversely as the square of the distance r of the surface from the source. What is the effect on the illumination if the intensity and distance are both doubled?

12. Coulomb's law states that the force F of attraction or repulsion between two electrostatic point charges of magnitudes q_1 and q_2 is directly proportional to the product of the magnitudes of the charges and inversely proportional to the square of the distance r between them. If the magnitude of one charge is doubled and the distance between charges reduced by a factor of one-half, how is the force affected?

13. In Example 2, at what altitude above the earth's surface must the astronaut be if his weight is to be 1 percent of his weight on the earth's surface?

14. The capacitance of a parallel-plate capacitor varies directly as the area of either of its plates and inversely as the separation of its plates. If the plates are 5 mm apart and 2 m² in area, the capacitance is 3.54×10^{-9} F. For square plates separated by 1 mm, what must be the length of a side for the capacitance to be 1 F? Based on your answer, would you expect to find a 1-F parallel-plate capacitor in practice?

15. Newton's law of gravitation states that the attractive force F between masses m_1 and m_2 varies directly as the product of the masses and inversely as the square of the distance r between their centers. If the centers of two 10-kg masses are 1 m apart, then $F = 6.67 \times 10^{-9}$ N. Find F when two 100-kg masses are 1 m apart.

16. Given a volume V containing n moles of gas at temperature T, the ideal gas law states that the pressure P of the gas is directly proportional to the product of n and T and inversely proportional to V. If the volume of a particular sample of an ideal gas is reduced to one-third its original value during an isothermal process, one that takes place at constant temperature, what happens to the pressure of the gas?

17. Suppose that in a laboratory experiment you took measurements of two related quantities, x and y, and obtained the following pairs of values:

x	3	6	12
y	240	60	15

Based on these data, would you conjecture that x varies inversely as y, or inversely as $\sqrt{y}$? To support your conclusion, find an equation that relates x and y.

18. In studies of electric fields, it is shown that the electric field intensity E at a distance r from an isolated point charge varies directly as the charge q and inversely as the

square of the distance r. If a point charge of 2×10^{-9} C sets up an electric field intensity of 2 N/C at a distance of 3 m from the charge, what is the electric field intensity for the same charge at a distance of 6 m from the charge?

10-3 Review

Review Questions

1. The statement that y varies directly as x means that the ratio of y to x is a

   _____.

2. If y is directly proportional to the product of x and w, then $y = kxw$. For this statement we can also say that y varies _____ as x and w.

3. If $y = kL^2/\sqrt{w}$, then y varies _____(a)_____ as L^2 and _____(b)_____ as $\sqrt{w}$.

4. If y varies jointly as x^2 and w and inversely as the product of w^2 and x, then in more simple terms we can say that y varies directly as __(a)__ and inversely as __(b)__.

Answers to Review Questions

1. Constant.   2. Jointly.   3. (a) Directly, (b) Inversely.   4. (a) x, (b) w.

Review Problems

1. If y varies directly as x and inversely as w, and $y = 7$ when $x = 2$ and $w = 3$, find y when $x = 1$ and $w = 4$.

2. If y varies directly as x^2 and inversely as $\sqrt{w}$, and $y = 2$ when $x = 3$ and $w = 4$, find y when $x = \frac{1}{3}$ and $w = 9$.

3. If y varies jointly as x^2 and w and inversely as z, and $y = 1$ when $x = 1$, $w = 2$, and $z = 3$, find y when $x = 3$, $w = 2$, and $z = 1$.

4. If y varies directly as $x^{3/2}$ and inversely as $\sqrt{z}$, and $y = 8$ when $x = 4$ and $z = 3$, find y when $x = 2$ and $z = 12$.

5. When a rod or cable is subjected to a stretching force, the stress is directly proportional to the strain produced. If, for a particular steel wire, the stress is 6.9×10^7 N/m^2 when the strain is 1/3000, what is the stress when the strain is 1/2000?

6. When an object is released from rest and falls freely, its speed varies directly as the square root of the product of the acceleration due to gravity and the distance fallen. Take the acceleration due to gravity to be 9.8 m/s^2. If a body acquires a speed of 9.9 m/s after falling a distance of 5 m, what is its speed after falling 8 m?

7. When a body travels in a circle at a constant speed, it is acted upon by a centripetal force which varies jointly as the mass of the body and the square of its speed and inversely as the radius of the circle. If a 2-kg mass traveling in a circle of radius 5 m with a speed of 10 m/s is acted upon by a centripetal force of 40 N, what force acts upon a 3-kg mass traveling in a circle of radius 6 m at a speed of 8 m/s?

8. In some spectrographic instruments, a charged particle is projected perpendicularly in a field of magnetic induction B. Under this condition the particle travels in a circle of radius R. The radius is directly proportional to the product of the mass m and speed v of the particle and inversely proportional to the product of the charge q on the particle and the magnetic induction B. If a charge of mass m_0 travels in a circle of radius 2 m in a magnetic field, what must be the mass of a charged particle with three times the charge if it is to travel in the same circle in the same field with the same speed?

9. The rate at which heat is transferred through a metal rod varies jointly as the cross-sectional area of the rod and the difference in temperature between its ends and inversely as the length of the rod. If 12,500 cal/s (calories per second) is transmitted through an aluminum rod 0.5 cm long of cross-sectional area 500 cm² when the temperature difference between its ends is 25 C°, at what rate is heat transferred through a rod of the same material and length if its cross-sectional area is 600 cm² and the temperature difference is 80 C°?

10. Under certain conditions, the velocity of an object varies jointly as its acceleration, which is constant, and the time it has been in motion. (a) If the velocity is 29.4 m/s after 3 s, what is the velocity after $\frac{1}{2}$ s? (b) If the acceleration is 9.8 m/s², what is the constant of variation?

complex numbers

11-1 Introduction

Every applied problem encountered thus far in our study of technical mathematics has had a solution in the real number system. There are, however, many problems in applied mathematics that have *no* solution in that system. To satisfy the practical requirement that we have solutions to such problems, the real number system can be extended to create the *system of complex numbers*. This new system, which includes the real numbers, provides solutions to previously unsolvable problems.

Moreover, there are problems in science and engineering where, although a solution in the real number system does exist, the characteristics of that system make obtaining the solution tedious. In such problems, for example the analysis of alternating-current circuits in electrical engineering, the complex number system permits a much simpler and more compact solution. In the following section you will see that the need for complex numbers arises quite naturally from consideration of solving certain equations.

11-2 The j-Operator and Complex Numbers

To solve the equation $x^2 = 1$, we must find all real numbers x having a square of 1. Because only 1 and -1 meet that condition, they are the only solutions.

Now, suppose we consider the equation $x^2 = -1$. We know that the square of every real number is positive or zero. Thus there is no real number x whose square is -1; that is, the symbol $\sqrt{-1}$ is not meaningful in the system of real numbers. Similarly, the real number system provides no solutions to the equations $x^2 = -2$ and more generally $x^2 = -a$, where $a > 0$. To overcome this situation, we shall extend the real number system so that the new system will indeed provide solutions to equations such as $x^2 = -1$. In fact, by considering only $\sqrt{-1}$, we shall be able to handle a square root of *any* negative number.

To begin, we introduce (or invent, so to speak) a new type of number that, by its definition, is a solution of the equation $x^2 = -1$.

> The ***j*-operator,** denoted by j, is that number which when squared is equal to -1; that is,
>
> $$j^2 = -1.$$

From the definition of j, it seems reasonable to express j as $\sqrt{-1}$; that is, j is a square root of -1. Since j is not a real number, we call it (according to custom) the **imaginary unit.** The term *imaginary* does not mean that j is "impossible" or "does not exist," but only that it does not belong to the set of real numbers. Indeed, the practical applications of j to topics such as electrical theory are extensive.*

By taking the product of j and a real number, such as $2j$, $-5j$, and $6.4j$, we obtain what is referred to as a *pure imaginary number.*

> **A pure imaginary number** is a number that can be expressed in the form bj, where b is a real number.†

To generalize the notion of $\sqrt{-1}$, we express a square root of *any* negative number as the product of a real number and j in the following manner:

> If a is a positive number, then
>
> $$\sqrt{-a} = j\sqrt{a}.$$

Thus

$$\sqrt{-4} = j\sqrt{4} = j(2) = 2j.$$

---

*In mathematics, the symbol i is preferred instead of j. However, in electrical theory the use of j avoids confusion with the use of i for electrical current. We adopt that symbol here.

†In electrical theory, bj is usually written jb. For example, $2j$ is written $j2$, which should not be confused with j^2.

example 1

Write the following pure imaginary numbers in terms of j.

a. $\sqrt{-2} = j\sqrt{2}$.

b. $-\sqrt{-9} = -(j\sqrt{9}) = -[j(3)] = -3j$.

c. $\sqrt{-32} = j\sqrt{32} = j(4\sqrt{2}) = 4j\sqrt{2}$.

d. $\sqrt{-\frac{1}{16}} = j\sqrt{\frac{1}{16}} = \frac{1}{4}j = \frac{j}{4}$.

Algebraic operations with j obey the usual rules for manipulating real numbers. The following example illustrates that any positive integral power of j has one of four possible values: j, -1, $-j$, or 1.

example 2

a. $j^1 = j$.

b. $j^2 = -1$.

A note of caution! *The rule $\sqrt{a}\sqrt{b} = \sqrt{ab}$, which is true for nonnegative real numbers, is **false** when **both** a and b are negative.* By that rule we have

$$\sqrt{-1}\sqrt{-1} = \sqrt{(-1)(-1)} = \sqrt{1} = 1,$$

which is *false*, since $(\sqrt{-1})^2$ must be -1 because of the meaning of the square-root symbol. By definition, however, the following *is* correct:

$$\sqrt{-1}\sqrt{-1} = j \cdot j = j^2 = -1.$$

Thus, to help prevent any errors in computations, **always express square roots of negative numbers in the bj-form** *before* **performing any algebraic operations with them.**

c. $j^3 = j^2 \cdot j = (-1)j = -j$.

d. $j^4 = j^2 \cdot j^2 = (-1)(-1) = 1$.

e. $j^5 = j^4 \cdot j = 1 \cdot j = j$.

f. $j^6 = j^4 \cdot j^2 = 1 \cdot j^2 = -1$, and so on.

From the pattern in Example 2, we can infer that the values of j^n, where n is a positive integer, can easily be obtained. First, find the remainder r when n is divided by 4. Then raise j to the rth power.

example 3

Evaluate each of the following:

a. j^{507}.

Since $507 \div 4$ is 126 with a remainder of 3,

$$j^{507} = j^3 = -j.$$

b. j^{26}.

Since $26 = (6)(4) + 2$,

$$j^{26} = j^2 = -1.$$

c. j^{1000}.

Since $1000 = (250)(4) + 0$,

$$j^{1000} = j^0 = 1.$$

Our claim that $j^0 = 1$ is reasonable because

$$j^{1000} = (j^4)^{250} = 1^{250} = 1.$$

d. $j = j^5 = j^9 = j^{13} = j^{17} = j^{21}$, and so on.

By combining the real number system with the concept of a pure imaginary number, we are led to the notion of a *complex number*, namely the sum of a real number and a pure imaginary number.

> A **complex number** is one of the form $a + bj$, where a and b are real numbers. The number a is called the **real part** of $a + bj$, and b is called the **imaginary part**.

Some examples of complex numbers are $2 + 3j$, $-4 + j$, and $-3 - 5j$, which is $-3 + (-5)j$. The real part of $-3 - 5j$ is -3 and the imaginary part is -5. If $a = 0$, then $a + bj$ is bj, a *pure imaginary number*. If $b = 0$, then $a + bj$ is a, a *real number*. Thus, *every real number is also a complex number with imaginary part zero*. For example, the real number 3 is the complex number $3 + 0j$. Complex numbers that are not real are called **imaginary numbers**. Thus the complex number 7 is real, but the complex number $7 + 2j$ is imaginary.

The complex numbers $a + bj$ and $a - bj$ are said to be (complex) **conjugates** of each other. For example, the conjugate of $2 + 3j$ is $2 - 3j$, the conjugate of $-3 - 4j$ is $-3 + 4j$, and the conjugate of 6 is 6 because the conjugate of $6 + 0j$ is $6 - 0j$, or 6.

example 4

Complex number	Real part	Imaginary part	Conjugate
a. $3 + 4j$	3	4	$3 - 4j$
b. $-3 - j$	-3	-1	$-3 + j$
c. -7	-7	0	-7
d. $-j$	0	-1	j
e. $\sqrt{-4}$	0	2	$-2j$
f. $\sqrt[3]{-1}$	-1	0	-1
g. 0	0	0	0

Observe in complex number f that $\sqrt[3]{-1}$ is a real number; $(-1)^3 = -1$ and thus $\sqrt[3]{-1} = -1$. Note in complex numbers c, f, and g that a real number is equal to its conjugate. Finally, in g we note that *zero is the only complex number that is both real and pure imaginary.*

A proper definition of a complex number requires that we be precise about when two complex numbers are equal. We say that $a + bj = c + dj$ if and only if $a = c$ and $b = d$. This means that **two complex numbers are equal if and only if they have the same real parts and the same imaginary parts.** Thus $2 - 3j = -3j + 2$ and $0.2 + j = j + \frac{1}{5}$, but $4 + 2j \neq 2 + 4j$ and $3 - j \neq j - 3$.

example 5

Solve each of the following equations if x and y are real numbers.

a. $2 - 5j = x + yj$.

By the definition of equality of complex numbers, we can equate the real parts of both sides of the equation:

$$2 = x.$$

Equating imaginary parts gives

$$-5 = y.$$

The solution is $x = 2$ and $y = -5$.

b. $x - y + xj = 3 + 2j$.

Equating real parts of both sides of the equation gives

$$x - y = 3. \tag{1}$$

Equating imaginary parts gives

$$x = 2.$$

Substituting this value of x in Eq. 1 gives $2 - y = 3$, from which $y = -1$. The solution is $x = 2$ and $y = -1$.

Exercise 11-2

Simplify the expressions in Problems 1–8.

1. j^9.
2. j^{14}.
3. j^{15}.
4. j^{488}.
5. j^{66}.
6. j^{243}.
7. j^{324}.
8. $j^2 \cdot j^3 \cdot j^4$.

In Problems 9–20, write each number in terms of j.

9. $\sqrt{-81}$.
10. $\sqrt{-36}$.
11. $-\sqrt{-25}$.
12. $\sqrt{-27}$.
13. $\sqrt{-32}$.
14. $\sqrt{-144}$.
15. $\sqrt{-\frac{1}{4}}$.
16. $-\sqrt{-\frac{1}{100}}$.
17. $\sqrt{-.09}$.
18. $\sqrt{-.04}$.
19. $\sqrt{-\pi^6}$.
20. $\sqrt{-4^{10}}$.

For each of the complex numbers in Problems 21–36, state (a) the real part, (b) the imaginary part, and (c) the conjugate. Simplify first, if necessary.

21. $-6 + 5j$.
22. -2.
23. $-31j - 2$.
24. $-3 + 5j$.
25. $-3j$.
26. $2 - \sqrt{-9}$.
27. $7 + \frac{3}{5}j$.
28. πj.
29. j^{17}.
30. j^2.
31. 7.
32. $-\sqrt[3]{-64}$.
33. $\sqrt[3]{-8}$.
34. $6 + \sqrt{-3}$.
35. $-\sqrt{-49}$.
36. 0.

If x and y are real numbers, solve the equations in Problems 37–42.

37. $2x + yj = 4 - 6j$.
38. $x - 2j = 17 + yj$.
39. $x + 4j = 17 + yj$.
40. $x + (x - y)j = 4j$.
41. $(x + y) + (x - y)j = 18 - 14j$.
42. $x + yj = a - bj$.

43. Two alternating-current voltages are given by the expression $\frac{3}{2} + (y + 1)j$ and $(7 + x) - 3j$, respectively. If the voltages are equal, what are the values of x and y? (Assume that x and y are real numbers.)

44. What can be said about a complex number that is equal to its conjugate?

45. Determine whether the following statements are true or false.
    (a) $\frac{1}{2} + 2j = 2j + 0.5$.

(b) $3 - \sqrt{-5} = 3 - j\sqrt{5}$.

(c) $\sqrt[3]{-27} = 3j$.

(d) $5 - 6j = (7 - 2) + (4 - 10)j$.

46. Suppose $a + bj = 0$. To what must $a^2 + b^2$ be equal?

47. A Maxwell bridge is an ac bridge circuit that permits the inductance L_x and resistance R_x of a coil to be measured. A theoretical analysis of the circuit yields the equation

$$R_x + j\omega L_x = R_2 R_3 \left(\frac{1}{R_1} + j\omega C_1 \right).$$

Determine the resistance and inductance of a coil in terms of the circuit constants R_1, R_2, R_3, C_1, and ω.

11-3 Geometrical Representation of Complex Numbers

Complex numbers can be geometrically represented in a plane with the use of a rectangular coordinate system. By one method, the complex number $a + bj$ is represented by the point (a, b). The abscissa a corresponds to the real part of $a + bj$, and the ordinate b corresponds to the imaginary part of $a + bj$ [Fig. 11-1(a)]. For example, in Fig. 11-1(b) the number $2 + 3j$ is represented by the point $(2, 3)$ in the first quadrant; the number $-3 - j$ is represented by the point $(-3, -1)$ in the third quadrant.

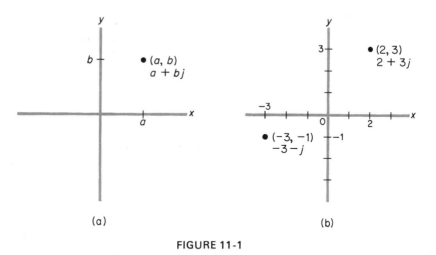

(a)   (b)

FIGURE 11-1

The origin $(0, 0)$ corresponds to 0 or $0 + 0j$. Since the points in the plane are considered here to represent complex numbers, we refer to the plane as the **complex plane** (also called the *Argand plane*).

Observe in Fig. 11-2 that the point $(a, 0)$ on the x-axis corresponds to the real number $a = a + 0j$, while the point $(0, b)$ on the y-axis corresponds to the pure

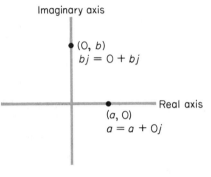

FIGURE 11-2

imaginary number $bj = 0 + bj$. For these reasons, the x-axis is called the **real axis** and the y-axis is called the (pure) **imaginary axis**. The fact that $(0, 0)$ lies both on the real axis *and* the imaginary axis gives a geometric picture of the previous statement in Example 4 that zero is both a real and a pure imaginary number.

Since the complex number $a + bj$ can be represented by the point (a, b), we can speak of the *point $a + bj$* and no confusion should arise. Also, $a + bj$ is called the **rectangular form** of a complex number.

example 1

Locate the points in the complex plane that correspond to the complex numbers $2 + j, 3 - 2j, -1 - 2j, -1 + 3j, -3, 2, j,$ and $-2j$. (See Fig. 11-3.)

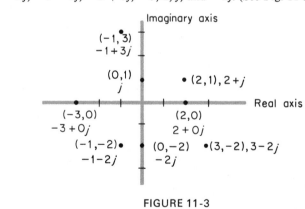

FIGURE 11-3

The complex number $a + bj$ can also be represented in the plane by the vector **OP** from the origin to the point $P(a, b)$, as indicated in Fig. 11-4. Hence, we can speak

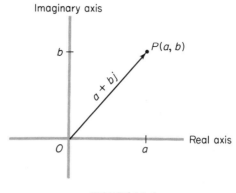

FIGURE 11-4

interchangeably of the *complex number a + bj*, the *point a + bj*, and the *vector a + bj*.

In Fig. 11-5, the angle θ that the vector **OP** makes with the positive real axis is called an **amplitude** or **argument** of $a + bj$. The length r of **OP** is called the **absolute value** or **modulus** of $a + bj$ and is always positive or zero. From an observation of

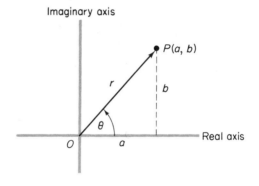

FIGURE 11-5

Fig. 11-5, we can conclude that $\cos \theta = \dfrac{a}{r}$ or

$$a = r \cos \theta. \tag{1}$$

Similarly, $\sin \theta = \dfrac{b}{r}$ or

$$b = r \sin \theta, \tag{2}$$

and

$$\tan \theta = \frac{b}{a}, \tag{3}$$

$$r = \sqrt{a^2 + b^2}. \tag{4}$$

By using Eqs. (1) and (2), we can express $a + bj$ in terms of r and θ:

$$a + bj = r \cos \theta + (r \sin \theta)j = r(\cos \theta + j \sin \theta).$$

We speak of $r(\cos \theta + j \sin \theta)$ as a **trigonometric** or **polar form** of $a + bj$. Polar form is often denoted by the symbol $r\underline{/\theta}$, which is read r *at angle* θ. Another abbreviation is r cis θ.

$$a + bj = r(\cos \theta + j \sin \theta) = r\underline{/\theta}.$$

example 2

Locate the number $2(\cos 300° + j \sin 300°)$ in the complex plane and express the number in rectangular form.

Because the absolute value r is 2 and the amplitude θ is 300°, the number is represented by the vector of length 2 (units) that makes an angle of 300° with the positive x-axis (Fig. 11-6). The number can also be written as $2\underline{/300°}$.

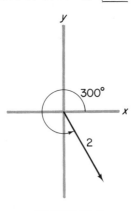

FIGURE 11-6

In rectangular form, $a = r \cos \theta = 2(1/2) = 1$ and $b = r \sin \theta = 2(-\sqrt{3}/2) = -\sqrt{3}$. Thus

$$2(\cos 300° + j \sin 300°) = a + bj = 1 - j\sqrt{3}.$$

More directly, we can write

$$2(\cos 300° + j \sin 300°) = 2\left[\frac{1}{2} + j\left(-\frac{\sqrt{3}}{2}\right)\right] = 1 - j\sqrt{3}.$$

example 3

Express each of the following complex numbers in rectangular form.

a. $4(\cos 45° + j \sin 45°)$.

$$4(\cos 45° + j \sin 45°) = 4\left(\frac{\sqrt{2}}{2} + j \cdot \frac{\sqrt{2}}{2}\right) = 2\sqrt{2} + 2j\sqrt{2}.$$

b. $8(\cos 90° + j \sin 90°)$.

$$8(\cos 90° + j \sin 90°) = 8(0 + j \cdot 1) = 8j.$$

c. $3\underline{/150°}$.

$$3\underline{/150°} = 3(\cos 150° + j \sin 150°)$$

$$= 3\left(-\frac{\sqrt{3}}{2} + j \cdot \frac{1}{2}\right) = -\frac{3\sqrt{3}}{2} + \frac{3}{2}j.$$

d. $24.3\underline{/27.4°}$.

$$24.3\underline{/27.4°} = 24.3(\cos 27.4° + j \sin 27.4°)$$

$$= 24.3(0.8878 + 0.4602j)$$

$$= 21.6 + 11.2j.$$

To find a trigonometric form of the complex number $a + bj$, we make use of Eqs. 3 and 4:

$$\tan \theta = \frac{b}{a}, \qquad r = \sqrt{a^2 + b^2}.$$

The next example shows the procedure.

example 4

The impedance (in ohms) of an inductor is given by $2 + 2j$, where the real part represents the resistance of the inductor and the imaginary part represents the inductive reactance. Express the impedance in trigonometric form.

First, we note that $2 + 2j$ lies in the first quadrant. In Fig. 11-7, $2 + 2j$ is geometrically represented by both the point $P(2, 2)$ and the vector **OP** from the origin to $P(2, 2)$. Second, for the absolute value we have $a = 2$, $b = 2$, and

$$r = \sqrt{a^2 + b^2} = \sqrt{2^2 + 2^2} = \sqrt{8} = 2\sqrt{2} \ \Omega.$$

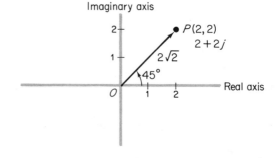

FIGURE 11-7

Now, to find the amplitude θ we have

$$\tan \theta = \frac{b}{a} = \frac{2}{2} = 1.$$

Thus θ is a first-quadrant angle with a tangent of 1. Using our knowledge of special angles, we conclude that θ could be $45°$, $45° + 360°$, $45° - 360°$, and so on for other coterminal angles. However, in general *we usually choose θ such that $0° \leq \theta < 360°$.* Thus we choose $\theta = 45°$. We can now write

$$2 + 2j = r(\cos \theta + j \sin \theta)$$
$$= 2\sqrt{2}(\cos 45° + j \sin 45°) \quad \text{or} \quad 2\sqrt{2}\underline{/45°}\ \Omega.$$

Because, in general, there are two choices for θ such that both $\tan \theta = b/a$ and $0° \leq \theta < 360°$, the correct choice will be evident by first determining the quadrant in which the point $a + bj$ lies. For our situation above, $\tan 45° = 1$ and $\tan 225° = 1$, but we must choose $\theta = 45°$ because $2 + 2j$ lies in the first quadrant.

example 5

Express $-3 + 3j\sqrt{3}$ in polar form.

The point $-3 + 3j\sqrt{3}$ lies in the second quadrant (Fig. 11-8).

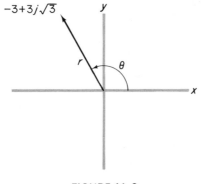

FIGURE 11-8

For $a = -3$ and $b = 3\sqrt{3}$, we have

$$r = \sqrt{a^2 + b^2} = \sqrt{(-3)^2 + (3\sqrt{3})^2} = \sqrt{9 + 27} = 6$$

and

$$\tan \theta = \frac{b}{a} = \frac{3\sqrt{3}}{-3} = -\sqrt{3}.$$

For $\tan \theta = -\sqrt{3}$, θ may be either 120° or 300° (from our knowledge of special angles). But $-3 + 3j\sqrt{3}$ is in the second quadrant, so the correct choice is 120°. Therefore

$$-3 + 3j\sqrt{3} = 6(\cos 120° + j \sin 120°).$$

In Example 5, a typical direct calculator result for an angle with a tangent of $-\sqrt{3}$ (or -1.732) is $-60°$. That result is *unacceptable* because the problem requires the amplitude to be a second-quadrant angle. As discussed in Sec. 7-6, we should first find the acute reference angle whose tangent is $\sqrt{3}$ (we omit the negative sign). A calculator result is 60°. Thus $\theta = 180° - 60° = 120°$. We emphasize that due to our preference for θ to lie between 0° and 360°, we choose $6/120°$ as our answer. You should realize, however, that $6/-240°$ could be used as a polar form for the given number. Similarly, in Example 4 another polar form for $2 + 2j$ is given by $2\sqrt{2}\ [\cos(-315°) + j \sin(-315°)]$. The amplitude for the complex number zero can be any angle.

example 6

The voltage across an inductor in an ac circuit is $3 - 4j$ volts. Express that voltage in polar form.

The vector $3 - 4j$ lies in the fourth quadrant. Here,

$$r = \sqrt{(3)^2 + (-4)^2} = \sqrt{25} = 5 \text{ V}$$

and

$$\tan \theta = \frac{b}{a} = \frac{-4}{3} = -\frac{4}{3} = -1.3333.$$

The reference angle with a tangent of 1.3333 is 53.1°. Because θ is a fourth-quadrant angle, we choose θ to be $360° - 53.1° = 306.9°$. We then have

$$3 - 4j = 5/306.9° \text{ V}.$$

The trigonometric form of a real number or a pure imaginary number is easy to find, as the following example shows.

example 7

Express each of the following complex numbers in trigonometric form.

a. 8.

The point 8, or $8 + 0j$, lies on the positive x-axis and is eight units from the origin [Fig. 11-9(a)]. Therefore $\theta = 0°$, $r = 8$, and we have $8 = 8(\cos 0° + j \sin 0°)$.

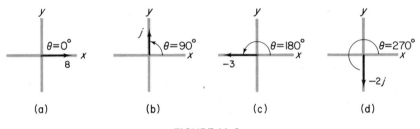

(a)   (b)   (c)   (d)

FIGURE 11-9

b. j.

The point j, or $0 + 1j$, lies on the positive y-axis and is one unit from the origin [Fig. 11-9(b)]. Thus $\theta = 90°$ and $r = 1$. Therefore $j = 1(\cos 90° + j \sin 90°)$.

c. -3.

By inspection of Fig. 11-9(c), clearly $r = 3$ and $\theta = 180°$, so $-3 = 3/180°$.

d. $-2j$.

By inspection of Fig. 11-9(d), we have $r = 2$ and $\theta = 270°$. Hence $-2j = 2/270°$.

Exercise 11-3

In Problems 1–18, locate the points in the complex plane that correspond to the given number and its conjugate and express the given number in trigonometric form. Do not use a calculator in 1–16.

1. $4 + 4j$.

2. $-\sqrt{3} + j$.

3. $2 - 2j\sqrt{3}$.

4. -4.

5. $5j$.

6. $1 + j\sqrt{3}$.

7. $-3 - 3j$.

8. $-8j$.

9. 1.

10. $\sqrt{2} - j\sqrt{2}$.

11. $-1 + j\sqrt{3}$.

12. $-3\sqrt{3} + 3j$.

13. $-\sqrt{3} - j$.

14. $6j$.

15. $-5j$.

16. 64.

17. $8 + 3j$.

18. $5 - 7j$.

*In Problems **19–34**, locate the given number in the complex plane and express it in rectangular form. Do not use a calculator in **19–30**.*

19. $2(\cos 30° + j \sin 30°)$.

20. $3(\cos 240° + j \sin 240°)$.

21. $6(\cos 120° + j \sin 120°)$.

22. $4(\cos 210° + j \sin 210°)$.

23. $2(\cos 315° + j \sin 315°)$.

24. $3(\cos 150° + j \sin 150°)$.

25. $3(\cos 270° + j \sin 270°)$.

26. $2(\cos 180° + j \sin 180°)$.

27. $4\underline{/0°}$.

28. $4\underline{/240°}$.

29. $3\underline{/330°}$.

30. $\frac{1}{2}\underline{/90°}$.

31. $2\underline{/15°}$.

32. $3\underline{/40°}$.

33. $2\underline{/245°}$.

34. $4\underline{/340°}$.

35. If all complex numbers with an absolute value of 1 were plotted in the complex plane, what geometric figure would they form?

36. If $3(\cos 220° + j \sin 220°) = a + bj$, find a and b.

37. If $4(\cos 500° + j \sin 500°) = a + bj$, find a and b.

38. If $2(\cos 0° + j \sin 0°) = a + \left(\dfrac{b}{c}\right)j$, find a.

*In Problems **39–42**, express the given number in rectangular form.*

39. $3[\cos (-205°) + j \sin (-205°)]$.

40. $7\left(\cos \dfrac{\pi}{5} + j \sin \dfrac{\pi}{5}\right)$.

41. $0.75\underline{/-42°}$.

42. $1\underline{/-100.3°}$.

43. The impedance of an inductor is $6.2 + 0.8j$ Ω. (a) Express the impedance in polar form. Find the (b) resistance and (c) inductive reactance of the inductor (see Example 4).

44. The impedance of a branch of a circuit is $1.5 - 2.3j$ ohms. Express that impedance in trigonometric form.

45. Express a voltage of $23 - 46j$ volts in polar form.

46. Find the polar form of the conjugate of the voltage in Problem 45.

47. The voltage across an inductor in an ac circuit is $11.2\underline{/72°}$ V. Express the voltage in rectangular form.

48. The electric current in a circuit is $0.026\underline{/26°}$ A. Express that current in rectangular form.

49. Find the acute angle between $V = 2 + 3j$ and $I = 4 + j$.

50. Arrange the following numbers in order of decreasing absolute value: $4 + 3j$, $-6j$, and $5 - 5j$.

11-4 Operations in Rectangular Form

Algebraic operations with complex numbers in rectangular form are defined in a way so that the usual rules of real numbers hold, such as the commutative, associative, and distributive laws. We shall present definitions of all basic operations, each of which will be followed by a simple verbal explanation. Rather than memorize the definitions, you should make use of the verbal explanations, as the examples will show.

The sum (or difference) of two complex numbers is a complex number in which the real part is the sum (or difference) of their real parts and the imaginary part is the sum (or difference) of their imaginary parts. That is,

$$(a + bj) + (c + dj) = (a + c) + (b + d)j$$

and

$$(a + bj) - (c + dj) = (a - c) + (b - d)j.$$

> **Add or subtract complex numbers as you would ordinary algebraic expressions. Treat j like any other literal number.**

example 1

Perform the indicated operations.

a. $(2 + 3j) + (4 + j) = 2 + 3j + 4 + j = 6 + 4j.$

b. $2 + (8 - 3j) = 2 + 8 - 3j = 10 - 3j.$

c. $(6 + 3j) - (2 + 5j) = 6 + 3j - 2 - 5j = 4 - 2j.$

d. $2j - (4 + 2j) = 2j - 4 - 2j = -4.$

e. $5 - 2j - (-6 + j) = 5 - 2j + 6 - j = 11 - 3j.$

f. $\sqrt{8} + \sqrt{-\frac{3}{2}} - \sqrt{-24} = \sqrt{8} + j\sqrt{\frac{3}{2}} - j\sqrt{24}$

$$= 2\sqrt{2} + \frac{1}{2}j\sqrt{6} - 2j\sqrt{6}$$

$$= 2\sqrt{2} - \frac{3}{2}j\sqrt{6}.$$

Note that the complex numbers $\sqrt{-\frac{3}{2}}$ and $\sqrt{-24}$ were *first* placed in $a + bj$ form before we proceeded to other operations.

Addition and subtraction of complex numbers can be interpreted geometrically as addition and subtraction of vectors with their initial points at the origin. The vector representing $a + bj$ has terminal point $P_1(a, b)$ and the vector for $c + dj$ has terminal point $P_2(c, d)$, as indicated in Fig. 11-10. $\mathbf{OP}_1$ and $\mathbf{OP}_2$ are vectors representing $a + bj$ and $c + dj$, respectively. Vector $\mathbf{OQ}$ is the diagonal of the parallelogram having $\mathbf{OP}_1$ and $\mathbf{OP}_2$ as adjacent sides. We wish to show that $\mathbf{OQ}$ is

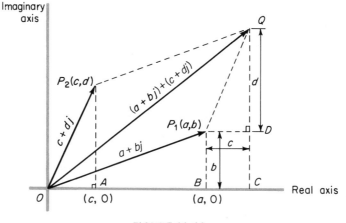

FIGURE 11-10

the vector representing the sum

$$(a + bj) + (c + dj) = (a + c) + (b + d)j.$$

Because triangle OAP_2 is congruent to triangle P_1DQ, it follows, by corresponding sides, that $\overline{P_1D} = \overline{OA} = c$ and $\overline{DQ} = \overline{AP_2} = d$. Thus $\overline{OC} = \overline{OB} + \overline{BC} = \overline{OB} + \overline{P_1D} = a + c$ and $\overline{CQ} = \overline{CD} + \overline{DQ} = \overline{BP_1} + \overline{DQ} = b + d$. As a result, **OQ** represents the vector $(a + c) + (b + d)j$, which is $(a + bj) + (c + dj)$.

example 2

Geometrically find the sum $(2 + 3j) + (3 + j)$.

The sum of $2 + 3j$ and $3 + j$ is represented geometrically by the diagonal vector $5 + 4j$ of the parallelogram with the given vectors for adjacent sides (Fig. 11-11).

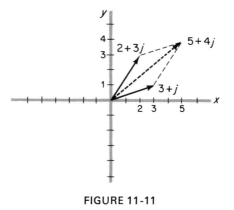

FIGURE 11-11

The subtraction $(a + bj) - (c + dj)$ can be expressed geometrically as the vector sum $(a + bj) + (-c - dj)$, where the vector representing $-c - dj$ is a vector equal in magnitude but opposite in direction to the vector $c + dj$.

example 3

Geometrically determine the difference $(2 + j) - (3 - 2j)$.

The difference $(2 + 3j) - (3 - 2j)$ is represented by the diagonal vector $-1 + 3j$ of the parallelogram which has as adjacent sides the vector for $2 + j$ and the vector which is equal in magnitude but opposite in direction to $3 - 2j$ (that is, $-3 + 2j$) (Fig. 11-12).

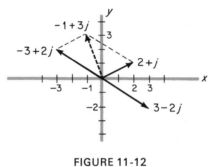

FIGURE 11-12

We define multiplication of complex numbers by making use of the distributive law and the fact that $j^2 = -1$. In general,

$$(a + bj)(c + dj) = a(c + dj) + bj(c + dj)$$
$$= ac + adj + bcj + bdj^2$$
$$= ac + (ad + bc)j + bd(-1).$$
$$(a + bj)(c + dj) = (ac - bd) + (ad + bc)j.$$

> **Multiply complex numbers as you would algebraic expressions. However, all complex numbers should be expressed in the form $a + bj$ before multiplying them, and whenever j^2 occurs, it should be replaced by -1.**

example 4

Perform the indicated operations.

a. $j(-2 + 3j) = -2j + 3j^2 = -2j + 3(-1) = -3 - 2j.$

b. $(8j)(4j) = 32j^2 = 32(-1) = -32.$

c. $(3 + 2j)(2 - 5j) = 3(2 - 5j) + 2j(2 - 5j)$
$$= 6 - 15j + 4j - 10j^2$$
$$= 6 - 11j - 10(-1)$$
$$= 16 - 11j.$$

d. $(-3 - 4j)(2 - j) = -3(2 - j) - 4j(2 - j)$
$$= -6 + 3j - 8j + 4j^2$$
$$= -6 - 5j + 4(-1) = -10 - 5j.$$

e. $(4 + 5j)^2.$

We treat this as a square of a binomial:
$$(4 + 5j)^2 = (4)^2 + 2(4)(5j) + (5j)^2$$
$$= 16 + 40j + 25j^2$$
$$= 16 + 40j + 25(-1) = -9 + 40j.$$

f. $2\sqrt{-4}(3 - 2\sqrt{-3}) + j = 2(2j)(3 - 2j\sqrt{3}) + j$
$$= (4j)(3 - 2j\sqrt{3}) + j$$
$$= 12j - 8j^2\sqrt{3} + j$$
$$= 13j - 8(-1)\sqrt{3}$$
$$= 8\sqrt{3} + 13j.$$

g. $(2 + 3j)(2 - 3j) = (2)^2 - (3j)^2 = 4 - 9j^2 = 4 - 9(-1) = 13.$

h. $(a + bj)(a - bj) = a^2 - (bj)^2 = a^2 - b^2j^2 = a^2 - b^2(-1) = a^2 + b^2.$ Therefore
$$(a + bj)(a - bj) = a^2 + b^2,$$

which is *always* a real number. A common *error* that students make is to write $(a + bj)(a - bj) = a^2 - b^2$, which is generally false.

As shown in (g) and (h) of Example 4, the product of a complex number and its conjugate is always a real number. For this reason, to find $(a + bj)/(c + dj)$, we are motivated to multiply *both* the numerator and denominator by the conjugate of the *denominator*. The resulting denominator will be a real number, and the quotient therefore can easily be put in rectangular form. The procedure resembles that of rationalizing the denominator of an algebraic expression.

$$\frac{a + bj}{c + dj} = \frac{a + bj}{c + dj} \cdot \frac{c - dj}{c - dj}, \quad c + dj \neq 0$$
$$= \frac{ac - adj + bcj - bdj^2}{c^2 - d^2j^2}$$
$$= \frac{(ac + bd) + (bc - ad)j}{c^2 + d^2}$$
$$= \frac{ac + bd}{c^2 + d^2} + \frac{bc - ad}{c^2 + d^2}j.$$

To find the quotient of two complex numbers, multiply both the numerator and denominator by the conjugate of the denominator and simplify. As a result, the denominator will be a real number.

example 5

Perform the indicated operations.

a. $\dfrac{2-j}{3+2j}$.

We multiply both the numerator and denominator by the conjugate of the denominator, namely, $3 - 2j$:

$$\frac{2-j}{3+2j} = \frac{2-j}{3+2j} \cdot \frac{3-2j}{3-2j} = \frac{(2-j)(3-2j)}{(3+2j)(3-2j)}$$

$$= \frac{6-4j-3j+2j^2}{9-4j^2} = \frac{6-7j+2(-1)}{9-4(-1)} = \frac{4-7j}{13} = \frac{4}{13} - \frac{7}{13}j.$$

b. $\dfrac{2}{1-j} = \dfrac{2}{1-j} \cdot \dfrac{1+j}{1+j} = \dfrac{2(1+j)}{(1-j)(1+j)} = \dfrac{2+2j}{1-j^2}$

$$= \frac{2+2j}{1-(-1)} = \frac{2+2j}{2} = 1+j.$$

c. $\dfrac{6}{5j} = \dfrac{6}{5j} \cdot \dfrac{-5j}{-5j} = \dfrac{-30j}{-25j^2} = \dfrac{-30j}{-25(-1)} = -\dfrac{6}{5}j.$ Alternatively, if the denominator is a pure imaginary number, it suffices to multiply the given fraction by j/j. Thus

$$\frac{6}{5j} = \frac{6}{5j} \cdot \frac{j}{j} = \frac{6j}{5j^2} = \frac{6j}{5(-1)} = -\frac{6}{5}j.$$

example 6

If $f(z) = z^2 + 6z + \dfrac{1}{z}$, find $f(3j)$.

$$f(3j) = (3j)^2 + 6(3j) + \frac{1}{3j}$$

$$= 9j^2 + 18j + \frac{1}{3j} \cdot \frac{j}{j} = 9(-1) + 18j + \frac{j}{3(-1)}$$

$$= -9 + 18j - \frac{1}{3}j = -9 + \frac{53}{3}j.$$

example 7

When elements of a circuit are connected in *series*, the total impedance Z of the circuit is the *sum* of the individual impedances. Suppose that a resistor, a capacitor, and an inductor are connected in series. If their impedances, in ohms, are 180, $10 + 60j$, and $22 - 110j$, respectively, find the magnitude (or absolute value) of the circuit impedance and express the circuit impedance in polar form.

Letting $180 = Z_1$, $10 + 60j = Z_2$, and $22 - 110j = Z_3$, we have

$$Z = Z_1 + Z_2 + Z_3$$
$$= (180) + (10 + 60j) + (22 - 110j)$$
$$= 212 - 50j \ \Omega.$$

The absolute value of Z is

$$r = \sqrt{(212)^2 + (-50)^2} = 217.8 \ \Omega.$$

Also,

$$\tan \theta = \frac{-50}{212},$$

from which we find that $\theta = 346.7°$, because Z is in the fourth quadrant. Thus the magnitude (absolute value) of the circuit impedance is 217.8 Ω, and in polar form we have $Z = 217.8\underline{/346.7°} \ \Omega$.

example 8

When two elements of an electrical circuit are connected in *parallel*, the total impedance Z of the circuit is given by

$$Z = \frac{Z_1 Z_2}{Z_1 + Z_2},$$

where Z_1 and Z_2 are the impedances of the two elements. Suppose capacitive and inductive elements are connected in parallel. If their impedances (in ohms) are $7 - 12j$ and $3 + 26j$, find the magnitude (in ohms) of the circuit impedance and the *phase angle* θ, which is the amplitude of Z.

Letting $7 - 12j = Z_1$ and $3 + 26j = Z_2$, we have

$$Z = \frac{(7 - 12j)(3 + 26j)}{(7 - 12j) + (3 + 26j)} = \frac{21 + 182j - 36j + 312}{10 + 14j}$$

$$= \frac{333 + 146j}{10 + 14j} \cdot \frac{10 - 14j}{10 - 14j} = \frac{3330 - 4662j + 1460j + 2044}{100 + 196}$$

$$= \frac{5374 - 3202j}{296} = 18.16 - 10.82j.$$

The magnitude of the circuit impedance is

$$\sqrt{(18.16)^2 + (-10.82)^2} = 21.1.$$

The phase angle θ is given by

$$\tan \theta = \frac{-10.82}{18.16} = -0.5958$$

from which $\theta = 329.2°$, because Z lies in the fourth quadrant.

Just as complex numbers can be represented by vectors, liberal adaptation permits vector quantities such as force and velocity to be represented by complex numbers. As a result, problems which involve finding the resultant of a number of vector quantities may be solved by means of algebra of complex numbers. That is, the resultant of two or more vectors can be obtained by first expressing each vector as a complex number and then adding these numbers in the usual manner. In the following example, we shall find the resultant of three forces acting at the same point (that is, *concurrent forces*).

example 9

Use complex algebra to find the resultant of the following system of forces that act at the origin:

$$A = 30 \text{ N}, \qquad \theta_A = 44°,$$
$$B = 40 \text{ N}, \qquad \theta_B = 121°,$$
$$C = 20 \text{ N}, \qquad \theta_C = 209°,$$

where θ is the angle that the given force makes with the positive x-axis. The system is shown in Fig. 11-13.

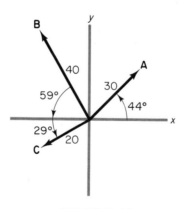

FIGURE 11-13

After first writing each force in trigonometric form, we express them in rectangular form:

$$\mathbf{A} = 30(\cos 44° + j \sin 44°) = 21.58 + 20.84j,$$
$$\mathbf{B} = 40(\cos 121° + j \sin 121°) = -20.60 + 34.29j,$$
$$\mathbf{C} = 20(\cos 209° + j \sin 209°) = -17.49 - 9.70j.$$

We now add to obtain the resultant.

$$\mathbf{A} + \mathbf{B} + \mathbf{C} = -16.51 + 45.43j = 48.3\underline{/110.0°}.$$

Thus the magnitude of the resultant is 48.3 N and its direction is $\theta = 110.0°$.

Exercise 11-4

In Problems **1–48,** *perform the indicated operations and express the answer in rectangular form.*

1. $2j + 3j - 3.$

2. $2j - 6j + 4j.$

3. $(3 - 5j) + (-6 + 4j).$

4. $(6j - 2) + (7 + 4j).$

5. $(7 - 3j) - (9 - 6j).$

6. $(4 + 3j) - (5j - 6).$

7. $\sqrt{-4} + 2\sqrt{-8} + 3\sqrt{12}.$

8. $j^2 - 2j + j\sqrt{-16} + j^3\sqrt{-5}.$

9. $(8 - \sqrt{-16}) - (\sqrt{-1} + 4j).$

10. $\sqrt{-5} - 2\sqrt{-16} + (3 - \sqrt{-2}) - (j\sqrt{2} + 1).$

11. $\sqrt{-5}\sqrt{-2}\sqrt{-20}.$

12. $(8j)(2j) - (6j)(2j) + j^3(j^6).$

13. $3(2j)^3(3j)^2(j)^5.$

14. $(-\sqrt{-4})(-\sqrt{-5})(-\sqrt{-20}).$

15. $(2j)^4(-2j)^2(j)^6.$

16. $j(2j)(3j)(4j).$

17. $(2 + j)(3 + 2j).$

18. $(1 + j)(6 - 2j).$

19. $(4 + 3j)(5 - 2j).$

20. $(-2 - j)(-3 + j).$

21. $2(2 - j)(3 + 2j).$

22. $2(-5 + j)(-5 - j).$

23. $(6 + 2j)(-7 - \sqrt{-4}).$

24. $(2 - \sqrt{-3})(3 + \sqrt{-12}).$

25. $(3 + 2j)^2.$

26. $(8 - 4j)^2.$

27. $(3 - \sqrt{-25})^2.$

28. $(2 - \sqrt{-64})^2.$

29. $(\frac{1}{3} - \frac{4}{5}j)(\frac{3}{8} + \frac{2}{7}j).$

30. $2(3 + \sqrt{-36})(2 + \sqrt{-72})(\sqrt{-4}).$

31. $\dfrac{3 - j}{4 + j}.$

32. $\dfrac{1 - j}{1 + j}.$

33. $\dfrac{2 - j}{3 - j}.$

34. $\dfrac{2 - j}{2 + j}.$

35. $\dfrac{2}{2 + 3j}.$

36. $\dfrac{\sqrt{-12}}{\sqrt{-9}}.$

37. $2j + \dfrac{2}{j}.$

38. $\dfrac{2 + 3j}{4 - 2j}.$

39. $\dfrac{5 + 3j}{5 - 6j}.$

40. $\dfrac{3}{2(1 - j)}.$

41. $\dfrac{1}{(-4 + 3j)(2 + 4j)}.$

42. $\dfrac{5}{(2 + j)(2 - j)}.$

43. $(2 - j)(3 + j)(1 + j).$

44. $(1 + j)^2(1 - j).$

45. $\dfrac{\dfrac{2}{3} - \dfrac{j}{2}}{\dfrac{1}{3} + \dfrac{j}{4}}.$

46. $\dfrac{\dfrac{1}{3} + \dfrac{j}{4}}{\dfrac{2}{3} + \dfrac{j}{2}}.$

47. $\dfrac{(6 + 2j)(4 - 3j)}{(1 + j)^2}.$

48. $5 + 2j + (1 + j)^{-2}.$

49. If $f(z) = z^2 - 2z + 1$, find $f(1 + j)$.

50. If $f(z) = 2z^2 - z + 1$, find $f(2 - j)$.

Geometrically construct the sums and differences in Problems **51–54.**

51. $(2 - 3j) + (-4 + 3j).$　　　　　**52.** $(8 - 4j) + (-6 - 2j).$

53. $(3 + 2j) - (2 + 4j).$　　　　　**54.** $(3 + 5j) - (5 + 2j).$

55. In electrical theory, impedance Z (in ohms) is given by

$$Z = \frac{V}{I},$$

where V is voltage (in volts) and I is current (in amperes). (a) Find Z if $V = 5 + 5j$ and $I = 3 + 4j$. (b) Find V if $Z = 1 + j$ and $I = 1 - j$.

56. The voltage V across a circuit element is given by $V = IZ$, where V is in volts, I is in amperes, and Z is in ohms. Find the magnitude of the voltage across an element if $I = 4 - 3j$ and $Z = 8 - 15j$.

57. Figure 11-14 indicates part of an electrical circuit. Kirchhoff's laws imply that $I_1 + I_2 = I_3$. Find I_2 if $I_1 = 7 + 2j$ and $I_3 = 9 - 5j$.

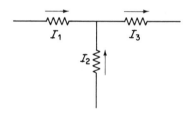

FIGURE 11-14

58. A student said that $-1/j = j^2/j = j$. Is this correct?

59. A resistor, a capacitor, and an inductor are connected is *series*. Their impedances (in ohms) are 8, $3 - 7j$, and $2 + 15j$, respectively. Find the magnitude of the circuit impedance and the angle θ (see Example 7).

60. If the resistor and capacitor in Problem 59 were connected in *parallel*, find the impedance of the combination and the phase angle θ (see Example 8).

61. If the capacitor and inductor in Problem 59 were connected in *parallel*, find the circuit impedance and the phase angle θ (see Example 8).

62. The impedance Z of a combination series-parallel circuit is given by

$$Z = Z_1 + \frac{Z_2 Z_3}{Z_2 + Z_3},$$

where $Z_1 = 1 + 3j$, $Z_2 = 1 + j$, and $Z_3 = 1 + 2j$. Find Z (in ohms).

In Problems 63–66, find the resultant of the given vectors in the manner of Example 9. Give answer in polar form.

63. $A = 100$, $\theta_A = 310°$,
$\quad B = 120$, $\theta_B = 35°$,
$\quad C = 50$, $\theta_C = 40°$.

64. $A = 20$, $\theta_A = 125°$,
$\quad B = 30$, $\theta_B = 315°$,
$\quad C = 10$, $\theta_C = 70°$.

65. $A = 120$, $\theta_A = 80°$,
$\quad B = 49$, $\theta_B = 125°$,
$\quad C = 85$, $\theta_C = 215°$.

66. $A = 200$, $\theta_A = 42°$,
$\quad B = 100$, $\theta_B = 85°$,
$\quad C = 50$, $\theta_C = 155°$.

67. In finding the Thévenin equivalent for a complex circuit, the open-circuit voltage V_0 must be found, where

$$V_0 = V_2 + \frac{Z_2}{Z_1 + Z_2}(V_1 - V_2).$$

Given that $V_1 = 2 + 0j$, $V_2 = 0.707 + 0.707j$, $Z_1 = 1 + 2j$, and $Z_2 = 2 + 3j$, find V_0.

68. The Hay bridge is an ac circuit used in electrical measurements. It is governed by the equation

$$\left(R_1 - j\frac{1}{\omega C_1}\right)(R_x + j\omega L_x) = R_2 R_3.$$

Express R_x and L_x in terms of the other circuit constants.

11-5   Exponential Form of a Complex Number

It is not uncommon for an engineer to encounter, and indeed perform, computations involving the *exponential form* of a complex number. This form makes use of a special *irrational number* that is symbolized by the letter e and is approximated by

$$e \approx 2.71828 \ldots.$$

The number e plays an important role in mathematics; you will encounter it again in Chapter 13.

A complex number $z = a + bj$ having trigonometric form $r(\cos \theta + j \sin \theta)$ can also be expressed in the **exponential form**

$$\boxed{z = re^{j\theta},}$$

where

$$\boxed{e^{j\theta} = \cos \theta + j \sin \theta.}$$

The last equation is called **Euler's formula** and requires that θ be in radians. Our definition of the exponential form $re^{j\theta}$ allows the usual rules for exponents to hold, as will be illustrated in the next section.

example 1

Express $4 - 4j$ in exponential form.

In trigonometric form we have $4 - 4j = 4\sqrt{2}(\cos 315° + j \sin 315°)$, which in terms of *radians* is $4\sqrt{2}\left(\cos \frac{7\pi}{4} + j \sin \frac{7\pi}{4}\right)$. Thus $r = 4\sqrt{2}$, $\theta = \frac{7\pi}{4}$, and

$$4 - 4j = re^{j\theta} = 4\sqrt{2}\, e^{(7\pi/4)j}.$$

example 2

Express $3.2(\cos 23.6° + j \sin 23.6°)$ in exponential form.

Here $r = 3.2$ and in terms of radians we have $\theta = 23.6° = 0.412$. Thus

$$3.2\,(\cos 23.6° + j \sin 23.6°) = 3.2e^{0.412j}.$$

example 3

Express $3.5e^{1.65j}$ in polar and rectangular forms.

We can immediately write a polar form, which is then used to obtain the rectangular form.

$$3.5e^{1.65j} = 3.5\,(\cos 1.65 + j \sin 1.65)$$
$$= 3.5\,(-0.0791 + 0.9969j) = -0.28 + 3.49j.$$

Exercise 11-5

In Problems 1–12, express the given complex numbers in exponential form. If possible, do not use a calculator.

1. $1 + j$.   **2.** -6.   **3.** $-2\sqrt{3} + 2j$.

4. $-3 - 3j$.   **5.** $-7j$.   **6.** $1 - j\sqrt{3}$.

7. $-4.6 - 7.8j$.   **8.** $-0.46 + 1.53j$.

9. $2.8\,(\cos 14.6° + j \sin 14.6°)$.   **10.** $7.3\,(\cos 123.6° + j \sin 123.6°)$.

11. $3.7\,(\cos 2.46 + j \sin 2.46)$.   **12.** $3\left(\cos \frac{\pi}{5} + j \sin \frac{\pi}{5}\right)$.

In Problems **13–20**, *express the given complex number in polar and rectangular forms. If possible, do not use a calculator.*

13. $e^{\pi j/2}$.

14. $2e^{(4/3)\pi j}$.

15. $3e^{3\pi j/4}$.

16. $4e^{\pi j}$.

17. $2e^{(5\pi/6)j}$.

18. $e^{(3\pi/2)j}$.

19. $4e^{2.35j}$.

20. $1.6e^{3.01j}$.

21. Express $e^{j\omega t}$ in polar form.

11-6 Operations in Polar Form

Multiplication or division of complex numbers is easily performed when the numbers are in polar form. We can determine a formula for the product of two complex numbers by considering the product of the exponential forms $r_1 e^{j\theta_1}$ and $r_2 e^{j\theta_2}$. From rules of exponents, we have

$$(r_1 e^{j\theta_1})(r_2 e^{j\theta_2}) = r_1 r_2 e^{j\theta_1 + j\theta_2} = r_1 r_2 e^{j(\theta_1 + \theta_2)}.$$

In polar form this means that

$$r_1(\cos\theta_1 + j\sin\theta_1) \cdot r_2(\cos\theta_2 + j\sin\theta_2) = r_1 r_2[\cos(\theta_1 + \theta_2) + j\sin(\theta_1 + \theta_2)].$$

Therefore *the product of two complex numbers in polar form is a complex number in which the absolute value is the product of the absolute values of the given numbers and the amplitude is the sum of the amplitudes of the given numbers.* More compactly, we have

$$(r_1\underline{/\theta_1})(r_2\underline{/\theta_2}) = r_1 r_2\underline{/\theta_1 + \theta_2}.$$

example 1

Find each of the following products and express the answer in rectangular form.

a. $2(\cos 10° + j\sin 10°) \cdot 4(\cos 20° + j\sin 20°)$.

The product of the absolute values is $2 \cdot 4 = 8$ and the sum of the amplitudes is $10° + 20° = 30°$. Thus

$$2(\cos 10° + j\sin 10°) \cdot 4(\cos 20° + j\sin 20°) = 8(\cos 30° + j\sin 30°)$$

$$= 8\left(\frac{\sqrt{3}}{2} + \frac{1}{2}j\right)$$

$$= 4\sqrt{3} + 4j.$$

b. $(3\underline{/5°})(4\underline{/20°})(2\underline{/8°}) = (12\underline{/25°})(2\underline{/8°}) = 24\underline{/33°}$

$$= 24(\cos 33° + j\sin 33°) = 20.1 + 13.1j.$$

In actual practice we multiply the three absolute values immediately as well as take the sum of the three amplitudes.

Multiplication of a complex number $a + bj$ by j has special geometrical significance. If $a + bj = r(\cos \theta + j \sin \theta)$ and $j = 1(\cos 90° + j \sin 90°)$, then by the preceding rule we obtain

$$(a + bj)j = r[\cos (\theta + 90°) + j \sin (\theta + 90°)],$$

which is the vector obtained by rotating $a + bj$ counterclockwise through an angle of 90°. Thus the effect of multiplying a vector by j is to rotate the vector counterclockwise by 90°. It is based on this rotational effect that we speak of j as an *operator*.

We now turn our attention to the quotient of two complex numbers. Using laws of exponents gives

$$\frac{r_1 e^{j\theta_1}}{r_2 e^{j\theta_2}} = \frac{r_1}{r_2} e^{j\theta_1 - j\theta_2} = \frac{r_1}{r_2} e^{j(\theta_1 - \theta_2)}.$$

In polar form this means that

$$\frac{r_1(\cos \theta_1 + j \sin \theta_1)}{r_2(\cos \theta_2 + j \sin \theta_2)} = \frac{r_1}{r_2}[(\cos(\theta_1 - \theta_2) + j \sin(\theta_1 - \theta_2)].$$

Therefore *the quotient of two complex numbers in polar form is a complex number in which the absolute value is the absolute value of the numerator divided by the absolute value of the denominator and the amplitude is the result of subtracting the amplitude of the denominator from that of the numerator.* More compactly we have

$$\frac{r_1 /\theta_1}{r_2 /\theta_2} = \frac{r_1}{r_2} /\theta_1 - \theta_2.$$

example 2

Perform the indicated operations and express the answer in rectangular form.

a. $\dfrac{3(\cos 75° + j \sin 75°)}{6(\cos 15° + j \sin 15°)} = \dfrac{3}{6}[\cos (75° - 15°) + j \sin (75° - 15°)]$

$$= \frac{1}{2}(\cos 60° + j \sin 60°)$$

$$= \frac{1}{2}\left(\frac{1}{2} + j\frac{\sqrt{3}}{2}\right) = \frac{1}{4} + j\frac{\sqrt{3}}{4}.$$

b. $\dfrac{(3\underline{/10°})(5\underline{/140°})}{7\underline{/230°}} = \dfrac{15\underline{/150°}}{7\underline{/230°}} = \dfrac{15}{7}\underline{/150° - 230°}$

$\qquad = \dfrac{15}{7}\underline{/-80°} = \dfrac{15}{7}\ [\cos(-80°) + j\sin(-80°)]$

$\qquad = 0.37 - 2.11j.$

example 3

Perform the indicated operations and express the answers in polar form.

a. $\dfrac{24\underline{/10°}}{4\underline{/100°}} + \dfrac{25\underline{/0°}}{2.5\underline{/-123°}} = 6\underline{/-90°} + 10\underline{/123°}$

$\qquad\qquad = (0 - 6j) + (-5.45 + 8.39j)$

$\qquad\qquad = -5.45 + 2.39j = 5.95\underline{/156.3°}.$

b. $\dfrac{1}{(2.3\underline{/15.4°})(1.8\underline{/13.8°})} = \dfrac{1\underline{/0°}}{4.14\underline{/29.2°}} = 0.24\underline{/-29.2°} = 0.24\underline{/330.8°}.$

example 4

A capacitive element with impedance $Z_1 = 13.9\underline{/-59.7°}\ \Omega$ and an inductor with impedance $Z_2 = 26.2\underline{/83.4°}\ \Omega$ are connected in parallel. Find the circuit impedance Z.

From Example 8 of Sec. 11-4,

$$Z = \dfrac{Z_1 Z_2}{Z_1 + Z_2} = \dfrac{(13.9\underline{/-59.7°})(26.2\underline{/83.4°})}{13.9\underline{/-59.7°} + 26.2\underline{/83.4°}}$$

$$= \dfrac{364.2\underline{/23.7°}}{(7.01 - 12.0j) + (3.01 + 26.0j)}$$

$$= \dfrac{364.2\underline{/23.7°}}{10.02 + 14.0j} = \dfrac{364.2\underline{/23.7°}}{17.2\underline{/54.4°}}$$

$$= 21.2\underline{/-30.7°} = 21.2\underline{/329.3°}.$$

Exercise 11-6

In Problems 1–14, perform the indicated operations and give the answers in polar form.

1. $2(\cos 17° + j\sin 17°)\cdot 4(\cos 43° + j\sin 43°).$

2. $4(\cos 125° + j\sin 125°)\cdot 5(\cos 85° + j\sin 85°).$

3. $3(\cos 105° + j\sin 105°)\cdot 2(\cos 105° + j\sin 105°).$

4. $5(\cos 324° + j\sin 324°)\cdot 3(\cos 126° + j\sin 126°).$

5. $\dfrac{30(\cos 145° + j\sin 145°)}{3(\cos 100° + j\sin 100°)}.$

6. $\dfrac{25(\cos 384° + j\sin 384°)}{5(\cos 174° + j\sin 174°)}.$

7. $\dfrac{18(\cos 284° + j \sin 284°)}{3(\cos 59° + j \sin 59°)}$.

8. $\dfrac{32(\cos 125° + j \sin 125°)}{16(\cos 170° + j \sin 170°)}$.

9. $2\underline{/44°} \cdot 2\underline{/11°}$.

10. $9\underline{/39°} \cdot 8\underline{/28°}$.

11. $1\underline{/46°} \cdot 3\underline{/-12°} \cdot 7\underline{/37°}$.

12. $3\underline{/-45°} \cdot 4\underline{/-87°} \cdot 0.5\underline{/64°}$.

13. $\dfrac{2\underline{/134°}}{4\underline{/-250°}}$.

14. $\dfrac{4\underline{/251°}}{5\underline{/264°}}$.

*In Problems **15–22**, perform the indicated operations and give the answers in rectangular form.*

15. $\dfrac{3\underline{/325°} \cdot 12\underline{/254°}}{18\underline{/9°}}$.

16. $\dfrac{4\underline{/275°}}{2\underline{/44°} \cdot 50\underline{/19°}}$.

17. $\dfrac{(4\underline{/77°})(4\underline{/157°})}{(3\underline{/200°})(2\underline{/50°})}$.

18. $\dfrac{(3\underline{/46°})(5\underline{/295°})}{(4\underline{/200°})(3\underline{/23°})}$.

19. $\dfrac{(7\underline{/-10°})(4\underline{/15°})}{(3\underline{/41°})(2\underline{/-63°})}$.

20. $8\underline{/-10°} + 4\underline{/15°}$.

21. $\dfrac{10\underline{/10°}}{4\underline{/60°}} + \dfrac{15\underline{/5°}}{3\underline{/0°}}$.

22. $\dfrac{5\underline{/-4°} + 6\underline{/5.6°}}{(5\underline{/-4°})(6\underline{/5.6°})}$.

23. If a capacitor of impedance $6\underline{/275°}$ (Ω) and an inductor of impedance $8\underline{/40°}$ (Ω) are connected in parallel, find the circuit impedance and express the answer in rectangular form. (See Example 4.)

24. The voltage V (in volts) across a circuit with an impedance Z (in ohms) and carrying a current I (in amperes) is given by $V = IZ$. Find V if $I = 1.5\underline{/38°}$ and $Z = 6\underline{/48°}$. Express the answer in both polar and rectangular forms.

25. In Problem 24, if the current in the circuit is $4\underline{/50°}$ and the voltage is $20\underline{/30°}$, find the impedance of the circuit and express the answer in polar form.

26. Given that the impedance Z of a circuit element is the reciprocal of its admittance Y, find the impedance if $Y = 0.5\underline{/30°}$. Give your answer in polar form.

27. In the analysis of a mechanical network, the following determinant was encountered:

$$\Delta = \begin{vmatrix} 10 & -0.5 & 0.25\underline{/90°} \\ 0 & 1.3\underline{/20.1°} & -0.8\underline{/71.2°} \\ 0 & -0.8\underline{/72.3°} & 0.6\underline{/62.6°} \end{vmatrix}.$$

Find Δ in rectangular form. *Hint*: Expand along the first column.

28. Show that the effect of dividing a complex number by j is to rotate the vector clockwise by 90°.

11-7 de Moivre's Formula

To evaluate an expression such as $(\sqrt{3} + j)^5$, it is obvious that using repeated multiplication would be rather laborious. Fortunately, using polar form reduces the work considerably. To see why, observe that the nth power of $r(\cos \theta + j \sin \theta)$ is given by

$$[r(\cos\theta + j\sin\theta)]^n = (re^{j\theta})^n = r^n e^{n\theta j}$$
$$= r^n(\cos n\theta + j\sin n\theta).$$

That is, **to raise a complex number to a power _n_, we raise its absolute value to the _n_th power and multiply its amplitude by _n_.** Thus we have the following important formula, which is true for any integer n:

DE MOIVRE'S FORMULA

$$[r(\cos\theta + j\sin\theta)]^n = r^n(\cos n\theta + j\sin n\theta).$$

For example, because $\sqrt{3} + j = 2(\cos 30° + j\sin 30°)$, we have

$$(\sqrt{3} + j)^5 = [2(\cos 30° + j\sin 30°)]^5$$
$$= 2^5[\cos(5\cdot30°) + j\sin(5\cdot30°)]$$
$$= 32(\cos 150° + j\sin 150°)$$
$$= 32\left(-\frac{\sqrt{3}}{2} + \frac{1}{2}j\right)$$
$$= -16\sqrt{3} + 16j.$$

example 1

Use de Moivre's formula to express the given number in $a + bj$ form.

a. $[2(\cos 10° + j\sin 10°)]^6 = 2^6[\cos(6\cdot10°) + j\sin(6\cdot10°)]$
$$= 64(\cos 60° + j\sin 60°)$$
$$= 64\left(\frac{1}{2} + j\frac{\sqrt{3}}{2}\right) = 32 + 32j\sqrt{3}.$$

b. $(3\underline{/30°})^{-3} = 3^{-3}\underline{/-3\cdot30°} = \frac{1}{27}\underline{/-90°} = \frac{1}{27}[0 + j(-1)] = -\frac{1}{27}j.$

example 2

Use de Moivre's formula to express the given number in $a + bj$ form.

a. $(3 + 2j)^4 = (\sqrt{13}\underline{/33.7°})^4 = (\sqrt{13})^4\underline{/4\cdot33.7°}$
$$= 13^2\underline{/134.8°} = -119.1 + 119.9j.$$

b. $\dfrac{(2 + 2j)^{15}}{(\sqrt{3} + j)^{21}} = \dfrac{(\sqrt{8}\underline{/45°})^{15}}{(2\underline{/30°})^{21}} = \dfrac{(2^{3/2})^{15}\underline{/15\cdot45°}}{2^{21}\underline{/21\cdot30°}}$ \quad (since $\sqrt{8} = 2\sqrt{2} = 2^{3/2}$)

$$= \frac{2^{45/2}\underline{/675°}}{2^{21}\underline{/630°}} = 2^{3/2}\underline{/45°}$$

$$= 2\sqrt{2}\left(\frac{\sqrt{2}}{2} + j\frac{\sqrt{2}}{2}\right)$$

$$= 2 + 2j.$$

We conclude this section by using de Moivre's formula to solve the equation $w^n = z$ for w, where w and z are complex numbers and n is a positive integer. That is, we want to find an nth root of a complex number z. Suppose $z = r(\cos \theta + j \sin \theta)$ and $w = \rho(\cos \varphi + j \sin \varphi)$, where ρ and φ are the Greek letters rho and phi, respectively. Then substituting into $w^n = z$ gives

$$[\rho(\cos \varphi + j \sin \varphi)]^n = r(\cos \theta + j \sin \theta),$$

or, by de Moivre's formula,

$$\rho^n(\cos n\varphi + j \sin n\varphi) = r(\cos \theta + j \sin \theta).$$

Both sides of this equation represent the same number. But two numbers in polar form represent the same number if, in addition to having the same absolute value, their amplitudes are coterminal angles. In other words, $n\varphi$ can differ from θ by any integral multiple of $360°$ (or 2π if θ is in radians). Symbolically, this means that

$$n\varphi = \theta + k \cdot 360°,$$

$$\varphi = \frac{\theta}{n} + \frac{k \cdot 360°}{n}, \text{ where } k \text{ is an integer.}$$

Also, $\rho^n = r$ is true if $\rho = \sqrt[n]{r}$, the positive nth root of r. Thus the nth roots of z are given by the formula

$$\boxed{\begin{array}{c} w_k = \sqrt[n]{r}\left[\cos\left(\frac{\theta}{n} + \frac{k \cdot 360°}{n}\right) + j \sin\left(\frac{\theta}{n} + \frac{k \cdot 360°}{n}\right)\right], \\ \text{where } k = 0, 1, 2, \ldots, n - 1. \end{array}}$$

Each of the n values of k from zero to $n - 1$ gives a different value of w. For other values of k, repetition of the previous values of z occurs. In summary, there are exactly n different complex nth roots of a nonzero complex number. These roots have the same absolute value.

example 3

Find the six sixth roots of -64. That is, find the six solutions of $x^6 = -64$.

We first express -64 in trigonometric form:

$$-64 = 64(\cos 180° + j \sin 180°).$$

If we denote the sixth roots by w_k, substituting in the preceding formula gives

$$w_k = \sqrt[6]{64}\left[\cos\left(\frac{180°}{6} + \frac{k \cdot 360°}{6}\right) + j\sin\left(\frac{180°}{6} + \frac{k \cdot 360°}{6}\right)\right]$$

$$= 2[\cos(30° + k \cdot 60°) + j\sin(30° + k \cdot 60°)], \qquad k = 0, 1, \ldots, 5.$$

Next we successively replace k by $0, 1, \ldots, 5$. This gives the roots $w_0, w_1, \ldots, w_5$. If $k = 0$,

$$w_0 = 2(\cos 30° + j\sin 30°) = 2\left(\frac{\sqrt{3}}{2} + \frac{1}{2}j\right) = \sqrt{3} + j.$$

If $k = 1$,

$$w_1 = 2(\cos 90° + j\sin 90°) = 2(0 + j) = 2j.$$

If $k = 2$,

$$w_2 = 2(\cos 150° + j\sin 150°) = 2\left(-\frac{\sqrt{3}}{2} + \frac{1}{2}j\right) = -\sqrt{3} + j.$$

If $k = 3$,

$$w_3 = 2(\cos 210° + j\sin 210°) = 2\left(-\frac{\sqrt{3}}{2} - \frac{1}{2}j\right) = -\sqrt{3} - j.$$

If $k = 4$,

$$w_4 = 2(\cos 270° + j\sin 270°) = 2(0 - j) = -2j.$$

If $k = 5$,

$$w_5 = 2(\cos 330° + j\sin 330°) = 2\left(\frac{\sqrt{3}}{2} - \frac{1}{2}j\right) = \sqrt{3} - j.$$

You may verify that for $k > 5$, no new roots will be obtained. As geometrically shown in Fig. 11-15, the roots are equally spaced points on a circle of radius 2. They appear as vertices of a regular six-sided polygon in the complex plane.

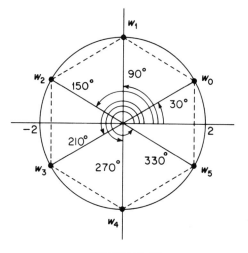

FIGURE 11-15

example 4

Find the three cube roots of $-1 + j\sqrt{3}$.

$-1 + j\sqrt{3} = 2(\cos 120° + j \sin 120°),$

$$w_k = \sqrt[3]{2} \left[\cos \left(\frac{120°}{3} + \frac{k \cdot 360°}{3} \right) + j \sin \left(\frac{120°}{3} + \frac{k \cdot 360°}{3} \right) \right]$$

$$= \sqrt[3]{2} \left[\cos (40° + k \cdot 120°) + j \sin (40° + k \cdot 120°), \qquad k = 0, 1, 2. \right.$$

Thus

if $k = 0,$ $w_0 = \sqrt[3]{2}(\cos 40° + j \sin 40°),$

if $k = 1,$ $w_1 = \sqrt[3]{2}(\cos 160° + j \sin 160°),$

if $k = 2,$ $w_2 = \sqrt[3]{2}(\cos 280° + j \sin 280°).$

See Fig. 11-16. Note that this problem could have been posed by saying, "Solve the equation $x^3 = -1 + j\sqrt{3}$."

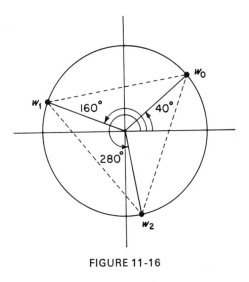

FIGURE 11-16

Exercise 11-7

Use de Moivre's formula to evaluate the expressions in Problems 1-20. Give your answer in both trigonometric and rectangular forms. Do not use a calculator.

1. $[2(\cos 10° + j \sin 10°)]^3.$

2. $[3(\cos 25° + j \sin 25°)]^6.$

3. $[\sqrt{2}(\cos 15° + j \sin 15°)]^8.$

4. $[2(\cos 150° + j \sin 150°)]^4.$

5. $(\cos 40° + j \sin 40°)^{-6}.$

6. $[2(\cos 45° + j \sin 45°)]^{-3}.$

7. $(\sqrt{2} + j\sqrt{2})^5.$

8. $(-\sqrt{2} - j\sqrt{2})^4.$

9. $(-\sqrt{3} + j)^4$.

10. $\left(-\dfrac{\sqrt{3}}{2} - \dfrac{1}{2}j\right)^5$.

11. $(\sqrt{3} + j)^4$.

12. $\left(-\dfrac{1}{2} - j\dfrac{\sqrt{3}}{2}\right)^4$.

13. $(-\sqrt{2} + j\sqrt{2})^6$.

14. $(1 + j)^7$.

15. $(1 - j)^{10}$.

16. $(-\sqrt{2} + j\sqrt{2})^4$.

17. $\dfrac{(\sqrt{2} + j\sqrt{2})^{10}}{(\sqrt{3} + j)^{10}}$.

18. $\dfrac{(1 - j)^{15}}{(1 + j)^{12}}$.

19. $(-2 + 2j)^{-8}$.

20. $(1 - j\sqrt{3})^{-4}$.

*Find the indicated roots in Problems **21–30**. Give the answers in rectangular form if you can do so without using a calculator.*

21. Cube roots of 1.

22. Fourth roots of 16.

23. Square roots of $-8j$.

24. Cube roots of -4.

25. Square roots of j.

26. Fourth roots of $\frac{1}{2}(1 - j\sqrt{3})$.

27. Fourth roots of $2(-1 + j\sqrt{3})$.

28. Fifth roots of $1 + j$.

29. Sixth roots of $2 - 2j\sqrt{3}$.

30. Sixth roots of $-1 - j$.

*In Problems **31–36**, solve the given equations. Express your answers in rectangular form if you can do so without a calculator.*

31. $x^3 = 1$.

32. $x^4 = 1$.

33. $x^5 - 1 = 0$.

34. $x^6 - 1 = 0$.

35. $x^3 = 1 + j$.

36. $x^3 = -\sqrt{2} - j\sqrt{2}$.

11-8   Review

Review Questions

1. The powers j^2, j^3, j^4, j^5, and j^{-2} are equal, respectively, to _____.

2. The real part of $3 - 4j$ is ___(a)___ and the imaginary part is ___(b)___.

3. Among the numbers $\sqrt[3]{-8}$, $\sqrt{-2}$, and $\sqrt{(-2)(-2)}$, which are pure imaginary? _____

4. The number $a + bj$ is the conjugate of what number? _____

5. The product of a complex number and its conjugate is _(always)(sometimes)_ a real number.

6. In the representation of a complex number $a + bj$ in the complex plane, the absolute value of $a + bj$ is the distance from $(0, 0)$ to the point _____(a)_____. This distance is given by the expression _____(b)_____.

7. Representation of a complex number in polar form _(is)(is not)_ unique.

8. A trigonometric form for $z = 8$ is _____.

9. In rectangular form, $3(\cos 270° + j \sin 270°)$ is equal to _____.

10. The division $\dfrac{1}{1-j}$ is performed by multiplying the numerator and denominator by _____.

11. $\sqrt{(-2)(-2)}$ equals __(a)__ but $\sqrt{-2}\sqrt{-2}$ equals __(b)__.

12. The nth roots of 1 lie on a circle of radius __(a)__ and determine the vertices of a regular polygon of __(b)__ sides.

13. The imaginary part of a complex number _(is)(is not)_ a real number.

14. If $1 + zj = 0$, then z equals _____.

15. The square of a pure imaginary number _(is)(is not)_ a real number.

16. In the complex plane, the vector representing the number $-2 + j\sqrt{3}$ has its initial point at __(a)__ and terminates at the point __(b)__.

17. If z is a sixth root of $-2 + j\sqrt{3}$, then z^6 equals _____.

18. In the complex plane, $e^{j\theta}$ is a point on a circle with radius _____.

Answers to Review Questions

1. $-1, -j, 1, j, -1.$ **2.** (a) 3, (b) -4.   **3.** $\sqrt{-2}$.   **4.** $a - bj$.   **5.** Always.
6. (a) (a, b), (b) $\sqrt{a^2 + b^2}$.   **7.** Is not.   **8.** $8(\cos 0° + j \sin 0°)$.   **9.** $-3j$.   **10.** $1 + j$.
11. (a) 2, (b) -2.   **12.** (a) 1, (b) n.   **13.** Is.   **14.** j.   **15.** Is.
16. (a) $(0, 0)$, (b) $(-2, \sqrt{3})$.   **17.** $-2 + j\sqrt{3}$.   **18.** 1.

Review Problems

In Problems 1–6, simplify the expressions.

1. $8 + 2j - j(2 + j) + 5j^3 - \sqrt{-4}$.

2. $(2 + j)(3 - 3j) - 6j(j + 7)$.

3. $\dfrac{7}{j + 2}$.

4. $\dfrac{j - 6}{5 + 2j}$.

5. $\dfrac{2 + j}{(1 + j)(2 - j)}$.

6. $(3 + 2j)(3 - 2j) - (1 + 3j)^2$.

In Problems 7–14, transform to polar form.

7. $4\sqrt{2} + 4j\sqrt{2}$.

8. $\dfrac{3}{5} - \dfrac{3\sqrt{3}}{5}j$.

9. $-\dfrac{\sqrt{3}}{2} + \dfrac{j}{2}$.

10. $-27j$.

11. $7 - 8j$.

12. $-0.3 - 0.2j$.

13. $3e^{\pi j/4}$.

14. $2e^{1.5j}$.

In Problems 15–20, transform to rectangular form.

15. $\sqrt{3}(\cos 315° + j \sin 315°)$.

16. $\tfrac{1}{2}(\cos 210° + j \sin 210°)$.

17. $\sqrt{2}(\cos 135° + j \sin 135°)$.

18. $\tfrac{2}{3}(\cos 60° + j \sin 60°)$.

19. $3(\cos 22.1° + j \sin 22.1°)$.

20. $2.4/\underline{320.7°}$.

In Problems **21–27,** *perform the indicated operations and give the answers in polar and rectangular forms.*

21. $2(\cos 341° + j \sin 341°) \cdot 3(\cos 109° + j \sin 109°)$.

22. $(1.4\underline{/40°})(7.5\underline{/75.2°})$.

23. $\dfrac{\sqrt{8}\,(\cos 284° + j \sin 284°)}{\sqrt{2}\,(\cos 59° + j \sin 59°)}$.

24. $\dfrac{0.780\underline{/42°}}{0.156\underline{/73°}}$.

25. $[2.4(\cos 10° + j \sin 10°)]^5$.

26. $\dfrac{(3\underline{/23°})^4}{(2\underline{/17°})^5}$.

27. $\dfrac{[2(\cos 22° + j \sin 22°)]^8 \cdot [3(\cos 125° + j \sin 125°)]^5}{[3(\cos 78° + j \sin 78°)]^4 \cdot [2(\cos 139° + j \sin 139°)]^2}$.

In Problems **28–31,** *give all answers in polar coordinates.*

28. Find all square roots of $-1 + j\sqrt{3}$.

29. Find all fifth roots of $-\sqrt{2} - j\sqrt{2}$.

30. Find all eighth roots of 1.

31. In the analysis of a circuit, the current was found to be $100/(4 + 6j)$ amperes. What is the absolute value of the current?

32. In an alternating current series circuit, the admittance Y is expressed as the reciprocal of the impedance Z. If $Z = 16.8 - 22.1j$, find Y.

33. The current I through a particular circuit is given by $I = V/Z$, where I is in amperes, voltage V is in volts, and impedance Z is in ohms. (a) Find I if $V = 8.1 - 2.0j$ and $Z = 5.6 - 0.3j$. (b) Find Z if $I = 1 + j$ and $V = 1 - j$.

34. Suppose $R + \left(\omega L - \dfrac{1}{\omega C}\right)j = re^{j\theta}$. Find r and $\tan\theta$.

12

quadratic equations

12-1 Solving Quadratic Equations by Factoring

If a ball is thrown vertically upward from ground level at a speed of 19.6 m/s, then (neglecting air resistance) its height s (in meters) after t seconds have elapsed is given by

$$s = -4.9t^2 + 19.6t.$$

For example, after 1 second its height is $-4.9(1)^2 + 19.6(1) = 14.7$ m. When does the ball hit the ground?

The ball hits the ground when s is 0. Thus we want to solve

$$-4.9t^2 + 19.6t = 0. \tag{1}$$

In Eq. 1, note that the highest power of the variable t that occurs is the second. For this reason, Eq. 1 is called a **second-degree equation** or an **equation of degree 2**. It is most commonly referred to as a *quadratic equation*.

> A **quadratic equation** in the variable x is an equation that can be written in the form
>
> $$ax^2 + bx + c = 0$$
>
> where a, b, and c are constants and $a \neq 0$.

example 1

The following are quadratic equations of the form $ax^2 + bx + c = 0$.

a. $3x^2 - 5x + 2 = 0$ $a = 3, b = -5, c = 2$.   *Note that $b \neq 5$.*

b. $x^2 - 4 = 0$ $a = 1, b = 0, c = -4$.

c. $x^2 - x = 0$ $a = 1, b = -1, c = 0$.

d. $2x^2 = x - 4$ Rewrite this as $2x^2 - x + 4 = 0$; then $a = 2, b = -1, c = 4$.

A method of solving quadratic equations involves factoring $ax^2 + bx + c$ into *first-degree* factors. For example, returning to the ball problem, we can rewrite Eq. 1 as

$$4.9t^2 - 19.6t = 0 \qquad (2)$$

$$t(4.9t - 19.6) = 0.$$

Think of this as two numbers, t and $4.9t - 19.6$, having a product of zero. *But whenever a product of two or more numbers is zero, at least one of the numbers must be zero.* This means that we must have either

$$t = 0 \quad \text{or} \quad 4.9t - 19.6 = 0,$$

from which

$$t = 0 \quad \text{or} \quad t = \frac{19.6}{4.9} = 4.$$

Thus Eq. 2 has two roots: 0 and 4. You should verify by substitution that these values satisfy the given equation. However, due to the physical situation involved in the problem, we must reject $t = 0$, because that is the time the ball *left* the ground. Thus the ball *strikes* the ground 4 seconds later. In summary, 0 and 4 are solutions of Eq. 2, but $t = 4$ seconds is the solution to the problem posed.

example 2

Solve $6w^2 = 4w$.

We *do not* divide both sides by w (a variable), because equivalence is not guaranteed and we may lose a root. Instead, we rewrite the equation as

$$6w^2 - 4w = 0.$$

Factoring gives

$$2w(3w - 2) = 0.$$

Setting each factor equal to zero and solving the equations give

$2w = 0$	$3w - 2 = 0$
$w = 0.$	$3w = 2$
	$w = \frac{2}{3}.$

Thus the solutions are 0 and $\frac{2}{3}$. Note that if we had divided both sides of $6w^2 = 4w$ by w and obtained $6w = 4$, our only solution would have been $\frac{2}{3}$. That is, we would lose the root 0. This confirms our discussion of Operation 4 in Sec. 5-2. Initially, however, we could have divided both sides of the given equation by 2, obtaining the equivalent equation $3w^2 = 2w$. *This type of simplifying operation is a great aid in solving equations and should not be overlooked.*

example 3

Solve $x^2 - 3x + 2 = 0$ by factoring.

$$x^2 - 3x + 2 = 0$$
$$(x - 1)(x - 2) = 0.$$

$x - 1 = 0$	$x - 2 = 0$
$x = 1.$	$x = 2.$

The solutions are 1 and 2. The equation $x^2 - 3x + 2 = 0$ can be solved graphically by sketching the graph of the function $y = f(x) = x^2 - 3x + 2$ and observing the zeros of the function, that is, those values of x for which $y = 0$. A sketch is shown in Fig. 12-1.

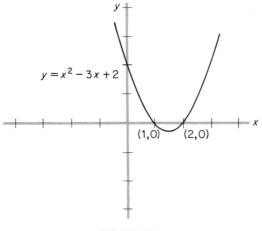

FIGURE 12-1

example 4

Solve $x - 3 = \dfrac{x^2}{3} + 3x$ by factoring.

First, to clear the equation of fractions, we multiply both sides by 3.

$$3(x - 3) = 3\left(\frac{x^2}{3} + 3x\right)$$

$$3x - 9 = x^2 + 9x.$$

Next we rewrite the equation so that one side is zero and then we factor:

$$0 = x^2 + 6x + 9$$

$$0 = (x + 3)(x + 3).$$

$$x + 3 = 0 \qquad\qquad x + 3 = 0$$
$$x = -3. \qquad\qquad x = -3.$$

The solution is -3. Because two factors gave rise to the same root, -3, we say that there are two *equal roots* of -3 or that -3 is a **repeated** (or **double**) **root**. The graph of $y = x^2 + 6x + 9$ touches, but does not cross, the x-axis when $x = -3$ (Fig. 12-2).

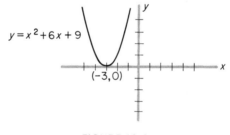

FIGURE 12-2

example 5

Solve $(3x - 4)(x + 1) = -2$.

You should approach a problem like this with caution. If the product of two numbers is equal to -2, it is *not* true that at least one of the numbers must be -2. That is, you *must not* set each factor equal to -2. *Do not write* $3x - 4 = -2$ and $x + 1 = -2$. To solve the equation, we first multiply the factors in the left side. Then we combine terms so that one side is zero.

$$(3x - 4)(x + 1) = -2$$

$$3x^2 - x - 4 = -2$$

$$3x^2 - x - 2 = 0$$

$$(3x + 2)(x - 1) = 0.$$

$$3x + 2 = 0 \qquad\bigg|\qquad x - 1 = 0$$
$$3x = -2 \qquad\qquad x = 1.$$
$$x = -\tfrac{2}{3}.$$

The solutions are $-\tfrac{2}{3}$ and 1.

example 6

Solve $u^2 = 3$.

This equation is equivalent to $u^2 - 3 = 0$. Factoring gives

$$(u - \sqrt{3})(u + \sqrt{3}) = 0,$$

from which $u = \sqrt{3}$ or $u = -\sqrt{3}$. The pair of roots $\sqrt{3}$ and $-\sqrt{3}$ may be written $\pm\sqrt{3}$, which is read *plus or minus* 3. More generally,

$$\boxed{\text{if } u^2 = k, \quad \text{then} \quad u = \pm\sqrt{k}.}$$

If k is negative, the roots are imaginary and are conjugates of each other. Otherwise, the roots are real. For example, the roots of $x^2 = 4$ are $\pm\sqrt{4} = \pm 2$, but $x^2 = -4$ has roots $\pm\sqrt{-4} = \pm 2j$. For the latter case, the graph of $y = x^2 + 4$ will not intersect the x-axis: This indicates that there are no real roots (Fig. 12-3).

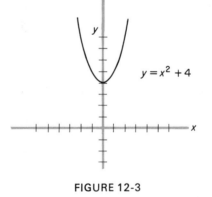

$$y = x^2 + 4$$

FIGURE 12-3

The boxed rule in Example 6 easily allows us to solve quadratic equations that do not contain a first-degree term. We simply solve for x^2 and apply the rule. For example, to solve $5x^2 - 11 = 0$ we have

$$5x^2 = 11, \qquad x^2 = \tfrac{11}{5}, \qquad x = \pm\sqrt{\tfrac{11}{5}} = \pm\frac{\sqrt{55}}{5}.$$

Do not forget the $\pm$ sign.

From the examples presented thus far and the fact that a second-degree polynomial can be expressed as a product of two first-degree polynomials, it is reasonable to infer that **every quadratic equation has two roots, although they may not necessarily be different.**

Some equations that are not quadratic may also be solved by factoring, as Example 7 shows.

example 7

Solve $4x^4 - 16x^2 = 0$.

This is called a fourth-degree equation. (Why?) Dividing both sides by 4, we have

$$x^4 - 4x^2 = 0$$
$$x^2(x^2 - 4) = 0$$
$$x^2(x + 2)(x - 2) = 0$$
$$x \cdot x(x + 2)(x - 2) = 0.$$

Setting each of the *four* factors equal to 0 and solving the resulting equations give

$x = 0.$	$x = 0.$	$x + 2 = 0$	$x - 2 = 0$
		$x = -2.$	$x = 2.$

Thus the roots are 0 and ± 2. Here 0 is a repeated root.

example 8

A rectangular observation deck overlooking a scenic valley is to be built. It is to have dimensions 6 m by 12 m. A rectangular shelter of area 40 m² is to be centered over the deck. The uncovered part of the deck is to serve as a walkway of uniform width. How wide should this walkway be?

Let w be the width (in meters) of the walkway (Fig. 12-4). Then the part of the deck for the shelter has dimensions $12 - 2w$ by $6 - 2w$. Since this area must be 40 m², where area = (length)(width), we have

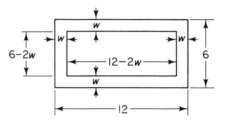

FIGURE 12-4

$$(12 - 2w)(6 - 2w) = 40$$
$$72 - 36w + 4w^2 = 40$$
$$4w^2 - 36w + 32 = 0$$
$$w^2 - 9w + 8 = 0 \qquad \text{(dividing both sides by 4)}$$
$$(w - 8)(w - 1) = 0$$
$$w = 8, 1.$$

Although 8 is a solution to the equation, it is not a solution to our problem, because one of the dimensions of the deck itself is only 6 m. Thus the only possible solution is 1 m.

Exercise 12-1

In Problems **1–68,** *solve by the methods of this section.*

1. $x^2 + 3x + 2 = 0.$ **2.** $x^2 - 5x + 6 = 0.$ **3.** $x^2 + 9x + 14 = 0.$

4. $x^2 + 8x + 15 = 0.$ **5.** $t^2 - 7t + 12 = 0.$ **6.** $t^2 - 4t + 4 = 0.$

7. $z^2 + 2z - 3 = 0.$ **8.** $z^2 + z - 12 = 0.$ **9.** $x^2 - 12x + 36 = 0.$

10. $x^2 - 1 = 0.$ **11.** $x^2 - 8x = 0.$ **12.** $t^2 = 16.$

13. $2x^2 + 10x = 0.$ **14.** $0 = 3x - x^2.$ **15.** $0 = 3t^2 - 6t.$

16. $x^2 = 32.$ **17.** $4 - x^2 = 0.$ **18.** $10x^2 - x - 3 = 0.$

19. $x^2 = 25.$ **20.** $x^2 = 8.$ **21.** $x^2 = 2x.$

22. $9x^2 + 36 = 0.$ **23.** $\dfrac{x^2}{3} = -4.$ **24.** $\dfrac{x^2}{7} = 1.$

25. $9z^2 = 81.$ **26.** $3x^2 - 12x + 12 = 0.$ **27.** $6x^2 + 7x - 3 = 0.$

28. $3 = z^2.$ **29.** $\dfrac{2}{3}t^2 - 6 = 0.$ **30.** $7t^2 = 7t.$

31. $2x^2 - 14 = 0.$ **32.** $x^2 + 21 = 18.$ **33.** $2x^2 + 7x = 4.$

34. $x^2 = 2x + 3.$ **35.** $-x^2 + 3x + 10 = 0.$ **36.** $2x^2 + 3x - 2 = 0.$

37. $4x^2 + 4x = -1.$ **38.** $9x^2 - 1 = 0.$ **39.** $6(x^2 + 2x) + 6 = 0.$

40. $4x^2 - 12x + 9 = 0.$ **41.** $t(t + 4) = 5.$ **42.** $2y^2 = 4y.$

43. $3x^2 + 5(2 - x) = 2x^2 + 4.$ **44.** $2(x^2 - 5) - 3(x^2 - 7) = 3.$

45. $4 - x^2 = (x + 1)^2 + 3.$ **46.** $(2x - 5)(x + 5) = -22.$

47. $\dfrac{x^2}{2} - x - 4 = 0.$ **48.** $x^2 + \dfrac{7}{2}x - 2 = 0.$

49. $6y^2 + \dfrac{5}{2}y + \dfrac{1}{4} = 0.$ **50.** $\dfrac{x^2}{2} + \dfrac{10}{3}x + 2 = 0.$

51. $x(x - 1)(x + 2) = 0.$ **52.** $x^2(x - 4) = 0.$

53. $(x - 2)^2(x + 1)^2 = 0.$ **54.** $x(x - 1)(x + 1) = 0.$

55. $7x^2(x - 2)^2(x + 3)(x - 4) = 0.$

56. $x(x^2 - 1)(x^2 - 4) = 0.$

57. $x(x^2 - 1)(x^2 - 1) = 0.$

58. $x^3 - x = 0.$

59. $x^3 - 64x = 0.$

60. $x^3 - 4x^2 - 5x = 0.$

61. $3y^3 + 18y^2 + 24y = 0.$

62. $3x^4 + 11x^3 - 4x^2 = 0.$

63. $x^4 - 10x^2 + 9 = 0.$

64. $x^4 - 29x^2 + 100 = 0.$

65. $x^2(x^4 - 2x^2 + 1) = 0.$

66. $x^5 - 6x^3 + 8x = 0.$

67. $x^4 - 13x^2 + 36 = 0.$

68. $x^5 - 4x^3 + 4x = 0.$

In Problems 69–72, solve the given equation for the indicated letter.

69. $T^2 = 4\pi^2\left(\dfrac{L}{g}\right); \quad T.$

70. $s = \dfrac{1}{2}at^2; \quad t.$

71. $mgh = \dfrac{1}{2}mv^2 + \dfrac{1}{2}I\omega^2; \quad \omega.$

72. $P = \dfrac{E^2}{R + r} - \dfrac{E^2r}{(R + r)^2}; \quad E.$

73. When an object is thrown straight upward with a speed of 49 m/s, at time t its height s above its starting point is given by $s = 49t - 4.9t^2$, where s is in meters and t is in seconds. How long after it is thrown will the object return to its starting point?

74. The force F acting on an object is a function of time t and is given by $F = f(t) = 2t^2 - 19t + 29$, where F is in newtons and t is in seconds. At what values of t is $F = 5$ N?

75. The formula

$$S = 2\pi r^2 + 2\pi rh$$

gives the total surface area S of a cylinder of radius r and height h. Find r in order that a cylinder of height 2 cm will have an area of 48π cm^2.

76. A rectangular field has an area of 120 m^2, and its length is 2 m greater than its width. What are its length and width?

77. The differences between the lengths of the hypotenuse and the other two sides of a triangle are, respectively, 8 and 4 cm. Find the other two sides.

78. The length, width, and height of a shipping crate are in the ratio of 3 : 2 : 1. Another crate has the same volume as the first crate, but it is 2 m longer, 2 m wider, and half as high. Find the dimensions of the *second* crate.

79. The distance s (in meters) that a free-falling object falls from rest in t seconds is given by $s = 4.9t^2$. How long will it take for such an object to hit the ground if it is dropped from a cliff 100 m high?

80. A lumber company owns a lot that is of rectangular shape, 1 km by 2 km. If the company cuts a uniform strip of trees along the outer edges of this lot, how wide should the strip be if $\frac{3}{4}$ km^2 of the lot is to remain?

81. A rectangular plot, 4 m by 8 m, is to be used for a garden. It is decided to put a pavement inside the entire border so that 12 m^2 of the plot is left for flowers. How wide should the pavement be?

12-2 Completing the Square— The Quadratic Formula

Solving quadratic equations by factoring can be quite difficult, as you can see by trying that method on $x^2 - 6x + 3 = 0$. However, there are other methods available that will now be considered.

In Example 6 of the previous section, the roots of $u^2 = k$ were shown to be $\pm\sqrt{k}$. We call $u^2 = k$ a **pure quadratic equation**, because it does not contain a first-degree term. We shall now show how *any* quadratic equation can be written in a pure form and, as a result, easily solved.

In general, in the square of the binomial $x + k$, namely

$$(x + k)^2 = x^2 + 2kx + k^2.$$

the constant term k^2 is equal to the square of one-half the coefficient of x, that is, the square of one-half of $2k$. Thus the sum of an x^2-term and an x-term can be made into the square of a binomial by **adding to it the square of one-half the coefficient of x.** This is true *only* if the coefficient of the x^2-term is 1.

To illustrate these ideas, consider the equation

$$x^2 - 6x + 3 = 0.$$

This is not a pure quadratic equation due to the first-degree term $-6x$; also, the equation cannot easily be factored. You should carefully study the following steps in the solution of the equation. We first rewrite the equation in an equivalent form so that the left side consists only of an x^2-term and an x-term:

$$x^2 - 6x = -3.$$

Next, to **both** sides we add the square of one-half the coefficient of the x-term, namely, $[\frac{1}{2}(-6)]^2 = 9$. As a result, the left side is the *square of a binomial:*

$$x^2 - 6x + 9 = -3 + 9$$
$$(x - 3)^2 = 6.$$

This equation has the pure form $u^2 = k$, where u is $x - 3$ and k is 6. Because $u = \pm\sqrt{k}$, we have

$$x - 3 = \pm\sqrt{6}$$
$$x = 3 \pm \sqrt{6} \qquad \text{(adding 3 to both sides).}$$

Therefore the roots are $3 + \sqrt{6}$ and $3 - \sqrt{6}$. Although these roots can be put in decimal form (a common practice in technology), in this text a radical form is acceptable. The technique we have used to solve the quadratic equation is called **completing the square.**

example 1

Solve $2x^2 + 3x - 4 = 0$ by completing the square.

$$2x^2 + 3x - 4 = 0$$
$$2x^2 + 3x = 4.$$

Dividing both sides by 2 so that the coefficient of the x^2-term is 1, we have

$$x^2 + \frac{3}{2}x = 2.$$

Adding $[\frac{1}{2}(\frac{3}{2})]^2$, or $\frac{9}{16}$, to both sides gives

$$x^2 + \frac{3}{2}x + \frac{9}{16} = 2 + \frac{9}{16}$$
$$\left(x + \frac{3}{4}\right)^2 = \frac{41}{16}.$$

This equation is in pure form. Thus

$$x + \frac{3}{4} = \pm\sqrt{\frac{41}{16}} = \pm\frac{\sqrt{41}}{4}$$
$$x = -\frac{3}{4} \pm \frac{\sqrt{41}}{4}$$
$$= \frac{-3 \pm \sqrt{41}}{4}.$$

The roots are $\dfrac{-3 + \sqrt{41}}{4}$ and $\dfrac{-3 - \sqrt{41}}{4}$.

Applying the method of completing the square to the general quadratic equation $ax^2 + bx + c = 0$ results in a formula that gives the roots of any quadratic equation. Let

$$ax^2 + bx + c = 0, \qquad a \neq 0.$$

Then

$$ax^2 + bx = -c.$$

We can divide both sides by a because $a \neq 0$;

$$x^2 + \frac{b}{a}x = -\frac{c}{a}.$$

Because the coefficient of the x-term is b/a, we add the square of $\frac{1}{2}(b/a)$ to both sides:

$$x^2 + \frac{b}{a}x + \left(\frac{b}{2a}\right)^2 = \left(\frac{b}{2a}\right)^2 - \frac{c}{a}.$$

The left side factors into $\left(x + \dfrac{b}{2a}\right)^2$ and the right side simplifies into $\dfrac{b^2 - 4ac}{4a^2}$. Thus

$$\left(x + \frac{b}{2a}\right)^2 = \frac{b^2 - 4ac}{4a^2}.$$

This equation has the form $u^2 = k$, where $u = x + \frac{b}{2a}$ and $k = \frac{b^2 - 4ac}{4a^2}$. Therefore

$$x + \frac{b}{2a} = \pm\sqrt{\frac{b^2 - 4ac}{4a^2}} = \pm\frac{\sqrt{b^2 - 4ac}}{2a}.$$

Solving for x, we obtain

$$x = -\frac{b}{2a} \pm \frac{\sqrt{b^2 - 4ac}}{2a}$$

$$x = \frac{-b \pm \sqrt{b^2 - 4ac}}{2a}. \tag{1}$$

It can be shown that the two values $\dfrac{-b + \sqrt{b^2 - 4ac}}{2a}$ and $\dfrac{-b - \sqrt{b^2 - 4ac}}{2a}$ do indeed satisfy $ax^2 + bx + c = 0$. Equation (1) is called the **quadratic formula**.

QUADRATIC FORMULA

If $ax^2 + bx + c = 0$, where a, b, and c are constants and $a \neq 0$, then

$$x = \frac{-b \pm \sqrt{b^2 - 4ac}}{2a}.$$

These values of x are the roots of the quadratic equation above.

The quadratic formula, along with the hypothesis that precedes it, should be memorized. Be sure to use it correctly. *Do not write* $x = -b \pm \dfrac{\sqrt{b^2 - 4ac}}{2a}$.

example 2

Solve $4x^2 - 17x + 15 = 0$ by the quadratic formula.

Here $a = 4$, $b = -17$ (not 17), and $c = 15$.

$$x = \frac{-b \pm \sqrt{b^2 - 4ac}}{2a} = \frac{-(-17) \pm \sqrt{(-17)^2 - 4(4)(15)}}{2(4)}$$

$$= \frac{17 \pm \sqrt{49}}{8} = \frac{17 \pm 7}{8}.$$

The roots are $\dfrac{17 + 7}{8} = \dfrac{24}{8} = 3$ and $\dfrac{17 - 7}{8} = \dfrac{10}{8} = \dfrac{5}{4}$.

If a, b, and c are real numbers, the expression $b^2 - 4ac$ under the radical sign in the quadratic formula is called the **discriminant** of the general quadratic equation $ax^2 + bx + c = 0$. In Example 2 the discriminant, 49, is positive, so its square root is positive. Thus the equation has two different real roots. More generally, here are the possibilities of the discriminant and the corresponding roots of a quadratic equation.

$b^2 - 4ac$	*Type of solutions*
positive	two different real roots
zero	one real root (double root)
negative	two different imaginary roots (conjugates)

The discriminant is useful because it tells you something about the roots of a quadratic equation without you actually having to find the roots.

example 3

a. Solve $9t^2 + 12t + 4 = 0$ by the quadratic formula. First examine the discriminant. Here $a = 9$, $b = 12$, and $c = 4$. Because $b^2 - 4ac = 12^2 - 4(9)(4) = 0$, the equation has one real root.

$$t = \frac{-b \pm \sqrt{b^2 - 4ac}}{2a} = \frac{-12 \pm \sqrt{0}}{2(9)}.$$

Thus

$$t = \frac{-12 + 0}{18} = -\frac{2}{3} \quad \text{or} \quad t = \frac{-12 - 0}{18} = -\frac{2}{3}.$$

The only solution is $-\frac{2}{3}$.

b. Solve $x^2 = -x - 1$ by the quadratic formula. First examine the discriminant. To determine a, b, and c, we first rewrite the equation as $x^2 + x + 1 = 0$. Thus $a = 1$, $b = 1$, and $c = 1$. Because $b^2 - 4ac = 1^2 - 4(1)(1) = -3 < 0$, there are two different imaginary roots:

$$x = \frac{-b \pm \sqrt{b^2 - 4ac}}{2a} = \frac{-1 \pm \sqrt{-3}}{2} = \frac{-1 \pm j\sqrt{3}}{2} = -\frac{1}{2} \pm \frac{j\sqrt{3}}{2}.$$

Note that the roots are a pair of conjugates.

Exercise 12-2

In Problems 1–6, solve the given equation by completing the square.

1. $x^2 + 4x - 3 = 0$.   **2.** $x^2 - 6x + 2 = 0$.   **3.** $x^2 + x - 1 = 0$.

4. $x^2 - x + 1 = 0$.   **5.** $2x^2 + 4x - 5 = 0$.   **6.** $3x^2 - 9x + 4 = 0$.

In Problems 7–42, solve the given equation by the quadratic formula. In Problems 7–12, first determine the nature of the roots by examination of the discriminant.

7. $x^2 + 3x + 1 = 0$.   **8.** $x^2 - 4x + 2 = 0$.   **9.** $x^2 - 6x + 9 = 0$.

10. $x^2 + x - 3 = 0$.   **11.** $t^2 - 4t + 5 = 0$.   **12.** $x^2 - 2x + 2 = 0$.

13. $x^2 + 2x + 3 = 0$.   **14.** $x^2 - 2x + 4 = 0$.   **15.** $2y^2 + 3y - 4 = 0$.

16. $3t^2 - 3t + 1 = 0$.   **17.** $6r^2 + 8r + 3 = 0$.   **18.** $3x^2 + 6x - 2 = 0$.

19. $x^2 + 4 = 0$.   **20.** $x^2 + 8 = 0$.   **21.** $4x^2 = -20x - 25$.

22. $z^2 = z - 1$.   **23.** $1 + x^2 = 0$.   **24.** $9z(z - 1) = 3z - 4$.

25. $5x(x + 2) + 6 = 3$.   **26.** $(4x - 1)(2x + 3) = 18x - 4$.

27. $2 - 2x - 3x^2 = 0$.   **28.** $1 + 8w - 4w^2 = 0$.

29. $-3r^2 + 5r = 4$.   **30.** $x(x + 5) = 5(x - 5)$.

31. $\frac{2}{3}x^2 - \frac{1}{9}x + 2 = 0$.   **32.** $\frac{3}{5}x^2 + \frac{1}{15}x - 3 = 0$.

33. $0.01x^2 + 0.2x - 0.6 = 0$.   **34.** $0.04x^2 - 0.1x - 0.09 = 0$.

35. $2x^2 - \sqrt{3}x + 4 = 0$.   **36.** $\sqrt{8}x^2 + \sqrt{5}x - \sqrt{2} = 0$.

37. $x^2 = \dfrac{x + 5}{6}$.   **38.** $\dfrac{x - 5}{7} = 2x^2$.

39. $\dfrac{2x^2 - 5x}{3} = x - 1$.   **40.** $\dfrac{x^2}{3} + 2x = x + 1$.

41. $\dfrac{x^2}{3} = \dfrac{11}{6}x + 1$.   **42.** $5x^2 - \dfrac{7}{2}x = \dfrac{x + 2}{2}$.

In Problems 43 and 44, solve for x.

43. $x^2 - jx + 6 = 0$.   **44.** $6x^3 + 8x^2 - 10x = 0$.

45. If $3x^2 - 5xy - 4y^2 = 0$, solve for x by treating y as a constant.

46. If $2x^2 + 6xy - 9y^2 = 0$, solve for y by treating x as a constant.

47. Given the equation of motion

$$s = v_0 t + \tfrac{1}{2}at^2,$$

find t (in seconds) if $s = 15$ m, $v_0 = 18$ m/s, and $a = -9.8$ m/s^2. Here s, v_0, and a are displacement, initial velocity, and acceleration, respectively.

48. When a projectile is fired so that its initial velocity in the vertical direction is 30 m/s, its height s above its starting level after t seconds is given by

$$s = 30t - 4.9t^2.$$

When will the projectile be at a height of 32 m above its starting level?

49. A chemist took some acid from a full beaker containing 81 cm^3 and then filled up the beaker with pure water. He then took the same amount from the mixture that he had taken the first time and found that 64 cm^3 of *pure* acid remained in the beaker. How many cubic centimeters did he take each time?

50. An open box is to be made from a square piece of tin by cutting out a 3-cm square from each corner and folding up the sides. See Fig. 12-5. The box is to contain 75 cm³. Find the dimensions of the square piece of tin that must be used.

FIGURE 12-5

51. In a circuit carrying a current i (in amperes), the power P dissipated (in watts) is given by

$$P = i^2R + iV.$$

In one circuit, $R = 10\ \Omega$, $V = 24$ V, and $P = 30$ W. Find i (assume $i > 0$).

52. A platinum resistance thermomometer of certain specifications operates according to the equation

$$R = 10.000 + (4.124 \times 10^{-2})T - (1.779 \times 10^{-5})T^2,$$

where R is the resistance of the thermometer at temperature T (in degrees Celsius). If $R = 13.946\ \Omega$, find the corresponding value of T. Assume that such a thermometer is useable only if $T < 600°C$.

53. In studying the dynamic behavior of galvanometers, one encounters the equation

$$Jm^2 + Dm + S = 0,$$

where J, D, and S are physical quantities that determine the characteristics of the motion of the galvanometer coil. Solve the equation for m.

54. In Problem 53, a galvanometer is said to be *overdamped* when $\dfrac{D^2}{4J^2} > \dfrac{S}{J}$, *underdamped* when $\dfrac{D^2}{4J^2} < \dfrac{S}{J}$, and *critically damped* when $\dfrac{D^2}{4J^2} = \dfrac{S}{J}$. For each case, what is the nature of the roots of the equation in Problem 53?

12-3   Quadratic Functions

Now that we have considered methods of solving quadratic equations, we turn our attention to properties of the graph of a *quadratic function*.

> A function that can be written in the form
> $$y = f(x) = ax^2 + bx + c,$$
> where a, b, and c are constants and $a \neq 0$, is called a **quadratic function**.

For example, the functions $f(x) = x^2 - 3x + 2$ and $y = -3t^2$ are quadratic, but $g(x) = \dfrac{1}{x^2}$ is not.

The graph of the quadratic function $y = f(x) = ax^2 + bx + c$ is called a **parabola** and has a shape such as the curves in Fig. 12-6. If $a > 0$, the parabola extends upward indefinitely, and we say that the parabola *opens upward* or is *concave up* [Fig. 12-6(a)]. If $a < 0$, then the parabola *opens downward* or is *concave down* [Fig. 12-6(b)].

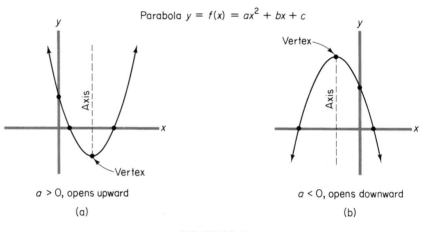

Parabola $y = f(x) = ax^2 + bx + c$

$a > 0$, opens upward

(a)

$a < 0$, opens downward

(b)

FIGURE 12-6

Observe in Fig. 12-6 that each parabola is *symmetric* about a vertical line, called the **axis** of the parabola. This means that if a mirror were placed on the line, then the left half of the parabola would be the mirror image of the right half, and vice versa. The axis is *not* part of the parabola.

Figure 12-6 also shows points labeled **vertex**. At such a point, the axis cuts the parabola. If $a > 0$, the vertex is the "lowest" point on the parabola. This means that at this point $f(x)$ has a minimum value. By performing algebraic manipulations on $ax^2 + bx + c$, we can determine not only this minimum value but also where it occurs.

$$f(x) = ax^2 + bx + c = (ax^2 + bx) + c.$$

Adding and subtracting $b^2/(4a)$ gives

$$f(x) = \left(ax^2 + bx + \frac{b^2}{4a}\right) + c - \frac{b^2}{4a}$$

$$= a\left(x^2 + \frac{b}{a}x + \frac{b^2}{4a^2}\right) + c - \frac{b^2}{4a}$$

$$= a\left(x + \frac{b}{2a}\right)^2 + \frac{4ac - b^2}{4a}.$$

Because $\left(x + \dfrac{b}{2a}\right)^2 \geq 0$ and $a > 0$, it follows that $f(x)$ has a minimum value when $x + \dfrac{b}{2a} = 0$, that is, when $x = -\dfrac{b}{2a}$. The minimum value is $\dfrac{4ac - b^2}{4a}$. Thus the vertex is the point $\left(-\dfrac{b}{2a}, \dfrac{4ac - b^2}{4a}\right)$. Because the y-coordinate of this point is the same as $f\left(-\dfrac{b}{2a}\right)$, we have

$$\text{vertex} = \left(-\frac{b}{2a},\ f\left(-\frac{b}{2a}\right)\right).$$

This is also the vertex of a parabola that opens downward ($a < 0$), but in this case $f\left(-\dfrac{b}{2a}\right)$ is the *maximum* value of $f(x)$ [Fig. 12-6(b)]. In summary:

> The graph of the quadratic function $y = f(x) = ax^2 + bx + c$ is a parabola.
>
> 1. If $a > 0$, the parabola opens upward.
>   If $a < 0$, it opens downward.
> 2. The vertex occurs at $\left(-\dfrac{b}{2a}, f\left(-\dfrac{b}{2a}\right)\right)$.
> 3. The equation of the axis is $x = -\dfrac{b}{2a}$.

We can quickly sketch the graph of a quadratic function by first locating the vertex and a few other points on the graph. Frequently it is convenient to choose these other points to be those where the parabola intersects the x- and y-axes. These are called x- and y-**intercepts**, respectively. A y-intercept is obtained by setting $x = 0$ in $y = ax^2 + bx + c$ and solving for y. The x-intercepts are obtained by setting $y = 0$ and solving for x. Once the intercepts and vertex are found, it is then relatively easy to draw the appropriate parabola through these points. In case the x-intercepts are very close to the vertex, or no x-intercepts exist, we find a point on each side of the vertex so that we can give a reasonable sketch of the parabola.

example 1

Graph the following quadratic functions.

a. $y = f(x) = 12 - 4x - x^2$.

Here $a = -1$, $b = -4$, and $c = 12$. Because $a < 0$ the parabola opens downward. To find the vertex, we have

$$-\frac{b}{2a} = -\frac{-4}{2(-1)} = -2,$$

and

$$f\left(-\frac{b}{2a}\right) = f(-2) = 12 - 4(-2) - (-2)^2 = 16.$$

Thus the vertex (highest point) is $(-2, 16)$.

To find the y-intercept, we set $x = 0$. Then $y = 12 - 4(0) - 0^2 = 12$. Hence the y-intercept is 12. [More precisely, the y-intercept is the *point* $(0, 12)$.] To find the x-intercepts, we set $y = 0$. Then

$$0 = 12 - 4x - x^2$$
$$= (6 + x)(2 - x).$$

Thus $x = -6$ or $x = 2$, so the x-intercepts are -6 and 2. [That is, $(-6, 0)$ and $(2, 0)$.]

Now we plot the vertex and intercepts [Fig. 12-7(a)]. Through these points we draw a parabola opening downward [Fig. 12-7(b)].

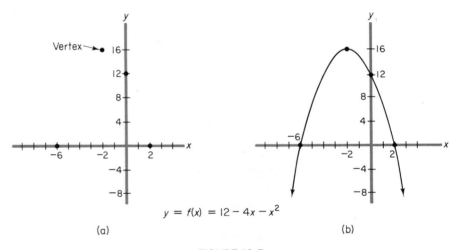

$$y = f(x) = 12 - 4x - x^2$$

(a)   (b)

FIGURE 12-7

b. $g(x) = x(x - 6) + 7$.

Because $g(x) = x^2 - 6x + 7$, g is a quadratic function where $a = 1$, $b = -6$, and $c = 7$. The parabola opens upward, since $a > 0$. Now,

$$-\frac{b}{2a} = -\frac{-6}{2(1)} = 3$$

and $g(3) = 3^2 - 6(3) + 7 = -2$. Thus the vertex (lowest point) is $(3, -2)$.

If $x = 0$, then $g(x) = 7$. Thus the vertical-axis intercept is 7. If $g(x) = 0$, then

$$0 = x^2 - 6x + 7.$$

Because the right side of this equation does not factor easily, we shall use the quadratic formula to solve for x.

$$x = \frac{-b \pm \sqrt{b^2 - 4ac}}{2a} = \frac{-(-6) \pm \sqrt{(-6)^2 - 4(1)(7)}}{2(1)}$$

$$= \frac{6 \pm \sqrt{8}}{2} = \frac{6 \pm \sqrt{4 \cdot 2}}{2} = \frac{6 \pm 2\sqrt{2}}{2}$$

$$= \frac{6}{2} \pm \frac{2\sqrt{2}}{2} = 3 \pm \sqrt{2}.$$

Thus the x-intercepts are $3 + \sqrt{2}$ and $3 - \sqrt{2}$, which are approximately 4.4 and 1.6, respectively.

After plotting the vertex and intercepts, we draw a parabola opening upward. See Fig. 12-8.

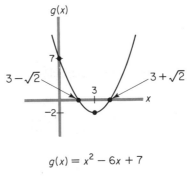

$$g(x) = x^2 - 6x + 7$$

FIGURE 12-8

example 2

The height s of a ball thrown vertically upward from the ground is given by the equation of motion

$$s = 19.6t - 4.9t^2,$$

where s is in meters and t is elapsed time in seconds. When does the ball reach its greatest height and what is that height?

Note that s is a quadratic function of t, where $a = -4.9$, $b = 19.6$, and $c = 0$. Because $a < 0$ (the parabola opens downward), then s is a maximum when

$$t = -\frac{b}{2a} = -\frac{19.6}{2(-4.9)} = 2.$$

The maximum value of s is

$$s = 19.6(2) - 4.9(2)^2 = 19.6.$$

Thus the maximum height is 19.6 m, which occurs after 2 s. Figure 12-9 shows the graph of the given function. Only the portion for which $s \geq 0$ is drawn, as the height cannot be negative.

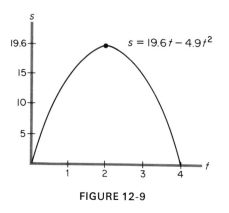

FIGURE 12-9

example 3

Find the dimensions of the rectangular region with perimeter 20 m that has the largest area.

We first point out that both rectangles in Fig. 12-10 have a perimeter of 20 m, but in (a) the area is 16 m² and in (b) it is 24 m². We want to obtain the *largest* possible area.

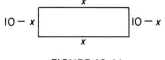

FIGURE 12-10

Suppose we denote the length of one side of the rectangle by x. Then the opposite side also has length x. This leaves a total of $20 - 2x$ to be divided equally between the other two sides. Hence each of these sides has length $(20 - 2x)/2$ or $10 - x$. An appropriate rectangle is shown in Fig. 12-11. You should verify that the perimeter is

FIGURE 12-11

20 m. Let A denote the area of the rectangle. Then

$$A = x(10 - x)$$
$$= 10x - x^2.$$

Here A is a quadratic function of x, where $a = -1$ and $b = 10$. Thus A has a maximum value when

$$x = -\frac{b}{2a} = -\frac{10}{2(-1)} = 5.$$

Therefore, to obtain the maximum area, the dimensions should be 5 by $10 - 5$, or simply 5 m by 5 m. In short, the rectangle should be a square. In this case, the area is 25 m².

Exercise 12-3

In Problems **1–8**, *state whether or not the function is quadratic.*

1. $f(x) = 26 - 3x$.

2. $g(x) = (7 - x)^2$.

3. $g(x) = 4x^2$.

4. $h(s) = 6(4s + 1)$.

5. $h(q) = \dfrac{1}{2q - 4}$.

6. $f(t) = 2t(3 - t) + 4t$.

7. $f(s) = \dfrac{s^2 - 4}{2}$.

8. $g(t) = (t^2 - 1)^2$.

In Problems **9–12**, *do not include a graph.*

9. For the parabola $y = f(x) = -4x^2 + 8x + 7$, (a) find the vertex. (b) Does the vertex correspond to the highest point, or the lowest point, on the graph?

10. Repeat Problem 9 if $y = f(x) = 8x^2 + 4x - 1$.

11. For the parabola $y = f(x) = x^2 + 2x - 8$, find (a) the y-intercept, (b) the x-intercepts, (c) the vertex, and (d) the equation of the axis.

12. Repeat Problem 11 if $y = f(x) = 3 + x - 2x^2$.

In Problems **13–22**, *graph the functions. Give the vertex and intercepts.*

13. $y = f(x) = x^2 - 6x + 5$.

14. $y = f(x) = -3x^2$.

15. $y = g(x) = -2x^2 - 6x$.

16. $y = f(x) = x^2 - 1$.

17. $s = h(t) = (t + 1)^2$.

18. $s = h(t) = 2t^2 + 3t - 2$.

19. $y = f(x) = 2x(4 - x) - 9$.

20. $y = H(x) = 1 - x - x^2$.

21. $t = f(s) = s^2 - 8s + 13$.

22. $t = f(s) = s^2 + 6s + 11$.

In Problems **23–26**, *state whether the function has a maximum value or a minimum value and find that value.*

23. $f(x) = 100x^2 - 20x + 25$.

24. $g(x) = -2x^2 - 16x + 3$.

25. $g(t) = 4t - (50 + 0.1t^2)$.

26. $y = x(x + 3) - 12$.

27. For the rectangle shown in Fig. 12-12, express its area as a quadratic function of x. For what value of x will the area be a maximum?

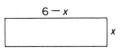

$6 - x$

x

FIGURE 12-12

28. An object is thrown vertically upward from the ground with an initial velocity of 58.8 m/s. Its displacement s from its starting point after t seconds have elapsed is given by

$$s = f(t) = -4.9t^2 + 58.8t,$$

where s is in meters. After how many seconds will the object reach its maximum height? What will this maximum height be? Sketch the graph of f.

29. A man wishes to fence in a rectangular plot adjacent to a building by using the building as one side of the enclosed area. If he has 200 m of fence, what should be the dimensions of the enclosed plot if the area is to be a maximum?

30. During a collision the force F (in newtons) that acted on an object varied with time t according to the equation $F = 87t - 21t^2$, where t is in seconds. (a) For what value of t was the force a maximum? (b) What was the maximum value of the force?

31. The displacement s of an object from a reference point at time t is given by

$$s = 3.2t^2 - 16t + 28.7,$$

where s in is meters and t is in seconds. (a) For what value of t does the minimum displacement occur? (b) What is the minimum displacement of the object from the reference point?

32. An 8 μC charge is divided into two parts having charges of q and $(8 - q)\,\mu$C. When placed 1 m apart, the Coulomb electrical force F between these charges is given by

$$F = 8kq - kq^2,$$

where k is a positive constant. For what value of q will F be a maximum?

33. When a horizontal beam of length l is uniformly loaded, the moment equation is

$$M = \frac{wlx}{2} - \frac{wx^2}{2},$$

where w is related to the load and x is measured from the left end of the beam. (a) For what value of x is M a maximum (assume $w > 0$)? (b) What is the maximum value of M? (c) For what values of x is $M = 0$?

12-4 Equations Leading to Quadratic Equations

Some types of equations that are not quadratic can lead to quadratic equations by algebraic operations. We shall consider three such types: fractional equations, radical equations, and equations in *quadratic form*.

A. Fractional Equations

Recall that to solve a fractional equation, we first clear the equation of fractions by multiplying both sides by the L.C.D. of the fractions involved. Since this operation does not guarantee that the resulting equation is equivalent to the original equation, it is important that any roots of the resulting equation be checked by substituting them in the original equation.

example 1

Solve $\dfrac{y+1}{y+3} + \dfrac{y+5}{y-2} = \dfrac{7(2y+1)}{y^2+y-6}$. (1)

Because $y^2 + y - 6 = (y+3)(y-2)$, we see that the L.C.D. is $(y+3)(y-2)$. Multiplying both sides by the L.C.D. gives

$$(y+3)(y-2)\left[\frac{y+1}{y+3} + \frac{y+5}{y-2}\right] = (y+3)(y-2)\left[\frac{7(2y+1)}{(y+3)(y-2)}\right]. \quad (2)$$

Because Eq. 1 was multiplied by an expression involving the variable y, remember that Eq. 2 is not necessarily equivalent to Eq. 1. After simplifying Eq. 2, we have

$$(y-2)(y+1) + (y+3)(y+5) = 7(2y+1)$$
$$y^2 - y - 2 + y^2 + 8y + 15 = 14y + 7$$
$$2y^2 + 7y + 13 = 14y + 7$$
$$2y^2 - 7y + 6 = 0 \qquad \text{(quadratic)}$$
$$(2y-3)(y-2) = 0.$$

$$
\begin{array}{c|c}
2y - 3 = 0 & y - 2 = 0 \\
2y = 3 & y = 2. \\
y = \tfrac{3}{2}. &
\end{array}
$$

Thus $\tfrac{3}{2}$ and 2 are *possible* roots of the given equation. But 2 cannot be a root of Eq. 1, as substitution leads to a denominator of 0. However, you should check that $\tfrac{3}{2}$ does indeed satisfy the *original* equation. Thus the only solution is $\tfrac{3}{2}$.

example 2

The rate of the current in a stream is 3 km/h. A man rowed upstream for 3 km and then returned to his starting point. The round trip took a total of one hour and twenty minutes. How fast could the man row in still water?

Let r be the rate (in kilometers per hour) at which the man can row in still water. Since the rate of the current is 3 km/h, the man's rate upstream was $r - 3$ and downstream it was $r + 3$. Since time = distance/rate and distance = 3 for each rate, we have

$$\left(\begin{array}{c}\text{time}\\\text{upstream}\end{array}\right) + \left(\begin{array}{c}\text{time}\\\text{downstream}\end{array}\right) = \text{total time}$$

$$\frac{3}{r-3} + \frac{3}{r+3} = \frac{4}{3}. \qquad \left(1\text{ h }20\text{ min} = \frac{4}{3}\text{ h}\right)$$

Multiplying both sides by $3(r-3)(r+3)$ and simplifying, we obtain

$$3(3)(r + 3) + 3(3)(r - 3) = 4(r - 3)(r + 3)$$
$$9r + 27 + 9r - 27 = 4[r^2 - 9]$$
$$18r = 4r^2 - 36$$
$$0 = 4r^2 - 18r - 36$$
$$0 = 2r^2 - 9r - 18 \quad \text{(dividing both sides by 2)}$$
$$0 = (2r + 3)(r - 6).$$

$$
\begin{array}{c|c}
2r + 3 = 0 & r - 6 = 0 \\
r = -\tfrac{3}{2}. & r = 6.
\end{array}
$$

The values $-\frac{3}{2}$ and 6 satisfy the original equation. But r is a rate, a positive number, so the only acceptable answer is 6 km/h.

B. Radical Equations

Recall that when solving a radical equation, we raise both sides to the same power to eliminate the radical. Again, you must check that any solutions obtained satisfy the original equation.

example 3

Solve $\sqrt{x + 2} - x + 4 = 0$.

It is best to rewrite the equation so that the radical is by itself on one side.

$$\sqrt{x + 2} = x - 4$$
$$x + 2 = (x - 4)^2 \qquad \text{(squaring both sides)}$$
$$x + 2 = x^2 - 8x + 16$$
$$0 = x^2 - 9x + 14$$
$$0 = (x - 7)(x - 2).$$

Thus

$$x = 7 \quad \text{or} \quad x = 2.$$

Now we check these values in the *original* equation.

Replacing x by 7 gives $\sqrt{7 + 2} - 7 + 4 = 0$ or $3 - 7 + 4 = 0$, which is *true*.
Replacing x by 2 gives $\sqrt{2 + 2} - 2 + 4 = 0$ or $2 - 2 + 4 = 0$, which is *false*.

Thus the solution is 7.

example 4

Solve $\sqrt{x + 6} - \sqrt{2x + 5} = -1$.

It is best to rewrite the equation so that only one radical expression appears in the left side:

$$\sqrt{x + 6} = \sqrt{2x + 5} - 1.$$

Squaring both sides and simplifying, we have

$$x + 6 = 2x + 5 - 2\sqrt{2x + 5} + 1$$
$$2\sqrt{2x + 5} = x.$$

Squaring both sides again gives

$$4(2x + 5) = x^2$$
$$8x + 20 = x^2.$$

Thus
$$x^2 - 8x - 20 = 0$$
$$(x - 10)(x + 2) = 0.$$
$$x = 10 \quad \text{or} \quad x = -2.$$

Substitution shows that the original equation is satisfied only for $x = 10$. Thus the solution is 10.

example 5

Solve $\sqrt[3]{x^2 + 18} = 3$.

Cubing both sides (because the index is 3), we have

$$x^2 + 18 = 27$$
$$x^2 = 9$$
$$x = \pm 3.$$

You may check that ± 3 are indeed solutions.

C. Equations in Quadratic Form

In some cases, an equation that is not quadratic can, by an appropriate substitution, be transformed into a quadratic equation. A few examples will illustrate how to solve such equations, which are said to be in **quadratic form**. In each case, a change of variable will be made.

example 6

Solve $x^4 - x^2 - 6 = 0$.

The equation is of the fourth degree but is quadratic in the variable x^2 because it can be written as

$$(x^2)^2 - (x^2) - 6 = 0.$$

By substituting the variable w for x^2, we obtain a quadratic equation in the variable w.

$$w^2 - w - 6 = 0$$
$$(w - 3)(w + 2) = 0$$
$$w = 3 \quad \text{or} \quad w = -2.$$

Since $w = x^2$, this means that either $x^2 = 3$ or $x^2 = -2$. Thus

$$x = \pm\sqrt{3}, \pm j\sqrt{2}.$$

By checking, we find that all four values of x satisfy the original equation. The solution can also be obtained by factoring the left side of the original equation, which gives $(x^2 - 3)(x^2 + 2) = 0$. Setting each of the factors equal to zero gives $x^2 - 3 = 0$ and $x^2 + 2 = 0$, from which $x = \pm\sqrt{3}, \pm j\sqrt{2}$.

example 7

Find all real roots of $\dfrac{1}{x^6} + \dfrac{9}{x^3} + 8 = 0$.

The equation is quadratic in form because it can be written as

$$\left(\frac{1}{x^3}\right)^2 + 9\left(\frac{1}{x^3}\right) + 8 = 0.$$

By substituting the variable w for $1/x^3$, we obtain a quadratic equation in w.

$$w^2 + 9w + 8 = 0$$
$$(w + 8)(w + 1) = 0$$
$$w = -8 \quad \text{or} \quad w = -1.$$

Returning to the variable x, we have

$$\frac{1}{x^3} = -8 \quad \text{or} \quad \frac{1}{x^3} = -1.$$

Equivalently,

$$x^3 = -\tfrac{1}{8} \quad \text{or} \quad x^3 = -1,$$

from which

$$x = -\tfrac{1}{2}, -1.$$

Checking, we find that these values of x satisfy the original equation. We point out that other cube roots of $-\tfrac{1}{8}$ or -1 can be found by using polar form and the method discussed previously for finding roots of a complex number.

Exercise 12-4

In Problems 1–16, solve the given fractional equation.

1. $\dfrac{x}{3} = \dfrac{6}{x} - 1.$

2. $\dfrac{1}{2x} - \dfrac{2x - 3}{4x} = \dfrac{3x}{4}.$

3. $\dfrac{1}{x^2} + \dfrac{6}{x} + 8 = 0.$

4. $\dfrac{1}{x} - \dfrac{2}{3x} = 3x.$

5. $\dfrac{3}{x-4} + \dfrac{x-3}{x} = 2.$

6. $\dfrac{1}{x^2} + \dfrac{1}{x} - 12 = 0.$

7. $\dfrac{2}{x-2} = \dfrac{x+1}{x+4}.$

8. $\dfrac{x}{x-1} = \dfrac{4}{x}.$

9. $\dfrac{x^2}{x-1} + 1 = \dfrac{1}{x-1}.$

10. $\dfrac{4-x}{x} + \dfrac{8}{4+x} = 1.$

11. $\dfrac{2}{x-1} - \dfrac{6}{2x+1} = 5.$

12. $\dfrac{x+1}{x} - \dfrac{6}{x+5} = \dfrac{3}{x}.$

13. $\dfrac{3}{x} - \dfrac{4}{x+2} = \dfrac{5}{3}.$

14. $x + \dfrac{2x}{x-2} = \dfrac{4}{x-2}.$

15. $\dfrac{3}{x+1} + \dfrac{4}{x} = \dfrac{12}{x+2}.$

16. $\dfrac{2}{x^2-1} - \dfrac{1}{x(x-1)} = \dfrac{2}{x^2}.$

In Problems 17–28, solve the given radical equation.

17. $\sqrt{x+2} = x - 4.$

18. $3\sqrt{x+4} = x - 6.$

19. $z + 2 = 2\sqrt{4z-7}.$

20. $x + \sqrt{x} - 2 = 0.$

21. $\sqrt{x+7} - \sqrt{2x} = 1.$

22. $\sqrt{3x} - \sqrt{5x+1} = -1.$

23. $\sqrt[3]{x^2+2} = 3.$

24. $\sqrt{x} + \sqrt{2x+7} - 8 = 0.$

25. $\sqrt{x} - \sqrt{2x+1} + 1 = 0.$

26. $\sqrt{x-2} + 2 = \sqrt{2x+3}.$

27. $\sqrt{x+5} + 1 = 2\sqrt{x}.$

28. $\sqrt{\sqrt{x}+2} = \sqrt{2x-4}.$

In Problems 29–44, solve the given quadratic-form equation.

29. $x^4 - x^2 - 6 = 0.$

30. $x^4 - 3x^2 - 10 = 0.$

31. $\dfrac{1}{x^2} + \dfrac{6}{x} + 8 = 0.$

32. $\dfrac{1}{x^2} + \dfrac{1}{x} - 12 = 0.$

33. $\dfrac{1}{x^4} - \dfrac{9}{x^2} + 14 = 0.$

34. $\dfrac{1}{x^4} - \dfrac{9}{x^2} + 8 = 0.$

35. $x - 2\sqrt{x} - 3 = 0.$

36. $6x - 5\sqrt{x} + 1 = 0.$

37. $(x-3)^2 + 9(x-3) + 14 = 0.$

38. $(x+5)^2 - 8(x+5) = 0.$

39. $\dfrac{1}{(x-2)^2} - \dfrac{12}{x-2} + 35 = 0.$

40. $\dfrac{2}{(x+4)^2} + \dfrac{7}{x+4} + 3 = 0.$

41. $(x^2+2)^2 + 12(x^2+2) + 11 = 0.$

42. $(x^2-5)^2 - 9(x^2-5) - 36 = 0.$

43. $y^{2/3} + y^{1/3} - 2 = 0.$

44. $2y^{-2/3} - 5y^{-1/3} - 3 = 0.$

45. In the ac circuit shown in Fig. 12-13, the impedance Z (in ohms) is given by

$$Z = \sqrt{R^2 + X^2},$$

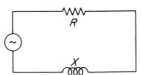

FIGURE 12-13

where R is the resistance (in ohms) and X is the reactance (in ohms). If $Z = 10$ and $R = 8$, find X if $X > 0$.

46. In a series ac circuit, resonance occurs when

$$2\pi f_r L = \frac{1}{2\pi f_r C},$$

where f_r is a resonant frequency, L is inductance, and C is capacitance. Solve for f_r if $f_r > 0$.

47. An object is 120 cm from a wall. In order to focus the image of the object on the wall, a converging lens with a focal length of 24 cm is to be used. The lens is placed between the object and the wall at a distance of p cm from the object, where

$$\frac{1}{p} + \frac{1}{120 - p} = \frac{1}{24}.$$

Find p to one decimal place.

48. If $\omega L = \dfrac{1}{\omega C}$ and $2\pi f_r = \omega$, show that

$$f_r = \frac{1}{2\pi\sqrt{LC}}.$$

Assume that all quantities are positive.

49. A boat traveled 36 km upstream on a river where the rate of the current was 3 km/h. It then returned. The round trip took 5 hours. Find the speed of the boat in still water.

50. A tank can be filled by two pipes used together in $3\frac{3}{4}$ hours. When used alone to fill the tank, the larger pipe can do it in 4 hours less time than the smaller pipe. What time is required for each pipe to fill it alone?

51. A small boat moving easterly out to sea with a speed of 10 m/s is 100 m from the nearest point A of a straight shoreline. A faster boat with a speed of 15 m/s starts from point B, which is 100 m south of A, to meet it. After how many seconds will the boats meet?

52. If a resistance R and reactance X are connected in parallel, the impedance Z of the circuit is given by

$$Z = \frac{RX}{\sqrt{R^2 + X^2}}.$$

Solve this equation for X.

53. The frequency of a damped vibration, ω_d (in radians per second), is given by

$$\omega_d = \sqrt{1 - d^2}\,\omega_n,$$

where ω_n is the natural frequency of the undamped vibration and d, a unitless constant, is called the *damping factor*. If $\omega_n = 25.4$ rad/s and $\omega_d = 24.1$ rad/s, find the damping factor, which is positive.

54. The mass m of an object moving with speed v (in meters per second) is given by

$$m = \frac{m_0}{\sqrt{1 - \dfrac{v^2}{c^2}}},$$

where m_0 is the rest mass of the object and $c = 3 \times 10^8$ m/s is the speed of light in vacuum. If $m = 1.5m_0$, find v.

12-5 Nonlinear Systems

A system of equations in which at least one equation is not linear is called a **nonlinear system**. Solutions of such systems may often be found algebraically by elimination by addition or elimination by substitution. Of course, the systems may be solved graphically, but one can only approximate the solutions in that case, and finding imaginary solutions (if desired) is impossible.

example 1

Solve
$$\begin{cases} x^2 - 2x + y - 7 = 0 & (1) \\ 3x - y + 1 = 0. & (2) \end{cases}$$

Solving Eq. 2 for y gives
$$y = 3x + 1. \qquad (3)$$
Substituting in Eq. 1 and simplifying, we have
$$x^2 - 2x + (3x + 1) - 7 = 0$$
$$x^2 + x - 6 = 0$$
$$(x + 3)(x - 2) = 0$$
$$x = -3 \quad \text{or} \quad x = 2.$$

From Eq. 3, if $x = -3$ then $y = -8$; if $x = 2$ then $y = 7$. You should verify that each pair of values satisfies the given system. Hence the solutions are $x = -3, y = -8$ and $x = 2, y = 7$. These solutions can be seen geometrically in the graph of the system in Fig. 12-14. Notice that the graph of Eq. 1 is a parabola and the graph of Eq. 2 is a line. The solutions correspond to the intersection points $(-3, -8)$ and $(2, 7)$.

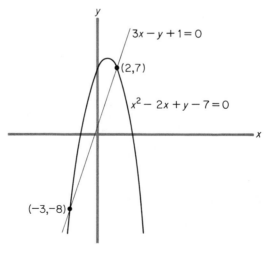

FIGURE 12-14

example 2

Solve

$$\begin{cases} y = \sqrt{x + 2} \\ x + y = 4. \end{cases}$$

Solving the second equation for y gives

$$y = 4 - x. \tag{4}$$

Substituting into the first equation gives

$$4 - x = \sqrt{x + 2}$$

$$16 - 8x + x^2 = x + 2 \qquad \text{(squaring both sides)}$$

$$x^2 - 9x + 14 = 0$$

$$(x - 2)(x - 7) = 0.$$

Thus $x = 2$ or $x = 7$. From Eq. 4, if $x = 2$, then $y = 2$; if $x = 7$, then $y = -3$. Although $x = 2$ and $y = 2$ satisfy the original equations, $x = 7$ and $y = -3$ do not. Thus the solution is $x = 2$, $y = 2$.

example 3

Solve

$$\begin{cases} x^2 + y^2 = 4 & (5) \\ 9x^2 + y^2 = 9. & (6) \end{cases}$$

Multiplying each side of Eq. 5 by -1 and adding to Eq. 6 gives

$$8x^2 = 5$$

$$x^2 = \frac{5}{8}$$

$$x = \pm\sqrt{\frac{5}{8}} = \pm\frac{\sqrt{10}}{4}.$$

Substituting $x = \sqrt{10}/4$ in Eq. 5 gives $y = \pm\frac{3}{4}\sqrt{6}$. Substituting $x = -\sqrt{10}/4$ in Eq. 5 gives $y = \pm\frac{3}{4}\sqrt{6}$. The four solutions are $x = \sqrt{10}/4$, $y = \pm3\sqrt{6}/4$ and $x = -\sqrt{10}/4$, $y = \pm3\sqrt{6}/4$. For illustrative purposes, the graphs of the given equations are shown in Fig. 12-15. The four points of intersection correspond to the four solutions.

example 4

Find all real solutions of

$$\begin{cases} 2x^2 + xy - y^2 = 20 & (7) \\ \qquad\qquad xy = 6. & (8) \end{cases}$$

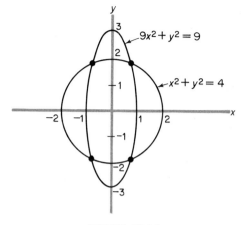

FIGURE 12-15

From Eq. 8, if $x \neq 0$, then $y = 6/x$. Substituting in Eq. 7, we have

$$2x^2 + x\left(\frac{6}{x}\right) - \left(\frac{6}{x}\right)^2 = 20$$

$$2x^2 + 6 - \frac{36}{x^2} = 20$$

$$2x^4 + 6x^2 - 36 = 20x^2 \qquad \text{(multiplying both sides by } x^2\text{)}$$

$$2x^4 - 14x^2 - 36 = 0$$

$$x^4 - 7x^2 - 18 = 0 \qquad \text{(dividing both sides by 2)}$$

$$(x^2 - 9)(x^2 + 2) = 0$$

$$(x + 3)(x - 3)(x^2 + 2) = 0.$$

Setting the first two factors equal to zero gives $x = \pm 3$. Substituting these values of x into the equation $y = 6/x$ gives the solutions $x = 3$, $y = 2$ and $x = -3$, $y = -2$, which check in the given system. The factor $x^2 + 2$ does not give rise to real solutions.

Exercise 12-5

In Problems **1–16**, *solve the nonlinear systems.*

1. $\begin{cases} 2x^2 - 3y^2 = 6 \\ 3x^2 - 2y^2 = 19. \end{cases}$ **2.** $\begin{cases} 2x^2 - 5y^2 = 10 \\ 3x^2 + 15y^2 = 195. \end{cases}$ **3.** $\begin{cases} y = 4 - x^2 \\ 3x + y = 0. \end{cases}$

4. $\begin{cases} y = x^3 \\ x - y = 0. \end{cases}$ **5.** $\begin{cases} p^2 = 4 - q \\ p = q + 2. \end{cases}$ **6.** $\begin{cases} y^2 - x^2 = 28 \\ x - y = 14. \end{cases}$

7. $\begin{cases} x = y^2 \\ y = x^2. \end{cases}$ **8.** $\begin{cases} p^2 - q = 0 \\ 3q - 2p - 1 = 0. \end{cases}$ **9.** $\begin{cases} y = 4x - x^2 + 8 \\ y = x^2 - 2x. \end{cases}$

10. $\begin{cases} x^2 - y = 8 \\ y - x^2 = 0. \end{cases}$ **11.** $\begin{cases} p = \sqrt{q} \\ p = q^2. \end{cases}$ **12.** $\begin{cases} z = \dfrac{4}{w} \\ 3z = 2w + 2. \end{cases}$

13. $\begin{cases} x^2 = y^2 + 14 \\ y = x^2 - 16. \end{cases}$ _hyperbola_   _parabola_

14. $\begin{cases} x^2 + y^2 - 2xy = 1 \\ 3x - y = 5. \end{cases}$

15. $\begin{cases} y = \dfrac{x^2}{x-1} + 1 \\ y = \dfrac{1}{x-1}. \end{cases}$

16. $\begin{cases} x = y + 6 \\ y = 3\sqrt{x+4}. \end{cases}$

17. In making stress tests, a technician uses four square sheets of glass. Exactly three of the sheets are identical in size. If the sum of the areas of the four sheets is 156 m² and the sum of their perimeters is 96 m, find the possible sizes of the sheets.

18. When wet, a rectangular cloth shrank one-eighth in length and one-sixteenth in width. If the original area of the cloth was reduced by 5.75 m² and the total length of the four sides was reduced by 4.25 m, find the original length and width of the cloth.

19. When a body A of mass 5 kg moving with a speed of 3 m/s undergoes a completely elastic collision with a body B of mass 2 kg initially at rest, the principles of conservation of linear momentum and kinetic energy yield the system of equations

$$\begin{cases} 5(3) = 5V_A + 2V_B \\ \tfrac{1}{2}(5)(3^2) = \tfrac{1}{2}(5)V_A^2 + \tfrac{1}{2}(2)(V_B^2), \end{cases}$$

where V_A and V_B are the speeds of bodies A and B after the collision. Find V_A and V_B.

20. Two bodies A and B are moving at constant rates and in the same direction around a circle 36 m in circumference. A makes one revolution in 3 seconds less time than B, and A and B meet every 18 seconds. What are their rates?

21. The equivalent capacitance C of two capacitors C_1 and C_2 connected in parallel is given by

$$C = C_1 + C_2.$$

If the capacitors are connected in series, the equivalent capacitance is given by

$$C = \frac{C_1 C_2}{C_1 + C_2}.$$

When two capacitors are connected in parallel, the equivalent capacitance in 9 μF; when connected in series the equivalent capacitance is 2 μF. Find the values of C_1 and C_2.

22. When two capacitors C_1 and C_2 are connected in parallel, the equivalent capacitance is 3.90 μF. When the same capacitors are connected in series, the equivalent capacitance is 0.867 μF. Find C_1 and C_2. (See Problem 21.)

23. A uniform beam is l meters long and weighs W newtons. When a pivot is placed 2.5 m from the left end, the beam can be balanced by a 30-N force applied at its left end [Fig. 12-16(a)]. When the 30-N force is applied to the right end of the beam, the beam can again be balanced at the same pivot when a force of 96 N is applied to the left end [Fig. 12-16(b)]. Find l and W. _Hint_: It may help to review Example 5 in Sec. 5-6.

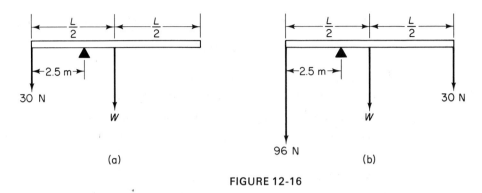

FIGURE 12-16

12-6   Review

Review Questions

1. A quadratic equation is of the _____(a)_____ degree and can be written in the form _____(b)_____ .

2. True or false: Every quadratic equation has two different roots. _____

3. The discriminant of $ax^2 + bx + c = 0$ is $(b^2 - 4ac)(\sqrt{b^2 - 4ac})$.

4. If the discriminant of a quadratic equation is (positive)(negative)(zero) , then the roots are imaginary.

5. If the discriminant of $ax^2 + bx + c = 0$ is (positive)(zero) , then the equation has only one solution.

6. The roots of $x^2(x - 2)(2x + 1)$ are equal to _____.

7. The roots of $x^2 - 4 = 0$ are equal to _____.

8. In the equation $(x - 5)(x - 5) = 0$, the root 5 is called a _____ root.

9. If the graph of $f(x) = ax^2 + bx + c = 0$ does not intersect the x-axis, then the equation $f(x) = 0$ has two (real)(imaginary) roots.

10. The roots of $x^2 + 100x = 0$ are equal to _____.

11. The equation $x^{2/3} + 3x^{1/3} - 6 = 0$ has quadratic form. We can transform the equation into a quadratic equation in w if we substitute w for _____.

12. To complete the square in the equation $x^2 - 7x = 0$, you would add the number _____ to both sides.

13. The discriminant of $2x^2 - 4x + 3 = 0$ is equal to _____.

14. Both roots of $2x^2 - 4x + 3 = 0$ are (real)(imaginary) .

15. The nonlinear system

$$\begin{cases} x^2 - 2xy - y^2 = 6 \\ 2x - y = 3 \end{cases}$$

can be solved easily for x by solving the   (first)(second)   equation for y and sub-
$$\text{(a)}$$
stituting this value in the   (first)(second)   equation.
$$\text{(b)}$$

16. The graph of $f(x) = 7x^2 + 3x - 5$ is called a _____.

17. The parabola $g(x) = x^2 - 1$ opens   (upward)(downward) .

18. The vertex of the parabola $f(x) = x^2 - 6x + 1$ occurs when $x =$ ____.

19. The graph of $y = -2x^2 + 4x - 3$ has a   (high)(low)   point when $x =$ (b) .
$$\text{(a)}$$

Answers to Review Questions

1. (a) Second,   (b) $ax^2 + bx + c = 0, a \neq 0$.   **2.** False.   **3.** $b^2 - 4ac$.   **4.** Negative.
5. Zero.   **6.** $0, 2, -\frac{1}{2}$.   **7.** ± 2.   **8.** Double, or repeated.   **9.** Imaginary.
10. $0, -100$.   **11.** $x^{1/3}$.   **12.** $\frac{49}{4}$.   **13.** -8.   **14.** Imaginary.
15. (a) Second,   (b) First.   **16.** Parabola.   **17.** Upward.   **18.** 3.   **19.** (a) High,   (b) 1.

Review Problems

In Problems 1–10, solve by factoring.

1. $x^2 - 10x + 25 = 0$.   2. $x^2 - 2x - 8 = 0$.   3. $x^2 - 2x - 24 = 0$.

4. $x^2 + 6x + 9 = 0$.   5. $12x^2 - 20x + 3 = 0$.   6. $4x^2 - 5x - 6 = 0$.

7. $x^2 - 12 = 0$.   8. $x^2 - 28 = 0$.   9. $2x^3 - x^2 = 0$.

10. $x^4 - 9x^2 = 0$.

In Problems 11–14, solve by completing the square.

11. $x^2 - 10x + 1 = 0$.   12. $x^2 + 8x - 5 = 0$.

13. $4x^2 + 12x - 2 = 0$.   14. $2x^2 - 2x - 3 = 0$.

In Problems 15–20, solve by the quadratic formula.

15. $x^2 - 6x + 7 = 0$.   16. $x^2 + 3x - 5 = 0$.   17. $4x^2 + 4x + 1 = 0$.

18. $3x^2 - 2x + 6 = 0$.   19. $2x - 5 - 2x^2 = 0$.   20. $25 - 20x + 4x^2 = 0$.

In Problems 21–48, solve.

21. $16x^2 - 9 = 0$.   22. $25x^2 - 3 = 1$.

23. $y^2 + 2y - 24 = 0$.   24. $y^2 + 4y - 21 = 0$.

25. $(z + 4)^2 = 36$.   26. $4z(z + 2) = -8 - 4z$.

27. $3(t - 1) = 2t^2$.   28. $100t^2 = 100t$.

29. $(x + 1)(x + 2) = 4$.   30. $x^2 + 5 = -(1 - x)$.

31. $4x^2 + 10x = -\dfrac{25}{4}$.   32. $\dfrac{3}{4}(x^2 - 2) = x$.

33. $\dfrac{x}{x-1} - \dfrac{9}{x+3} = 0.$

34. $\dfrac{1}{x^2} - \dfrac{9}{x} + 8 = 0.$

35. $\dfrac{x+1}{x} + \dfrac{2x}{x-2} = \dfrac{5x+1}{x}.$

36. $\dfrac{6x+7}{2x+1} - \dfrac{6x+1}{2x} = 1.$

37. $\dfrac{x}{x-1} - \dfrac{2}{x} + \dfrac{x-2}{x^2-x} = 0.$

38. $\sqrt{z^2+9} = 5.$

39. $\sqrt{2x+1} = x - 7.$

40. $\sqrt{x} - \sqrt{x+1} = 6.$

41. $x^{2/3} - x^{1/3} - 12 = 0.$

42. $x^4 + 5x^2 + 6 = 0.$

43. $x^{-2} + 10x^{-1} + 25 = 0.$

44. $x + 1 + 2\sqrt{x} = 0.$

45. $\begin{cases} y = \dfrac{18}{x+4} \\ x - y + 7 = 0. \end{cases}$

46. $\begin{cases} x^2 + y^2 = 15 \\ x^2 - y^2 = 13. \end{cases}$

47. $\begin{cases} x^2 - 2x + y = 36 \\ x - y = -6. \end{cases}$

48. $\begin{cases} x^2 - y + 2x = 7 \\ x^2 + y = 5. \end{cases}$

In Problems **49–52,** *graph each quadratic function. Give all intercepts and the vertex.*

49. $y = f(x) = 9 - x^2.$

50. $s = g(t) = 8 - 2t - t^2.$

51. $y = h(t) = t^2 - 4t - 5.$

52. $y = (2x - 1)^2.$

53. Find the maximum value of the function $y = -3x^2 + 6x - 4.$

54. Find the minimum value of the function $y = 4x^2 + 16x - 6.$

55. In studies of electrical networks, the following equation occurs:

$$S^2 + \dfrac{R}{L}S + \dfrac{1}{LC} = 0.$$

Show that

$$S = -\dfrac{R}{2L} \pm \sqrt{\left(\dfrac{R}{2L}\right)^2 - \dfrac{1}{LC}}.$$

56. In the kinetic theory of gases, it is shown that at a given temperature the kinetic energy of different gas molecules is the same. Given that

$$\tfrac{1}{2}m_1 v_1^2 = \tfrac{1}{2}m_2 v_2^2,$$

show that if $\dfrac{v_2}{v_1} > 0$, then

$$\dfrac{v_2}{v_1} = \sqrt{\dfrac{m_1}{m_2}}.$$

57. The height h of an object thrown straight upward from the ground is given by

$$h = 44.1t - 4.9t^2,$$

where h is in meters and t is elapsed time in seconds. (a) After how many seconds does the object strike the ground? (b) When is the object at a height of 88.2 m? (c) After how many seconds is the object at its maximum height? (d) What is the maximum height of the object?

58. The kinetic energy K of a particle is given by $K = \frac{1}{2}mv^2$, where m is the mass and v ($v > 0$) is the speed of the particle. The momentum p of the same particle is given by $p = mv$. Show that $p = \sqrt{2mK}$.

59. An open box is to be made from a square piece of tin by cutting out a 6-cm square from each corner and turning up the sides. The box will contain 150 cm^3. Find the *area* of the original square.

60. A square plot, 12 m by 12 m, is to be used for a garden. It is decided to put a pavement of uniform width inside the plot bordering three of the sides so that 80 m^2 of the plot is left for flowers. How wide should the pavement be?

13

exponential
and logarithmic
functions

13-1 Exponential Functions

Many physical quantities, such as the charge on a discharging capacitor, the temperature of a cooling body, and the amount of a radioactive substance, can be described mathematically by functions involving a constant raised to a variable power. These are called *exponential functions*. An example is $y = 2^x$. Do not confuse the exponential function $y = 2^x$ with the polynomial function $y = x^2$, which has a variable base and a constant exponent.

> The function f defined by
> $$y = f(x) = b^x,$$
> where $b > 0$, $b \neq 1$, and the exponent x is any real number, is called an **exponential function** to the base b.

We made the restriction $b \neq 1$ to exclude the rather simple constant function $f(x) = 1^x = 1$. Because the exponent in b^x can be any real number, the question arises concerning how we define something like $6^{\sqrt{2}}$. Stated simply, we use an approximation method. First, $6^{\sqrt{2}}$ is approximately $6^{1.4} = 6^{7/5} = \sqrt[5]{6^7}$, which *is* defined. Better approximations are $6^{1.41} = \sqrt[100]{6^{141}}$ and $6^{1.414}$. In this way a meaning of $6^{\sqrt{2}}$ becomes evident.

Figure 13-1 shows the graphs of the exponential functions $y = 2^x$, $y = 3^x$, and $y = \left(\frac{1}{2}\right)^x = \frac{1}{2^x} = 2^{-x}$. Notice that all the graphs contain the point $(0, 1)$, because $b^0 = 1$ for any base b.

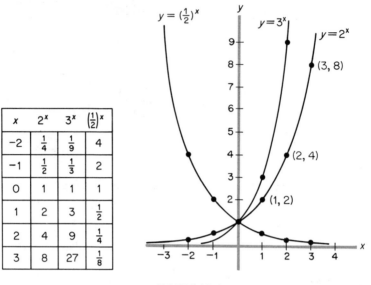

x	2^x	3^x	$\left(\frac{1}{2}\right)^x$
−2	$\frac{1}{4}$	$\frac{1}{9}$	4
−1	$\frac{1}{2}$	$\frac{1}{3}$	2
0	1	1	1
1	2	3	$\frac{1}{2}$
2	4	9	$\frac{1}{4}$
3	8	27	$\frac{1}{8}$

FIGURE 13-1

You can also see in Fig. 13-1 that the graph of $y = b^x$ has one of two basic shapes, depending on whether $b > 1$ or $0 < b < 1$. If $b > 1$ as in $y = 2^x$ and $y = 3^x$, then as x increases, y also increases. That is, the graph rises to the right. The larger the base, the more quickly the graph rises. But y can also take on values very close to zero. Notice how the graph of $y = 3^x$ gets close to the x-axis on the left. For example, if $x = -100$, then $3^x = 3^{-100} = 1/3^{100}$ is a number close to zero. On the other hand, suppose $0 < b < 1$, as in $y = (\frac{1}{2})^x$. Then as x increases, y *decreases*, taking on values close to zero. In all cases note that the graph of $y = b^x$ always lies above the x-axis. There is no x-intercept. Finally, we note that the domain of $y = b^x$ consists of all real numbers, and the range consists of all positive numbers.

One of the most important bases in $y = b^x$ is an irrational number denoted by the letter e, in honor of the Swiss mathematician and physicist Leonhard Euler (1707–1783):

e is approximately 2.71828. . . .

Although e seems to be a strange number to use as a base in an exponential function, it arises quite naturally in applied mathematics, science, and engineering technology. Values of e^x can be obtained conveniently by using the e^x key on a calculator. Figure 13-2 shows the graph of $y = e^x$.

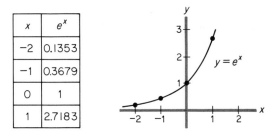

x	e^x
-2	0.1353
-1	0.3679
0	1
1	2.7183

FIGURE 13-2

There are many physical quantities for which the rate of growth or decay at any time is proportional to the amount of the quantity present at that time. Examples are bacteria growth, decay of a radioactive element, and the decay of a current in some electrical circuits. Such growth or decay can be described in terms of a function of the form

$$Q = Q(t) = Q_0 e^{kt}, \tag{1}$$

where Q is the amount of the quantity at time t, and Q_0 and k are constants. Due to the form of Eq. 1, we say that the quantity has **exponential growth** if $k > 0$ and **exponential decay** if $k < 0$.* If $t = 0$ in Eq. 1, then

$$Q = Q_0 e^0 = Q_0(1) = Q_0.$$

Thus Q_0 represents the amount of the quantity present when $t = 0$; that is, Q_0 is the initial amount.

With exponential decay, to stress that k is negative it is customary to replace k by $-\lambda$, where λ (lambda) is a positive constant called the **decay constant**. Thus Eq. 1 becomes

$$\boxed{Q = Q(t) = Q_0 e^{-\lambda t}.} \tag{2}$$

example 1

The number Q of milligrams of a radioactive substance present after t years is given by the exponential decay function

$$Q = Q(t) = 100e^{-0.035t}.$$

(a) How much of the substance is present initially? (b) How many milligrams are present after 20 years?

*Note that $e^{kt} = (e^k)^t = b^t$, where $b = e^k$. If $k > 0$, then $b > 1$ and so e^{kt} increases as t increases. If $k < 0$, then $b < 1$ and e^{kt} decreases as t increases.

a. Comparing the given equation to Eq. 2 gives $Q_0 = 100$. Thus there are 100 mg present initially. That is, the value of $Q(t)$ is 100 when $t = 0$.

b. After 20 years the amount present is $Q(20)$:

$$Q(20) = 100e^{-0.035(20)} = 100e^{-0.7}$$
$$= 100(0.4966) = 49.66 \text{ mg.}$$

The time required for one-half of a radioactive substance to decay is called the **half-life** of the substance. It is the value of t for which $Q = Q_0/2$ in Eq. 2. For example, the half-life of radioactive carbon 14 (^{14}C) is approximately 5600 years. Figure 13-3 shows the graph of radioactive decay.

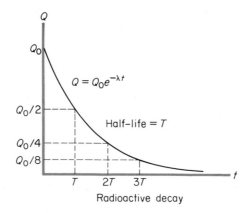

Radioactive decay

FIGURE 13-3

Exercise 13-1

In Problems 1–4, graph the function.

1. $y = 4^x$.

2. $y = (\frac{1}{3})^x$.

3. $f(t) = (\frac{1}{4})^t$.

4. $f(t) = 3^{t/2}$.

In Problems 5–8, use a calculator to find the value of the given number to four decimal places.

5. $e^{2.4}$.

6. $e^{0.06}$.

7. $e^{-4.2}$.

8. $e^{-3.67}e^{2.87}$.

In Problems 9–14, find the functional values without the use of a calculator.

9. $f(x) = 9^x$; $f(2)$, $f(-2)$, $f(\frac{1}{2})$.

10. $g(x) = 4(3)^x$; $g(0)$, $g(2)$, $g(-1)$.

11. $h(t) = 3(16)^{t/2}$; $h(1)$, $h(\frac{1}{2})$, $h(-\frac{1}{2})$.

12. $f(t) = 5 - (\frac{1}{2})^t$; $f(2)$, $f(3)$, $f(-3)$.

13. $g(x) = 1 + 2(\frac{1}{8})^{1-x}$; $\quad g(1)$, $\quad g(-1)$, $\quad g(\frac{1}{3})$.

14. $h(x) = \dfrac{6(.25)^{(4-x)/2}}{5}$; $\quad h(0)$, $\quad h(2)$, $\quad h(3)$.

15. The number Q of milligrams of a radioactive substance present after t years is given by $Q = 75e^{-0.0244t}$. (a) How much of the substance is present initially? (b) How many milligrams are present after 14 years?

16. Show that the exponential decay function in Problem 15 can be expressed as $Q = 75(0.976)^t$.

17. The decaying current i, in amperes, in an ac circuit is given by $i = 10e^{-2t} \sin (100t)$, where time t is in seconds and the angle $100t$ is in radians. Find the current when $t = 1.2$ s.

18. The charge q on a discharging capacitor is given by $q = 8e^{-2.8t}$, where t is time in seconds and q is in microcoulombs. Find q when $t = 0.3$ s.

13-2 Logarithmic Functions

Another important type of function is a *logarithmic function*, which is related to an exponential function. Figure 13-4 shows the graph of the exponential function $s = f(t) = 2^t$. The function f sends an input number t into a *positive* output number s. For example, f sends 2 into 4: $f(2) = 4$.

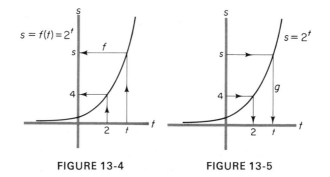

FIGURE 13-4   FIGURE 13-5

Now look at the same curve in Fig. 13-5. You can see that with each positive number s, we can associate exactly one value of t. Notice that with $s = 4$, we associate $t = 2$. If we think here of s as an input and t as an output, then we have a function that sends values of s into values of t. We shall denote this function by g. Thus

$$g(s) = t, \quad \text{where} \quad s = 2^t.$$

The functions f and g are related. In Fig. 13-6 you can see that g *reverses* the action of f, and vice versa. For example,

f sends 2 into 4, and g sends 4 into 2.

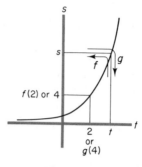

FIGURE 13-6

Notice that the domain of g is the range of f (all positive numbers), and the range of g is the domain of f (all real numbers).

We give a special name to g. It is called the **logarithmic function base 2**. Usually we write g as $\log_2$ (read *log base* 2). Thus $\log_2$ is merely a symbol for a special function.

In summary, if

$$s = f(t) = 2^t, \quad \text{then} \quad g(s) = \log_2(s) = t. \tag{1}$$

For example, $\log_2 4 = 2$.

Generalizing to other bases and replacing s by x and t by y in (1), we have the following definition.

> The **logarithmic function base b** is denoted by $\log_b$ and
> $$y = \log_b x \quad \text{if and only if} \quad b^y = x.$$
> The domain of $\log_b$ is all positive numbers, and the range is all real numbers.

Because the logarithmic function reverses the action of the exponential function, we say that the logarithmic function is the *inverse* of the exponential function. Similarly, the exponential function is the inverse of the logarithmic function.

Remember: When we say that the logarithm base b of x is the number y, we mean that b raised to the y power is x.

> $$\log_b x = y \quad \textbf{means} \quad b^y = x.$$

In this sense, *the logarithm of a number is an exponent*. It is the power to which we must raise the base to obtain the given number. For example,

$$\log_2 8 = 3 \quad \text{because} \quad 2^3 = 8.$$

We say that $\log_2 8 = 3$ is the **logarithmic form** of the **exponential form** $2^3 = 8$.

example 1

		Exponential form		Logarithmic form
a.	Since	$5^2 = 25,$	then	$\log_5 25 = 2.$
b.	Since	$3^4 = 81,$	then	$\log_3 81 = 4.$
c.	Since	$10^0 = 1,$	then	$\log_{10} 1 = 0.$

example 2

	Logarithmic form		Exponential form
a.	$\log_{10} 1000 = 3$	means	$10^3 = 1000.$
b.	$\log_{64} 8 = \frac{1}{2}$	means	$64^{1/2} = 8.$
c.	$\log_2 \frac{1}{16} = -4$	means	$2^{-4} = \frac{1}{16}.$

example 3

Graph the function $y = \log_2 x$.

To determine points, it is convenient to use the equivalent exponential form $x = 2^y$. If $y = 0$, then $x = 2^0 = 1$. This gives the point $(1, 0)$. When $y = 2$, then $x = 2^2 = 4$, and when $y = -1$, we have $x = 2^{-1} = \frac{1}{2}$. This gives the points $(4, 2)$ and $(\frac{1}{2}, -1)$. Other points are shown in Fig. 13-7. Note that the domain is all positive numbers; *negative numbers and zero do not have logarithms*, because any power of 2 is positive. The range is all real numbers. Observe that as x increases, y increases. Finally, we emphasize that *the graph of $y = \log_2 x$ is identical to the graph of $x = 2^y$.*

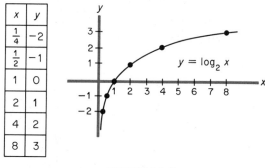

x	y
$\frac{1}{4}$	-2
$\frac{1}{2}$	-1
1	0
2	1
4	2
8	3

FIGURE 13-7

Figure 13-8 shows the graphs of the basic exponential and logarithmic functions $y = b^x$ and $y = \log_b x$ for $b > 1$. Notice that the graph of $y = \log_b x$ has the same shape as that of $y = \log_2 x$ in Fig 13-7. It is also clear from Fig. 13-8 that if $0 < x < 1$, then $\log_b x$ is negative; if $x > 1$, then $\log_b x$ is positive; if $x = 1$, then $\log_b x = 0$.

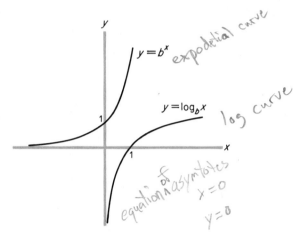

FIGURE 13-8

Because the graph of $y = \log_b x$ in Fig. 13-8 is always rising, it is obvious that if two numbers are different, then their logarithms are different. This means that:

> If $\log_b m = \log_b n$, then $m = n$. (1)

There is a similar property for the exponential function:

> If $b^m = b^n$, then $m = n$. (2)

Logarithms to the base 10 are called **common logarithms**. The subscript 10 is generally omitted from the notation. Thus

> $\log x$ means $\log_{10} x$.

Logarithms to the base e are called **natural** (or Naperian) **logarithms**. We use the symbol ln for such logarithms. Thus

> $\ln x$ means $\log_e x$.

Common and natural logarithms of numbers can be found with a calculator by using the log and ln keys, respectively. For example, you should verify that $\ln 2 \approx 0.69315$. This means that $e^{0.69315} \approx 2$.

example 4

Find each of the following without the aid of a calculator.

a. log 1000.

Here the base is 10. Thus log 1000 is the power to which we must raise 10 in order to get 1000. Because $10^3 = 1000$, we have log 1000 = 3.

b. log 0.0001.

Because $0.0001 = 10^{-4}$, then log 0.0001 = −4.

c. ln e.

Here the base is e. Because $e^1 = e$, ln e = 1.

d. ln 0.

For *any* base b, $\log_b 0$ is undefined.

e. $\log_{36} 6$.

Because $\sqrt{36} = 36^{1/2} = 6$, $\log_{36} 6 = \frac{1}{2}$.

example 5

Solve each equation for x.

a. $e^{0.2x} = 6$.

In logarithmic form,

$$0.2x = \ln 6$$

$$x = \frac{\ln 6}{0.2} = \frac{1.7918}{0.2} = 8.959.$$

b. $\log_3 x = 4$.

In exponential form, $3^4 = x$. Thus $x = 81$.

c. $x + 1 = \log_4 16$.

Because $\log_4 16$ is 2, we have $x + 1 = 2$, from which $x = 1$. If you did not recognize that $\log_4 16 = 2$, then you could solve the equation in the following way.

$$x + 1 = \log_4 16$$

$$4^{x+1} = 16 \qquad \text{(converting to exponential form).}$$

$$4^{x+1} = 4^2.$$

From property (2), $x + 1 = 2$, so $x = 1$.

d. $\log_x 49 = 2$.

$$\log_x 49 = 2$$
$$x^2 = 49$$
$$x = \pm 7.$$

A negative number cannot be a base for a logarithm, so we disregard $x = -7$ and choose $x = 7$.

When the logarithm of a number N is known, the process of finding N is referred to as finding the **antilogarithm**. Because this involves reversing the action of the logarithmic function, we can make use of the 10^x, e^x, or y^x exponential keys on a calculator, as the following examples show.

example 6

a. If $\log N = 4.86052$, find N. That is, find antilog 4.86052.

Because $\log N = 4.86052$, in exponential form we have

$$N = 10^{4.86052} = 72{,}530.$$

That is, antilog 4.86052 = 72,530.

b. If $\ln N = -5.37737$, find N. That is, find antilog$_e$ (-5.37737).

$$\text{antilog}_e\,(-5.37737) = e^{-5.37737} = 4.62 \times 10^{-3}.$$

Thus $N = 4.62 \times 10^{-3}$.

In the previous section the exponential decay function $Q = Q_0 e^{-\lambda t}$ was discussed. Recall that the value of t when $Q = Q_0/2$ is the half-life of a radioactive substance. We wish to find a formula for this value of t.

$$\frac{Q_0}{2} = Q_0 e^{-\lambda t},$$

$$\frac{1}{2} = e^{-\lambda t} \qquad \text{(dividing both sides by } Q_0\text{)}.$$

In logarithmic form we have

$$-\lambda t = \ln \frac{1}{2} = -0.69315,$$

which means

$$\boxed{t = \frac{0.69315}{\lambda}.}$$

(3)

Note that the half-life depends on λ. That is, it depends on the substance and not on the amount of the substance.

example 7

If 60 percent of a radioactive element remains after 50 days, find the decay constant and the half-life of the element.

We use the function $Q = Q_0 e^{-\lambda t}$, where Q_0 is the amount of the element present at $t = 0$ and λ is the decay constant. Because $Q = 0.6Q_0$ when $t = 50$, we have

$$0.6Q_0 = Q_0 e^{-50\lambda}$$
$$0.6 = e^{-50\lambda}$$
$$-50\lambda = \ln 0.6 \qquad \text{(logarithmic form)}$$
$$\lambda = -\frac{1}{50}\ln 0.6 = -\frac{1}{50}(-0.51083)$$
$$= 0.01022.$$

Thus $Q = Q_0 e^{-0.01022t}$. The half-life, from Eq. 3, is

$$\frac{0.69315}{\lambda} = \frac{0.69315}{0.01022} = 67.82 \text{ days.}$$

Note that the unit of λ is the unit of $1/\text{time}$. Here the unit is $1/\text{day} = (\text{day})^{-1}$.

Exercise 13-2

In Problems 1–16, write each exponential form logarithmically and each logarithmic form exponentially.

1. $4^3 = 64$.

2. $2 = \log_{12} 144$.

3. $10^5 = 100{,}000$.

4. $\log_9 3 = \frac{1}{2}$.

5. $\log_2 64 = 6$.

6. $4^4 = 256$.

7. $\log_8 2 = \frac{1}{3}$.

8. $8^{2/3} = 4$.

9. $6^0 = 1$.

10. $\log_{1/2} 4 = -2$.

11. $\log_2 x = 14$.

12. $10^{0.48302} = 3.041$.

13. $e^2 = 7.3891$.

14. $e^{0.33647} = 1.4$.

15. $\ln 3 = 1.0986$.

16. $\log 5 = 0.6990$.

In Problems 17 and 18, graph the function.

17. $y = f(x) = \log_3 x$.

18. $y = f(x) = \log_{1/2} x$.

In Problems 19–22, use a calculator to find the value of the given number to four decimal places.

19. $\ln 7.34$

20. $\ln 3.1$

21. $\log 0.2538$

22. $\log 5988$

In Problems 23–36, find the value of each number without the aid of a calculator.

23. $\log_6 36$.

24. $\log_2 32$.

25. $\log_3 27$.

26. $\log_{27} 3$.

27. $\log_{16} 4$.

28. $\log_7 7$.

29. $\log 10$.

30. $\log 10{,}000$.

31. $\log 0.01$.

32. $\ln (e^4)$.

33. $\log_5 1$.

34. $\log_2 \sqrt{2}$.

35. $\log_2 \frac{1}{8}$.

36. $\log_5 \frac{1}{25}$.

In Problems 37–60, find x without the aid of a calculator.

37. $\log_3 x = 2$.

38. $\log_2 x = 4$.

39. $\log_5 x = 3$.

40. $\log_4 x = 0$.

41. $\log x = -1$.

42. $\ln x = 1$.

43. $\ln x = 2$.

44. $\log_x 100 = 2$.

45. $\log_x 8 = 3$.

46. $\log_x 3 = \frac{1}{2}$.

47. $\log_x \frac{1}{6} = -1$.

48. $\log_x y = 1$.

49. $\log_4 16 = x$.

50. $\log_3 1 = x$.

51. $\log 10^{-7} = x$.

52. $\log_2 \frac{1}{16} = x$.

53. $\log_{25} 5 = x$.

54. $\log_9 9 = x$.

55. $\log_3 x = -4$.

56. $\log_x (2x - 3) = 1$.

57. $\log_x (6 - x) = 2$.

58. $\log_8 64 = x - 1$.

59. $2 + \log_2 4 = 3x - 1$.

60. $\log_3 (x + 2) = -2$.

In Problems 61–68, find x to three decimal places.

61. $e^{3x} = 2$.

62. $e^{2x-5} + 1 = 4$.

63. $0.1e^{0.1x} = 0.5$.

64. $3e^{2x} - 1 = \frac{1}{2}$.

65. $\log x = 2.35$.

66. $\log x = -0.78$.

67. $\ln x = -0.03$.

68. $\ln x = 4.295$.

69. In chemistry, the acidity or basicity of an aqueous solution at room temperature is determined by finding the pH of the solution. If the hydrogen-ion concentration is denoted by $[H^+]$, then the pH is given by

$$pH = -\log [H^+].$$

If pH < 7, the solution is acidic. If pH > 7, it is basic. If pH $= 7$, the solution is said to be neutral.

(a) What is the pH of vinegar with $[H^+]$ equal to 3×10^{-4}?

(b) An ammonia cleaning solution has a pH of 7.85. What is the $[H^+]$ of this solution?

70. If $\ln \dfrac{V}{V_0} = -\dfrac{t}{RC}$, solve for V.

71. The intensity level β of a sound wave of intensity I is defined by

$$\beta = 10 \log \frac{I}{I_0},$$

where I_0 is a reference intensity taken to be 10^{-12} W/m^2, which corresponds, approximately, to the faintest audible sound. The intensity level is measured in decibels (db). If a second source has an intensity of 3×10^{-10} W/m^2, what is its intensity level to the nearest tenth of a decibel?

72. The work, in joules, done by a 1-kg sample of nitrogen gas as its volume changes from an initial value V_i to a final value V_f during an isothermal (constant-temperature) process is given by

$$W = 8.1 \times 10^4 \ln \frac{V_f}{V_i}.$$

If such a sample expands isothermally from a volume of 3 liters to a volume of 7 liters, determine the work done by the gas to the nearest hundred joules.

73. Atmospheric pressure p varies with the altitude h above the earth's surface. For altitudes up to about 10 km, the pressure p (in millimeters of mercury) is given approximately by

$$p = 760e^{-0.125h},$$

where h is in kilometers. (a) Find p at an altitude of 7.3 km. (b) At what altitude will the pressure be 400 mm of mercury?

74. In studies of electric fields, one may encounter a device called a cylindrical capacitor, two concentric cylindrical conductors. The capacitance per unit length of such a device, in microfarads per meter, can be shown to be *inversely* proportional to

$$\ln \frac{r_0}{r_i},$$

where r_0 and r_i are the radii of the outer and inner cylinders, respectively. If the capacitance per unit length of a particular cylindrical capacitor is 10 μF/m when the outer radius is twice the inner radius, find the capacitance per unit length when it is three times the inner radius.

75. If 30 percent of the initial amount of a radioactive sample *remains* after 100 seconds, find the decay constant and the half-life of the element. (Refer to Example 7.)

76. If 30 percent of the initial amount of a radioactive sample *has decayed* after 100 seconds, find the decay constant and the half-life of the element. (Refer to Example 7.)

77. Radon has a half-life of 3.82 days. (a) Find the decay constant. (b) What fraction of the original amount of it remains after 7.64 days? *Hint*: The fraction of the original amount at any time is given by Q/Q_0.

13-3   Properties of Logarithms

Because logarithms are exponents, their properties can be obtained by using properties of exponents. For example, we shall consider the logarithm of a product, such as $\log_b (mn)$. If we let $x = \log_b m$ and $y = \log_b n$, then $b^x = m$ and $b^y = n$. Therefore,

$$mn = b^x b^y = b^{x+y}.$$

Thus $mn = b^{x+y}$. Converting this to logarithmic form gives $\log_b (mn) = x + y$. But, from above, $x = \log_b m$ and $y = \log_b n$. Thus we have our first property.

PROPERTY 1

$$\log_b (mn) = \log_b m + \log_b n.$$

That is, *the logarithm of the product of two numbers is the sum of the logarithms of the numbers.* For example, $\log (3 \cdot 5) = \log 3 + \log 5$.

In some of the examples and exercises that follow, we shall use Table 13-1, which gives the values of a few common logarithms. This table, which you should verify with a calculator, is useful in illustrating the many properties of logarithms.

Table 13-1 Common logarithms

x	log x	x	log x
2	0.3010	7	0.8451
3	0.4771	8	0.9031
4	0.6021	9	0.9542
5	0.6990	10	1.0000
6	0.7782	e	0.4343

example 1

Use Table 13-1 to find each of the following.

a. log 15.

Log 15 is not in Table 13-1. But we can write 15 as the product $3 \cdot 5$. Thus

$$\log 15 = \log (3 \cdot 5)$$
$$= \log 3 + \log 5 \qquad \text{(Property 1)}$$
$$= 0.4771 + 0.6990 \qquad \text{(Table 13-1)}$$
$$\log 15 = 1.1761.$$

b. log 56.

$$\log 56 = \log (8 \cdot 7) = \log 8 + \log 7 = 0.9031 + 0.8451 = 1.7482.$$

The next two properties can be proved in the same way as Property 1.

PROPERTY 2

$$\log_b \frac{m}{n} = \log_b m - \log_b n.$$

That is, *the logarithm of a quotient is equal to the logarithm of the numerator minus the logarithm of the denominator.* For example, $\log \frac{2}{3} = \log 2 - \log 3$.

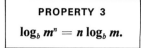

PROPERTY 3

$\log_b m^n = n \log_b m.$

That is, *the logarithm of the nth power of a number is equal to n times the logarithm of the number.* For example, $\log 2^8 = 8 \log 2$. Note that $\log 2^8 \neq (\log 2)^8$.

We point out that the logarithm of a sum is *not* the sum of logarithms. In general,

$$\log_b (m + n) \neq \log_b m + \log_b n$$

and

$$\log_b (m - n) \neq \log_b m - \log_b n.$$

Also,

$$\log_b (mn) \neq (\log_b m)(\log_b n)$$

and

$$\log_b \frac{m}{n} \neq \frac{\log_b m}{\log_b n}.$$

example 2

Use Table 13-1 to find each of the following.

a. $\log \frac{9}{2}$.

$$\log \frac{9}{2} = \log 9 - \log 2 \qquad \text{(Property 2)}$$
$$= 0.9542 - 0.3010 \qquad \text{(Table 13-1)}.$$
$$\log \frac{9}{2} = 0.6532.$$

b. $\log 64$.

$$\log 64 = \log (8^2)$$
$$= 2 \log 8 \qquad \text{(Property 3)}$$
$$= 2(0.9031) \qquad \text{(Table 13-1)}.$$
$$\log 64 = 1.8062.$$

c. $\log \sqrt{5}$.

$$\log \sqrt{5} = \log (5^{1/2}) = \frac{1}{2} \log 5 = \frac{1}{2}(0.6990) = 0.3495.$$

d. $\log \frac{15}{7}$.

$$\log \frac{15}{7} = \log 15 - \log 7 = \log (3 \cdot 5) - \log 7$$
$$= [\log 3 + \log 5] - \log 7$$
$$= [0.4771 + 0.6990] - 0.8451 = 0.3310.$$

e. $\log \frac{16}{21}$.

$$\log \frac{16}{21} = \log 16 - \log 21 = \log (4^2) - \log (3 \cdot 7)$$
$$= 2 \log 4 - [\log 3 + \log 7]$$
$$= 2(0.6021) - [0.4771 + 0.8451] = -0.1180.$$

example 3

a. $\log [(a)(b)(c)] = \log [(ab)(c)]$
$$= \log (ab) + \log c$$
$$= \log a + \log b + \log c.$$

This technique can, of course, be extended to the logarithm of any number of factors.

b. Do not confuse $\log x^2$ with $(\log x)^2$. We have $\log x^2 = 2 \log x$, but $(\log x)^2 = (\log x)(\log x)$.

c. $\log [a(b + c)] = \log a + \log (b + c)$. Note that $\log (b + c)$ cannot be simplified; $\log (b + c) \neq \log b + \log c$.

example 4

a. Write $\log_3 \frac{1}{x^2}$ in terms of $\log_3 x$.

$$\log_3 \frac{1}{x^2} = \log_3 x^{-2} = -2 \log_3 x \qquad \text{(Property 3)}.$$

b. Write $\log_4 x - \log_4 (x + 3)$ as a single logarithm.

$$\log_4 x - \log_4 (x + 3) = \log_4 \frac{x}{x + 3} \qquad \text{(Property 2)}.$$

c. Write $3 \log_2 10 + \log_2 15$ as a single logarithm.

$$3 \log_2 10 + \log_2 15 = \log_2 (10^3) + \log_2 15 \qquad \text{(Property 3)}$$
$$= \log_2 [(10^3)15] \qquad \text{(Property 1)}$$
$$= \log_2 15,000.$$

d. Write $\ln 3 + \ln 7 - \ln 2 - 2 \ln 4$ as a single logarithm.

$$\ln 3 + \ln 7 - \ln 2 - 2 \ln 4 = \ln 3 + \ln 7 - \ln 2 - \ln (4^2)$$
$$= \ln 3 + \ln 7 - [\ln 2 + \ln (4^2)]$$
$$= \ln (3 \cdot 7) - \ln [2 \cdot 4^2]$$
$$= \ln 21 - \ln 32$$
$$= \ln \frac{21}{32}.$$

e. Write $-\log \frac{x}{2}$ without using a minus sign.

$$-\log \frac{x}{2} = (-1) \log \frac{x}{2}$$
$$= \log \left(\frac{x}{2}\right)^{-1} \qquad \text{(Property 3)}$$
$$= \log \frac{2}{x}$$

example 5

a. Write $\log_6 \frac{x^5 y}{zw}$ in terms of $\log_6 x$, $\log_6 y$, $\log_6 z$, and $\log_6 w$.

$$\log_6 \frac{x^5 y}{zw} = \log_6 (x^5 y) - \log_6 (zw)$$
$$= \log_6 (x^5) + \log_6 y - (\log_6 z + \log_6 w)$$
$$= 5 \log_6 x + \log_6 y - \log_6 z - \log_6 w.$$

b. Write $\ln \sqrt[3]{\frac{x^5(x-2)^8}{x-3}}$ in terms of $\ln x$, $\ln (x-2)$, and $\ln (x-3)$.

$$\ln \sqrt[3]{\frac{x^5(x-2)^8}{x-3}} = \ln \left[\frac{x^5(x-2)^8}{x-3}\right]^{1/3} = \frac{1}{3} \ln \frac{x^5(x-2)^8}{x-3}$$
$$= \frac{1}{3}\{\ln [x^5(x-2)^8] - \ln (x-3)\}$$
$$= \frac{1}{3}[\ln x^5 + \ln (x-2)^8 - \ln (x-3)]$$
$$= \frac{1}{3}[5 \ln x + 8 \ln (x-2) - \ln (x-3)].$$

Because $b^0 = 1$ and $b^1 = b$, then by converting to logarithmic forms we have the following properties:

> **PROPERTY 4**
>
> $\log_b 1 = 0$.
>
> **PROPERTY 5**
>
> $\log_b b = 1$.

example 6

Find each of the following.

a. $\log 1$.

$$\log 1 = \log_{10} 1 = 0 \qquad \text{(Property 4)}.$$

b. $\ln e$.

$$\ln e = \log_e e = 1 \qquad \text{(Property 5)}.$$

c. $\log 1000$.

$$\log 1000 = \log_{10} 10^3 = 3 \log_{10} 10$$
$$= 3 \cdot 1 \qquad \text{(Property 5)}$$
$$= 3.$$

d. $\log (10^n)$.

$$\log (10^n) = n \log_{10} 10 = n \cdot 1 = n.$$

In general, for any base b and any real number n we have

> **PROPERTY 6**
>
> $\log_b b^n = n$.

example 7

a. Find $\log_7 \sqrt[9]{7^8}$.

$$\log_7 \sqrt[9]{7^8} = \log_7 (7^{8/9}) = \frac{8}{9} \qquad \text{(Property 6)}.$$

b. Find $\log_3 \dfrac{27}{81}$.

$$\log_3 \frac{27}{81} = \log_3 \frac{3^3}{3^4} = \log_3 (3^{-1}) = -1.$$

c. Find $\ln (e^2) + \log \dfrac{1}{10}$.

$$\ln (e^2) + \log \frac{1}{10} = 2 + \log 10^{-1} = 2 + (-1) = 1.$$

d. Find $\log \frac{200}{21}$ by using Table 13-1.

$$\log \frac{200}{21} = \log 200 - \log 21 = \log (2 \cdot 10^2) - \log (3 \cdot 7)$$
$$= \log 2 + \log (10^2) - (\log 3 + \log 7)$$
$$= \log 2 + 2 - \log 3 - \log 7$$
$$= 0.3010 + 2 - 0.4771 - 0.8451$$
$$= 0.9788.$$

Exercise 13-3

In Problems 1–18, use Table 13-1 and properties of logarithms to find the given values.

1. $\log 35$.

2. $\log 12$.

3. $\log \frac{9}{4}$.

4. $\log \frac{7}{10}$.

5. $\log 25$.

6. $\log 0.0001$.

7. $\log 2000$.

8. $\log (3 \times 10^4)$.

9. $\log 10^5$.

10. $\log_5 (5\sqrt{5})^5$.

11. $\log_2 (2^6/2^{10})$.

12. $\log \sqrt[3]{400}$.

13. $\ln \frac{1}{e}$.

14. $\ln e^4$.

15. $\log_3 \sqrt[3]{3}$.

16. $\log 10^{10}$.

17. $\log 10 + \ln e^3$.

18. $\log 10^e$.

In Problems 19–28, write the given expression in terms of $\log x$, $\log y$, and $\log z$.

19. $\log (xy)$.

20. $\log (x^2 yz)$.

21. $\log \frac{x}{z^2}$.

22. $\log x^6$.

23. $\log \sqrt{x}$.

24. $\log \frac{xy^2}{z^3}$.

25. $\log (xy^2)^6$.

26. $\log \frac{y\sqrt[3]{x}}{z^2}$.

27. $\log \sqrt[6]{\frac{x^2 y^3}{z^5}}$.

28. $\log \frac{1}{y\sqrt{z}}$.

In Problems 29–34, write each expression in terms of log x, log (x + 2), and log (x − 3).

29. $\log [x(x + 2)(x − 3)]$.

30. $\log \dfrac{x^2(x + 2)}{x − 3}$.

31. $\log \dfrac{\sqrt{x}}{(x + 2)(x − 3)^2}$.

32. $\log [(x − 3)\sqrt{x(x + 2)}]$.

33. $\log \sqrt{\dfrac{x^2(x − 3)^3}{x + 2}}$.

34. $\log \dfrac{1}{x(x − 3)^2(x + 2)^3}$.

In Problems 35–46, write each expression as a single logarithm.

35. $\log_2 7 + \log_2 3$.

36. $\log_3 32 − \log_3 2$.

37. $3 \log_{10} 7 − 5 \log_{10} 23$.

38. $2 \log_{10} 39 − \tfrac{1}{2} \log_{10} 3$.

39. $2 \log_3 4 + \log_3 2$.

40. $4 \log_4 3 − \log_4 9$.

41. $\log_4 4 − \log_4 200$.

42. $3 \log_2 10 + \log_2 15$.

43. $12 \log_4 3 + \log_4 3^{-2}$.

44. $\log \sqrt[3]{x} − 3 \log x^2$.

45. $\log_2 2x − \log_2 (x + 1)$.

46. $2 \log x − \tfrac{1}{2} \log (x − 2)$.

47. The intensity level β of a sound wave of intensity I is given by

$$\beta = 10 \log \frac{I}{I_0}.$$

where I_0 is a constant reference intensity. If two sound sources have intensities I_1 and I_2, show that the *difference* in the intensity levels of the sounds is given by

$$\beta_2 − \beta_1 = 10 \log \frac{I_2}{I_1}.$$

13-4   Change of Base

Our next property of logarithms allows us to convert logarithms from one base to another. Let

$$x = \log_b N.$$

Then, in exponential form,

$$b^x = N.$$

Taking the logarithm (base a) of both sides, we have

$$\log_a (b^x) = \log_a N$$
$$x \log_a b = \log_a N$$
$$x = \frac{\log_a N}{\log_a b}.$$

However, from before, $x = \log_b N$. Thus we have the *change of base formula*:

CHANGE OF BASE FORMULA

$$\log_b N = \frac{\log_a N}{\log_a b}.$$

This formula allows us to express a logarithm base b of a number in terms of logarithms base a.

example 1

a. Find $\log_5 100$ by using common logarithms.

Using the change of base formula with $b = 5$, $N = 100$, and $a = 10$ gives

$$\log_5 100 = \frac{\log 100}{\log 5} = \frac{2}{0.69897} = 2.8614.$$

We point out that $\dfrac{\log 100}{\log 5} \neq \log(100 - 5)$ and $\dfrac{\log 100}{\log 5} \neq \log \dfrac{100}{5}$.

b. Find $\log_4 20$ by using natural logarithms.

Using the change of base formula with $b = 4$, $N = 20$, and $a = e$, we have

$$\log_4 20 = \frac{\log_e 20}{\log_e 4} = \frac{\ln 20}{\ln 4} = \frac{2.99573}{1.38629} = 2.1610.$$

c. From the change of base formula with $b = 10$ and $a = e$, we have

$$\log N = \frac{\ln N}{\ln 10}.$$

Thus

$$\ln N = (\ln 10)(\log N),$$

or

$$\ln N = 2.30259 \log N. \tag{1}$$

It also follows that

$$\log N = 0.43429 \ln N. \tag{2}$$

Exercise 13-4

In Problems 1–6, find the values of the logarithms.

1. $\log_5 27$.

2. $\log_2 15$.

3. $\log_7 0.67$.

4. $\log_{100} 25$.

5. $\log_6 0.00032$.

6. $\log_5 0.5$.

13-5 Exponential and Logarithmic Equations

An exponential equation can generally be solved by first taking logarithms of both sides, as the following examples show.

example 1

Solve $5^{2x+1} = 36$.

Taking common logarithms of both sides, we have

$$\log 5^{2x+1} = \log 36$$
$$(2x + 1)(\log 5) = \log 36$$
$$2x + 1 = \frac{\log 36}{\log 5}$$
$$2x = \frac{\log 36}{\log 5} - 1$$
$$x = \frac{\log 36}{2 \log 5} - \frac{1}{2}$$
$$= \frac{1.55630}{2(0.69897)} - \frac{1}{2}$$
$$= 0.61328.$$

example 2

Solve $x^{3.4} = 12$.

Taking common logarithms of both sides gives

$$\log x^{3.4} = \log 12$$
$$3.4 \log x = \log 12$$
$$\log x = \frac{\log 12}{3.4} = 0.31741$$
$$x = \text{antilog } 0.31741$$
$$= 10^{0.31741} = 2.077.$$

example 3

A 6-μF capacitor is charged by connecting it in series with a 2-MΩ resistor and a 100-V battery. In the charging circuit the current i (in amperes) follows an exponential decay given by

$$i = \frac{\mathcal{E}}{R} e^{-t/(RC)}, \tag{1}$$

where C is the capacitance (in farads), R is the resistance (in ohms), and $\mathcal{E}$ is the emf (in volts). In how many seconds after the connection is made will the current in the circuit be 20 μA?

Substituting the given values into Eq. 1 gives

$$20 \times 10^{-6} = \frac{100}{2 \times 10^6} e^{-t/[(2 \times 10^6)(6 \times 10^{-6})]}$$

$$0.4 = e^{-t/12}. \tag{2}$$

Taking natural logarithms of both sides gives

$$\ln 0.4 = \ln e^{-t/12}$$

$$= -\frac{t}{12} \ln e = -\frac{t}{12}(1) = -\frac{t}{12}.$$

Thus

$$t = -12 \ln 0.4 = -12(-0.91629) = 11.0 \text{ s.}$$

Equation 2 can also be solved by first expressing it in an equivalent logarithmic form.

$$-\frac{t}{12} = \ln 0.4$$

$$t = -12 \ln 0.4 = 11.0 \text{ s.}$$

A logarithmic equation can often be solved by expressing it in exponential form, as the following examples show.

example 4

Solve $\log_2 x + \log_2 (x + 4) = 5$.

We first write the left side as a single logarithm by using Property 1:

$$\log_2 [x(x + 4)] = 5.$$

In exponential form, we have

$$x(x + 4) = 2^5$$

$$x^2 + 4x = 32$$

$$x^2 + 4x - 32 = 0$$

$$(x - 4)(x + 8) = 0$$

$$x = 4 \quad \text{or} \quad x = -8.$$

We must reject $x = -8$ because the given equation is not defined for negative x (the logarithm of a negative number is not defined). Thus we choose $x = 4$.

example 5

Solve $\log_{(4x+1)} 5 = 2.32193$.

In exponential form, we have

$$(4x + 1)^{2.32193} = 5.$$

Taking common logarithms of both sides yields

$$2.32193 \log (4x + 1) = \log 5$$

$$\log (4x + 1) = \frac{\log 5}{2.31293} = \frac{0.69897}{2.32193} = 0.30103.$$

Thus

$$4x + 1 = \text{antilog } 0.30103 = 2.00$$

$$x = 0.25$$

example 6

Solve $\log (x + 1) - \log (x - 1) = \log x$.

Simplifying the left side gives

$$\log \frac{x + 1}{x - 1} = \log x.$$

Recall that if the logarithms of two numbers are equal, then the numbers are equal. Thus

$$\frac{x + 1}{x - 1} = x$$

$$x + 1 = x(x - 1)$$

$$= x^2 - x$$

$$0 = x^2 - 2x - 1.$$

Using the quadratic formula gives $x = 1 \pm \sqrt{2}$. However, the given equation is not defined for $x = 1 - \sqrt{2}$. The solution is $1 + \sqrt{2}$.

Exercise 13-5

In Problems **1–18**, *solve each equation.*

1. $12^x = 17$. **2.** $2^{8x} = 9$. **3.** $3^{x-2} = 14$.

4. $5^{2x-4} = 96$. **5.** $2^{-t} = 9$. **6.** $3^{t/2} = 0.056$.

7. $e^{3t+1} = 35$. **8.** $e^{1-t} = 354$.

9. $x^{2.56} = 26$. **10.** $t^{2.5} = 24.71$.

11. $\log (2x + 1) = \log (x + 6)$.

12. $\log x + \log 3 = \log 5$.

13. $\log x - \log (x - 1) = \log 4$.

14. $\log_2 x + 3 \log_2 2 = \log_2 (2/x)$.

15. $\log_x (2x + 3) = 2$.

16. $\log_x 4.3 = 1.3$.

17. $\log (3x - 1) - \log (x - 3) = 2$.

18. $\log_3 (2x + 3) = 4 - \log_3 (x + 6)$.

19. The magnitude of the force F (in newtons) driving a piston varies with the distance x (in meters) of the piston from its central position according to the equation

$$F = 135x^{-7/5}.$$

(a) Find the force acting when the piston is 8.0 cm from its central position. (b) How far is the piston from its central position when $F = 1000$ N?

20. A sound source has an intensity level of 100 db. Find its intensity in watts per square meter. Refer to the formula in Problem 71 in Sec. 13-2.

21. A 2-μF capacitor is charged by connecting it in series with a 4-MΩ resistor and a 200-V source. (a) Find the current in the circuit at $t = 0$, which is the instant the connections are made. (Refer to Example 3.) (b) For what value of t will the current in the circuit be 10 μA?

22. A capacitance C is charged by connecting it in series with a resistance R and an emf $\mathcal{E}$. (a) Show that the initial current in the circuit (at $t = 0$) is $\mathcal{E}/R$. (See Example 3.) (b) The *capacitive time constant* τ_C is given by $\tau_C = RC$. Show that when $t = \tau_C$, the current has decayed to $1/e$ of its initial value. (c) In (b), approximately what percentage of the initial current does that represent?

13-6 Logarithmic and Semilogarithmic Graph Paper

In technical work there is sometimes a need to conveniently graph a function $y = f(x)$ when both x and y range over wide intervals of values. In such cases it may be best to show not how y varies with x, but how $\log y$ varies with $\log x$. For example, if $10 \le x \le 1000$, then $1 \le \log x \le 3$. Clearly, the latter interval is easier to work with on an axis.

If such a graph is desired, we can sketch it without having to determine the logarithms of any numbers. We use a special **logarithmic graph paper** (or **log paper**) on which both axes are ruled with logarithmic scales in base 10 (Fig. 13-9). Plotting a point (x, y) on log paper is equivalent to plotting the point $(\log x, \log y)$ on ordinary graph paper. The 1 that is preprinted on log paper can represent only an integral power of 10, such as 1, 10, 100, 0.1, 0.01, and so on. If the 1 represents 10, then the 2 represents 20. A **cycle** is the distance between two numbers having logarithms that are consecutive integers. For example, from 1 to 10 is one cycle; from 10 to 100 is one cycle. Log paper is described by the number of cycles on each axis. For example, Fig. 13-9 has two cycles on the vertical axis.

A similar type of graph paper, called **semilogarithmic graph paper**, is shown in Fig. 13-10. One axis is ruled logarithmically (base 10) and the other axis is ruled linearly, like ordinary graph paper. This paper is used when only *one* variable has a wide range of values.

A significant advantage of log paper is that the graph of the **power function** $y = ax^m$, where a and x are positive, appears as a straight line on log paper. To show why, we take the common logarithm of both sides and simplify:

$$\log y = \log ax^m$$
$$\log y = \log a + \log x^m$$
$$\log y = \log a + m \log x. \tag{1}$$

If we substitute y_L for $\log y$, x_L for $\log x$, and b for the constant $\log a$, then Eq. 1 becomes

$$y_L = mx_L + b,$$

which is an equation of a straight line. Thus equations of the form $y = ax^m$ appear as straight lines on log paper. The exponent m of $y = ax^m$ is the slope of the line. *If the graph of data is a straight line on log paper, then the data are related by a function of the form $y = ax^m$.*

Similarly, the graph of the exponential function $y = ab^x$, where a and b are positive, is a straight line on semilog paper if y is on the logarithmic scale. Taking logarithms of both sides gives

$$\log y = \log a + x \log b.$$

Substituting y_L for $\log y$, k for the constant $\log a$, and m for the constant $\log b$ gives

$$y_L = mx + k,$$

which is a straight line. *If the graph of data is a straight line on semilog paper, then the data are related by a function of the form $y = ab^x$.*

example 1

Sketch the graph of the power function $y = 3x^2$, for $1 \leq x \leq 5$, on log paper.

Using Table 13-1, we note that two logarithmic cycles will be needed for y: one cycle

Table 13-1

x	1	2	3	4	5
y	3	12	27	48	75

for 3 and one cycle for 12, 27, 48, and 75. The graph, shown in Fig. 13-9, is a straight line, as expected. *Using a ruler* to measure Δx and Δy, you should verify that $\Delta y / \Delta x = 2$. The slope may also be found analytically. Choosing the points $(1, 3)$ and $(5, 75)$,

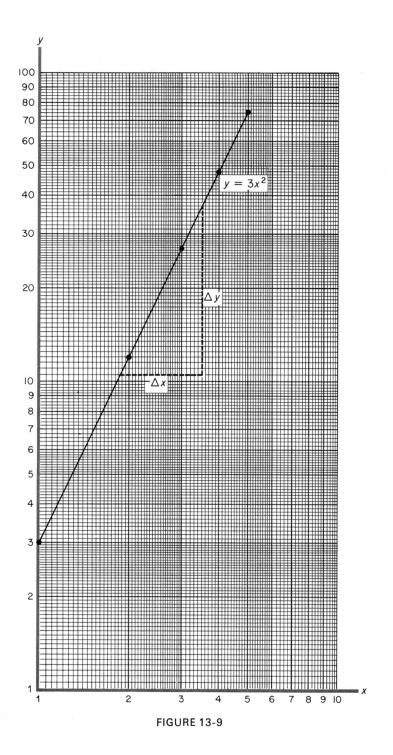

FIGURE 13-9

we have

$$\frac{\Delta y}{\Delta x} = \frac{\log y_2 - \log y_1}{\log x_2 - \log x_1} = \frac{\log 75 - \log 3}{\log 5 - \log 1} = 2.$$

In particular, note that using the same points you *must not* write

$$\frac{\Delta y}{\Delta x} = \frac{75 - 3}{5 - 1} = 18,$$

for the data do not give a straight line on ordinary graph paper.

example 2

Suppose that the data in Table 13-2 are plotted on log paper and the resulting points lie on a straight line. Determine an equation that relates y as a function of x.

Table 13-2

x	1.4	2.5	6.1	11.4	17.5
y	24.5	7.68	1.29	0.369	0.157

Because the data determine a straight line on log paper, the equation is a power function of the form $y = ax^m$. To find the slope m of the line, we may use the slope formula

$$m = \frac{\log y_2 - \log y_1}{\log x_2 - \log x_1}$$

and two of the data points, such as $(17.5, 0.157)$ and $(1.4, 24.5)$. This gives

$$m = \frac{\log 24.5 - \log 0.157}{\log 1.4 - \log 17.5}$$

$$= \frac{2.1933}{-1.0969} = -2.0.$$

Thus $y = ax^{-2} = a/x^2$. To find a, we substitute a data point, such as $(1.4, 24.5)$, into the equation and solve for a.

$$24.5 = \frac{a}{(1.4)^2}$$

$$a = 24.5(1.4)^2 = 48.0.$$

Thus $y = \dfrac{48}{x^2}$.

example 3

Sketch the graph of the exponential function $y = e^x$, for $-1 \le x \le 4$, on semilog paper.

From Table 13-3, we note that three cycles will be needed for y. The graph, shown in Fig. 13-10, is a straight line as expected.

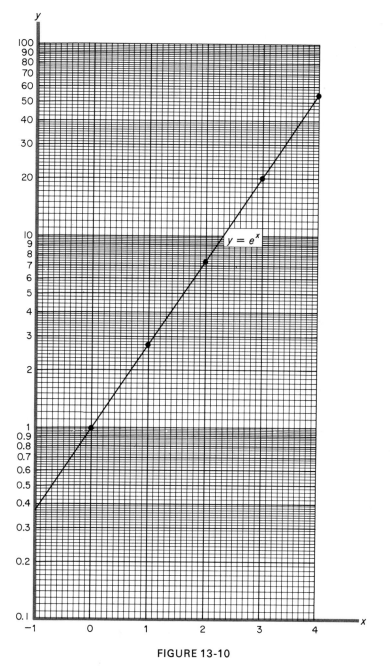

FIGURE 13-10

Table 13-3

x	-1	0	1	2	3	4
y	0.37	1	2.72	7.39	20.1	54.6

example 4

A student found that data from an experiment resulted in a straight-line graph on semilog paper. If two of the data points are $x = 1$, $y = 2.81$, and $x = 4$, $y = 5.12$, find an equation that approximates the data.

We assume that the equation is of the form $y = ab^x$. Substituting the given values gives the system

$$2.81 = ab \tag{1}$$

$$5.12 = ab^4. \tag{2}$$

From Eq. 1, $a = 2.81/b$. Substituting into Eq. 2 gives

$$5.12 = 2.81b^3$$

$$b^3 = \frac{5.12}{2.81}$$

$$b = 1.22.$$

Thus $y = a(1.22)^x$. At $(1, 2.81)$ we have

$$2.81 = a(1.22)$$

$$a = 2.30.$$

Therefore the data are approximated by the equation

$$y = 2.3(1.22)^x.$$

We point out that because $\ln 1.22 = 0.199$, then $1.22 = e^{0.199}$ and the answer can be expressed as $y = 2.3e^{0.199x}$.

Exercise 13-6

1. Consider the function $y = e^{-x}$ for $1 \leq x \leq 6$. (a) Will the graph be a straight line on semilog paper or on log paper? (b) On the appropriate paper, use the points corresponding to $x = 1$ and $x = 6$ to sketch the straight-line graph. (c) From your graph, estimate e^{-x} for various values of x between 1 and 6 and compare your results to values found with a calculator.

2. Consider the function $y = \sqrt{x}$. (a) Will the graph be a straight line on semilog paper or on log paper? (b) On the appropriate paper, use the points corresponding to $x = 1$ and $x = 100$ to sketch the straight-line graph. (c) From your graph, estimate the square roots of various numbers between 1 and 100 and compare your results to values found with a calculator.

3. During an experiment the data shown in Table 13-4 were recorded. Plot the data on log paper and semilog paper. (a) On which paper do the points lie on a straight line? (b) Find an equation that approximates the data.

Table 13-4

x	1	4	8	12	16	20	24
y	600	150	75	50	37.5	30	25

4. Table 13-5 gives the barometric pressure p, in millimeters of mercury, at various altitudes h, in meters. (a) Plot the data on semilog paper. (b) Determine an equation for p as a function of h. Give your answer in two forms, like in Example 4.

Table 13-5

h (m)	0	500	1000	1500	2000	2500
p (mm)	760	716	674	635	598	563

5. Data from an experiment produced a straight line on semilog paper. If two of the data points are $x = 2$, $y = 3.61$ and $x = 4$, $y = 32.6$, find an equation that approximates the data.

6. Data from an experiment produced a straight line on log paper. If two of the data points are $x = 3$, $y = 3.46$ and $x = 8$, $y = 4.80$, find an equation that approximates the data.

7. The period T of a simple pendulum was measured for various lengths L. The results are given in Table 13-6. Plot the data on log paper and semilog paper. (a) On which paper do the points lie on a straight line? (b) Find an equation for T as a function of L.

Table 13-6

L (m)	0.2	0.4	0.6	0.8	1.0	1.2
T (s)	0.89	1.26	1.55	1.79	2.00	2.20

13-7 Review

Review Questions

1. A function of the form $f(x) = b^x$ is called an _____ function.

2. Is the value of e closer to 2 or to 3? _____

3. If $\log_b x = y$, then $b^y =$ _____.

4. The base in $\log x$ is _10_.

5. The base in $\ln x$ is __e or 2.7__

6. The domain of the exponential function $f(x) = b^x$ is _____(a)_____ and its range is _____(b)_____.

7. The domain of the logarithmic function $g(x) = \log_b x$ is _____(a)_____ and its range is _____(b)_____.

8. The graph in Fig. 13-11 is typical of a(n) _(exponential)(logarithmic)_ function.

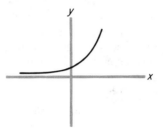

FIGURE 13-11

9. If $\log_2 (x + 1) = \log_2 4$, then $x =$ _____.

10. If $\log x = 1.2222$, then $\log \sqrt{x} =$ _____.

11. $\log 10^{5x} =$ _____.

12. $\ln \dfrac{x^2 y^3}{z^4} =$ __(a)__ $\ln x +$ __(b)__ $\ln y -$ __(c)__ $\ln z$.

13. The graphs of $y = e^{x+2}$ and $y = e^2 e^x$ _(are)(are not)_ identical.

14. $\log_5 5 =$ _____.

15. $\log_3 1 =$ _____.

16. If $\log x = 0.62148$, then $10^{0.62148} =$ _____.

Answers to Review Questions

1. Exponential. **2.** 3. **3.** x. **4.** 10. **5.** e.
6. (a) All real numbers, (b) All positive numbers.
7. (a) All positive numbers, (b) All real numbers. **8.** Exponential. **9.** 3.
10. 0.6111. **11.** $5x$. **12.** (a) 2, (b) 3, (c) 4. **13.** Are. **14.** 1. **15.** 0. **16.** x.

Review Problems

In Problems 1–4, find the given functional values.

1. $f(x) = 4 + 3^{2x}$; $f(0)$, $f(1)$, $f(-\tfrac{1}{2})$.

2. $g(t) = 4(9)^{t/2}$; $g(1)$, $g(-1)$, $g(3)$.

3. $h(s) = 100e^{(s+3)/2}$; $h(-3)$, $h(5)$, $h(-6)$.

4. $F(x) = 6 - 3(\tfrac{1}{2})^{x+4}$; $F(-3)$, $F(-1)$, $F(-6)$.

In Problems 5 and 6, graph the given function.

5. $y = \log_5 x$.   **6.** $y = 5^x$.

*In Problems **7–12**, write each exponential form logarithmically and each logarithmic form exponentially.*

7. $3^5 = 243$.

8. $\log_7 343 = 3$.

9. $\log_{16} 2 = \dfrac{1}{4}$.

10. $10^5 = 100{,}000$.

11. $e^4 = 54.598$.

12. $\log_9 9 = 1$.

*In Problems **13–18**, find the values.*

13. $\log_5 125$.

14. $\log_4 16$.

15. $\log_2 \dfrac{1}{16}$.

16. $\log_{1/3} \dfrac{1}{9}$.

17. $\log_{1/3} 9$.

18. $\log_4 2$.

*In Problems **19–24**, determine the common logarithms of the given numbers to five decimal places.*

19. 634.82.

20. 0.00064321.

21. 8.62×10^{16}.

22. 0.084138.

23. 6047.1.

24. 9.72×10^{-3}.

*In Problems **25–28**, determine the natural logarithms of the given numbers to five decimal places.*

25. 0.632.

26. 468.

27. 4.72.

28. 0.000014.

*In Problems **29–32**, determine the value of N to four decimal places.*

29. $\ln N = 1.13465$.

30. $\log N = 8.19893$.

31. $\log N = -0.68078$.

32. $\log N = 3.69037$.

*In Problems **33–50**, find x.*

33. $\log_5 \dfrac{1}{25} = x$.

34. $\log_x 1000 = 3$.

35. $\log x = -2$.

36. $\log_8 64 = x$.

37. $\log_x 81 = 2$.

38. $\log_3 x = \dfrac{1}{2}$.

39. $\log_x (4x - 9) = 1$.

40. $\log_4 (x - 6) = 2$.

41. $\log_6 x = 3.265$.

42. $e^{0.3x+1} = 6$.

43. $7^{1.6x} = 3.429$.

44. $\log_e \pi = x$.

45. $\log x = 0$.

46. $\ln \dfrac{1}{e} = x$.

47. $\log_x (2x + 3) = 2$.

48. $\log (4x + 1) = \log (x + 2)$.

49. $e^{\ln(x+4)} = 7$.

50. $\log x + \log 2 = 1$.

*In Problems **51–56**, write each expression as a single logarithm.*

51. $2 \log 5 - 3 \log 3$

52. $6 \ln x + 4 \ln y$

53. $2 \ln x + \ln y - 3 \ln z$

54. $\log_6 2 - \log_6 4 - 2 \log_6 3$

55. $\frac{1}{2} \log_2 x + 2 \log_2 (x^2) - 3 \log_2 (x + 1) - 4 \log_2 (x + 2)$

56. $3 \log x + \log y - 2(\log z + \log w)$

*In Problems **57–62**, write the expressions in terms of* $\ln x$, $\ln y$, *and* $\ln z$.

57. $\ln \frac{x^2 y}{z^3}$.

58. $\ln \frac{\sqrt{x}}{(yz)^2}$

59. $\ln \sqrt[3]{xyz}$.

60. $\ln \left[\frac{xy^3}{z^2} \right]^4$

61. $\ln \left[\frac{1}{x} \sqrt{\frac{y}{z}} \right]$.

62. $\ln \left[\left(\frac{x}{y} \right)^2 \left(\frac{x}{z} \right)^3 \right]$.

63. If $\log 3 = x$ and $\log 4 = y$, express $\log (16\sqrt{3})$ in terms of x and y.

64. Express

$$\log \frac{x^2 \sqrt{x + 1}}{\sqrt[3]{x^2 + 2}}$$

in terms of $\log x$, $\log (x + 1)$, and $\log (x^2 + 2)$.

65. Find $\log_3 4$.

66. Data from an experiment produced a straight line on log paper. If two of the data points are $x = 2$, $y = 26.4$ and $x = 4$, $y = 278.6$, find an equation that approximates the data.

67. Data from an experiment produced a straight line on semilog paper. If two of the data points are $x = 2$, $y = 49$ and $x = 3$, $y = 171.5$, find an equation that approximates the data.

68. If 95 percent of a radioactive substance remains after 100 years, find the decay constant and, to the nearest percent, give the percentage of the original amount present after 200 years.

69. The following equation was encountered in statistical biology:

$$R = 2\sigma \sqrt{2 \log \left(\frac{n}{\sigma \sqrt{2\pi}} \right)}.$$

Find R if $\sigma = 2.378$ and $n = 1000$.

70. When a solenoid of inductance L (in henrys) and resistance R (in ohms) is connected to a battery of emf $\mathcal{E}$ (in volts), the current i (in amperes) in the circuit is given by

$$i = \frac{\mathcal{E}}{R}(1 - e^{-Rt/L}).$$

A solenoid with an inductance of 60 H and a resistance of 20 Ω is connected to a 100-V battery. For what value of t will the current be 2.5 A?

trigonometric graphs and polar coordinates

14-1 Introduction

In Chapter 7 the trigonometric functions were introduced, but no consideration was given to their graphical characteristics. To properly understand the behavior of the trigonometric functions, an analysis of their graphs is essential. These graphs have wide application in mathematically describing several occurrences in nature, such as wave motion, vibrations and simple harmonic motion, and certain electrical phenomena. In this chapter we shall consider the graphs of the six trigonometric functions and some of their variations. You will see that, in comparison to the graphs of algebraic functions, these graphs have strikingly unique features.

14-2 The Graph of the Sine Function

To sketch the graph of the basic sine function $y = \sin x$, we shall first determine some points that lie on it. Table 14-1 lists some values of x between 0 and 2π radians and also the corresponding y-values. These points are plotted in Fig 14-1 and then connected by a smooth curve.

Recall that the angles x and $x + 2\pi$ are coterminal angles. Because trigonometric function values of coterminal angles are equal, we have $\sin x = \sin (x + 2\pi)$. For example, $\sin \pi = \sin (\pi + 2\pi)$. This means that the graph of $y = \sin x$ repeats itself every 2π radians. That is, as x increases from 2π to 4π, from 4π to 6π, and so forth, $\sin x$ behaves exactly as it does from zero to 2π. This is indicated by the broken

461

Table 14-1

x (rad)	y = sin x	x (rad)	y = sin x
0	0	$\frac{7\pi}{6}$	$-\frac{1}{2} = -0.5$
$\frac{\pi}{6}$	$\frac{1}{2} = 0.5$	$\frac{4\pi}{3}$	$-\frac{\sqrt{3}}{2} \approx -0.87$
$\frac{\pi}{3}$	$\frac{\sqrt{3}}{2} \approx 0.87$	$\frac{3\pi}{2}$	-1
$\frac{\pi}{2}$	1	$\frac{5\pi}{3}$	$-\frac{\sqrt{3}}{2} \approx -0.87$
$\frac{2\pi}{3}$	$\frac{\sqrt{3}}{2} \approx 0.87$	$\frac{11\pi}{6}$	$-\frac{1}{2} = -0.5$
$\frac{5\pi}{6}$	$\frac{1}{2} = 0.5$	2π	0
π	0		

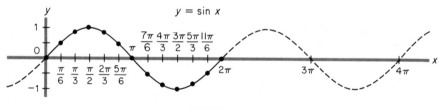

FIGURE 14-1

curve in Fig. 14-1. Note the characteristic wavelike nature of the sine curve. To describe the repetition, or *periodicity*, we say that $y = \sin x$ is a **periodic function** with **period** 2π. Actually, because $\sin (x + 4\pi) = \sin x$, the number 4π is also a period of $y = \sin x$. However, because 2π is the *smallest* positive number p such that $\sin (x + p) = \sin x$, we call 2π *the* period of $y = \sin x$.

We emphasize that Fig. 14-1 shows merely a portion of the basic sine curve, for $y = \sin x$ is defined for all values of x and its graph extends indefinitely to the right and to the left.

The graph of $y = \sin x$ over an interval of one period (2π) is called a **cycle** of the sine curve. Notice in Fig. 14-1 that the cycle from $x = 0$ to $x = 2\pi$ has four basic parts in its pattern:

1. From $x = 0$ to $x = \pi/2$, the curve *rises* from $y = 0$ to $y = 1$.

2. From $x = \pi/2$ to $x = \pi$, the curve *falls* from $y = 1$ to $y = 0$.

3. From $x = \pi$ to $x = 3\pi/2$, the curve continues to *fall* from $y = 0$ to $y = -1$.

4. From $x = 3\pi/2$ to $x = 2\pi$, the curve *rises* from $y = -1$ to $y = 0$.

Thus, the zeros of the sine function are $0, \pi, 2\pi$, and so on.

The values of $\sin x$ range between a maximum of 1 and a minimum of -1. In general, *one-half of the difference of the maximum and minimum values of a periodic function over one cycle is called the* **amplitude** *of the function.* Thus *the amplitude of* $y = \sin x$ *is* 1, because $\frac{1}{2}[1 - (-1)] = 1$.

In the following examples you will learn how to sketch variations of the sine function. We begin with functions of the form $y = a \sin x$, where a is a constant. You will see that although the function $y = a \sin x$ has the same period, 2π, as the basic sine function $y = \sin x$, its graph may differ in a *vertical* sense from that of $y = \sin x$. This difference depends on a.

example 1

Sketch the graph of $y = 2 \sin x$.

The y-value of each point on the curve $y = 2 \sin x$ is two times the corresponding y-value on the curve $y = \sin x$. That is, as the values of $\sin x$ vary between 1 and -1, the values of two times $\sin x$ vary between 2 and -2. This means that the graphs of $y = 2 \sin x$ and $y = \sin x$ differ in a vertical sense, but not in a horizontal sense. The amplitude of $y = 2 \sin x$ is $\frac{1}{2}[2 - (-2)] = 2$, but the period is still 2π. To sketch the graph, we draw a basic sine curve pattern and label the axes to indicate the amplitude 2 and period 2π. Two cycles are shown in Fig. 14-2.

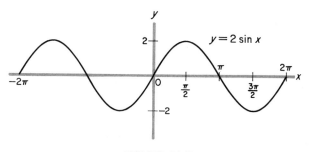

FIGURE 14-2

example 2

Sketch the graph of $y = -2 \sin x$.

The y-value of each point on the curve $y = -2 \sin x$ is the negative of the corresponding y-value on the curve $y = 2 \sin x$ in Example 1. Whenever $2 \sin x$ is positive, then $-2 \sin x$ is negative; whenever $2 \sin x$ is negative, then $-2 \sin x$ is positive. The effect is to *invert* the curve in Fig. 14-2. Thus we get two cycles of the graph of $y = -2 \sin x$ in Fig. 14-3. It shows that the amplitude of $y = -2 \sin x$ is 2 (which is $|-2|$) and the period is 2π.

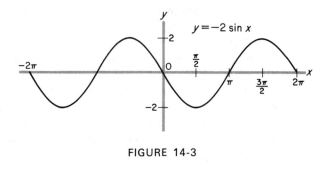

FIGURE 14-3

From Examples 1 and 2 we conclude that **the amplitude of** $y = a \sin x$ **is** $|a|$ **and its period is** 2π. **The shape is that of a basic sine curve if** $a > 0$ **or an inverted sine curve if** $a < 0$.

A more general form of a sine function is

$$y = a \sin (bx + c) \qquad a, b, c \text{ constants}, b > 0.$$

(The equation $y = a \sin x$ is a special case where $b = 1$ and $c = 0$.) The quantity $bx + c$, which represents an angle, is called the **argument** of the sine function. As before, the amplitude is $|a|$, and the graph has a basic sine curve pattern if $a > 0$, or an inverted sine curve pattern if $a < 0$. But the graph may be affected in a *horizontal* way, depending on $bx + c$.

To show why, we examine the function $y = 3 \sin \left(2x + \dfrac{\pi}{2}\right)$. Here $a = 3, b = 2$, and $c = \pi/2$. The amplitude is 3, and the shape is that of a basic sine curve because $a > 0$. Recall that we obtain one cycle of the curve $y = \sin \theta$ whenever θ ranges over an interval of length 2π. Similarly, we obtain one cycle of $y = 3 \sin \left(2x + \dfrac{\pi}{2}\right)$ whenever the argument $2x + \dfrac{\pi}{2}$ ranges over an interval of length 2π, such as from zero to 2π. Thus a cycle *begins* when

$$2x + \frac{\pi}{2} = 0$$

$$2x = -\frac{\pi}{2}$$

$$x = -\frac{\pi}{4}.$$

The previous cycle *ends* when

$$2x + \frac{\pi}{2} = 2\pi$$

$$2x = \frac{3\pi}{2}$$

$$x = \frac{3\pi}{4}.$$

To sketch a cycle of $y = 3 \sin \left(2x + \frac{\pi}{2} \right)$, we first draw one cycle of the basic sine curve pattern beginning at $-\pi/4$ and ending at $3\pi/4$. The graph is shown in Fig. 14-4. The y-axis is labeled with a 3 and -3 so that maximum and minimum values are indicated. The curve, of course, repeats itself indefinitely both to the right and left.

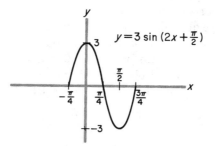

FIGURE 14-4

The period is the length of the interval from $-\pi/4$ to $3\pi/4$, which is

$$\frac{3\pi}{4} - \left(-\frac{\pi}{4} \right) = \pi.$$

Thus the curve completes one cycle as x varies over an interval of length π, for over that interval the argument $2x + \frac{\pi}{2}$ varies over an interval of length 2π.

Finally, on the x-axis we also label the values of x where $3 \sin \left(2x + \frac{\pi}{2} \right)$ has a maximum value (3), or minimum value (-3), or is zero. We find these values by dividing the period p by 4,

$$\frac{p}{4} = \frac{\pi}{4},$$

and successively adding the result to the beginning x-value, $-\pi/4$.

$$-\frac{\pi}{4} + \frac{\pi}{4} = 0; \qquad 0 + \frac{\pi}{4} = \frac{\pi}{4}; \qquad \frac{\pi}{4} + \frac{\pi}{4} = \frac{2\pi}{4} = \frac{\pi}{2}; \qquad \frac{\pi}{2} + \frac{\pi}{4} = \frac{3\pi}{4}.$$

More generally, a cycle of $y = a \sin (bx + c)$ begins when

$$bx + c = 0, \quad \text{or} \quad x = -\frac{c}{b},$$

and it ends when

$$bx + c = 2\pi, \quad \text{or} \quad x = -\frac{c}{b} + \frac{2\pi}{b}.$$

Thus the period is

$$\left(-\frac{c}{b} + \frac{2\pi}{b}\right) - \left(-\frac{c}{b}\right) = \frac{2\pi}{b}.$$

This result means that b gives the number of cycles in the interval from zero to 2π.

Furthermore, depending on the values of b and c, the graph of $y = a \sin (bx + c)$ may be shifted horizontally to the right or left with respect to the graph of the basic sine function. The quantity $-c/b$ is called the **displacement** and represents the amount by which $y = a \sin (bx + c)$ is shifted in comparison to the basic sine curve. That is, a cycle of $y = \sin x$ begins when $x = 0$, but a cycle of $y = a \sin (bx + c)$ begins when $x = -c/b$. If the displacement is positive, the shift is to the right; if the displacement is negative, the shift is to the left. For example, given the function $y = 3 \sin \left(2x + \frac{\pi}{2}\right)$, the displacement d is

$$d = -\frac{c}{b} = -\frac{\pi/2}{2} = -\frac{\pi}{4} < 0,$$

which agrees with the fact that the cycle shown in Fig. 14-4 begins to the *left* of the origin at $x = -\pi/4$.

The preceding discussion leads to a procedure for sketching the graph of $y = a \sin (bx + c)$, where $b > 0$.

1. *Find the amplitude. It is* $|a|$.

2. *Find the shape of the curve, that is, regular sine curve pattern ($a > 0$) or inverted sine curve pattern ($a < 0$).*

3. *Solve $bx + c = 0$ to find a value of x when a cycle begins. Call this value x_b.*

4. *Solve $bx + c = 2\pi$ to find the value of x when the cycle in Step 3 ends. Call this x_e.*

5. *Find the period p:*

    $$p = \frac{2\pi}{b}.$$

6. *Find the x-values of "important" points. By important, we mean those points where the function has a maximum, minimum, or zero-value. One of these is*

x_b. *To find the others, divide p by* 4 *and successively add this result to* x_b. *Also, label the y-axis to show the maximum and minimum values.*

A general sketch of $y = a \sin(bx + c)$ appears in Fig. 14-5. The following things should be noted.

1. *a* affects amplitude and shape (that is, regular or inverted pattern).

2. *b* affects the period.

3. *b* and *c* affect displacement.

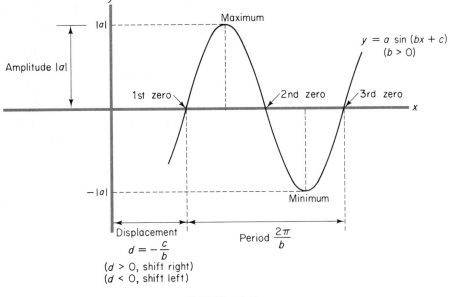

FIGURE 14-5

---

example 3

Sketch the graph of $y = \sin\left(\pi x - \dfrac{\pi}{4}\right)$.

1. The amplitude is $|a| = |1| = 1$.

2. Because $a > 0$, the shape is that of a regular sine curve pattern.

3. If $\pi x - \dfrac{\pi}{4} = 0$, then $\pi x = \dfrac{\pi}{4}$ and so $x = \dfrac{1}{4}$. Thus a cycle begins when $x = \dfrac{1}{4}$,

so $x_b = \dfrac{1}{4}$.

4. If $\pi x - \frac{\pi}{4} = 2\pi$, then $\pi x = \frac{9\pi}{4}$, so $x = \frac{9}{4}$. The previous cycle ends when $x = \frac{9}{4}$, so $x_e = \frac{9}{4}$.

5. The period p is

$$p = \frac{2\pi}{b} = \frac{2\pi}{\pi} = 2.$$

6. Since $\frac{p}{4}$ is $\frac{2}{4}$, the x-values of important points are: $\frac{1}{4}, \frac{1}{4} + \frac{2}{4} = \frac{3}{4}, \frac{3}{4} + \frac{2}{4} = \frac{5}{4}$, and so on.

Important points: when $x = \frac{1}{4}, \frac{3}{4}, \frac{5}{4}, \frac{7}{4}$, and $\frac{9}{4}$.

One cycle of the graph is shown in Fig. 14-6.

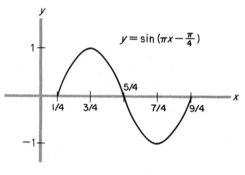

FIGURE 14-6

example 4

Sketch the graph of $y = -2 \sin (\frac{1}{2}x)$.

1. The amplitude is $|a| = |-2| = 2$.

2. Since $a < 0$, the shape is that of an *inverted* sine curve pattern.

3. If $\frac{1}{2}x = 0$, then $x = 0$. A cycle begins when $x_b = 0$.

4. If $\frac{1}{2}x = 2\pi$, then $x = 4\pi$. The cycle above ends when $x_e = 4\pi$.

5. The period p is

$$p = \frac{2\pi}{b} = \frac{2\pi}{\frac{1}{2}} = 4\pi.$$

6. Important points: when $x = 0, \pi, 2\pi, 3\pi$, and 4π.

One cycle of the graph is drawn in Fig. 14-7. Note that in the interval from zero to 2π, there is one-half ($b = \frac{1}{2}$) cycle of $y = -2 \sin (\frac{1}{2}x)$.

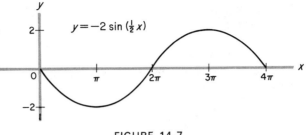

FIGURE 14-7

example 5

Sketch the graphs of $y = \sin x$ and $y = \sin 3x$ on the same coordinate plane.

The graphs appear in Fig. 14-8. The period of $y = \sin 3x$ is $2\pi/b = 2\pi/3$. Note that in the interval from zero to 2π, there are three ($b = 3$) cycles of $y = \sin 3x$.

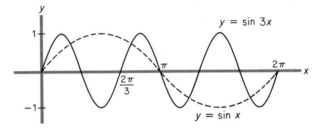

FIGURE 14-8

example 6

When an object vibrates in simple harmonic motion, its displacement y from its equilibrium position as a function of time t can be written in the general form

$$y = A \sin (2\pi f t + \varphi),$$

where $|A|$ is the *amplitude* of the motion, f is the *frequency* in cycles per second (or hertz), and φ is the *phase constant*. Suppose a mass attached to a spring undergoes simple harmonic motion according to the equation

$$y = 0.60 \sin \left(\frac{\pi}{2} t - \frac{\pi}{4} \right),$$

where y is in meters and t is in seconds. Find the amplitude, frequency, and period of the motion.

Comparing the given equation to the general form above, we have an amplitude of $A = 0.60$ m. Because the coefficient of t must correspond to $2\pi f$, we have

$$2\pi f = \frac{\pi}{2}, \qquad f = \frac{1}{4}.$$

Thus the frequency of the motion is $f = \frac{1}{4}$ cycle per second or $\frac{1}{4}$ hertz. The period p is given by

$$p = \frac{2\pi}{b} = \frac{2\pi}{\pi/2} = 4 \text{ s.}$$

Note that the period and frequency of a simple harmonic motion are reciprocals of one another.

Exercise 14-2

In Problems 1–18, draw one cycle of each curve. Give the amplitude A and period p.

1. $y = 3 \sin x$.   **2.** $y = \frac{1}{2} \sin x$.   **3.** $y = -4 \sin x$.

4. $y = -1.2 \sin t$.   **5.** $y = \sin 2x$.   **6.** $y = \sin \frac{x}{2}$.

7. $y = 2 \sin \frac{1}{3} t$.   **8.** $y = 3 \sin 6x$.   **9.** $y = -4 \sin 3x$.

10. $y = 1.2 \sin \frac{3\pi x}{2}$ **11.** $y = \sin \left(x + \frac{\pi}{4} \right)$ **12.** $y = -3 \sin \left(x - \frac{\pi}{6} \right)$.

13. $y = 4 \sin \left(2t - \frac{\pi}{2} \right)$.   **14.** $y = -\frac{1}{4} \sin \left(t + \frac{\pi}{2} \right)$.

15. $y = -2 \sin \left(\frac{x}{2} - \frac{2\pi}{3} \right)$.   **16.** $y = 2 \sin \left(2x - \frac{2\pi}{3} \right)$.

17. $y = \sin \left(\pi x - \frac{\pi}{2} \right)$.   **18.** $y = 3 \sin \left(\frac{2}{3} \pi x - \frac{3\pi}{2} \right)$.

19. Draw the graphs of $y = \sin x$ and $y = \sin 2x$ on the same coordinate plane. How many cycles of $y = \sin 2x$ are there for each cycle of $y = \sin x$?

20. Draw the graph of $y = 2 \sin \frac{x}{4}$ from $x = -2\pi$ to $x = 4\pi$.

21. If $y = 2.3 \sin (8.7t - 1.2)$ describes the harmonic motion of a particle, where t is in seconds and y is in meters, find (a) the period and (b) the frequency. (See Example 6.)

22. Repeat Problem 21 if $y = 4 \sin \omega t$, where ω is a constant.

23. The transverse wave traveling on a stretched string is of the form $y = 2 \sin [\pi(2x - 20t)]$, where t is time in seconds. Sketch one cycle of this wave when $t = 2$ s.

24. The velocity v of a particle undergoing simple harmonic motion is given by the relation $v = -2\pi fA \sin (2\pi ft)$, where f is the frequency in hertz, A is the maximum displacement from the equilibrium point, and t is time in seconds. Sketch the graph of this equation for a frequency of 50 Hz and $A = 10$ m.

25. The horizontal range R of a projectile having an initial speed v_0 and projected at an angle θ above the horizontal is given by

$$R = \frac{v_0^2}{g} \sin 2\theta.$$

(a) Draw one cycle of the graph of this equation.

(b) At what angle of projection, θ, does your graph indicate the horizontal range is maximum? We point out that the graph has physical significance for the first half-cycle only, for an object must be projected *above* the horizontal.

26. When the coil of a generator rotates in a magnetic field, the induced voltage $\mathcal{E}$ in the coil as a function of time is given by the expression

$$\mathcal{E} = \mathcal{E}_m \sin(\omega t - \varphi),$$

where $\mathcal{E}_m$ is the maximum induced voltage, ω is the angular speed of the coil in radians per second, t is the time in seconds, and φ is the phase angle in radians. Let $\mathcal{E}_m = 20$ volts, $\omega = \frac{\pi}{4}$ rad/s, and $\varphi = \frac{\pi}{2}$ rad. Sketch one cycle of the curve and determine, from your graph, the induced voltage when $t = 6$ s.

14-3 The Graph of the Cosine Function

The graph of the basic cosine function $y = \cos x$ appears in Fig. 14-9. Like the sine function, the period of $y = \cos x$ is 2π and the amplitude is 1. For the cycle from

Table 14-2

x	0	$\frac{\pi}{6}$	$\frac{\pi}{3}$	$\frac{\pi}{2}$	$\frac{2\pi}{3}$	$\frac{5\pi}{6}$	π	$\frac{7\pi}{6}$	$\frac{4\pi}{3}$	$\frac{3\pi}{2}$	$\frac{5\pi}{3}$	$\frac{11\pi}{6}$	2π
$y = \cos x$	1	0.87	0.5	0	-0.5	-0.87	-1	-0.87	-0.5	0	0.5	0.87	1

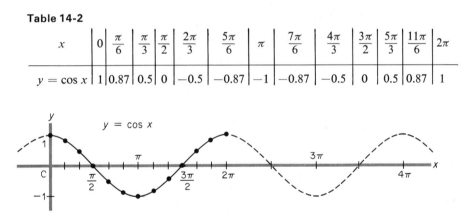

FIGURE 14-9

$x = 0$ to $x = 2\pi$, there are four basic parts.

1. From $x = 0$ to $x = \pi/2$, the curve *falls* from $y = 1$ to $y = 0$.

2. From $x = \pi/2$ to $x = \pi$, the curve continues to *fall* from $y = 0$ to $y = -1$.

3. From $x = \pi$ to $x = 3\pi/2$, the curve *rises* from $y = -1$ to $y = 0$.

4. From $x = 3\pi/2$ to $x = 2\pi$, the curve continues to *rise* from $y = 0$ to $y = 1$.

Comparing the basic cosine curve in Fig. 14-9 to the basic sine curve in Fig. 14-1, you can see that the cosine curve is simply the sine curve shifted $\pi/2$ to the left. More generally, $\sin\left(x + \dfrac{\pi}{2}\right) = \cos x$. In fact, the complete discussion in Sec. 14-2 of amplitude, inversion, period, and displacement also applies to variations of the cosine function, that is, to functions having the form $y = a\cos(bx + c)$ where $b > 0$. The following examples will illustrate this.

example 1

Sketch the graph of $y = 3\cos 6x$.

1. The amplitude is $|a| = |3| = 3$.

2. Because $a > 0$, the shape is that of a regular cosine curve.

3. If $6x = 0$, then $x = 0$. A cycle begins when $x_b = 0$.

4. If $6x = 2\pi$, then $x = \pi/3$. The cycle above ends when $x_e = \pi/3$.

5. The period p is

$$p = \frac{2\pi}{b} = \frac{2\pi}{6} = \frac{\pi}{3}.$$

6. Important points: when $x = 0$, $\dfrac{\pi}{12}$, $\dfrac{\pi}{6}$, $\dfrac{\pi}{4}$, and $\dfrac{\pi}{3}$.

   One cycle of the graph is drawn in Fig. 14-10.

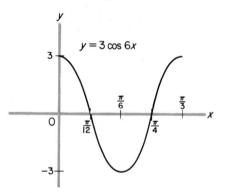

FIGURE 14-10

example 2

Sketch the graph of $y = -2\cos(7x - \pi)$.

1. The amplitude is $|a| = |-2| = 2$.

2. Because $a < 0$, the curve has an *inverted* cosine curve pattern.

3. If $7x - \pi = 0$, then $x = \pi/7$. A cycle begins when $x_b = \pi/7$.

4. If $7x - \pi = 2\pi$, then $x = 3\pi/7$. The cycle above ends when $x_e = 3\pi/7$.

5. The period p is

$$p = \frac{2\pi}{b} = \frac{2\pi}{7}.$$

6. Important points: when $x = \dfrac{\pi}{7}, \dfrac{3\pi}{14}, \dfrac{2\pi}{7}, \dfrac{5\pi}{14},$ and $\dfrac{3\pi}{7}$.

One cycle of the graph is drawn in Fig. 14-11.

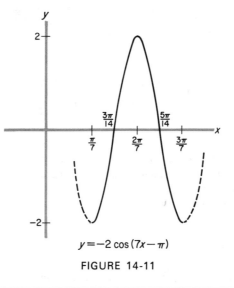

$$y = -2 \cos(7x - \pi)$$

FIGURE 14-11

In electrical circuits it is often necessary to deal with the *phase relationship* between trigonometric functions having the same period. For example, in ac circuits the voltage and current are both expressible as cosine or sine functions. The graphs of these functions do not necessarily pass through their zero (or maximum) values at the same instant of time. If they do not rise and fall together, a *phase difference* is said to exist between them.

In Fig. 14-12, we have indicated three different phase relationships that exist between a voltage V and a current I in an ac circuit. Figures 14-12 (a), (b), and (c), respectively, represent an ac generator connected in series to a pure resistor R, a pure capacitor C, and a pure inductor L. In (a), the current and voltage are said to be *in phase* because they pass through their zero values and maximum values at the same instant of time. This relationship is characteristic of a purely resistive ac circuit. In (b), the current and voltage are said to be 90° *out of phase* because their corresponding maximum values and zero values occur $\frac{1}{4}$ cycle apart. Note that in discussing phase relationships the engineer speaks in terms of *electrical degrees*, where 1 cycle represents 360 electrical degrees. More specifically we say that in (b) the current *leads*

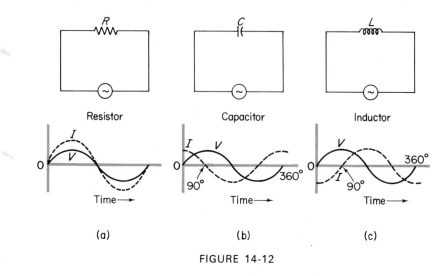

FIGURE 14-12

the voltage by 90° because it reaches its maximum (or zero) value $\frac{1}{4}$ cycle, or 90 electrical degrees, earlier than the voltage does as we view the curves from left to right. Equivalently, we can say that the voltage *lags* the current by 90°. This is characteristic of a purely capacitive ac circuit. Finally, in (c) the voltage *leads* the current by 90°—characteristic of a purely inductive ac circuit.

Exercise 14-3

*In Problems **1–12**, draw one cycle of each curve. Give the amplitude A and the period p.*

1. $y = \frac{1}{2} \cos x.$

2. $y = -3 \cos x.$

3. $y = 4 \cos 4t.$

4. $y = \frac{1}{2} \cos 5x.$

5. $y = -4 \cos 3x.$

6. $y = \cos \left(4x - \frac{\pi}{2} \right).$

7. $y = 2 \cos \left(x + \frac{\pi}{3} \right).$

8. $y = \cos \left(\frac{1}{4} x \right).$

9. $y = -2 \cos \left(\frac{x}{2} - \frac{2\pi}{3} \right).$

10. $y = 3 \cos \left(x - \frac{\pi}{6} \right).$

11. $y = \cos \left(\pi x - \frac{\pi}{2} \right).$

12. $y = 2 \cos (3x + 1).$

13. The voltage across an inductor in an ac circuit can be described mathematically by the equation $y_1 = 2 \cos 3x$. The voltage across another component in the same circuit is given by $y_2 = \cos \left(3x - \frac{\pi}{2} \right)$. What is the phase relationship between these two voltage signals—that is, which of the curves leads the other and by how many electrical degrees?

14. If a uniform metal disk with its plane horizontal is suspended by a wire attached to its center, the device is called a torsional pendulum. If the disk is now rotated through an angle in the horizontal plane and released, it will execute simple angular harmonic motion. For such motion the angular displacement θ from the equilibrium position is given by the equation

$$\theta = \theta_m \cos(\omega t + \alpha),$$

where θ_m is the maximum displacement in radians, ω is the angular frequency in radians per second, t is time in seconds, and α is the phase angle in radians. Draw one cycle of the graph of this equation if $\omega = \pi$ and $\alpha = \pi/2$.

15. In a series ac circuit having a current $I = 2 \sin(120\,\pi t)$, the voltage across a pure capacitor as a function of time is $V = -3 \cos(120\,\pi t)$. Sketch the graph of both of these equations on the same coordinate plane and determine the phase difference between I and V.

14-4 The Sine Curve and Harmonic Motion

When a particle moves around a circle at a constant speed, the projection of the particle on a diameter of the circle, which we shall describe, is said to be in *simple harmonic motion*. In physics, a discussion of simple harmonic motion (SHM) is often presented with a geometric approach. Because that technique illustrates the natural occurrence of sine and cosine curves in a technical context, it is worthy of our brief consideration.

Figure 14-13 shows a particle P on a circle with radius A and center at the origin. We shall assume that the particle is moving counterclockwise around the

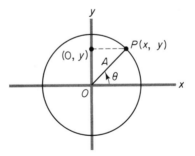

FIGURE 14-13

circle at a constant angular speed ω, which is measured in radians per second. The radius vector from O to P represents the position of P with respect to O.

As the radius vector rotates counterclockwise from an initial position along the positive x-axis, it generates a positive angle θ. If $\theta = 0$ when time $t = 0$, then at some later time t we have

$$\theta = \omega t. \tag{1}$$

Because there are 2π rad in one revolution, the angular speed ω is related to the frequency f (the number of revolutions completed by P in a second) by the equation

$$\omega = 2\pi f. \tag{2}$$

From Eqs. 1 and 2, we can write

$$\theta = 2\pi f t \tag{3}$$

When the particle, and therefore the endpoint of the radius vector, is at (x_1, y_1), then $\sin \theta_1 = y_1/A$ (Fig. 14-14). When the particle is at (x_2, y_2), then $\sin \theta_2 = y_2/A$. In fact, regardless of the position (x, y) of particle P we have

$$\sin \theta = \frac{y}{A} \quad \text{or} \quad y = A \sin \theta. \tag{4}$$

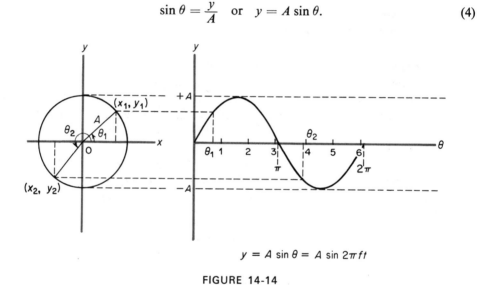

$$y = A \sin \theta = A \sin 2\pi f t$$

FIGURE 14-14

Thus we conclude that for any position (x, y) of particle P, the value of the ordinate y is expressible in terms of the sine of the generated angle. Moreover, from (4) and (3), we have

$$y = A \sin \theta = A \sin 2\pi f t. \tag{5}$$

The resulting graph of $y = A \sin \theta$ for one counterclockwise revolution of the radius vector is also shown in Fig. 14-14. This sine curve was obtained as follows: For a given value of θ, the ordinate of a point on the curve $y = A \sin \theta$ is the same as the ordinate of the position of the particle for the same value of θ. This is indicated by the broken lines. The values of θ along the horizontal axis are in radians. Observe, for example, that when the particle moves in the third or fourth quadrants, its ordinate is negative. Therefore, the graph of $y = A \sin \theta$ falls below the θ-axis for θ between π and 2π. Although only a portion of the curve is shown, it should be realized that the curve continues in this manner indefinitely. Similarly, you should realize that values of $A \sin \theta$ for negative angles could be found by considering *clockwise* rotation of the radius vector.

When the particle P is at point (x, y), the point $(0, y)$ is called the **projection** of P on the y-axis (refer back to Fig. 14-13). If P begins at $(A, 0)$ and travels once around the circle, then its projection travels on the y-axis from $(0, 0)$ to $(0, A)$, then to $(0, -A)$, and back to $(0, 0)$. Thus, the projection will move up and down on the diameter of the circle between $(0, A)$ and $(0, -A)$. The motion of the projection on the y-axis is an example of simple harmonic motion (SHM). The period of the SHM is the same as the time of one revolution of P around the circle. The frequency of the SHM is the same as the number of revolutions per second that P makes around the circle.

Equation 5, which gives the y-axis position of the projection executing SHM along the y-axis, is restricted in the sense that if $t = 0$, then $y = 0$. For a real motion we might expect that if $t = 0$, then y could have some other value between $-A$ and A. That is taken care of in the following more general form for the equation of SHM.

$$y = A \sin (2\pi ft + \varphi), \tag{6}$$

where φ is called the phase constant. In particular we note that if $\varphi = \pi/2$, then the curve generated in the manner of Fig. 14-14 is

$$y = A \sin \left(2\pi ft + \frac{\pi}{2}\right) = A \cos 2\pi ft,$$

a cosine curve (this follows from the fact that $\sin \left(x + \frac{\pi}{2}\right) = \cos x$, which was stated in Sec. 14-3). Simple harmonic motions are described in terms of both sine and cosine functions.

14-5   Graphs of Tangent, Cotangent, Secant, and Cosecant

While the graphs of the sine and cosine functions were both smooth curves exhibiting wavelike appearances, the graphs of the remaining trigonometric functions are strikingly different. Consider the function

$$y = \tan x.$$

In Table 14-3 are x- and y-values for $y = \tan x$ (some y-values are approximate). The dashes when $x = \pm \pi/2$ and $x = \pm 3\pi/2$ mean that $\tan x$ is not defined there.

Figure 14-15 shows the graph of $y = \tan x$. As expected, there are no points on the graph when $x = \pm\pi/2, \pm 3\pi/2$. But for x near these values, $\tan x$ increases or de-

Table 14-3

x	0	$\dfrac{\pi}{6}$	$\dfrac{\pi}{3}$	$\dfrac{\pi}{2}$	$\dfrac{2\pi}{3}$	$\dfrac{5\pi}{6}$	π	$\dfrac{7\pi}{6}$	$\dfrac{4\pi}{3}$	$\dfrac{3\pi}{2}$
$y = \tan x$	0	0.6	1.7	—	−1.7	−0.6	0	0.6	1.7	—

x	$-\dfrac{\pi}{6}$	$-\dfrac{\pi}{3}$	$-\dfrac{\pi}{2}$	$-\dfrac{2\pi}{3}$	$-\dfrac{5\pi}{6}$	$-\pi$	$-\dfrac{7\pi}{6}$	$-\dfrac{4\pi}{3}$	$-\dfrac{3\pi}{2}$
$y = \tan x$	−0.6	−1.7	—	1.7	0.6	0	−0.6	−1.7	—

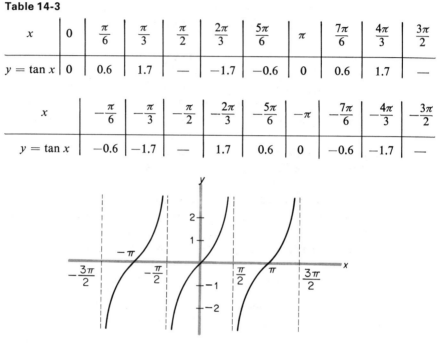

$y = \tan x$

FIGURE 14-15

creases without bound. The graph gets very close to the vertical lines $x = \pm\pi/2$, $\pm 3\pi/2$, but does not touch them. These lines are called **vertical asymptotes** of the curve; they are lines near which the function "blows up." However, they are *not* part of the graph. We also see that the portion of the graph between $x = -\pi/2$ and $x = \pi/2$ repeats itself. Thus

$$\boxed{y = \tan x \text{ has period } \pi.}$$

That is, $\tan (x + \pi) = \tan x$. Only three cycles of $y = \tan x$ are shown in Fig. 14-15, but it should be clear that the graph continues both to the left and right. Because $\tan x$ has no maximum or minimum values, no amplitude is assigned to it.

The graph of $y = \csc x$ can be conveniently sketched if we use the reciprocal relationship

$$\csc x = \frac{1}{\sin x}.$$

We first sketch the sine function (see the broken curve in Fig. 14-16). For a point (x, y) on the graph of $y = \sin x$, we estimate the value of y. The reciprocal of this value is then the ordinate of the corresponding point on $y = \csc x$ with the same

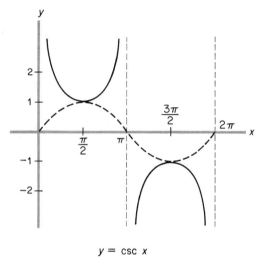

$$y = \csc x$$

FIGURE 14-16

abscissa. For example, when $\sin x = \frac{1}{2}$, then $\csc x = 2$; when $\sin x = 1$, then $\csc x = 1$; and so on. In this way we can get the entire graph of $y = \csc x$. The solid curve in Fig. 14-16 shows one cycle. Just as $\sin x$ has period 2π,

$$\boxed{y = \csc x \text{ has period } 2\pi.}$$

For $x = 0, \pi, 2\pi$, and so on, $\sin x = 0$. Thus $\csc x$ is not defined for these values. The lines $x = 0, \pi, 2\pi$, and so forth are vertical asymptotes. No amplitude is assigned to $y = \csc x$.

By similar reasoning we can also sketch the graphs of

$$y = \cot x = \frac{1}{\tan x} \quad \text{and} \quad y = \sec x = \frac{1}{\cos x}.$$

These graphs, with the graphs of the corresponding reciprocal functions shown in broken curves, are indicated in Figs. 14-17 and 14-18. Note that when $\tan x = 0$, $\cot x$ is undefined; when $\tan x$ is undefined, $\cot x = 0$. It should be clear that

$\cot (x + \pi) = \cot x$ and $\sec (x + 2\pi) = \sec x$. That is,

$y = \cot x$ has period π.

$y = \sec x$ has period 2π.

No amplitudes are assigned to these functions.

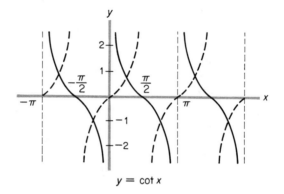

$y = \cot x$

FIGURE 14-17

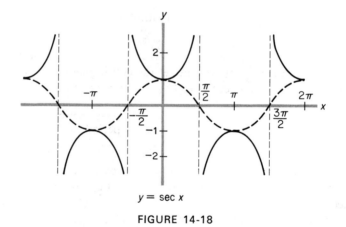

$y = \sec x$

FIGURE 14-18

Exercise 14-5

1. Draw the graph of $y = \csc x$. Use this graph to find all angles x between zero and 4π for which $\csc x = -1$.

2. Draw the graph of $y = \cot x$. Use this graph to find all angles x between zero and 2π for which $\cot x = 0$.

3. Draw the graph of $y = \tan x$. Use this graph to find all angles x between $-\pi/2$ and $5\pi/2$ for which $\tan x = 0$.

4. Draw the graph of $y = \sec x$. Use this graph to find all angles x between $-5\pi/2$ and $5\pi/2$ for which $\sec x = 1$.

14-6 Combinations of Trigonometric Functions— Addition of Ordinates

In certain applications, physical phenomena are representable mathematically as sums or differences of trigonometric functions. The graphs of such combinations of trigonometric functions may be sketched by a technique known as **addition of ordinates**. We shall illustrate this method by sketching the graph of $y = \sin x + \cos x$. This equation can be thought of as representing the sum of two functions:

$$y = y_1 + y_2, \quad \text{where } y_1 = \sin x \quad \text{and} \quad y_2 = \cos x.$$

We first sketch the graphs of $y_1 = \sin x$ and $y_2 = \cos x$ on the same coordinate plane, as shown in Fig. 14-19. These graphs are then combined by adding the ordinates (y-values) corresponding to the same abscissa (x-value). For example, point P is

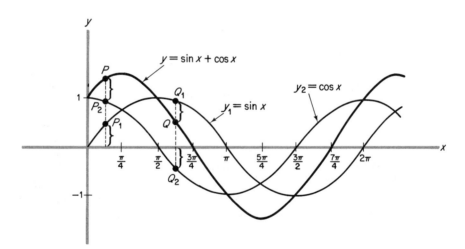

FIGURE 14-19

obtained by measuring the ordinate of P_1 (see the lower brace) and adding it algebraically to the ordinate of P_2 (see the upper brace). To obtain point Q, we add the negative ordinate of point Q_2 to the ordinate of Q_1. After a suitable number of points are obtained in this manner, they are connected by a smooth curve. Thus we obtain the graph of $y = \sin x + \cos x$. Engineers often speak of this addition of ordinates as the *principle of superposition*.

example 1

Sketch the graph of $y = \sin x + \frac{1}{3} \sin 3x$.

We first sketch the graphs of $y_1 = \sin x$ and $y_2 = \frac{1}{3} \sin 3x$ on the same coordinate plane (Fig. 14-20) using the facts that $\sin x$ has amplitude 1 and period 2π, but $\frac{1}{3} \sin 3x$

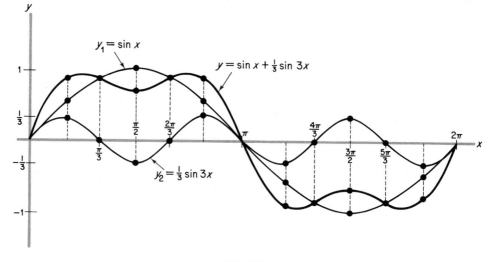

FIGURE 14-20

has amplitude $\frac{1}{3}$ and period $2\pi/3$. Next, at various values of x we add the y-values of the two graphs. We then connect the points by a smooth curve.

The French mathematician J. Fourier (1768–1830) showed that we can analyze extremely complicated periodic waves as a combination of relatively simple waves. By his technique, well known in engineering as Fourier analysis, it can be shown that a periodic function can be represented as an infinite series—that is, an unending sum of terms—each term of which is a sine or cosine function. Example 2 gives an illustration.

example 2

The broken curve of Fig. 14-21(a) is a sawtooth waveform, a periodic curve commonly associated with the oscilloscope. Figure 14-21(b) shows the graphs of the first six terms of the Fourier series for that periodic wave. The solid curve in Fig. 14-21(a) is the sum of the first six terms of the Fourier series found from the graphs in (b) by the technique of addition of ordinates. The solid curve can be seen to be a fairly close approximation of the sawtooth waveform. As additional terms of the Fourier series are included, the approximation continually improves. Hence, the sawtooth waveform has been expressed as a sum of relatively simple sine curves.

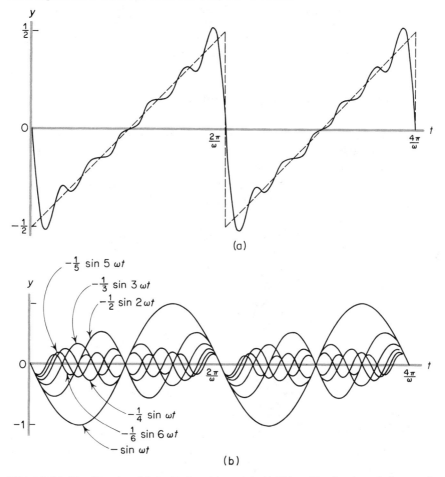

FIGURE 14-21 (Reprinted from R. Resnick and D. Halliday, *Physics,* 1st ed., by permission of John Wiley & Sons, Inc.)

Exercise 14-6

In Problems 1-8, sketch the graph of the given equation over the given interval by means of addition of ordinates.

1. $y = 2 + \sin x$; 0 to 2π.

2. $y = 1 + \cos x$; 0 to 2π.

3. $y = \sin x + \sin 2x$; 0 to 2π.

4. $y = \sin 2x + 2 \sin x$; 0 to 2π.

5. $y = \sin 2x + \cos 3x$; 0 to π.

6. $y = 4 \sin x - 3 \cos x$; 0 to 2π.

7. $y = x + \sin x$; 0 to 3π.

8. $y = \cos 3x - \sin 2x$; 0 to π.

9. Consider a string fixed at both ends in which a wavetrain is initiated by plucking the string. Waves will be reflected from both ends of the string with the resulting shape of the string determined by the sum of the two waves, one traveling to the right and the other traveling to the left. If the wave traveling to the right is given by $y_1 = 2 \sin \pi(x - t)$ and the one to the left by $y_2 = 2 \sin \pi(x + t)$, find the shape of the string as a function of position at $t = 3$ s.

14-7 Inverse Trigonometric Functions

For the function $w = f(t) = \sin t$, the inputs are t's and the outputs are w's. Suppose we reverse these roles by thinking of the number w as an *input*, where $-1 \le w \le 1$, and the angle t as an *output*. For example, if the input is $w = \frac{1}{2}$, then the output is an angle t such that $\frac{1}{2} = \sin t$. There are many values of t that we can choose here, such as $-7\pi/6$, $\pi/6$, $5\pi/6$, and $13\pi/6$, as shown in Fig. 14-22.

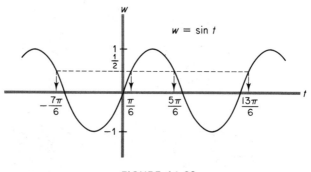

FIGURE 14-22

Because there is more than one output for one input, the equation $w = \sin t$ does *not* define t as a function of w. However, if we restrict the values of t so that

$$-\frac{\pi}{2} \le t \le \frac{\pi}{2},$$

then to each input w there corresponds exactly one value of t and we *do* have a function of w (Fig. 14-23). Thus if $\frac{1}{2}$ is the input, then the output is $\pi/6$ because

$$\sin \frac{\pi}{6} = \frac{1}{2} \quad \text{and} \quad -\frac{\pi}{2} \le \frac{\pi}{6} \le \frac{\pi}{2}.$$

Similarly, if -1 is the input, then $-\pi/2$ is the output because

$$\sin\left(-\frac{\pi}{2}\right) = -1 \quad \text{and} \quad -\frac{\pi}{2} \le -\frac{\pi}{2} \le \frac{\pi}{2}.$$

This function that reverses the action of the sine function and sends numbers into angles is called the **arcsine function** or **inverse sine function**. It is written arcsin

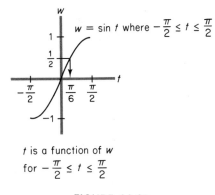

t is a function of w

for $-\dfrac{\pi}{2} \leq t \leq \dfrac{\pi}{2}$

FIGURE 14-23

or $\sin^{-1}$, where the -1 is not an exponent but simply part of this new symbol. (This function is also written with capital letters as Arcsin or Sin^{-1}.) Thus

$$t = \arcsin w = \sin^{-1} w.$$

In the discussion above, let us replace the input number w by x and the output angle t by y. Then to say that

$$y = \arcsin x$$

means that y is the angle (*in radians*) having a sine of x (that is, $\sin y = x$) such that

$$-\frac{\pi}{2} \leq y \leq \frac{\pi}{2}.$$

Note that the domain of $y = \arcsin x$ consists of all x such that $-1 \leq x \leq 1$.

> $y = \arcsin x$ means $x = \sin y$,
>
> where $-\dfrac{\pi}{2} \leq y \leq \dfrac{\pi}{2}$ and $-1 \leq x \leq 1$.

We define inverse trigonometric functions for the cosine and tangent functions as follows.

> $y = \arccos x$ means $x = \cos y$,
>
> where $0 \leq y \leq \pi$ and $-1 \leq x \leq 1$.

> $y = \arctan x$ means $x = \tan y$,
>
> where $-\dfrac{\pi}{2} < y < \dfrac{\pi}{2}$ and x is any real number.

For the inverse tangent function, note that the values $\pm\pi/2$ are excluded for y, because the tangent function is not defined at these values.

example 1

Find each of the following.

a. $\arcsin \dfrac{\sqrt{2}}{2}$.

Arcsin $\dfrac{\sqrt{2}}{2}$ is *the* angle between $-\dfrac{\pi}{2}$ and $\dfrac{\pi}{2}$ with a sine of $\dfrac{\sqrt{2}}{2}$. Clearly, we have $\arcsin \dfrac{\sqrt{2}}{2} = \dfrac{\pi}{4}$.

b. $\arccos \dfrac{1}{2}$.

Arccos $\dfrac{1}{2}$ is *the* angle between 0 and π with a cosine of $\dfrac{1}{2}$. Thus $\arccos \dfrac{1}{2} = \dfrac{\pi}{3}$.

c. $\arccos \left(-\dfrac{\sqrt{3}}{2} \right)$.

Arccos $\left(-\dfrac{\sqrt{3}}{2} \right)$ is *the* angle, call it y, between 0 and π such that $\cos y = -\dfrac{\sqrt{3}}{2}$. Because $\cos y$ is negative, then y must be a second-quadrant angle. If its reference angle is y_{ref}, then $\cos y_{\text{ref}} = \dfrac{\sqrt{3}}{2}$. Clearly, y_{ref} must be $\dfrac{\pi}{6}$, so $y = \pi - \dfrac{\pi}{6} = \dfrac{5\pi}{6}$. Thus $\arccos \left(-\dfrac{\sqrt{3}}{2} \right) = \dfrac{5\pi}{6}$.

d. $\arctan (-1)$.

Arctan (-1) is *the* angle between $-\dfrac{\pi}{2}$ and $\dfrac{\pi}{2}$ with a tangent of -1. Therefore, $\arctan (-1) = -\dfrac{\pi}{4}$.

example 2

Find each of the following.

a. $\sin (\arcsin \tfrac{1}{4})$.

Arcsin $\tfrac{1}{4}$ is an angle with a sine of $\tfrac{1}{4}$. Thus the sine of this angle is $\tfrac{1}{4}$, so

$$\sin \left(\arcsin \frac{1}{4} \right) = \frac{1}{4}.$$

In general, $\sin (\arcsin x) = x$.

b. $\cos (\arcsin 0)$.

Because arcsin $0 = 0$, then

$$\cos (\arcsin 0) = \cos (0) = 1.$$

c. $\arcsin \left(\sin \dfrac{5\pi}{6} \right).$

$$\arcsin \left(\sin \dfrac{5\pi}{6} \right) = \arcsin \left(\dfrac{1}{2} \right) = \dfrac{\pi}{6}.$$

Note that $\arcsin \left(\sin \dfrac{5\pi}{6} \right) \neq \dfrac{5\pi}{6}.$

The remaining inverse trigonometric functions, which are not frequently used, can be defined as follows.

$y = \text{arccot } x \quad \text{means} \quad x = \cot y \text{ and } 0 < y < \pi.$

$y = \text{arcsec } x \quad \text{means} \quad x = \sec y \text{ and } 0 \leq y \leq \pi, \, y \neq \pi/2.$

$y = \text{arccsc } x \quad \text{means} \quad x = \csc y \text{ and } -\pi/2 \leq y \leq \pi/2, \, y \neq 0.$

The graphs of some inverse trigonometric functions are shown in Fig. 14-24.

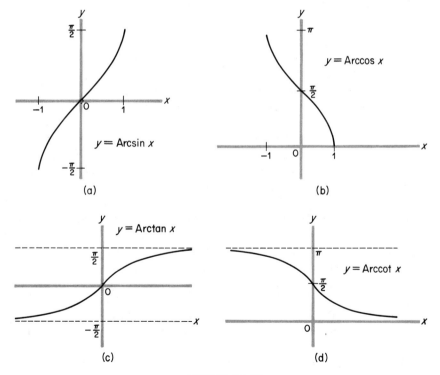

FIGURE 14-24

Exercise 14-7

Find the value of each of the following.

1. arcsin 1.

2. arcsin $\dfrac{\sqrt{3}}{2}$.

3. arccos $\dfrac{\sqrt{3}}{2}$.

4. arccos (-1).

5. arctan 0.

6. arcsin $\left(-\dfrac{\sqrt{2}}{2}\right)$.

7. arcsin $\left(-\dfrac{1}{2}\right)$.

8. arccos 0.

9. arctan 1.

10. arctan $(-\sqrt{3})$.

11. arccos $\left(-\dfrac{\sqrt{2}}{2}\right)$.

12. arccos $(-\frac{1}{2})$.

13. sin (arcsin $\frac{1}{3}$).

14. cos [arccos $(-\frac{1}{5})$].

15. cos (arcsin $\frac{1}{2}$).

16. sin [arccos (-1)].

17. cot (arccos 0).

18. tan (arccos 1).

19. cos [arctan (-1)].

20. sin $\left(\text{arctan } \dfrac{\sqrt{3}}{3}\right)$.

21. arcsin $\left(\sin \dfrac{2\pi}{3}\right)$.

22. arcsin $\left(\sin \dfrac{\pi}{3}\right)$.

14-8   The Oscilloscope—Lissajous Figures

We now consider the generation of *Lissajous figures* on the screen of a cathode-ray oscilloscope. The oscilloscope is one of the most useful and versatile instruments available to the engineer.

The heart of an oscilloscope is the cathode-ray tube in which a narrow beam of high-speed electrons strikes a special screen which fluoresces; that is, it gives off visible light at the point where the beam strikes the screen. The position at which the beam strikes the screen can be controlled by two pairs of *deflection plates*. Depending on its polarity, a voltage signal applied to the horizontal deflection plates will cause the beam to move to the right or to the left; a signal applied to the vertical deflection plates will cause the beam to move up or down.

When sinusoidal signals (that is, signals represented by sine or cosine curves) are applied to the two pairs of deflecting plates, the path traced out by the flourescent dot formed by the impinging electron beam forms a pattern on the screen of the oscilloscope. Furthermore, the pattern will remain stationary as long as the amplitudes and phase relationships of the signals applied to the deflection plates do not change.

Let us consider a simple situation. Suppose a voltage signal in the shape of a sine curve is applied to the vertical deflection plates with *no signal* applied to the horizontal deflection plates. This situation is illustrated in Fig. 14-25 where, for convenience, we show rectangular coordinate axes on the screen of the oscilloscope. With no signal applied to the horizontal deflection plates, the dot will not move to the left or right and, hence, it will remain on the *y*-axis. Its motion on the *y*-axis is

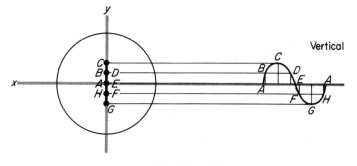

FIGURE 14-25

controlled by the signal applied to the vertical deflection plates as shown in Fig. 14-25. The dot is at the center of the screen when the voltage applied to the vertical deflection plates is at point A on the voltage signal. The dot moves upward along the y-axis and reaches a maximum height at point C as the voltage applied to the deflection plates reaches its maximum value at point C.* Then, corresponding to a decreasing voltage signal between points C and G, the dot moves downward along the y-axis, reaching its lowest position at point G. Since the voltage signal increases to its original value in the last quarter of the cycle between points G and A, the dot will rise along the y-axis and return to its initial position. If the frequency of the signal to the vertical deflection plates were, for example, 60 cycles per second, the travels of the dot outlined above would be repeated 60 times each second. It is not surprising then that we should "see" a *stationary* vertical line on the oscilloscope screen.

It should be clear that if the sinusoidal voltage shown in Fig. 14-25 were applied to the horizontal deflection plates with no signal applied to the vertical deflection plates, the dot would trace a path back and forth along the x-axis and we should "see" a horizontal line on the oscilloscope screen.

When sinusoidal signals are simultaneously applied to both sets of deflection plates, the pattern which results depends on the amplitudes, frequencies, and phase relationships of the two signals. The patterns observed on the screen when the ratio of the frequencies of the two signals can be expressed as a ratio of integers are called **Lissajous figures.**

As an example let us consider voltage signals that have the *same* frequency f, *different* amplitudes, and are 90° out of phase with one another. The mathematical form of such voltage signals applied to the horizontal and vertical deflection plates are given by Eqs. (1) and (2),

$$V_x = 4 \sin (\omega t) \tag{1}$$

$$V_y = 2 \cos (\omega t) \tag{2}$$

*Because of a scaling factor, these heights may not necessarily be the same.

In each case we assume the value of ω is the same; it represents the constant quantity $2\pi f$, called the *angular frequency*. The physical situation is illustrated in Fig. 14-26. By considering the horizontal and vertical deflections simultaneously, it should be

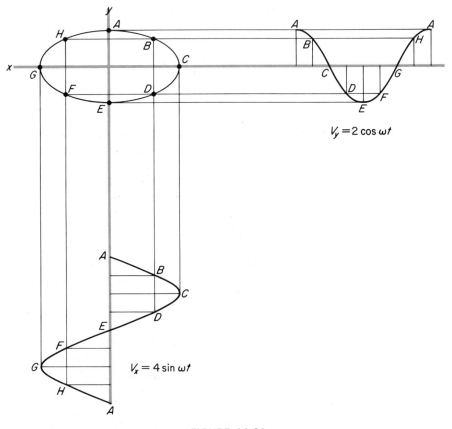

$$V_y = 2 \cos \omega t$$

$$V_x = 4 \sin \omega t$$

FIGURE 14-26

clear that these voltage signals will result in the generation of the Lissajous figure shown, which is called an ellipse. Moreover, it should be apparent that if the amplitudes of the two signals were the same, the Lissajous figure would be a circle.

An important application of Lissajous figures is in the calibration of signal generators or, indeed, in any instance where a frequency comparison is desired. Photographs of actual Lissajous patterns for various values of the ratio f_y/f_x, where f_y and f_x are the frequencies of the vertical and horizontal signals, respectively, are shown in Fig. 14-27. Each of these patterns was generated by using signals of equal amplitudes to the vertical and horizontal deflection plates.

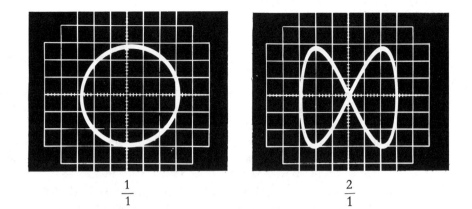

$$\frac{1}{1} \qquad \frac{2}{1}$$

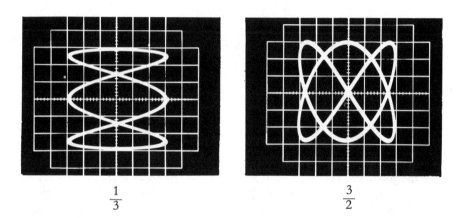

$$\frac{1}{3} \qquad \frac{3}{2}$$

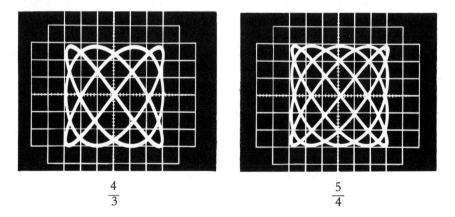

$$\frac{4}{3} \qquad \frac{5}{4}$$

FIGURE 14-27 (Courtesy Donald Lyons)

Exercise 14-8

1. Construct a diagram similar to Fig. 14-26 and determine the resulting pattern on the screen if $V_x = 2 \sin \omega t$ and $V_y = 2 \sin \omega t$.

2. In Problem 1, if the amplitude of the vertical deflection signal were increased while that of the horizontal deflection signal remained the same, how would the pattern on the screen change?

3. How would the pattern of Fig. 14-26 appear if the deflection voltages were switched, that is, if the vertical signal were applied to the horizontal deflection plates and the horizontal signal were applied to the vertical deflection plates?

4. As an example of the Lissajous patterns generated for ratios of vertical to horizontal frequencies which are expressible by integers, construct a diagram for

$$V_x = \sin 2\pi t$$

and

$$V_y = \sin 4\pi t,$$

which illustrates the ratio $f_y/f_x = 2/1$.

14-9 Polar Coordinates

Besides representing a point in a plane by its rectangular coordinates (x, y), we can use another system called the **polar coordinate system** to represent points. We shall impose such a system on a rectangular coordinate plane. Here the origin O is called the **pole**, and the positive x-axis is called the **polar axis** (Fig. 14-28). For any point P (except the pole), let r be the distance from the pole to P, and let θ be the angle (in radians or degrees) from the polar axis to the line segment OP. The pair of numbers r and θ locate P, and we refer to the ordered pair (r, θ) as **polar coordinates** for P. For example, Fig. 14-29 gives some points and a polar-coordinate representation of each point. Note that θ can be negative. The pole has polar coordinates $(0, \theta)$, where θ is any angle.

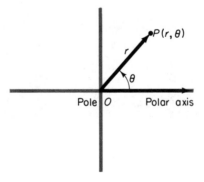

FIGURE 14-28

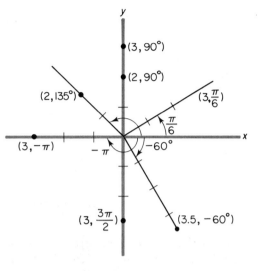

FIGURE 14-29

As opposed to rectangular coordinates in which each point has exactly one representation, with polar coordinates there are infinitely many ways to represent a given point. For example, the point $(3, \pi/6)$ in Fig. 14-30(a) can also be represented by $(3, \frac{\pi}{6} + 2\pi)$. Similarly, $(2, 90°)$ and $(2, -270°)$ are polar coordinates for the same point [Fig. 14-30(b)].

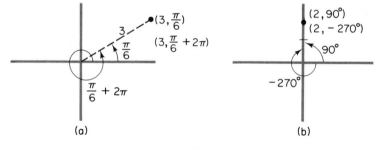

FIGURE 14-30

For positive values of the r-coordinate, the point located by (r, θ) is on the terminal side of θ. Actually, we can also permit negative values of the r-coordinate. We consider the polar coordinates $(-r, \theta)$, where $r > 0$, to locate the point that is a distance of r from the pole but that is on the backward extension of the terminal side of θ drawn through the pole. This means that if θ is in degrees, then $(-r, \theta)$ and $(r, \theta + 180°)$ represent the same point, as shown in Fig. 14-31(a). Some other examples are given in Fig. 14-31(b).

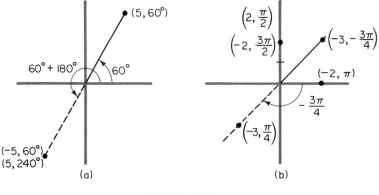

(a)   (b)

FIGURE 14-31

From Fig. 14-32 and our knowledge of trigonometry, it follows that if P has rectangular coordinates (x, y) and polar coordinates (r, θ), then

$$x = r \cos \theta, \qquad y = r \sin \theta,$$
$$r^2 = x^2 + y^2,$$
$$\tan \theta = \frac{y}{x}, \quad \text{for } x \neq 0.$$

These relations are used to convert from polar form to rectangular form, and vice versa, as Example 1 shows.

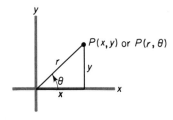

FIGURE 14-32

example 1

Find the rectangular coordinates of the point having polar coordinates $(4, 3\pi/4)$.

We have

$$x = r \cos \theta = 4 \cos \frac{3\pi}{4} = 4\left(-\frac{\sqrt{2}}{2}\right) = -2\sqrt{2}.$$

$$y = r \sin \theta = 4 \sin \frac{3\pi}{4} = 4\left(\frac{\sqrt{2}}{2}\right) = 2\sqrt{2}.$$

The rectangular coordinates are $(-2\sqrt{2}, 2\sqrt{2})$.

example 2

Find polar coordinates of the point having the rectangular coordinates $(3, -5)$. See Fig. 14-33.

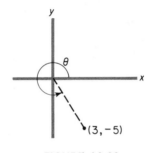

FIGURE 14-33

We have

$$r^2 = x^2 + y^2 = 3^2 + (-5)^2 = 34.$$

Choosing a positive value of r for convenience gives

$$r = \sqrt{34} = 5.83.$$

Also,

$$\tan \theta = \frac{y}{x} = \frac{-5}{3} = -1.66667.$$

Since $\tan \theta$ is negative and $(3, -5)$ lies in the fourth quadrant, we can choose $\theta = 300.96°$. Thus the point has polar coordinates $(5.83, 300.96°)$. Choosing $r = -\sqrt{34}$ and $\theta = 120.96°$ also gives a polar representation of the point.

The graph of a polar equation in the variables r and θ consists of all points (r, θ) that satisfy the equation. The remaining examples illustrate the sketching of polar equations.

example 3

Sketch the graph of the polar equation $r = 2$.

The equation can be thought of as $r = 2 + 0\theta$. Thus, for *any* value of θ, we have $r = 2$. Therefore the graph is a circle of radius 2 (Fig. 14-34).

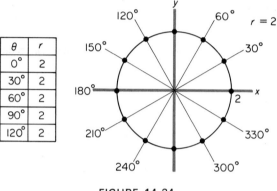

θ	r
$0°$	2
$30°$	2
$60°$	2
$90°$	2
$120°$	2

FIGURE 14-34

example 4

Sketch the polar graph of $r = 2 \sin \theta$.

Choosing some values of θ between $0°$ and $360°$ and finding the corresponding values of r, we obtain Table 14-4.

Table 14-4

θ	$0°$	$30°$	$45°$	$60°$	$90°$	$120°$	$135°$	$150°$	$180°$
r	0	1	$\sqrt{2}$	$\sqrt{3}$	2	$\sqrt{3}$	$\sqrt{2}$	1	0

θ	$210°$	$225°$	$240°$	$270°$	$300°$	$315°$	$330°$	$360°$
r	-1	$-\sqrt{2}$	$-\sqrt{3}$	-2	$-\sqrt{3}$	$-\sqrt{2}$	-1	0

Connecting the points by a smooth curve gives Fig. 14-35. Because the sine function has period $360°$, we shall not obtain any new points for $\theta > 360°$ or $\theta < 0°$. In fact, for θ between $180°$ and $360°$, note that $r < 0$ and the corresponding points are the same as those for θ between $0°$ and $180°$. It can be shown that the graph is a circle.

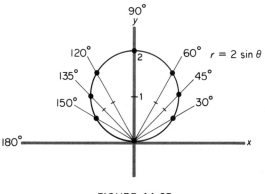

FIGURE 14-35

example 5

Sketch the graph of the polar equation $r = \theta$, where $\theta \geq 0$.

See Fig. 14-36. The graph, which is an unending spiral, is called the *spiral of Archimedes*. Here, θ must be in radians. Observe that as θ increases, r increases.

θ	r
0	0
$\dfrac{\pi}{4}$	0.8
$\dfrac{\pi}{2}$	1.6
π	3.1
$\dfrac{3\pi}{2}$	4.7
2π	6.3
$\dfrac{5\pi}{2}$	7.9

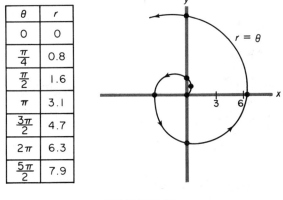

FIGURE 14-36

Sketching polar graphs can be made less time consuming if *polar coordinate graph paper* is used. This paper consists of concentric circles and rays (like spokes on a wheel) (Fig. 14-37).

example 6

Sketch the graph of $r = 2(1 + \cos \theta)$.

Figure 14-37 shows the graph, which is called a *cardioid*.

497

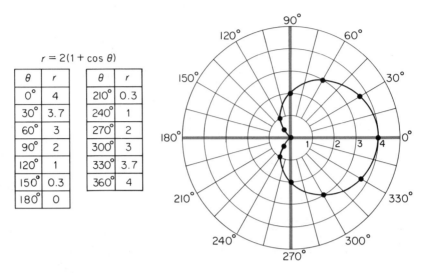

$$r = 2(1 + \cos \theta)$$

θ	r
$0°$	4
$30°$	3.7
$60°$	3
$90°$	2
$120°$	1
$150°$	0.3
$180°$	0

θ	r
$210°$	0.3
$240°$	1
$270°$	2
$300°$	3
$330°$	3.7
$360°$	4

FIGURE 14-37

Exercise 14-9

In Problems **1–12**, plot the points with the given polar coordinates.

1. $(1, 30°)$. **2.** $\left(2, \frac{\pi}{2}\right)$. **3.** $(2, -60°)$. **4.** $(3, 45°)$.

5. $(1.5, 180°)$. **6.** $\left(3, \frac{3\pi}{4}\right)$. **7.** $\left(-3, \frac{5\pi}{6}\right)$. **8.** $\left(2, \frac{5\pi}{4}\right)$.

9. $(-2, -60°)$. **10.** $(-3, 0)$. **11.** $(2.5, 195°)$. **12.** $\left(-4, -\frac{\pi}{2}\right)$.

In Problems **13–22**, find rectangular coordinates for each point with the given polar coordinates.

13. $(3, 60°)$. **14.** $(0, -\pi)$. **15.** $\left(2, \frac{3\pi}{4}\right)$. **16.** $(4, 0)$.

17. $(5, -150°)$. **18.** $\left(\frac{3}{5}, -\frac{5\pi}{3}\right)$. **19.** $\left(-2, \frac{7\pi}{4}\right)$. **20.** $(3, 270°)$.

21. $(-5, -20.6°)$. **22.** $(0, 0)$.

In Problems **23–34**, find polar coordinates (with $r > 0$) for the points with the given rectangular coordinates.

23. $(0, 2)$. **24.** $(2, 2)$. **25.** $(1, -\sqrt{3})$. **26.** $(3, -3)$.

27. $(-4, 0)$. **28.** $(-4, -4)$. **29.** $(-2, 2\sqrt{3})$. **30.** $(0, -8)$.

31. $(2.41, 5.64)$. **32.** $(-2.1, 5.3)$. **33.** $(-4, -6)$. **34.** $(5, -6)$.

*In Problems **35–46**, sketch the graphs of the equations in polar coordinates.*

35. $r = 1$. **36.** $\theta = \pi/3$. **37.** $r = 2\cos\theta$.

38. $r = \sin\theta$. **39.** $r = 2\theta$, where $\theta \geq 0$. **40.** $r = 1 + \cos\theta$.

41. $r = 2(1 - \cos\theta)$. **42.** $r = 1 + 2\cos\theta$. **43.** $r = \sin 3\theta$.

44. $r = \cos 2\theta$. **45.** $r^2 = \cos 2\theta$. **46.** $r = 1 + 2\sin\theta$.

14-10 Review

Review Questions

1. The period of $y = 4\sin 18x$ is equal to __(a)__ . The amplitude is __(b)__ .

2. The values of $y = 3\sin\left(\dfrac{6}{97}x - \dfrac{2\pi}{63}\right)$ range from a minimum of __(a)__ to a maximum of __(b)__ .

3. In comparison to the graph of $y = \sin x$, the graph of $y = \sin\left(x + \dfrac{\pi}{2}\right)$ _(leads)(lags)_ by $\pi/2$.

4. The periods of $y = \sin x$ and $y = \cos x$ are both equal to __(a)__ , but the periods of $y = \tan x$ and $y = \cot x$ are both equal to __(b)__ .

5. The graph of $y = \sin x$ is the same as the graph of $y = -\cos x$ displaced $\pi/2$ radians to the _(left)(right)_ .

6. Arcsin x is the angle in the interval from $-\dfrac{\pi}{2}$ to $\dfrac{\pi}{2}$ with sine of ____ .

7. Arccos x is the angle in the interval from __(a)__ to __(b)__ with cosine of __(c)__ .

8. Arctan x is the angle in the interval from __(a)__ to __(b)__ with tangent of __(c)__ .

9. The angles 0, $\pm 2\pi$, $\pm 4\pi$, and so on, all have a cosine of 1. But arccos $1 =$ ____ .

10. True or False: Every point in the plane has one and only one representation in polar coordinates. _____

Answers to Review Questions

1. (a) $\pi/9$, (b) 4. **2.** (a) -3, (b) 3. **3.** Leads. **4.** (a) 2π, (b) π. **5.** Left. **6.** x.
7. (a) 0, (b) π, (c) x. **8.** (a) $-\pi/2$, (b) $\pi/2$, (c) x. **9.** 0. **10.** False.

Review Problems

*In Problems **1–10**, sketch one cycle of each curve. In **1–8**, give the amplitude A and period p.*

1. $y = -\sin 3x$. **2.** $y = 3\cos 6x$.

3. $y = 4\cos\left(x - \dfrac{\pi}{2}\right)$. **4.** $y = 2\sin\left(3x + \dfrac{\pi}{2}\right)$.

5. $y = 3 \cos \left(2x + \dfrac{\pi}{6}\right).$

6. $y = -\cos \left(\dfrac{x}{2} - \dfrac{\pi}{3}\right).$

7. $y = \tan x.$

8. $y = \sec x.$

9. $y = \sin 2x + 2 \cos x.$

10. $y = 2 \sin x - \cos x.$

In Problems 11–24, find the value of the given expression.

11. $\arcsin(-1).$

12. $\arccos \dfrac{1}{2}.$

13. $\arctan \dfrac{\sqrt{3}}{3}.$

14. $\arcsin \left(-\dfrac{\sqrt{3}}{2}\right).$

15. $\arccos \left(-\dfrac{\sqrt{3}}{2}\right).$

16. $\arctan(-1).$

17. $\tan(\arccos 1).$

18. $\cos \left(\arcsin \dfrac{\sqrt{2}}{2}\right).$

19. $\sin[\arctan(-\sqrt{3})].$

20. $\csc(\arccos 0).$

21. $\sin(\arcsin 0.8).$

22. $\arctan(\tan 2\pi).$

23. $\arccos(\cos 3\pi).$

24. $\cos \left[\arccos \left(-\dfrac{1}{10}\right)\right].$

In Problems 25–28, find rectangular coordinates for the points with the given polar coordinates.

25. $(1, 315°).$

26. $(-3, 50°).$

27. $(5, -210°).$

28. $(2, \pi).$

In Problems 29–32, find polar coordinates for the points with the given rectangular coordinates.

29. $(1, -1).$

30. $(-7, 8).$

31. $(-4, 0).$

32. $(1, \sqrt{3}).$

In Problems 33–36, sketch the given curve in polar coordinates.

33. $r = 2(1 - \sin \theta).$

34. $r = 1 - 2 \sin \theta.$

35. $r = 2 - \sin \theta.$

36. $r = e^{\theta/6}$, for $\theta \geq 0.$

trigonometric formulas and equations

15-1 Basic Identities

In Chapter 7 the following basic trigonometric relations were given:

1. $\csc \theta = \dfrac{1}{\sin \theta}$, $\qquad \sin \theta = \dfrac{1}{\csc \theta}$.

2. $\sec \theta = \dfrac{1}{\cos \theta}$, $\qquad \cos \theta = \dfrac{1}{\sec \theta}$.

3. $\cot \theta = \dfrac{1}{\tan \theta}$, $\qquad \tan \theta = \dfrac{1}{\cot \theta}$.

4. $\tan \theta = \dfrac{\sin \theta}{\cos \theta}$.

5. $\cot \theta = \dfrac{\cos \theta}{\sin \theta}$.

Each of the above equations is called a **trigonometric identity**. That is, each equation is true for *all* values of the variable θ for which both sides are defined.

There are three more basic identities: Each involves a *power* of a trigonometric function. In stating them, we shall abbreviate $(\sin \theta)^2$ by writing $\sin^2 \theta$ (read *sine squared theta*). The squares of the other trigonometric functions are abbreviated in a similar fashion. Do not confuse $\sin^2 \theta$ with $\sin \theta^2$, which means $\sin (\theta^2)$. The three identities in their various forms are:

$$
\begin{aligned}
&\textbf{6.} \quad \sin^2 \theta + \cos^2 \theta = 1 \quad \textbf{or} \quad
\begin{cases}
\sin^2 \theta = 1 - \cos^2 \theta, \\
\cos^2 \theta = 1 - \sin^2 \theta.
\end{cases} \\[2mm]
&\textbf{7.} \quad 1 + \tan^2 \theta = \sec^2 \theta \quad \textbf{or} \quad
\begin{cases}
\tan^2 \theta = \sec^2 \theta - 1, \\
\sec^2 \theta - \tan^2 \theta = 1.
\end{cases} \\[2mm]
&\textbf{8.} \quad 1 + \cot^2 \theta = \csc^2 \theta \quad \textbf{or} \quad
\begin{cases}
\cot^2 \theta = \csc^2 \theta - 1, \\
\csc^2 \theta - \cot^2 \theta = 1.
\end{cases}
\end{aligned}
$$

To prove these identities, let θ be any angle in standard position and (x, y) be a point on its terminal side (Fig. 15-1). Then

$$x^2 + y^2 = r^2.$$

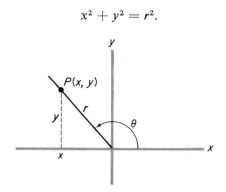

FIGURE 15-1

Successively dividing both sides of this equation by r^2, x^2, and y^2, respectively, we obtain three equations.

$$\frac{x^2}{r^2} + \frac{y^2}{r^2} = 1, \qquad 1 + \frac{y^2}{x^2} = \frac{r^2}{x^2}, \qquad \frac{x^2}{y^2} + 1 = \frac{r^2}{y^2}$$

or, equivalently,

$$\left(\frac{x}{r}\right)^2 + \left(\frac{y}{r}\right)^2 = 1, \qquad 1 + \left(\frac{y}{x}\right)^2 = \left(\frac{r}{x}\right)^2, \qquad \left(\frac{x}{y}\right)^2 + 1 = \left(\frac{r}{y}\right)^2.$$

Using the definitions of the trigonometric functions, we see that these three equations are equivalent, respectively, to the identities

$$\cos^2 \theta + \sin^2 \theta = 1, \qquad 1 + \tan^2 \theta = \sec^2 \theta, \qquad \cot^2 \theta + 1 = \csc^2 \theta.$$

When using Identities 6 to 8 to express one trigonometric function in terms of the other, you must consider signs. Identity 6, for example, implies that $\sin \theta = \pm\sqrt{1 - \cos^2 \theta}$. The choice of whether to use the plus sign or minus sign depends on the sign of $\sin \theta$. If θ is a first- or second-quadrant angle, use the plus sign. For a third- or fourth-quadrant angle, use the minus sign.

example 1

a. $\sin^2 20° + \cos^2 20° = 1$, by Identity 6.

b. $1 + \tan^2 \dfrac{\pi}{3} = \sec^2 \dfrac{\pi}{3}$, by Identity 7.

c. $1 + \cot^2 4x = \csc^2 4x$, by Identity 8.

Identities 1–8 are considered to be the basic trigonometric identities and their variations, and you should become familiar with them. They are used to simplify expressions involving trigonometric functions and to prove (or verify) other identities. In physical situations, this can mean dealing with a simpler and more suitable form of a trigonometric expression.

To illustrate, we shall prove the identity

$$\cot x \sin x = \cos x.$$

We usually choose one side of an identity and make substitutions until it is the same as the other side. Frequently it is best to choose the more complicated side, which in our case is $\cot x \sin x$. Using Identity 5, we can replace $\cot x$ by $(\cos x)/(\sin x)$. Thus

$$\cot x \sin x \quad \text{becomes} \quad \frac{\cos x}{\sin x} \cdot \sin x.$$

This reduces to $\cos x$, which is the same as the right side of the given identity. Thus the identity is proved. We usually write our work in a vertical arrangement as follows:

Left side	Right side
$\cot x \sin x$	$\cos x.$
$= \dfrac{\cos x}{\sin x} \sin x$	
$= \cos x.$	

example 2

Prove the identity $\sec \theta - \tan \theta \sin \theta = \cos \theta$.

Because the left side is the more complicated side, we shall try to transform it into the right side. In each step of the proof below, the number of the basic identity being used is indicated.

$$\sec \theta - \tan \theta \sin \theta \quad\quad\quad\quad \cos \theta.$$

$$= \frac{1}{\cos \theta} - \frac{\sin \theta}{\cos \theta} \sin \theta \quad (2, 4)$$

$$= \frac{1}{\cos \theta} - \frac{\sin^2 \theta}{\cos \theta}$$

$$= \frac{1 - \sin^2 \theta}{\cos \theta} \quad\quad (\text{combining})$$

$$= \frac{\cos^2 \theta}{\cos \theta} \quad\quad (6)$$

$$= \cos \theta.$$

The approach we took here of expressing the more complicated side in terms of sines and cosines and then simplifying is often used when no other procedure is evident.

example 3

Prove the identity $\dfrac{\tan^2 x}{1 + \sec x} = \sec x - 1$.

$$\frac{\tan^2 x}{1 + \sec x} \quad\quad\quad\quad \sec x - 1.$$

$$= \frac{\sec^2 x - 1}{1 + \sec x} \quad\quad (7)$$

$$= \frac{(\sec x + 1)(\sec x - 1)}{1 + \sec x} \quad (\text{factoring})$$

$$= \sec x - 1.$$

example 4

Prove $\csc^2 x - \dfrac{\cos^2 x}{\sin^2 x} = 1$.

Here we can write $\dfrac{\cos^2 x}{\sin^2 x}$ as $\left(\dfrac{\cos x}{\sin x}\right)^2$ or $\cot^2 x$ (by Identity 5).

$$\csc^2 x - \frac{\cos^2 x}{\sin^2 x} \quad\quad\quad 1.$$

$$= \csc^2 x - \cot^2 x \quad (5)$$

$$= 1. \quad\quad\quad\quad\quad (8)$$

example 5

Prove the identity $1 - \cot^4 x = 2 \csc^2 x - \csc^4 x$.

$$1 - \cot^4 x. \quad \left| \begin{aligned} & 2 \csc^2 x - \csc^4 x \\ &= (\csc^2 x)(2 - \csc^2 x) && \text{(factoring)} \\ &= (1 + \cot^2 x)[2 - (1 + \cot^2 x)] && \text{(8)} \\ &= (1 + \cot^2 x)[1 - \cot^2 x] \\ &= 1 - \cot^4 x && \text{(multiplying)}. \end{aligned} \right.$$

You may also prove an identity by *separately* manipulating *both* sides until they are the same. Usually we write both sides in terms of sines and cosines when no other approach to the problem is obvious. Example 6 shows this method.

example 6

Prove the identity $\tan x + \cot x = \csc x \sec x$.

$$\begin{aligned} & \tan x + \cot x \\ &= \frac{\sin x}{\cos x} + \frac{\cos x}{\sin x} && \text{(4, 5)} \\ &= \frac{\sin^2 x + \cos^2 x}{\cos x \sin x} && \text{(combining)} \\ &= \frac{1}{\cos x \sin x}. && \text{(6)} \end{aligned} \quad \left| \quad \begin{aligned} & \csc x \sec x \\ &= \frac{1}{\sin x} \cdot \frac{1}{\cos x} && \text{(1, 2)} \\ &= \frac{1}{\sin x \cos x}. \end{aligned} \right.$$

In Example 6 there was really no need to manipulate the right side, because we can take the last line on the left and write

$$\frac{1}{\cos x \sin x} = \frac{1}{\cos x} \cdot \frac{1}{\sin x} = \sec x \csc x,$$

which agrees with the right side of the identity.

example 7

When a ball of mass m is suspended from a string and pulled aside by a horizontal force F until the string makes an angle θ with the vertical, three forces are acting on the ball, as shown in Fig. 15-2. The downward gravitational force is mg, the tension in

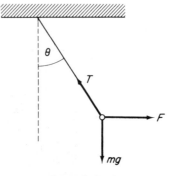

FIGURE 15-2

the string is T, and F is the supporting force. The system, being stationary, is said to be in equilibrium, and the relationships between the forces are determined by applying Newton's second law. By summing vertical and horizontal components, it can be shown that

$$T \cos \theta - mg = 0 \quad \text{and} \quad F - T \sin \theta = 0.$$

Show that $F = mg \tan \theta$.

Solving the first equation for T, we obtain $T = mg/(\cos \theta)$; substituting this value into the second equation gives

$$F - \left(\frac{mg}{\cos \theta}\right) \sin \theta = 0$$

$$F = mg \left(\frac{\sin \theta}{\cos \theta}\right).$$

Finally, by Identity 4, we have

$$F = mg \tan \theta.$$

Exercise 15-1

In Problems 1–40, prove the identities.

1. $\tan x \cos x = \sin x$.

2. $\cot x \tan x = 1$.

3. $\dfrac{\sin x}{\tan x} = \cos x$.

4. $\csc x \cos x = \cot x$.

5. $\dfrac{1 - \sin^2 x}{\cos x} = \cos x$.

6. $\dfrac{\cos x \tan x}{\sin x} = 1$.

7. $(1 + \cos x)(1 - \cos x) = \sin^2 x$.

8. $(\tan x)(1 - \sin^2 x) = \sin x \cos x$.

9. $\dfrac{\csc x}{\sec x} = \cot x$.

10. $\dfrac{\sin^2 x}{1 - \sin^2 x} = \tan^2 x$.

11. $\dfrac{\cos^2 \theta}{1 - \sin \theta} = 1 + \sin \theta$.

12. $\sec^2 \theta - \dfrac{\sin^2 \theta}{\cos^2 \theta} = 1$.

13. $\dfrac{1}{1 - \cos^2 \theta} = \csc^2 \theta.$

14. $\dfrac{1}{1 + \tan^2 \theta} = \cos^2 \theta.$

15. $\dfrac{1 - \cos^2 x}{1 - \sin^2 x} = \tan^2 x.$

16. $\dfrac{1}{\csc^2 x - 1} = \tan^2 x.$

17. $\dfrac{1 - \sin x}{\cos x} = \sec x - \tan x.$

18. $\dfrac{\cos^2 x}{1 - \sin^2 x} = 1.$

19. $\dfrac{1 + \tan^2 x}{\csc x} = \tan x \sec x.$

20. $\dfrac{1 + \cot^2 x}{\sec x} = \cot x \csc x.$

21. $(\sin x)(1 + \cot^2 x) = \csc x.$

22. $(1 + \tan^2 x) \cos x = \sec x.$

23. $\csc^4 \theta - \cot^4 \theta = \csc^2 \theta + \cot^2 \theta.$

24. $\dfrac{\csc^4 \theta - 1}{\cot^2 \theta} = \csc^2 \theta + 1.$

25. $\dfrac{2}{1 - \cos x} = \dfrac{2 \sec x}{\sec x - 1}.$

26. $\dfrac{\sin^2 x + \cos^2 x}{\cos^2 x} = \sec^2 x.$

27. $\dfrac{\sin x \cos y}{\sin y \cos x} = \tan x \cot y.$

28. $\dfrac{\cot x}{1 + \cot^2 x} = \sin x \cos x.$

29. $\dfrac{1}{\tan x + \cot x} = \cos x \sin x.$

30. $\dfrac{1 + \cot^2 x}{\cos^2 x \csc^2 x + 1} = 1.$

31. $\dfrac{1 + \tan x}{\sec x + \csc x} = \sin x.$

32. $\dfrac{\sin^2 x}{\cos^4 x + \cos^2 x \sin^2 x} = \tan^2 x.$

33. $\dfrac{1}{\sec x - \tan x} - \dfrac{1}{\sec x + \tan x} = 2 \tan x.$

34. $\dfrac{\cos x}{\tan x + \sec x} - \dfrac{\cos x}{\tan x - \sec x} = 2.$

35. $\dfrac{\cos^2 x - \cos^2 x \sin^2 x}{\sin^2 x - \cos^2 x \sin^2 x} = \cot^4 x.$

36. $\sin^2 x + 1 - \cos^2 x - 2 \sin^2 x \cos^2 x = 2 \sin^4 x.$

37. $\dfrac{\sin^2 x}{\cos x}(\tan x - \cos x \cot x) = (\sin x)(\tan^2 x - \cos x).$

38. $\dfrac{\sin x + \tan x}{1 + \cos x} = \tan x.$

39. $\cos^4 x - \sin^4 x + 1 = 2 \cos^2 x.$

40. $(1 + \cos x) \csc x + \dfrac{1}{\csc x(1 + \cos x)} = 2 \csc x.$

41. Suppose a weight W slides down a plane, inclined at an angle θ, at constant speed. Such a situation leads to the system of equations

$$\begin{cases} W \sin \theta - \mu N = 0 \\ N - W \cos \theta = 0, \end{cases}$$

where N is a force that the plane exerts on the block and μ is a constant involved with friction. Solve this system for μ and show that $\mu = \tan \theta$.

42. When a beam of circularly polarized light falls on a polarizing sheet, the resulting amplitude E of the electric field component is given by

$$E = \sqrt{E_x^2 + E_y^2},$$

where $E_x = E_m \sin(\omega t)$ and $E_y = E_m \cos(\omega t)$. Prove that $E = E_m$. You may assume that $E_m > 0$.

15-2   Functions of the Sum and Difference of Angles

In the theory of the interference and diffraction of electromagnetic waves, it is usual to assume that the electric field component of such a wave is of the form $E_0 \sin(\omega t + \varphi)$. In this and many other situations, it is useful to express a trigonometric function of the sum of two angles in terms of functions of the individual angles. We can do this by using the following identities, which are called the **addition formulas**.

> **9.** $\sin(x + y) = \sin x \cos y + \cos x \sin y.$
>
> **10.** $\cos(x + y) = \cos x \cos y - \sin x \sin y.$
>
> **11.** $\tan(x + y) = \dfrac{\tan x + \tan y}{1 - \tan x \tan y}.$

Identity 9 states that *the sine of the sum of two angles is the sine of the first angle times the cosine of the second angle, plus the cosine of the first angle times the sine of the second angle.*

In general, $\sin(x + y) \neq \sin x + \sin y$, and similarly for $\cos(x + y)$ and for $\tan(x + y)$. For example,

$$\sin(30° + 60°) = \sin 90° = 1,$$

but

$$\sin 30° + \sin 60° = \frac{1}{2} + \frac{\sqrt{3}}{2} = \frac{1 + \sqrt{3}}{2}.$$

The proofs of Identities 9–11 are given at the end of this section.

example 1

Find $\sin 75°$ by using the trigonometric values of $45°$ and $30°$.

Because $75° = 45° + 30°$, we may use Identity 9 with $x = 45°$ and $y = 30°$.

$$\sin 75° = \sin(45° + 30°)$$
$$= \sin 45° \cos 30° + \cos 45° \sin 30°$$
$$= \frac{\sqrt{2}}{2} \cdot \frac{\sqrt{3}}{2} + \frac{\sqrt{2}}{2} \cdot \frac{1}{2}$$
$$= \frac{\sqrt{6}}{4} + \frac{\sqrt{2}}{4} = \frac{\sqrt{6} + \sqrt{2}}{4}.$$

example 2

Simplify the equation $y = \cos\left(x + \frac{\pi}{2}\right)$.

We expand $\cos\left(x + \frac{\pi}{2}\right)$ by using Identity 10.

$$y = \cos\left(x + \frac{\pi}{2}\right) = \cos x \cos \frac{\pi}{2} - \sin x \sin \frac{\pi}{2}$$

$$= (\cos x)(0) - (\sin x)(1) = -\sin x.$$

Thus $y = -\sin x$.

The formulas for the functions of the *difference* of two angles can be easily obtained if we first express a trigonometric function of $-\theta$ in terms of a trigonometric function of θ. We shall do this for the case where θ is a second-quadrant angle, but the results are true for any angle θ.

Figure 15-3 shows the angles θ and $-\theta$, both in standard position, along with points on their terminal sides. These points are chosen so that they give the same

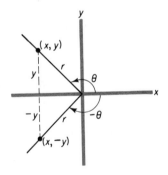

FIGURE 15-3

value of r. Notice that their first coordinates are equal, but their second coordinates differ in sign. We have

$$\sin(-\theta) = \frac{-y}{r} = -\frac{y}{r} = -\sin\theta,$$

$$\cos(-\theta) = \frac{x}{r} = \cos\theta,$$

$$\tan(-\theta) = \frac{-y}{x} = -\frac{y}{x} = -\tan\theta.$$

Because cosecant and sine are reciprocals of each other, we also have

$$\csc(-\theta) = \frac{1}{\sin(-\theta)} = \frac{1}{-\sin\theta} = -\csc\theta.$$

We can do the same for secant and cotangent. In summary, we have

$$
\textbf{12.} \quad
\begin{cases}
\sin(-\boldsymbol{\theta}) = -\sin\boldsymbol{\theta}, & \csc(-\boldsymbol{\theta}) = -\csc\boldsymbol{\theta}. \\
\cos(-\boldsymbol{\theta}) = \cos\boldsymbol{\theta}, & \sec(-\boldsymbol{\theta}) = \sec\boldsymbol{\theta}, \\
\tan(-\boldsymbol{\theta}) = -\tan\boldsymbol{\theta}, & \cot(-\boldsymbol{\theta}) = -\cot\boldsymbol{\theta}.
\end{cases}
$$

For example, $\sin(-30°) = -\sin 30° = -(\frac{1}{2}) = -\frac{1}{2}$, and $\cos(-\pi/4) = \cos(\pi/4) = \sqrt{2}/2$.

Using the identities above, we may find formulas for the trigonometric functions of the *difference* of two angles. For example, to find $\sin(x - y)$ we have

$$
\begin{aligned}
\sin(x - y) &= \sin[x + (-y)] \\
&= \sin x \cos(-y) + \cos x \sin(-y) &\text{(from 9)} \\
&= \sin x \cos y + (\cos x)(-\sin y) &\text{(from 12)} \\
&= \sin x \cos y - \cos x \sin y.
\end{aligned}
$$

We can do the same kind of thing to Identities 10 and 11. Thus we have the **subtraction formulas**:

$$
\begin{aligned}
&\textbf{13.} \quad \sin(x - y) = \sin x \cos y - \cos x \sin y. \\
&\textbf{14.} \quad \cos(x - y) = \cos x \cos y + \sin x \sin y. \\
&\textbf{15.} \quad \tan(x - y) = \frac{\tan x - \tan y}{1 + \tan x \tan y}.
\end{aligned}
$$

It is worth pointing out that mathematical reference handbooks often combine identities of similar form. For example, in a typical reference source, Identities 9 and 13 might appear as follows:

$$\sin(x \pm y) = \sin x \cos y \pm \cos x \sin y.$$

Here, *either* the upper signs ($+$ and $+$) in both sides *or* the lower signs ($-$ and $-$) in both sides are chosen. Similarly, Identities 10 and 14 can be given as

$$\cos(x \pm y) = \cos x \cos y \mp \sin x \sin y.$$

Here, if the plus sign is chosen in the left side, then the minus sign is chosen in the right side, and so on.

example **3**

Find $\cos 15°$ by using a subtraction formula.

Because $15° = 45° - 30°$, using Identity 14 we have

$$\cos 15° = \cos (45° - 30°)$$
$$= \cos 45° \cos 30° + \sin 45° \sin 30°$$
$$= \frac{\sqrt{2}}{2} \cdot \frac{\sqrt{3}}{2} + \frac{\sqrt{2}}{2} \cdot \frac{1}{2}$$
$$= \frac{\sqrt{6}}{4} + \frac{\sqrt{2}}{4} = \frac{\sqrt{6} + \sqrt{2}}{4}.$$

example 4

Show that $\tan (\pi - x) = -\tan x$.

From Identity 15 we have

$$\tan (\pi - x) = \frac{\tan \pi - \tan x}{1 + \tan \pi \tan x}$$
$$= \frac{0 - \tan x}{1 + (0) \tan x} = \frac{-\tan x}{1} = -\tan x.$$

example 5

Prove the identity $\dfrac{\cos (A + B)}{\sin A \cos B} = \cot A - \tan B$.

Using Identity 10 we have

$$\frac{\cos (A + B)}{\sin A \cos B} \qquad \Big| \qquad \cot A - \tan B.$$

$$= \frac{\cos A \cos B - \sin A \sin B}{\sin A \cos B}$$

$$= \frac{\cos A \cos B}{\sin A \cos B} - \frac{\sin A \sin B}{\sin A \cos B}$$

$$= \frac{\cos A}{\sin A} - \frac{\sin B}{\cos B}$$

$$= \cot A - \tan B.$$

example 6

If $\sin \alpha = \frac{1}{3}$, $\cos \beta = \frac{3}{4}$, and α is a first-quadrant angle and β is a fourth-quadrant angle, find $\cos (\alpha - \beta)$.

Angles α and β are sketched in Fig. 15-4. First we shall obtain values of x, y, and r for each angle. Since $\sin \alpha = y/r = \frac{1}{3}$, we can choose a point (x, y) on the terminal side

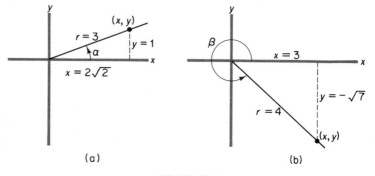

FIGURE 15-4

of α so that $y = 1$ and $r = 3$ [Fig. 15-4(a)]. By the Pythagorean theorem, $x^2 + 1^2 = 3^2$. Thus $x^2 = 3^2 - 1^2 = 8$ and so $x = 2\sqrt{2}$, because x is positive in Quadrant I. Similarly, we can get values for x, y, and r for β [Fig. 15-4(b)]. By Identity 14 we have

$$\cos(\alpha - \beta) = \cos \alpha \cos \beta + \sin \alpha \sin \beta$$

$$= \left(\frac{2\sqrt{2}}{3}\right)\left(\frac{3}{4}\right) + \left(\frac{1}{3}\right)\left(-\frac{\sqrt{7}}{4}\right)$$

$$= \frac{6\sqrt{2}}{12} - \frac{\sqrt{7}}{12} = \frac{6\sqrt{2} - \sqrt{7}}{12}.$$

example 7

Parallel and perpendicular lines: Section 6-4 made use of the facts that if two nonvertical lines L_1 and L_2 are parallel, then their slopes m_1 and m_2 are equal, and if the two lines are perpendicular, the slope of one line is the negative reciprocal of the slope of the other line—that is, $m_2 = -1/m_1$. We are now able to prove both statements.

Figure 15-5(a) shows two parallel lines, L_1 and L_2, which are not horizontal. For each line we can determine the slope by selecting two arbitrary points on the line. We choose for these points the intersections of the line with the x- and y-axes, and we define the angle α formed from the x-axis in a positive direction to the line as the **angle of inclination** of the line. Clearly, if the two lines are parallel, they must have the same angle of inclination. Furthermore,

$$m_2 = \frac{y_4 - y_3}{x_4 - x_3} = \tan \alpha$$

and

$$m_1 = \frac{y_2 - y_1}{x_2 - x_1} = \tan \alpha.$$

Hence, for parallel lines, $m_1 = m_2$. Note that if L_1 and L_2 are horizontal lines, they both have slopes of zero.

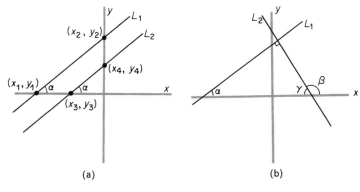

(a)   (b)

FIGURE 15-5

Figure 15-5(b) shows two perpendicular lines with angles of inclination α and β. Now,

$$\alpha + \gamma + 90° = 180°,$$

and

$$\gamma + \beta = 180°.$$

Therefore

$$\alpha + \gamma + 90° = \gamma + \beta,$$

so

$$\alpha + 90° = \beta.$$

Thus

$$\tan (\alpha + 90°) = \tan \beta.$$

Using Identities 4, 9, and 10 gives

$$\tan (\alpha + 90°) = \frac{\sin (\alpha + 90°)}{\cos (\alpha + 90°)} = \frac{\sin \alpha \cos 90° + \cos \alpha \sin 90°}{\cos \alpha \cos 90° - \sin \alpha \sin 90°}$$

$$= \frac{0 + \cos \alpha}{0 - \sin \alpha} = -\cot \alpha.$$

Thus

$$-\cot \alpha = \tan \beta \quad \text{or} \quad -\frac{1}{\tan \alpha} = \tan \beta.$$

Because $m_1 = \tan \alpha$ and $m_2 = \tan \beta$,

$$m_2 = -\frac{1}{m_1}.$$

We now consider the proofs of Identities 9–11. If α and β are two positive acute angles, then the sum $\alpha + \beta$ may be a first- or second-quadrant angle; these two cases are illustrated in Figs. 15-6 and 15-7. The discussion that follows refers to both figures.

From any point P on the terminal side of $\alpha + \beta$, perpendiculars are constructed both to the x-axis at A and to the terminal side of α at B. From B, perpendiculars are constructed to the x-axis at C and to AP at D. Note that $\overline{AD} = \overline{CB}$. Furthermore,

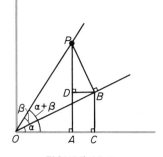

FIGURE 15-6

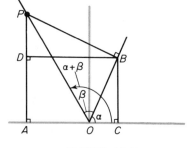

FIGURE 15-7

because

$$\sphericalangle BPD + \sphericalangle PBD = 90°$$

and

$$\sphericalangle DBO + \sphericalangle PBD = 90°,$$

it follows that

$$\sphericalangle BPD = \sphericalangle DBO.$$

However, $\sphericalangle DBO = \sphericalangle \alpha$, because they are alternate interior angles formed by parallel lines cut by a transversal. Thus $\sphericalangle BPD = \sphericalangle \alpha$.

Now, from $\triangle OCB$, $\sin \alpha = \overline{CB}/\overline{OB}$, or $\overline{CB} = \overline{OB} \sin \alpha$; from $\triangle PDB$, $\cos \alpha = \overline{DP}/\overline{PB}$, or $\overline{DP} = \overline{PB} \cos \alpha$. Therefore

$$\sin (\alpha + \beta) = \frac{\overline{AP}}{\overline{OP}} = \frac{\overline{AD} + \overline{DP}}{\overline{OP}} = \frac{\overline{CB} + \overline{DP}}{\overline{OP}}$$

$$= \frac{\overline{OB} \sin \alpha + \overline{PB} \cos \alpha}{\overline{OP}}$$

$$= \frac{\overline{OB}}{\overline{OP}} \sin \alpha + \frac{\overline{PB}}{\overline{OP}} \cos \alpha$$

$$\mathbf{\sin (\alpha + \beta) = \sin \alpha \cos \beta + \cos \alpha \sin \beta.}$$

Similarly,

$$\cos (\alpha + \beta) = \frac{\overline{OA}}{\overline{OP}} = \frac{\overline{OC} - \overline{DB}}{\overline{OP}}.$$

From $\triangle OCB$, $\cos \alpha = \overline{OC}/\overline{OB}$, or $\overline{OC} = \overline{OB} \cos \alpha$; from $\triangle BPD$, $\sin \alpha = \overline{DB}/\overline{BP}$, or $\overline{DB} = \overline{BP} \sin \alpha$. Therefore

$$\cos (\alpha + \beta) = \frac{\overline{OC} - \overline{DB}}{\overline{OP}} = \frac{\overline{OB} \cos \alpha - \overline{BP} \sin \alpha}{\overline{OP}}$$

$$= \frac{\overline{OB}}{\overline{OP}} \cos \alpha - \frac{\overline{BP}}{\overline{OP}} \sin \alpha$$

$$= \cos \beta \cos \alpha - \sin \beta \sin \alpha$$

$$\mathbf{\cos (\alpha + \beta) = \cos \alpha \cos \beta - \sin \alpha \sin \beta.}$$

Although in our proofs we assumed *positive acute* angles α and β, it can be shown that the identities are true for any values of α and β whatsoever. Finally,

$$\tan(\alpha + \beta) = \frac{\sin(\alpha + \beta)}{\cos(\alpha + \beta)}$$

$$= \frac{\sin\alpha\cos\beta + \cos\alpha\sin\beta}{\cos\alpha\cos\beta - \sin\alpha\sin\beta}.$$

Dividing the numerator and denominator by $\cos\alpha\cos\beta$ gives

$$\tan(\alpha + \beta) = \frac{\dfrac{\sin\alpha\cos\beta}{\cos\alpha\cos\beta} + \dfrac{\cos\alpha\sin\beta}{\cos\alpha\cos\beta}}{1 - \dfrac{\sin\alpha\sin\beta}{\cos\alpha\cos\beta}}$$

$$\boldsymbol{\tan(\alpha + \beta) = \frac{\tan\alpha + \tan\beta}{1 - \tan\alpha\tan\beta}.}$$

Although we could derive formulas for $\cot(\alpha + \beta)$, $\sec(\alpha + \beta)$, and $\csc(\alpha + \beta)$, they are rarely used.

Exercise 15-2

1. Find $\cos 75°$ by using functions of $30°$ and $45°$.

2. Find $\sin 15°$ by using functions of $30°$ and $45°$.

3. Find $\sin 195°$ by using functions of $225°$ and $30°$.

4. Find $\cos 165°$ by using functions of $120°$ and $45°$.

*In Problems **5–12**, use the formulas of this section to find the given values. Rationalize your answers.*

5. $\tan 15°$.   **6.** $\tan 75°$.   **7.** $\cos 105°$.

8. $\sin 105°$.   **9.** $\sin 255°$.   **10.** $\cos 255°$.

11. $\tan 255°$.   **12.** $\tan 345°$.

13. If α and β are second-quadrant angles and $\tan\alpha = -\frac{1}{2}$ and $\tan\beta = -\frac{2}{3}$, find (a) $\sin(\alpha + \beta)$, (b) $\cos(\alpha + \beta)$, (c) $\tan(\alpha + \beta)$, and (d) the quadrant in which $\alpha + \beta$ lies.

14. If α is a first-quadrant angle and $\sin\alpha = \frac{3}{5}$, and β is a second-quadrant angle and $\cos\beta = -\frac{3}{4}$, find (a) $\sin(\alpha - \beta)$, (b) $\cos(\alpha - \beta)$, and (c) $\tan(\alpha - \beta)$.

*In Problems **15–20**, write each expression in terms of $\sin x$, $\cos x$, or $\tan x$, as in Example 4.*

15. $\sin(x + \pi)$.   **16.** $\cos(x + \pi)$.   **17.** $\cos\left(\dfrac{\pi}{2} - x\right)$.

18. $\sin\left(\dfrac{\pi}{2} - x\right)$.   **19.** $\tan\left(x + \dfrac{\pi}{4}\right)$.   **20.** $3\sin\left(x + \dfrac{\pi}{2}\right)$.

21. Express $\cos 23° \cos 47° - \sin 23° \sin 47°$ as a trigonometric value of one angle only.

22. Express $\sin 18° \cos 10° - \cos 18° \sin 10°$ as a trigonometric value of one angle only.

In Problems 23–28, prove the given identities.

23. $\dfrac{\sin (\alpha + \beta)}{\cos \alpha \cos \beta} = \tan \alpha + \tan \beta.$

24. $\cos (\alpha + \beta) - \cos (\alpha - \beta) = -2 \sin \alpha \sin \beta.$

25. $\sin (x + y) + \sin (x - y) = 2 \sin x \cos y.$

26. $\sin (A + B) \sin (A - B) = \sin^2 A - \sin^2 B.$

27. $\dfrac{\sin (x + y)}{\sin (x - y)} = \dfrac{\tan x + \tan y}{\tan x - \tan y}.$

28. $\dfrac{\sin (x + y)}{\cos (x - y)} = \dfrac{\tan x + \tan y}{1 + \tan x \tan y}.$

29. Derive Identity 14.

30. Derive Identity 15.

In Problems 31–36, without performing any calculations, determine whether the given statement is true or false.

31. $\sin (-85°) = -\sin 85°.$

32. $\sin (-225°) = -\sin 225°.$

33. $\cos (-225°) = \cos 225°.$

34. $\cos (-225°) = -\cos 45°.$

35. In a certain three-phase ac generator, the phases are expressed as $I \cos \theta$, $I \cos (\theta + 120°)$, and $I \cos (\theta + 240°)$. It is to be shown that each phase is numerically equal to the sum of the other phases but opposite in sign. To do this it suffices to show that

$$I \cos \theta + I \cos (\theta + 120°) + I \cos (\theta + 240°) = 0.$$

Show that this is indeed the case.

36. The displacement x of a certain object, undergoing harmonic motion, as a function of time t is given by

$$x = 2\sqrt{2} \cos \left(2t - \frac{\pi}{4}\right).$$

(a) By expanding the right side, show that the displacement is the sum of two different motions: a sine function and a cosine function.

(b) For the two different motions in part a, find the contribution of each to the displacement when $t = \dfrac{\pi}{4}$.

37. For light passing symmetrically through a prism, the index of refraction, n, of glass with respect to air is given by

$$n = \frac{\sin \left[\frac{1}{2}(\alpha + \beta)\right]}{\sin (\beta/2)},$$

where α is the deviation angle and β is the angle of the apex of the prism. If $\beta = 60°$, show that $n = \sqrt{3} \sin (\alpha/2) + \cos (\alpha/2)$.

38. The electric field components of two light waves vary with time at a given point as

$$E_1 = E_0 \sin (\omega t),$$
$$E_2 = E_0 \sin (\omega t + \varphi).$$

The electric field component is associated with the disturbance caused by the waves. Show that $E_1 + E_2 = E_0 (\sin \omega t)(1 + \cos \varphi) + E_0(\cos \omega t) \sin \varphi$.

39. The equation of a standing wave can be obtained by adding the displacements y_1 and y_2 associated with two waves traveling in opposite directions. Given

$$y_1 = A \sin (\omega t - kx),$$
$$y_2 = -A \sin (\omega t + kx),$$

show that the equation of the standing wave is

$$y = y_1 + y_2 = -2A \cos (\omega t) \sin (kx).$$

15-3 Double- and Half-Angle Formulas

Using the addition formulas, we can derive formulas that express the trigonometric functions of twice an angle in terms of functions of the angle itself. By letting $y = x$ in Identity 9, we obtain

$$\sin 2x = \sin (x + x) = \sin x \cos x + \cos x \sin x$$
$$= 2 \sin x \cos x.$$

Thus,

> **16.** $\sin 2x = 2 \sin x \cos x.$

Letting $y = x$ in Identity 10, we have

$$\cos 2x = \cos (x + x) = \cos x \cos x - \sin x \sin x$$
$$= \cos^2 x - \sin^2 x.$$

But since $\sin^2 x + \cos^2 x = 1$, the last expression can be written either as

$$\cos^2 x - \sin^2 x = \cos^2 x - (1 - \cos^2 x) = 2 \cos^2 x - 1,$$

or as

$$\cos^2 x - \sin^2 x = (1 - \sin^2 x) - \sin^2 x = 1 - 2 \sin^2 x.$$

Thus we have

> **17.** $\begin{cases} \cos 2x = \cos^2 x - \sin^2 x \\ \qquad = 2 \cos^2 x - 1 \\ \qquad = 1 - 2 \sin^2 x. \end{cases}$

Similarly, letting $y = x$ in Identity 11 gives

> **18.** $\tan 2x = \dfrac{2 \tan x}{1 - \tan^2 x}.$

Identities 16–18 are called the **double-angle formulas.**

Do not confuse sin 2θ with 2 sin θ; they are *not* the same for all values of θ. If $\theta = 30°$, then sin $2\theta = \sin 60° = \sqrt{3}/2$, but 2 sin $\theta = 2 \sin 30° = 2(\frac{1}{2}) = 1$.

example 1

Use a double-angle formula to evaluate sin 60°.

Because we want sin $2x = \sin 60°$, we let $x = 30°$. From Identity 16 we have

$$\sin 2x = 2 \sin x \cos x,$$
$$\sin 60° = \sin (2 \cdot 30°) = 2 \sin 30° \cos 30°$$
$$= 2\left(\frac{1}{2}\right)\left(\frac{\sqrt{3}}{2}\right) = \frac{\sqrt{3}}{2}.$$

example 2

If θ is a second-quadrant angle and sin $\theta = \frac{3}{5}$, find tan 2θ.

Figure 15-8 shows the result of drawing a second-quadrant angle θ such that sin $\theta = \frac{3}{5}$. To find x we solve $x^2 + 3^2 = 5^2$, which gives $x = -4$ (negative, because x is negative

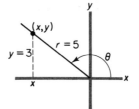

FIGURE 15-8

in the second quadrant). Using Identity 18 with tan $\theta = 3/x = 3/(-4) = -\frac{3}{4}$, we have

$$\tan 2\theta = \frac{2 \tan \theta}{1 - \tan^2 \theta} = \frac{2\left(-\frac{3}{4}\right)}{1 - \left(-\frac{3}{4}\right)^2}$$
$$= \frac{-\frac{3}{2}}{1 - \frac{9}{16}} = \frac{-\frac{3}{2}}{\frac{7}{16}} = -\frac{24}{7}.$$

There are formulas, called **half-angle formulas**, that express a trigonometric function of half an angle, $\theta/2$, in terms of the angle θ itself. To derive one of them, we use the double-angle formula

$$\cos 2x = 1 - 2 \sin^2 x.$$

Letting $x = \theta/2$ gives

$$\cos\left[2\left(\frac{\theta}{2}\right)\right] = 1 - 2 \sin^2 \frac{\theta}{2}$$

$$\cos \theta = 1 - 2 \sin^2 \frac{\theta}{2},$$

which can be written

$$2 \sin^2 \frac{\theta}{2} = 1 - \cos \theta$$

$$\sin^2 \frac{\theta}{2} = \frac{1 - \cos \theta}{2}.$$

Solving for $\sin (\theta/2)$ gives the identity

$$\boxed{\textbf{19.} \quad \sin \frac{\theta}{2} = \pm \sqrt{\frac{1 - \cos \theta}{2}}.}$$

The choice of whether to use the plus sign or minus sign depends on the sign of $\sin (\theta/2)$. If $\theta/2$ is a first- or second-quadrant angle, use the plus sign. For a third- or fourth-quadrant angle, use the minus sign.

Using the double-angle formula

$$\cos 2x = 2 \cos^2 x - 1$$

and again letting $x = \theta/2$ yields

$$\cos\left[2\left(\frac{\theta}{2}\right)\right] = 2 \cos^2 \frac{\theta}{2} - 1.$$

Rearranging terms and dividing by 2, we have

$$\cos^2 \frac{\theta}{2} = \frac{1 + \cos \theta}{2}. \tag{1}$$

Thus we have the identity

$$\cos \frac{\theta}{2} = \pm \sqrt{\frac{1 + \cos \theta}{2}}.$$

Also, because

$$\tan \frac{\theta}{2} = \frac{\sin \dfrac{\theta}{2}}{\cos \dfrac{\theta}{2}} = \frac{\sin \dfrac{\theta}{2}}{\cos \dfrac{\theta}{2}} \cdot \frac{2 \cos \dfrac{\theta}{2}}{2 \cos \dfrac{\theta}{2}}$$

$$= \frac{2 \sin \dfrac{\theta}{2} \cos \dfrac{\theta}{2}}{2 \cos^2 \dfrac{\theta}{2}},$$

we have, from Identity 16 and Eq. 1, the identity

$$\tan \frac{\theta}{2} = \frac{\sin \theta}{1 + \cos \theta}.$$

The last two identities, then, are:

---

20. $\cos \dfrac{\theta}{2} = \pm \sqrt{\dfrac{1 + \cos \theta}{2}}.$

21. $\tan \dfrac{\theta}{2} = \dfrac{\sin \theta}{1 + \cos \theta}.$

In Identity 20, use the plus sign if $\theta/2$ is a first- or fourth-quadrant angle; in these quadrants the cosine function is positive. Use the minus sign for the other quadrants. Again, the proper sign depends on $\theta/2$, not θ. Note that $\tan (\theta/2)$ is expressed without radicals. Another form for $\tan (\theta/2)$ is

$$\tan \frac{\theta}{2} = \frac{\sin \theta}{1 + \cos \theta} \cdot \frac{1 - \cos \theta}{1 - \cos \theta} = \frac{(\sin \theta)(1 - \cos \theta)}{1 - \cos^2 \theta}$$

$$= \frac{(\sin \theta)(1 - \cos \theta)}{\sin^2 \theta}$$

$$= \frac{1 - \cos \theta}{\sin \theta}.$$

example 3

Use a half-angle formula to determine $\sin 75°$.

We want $\dfrac{\theta}{2} = 75°$, so $\theta = 150°$. Because $\sin 75°$ is positive, we use the plus sign with Identity 19.

$$\sin 75° = \sin \frac{150°}{2} = \sqrt{\frac{1 - \cos 150°}{2}}$$

$$= \sqrt{\frac{1 - \left(-\frac{\sqrt{3}}{2}\right)}{2}} = \sqrt{\frac{2 + \sqrt{3}}{4}}$$

$$= \frac{\sqrt{2 + \sqrt{3}}}{2}.$$

example 4

Find $\tan 105°$ from the trigonometric functions of $210°$.

We use Identity 21 with $\theta = 210°$.

$$\tan 105° = \tan \frac{210°}{2} = \frac{\sin 210°}{1 + \cos 210°}$$

$$= \frac{-\frac{1}{2}}{1 + \left(-\frac{\sqrt{3}}{2}\right)} = -\frac{\frac{1}{2}}{\frac{2 - \sqrt{3}}{2}}$$

$$= -\frac{1}{2 - \sqrt{3}} = -\frac{1}{2 - \sqrt{3}} \cdot \frac{2 + \sqrt{3}}{2 + \sqrt{3}}$$

$$= -\frac{2 + \sqrt{3}}{4 - 3} = -(2 + \sqrt{3}).$$

As an aid to you, Table 15-1 gives a summary of the identities of this chapter, along with some other identities for future reference.

Table 15-1 Trigonometric identities

1. $\csc \theta = \frac{1}{\sin \theta}.$

2. $\sec \theta = \frac{1}{\cos \theta}.$

3. $\cot \theta = \frac{1}{\tan \theta}.$

4. $\tan \theta = \frac{\sin \theta}{\cos \theta}.$

5. $\cot \theta = \frac{\cos \theta}{\sin \theta}.$

6. $\sin^2 \theta + \cos^2 \theta = 1.$

7. $1 + \tan^2 \theta = \sec^2 \theta.$

8. $1 + \cot^2 \theta = \csc^2 \theta.$

9. $\sin (x + y) = \sin x \cos y + \cos x \sin y.$

10. $\cos (x + y) = \cos x \cos y - \sin x \sin y.$

11. $\tan (x + y) = \frac{\tan x + \tan y}{1 - \tan x \tan y}.$

12. $\sin (-\theta) = -\sin \theta, \quad \csc (-\theta) = -\csc \theta.$
    $\cos (-\theta) = \cos \theta, \quad \sec (-\theta) = \sec \theta$
    $\tan (-\theta) = -\tan \theta, \quad \cot (-\theta) = -\cot \theta.$

13. $\sin (x - y) = \sin x \cos y - \cos x \sin y.$

14. $\cos (x - y) = \cos x \cos y + \sin x \sin y.$

15. $\tan (x - y) = \frac{\tan x - \tan y}{1 + \tan x \tan y}.$

16. $\sin 2x = 2 \sin x \cos x.$

17. $\cos 2x = \cos^2 x - \sin^2 x$
    $\quad\quad\quad = 2 \cos^2 x - 1$
    $\quad\quad\quad = 1 - 2 \sin^2 x.$

continued

Table 15-1 Continued

18. $\tan 2x = \dfrac{2 \tan x}{1 - \tan^2 x}$.

19. $\sin \dfrac{\theta}{2} = \pm\sqrt{\dfrac{1 - \cos \theta}{2}}$.

20. $\cos \dfrac{\theta}{2} = \pm\sqrt{\dfrac{1 + \cos \theta}{2}}$.

21. $\tan \dfrac{\theta}{2} = \dfrac{\sin \theta}{1 + \cos \theta} = \dfrac{1 - \cos \theta}{\sin \theta}$.

22. $\sin (x + y) + \sin (x - y) = 2 \sin x \cos y$.

23. $\cos (x + y) + \cos (x - y) = 2 \cos x \cos y$.

24. $\sin (x + y) - \sin (x - y) = 2 \cos x \sin y$.

25. $\cos (x + y) - \cos (x - y) = -2 \sin x \sin y$.

26. $\sin x + \sin y = 2 \sin \dfrac{x + y}{2} \cos \dfrac{x - y}{2}$.

27. $\cos x + \cos y = 2 \cos \dfrac{x + y}{2} \cos \dfrac{x - y}{2}$.

28. $\sin x - \sin y = 2 \cos \dfrac{x + y}{2} \sin \dfrac{x - y}{2}$.

29. $\cos x - \cos y = -2 \sin \dfrac{x + y}{2} \sin \dfrac{x - y}{2}$.

Exercise 15-3

In Problems 1–6, use a double-angle formula to evaluate the given trigonometric value. A calculator should not be needed.

1. $\sin 60°$.
2. $\cos 60°$.
3. $\cos 240°$.
4. $\sin 240°$.
5. $\tan 120°$.
6. $\tan 240°$.

In Problems 7–12, use a half-angle formula to evaluate the given trigonometric value. A calculator should not be needed.

7. $\sin 15°$.
8. $\cos 75°$.
9. $\cos 22.5°$.
10. $\sin 157.5°$.
11. $\tan 112.5°$.
12. $\sin 67.5°$.

In Problems 13–16, find $\sin x$, $\cos x$, $\tan x$, $\sin 2x$, $\cos 2x$, and $\tan 2x$ from the given information.

13. $\cos x = \frac{3}{5}$, $\sin x$ is positive.
14. $\sec x = 5$, $\sin x$ is negative.
15. $\sin x = -\frac{1}{3}$, $\cot x$ is positive.
16. $\cos x = -\frac{1}{4}$, $\tan x$ is negative.

In Problems 17–20, find $\sin x$, $\cos x$, $\tan x$, $\sin (x/2)$, $\cos (x/2)$, and $\tan (x/2)$ from the given information. Assume that $0° < x < 360°$ and use the facts that if $0° < x < 180°$, then $0° < \dfrac{x}{2} < 90°$, and if $180° < x < 360°$, then $90° < \dfrac{x}{2} < 180°$.

17. $\cos x = \frac{12}{13}$, $\sin x$ is positive.

18. $\cot x = -\frac{8}{15}$, $\sin x$ is positive.

19. $\sin x = -\frac{3}{5}$, $\tan x$ is positive.

20. $\cos x = \frac{5}{13}$, $\sin x$ is negative.

In Problems 21–26, prove the identities.

21. $\cos^4 x - \sin^4 x = \cos 2x$.

22. $1 + \sin 2x = (\sin x + \cos x)^2$.

23. $\sin 2x \cot x = \cos 2x + 1$.

24. $\tan \frac{x}{2} = \csc x - \cot x$.

25. $2 \sin \frac{\theta}{2} \cos \frac{\theta}{2} = \sin \theta$.

26. $\tan x + \cot x = 2 \csc 2x$.

27. Show that $\sin 3x = 3 \sin x - 4 \sin^3 x$. *Hint*: $\sin 3x = \sin (2x + x)$.

28. The index of refraction, n, of a prism whose apex angle is α and whose angle of minimum deviation is φ is given by

$$n = \frac{\sin [(\alpha + \varphi)/2]}{\sin (\alpha/2)} \qquad (n > 0).$$

Show that

$$n = \sqrt{\frac{1 - \cos \alpha \cos \varphi + \sin \alpha \sin \varphi}{1 - \cos \alpha}}.$$

29. If a projectile is fired from the ground at an angle θ with the horizontal with an initial speed v_0, the horizontal range of the projectile is given by

$$R = \frac{v_0^2 \sin 2\theta}{g}.$$

Determine another expression for R in terms of θ.

30. Two tuning forks of nearly equal frequencies f_1 and f_2 are heard by a listener. The air-pressure variations p_1 and p_2 on the listener's eardrum are given by

$$p_1 = p_0 \cos 2\pi f_1 t$$

and

$$p_2 = p_0 \cos 2\pi f_2 t,$$

where p_0, f_1, and f_2 are constants. Use Identity 27 in Table 15-1 to show that the total pressure $p = p_1 + p_2$ can be expressed as

$$p = 2p_0 \cos \left[2\pi \left(\frac{f_1 + f_2}{2} \right) t \right] \cos \left[2\pi \left(\frac{f_1 - f_2}{2} \right) t \right].$$

15-4 Trigonometric Equations

A **trigonometric equation** is an equation involving trigonometric functions of unknown angles. An example is $2 \sin x = 1$. Solving this equation means to find all *angles* x for which the equation is true. We shall consider as solutions only those angles x such that $0° \leq x < 360°$. To solve a trigonometric equation we use algebra (as we would with any equation) and also trigonometric identities when they seem useful.

example 1

Solve $2 \sin x = 1$.

$$2 \sin x = 1$$
$$\sin x = \frac{1}{2}.$$

From our knowledge of special angles, clearly $30°$ is a solution. But $\sin x$ is also positive if x is a second-quadrant angle. Thus a solution exists there, and it has $30°$ as its reference angle. It must be $180° - 30° = 150°$. The solutions are $30°$ and $150°$.

Some trigonometric equations can be solved by factoring, as Example 2 shows.

example 2

Solve $2 \sin^2 x - \sin x - 1 = 0$.

$$2 \sin^2 x - \sin x - 1 = 0$$
$$(2 \sin x + 1)(\sin x - 1) = 0 \qquad \text{(factoring)}.$$

$2 \sin x + 1 = 0$	$\sin x - 1 = 0$
$2 \sin x = -1$	$\sin x = 1.$
$\sin x = -\dfrac{1}{2}.$	

Thus either $\sin x = -\frac{1}{2}$ or $\sin x = 1$. If $\sin x = -\frac{1}{2}$, then x is a third- or fourth-quadrant angle with $30°$ as its reference angle; so $x = 210°$ or $x = 330°$. If $\sin x = 1$, then $x = 90°$. The solutions are $90°$, $210°$, and $330°$.

Some trigonometric equations can be solved by writing the equation in terms of one trigonometric function only, as Example 3 shows.

example 3

Solve $2 \cos x - \sec x = 1$.

We can write this equation in terms of $\cos x$ only.

$$2 \cos x - \sec x = 1$$
$$2 \cos x - \frac{1}{\cos x} = 1 \qquad \text{(Identity 2)}.$$

To clear of fractions, we multiply both sides by $\cos x$.

$$2 \cos^2 x - 1 = \cos x$$

$$2 \cos^2 x - \cos x - 1 = 0$$

$$(2 \cos x + 1)(\cos x - 1) = 0 \qquad \text{(factoring).}$$

$2 \cos x + 1 = 0$	$\cos x - 1 = 0$
$2 \cos x = -1$	$\cos x = 1.$
$\cos x = -\dfrac{1}{2}.$	

If $\cos x = -\frac{1}{2}$, then $x = 120°$ or $240°$. If $\cos x = 1$, then $x = 0°$. *We are not done yet!* Because we multiplied both sides by $\cos x$—which involves a variable—we must check each value of x in the original equation.

If $x = 0°$, then $2 \cos 0° - \sec 0° = 2(1) - 1 = 1 = $ right side.

If $x = 120°$, then $2 \cos 120° - \sec 120° = 2(-\frac{1}{2}) - (-2) = 1 = $ right side.

If $x = 240°$, then $2 \cos 240° - \sec 240° = 2(-\frac{1}{2}) - (-2) = 1 = $ right side.

Thus the solutions are $0°$, $120°$, and $240°$.

Another method of solving trigonometric equations involves squaring both sides, as Example 4 shows.

example 4

Solve $\sin x + \cos x = 1$.

In this equation, no worthwhile substitution seems obvious. One way out of this situation is to square both sides. Before the squaring, a common practice is to rewrite the equation so that there is a trigonometric function on each side.

$$\sin x + \cos x = 1$$

$$\sin x = 1 - \cos x$$

$$(\sin x)^2 = (1 - \cos x)^2$$

$$\sin^2 x = 1 - 2 \cos x + \cos^2 x$$

$$1 - \cos^2 x = 1 - 2 \cos x + \cos^2 x \qquad \text{(Identity 6).}$$

Now we combine terms.

$$0 = 2 \cos^2 x - 2 \cos x$$

$$0 = (2 \cos x)(\cos x - 1) \qquad \text{(factoring).}$$

$2 \cos x = 0$	$\cos x - 1 = 0$
$\cos x = 0$	$\cos x = 1$
$x = 90°, 270°.$	$x = 0°.$

Because we squared both sides, we must check all values of x in the given equation.

If $x = 0°$, then $\sin 0° + \cos 0° = 0 + 1 = 1 = $ right side.

If $x = 90°$, then $\sin 90° + \cos 90° = 1 + 0 = 1 = $ right side.

If $x = 270°$, then $\sin 270° + \cos 270° = -1 + 0 = -1 \neq $ right side.

Thus the solutions are $0°$ and $90°$.

In Example 4 we solved $0 = (2 \cos x)(\cos x - 1)$ by setting each factor equal to 0. You may be tempted to first divide both sides by $2 \cos x$. Doing this division gives $0 = (\cos x - 1)$, which has $0°$ as its only solution. However, from Example 4 we know that the original equation is true not only for $0°$, but for $90°$ as well. Thus, by dividing by $2 \cos x$ we lose a solution. In general, it is best not to divide both sides of an equation by an expression involving a variable.

example 5

Solve $2 \sin x \cos x = 1$.

$$2 \sin x \cos x = 1$$

$$\sin 2x = 1 \qquad \text{(Identity 16)}.$$

Because $\sin 90° = 1$, then $2x = 90°$ and so $x = 45°$. Also, $\sin 450° = 1$. Solving $2x = 450°$ gives $x = 225°$. Thus $x = 45°, 225°$. Note that although $450°$ is beyond our usual considerations, after dividing by 2 we obtain an appropriate solution. More generally, to solve $\sin nx = k$, we consider all angles nx between $0°$ and $(360n)°$ with a sine of k so that we find all solutions x between $0°$ and $360°$.

Exercise 15-4

In Problems **1–32**, *solve for x, where* $0° \leq x < 360°$.

1. $\sin x = \dfrac{\sqrt{2}}{2}$.

2. $\cos x = -\dfrac{\sqrt{3}}{2}$.

3. $\tan x = -1$.

4. $\sin x = 0$.

5. $2 \cos x = 1$.

6. $\sin (x + 10°) = -\dfrac{1}{2}$.

7. $2 \cos^2 x - \cos x - 1 = 0$.

8. $\sin^2 x - 2 \sin x + 1 = 0$.

9. $\sin x + \sin x \cos x = 0$.

10. $\sin^2 x - 1 = 0$.

11. $\sin x = 2 \cos x$.

12. $2 \tan^2 x = 5$.

13. $\sin^2 x + \sin x - 1 = 0$.

14. $(\sin x)(3 \cos x - 2) = 0$.

15. $2 \sin x - \csc x = 1$.

16. $\tan x \cos x = \dfrac{1}{2}$.

17. $\sin 2x = \dfrac{\sqrt{3}}{2}$.

18. $\cos 3x = 1$.

19. $\cos x - 1 - \sqrt{3}\,\sin x = 0$.

20. $\cos x - \sin x - 1 = 0$.

21. $2\sin x \cos x = -\dfrac{\sqrt{2}}{2}$.

22. $\sin 2x = \sin x$.

23. $\cos x - \cos 2x = 1$.

24. $\sin 2x \cos x = 0$.

25. $2\sin x - \tan x = 0$.

26. $\sin x + \cos 2x = 4\sin^2 x$.

27. $2\tan^2 x + \sec^2 x = 2$.

28. $\sqrt{2 - \csc^2 x} = \csc x$.

29. $\sin 2x + \cos x = 0$.

30. $\tan 2x + \sec 2x = 1$.

31. $\sec^2 x + \tan x = 1$.

32. $\cot x - \csc^2 x = -1$.

15-5   Review

Review Questions

1. How many of the following expressions always have a value of 1? _____

$$\sin^2 \theta + \cos^2 \theta, \qquad \csc^2 3° - \cot^2 3°, \qquad \sec^2 \theta + \tan^2 \theta$$

2. Which of the following statements are identities? _____

(a) $\sin^2 \theta = 1 + \cos^2 \theta$.

(b) $\dfrac{1}{\sec \theta} = \cos \theta$.

(c) $\sin \theta \csc \theta = 1$.

(d) $1 + \sec^2 \theta = \tan \theta$.

3. True or false: $\sin(-15°) = -\sin 15°$. _____

4. True or false: $\cos(A + B) = \cos A \cos B + \sin A \sin B$ for all values of A and B.

_____

5. If $A = 130°$, then $\cos(A/2)$ is _(positive)(negative)_ .

6. $\dfrac{2\tan 40°}{1 - \tan 40°} = \tan$ _____°.

Answers to Review Questions

1. Two.   **2.** b, c.   **3.** True.   **4.** False.   **5.** Positive.   **6.** 80.

Review Problems

In Problems 1–10, prove the given identities.

1. $\tan x + \cot x = \sec x \csc x$.

2. $\cot^2 x \sin^2 x + \tan^2 x \cos^2 x = 1$.

3. $\csc^2 \theta \tan^2 \theta - \sec \theta \cos \theta = \tan^2 \theta$.

4. $\dfrac{\sec^2 \theta}{\cot \theta} - \tan^3 \theta = \tan \theta$.

5. $\dfrac{\sin^2 x}{1 - \cos x} = 1 + \cos x$.

6. $\sec^2 x + \csc^2 x = \sec^2 x \csc^2 x$.

7. $\cos x + \sin x \tan x = \sec x$.

8. $\sin 2x \tan x = 2\sin^2 x$.

9. $\dfrac{1 + \cos 2x}{\sin 2x} = \cot x$.

10. $\sin^2 \dfrac{x}{2} = \dfrac{\tan x - \sin x}{2\tan x}$.

*In Problems **11–18**, evaluate the given expressions if α and β are first-quadrant angles and* $\sin \alpha = \frac{1}{2}$ *and* $\sin \beta = \frac{4}{5}$.

11. $\sin (\alpha + \beta)$.   **12.** $\cos (\alpha - \beta)$.   **13.** $\tan \frac{\beta}{2}$.

14. $\cos (\alpha + \beta)$.   **15.** $\cos 2\alpha$.   **16.** $\sin 2\alpha$.

17. $\tan (\beta - 45°)$.   **18.** $\cos \frac{\beta}{2}$.

19. If $\tan x = \frac{15}{8}$ find $\sin x$, $\cos x$, $\tan x$, $\sin (-x)$, $\cos (-x)$, $\sin 2x$, $\cos 2x$, $\tan 2x$, $\sin \frac{x}{2}$, $\cos \frac{x}{2}$, and $\tan \frac{x}{2}$. Assume x is acute.

20. If $\sin x = \frac{3}{5}$, find the values asked for in Problem 19. Assume x is acute.

*In Problems **21–24**, solve the equation for x, where $0° \leq x < 360°$.*

21. $\sin x \cos x - \cot x = 0$.

22. $\sin 2x - \sqrt{2} \sin x = 0$.

23. $\frac{\sqrt{3}}{2} + \tan^2 x + \sin x - \sec^2 x = -1$.

24. $1 + \sin 2x = 0$.

25. (a) Prove that $\sin x = \cos \left(x - \frac{\pi}{2} \right)$.

  (b) Use your result in (a) to show that
$$\sin \left(\omega t + \frac{\pi}{5} \right) = \cos \left(\omega t - \frac{3\pi}{10} \right).$$

oblique triangles
and applications
of angular measurement

16-1 The Law of Sines

In Sec. 7-5 we solved right triangles by applying the basic definitions of the trigonometric functions. We now turn our attention to formulas that allow us to solve triangles that do not contain right angles. Such triangles, called **oblique triangles**, are of two types, depending on the angles they contain. An **acute triangle** has three acute angles [Fig. 16-1(a)]. An **obtuse triangle** has one obtuse angle, and this angle must be opposite the longest side [Fig. 16-1(b)].

Oblique triangles

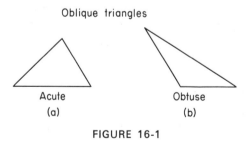

Acute   Obtuse
(a)   (b)

FIGURE 16-1

Figure 16-2 shows both types of oblique triangles; an altitude CD has been constructed in each. Each altitude is taken to be of length h. In Fig. 16-2(b), $\sin A = \sin(180° - A) = \sin \angle CAD$. Therefore, for both triangles we have

$$\sin A = \frac{h}{b} \qquad \text{or} \qquad h = b \sin A,$$

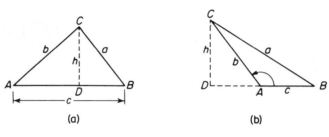

FIGURE 16-2

and

$$\sin B = \frac{h}{a} \quad \text{or} \quad h = a \sin B.$$

Hence

$$a \sin B = b \sin A.$$

Dividing both sides by $\sin A \sin B$ gives

$$\frac{a}{\sin A} = \frac{b}{\sin B}. \tag{1}$$

In a similar way it can be shown that

$$\frac{b}{\sin B} = \frac{c}{\sin C}. \tag{2}$$

Combining Eqs. 1 and 2, we have the **law of sines** (or *sine law*):

LAW OF SINES
$\dfrac{a}{\sin A} = \dfrac{b}{\sin B} = \dfrac{c}{\sin C}.$

The sine law is used to solve a triangle when you know *either* of the following:

1. Two angles and any side.
2. Two sides and the angle opposite one of them.

Note that three specific parts must be known in order to use the sine law.

example 1

Given two angles and any side.

Solve triangle ABC if $A = 30°$, $B = 70°$, and $a = 4$.

A sketch of the triangle is in Fig. 16-3. Angle C is easily found.

$$C = 180° - A - B = 180° - 30° - 70° = 80°.$$

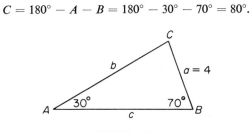

FIGURE 16-3

To find b, we pair the first and second expressions in the sine law and substitute in our data. This leads to an equation with one unknown.

$$\frac{b}{\sin B} = \frac{a}{\sin A}$$

$$b = \frac{a \sin B}{\sin A} = \frac{4(\sin 70°)}{\sin 30°} = 7.52.$$

Applying the law of sines once again to find c, we have

$$\frac{c}{\sin C} = \frac{a}{\sin A}$$

$$c = \frac{a \sin C}{\sin A} = \frac{4(\sin 80°)}{\sin 30°} = 7.88.$$

Thus $C = 80°$, $b = 7.52$, and $c = 7.88$.

If you are given two sides and the angle opposite one of them, there may be two, one, or no triangles fitting the data. Because of these possibilities, we say that this kind of problem falls in the **ambiguous case**. To see why these situations may occur, let us assume that the given parts are a, b, and A. We shall consider the situations when $A < 90°$ or when $A \geq 90°$.

Angle $A < 90°$: If A is an acute angle, there are five possible situations:

1. If $a < b \sin A$, then side a is shorter than the altitude $b \sin a$ and will not meet the lower side of angle A (Fig. 16-4). Thus there is no triangle and, hence, *no solution.*

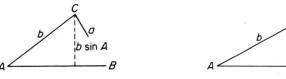

FIGURE 16-4   FIGURE 16-5

2. If $a = b \sin A$, then a corresponds to the altitude and there is only *one solution*, which is the right triangle ABC (Fig. 16-5).

3. If $a > b$, then as a consequence $a > b \sin A$ and a meets the lower side of A at exactly one point (Fig. 16-6). In this case only *one triangle* is determined.

4. If $a > b \sin A$ *and* $a < b$, there are *two solutions*. As shown in Fig. 16-7, triangles ABC and $AB'C$ both meet the given conditions. Note that angles B and $AB'C$ are supplementary, but B is acute and $AB'C$ is obtuse.

5. If $a = b$, there is *one solution*, which is an isosceles triangle (Fig. 16-8).

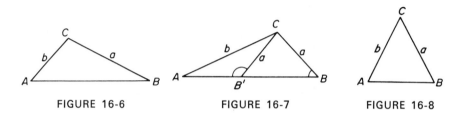

FIGURE 16-6   FIGURE 16-7   FIGURE 16-8

Angle $A \geq 90°$: If A is either a right angle or an obtuse angle, there are two possible situations:

1. If $a \leq b$, there is *no solution* (Fig. 16-9).

2. If $a > b$, there is *one solution* (Fig. 16-10).

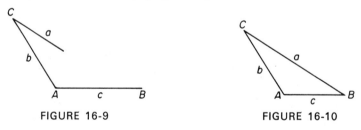

FIGURE 16-9   FIGURE 16-10

When you have a problem involving the ambiguous case, a fairly accurate sketch based on the given data will often make the number of solutions obvious. Moreover, the particular situation occurring should become clear to you after applying the sine law. For example, obtaining the result that $\sin B = 1.3$ indicates that no triangle exists, because the sine of any angle cannot be greater than 1.

example 2

Given two sides and the angle opposite one of them.

Solve triangle ABC if $a = 6$, $b = 10$, and $A = 30°$.

We first find B. By the sine law, $\dfrac{b}{\sin B} = \dfrac{a}{\sin A}$, which may be written

$$\frac{\sin B}{b} = \frac{\sin A}{a}.$$

Thus

$$\sin B = \frac{b \sin A}{a} = \frac{10 \sin 30°}{6} = 0.83333.$$

Two angles with sines of 0.83333 are $B = 56.44°$ and $B = 180° - 56.44° = 123.56°$. Thus two triangles are determined (Fig. 16-11).

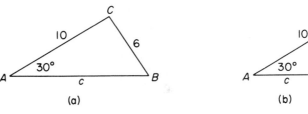

(a)   (b)

FIGURE 16-11

Case 1.   If $B = 56.44°$ [Fig. 16-11(a)], then

$$C = 180° - A - B = 180° - 30° - 56.44° = 93.56°.$$

Thus

$$\frac{c}{\sin C} = \frac{a}{\sin A}$$

$$c = \frac{a \sin C}{\sin A} = \frac{6 \sin 93.56°}{\sin 30°} = 11.98.$$

The solution for Fig. 16-11(a) is $c = 11.98$, $B = 56.44°$, and $C = 93.56°$.

Case 2.   If $B = 123.56°$ [Fig. 16-11(b)], then

$$C = 180° - A - B = 180° - 30° - 123.56° = 26.44°.$$

Thus

$$\frac{c}{\sin C} = \frac{a}{\sin A}$$

$$c = \frac{a \sin C}{\sin A} = \frac{6(\sin 26.44°)}{\sin 30°} = 5.34.$$

Thus, the solution for Fig. 16-11(b) is $c = 5.34$, $B = 123.56°$, and $C = 26.44°$.

example 3

Given two sides and the angle opposite one of them.

Solve triangle ABC if $b = 10$, $c = 5$, and $B = 60°$.

By the sine law,

$$\frac{\sin C}{c} = \frac{\sin B}{b}$$

$$\sin C = \frac{5 \sin 60°}{10} = 0.43301.$$

At this point you might be tempted to think that there are two choices for C, as in Example 2. This is *not* the case here. Because C is opposite side c, and c is *not* the longest side $(10 > 5)$, then C *cannot* be obtuse. C must be acute. Thus we find that

$$C = 25.66°.$$

A sketch of the triangle is in Fig. 16-12.

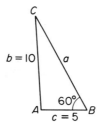

FIGURE 16-12

Now,

$$A = 180° - 60° - 25.66° = 94.34°.$$

Thus

$$\frac{a}{\sin A} = \frac{b}{\sin B}$$

$$a = \frac{b \sin A}{\sin B} = \frac{10(\sin 94.34°)}{\sin 60°} = 11.51.$$

Therefore $A = 94.34°$, $C = 25.66°$, and $a = 11.51$.

example 4

Given two sides and the angle opposite one of them.

Solve triangle ABC if $a = 2$, $b = 6$, and $A = 20°$.

By the sine law,

$$\frac{\sin B}{b} = \frac{\sin A}{a}$$

$$\sin B = \frac{6(\sin 20°)}{2} = 1.02606.$$

But the sine of an angle cannot be greater than 1. Thus there is no triangle and therefore **no solution.**

Exercise 16-1

In Problems **1–16**, *solve triangle ABC from the given information.*

1. $A = 50.1°$, $B = 98.4°$, $a = 20.31$.   **2.** $A = 78.3°$, $C = 41.3°$, $c = 101.12$.

3. $a = 9.23$, $b = 7.22$, $A = 80.42°$.   **4.** $a = 20.41$, $b = 10.72$, $A = 55.68°$.

5. $a = 7.46$, $b = 9.62$, $A = 20.46°$.   **6.** $a = 67.01$, $b = 95.62$, $A = 24.63°$.

7. $a = 50.41$, $b = 97.42$, $A = 58.82°$.   **8.** $b = 30.7$, $c = 70.5$, $B = 28.97°$.

9. $a = 7.12$, $c = 20.19$, $C = 138.82°$.   **10.** $b = 109$, $c = 90.5$, $B = 110.53°$.

11. $B = 60.3°$, $C = 72.1°$, $a = 80.3$.   **12.** $C = 20.4°$, $A = 40.4°$, $b = 50.4$.

13. $c = 5.00$, $b = 10.00$, $C = 30°$.   **14.** $b = 70.3$, $c = 70.3$, $C = 68.18°$.

15. $a = 6.04$, $b = 7.05$, $A = 104.24°$.   **16.** $a = 60.6$, $b = 60.6$, $A = 99.66°$.

17. A boat B can be seen from points A and C on the shore. A and C are 1650 m apart. Angles BAC and BCA are found to be 65° and 75°, respectively. How far is the boat from A?

18. In order to find the distance between points A and B, another point C is marked off. The distance from B to C is known to be 65 m. Angle ABC is measured to be 120°, and angle BCA is found to be 35°. Find the distance between A and B.

19. Two students send up a balloon with a remote-controlled camera to take a picture of the countryside. They position themselves 1.6 km apart. When the picture is taken, the balloon is between the students and the angles of elevation from the students are 46° and 70°. Find the height of the balloon.

20. From a point on the ground, the angle of elevation of the top of a building is 60°. From another point 33 m *farther* away from the building, the angle of elevation is 40°. Find the height of the building.

21. Suppose forces $F_1 = 500$ N and $F_2 = 700$ N act on a body such that the resultant force **F** forms an angle of 42° with **F**$_1$. Find F and the angle θ that **F**$_2$ makes with **F**$_1$.

22. In one of the locks of the St. Lawrence Seaway, the angle of elevation α of the top C of a Canadian landmark from a ship at point A is $\alpha = 55°$ (Fig. 16-13). As the lock fills, the ship rises from A to B and the angle of elevation decreases to $\beta = 50°$. If the ship is 135 m from the base of the landmark when at B, through what distance did the ship rise?

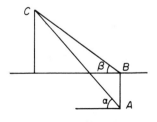

FIGURE 16-13

16-2   The Law of Cosines

To develop another formula that is important in the solution of oblique triangles, consider the oblique triangle ABC in Fig. 16-14. (Although angle A is acute, our results will also be true when A is obtuse.) If we let the length of the line segment AD

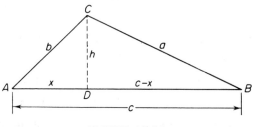

FIGURE 16-14

be x, then the length of segment DB must be $c - x$. Note that constructing the altitude CD has divided the oblique triangle into two right triangles. Applying the Pythagorean theorem, from $\triangle BCD$ we have

$$a^2 = h^2 + (c - x)^2, \tag{1}$$

and from $\triangle ACD$ we obtain

$$b^2 = h^2 + x^2. \tag{2}$$

Subtracting Eq. 2 from Eq. 1 yields

$$a^2 - b^2 = h^2 + (c - x)^2 - (h^2 + x^2)$$
$$= h^2 + c^2 - 2cx + x^2 - h^2 - x^2$$
$$a^2 - b^2 = c^2 - 2cx. \tag{3}$$

However, $\cos A = x/b$ and, therefore, $x = b \cos A$. Substituting this value for x in Eq. 3 and rearranging terms yields

$$a^2 = b^2 + c^2 - 2bc \cos A. \tag{4}$$

In a similar manner it can be shown that

$$b^2 = a^2 + c^2 - 2ac \cos B \tag{5}$$

and

$$c^2 = a^2 + b^2 - 2ab \cos C. \tag{6}$$

Equations 4–6 are known collectively as the **law of cosines**, or *cosine law*.

> **LAW OF COSINES**
>
> $a^2 = b^2 + c^2 - 2bc \cos A.$
>
> $b^2 = a^2 + c^2 - 2ac \cos B.$
>
> $c^2 = a^2 + b^2 - 2ab \cos C.$

In words, the cosine law states that *the square of the length of any side of a triangle is equal to the sum of the squares of the lengths of the other two sides minus twice the product of the lengths of these sides times the cosine of their included angle.* The cosine law is used in solving an oblique triangle when you know *either* of the following.

1. Two sides and their included angle.

2. Three sides.

Note that three specific parts must be known in order to use the cosine law.

example 1

Given two sides and their included angle.

Solve triangle ABC if $a = 10$, $b = 40$, and $C = 120°$ (Fig. 16-15).

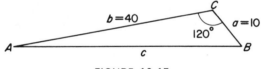

FIGURE 16-15

By the cosine law,

$$c^2 = a^2 + b^2 - 2ab \cos C$$
$$= 10^2 + 40^2 - 2(10)(40) \cos 120°$$
$$= 100 + 1600 - 800(-0.5)$$
$$= 2100$$
$$c = 45.8258.$$

Although A and B can be found with the cosine law, we shall use the sine law for convenience. For A we have

$$\frac{\sin A}{a} = \frac{\sin C}{c}$$
$$\sin A = \frac{a \sin C}{c} = \frac{10 \sin 120°}{45.8258} = 0.18898$$
$$A = 10.89°.$$

Note that A must be acute, since C is obtuse. Even if C were not obtuse, A must be acute here because a is the smallest side. Only the angle opposite the longest side has *any* chance of being obtuse. Finally,

$$B = 180° - A - C = 180° - 10.89° - 120° = 49.11°.$$

Thus $c = 45.83$, $A = 10.89°$, and $B = 49.11°$. Although the value of c to four decimal places was used to find A, it has been rounded to two decimal places in our final answer.

example 2

Given three sides.

Solve triangle ABC if $a = 7$, $b = 6$, and $c = 8$ (Fig. 16-16).

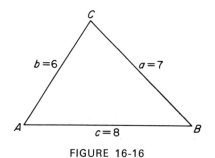

FIGURE 16-16

We first find the largest angle. That will tell us whether or not the triangle contains an obtuse angle. Because the largest angle must be opposite the longest side, here it is C.

$$c^2 = a^2 + b^2 - 2ab \cos C$$
$$8^2 = 7^2 + 6^2 - 2(7)(6) \cos C$$
$$64 = 85 - 84 \cos C$$
$$84 \cos C = 21$$
$$\cos C = 0.25000.$$

Since $\cos C$ is positive, C is acute:

$$C = 75.52°.$$

To solve for A and B, we choose to use the sine law instead of the cosine law.

$$\frac{\sin B}{b} = \frac{\sin C}{c}$$
$$\sin B = \frac{b \sin C}{c} = \frac{6 \sin 75.52°}{8} = 0.72618$$
$$B = 46.57° \qquad (B \text{ must be acute}).$$

Finally,

$$A = 180° - B - C = 180° - 46.57° - 75.52° = 57.91°.$$

Therefore $A = 57.91°$, $B = 46.57°$, and $C = 75.52°$.

In Example 2, with efficient use of a calculator we can find C without performing intermediate steps. The following alternative forms of the cosine law are used for such purposes:

$$\cos A = \frac{b^2 + c^2 - a^2}{2bc},$$

$$\cos B = \frac{a^2 + c^2 - b^2}{2ac},$$

$$\cos C = \frac{a^2 + b^2 - c^2}{2ab}.$$

The $\cos^{-1}$ key will give the proper angle even if it is obtuse, that is, a second-quadrant angle. In Example 2 we have

$$\cos C = \frac{7^2 + 6^2 - 8^2}{2(7)(6)}$$

$$C = \cos^{-1}\left[\frac{7^2 + 6^2 - 8^2}{2(7)(6)}\right] = 75.52°.$$

example 3

Given triangle ABC such that $a = 9$, $b = 8$, and $c = 2$, solve for A.

By the cosine law,

$$a^2 = b^2 + c^2 - 2bc \cos A$$
$$9^2 = 8^2 + 2^2 - 2(8)(2) \cos A$$
$$81 = 68 - 32 \cos A$$
$$32 \cos A = -13$$
$$\cos A = -\frac{13}{32} = -0.40625.$$

Because $\cos A$ is negative, angle A is obtuse. The reference angle for A is $66.03°$ and thus

$$A = 113.97°.$$

Alternatively, we have

$$\cos A = \frac{8^2 + 2^2 - 9^2}{2(8)(2)}$$

$$A = \cos^{-1}\left[\frac{8^2 + 2^2 - 9^2}{2(8)(2)}\right] = 113.97°.$$

Exercise 16-2

In Problems 1–10, solve triangle ABC from the given data.

1. $a = 20$, $b = 40$, $C = 28°$.   **2.** $b = 7$, $c = 13$, $A = 135°$.

3. $a = 16.1$, $b = 17.2$, $c = 18.3$.   **4.** $a = 7$, $b = 4$, $c = 1$.

5. $a = 14.86$, $c = 12.24$, $B = 115.23°$.   6. $a = 18.10$, $b = 24.53$, $c = 26.41$.

7. $a = 110$, $b = 85$, $c = 90$.   8. $a = 10.45$, $c = 9.83$, $B = 62.45°$.

9. $a = 116.32$, $b = 82.64$, $c = 95.24$.   10. $b = 145.87$, $c = 231.56$, $A = 29.44°$.

11. Figure 16-17 shows two forces represented by the vectors **OA** and **AB**. Find the length r of the resultant **OB** and find θ.

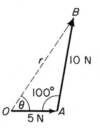

FIGURE 16-17

12. Repeat Problem 11 for the data in Fig. 16-18.

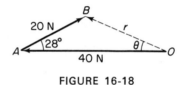

FIGURE 16-18

13. Two boats leave a dock at the same time. One travels north at 10 km/h. The other travels northeast at 20 km/h. After 3 hours, how far apart are the boats?

14. Points A and B are on opposite sides of a lake. To find the distance $\overline{AB}$, another point C on the same side of the lake as A is used. It is known that $\overline{BC} = 200$ m and $\overline{AC} = 500$ m. Angle BCA is measured to be 35°. Find $\overline{AB}$.

15. Two forces act simultaneously on an object: $F_1 = 40$ N and acts due west; $F_2 = 20$ N and acts 62° east of north. Find the magnitude and direction of the resultant force acting on the object.

16. Forces acting on an object tend to give it simultaneous velocities in two directions. If $v_1 = 12$ cm/s directed due east, and $v_2 = 12$ cm/s directed 25° east of north, what is the magnitude and direction of the resultant velocity?

17. A student claims that he underwent two separate displacements of 5 m and 8 m respectively, and ended up exactly 10 m from his starting point. Find the angle between the 5-m displacement and the resultant displacement of 10 m. What is the angle between the original two displacements?

18. Two engines and separate steering mechanisms of a speedboat effectively create two velocities: one, 22 km/h, 65° east of north, and a second, 50 km/h, 52° east of north. Determine the magnitude and direction of the resultant velocity.

19. Figure 16-19 shows a cross-sectional view of a roadside sign. The sign is 7 m tall

and three sections of supporting beams are 2.5, 3.5, and 4.5 m, respectively. Find the distance x from the base of the sign to the bottom of the back leg.

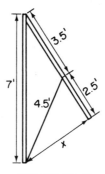

FIGURE 16-19

16-3   Areas and Angular Speed

A.   Area of a Triangle

Recall from geometry that the area of any triangle is equal to one-half the product of the lengths of its base and altitude. For each triangle ABC in Fig. 16-20,

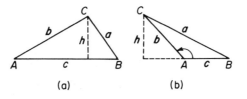

(a)   (b)

FIGURE 16-20

c is the base and h is the altitude. Moreover, in each case

$$\sin A = \frac{h}{b},$$

or

$$h = b \sin A.$$

Thus

$$\text{area} = \tfrac{1}{2}(\text{base})(\text{altitude})$$
$$= \tfrac{1}{2}c(b \sin A).$$

$$\boxed{\text{area} = \tfrac{1}{2}bc \sin A.}$$

By appropriate labeling we can also show area $= \frac{1}{2}ac \sin B = \frac{1}{2}ab \sin C$. That is, **the area of a triangle is equal to one-half the product of the lengths of any two sides and the sine of their included angle.**

example 1

Find the area of triangle ABC if $b = 10$, $c = 15$, and $A = 35°$.

$$\text{area} = \tfrac{1}{2}bc \sin A$$
$$= \tfrac{1}{2}(10)(15) \sin 35°$$
$$= 43.02 \quad \text{square units.}$$

example 2

Find the area of the triangle in Fig. 16-21.

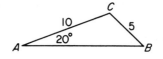

FIGURE 16-21

The area is given by $\frac{1}{2}ab \sin C$. To find C we first note that by the sine law,

$$\sin B = \frac{b \sin A}{a} = \frac{10 \sin 20°}{5} = 0.68404$$

$$B = 43.16°.$$

Thus $C = 180° - 20° - 43.16° = 116.84°$. Therefore

$$\text{area} = \tfrac{1}{2}(5)(10) \sin 116.84°$$
$$= 22.31 \quad \text{square units.}$$

B.   Area of a Sector of a Circle

From geometry, the area A of a sector of a circle determined by a central angle θ (the shaded region in Fig. 16-22) is directly proportional to θ. Symbolically,

$$A = k\theta.$$

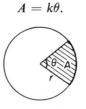

FIGURE 16-22

But when $\theta = 2\pi$, we know that $A = \pi r^2$. Therefore

$$\pi r^2 = k(2\pi)$$
$$k = \tfrac{1}{2}r^2.$$

Thus

$$\boxed{A = \tfrac{1}{2}r^2\theta, \qquad \theta \text{ in radians.}}$$

example 3

For a circle of radius 2 m, find the area of a sector determined by a central angle of 30°.

$$30° = 30°\left(\frac{\pi}{180°}\right) = \frac{\pi}{6} \text{ rad.}$$

$$A = \frac{1}{2}r^2\theta = \frac{1}{2}(2^2)\left(\frac{\pi}{6}\right) = \frac{\pi}{3} \text{ m}^2.$$

C. Angular Speed

The average linear speed $\bar{v}$ of an object is the average rate of change of distance with respect to time—that is, the average speed is the ratio of distance s to time t:

$$\boxed{\bar{v} = \frac{s}{t}.} \tag{1}$$

Let Fig. 16-23 represent a disk of radius r rotating counterclockwise. The segment OP serves as a reference. The **angular displacement** is the angle θ, in radians,

FIGURE 16-23

through which the disk rotates, and the **average angular speed** $\bar{\omega}$ is the ratio of the angular displacement to time—that is,

$$\bar{\omega} = \frac{\theta}{t},$$

or

$$\theta = \bar{\omega}t.$$ (2)

If we assume that time is measured in seconds, the unit of $\bar{\omega}$ is radians per second. While the disk rotates through an angle θ, in radians, the point P on the rim moves a distance s given by (here we use the formula for arc length)

$$s = r\theta.$$

Thus, using Eq. 2 to substitute for θ, we have

$$s = r(\bar{\omega}t).$$

$$s = r\bar{\omega}t \qquad (\bar{\omega} \text{ in radians per second}).$$ (3)

To relate angular speed $\bar{\omega}$ to linear speed $\bar{v}$, we need only to take the value of s from Eq. 1 and substitute it into Eq. 3:

$$\bar{v}t = r\bar{\omega}t$$

$$\bar{v} = r\bar{\omega},$$ (4)

where $\bar{\omega}$ is in radians per second.

example 4

A rotating circular disk of radius 2 m makes 10 revolutions per second. Find (a) the angular speed of the disk, (b) the linear speed of a point on the rim, and (c) the distance moved by that point in 10 s.

a. $\bar{\omega} = \dfrac{10 \text{ rev}}{\text{s}} = 10\dfrac{\text{rev}}{\text{s}} \left(2\pi\dfrac{\text{rad}}{\text{rev}}\right) = 20\pi \text{ rad/s}.$

b. $\bar{v} = r\bar{\omega} = (2)(20\pi) = 40\pi \text{ m/s}.$

c. $s = r\bar{\omega}t = (2)(20\pi)(10) = 400\pi \text{ m}.$

Exercise 16-3

In Problems 1–6, find the area of the triangle ABC having the given parts.

1. $b = 6$, $c = 8$, $A = 20°$.
2. $a = 10$, $b = 5$, $C = 14°$.
3. $a = 7$, $c = 12$, $B = 130°$.
4. $a = 20$, $b = 13$, $A = 55°$.
5. $a = 40$, $A = 70°$, $b = 40$.
6. $A = 100°$, $a = 100$, $b = 80$.

In Problems **7–10**, *the radius r* (*in centimeters*) *and central angle* θ *of a circle are given. Find the area of the sector determined by* θ. *You may express your answer in terms of* π.

7. $r = 12$, $\theta = \pi/6$.   **8.** $r = 25$, $\theta = \pi/3$.

9. $r = 18$, $\theta = 40°$.   **10.** $r = 20$, $\theta = 171°$.

11. What is the angular speed, in radians per second, of a wheel that makes 900 rev/min?

12. Three concentric circles have radii of 1, 1.5, and 3 m. What is the area of the segment between the inner and middle circles bounded by radii forming a central angle of 87°?

13. A semicircular traffic rotary is to be built so that an automobile traveling at a constant speed of 30 km/h can traverse the semicircle in 12 s. What is the required radius, in meters?

14. In the traffic rotary of Problem 13, what is the average angular speed of the automobile?

15. A wheel of an automobile has a radius of 43 cm. If the automobile is traveling at a constant speed of 30 km/h, what is the angular speed of the wheel, in radians per second?

16. A drive belt runs around two pulleys which have diameters of 20 cm and 80 cm. If the larger pulley makes 3 revolutions every second, determine each of the following.
(a) The angular speed of the small pulley, in radians per second.
(b) The linear speed of a point on the rim of each pulley, in centimeters per second.
(c) The area, in square centimeters, of a sector swept out by a radius line on each pulley in 2 s.

17. The propeller of a fan rotates at a constant angular speed of 1200 rev/min. The radius of the propeller is 10 cm. Determine (a) the angular speed, in radians per second, (b) the angular displacement after 28 s, (c) the linear and angular speeds of a point on the propeller 2 cm from the center, and (d) the linear and angular speeds of a point on the rim of the propeller.

18. A circular road surrounds a lake. The road can be considered as the region between two concentric circles having radii of 60 m and 67 m. Reflective material is to be applied to a portion of the road that is used as a pedestrian crossway. This portion can be considered as the region between the circles and bounded by a central angle of 5°. How many square meters of reflective material are required?

16-4   Review

Review Questions

1. True or false: Given two sides and the included angle of an oblique triangle, two solutions may occur. _____

2. The law of _____ is the first relation that is used to solve an oblique triangle when three sides are given.

3. When solving an oblique triangle where the lengths of three sides are given, you should solve first for the __(largest)(smallest)__ angle.

4. The largest angle of a triangle is found opposite the side of __(greatest)(least)__ length.

5. State in the order given, that is, a, b, and c, how many triangles are possible in each case.
   (a) $a = 30$, $b = 25$, $A = 45°$.
   (b) $a = 20$, $b = 30$, $A = 45°$.
   (c) $a = 2\sqrt{3}$, $b = 4$, $A = 60°$.   _____

Answers to Review Questions

1. False.   **2.** Cosines.   **3.** Largest.   **4.** Greatest.   **5.** 1, 0, 1.

Review Problems

*In Problems **1–10**, solve the triangles ABC from the given data.*

1. $a = 5$, $b = 4$, $C = 30°$. 　　　　**2.** $a = 2$, $c = 3$, $B = 60°$.

3. $B = 30°$, $C = 70°$, $b = 3$. 　　　**4.** $A = 110°$, $B = 40°$, $a = 9$.

5. $a = 8$, $b = 6$, $c = 3$. 　　　　　**6.** $a = 5$, $b = 7$, $c = 9$.

7. $A = 60°$, $a = 20$, $b = 10$. 　　　**8.** $b = 5$, $c = 8$, $C = 40°$.

9. $a = 6$, $b = 8$, $A = 10°$. 　　　　**10.** $A = 130°$, $b = 20$, $a = 10$.

11. It is required that a circular track in the shape of a washer have an area of 2500 m². Determine the inside and outside radii of the track if the circumference of the inner edge is 91 m. If a woman runs along the very center of the track, how many revolutions must she make to run 3.2 km?

12. A phonograph turntable rotates at $33\frac{1}{3}$ rev/min. What is the linear speed of a point 2 cm from the center of the turntable?

13. Find the area of triangle *ABC* if $a = 25$, $b = 12$, and $C = 120°$.

14. In Fig. 16-24 are forces **AB** and **BC** represented by vectors. Find the length r of the resultant **AC**.

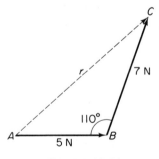

FIGURE 16-24

17

inequalities

17-1 Linear Inequalities in One Variable

In Sec. 1-1 the inequality symbols $<$, $>$, $\leq$, and $\geq$ were introduced. In defining an inequality below, we shall use the less than relation ($<$), but the others ($>$, $\geq$, $\leq$) also apply.

> An **inequality** is a statement that one number is less than another number.

Inequalities are represented by means of inequality symbols. If two inequalities have their inequality symbols pointing in the same direction, then the inequalities are said to have the *same sense*. However, if the symbols point in opposite directions, the inequalities are said to be *opposite in sense*, or one is said to have the *reverse sense* of the other. Thus, the inequalities $a < b$ and $c < d$ have the same sense, but $a < b$ and $c > d$ are opposite in sense.

As with equations, there are various types of inequalities. An **absolute inequality** is one that is true for *all* allowable values of the variables involved. A **conditional inequality** is one that is true for *some*, but not all, of the allowable values.

547

example 1

a. $x^2 \geq 0$ is an absolute inequality because the square of *any* real number x is positive or zero.

b. $x^2 > 0$ is a conditional inequality because it is true if and only if x is not zero.

Solving an inequality, such as $2(x - 3) > -10$, means to find all values of the variable for which the inequality is true. This involves the application of certain rules, which we now state.

1. **If the same number is added to or subtracted from both sides of an inequality, then the resulting inequality has the same sense as the original inequality.**

   Symbolically, if $a < b$, then $a + c < b + c$ and $a - c < b - c$.

   For example, because $7 < 10$, then $7 + 3 < 10 + 3$ or, simply, $10 < 13$.

2. **If both sides of an inequality are multiplied or divided by the same *positive* number, then the resulting inequality has the same sense as the original inequality.**

   Symbolically, if $a < b$ and $c > 0$, then $ac < bc$ and $\dfrac{a}{c} < \dfrac{b}{c}$.

   For example, because $3 < 7$ and $2 > 0$, then $3(2) < 7(2)$ and $\dfrac{3}{2} < \dfrac{7}{2}$.

3. **If both sides of an inequality are multiplied or divided by the same *negative* number, then the resulting inequality has the *reverse* sense of the original inequality.**

   Symbolically, if $a < b$ and $c > 0$, then $a(-c) > b(-c)$ and $\dfrac{a}{-c} > \dfrac{b}{-c}$.

   For example, $4 < 7$ but $4(-2) > 7(-2)$ or, equivalently, $-8 > -14$. Also $\dfrac{4}{-2} > \dfrac{7}{-2}$.

The result of applying Rules 1–3 to an inequality is called an **equivalent inequality**. It is an inequality for which the solution is exactly the same as that of the original inequality. We shall apply these rules to solve a *linear inequality*.

> A **linear inequality** in the variable x is an inequality that can be written in the form
> $$ax + b < 0 \quad (\text{or } >, \leq, \geq),$$
> where a and b are constants and $a \neq 0$.

In the following examples, the given inequality will be replaced by an equivalent inequality until the solution is obvious. Our goal is to isolate the variable on one side of the inequality symbol. Whereas a linear *equation* has exactly one solution, you will see that a linear *inequality* gives rise to infinitely many solutions.

example 2

a. Solve $2(x - 3) > -10$.

$$2(x - 3) > -10$$
$$2x - 6 > -10 \quad \text{(distributive law)}$$
$$2x - 6 + 6 > -10 + 6 \quad \text{(adding 6 to both sides [Rule 1])}$$
$$2x > -4 \quad \text{(simplifying)}$$
$$\frac{2x}{2} > \frac{-4}{2} \quad \text{(dividing both sides by 2 [Rule 2])}$$
$$x > -2 \quad \text{(simplifying).}$$

Because all of the inequalities are equivalent, the original inequality is true for all real numbers x such that $x > -2$. We shall write our solution simply as $x > -2$. Geometrically, we can represent the solution by a bold line segment on a number line, as in Fig. 17-1. The hollow dot indicates that -2 *is not included* in the solution.

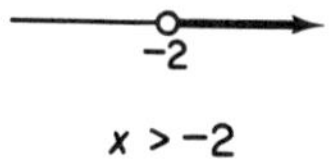

$$x > -2$$

FIGURE 17-1

b. Solve $5 - 2x \geq 4$.

$$5 - 2x \geq 4$$
$$-2x \geq -1 \quad \text{(subtracting 5 from both sides [Rule 1])}$$
$$\frac{-2x}{-2} \leq \frac{-1}{-2} \quad \begin{array}{l}\text{(dividing both sides by } -2 \text{ and}\\ \text{changing direction of inequality [Rule 3])}\end{array}$$
$$x \leq \frac{1}{2}.$$

The solution is $x \leq \frac{1}{2}$, which is represented geometrically by the bold line segment in Fig. 17-2. The solid dot means that $\frac{1}{2}$ *is included* in the solution.

$$x \leq \frac{1}{2}$$

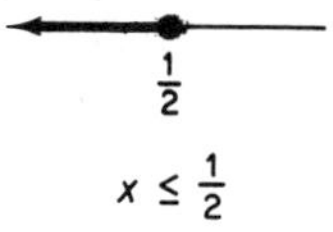

FIGURE 17-2

example 3

Solve $\frac{3}{2}t - 1 \le \frac{5}{3}(-3 + t)$.

To clear of fractions, we multiply both sides by the L.C.D., which is 6.

$$6\left(\frac{3}{2}t - 1\right) \le 6 \cdot \frac{5}{3}(-3 + t) \qquad \text{(Rule 2)}$$

$$9t - 6 \le 10(-3 + t)$$

$$9t - 6 \le -30 + 10t$$

$$-6 \le -30 + t \qquad \text{(subtracting } 9t \text{ from both sides [Rule 1])}$$

$$24 \le t \qquad \text{(adding 30 to both sides [Rule 1])}$$

$$t \ge 24 \qquad \text{(rewriting).}$$

See Fig. 17-3.

$t \ge 24$

FIGURE 17-3

example 4

a. Solve $2(x - 4) - 3 > 2x + 1$.

$$2(x - 4) - 3 > 2x + 1$$

$$2x - 8 - 3 > 2x + 1$$

$$-11 > 1 \qquad \text{(subtracting } 2x \text{ from both sides).}$$

The inequality $-11 > 1$ is never true, so there is *no solution*. Here the solution set can be written $\varnothing$, the empty set.

b. Solve $3z + 7 > 8z - (5z - 2)$.

$$3z + 7 > 8z - (5z - 2)$$

$$3z + 7 > 3z + 2$$

$$7 > 2 \qquad \text{(subtracting } 3z \text{ from both sides).}$$

Because the inequality $7 > 2$ is always true (true for any value of z), the solution is *all real numbers*. We write this solution as $-\infty < z < \infty$. See Fig. 17-4. The symbols $-\infty$ and ∞ are not numbers, but are merely a convenience for indicating that the solution is all real numbers.

$-\infty < z < \infty$

FIGURE 17-4

Frequently we shall use the word *interval* to describe certain sets of real numbers. For example, the set of all numbers x for which $a \le x \le b$ is called a **closed interval** because it *includes* the endpoints a and b. We denote it by $[a, b]$. The set of all x for which $a < x < b$ is called an **open interval** and is denoted by (a, b). The endpoints are *not* part of this set. See Fig. 17-5.

Closed interval $[a,b]$ Open interval (a,b)

FIGURE 17-5

Extending these concepts, we have the intervals shown in Fig. 17-6, where the symbols ∞ and $-\infty$ are not numbers but are merely a convenience for indicating that an interval extends indefinitely in some direction.

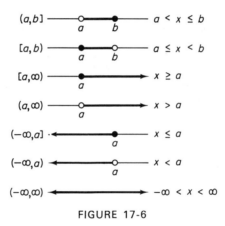

FIGURE 17-6

Exercise 17-1

In Problems **1–34**, *solve the inequalities and indicate your answers geometrically on the real number line.*

1. $4x > 8$.   **2.** $8x < -2$.   **3.** $3x - 4 \le 5$.

4. $5x \ge 0$.   **5.** $-4x \ge 2$.   **6.** $6 \le 5 - 3y$.

7. $3 - 5s > 5$.   **8.** $4s - 1 < -5$.   **9.** $6x - 15 < 2x - 3$.

10. $3x + 1 > 2(x + 4)$.   **11.** $2x - 3 \le 4 + 7x$.   **12.** $-3 \ge 8(2 - x)$.

13. $3 < 2y + 3$.   **14.** $2y + 3 \le 1 + 2y$.

15. $3(2 - 3x) > 4(1 - 4x)$.   **16.** $8(x + 1) + 1 < 3(2x) + 1$.

17. $2(3x - 2) > 3(2x - 1)$.   **18.** $3 - 2(x - 1) \le 2(4 + x)$.

19. $\frac{5}{3}x < 10$.   **20.** $-\frac{1}{2}x > 6$.

21. $\dfrac{9y+1}{4} \le 2y - 1.$

22. $\dfrac{4y-3}{2} \ge \dfrac{1}{3}.$

23. $4x - 1 \ge 4(x-2) + 7.$

24. $0x \le 0.$

25. $\dfrac{1-t}{2} < \dfrac{3t-7}{3}.$

26. $\dfrac{3(2t-2)}{2} > \dfrac{6t-3}{5} + \dfrac{t}{10}.$

27. $2x + 3 \ge \frac{1}{2}x - 4.$

28. $4x - \frac{1}{2} \le \frac{3}{2}x.$

29. $\frac{2}{3}r < \frac{5}{6}r.$

30. $\frac{7}{4}t > -\frac{2}{3}t.$

31. $\dfrac{y}{2} + \dfrac{y}{3} > y + \dfrac{y}{5}.$

32. $\dfrac{5y-1}{-3} > \dfrac{7(y+1)}{-2}.$

33. $0.1(0.03x + 4) \ge 0.02x + 0.434.$

34. $0.02(x+3) < 0.5(x - 0.08).$

35. The amount of current needed for a certain electrical appliance is more than 7 A but less than 9.5 A. If 12 such appliances are to be used, and I represents the total number of amperes needed, describe I by using inequalities.

36. Using inequalities, symbolize the following statement: The number of working hours x to produce a blueprint is at least 15 but not more than 18.

37. If a block slides down a rough inclined plane, it can be deduced from the principle of conservation of energy that the gravitational potential energy P of the block at the top of the inclined plane is greater than the kinetic energy K of the block at the bottom of the plane. If $K = 36$ J, geometrically indicate the possible values of P on the real number line.

17-2   Nonlinear Inequalities

Let us consider how we would go about solving the inequality

$$x^2 - x - 2 > 0,$$

which is not linear. One method is to graph the equation $y = f(x) = x^2 - x - 2$ and note when y is greater than 0. In Fig. 17-7 we see that $y > 0$ if $x < -1$ or $x > 2$.

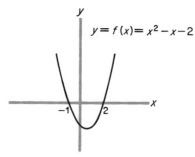

FIGURE 17-7

That is, the solution of $x^2 - x - 2 > 0$ is $x < -1$ or $x > 2$. Although this approach is easy to understand, the accuracy of the graphical technique is too limited. A more accurate method is needed.

Consider again the inequality $x^2 - x - 2 > 0$. We begin solving it by finding the roots of the corresponding *equation* $x^2 - x - 2 = 0$. Because $x^2 - x - 2 = (x + 1)(x - 2) = 0$, the roots are -1 and 2, which are shown in Fig. 17-8.

FIGURE 17-8

These roots determine three intervals on the number line:

$$(-\infty, -1), \qquad (-1, 2), \quad \text{and} \quad (2, \infty).$$

Referring back to Fig. 17-7, notice that if x is *any* number in the interval $(-\infty, -1)$, then $f(x) > 0$. If x is *any* number in the interval $(-1, 2)$, then $f(x) < 0$, and so on. That is, given any of these three intervals, $f(x)$ does not change sign *throughout* the interval. This means that to determine the sign of $f(x)$ on one of these intervals, it is sufficient to determine its sign at *any* point in that interval. For instance, -2 is in $(-\infty, -1)$ and $f(-2) = 4 > 0$. Thus $f(x) > 0$ on the *entire* interval $(-\infty, -1)$. Because zero is in $(-1, 2)$ and $f(0) = -2 < 0$, then $f(x) < 0$ on the *entire* interval $(-1, 2)$. Similarly, 3 is in $(2, \infty)$ and $f(3) = 4 > 0$; thus, $f(x) > 0$ on the *entire* interval $(2, \infty)$. (Fig. 17-9). Therefore $x^2 - x - 2 > 0$ for $x < -1$ or for $x > 2$, and so we have solved the inequality.

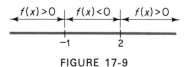

FIGURE 17-9

example 1

Solve $x^2 - 4x - 12 < 0$.

Let $f(x) = x^2 - 4x - 12 = (x + 2)(x - 6)$. The roots of $f(x) = 0$ are -2 and 6, which are shown in Fig. 17-10.

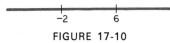

FIGURE 17-10

These roots determine three intervals:

$$(-\infty, -2), \qquad (-2, 6), \quad \text{and} \quad (6, \infty).$$

Because -8 is in $(-\infty, -2)$, the sign of $f(x)$ on $(-\infty, -2)$ is the same as the sign of $f(-8)$. Given

$$f(x) = (x + 2)(x - 6),$$

then

$$f(-8) = (-8 + 2)(-8 - 6) = (-)(-) = (+),$$

so $f(x) > 0$ on $(-\infty, -2)$. Note that it is not necessary to actually evaluate $f(-8)$. Knowing the signs of the factors is enough. For the other intervals we find that

$$f(0) = (+)(-) = (-), \qquad \text{so } f(x) < 0 \text{ on } (-2, 6),$$
$$f(10) = (+)(+) = (+), \qquad \text{so } f(x) > 0 \text{ on } (6, \infty).$$

A summary of our results is given by the sign chart in Fig. 17-11. Thus the solution of $x^2 - 4x - 12 < 0$ is $-2 < x < 6$, because that is the only one of the three intervals on which $f(x) < 0$.

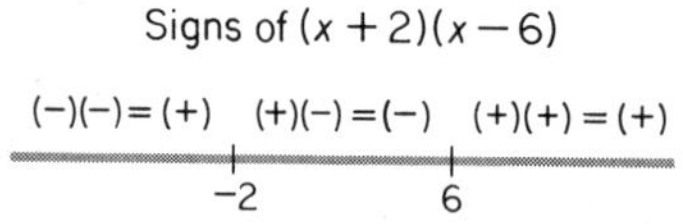

Signs of $(x + 2)(x - 6)$

$$(-)(-) = (+) \quad (+)(-) = (-) \quad (+)(+) = (+)$$

$$-2 \qquad\qquad 6$$

FIGURE 17-11

example 2

Solve $x(x - 1)(x + 4) \leq 0$.

If $f(x) = x(x - 1)(x + 4)$, then the roots of the equation $f(x) = 0$ are 0, 1, and -4, which are shown in Fig. 17-12.

$$-4 \qquad\qquad 0 \quad 1$$

FIGURE 17-12

These three roots determine four intervals:

$$(-\infty, -4), \qquad (-4, 0), \qquad (0, 1), \quad \text{and} \quad (1, \infty).$$

Because -5 is in $(-\infty, -4)$, the sign of $f(x)$ on $(-\infty, -4)$ is the same as that of $f(-5)$. Given

$$f(x) = x(x - 1)(x + 4),$$

then

$$f(-5) = -5(-5 - 1)(-5 + 4) = (-)(-)(-) = (-),$$

so $f(x) < 0$ on $(-\infty, -4)$. For the other intervals we find that

$$f(-2) = (-)(-)(+) = (+), \qquad \text{so } f(x) > 0 \text{ on } (-4, 0),$$
$$f(\tfrac{1}{2}) = (+)(-)(+) = (-), \qquad \text{so } f(x) < 0 \text{ on } (0, 1),$$
$$f(2) = (+)(+)(+) = (+), \qquad \text{so } f(x) > 0 \text{ on } (1, \infty).$$

Our results are summarized by the sign chart in Fig. 17-13. Thus $x(x - 1)(x + 4) \leq 0$

for $x \le -4$ or $0 \le x \le 1$. Note that -4, 0, and 1 are included in the solution because these roots satisfy the equality ($=$) part of the inequality ($\le$).

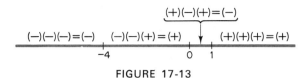

FIGURE 17-13

example 3

Solve $\dfrac{x^2 - 6x + 5}{x} \ge 0.$

Let

$$f(x) = \frac{x^2 - 6x + 5}{x} = \frac{(x-1)(x-5)}{x}.$$

For a quotient we solve the inequality by considering the intervals determined by the roots of $f(x) = 0$, namely 1 and 5, and those values of x for which f is undefined. Here f is undefined when $x = 0$. In Fig. 17-14 we have placed a hollow dot at zero

FIGURE 17-14

to indicate that f is not defined there. We thus consider the intervals

$$(-\infty, 0), \quad (0, 1), \quad (1, 5), \quad \text{and} \quad (5, \infty).$$

Determining the sign of $f(x)$ at a point in each interval, we find that

$$f(-1) = \frac{(-)(-)}{(-)} = (-), \qquad \text{so } f(x) < 0 \text{ on } (-\infty, 0),$$

$$f\left(\tfrac{1}{2}\right) = \frac{(-)(-)}{(+)} = (+), \qquad \text{so } f(x) > 0 \text{ on } (0, 1),$$

$$f(2) = \frac{(+)(-)}{(+)} = (-), \qquad \text{so } f(x) < 0 \text{ on } (1, 5),$$

$$f(6) = \frac{(+)(+)}{(+)} = (+), \qquad \text{so } f(x) > 0 \text{ on } (5, \infty).$$

The sign chart is given in Fig. 17-15. Therefore $f(x) \ge 0$ for $0 < x \le 1$ or $x \ge 5$ (Fig. 17-16). Why are 1 and 5 included, but zero excluded?

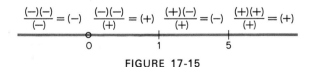

FIGURE 17-15

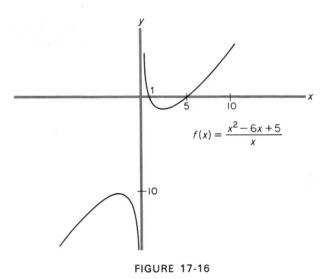

$$f(x) = \frac{x^2 - 6x + 5}{x}$$

FIGURE 17-16

example 4

Solve $t^3 + 16t > 8t^2$.

We first rewrite the inequality so that one side is zero and then we factor.

$$t^3 - 8t^2 + 16t > 0$$
$$t(t^2 - 8t + 16) > 0$$
$$t(t - 4)^2 > 0.$$

The roots of $t(t - 4)^2 = 0$ are 0 and 4. From the sign chart in Fig. 17-17, we conclude that the solution is $0 < t < 4$ or $t > 4$.

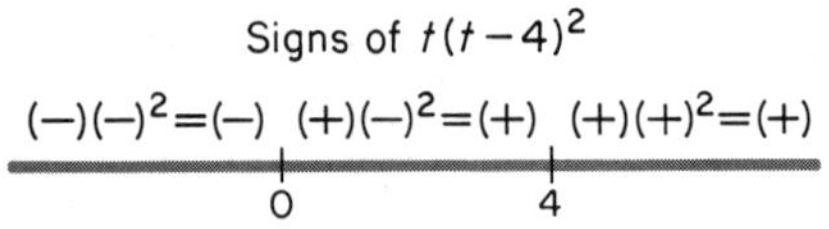

Signs of $t(t-4)^2$

$$(-)(-)^2=(-) \quad (+)(-)^2=(+) \quad (+)(+)^2=(+)$$

0   4

FIGURE 17-17

example 5

a. Solve the inequality $x^2 + x + 1 > 0$.

Using the quadratic formula, we find the roots of $x^2 + x + 1 = 0$ to be imaginary. We therefore turn to the graph of $y = x^2 + x + 1$ for any information it may yield (Fig. 17-18). Because for all x we have $y > 0$, the solution of $x^2 + x + 1 > 0$ is $-\infty < x < \infty$.

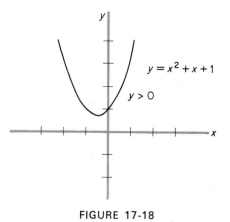

FIGURE 17-18

b. Solve $x^2 + x + 1 < 0$.

From Part a, $x^2 + x + 1$ is always positive. Thus the inequality $x^2 + x + 1 < 0$ has no solution.

Exercise 17-2

In Problems **1–38**, *solve the inequalities.*

1. $(x - 1)(x - 5) < 0$.   **2.** $(x + 3)(x - 8) > 0$.   **3.** $(x + 1)(x - 3) > 0$.

4. $(x + 4)(x + 5) < 0$.   **5.** $x^2 - 1 < 0$.   **6.** $x^2 > 9$.

7. $x^2 - x - 6 > 0$.   **8.** $x^2 - 2x - 3 \leq 0$.   **9.** $5s - s^2 \leq 0$.

10. $t^2 + 9t + 18 \geq 0$.   **11.** $x^2 + 5x < -6$.   **12.** $x^2 - 12 > x$.

13. $x^2 + 4x - 5 \geq 3x + 15$.   **14.** $x^2 + 9x + 9 \leq 2 - x^2$.

15. $2z^2 - 5z - 12 < 0$.   **16.** $5t^2 - 1 > 4t$.

17. $x^2 + 2x + 1 > 0$.   **18.** $x^2 + 9 \leq 6x$.

19. $4(t^2 + t) - 1 \geq 2$.   **20.** $3s^2 \leq 11s - 10$.

21. $(x + 2)(x - 1)(x - 4) > 0$.   **22.** $x(x + 3)(5 - x) < 0$.

23. $(x + 5)(x - 3)^2 < 0$.   **24.** $(x + 1)^2(x - 4)^2 > 0$.

25. $y^3 - y \leq 0$.   **26.** $x^3 + 8x^2 + 15x \geq 0$.

27. $x^3 - 2x^2 \geq 0$.   **28.** $p^4 - 2p^3 - 3p^2 \leq 0$.   **29.** $\dfrac{x - 4}{x + 8} > 0$.

30. $\dfrac{x + 3}{x + 5} < 0$.   **31.** $\dfrac{t}{3 - t} \leq 0$.   **32.** $\dfrac{s - 1}{2s - 1} > 0$.

33. $\dfrac{5}{x + 2} > 0$.   **34.** $\dfrac{3}{9(x - 8)} < 0$.   **35.** $\dfrac{x + 3}{x^2 - 1} < 0$.

36. $\dfrac{x^2 - x - 6}{x + 4} > 0.$ **37.** $\dfrac{x^2 - 5x + 4}{x^2 + 5x + 4} \geq 0.$ **38.** $\dfrac{x^2 - 4}{x^2 + 2x + 1} \leq 0.$

39. A company owns a 1 km by 2 km rectangular lot and needs to cut a uniform strip of trees along the outer edges of the lot. At most, how wide can the strip be if at least $\frac{3}{4}$ km² of the lot must remain?

40. A container manufacturer wishes to make an open box by cutting a 4-cm square from each corner of a square sheet of aluminum and then turning up the sides. The box is to contain at least 324 cm². Find the dimensions of the smallest sheet of aluminum that can be used.

17-3 Absolute-Value Inequalities

Recall that the absolute value of a real number is the distance on the number line between the number and zero. If x is any positive number, clearly $|x| = x$. Just as $|-5| = 5 = -(-5)$, it should not be difficult to convince yourself that if x is any negative number, then $|x|$ is the positive number $-x$. The minus sign indicates that we have changed the sign of x. Thus, aside from its geometrical interpretation, absolute value can be defined as follows.

> The **absolute value** of a real number x, written $|x|$, is
> $$|x| = \begin{cases} x, & \text{if } x > 0, \\ 0, & \text{if } x = 0, \\ -x, & \text{if } x < 0. \end{cases}$$

Applying the definition gives $|5| = 5$, $|-4| = -(-4) = 4$, $-|2| = -2$, and $-|-6| = -6$. Note that $|\pi - 4| = 4 - \pi$, not $\pi - 4$. Why?

example 1

a. Solve $|x - 4| = 3$.

This equation states that $x - 4$ is a number three units from zero. Thus either
$$x - 4 = 3 \quad \text{or} \quad x - 4 = -3.$$
If $x - 4 = 3$, then $x = 7$; if $x - 4 = -3$, then $x = 1$. Thus $x = 1, 7$.

b. Solve $|8 - 5x| = 6$.

The equation is true if $8 - 5x = 6$ or if $8 - 5x = -6$. Solving these gives $x = \frac{2}{5}$ and $x = \frac{14}{5}$.

c. Solve $|x - 5| = -2$.

Because the absolute value of a number is never negative, there is no solution.

The numbers 5 and 9 are 4 units apart. Also,

$$|9 - 5| = |4| = 4,$$
$$|5 - 9| = |-4| = 4.$$

In general, we may interpret $|a - b|$ or $|b - a|$ as the *distance* between a and b. For example, to solve the equation $|x - 4| = 3$ in (a) of Example 1 means to find all numbers x that are exactly three units from 4. Thus x can be 1 or 7. We also remark that $|a - b| = |b - a|$.

Let us turn now to inequalities. If $|x| < 3$, then x is less than 3 units from 0. Thus x must lie between -3 and 3. That is, $-3 < x < 3$ [Fig. 17-19(a)]. However, if $|x| > 3$, then x must be more than 3 units from 0. Thus, one of two things must be true: either $x > 3$ *or* $x < -3$ [Fig. 17-19(b)]. We can extend these ideas. Given that $|x| \leq 3$, then $-3 \leq x \leq 3$. If $|x| \geq 3$, then $x \geq 3$ or $x \leq -3$.

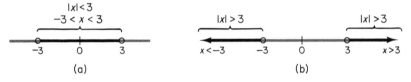

Paul & Shaevel 17-19

FIGURE 17-19

In general, the solutions of $|x| < d$ or $|x| \leq d$, where d is a positive number, consist of one interval, namely $-d < x < d$ or $-d \leq x \leq d$, respectively. However, when $|x| > d$ or $|x| \geq d$ there are two intervals in the solution, namely $x < -d$ and $x > d$, or $x \leq -d$ and $x \geq d$, respectively.

example 2

a. Solve $|x - 2| < 4$.

The number $x - 2$ must be less than 4 units from 0. From our discussion above this means that $-4 < x - 2 < 4$. We may set up the procedure for solving this inequality as follows:

$$-4 < x - 2 < 4$$
$$-4 + 2 < x < 4 + 2 \qquad \text{(adding 2 to each member)}$$
$$-2 < x < 6.$$

b. Solve $|3 - 2x| \leq 5$.

$$-5 \leq 3 - 2x \leq 5$$
$$-5 - 3 \leq -2x \leq 5 - 3 \qquad \text{(subtracting 3 from each member)}$$
$$-8 \leq -2x \leq 2$$

$$4 \geq x \geq -1 \qquad \text{(dividing each member by } -2\text{),}$$
$$-1 \leq x \leq 4 \qquad \text{(rewriting).}$$

Note that the sense of the original inequality was reversed in the next-to-last step where we divided by a negative number.

example 3

a. Solve $|x + 5| \geq 7$.

The number $x + 5$ must be *at least* 7 units from 0. Thus, either $x + 5 \leq -7$ or $x + 5 \geq 7$. This means that either $x \leq -12$ or $x \geq 2$.

b. Solve $|3x - 4| > 1$.

Either $3x - 4 < -1$ or $3x - 4 > 1$. Thus either $3x < 3$ or $3x > 5$. Therefore, either $x < 1$ or $x > \frac{5}{3}$.

example 4

Using absolute value notation, express the following statements.

a. x is less than four units from 7.

$$|x - 7| < 4.$$

b. x differs from 2 by at least 3.

$$|x - 2| \geq 3.$$

c. $x < 9$ and $x > -9$ simultaneously.

$$|x| < 9.$$

d. x is strictly within two units of -3.

$$|x - (-3)| < 2,$$
$$|x + 3| < 2.$$

e. x is strictly within σ (sigma) units of μ (mu).

$$|x - \mu| < \sigma.$$

Exercise 17-3

*In Problems **1–8**, write an equivalent form without the absolute value symbol.*

1. $|-6|$.   **2.** $|\pi^{-2}|$.   **3.** $|7 - 3|$.

4. $|(-6 - 4)/2|$.   **5.** $|4(-7/3)|$.   **6.** $|3 - 8| - |8 - 3|$.

7. $|x| < 4$.   **8.** $|x| < 8$.

9. Using the absolute value symbol, express each fact.
   (a) x is strictly within three units of 7.
   (b) x differs from 2 by less than 3.
   (c) x is no more than five units from 7.
   (d) the distance between 7 and x is 4.
   (e) $x + 4$ is strictly within two units of the origin.
   (f) x is strictly between -3 and 3.
   (g) $x < -6$ or $x > 6$.
   (h) $x - 6 > 4$ or $x - 6 < -4$.
   (i) the number of hours, x, that a machine will operate efficiently differs from 105 by less than 3.

10. Show that if $|x - \mu| \leq 2\sigma$, then $-2\sigma + \mu \leq x \leq 2\sigma + \mu$.

In Problems 11–40, solve the given equation or inequality.

11. $|x| = 6$.

12. $|-x| = 3$.

13. $\left|\dfrac{x}{3}\right| = 2$.

14. $\left|\dfrac{4}{x}\right| = 8$.

15. $|x - 5| = 8$.

16. $|4 + 3x| = 2$.

17. $|5x - 2| = 0$.

18. $|7x + 3| = x$.

19. $|7 - 4x| = 5$.

20. $|1 - 2x| = 1$.

21. $|x| < 3$.

22. $|x| < 10$.

23. $|x| > 6$.

24. $|x| > 3$.

25. $|2x| \leq 2$.

26. $|4x| \leq 3$.

27. $|3x| \geq 9$.

28. $\left|\dfrac{x}{2}\right| \geq 3$.

29. $|x - 4| < 16$.

30. $|y + 5| \leq 6$.

31. $|y + 1| \geq 6$.

32. $|x - 2| \geq 4$.

33. $|3x - 5| \leq 1$.

34. $\left|\dfrac{x}{3} - 5\right| < 4$.

35. $|1 - 3x| < 2$.

36. $|4x - 1| > 7$.

37. $|\tfrac{1}{2} - t| > \tfrac{1}{2}$.

38. $|5 - 2x| > 1$.

39. $\left|\dfrac{3x - 8}{2}\right| \geq 4$.

40. $\left|\dfrac{x - 8}{4}\right| \leq 2$.

41. In the manufacture of a certain machine, the average dimension of a part is 0.01 cm. Using the absolute value symbol, express the fact that an individual measurement x of a part does not differ from the average by more than 0.005 cm.

17-4 Linear Inequalities in Two Variables

Suppose that a chemical manufacturer has available 60 kg of a certain chemical element and uses it all to manufacture x units of compound A and y units of compound B. If each unit of A requires 2 kg of the element and each unit of B requires 3 kg, then the possible combinations of A and B that can be produced must satisfy the equation

$$2x + 3y = 60, \quad \text{where } x, y \geq 0,$$

The solution is represented by the line segment in Fig. 17-20. For example, if 15

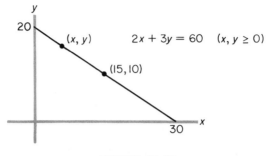

FIGURE 17-20

units of A are made, which require 30 kg of the element, then because all 60 kg of the element must be used, 10 kg of B must be made, which require 30 kg of the element. Thus (15, 10) is on the line.

On the other hand, suppose the manufacturer does not necessarily wish to use the *total* supply of the element. The possible combinations are now described by the inequality

$$2x + 3y \leq 60, \quad \text{where } x, y \geq 0. \tag{1}$$

When linear inequalities in *one* variable were discussed, their solutions were represented geometrically by *intervals* on the real number line. However, for an inequality in *two* variables, as in (1), the solution is usually represented by a *region* in the coordinate plane. We shall find the region corresponding to (1) after considering such inequalities in general.

A **linear inequality** in the variables x and y is an inequality that can be written in the form

$$ax + by + c < 0 \quad (\text{or} \leq 0, \geq 0, > 0),$$

where a, b and c are constants and a and b are not both zero.

Geometrically, the solution of a linear inequality in x and y consists of all points in the plane with coordinates that satisfy the inequality. In particular, the graph of a nonvertical line $y = mx + b$ separates the plane into three distinct parts (Fig. 17–21).

1. The line itself, consisting of all points (x, y) with coordinates that satisfy $y = mx + b$.

2. The region lying above the line, consisting of all points (x, y) that satisfy $y > mx + b$.

3. The region below the line, consisting of all points (x, y) satisfying $y < mx + b$.

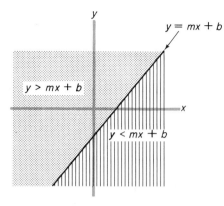

FIGURE 17-21

For a vertical line $x = a$, we speak of regions to the right $(x > a)$ or the left $(x < a)$ of the line (Fig. 17-22).

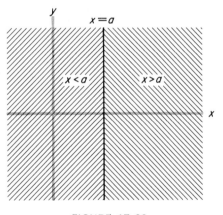

FIGURE 17-22

To apply these facts, we shall solve $x + y < 4$. We first sketch the corresponding line $x + y = 4$ by choosing two points on it, for instance $(4, 0)$ and $(0, 4)$ (Fig. 17-23). By writing the inequality in the equivalent form $y < -x + 4$, we conclude from (3) that the solution consists of all points below this line. Part of this region is shaded in the diagram. Thus, if (x, y) is *any* point in this region, then $y < -x + 4$. For example, the point $(-2, 1)$ is in the region and $1 < -(-2) + 4$. You must realize that this check with a single point *does not* guarantee that our solution is correct. However, if the given inequality were *not* satisfied by the chosen point, then our solution is not correct. Moreover, if we had required that $y \leq -x + 4$ instead of $y < -x + 4$, then the line $y = -x + 4$ would also have been included in the solution as indicated by the solid line in Fig. 17-24. **We shall adopt the conventions that a solid line *is included* and that a broken line *is not* included in the solution.**

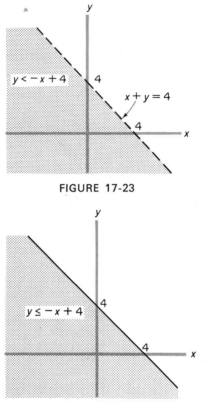

FIGURE 17-23

FIGURE 17-24

example 1

Find the region described by $y \leq 3$.

Because x does not appear, the inequality is assumed to be true for all values of x. Thus the solution consists of the line $y = 3$ *and* the region below it (Fig. 17-25), because the y-coordinate of each point in that region is less than 3.

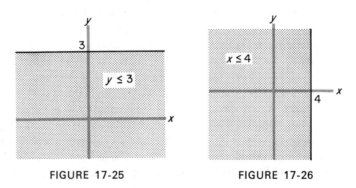

FIGURE 17-25   FIGURE 17-26

example 2

Find the region described by $x \leq 4$.

Because y does not appear, the inequality is assumed to be true for all values of y. The solution consists of the line $x = 4$ and the region to the left of the line (Fig. 17-26).

example 3

Solve $2(2x - y) < 2(x + y) + 4$.

We first rewrite the inequality in an equivalent form so that y alone appears to the left of the inequality symbol:

$$2(2x - y) < 2(x + y) + 4$$
$$4x - 2y < 2x + 2y + 4$$
$$-4y < -2x + 4$$
$$-y < -\frac{x}{2} + 1$$
$$y > \frac{x}{2} - 1.$$

In the last step, the sense of the original inequality was changed because we multiplied both sides by -1, a negative number. We now sketch the line $y = (x/2) - 1$ by using the points $(2, 0)$ and $(0, -1)$. Then we shade the region above the line (Fig. 17-27). This region is the solution.

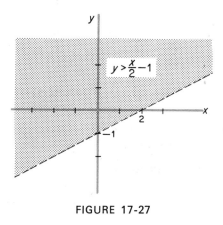

FIGURE 17-27

The solution of a *system* of inequalities consists of all points with coordinates that simultaneously satisfy all the given inequalities. Geometrically, it is the region that is common to all the regions determined by the given inequalities. For example, let us solve

$$\begin{cases} y - 3x < 6 \\ x - y \le -3. \end{cases}$$

The system is equivalent to

$$\begin{cases} y < 3x + 6 \\ y \ge x + 3. \end{cases}$$

Note that each inequality has been written so that y is isolated on one side. Thus the appropriate regions with respect to the corresponding lines will be apparent. We first sketch the lines $y = 3x + 6$ and $y = x + 3$ and then shade the region that is simultaneously *below* the first line and *on or above* the second line (Fig. 17-28). This region is the solution. When sketching the lines, **you should draw broken lines everywhere until it is clear which portions of the lines are to be included in the solution.**

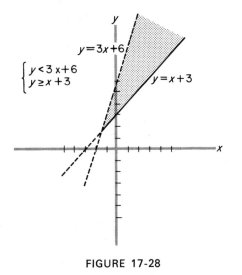

FIGURE 17-28

example 4

Find the region described by

$$\begin{cases} 2x + 3y \le 60 \\ x \ge 0 \\ y \ge 0. \end{cases}$$

This system relates to Inequality 1 in the discussion at the beginning of this section. The latter two inequalities restrict the solution to points that are both on or to the right of the y-axis *and* on or above the x-axis. The desired region is indicated in Fig. 17-29.

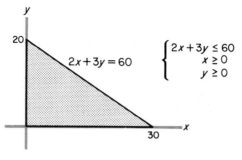

$$\begin{cases} 2x + 3y \le 60 \\ x \ge 0 \\ y \ge 0 \end{cases}$$

FIGURE 17-29

example 5

Solve

$$\begin{cases} 2x + y > 3 \\ x \ge y \\ 2y - 1 > 0. \end{cases}$$

The system is equivalent to

$$\begin{cases} y > -2x + 3 \\ y \le x \\ y > \tfrac{1}{2}. \end{cases}$$

We sketch the lines $y = -2x + 3$, $y = x$, and $y = \tfrac{1}{2}$ and then shade the region that is simultaneously *above* the first line, *on or below* the second line, and *above* the third line (Fig. 17-30). This region is the solution.

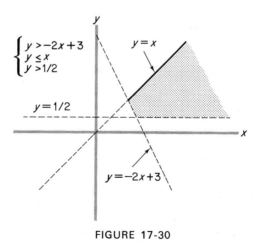

FIGURE 17-30

Exercise 17-4

Sketch the region described by the following inequalities.

1. $y > 2x$.   **2.** $y < 3x - 4$.   **3.** $2x + 3y \leq 6$.

4. $x + 3y > 12$.   **5.** $x + 5y < -5$.   **6.** $3x + y \leq 0$.

7. $-x \geq 2y - 4$.   **8.** $2x + y \geq 10$.

9. $2(x + y) > 2(2x - y)$.   **10.** $-x < 2$.

11. $\frac{3}{2}x + \frac{4}{3}y > \frac{3}{2}(x - y)$.

12. $2(x^2 + 4x + y) > 4(x^2 - y + 1) - 2x^2$.

13. $\begin{cases} y \leq 2x \\ x > 2y. \end{cases}$ **14.** $\begin{cases} x - y < 1 \\ y - x \leq 1. \end{cases}$ **15.** $\begin{cases} 3x - 2y < 6 \\ x - 3y > 9. \end{cases}$

16. $\begin{cases} 2x + 3y > -6 \\ 3x - y < 6. \end{cases}$ **17.** $\begin{cases} 2x + 3y \leq 6 \\ x \geq 0. \end{cases}$ **18.** $\begin{cases} 2y - 3x < 6 \\ x < 0. \end{cases}$

19. $\begin{cases} 2x - 2 \geq y \\ 2x \leq 3 - 2y. \end{cases}$ **20.** $\begin{cases} \frac{3}{2}x - \frac{3}{4}y \geq 1 \\ x(x + 1) - 5 \leq xy - x(y - x). \end{cases}$

21. $\begin{cases} x - y > 4 \\ x < 2 \\ y > 1. \end{cases}$ **22.** $\begin{cases} 2x + y < -1 \\ y > -x \\ 2x + 4 < 0. \end{cases}$ **23.** $\begin{cases} y < 2x + 1 \\ y > 1 \\ x > \frac{1}{2}. \end{cases}$

24. $\begin{cases} 4x + 3y \geq 12 \\ y \geq x \\ 2y \leq 3x + 6. \end{cases}$ **25.** $\begin{cases} 5y - 2x \leq 10 \\ 4x - 6y \leq 12 \\ y \geq 2. \end{cases}$ **26.** $\begin{cases} 3x + y > -6 \\ x - y > -5 \\ x \geq 0. \end{cases}$

17-5 Review

Review Questions

1. True or false: If $x > -3$, then $-x > 3$. _____(a)_____

If $x > 4$, then $2x > 8$. _____(b)_____

If $2 < x < 3$, then both $x > 2$ and $x < 3$. _____(c)_____

2. The solution of $4x \leq 12$ is _____.

3. The solution of $x + 1 < x + 2$ is _____.

4. The solution of $x - 2 \geq x + 1$ is _____.

5. The solution of $|x - 5| = 0$ is _____.

6. The solution of $-3 \leq x - 4 \leq 3$ is _____.

7. If $-x > 0$, then $|x| =$ _____.

8. In absolute value notation, the fact that $2x$ is strictly within seven units of 4 would be written _____.

9. True or false: The inequality $x > 2$ is equivalent to $x^2 > 4$. _____

10. The inequality $x \geq 4$ is satisfied by all points to the (right)(left) of the line
$$\overline{\text{(a)}}$$
$x = 4$ and (includes)(excludes) the line itself.
$$\overline{\text{(b)}}$$

11. If $y_1 \geq m_1x + b_1$ and $y_2 \leq m_2x + b_2$ is a system of inequalities, which of the regions 1, 2, 3, or 4 in Fig. 17-31 would correspond to the solution? _____

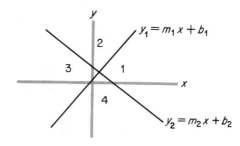

FIGURE 17-31

Answers to Review Questions

1. (a) False, (b) True, (c) True. **2.** $x \leq 3$. **3.** $-\infty < x < \infty$. **4.** $\varnothing$. **5.** 5.
6. $1 \leq x \leq 7$. **7.** $-x$. **8.** $|2x - 4| < 7$. **9.** False. **10.** (a) right, (b) Includes.
11. 3.

Review Problems

In Problems 1–34, solve the inequalities and equations.

1. $3x + 5 < 6$.

2. $3(x + 1) > 9$.

3. $4 - 2x \geq 8$.

4. $-2(x + 6) \leq x + 4$.

5. $3(t + 4) < 9 + 6t$.

6. $5(s + 3) > 2(s - 1)$.

7. $\frac{1}{3}(x + 2) \geq \frac{1}{4}x + 4$.

8. $\frac{x + 1}{5} \leq \frac{x}{10} + 2$.

9. $x^2 + 4x - 12 < 0$.

10. $x^2 + 11x + 28 > 0$.

11. $y^2 > 6y$.

12. $z^2 + 6z < -5$.

13. $2x^2 + 5x \geq x^2 - 4x - 20$.

14. $3x(x - 4) \leq 2x^2 - 27$.

15. $x(3x + 2) < 1$.

16. $6x(x - 1) > 1 - 5x$.

17. $(x + 4)(x - 5)(x - 9) > 0$.

18. $(x + 2)(x + 4)^2 < 0$.

19. $p^3 - 8p^2 \leq 0$.

20. $r^3 - 9r \geq 0$.

21. $\frac{x + 9}{x + 2} \geq 0$.

22. $\frac{x + 3}{x^2 - 3x + 2} \leq 0$.

23. $\frac{x^2 - 6x + 9}{x^2 + 7x + 10} > 0$.

24. $\frac{x^2 + 2x - 8}{x^2 - 25} < 0$.

25. $|3 - 2x| = 7$.

26. $\left|\frac{5x - 8}{13}\right| = 0$.

27. $|3x| > 6$.

28. $|x + 4| \leq 6$.

29. $|4x - 1| < 1$.

30. $\left|\dfrac{5x-8}{12}\right| \geq 1.$ **31.** $|4-2x| \geq 4.$ **32.** $|-1-x| < 1.$

33. $|x+\frac{1}{2}| \leq \frac{3}{2}.$ **34.** $|\frac{2}{3}x-5| > 4.$

In Problems 35–38, sketch the region described by the given system.

35. $\begin{cases} 2x+y < 4 \\ -y+2x > 5. \end{cases}$ **36.** $\begin{cases} 3x+2y > 5 \\ -3y+5x < 7. \end{cases}$ **37.** $\begin{cases} 3x+y < 4 \\ 8x-y > -2. \end{cases}$

37. $\begin{cases} y \geq 5 \\ 2x-y < -2. \end{cases}$ **39.** $\begin{cases} x+y > 1 \\ 3x-5 \geq y \\ y > 2x. \end{cases}$ **40.** $\begin{cases} 3x+y > -4 \\ x-y < -5 \\ x > 0. \end{cases}$

18

analytic geometry

18-1   The Conic Sections

In Chapter 6 the rectangular coordinate system was introduced and the graphs of equations and functions were considered. In particular, the properties of straight lines were determined from their algebraic equations. In the following sections we extend the concepts of analytic geometry and concern ourselves with four curves that may be formed by the intersection of a plane with a right circular cone. These **conic sections**, or **conics**, are the *circle*, the *parabola*, the *ellipse*, and the *hyperbola*. They are shown in Fig. 18-1, where the type of curve obtained depends on how the intersecting plane cuts the cone.

A right circular cone can be thought of as the surface generated by a rotating line that passes through a certain point, called the **vertex** of the cone, and a certain circle. Any line on the surface of the cone that intersects the vertex is called an **element**, or **generator**, of the cone. The **axis** of the cone is the line through the vertex that makes equal angles with all elements of the cone. The cone extends indefinitely on both sides of its vertex and can be spoken of as a *double right circular cone*. The part of the cone on one side of the vertex is called a **nappe**; the cone has an *upper nappe* and a *lower nappe*.

An **ellipse** occurs when an intersecting plane is not parallel to any generator, as in Fig. 18-1(c). If, in addition, the intersecting plane is perpendicular to the axis of the cone, a **circle** occurs, as in (a). In a sense, a circle can be considered a special case of an ellipse. A **parabola** occurs when the intersecting plane is parallel to an

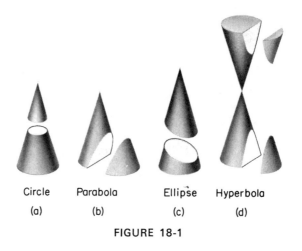

Circle   Parabola   Ellipse   Hyperbola

(a)   (b)   (c)   (d)

FIGURE 18-1

element of the cone, as in (b). The **hyperbola** in (d) occurs when the intersecting plane cuts both nappes.

In comparison to these **regular conics**, certain special cuts in which the intersecting plane passes through the vertex give rise to the **degenerate conics**. If, in the case of Fig. 18-1(a), the intersecting plane also passes through the vertex, the resulting intersection is merely a point. The degenerate case of the hyperbola, namely two intersecting straight lines, occurs when the intersecting plane also contains the axis of the cone, as shown in Fig. 18-2(a). Finally, the parabola degenerates to a straight line if the intersecting plane also passes through the vertex, as shown in Fig. 18-2(b).

(a)   (b)

FIGURE 18-2

18-2   The Distance Formula

If $P_1(x_1, y_1)$ and $P_2(x_2, y_2)$ are two points in the xy-plane, a formula can be derived for the distance between them—that is, for the length d of the line segment joining the points (Fig. 18-3). Through P_1 and P_2 we construct horizontal and vertical seg-

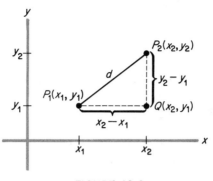

FIGURE 18-3

ments, respectively, which intersect at $Q(x_2, y_1)$. Thus a right triangle P_1QP_2 is formed; its hypotenuse has length d and its sides have lengths $x_2 - x_1$ and $y_2 - y_1$. By the Pythagorean theorem,

$$d^2 = (x_2 - x_1)^2 + (y_2 - y_1)^2.$$

Because d cannot be negative, we must have

$$\boxed{d = \sqrt{(x_2 - x_1)^2 + (y_2 - y_1)^2},}$$

which is called the **distance formula**. Since $(x_2 - x_1)^2 = (x_1 - x_2)^2$ and $(y_2 - y_1)^2 = (y_1 - y_2)^2$, the order of the subscripts in the distance formula is immaterial. Thus, given any two points, the distance between these points can be determined by choosing either point as (x_1, y_1) in the formula.

example 1

Find the distance between the given points.

a. $(5, -2)$ and $(-3, 4)$.

Letting $(5, -2) = (x_1, y_1)$ and $(-3, 4) = (x_2, y_2)$, by the distance formula we have

$$d = \sqrt{(x_2 - x_1)^2 + (y_2 - y_1)^2}$$
$$= \sqrt{(-3 - 5)^2 + [4 - (-2)]^2}$$
$$= \sqrt{(-8)^2 + (6)^2} = \sqrt{64 + 36}$$
$$= \sqrt{100} = 10.$$

If we chose $(-3, 4)$ as (x_1, y_1), we would get the same result.

b. $(3, -6)$ and the origin.

Let $(0, 0) = (x_1, y_1)$ and $(3, -6) = (x_2, y_2)$. Then

$$d = \sqrt{(x_2 - x_1)^2 + (y_2 - y_1)^2}$$
$$= \sqrt{(3 - 0)^2 + (-6 - 0)^2}$$
$$= \sqrt{9 + 36} = \sqrt{45} = 3\sqrt{5}.$$

Exercise 18-2

Find the distance between the given points.

1. $(2, 3), (5, 7)$. $3^2 + 4^2 = \sqrt{35} = 5$

2. $(4, 5), (12, 11)$.

3. $(0, 5), (2, -2)$.

4. $(1, 3), (1, 4)$.

5. $(-1, -2), (-3, -4)$.

6. $(-4, 4)$, origin.

7. $(2, -3), (-5, -3)$.

8. $(-\frac{3}{2}, \frac{1}{2}), (\frac{1}{2}, \frac{3}{2})$.

9. $(1, -\frac{1}{2})$, origin.

10. $(4, 0), (-1, \sqrt{11})$.

11. $(-5, 0), (0, -12)$.

12. $(0, -2), (-5, -2)$.

18-3   The Circle

> A **circle** is the set of all points in a plane that are at a given distance from a fixed point in the plane.

The fixed point is called the **center**, and the given distance is the **radius** of the circle. In general, suppose that a circle has a radius of r and has its center at (h, k), as in Fig. 18-4. Let (x, y) be any point on the circle. Then its distance from (h, k)

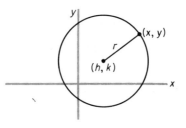

FIGURE 18-4

must be r. Applying the distance formula to (h, k) and (x, y) gives

$$\sqrt{(x - h)^2 + (y - k)^2} = r.$$

Squaring both sides, we have

$$(x - h)^2 + (y - k)^2 = r^2.$$

Any point on the circle must satisfy this equation. Also, it can be shown that all points satisfying the equation lie on the circle. Thus we say that

$$(x - h)^2 + (y - k)^2 = r^2 \qquad (1)$$

is the **standard form** of an equation of the circle with center (h, k) and radius r.

example 1

Find the standard form of an equation of the circle with the given center and radius.

a. Center $(0, 0)$ and radius $\sqrt{3}$.

We use Eq. 1 with $h = 0$, $k = 0$, and $r = \sqrt{3}$.

$$(x - h)^2 + (y - k)^2 = r^2$$
$$(x - 0)^2 + (y - 0)^2 = (\sqrt{3})^2$$
$$x^2 + y^2 = 3.$$

In general,

$$x^2 + y^2 = r^2 \qquad (2)$$

is the standard form of an equation of the circle with center at the origin and radius r.

b. Center $(-3, 2)$ and radius 4.

We use Eq. 1 with $h = -3$, $k = 2$, and $r = 4$.

$$(x - h)^2 + (y - k)^2 = r^2$$
$$[x - (-3)]^2 + (y - 2)^2 = 4^2$$
$$(x + 3)^2 + (y - 2)^2 = 16.$$

example 2

Describe the graph of the given equation.

a. $(x - 1)^2 + (y + 4)^2 = 9$.

This has the form of Eq. 1. By writing this equation as

$$(x - 1)^2 + [y - (-4)]^2 = (3)^2,$$

we see that $h = 1$, $k = -4$, and $r = 3$. Thus the graph is a circle with center $(1, -4)$ and radius 3.

b. $x^2 + y^2 = 5$.

This has the form of Eq. 2 with $r^2 = 5$. Thus $r = \sqrt{5}$. The graph is a circle with center at the origin and radius $\sqrt{5}$.

If we expand the terms in the standard form of a circle, we have

$$(x - h)^2 + (y - k)^2 = r^2$$
$$x^2 - 2hx + h^2 + y^2 - 2ky + k^2 = r^2$$
$$x^2 + y^2 + (-2h)x + (-2k)y + (h^2 + k^2 - r^2) = 0 \quad \text{(rearranging).}$$

Because h, k, and r are constants, the last equation has the form

$$\boxed{x^2 + y^2 + Dx + Ey + F = 0,} \tag{3}$$

where D, E, and F are constants. Equation 3 is called the **general form** of an equation of a circle. If an equation cannot be put in this form, its graph is not a circle.

example 3

Find the general form of an equation of the circle with center (1, 4) and radius 2.

The standard form is

$$(x - 1)^2 + (y - 4)^2 = 2^2.$$

Expanding gives

$$x^2 - 2x + 1 + y^2 - 8y + 16 = 4$$
$$x^2 + y^2 - 2x - 8y + 13 = 0,$$

which is the general form.

We can determine the center and radius of a circle given in general form by using the method of completing the square to express the circle in standard form. For example, the equation

$$x^2 + y^2 - 6x + 10y + 5 = 0$$

has the general form of Eq. 3. Regrouping gives

$$(x^2 - 6x) + (y^2 + 10y) = -5.$$

Completing the squares in x and y, we have

$$(x^2 - 6x + 9) + (y^2 + 10y + 25) = -5 + 9 + 25,$$

or the standard form

$$(x - 3)^2 + (y + 5)^2 = 29.$$

Thus the graph of the given equation is a circle with center $(3, -5)$ and radius $\sqrt{29}$.

example 4

Describe the graphs of the following equations.

a. $x^2 + y^2 - y = 0$.

$$x^2 + y^2 - y = 0$$
$$x^2 + (y^2 - y) = 0$$
$$x^2 + (y^2 - y + \tfrac{1}{4}) = \tfrac{1}{4} \qquad \text{(completing the square)}$$
$$(x - 0)^2 + (y - \tfrac{1}{2})^2 = (\tfrac{1}{2})^2 \qquad \text{(standard form)}.$$

The graph is a circle with center $(0, \tfrac{1}{2})$ and radius $\tfrac{1}{2}$.

b. $2x^2 + 2y^2 + 8x - 3y + 5 = 0$.

To complete the squares, we first get the coefficients of the x^2- and y^2-terms to be 1. Thus we divide both sides by 2.

$$x^2 + y^2 + 4x - \tfrac{3}{2}y + \tfrac{5}{2} = 0$$
$$(x^2 + 4x) + (y^2 - \tfrac{3}{2}y) = -\tfrac{5}{2} \qquad \text{(regrouping)}$$
$$(x^2 + 4x + 4) + (y^2 - \tfrac{3}{2}y + \tfrac{9}{16}) = -\tfrac{5}{2} + 4 + \tfrac{9}{16} \qquad \text{(completing the squares)}$$
$$(x + 2)^2 + (y - \tfrac{3}{4})^2 = \tfrac{33}{16}.$$

Thus the graph is a circle with center $(-2, \tfrac{3}{4})$ and radius $\sqrt{\tfrac{33}{16}}$ or $\sqrt{33}/4$.

Every circle has an equation of the general form $x^2 + y^2 + Dx + Ey + F = 0$. But an equation of this form does not always have a circle as its graph. The graph could be a point, or there may not be any graph at all. For example, the equation

$$x^2 + y^2 - 2x - 6y + 10 = 0 \qquad (4)$$

may be written

$$(x^2 - 2x + 1) + (y^2 - 6y + 9) = -10 + 1 + 9$$
$$(x - 1)^2 + (y - 3)^2 = 0.$$

This implies a center at $(1, 3)$, but a radius of 0. Thus the graph is the single point $(1, 3)$. Also, if the 10 in Eq. 4 were replaced by 11, then we would have the equation

$$(x - 1)^2 + (y - 3)^2 = -1.$$

This implies that r^2 is -1, a negative number. But for a circle r^2 cannot be negative. Thus the equation does not define a circle. In fact, because the left side of the equation is a sum of squares, it can never have a negative value. Therefore the equation has no graph.

Exercise 18-3

In Problems 1–6, find the standard and general forms of an equation of the circle with the given center C and radius r.

1. $C = (2, 3), r = 6$.
2. $C = (4, -5), r = 2$.
3. $C = (-1, 6), r = 4$.
4. $C = (-2, -3), r = 1$.
5. $C = (0, 0), r = \frac{1}{2}$.
6. $C = (3, 0), r = \sqrt{3}$.

In Problems 7–12, give the center C and radius r of the circle with the given equation. Also, sketch the circle.

7. $x^2 + y^2 = 9$.
8. $(x - 1)^2 + (y - 2)^2 = 1$.
9. $(x - 3)^2 + (y + 4)^2 = 2$.
10. $(x + 6)^2 + (y + 1)^2 = 3^2$.
11. $(x + 2)^2 + y^2 = 1$.
12. $x^2 + (y - 3)^2 = 16$.

In Problems 13–24, describe the graph of the given equation.

13. $x^2 + y^2 - 2x - 4y - 4 = 0$.
14. $x^2 + y^2 + 4x - 6y + 9 = 0$.
15. $x^2 + y^2 + 6y + 5 = 0$.
16. $x^2 + y^2 - 12x + 27 = 0$.
17. $x^2 + y^2 + 2x - 2y + 3 = 0$.
18. $x^2 + y^2 + 6x - 2y - 15 = 0$.
19. $x^2 + y^2 - 14x + 4y + 38 = 0$.
20. $x^2 + y^2 + 4y - 8x + 21 = 0$.
21. $x^2 + y^2 - 3x + y + \frac{5}{2} = 0$.
22. $9x^2 + 9y^2 - 6x + 18y + 9 = 0$.
23. $2x^2 + 2y^2 - 4x + 7y + 2 = 0$.
24. $16x^2 + 16y^2 + 24x - 48y - 3 = 0$.

Recall that in Chapter 12 we considered nonlinear systems of equations. In Problems 25–28, you are given a system of two equations. Use a rough sketch to predict the number of different real solutions of each system.

25. $\begin{cases} x^2 + y^4 = 4 \\ x^2 - 2x + y^2 - 2y = 2. \end{cases}$
26. $\begin{cases} x^2 - 4x + y^2 = -3 \\ x^2 - 10x + y^2 = -21. \end{cases}$
27. $\begin{cases} x^2 + y^2 = 1 \\ x^2 - 6x + y^2 = -8. \end{cases}$
28. $\begin{cases} x^2 + y^2 = 9 \\ x - y = 1. \end{cases}$

29. Which of the following equations are *not* equations of circles?
    (a) $x^2 + y^2 = 4$.
    (b) $x^2 + 2y^2 = 4$.
    (c) $x^2 - (y - 2)^2 = 4$.
    (d) $x^2 + 2xy + y^2 = 4$.
    (e) $2x^2 + 2y^2 = 4$.
    (f) $2x + 2y = 4$.
    (g) $\dfrac{1}{x^2} + \dfrac{1}{y^2} = \dfrac{1}{4}$.

30. A particle moves in a coordinate plane so that it it always twice as far from $(4, 0)$ as from $(1, 0)$. Determine whether its path is a circle.

31. A racing automobile travels around a circular track at a speed of 52.80 m/s and makes one revolution every 39.25 s. Taking the origin of a coordinate system at the center of the track and approximating π by 3.14, determine an equation of the path of the automobile.

32. When a particle with mass m and charge q enters a magnetic field of induction B with a velocity v at right angles to B, it can be shown that the particle will travel in a circle of radius r, where

$$r = \frac{mv}{qB}.$$

This is one of the basic operating principles of a mass spectrograph and an important consideration in the design of cyclotrons. If a singly charged lithium ion enters a magnetic field of induction $B = 0.4$ webers/m² with a speed of 1.17×10^5 m/s, determine an equation of its circular path. For this ion, $q = 1.60 \times 10^{-19}$ C and $m = 1.16 \times 10^{-26}$ kg. (Assume that r is in meters.)

18-4 The Parabola

> A **parabola** is the set of all points in a plane that are equidistant from a given straight line and a given point not on the line.

The given point is called the **focus** and the given line the **directrix**. Let $2p$, where $p > 0$, be the distance from the focus to the directrix. In Fig. 18-5, for convenience we choose the focus at $F(0, p)$ and the directrix having equation $y = -p$.

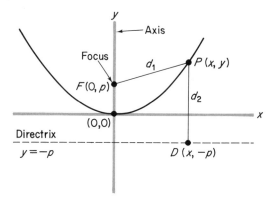

FIGURE 18-5

The line through the focus and perpendicular to the directrix is called the **axis** of the parabola. The origin lies on the parabola, since it is the midpoint of the segment of the axis that connects the focus and the directrix. The axis is a *line of symmetry* in the sense that if a mirror were placed along the axis, then half of the parabola is the mirror image of the other half.

To find an equation of the parabola, we first select an arbitrary point $P(x, y)$ on the parabola. It should be clear that the point of intersection of the directrix and the perpendicular to the directrix from P is $D(x, -p)$, as shown. From the definition of a parabola and the distance formula, we have

$$d_1 = d_2,$$
$$\sqrt{(x-0)^2 + (y-p)^2} = \sqrt{(x-x)^2 + (y+p)^2}.$$

Squaring both sides yields

$$x^2 + (y-p)^2 = (y+p)^2$$
$$x^2 + y^2 - 2py + p^2 = y^2 + 2py + p^2.$$

Simplifying gives

$$x^2 = 4py.$$

The coordinates of every point on the parabola satisfy this equation. It can also be shown that any point with coordinates that satisfy $x^2 = 4py$ is a point on the parabola. The equation $x^2 = 4py$ is called the **standard form** of an equation of the parabola with focus at $(0, p)$ and directrix $y = -p$.

The point at which a parabola intersects its axis is called the **vertex** of the parabola. It is the midpoint of the segment of the axis that joins the focus and the directrix. The vertex of the parabola above is at the origin.

More generally, a parabola with vertex at the origin and a coordinate axis for its axis has four possible orientations, the equations of which can be derived in the manner above. The possibilities are indicated in Fig. 18-6. There is no need for you to

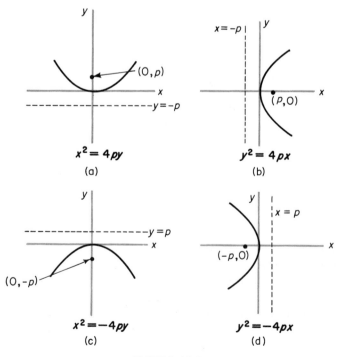

FIGURE 18-6

memorize which type of parabola corresponds to each equation, for the equation itself reveals the orientation of the parabola it represents. Consider, for example, Fig. 18-6(b) and the equation $y^2 = 4px$. Because p is considered positive and y^2 is never negative, it follows that x [or $y^2/(4p)$] is never negative. Thus the parabola opens to the right, as the graph indicates. You are urged to interpret mentally the remaining graphs and equations of Fig. 18-6 in a similar manner. In each case, p *is the distance from the vertex to the focus.* Note that Figs. 18-6(b) and (d) are *not* graphs of functions of x.

example 1

a. Determine the vertex, focus, and equation of the directrix of the parabola given by $y^2 = -16x$. Sketch the graph.

This equation has the standard form $y^2 = -4px$, so the vertex of the parabola is at the origin. Because $x = y^2/-16$, x is never positive and the parabola must open to the left, as shown in Fig. 18-7. Also,

$$4p = 16$$
$$p = 4.$$

Thus the distance from the vertex to the focus is 4, so the focus is at $(-4, 0)$. The equation of the directrix is $x = 4$. To aid you in sketching the graph, we remark that *the "width" of a parabola at its focus is 4p.** This means that the parabola $y^2 = -16x$ is 16 units wide along a line perpendicular to its axis and passing through $(-4, 0)$. From this information we plot the points $(-4, 8)$ and $(-4, -8)$. The graph is given in Fig. 18-7.

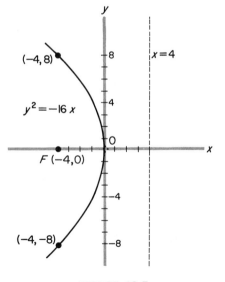

FIGURE 18-7

*The line segment passing through the focus, perpendicular to the axis, and with its ends on the parabola is called the *latus rectum*. Thus the width of the latus rectum is 4p.

b. Determine an equation of the parabola with vertex at $V(0, 0)$ and focus at $F(0, -\frac{3}{2})$.

Refer to Fig. 18-8. From the locations of the focus and vertex, the parabola must open downward and, as a result, y is never positive. Hence, an equation is of the form $x^2 = -4py$. Because p, the distance from the focus to the vertex, is $\frac{3}{2}$, the required equation is

$$x^2 = -4(\tfrac{3}{2})y$$
$$x^2 = -6y.$$

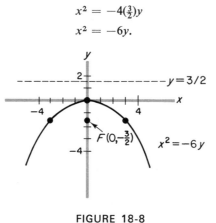

FIGURE 18-8

Consider the parabola with its axis parallel to the x-axis and its vertex at the point $V(h, k)$ as shown in Fig. 18-9, where $2p$, $p > 0$, is the distance from the focus to the directrix. The focus must be at $F(h + p, k)$ and the directrix must be the line

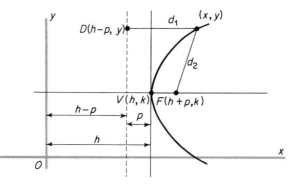

FIGURE 18-9

$x = h - p$. From the dimensions shown in the diagram, we can deduce that the point of intersection of the directrix and a perpendicular to the directrix from an arbitrary point (x, y) on the parabola is $D(h - p, y)$. From the definition of a parabola,

$$d_2 = d_1$$
$$\sqrt{[x - (h + p)]^2 + (y - k)^2} = \sqrt{[x - (h - p)]^2 + (y - y)^2}.$$

Squaring both sides and simplifying yields

$$y^2 - 2ky + k^2 = 4px - 4hp,$$

which can be written in the *standard form*

$$(y - k)^2 = 4p(x - h).$$

In a similar manner the standard forms of equations of other parabolas with vertex at (h, k) and axis parallel to a coordinate axis can be derived. The four possibilities are shown in Fig. 18-10.

You should carefully compare the graphs and equations in Figs. 18-6 and 18-10 and observe the obvious patterns. For example, moving (or *translating*) the vertex

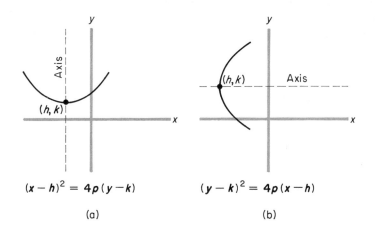

$$(x - h)^2 = 4p(y - k)$$

(a)

$$(y - k)^2 = 4p(x - h)$$

(b)

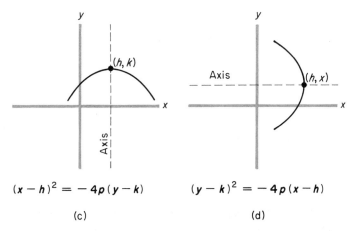

$$(x - h)^2 = -4p(y - k)$$

(c)

$$(y - k)^2 = -4p(x - h)$$

(d)

FIGURE 18-10

of the parabola $y^2 = 4px$ from the point $(0, 0)$ to the point (h, k) gives the parabola $(y - k)^2 = 4p(x - h)$. Both parabolas open to the right.

It is left as an exercise for you to expand the standard forms and show that a general form of an equation of a parabola can be written

$$Ax^2 + Dx + Ey + F = 0, \quad A, E \neq 0 \tag{1}$$

for a parabola with axis parallel to the y-axis, and

$$Cy^2 + Dx + Ey + F = 0, \quad C, D \neq 0 \tag{2}$$

for a parabola with axis parallel to the x-axis. Conversely, for A, C, D, and E unequal to zero, Eqs. 1 and 2 satisfy the requirements of the locus for a parabola and can be transformed into standard form.

In the case that $E = 0$ in Eq. 1 or $D = 0$ in Eq. 2, three degenerate cases may arise. For example, if $E = 0$ in Eq. 1, then

$$Ax^2 + Dx + F = 0.$$

Let us consider different values of A, D, and F.

1. For $x^2 + 4x + 4 = 0$,

$$(x + 2)(x + 2) = 0$$
$$x = -2.$$

Thus the set of all points satisfying the given equation is the straight line $x = -2$.

2. For $x^2 - 2x - 8 = 0$,

$$(x - 4)(x + 2) = 0$$
$$x = 4 \quad \text{or} \quad x = -2.$$

Thus two distinct parallel straight lines occur. This is the only degenerate case that cannot be illustrated by a conic section.

3. For $x^2 + 4x + 5 = 0$,

$$x^2 + 4x + 4 = -1$$
$$(x + 2)^2 = -1$$

and, hence, no parabola exists.

example 2

Find the standard form of an equation of the parabola with vertex at $V(-1, 4)$ and focus at $F(-1, 1)$.

By indicating the data in the plane (Fig. 18-11), we conclude that the parabola must open downward. The equation is of the form $(x - h)^2 = -4p(y - k)$ with $h = -1$, $k = 4$, and $p = 4 - 1 = 3$. Thus the equation is

$$(x + 1)^2 = -4(3)(y - 4)$$
$$(x + 1)^2 = -12(y - 4).$$

The graph and directrix are shown in Fig. 18-11. Note that the equation of the directrix is $y = 7$.

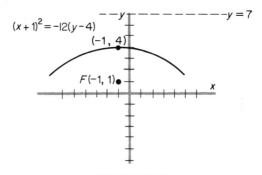

FIGURE 18-11

example 3

Find the coordinates of the focus and vertex and the equation of the directrix of the parabola

$$y^2 - 8y - 8x + 24 = 0.$$

Rearranging terms and completing the square in y we have

$$y^2 - 8y + 16 = 8x - 24 + 16$$
$$= 8x - 8$$
$$(y - 4)^2 = 8(x - 1).$$

Hence, the vertex is the point $(1, 4)$ and the parabola opens to the right. Also, since $4p = 8$, $p = 2$ and the focus lies two units to the right of the vertex at the point $(3, 4)$. A point on the directrix lies two units to the left of the vertex and so the equation of the directrix is $x = -1$.

example 4

The height s of a ball thrown vertically upward from the ground is given by the equation of motion

$$s = 19.6t - 4.9t^2,$$

where s is in meters and t is elapsed time in seconds Find the maximum height of the ball.

Note that s is a quadratic function of t. Observe that we can write

$$s = 19.6t - 4.9t^2$$

$$s = -4.9(t^2 - 4t)$$

$$s - 19.6 = -4.9(t^2 - 4t + 4).$$

Thus

$$(t - 2)^2 = -\frac{1}{4.9}(s - 19.6).$$

This is the equation of a parabola, opening downward, with vertex at (2, 19.6), as shown in Fig. 12-9 in Sec. 12-3. Hence the maximum height of the ball is 19.6 m.

Example 4 supplements our discussion of quadratic functions in Sec. 12-3, where it was stated that the graph of a quadratic function is a parabola. It can be shown that if the graph of a quadratic function $y = f(x)$ crosses the x-axis at the points $(x_1, 0)$ and $(x_2, 0)$ then the variable y has its maximum (or minimum) value when

$$x = \frac{x_1 + x_2}{2}. \tag{3}$$

This fact will be used in the following example.

example 5

Find the maximum value of the quadratic function $y = 20x - x^2$.

To determine the values of x for which its graph crosses the x-axis, we set $y = 0$. Then

$$0 = 20x - x^2$$

$$0 = x(20 - x),$$

so

$$x = 0 \quad \text{or} \quad x = 20.$$

By Eq. 3, the maximum value is attained when

$$x = \frac{0 + 20}{2} = 10.$$

Hence the maximum value is

$$y = 20x - x^2$$

$$= 20(10) - (10)^2$$

$$= 100.$$

You should use this technique to verify the result in Example 4.

Exercise 18-4

In Problems **1–12,** *find the coordinates of the vertex V and focus F, an equation of the directrix D, and sketch each parabola.*

1. $y^2 = 4x.$

2. $y^2 = -6x.$

3. $x^2 = -8y.$

4. $y^2 = -x.$

5. $x^2 = 2y.$

6. $(x + 2)^2 = 4(y - 7).$

7. $(y + 2)^2 = \frac{1}{2}x.$

8. $4x^2 = 3(y - 1).$

9. $(x - 4)^2 = 8(y + 3).$

10. $(y - 7)^2 = 12(x - 4).$

11. $(y + 2)^2 = -\frac{1}{4}(x - 1).$

12. $y = x^2.$

In Problems **13–22,** *determine the standard form of an equation of the parabola that has the given properties.*

13. Focus $(0, 3)$, directrix $y = -5$.

14. Vertex $(2, 4)$, directrix $y = 6$.

15. Focus $(1, 4)$, vertex $(3, 4)$.

16. Focus $(0, 5)$, directrix $x = -10$.

17. Vertex $(-3, 2)$, directrix $y = 4$.

18. Focus $(-2, -2)$, vertex $(-2, -6)$.

19. Focus $(0, \frac{3}{2})$, directrix $y = -\frac{3}{2}$.

20. Vertex $(3, 1)$, directrix $x = 6$.

21. Focus $(-3, -2)$, vertex $(-4, -2)$.

22. Focus $(0, -4)$, directrix $y = 4$.

In Problems **23–27,** *transform the given equation into standard form and determine the coordinates of the focus and vertex.*

23. $y^2 - 6y + 4x + 1 = 0.$

24. $2y^2 + 4y - x - 4 = 0.$

25. $3x^2 - 12x - y + 12 = 0.$

26. $x^2 + 3y - 8x + 19 = 0.$

27. $y^2 + 4y - x + 5 = 0.$

In Problems **28–31,** *use a rough graph of the given system to predict how many different real solutions exist.*

28. $\begin{cases} y^2 = x - 1 \\ y = x^2 - 2x + 1. \end{cases}$

29. $\begin{cases} y = x^2 - 3x \\ x + y = -4. \end{cases}$

30. $\begin{cases} x = (y - 1)^2 \\ x - y = 2. \end{cases}$

31. $\begin{cases} y^2 = 2x + 1 \\ x^2 + y^2 = 9. \end{cases}$

32. The power P developed in a resistor of resistance R ohms carrying a current of i amperes is given by $P = i^2R$. If a resistor has a resistance of 10 Ω, sketch a graph of power as a function of current.

33. When an object is thrown straight upward with an initial velocity of 58.8 m/s, its height h, in meters, as a function of time t, in seconds, is given by $h = 58.8t - 4.9t^2$. At what time does the object reach its maximum height and what is that height?

34. The displacement s of an object from a reference point is given by the equation $s = 3t^2 - 24t + 103$, where s is in meters and t is in seconds. What is the minimum displacement of the particle from the reference point?

35. If a light source is placed between the focus and vertex of a parabolic mirror, the rays of light diverge after reflection, while if the light source is placed outside the focus, the rays converge after reflection. This is how automobile headlights can give a broad beam of light (high beams) from one filament and a narrow beam of light (low beams) from a second filament. If the equation of a cross-sectional view of a parabolic mirror is $y^2 = 20x$, where x and y are in centimeters, what may the distance be between the vertex of the mirror and a filament if the light rays are to diverge after reflection from the mirror?

36. When an object of mass $\frac{1}{8}$ kg moves in a straight line on a horizontal surface 4 m above the ground, its energy E, in the absence of rotation, can be given by $E = 4.9 + \frac{1}{16}v^2$, where v is the speed of the object in meters per second, and E is measured in joules. The value of v is taken to be positive for one direction of motion and negative for the opposite direction. Sketch a graph of this energy function for the values of v from $v = -4$ m/s to $v = 4$ m/s.

18-5 The Ellipse

An **ellipse** is the set of all points in a plane such that for each point the sum of its distances from two fixed points is a constant.

The two fixed points in the definition are called the **foci** (the plural of focus) of the ellipse. Let $2c$, where $c > 0$, be the distance between the foci. For convenience we shall locate the foci on the x-axis at points $F_1(c, 0)$ and $F_2(-c, 0)$ (Fig. 18-12).

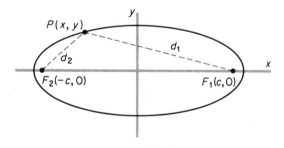

FIGURE 18-12

Furthermore, let the constant sum referred to in the definition be $2a$. To eliminate from our consideration those points on the line segment joining the foci, we must require that $2a > 2c$, or $a > c$. Selecting an arbitrary point $P(x, y)$ on the ellipse and applying the definition, we have

$$d_1 + d_2 = \text{constant},$$
$$\sqrt{(x - c)^2 + (y - 0)^2} + \sqrt{(x + c)^2 + (y - 0)^2} = 2a.$$

Rearranging terms, we have

$$\sqrt{(x - c)^2 + y^2} = 2a - \sqrt{(x + c)^2 + y^2}.$$

Squaring both sides gives

$$x^2 - 2cx + c^2 + y^2 = 4a^2 - 4a\sqrt{(x + c)^2 + y^2} + x^2 + 2cx + c^2 + y^2,$$

which simplifies to

$$a^2 + cx = a\sqrt{(x + c)^2 + y^2}.$$

Squaring both sides, we have

$$a^4 + 2a^2cx + c^2x^2 = a^2(x^2 + 2cx + c^2 + y^2).$$

Rearranging terms and grouping gives

$$a^4 - a^2c^2 + c^2x^2 - a^2x^2 - a^2y^2 = 0$$
$$a^2(a^2 - c^2) + x^2(c^2 - a^2) - a^2y^2 = 0.$$

Dividing both sides by $a^2(a^2 - c^2)$ gives

$$1 - \frac{x^2}{a^2} - \frac{y^2}{a^2 - c^2} = 0,$$

which can be written as

$$\frac{x^2}{a^2} + \frac{y^2}{a^2 - c^2} = 1.$$

Because $a > c$, the number $a^2 - c^2$ is positive. If we introduce a new positive number b such that

$$a^2 - c^2 = b^2, \tag{1}$$

then we can write the equation above in the form

$$\frac{x^2}{a^2} + \frac{y^2}{b^2} = 1. \qquad \textit{ellipse} \tag{2}$$

Thus the coordinates of every point on the given ellipse satisfy Eq. 2. Conversely it can be shown that any point whose coordinates satisfy Eq. 2 is a point on the ellipse. Equation 2 is called the **standard form** of an equation of the ellipse with foci on the x-axis at $F_1(c, 0)$ and $F_2(-c, 0)$, where $a^2 = b^2 + c^2$.

The relationship between a, b, and c is easily seen from triangle OP_1F_1 in Fig. 18-13. From Eq. 2, if $y = 0$, then $x = \pm a$; thus the x-intercepts are $(\pm a, 0)$. If $x = 0$, then $y = \pm b$; the y-intercepts are $(0, \pm b)$. Segment V_1V_2, which has length $2a$ and passes through the foci, is called the **major axis** and its midpoint is called the **center** of the ellipse. For the ellipse described above, the center is at the origin. Segment

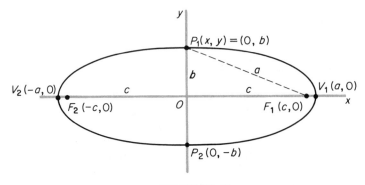

FIGURE 18-13

P_1P_2, which has length $2b$, is called the **minor axis**. We speak of a as the **semimajor axis**; *it is the distance from the center of the ellipse to the end of the major axis*. Similarly, we speak of b as the **semiminor axis**. The endpoints of the major axis, namely V_1 and V_2, are called the **vertices** of the ellipse.

For an ellipse having center at the origin and foci on the y-axis [at $(0, c)$ and $(0, -c)$], the standard form is

$$\frac{x^2}{b^2} + \frac{y^2}{a^2} = 1. \qquad (3)$$

Here, the major axis lies on the y-axis. The vertices are $(0, \pm a)$. Again, $b^2 = a^2 - c^2$.

In Eqs. 2 and 3, remember that since $a > b$, **the larger denominator is always a^2**. Thus, if the larger denominator is in the x^2-term, the major axis is horizontal. If it is in the y^2-term, the major axis is vertical.

In general, it can be shown that the standard form of an equation of an ellipse with center (h, k) and major axis horizontal is given by

$$\frac{(x - h)^2}{a^2} + \frac{(y - k)^2}{b^2} = 1, \qquad (4)$$

and for one where the major axis is vertical, the equation is

$$\frac{(x - h)^2}{b^2} + \frac{(y - k)^2}{a^2} = 1. \qquad (5)$$

example 1

For the ellipse $4x^2 + 9y^2 = 36$, find the center, vertices, foci, and endpoints of the minor axis. Sketch the ellipse.

To obtain the standard form, we divide both sides by 36:

$$\frac{x^2}{9} + \frac{y^2}{4} = 1.$$

The center is at the origin. Because the larger denominator (9) is under x^2, the major axis lies on the x-axis. Since $a^2 = 9$ and $b^2 = 4$, then $a = 3$ and $b = 2$. Hence, the vertices are $(\pm 3, 0)$ and the endpoints of the minor axis are at $(0, \pm 2)$. From this information we can sketch the graph, as in Fig. 18-14. Also, by rewriting Eq. 1 we can find c:

$$c^2 = a^2 - b^2 = 9 - 4 = 5$$
$$c = \sqrt{5}.$$

Thus the foci are at $(\pm\sqrt{5}, 0)$.

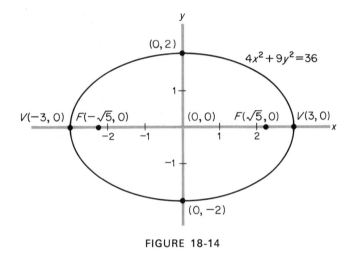

FIGURE 18-14

example 2

Find an equation of the ellipse with a major axis of length eight units, a focus at $(2, 8)$, and center at $(2, 5)$.

An ellipse with a center at $(2, 5)$ and a focus at $(2, 8)$ must have a vertical major axis. The distance from the center to the given focus is three units. Thus $c = 3$. Also, since the length of the major axis is $2a \ (= 8)$, then $a = 4$. Therefore, by Eq. 1, we have $b^2 = a^2 - c^2 = 16 - 9 = 7$. Thus, because $h = 2$ and $k = 5$, from Eq. 5 the standard form is

$$\frac{(x-2)^2}{7} + \frac{(y-5)^2}{16} = 1.$$

The graph is shown in Fig. 18-15.

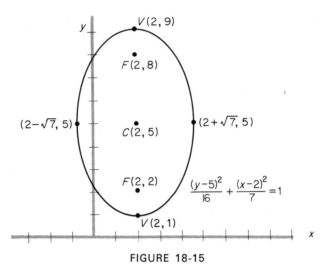

FIGURE 18-15

example 3

Determine the center, foci, vertices, and endpoints of the minor axes of the ellipse

$$x^2 + 2y^2 + 4x - 4y + 2 = 0.$$

First we put the equation into standard form. Rearranging and grouping terms, we can write

$$(x^2 + 4x) + 2(y^2 - 2y) = -2.$$

Completing the squares in x and y, we have

$$(x^2 + 4x + 4) + 2(y^2 - 2y + 1) = -2 + 4 + 2.$$

Note that when 1 was added to $y^2 - 2y$ to complete the square in y, it was equivalent to adding 2 to the left side of the equation. Hence 2 had to be added to the right side. This gives

$$(x + 2)^2 + 2(y - 1)^2 = 4.$$

Finally, dividing by 4 gives the standard form.

$$\frac{(x + 2)^2}{4} + \frac{(y - 1)^2}{2} = 1.$$

Clearly $a^2 = 4$, $b^2 = 2$, and $c^2 = a^2 - b^2 = 2$. Thus $a = 2$, $b = \sqrt{2}$, and $c = \sqrt{2}$. Because $h = -2$ and $k = 1$, the center is at $(-2, 1)$. Also, the major axis is horizontal. Because $c = \sqrt{2}$, the foci are at $(-2 \pm \sqrt{2}, 1)$. Also, because $a = 2$, the vertices are $(-2 \pm 2, 1)$, that is, at $(0, 1)$ and $(-4, 1)$. Lastly, because $b = \sqrt{2}$, the endpoints of the minor axis are at $(-2, 1 \pm \sqrt{2})$.

Exercise 18-5

In Problems 1–8, find the center C, vertices V, and endpoints E of the minor axis of the given ellipse. Sketch each ellipse.

1. $\dfrac{x^2}{25} + \dfrac{y^2}{16} = 1.$
 2. $\dfrac{x^2}{144} + \dfrac{y^2}{169} = 1.$

3. $\dfrac{x^2}{100} + \dfrac{y^2}{144} = 1.$
 4. $\dfrac{x^2}{49} + \dfrac{y^2}{4} = 1.$

5. $4x^2 + y^2 = 4.$
 6. $16x^2 + 9y^2 = 144.$

7. $\dfrac{(x-2)^2}{9} + \dfrac{(y+3)^2}{4} = 1.$
 8. $\dfrac{(x+2)^2}{9} + \dfrac{(y-3)^2}{25} = 1.$

In Problems 9–12, for each ellipse find the center C, vertices V, and endpoints E of the minor axis.

9. $4x^2 + y^2 - 16x = 0.$
 10. $2x^2 + y^2 + 8x + 4y + 6 = 0.$

11. $9x^2 + 25y^2 - 54x + 100y = 44.$
 12. $x^2 + 2y^2 + 4x - 8y - 6 = 0.$

In Problems 13–21, determine the standard form of an equation of the ellipse with the given properties. Assume the center is at the origin unless otherwise stated.

13. Vertex (6, 0), focus (5, 0).

14. Major axis of length 16, focus (6, 0).

15. Focus (−8, 1), minor axis of length 4, center (0, 1).

16. Focus (3, 3), center on *y*-axis, vertex (−5, 3).

17. Major axis of length 16 and horizontal, minor axis of length 8.

18. Vertex (3, 10), focus (3, −6), center on *x*-axis.

19. Vertex (0, 0), center (0, −8), minor axis of length 5.

20. Focus (−4, −5), major axis of length 14, center (−4, 1).

21. Minor axis horizontal and of length 4, focus (−2, −8), center (−2, −1).

22. The arch of a bridge has the shape of one-half an ellipse. The maximum height of the bridge is 50 m and the bridge has a span at water level of 120 m. If the origin of a coordinate system is midway between the ends of the bridge at water level, what is the equation of the ellipse? What is the equation if the origin of the coordinate system is at one end of the bridge at water level?

23. Satellites can be made to orbit the earth in an elliptical path whose center is at the center of the earth. If the altitude of such a satellite—that is, its distance above the surface of the earth—ranges from 1.6×10^6 to 6.4×10^6 m, find an equation of its path. The radius of the earth is approximately 6.4×10^6 m. Choose a horizontal major axis and the center of the earth as the origin of the coordinate system.

> A **hyperbola** is the set of all points in a plane such that for each point the difference between its distances from two fixed points, called foci, is a positive constant.

Suppose the distance between the two foci is $2c$, where $c > 0$. For convenience we shall locate the foci on the x-axis at points $F_1(c, 0)$ and $F_2(-c, 0)$ (Fig. 18-16).

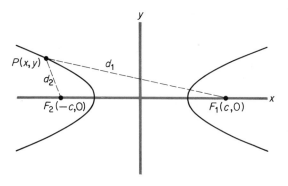

FIGURE 18-16

Let the constant difference referred to in the definition be $2a$, where $a > 0$. Selecting a point $P(x, y)$ on the hyperbola, we have (by definition)

$$d_1 - d_2 = \pm 2a,$$

where the $\pm$ sign depends on which of d_1 or d_2 is the larger. Therefore, by the distance formula,

$$\sqrt{(x - c)^2 + (y - 0)^2} - \sqrt{(x + c)^2 + (y - 0)^2} = \pm 2a.$$

Using the same techniques as those used in the preceding section, we obtain

$$c^2x^2 - a^2x^2 - a^2y^2 = a^2c^2 - a^4,$$

or

$$x^2(c^2 - a^2) - a^2y^2 = a^2(c^2 - a^2).$$

Dividing both sides by $a^2(c^2 - a^2)$ gives

$$\frac{x^2}{a^2} - \frac{y^2}{c^2 - a^2} = 1. \tag{1}$$

As in the case of the derivation of an equation of an ellipse, it would seem natural to introduce a positive number b such that

$$b^2 = c^2 - a^2. \tag{2}$$

(Do not confuse this with $b^2 = a^2 - c^2$ for an ellipse.) However, we must be sure that $c^2 - a^2$ is always positive. It is shown in geometry that the difference between any two sides of a triangle is less than the third side. Hence, from Fig. 18-16, for the triangle F_1F_2P with $d_1 > d_2$ we have

$$2c > d_1 - d_2,$$

and by definition it follows that

$$2c > 2a, \quad \text{or} \quad c > a.$$

Thus $c^2 > a^2$ and $c^2 - a^2 > 0$. The proof if $d_2 > d_1$ is similar.

Using Eq. 2, from Eq. 1 we obtain the **standard form** of an equation of the hyperbola with foci at $(\pm c, 0)$:

$$\frac{x^2}{a^2} - \frac{y^2}{b^2} = 1, \tag{3}$$

where $c^2 = a^2 + b^2$.

When $y = 0$, then $x = \pm a$ and hence the hyperbola crosses the x-axis at the points $V_1(a, 0)$ and $V_2(-a, 0)$ (refer to Fig. 18-17). These points, those for which the

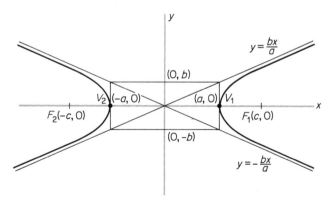

FIGURE 18-17

hyperbola cuts the line through the two foci, are called the **vertices** of the hyperbola. The line segment V_1V_2 that joins the vertices is $2a$ units long and is called the **transverse axis**. The midpoint of the transverse axis is called the **center** of the hyperbola. In Fig. 18-17 the center is at the origin.

To determine more precisely the nature of a hyperbola and the geometrical significance of b, we solve Eq. 3 for y:

$$b^2x^2 - a^2y^2 = a^2b^2$$

$$y^2 = \frac{b^2x^2 - a^2b^2}{a^2} = \frac{b^2x^2}{a^2}\left(1 - \frac{a^2}{x^2}\right)$$

$$y = \pm\frac{b}{a}x\sqrt{1 - \frac{a^2}{x^2}}.$$

As x increases or decreases without bound, then the values of a^2/x^2 get closer to zero and the expression under the radical sign approaches a value of 1. We can conclude that y will approach the values $(b/a)x$ and $-(b/a)x$. The straight lines $y = (b/a)x$ and $y = -(b/a)x$ are called **asymptotes** for the hyperbola. That is, they are straight lines that the hyperbola approaches as a limiting position. These results are indicated in Fig. 18-17.

From the diagram it should be clear that the asymptotes coincide, so to speak, with the diagonals of a rectangle of length $2a$ and width $2b$ and whose vertices are $(a, b), (-a, b), (-a, -b)$, and $(a, -b)$. The line segment on the y-axis joining the points $(0, b)$ and $(0, -b)$ has length $2b$ and is called the **conjugate axis** of the hyperbola. Clearly, the asymptotes provide convenient guide lines for sketching a hyperbola. They are most easily sketched by drawing extended diagonals of the rectangle whose sides pass through the vertices and the endpoints of the conjugate axis. The rectangle and asymptotes are *not* part of the graph. It can be shown that *the equations of the asymptotes of the hyperbola can be found by replacing the 1 in the standard form by zero and solving for y.*

In a similar manner, it can be shown that an equation of a hyperbola with center at the origin, transverse axis along the y-axis, and conjugate axis along the x-axis, is

$$\frac{y^2}{a^2} - \frac{x^2}{b^2} = 1. \tag{4}$$

In this case the vertices are located at $V_1(0, a)$ and $V_2(0, -a)$, the foci are at $F_1(0, c)$ and $F_2(0, -c)$, and the lines $y = \pm ax/b$ are asymptotes.

Using the definition, we can show that the standard form of an equation of a hyperbola with center at (h, k) and transverse axis horizontal is given by

$$\frac{(x - h)^2}{a^2} - \frac{(y - k)^2}{b^2} = 1, \tag{5}$$

while if the transverse axis is vertical, the equation is

$$\frac{(y - k)^2}{a^2} - \frac{(x - h)^2}{b^2} = 1. \tag{6}$$

Note that a^2 is always associated with the positive term. Again, the equations of the asymptotes can be found by replacing the 1 in the standard form by zero and solving for y.

Finally, a general form of an equation of a hyperbola can be written

$$Ax^2 + Cy^2 + Dx + Ey + F = 0,$$ (7)

where A and C have opposite signs.

example 1

Discuss and sketch the graph of the hyperbola $\frac{y^2}{4} - x^2 = 1$.

From the standard forms of an equation of a hyperbola, a^2 is always associated with the positive term. In this case, $a^2 = 4$ and $b^2 = 1$; that is, $a = 2$, and $b = 1$. Also, $c^2 = a^2 + b^2 = 4 + 1 = 5$, or $c = \sqrt{5}$. Because the equation is of the form of Eq. 4, or, equivalently, the form of Eq. 6 with $h = k = 0$, we deduce that the hyperbola has vertices $V_1(0, 2)$ and $V_2(0, -2)$, foci $F_1(0, \sqrt{5})$ and $F_2(0, -\sqrt{5})$, a vertical transverse axis of length 4, and a horizontal conjugate axis of length 2. We can easily sketch the graph by first locating the vertices and endpoints of the conjugate axis. Then we construct the rectangle whose sides pass through these points. Next, we sketch the asymptotes by drawing extended diagonals of the rectangle. Finally, we draw the hyperbola which passes through the vertices and approaches the asymptotes. The results are shown in Fig. 18-18. Note that the equations of the asymptotes are $y = 2x$ and $y = -2x$. They are obtained by solving the equation $y^2/(4) - x^2 = 0$ for y.

$$\frac{y^2}{4} = x^2, \quad y^2 = 4x^2, \quad y = \pm 2x.$$

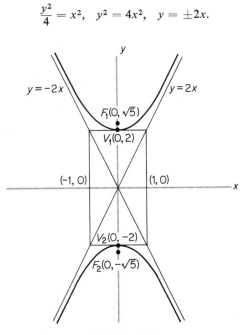

FIGURE 18-18

example 2

Discuss and sketch the graph of the hyperbola

$$2x^2 - y^2 - 16x + 4y + 24 = 0.$$

First we put the equation into standard form. The equation can be written

$$(2x^2 - 16x) - (y^2 - 4y) = -24.$$

Completing the squares and simplifying, we have

$$2(x^2 - 8x + 16) - (y^2 - 4y + 4) = -24 + 32 - 4$$

$$2(x - 4)^2 - (y - 2)^2 = 4$$

$$\frac{(x - 4)^2}{2} - \frac{(y - 2)^2}{4} = 1. \tag{8}$$

Equation 8 matches Eq. 5 where $h = 4$ and $k = 2$. Thus the center of the hyperbola is at (4, 2) and the transverse axis is horizontal. Since $a^2 = 2$ and $b^2 = 4$, then $a = \sqrt{2}$, $b = 2$, and $c^2 = 4 + 2$ or $c = \sqrt{6}$. In Fig. 18-19 we locate the center of the hyperbola, the vertices $(4 \pm \sqrt{2}, 2)$, and the endpoints of the conjugate axis $(4, 2 \pm 2)$. Then

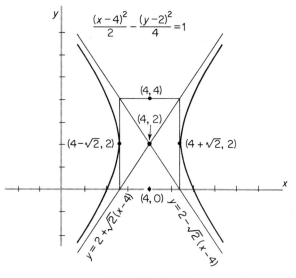

FIGURE 18-19

the corresponding rectangle is completed and the asymptotes are drawn. The graph is then sketched. As previously mentioned, to find the equations of the asymptotes we set the left side of Eq. 8 equal to zero and solve for y:

$$\frac{(y - 2)^2}{4} = \frac{(x - 4)^2}{2}$$

$$\frac{y-2}{2} = \pm\frac{x-4}{\sqrt{2}}$$

$$y - 2 = \pm\sqrt{2}(x-4)$$

$$y = 2 \pm \sqrt{2}(x-4).$$

The standard form of an equation of a hyperbola with center at the origin and transverse axis along the x-axis is

$$\frac{x^2}{a^2} - \frac{y^2}{b^2} = 1.$$

If $b = a$, the result $x^2 - y^2 = a^2$ is a hyperbola with mutually perpendicular asymptotes, $y = \pm x$. The corresponding rectangle is, in this case, a square and the curve is called an **equilateral hyperbola**.

We conclude our discussion here by stating that there is one special form of an equation of an equilateral hyperbola. The equation

$$xy = c, \qquad (9)$$

where c is a nonzero constant, is an equation of an equilateral hyperbola whose asymptotes are the coordinate axes. The general shapes of the graphs of $xy = c$ for $c > 0$ and $c < 0$ are shown in Figs. 18-20 and 18-21, respectively. If c is positive, the foci lie on the line $y = x$, while if c is negative, they lie on the line $y = -x$. The graphs of hyperbolas for which the equations are in such forms can be easily sketched by assuming values for one variable and determining the corresponding values of the other variable.

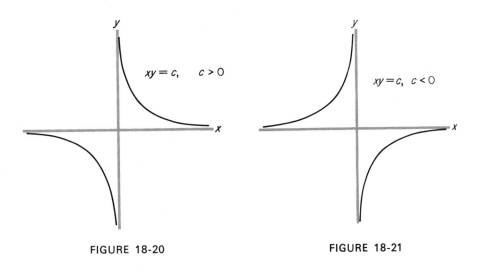

FIGURE 18-20   FIGURE 18-21

Exercise 18-6

*In Problems **1–10**, find the center C, vertices V, focus F, endpoints E of the conjugate axis, and asymptotes A of each hyperbola. Sketch each hyperbola.*

1. $\dfrac{x^2}{16} - \dfrac{y^2}{9} = 1.$

2. $\dfrac{y^2}{25} - \dfrac{x^2}{144} = 1.$

3. $\dfrac{y^2}{36} - x^2 = 1.$

4. $4x^2 - 9y^2 = 36.$

5. $x^2 - y^2 = 4.$

6. $\dfrac{x^2}{16} - \dfrac{(y-2)^2}{16} = 1.$

7. $4(y+3)^2 - 25(x-2)^2 = 100.$

8. $(x+3)^2 - 2y^2 + 8 = 0.$

9. $9x^2 - 36x - 16y^2 - 32y - 124 = 0.$

10. $y^2 - 4x^2 - 10y + 16x - 7 = 0.$

*In Problems **11–20**, determine the standard form of an equation of the hyperbola satisfying the given conditions. Assume the center is at $(0,0)$ unless otherwise stated.*

11. Focus $(0, 3)$, vertex $(0, 2)$.

12. Transverse axis of length 10, focus $(7, 0)$.

13. Vertex $(4, 0)$, conjugate axis of length 2.

14. Conjugate axis of length 4, focus $(0, 6)$.

15. Center $(-4, 2)$, focus $(-4, 6)$, vertex on x-axis.

16. Center $(-7, 0)$, focus at origin, transverse axis of length 6.

17. Vertex on y-axis, center $(-2, 4)$, conjugate axis of length 3.

18. Vertex at $(4, 0)$, center $(4, 2)$, conjugate axis of length 4.

19. Center on line $y = 4$, vertex $(0, 2)$, focus $(0, 1)$.

20. Vertex $(2, 6)$, focus $(4, 6)$, center on y-axis.

*In Problems **21–26**, sketch the graph of each hyperbola and state the equations of the asymptotes.*

21. $xy = 3.$

22. $xy = -3.$

23. $xy = -5.$

24. $5xy = 6.$

25. $4xy = 1.$

26. $xy = 120.$

27. The speed v of a wave is a function of the frequency f and the wavelength λ, where $v = f\lambda$. For visible light in a vacuum, $v = 3 \times 10^8$ m/s and values of λ range from about 4×10^{-7} to about 7×10^{-7} m. Sketch a graph of frequency versus wavelength for the visible portion of the spectrum.

28. The relationship between the index of refraction of a material, n, the wavelength of light in the material, λ, and the wavelength of light in air, λ_a, is $\lambda_a = n\lambda$. If the wavelength of blue-green light in air is 5000 angstroms, sketch a graph of λ versus n for values of n from 1.5 to 2.5, in increments of 0.1.

29. For an ideal gas at constant temperature, the product of the pressure p and volume v is a constant. A particular sample of such a gas has a pressure of 4 atmospheres and a volume of 5 liters. Sketch a graph of pressure versus volume.

18-7 Summary of Conic Sections

It is often important to be able to identify a curve from a brief examination of its equation. Assuming no degenerate cases, from the results of the preceding sections we conclude that the graph of

$$Ax^2 + Bxy + Cy^2 + Dx + Ey + F = 0$$

will be:

1. A circle if $A = C$, and $B = 0$.

2. A parabola if $A = 0$ or $C = 0$ but not both, and $B = 0$.

3. An ellipse if $A \neq C$ but A and C have the same sign, and $B = 0$.

4. A hyperbola if either

    a. A and C have opposite signs, and $B = 0$, or
    b. $A = C = 0$, and $B \neq 0$.

example 1

Classify each of the following equations as that of a circle, parabola, ellipse, or hyperbola.

a. $x^2 + y^2 + 3x - 6y - 7 = 0$.

Because the coefficients of the x^2- and y^2-terms are equal ($A = C = 1$), the equation is that of a circle.

b. $2y^2 + x^2 - 4y - 4x - 10 = 0$.

Because the coefficients of the x^2- and y^2-terms are unequal but have the same sign ($A = 1 \neq 2 = C$), the equation is that of an ellipse.

c. $2y^2 + 3y - 4x + 9 = 0$.

As there is a y^2-term but no x^2-term ($A = 0, C = 2$), the equation is that of a parabola.

d. $5x^2 - 3y^2 - 5x + 2y + 16 = 0$.

Because the x^2- and y^2-terms are opposite in sign, the equation is that of a hyperbola.

e. $xy = 7$.

Because $A = C = 0$ and $B = 1 \neq 0$, the equation is that of an (equilateral) hyperbola.

Exercise 18-7

By inspection, classify each of the following equations as a circle, parabola, ellipse, or hyperbola.

1. $3x^2 + 3y^2 + 2x + 5y - 6 = 0$.   **2.** $3x^2 + 2y^2 + 2x - 7 = 0$.

3. $2y^2 + 3x + 2y + 1 = 0$.   **4.** $3xy = 18.21$.

5. $x^2 + 3x + 14y - 17 = 0$.   **6.** $-2x^2 - 2y^2 + 3x - 4y + 17 = 0$.

7. $2x^2 - 3y^2 + 2x + 6 = 0$.   **8.** $3y^2 - 2x = 4$.

9. $4x^2 + 2y^2 + 3y = 8$.   **10.** $2x^2 + 3y = 7$.

11. $xy = -3$.   **12.** $4x^2 + 4y^2 - 6x + 3y + 7 = 0$.

13. $x^2 + 2y^2 + 3 = 2y - y^2$.   **14.** $4x^2 - 2y^2 - 3x + 4y + 182 = 0$.

15. $x^2 + 5y^2 + x + 17y = 1$.   **16.** $1.3x^2 - 7.2 = -8.6y^2$.

17. $x^2 + 3x - 4y + 6 = 4$.   **18.** $3x^2 + 3y^2 - 4 = 0$.

19. $4x^2 - 7y^2 = 16$.   **20.** $1.2x^2 = 3y + 7.4$.

18-8   Parametric Equations

Whenever we graphed an equation in the variables x and y, we obtained points (x, y) by assigning values to one variable and determing corresponding values of the other variable. It is often convenient, however, to express both x and y as functions of a third variable, called a **parameter**.

For example, the equations

$$x = t + 1 \tag{1}$$

$$y = t^2 - 3 \tag{2}$$

define a curve. Here t is the parameter and the pair of equations are called **parametric equations** of the curve.* If $t = 0$, then $x = 1$ and $y = -3$. Thus $(1, -3)$ is a point on the curve. By choosing other values for t, we obtain the table and graph in Fig. 18-22. We connected the points in order of increasing values of t, as shown by the arrows in the graph. Thus the curve is given a directional sense. This is meaningful because the parametric equations could be looked upon as giving the position of a moving particle at time t. Although Fig. 18-22 shows the t-values associated with some points, *the parameter usually does not appear in such a graph at all.*

---

*See, for example, Eqs. 1 and 2 in Sec. 14-8, which concern Lissajous figures.

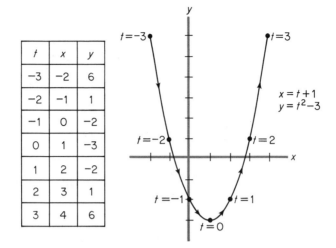

t	*x*	*y*
−3	−2	6
−2	−1	1
−1	0	−2
0	1	−3
1	2	−2
2	3	1
3	4	6

FIGURE 18-22

You may have noticed that the curve in Fig. 18-22 appears to be a parabola. To prove that this is indeed the case, we can find a single equation in x and y by *eliminating the parameter*. Because $t = x - 1$ from Eq. 1, by substituting into Eq. 2 we get the direct relationship between x and y.

$$y = (x - 1)^2 - 3$$
$$y = x^2 - 2x - 2, \tag{3}$$

which is a familiar form of a parabola. Equation 3 is called a **rectangular form** of the curve. In many cases it is not so simple and sometimes next to impossible to eliminate the parameter. In fact, one of the advantages of parametric equations is that a curve with a complicated equation in x and y may have a very simple parametric form.

When eliminating the parameter, you must be careful about the domain of the resulting rectangular form, as Example 1 will show.

example 1

Sketch the graph of

$$x = t^2, \qquad y = t^2$$

and eliminate the parameter.

The graph appears in Fig. 18-23(a). Because $x = t^2 = y$, a rectangular form is $y = x$; its graph is the straight line in Fig. 18-23(b). Note that the graph in (a) is not the complete graph in (b), but only a portion of it. To see why, observe that in the parametric equations, for all values of t we have $x \geq 0$. In (b) we have $-\infty < x < \infty$. That is, we obtain the graph in (a) from the rectangular form $y = x$ by restricting the domain so that $x \geq 0$. The graph in (a) is the correct representation of the parametric equations.

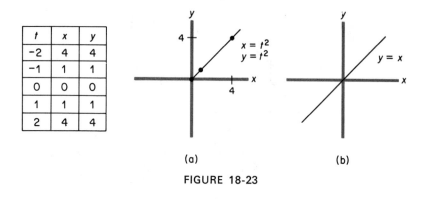

t	x	y
-2	4	4
-1	1	1
0	0	0
1	1	1
2	4	4

(a)   (b)

FIGURE 18-23

example 2

Sketch the graph of

$$x = 3 \sin \theta, \qquad y = 4 \cos \theta,$$

and eliminate the parameter.

Here the parameter is θ. Because the sine and cosine functions have period 2π, we need consider θ only in the interval from zero to 2π. We also note that $|x| \le 3$ and $|y| \le 4$, because the sine and cosine functions have values between -1 and 1. The graph appears in Fig. 18-24.

θ	x	y
0	0	4
$\frac{\pi}{4}$	2.1	2.8
$\frac{\pi}{2}$	3	0
$\frac{3\pi}{4}$	2.1	-2.8
π	0	-4
$\frac{5\pi}{4}$	-2.1	-2.8
$\frac{3\pi}{2}$	-3	0
$\frac{7\pi}{4}$	-2.1	2.8
2π	0	4

FIGURE 18-24

To eliminate the parameter we write

$$\sin \theta = \frac{x}{3} \quad \text{and} \quad \cos \theta = \frac{y}{4}.$$

Thus

$$\left(\frac{x}{3}\right)^2 + \left(\frac{y}{4}\right)^2 = \sin^2 \theta + \cos^2 \theta$$

$$\frac{x^2}{9} + \frac{y^2}{16} = 1.$$

This is a familiar form of an ellipse.

example 3

Sketch the graph of

$$x = t^3 - 3t, \quad y = t^2.$$

See Fig. 18-25. We included the parameter values $\pm\sqrt{3}$ because they give x a value of zero, since $0 = t(t^2 - 3) = t(t + \sqrt{3})(t - \sqrt{3})$.

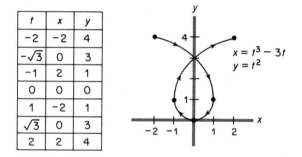

t	x	y
-2	-2	4
$-\sqrt{3}$	0	3
-1	2	1
0	0	0
1	-2	1
$\sqrt{3}$	0	3
2	2	4

FIGURE 18-25

example 4

Determine a set of parametric equations for

$$x^3 + y^3 = xy.$$

One technique is to let $y = tx$. Then

$$x^3 + t^3x^3 = x(tx),$$

or

$$x + t^3x = t$$

$$x = \frac{t}{1 + t^3}.$$

Hence,

$$y = tx$$
$$= \frac{t^2}{1 + t^3}.$$

The parametric equations are $x = \dfrac{t}{1 + t^3}$ and $y = \dfrac{t^2}{1 + t^3}$.

example 5

In the absence of air resistance, when a projectile with initial velocity v_0 is fired at an angle α with the ground, the coordinates of its position at time t are given by the parametric equations

$$x = (v_0 \cos \alpha)t \tag{4}$$

$$y = (v_0 \sin \alpha)t - \tfrac{1}{2}gt^2, \tag{5}$$

for which the graph is a parabola (Fig. 18-26). Here, g is the constant acceleration due to gravity, h is the maximum height of the projectile, and R is the (horizontal) range.

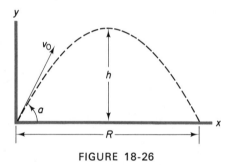

FIGURE 18-26

If $v_0 = 20$ m/s, $\alpha = 30°$, and $g = 9.8$ m/s², (a) find when the projectile strikes the ground (that is, the time of flight), (b) find the range R, and (c) find the maximum height h.

Substituting the given data into Eqs. 4 and 5, we obtain

$$x = (20 \cos 30°)t \tag{6}$$

$$y = (20 \sin 30°)t - 4.9t^2. \tag{7}$$

a. When the projectile strikes the ground, then $y = 0$. Thus, from Eq. 7,

$$(20 \sin 30°)t - 4.9t^2 = 0$$

$$t(20 \sin 30° - 4.9t) = 0.$$

Hence either $t = 0$ or $t = (20 \sin 30°)/4.9 = 2.04$. We choose $t = 2.04$ s.

b. The range R is obtained by substituting $t = 2.04$ from (a) into Eq. 6:

$$R = (20 \cos 30°)(2.04) = 35.3 \text{ m}.$$

c. To find h we note that the path of the projectile is a parabola that meets the x-axis when $t = 0$ and $t = 2.04$. From Example 7 of Sec. 18-4 and the discussion immediately preceding it, we conclude that the maximum height is obtained when

$$t = \frac{0 + 2.04}{2} = 1.02 \text{ s.}$$

Thus, from Eq. 7, the maximum height h is given by

$$h = (20 \sin 30°)(1.02) - 4.9(1.02)^2 = 5.10 \text{ m.}$$

Exercise 18-8

In Problems **1–10**, *sketch the graph of the curve represented by the given parametric equations. Eliminate the parameter in **1–9**.*

1. $x = 2t, y = t + 1$.
2. $x = t - 3, y = 3t + 1$.

3. $x = t, y = \dfrac{1}{t}$.
4. $x = t - 1, y = t^2 - 2t$.

5. $x = 3 - t, y = t - t^2$.
6. $x = \cos t, y = 2 \sin t$.

7. $x = 4 \cos t, y = 2 \cos t$.
8. $x = \cos 2t, y = \cos t$.

9. $x = 2 \cos t - 1, y = 2 \sin t - 2$.
10. $x = t^3 - 3t - 2, y = t^2 - t - 2$.

In Problems **11–16**, *find parametric representations for the curves given by the equations in the same manner as in Example 4.*

11. $x = y + xy$. **12.** $x^2 + y^2 = 9x$. **13.** $x^3 + y^3 = 2xy$.

14. $y^2 - 2x^2 = 8y$. **15.** $x^2 + 2xy + y = x$. **16.** $x^3 - 3xy + y^3 = 0$.

17. By eliminating the parameter, show that a projectile with motion as given by Eqs. 4 and 5 of Example 5 has a parabolic path.

18. A particle moves in the xy-plane such that the coordinates of its position as functions of time are given by

$$x = r \cos \omega t,$$
$$y = r \sin \omega t,$$

where r and ω are constants. By eliminating the parameter, determine the type of path the body follows.

19. Sketch the graph of the projectile in Example 5 with the path as given by Eqs. 6 and 7. Choose parameter values of $t = 0, 0.25, 0.50, 0.75$, and so on.

20. Show that the parametric equations

$$x = a \cos \theta,$$
$$y = b \sin \theta$$

describe an ellipse for $a \neq b$.

21. A projectile is fired from ground level with an initial velocity of 300 m/s at an angle of 40° with the ground (see Example 5). Assume $g = 9.8$ m/s². (a) After 3 s, how far has the projectile traveled horizontally and how far vertically?

(b) Find when the projectile strikes the ground. (c) Find the range (to the nearest meter). (d) Find the maximum height (to the nearest meter) and the time when it occurs.

22. A body is fired from the ground at an angle of 45° with an initial velocity of 120 m/s. To the nearest meter, find the range of the body (see Example 5). Assume that $g = 9.8$ m/s².

23. The coordinates of the position of a particle at time t are given parametrically by

$$x = 2t, \qquad y = t + 1,$$

where x and y are in meters and t is in seconds. Show that the distance d of the particle from the origin is given by $d = \sqrt{x^2 + y^2}$. Determine at what time(s) t the particle will be 4 m from the origin.

24. The coordinates of the position of a particle (in meters) as functions of time t (in seconds) are given parametrically by

$$x = 2 - t, \qquad y = 3t + 1.$$

For what value(s) of t will the particle be 3 m from the origin? (See Problem 23.)

18-9   Review

Review Questions

1. The set of all points in a plane that are equidistant from a fixed point in the plane is called a(n) _____ .

2. The only conic section with asymptotes is the _____ .

3. The equation $(x - 2)^2 + (y + 4)^2 = 3$ defines a circle of radius __(a)__ whose center is at __(b)__ .

4. The graph of $y^2 = x$ is called a _____ .

5. The vertex of the graph of $(y - 2)^2 = 9x$ is at _____ .

6. The parabola $x^2 = -4y$ opens _(downward)(to the left)_ .

7. The graph of $\dfrac{x^2}{4} - \dfrac{y^2}{9} = 1$ is called a(n) _____(a)_____ , and the graph of $\dfrac{x^2}{4} + \dfrac{y^2}{9} = 1$ is called a(n) _____(b)_____ .

8. The major axis of $\dfrac{(x + 3)^2}{4} + \dfrac{(y - 2)^2}{9} = 1$ is _(horizontal)(vertical)_ .

9 The graph of $xy = -7$ is a(n) _____ .

10. In sketching the graph determined by parametric equations, the parameter _(does)(does not)_ have to appear in the graph.

11. The graph of a parabola is that of a function of x if the directrix is _(parallel)(perpendicular)_ to the x-axis.

12. In a plane, the set of all points the sum of whose distances from two fixed points is a constant is called a(n) _____.

13. In a plane the equation $\frac{x^2}{5} + \frac{y^2}{5} = 1$ defines a(n) _____.

Answers to Review Questions

1. Circle. **2.** Hyperbola. **3.** (a) $\sqrt{3}$, (b) $(2, -4)$. **4.** Parabola. **5.** $(0, 2)$.
6. Downward. **7.** (a) Hyperbola, (b) Ellipse. **8.** Vertical. **9.** Hyperbola (equilateral).
10. Does not. **11.** Parallel. **12.** Ellipse. **13.** Circle.

Review Problems

In Problems 1–4, find the distance between the given points.

1. $(1, 4)$, $(-3, 2)$.   **2.** $(-1, -1)$, $(-6, -1)$.

3. $(-8, 2)$, $(0, -4)$.   **4.** $(-3, -4)$, $(-1, 1)$.

In Problems 5–8, find the standard and general forms of an equation of a circle having the given center C and radius r.

5. $C = (0, 0)$, $r = 5$.   **6.** $C = (0, -2)$, $r = \sqrt{2}$.

7. $C = (1, -1)$, $r = \frac{1}{2}$.   **8.** $C = (\frac{1}{2}, \frac{1}{4})$, $r = 1$.

In Problems 9–36, discuss and sketch the graph of each equation.

9. $x^2 + y^2 = 16$.   **10.** $(x - 4)^2 + (y - 3)^2 = 1$.

11. $(x + 2)^2 + (y - 1)^2 = 7$.   **12.** $x^2 + (y - 1)^2 - 12 = 0$.

13. $9x^2 - 100y^2 = 900$.   **14.** $3x - 4y^2 = 0$.

15. $36x^2 + y^2 = 36$.   **16.** $36y^2 - x^2 = 4$.

17. $5x^2 + 2y = 0$.   **18.** $x^2 + \frac{1}{2}y^2 = 1$.

19. $6x^2 - 1 = -6y^2$.   **20.** $\frac{1}{49}x^2 - \frac{1}{49}y^2 = 1$.

21. $\frac{(x + 1)^2}{2} - \frac{y^2}{8} = 2$.   **22.** $(y - 6)^2 - (x + 2)^2 = 1$.

23. $(y - 2)^2 = 12x$.   **24.** $\frac{1}{2}y - (x - 3)^2 = \frac{3}{2}y$.

25. $xy = -8$.   **26.** $x^2 = \frac{1}{3}y$.

27. $(x + 5)^2 + \frac{1}{2}(y - 2)^2 = 4$.   **28.** $x^2 = 36 - (y + 2)^2$.

29. $x^2 + y^2 + 5x - 6y + 2 = 0$.   **30.** $x^2 + y^2 - x - 1 = 0$.

31. $9x^2 + 9y^2 - 18x - 6y + 10 = 0$.   **32.** $3x^2 + 3y^2 - 6x + 12y + 16 = 0$.

33. $y^2 - 2x - 2y = 4$.   **34.** $4x^2 + 9y^2 - 16x + 18y = 11$.

35. $2x^2 - 2y^2 + 4x + 10 = 0$.   **36.** $25x^2 - 2y^2 = -100$.

In Problems 37–39, find the standard form of an equation of the given conic.

37. parabola: vertex $(2, 1)$ and focus $(2, 4)$.

38. hyperbola: vertices $(1, 1)$ and $(1, -5)$, and foci $(1, -2 \pm \sqrt{13})$.

39. ellipse: vertices $(-2, -2)$ and $(-2, 8)$, and foci $(-2, 0)$ and $(-2, 6)$.

40. Sketch the curve and eliminate the parameter:

$$x = 2(2 - t)$$
$$y = t + t^2.$$

41. In the manner of Example 4 in Sec. 18-8, find a parametric representation for the curve given by the equation

$$2x^3 - y^3 = 3xy.$$

19

sequences and series

19-1 Sequences

For an object starting from rest and traveling in a straight-line path with a constant acceleration of 4 m/s², it is shown in physics that the distance s (in meters) of the object from its starting point at time t (in seconds) is given by the function $s = f(t) = 2t^2$. Let us restrict t to positive integral values; that is, we take the domain of f to be the positive integers. We find that if $t = 1$, then $s = 2$; if $t = 2$, then $s = 8$; and so on. Thus we have the following correspondence:

$$\begin{array}{ccccccc}
\text{Domain} & 1 & 2 & 3 & 4 & \cdots & n & \cdots \\
& \downarrow & \downarrow & \downarrow & \downarrow & & \downarrow & \\
\text{Range} & 2 & 8 & 18 & 32 & \cdots & 2n^2 & \cdots .
\end{array}$$

In general, any function f such as this which has as its domain the positive integers is called an *infinite sequence*. By considering the natural ordering of the positive integers, we can list the functional values of f in an orderly fashion as follows:

$$f(1), f(2), f(3), f(4), \ldots , f(n), \ldots . \tag{1}$$

In fact, we can go one step further if we drop the functional notation in (1) and, instead, adopt a subscript notation. That is, for (1) we can equivalently write

$$a_1, a_2, a_3, a_4, \ldots , a_n, \ldots , \tag{2}$$

where $a_n = f(n)$. Thus, if $f(n) = 2n^2$, then $a_1 = f(1) = 2$, $a_2 = f(2) = 8$, $a_3 = 18$,

611

and so on, and the functional values are

$$2, 8, 18, 32, \ldots, 2n^2, \ldots. \tag{3}$$

Because (3) essentially defines a particular sequence, it is commonly referred to as an infinite sequence itself. Similarly, by the infinite sequence

$$\frac{3}{1}, \frac{4}{2}, \frac{5}{3}, \ldots, \frac{n+2}{n}, \ldots$$

we mean the function, say g, defined by $g(n) = (n + 2)/n$, where n is a positive integer. In summary, we have the following definition.

An **infinite sequence**, denoted

$$a_1, a_2, a_3, \ldots, a_n, \ldots,$$

is a function f with domain the positive integers and such that $a_n = f(n)$.

Corresponding to the integer 1 is the **first term** a_1, to 2 corresponds the **second term** a_2, and so forth. The **nth term**, or **general term**, is a_n and usually defines the function; that is, $a_n = f(n)$. A sequence with the general term a_n is often denoted by the symbol $\{a_n\}$. For example, the infinite sequence in (3) can be denoted $\{2n^2\}$.

example 1

Determine the first four terms of the infinite sequence having the general term $a_n = 2n + 3$.

In the expression $2n + 3$, we successively replace n by the integers 1, 2, 3, and 4.

$$n = 1, \quad a_1 = 2(1) + 3 = 5.$$
$$n = 2, \quad a_2 = 2(2) + 3 = 7.$$
$$n = 3, \quad a_3 = 2(3) + 3 = 9.$$
$$n = 4, \quad a_4 = 2(4) + 3 = 11.$$

Therefore

$$\{2n + 3\} = 5, 7, 9, 11, \ldots.$$

example 2

Determine the first four terms of the infinite sequence $\{(-1)^n(n^2 + 1)\}$.

$$n = 1, \quad a_1 = (-1)^1(1^2 + 1) = -2.$$
$$n = 2, \quad a_2 = (-1)^2(2^2 + 1) = 5.$$

$$n = 3, \quad a_3 = (-1)^3(3^2 + 1) = -10.$$
$$n = 4, \quad a_4 = (-1)^4(4^2 + 1) = 17.$$

Hence

$$\{(-1)^n(n^2 + 1)\} = -2, 5, -10, 17, \ldots.$$

example 3

Find a general term for an infinite sequence such that its first six terms are

$$1, \sqrt{2}, \sqrt{3}, 2, \sqrt{5}, \sqrt{6}, \ldots.$$

By inspection, a general term is $a_n = \sqrt{n}$.

example 4

Write *all* the terms of the **finite sequence**

$$\{n(n + 1)\}, \quad \text{where } n = 1, 2, 3, 4.$$

In this case, the domain of the sequence is a *finite* set of consecutive positive integers. Successively substituting 1, 2, 3, and 4 for n in the general term, we have

$$\{n(n + 1)\} = 2, 6, 12, 20.$$

Note that there are exactly four terms. Similarly, the finite sequence $a_1, a_2, \ldots, a_{25}$ has 25 terms. In contrast to an infinite sequence, note that a finite sequence has a first term *and* a last term.

Exercise 19-1

In Problems **1–16**, *write the first four terms of the given infinite sequence.*

1. $\{3n\}$.

2. $\{\frac{1}{2}n\}$.

3. $\{2n - 1\}$.

4. $\{n^2 + 4\}$.

5. $\left\{\dfrac{n}{n + 1}\right\}$.

6. $\left\{\dfrac{n - 1}{n}\right\}$.

7. $\left\{\dfrac{n - 1}{n + 1}\right\}$.

8. $\left\{\dfrac{n^2 + 1}{n^2 - 2}\right\}$.

9. $\left\{\dfrac{n}{2^n}\right\}$.

10. $\left\{\dfrac{3^n}{n}\right\}$.

11. $\left\{\sin\dfrac{n\pi}{2}\right\}$.

12. $\left\{\cos\left(\dfrac{n\pi}{2}\right)\right\}$.

13. $\left\{\dfrac{e^n}{2}\right\}$.

14. $\left\{\dfrac{\sin nx}{n^2}\right\}$.

15. $\{(-1)^{n+1}(n^2)\}$

16. $\{(-1)^n(2n)^2\}$.

In Problems **17–24**, *find, by inspection, a general term for the given infinite sequence.*

17. $4, 8, 12, 16, \ldots.$

18. $0, -1, -2, -3, \ldots.$

19. $4, 6, 8, 10, \ldots.$

20. $1, \frac{3}{2}, 2, \frac{5}{2}, \dots$ **21.** $1, \frac{1}{3}, \frac{1}{9}, \frac{1}{27}, \dots$ **22.** $1, \frac{1}{2}, \frac{1}{4}, \frac{1}{8}, \dots$

23. $\frac{1}{2}, -\frac{1}{3}, \frac{1}{4}, -\frac{1}{5}, \dots$ **24.** $-\frac{1}{2}, \frac{1}{3}, -\frac{1}{4}, \frac{1}{5}, \dots$

19-2   Arithmetic and Geometric Progressions

A. Arithmetic Progressions

If the difference between every two consecutive terms of a sequence is the same number d, that is,

$$a_2 - a_1 = a_3 - a_2 = \cdots = a_{n+1} - a_n = d,$$

then the sequence is called an **arithmetic sequence** or **arithmetic progression** with **common difference** d. This means that in an arithmetic progression, each term after the first can be obtained by adding the common difference d to the preceding term.

example 1

a. The arithmetic progression $1, 3, 5, 7, \dots$ has a common difference $d = 2$, since the differences $3 - 1$, $5 - 3$, $7 - 5$, and so on, are all 2.

b. The arithmetic progression $6, 11, 16, 21, \dots$ has $d = 5$. Verify this.

c. The arithmetic progression $2, -1, -4, \dots$ has $d = -3$. Verify this.

We can list the terms of an arithmetic progression as follows:

$$a_1, a_1 + d, a_1 + 2d, \dots, a_1 + (n - 1)d, \dots.$$

Thus the formula

$$\boxed{a_n = a_1 + (n - 1)d} \tag{1}$$

gives *the nth term, a_n, of an arithmetic progression with first term a_1 and common difference d.*

example 2

Find the eighteenth term of the arithmetic progression

$$7, 13, 19, \dots.$$

Here $a_1 = 7$ and $d = 13 - 7 = 6$. We want a_n for $n = 18$. By Eq. (1),

$$a_n = a_1 + (n - 1)d$$
$$a_{18} = 7 + (18 - 1)6 = 109.$$

example 3

The first term of an arithmetic progression is 3 and the thirteenth term is -45. Find the common difference and the first four terms.

Here $a_1 = 3$, and for $n = 13$ we have $a_n = -45$. Substituting in Eq. 1 we obtain

$$a_n = a_1 + (n - 1)d$$
$$-45 = 3 + (13 - 1)d$$
$$-45 = 3 + 12d$$
$$d = -4.$$

Thus the sequence is $3, -1, -5, -9, \ldots$.

example 4

A particle has an initial speed of 5 m/s and travels in a straight line with an acceleration of 2 m/s². The values of the speed of the particle, in meters per second, at positive integral values of time (in seconds) form the arithmetic progression

$$7, 9, 11, 13, \ldots, 5 + 2t, \ldots.$$

Find the speed of the particle when $t = 100$ s.

Here the first term $a_1 = 7$ corresponds to the time $t = 1$, the second term $a_2 = 9$ corresponds to $t = 2$, and so on, and $d = 2$. We need to find a_{100}, which corresponds to $t = 100$. In Eq. 1 we set $a_1 = 7$, $d = 2$, and $n = 100$.

$$a_n = a_1 + (n - 1)d$$
$$a_{100} = 7 + (100 - 1)(2) = 205.$$

Thus the speed is 205 m/s.

B. Geometric Progressions

If the ratio of every two consecutive terms in a sequence is the same number r, that is,

$$\frac{a_2}{a_1} = \frac{a_3}{a_2} = \cdots = \frac{a_{n+1}}{a_n} = r,$$

then the sequence is called a **geometric sequence** or **geometric progression** with **common ratio r**. In this case each term after the first can be obtained by multiplying the preceding term by the common ratio r. Thus a geometric progression has the form

$$a_1, a_1 r, a_1 r^2, \ldots, a_1 r^{n-1}, \ldots.$$

Note that *the nth term a_n of a geometric progression with first term a_1 and common ratio r is given by*

$$\boxed{a_n = a_1 r^{n-1}.}$$ (2)

example 5

a. The first five terms of the geometric progression having $a_1 = 3$ and common ratio $\frac{1}{2}$ are

$$3, 3\left(\frac{1}{2}\right), 3\left(\frac{1}{2}\right)^2, 3\left(\frac{1}{2}\right)^3, 3\left(\frac{1}{2}\right)^4, \ldots$$

or

$$3, \frac{3}{2}, \frac{3}{4}, \frac{3}{8}, \frac{3}{16}, \ldots$$

b. If the first term of a geometric progression with common ratio -2 is -1, then the progression is

$$-1, (-1)(-2), (-1)(-2)^2, (-1)(-2)^3, \ldots$$

or

$$-1, 2, -4, 8, \ldots.$$

c. The geometric progression $1, \frac{1}{2}, \frac{1}{4}, \frac{1}{8}, \ldots$ has common ratio $r = \frac{1}{2}$. The ratios

$$\frac{\frac{1}{2}}{1}, \frac{\frac{1}{4}}{\frac{1}{2}}, \frac{\frac{1}{8}}{\frac{1}{4}}, \text{ and so on, are all equal to } \frac{1}{2}.$$

d. In the geometric progression $1, 0.1, 0.01, 0.001, \ldots,$ we have $a_1 = 1$ and $r = 0.1$.

example 6

a. Find the fifth term of the geometric progression $1, -3, 9, \ldots.$

Here $a_1 = 1$, $r = -3/1 = -3$, and we want a_n for $n = 5$. By Eq. 2 we have

$$a_n = a_1 r^{n-1}$$
$$a_5 = 1(-3)^{5-1} = 1(-3)^4 = 81.$$

b. Find the seventh term of the geometric progression $\sqrt{2}, 2, 2\sqrt{2}, 4, \ldots.$

Here $a_1 = \sqrt{2}$, $r = 2/\sqrt{2} = \sqrt{2}$, and we want a_n for $n = 7$.

$$a_n = a_1 r^{n-1}$$
$$a_7 = \sqrt{2}(\sqrt{2})^{7-1} = (\sqrt{2})^7 = 8\sqrt{2}.$$

example 7

The first term of a geometric progression is 3 and the sixth term is $\frac{3}{32}$. Find the common ratio.

Here $a_1 = 3$, and for $n = 6$ we have $a_n = \frac{3}{32}$. From Eq. (2) we obtain

$$a_n = a_1 r^{n-1}$$

$$a_6 = 3r^{6-1} = \frac{3}{32}$$

$$r^5 = \frac{3}{3(32)} = \frac{1}{32}$$

$$r = \sqrt[5]{\frac{1}{32}} = \frac{1}{2}.$$

Exercise 19-2

In Problems **1–16**, *determine whether the given sequence is an arithmetic progression, a geometric progression, or neither. For those that are arithmetic or geometric progressions, find the indicated term.*

1. $13, 1, -11, \ldots$; eighth term.

2. $13, 0, -13, \ldots$; seventh term.

3. $6, -3, \frac{3}{2}, \ldots$; sixth term.

4. $4, 1, \frac{1}{4}, \ldots$; seventh term.

5. $-1, 3, -9, \ldots$; sixth term.

6. $12, 16, 20, \ldots$; tenth term.

7. $\frac{1}{3}, \frac{2}{3}, 1, \ldots$; eleventh term.

8. $a, -a, -3a, \ldots$; ninth term.

9. $-4, 2, -1, \ldots$; tenth term.

10. $0.3, 0.03, 0.003, \ldots$; seventh term.

11. $3, 15, 24, \ldots$; tenth term.

12. $12, -4, \frac{4}{3}, \ldots$; seventh term.

13. $0.4, 0.8, 1.2, \ldots$; tenth term.

14. $0.9, 1, 1.1, \ldots$; sixth term.

15. $\frac{3}{2}, \frac{9}{4}, \frac{27}{8}, \ldots$; sixth term.

16. $6, 2, \frac{1}{3}, \ldots$; fifth term.

17. The fourth term of an arithmetic progression with common difference 14 is 86. Find the first term.

18. The first term of an arithmetic progression is 6. The tenth term is 10. Find the common difference.

19. The sixth term of a geometric progression is 16. The seventh term is 32. Find the first term.

20. The sixteenth term of an arithmetic progression is 28. The first term is -4. Find the common difference.

21. In an arithmetic progression, $a_1 = 6$, $a_n = 26$, and $d = 4$. Find n.

22. If the first term of a geometric progression is 18 and the fourth term is $\frac{2}{81}$, find the second term.

23. The first swing of a pendulum is 10 cm, and because of resistive effects each succeeding swing is $\frac{1}{4}$ cm less. What is the length of the thirteenth pendulum swing?

24. How many swings of the pendulum in Problem 23 are completed before the pendulum comes to rest?

25. A distant star now has a surface temperature of 10,000°C, and observations indicate that the temperature decreases by 10 percent every 1000 years. What will be the temperature 4000 years from now?

26. For the star of Problem 25, in how many years will the surface temperature be 7290°C?

19-3   Series

If we are given a sequence, either finite or infinite, then an indicated sum of its terms is called a **series**. For example, the expression

$$a_1 + a_2 + a_3$$

is a *finite series* with three terms, and the expression

$$a_1 + a_2 + a_3 + \cdots$$

is called an *infinite series*, because there are infinitely many terms.

You might at first be alarmed by the notion of an "infinite sum" as indicated above. The word *sum* probably has meaning to you only as far as a finite number of quantities is concerned, and the thought of infinitely many additions may seem awesome. Be assured that we can, in a reasonable way, attach a meaning to such a sum. In fact, it will be done, in part, in terms of finite sums. First, however, other topics must be considered.

For convenience, to indicate a sum we shall introduce **summation** or **sigma notation**, so named because the capital Greek letter $\sum$ (sigma) is used. For example,

$$\sum_{k=1}^{3} (2k + 5)$$

denotes the sum of those numbers obtained from the expression $2k + 5$ by first replacing k by 1, then by 2, and finally by 3. That is, k takes on consecutive integer values from 1 to 3. Thus

$$\sum_{k=1}^{3} (2k + 5) = [2(1) + 5] + [2(2) + 5] + [2(3) + 5]$$
$$= 7 + 9 + 11 = 27.$$

The letter k is called the **index of summation**; the numbers 1 and 3 are the **limits of summation** (1 is the *lower limit* and 3 is the *upper limit*). The symbol used for the index is a "dummy" symbol in the sense that it does not affect the sum of the terms. Any other letter can be used. For example,

$$\sum_{j=1}^{3} (2j + 5) = 7 + 9 + 11 = \sum_{k=1}^{3} (2k + 5).$$

The expression $\sum_{k=1}^{3} (2k + 5)$ may be read *the sum of $2k + 5$ from $k = 1$ to $k = 3$.*

example 1

Evaluate each of the following.

a. $\sum_{k=4}^{7} \dfrac{k^2 + 3}{2}$.

Here the sum begins with $k = 4$.

$$\sum_{k=4}^{7} \frac{k^2 + 3}{2} = \frac{4^2 + 3}{2} + \frac{5^2 + 3}{2} + \frac{6^2 + 3}{2} + \frac{7^2 + 3}{2}$$

$$= \frac{19}{2} + \frac{28}{2} + \frac{39}{2} + \frac{52}{2} = 69.$$

b. $\sum_{j=0}^{2} (-1)^{j+1}(j - 1)^2$.

Here the sum begins with $j = 0$.

$$\sum_{j=0}^{2} (-1)^{j+1}(j - 1)^2 = (-1)^{0+1}(0 - 1)^2 + (-1)^{1+1}(1 - 1)^2 + (-1)^{2+1}(2 - 1)^2$$

$$= (-1) + 0 + (-1) = -2.$$

c. $\sum_{n=1}^{4} 2$.

The 2 can be thought of as $2 + 0n$.

$$\sum_{n=1}^{4} 2 = 2 + 2 + 2 + 2 = 8$$

An infinite series can be represented by the sigma notation

$$\sum_{n=1}^{\infty} a_n = a_1 + a_2 + a_3 + \cdots + a_n + \cdots,$$

where the index n is replaced successively by the integers $1, 2, 3, \ldots$. For example,

$$\sum_{n=1}^{\infty} \left(\frac{1}{2}\right)^n = \frac{1}{2} + \left(\frac{1}{2}\right)^2 + \left(\frac{1}{2}\right)^3 + \cdots.$$

Let us now consider how to find the sum S_n of the first n terms of an arithmetic progression with common difference d. We have

$$S_n = a_1 + a_2 + a_3 + \cdots + a_n,$$

where $a_2 = a_1 + d, a_3 = a_1 + 2d$, and so on. Thus

$$S_n = a_1 + (a_1 + d) + (a_1 + 2d) + \cdots + [a_1 + (n - 1)d]. \tag{1}$$

If we write the nth term a_n first, then S_n can be written in the alternative form

$$S_n = a_n + (a_n - d) + (a_n - 2d) + \cdots + [a_n - (n - 1)d]. \tag{2}$$

Adding corresponding sides of Eq. 1 and Eq. 2 yields

$$S_n = a_1 + (a_1 + d) + \cdots + [a_1 + (n-1)d]$$
$$S_n = a_n + (a_n - d) + \cdots + [a_n - (n-1)d]$$
$$2S_n = (a_1 + a_n) + (a_1 + a_n) + \cdots + (a_1 + a_n).$$

On the right side of the last equation, the term $a_1 + a_n$ occurs n times. Therefore

$$2S_n = n(a_1 + a_n).$$

Thus *the sum S_n of the first n terms of an arithmetic progression is given by*

$$S_n = \frac{n(a_1 + a_n)}{2}, \tag{3}$$

where a_1 is the first term and a_n is the nth term.

example 2

Find the sum of the first eight terms of the series

$$1 + 4 + 7 + \cdots.$$

The terms form an arithmetic progression with $d = 3$ and eighth term given by

$$a_n = a_1 + (n-1)d$$
$$a_8 = 1 + (8-1)3 = 22.$$

The sum can now be determined by using Eq. 3:

$$S_8 = \frac{8(a_1 + a_8)}{2} = \frac{8(1 + 22)}{2} = 92.$$

example 3

Find the sum of the odd integers between 20 and 60.

The odd integers between 20 and 60 form an arithmetic progression with $d = 2$. For $a_1 = 21$ and $a_n = 59$, to find n we have

$$a_n = a_1 + (n-1)d$$
$$59 = 21 + (n-1)2,$$

from which $n = 20$. That is, 59 is the twentieth term of the arithmetic progression. Hence, using Eq. 3 gives

$$S_{20} = \frac{20(21 + 59)}{2} = 800.$$

example 4

Derive a formula for the sum of the first k positive integers.

The terms of the series

$$\sum_{n=1}^{k} n = 1 + 2 + 3 + \cdots + k$$

form an arithmetic progression with $a_1 = 1$, $d = 1$, and k terms. Thus, by Eq. 3, we have

$$\boxed{\sum_{n=1}^{k} n = \frac{k(k + 1)}{2}.}$$ (4)

For example, to find the sum of the first 25 positive integers we set $k = 25$:

$$\sum_{n=1}^{25} n = \frac{25(25 + 1)}{2} = 325.$$

Let us now determine a formula that gives the sum of the first n terms of a geometric progression. Such an indicated sum is called a (*finite*) *geometric series*. If the first term is a_1 and the common ratio is r, then the sum S_n is given by

$$S_n = a_1 + a_1 r + a_1 r^2 + \cdots + a_1 r^{n-1}.$$ (5)

Multiplying both sides by r gives

$$r S_n = a_1 r + a_1 r^2 + a_1 r^3 + \cdots + a_1 r^n.$$ (6)

Subtracting corresponding sides of Eq. 6 from Eq. 5 and factoring gives

$$S_n - r S_n = a_1 - a_1 r^n$$
$$S_n(1 - r) = a_1(1 - r^n).$$

Thus, for $r \neq 1$, we have

$$\boxed{S_n = \frac{a_1(1 - r^n)}{1 - r},}$$ (7)

which gives *the sum S_n of the first n terms of a geometric progression with first term a_1 and common ratio r.* Equivalently,

$$S_n = \frac{a_1 - a_1 r^n}{1 - r} = \frac{a_1 - (a_1 r^{n-1})r}{1 - r}.$$

Hence an alternative formula for S_n is

$$S_n = \frac{a_1 - ra_n}{1 - r}.$$ (8)

If $r = 1$, then Eqs. 7 and 8 cannot be used. However, in that case, we have quite simply

$$S_n = a_1 + a_1 + \cdots + a_1 = na_1.$$

example 5

Find the sum of the first ten terms of the geometric progression 12, 6, 3, ...

Here we have $a_1 = 12$, $r = \frac{1}{2}$, and $n = 10$. From Eq. 7,

$$S_n = \frac{a_1(1 - r^n)}{1 - r}$$

$$S_{10} = \frac{12[1 - (\frac{1}{2})^{10}]}{1 - \frac{1}{2}} = \frac{12(1 - \frac{1}{1024})}{\frac{1}{2}} = \frac{3069}{128}.$$

example 6

Find the sum of the geometric series $1 + \frac{1}{2} + (\frac{1}{2})^2 + \cdots + (\frac{1}{2})^6$.

Here $a_1 = 1$, $r = \frac{1}{2}$, and $n = 7$. From Eq. 7 we have

$$S_7 = \frac{1[1 - (\frac{1}{2})^7]}{1 - \frac{1}{2}} = \frac{\frac{127}{128}}{\frac{1}{2}} = \frac{127}{64}.$$

Exercise 19-3

In Problems 1–8, evaluate the given sum.

1. $\sum_{k=1}^{5} (k + 4)$.

2. $\sum_{k=12}^{15} (5 - 2k)$.

3. $\sum_{n=2}^{3} (3n^2 - 7)$.

4. $\sum_{n=2}^{4} \frac{n + 1}{n - 1}$.

5. $\sum_{k=3}^{4} \frac{(-1)^k(k + 1)}{2^k}$.

6. $\sum_{n=1}^{5} 1$.

7. $\sum_{k=1}^{3} \frac{(-1)^{k-1}(1 - k^2)}{k}$.

8. $\sum_{n=1}^{4} (n^2 + n)$.

In Problems 9 and 10, write the first four terms of the series.

9. $\sum_{n=1}^{\infty} 2\left(\frac{1}{2}\right)^n$.

10. $\sum_{n=0}^{\infty} (-1)^n \frac{1}{n + 1}$.

In Problems **11–26**, *determine whether the terms of the given series form an arithmetic or geometric progression and find the indicated sum.*

11. $2 + 4 + 6 + \cdots$; S_{10}.

12. $1 + 5 + 9 + \cdots$; S_9.

13. $15 + 10 + 5 + \cdots$; S_{16}.

14. $-\frac{1}{3} + \frac{1}{3} + 1 + \cdots$; S_{12}.

15. $2 + 0 - 2 - 4 + \cdots$; S_{12}.

16. $14 + 7 + 0 + \cdots$; S_{10}.

17. $-10 + 6 + 22 + \cdots$; S_{10}.

18. $\frac{3}{6} + \frac{2}{6} + \frac{1}{6} + \cdots$; S_9.

19. $3 + 9 + 27 + \cdots$; S_6.

20. $1 - \frac{1}{4} + \frac{1}{16} - \cdots$; S_6.

21. $6 - 12 + 24 - \cdots$; S_6.

22. $0.1 + 0.02 + 0.004 + \cdots$; S_{11}.

23. $0.3 + 0.03 + 0.003 + \cdots$; S_{10}.

24. $24 + 12 + 6 + \cdots$; S_{10}.

25. $2 + 2\sqrt{2} + 4 + \cdots$; S_{10}.

26. $2\sqrt{3} + 6 + 6\sqrt{3} + \cdots$; S_8.

In Problems **27–32**, *find the values of the indicated quantities if an arithmetic progression has the given properties.*

27. $a_n = 12, d = \frac{1}{4}, S_n = 99$; a_1, n.

28. $a_9 = 20, d = 1$; a_{16}, S_{16}.

29. $a_{13} = 42, d = 2$; a_{16}, S_{16}.

30. $a_1 = 12, a_n = 42, d = 2$; n, S_n.

31. $a_1 = -30, d = 3, S_n = 69$; n, a_n.

32. $a_n = 14, d = \frac{1}{2}, S_n = 98$; n.

In Problems **33–38**, *find the values of the indicated quantities if a geometric progression has the given properties.*

33. $r = \frac{1}{2}, S_6 = 126$; a_1, a_6.

34. $a_1 = 1, a_6 = 32$; r, S_6.

35. $a_1 = \frac{3}{4}, a_n = -96, S_n = -\frac{255}{4}$; r.

36. $a_1 = \frac{1}{2}, a_{10} = 256$; a_{12}, S_{12}.

37. $a_6 = 1, a_8 = 9$; S_5.

38. $r = \frac{1}{3}, S_5 = 121$; a_1, a_5.

39. If a person saves 1¢ the first day, 2¢ the next day, 3¢ the next day, and so on, how much money will have been saved after 30 days?

40. If a person saves 1¢ the first day, 2¢ the next day, 4¢ the next, 8¢ the next, and so on, how much money will have been saved after 30 days?

41. It can be shown that the sum of the squares of the first k positive integers is given by

$$\sum_{n=1}^{k} n^2 = \frac{k(k + 1)(2k + 1)}{6}.$$

Find the sum of the squares of the first ten positive integers.

42. It can be shown that the sum of the cubes of the first k positive integers is given by

$$\sum_{n=1}^{k} n^3 = \frac{k^2(k + 1)^2}{4}.$$

Find the sum of the cubes of the first ten positive integers.

43. Find the sum of the first 100 positive integers.

44. A 12-hour clock strikes once at 1 o'clock, twice at 2 o'clock, and so on. How many strikes will it make in 24 *consecutive* hours?

45. In a vacuum, an object falls approximately 4.9 m the first second, 14.7 m the next, 24.5 m the next, and so on. How far does it fall in 12 s?

46. The tip of a pendulum moves 4 cm the first second, 2 cm the next, 1 cm the next, and so on. How far does it move in 10 s?

47. A tank full of alcohol is emptied of one-fourth of its contents. The tank is then filled with water. This is repeated three more times. What part of the volume of the tank is now alcohol?

48. By means of a pump, air is being removed from a container in such a way that each second one-tenth of the remaining air in the container is removed. After 5 s, what percentage of air is left?

19-4   Limits of Sequences

We now consider one of the very fundamental ideas of mathematics—the concept of a limit. The ideas and techniques we shall develop here are useful in both the main topics of calculus, namely finding derivatives and finding integrals.

We begin by examining rather closely a sequence that conveniently typifies a situation which arises quite naturally in mechanics. Consider a pendulum that is displaced from its equilibrium (rest) position and then released. The pendulum will oscillate back and forth. Let us assume that the length of the first swing was $\frac{1}{2}$ m and that the length of any subsequent swing was exactly one-half the length of the swing that preceded it. If we let a_1 be the length of the first swing, a_2 the length of the second swing, and so on, we have

$$a_1 = \frac{1}{2} = \frac{1}{2^1}$$

$$a_2 = \frac{1}{2}\left(\frac{1}{2}\right) = \frac{1}{2^2}$$

$$a_3 = \frac{1}{2}\left(\frac{1}{2^2}\right) = \frac{1}{2^3}$$

$$a_4 = \frac{1}{2}\left(\frac{1}{2^3}\right) = \frac{1}{2^4}.$$

Clearly, for the nth swing of the pendulum,

$$a_n = \frac{1}{2^n}.$$

Thus the sequence with terms corresponding to the lengths of the swings is

$$\left\{\frac{1}{2^n}\right\} = \frac{1}{2^1}, \frac{1}{2^2}, \frac{1}{2^3}, \frac{1}{2^4}, \cdots, \frac{1}{2^n}, \cdots$$

$$= \frac{1}{2}, \frac{1}{4}, \frac{1}{8}, \frac{1}{16}, \cdots, \frac{1}{2^n}, \cdots.$$

Some of the terms of this sequence are indicated on the real number line in Fig. 19-1. Observe that as n increases, the terms get closer to zero. Moreover, although

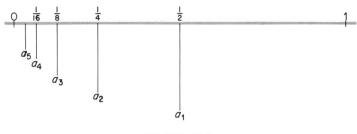

FIGURE 19-1

$1/2^n$ will never equal zero, for large values of n the corresponding terms will come as close to zero as we wish. For example, suppose we wish to find when the length of a swing will be less than $\frac{1}{10,000}$ m. Then we must have the inequality

$$\frac{1}{2^n} < \frac{1}{10,000},$$

which is true for $n > 13$. That is, beginning with the fourteenth term (the fourteenth swing of the pendulum), each term in the sequence $\{1/2^n\}$ will be less than $\frac{1}{10,000}$ m.

The ideas of the preceding discussion are verbally expressed by saying that as n increases indefinitely, the sequence $\{1/2^n\}$ has zero for a **limit**, or $\{1/2^n\}$ *converges* to zero. Symbolically we write

$$\lim_{n \to \infty} \frac{1}{2^n} = 0. \tag{1}$$

Here the notation $n \to \infty$ means that n is increasing indefinitely through positive integral values. Equation 1 can be read *the limit of the sequence $\{1/2^n\}$ as n increases without bound is equal to zero*. Equivalently, we can state that every interval containing zero, no matter how small, contains all the terms of the sequence $\{1/2^n\}$ from some term on.

More generally we write

$$\lim_{n \to \infty} a_n = a,$$

which means that the limit of the sequence $\{a_n\}$ as $n \to \infty$ is the number a. That is, every interval containing a contains all the terms of the sequence $\{a_n\}$ from some term on. For n sufficiently large, a_n is arbitrarily close to a.

Not every sequence has a limit. For example, the terms of the sequence $\{n^2\} = 1, 4, 9, \ldots$ increase without bound as $n \to \infty$, so the sequence has no limit. We denote this situation by writing

$$\lim_{n \to \infty} n^2 = \infty,$$

which can be read *as n increases without bound, the terms of the sequence $\{n^2\}$ increase without bound*. The use of the "equals" sign in this situation does not mean that the limit exists. On the contrary, the symbolism here (∞) is a way of saying specifically that there is no limit and it indicates **why** there is no limit. A sequence that has a finite limit is said to **converge** or be **convergent**; otherwise, it **diverges** or is **divergent**. Thus $\{1/2^n\}$ is a convergent sequence, but $\{n^2\}$ is a divergent sequence. When a sequence converges, its limit must be unique.

example 1

The sequence

$$3, 2, -5, -5, \ldots, -5, \ldots$$

converges to -5, since *every* interval containing -5 must contain all the terms of the sequence from the third term on. For most convergent sequences, however, you may have to ignore many, perhaps a million, of the terms in the sequence before all the remaining terms lie in a given interval if the interval is quite small.

example 2

a. The terms of the arithmetic sequence $\{-5n\} = -5, -10, -15, \ldots$ decrease without bound and so the sequence diverges; that is, it has no finite limit. Symbolically, we denote this situation by writing

$$\lim_{n \to \infty} (-5n) = -\infty.$$

In fact, because of the common difference d, where $|d| > 0$, *every arithmetic progression is divergent.*

b. The sequence $\{(-1)^n\} = -1, 1, -1, 1, \ldots$ has no limit as $n \to \infty$ and hence is divergent.

example 3

The terms of the sequence

$$\left\{\frac{n+1}{n}\right\} = 2, \frac{3}{2}, \frac{4}{3}, \frac{5}{4}, \frac{6}{5}, \ldots$$

are clearly getting closer to 1 as n increases. In fact, for $n = 1000$,

$$a_{1000} = \frac{1001}{1000} = 1 + \frac{1}{1000}.$$

In Example 6 it will be shown that 1 is indeed the limit.

Without going into their proofs, we shall state some theorems on limits and illustrate their use in determining the behavior of various sequences.

THEOREM 1.

If $|r| < 1$, then $\lim_{n \to \infty} r^n = 0$. If $|r| > 1$, then $\lim_{n \to \infty} r^n$ does not exist and $\{r^n\}$ diverges.

THEOREM 2.

$\lim_{n \to \infty} c = c$, where c is a constant.

THEOREM 3.

$\lim_{n \to \infty} ca_n = c \lim_{n \to \infty} a_n$ if $\{a_n\}$ is convergent.

THEOREM 4.

If each term of a divergent sequence is multiplied by the same nonzero constant, the resulting sequence is also divergent.

---

example 4

Establish the convergence or divergence of the following sequences. In the case of convergence, find the limit.

a. $\{(-\frac{1}{2})^n\} = -\frac{1}{2}, \frac{1}{4}, -\frac{1}{8}, \ldots$.

Because $|-\frac{1}{2}| < 1$, by Theorem 1 we have

$$\lim_{n \to \infty} (-\tfrac{1}{2})^n = 0.$$

The sequence converges to 0.

b. $\{3\} = 3, 3, 3, \ldots$.

From Theorem 2, we have

$$\lim_{n \to \infty} 3 = 3.$$

The sequence converges to 3.

c. $\left\{\frac{3}{4^n}\right\}$.

Because $\frac{3}{4^n} = 3\left(\frac{1}{4}\right)^n$ and $\left|\frac{1}{4}\right| < 1$, by Theorems 3 and 1 we have

$$\lim_{n \to \infty} \frac{3}{4^n} = 3 \lim_{n \to \infty} \left(\frac{1}{4}\right)^n = 3(0) = 0.$$

d. $\{2(\frac{4}{3})^n\}$.

Because $|\frac{4}{3}| > 1$, Theorem 1 asserts that $\{(\frac{4}{3})^n\}$ diverges. By Theorem 4, $\{2(\frac{4}{3})^n\}$ also diverges. Note how the terms in the sequence increase without bound as

$n \longrightarrow \infty$:

$$\left\{2\left(\frac{4}{3}\right)^n\right\} = \frac{8}{3}, \frac{32}{9}, \frac{128}{27}, \frac{512}{81}, \ldots.$$

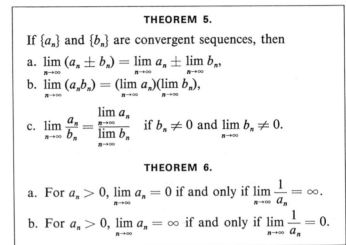

THEOREM 5.

If $\{a_n\}$ and $\{b_n\}$ are convergent sequences, then

a. $\lim\limits_{n \to \infty} (a_n \pm b_n) = \lim\limits_{n \to \infty} a_n \pm \lim\limits_{n \to \infty} b_n,$

b. $\lim\limits_{n \to \infty} (a_n b_n) = (\lim\limits_{n \to \infty} a_n)(\lim\limits_{n \to \infty} b_n),$

c. $\lim\limits_{n \to \infty} \dfrac{a_n}{b_n} = \dfrac{\lim\limits_{n \to \infty} a_n}{\lim\limits_{n \to \infty} b_n}$ if $b_n \neq 0$ and $\lim\limits_{n \to \infty} b_n \neq 0.$

THEOREM 6.

a. For $a_n > 0$, $\lim\limits_{n \to \infty} a_n = 0$ if and only if $\lim\limits_{n \to \infty} \dfrac{1}{a_n} = \infty.$

b. For $a_n > 0$, $\lim\limits_{n \to \infty} a_n = \infty$ if and only if $\lim\limits_{n \to \infty} \dfrac{1}{a_n} = 0.$

example 5

a. Because $\lim\limits_{n \to \infty} n^3 = \infty$, then by Theorem 6(b), $\lim\limits_{n \to \infty} \dfrac{1}{n^3} = 0.$

b.
$$\lim\limits_{n \to \infty} \left(2 + \frac{1}{n^3}\right) = \lim\limits_{n \to \infty} 2 + \lim\limits_{n \to \infty} \frac{1}{n^3} \qquad \text{(Theorem 5(a))}$$
$$= 2 + 0 = 2 \qquad \text{(Theorem 2 and Example 5a).}$$

example 6

Find $\lim\limits_{n \to \infty} \dfrac{n + 1}{n}.$

As $n \longrightarrow \infty$, the numerator and denominator get arbitrarily large and we say that the quotient $(n + 1)/n$ has the form ∞/∞. However, we can find the limit by first performing an algebraic operation.

$$\lim\limits_{n \to \infty} \frac{n + 1}{n} = \lim\limits_{n \to \infty} \left(\frac{n}{n} + \frac{1}{n}\right)$$
$$= \lim\limits_{n \to \infty} 1 + \lim\limits_{n \to \infty} \frac{1}{n} \qquad \text{(Theorem 5(a))}$$
$$= 1 + 0 = 1 \qquad \text{(Theorems 2 and 6(b)).}$$

Our result means that as $n \longrightarrow \infty$, the number $(n + 1)/n$ gets arbitrarily close to 1.

example 7

Find $\lim\limits_{n\to\infty} \dfrac{2n^2 + 3n}{3n^2 + 4n}$.

As $n \longrightarrow \infty$, the quotient takes on the form ∞/∞. A situation such as this can be remedied by dividing the numerator and denominator by the greatest power of n that occurs (in our case, n^2) and applying Theorem 5. We have

$$\lim_{n\to\infty} \frac{2n^2 + 3n}{3n^2 + 4n} = \lim_{n\to\infty} \frac{\dfrac{2n^2 + 3n}{n^2}}{\dfrac{3n^2 + 4n}{n^2}}$$

$$= \lim_{n\to\infty} \frac{2 + \dfrac{3}{n}}{3 + \dfrac{4}{n}}$$

$$= \frac{\lim\limits_{n\to\infty} \left(2 + \dfrac{3}{n}\right)}{\lim\limits_{n\to\infty} \left(3 + \dfrac{4}{n}\right)} \qquad \text{(Theorem 5(c))}$$

$$= \frac{\lim\limits_{n\to\infty} 2 + 3 \lim\limits_{n\to\infty} \dfrac{1}{n}}{\lim\limits_{n\to\infty} 3 + 4 \lim\limits_{n\to\infty} \dfrac{1}{n}} \qquad \text{(Theorems 5(a) and 3)}$$

$$= \frac{2 + 0}{3 + 0} = \frac{2}{3} \qquad \text{(Theorems 2 and 6(b))}.$$

example 8

Find $\lim\limits_{n\to\infty} \dfrac{2n^2}{n^3 + 1}$

The quotient has the form ∞/∞ as $n \longrightarrow \infty$.

$$\lim_{n\to\infty} \frac{2n^2}{n^3 + 1} = \lim_{n\to\infty} \frac{\dfrac{2n^2}{n^3}}{\dfrac{n^3 + 1}{n^3}} = \lim_{n\to\infty} \frac{\dfrac{2}{n}}{1 + \dfrac{1}{n^3}}$$

$$= \frac{2 \lim\limits_{n\to\infty} \dfrac{1}{n}}{\lim\limits_{n\to\infty} 1 + \lim\limits_{n\to\infty} \dfrac{1}{n^3}}$$

$$= \frac{2 \cdot 0}{1 + 0} = \frac{0}{1} = 0.$$

Our approach to the concept of a limit has been intuitive and is in no way rigorous. However, because the limit concept is fundamental in mathematics and lies at the very foundation of higher mathematics, you should have some "feeling" for this notion.

Exercise 19-4

Find the following limits. In the case of divergence, so state.

1. $\lim\limits_{n\to\infty} (2n)$.

2. $\lim\limits_{n\to\infty} (3n + 4)$.

3. $\lim\limits_{n\to\infty} \left(\dfrac{6}{n}\right)$.

4. $\lim\limits_{n\to\infty} (7 + \tfrac{1}{3})$.

5. $\lim\limits_{n\to\infty} (3 - \tfrac{1}{4})$.

6. $\lim\limits_{n\to\infty} \left(\dfrac{-6}{n}\right)$.

7. $\lim\limits_{n\to\infty} (\tfrac{3}{4})^n$.

8. $\lim\limits_{n\to\infty} (\tfrac{17}{16})^n$.

9. $\lim\limits_{n\to\infty} [3(\tfrac{1}{2})^n]$.

10. $\lim\limits_{n\to\infty} \left(\dfrac{n+1}{2n}\right)$.

11. $\lim\limits_{n\to\infty} \left(\dfrac{3n-1}{2n}\right)$.

12. $\lim\limits_{n\to\infty} \left(1 + \dfrac{n-1}{n}\right)$.

13. $\lim\limits_{n\to\infty} \left(\dfrac{n+3}{4-n}\right)$.

14. $\lim\limits_{n\to\infty} \left(\dfrac{n^2-n+1}{2n^2}\right)$.

15. $\lim\limits_{n\to\infty} \left[\dfrac{1}{5}\left(\dfrac{7}{4}\right)^n\right]$.

16. $\lim\limits_{n\to\infty} \left[8\left(\dfrac{1}{3^n}\right)\right]$.

17. $\lim\limits_{n\to\infty} \dfrac{(100)^n}{(101)^n}$.

18. $\lim\limits_{n\to\infty} \left(\dfrac{3n^2+2n+5}{4n^2}\right)$.

19. $\lim\limits_{n\to\infty} \left(\dfrac{2n^4-6n^2+5}{n^5}\right)$.

20. $\lim\limits_{n\to\infty} \dfrac{8n^5-6n^4+3n^3+1}{n^6-4n^3+1}$.

19-5   The Infinite Geometric Series

If we are given a series $\sum\limits_{n=1}^{\infty} a_n$, then the sum of its first n terms is called the **nth partial sum** of the series and is denoted by S_n:

$$S_1 = a_1,$$
$$S_2 = a_1 + a_2 = S_1 + a_2,$$
$$S_3 = a_1 + a_2 + a_3 = S_2 + a_3,$$

.
.
.

$$S_n = a_1 + a_2 + \cdots + a_n = S_{n-1} + a_n,$$

where S_1 is the first partial sum, S_2 the second partial sum, and so on. Observe that $S_2 = S_1 + a_2$, $S_3 = S_2 + a_3, \ldots, S_n = S_{n-1} + a_n$, and $S_n = \sum\limits_{k=1}^{n} a_k$. The sequence

$$\{S_n\} = S_1, S_2, S_3, \ldots, S_n, \ldots,$$

is called the **sequence of partial sums** of the series.

example 1

Determine the first four terms of the sequence of partial sums for the series $\sum\limits_{n=1}^{\infty} \dfrac{1}{n(n+1)}$.

$$S_1 = \frac{1}{1(1+1)} = \frac{1}{2},$$

$$S_2 = S_1 + \frac{1}{2(2+1)} = \frac{1}{2} + \frac{1}{6} = \frac{2}{3},$$

$$S_3 = S_2 + \frac{1}{3(4)} = \frac{2}{3} + \frac{1}{12} = \frac{3}{4},$$

$$S_4 = S_3 + \frac{1}{4(5)} = \frac{3}{4} + \frac{1}{20} = \frac{4}{5}.$$

Thus $\{S_n\} = \dfrac{1}{2}, \dfrac{2}{3}, \dfrac{3}{4}, \dfrac{4}{5}, \ldots$.

If the sequence $\{S_n\}$ of partial sums of the series $\sum\limits_{n=1}^{\infty} a_n$ converges to a finite number L, this limit is defined to be the *sum* of the series. That is,

$$\sum_{n=1}^{\infty} a_n = \lim_{n \to \infty} S_n = L.$$

In this case $\sum\limits_{n=1}^{\infty} a_n$ is said to be **convergent** to L, or to **converge**. This means that by adding up a sufficient number of terms of the series, we can approach L as arbitrarily closely as we wish. If $\lim\limits_{n \to \infty} S_n$ does not exist, the series is said to **diverge** or be **divergent**.

We shall now determine the sum of the infinite geometric series

$$\sum_{n=1}^{\infty} a_1 r^{n-1} = a_1 + a_1 r + a_1 r^2 + \cdots + a_1 r^{n-1} + \cdots, \qquad \text{where } a_1 \neq 0^*.$$

The nth partial sum, S_n, is

$$S_n = a_1 + a_1 r + a_1 r^2 + \cdots + a_1 r^{n-1}$$

and was previously found to be

$$S_n = \frac{a_1(1 - r^n)}{1 - r}.$$

The limit of S_n as $n \to \infty$ is now considered for the possible values of r.

If $|r| < 1$, then by Theorem 1, $\lim\limits_{n \to \infty} r^n = 0$ and

*If $a_1 = 0$, then the series is $0 + 0 + \cdots + 0 + \cdots$. We shall not consider this uninteresting case.

$$\lim_{n \to \infty} S_n = \lim_{n \to \infty} \frac{a_1(1 - r^n)}{1 - r} = \frac{a_1}{1 - r}.$$

Thus if $|r| < 1$, the geometric series converges to the sum $a_1/(1 - r)$. But if $|r| > 1$, then $\lim_{n \to \infty} r^n$ does not exist and so neither does $\lim_{n \to \infty} S_n$. If $r = 1$, then

$$S_n = a_1 + a_1 + \cdots + a_1 = na_1,$$

which has no limit as $n \to \infty$. If $r = -1$, then

$$S_n = a_1 - a_1 + a_1 - a_1 + \cdots + (\pm a_1).$$

This is zero if n is even and is a_1 if n is odd. Hence the series diverges, because a limit of a sequence must be unique. In summary, we have:

The geometric series $\sum_{n=1}^{\infty} a_1 r^{n-1}$ converges if $|r| < 1$ and diverges if $|r| \geq 1$. If the series is convergent, its sum S is given by

$$S = \frac{a_1}{1 - r}.$$

---

example 2

Test the following series for convergence or divergence. In the case of convergence, find the sum.

a. $\sum_{n=1}^{\infty} 8(\frac{1}{2})^n = 4 + 2 + 1 + \frac{1}{2} + \cdots$.

The series is geometric with $a_1 = 4$ and $r = \frac{1}{2}$. Because $|r| < 1$, the series converges and the sum is

$$\frac{a_1}{1 - r} = \frac{4}{1 - \frac{1}{2}} = 8.$$

b. $6 - 1 + \frac{1}{6} - \frac{1}{36} + \cdots = \sum_{n=1}^{\infty} 6(-\frac{1}{6})^{n-1}$.

The series is geometric with $a_1 = 6$ and $r = -\frac{1}{6}$. Because $|-\frac{1}{6}| < 1$, the series converges and the sum is

$$\frac{6}{1 - (-\frac{1}{6})} = \frac{36}{7}.$$

c. $\sum_{n=1}^{\infty} 4(\frac{5}{3})^n$.

The series is geometric with $|r| = \frac{5}{3} > 1$ and hence diverges.

d. $\sum_{n=1}^{\infty} \frac{1}{4^n} = \frac{1}{4} + \frac{1}{16} + \frac{1}{64} + \cdots$.

The series is geometric with $a_1 = \frac{1}{4}$ and $r = \frac{1}{4}$. Since $|r| < 1$, the series converges and the sum is

$$\frac{\frac{1}{4}}{1 - \frac{1}{4}} = \frac{1}{3}.$$

example 3

The pendulum discussed in Sec. 19-4 had an initial swing of $\frac{1}{2}$ m; the length of any subsequent swing was one-half the length of the previous swing. How far did the tip of the pendulum move before coming to rest?

We showed that the sequence whose terms give the lengths of the swings is

$$\left\{ \frac{1}{2^n} \right\} = \frac{1}{2^1}, \frac{1}{2^2}, \frac{1}{2^3}, \frac{1}{2^4}, \cdots.$$

The corresponding geometric series is

$$\frac{1}{2} + \frac{1}{4} + \frac{1}{8} + \cdots \frac{1}{2^n} + \cdots.$$

Here $a_1 = \frac{1}{2}$ and $r = \frac{1}{2}$ and, hence,

$$S = \frac{\frac{1}{2}}{1 - \frac{1}{2}} = 1 \text{ m}.$$

example 4

Determine the rational number that corresponds to the repeating decimal $0.\overline{123}$.

The line above the digits 123 is called a **vinculum** and indicates those digits that repeat. Hence,

$$0.\overline{123} = 0.123123123\ldots$$

$$= 0.123 + 0.000123 + 0.000000123 + \cdots.$$

Thus the repeating decimal has been expressed as an infinite geometric series with $a_1 = 0.123$ and $r = 0.001$. Therefore

$$S = \frac{0.123}{1 - 0.001} = \frac{0.123}{0.999} = \frac{123}{999} = \frac{41}{333}.$$

That is $0.\overline{123} = 41/333$.

Exercise 19-5

In Problems 1–24, find the sum of the series if the sum exists.

1. $\displaystyle\sum_{n=1}^{\infty} (\tfrac{1}{2})^n.$

2. $\displaystyle\sum_{n=1}^{\infty} (\tfrac{3}{4})^n.$

3. $\displaystyle\sum_{n=1}^{\infty} (-\tfrac{2}{3})^n.$

4. $\sum\limits_{n=1}^{\infty} (1.2)^n$.

5. $\sum\limits_{n=1}^{\infty} \left(\frac{7}{6}\right)^n$.

6. $\sum\limits_{n=1}^{\infty} 4\left(\frac{1}{1.1}\right)^n$.

7. $\sum\limits_{k=3}^{\infty} (\frac{3}{5})^{k+2}$.

8. $\sum\limits_{i=5}^{\infty} (-\frac{4}{9})^i$.

9. $\sum\limits_{n=1}^{\infty} 3(-0.2)^n$.

10. $\sum\limits_{n=1}^{\infty} 3(1 - \frac{1}{3})^n$.

11. $\sum\limits_{n=1}^{\infty} 100\left(\frac{1}{4^n}\right)$.

12. $\sum\limits_{n=1}^{\infty} \frac{1}{4}(3^n)$.

13. $\sum\limits_{n=1}^{2} (\frac{1}{3})^n$.

14. $\sum\limits_{n=1}^{\infty} \frac{9}{4}(\frac{4}{9})^{n+3}$.

15. $3 + \frac{3}{2} + \frac{3}{4} + \cdots$.

16. $4 + 1 + \frac{1}{4} + \cdots$.

17. $12 + 4 + \frac{4}{3} + \cdots$.

18. $\frac{1}{1.2} + \frac{1}{(1.2)^2} + \frac{1}{(1.2)^3} + \cdots$.

19. $-4 + 2 - 1 + \cdots$.

20. $100 - 10 + 1 - 0.1 + \cdots$.

21. $\frac{5}{3} + \frac{1}{6} + \frac{1}{60} + \cdots$.

22. $\frac{3}{4} + \frac{3}{4^2} + \frac{3}{4^3} + \cdots$.

23. $\frac{1}{0.1} + \frac{1}{(0.1)^2} + \frac{1}{(0.1)^3} + \cdots$.

24. $0.02 + 0.002 + 0.0002 + \cdots$.

In Problems 21–26, determine the rational number that is represented by the given repeating decimal.

25. $0.\overline{24}$

26. $0.\overline{42}$

27. $3.\overline{212}$

28. $2.0\overline{46}$

29. $0.021\overline{32}$

30. $0.15\overline{6}$

31. When dropped from a height of 4 m, a ball after the first bounce reaches a height of 2 m, after the second bounce a height of 1 m, and so on. What is the total distance traveled by the ball before coming to rest?

32. The tip of a pendulum moves through a distance of 6 cm, after which the distance is constantly decreased on each swing by 10 percent. Before coming to rest, through what total distance has the tip moved?

33. The first oscillation of a mass suspended on a vertical spring is 20 cm long. If it is observed that the length of each succeeding oscillation decreases by 20 percent, how far does the mass travel before coming to rest?

34. When a motor is turned off, a flywheel attached to the motor is observed to "coast" to a stop. In the first second it made 190 revolutions, and in each succeeding second it made nine-tenths as many revolutions as the preceding second. How many revolutions did the flywheel make before coming to rest?

35. When a small object is projected up an inclined plane, it is observed to move 10 m in the first second and in any succeeding second it moves four-fifths as far as it did in the preceding second. How far does it travel before coming to rest?

36. The midpoints of the sides of a 10-cm square are joined to form an inscribed square, and this process is continued without end. Find the sum of the areas of all the squares including the original one.

In this section we shall develop a formula that gives the series of terms obtained by finding the product or *expansion* of $(a + b)^n$. By using direct multiplication, we can find some positive integral powers of the binomial $a + b$.

$$(a + b)^2 = a^2 + 2ab + b^2.$$
$$(a + b)^3 = a^3 + 3a^2b + 3ab^2 + b^3.$$
$$(a + b)^4 = a^4 + 4a^3b + 6a^2b^2 + 4ab^3 + b^4.$$

Looking at our results, we can point out similarities in the expansion of $(a + b)^n$ for $n = 2, 3, 4$.

1. The expansion has $n + 1$ terms. For example, in $(a + b)^4$ we have $n = 4$ and the expansion has five terms.

2. The first term is a^n and the last term is b^n.

3. As we move from one term to the next, the exponent for a successively *decreases* by 1 (from n to 1). From the second term on, the exponent for b successively *increases* by 1 (from 1 to n).

4. In each term involving a and b, the sum of the exponents for a and b is n. For example, the second term in the expansion of $(a + b)^4$ contains a^3b^1, and $3 + 1 = 4 = n$.

5. In any term involving b, the exponent for b is one less than the number of the term. For example, the *third* term for $(a + b)^4$ contains b^2, and $2 = 3 - 1$.

We can also find a pattern for the coefficients of the terms in the above expansions of $(a + b)^n$. If the coefficient of any term is multiplied by the exponent for a in that term and then divided by the number of that term, the result is the coefficient of the next term. For example, the first term in the expansion of $(a + b)^4$ is $a^4 = 1 \cdot a^4$. Multiplying the coefficient 1 by the exponent of a (4) and dividing by the number of the term (1), we obtain

$$\frac{1 \cdot 4}{1} = \frac{4}{1},$$

which is the coefficient 4 of the second term. Continuing in this manner, we have

$$(a + b)^4 = a^4 + \frac{4}{1}a^3b + \frac{4}{1} \cdot \frac{3}{2}a^2b^2 + \frac{4}{1} \cdot \frac{3}{2} \cdot \frac{2}{3}ab^3 + b^4 \qquad (1)$$

$$= a^4 + 4a^3b + 6a^2b^2 + 4ab^3 + b^4.$$

In Eq. 1, note that the numerator of the term in which the exponent for b is 2 contains the *two* factors $4 \cdot 3$, and the denominator contains the *two* factors $1 \cdot 2$.

Similarly, the numerator of the term in which the exponent for b is 3 contains the *three* factors $4 \cdot 3 \cdot 2$, and the denominator contains the *three* factors $1 \cdot 2 \cdot 3$. Both of these denominators consist of the product of consecutive positive integers and are usually represented by *factorial notation*. If n is a positive integer, then the symbol $n!$, read *n factorial*, represents the product of the first n positive integers:

$$n! = n(n-1)(n-2)(n-3) \cdots (2)(1).$$

For example,

$$3! = 3 \cdot 2 \cdot 1 = 6$$
$$4! = 4 \cdot 3 \cdot 2 \cdot 1 = 4 \cdot 3! = 4(6) = 24.$$

We define $0!$ to be 1. Using factorial notation, we can express the term involving b^r in the expansion of $(a+b)^n$ as

$$\frac{\overbrace{n(n-1)(n-2) \cdots (n-r+1)}^{r \text{ factors}} a^{n-r} b^r}{r!}.$$

All the patterns that we have observed carry over to the expansion of $(a+b)^n$, where n is *any* positive integer. In summary we have the **binomial theorem:**

BINOMIAL THEOREM

If n is a positive integer, then

$$(a+b)^n = a^n + \frac{n}{1!}a^{n-1}b + \frac{n(n-1)}{2!}a^{n-2}b^2 + \cdots +$$
$$\frac{n(n-1)(n-2) \cdots (n-r+1)}{r!}a^{n-r}b^r + \cdots + b^n.$$

---

example 1

Use the binomial theorem to expand $(x+2)^5$.

We replace a by x, b by 2, and n by 5. The expansion will have six terms.

$$(x+2)^5$$
$$= x^5 + \frac{5}{1!}x^4(2) + \frac{5 \cdot 4}{2!}x^3(2)^2 + \frac{5 \cdot 4 \cdot 3}{3!}x^2(2)^3 + \frac{5 \cdot 4 \cdot 3 \cdot 2}{4!}x(2)^4 + (2)^5.$$

This simplifies to

$$(x+2)^5 = x^5 + 10x^4 + 40x^3 + 80x^2 + 80x + 32.$$

example 2

Write the first four terms in the expansion of $(a + b)^{20}$.

Using the binomial theorem with $n = 20$ gives

$$(a + b)^{20} = a^{20} + \frac{20}{1!}a^{19}b + \frac{20 \cdot 19}{2!}a^{18}b^2 + \frac{20 \cdot 19 \cdot 18}{3!}a^{17}b^3 + \cdots$$

$$= a^{20} + 20a^{19}b + 190a^{18}b^2 + 1140a^{17}b^3 + \cdots.$$

example 3

Expand $(3x^2 - 1)^4$.

Noting that $(3x^2 - 1)^4 = [3x^2 + (-1)]^4$, we use the binomial theorem with $a = 3x^2$, $b = -1$, and $n = 4$.

$(3x^2 - 1)^4$

$$= (3x^2)^4 + \frac{4}{1!}(3x^2)^3(-1) + \frac{4 \cdot 3}{2!}(3x^2)^2(-1)^2 + \frac{4 \cdot 3 \cdot 2}{3!}(3x^2)(-1)^3 + (-1)^4$$

$$= 3^4x^8 + 4(3)^3x^6(-1) + 6(3)^2x^4(1) + 4(3)x^2(-1) + 1$$

$$= 81x^8 - 108x^6 + 54x^4 - 12x^2 + 1.$$

example 4

Find the sixth term in the expansion of $\left(x + \frac{2}{y}\right)^{15}$.

Here x plays the role of a, $2/y$ plays the role of b, and $n = 15$. In the sixth term, the exponent for $2/y$ is 5, so the exponent for x is 10. The numerator of the coefficient consists of five decreasing factors beginning with 15, and the denominator is 5! This gives

$$\frac{(15)(14)(13)(12)(11)}{5!}x^{10}\left(\frac{2}{y}\right)^5,$$

which simplifies to

$$\frac{96,096x^{10}}{y^5}.$$

Setting $a = 1$ and $b = x$ in the binomial theorem, we obtain the **binomial series**

$$(1 + x)^n = 1 + nx + \frac{n(n - 1)}{2!}x^2 + \cdots + \frac{n(n - 1) \cdots (n - r + 1)}{r!}x^r + \cdots,$$

which for $|x| < 1$ can be shown to be a valid equation for **any real number n**. When n is not a positive integer, the series is unending, but nevertheless we can get a reasonable approximation to $(1 + x)^n$ in most cases by considering a few terms only.

example 5

Write the first four terms of $(1 + x)^{-2}$.

$$(1 + x)^{-2} = 1 + (-2)x + \frac{(-2)(-3)}{2!}x^2 + \frac{(-2)(-3)(-4)}{3!}x^3 + \cdots$$

$$= 1 - 2x + 3x^2 - 4x^3 + \cdots.$$

example 6

Approximate $\sqrt{104}$ to three decimal places by using the binomial series.

We can write

$$\sqrt{104} = \sqrt{100 + 4} = \sqrt{100(1 + \tfrac{4}{100})}$$

$$= 10(1 + \tfrac{1}{25})^{1/2}.$$

Because $|\tfrac{1}{25}| < 1$, we can use the binomial series with $x = \tfrac{1}{25}$ and $n = \tfrac{1}{2}$:

$$\sqrt{104} = 10\left[1 + \frac{1}{2}\left(\frac{1}{25}\right) + \frac{\tfrac{1}{2}(-\tfrac{1}{2})}{2!}\left(\frac{1}{25}\right)^2 + \cdots\right]$$

$$= 10\left(1 + \frac{1}{50} - \frac{1}{5000} + \cdots\right)$$

$$= 10(1 + 0.02 - 0.0002 + \cdots)$$

$$\approx 10(1.0198).$$

$$\sqrt{104} \approx 10.198.$$

Considering more terms in this series would not have contributed to the accuracy of the desired approximation. Compare our answer to that obtained with a calculator.

Exercise 19-6

In Problems 1–12, use the binomial theorem to expand each expression and simplify.

1. $(x + 4)^3$.   **2.** $(x - 3)^3$.   **3.** $(y - 2)^4$.

4. $(y + 3)^5$.   **5.** $(3x + 1)^5$.   **6.** $(x + h)^6$.

7. $(2z - y)^4$.   **8.** $(z^2 - 2)^3$.   **9.** $\left(a - \dfrac{1}{b}\right)^5$.

10. $(x - 2y)^6$.   **11.** $\left(1 + \dfrac{x}{y^2}\right)^6$.   **12.** $\left(\dfrac{x}{y} + \dfrac{y}{x}\right)^4$.

In Problems **13–20,** *find the first three terms in the binomial expansion of each expression and simplify.*

13. $(x + 1)^{100}$. **14.** $(x - 1)^{45}$. **15.** $(2x - 3)^7$.

16. $(x + 2)^8$. **17.** $(y^2 - 5x)^{10}$. **18.** $(y^3 - 6)^{12}$.

19. $\left(3z^2 + \dfrac{x}{3}\right)^5$. **20.** $(a^2 + b^2)^{20}$.

In Problems **21–28,** *find only the indicated term(s) and simplify.*

21. The fourth term of $(x + y)^{15}$. **22.** The fifth term of $(\frac{1}{2}x - y)^{10}$.

23. The sixth term of $\left(2x - \dfrac{3}{y}\right)^8$. **24.** The fourth term of $\left(\dfrac{1}{x^2} - y\right)^7$.

25. The middle term of $(x - 2y)^6$. **26.** The middle terms of $\left(\dfrac{1}{x} + \dfrac{1}{y}\right)^5$.

27. The term involving x^6 in $(x^3 - y)^5$.

28. The term involving x^8 in $(2y - 3x^2)^7$.

In Problems **29–32,** *find the first four terms in the expansion of the given expression and simplify.*

29. $(1 + x)^{-3}$. **30.** $(1 + x)^{2/3}$.

31. $(1 - y)^{1/2}$. **32.** $(1 - x)^{1/4}$.

In Problems **33–40,** *approximate the given number to three decimal places by using the binomial series.*

33. $\sqrt{50}$. **34.** $\sqrt{26}$. **35.** $\sqrt{61}$. **36.** $\sqrt{99}$.

37. $\sqrt[3]{29}$. **38.** $\sqrt[3]{66}$. **39.** $\sqrt[4]{80}$. **40.** $(1.02)^{-4}$.

19-7 Review

Review Questions

1. An infinite sequence is a function whose domain is the set of _____.

2. The sixth term of the sequence $\left\{(-1)^{n+1}\dfrac{2n}{n+1}\right\}$ is _____.

3. The sequence $\frac{1}{2}, \frac{2}{4}, \frac{3}{8}, \ldots$ has a general term given by _____.

4. The sequence $-6, 2, 10, \ldots$ is a(n) _____(a)_____ progression whose _____(b)_____ is 8.

5. For an arithmetic progression, the nth term is given by the formula _____(a)_____ and the sum of the first n terms is given by the formula _____(b)_____.

6. For a geometric progression, the nth term is given by the formula _____(a)_____ and the sum of the first n terms is given by the formula _____(b)_____.

7. The sixth term of the series $\sum\limits_{i=1}^{10} (-1)^{i+1} x^{2i}$ is _____.

8. As n increases without bound, the sequence $\{1/n\}$ converges to _____.

9. The limit of any arithmetic progression with difference $d \neq 0$ _(does)(does not)_ exist.

10. $\sum\limits_{n=1}^{\infty} r^n$ converges if _____.

11. The last term of $(a + 2b)^{19}$ is _____.

12. True or false: For a sequence to have the number 2 as a limit, all the terms from some point on must be equal to 2. _____

13. The sequence $4, -4, 4, -4, \ldots$ _(does)(does not)_ converge.

14. For what value(s) of a does the sequence $a, -a, a, -a, \ldots$ converge? _____

15. The sum of the geometric series $2 + 1 + \frac{1}{2} + \cdots$ is _____.

16. The value of $4!$ is _____.

17. The number of terms in the expansion of $(4x - 1)^8$ is _____.

18. The geometric sequence $1, 1 + r, (1 + r)^2, (1 + r)^3$ has a common ratio of _____.

Answers to Review Questions

1. Positive integers.   **2.** $-\frac{12}{7}$.   **3.** $n/2^n$.   **4.** (a) Arithmetic,   (b) Common difference.
5. (a) $a_n = a_1 + (n - 1)d$,   (b) $S_n = n(a_1 + a_n)/2$.
6. (a) $a_n = a_1 r^{n-1}$,   (b) $S_n = a_1(1 - r^n)/(1 - r)$.   **7.** $-x^{12}$.   **8.** 0.   **9.** Does not.
10. $|r| < 1$.   **11.** $2^{19}b^{19}$.   **12.** False (to see this, consider the counterexample $\{2 - 1/n\}$).
13. Does not.   **14.** $a = 0$.   **15.** 4.   **16.** 24.   **17.** 9.   **18.** $1 + r$.

Review Problems

1. Find the tenth term of the arithmetic progression $3, 8, 13, \ldots$.

2. Find the sixth term of the geometric progression $12, -3, \frac{3}{4}, \ldots$.

3. Write the first three terms of $\sum\limits_{n=2}^{\infty} (n^2 - n)$.

4. Find the sum $\sum\limits_{n=1}^{4} (2n + n^2)$.

5. Find the sum $1 + \frac{1}{2} + (\frac{1}{2})^2 + \cdots + (\frac{1}{2})^6$.

6. Find the sum $1 + 3 + 5 + 7 + \cdots + 33$.

In Problems 7–10, find the limits, if they exist.

7. $\lim\limits_{n \to \infty} \dfrac{2}{n^2}$.

8. $\lim\limits_{n \to \infty} \left(\dfrac{3}{2}\right)^n$.

9. $\lim\limits_{n \to \infty} \dfrac{6n^2 + 5n}{1 - 2n^2}$.

10. $\lim\limits_{n \to \infty} \dfrac{4n^2 + 2n + 5}{n^3 + 4n}$.

In Problems **11–14,** *use the binomial theorem to expand each expression.*

11. $(x - 4)^4$.

12. $(2x + 1)^5$.

13. $(x^3 + 2y)^3$.

14. $\left(1 - \dfrac{x}{3}\right)^6$.

15. Find the sum of all integers between 29 and 124 that are divisible by 6.

16. How many terms of $-16, -12, -8, \ldots$ must be added to give a sum of 44?

17. Express $0.2\overline{32}$ as a rational number in fractional form.

18. The twelfth term and twenty-third term of an arithmetic progression are -12 and 20, respectively. Find the sixteenth term.

19. Find the middle term of $(2 - \frac{1}{2}x^2)^{12}$.

20. By using the binomial series, approximate $\sqrt[3]{124}$ to three decimal places.

21. Find $\sum\limits_{k=1}^{\infty} (\frac{4}{9})^k$.

22. In the series $1 + \frac{1}{2} + \frac{1}{4} + \cdots$, what is the numerical difference between the nth partial sum and the limit of the nth partial sum?

23. The sum of an infinite geometric series is 6 and the first term is 2. What is the second term?

24. The value of the fifth term in the expansion of $(a + 2)^5$ is 48 for a particular value of a. Find this value.

25. A ball is released from an initial height of 8 m and it is observed that after each contact with the floor the ball rebounds to a height equal to three-fourths of the height from which it last fell. What height does the ball reach on its fifth bounce?

26. For the ball of Problem 25, what total distance does it travel before coming to rest?

the scientific calculator

A

A-1 Introduction

Many of the numerical calculations required in this text can be performed with the simplest type of calculator available. However, the more complicated evaluations require the sophistication of a *scientific* calculator. In addition to the four basic arithmetic operations of addition, subtraction, multiplication, and division, a scientific calculator can handle squares, square roots, reciprocals, powers and roots, and trigonometric, inverse trigonometric, logarithmic, and exponential functions. Moreover, depending on the particular calculator model, a variety of additional features and capabilities may also be found.

The sequence of operations that allows one to perform a calculation is based, in part, on the type of logical system employed in the design of the calculator. Generally, one of two systems is used. The first is called **algebraic logic** (ALG). Most calculations done with algebraic logic can be entered just as they are stated in a given problem. For this reason the system is very easy to learn. The second logical system is called **reverse Polish notation** (RPN) in honor of Lukasiewicz, a Polish logician (1878–1956). Calculators with this logic are characterized by the absence of an equals key $\boxed{=}$. Although it may not be as easy to learn to use a calculator with this system, two advantages of RPN are the following: (1) intermediate results are displayed as they are calculated, and (2) the use of parentheses is eliminated when you are entering numbers in compound calculations. Furthermore, with RPN a complicated problem can sometimes be solved with fewer keystrokes than with ALG.

The choice of one logical system over the other, as well as choice of calculator model, is simply one of personal preference. Regardless of your choice, however, two points can be made. First, the only way to master the use of your particular calculator is to study the operator's manual that comes with it. Features and techniques of use do vary, and the manual will fully explain the capabilities of your calculator. Second, and most important, you must be aware that the ability to use a calculator does not replace your need to understand the underlying mathematical principles. After all, it is your *understanding* of the mathematics that enables you to solve a problem in the first place! Once a problem is set up, the calculator serves only to simplify the task of performing the numerical calculations.

This appendix is *not* intended to replace your calculator instruction manual. In the sections that follow, it is our purpose simply to illustrate some of the fundamental operations that can be performed with a scientific calculator. In particular, we are concerned with the type of calculations that occur throughout this text. In most numerical examples we give a *representative sequence* of key operations for both algebraic logic and reverse Polish notation. In general, these sequences apply to many calculator models. However, because wide variations in calculator logic do occur, you may find that changes in a particular sequence are necessary when using your own calculator. Although calculator displays of 8 or 10 digits are not unusual in practice, in all that follows *we shall give a rounded display* for our answers.

A-2 Data Entry and Scientific Notation

There are slight differences in the techniques for entering and displaying data in the two logical systems. Data entry with RPN logic uses an **enter key**, designated by ENTER ↑ . For convenience, we shall denote that key by ↑ . In both systems, a **change-sign key**, designated by +/− or CHS , is used to change the sign of the displayed number.

example 1

Enter the number −63.25.

ALG: 6 3 . 2 5 +/−   Display: −63.25

RPN: 6 3 . 2 5 CHS ↑   Display: −63.25

When only one number is keyed into the calculator, you do not need to use the ↑ key.

The approximate value of π can be entered directly as 3.1416. . . , or you can use the special **pi key**, designated by π , that is available on all scientific calculators. Pressing π immediately enters the value of π and it appears in the display.

The **enter-exponent** (of 10) **key**, designated by EE or EEX , is used to enter a number in scientific notation or any product, one of whose factors is a power of 10. There are two points to remember! First, the exponent for 10 is entered *after* the EE key is pressed. Second, for a negative exponent of 10, the +/− key is used *after* the exponent has been keyed in.

example 2

Enter the number 54.7×10^6.

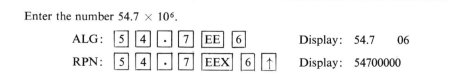

ALG: 5 4 . 7 EE 6   Display: 54.7   06

RPN: 5 4 . 7 EEX 6 ↑   Display: 54700000

If the exponent for 10 had been −6 instead of 6, then the keystroke sequence would remain the same, but the change-sign key would be pressed after the 6 is entered.

With RPN logic, you can avoid displaying a number with a string of zeros (such as in Example 2) by converting the displayed number to scientific notation display. This is done by pressing the **scientific notation key**, designated by $\boxed{\text{SCI}}$, followed by a number key. The number key specifies the number of decimal places to be retained in the display. There will, of course, be a single digit to the left of the decimal point. To change back to a standard decimal display, use the **fixed-decimal key**, designated by $\boxed{\text{FIX}}$, followed by a number key. The number key once again specifies the number of decimal places to be displayed. Some scientific calculators having ALG logic also allow the user to shift back and forth between fixed decimal and scientific notation displays. You should check the instruction manual for your calculator to see if this feature is available and, if so, how it is used.

example 3

Enter the number -6.81×10^{12}.

ALG: $\boxed{6}$ $\boxed{.}$ $\boxed{8}$ $\boxed{1}$ $\boxed{+/-}$ $\boxed{\text{EE}}$ $\boxed{1}$ $\boxed{2}$ Display: −6.81   12

RPN: $\boxed{6}$ $\boxed{.}$ $\boxed{8}$ $\boxed{1}$ $\boxed{\text{CHS}}$ $\boxed{\text{EE}}$ $\boxed{1}$ $\boxed{2}$ $\boxed{\uparrow}$ Display: −6.8100000   12

$\boxed{\text{SCI}}$ $\boxed{2}$ Display: −6.81   12

Throughout the rest of this appendix, we shall use a compact notation in which a number in a box represents a keystroke sequence. For example, $\boxed{12.3}$ represents the keystrokes $\boxed{1}$ $\boxed{2}$ $\boxed{.}$ $\boxed{3}$.

A-3 Arithmetic Operations

The four basic arithmetic operations are performed with the use of the four function keys designated by $\boxed{+}$, $\boxed{-}$, $\boxed{\times}$, and $\boxed{\div}$. With RPN logic, the result is displayed immediately after one of the four function keys is pressed; no $\boxed{=}$ key is needed as it is with ALG. In RPN, a function such as subtraction is executed as soon as the subtraction function key is pressed. The two numbers in the subtraction are essentially positioned or stacked *before* performing the subtraction. The numbers are separated by the use of the $\boxed{\uparrow}$ key.

example 1

Evaluate $17.2 - 6.9$.

ALG: $\boxed{17.2}$ $\boxed{-}$ $\boxed{6.9}$ $\boxed{=}$ Display: 10.30

RPN: $\boxed{17.2}$ $\boxed{\uparrow}$ $\boxed{6.9}$ $\boxed{-}$ Display: 10.30

Chain calculations pose unique situations because the way they are handled depends on the particular logic used in the calculator. *You must check the specific instructions in your owner's manual to learn how to use your calculator!* With ALG logic you may be able to use **parentheses keys**, designated by $\boxed{(}$ and $\boxed{)}$, whenever there is doubt in your mind as to how the calculator will treat a given expression.

example 2

Evaluate $(6.32 + 8.45) \div \pi$.

ALG: $\boxed{(}$ $\boxed{6.32}$ $\boxed{+}$ $\boxed{8.45}$ $\boxed{)}$ $\boxed{\div}$ $\boxed{\pi}$ $\boxed{=}$ Display: 4.70

RPN: $\boxed{6.32}$ $\boxed{\uparrow}$ $\boxed{8.45}$ $\boxed{+}$ $\boxed{\pi}$ $\boxed{\div}$ Display: 4.70

If the key sequence for ALG logic in Example 2 were performed without keying in the parentheses, the expression evaluated would be $6.32 + (8.45 \div \pi) = 9.01$. This is because of the hierarchy of operations in ALG logic, in which multiplications and divisions are performed before additions and subtractions. There is another way to accomplish the calculation in Example 2. We can use the $\boxed{=}$ key to perform the addition first; in this way the parentheses are not needed at all.

ALG: $\boxed{6.32}$ $\boxed{+}$ $\boxed{8.45}$ $\boxed{=}$ $\boxed{\div}$ $\boxed{\pi}$ $\boxed{=}$ Display: 4.70

example 3

Evaluate $(6.2 \times 9.0) - (8.0 \div 3.5)$.

ALG: $\boxed{6.2}$ $\boxed{\times}$ $\boxed{9}$ $\boxed{=}$ $\boxed{-}$ $\boxed{(}$ $\boxed{8}$ $\boxed{\div}$ $\boxed{3.5}$ $\boxed{)}$ $\boxed{=}$ Display: 53.51

RPN: $\boxed{6.2}$ $\boxed{\uparrow}$ $\boxed{9}$ $\boxed{\times}$ $\boxed{8}$ $\boxed{\uparrow}$ $\boxed{3.5}$ $\boxed{\div}$ $\boxed{-}$ Display: 53.51

In the RPN sequence, note that the key operations $\boxed{8}$ $\boxed{\uparrow}$ begin the entry of a new number string; the value of 6.2×9.0 has already been stored. The final keystroke operation, $\boxed{-}$, causes the difference between the stored value of 6.2×9.0 and the value of the last number string $8.0 - 3.5$ to be displayed.

example 4

Evaluate $\dfrac{40,000 \times 15.6}{12.6 + 15.7}$.

ALG: $\boxed{40000}$ $\boxed{\times}$ $\boxed{15.6}$ $\boxed{=}$ $\boxed{\div}$ $\boxed{(}$ $\boxed{12.6}$ $\boxed{+}$ $\boxed{15.7}$ $\boxed{)}$ $\boxed{=}$ Display: 22049.47

RPN: $\boxed{40000}$ $\boxed{\uparrow}$ $\boxed{15.6}$ $\boxed{\times}$ $\boxed{12.6}$ $\boxed{\uparrow}$ $\boxed{15.7}$ $\boxed{+}$ $\boxed{\div}$ Display: 22049.47

Exercise A-3

Evaluate each expression.

1. $8.735 \div -8.23$.

2. 33.65×0.0072.

3. $(8 \times 10^{-6})(62.3)$.

4. $-82.5 \div (5.2 \times 10^{-2})$.

5. $6.23 + (8.2 - 3)$.

6. $0.076 + (4.8 - 7)$.

7. $8\pi - 16.3$.

8. $5\pi - 4.2$.

9. $6.2\pi + [8.3(2)]$.

10. $(6.02 \times 10^{-23})(1.73)$.

11. $26.1 \times 13.2 \times 0.315$.

12. $0.064 \times 7.8 \times 10^{-13} \times \pi$.

13. $\dfrac{6.27 \times 10^{13}}{15.5 \times 8.3}$.

14. $\dfrac{18\pi \times 40,000}{14.9}$.

15. $\dfrac{1}{2}\left(\dfrac{\pi}{3.6}\right)(18.4)$.

16. $\dfrac{6(-3.92)}{0.047}$.

17. $10^4 - [(82.6)(5.3)]$.

18. $\dfrac{76.4}{10^{-2} + 4}$.

19. $\dfrac{5 \times 10^{13}}{26.3 - 18.1}$.

20. $2\pi(3 \times 10^4)(2.6 \times 10^3)$.

21. $\dfrac{(-0.183)\pi}{1.47} - 6$.

22. $\dfrac{4\pi}{3}(8.2 - 16.3)$.

23. $\dfrac{(9 \times 10^9)(8 \times 10^{-6})(5 \times 10^{-6})}{3.0}$.

24. $\dfrac{(9 \times 10^9)(6.2 \times 10^{-6})(-8.4 \times 10^{-6})}{5.1}$.

25. $\dfrac{(18.3\pi)(-7.23)}{13.7 + 6.83}$.

26. $\dfrac{[(1.6 \times 10^{-5}) + (4.2 \times 10^{-5})]\pi}{1100}$.

27. $\dfrac{5\pi + 72.83 - 13}{4.28\pi - 5.17}$.

28. $\dfrac{280,000 \times 0.0000421}{0.006 \times 7,000,000}$.

Answers to Exercise A-3

1. -1.06. **2.** 0.24. **3.** 4.98×10^{-4}. **4.** -1586.54. **5.** 11.43. **6.** -2.12.
7. 8.83. **8.** 11.51. **9.** 36.08. **10.** 1.04×10^{-22}. **11.** 108.52. **12.** 1.57×10^{-13}.
13. 4.87×10^{11}. **14.** 1.52×10^{5}. **15.** 8.03. **16.** -500.43. **17.** 9562.22.
18. 19.05. **19.** 6.10×10^{12}. **20.** 4.90×10^{8}. **21.** -6.39. **22.** -33.93. **23.** 0.12.
24. -0.09. **25.** -20.25. **26.** 1.66×10^{-7}. **27.** 9.13. **28.** 2.81×10^{-4}.

A-4 Reciprocal, Square, Square Root, and Factorial

The special function keys described in this section are all one-number function keys. They operate on only *one* number—the number that is displayed by the calculator. This displayed number could be keyed in or it could be the result of a previous calculation. If x is the displayed number, then:

1. The **reciprocal key**, designated by $\boxed{1/x}$, calculates the reciprocal of x for $x \neq 0$. If $x = 0$, an error message is displayed.

2. The **square key**, designated by $\boxed{x^2}$, calculates the square of x.

3. The **square-root key**, designated by $\boxed{\sqrt{x}}$, calculates the square root of x for $x \geq 0$. If $x < 0$, an error message is displayed.

4. The **factorial key**, designated by $\boxed{x!}$ or $\boxed{n!}$, calculates the factorial of a positive integer x, where $x! = x(x - 1)(x - 2) \cdots (2)(1)$. If x is not a positive integer, an error message is displayed. An error message may also be displayed if the factorial value exceeds the computational capabilities of the calculator.

The functions above are performed without the use of the $\boxed{=}$ or $\boxed{\uparrow}$ keys, so *the keystroke sequences are generally the same for both ALG and RPN logic.* However, differences in the displays for the two systems may occur.

example 1

Find the (a) reciprocal, (b) square, and (c) square root of 48.7.

a. ALG and RPN: $\boxed{48.7}$ $\boxed{1/x}$ Display: 0.0205

b. ALG and RPN: $\boxed{48.7}$ $\boxed{x^2}$ Display: 2371.69

c. ALG and RPN: $\boxed{48.7}$ $\boxed{\sqrt{x}}$ Display: 6.98

example 2

Evaluate $\frac{5\sqrt{2}}{2}$.

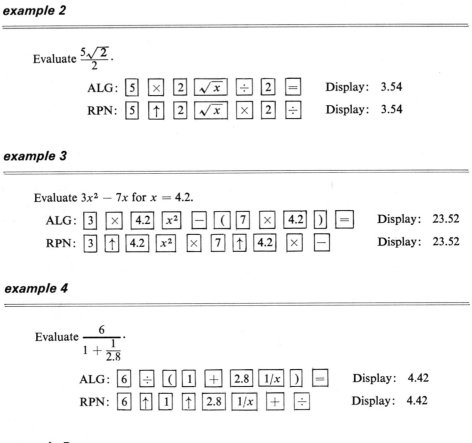

ALG: $\boxed{5}$ $\boxed{\times}$ $\boxed{2}$ $\boxed{\sqrt{x}}$ $\boxed{\div}$ $\boxed{2}$ $\boxed{=}$ Display: 3.54

RPN: $\boxed{5}$ $\boxed{\uparrow}$ $\boxed{2}$ $\boxed{\sqrt{x}}$ $\boxed{\times}$ $\boxed{2}$ $\boxed{\div}$ Display: 3.54

example 3

Evaluate $3x^2 - 7x$ for $x = 4.2$.

ALG: $\boxed{3}$ $\boxed{\times}$ $\boxed{4.2}$ $\boxed{x^2}$ $\boxed{-}$ $\boxed{(}$ $\boxed{7}$ $\boxed{\times}$ $\boxed{4.2}$ $\boxed{)}$ $\boxed{=}$ Display: 23.52

RPN: $\boxed{3}$ $\boxed{\uparrow}$ $\boxed{4.2}$ $\boxed{x^2}$ $\boxed{\times}$ $\boxed{7}$ $\boxed{\uparrow}$ $\boxed{4.2}$ $\boxed{\times}$ $\boxed{-}$ Display: 23.52

example 4

Evaluate $\dfrac{6}{1 + \dfrac{1}{2.8}}$.

ALG: $\boxed{6}$ $\boxed{\div}$ $\boxed{(}$ $\boxed{1}$ $\boxed{+}$ $\boxed{2.8}$ $\boxed{1/x}$ $\boxed{)}$ $\boxed{=}$ Display: 4.42

RPN: $\boxed{6}$ $\boxed{\uparrow}$ $\boxed{1}$ $\boxed{\uparrow}$ $\boxed{2.8}$ $\boxed{1/x}$ $\boxed{+}$ $\boxed{\div}$ Display: 4.42

example 5

Find the hypotenuse of a right triangle in which the legs have lengths of 9.2 cm and 18.6 cm.

Using the Pythagorean theorem, we have

$$c^2 = a^2 + b^2$$
$$= (9.2)^2 + (18.6)^2$$
$$c = \sqrt{(9.2)^2 + (18.6)^2}.$$

ALG: $\boxed{9.2}$ $\boxed{x^2}$ $\boxed{+}$ $\boxed{18.6}$ $\boxed{x^2}$ $\boxed{=}$ $\boxed{\sqrt{x}}$ Display: 20.75

RPN: $\boxed{9.2}$ $\boxed{x^2}$ $\boxed{18.6}$ $\boxed{x^2}$ $\boxed{+}$ $\boxed{\sqrt{x}}$ Display: 20.75

With RPN note that the intermediate result $(9.2)^2$ is automatically stored. You do not have to press the enter key to store it.

example 6

Find the surface area of a sphere of radius 1.25 m.

The surface area A of a sphere of radius r is given by

$$A = 4\pi r^2$$

$$A = 4\pi(1.25)^2.$$

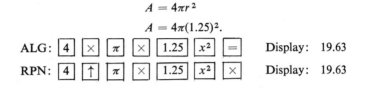

ALG: $\boxed{4}$ $\boxed{\times}$ $\boxed{\pi}$ $\boxed{\times}$ $\boxed{1.25}$ $\boxed{x^2}$ $\boxed{=}$ Display: 19.63

RPN: $\boxed{4}$ $\boxed{\uparrow}$ $\boxed{\pi}$ $\boxed{\times}$ $\boxed{1.25}$ $\boxed{x^2}$ $\boxed{\times}$ Display: 19.63

example 7

Find $\dfrac{5!}{4!\,3!}$.

ALG: $\boxed{5}$ $\boxed{x!}$ $\boxed{\div}$ $\boxed{4}$ $\boxed{x!}$ $\boxed{\div}$ $\boxed{3}$ $\boxed{x!}$ $\boxed{=}$ Display: 0.833

RPN: $\boxed{5}$ $\boxed{x!}$ $\boxed{4}$ $\boxed{x!}$ $\boxed{\div}$ $\boxed{3}$ $\boxed{x!}$ $\boxed{\div}$ Display: 0.833

Here we used the general fact that $\dfrac{a}{bc} = (a \div b) \div c$.

Exercise A-4

In Problems 1–30, perform the indicated operations.

1. $\dfrac{1}{0.01683}$.

2. $\dfrac{1}{\sqrt{137.4}}$.

3. $\dfrac{1}{3.2 \times 10^{-5}}$.

4. $5\sqrt{3}$.

5. $\dfrac{6\sqrt{17.2}}{5.1}$.

6. $(5.2)^2 + (6.3)^2$.

7. $(8.3^2 - 4.2)^2$.

8. $\left(\dfrac{1}{2.6 \times 10^{-3}}\right)^2$.

9. $4\pi(3.2)^2$.

10. $\pi(8.7)^2$.

11. $\sqrt{(8.1)^2 + (3.2)^2}$.

12. $\dfrac{(7.45 \times 10^{23})^2}{3\pi}$.

13. $\dfrac{1}{2}(6.23)^2\left(\dfrac{5.2}{3.1}\right)^2$.

14. $(15\pi)^2 + 15\pi^2$.

15. $\sqrt{6.5} - \sqrt{18}$.

16. $5\sqrt{18} - 4.6$.

17. $(3.2 + 5\pi)^2\sqrt{8.2}$.

18. $\dfrac{4 + 5\pi}{\sqrt{182}}$.

19. $\left(\dfrac{2}{\sqrt{5} - \sqrt{3}}\right)^2$.

20. $\left(\dfrac{3.6}{2\sqrt{7} - \sqrt{11}}\right)^2$.

21. $(0.032)\sqrt{(9.6)^2 - (5.2)^2}$.

22. $\left(\dfrac{1}{9\pi \times 16.2}\right)^2$.

23. $(\sqrt{13} - 3.6\pi)^2$.

24. $\dfrac{(6.02)^2 - 13.1}{\sqrt{15.2}}$.

25. $\left(\dfrac{2 + \sqrt{2}}{2 - \sqrt{2}}\right)^2$.

26. $2 + \dfrac{0.2}{4} - \dfrac{(0.2)^2}{64}$.

27. $\sqrt{3! + 5!}$.

28. $\left(\dfrac{4!}{3! \, 2!}\right)^2$.

29. $\dfrac{3 + \sqrt{(-3)^2 - 4(7)(-8)}}{2(7)}$.

30. $\dfrac{-5 - \sqrt{(5)^2 - 4(3)(-4)}}{2(3)}$.

31. $\sqrt{(6.8 - 3.7)^2 + (8.2 - 13.9)^2}$.

32. $(1.63 - 1)\left(\dfrac{1}{3.65} - \dfrac{1}{8.28}\right)$.

33. Evaluate $3(t + 2)^2$ if $t = \frac{1}{3}$.

34. Evaluate $3t^2 - 2t + 1$ if $t = 2.2$.

35. Evaluate $\sqrt{4.7t^2 - t}$ if $t = 4.58$.

Answers to Exercise A-4

1. 59.42. **2.** 0.085. **3.** 31,250. **4.** 8.66. **5.** 4.88. **6.** 66.73. **7.** 4184.80.
8. 1.48×10^5. **9.** 128.68. **10.** 237.79. **11.** 8.71. **12.** 5.89×10^{46}. **13.** 54.60.
14. 2368.71. **15.** −1.69. **16.** 16.61. **17.** 1023.76. **18.** 1.46. **19.** 15.75.
20. 3.32. **21.** 0.26. **22.** 4.77×10^{-6}. **23.** 59.35. **24.** 5.94. **25.** 33.97. **26.** 2.05.
27. 11.22. **28.** 4. **29.** 1.30. **30.** −2.26. **31.** 6.49. **32.** 0.097. **33.** 13.55.
34. 11.12. **35.** 9.70.

A-5 Powers and Roots

The **power-function key**, designated by $\boxed{y^x}$, is a two-number function key. It raises a positive number y to *any* xth power. For $y < 0$ (and on some calculators for $y \leq 0$), an error message is displayed. The keystroke sequence is slightly different for the two systems of logic. Typical sequences are

ALG: $\boxed{y}$ $\boxed{y^x}$ $\boxed{x}$ $\boxed{=}$ (The exponent is keyed in *after* the operation key.)

RPN: $\boxed{y}$ $\boxed{\uparrow}$ $\boxed{x}$ $\boxed{y^x}$ (Both numbers are keyed in *before* the operation. The $\boxed{\uparrow}$ key separates the numbers.)

example 1

Evaluate 2.6^9.

ALG: $\boxed{2.6}$ $\boxed{y^x}$ $\boxed{9}$ $\boxed{=}$ Display: 5429.50

RPN: $\boxed{2.6}$ $\boxed{\uparrow}$ $\boxed{9}$ $\boxed{y^x}$ Display: 5429.50

example 2

Find $3.94^{-1.26}$.

ALG: $\boxed{3.94}$ $\boxed{y^x}$ $\boxed{1.26}$ $\boxed{+/-}$ $\boxed{=}$ Display: 0.1777

RPN: $\boxed{3.94}$ $\boxed{\uparrow}$ $\boxed{1.26}$ $\boxed{CHS}$ $\boxed{y^x}$ Display: 0.1777

The $\boxed{y^x}$ key can be used to find roots if we use the relation

$$\sqrt[n]{y} = y^{1/n}.$$

The reciprocal key is also useful here.

example 3

Find $\sqrt[5]{138.7}$.

$$\sqrt[5]{138.7} = 138.7^{1/5}.$$

ALG: $\boxed{138.7}$ $\boxed{y^x}$ $\boxed{5}$ $\boxed{1/x}$ $\boxed{=}$ Display: 2.682

RPN: $\boxed{138.7}$ $\boxed{\uparrow}$ $\boxed{5}$ $\boxed{1/x}$ $\boxed{y^x}$ Display: 2.682

Some ALG logic calculators may have an **inverse key**, designated by $\boxed{INV}$. In such cases, roots can be obtained without the use of the reciprocal key. The keystroke sequence $\boxed{y}$ $\boxed{INV}$ $\boxed{y^x}$ $\boxed{x}$ calculates the xth root of y. Using this feature to redo Example 3, we have:

ALG: $\boxed{138.7}$ $\boxed{INV}$ $\boxed{y^x}$ $\boxed{5}$ $\boxed{=}$ Display: 2.682

The simplest and most direct method for finding roots is provided on some ALG logic calculators by a special **root key**, designated by $\boxed{\sqrt[x]{y}}$. To redo the problem of Example 3 with such a feature, the sequence is

ALG: $\boxed{138.7}$ $\boxed{\sqrt[x]{y}}$ $\boxed{5}$ $\boxed{=}$ Display: 2.682

In technical work it is often necessary to evaluate the forms 10^x and e^x, where $e = 2.7182.\ldots$. Even though these forms could be handled by the use of the power key $\boxed{y^x}$, nearly all scientific calculators have special provisions for handling them. A **natural-antilogarithm key**, designated by $\boxed{e^x}$, computes e raised to the xth power, where x is the displayed number. The exponent x may be any number. On some calculators with ALG logic, the natural antilogarithm function is accomplished by the keystroke sequence [INV] [LN]. The *natural-logarithm key* [LN] will be discussed separately in Sec. A-7.

Similarly, a **common-antilogarithm key**, designated by [10^x], computes 10 raised to the *x*th power. Alternatively, this common antilogarithm function might be accomplished by the keystroke sequence [INV] [LOG]. The *common-logarithm key* [LOG] will also be discussed in Sec. A-7.

example 4

Evaluate $2.5e^{-1.6}$.

ALG: [2.5] [×] [1.6] [+/−] [INV] [LN] [=]   Display: 0.5047

RPN: [2.5] [↑] [1.6] [CHS] [e^x] [×]   Display: 0.5047

example 5

Evaluate $-5.3(10)^{2.7}$.

ALG: [5.3] [+/−] [×] [2.7] [INV] [LOG] [=]   Display: −2656.29

RPN: [5.3] [CHS] [↑] [2.7] [10^x] [×]   Display: −2656.29

Exercise A-5

Evaluate each expression.

1. 3^5.
2. 4^7.
3. 5^{-4}.
4. 8^{-7}.
5. $(-6)^8$.
6. $(-5)^9$.
7. $10^{6.71}$.
8. $10^{-2.3}$.
9. $10^{-0.321}$.
10. e^7.
11. e^{-8}.
12. $e^{5.2}$.
13. $e^{-6.7}$.
14. $e^{\sqrt{3}}$.
15. $10^{\sqrt{6}}$.
16. $(6.32)^{1.74}$.
17. $(2.93)^{-3.4}$.
18. $(-7.6)^4$.
19. $(-8.3)^5$.
20. $(0.47)^{13.2}$.
21. $(6.2 \times 10^{-23})^4$.
22. $(7.93 \times 10^5)^{6.1}$.
23. $\sqrt[5]{13}$.
24. $\sqrt[7]{9}$.
25. $\sqrt[3]{174}$.
26. $\sqrt[3]{(18.3)^2}$.
27. $\sqrt[3]{7.23 \times 10^{19}}$.
28. $\sqrt[4]{8.6 \times 10^{-13}}$.
29. $6(10)^{2\sqrt{3}}$.
30. $\frac{4}{3}\pi(18.7)^3$.
31. $60e^{-1.5}$
32. $e^{0.63} + e^{-0.63}$.
33. $120(1 - e^{-3.2})$.
34. $\frac{160}{22}(1 - e^{-1.13})$.
35. $\frac{4}{3}\pi[(16.7)^3 - (6.2)^3]$.
36. $(1.6 \times 10^{-19})^4(1.67 \times 10^{27})^2$.

37. $\dfrac{6.27(1 - 1.03^{16})}{1 - 1.03}$.

38. $\dfrac{\sqrt[3]{7.38 \times 10^{10}} + \sqrt[5]{5.28 \times 10^{12}}}{13.3}$.

39. $\dfrac{2.6 \times 10^{-3}}{4\pi(8.85 \times 10^{-12})} \left(\dfrac{1}{7.2 \times 10^{-3}}\right)^{3/2}$.

40. $\pi(3.29 + 6.82)^5 \sqrt[3]{(7.2)^2 + (3.29 - 6.82)^2}$.

Answers to Exercise A-5

1. 243. **2.** 16,384. **3.** 1.6×10^{-3}. **4.** 4.77×10^{-7}. **5.** 1,679,616.0.
6. $-1,953,125.0$. **7.** 5,128,613.8. **8.** 0.0050. **9.** 0.478. **10.** 1096.6.
11. 3.35×10^{-4}. **12.** 181.27. **13.** 1.23×10^{-3}. **14.** 5.65. **15.** 281.51. **16.** 24.73.
17. 0.026. **18.** 3336.22. **19.** $-39,390.41$. **20.** 4.70×10^{-5}. **21.** 1.48×10^{-89}.
22. 9.67×10^{35}. **23.** 1.670. **24.** 1.369. **25.** 5.583. **26.** 6.944. **27.** 4.166×10^{6}.
28. 9.63×10^{-4}. **29.** 1.747×10^{4}. **30.** 27,391.35. **31.** 13.39. **32.** 2.41.
33. 115.11. **34.** 4.92. **35.** 18,510.83. **36.** 1.83×10^{-21}. **37.** 126.38.
38. 341.72. **39.** 3.83×10^{10}. **40.** 1.33×10^{6}.

A-6 Trigonometric and Inverse Trigonometric Functions

All scientific calculators feature special keys for finding values of trigonometric functions. These keys, designated by $\boxed{\text{SIN}}$, $\boxed{\text{COS}}$, $\boxed{\text{TAN}}$, are used to find the sine, cosine, and tangent, respectively, of the displayed number. When one of these keys is pressed, the calculator interprets the displayed number to be an angle and it determines the value of the appropriate trigonometric function. There may, however, be one necessary preliminary step. *You may have to set your calculator for the proper angular mode of operation.*

Typically, scientific calculators are capable of functioning in up to three different angular modes: degrees, radians, and grads (100 grads = 90°). The angular mode determines how the calculator "reads" the displayed number. For example, when the calculator is in the *degree* mode, it interprets the displayed number to be an angle measured in degrees. Calculators differ in the mechanical method used to set the angular mode. Your calculator may have a slide switch to change modes, it may have individual keys to set each mode, or it may have one key that, with repeated pressings, allows mode changes. In most cases, when a calculator is turned on it is in the degree mode. In all that follows we shall assume that the calculator is set in the appropriate angular mode before a trigonometric function key is used.

example 1

Evaluate (a) sin 52.7°, (b) cos $4\pi/3$, (c) tan² 70°, and (d) sec 110°.

a. ALG and RPN: $\boxed{52.7}\boxed{\text{SIN}}$ Display: 0.7955

b. ALG: $\boxed{4}$ $\boxed{\times}$ $\boxed{\pi}$ $\boxed{\div}$ $\boxed{3}$ $\boxed{=}$ $\boxed{\text{COS}}$ Display: -0.5000

  RPN: $\boxed{4}$ $\boxed{\uparrow}$ $\boxed{\pi}$ $\boxed{\times}$ $\boxed{3}$ $\boxed{\div}$ $\boxed{\text{COS}}$ Display: -0.5000

c. ALG and RPN: $\boxed{70}$ $\boxed{\text{TAN}}$ $\boxed{x^2}$ Display: 7.5486

d. Because sec 110° $= 1/(\cos 110°)$, the sequence is

ALG and RPN: $\boxed{110}$ $\boxed{\text{COS}}$ $\boxed{1/x}$ Display: -2.9238

Cosecants and cotangents of angles can also be found by using the reciprocal relations of Chapter 7.

example 2

Evaluate $\dfrac{6 \sin 26.44°}{\sin 30°}$.

This expression occurs in Example 2 of Sec. 16-1.

ALG: $\boxed{6}$ $\boxed{\times}$ $\boxed{26.44}$ $\boxed{\text{SIN}}$ $\boxed{\div}$ $\boxed{30}$ $\boxed{\text{SIN}}$ $\boxed{=}$ Display: 5.3431

RPN: $\boxed{6}$ $\boxed{\uparrow}$ $\boxed{26.44}$ $\boxed{\text{SIN}}$ $\boxed{\times}$ $\boxed{30}$ $\boxed{\text{SIN}}$ $\boxed{\div}$ Display: 5.3431

example 3

Find the value of c given that

$$c^2 = 10^2 + 40^2 - 2(10)(40) \cos 120°.$$

This equation occurs in Example 1 of Sec. 16-2. We must find the square root of the right side.

ALG: $\boxed{10}$ $\boxed{x^2}$ $\boxed{+}$ $\boxed{40}$ $\boxed{x^2}$ $\boxed{-}$ $\boxed{(}$ $\boxed{2}$ $\boxed{\times}$ $\boxed{10}$ $\boxed{\times}$ $\boxed{40}$ $\boxed{\times}$ $\boxed{120}$ $\boxed{\text{COS}}$ $\boxed{)}$ $\boxed{=}$ $\boxed{\sqrt{x}}$

Display: 45.8258

RPN: $\boxed{10}$ $\boxed{x^2}$ $\boxed{40}$ $\boxed{x^2}$ $\boxed{+}$ $\boxed{2}$ $\boxed{\uparrow}$ $\boxed{10}$ $\boxed{\times}$ $\boxed{40}$ $\boxed{\times}$ $\boxed{120}$ $\boxed{\text{COS}}$ $\boxed{\times}$ $\boxed{-}$ $\boxed{\sqrt{x}}$

Display: 45.8258

All scientific calculators are capable of determining an angle θ whose trigonometric value is shown in à display. Typically this is done by using the **inverse-trigonometric keys** designated $\boxed{\text{SIN}^{-1}}$, $\boxed{\text{COS}^{-1}}$, and $\boxed{\text{TAN}^{-1}}$. On some calculators a key sequence $\boxed{\text{INV}}$ $\boxed{\text{SIN}}$, $\boxed{\text{INV}}$ $\boxed{\text{COS}}$, or $\boxed{\text{INV}}$ $\boxed{\text{TAN}}$ is used instead. The inverse sine function, $\sin^{-1}$, is also called the arcsine function and the symbol arcsin x may be used instead of $\sin^{-1} x$. Generally, for a displayed trigonometric value, a corresponding angle θ determined by the calculator will be in the range (in degrees) shown in Table A-1.

It is important to keep in mind that the angle θ computed by the calculator is measured in degrees, radians, or grads, depending on the angular mode to which the calculator is set. We assume the degree mode is used in the following example.

Table A-1

Function	Range of x	Angle θ
$\sin^{-1}$	$-1 \leq x \leq 1$	$-90° \leq \theta \leq 90°$
$\cos^{-1}$	$-1 \leq x \leq 1$	$0° \leq \theta \leq 180°$
$\tan^{-1}$	$-\infty < x < \infty$	$-90° < \theta < 90°$

example 4

Find an angle B such that

$$\sin B = \frac{6 \sin 75.52°}{8}.$$

That is, find

$$\sin^{-1} \left[\frac{6 \sin 75.52°}{8} \right].$$

This expression occurs in Example 2, Sec. 16-2.

ALG: $\boxed{6}$ $\boxed{\times}$ $\boxed{75.52}$ $\boxed{\text{SIN}}$ $\boxed{\div}$ $\boxed{8}$ $\boxed{=}$ $\boxed{\text{INV}}$ $\boxed{\text{SIN}}$ Display: 46.57

Thus $B = 46.57°$.

RPN: $\boxed{6}$ $\boxed{\uparrow}$ $\boxed{75.52}$ $\boxed{\text{SIN}}$ $\boxed{\times}$ $\boxed{8}$ $\boxed{\div}$ $\boxed{\text{SIN}^{-1}}$ Display: 46.57

Thus $B = 46.57°$.

If the calculator is set to the radian mode just before the inverse trigonometric function key is used in Example 4, the calculator will compute a correct angular value of B in radians, namely 0.8127. However, if the radian mode is set *before* the 75.52 is entered, the final answer is 0.0912, which is an *incorrect* value for B. In the latter case the intermediate key sequence $\boxed{75.52}$ $\boxed{\text{SIN}}$ gives the sine of 75.52 *radians*, while the problem requires the sine of 75.52 *degrees*.

Exercise A-6

In Problems 1–22, find the value of the indicated expression. Given your answer rounded to four decimal places.

1. $\sin 56.8°$.

2. $\sin(-108.3°)$.

3. $\sin 2.68$.

4. $\sin\left(-\frac{6\pi}{7}\right)$.

5. $\cos 118°$.

6. $\cos(-113.5°)$.

7. $\cos 7.25$.

8. $\tan 72.9°$.

9. $\tan 352.1°$.

10. $\tan(-45°)$.

11. $\tan 2.83$.

12. $\sec 13.7°$.

13. sec 5.83.   **14.** csc $(-68.7°)$.   **15.** csc 137°.

16. cot 65°.   **17.** cot 3.8.   **18.** cot (-2.2π).

19. sin² 30.6°.   **20.** cos² $\left(\dfrac{\pi}{7.1}\right)$.   **21.** tan² 45.7°.

22. sin² 33° + cos² 33°.

In Problems 23–40, find the value of the given expression. Give all answers to two decimal places.

23. 26.7 sin 18.5°.   **24.** $\dfrac{32.6}{\cos 210°}$.   **25.** 36.9 tan 46°.

26. 18.3 sin² $\left(\dfrac{\pi}{8}\right)$.   **27.** $\dfrac{16.3}{\sin^2\left(\dfrac{\pi}{7}\right)}$.   **28.** $\dfrac{46 \sin 14.1°}{\sin 25°}$.

29. 110 cos 36.5° + 220 cos 94.3°.   **30.** 28.3 sin 62.1° + 43.1 sin 313°.

31. sin⁻¹ 0.6231.   **32.** cos⁻¹ 0.8392.   **33.** Arctan $\dfrac{17.6}{-13.2}$.

34. tan⁻¹ $\dfrac{-72.3}{93.4}$.   **35.** Arcsin $\left(\dfrac{7 \sin 47.2°}{20.9}\right)$.

36. sin⁻¹ $\left(\dfrac{6.2 \sin 60.3°}{8.4}\right)$.   **37.** cos⁻¹ $\left[\dfrac{85^2 + 90^2 - 110^2}{2(85)(90)}\right]$.

38. sin 32.3° cos 41.8° + cos 32.3° sin 41.8°.

39. $\dfrac{\tan 83.1° - \tan 22°}{1 + \tan 83.1° \tan 22°}$.   **40.** 62.4 $\left(\dfrac{\sin 46.3°}{1 + \cos 46.3°}\right)^2$.

Answers to Exercise A-6

1. 0.8368.   **2.** −0.9494.   **3.** 0.4454.   **4.** −0.4339.   **5.** −0.4695.   **6.** −0.3987.
7. 0.5679.   **8.** 3.2506.   **9.** −0.1388.   **10.** −1.0000.   **11.** −0.3221.   **12.** 1.0293.
13. 1.1123.   **14.** −1.0733.   **15.** 1.4663.   **16.** 0.4663.   **17.** 1.2927.   **18.** −1.3764.
19. 0.2591.   **20.** 0.8167.   **21.** 1.0501.   **22.** 1.0000.   **23.** 8.47.   **24.** −37.64.
25. 38.21.   **26.** 2.68.   **27.** 86.58.   **28.** 26.52.   **29.** 71.93.   **30.** −6.51.
31. 38.54°.   **32.** 32.94°.   **33.** −53.13°.   **34.** −37.74°.   **35.** 14.23°.   **36.** 39.88°.
37. 77.83°.   **38.** 0.96.   **39.** 1.81.   **40.** 11.41.

A-7 Common and Natural Logarithms

Logarithmic function keys, which are available on all scientific calculators, allow you to compute the values of logarithms to base e and base 10. The **common-logarithm key**, designated by $\boxed{\text{LOG}}$, computes the logarithm base 10 of the displayed number. The **natural-logarithm key**, designated by $\boxed{\text{LN}}$, computes the logarithm base e of the displayed number. In each case, the number whose logarithm is to be found must be greater than zero or an error message will be generated; the logarithm of a nonpositive number is not defined.

example 1

Find the (a) common and (b) natural logarithms of 362.7.

a. ALG and RPN: $\boxed{362.7}\,\boxed{\text{LOG}}$ Display: 2.55955

b. ALG and RPN: $\boxed{362.7}\,\boxed{\text{LN}}$ Display: 5.89358

example 2

Evaluate $3.7 \log 8^{2.3}$.

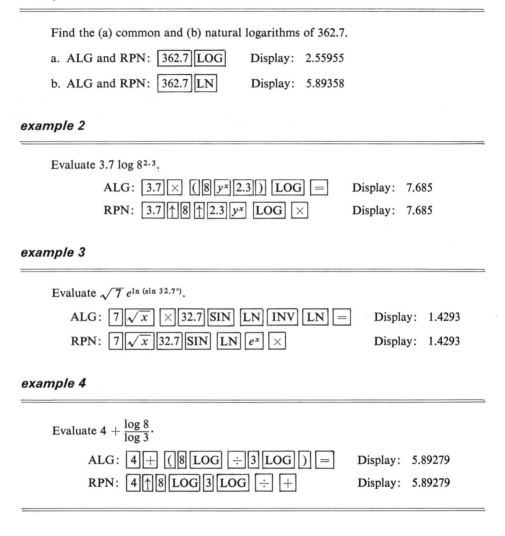

ALG: $\boxed{3.7}\,\boxed{\times}\,\boxed{(}\,\boxed{8}\,\boxed{y^x}\,\boxed{2.3}\,\boxed{)}\,\boxed{\text{LOG}}\,\boxed{=}$ Display: 7.685

RPN: $\boxed{3.7}\,\boxed{\uparrow}\,\boxed{8}\,\boxed{\uparrow}\,\boxed{2.3}\,\boxed{y^x}\,\boxed{\text{LOG}}\,\boxed{\times}$ Display: 7.685

example 3

Evaluate $\sqrt{7}\; e^{\ln(\sin 32.7°)}$.

ALG: $\boxed{7}\,\boxed{\sqrt{x}}\,\boxed{\times}\,\boxed{32.7}\,\boxed{\text{SIN}}\,\boxed{\text{LN}}\,\boxed{\text{INV}}\,\boxed{\text{LN}}\,\boxed{=}$ Display: 1.4293

RPN: $\boxed{7}\,\boxed{\sqrt{x}}\,\boxed{32.7}\,\boxed{\text{SIN}}\,\boxed{\text{LN}}\,\boxed{e^x}\,\boxed{\times}$ Display: 1.4293

example 4

Evaluate $4 + \dfrac{\log 8}{\log 3}$.

ALG: $\boxed{4}\,\boxed{+}\,\boxed{(}\,\boxed{8}\,\boxed{\text{LOG}}\,\boxed{\div}\,\boxed{3}\,\boxed{\text{LOG}}\,\boxed{)}\,\boxed{=}$ Display: 5.89279

RPN: $\boxed{4}\,\boxed{\uparrow}\,\boxed{8}\,\boxed{\text{LOG}}\,\boxed{3}\,\boxed{\text{LOG}}\,\boxed{\div}\,\boxed{+}$ Display: 5.89279

Exercise A-7

*In Problems **1–20**, evaluate the expression. Given all answers to five decimal places.*

1. $\log 4.837$.

2. $\log 0.932$.

3. $\log \sqrt{182.4}$.

4. $\ln 16.47$.

5. $\ln 0.8459$.

6. $\ln \sqrt{16.74}$.

7. $\log\left(\dfrac{36.7}{\sqrt{18.3}}\right)$.

8. $\ln(\sqrt{821} + 9.35)$.

9. $\dfrac{\log 16.3}{\log 5.9}$.

10. $7 + \dfrac{\log 9.2}{\log 4.6}$.

11. $\dfrac{4 + \log 18}{3}$.

12. $4 + \dfrac{\log 18}{3}$.

13. $\log (42.3^{8.1})$.   **14.** $\ln (16.3^{-3.2})$.   **15.** $\log \sin 52.7°$.

16. $\ln \cos 64.3°$.   **17.** $10 \log \dfrac{9.3 \times 10^{-10}}{10^{-12}}$.   **18.** $\sqrt{8.3}\, 10^{\ln 6.2}$.

19. $5.3 e^{\ln \sin 60°}$.   **20.** $(5 + \log 13) 17.3^{\ln 5.2}$.

Answers to Exercise A-7

1. 0.68458. **2.** −0.03058. **3.** 1.13051. **4.** 2.80154. **5.** −0.16735. **6.** 1.40890.
7. 0.93344. **8.** 3.63767. **9.** 1.57253. **10.** 8.45421. **11.** 1.75176. **12.** 4.41842.
13. 13.17336. **14.** −8.93173. **15.** −0.09937. **16.** −0.83550. **17.** 29.68483.
18. 192.34829. **19.** 4.58993. **20.** 672.10449.

values of trigonometric functions

Degrees	Radians	Sin	Cos	Tan	Cot		
0	0.0000	0.0000	1.0000	0.0000	. . . . . .	1.5708	90
1	0.0175	0.0175	0.9998	0.0175	57.290	1.5533	89
2	0.0349	0.0349	0.9994	0.0349	28.636	1.5359	88
3	0.0524	0.0523	0.9986	0.0524	19.081	1.5184	87
4	0.0698	0.0698	0.9976	0.0699	14.301	1.5010	86
5	0.0873	0.0872	0.9962	0.0875	11.430	1.4835	85
6	0.1047	0.1045	0.9945	0.1051	9.5144	1.4661	84
7	0.1222	0.1219	0.9925	0.1228	8.1443	1.4486	83
8	0.1396	0.1392	0.9903	0.1405	7.1154	1.4312	82
9	0.1571	0.1564	0.9877	0.1584	6.3138	1.4137	81
10	0.1745	0.1736	0.9848	0.1763	5.6713	1.3963	80
11	0.1920	0.1908	0.9816	0.1944	5.1446	1.3788	79
12	0.2094	0.2079	0.9781	0.2126	4.7046	1.3614	78
13	0.2269	0.2250	0.9744	0.2309	4.3315	1.3439	77
14	0.2443	0.2419	0.9703	0.2493	4.0108	1.3265	76
15	0.2618	0.2588	0.9659	0.2679	3.7321	1.3090	75
16	0.2793	0.2756	0.9613	0.2867	3.4874	1.2915	74
17	0.2967	0.2924	0.9563	0.3057	3.2709	1.2741	73
18	0.3142	0.3090	0.9511	0.3249	3.0777	1.2566	72
19	0.3316	0.3256	0.9455	0.3443	2.9042	1.2392	71
20	0.3491	0.3420	0.9397	0.3640	2.7475	1.2217	70
21	0.3665	0.3584	0.9336	0.3839	2.6051	1.2043	69
22	0.3840	0.3746	0.9272	0.4040	2.4751	1.1868	68
23	0.4014	0.3907	0.9205	0.4245	2.3559	1.1694	67
24	0.4189	0.4067	0.9135	0.4452	2.2460	1.1519	66
25	0.4363	0.4226	0.9063	0.4663	2.1445	1.1345	65
26	0.4538	0.4384	0.8988	0.4877	2.0503	1.1170	64
27	0.4712	0.4540	0.8910	0.5095	1.9626	1.0996	63
28	0.4887	0.4695	0.8829	0.5317	1.8807	1.0821	62
29	0.5061	0.4848	0.8746	0.5543	1.8040	1.0647	61
30	0.5236	0.5000	0.8660	0.5774	1.7321	1.0472	60
31	0.5411	0.5150	0.8572	0.6009	1.6643	1.0297	59
32	0.5585	0.5299	0.8480	0.6249	1.6003	1.0123	58
33	0.5760	0.5446	0.8387	0.6494	1.5399	0.9948	57
34	0.5934	0.5592	0.8290	0.6745	1.4826	0.9774	56
35	0.6109	0.5736	0.8192	0.7002	1.4281	0.9599	55
36	0.6283	0.5878	0.8090	0.7265	1.3764	0.9425	54
37	0.6458	0.6018	0.7986	0.7536	1.3270	0.9250	53
38	0.6632	0.6157	0.7880	0.7813	1.2799	0.9076	52
39	0.6807	0.6293	0.7771	0.8098	1.2349	0.8901	51
40	0.6981	0.6428	0.7660	0.8391	1.1918	0.8727	50
41	0.7156	0.6561	0.7547	0.8693	1.1504	0.8552	49
42	0.7330	0.6691	0.7431	0.9004	1.1106	0.8378	48
43	0.7505	0.6820	0.7314	0.9325	1.0724	0.8302	47
44	0.7679	0.6947	0.7193	0.9657	1.0355	0.8029	46
45	0.7854	0.7071	0.7071	1.0000	1.0000	0.7854	45
		Cos	Sin	Cot	Tan	Radians	Degrees

answers
to odd-numbered
problems

Exercise 0-2

1. 21. **3.** 1. **5.** 20. **7.** 3. **9.** 30. **11.** 20. **13.** 0. **15.** 2. **17.** 5. **19.** 13. **21.** 2. **23.** 1.
25. 12. **27.** 12. **29.** 11. **31.** 4. **33.** 8, 2. **35.** 5. **37.** 4. **39.** 36. **41.** Ten-thousands place.

Exercise 0-3

1. 8. **3.** 6. **5.** $\frac{8}{9}, \frac{7}{7}, \frac{8}{1}$. **7.** $7\frac{2}{3}$. **9.** $3\frac{3}{5}$. **11.** $1\frac{1}{2}$. **13.** $3\frac{1}{4}$. **15.** $\frac{12}{18}$. **17.** 20. **19.** 33. **21.** 3.
23. 3. **25.** 15. **27.** 49. **29.** $\frac{7}{3}$. **31.** $\frac{4}{3}$. **33.** $\frac{4}{5}$. **35.** $\frac{11}{24}$. **37.** $\frac{1}{4}$. **39.** $\frac{1}{10}$. **41.** $\frac{4}{3}$. **43.** $\frac{9}{2}$.
45. 20. **47.** $\frac{2}{77}$. **49.** $\frac{35}{8}$.

Exercise 0-4

1. 3. **3.** $\frac{1}{6}$. **5.** $\frac{12}{13}$. **7.** $\frac{1}{8}$. **9.** 18. **11.** 20. **13.** 36. **15.** 60. **17.** $\frac{23}{5}$. **19.** $\frac{51}{7}$. **21.** $\frac{19}{12}$.
23. $\frac{1}{56}$. **25.** $\frac{59}{36}$. **27.** $\frac{9}{20}$. **29.** $\frac{19}{30}$. **31.** $2\frac{11}{12}$. **33.** $1\frac{13}{24}$. **35.** $\frac{17}{6}$. **37.** $\frac{81}{40}$.

Exercise 0-5

1. $\frac{5}{3}$. **3.** $\frac{35}{36}$. **5.** 0. **7.** 2. **9.** $\frac{10}{27}$. **11.** $\frac{8}{15}$. **13.** $\frac{35}{11}$. **15.** $\frac{27}{10}$. **17.** $\frac{11}{6}$. **19.** $\frac{32}{15}$. **21.** $\frac{20}{3}$. **23.** $\frac{1}{6}$.
25. $\frac{27}{4}$. **27.** $\frac{3}{10}$. **29.** 20. **31.** $\frac{9}{2}$. **33.** $\frac{9}{175}$. **35.** $\frac{19}{21}$. **37.** $\frac{19}{44}$. **39.** $\frac{119}{135}$. **41.** $\frac{10}{27}$. **43.** $\frac{1}{6}$. **45.** $\frac{5}{3}$.
47. 9.

Exercise 0-6

1. 135.7416.   **3.** 75.7306.   **5.** 0.0273.   **7.** 0.016.   **9.** 2.   **11.** 3.   **13.** 5.   **15.** 0.326.   **17.** 0.00265.
19. 984.   **21.** 1.7.   **23.** 0.0002.   **25.** 79.1.   **27.** 0.0015.   **29.** $\frac{6241}{10,000}$.   **31.** $\frac{3}{500}$.   **33.** $\frac{12.483}{20.000}$.
35. 0.125.   **37.** 0.09375.

Exercise 0-7

1. 67.78 square centimeters.   **3.** 10.   **5.** 87.4 centimeters.   **7.** 30°.

Exercise 1-1

1. True.   **3.** False.   **5.** True.   **7.** False.   **9.** False.   **11.** 4.   **13.** −3.   **15.** 6.   **17.** −12.
19. <.   **21.** >.   **23.** >.   **25.** 4.   **27.** $\frac{2}{3}$.   **29.** 1.   **31.** 5.   **33.** −4.
35. (a) True,   (b) False,   (c) False,   (d) True.

Exercise 1-2

1. True.   **3.** False.   **5.** False.   **7.** False.   **9.** $x + 8$.   **11.** $11 + y$.   **13.** $12x$.   **15.** $2x$.   **17.** a.
19. $8 + 4t$.   **21.** $5z − yz$.   **23.** $7x − xy$.   **25.** $xy + xz − xw$.   **27.** $3ac$.   **29.** $\frac{3}{4}prs$.

Exercise 1-3

1. 3.   **3.** $\frac{10}{x}$.   **5.** 12.   **7.** −9.   **9.** 2.   **11.** −2.   **13.** −3.   **15.** −10.   **17.** −1.   **19.** 0.
21. 12.   **23.** −2.   **25.** 8.   **27.** −8.   **29.** 0.   **31.** −16.   **33.** 2.   **35.** $−\frac{1}{8}$.   **37.** −10.   **39.** 3.
41. $−a$.   **43.** $−12w$.   **45.** −3.   **47.** $\frac{1}{4}$.   **49.** 0.   **51.** −2.   **53.** 1.   **55.** 63.   **57.** −15.   **59.** $−\frac{2}{3}$.
61. $\frac{1}{6}$.   **63.** $−\frac{1}{2}$.   **65.** Not defined.   **67.** $−\frac{3}{4}$.   **69.** $\frac{1}{3}$.   **71.** $−\frac{4}{3}$.   **73.** $5xy$.   **75.** $\frac{x}{yz}$.   **77.** $6y$.
79. $−\frac{x}{yz}$.   **81.** −16.   **83.** 0.   **85.** 1959.   **87.** 4.   **89.** $\frac{3xy}{5z}$.   **91.** −0.0854.   **93.** 1.25.

Exercise 1-4

1. $\frac{1}{13}$.   **3.** $\frac{5}{4}$.   **5.** 8.   **7.** (a) 0.65°C,   (b) 437.8 cubic centimeters.   **9.** 68°F;   293 K.   **11.** $\frac{19}{9}$.
13. 478 meters per second.   **15.** 2% in each case.

Review Problems—Chapter 1

1. Commutative law.   **3.** Associative law.   **5.** Commutative law.   **7.** Distributive law.   **9.** True.
11. True.   **13.** False.   **15.** False.   **17.** $−\frac{1}{2}$.   **19.** $15x$.   **21.** $−10y$.   **23.** −1.   **25.** −12.   **27.** 1.
29. $20x − 12$.   **31.** $x − 1$.   **33.** −8.   **35.** $3xz$.   **37.** 15.   **39.** 5.   **41.** $28x$.   **43.** $\frac{2}{63}$.   **45.** 12.
47. 1.   **49.** $−12x$.   **51.** $8y − xy$.   **53.** (a) −6,   (b) $−\frac{13}{6}$.   **55.** (a) 11,   (b) 5,   (c) 11,   (d) −5.

Exercise 2-1

1. 8. **3.** -16. **5.** -16. **7.** -72. **9.** $\frac{1}{3}$. **11.** -64. **13.** x^{11}. **15.** y^9. **17.** x^7. **19.** $(x-2)^8$.
21. $\frac{x^7}{y^9}$. **23.** $14x^8$. **25.** $-12x^4$. **27.** x^{16}. **29.** x^9. **31.** t^{2n}. **33.** x^{29}. **35.** x^4. **37.** $\frac{1}{x}$.
39. $-y^6$. **41.** $\frac{1}{x^6}$. **43.** x^{13}. **45.** x. **47.** $\frac{1}{x^5}$. **49.** a^6b^6. **51.** $16x^4$. **53.** $16x^{16}y^8$. **55.** $\frac{a^3}{b^3}$.
57. $\frac{81}{x^4}$. **59.** x^4y^8. **61.** $\frac{8y^3}{z^3}$. **63.** $\frac{4}{9}a^4b^6c^{12}$. **65.** $\frac{x^6}{y^{15}}$. **67.** $\frac{x^8y^{12}}{16z^{16}}$. **69.** $-x^{13}$. **71.** $16x^8y^4$.
73. $-\frac{x^5y^5}{t^4}$. **75.** $-x^4$. **77.** 4. **79.** $x^{ac}y^{bc}$. **81.** -28.6.
83. (a) 18 watts, (b) 8 watts, (c) 0.05 watt. **85.** Power is (a) 4 times, (b) 9 times, (c) $\frac{1}{4}$ original value.
87. 7.10.

Exercise 2-2

1. 1. **3.** $\frac{1}{8}$. **5.** 54. **7.** 3. **9.** -4. **11.** -27. **13.** $\frac{1}{36}$. **15.** 1. **17.** $\frac{1}{x^6}$. **19.** x^3. **21.** $\frac{3}{y^4}$.
23. $16x$. **25.** $\frac{1}{x^5y^7}$. **27.** $\frac{2a^2c^5}{b^4}$. **29.** $\frac{x^9z^4}{w^2y^{12}}$. **31.** x. **33.** $\frac{1}{x^5}$. **35.** $\frac{y^{20}}{x^4}$. **37.** $\frac{2y^4}{x^2}$. **39.** $\frac{1}{9t^2}$.
41. $\frac{x^{15}}{y^{15}z^3}$. **43.** t^4. **45.** $\frac{y^5}{x^8}$. **47.** $\frac{xz^2w}{y^3}$. **49.** $\frac{8x^4y^{15}z^2}{3}$. **51.** x^2y^3. **53.** $\frac{64}{27}$. **55.** $\frac{5y^2}{8x^2}$.
57. $-xz$. **59.** $\frac{4x^8y^{10}}{z^4}$. **61.** $\frac{x^5}{y^{20}z^{20}}$. **63.** 14.2. **65.** 0.00920.

Exercise 2-3

1. 6.0214×10^{-6}. **3.** 1.04×10. **5.** 2.62451001×10^4. **7.** 1.42×10^2. **9.** 7.6×10^{-1}.
11. 262,000,000. **13.** 0.000000000624. **15.** 0.2020. **17.** 761,100. **19.** 5.983×10^{24} kilograms.
21. 6.67×10^{-11}. **23.** 2 newtons. **25.** 1.10×10^{30}. **27.** 2.6×10^2. **29.** 6.3×10^{-6}.
31. 4.0×10^6. **33.** 1.08×10^{21} cubic meters. **35.** 2.97×10^{-2} newton. **37.** 2.83×10^{-1} ohm.

Exercise 2-4

1. 7. **3.** 2. **5.** 6. **7.** -3. **9.** 4. **11.** 2. **13.** 0. **15.** -5. **17.** 2. **19.** 0.2 **21.** $\frac{1}{4}$. **23.** -5.
25. 11. **27.** $\frac{1}{3}$. **29.** 5. **31.** 4. **33.** 0. **35.** -1. **37.** 0.15. **39.** $5\sqrt{2}$. **41.** $2\sqrt{3}$. **43.** $2\sqrt{2}$.
45. $3\sqrt{6}$. **47.** $2\sqrt[4]{3}$. **49.** $2\sqrt[5]{2}$. **51.** $-5\sqrt[3]{4}$. **53.** $\frac{1}{5}$. **55.** $\frac{\sqrt{14}}{3}$. **57.** $\frac{\sqrt[3]{10}}{3}$. **59.** 5.
61. $-\frac{1}{2}$. **63.** 4. **65.** 4. **67.** $\frac{3\sqrt{2}}{2}$. **69.** $\frac{\sqrt{7}}{7}$. **71.** $\frac{2\sqrt{2}}{3}$. **73.** 13. **75.** 2. **77.** 13 ohms.
79. (a) 2 meters, (b) 2.2 centimeters.

Review Problems—Chapter 2

In Problems 1–23, T = *true* and F = *false*.
1. F. **3.** F. **5.** F. **7.** F. **9.** T. **11.** F. **13.** F. **15.** T. **17.** F. **19.** T. **21.** T. **23.** F.
25. x^{13}. **27.** $\frac{x^{10}}{y^{50}}$. **29.** $-32x^5y^{20}$. **31.** x^{14}. **33.** $-x^5$. **35.** $\frac{1}{25}$. **37.** $\frac{x^8z^{48}}{y^{12}}$. **39.** $\frac{1}{16t^4}$.
41. $\frac{z^2}{x^3y^5}$. **43.** 3. **45.** 0. **47.** 13. **49.** $\frac{1}{9}$. **51.** 0.15. **53.** $3\sqrt{5}$. **55.** $3\sqrt[4]{10}$. **57.** $\frac{\sqrt{7}}{4}$. **59.** 2.
61. 6. **63.** $2\sqrt{3}$. **65.** 5.64×10^{-5}. **67.** 2.8×10^7.
69. (a) 0.064 joule, (b) 0.08 joule, (c) 1.44 joules.

Exercise 3-1

1. (a) $3x^2$, (b) x^2. **3.** 2, 3, -4. **5.** 2, -2, 1. **7.** 4, 1, -2. **9.** 2, $\frac{7}{3}$. **11.** a; 2. **13.** b, d; 2.
15. b, c; 4. **17.** a; 1. **19.** b, d. **21.** b, c; 4. **23.** b. **25.** b; 5. **27.** a; 0.

Exercise 3-2

1. $11x - 2$. **3.** $11x - 2y - 3$. **5.** $-5x + 6y - 7$. **7.** $8y - 8$. **9.** $4x - 3y$. **11.** $7a - 8b + c$.
13. $a - b - c + d$. **15.** $2b + c$. **17.** $40x + 12y$. **19.** $-14x + 12y$. **21.** $a + 2b + 2c$.
23. $5x^2 + 15$. **25.** $2xy + 5z - 7$. **27.** $2x^2 - 9x - 13$. **29.** $-10 + 4x$. **31.** $5x + 50$.
33. $-a + 6$. **35.** $29x^2 - 22$. **37.** $8a - 11b - 13c$. **39.** $-2x - 4y - 3xy + 1$. **41.** $18x - 24$.
43. $3x - 6 + 6x^2 - 12y - x^3$. **45.** $9 - 100x + 60y$. **47.** $-(-x - 2x^2 + 3x^3) + 2b + 1$.
49. $-(2x^2 - 3x^2y + 5x + 3xy) - 6y - 1$. **51.** -2000θ. **53.** (a) $1.0268 - 0.0004T$, (b) 1.018.

Exercise 3-3

1. $15x^3$. **3.** $6x^2y$. **5.** $3a^3b^2$. **7.** $-8x^4y^4$. **9.** $a^3b^3c^2$. **11.** x^3yz^4. **13.** $24x^4y^5$. **15.** $90x^{10}$.
17. $ab^2c^4d^2$. **19.** $x^3 - 4x^2 + 7x$. **21.** $-3a^2b + a^3b^2 - a^3b$. **23.** $-5x^3y + 5xy^3 - 5x^2y^2$.
25. $4x^5y^2 + 8x^4y^4 - 12x^6y^2$. **27.** $-14xy + 8x^2y + 4xy^2 - 2x^3y$. **29.** $x^2 + 7x + 10$.
31. $3y^2 - 4y - 4$. **33.** $9x^2 - 6x + 1$. **35.** $16x^2 + 8xy + y^2$. **37.** $6x^4y + 6x^3y^2$. **39.** $t^3 - 8$.
41. $x^4 - 5x^3 - x^2 + 10x - 2$. **43.** $y^5 - y^4 + 5y^3 - 3y^2 + 6y$. **45.** $x^2 + 2xy + y^2 - 1$.
47. $16x^3 - 4x$. **49.** $4a^2b^2 + 4abrt + r^2t^2$. **51.** $2xy + y^2$. **53.** $6x$. **55.** $x^2 + x - 6$.
57. $-15x^2y^2$. **59.** $-2x^2 + 3x - 1$. **61.** 0. **63.** $3.64x^2 + 2.58x - 13.12$.
65. $b + c + 5ab + 5ac$. **67.** $r^2 - R^2$. **69.** $R_0 + R_0\alpha T - R_0\alpha T_0$.

Exercise 3-4

1. $\dfrac{b}{2}$. **3.** $-5x^2y$. **5.** $\dfrac{x}{2yz^2}$. **7.** $\dfrac{xw}{2}$. **9.** $-3y^3$. **11.** $9x^2y$. **13.** $\dfrac{abc^4}{2}$. **15.** $\dfrac{1}{x}$. **17.** $\dfrac{4x}{z^3}$.

19. $4a^8b^7$. **21.** $-xy^4$. **23.** $\dfrac{5}{x} - x + 2$. **25.** $-2 - \dfrac{y}{x}$. **27.** $\dfrac{3}{y} - x + \dfrac{1}{x^2y^2}$.

29. $x^5y + 3x - \dfrac{1}{y^3}$. **31.** $4y^2 + 2x^3y^2z - x^4y$. **33.** $-2xy + \dfrac{2y^2}{3x} - \dfrac{7}{3} + \dfrac{4}{3x}$. **35.** $\dfrac{2}{xy} - 4y^2 - 3xy$.

37. $-2x^6 - \dfrac{6x}{y^2} + \dfrac{1}{y^4}$. **39.** $2x + 7 + \dfrac{10}{x - 2}$. **41.** $1 + \dfrac{1}{x + 2}$. **43.** $x - 2 - \dfrac{3}{4x + 1}$.

45. $x^2 + 3x - 2$. **47.** $-x^3 + x^2 - 2x + 4 - \dfrac{19}{3x + 5}$. **49.** $2x^2 + 1 - \dfrac{2}{4x - 1}$.

51. $x^3 + x^2 - x - 1$. **53.** $x^3 - x^2y + xy^2 - y^3$. **55.** $5x^2 - 13x - 36 + \dfrac{39x + 220}{x^2 - x + 6}$.

57. $1 - \dfrac{T_2}{T_1}$; $T_1 \neq 0$. **59.** $\dfrac{1}{C_1} + \dfrac{1}{C_2} + \dfrac{1}{C_3}$. **61.** (a) $2t + 1$, (b) 5.

Exercise 3-5

1. $x^2 + 10x + 25$. **3.** $x^2 - 8x + 16$. **5.** $t^2 + t + \frac{1}{4}$. **7.** $x^2 + 4xy + 4y^2$. **9.** $4x^2 + 12x + 9$.
11. $9x^2 - 24xy + 16y^2$. **13.** $64x^2 + 32xy + 4y^2$. **15.** $9a^2b^2c^2 - 24abcef + 16e^2f^2$.
17. $36x^2 - 60xy + 25y^2$. **19.** $x^2 + 11x + 24$. **21.** $x^2 - x - 2$. **23.** $y^2 + 2y - 35$.
25. $x^2 - 5x + 6$. **27.** $x^2 - 9$. **29.** $9s^2 - 16$. **31.** $\frac{1}{4}x^2 - 4$. **33.** $10x^2 + 19x + 6$.
35. $12x^2 - 25x + 12$. **37.** $x^4 - 9$. **39.** $\frac{2}{9}a^2 - a - 2$. **41.** $2t^2 + 5t - 3$. **43.** $x^2y^2z^2 - a^2$.
45. $x^2 - 3$. **47.** $x^2y^4 + 2axy^2 + a^2$. **49.** $x^4 - 4x^2 + 4$. **51.** $4x^2 + 24x + 36$. **53.** $2xy^2 - 18x$.
55. $a^4b^2 - 4a^2bm^2n + 4m^4n^2$. **57.** $x^4 - 16$. **59.** 0. **61.** $5x^2 - 9x + 11$. **63.** $x^3 - 2x^2 - 4x + 8$.
65. $16x^4 - 96x^3 + 144x^2$. **67.** $6x + 1$. **69.** $x^2 - 2xy + y^2 - 4$. **71.** $a^2 + 2ab + b^2 - c^2$.
73. $x^3 + 6x^2 + 12x + 8$. **75.** $\frac{3}{4}RcZ^2 - \frac{3}{2}RcZ + \frac{3}{4}Rc$. **77.** $KE = 2mt^2 + 2mt + \frac{1}{2}m$.

Exercise 3-6

1. $8(x + 1)$. **3.** $2(7y - 4)$. **5.** $5(2x - y + 5)$. **7.** $x(5c + 9)$. **9.** $4y(1 - 4y)$. **11.** $3x(2y + z)$.
13. $x^2(2x - 1)$. **15.** $x^3y^3(2 + x^2y^2)$. **17.** $4mx^3(m - 2x)$. **19.** $3a^2y^3(3a^2 + y^2 - 2ayz)$.
21. $7zy(3z + w^2 + 2z^2y^2w^3)$. **23.** $(x + 4)(x - 4)$. **25.** $(x + 2)(x + 4)$. **27.** $(x + 5)(x - 3)$.
29. $(x - 4)(x - 5)$. **31.** $(y - 4)(y + 6)$. **33.** Prime. **35.** $(x + 6)^2$. **37.** $(x - 8)(x + 4)$.
39. $(y - 5)^2$. **41.** $(5x + 4)(5x - 4)$. **43.** $(y + \frac{2}{3})(y - \frac{2}{3})$. **45.** $(3x + 1)(x + 2)$.
47. $(2y - 1)(y - 3)$. **49.** $(4x + 1)^2$. **51.** $(3 + 2xy)(3 - 2xy)$. **53.** $(4y - 1)(y + 2)$.
55. $(2x - 5)(3x + 2)$. **57.** $(4x + 3)(3x - 2)$. **59.** $2(x + 3)(x - 1)$. **61.** $3x(x + 3)^2$.
63. $4s^2t(2t + 1)(2t - 1)$. **65.** $2(2y + 3)(y - 3)$. **67.** $x^2(x + 1)(x - 1)$.
69. $(9x^2 + y^2)(3x + y)(3x - y)$. **71.** $(t^2 + 2)(t + \sqrt{2})(t - \sqrt{2})$. **73.** $(x + 2)(x - 2)(x + 1)(x - 1)$.
75. $2x(2x + 1)(x - 2)$. **77.** $2(x + 3)^2(x - 1)(x + 1)$. **79.** $2(x + 4)(x + 1)$.
81. $(m + n)(m - n)(2n)$. **83.** $(x + y)(x - y + 1)$. **85.** $(3z + 2x - 1)(3z - 2x + 1)$.
87. $(x + 1)(x^2 + 1)$. **89.** $(a + b - c)(a - b + c)$. **91.** $(x - y)(x + y + 1)$.
93. $(x + 2)(x^2 - 2x + 4)$. **95.** $2\pi r(r + h)$. **97.** $(T_1 - T_2)(c + kT_1 + kT_2)$.

Review Problems—Chapter 3

1. $11x - 2y - 3$. **3.** $-2a + 19b + 4$. **5.** $-8xy + 26$. **7.** $9x - 18$. **9.** $3x^2 + 18x - 36$.
11. $2x^3y^4z^7$. **13.** $72a^5b^4$. **15.** $4x^8y^7$. **17.** $x^3 - 2x^2 + 4x$. **19.** $-2a^4b^2 + 2a^3b^2 - 3a^2b$.
21. $x^2 - x - 12$. **23.** $x^2 - 16$. **25.** $x^2 - 5x + 6$. **27.** $x^2 + 4xy + 4y^2$. **29.** $x^3 - 4x^2 + 3x - 12$.
31. $6x^4 - 11x^3 + 3x^2 + 15x - 5$. **33.** $2x^2 - xy + 5x - 3y^2 - 5y + 2$. **35.** $x^2 - 12x + 18$.
37. $\dfrac{ay^2}{x}$. **39.** $\dfrac{ab^2}{5}$. **41.** $-\dfrac{3}{8x}$. **43.** $x - 5 + \dfrac{7}{x}$. **45.** $\dfrac{x}{y} - 5y + \dfrac{7}{y}$.
47. $-x - 2xy^3w^2 + 2x^2y^2w$. **49.** $3x^2 + 3x - 1 - \dfrac{2}{2x - 1}$. **51.** $x^3 - 2x^2 + 6x - 10$.
53. $-x^3 + 2x^2 - x + 2 - \dfrac{2}{2x + 1}$. **55.** $x^2 + 12x + 36$. **57.** $x^2 - 10x + 25$.
59. $4x^2 + 16xy + 16y^2$. **61.** $x^2 - 64$. **63.** $9x^2 - 4$. **65.** $4x^2 - 16y^2$. **67.** $x^2 - 2x - 24$.
69. $x^2 - 13x + 42$. **71.** $4x^2 - 14x + 12$. **73.** $y^4 - 16$. **75.** $2x^4 + 2x^3 - 24x^2$. **77.** $8y - 18$.
79. $16x^3 + 32x^2 - 9x - 18$. **81.** $2xy^4(3x^2 + 2y^2)$. **83.** $(x - 5)(x - 6)$. **85.** $(4 + y)(4 - y)$.
87. $x(x - 8)(x + 7)$. **89.** $(3x - 2)(x + 4)$. **91.** $2(2x + 5)(2x - 5)$. **93.** $(3y - 2)(5y + 4)$.
95. $(x^2 + 2)(x + 2)(x - 2)$. **97.** $2x^3(x - 6)(x - 3)$. **99.** (a) Cannot be simplified, (b) $\dfrac{1}{f} - \dfrac{1}{p}$.
101. $\dfrac{2\pi^2 me^4}{h^3}\left(\dfrac{1}{n_2} + \dfrac{1}{n_1}\right)\left(\dfrac{1}{n_2} - \dfrac{1}{n_1}\right)$.

Exercise 4-1

1. $\dfrac{x}{y}$. **3.** $\dfrac{a}{bc}$. **5.** $-\dfrac{x}{y + z}$. **7.** True. **9.** True. **11.** False. **13.** True. **15.** False. **17.** $\dfrac{x + 2}{3x + 5}$.
19. 3. **21.** $\dfrac{1}{3a}$. **23.** $\dfrac{x - 9}{x}$. **25.** $\dfrac{3 + m}{4(1 - m)}$. **27.** $\dfrac{1}{x + 6}$. **29.** $\dfrac{2x + 3}{2x}$. **31.** $-\dfrac{t + 5}{t + 3}$.
33. $\dfrac{x - 12}{x - 3}$. **35.** $\dfrac{x + 3}{x - 4}$. **37.** -1. **39.** $\dfrac{x + 7}{7 - x}$. **41.** $3 - x$. **43.** $\dfrac{1}{2y - x}$. **45.** $(a^2 + b^2)(a - b)$.
47. $\dfrac{2x - 1}{3x - 2}$. **49.** $3w - 2x + 1$. **51.** $\bar{x} = \dfrac{x + 6}{8}$; $\bar{y} = y$.

Exercise 4-2

1. $\dfrac{7}{xy}$. **3.** $\dfrac{4}{x^3}$. **5.** $\dfrac{ab^2}{xy^2}$. **7.** $-\dfrac{y^2}{(y - 3)(y + 2)}$. **9.** $\dfrac{(x - 3)^2}{x^6}$. **11.** $-\dfrac{2x - 3}{2x + 3}$. **13.** $-(x + y)^2$.
15. $\dfrac{x}{2(x + 3)}$. **17.** $\dfrac{(x - 3)^2}{4}$. **19.** $\dfrac{x + 3}{x - 2}$. **21.** $\dfrac{x + 2}{(x - 3)(x + 1)}$. **23.** $\dfrac{x^2 + 4}{x(x - 2)}$.

25. $-\dfrac{(x-1)^2}{(x+2)(7+x)}.$ **27.** $\dfrac{3xyz^2}{5w}.$ **29.** $\dfrac{x+2}{x-4}.$ **31.** $4z^2.$ **33.** $-\dfrac{1}{x(x-y)}.$ **35.** $\dfrac{6y}{x}.$ **37.** $\dfrac{2}{9x^2}.$

39. $8x.$ **41.** $\dfrac{2(c+d)}{c-d}.$ **43.** $-27x^2.$ **45.** $\dfrac{x+3}{x}.$ **47.** $\dfrac{x-2}{x-1}.$ **49.** $\dfrac{3x-1}{x+1}.$ **51.** $\dfrac{8(x+2)}{15(x-2)}.$

53. $\dfrac{FL}{eA}.$ **55.** It decreases to $\frac{1}{4}$ its original value. **57.** $\dfrac{I+2mr^2}{I}.$ **59.** $\dfrac{2t+1}{3t^3}.$

Exercise 4-3

1. $(x-4)^5.$ **3.** $x^2y^3.$ **5.** $(x+3)^2(x-3).$ **7.** $2x(x+1).$ **9.** $\dfrac{x+5}{x-3}.$ **11.** $2.$ **13.** $\dfrac{2x-1}{x-1}.$

15. $\dfrac{2y+3x}{xy}.$ **17.** $\dfrac{x-8}{18}.$ **19.** $\dfrac{3y-4}{2xy}.$ **21.** $\dfrac{x^2+4}{2x}.$ **23.** $\dfrac{8x-21}{(x-2)(x-3)}.$ **25.** $\dfrac{5y^2-2x+3x^2}{x^2y}.$

27. $\dfrac{5x-1}{x-1}.$ **29.** $\dfrac{x^2+2xy-y^2}{(x-y)(x+y)}.$ **31.** $\dfrac{x^2+18x+9}{2(x-3)(x+3)}.$ **33.** $\dfrac{x+3}{x+1}.$

35. $\dfrac{-1}{(x+1)(x-1)}=-\dfrac{1}{(x+1)(x-1)}.$ **37.** $\dfrac{x^2-2x+9}{(x+3)^2(x-3)}.$ **39.** $\dfrac{-x^2-2x+1}{(x+5)(x+2)(x+1)}.$

41. $\dfrac{x^2+4x-4}{(x-2)(x+2)}.$ **43.** $\dfrac{2x^2+x-1}{x-1}=\dfrac{(2x-1)(x+1)}{x-1}.$ **45.** $\dfrac{-x^3+3x^2-x+3}{x^2(x+1)(x+2)}.$

47. $\dfrac{2y^2-y-6}{(2y+1)^2(y+3)}=\dfrac{(2y+3)(y-2)}{(2y+1)^2(y+3)}.$ **49.** $\dfrac{x^2+y^2+4xy}{(x+y)^2(x-y)}.$ **51.** $\dfrac{2x+3}{(x+y)(x-y)}.$

53. $\dfrac{9x-16a-17}{6}.$ **55.** $\dfrac{1}{y+2}.$ **57.** $\dfrac{kq_1(x+2)(x+3)+kq_2x(x+3)+kq_3x(x+2)}{x(x+2)(x+3)}.$

59. $\dfrac{q_1r_2-q_2r_1}{4\pi\epsilon_0 r_1 r_2}.$ **61.** $\dfrac{a(R_2+R_1)(R_2-R_1)}{kR_1^2 R_2^2}.$ **63.** $\varepsilon=\dfrac{(r_2+r_1)(\varepsilon_1 r_2+\varepsilon_2 r_1)}{r_1^2 r_2^2}.$

Exercise 4-4

1. $\dfrac{5}{3}.$ **3.** $\dfrac{1}{x}.$ **5.** $\dfrac{2x-3}{x}.$ **7.** $\dfrac{14}{6x-1}.$ **9.** $\dfrac{x(3y-1)}{y(2x+1)}.$ **11.** $\dfrac{x+3}{2x-3}.$ **13.** $x-y.$

15. $\dfrac{x^2+y^2}{(x+y)(x-y)}.$ **17.** $\dfrac{3(x+2)}{x+3}.$ **19.** $\dfrac{1}{x}.$ **21.** $\dfrac{a(2d+1)}{2d+2c+1}.$ **23.** $k=\dfrac{k_1k_2k_3}{k_2k_3+k_1k_3+k_1k_2}.$

25. $m^2=\dfrac{m_0^2c^2}{c^2-v^2}.$ **27.** $f=\dfrac{n_2R_1R_2}{(n_1-n_2)(R_1+R_2)}.$

Exercise 4-5

1. 2500 mm. **3.** 8.2×10^{-3} km. **5.** 0.15 m. **7.** 5 cm. **9.** 0.025 m. **11.** 6×10^{-6} F.
13. 2.1×10^{-6} μF. **15.** 7×10^{-4} mm. **17.** 6.2×10^{-3} mA. **19.** 40,000 g. **21.** 300,000 W.
23. 200 mW. **25.** 0.022 MΩ. **27.** 200 μV. **29.** 1.6×10^{-13} μC. **31.** 240 mm^2.
33. 5.1×10^6 cm^3. **35.** 5×10^{-4} m^3. **37.** 7.5×10^{-6} F. **39.** 1191.6 km/h. **41.** 2700 kg/m^3.
43. 9×10^{13} J. **45.** 3.1536×10^9 s. **47.** 3.84×10^{-2} m^2. **49.** 0.512 liter. **51.** 3.94×10^3 torr.

Review Problems—Chapter 4

1. $\dfrac{6(x-2)}{x(x-6)}.$ **3.** $\dfrac{x-8}{2x}.$ **5.** $\dfrac{3}{2}.$ **7.** $\dfrac{-x^2+3x-5}{(x-2)(x-3)}.$ **9.** $-3x(x+1).$ **11.** $\dfrac{3x^2-1}{(x-1)(x+1)}.$ **13.** $1.$

15. $-2.$ **17.** $\dfrac{x-2}{x+2}.$ **19.** $\dfrac{2x}{(x-1)^2}.$ **21.** $-\dfrac{3+x}{(x+4)(x+2)}.$ **23.** $\dfrac{x(x+1)}{x+2}.$ **25.** $-\dfrac{x+4}{x+3}.$

27. $\dfrac{i^2L}{2}.$ **29.** $\dfrac{R_1R_2R_3}{R_2R_3+R_1R_3+R_1R_2}.$ **31.** 10^{-10} μW/cm^2.

Exercise 5-1

1. 0.   **3.** $\frac{10}{3}$.   **5.** None.   **7.** Identity.   **9.** Not an identity.   **11.** $n - 10 = 0$.

13. $x(a + b) = bx + ax$.   **15.** $2(x + 3) = 5(x - 9)$.   **17.** $\dfrac{1}{t_1} + \dfrac{1}{t_2} = \dfrac{1}{T}$.   **19.** $s = vt$.

21. $F = \frac{9}{5}C + 32$.   **23.** $W = mg$.   **25.** $L = 20 + 5.3W$;   30.6 cm.   **27.** 8 A.

Exercise 5-2

1. Adding 5 to both sides; equivalence guaranteed.   **3.** Squaring both sides; equivalence *not* guaranteed.
5. Dividing both sides by x; equivalence *not* guaranteed.
7. Multiplying both sides by $x - 1$; equivalence *not* guaranteed.
9. Multiplying both sides by $(x - 5)/x$; equivalence *not* guaranteed.

Exercise 5-3

1. $x = -3$.   **3.** $x = 4$.   **5.** $x = \frac{9}{2}$.   **7.** $x = 24$.   **9.** $y = 0$.   **11.** $x = -\frac{6}{5}$.   **13.** $x = 2$.
15. $x = -14$.   **17.** $y = 3$.   **19.** $u = \frac{3}{2}$.   **21.** $x = 15$.   **23.** $x = 5$.   **25.** $x = -\frac{15}{4}$.   **27.** $y = -\frac{15}{4}$.
29. $x = \frac{7}{3}$.   **31.** $y = 11$.   **33.** $z = 2$.   **35.** $x = -2$.   **37.** $x = 2$.   **39.** $x = \frac{10}{3}$.   **41.** $x = 90$.
43. $y = 8$.   **45.** $x = -\frac{23}{9}$.   **47.** $x = -\frac{1}{4}$.   **49.** $x = \frac{8}{9}$.   **51.** $x = -\frac{26}{9}$.   **53.** $w = \frac{60}{17}$.   **55.** $x = \frac{14}{3}$.
57. $z = 3$.   **59.** $x = -\frac{23}{20}$.   **61.** $x = \frac{29}{12}$.   **63.** $y = 4$.   **65.** $V_2 = \dfrac{P_1 V_1}{P_2}$.   **67.** $a = \dfrac{v_0 - v}{t}$.

69. $m = \dfrac{2K}{v^2}$.   **71.** $h = \dfrac{V}{\pi r^2}$.   **73.** $R = \dfrac{P}{i^2}$.   **75.** $i = \dfrac{E_2 - E_1}{2R_1 + 3R_2 - 4R_4}$.   **77.** $Q' = \dfrac{Fr^2}{kQ}$.

79. $T_2 = \dfrac{VP_2 T_1}{V_0 P_1}$.   **81.** $E = \dfrac{IR}{1 - e^{-Rt/L}}$.

83. $t_2 = \dfrac{Q + mct_1 - mL}{mc}$, $t_1 = \dfrac{mct_2 + mL - Q}{mc}$, $c = \dfrac{Q - mL}{m(t_2 - t_1)}$.

85. $m = \dfrac{I\omega^2}{2gh - v^2}$, $I = \dfrac{m(2gh - v^2)}{\omega^2}$.   **87.** $h = \dfrac{V - 2\pi r^2}{2\pi r}$.   **89.** $f = \dfrac{f_0(v_0 U + \epsilon)}{\epsilon}$.   **91.** $m = \dfrac{Tr}{gr + v^2}$.

93. 53°C.   **95.** 6.7 kg.

Exercise 5-4

1. $x = \frac{1}{4}$.   **3.** No solution.   **5.** $x = \frac{8}{3}$.   **7.** $q = \frac{3}{2}$.   **9.** $p = 0$.   **11.** $x = \frac{10}{7}$.   **13.** $x = \frac{1}{8}$.   **15.** $y = 3$.

17. $x = \frac{5}{13}$.   **19.** No solution.   **21.** $x = \frac{7}{3}$.   **23.** $x = \dfrac{b(4a - 1)}{a(a + 2b)}$.   **25.** $T_1 = \dfrac{P_1 V_1 T_2}{P_2 V_2}$.

27. $P_2 = \dfrac{V_0 P_1 T_2}{V T_1}$.   **29.** $q = \dfrac{pf}{p - f}$, $f = \dfrac{pq}{p + q}$.   **31.** $R_1 = \dfrac{R_t R_2}{R_2 - R_t}$.   **33.** $m^2 = \dfrac{p^2}{v^2}$.

35. $R_1 = \dfrac{f(n - 1)R_2}{R_2 - f(n - 1)}$.   **37.** 149.4 Ω.   **39.** (a) 12 ohms.   **41.** 13.3 cm.

Exercise 5-5

1. $x = \frac{8}{5}$.   **3.** $x = \frac{8}{3}$.   **5.** $x = \frac{21}{19}$.   **7.** $x = -\frac{4}{3}$.   **9.** $x = \frac{3}{4}$.   **11.** $\frac{17}{9}$.   **13.** 1.   **15.** 7 m, $\frac{35}{3}$ m.
17. $\frac{32}{3}$.   **19.** 24 cm/s.   **21.** 273 cm³.   **23.** 400.   **25.** 93.3°C.   **27.** (a) 90°, (b) 2°.   **29.** 0.05 Ω.
31. 259 hertz   **33.** 543 hertz

Exercise 5-6

1. 18 kl. **3.** 420 liters of 20 percent solution, 280 liters of 30 percent solution. **5.** 32 ml.
7. $37\frac{1}{2}$ g of A, $137\frac{1}{2}$ g of B. **9.** 112 kg of A, 42 kg of B, 14 kg of C. **11.** $7\frac{1}{2}$ km. **13.** 1500 km.
15. 12 min. **17.** 3.75 N. **19.** 5.6 m. **21.** 632.2 m, 1.09 s. **23.** 27°C. **25.** 12 days, 5.52 m.
27. 80 m. **29.** 60 cm.

Review Problems—Chapter 5

1. $x = \frac{1}{2}$. **3.** $y = \frac{3}{2}$. **5.** $x = -\frac{3}{2}$. **7.** $z = -\frac{20}{9}$. **9.** $u = -\frac{11}{14}$. **11.** $x = -32$. **13.** $x = \frac{37}{21}$.
15. $x = -15$. **17.** No solution. **19.** $C = \dfrac{\lambda^2(n-1) - C'}{\lambda^2}$, $C' = \lambda^2(n - 1 - C)$. **21.** -15.
23. 200 ml. **25.** 18 days. **27.** 12 kg of A, 36 kg of B, 60 kg of C.

Exercise 6-1

1. x; all real numbers; $0, 12, -1, 4t, 4xy$.
3. x; all real numbers; $1, 1 + 2u, -13, 1 + 4x, 1 - 2(x + h) = 1 - 2x - 2h, 1 - 2xy$.
5. t; all real numbers; $1.02, 1.02, 1.02, 1.02, -0.0204$. **7.** p; all real numbers; $\dfrac{15}{2}, \dfrac{3(2p + 1)}{2}, \dfrac{3(4 + p)}{2p}$.
9. p; all real numbers; $1, 9, x_1^2 + 2x_1 + 1, w^2 + 2w + 1, p^2 + 2ph + h^2 + 2p + 2h + 1, \dfrac{x^2}{y^2} + \dfrac{2x}{y} + 1,$
$2x^2 - 1$.
11. t; all real numbers; $16, 36, h^2 + 12h + 36, h + 12$.
13. q; all real numbers; $5, 3, 0, |2x^2 + 3| = 2x^2 + 3$. **15.** x; all $x \geq -4$; $2, 0, 1, \sqrt{5 + x} - \sqrt{4 + x}$.
17. z; all $z \neq 1$; 1, not defined, $\dfrac{1}{9}, \dfrac{z^2}{z^2 - 4z + 4}$. **19.** x; all real numbers; $1, 1, 1.5, \dfrac{1}{2}$.
21. x; all $x \neq 2$ and -3; $\frac{3}{4}, \frac{7}{6}, -\frac{1}{6}$. **23.** Yes; no, because if $z = 4$, then $x = 1$ or -1.
25. (a) 13.7129, (b) 27.4258, (c) 44.7836. **27.** 0, 4.9, 19.6; all $t \geq 0$. **29.** $A = l^2$.
31. 9.8 m, 9.8 m; no; yes. **33.** $n = \dfrac{d}{12.7}$. **35.** $V = 4\pi(6 - t)$. **37.** $A = \dfrac{73a^2}{4}$.
39. (a) 9.81 m/s², (b) 2.8×10^{-3} m/s², (c) no.

Exercise 6-2

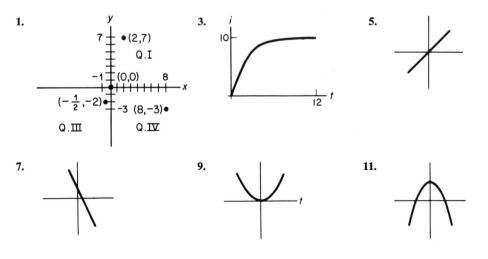

1.

3.

5.

7.

9.

11.

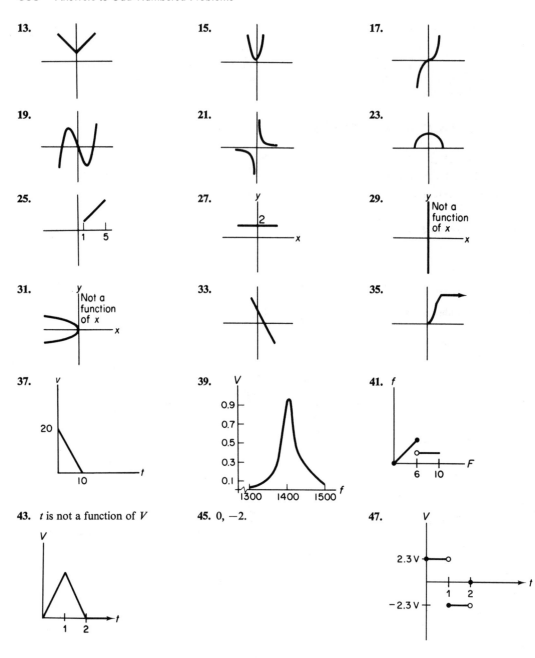

13.

15.

17.

19.

21.

23.

25.

27.

29. Not a function of x

31. Not a function of x

33.

35.

37.

39.

41. f

43. t is not a function of V

45. $0, -2$.

47.

Exercise 6-3

1. 2. **3.** $-\frac{8}{13}$. **5.** Not defined. **7.** 0. **9.** 9.8 m/s^2. **11.** $\frac{1}{2}$ ohm. **13.** $1.2 \times 10^{-5}/°$C.
15. -14 m/s.

Exercise 6-4

1. $y = 6x - 4$.

3. $y = -5x$.

5. $y = 9x - 23$.

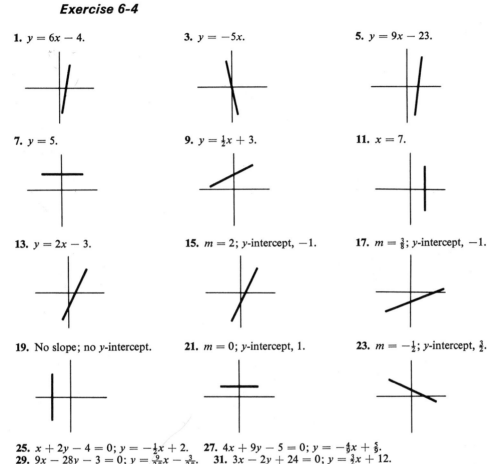

7. $y = 5$.

9. $y = \frac{1}{2}x + 3$.

11. $x = 7$.

13. $y = 2x - 3$.

15. $m = 2$; y-intercept, -1.

17. $m = \frac{3}{8}$; y-intercept, -1.

19. No slope; no y-intercept.

21. $m = 0$; y-intercept, 1.

23. $m = -\frac{1}{2}$; y-intercept, $\frac{3}{2}$.

25. $x + 2y - 4 = 0$; $y = -\frac{1}{2}x + 2$. **27.** $4x + 9y - 5 = 0$; $y = -\frac{4}{9}x + \frac{5}{9}$.
29. $9x - 28y - 3 = 0$; $y = \frac{9}{28}x - \frac{3}{28}$. **31.** $3x - 2y + 24 = 0$; $y = \frac{3}{2}x + 12$.
33. $x + y - 1 = 0$; $y = -x + 1$. **35.** 1. **37.** -3. **39.** Parallel. **41.** Parallel.
43. Perpendicular. **45.** Parallel. **47.** Neither. **49.** $(5, -4)$. **51.** Yes. **53.** $s = -\frac{5}{2}t + 70$; 10.
55. $V = \frac{1}{2}i$; 5 V. **57.** $P = \frac{T}{4} + 80$. **59.** (a) Yes, (b) 1.8704. **61.** (a) $v = 2t + 18$; (b) No.
63. (a) 4.0109, (b) 9.8.

Exercise 6-5

1. 1.33295. **3.** 1.33089. **5.** $24.9°C$. **7.** $35.5°C$. **9.** 7.670 mm Hg. **11.** $2.4°C$. **13.** 8154.3; 0.21.
15. 24.8. **17.** $47.3°C$.

Review Problems—Chapter 6

1. All real numbers. **3.** All real numbers except 1 and 2. **5.** All real numbers.
7. $7, 46, 62, 3t^2 - 4t + 7$. **9.** $0, 3, \sqrt{t}, \sqrt{x^2 - 1}$. **11.** $\frac{3}{5}, 0, \frac{\sqrt{x+4}}{x}, \frac{\sqrt{u}}{u-4}$. **13.** $-8, 4, 4, -92$.
15. $3 - 7x - 7h$.

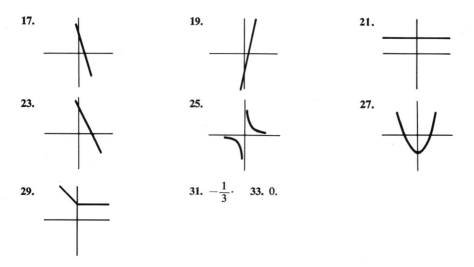

17.   **19.**   **21.**

23.   **25.**   **27.**

29.   **31.** $-\dfrac{1}{3}$.   **33.** 0.

35. $y = \frac{1}{3}x + \frac{11}{3}$; $x - 3y + 11 = 0$.   **37.** $y = 3x - 4$; $3x - y - 4 = 0$.
39. $y = 1$; $y - 1 = 0$.   **41.** Perpendicular.   **43.** Neither.   **45.** Parallel.   **47.** 2; -1.   **49.** -3; 2.
51. 4; 0.   **53.** $f(x) = -\frac{4}{3}x + \frac{19}{3}$.   **55.** $s + t - 3 = 0$; 0.   **57.** 0.3965; 0.9180.   **59.** 23.39.   **61.** 23.07.
63. 9800 N/m³.

Exercise 7-2

1. $\dfrac{\pi}{3}$.   **3.** 135°.   **5.** 90°.   **7.** $\dfrac{\pi}{4}$.   **9.** $-\dfrac{11\pi}{6}$.   **11.** 210°.   **13.** $-22\frac{1}{2}°$.   **15.** 4π.   **17.** 1080°.

19. $\left(\dfrac{720}{\pi}\right)°$.   **21.** Second.   **23.** Fourth.   **25.** Second.   **27.** Quadrantal.   **29.** First.   **31.** Third.

33. Quadrantal.   **35.** Fourth.   **37.** 208°.   **39.** 50°.   **41.** 395°, 755°, $-325°$, $-685°$.

43. 581.4°, 941.4°, $-138.6°$, $-498.6°$.   **45.** 290°, 650°, $-430°$, $-790°$.   **47.** $\dfrac{13\pi}{6}$, $\dfrac{25\pi}{6}$, $-\dfrac{11\pi}{6}$, $-\dfrac{23\pi}{6}$.

49. 60°.   **51.** $\dfrac{5\pi}{4}$.   **53.** $\dfrac{\pi}{2}$.   **55.** 0.611.   **57.** 1.470.   **59.** 135.218°.   **61.** $-214.401°$.   **63.** 6.81 km.

65. 14.14 cm.   **67.** 40°.   **69.** 69.3 rev/min.   **71.** 8.7×10^{-4}.   **73.** 40π, or 125.7.

75. $\left(\dfrac{108}{\pi}\right)°$, or 34.4°.   **77.** 200π m.

Exercise 7-3

Answers to Problems **1–13** *are in the order* sin θ, cos θ, tan θ, cot θ, sec θ, csc θ.

1. $\dfrac{3}{5}, \dfrac{4}{5}, \dfrac{3}{4}, \dfrac{4}{3}, \dfrac{5}{4}, \dfrac{5}{3}$.   **3.** $\dfrac{4}{5}, \dfrac{3}{5}, \dfrac{4}{3}, \dfrac{3}{4}, \dfrac{5}{3}, \dfrac{5}{4}$.   **5.** $\dfrac{\sqrt{3}}{2}, \dfrac{1}{2}, \sqrt{3}, \dfrac{\sqrt{3}}{3}, 2, \dfrac{2\sqrt{3}}{3}$.

7. $\dfrac{2}{3}, \dfrac{\sqrt{5}}{3}, \dfrac{2\sqrt{5}}{5}, \dfrac{\sqrt{5}}{2}, \dfrac{3\sqrt{5}}{5}, \dfrac{3}{2}$.   **9.** $\dfrac{1}{2}, \dfrac{\sqrt{3}}{2}, \dfrac{\sqrt{3}}{3}, \sqrt{3}, \dfrac{2\sqrt{3}}{3}, 2$.

11. $\dfrac{\sqrt{2}}{2}, \dfrac{\sqrt{2}}{2}, 1, 1, \sqrt{2}, \sqrt{2}$.   **13.** $\dfrac{\sqrt{3}}{3}, \dfrac{\sqrt{6}}{3}, \dfrac{\sqrt{2}}{2}, \sqrt{2}, \dfrac{\sqrt{6}}{2}, \sqrt{3}$.

15. $\cos\theta = \dfrac{\sqrt{21}}{5}$, $\tan\theta = \dfrac{2\sqrt{21}}{21}$, $\cot\theta = \dfrac{\sqrt{21}}{2}$, $\sec\theta = \dfrac{5\sqrt{21}}{21}$, $\csc\theta = \dfrac{5}{2}$.

17. $\sin\theta = \dfrac{4\sqrt{17}}{17}$, $\cos\theta = \dfrac{\sqrt{17}}{17}$, $\cot\theta = \dfrac{1}{4}$, $\sec\theta = \sqrt{17}$, $\csc\theta = \dfrac{\sqrt{17}}{4}$.   **19.** $\tan\theta = \dfrac{3}{4}$, $\sec\theta = \dfrac{5}{4}$.

21. $\sin A = \dfrac{\sqrt{7}}{4}$, $\cos A = \dfrac{3}{4}$, $\tan A = \dfrac{\sqrt{7}}{3}$, $\cot A = \dfrac{3\sqrt{7}}{7}$, $\sec A = \dfrac{4}{3}$, $\csc A = \dfrac{4\sqrt{7}}{7}$;

$\sin B = \dfrac{3}{4}$, $\cos B = \dfrac{\sqrt{7}}{4}$, $\tan B = \dfrac{3\sqrt{7}}{7}$, $\cot B = \dfrac{\sqrt{7}}{3}$, $\sec B = \dfrac{4\sqrt{7}}{7}$, $\csc B = \dfrac{4}{3}$.
29. 3.732.

Exercise 7-4

1. 0.5299. **3.** 0.9690. **5.** 1.3290. **7.** 4.5483. **9.** 1.4169. **11.** 1.8356. **13.** 0.5736. **15.** 0.3988.
17. 1.2349. **19.** 46.6°. **21.** 82.8°. **23.** 31.6°. **25.** 0.30. **27.** 1.22. **29.** $\frac{1}{2}$. **31.** 1. **33.** 18.4°.
35. 60°. **37.** $6\sqrt{3}$ V. **39.** (a) 163.3 m, (b) 153.4 m. **41.** 13.7°. **43.** (a) 57.5°, (b) 32.5°.

Exercise 7-5

1. $A = 30°$, $b = 3\sqrt{3}$, $c = 6$. **3.** $B = 45°$, $a = 3\sqrt{2}$, $b = 3\sqrt{2}$.
5. $A = 60°$, $B = 30°$, $a = 4\sqrt{3}$. **7.** $B = 56.5°$, $a = 6.84$, $b = 10.3$.
9. $A = 52.3°$, $B = 37.7°$, $c = 29.6$. **11.** $A = 62.6°$, $a = 47.5$, $c = 53.5$.
13. $A = 65.8°$, $B = 24.2°$, $a = 55.0$. **15.** $A = 77.4°$, $b = 5.16$, $c = 23.7$.
17. $R = 30.3\ \Omega$, $X_L = 19.4\ \Omega$. **19.** $P = 0.85$ W, $P_R = 1.41$ var. **21.** 201 m. **23.** 20.3 m. **25.** 6 min.
27. 88.7 m. **29.** 42.4 m. **31.** 10.96 m; 33.8°. **33.** 2540 km. **35.** 17.8 m.

Exercise 7-6

1. 65°. **3.** 47°. **5.** 22.6°. **7.** $\dfrac{\pi}{6}$. **9.** $\dfrac{1}{2}$. **11.** $-\dfrac{1}{2}$. **13.** -1. **15.** -1. **17.** $-\dfrac{2\sqrt{3}}{3}$. **19.** -1.

21. 1. **23.** $-\dfrac{\sqrt{2}}{2}$. **25.** $\sqrt{3}$. **27.** $\dfrac{\sqrt{3}}{2}$. **29.** -0.4245. **31.** 9.5668. **33.** 0.9839. **35.** 2.5257.

37. 9.5668. **39.** -0.9848. **41.** $\dfrac{\sqrt{3}}{3}$, or 0.5774. **43.** -0.3327. **45.** -0.3420. **47.** 0.1577.

49. 135°, 315°. **51.** 203.0°, 337.0°. **53.** 60°, 300°. **55.** 45°, 135°. **57.** 153.0°, 207.0°.
59. 40.0°, 140.0°. **61.** 82.8°, 262.8°. **63.** 76.4°. **65.** 322.0°. **67.** 1.42.

Exercise 7-7

1. 4.2 km, 45° south of east. **3.** $V_x = 122.87$, $V_y = 86.04$. **5.** $V_x = 0.53$, $V_y = -10.09$.
7. $V_x = -31.92$, $V_y = -2.23$. **9.** $V_x = -38.16$, $V_y = 196.33$. **11.** $V_x = 88.17$, $V_y = -121.35$.
13. $V = 8.60$, $\theta = 54.46°$. **15.** $V = 6.89$, $\theta = 332.32°$. **17.** $V = 5.24$, $\theta = 246.37°$.
19. $V = 3$, $\theta = 180°$. **21.** $V_h = 27.14$ m/s, $V_v = 16.96$ m/s. **23.** $a_h = 3.83$ m/s², $a_v = 3.21$ m/s².
25. (a) 28.19 N, (b) 10.26 N. **27.** (a) 53.24 N, (b) 37.28 N.

Exercise 7-8

1. $R = 141.1$, $\theta = 245.1°$. **3.** $R = 486.0$, $\theta = 109.4°$. **5.** $R = 363.0$, $\theta = 67.5°$.
7. $R = 507.3$, $\theta = 117.2°$. **9.** $R = 210.3$, $\theta = 49.5°$. **11.** $R = 74.4$ N, $\theta = 66.8°$. **13.** 440.0 km.
15. 488.4 km/h, 10.6° north of east. **17.** 43.6 km/h, 18.9° south of west. **19.** 46.8 km. **21.** 8.75 N.
23. 91.8 m/s; 19.3° above horizontal. **25.** 5.74° west of south.

Exercise 7-9

1. 0.3939. **3.** 0.7266. **5.** 0.0924. **7.** 1.0213. **9.** 0.6508. **11.** 41.7°. **13.** 74.3°. **15.** 12.2°.
17. 63.4°. **19.** 61.7°.

Review Problems—Chapter 7

1. $\frac{5\pi}{3}$.   **3.** 150°.   **5.** $-\frac{5\pi}{18}$.   **7.** 10°.   **9.** Third.   **11.** First.   **13.** 14π.   **15.** $\frac{3\pi}{2}$.   **17.** 140°.

19. $\sin\theta = -\frac{6\sqrt{37}}{37}$, $\cos\theta = \frac{\sqrt{37}}{37}$, $\tan\theta = -6$, $\cot\theta = -\frac{1}{6}$, $\sec\theta = \sqrt{37}$, $\csc\theta = -\frac{\sqrt{37}}{6}$.

21. $\sin\theta = -\frac{3\sqrt{5}}{7}$, $\cos\theta = -\frac{2}{7}$, $\tan\theta = \frac{3\sqrt{5}}{2}$, $\cot\theta = \frac{2\sqrt{5}}{15}$, $\sec\theta = -\frac{7}{2}$, $\csc\theta = -\frac{7\sqrt{5}}{15}$.

23. $\tan\theta = -\frac{\sqrt{6}}{12}$, $\cot\theta = -2\sqrt{6}$, $\sec\theta = -\frac{5\sqrt{6}}{12}$, $\csc\theta = 5$.

25. $\sin\theta = -\frac{2\sqrt{10}}{7}$, $\tan\theta = -\frac{2\sqrt{10}}{3}$, $\cot\theta = -\frac{3\sqrt{10}}{20}$, $\sec\theta = \frac{7}{3}$, $\csc\theta = -\frac{7\sqrt{10}}{20}$.   **27.** $-\frac{1}{2}$.

29. -1.   **31.** $\sqrt{2}$.   **33.** $\frac{\sqrt{3}}{3}$.   **35.** 0.   **37.** $-\frac{2\sqrt{3}}{3}$.   **39.** $A = 21.8°$, $B = 68.2°$, $c = 10.77$.

41. $A = 75°$, $b = 1.61$, $c = 6.21$.   **43.** $B = 44°$, $a = 7.25$, $c = 10.08$.

45. $B = 57.4°$, $a = 10.78$, $b = 16.85$.   **47.** $R = 204.4$, $\theta = 15.3°$.

49. (a) 95.3 V,   (b) -93.3 V,   (c) 87.8 V.   **51.** 101.3 m.   **53.** $d_x = -200.0$ km, $d_y = -346.4$ km.

Exercise 8-1

1. $x = -1$, $y = 1$.   **3.** No solution.   **5.** $x = 1$, $y = 2$.

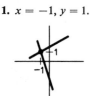

7. The coordinates of any point on the line $y = 6x - 3$.   **9.** $i_1 = 2.8$, $i_2 = 0.6$.

Exercise 8-2

1. $x = -1$, $y = 1$.   **3.** $T_1 = 3$, $T_2 = 2$.   **5.** $x = 2$, $y = -2$.   **7.** $x = \frac{1}{2}$, $y = \frac{3}{2}$.   **9.** $F_1 = 4$, $F_2 = -5$.

11. $x = 3$, $y = -1$.   **13.** $i_1 = 0$, $i_2 = 18$.   **15.** The coordinates of any point on the line $2x + 6y = 3$.

17. No solution.   **19.** $x = 12$, $y = -12$.   **21.** $F = 14.7$ N, $N = 49$ N.   **23.** $i_1 = \frac{13}{7}$ A, $i_2 = -\frac{12}{7}$ A.

25. $v_1 = -28$ m/s, $v_2 = -4$ m/s.   **27.** $F = 15.0$ N, $N = 40.0$ N.

Exercise 8-3

1. $x = 4$, $y = 2$, $z = 0$.   **3.** $x = 13$, $y = 22$, $z = -1$.   **5.** $x = \frac{1}{2}$, $y = \frac{1}{2}$, $z = \frac{1}{4}$.   **7.** $x = 0$, $y = \frac{4}{3}$, $z = 2$.

9. $x = -10$, $y = 56$, $z = -8$, $w = -98$.   **11.** $H = 50$, $T = 50\sqrt{2}$, $V = 50$ (all in newtons).

13. $i_1 = -2$, $i_2 = 1$, $i_3 = -1$ (all in amperes).

Exercise 8-4

1. (a) 1, (b) -2, (c) 0, (d) $-3b - a$, (e) $az - eh$, (f) $-4 - a^2$, (g) $-\frac{2}{7}$, (h) $\frac{7}{9}$.
3. $x = \frac{9}{5}, y = -\frac{2}{5}$. **5.** $x = \frac{6}{5}, z = \frac{16}{5}$. **7.** $i_1 = 3, i_2 = -5$. **9.** $x = \frac{16}{3}, y = \frac{2}{3}$. **11.** $x = \frac{7}{16}, y = \frac{13}{8}$.
13. No solution.

Exercise 8-5

1. -16. **3.** 98. **5.** -89. **7.** $x = 4, y = 2, z = 0$. **9.** $i_1 = \frac{2}{3}, i_2 = -\frac{28}{15}, i_3 = -\frac{26}{15}$.
11. $x = 1, y = 3, z = 5$. **13.** $a = \frac{1}{2}, b = \frac{1}{2}, c = \frac{1}{4}$. **15.** $y = 1$.
17. $T_1 = 327.3$ N, $T_2 = 163.6$ N, $a = 1.78$ m/s^2.

Exercise 8-6

1. 0. **3.** 0. **5.** 1. **7.** 24. **9.** -90.

Exercise 8-7

1. 8 m by 5 m. **3.** $56.25°$ and $33.75°$. **5.** 420 ℓ of 20 percent solution, 280 ℓ of 30 percent solution.
7. 3880 ℓ from tank A, 6120 ℓ from tank B. **9.** 30 kg of A, 50 kg of B, 20 kg of C.
11. $a = 1, b = -2, c = 0$. **13.** 164.5 m. **15.** $T_1 = 7.98$ N, $T_2 = 10.26$ N.
17. $T_1 = 493.8$ N, $T_2 = 224.2$ N.

Review Problems—Chapter 8

1. $x = \frac{17}{7}, y = -\frac{8}{7}$. **3.** $x = 0, y = 18$. **5.** No solution. **7.** $x = \frac{1}{2}, y = 1$.
9. The coordinates of any point on the line $6x = 3 - 9y$. **11.** $x = \frac{17}{20}, y = \frac{31}{20}$.
13. $x = 3, y = 1, z = -2$. **15.** $r = 1, s = 3, t = \frac{1}{2}$. **17.** 18. **19.** 3. **21.** $x = 1, y = 2$.
23. 2.5 kg of 20 percent copper alloy, 12.5 kg of 50 percent copper alloy.

Exercise 9-1

1. 5. **3.** $\frac{1}{9}$. **5.** 9. **7.** $\frac{1}{5}$. **9.** 16. **11.** 8. **13.** -2. **15.** 16. **17.** $x^{1/2}$. **19.** $x^{2/3}$. **21.** $x^{3/4}y^{5/4}$.
23. $x^{5/6}y^2$. **25.** $x^{9/4}$. **27.** $\frac{3}{x^{1/2}}$. **29.** $(x^2 - 5x)^{2/3}$. **31.** x^2. **33.** x. **35.** x^4. **37.** $x^{3/4}$.
39. $3xy$. **41.** $x^{3/2}$. **43.** y^2. **45.** $\frac{2}{x^4}$. **47.** $\frac{8y}{x^6}$. **49.** $a^2b^{21/4}c^{9/4}$. **51.** $\frac{1}{3x^5}$. **53.** $-\frac{2}{x^2}$. **55.** $\frac{x^4}{y^2}$.
57. $\frac{1}{x^{8/3}}$. **59.** $4x^2$. **61.** $\frac{x^{1/3}}{y}$. **63.** $\frac{x^2}{y^2}$. **65.** $4y^3$. **67.** $\frac{18y^4w^2}{x^2}$. **69.** 1.59; 5.81; 7.92.
71. 6×10^{-13} cm. **73.** 12.2 m^3/s. **75.** $p = 4.68 \times 10^7$ N/m^3; $T = 1.33 \times 10^5$ K.

Exercise 9-2

1. $-3x^{1/2}$. **3.** $\frac{2}{x^{1/3}}$. **5.** $x + 3x^{1/3}$. **7.** $\frac{3 + 3xy}{x^3}$. **9.** $\frac{y + x}{xy}$. **11.** $\frac{2x + 2}{x}$. **13.** $\frac{3 + xy}{x}$.

15. $\dfrac{x^2y^2 + 2xy + 1}{y^2}$. **17.** $x^3 + 4x^{3/2} + 4$. **19.** $x^2 - 2x^{1/2} + x^{3/2} - 2$ **21.** $x + 2x^2 + x^3$.
23. $x + 2x^{1/2}y^{1/2} + y$. **25.** $x^{1/3} + x - x^3$. **27.** $x + x^{5/3} - x^{11/3}$. **29.** $x^{1/4} - 3x^{1/12}$. **31.** $\frac{22}{3}$.
33. $\dfrac{x + y}{x}$. **35.** $\dfrac{b^2 - x^2}{b^2x^2}$. **37.** $y^2 + 8$.

Exercise 9-3

1. x^2. **3.** $2x^4$. **5.** $3x^8y^9$. **7.** xy^2z^3. **9.** $\dfrac{x^3}{y^4}$. **11.** x^2. **13.** x. **15.** $2\sqrt{3}$. **17.** $4\sqrt{2}$.
19. $2\sqrt[3]{2}$. **21.** $x^3\sqrt{x}$. **23.** $2x^2\sqrt[3]{3}$. **25.** $x^2\sqrt[4]{xy^2}$. **27.** $x^2z\sqrt[3]{yz}$. **29.** $2ay\sqrt[3]{y^2}$. **31.** $x^4y^2z\sqrt[5]{x^3z}$.
33. $9yzw^2\sqrt{xz}$. **35.** $\dfrac{\sqrt{2}}{2}$. **37.** $\dfrac{\sqrt[3]{50}}{5}$. **39.** $\dfrac{\sqrt[3]{x^2}}{y}$. **41.** $\dfrac{\sqrt{x}}{y^2}$. **43.** $\dfrac{\sqrt{2xy}}{y}$. **45.** $\dfrac{\sqrt[3]{2x^2y}}{xy}$.
47. $\dfrac{\sqrt[4]{24xy^3z^2}}{2x^2yz}$. **49.** $\sqrt[3]{x}$. **51.** $\sqrt{3}$. **53.** $2x\sqrt{y}$. **55.** $\dfrac{\sqrt{xy}}{y}$. **57.** $\sqrt[6]{xyz^5}$. **59.** $x^2\sqrt{xy}$.
61. $x^7\sqrt[3]{x^2}$. **63.** $x^2w^4\sqrt[6]{y^5w}$. **65.** $\dfrac{2x\sqrt[4]{x}}{y^2}$. **67.** $\dfrac{\sqrt{2}}{2}$. **69.** $\dfrac{\sqrt{xy}}{y^2}$. **71.** $\sqrt{x}$. **73.** $\dfrac{3\sqrt{7}}{7}$.
75. $\dfrac{2\sqrt{2x}}{x}$. **77.** $\dfrac{\sqrt[3]{4}}{2}$. **79.** $\dfrac{\sqrt[3]{9x^2}}{3x}$. **81.** $\dfrac{2\sqrt[5]{x^4y^2z^4}}{3z^2}$. **83.** $2b\sqrt[4]{8a^3b}$. **85.** $v = \dfrac{\sqrt{70gh}}{7}$.
87. It is halved. **89.** $E = \dfrac{\lambda ry\sqrt{r^2 + y^2}}{2\epsilon_0(r^2 + y^2)^2}$.

Exercise 9-4

1. $3\sqrt[3]{3}$. **3.** $2x^2\sqrt{2x}$. **5.** $11\sqrt{3}$. **7.** $20\sqrt{2}$. **9.** $-y\sqrt{x}$. **11.** $-8\sqrt[3]{2}$. **13.** 0. **15.** $\sqrt[3]{4}$.
17. $5x\sqrt{2}$. **19.** $42x\sqrt[3]{3y}$.

Exercise 9-5

1. $2\sqrt{3}$. **3.** $18\sqrt{2}$. **5.** $3\sqrt[3]{12}$. **7.** $x\sqrt{6x}$. **9.** 3. **11.** $16x\sqrt[3]{x}$. **13.** $2\sqrt{5}$. **15.** $6\sqrt{2} - 12$.
17. $-10 - 2\sqrt{3}$. **19.** -3. **21.** $9 + 4\sqrt{5}$. **23.** $2x + 3\sqrt{x} - 5$. **25.** $3xy^3\sqrt{2x}$.
27. $31 - 10\sqrt{6}$. **29.** $46\sqrt{6}$. **31.** $2y + 6\sqrt{2y} + 9$. **33.** $4x^5y^2\sqrt{2y}$. **35.** $\sqrt[4]{125}$. **37.** $x\sqrt[6]{27x}$.
39. $3\sqrt[6]{3x^5}$. **41.** $6x\sqrt[6]{8xy^2}$. **43.** $y\sqrt[20]{x^{13}y^2}$. **45.** $x^2\sqrt[6]{xy^5}$.

Exercise 9-6

1. 4. **3.** $\dfrac{\sqrt{21}}{7}$. **5.** $\sqrt{6}$. **7.** $a\sqrt{2}$. **9.** $\dfrac{2\sqrt[4]{x^3}}{x}$. **11.** $\dfrac{\sqrt[3]{12x^2}}{2x}$. **13.** $\dfrac{\sqrt[3]{50y}}{5y}$. **15.** $2 - \sqrt{3}$.
17. $2(\sqrt{3} + \sqrt{2})$. **19.** $-4 - 2\sqrt{6}$. **21.** $\dfrac{\sqrt{3}}{3}$. **23.** $3 - 2\sqrt{2}$. **25.** $\dfrac{x - \sqrt{5}}{x^2 - 5}$.
27. $\dfrac{5\sqrt{3} - 4\sqrt{2} - 13}{2}$. **29.** $\sqrt[4]{6}$. **31.** $\dfrac{\sqrt[6]{72}}{2}$. **33.** $\sqrt[6]{8x}$. **35.** $\dfrac{\sqrt[9]{2y^7}}{y}$. **37.** $2\sqrt[4]{xy}$. **39.** $\dfrac{\sqrt{35}}{5}$.

Exercise 9-7

1. $x = 27$. **3.** $y = \frac{41}{2}$. **5.** $x = 4$. **7.** $x = -\frac{15}{8}$. **9.** $z = 7$. **11.** $x = 4$. **13.** No solution.
15. $x = 0$. **17.** $y = \frac{49}{36}$. **19.** $g = \dfrac{4\pi^2L}{T^2}$. **21.** 3.9 m. **23.** 1.76 m.

Review Problems—Chapter 9

1. 1. **3.** $\frac{1}{5}$. **5.** 9. **7.** 10. **9.** 8. **11.** $\frac{1}{4}$. **13.** $\frac{1}{32}$. **15.** $4\sqrt{2}$. **17.** $x\sqrt[3]{2}$. **19.** $4x^2$. **21.** $3z^3$.

23. $\frac{9t^2}{4}$. **25.** $\frac{1}{x^2 y^2 z^2}$. **27.** $\frac{2}{x^4}$. **29.** $\frac{1}{16t^4}$. **31.** $\frac{y^6}{x^6}$. **33.** $\frac{z^2}{x^3 y^5}$. **35.** $2xy^2\sqrt[4]{x^3}$. **37.** $\frac{2x}{y^2}$.

39. $-27xy^2\sqrt{x}$. **41.** $\frac{2\sqrt[6]{x^5}}{y^3}$. **43.** $14\sqrt{2}$. **45.** $\sqrt[3]{t^2}$. **47.** $\frac{64y^6\sqrt{x}}{x^2}$. **49.** $\frac{y^4}{z^2}$. **51.** $2\sqrt{2}$.

53. $\sqrt{2} - 2\sqrt{3}$. **55.** 4. **57.** $\frac{2\sqrt{7}}{7}$. **59.** $\frac{3\sqrt[4]{x^3}}{x}$. **61.** $3x\sqrt{x}$. **63.** x^2. **65.** $x\sqrt{3}$.

67. $\frac{x\sqrt{y}}{y^2}$. **69.** $\frac{3\sqrt[3]{x^2 y}}{xy}$. **71.** $\frac{\sqrt[3]{12x}}{2}$. **73.** $\frac{\sqrt{6} + 2}{2}$. **75.** $x = 10$. **77.** $x = 5$. **79.** No solution.

81. $x = 10$. **83.** $E_{1y} = \frac{kq_1\sqrt{35}}{49}$, $E_{2y} = \frac{kq_2\sqrt{85}}{289}$.

Exercise 10-1

1. (a) $y = 4x$, (b) 24. **3.** $\frac{9}{2}$. **5.** 96. **7.** 2 cm. **9.** (a) $W = mg$, (b) 3.34 N. **11.** 30 cal.
13. 90 V. **15.** 2.3 km/s.

Exercise 10-2

1. (a) $y = \frac{36}{x}$, (b) 9. **3.** (a) $r = \frac{40s}{t^2}$, (b) $\frac{160}{81}$. **5.** 9. **7.** 225.
9. 2250 N; in simplified form, $k = 1$. **11.** The result is half the original illumination.
13. 5.74×10^7 m. **15.** 6.67×10^{-7} N. **17.** $x = \frac{12\sqrt{15}}{\sqrt{y}}$.

Review Problems—Chapter 10

1. $\frac{21}{8}$. **3.** 27. **5.** 1.035×10^8 N/m². **7.** 32 N. **9.** 48,000 cal/s.

Exercise 11-2

1. j. **3.** $-j$. **5.** -1. **7.** 1. **9.** $9j$. **11.** $-5j$. **13.** $4j\sqrt{2}$. **15.** $\frac{1}{2}j$. **17.** $0.3j$. **19.** $\pi^3 j$.
21. (a) -6, (b) 5, (c) $-6 - 5j$. **23.** (a) -2, (b) -31, (c) $-2 + 31j$. **25.** (a) 0, (b) -3, (c) $3j$.
27. (a) 7, (b) $\frac{2}{3}$, (c) $7 - \frac{2}{3}j$. **29.** (a) 0, (b) 1, (c) $-j$. **31.** (a) 7, (b) 0, (c) 7.
33. (a) -2, (b) 0, (c) -2. **35.** (a) 0, (b) -7, (c) $7j$. **37.** $x = 2, y = -6$. **39.** $x = 17, y = 4$.
41. $x = 2, y = 16$. **43.** $x = -\frac{11}{2}, y = -4$. **45.** (a) True, (b) True, (c) False, (d) True.
47. $R_x = \frac{R_2 R_3}{R_1}$, $L_x = R_2 R_3 C_1$.

Exercise 11-3

1. $4\sqrt{2}(\cos 45° + j\sin 45°)$. **3.** $4(\cos 300° + j\sin 300°)$. **5.** $5(\cos 90° + j\sin 90°)$.
7. $3\sqrt{2}(\cos 225° + j\sin 225°)$. **9.** $\cos 0° + j\sin 0°$. **11.** $2(\cos 120° + j\sin 120°)$.
13. $2(\cos 210° + j\sin 210°)$. **15.** $5(\cos 270° + j\sin 270°)$. **17.** $8.54(\cos 20.6° + j\sin 20.6°)$.
19. $\sqrt{3} + j$. **21.** $-3 + 3j\sqrt{3}$. **23.** $\sqrt{2} - j\sqrt{2}$. **25.** $-3j$. **27.** 4. **29.** $\frac{3\sqrt{3}}{2} - \frac{3j}{2}$.
31. $1.932 + 0.518j$. **33.** $-0.845 - 1.813j$. **35.** A circle of radius 1 with its center at the origin.
37. $a = -3.064$, $b = 2.571$. **39.** $-2.719 + 1.268j$. **41.** $0.557 - 0.502j$.
43. (a) $6.25 \underline{/7.35°}$ Ω, (b) 6.2 Ω, (c) 0.8 Ω. **45.** $51.43 \underline{/296.57°}$ V. **47.** $3.46 + 10.65j$ V. **49.** $42.27°$.

Exercise 11-4

1. $5j - 3$. **3.** $-3 - j$. **5.** $-2 + 3j$. **7.** $6\sqrt{3} + (2 + 4\sqrt{2})j$. **9.** $8 - 9j$. **11.** $-10j\sqrt{2}$.
13. -216. **15.** 64. **17.** $4 + 7j$. **19.** $26 + 7j$. **21.** $16 + 2j$. **23.** $-38 - 26j$. **25.** $5 + 12j$.
27. $-16 - 30j$. **29.** $\frac{99}{280} - \frac{43}{210}j$. **31.** $\frac{11}{17} - \frac{7}{17}j$. **33.** $\frac{7}{10} - \frac{1}{10}j$. **35.** $\frac{4}{13} - \frac{6}{13}j$. **37.** 0.
39. $\frac{7}{61} + \frac{45}{61}j$. **41.** $-\frac{1}{25} + \frac{1}{50}j$. **43.** $8 + 6j$. **45.** $\frac{14}{25} - \frac{48}{25}j$. **47.** $-5 - 15j$. **49.** -1. **51.** -2.
53. $1 - 2j$. **55.** (a) $\frac{7}{3} - \frac{1}{3}j\,\Omega$, (b) 2 V. **57.** $2 - 7j$. **59.** $15.3\,\Omega$, $\theta = 31.6°$. **61.** $12.22\,\Omega$, $\theta = 317.6°$.
63. $202.35 \,\underline{/6.92°}$. **65.** $133.85 \,\underline{/125.06°}$. **67.** $1.48 + 0.23j$.

Exercise 11-5

1. $\sqrt{2}\,e^{\pi j/4}$. **3.** $4e^{5\pi j/6}$. **5.** $7e^{3\pi j/2}$. **7.** $9.06e^{4.18j}$. **9.** $2.8e^{0.25j}$. **11.** $3.7e^{2.46j}$.
13. $\cos\frac{\pi}{2} + j\sin\frac{\pi}{2}$; j. **15.** $3\,\underline{/3\pi/4}$; $\frac{-3\sqrt{2}}{2} + \frac{3j\sqrt{2}}{2}$. **17.** $2\,\underline{/5\pi/6}$; $-\sqrt{3} + j$.
19. $4\,\underline{/2.35}$; $-2.81 + 2.85j$. **21.** $1(\cos\omega t + j\sin\omega t)$.

Exercise 11-6

1. $8\,\underline{/60°}$. **3.** $6\,\underline{/210°}$. **5.** $10\,\underline{/45°}$. **7.** $6\,\underline{/225°}$. **9.** $4\,\underline{/55°}$. **11.** $21\,\underline{/71°}$. **13.** $\frac{1}{2}\,\underline{/24°}$. **15.** $-\sqrt{3} - j$.
17. $2.56 - 0.74j$. **19.** $4.16 + 2.12j$. **21.** $6.59 - 1.48j$. **23.** $5.65 - 4.39j$. **25.** $5\,\underline{/340°}$.
27. $6.1 + 3.9j$.

Exercise 11-7

1. $8(\cos 30° + j\sin 30°)$, $4\sqrt{3} + 4j$. **3.** $16(\cos 120° + j\sin 120°)$, $-8 + 8j\sqrt{3}$.
5. $\cos(-240°) + j\sin(-240°)$, $-\frac{1}{2} + \frac{j\sqrt{3}}{2}$. **7.** $32(\cos 225° + j\sin 225°)$, $-16\sqrt{2} - 16j\sqrt{2}$.
9. $16(\cos 240° + j\sin 240°)$, $-8 - 8j\sqrt{3}$. **11.** $16(\cos 120° + j\sin 120°)$, $-8 + 8j\sqrt{3}$.
13. $64(\cos 90° + j\sin 90°)$, $64j$. **15.** $32(\cos 270° + j\sin 270°)$, $-32j$.
17. $1(\cos 150° + j\sin 150°)$, $-\frac{\sqrt{3}}{2} + \frac{j}{2}$. **19.** $\left(\frac{1}{2^{12}}\right)(\cos 0° + j\sin 0°)$, $\frac{1}{4096}$.
21. 1, $-\frac{1}{2} + \frac{j\sqrt{3}}{2}$, $-\frac{1}{2} - \frac{j\sqrt{3}}{2}$. **23.** $-2 + 2j$, $2 - 2j$. **25.** $\frac{\sqrt{2}}{2} + \frac{j\sqrt{2}}{2}$, $-\frac{\sqrt{2}}{2} - \frac{j\sqrt{2}}{2}$.
27. $\frac{\sqrt{6}}{2} + \frac{j\sqrt{2}}{2}$, $-\frac{\sqrt{2}}{2} + \frac{j\sqrt{6}}{2}$, $-\frac{\sqrt{6}}{2} - \frac{j\sqrt{2}}{2}$, $\frac{\sqrt{2}}{2} - \frac{j\sqrt{6}}{2}$.
29. $\sqrt[3]{2}(\cos 50° + j\sin 50°)$, $\sqrt[3]{2}(\cos 110° + j\sin 110°)$, $\sqrt[3]{2}(\cos 170° + j\sin 170°)$,
$\sqrt[3]{2}(\cos 230° + j\sin 230°)$, $\sqrt[3]{2}(\cos 290° + j\sin 290°)$, $\sqrt[3]{2}(\cos 350° + j\sin 350°)$.
31. 1, $-\frac{1}{2} + \frac{j\sqrt{3}}{2}$, $-\frac{1}{2} - \frac{j\sqrt{3}}{2}$.
33. $(\cos 0° + j\sin 0°) = 1$, $(\cos 72° + j\sin 72°)$, $(\cos 144° + j\sin 144°)$, $(\cos 216° + j\sin 216°)$,
$(\cos 288° + j\sin 288°)$
35. $\sqrt[6]{2}(\cos 15° + j\sin 15°)$, $\sqrt[6]{2}(\cos 135° + j\sin 135°)$, $\sqrt[6]{2}(\cos 255° + j\sin 255°)$.

Review Problems—Chapter 11

1. $9 - 7j$. **3.** $\frac{14}{5} - \frac{7}{5}j$. **5.** $\frac{7}{10} + \frac{1}{10}j$. **7.** $8\,\underline{/45°}$. **9.** $1\,\underline{/150°}$. **11.** $10.6\,\underline{/311.2°}$. **13.** $3\,\underline{/45°}$.
15. $\frac{\sqrt{6}}{2} - \frac{j\sqrt{6}}{2}$. **17.** $-1 + j$. **19.** $2.78 + 1.13j$. **21.** $6\,\underline{/90°}$; $6j$. **23.** $2\,\underline{/225°}$; $-\sqrt{2} - j\sqrt{2}$
25. $79.626\,\underline{/50°}$; $51.18 + 61.00j$. **27.** $192\,\underline{/211°}$; $-164.58 - 98.89j$.

29. $\sqrt[5]{2} \ \underline{/45°}, \ \sqrt[5]{2} \ \underline{/117°}, \ \sqrt[5]{2} \ \underline{/189°}, \ \sqrt[5]{2} \ \underline{/261°}, \ \sqrt[5]{2} \ \underline{/333°}.$ **31.** 13.9 A.
33. (a) $1.46 - 0.28j$,   (b) $-j\,\Omega$.

Exercise 12-1

1. $x = -2, -1.$ **3.** $x = -2, -7.$ **5.** $t = 3, 4.$ **7.** $z = -3, 1.$ **9.** $x = 6.$ **11.** $x = 0, 8.$
13. $x = 0, -5.$ **15.** $t = 0, 2.$ **17.** $x = \pm 2.$ **19.** $x = \pm 5.$ **21.** $x = 0, 2.$ **23.** $x = \pm 2j\sqrt{3}.$
25. $z = \pm 3.$ **27.** $x = \frac{1}{3}, -\frac{3}{2}.$ **29.** $t = \pm 3.$ **31.** $x = \pm\sqrt{7}.$ **33.** $x = \frac{1}{2}, -4.$ **35.** $x = 5, -2.$
37. $x = -\frac{1}{2}.$ **39.** $x = -1.$ **41.** $t = -5, 1.$ **43.** $x = 2, 3.$ **45.** $x = 0, -1.$ **47.** $x = 4, -2.$
49. $y = -\frac{1}{6}, -\frac{1}{4}.$ **51.** $x = 0, 1, -2.$ **53.** $x = 2, -1.$ **55.** $x = 0, 2, -3, 4.$ **57.** $x = 0, \pm 1.$
59. $x = 0, \pm 8.$ **61.** $y = 0, -4, -2.$ **63.** $x = \pm 1, \pm 3.$ **65.** $x = 0, \pm 1.$ **67.** $x = \pm 3, \pm 2.$

69. $\pm 2\pi \sqrt{\dfrac{L}{g}}.$ **71.** $\pm \sqrt{\dfrac{2mgh - mv^2}{I}}.$ **73.** $t = 10$ s.   **75.** 4 cm.   **77.** 16 cm, 12 cm.   **79.** 4.5 s.
81. 1 m.

Exercise 12-2

1. $x = -2 \pm \sqrt{7}.$ **3.** $x = -\dfrac{1}{2} \pm \dfrac{\sqrt{5}}{2}.$ **5.** $x = -1 \pm \dfrac{\sqrt{14}}{2}.$ **7.** $x = -\dfrac{3}{2} \pm \dfrac{\sqrt{5}}{2}.$ **9.** $x = 3.$

11. $t = 2 \pm j.$ **13.** $x = -1 \pm j\sqrt{2}.$ **15.** $y = -\dfrac{3}{4} \pm \dfrac{\sqrt{41}}{4}.$ **17.** $r = -\dfrac{2}{3} \pm \dfrac{j\sqrt{2}}{6}.$

19. $x = \pm 2j.$ **21.** $x = -\dfrac{5}{2}.$ **23.** $x = \pm j.$ **25.** $x = -1 \pm \dfrac{\sqrt{10}}{5}.$ **27.** $x = -\dfrac{1}{3} \pm \dfrac{\sqrt{7}}{3}.$

29. $r = \dfrac{5}{6} \pm \dfrac{j\sqrt{23}}{6}.$ **31.** $x = \dfrac{1}{12} \pm \dfrac{j\sqrt{431}}{12}.$ **33.** $x = -10 \pm 4\sqrt{10}.$ **35.** $x = \dfrac{\sqrt{3}}{4} \pm \dfrac{j\sqrt{29}}{4}.$

37. $x = 1, -\dfrac{5}{6}.$ **39.** $x = 2 \pm \dfrac{\sqrt{10}}{2}.$ **41.** $x = -\dfrac{1}{2}, 6.$ **43.** $x = 3j, -2j.$ **45.** $x = \dfrac{5y \pm y\sqrt{73}}{6}.$

47. 1.28 s or 2.40 s.   **49.** 9 cm³.   **51.** 0.91 A.   **53.** $m = \dfrac{-D \pm \sqrt{D^2 - 4JS}}{2J}.$

Exercise 12-3

1. Not quadratic.   **3.** Quadratic.   **5.** Not quadratic.   **7.** Quadratic.   **9.** (a) $(1, 11)$,   (b) Highest.
11. (a) -8,   (b) -4 and 2,   (c) $(-1, -9)$, $x = -1$.
13. Vertex: $(3, -4)$; intercepts: $(1, 0)$, $(5, 0)$, $(0, 5)$.   **15.** Vertex: $(-\frac{3}{2}, \frac{9}{2})$; intercepts: $(0, 0)$, $(-3, 0)$.

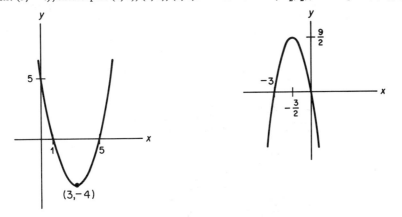

17. Vertex: $(-1, 0)$; intercepts: $(-1, 0)$, $(0, 1)$.

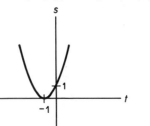

19. Vertex: $(2, -1)$; intercept: $(0, -9)$.

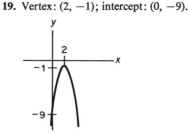

21. Vertex: $(4, -3)$; intercepts: $(4 + \sqrt{3}, 0)$, $(4 - \sqrt{3}, 0)$, $(0, 13)$. **23.** Minimum; 24. **25.** Maximum; -10.

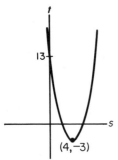

27. $x = 3$. **29.** 50 m by 100 m. **31.** (a) $t = 2.50$ s, (b) $s = 8.70$ m.

33. (a) $x = \dfrac{l}{2}$, (b) $M = \dfrac{wl^2}{8}$, (c) $x = 0$, $x = l$.

Exercise 12-4

1. $x = 3, -6$. **3.** $x = -\frac{1}{4}, -\frac{1}{2}$. **5.** $x = 6, -2$. **7.** $x = 5, -2$. **9.** $x = -2$. **11.** $x = -1, \frac{13}{10}$.
13. $x = 1, -\frac{18}{5}$. **15.** $x = 2, -\frac{4}{3}$. **17.** $x = 7$. **19.** $z = 4, 8$. **21.** $x = 2$. **23.** $x = \pm 5$.
25. $x = 0, 4$. **27.** $x = 4$. **29.** $x = \pm\sqrt{3}, \pm j\sqrt{2}$. **31.** $x = -\frac{1}{4}, -\frac{1}{2}$. **33.** $x = \pm\dfrac{\sqrt{7}}{7}, \pm\dfrac{\sqrt{2}}{2}$.
35. $x = 9$. **37.** $x = -4, 1$. **39.** $x = \frac{15}{7}, \frac{11}{5}$. **41.** $x = \pm j\sqrt{13}, \pm j\sqrt{3}$. **43.** $y = -8, 1$. **45.** 6 Ω.
47. 86.8 cm or 33.2 cm. **49.** 15 km/h. **51.** 23.0 s. **53.** 0.316.

Exercise 12-5

1. $x = 3, y = 2$; $x = 3, y = -2$; $x = -3, y = 2$; $x = -3, y = -2$.
3. $x = 4, y = -12$; $x = -1, y = 3$. **5.** $p = -3, q = -5$; $p = 2, q = 0$.
7. $x = 0, y = 0$; $x = 1, y = 1$. **9.** $x = 4, y = 8$; $x = -1, y = 3$.
11. $p = 0, q = 0$; $p = 1, q = 1$.
13. $x = 3\sqrt{2}, y = 2$; $x = -3\sqrt{2}, y = 2$; $x = \sqrt{15}, y = -1$; $x = -\sqrt{15}, y = -1$.
15. $x = -2, y = -\frac{1}{3}$. **17.** 7 by 7 and 3 by 3, or 5 by 5 and 9 by 9 (all in meters).
19. $V_A = \frac{9}{7}$ m/s, $V_B = \frac{30}{7}$ m/s. **21.** 3 μF and 6 μF, or 6 μF and 3 μF. **23.** $L = 8$ m, $W = 50$ N.

Review Problems—Chapter 12

1. $x = 5$. **3.** $x = 6, -4$. **5.** $x = \frac{1}{6}, \frac{3}{2}$. **7.** $x = \pm 2\sqrt{3}$. **9.** $x = 0, \frac{1}{2}$. **11.** $x = 5 \pm 2\sqrt{6}$.
13. $x = -\dfrac{3}{2} \pm \dfrac{\sqrt{11}}{2}$. **15.** $x = 3 \pm \sqrt{2}$. **17.** $x = -\frac{1}{2}$. **19.** $x = \dfrac{1}{2} \pm \dfrac{3j}{2}$. **21.** $x = \pm\frac{3}{4}$.

23. $y = 4, -6$.   **25.** $z = 2, -10$.   **27.** $t = \frac{3}{4} \pm \frac{i\sqrt{15}}{4}$.   **29.** $x = -\frac{3}{2} \pm \frac{\sqrt{17}}{2}$.   **31.** $x = -\frac{5}{4}$.

33. $x = 3$.   **35.** $x = 4$.   **37.** No solution.   **39.** $x = 12$.   **41.** $x = 64, -27$.   **43.** $x = -\frac{1}{5}$.

45. $x = -10, y = -3; x = -1, y = 6$.

47. $x = 1, y = 7; x = -1, y = -7; x = 3, y = -3, x = -3, y = 3$.

49. Intercepts: $(3, 0), (-3, 0)$; Vertex: $(0, 9)$.   **51.** Intercepts: $(5, 0), (-1, 0), (0, -5)$; vertex: $(2, -9)$.

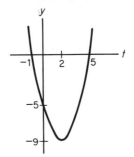

53. -1.   **57.** (a) 9 s, (b) $t = 3$ s or $t = 6$ s, (c) 4.5 s, (d) 99.23 m.   **59.** 289 cm².

Exercise 13-1

1.

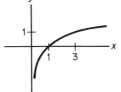

3.

5. 11.0232.   **7.** 0.0150.   **9.** 81, $\frac{1}{81}$, 3.   **11.** 12, 6, $\frac{3}{2}$.   **13.** 3, $\frac{33}{32}$, $\frac{3}{2}$.   **15.** (a) 75 mg, (b) 53.3.

17. 0.53 A.

Exercise 13-2

1. $\log_4 64 = 3$.   **3.** $\log 100{,}000 = 5$.   **5.** $2^6 = 64$.   **7.** $8^{1/3} = 2$.   **9.** $\log_6 1 = 0$.   **11.** $2^{14} = x$.

13. $\ln 7.3891 = 2$.   **15.** $e^{1.0986} = 3$.   **17.**

19. 1.9933.   **21.** -0.5955.

23. 2.   **25.** 3.   **27.** $\frac{1}{2}$.   **29.** 1.   **31.** -2.   **33.** 0.   **35.** -3.   **37.** 9.   **39.** 125.   **41.** $\frac{1}{10}$.   **43.** e^2.

45. 2.   **47.** 6.   **49.** 2.   **51.** -7.   **53.** $\frac{1}{2}$.   **55.** $\frac{1}{81}$.   **57.** 2.   **59.** $\frac{5}{3}$.   **61.** 0.231.   **63.** 16.094.

65. 223.872.   **67.** 0.970.   **69.** (a) 3.52, (b) 1.41×10^{-8}.   **71.** 24.8 db.

73. (a) 305.2 mm Hg, (b) 5.13 km.   **75.** 0.01204; 57.57 s.   **77.** (a) 0.18145, (b) 0.25.

Exercise 13-3

1. 1.5441. **3.** 0.3521. **5.** 1.3980. **7.** 3.3010. **9.** 5. **11.** −4. **13.** −1. **15.** $\frac{1}{3}$. **17.** 4.
19. $\log x + \log y$. **21.** $\log x - 2 \log z$. **23.** $\frac{1}{2} \log x$. **25.** $6(\log x + 2 \log y)$.
27. $\frac{1}{6}(2 \log x + 3 \log y - 5 \log z)$. **29.** $\log x + \log (x + 2) + \log (x - 3)$.
31. $\frac{1}{2} \log x - \log (x + 2) - 2 \log (x - 3)$. **33.** $\frac{1}{2}[2 \log x + 3 \log (x - 3) - \log (x + 2)]$.
35. $\log_2 21$. **37.** $\log \left(\frac{73}{23^5}\right)$. **39.** $\log_3 32$. **41.** $\log_4 \left(\frac{1}{50}\right)$. **43.** $\log_4 3^{10}$. **45.** $\log_2 \left(\frac{2x}{x+1}\right)$.

Exercise 13-4

1. 2.0478. **3.** −0.2058. **5.** −4.4912.

Exercise 13-5

1. 1.1402. **3.** 4.4022. **5.** −3.1699. **7.** 0.8518. **9.** 3.5705. **11.** 5. **13.** $\frac{4}{3}$. **15.** 3. **17.** $\frac{299}{97}$.
19. (a) 4634.6 N, (b) 0.24 m. **21.** (a) 5×10^{-5} A, (b) 12.88 s.

Exercise 13-6

1. (a) Semilog paper. **3.** (a) Log paper, (b) $y = \dfrac{600}{x}$. **5.** $y = 0.4(3.01)^x$.
7. (a) Log paper, (b) $T = 2.0L^{0.5}$.

Review Problems—Chapter 13

1. 5, 13, $\frac{13}{3}$. **3.** 100, $100e^4 = 5459.8$, $100e^{-3/2} = 22.31$. **5.**

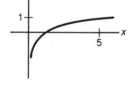

7. $\log_3 243 = 5$. **9.** $16^{1/4} = 2$. **11.** $\ln 54.598 = 4$. **13.** 3. **15.** −4. **17.** −2. **19.** 2.80265.
21. 16.93551. **23.** 3.78155. **25.** −0.45887. **27.** 1.55181. **29.** 3.1101. **31.** 0.2086. **33.** −2.
35. $\frac{1}{100}$. **37.** 9. **39.** 3. **41.** 347.27. **43.** 0.3958. **45.** 1. **47.** 3. **49.** 3. **51.** $\log \frac{25}{27}$.
53. $\ln \dfrac{x^2 y}{z^3}$. **55.** $\log_2 \dfrac{x^{9/2}}{(x+1)^3(x+2)^4}$. **57.** $2 \ln x + \ln y - 3 \ln z$. **59.** $\frac{1}{3}(\ln x + \ln y + \ln z)$.
61. $\frac{1}{2}(\ln y - \ln z) - \ln x$. **63.** $2y + \frac{1}{2}x$. **65.** 1.2619. **67.** $y = 4(3.5)^x$. **69.** 10.0.

Exercise 14-2

1. $A = 3, p = 2\pi$.   **3.** $A = 4, p = 2\pi$.

5. $A = 1, p = \pi$.

7. $A = 2, p = 6\pi$.

9. $A = 4, p = \dfrac{2\pi}{3}$.

11. $A = 1, p = 2\pi$.

13. $A = 4, p = \pi$.

15. $A = 2, p = 4\pi$.

17. $A = 1, p = 2$.

19. Two.   **21.** (a) 0.72 s,   (b) 1.38 hertz.

23.

25. (a)   (b) 45°

Exercise 14-3

1. $A = \tfrac{1}{2}, p = 2\pi$.

3. $A = 4, p = \dfrac{\pi}{2}$.

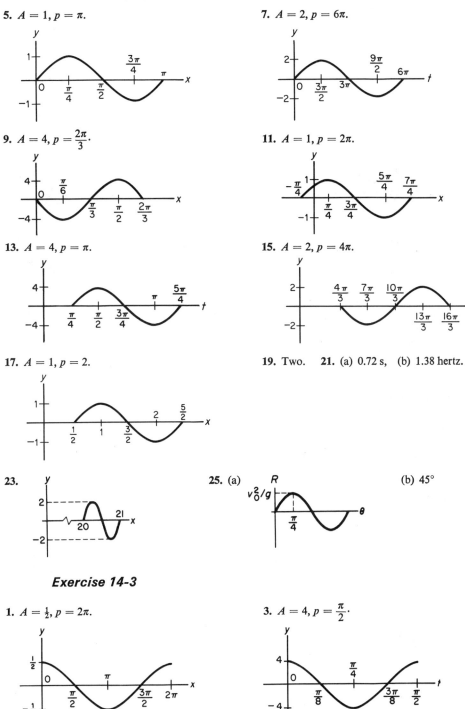

5. $A = 4, p = \dfrac{2\pi}{3}.$

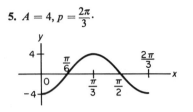

7. $A = 2, p = 2\pi.$

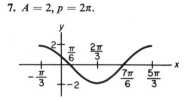

9. $A = 2, p = 4\pi.$

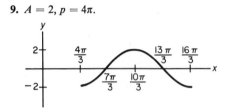

11. $A = 1, p = 2.$

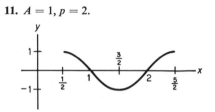

13. y_1 leads y_2 by $\frac{1}{4}$ cycle or 90°.   **15.** 90°.

Exercise 14-5

1. $\dfrac{3\pi}{2}, \dfrac{7\pi}{2}.$ **3.** $0, \pi, 2\pi.$

Exercise 14-6

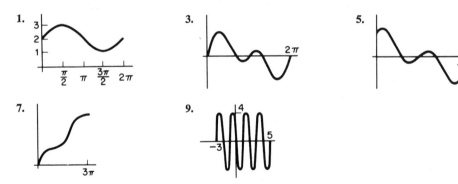

Exercise 14-7

1. $\dfrac{\pi}{2}.$ **3.** $\dfrac{\pi}{6}.$ **5.** 0.   **7.** $-\dfrac{\pi}{6}.$ **9.** $\dfrac{\pi}{4}.$ **11.** $\dfrac{3\pi}{4}.$ **13.** $\dfrac{1}{3}.$ **15.** $\dfrac{\sqrt{3}}{2}.$ **17.** 0.   **19.** $\dfrac{\sqrt{2}}{2}.$

21. $\dfrac{\pi}{3}.$

Exercise 14-8

1.

3.

Exercise 14-9

13. $\left(\frac{3}{2}, \frac{3\sqrt{3}}{2}\right)$. **15.** $(-\sqrt{2}, \sqrt{2})$. **17.** $\left(-\frac{5\sqrt{3}}{2}, -\frac{5}{2}\right)$. **19.** $(-\sqrt{2}, \sqrt{2})$.
21. $(-4.68, 1.76)$. **23.** $(2, 90°)$. **25.** $(2, 300°)$. **27.** $(4, 180°)$. **29.** $(4, 120°)$. **31.** $(6.13, 66.86°)$.
33. $(7.21, 236.31°)$.

35.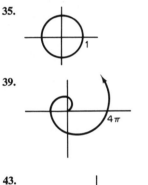

37.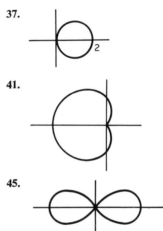

39.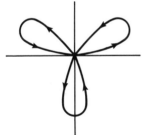

41.

43.

45.

Review Problems—Chapter 14

1. $A = 1, p = \frac{2\pi}{3}$.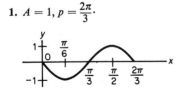

3. $A = 4, p = 2\pi$.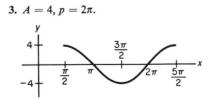

5. $A = 3$, $p = \pi$.

7. $p = \pi$.

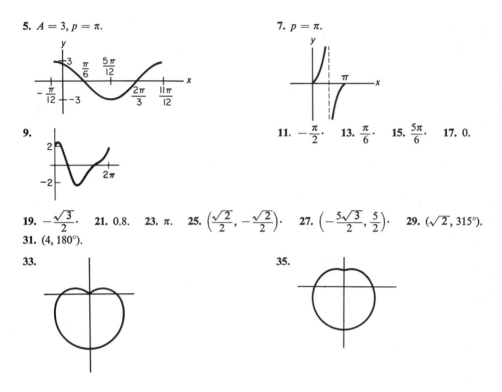

9.

11. $-\dfrac{\pi}{2}$. **13.** $\dfrac{\pi}{6}$. **15.** $\dfrac{5\pi}{6}$. **17.** 0.

19. $-\dfrac{\sqrt{3}}{2}$. **21.** 0.8. **23.** π. **25.** $\left(\dfrac{\sqrt{2}}{2}, -\dfrac{\sqrt{2}}{2}\right)$. **27.** $\left(-\dfrac{5\sqrt{3}}{2}, \dfrac{5}{2}\right)$. **29.** $(\sqrt{2}, 315°)$.
31. $(4, 180°)$.

33.

35.

Exercise 15-2

1. $\dfrac{\sqrt{6} - \sqrt{2}}{4}$. **3.** $\dfrac{\sqrt{2} - \sqrt{6}}{4}$. **5.** $2 - \sqrt{3}$. **7.** $\dfrac{\sqrt{2} - \sqrt{6}}{4}$. **9.** $\dfrac{-\sqrt{6} - \sqrt{2}}{4}$.

11. $2 + \sqrt{3}$. **13.** (a) $-\dfrac{7\sqrt{65}}{65}$, (b) $\dfrac{4\sqrt{65}}{65}$, (c) $-\dfrac{7}{4}$, (d) fourth. **15.** $-\sin x$. **17.** $\sin x$.

19. $\dfrac{1 + \tan x}{1 - \tan x}$. **21.** $\cos 70°$. **31.** True. **33.** True.

Exercise 15-3

1. $\dfrac{\sqrt{3}}{2}$. **3.** $-\dfrac{1}{2}$. **5.** $-\sqrt{3}$. **7.** $\dfrac{\sqrt{2 - \sqrt{3}}}{2}$. **9.** $\dfrac{\sqrt{2 + \sqrt{2}}}{2}$. **11.** $-\sqrt{2} - 1$.

13. $\sin x = \dfrac{4}{5}$, $\cos x = \dfrac{3}{5}$, $\tan x = \dfrac{4}{3}$, $\sin 2x = \dfrac{24}{25}$, $\cos 2x = -\dfrac{7}{25}$, $\tan 2x = -\dfrac{24}{7}$.

15. $\sin x = -\dfrac{1}{3}$, $\cos x = -\dfrac{2\sqrt{2}}{3}$, $\tan x = \dfrac{\sqrt{2}}{4}$, $\sin 2x = \dfrac{4\sqrt{2}}{9}$, $\cos 2x = \dfrac{7}{9}$, $\tan 2x = \dfrac{4\sqrt{2}}{7}$.

17. $\sin x = \dfrac{5}{13}$, $\cos x = \dfrac{12}{13}$, $\tan x = \dfrac{5}{12}$, $\sin \dfrac{x}{2} = \dfrac{\sqrt{26}}{26}$, $\cos \dfrac{x}{2} = \dfrac{5\sqrt{26}}{26}$, $\tan \dfrac{x}{2} = \dfrac{1}{5}$.

19. $\sin x = -\dfrac{3}{5}$, $\cos x = -\dfrac{4}{5}$, $\tan x = \dfrac{3}{4}$, $\sin \dfrac{x}{2} = \dfrac{3\sqrt{10}}{10}$, $\cos \dfrac{x}{2} = -\dfrac{\sqrt{10}}{10}$, $\tan \dfrac{x}{2} = -3$.

29. $R = \dfrac{2v_0^2 \sin \theta \cos \theta}{g}$.

Exercise 15-4

1. 45°, 135°.　**3.** 135°, 315°.　**5.** 60°, 300°.　**7.** 0°, 120°, 240°.　**9.** 0°, 180°.　**11.** 63.43°, 243.43°.
13. 38.17°, 141.83°.　**15.** 90°, 210°, 330°.　**17.** 30°, 60°, 210°, 240°.　**19.** 0°, 240°.
21. 112.5°, 157.5°, 292.5°, 337.5°.　**23.** 60°, 90°, 270°, 300°.　**25.** 0°, 60°, 180°, 300°.
27. 30°, 150°, 210°, 330°.　**29.** 90°, 210°, 270°, 330°.　**31.** 0°, 135°, 180°, 315°.

Review Problems—Chapter 15

11. $\dfrac{3 + 4\sqrt{3}}{10}$.　**13.** $\dfrac{1}{2}$.　**15.** $\dfrac{1}{2}$.　**17.** $\dfrac{1}{7}$.

19. $\sin x = \dfrac{15}{17}$, $\cos x = \dfrac{8}{17}$, $\tan x = \dfrac{15}{8}$, $\sin(-x) = -\dfrac{15}{17}$, $\cos(-x) = \dfrac{8}{17}$, $\sin 2x = \dfrac{240}{289}$, $\cos 2x = -\dfrac{161}{289}$,

$\tan 2x = -\dfrac{240}{161}$, $\sin \dfrac{x}{2} = \dfrac{3\sqrt{34}}{34}$, $\cos \dfrac{x}{2} = \dfrac{5\sqrt{34}}{34}$, $\tan \dfrac{x}{2} = \dfrac{3}{5}$.

21. 90°, 270°.　**23.** 240°, 300°.

Exercise 16-1

1. $C = 31.5°$, $b = 26.19$, $c = 13.83$.　**3.** $B = 50.47°$, $C = 49.11°$, $c = 7.08$.
5. (a) $B = 26.79°$, $C = 132.75°$, $c = 15.67$, (b) $B = 153.21°$, $C = 6.33°$, $c = 2.35$.　**7.** No triangle.
9. $A = 13.43°$, $B = 27.75°$, $b = 14.28$.　**11.** $A = 47.6°$, $b = 94.46$, $c = 103.48$.
13. $A = 60°$, $B = 90°$, $a = 8.66$.　**15.** No triangle.　**17.** 2479.5 m.　**19.** 1.2 km.
21. $F = 986.4$ N, $\theta = 70.55°$.

Exercise 16-2

1. $A = 22.80°$, $B = 129.20°$, $c = 24.23$.　**3.** $A = 53.83°$, $B = 59.59°$, $C = 66.58°$.
5. $A = 35.89°$, $C = 28.88°$, $b = 22.93$.　**7.** $A = 77.83°$, $B = 49.06°$, $C = 53.11°$.
9. $A = 81.34°$, $B = 44.62°$, $C = 54.04°$.　**11.** $r = 11.93$ N, $\theta = 55.6°$.　**13.** 44.2 km.
15. 24.23 N, 67.2° west of north.　**17.** 52.41°, 82.10°.　**19.** 3.84 m.

Exercise 16-3

1. 8.21 (units)².　**3.** 32.17 (units)².　**5.** 514.23 (units)².　**7.** 12π cm².　**9.** 36π cm².　**11.** 30π rad/s.
13. 31.8 m.　**15.** 19.4 rad/s.
17. (a) 40π rad/s, (b) 1120π rad, (c) $\bar{\omega} = 40\pi$ rad/s, $\bar{v} = 80\pi$ cm/s, (d) $\bar{\omega} = 40\pi$ rad/s, $\bar{v} = 400\pi$ cm/s.

Review Problems—Chapter 16

1. $A = 97.52°$, $B = 52.48°$, $c = 2.52$.　**3.** $A = 80°$, $a = 5.91$, $b = 5.64$.
5. $A = 121.86°$, $B = 39.57°$, $C = 18.57°$.　**7.** $B = 25.66°$, $C = 94.34°$, $c = 23.03$.
9. (a) $B = 13.39°$, $C = 156.61°$, $c = 13.72$, (b) $B = 166.61°$, $C = 3.39°$, $c = 2.04$.
11. 14.48 m, 31.71 m; 22.1 rev.　**13.** 129.9 (units)².

Exercise 17-1

1. $x > 2$.　**3.** $x \leq 3$.　**5.** $x \leq -\frac{1}{2}$.　**7.** $s < -\frac{2}{3}$.　**9.** $x < 3$.　**11.** $x \geq -\frac{7}{3}$.　**13.** $y > 0$.
15. $x > -\frac{2}{3}$.　**17.** No solution.　**19.** $x < 6$.　**21.** $y \leq -5$.　**23.** All real numbers.　**25.** $t > \frac{17}{9}$.
27. $x \geq -\frac{14}{3}$.　**29.** $r > 0$.　**31.** $y < 0$.　**33.** $x \leq -2$.　**35.** $84 < I < 114$.　**37.** ⟶
$$36$$

Exercise 17-2

1. $1 < x < 5$.   **3.** $x < -1$ or $x > 3$.   **5.** $-1 < x < 1$.   **7.** $x < -2$ or $x > 3$.   **9.** $s \leq 0$ or $s \geq 5$.
11. $-3 < x < -2$.   **13.** $x \leq -5$ or $x \geq 4$.   **15.** $-\frac{3}{2} < z < 4$.   **17.** $x < -1$ or $x > -1$.
19. $t \leq -\frac{3}{2}$ or $t \geq \frac{1}{2}$.   **21.** $-2 < x < 1$ or $x > 4$.   **23.** $x < -5$.   **25.** $y \leq -1$ or $0 \leq y \leq 1$.
27. $x = 0$ or $x \geq 2$.   **29.** $x < -8$ or $x > 4$.   **31.** $t \leq 0$ or $t > 3$.   **33.** $x > -2$.
35. $x < -3$ or $-1 < x < 1$.   **37.** $x < -4$ or $-1 < x \leq 1$ or $x \geq 4$.   **39.** $\frac{1}{4}$ km.

Exercise 17-3

1. $x = 6$.   **3.** $x = 4$.   **5.** $x = \frac{28}{3}$.   **7.** $-4 < x < 4$.
9. (a) $|x - 7| < 3$,   (b) $|x - 2| < 3$,   (c) $|x - 7| \leq 5$,   (d) $|x - 7| = 4$,   (e) $|x + 4| < 2$,
(f) $|x| < 3$,   (g) $|x| > 6$,   (h) $|x - 6| > 4$,   (i) $|x - 105| < 3$.
11. $x = \pm 6$.   '**13.** $x = \pm 6$.   **15.** $x = -3, 13$.   **17.** $x = \frac{2}{5}$.   **19.** $x = \frac{1}{2}, 3$.   **21.** $-3 < x < 3$.
23. $x > 6$ or $x < -6$.   **25.** $-1 \leq x \leq 1$.   **27.** $x \geq 3$ or $x \leq -3$.   **29.** $-12 < x < 20$.
31. $y \geq 5$ or $y \leq -7$.   **33.** $-\frac{4}{3} \leq x \leq 2$.   **35.** $-\frac{1}{3} < x < 1$.   **37.** $t < 0$ or $t > 1$.
39. $x \leq 0$ or $x \geq \frac{16}{3}$.   **41.** $|x - 0.01| \leq 0.005$.

Exercise 17-4

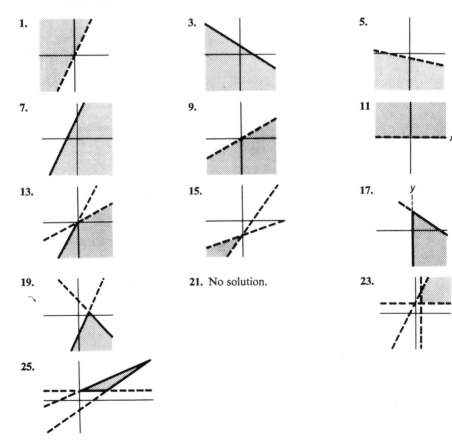

1.

3.

5.

7.

9.

11

13.

15.

17.

19.

21. No solution.

23.

25.

Review Problems—Chapter 17

1. $x < \frac{1}{3}$.   **3.** $x \leq -2$.   **5.** $t > 1$.   **7.** $x \geq 40$.   **9.** $-6 < x < 2$.   **11.** $y < 0$ or $y > 6$.
13. $x \leq -5$ or $x \geq -4$.   **15.** $-1 < x < \frac{1}{3}$.   **17.** $-4 < x < 5$ or $x > 9$.
19. $p \leq 0$ or $0 \leq p \leq 8$; more simply $p \leq 8$.   **21.** $x \leq -9$ or $x > -2$.
23. $x < -5$ or $-2 < x < 3$ or $x > 3$.   **25.** $x = -2, 5$.   **27.** $x > 2$ or $x < -2$.   **29.** $0 < x < \frac{1}{2}$.
31. $x \leq 0$ or $x \geq 4$.   **33.** $-2 \leq x \leq 1$.

35.    **37.**   **39.** No solution.

Exercise 18-2

1. 5.   **3.** $\sqrt{53}$.   **5.** $2\sqrt{2}$.   **7.** 7.   **9.** $\dfrac{\sqrt{5}}{2}$.   **11.** 13.

Exercise 18-3

1. $(x - 2)^2 + (y - 3)^2 = 36$; $x^2 + y^2 - 4x - 6y - 23 = 0$.
3. $(x + 1)^2 + (y - 6)^2 = 16$; $x^2 + y^2 + 2x - 12y + 21 = 0$.
5. $x^2 + y^2 = \frac{1}{4}$; $x^2 + y^2 - \frac{1}{4} = 0$.   **7.** $C = (0, 0)$, $r = 3$.   **9.** $C = (3, -4)$, $r = \sqrt{2}$.
11. $C = (-2, 0)$, $r = 1$.   **13.** Circle; $C = (1, 2)$, $r = 3$.   **15.** Circle; $C = (0, -3)$, $r = 2$.
17. No graph.   **19.** Circle; $C = (7, -2)$, $r = \sqrt{15}$.   **21.** Point $(\frac{3}{2}, -\frac{1}{2})$.
23. Circle; $C = (1, -\frac{7}{4})$, $r = \frac{7}{4}$.   **25.** Two.   **27.** None.   **29.** b, c, d, f, g.   **31.** $x^2 + y^2 = 330^2$.

Exercise 18-4

1. $V(0, 0)$, $F(1, 0)$, $D: x = -1$.   **3.** $V(0, 0)$, $F(0, -2)$, $D: y = 2$.   **5.** $V(0, 0)$, $F(0, \frac{1}{2})$, $D: y = -\frac{1}{2}$.
7. $V(0, -2)$, $F(\frac{1}{8}, -2)$, $D: x = -\frac{1}{8}$.   **9.** $V(4, -3)$, $F(4, -1)$, $D: y = -5$.
11. $V(1, -2)$, $F(\frac{15}{16}, -2)$, $D: x = \frac{17}{16}$.   **13.** $x^2 = 16(y + 1)$.   **15.** $(y - 4)^2 = -8(x - 3)$.
17. $(x + 3)^2 = -8(y - 2)$.   **19.** $x^2 = 6y$.   **21.** $(y + 2)^2 = 4(x + 4)$.
23. $(y - 3)^2 = -4(x - 2)$, $V(2, 3)$, $F(1, 3)$.   **25.** $(x - 2)^2 = \frac{1}{3}y$, $V(2, 0)$, $F(2, \frac{1}{12})$.
27. $(y + 2)^2 = x - 1$, $V(1, -2)$, $F(\frac{5}{4}, -2)$.   **29.** None.   **31.** Two.   **33.** 6 s; 176.4 m.
35. Less than 5 cm.

Exercise 18-5

1. $C(0, 0)$, $V(\pm 5, 0)$, $F(\pm 3, 0)$, $E(0, \pm 4)$.   **3.** $C(0, 0)$, $V(0, \pm 12)$, $F(0, \pm 2\sqrt{11})$, $E(\pm 10, 0)$.
5. $C(0, 0)$, $V(0, \pm 2)$, $F(0, \pm\sqrt{3})$, $E(\pm 1, 0)$.
7. $C(2, -3)$, $V(2 \pm 3, -3)$, $F(2 \pm \sqrt{5}, -3)$, $E(2, -3 \pm 2)$.   **9.** $C(2, 0)$, $V(2, \pm 4)$, $E(2 \pm 2, 0)$.
11. $C(3, -2)$, $V(3 \pm 5, -2)$, $E(3, -2 \pm 3)$.   **13.** $\dfrac{x^2}{36} + \dfrac{y^2}{11} = 1$.
15. $\dfrac{x^2}{68} + \dfrac{(y - 1)^2}{4} = 1$.   **17.** $\dfrac{x^2}{64} + \dfrac{y^2}{16} = 1$.   **19.** $\dfrac{x^2}{\frac{23}{4}} + \dfrac{(y + 8)^2}{64} = 1$.   **21.** $\dfrac{(x + 2)^2}{4} + \dfrac{(y + 1)^2}{53} = 1$.
23. $\dfrac{x^2}{(1.28 \times 10^7)^2} + \dfrac{y^2}{(8 \times 10^6)^2} = 1$, choosing the center of the earth as the center of the coordinate system.

Exercise 18-6

1. $C(0, 0)$, $V(\pm 4, 0)$, $F(\pm 5, 0)$, $E(0, \pm 3)$, $A: y = \pm \frac{3}{4}x$.
3. $C(0, 0)$, $V(0, \pm 6)$, $F(0, \pm\sqrt{37})$, $E(\pm 1, 0)$, $A: y = \pm 6x$.
5. $C(0, 0)$, $V(\pm 2, 0)$, $F(\pm 2\sqrt{2}, 0)$, $E(0, \pm 2)$, $A: y = \pm x$.
7. $C(2, -3)$, $V(2, -3 \pm 5)$, $F(2, -3 \pm \sqrt{29})$, $E(2 \pm 2, -3)$, $A: y = -3 \pm \frac{5}{2}(x - 2)$.
9. $C(2, -1)$, $V(2 \pm 4, -1)$, $F(2 \pm 5, -1)$, $E(2, -1 \pm 3)$, $A: y = -1 \pm \frac{3}{4}(x - 2)$.
11. $\dfrac{y^2}{4} - \dfrac{x^2}{5} = 1$.   **13.** $\dfrac{x^2}{16} - y^2 = 1$.   **15.** $\dfrac{(y - 2)^2}{4} - \dfrac{(x + 4)^2}{12} = 1$.
17. $\dfrac{(x + 2)^2}{4} - \dfrac{(y - 4)^2}{\frac{9}{4}} = 1$.   **19.** $\dfrac{(y - 4)^2}{4} - \dfrac{x^2}{5} = 1$.   **21.** $x = 0$, $y = 0$.   **23.** $x = 0$, $y = 0$.

25. $x = 0$, $y = 0$.

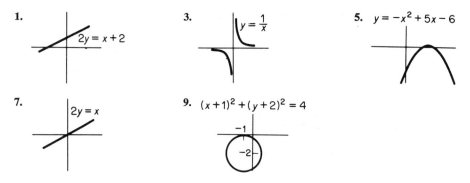

27. $f\lambda = 3(10^8)$

29. $pv = 20$

Exercise 18-7

1. Circle.   **3.** Parabola.   **5.** Parabola.   **7.** Hyperbola.   **9.** Ellipse.   **11.** Hyperbola.   **13.** Ellipse.
15. Ellipse.   **17.** Parabola.   **19.** Hyperbola.

Exercise 18-8

1. $2y = x + 2$

3. $y = \frac{1}{x}$

5. $y = -x^2 + 5x - 6$

7. $2y = x$

9. $(x + 1)^2 + (y + 2)^2 = 4$

11. $x = \dfrac{1 - t}{t}$, $y = 1 - t$.   **13.** $x = \dfrac{2t}{1 + t^3}$, $y = \dfrac{2t^2}{1 + t^3}$.   **15.** $x = \dfrac{1 - t}{1 + 2t}$, $y = \dfrac{t(1 - t)}{1 + 2t}$.
21. (a) 689.4 m; 534.4 m,   (b) 39.35 s,   (c) 9043 m,   (d) 1897 m when $t = 19.68$ s.   **23.** 1.54 s.

Review Problems—Chapter 18

1. $2\sqrt{5}$.   **3.** 10.   **5.** $x^2 + y^2 = 25$; $x^2 + y^2 - 25 = 0$.
7. $(x - 1)^2 + (y + 1)^2 = \frac{1}{4}$; $x^2 + y^2 - 2x + 2y + \frac{7}{4} = 0$.   **9.** Circle, $C(0, 0)$, $r = 4$.
11. Circle, $C(-2, 1)$, $r = \sqrt{7}$.
13. Hyperbola, $C(0, 0)$, $V(\pm 10, 0)$, $F(\pm\sqrt{109}, 0)$, endpts. of conjugate axis $(0, \pm 3)$, asym. $y = \pm\frac{3}{10}x$.
15. Ellipse, $C(0, 0)$, $V(0, \pm 6)$, $F(0, \pm\sqrt{35})$, endpts. of minor axis $(\pm 1, 0)$.

17. Parabola, $V(0, 0)$, $F(0, -\frac{5}{8})$, directrix $y = \frac{5}{8}$. **19.** Circle, $C(0, 0)$, $r = 1/\sqrt{6}$.
21. Hyperbola, $C(-1, 0)$, $V(-1 \pm 2, 0)$, $F(-1 \pm 2\sqrt{5}, 0)$, endpts. of conjugate axis $(-1, \pm 4)$, asym.
$y = \pm 2(x + 1)$.
23. Parabola, $V(0, 2)$, $F(3, 2)$, directrix $x = -3$. **25.** Hyperbola, $C(0, 0)$, asym. $x = 0$, $y = 0$.
27. Ellipse, $C(-5, 2)$, $V(-5, 2 \pm 2\sqrt{2})$, $F(-5, 2 \pm 2)$, endpts. of minor axis $(-5 \pm 2, 2)$.
29. Circle, $C(-\frac{5}{2}, 3)$, $r = \frac{\sqrt{53}}{2}$. **31.** Point $(1, \frac{1}{3})$. **33.** Parabola, $V(-\frac{5}{2}, 1)$, $F(-2, 1)$, directrix $x = -3$.
35. Hyperbola, $C(-1, 0)$, $V(-1, \pm 2)$, $F(-1, \pm 2\sqrt{2})$, endpts. of conjugate axis $(-1 \pm 2, 0)$.
37. $(x - 2)^2 = 12(y - 1)$. **39.** $\dfrac{(x + 2)^2}{9} + \dfrac{(y - 3)^2}{25} = 1$. **41.** $x = \dfrac{3t}{2 - t^3}$, $y = \dfrac{3t^2}{2 - t^3}$.

Exercise 19-1

1. 3, 6, 9, 12. **3.** 1, 3, 5, 7. **5.** $\frac{1}{2}, \frac{2}{3}, \frac{3}{4}, \frac{4}{5}$. **7.** $0, \frac{1}{3}, \frac{1}{2}, \frac{3}{5}$. **9.** $\frac{1}{2}, \frac{1}{2}, \frac{3}{8}, \frac{1}{4}$. **11.** 1, 0, -1, 0.
13. $\dfrac{e}{2}, \dfrac{e^2}{2}, \dfrac{e^3}{2}, \dfrac{e^4}{2}$. **15.** 1, -4, 9, -16. **17.** $4n$. **19.** $2(n + 1)$. **21.** $\left(\dfrac{1}{3}\right)^{n-1}$. **23.** $\dfrac{(-1)^{n+1}}{n + 1}$.

Exercise 19-2

1. Arith., -71. **3.** Geom., $-\frac{3}{16}$. **5.** Geom., 243. **7.** Arith., $\frac{11}{3}$. **9.** Geom., $\frac{1}{128}$. **11.** Neither.
13. Arith., 4. **15.** Geom., $\frac{729}{64}$. **17.** 44. **19.** $\frac{1}{2}$. **21.** 6. **23.** 7 cm. **25.** $6561°$C.

Exercise 19-3

1. 35. **3.** 25. **5.** $-\frac{3}{16}$. **7.** $-\frac{7}{6}$. **9.** $1 + \frac{1}{2} + \frac{1}{4} + \frac{1}{8}$. **11.** 110. **13.** -360. **15.** -108.
17. 620. **19.** 1092. **21.** -126. **23.** 0.3333333333. **25.** $62(1 + \sqrt{2})$.
27. $a_1 = 10$, $n = 9$; $a_1 = -\frac{39}{4}$, $n = 88$. **29.** $S_{16} = 528$, $a_{16} = 48$. **31.** $n = 23$, $a_n = 36$.
33. $a_1 = 64$, $a_6 = 2$. **35.** -2. **37.** $\frac{121}{243}$ or $-\frac{61}{243}$. **39.** $4.65. **41.** 385. **43.** 5050. **45.** 705.6 m.
47. $\frac{81}{256}$.

Exercise 19-4

1. Div. **3.** 0. **5.** $\frac{11}{4}$. **7.** 0. **9.** 0. **11.** $\frac{3}{2}$. **13.** -1. **15.** Div. **17.** 0. **19.** 0.

Exercise 19-5

1. 1. **3.** $-\frac{2}{3}$. **5.** Div. **7.** $\frac{243}{1250}$. **9.** $-\frac{1}{2}$. **11.** $\frac{100}{3}$. **13.** $\frac{4}{9}$. **15.** 6. **17.** 18. **19.** $-\frac{8}{3}$.
21. $\frac{50}{27}$. **23.** Div. **25.** $\frac{8}{33}$. **27.** $\frac{3209}{999}$. **29.** $\frac{2111}{99.000}$. **31.** 12 m. **33.** 100 cm. **35.** 50 m.

Exercise 19-6

1. $x^3 + 12x^2 + 48x + 64$. **3.** $y^4 - 8y^3 + 24y^2 - 32y + 16$.
5. $243x^5 + 405x^4 + 270x^3 + 90x^2 + 15x + 1$. **7.** $16z^4 - 32z^3y + 24z^2y^2 - 8zy^3 + y^4$.
9. $a^5 - \dfrac{5a^4}{b} + \dfrac{10a^3}{b^2} - \dfrac{10a^2}{b^3} + \dfrac{5a}{b^4} - \dfrac{1}{b^5}$. **11.** $1 + \dfrac{6x}{y^2} + \dfrac{15x^2}{y^4} + \dfrac{20x^3}{y^6} + \dfrac{15x^4}{y^8} + \dfrac{6x^5}{y^{10}} + \dfrac{x^6}{y^{12}}$.
13. $x^{100} + 100x^{99} + 4950x^{98}$. **15.** $128x^7 - 1344x^6 + 6048x^5$. **17.** $y^{20} - 50xy^{18} + 1125x^2y^{16}$.
19. $243z^{10} + 135xz^8 + 30x^2z^6$. **21.** $455x^{12}y^3$. **23.** $-\dfrac{108,864x^3}{y^5}$. **25.** $-160x^3y^3$. **27.** $-10x^6y^3$.
29. $1 - 3x + 6x^2 - 10x^3$. **31.** $1 - \dfrac{y}{2} - \dfrac{y^2}{8} - \dfrac{y^3}{16}$. **33.** 7.071. **35.** 7.810. **37.** 3.072. **39.** 2.991.

Review Problems—Chapter 19

1. 48. **3.** $2 + 6 + 12$. **5.** $\frac{127}{64}$. **7.** 0. **9.** -3. **11.** $x^4 - 16x^3 + 96x^2 - 256x + 256$.
13. $x^9 + 6x^6y + 12x^3y^2 + 8y^3$. **15.** 1200. **17.** $\frac{23}{99}$. **19.** $924x^{12}$. **21.** $\frac{4}{5}$. **23.** $\frac{4}{3}$. **25.** $\frac{243}{128}$ m.

index

A

Radians and Degrees

$$1° = \frac{\pi}{180} \text{ radians}$$

$$1 \text{ radian} = \left(\frac{180}{\pi}\right)°$$

Positive Trigonometric Functions

Quadrant	I	II	III	IV
	all	sin csc	tan cot	cos sec

Trigonometric Functions of Any Angle

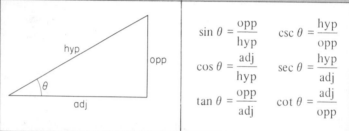

$$\sin\theta = \frac{y}{r} \qquad \csc\theta = \frac{r}{y}$$

$$\cos\theta = \frac{x}{r} \qquad \sec\theta = \frac{r}{x}$$

$$\tan\theta = \frac{y}{x} \qquad \cot\theta = \frac{x}{y}$$

where $r = \sqrt{x^2 + y^2}$, $r \neq 0$

Right-Triangle Trigonometry

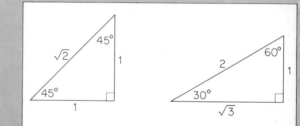

$$\sin\theta = \frac{\text{opp}}{\text{hyp}} \qquad \csc\theta = \frac{\text{hyp}}{\text{opp}}$$

$$\cos\theta = \frac{\text{adj}}{\text{hyp}} \qquad \sec\theta = \frac{\text{hyp}}{\text{adj}}$$

$$\tan\theta = \frac{\text{opp}}{\text{adj}} \qquad \cot\theta = \frac{\text{adj}}{\text{opp}}$$

Special Triangles

Special Angles

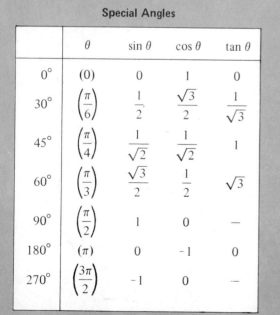

	θ	$\sin\theta$	$\cos\theta$	$\tan\theta$
0°	(0)	0	1	0
30°	$\left(\dfrac{\pi}{6}\right)$	$\dfrac{1}{2}$	$\dfrac{\sqrt{3}}{2}$	$\dfrac{1}{\sqrt{3}}$
45°	$\left(\dfrac{\pi}{4}\right)$	$\dfrac{1}{\sqrt{2}}$	$\dfrac{1}{\sqrt{2}}$	1
60°	$\left(\dfrac{\pi}{3}\right)$	$\dfrac{\sqrt{3}}{2}$	$\dfrac{1}{2}$	$\sqrt{3}$
90°	$\left(\dfrac{\pi}{2}\right)$	1	0	—
180°	(π)	0	-1	0
270°	$\left(\dfrac{3\pi}{2}\right)$	-1	0	—

Inverse Trigonometric Functions

$$y = \arcsin x = \sin^{-1} x \text{ where } x = \sin y$$

$$\text{and } -\frac{\pi}{2} \leq y \leq \frac{\pi}{2}$$

$$y = \arccos x = \cos^{-1} x \text{ where } x = \cos y$$

$$\text{and } 0 \leq y \leq \pi$$

$$y = \arctan x = \tan^{-1} x \text{ where } x = \tan y$$

$$\text{and } -\frac{\pi}{2} < y < \frac{\pi}{2}$$